ENCYCLOPEDIA OF
CONTEMPORARY LITERARY THEORY
Approaches, Scholars, Terms

The last half of the twentieth century has witnessed a revolution in literary studies. Drawing on a vast network of other disciplines – such as philosophy, anthropology, linguistics, political economy, sociology, women's studies, religion – the new literary theories are not only changing traditional boundaries and issues of literary study, but also questioning the very foundations of Western thought.

Irena R. Makaryk has compiled a welcome guide to this complex field. The *Encyclopedia of Contemporary Literary Theory* surveys this enormous range of literary theories, theorists, and critical terms, and provides lucid explanations of each.

A distinguished international group of 170 scholars has contributed to this three-part volume. In Part 1, forty-eight evaluative essays examine the historical and cultural context out of which new schools and approaches to literature arose, the uses and limitations of each, and the key issues they address. A bibliographical essay on theory and pedagogy concludes this section; it suggests some of the ways that the theoretical issues have altered and will continue to alter ways of teaching literature.

Focusing on individual theorists, Part 2 examines their achievements, influence, and their place in the larger critical context.

Part 3 deals with the vocabulary of literary theory. It identifies significant, complex terms, and explains their origins and use.

Accessibility is a key feature of the work. Bibliographies for each entry and extensive cross-referencing throughout make the *Encyclopedia of Contemporary Literary Theory* an indispensable tool for literary theorists and historians, and for all scholars of contemporary criticism and culture.

IRENA R. MAKARYK is Chair of Graduate English Studies at the University of Ottawa. She is the author of *Comic Justice in Shakespeare*, editor of and contributor to '*Living Record': Essays in Memory of Constantine Bida*, and translator and editor of *About the Harrowing of Hell: A 17th-Century Ukrainian Play in Its European Context*.

ENCYCLOPEDIA OF CONTEMPORARY LITERARY THEORY

Approaches, Scholars, Terms

IRENA R. MAKARYK

General Editor and Compiler

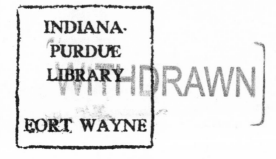
UNIVERSITY OF TORONTO PRESS

Toronto Buffalo London

© University of Toronto Press Incorporated 1993
Toronto Buffalo London
Printed in Canada

Paperback reprinted 1993

ISBN 0-8020-5914-7 (cloth)
ISBN 0-8020-6860-X (paper)

∞

Printed on acid-free paper

Theory / Culture
General editors: Linda Hutcheon and Paul Perron

Canadian Cataloguing in Publication Data

Main entry under title:

Encyclopedia of contemporary literary theory

(Theory/culture)
Includes index.
ISBN 0-8020-5914-7 (bound)
ISBN 0-8020-6860-X (pbk.)

1. Criticism – Encyclopedias.
I. Makaryk, Irena Rima, 1951–
II. Series.

PN81.E63 1993   801'.95   C92-095270-4

Contents

Introduction

'A man with one theory is lost. He needs several of them, or lots!
He should stuff them in his pockets like newspapers.'
Bertolt Brecht

One hundred and seventy eminent scholars from around the world have helped create this book. Gathered from various departments – Religion, Philosophy, Sociology, Psychology, Linguistics, Women's Studies, English, Modern Languages, French, Political Science, Comparative Literature, Slavic Studies, Translation, Administration – the contributors to this encyclopedia suggest, by the very diversity of their affiliations, the rich variety of contemporary theory.

Yet this book in itself may be perceived as a kind of literary paradox – a strange platypus – for the beast described here not only resists classification (not an uncommon characteristic of any discipline) but even rejects the very nature of this task. Simply by being, this encyclopedia is an offence to some of the very subject-matter with which it deals – the 'new new theory' which questions the apparent tradition into which this genre of work falls: the encyclopedia. Many schools, approaches and theorists discussed here attack such 'magisterial' products, as well as presuppositions concerning the neutrality and disinterestedness of scholarship, the idea of literary canons, the transparency of language, and even the notion of clarity itself as a desirable or necessary feature of argument. Issues discussed reappear from a variety of points of view, some that overlap, others that contradict each other; all in combination suggest the contestatory nature of the current critical and theoretical scene.

Selection of entries

The present-day field of literary theory and criticism is as vast as it is varied. Though it is not meant to be complete, this volume is intended to suggest something of the immense scope of current theoretical approaches. In establishing the list of entries, the editor consulted a variety of sources, including the *PMLA* annual bibliographical listings under literary criticism and theory, the most-cited authors in the *Arts and Humanities Citation Index*, *Current Comments*, and an array of monographs and bibliographies on contemporary theory. The schools, approaches and theorists were generally selected on the basis of their most-frequently cited status. In a few other cases, such as Quebec feminism and some European approaches, the decision for inclusion was based on the desire to make more widely known to an anglophone audience the work of lesser-known but important theories.

At the core of this volume is the attempt to delineate the different kinds of approaches and schools since New Criticism, that is, the trends, tendencies and critics who have commanded attention over the past 50 years. Yet many of these approaches are grounded in earlier theoretical work. For this reason, a number of important precursors appear in this volume – Virginia Woolf, Sigmund Freud, Wilhelm Dilthey, Friedrich Nietzsche, among others – and a number of schools, such as the Neo-Aristotelians, the Russian formalists, the Prague School. While the original list of entries for this volume was considerably shorter, expansion and revision have occurred after extensive correspondence with scholars from around the world. Unfortunately, some entries had to be abandoned either when it proved impossible to find a contributor who could prepare an entry within the time constraints of the project, or, in much rarer cases, when the entry did not meet the standards of the volume.

Evaluation

Each of the entries has undergone a rigorous evaluation procedure. In some cases, this has meant that as many as nine readers commented on a single article. Revisions following these numerous reports were often extensive. The contributor alone, however, is responsible for the final version of the entry.

Organization

Constructed as both dictionary and analytic compendium, this book includes three sections designed to serve as either building blocks or as separate points of entry. Each section is alphabetically arranged.

Part 1 of this volume, 'Approaches' – 48 evaluative essays – examines the great variety of schools and approaches to literary studies, providing a sense of their historical, social and cultural contexts, an overview of the basic issues and of their major practitioners. Some of these essays examine large, systemic theories shared by scholars working in different parts of the world. Others are affiliated with particular schools (and hence with specific geographical locations) which have developed a common point of view. Still others merely share some general assumptions but employ a plethora of different methodologies. This section concludes with a bibliographical essay on the connections between theory and pedagogy. In particular, it examines the nature of the evolution of English studies as a case study of the development of literary theory.

Part 2, 'Scholars,' focuses on those who have helped transform the study of literature. The list includes not only literary theorists and critics but also historians, philosophers, linguists, social scientists, theologians, polemicists, authors. Not always neatly pigeon-holed into any particular school or approach, the work of these theorists and critics is explored and assessed.

Part 3, 'Terms,' deals with the vocabulary of literary theory. A selected list, it encompasses what Oswald Ducrot and Tzvetan Todorov have called both methodological and descriptive concepts. These have been chosen on the basis of difficulty, the frequency with which

students may encounter these terms or their centrality to an understanding of a particular theory or approach. Throughout the volume, the contributors have attempted to make the language as straightforward as possible, recognizing that here literary scholars are speaking to each other and thus are still heavily dependent upon their own dialect. Thus, the implied reader to whom this book is directed is not the general reader, but the advanced student of literature, the reader already engaged in literary criticism, and often either on the way to or already in the profession. In some cases, where the very nature of the material deliberately confounds logic, and where the theorists themselves refuse linearity of argument and espouse what used to be called a more poetic manner of writing, the density and flavour of the work have been retained. While some uniformity of style has been imposed on the entries, the individuality of the scholars has not, I hope, been entirely suppressed.

Transliteration

The transliteration of Slavic languages follows the Library of Congress system, except where bibliographical information provides alternative spellings, or when a more commonly used spelling would be more readily identified by the reader.

Directions for use

1 Articles are arranged alphabetically within each of the three sections.
2 Asterisks refer the reader to another article in the volume.
3 Bibliographies at the end of each entry suggest material for further study.

Acknowledgments

This volume is unusual in having received all of its support from the University of Ottawa. The Research Committee of the School of Graduate Studies and Research provided the initial funding for the project in late 1986. Subsequently, the Committee's additional grants were augmented by the generosity of three consecutive deans: Dr. Marcel Hamelin (now Rector of the University), Dr. Nigel Dennis, and Dr. Jean-Louis Major, who chaired the Research Committee of the Faculty of Arts.

Such assistance would not be possible without the unflagging enthusiasm and encouragement of Dr. Frank Tierney, then Chair of the Department of English, who first listened to the idea many years ago, and then convinced the appropriate committees of the necessity of their financial support. With similar zeal, Dr. David Staines, his successor, helped see the project to its completion and, like Dr. Tierney, supplied the project with much-needed graduate assistants, and with larger office space for the growing number of files.

A number of colleagues provided very helpful suggestions and criticisms. In the first few years of the project Dr. Peter McCormick was particularly invaluable in areas where the literary crossed with the philosophical. Also, much profit was derived from conversations with Professors Ina Ferris, David L. Jeffrey, Sheldon P. Zitner, Linda Hutcheon, and, especially, Camille R. La Bossière.

Instrumental to the success of this book has been the work of the members of the Advisory Board: Linda Hutcheon (Toronto), Louis Kelly (Ottawa), Patrick Imbert (Ottawa), Camille R. La Bossière (Ottawa), and Sheldon P. Zitner (Toronto), who read all of the material and made valuable comments and suggestions. They have also helped encourage this harmless drudge when my resolution became sluggish, and my patience dull.

The difficult and very important task of reading and evaluating the entries fell to Naomi Black (York), William Bonney (Mississippi), Donald J. Childs (Ottawa), J. Douglas Clayton (Ottawa), Andrew Donskov (Ottawa), David Dooley (Toronto), Ina Ferris (Ottawa), Len Findlay (Saskatchewan), Terry Goldie (York), Rosmarin Heidenreich (St. Boniface), John S. Hill (Ottawa), Nina Kolesnikoff (McMaster), Peter McCormick (Ottawa), Dominic

Manganiello (Ottawa), Reed Merrill (Washington), Heather Murray (Toronto), Bernhard Radloff (Ottawa), David Raynor (Ottawa), Ronald de Souza (Toronto), and John Thurston (Ottawa).

The English Department's Secretariat – especially Mrs. Marie Tremblay-Chénier, Mrs. Julie Sévigny-Roy and Mrs. Paula Greenwood – passed on the great many faxes, telephone messages and photocopying orders with equanimity and good humour.

Roy Gibbons, then of Research Services, set up the computer program for the project. Additional programing and a great deal of technical troubleshooting were graciously handled by Professor George White of the Computer Science Department. Mr. Roland Serrat, Computing and Communications Services, authoritatively directed the preparation of the machine-readable copy for the University of Toronto Press.

Finally, an enormous amount of credit must be given to our University of Ottawa English Department graduate students, especially Anne-Louise Gibbons, who acted as my research assistant for over three years, inputting material and making helpful suggestions of her own. Marilyn Geary took upon herself the task of making our relatively orderly filing system truly so. Rhonda Waukhonen, Steven de Paul, Debbie James, and Chris Maguire were all at one time or another involved in the tedious business of photocopying, checking and dispatching materials. Sandra Schaeken and Cheryl Ringor (from Law) acted as inputters in the last months of the project. But most thanks are due to the diligence, astonishing cheerfulness, patience, and professionalism of Micheline White, the assistant who conquered the computer and in the last year of the project brought the whole volume together. The task literally could not have been done without her.

Contributors

Adamson, Joseph (McMaster): deconstruction, *différance/différence*, grammatology, metaphysics of presence, supplementarity, white mythology, Jacques Derrida

Adey, Lionel (Victoria): C(live) S(taples) Lewis

van Alphen, Ernst (Utrecht): narratology (with Marie-Laure Ryan)

Allen, Douglas (Maine): Mircea Eliade

Anderson, Roland (Alberta): liminality (with Linda Woodbridge)

Balfour, Ian (York): synecdoche

Barasch, Frances K. (Baruch): theories of the grotesque

Baross, Zsuzsa (Trent): poststructuralism

Barsky, Robert (McGill): discourse analysis theory

Baxter, John (Dalhousie): mimesis

Beddoes, Julie (Saskatchewan): recuperation

Belleguic, Thierry (Queen's): dialogical criticism (with Clive Thomson)

Best, Steven (Texas): Jean Baudrillard

Biron, Michel (Ottawa): sociocriticism

Bonney, William (Mississippi): J(oseph) Hillis Miller

Bonnycastle, Stephen (RMC): Roland Barthes

Bowen, Deborah (Ottawa): W(illiam) K(urtz) Wimsatt, Jr.

Boyman, Anne (Barnard): Jean-François Lyotard

Brady, Kristin (Western): Simone de Beauvoir

Bristol, Michael D. (McGill): subversion

Brown, Russell (Toronto): theme

de Bruyn, Frans (Ottawa): genre criticism, Terry Eagleton, Fredric R. Jameson

Buitenhuis, Peter (Simon Fraser): Lionel Trilling

Burnham, Clint (York): Pierre Macherey

Camden, Vera J. (Kent): psychoanalytic theory

Campbell, Gregor (Toronto): imaginary/symbolic/real, *langue/parole*, mirror stage (with Gordon E. Slethaug), Name-of-the-Father,

signified/signifier/signification, structuralism, Norman N. Holland, John R. Searle

Capozzi, Rocco (Toronto): Umberto Eco

Carr, David (Emory): Hayden White

Cavell, Richard (UBC): spatial form, Antonio Gramsci

Chaitin, Gilbert D. (Indiana): metonymy/metaphor

Chamberlain, Daniel (Queen's): Oswald Ducrot, Maurice Merleau-Ponty

Childs, Donald J. (Ottawa): New Criticism

Chisholm, Dianne (Alberta): Toril Moi

Clark, Michael (California, Irvine): Michel Foucault

Cleary, Jean Coates (Victoria): Carl Gustav Jung

Collins, Robert G. (Ottawa): Cleanth Brooks

Cooke, Nathalie (McGill): closure/dis-closure

Cuddy-Keane, Melba (Toronto): Virginia Stephen Woolf

Cunningham, Valentine (Oxford): logocentrism

Danesi, Marcel (Toronto): semiosis

Diedrick, James (Albion): heteroglossia, polyphonic novel

Dimić, Milan (Alberta): polysystem theory

Doležel, Lubomír (Toronto): Semiotic Poetics of the Prague School (Prague School)

Dooley, David J. (Toronto): Jacques Maritain

Dopp, Jamie (Victoria); ideologeme, materialist criticism, metalanguage

Eggers, Walter (New Hampshire): Ernst Alfred Cassirer

Eldridge, Richard (Swarthmore): Ludwig Wittgenstein

Emerson, Caryl (Princeton): Mikhail Mikhailovich Bakhtin

Endo, Paul (Toronto): anxiety of influence, Harold Bloom

Falconer, Graham (Toronto): genetic criticism

Faraday, Nancy (Ottawa): Claude Lévi-Strauss

Fekete, John (Trent): Raymond Williams

Ferns, John (McMaster): William Empson, (Arthur) Yvor Winters

Findlay, Len (Saskatchewan): Paul Ricoeur

Fizer, John (Rutgers): Alexander A. Potebnia

Fortier, Mark (Toronto): Pierre Félix Guattari

Gallays, François (Ottawa): disnarrated, ideal reader, Gerald Prince

Gamache, Lawrence (Ottawa): D(avid) H(erbert) Lawrence

Garrett, Julia M. (California, Santa Barbara): Clifford Geertz

Gelfand, Elissa (Mount Holyoke): French feminist criticism

Godard, Barbara (York): intertextuality, Hélène Cixous, Luce Irigaray

Goellnicht, Donald C. (McMaster): Black criticism, Houston A. Baker, Jr., Henry Louis Gates, Jr.

Goldie, Terry (York): ideological horizon, post-colonial theory (with Jonathan Hart), Edward W. Said

Goodwin, David (Western): rhetorical criticism

Harris, Wendell V. (Penn. State): E(ric) D(onald) Hirsch, Jr., Robert Scholes

Hart, Jonathan (Alberta): post-colonial theory (with Terry Goldie)

Harvey, Elizabeth (Western): gynesis, trope

Harvey, Robert (Stony Brook): Jean-Paul Sartre

Hatch, Ronald B. (UBC): David Bleich

Hauch, Linda (Ottawa): diegesis

Havercroft, Barbara (Québec, Montréal): *énonciation/énoncé*, Gérard Genette

Hébert, Pierre (Sherbrooke): Claude Bremond, Jean Rousset

Heble, Ajay (Guelph): trace

Heidenreich, Rosmarin (St. Boniface): Wolfgang Iser

Henderson, Greig (Toronto): J(ohn) L(angshaw) Austin, Kenneth Duva Burke, T(homas) S(tearns) Eliot, I(vor) A(rmstrong) Richards

Henricksen, Bruce (Loyola): Murray Krieger

Hill, John Spencer (Ottawa): Wilhelm Dilthey

Holub, Robert C. (Berkeley): Constance School of Reception Aesthetics (Reception Theory), horizon of expectation, implied reader, indeterminacy, Hans Robert Jauss

Hutcheon, Linda (Toronto): postmodernism, Charles Mauron

Imbert, Patrick (Ottawa): Charles Grivel

Jeffrey, David Lyle (Ottawa): Frank Kermode, Durant Waite Robertson, Jr.

Jirgens, Karl E. (Toronto): Jacques-Marie Emile Lacan, Walter Jackson Ong

Jones, Heather (Mount Allison): patriarchy, phallocentrism

Jones, Manina (Waterloo): textuality

Keith, W.J. (Toronto): F(rank) R(aymond) Leavis

Kellner, Douglas (Texas): Marxist criticism

Kelly, Louis G. (Ottawa): theories of translation, Erich Auerbach

Kerby, Anthony (Ottawa): hermeneutics

Kidder, Richard (Toronto): Roman Jakobson

King, Ross (University College): interpellation, reification

Kneale, J. Douglas (Western): Geoffrey H. Hartman

Kolesnikoff, Nina (McMaster): defamiliarization, Russian formalism, story/plot, Boris Mikhailovich Eikhenbaum, Vladimir Iakovlevich Propp, Viktor Borisovich Shklovskii, Boris Viktorovich Tomashevskii, Iurii Nikolaevich Tynianov

Kompridis, Nikolas (York): Theodor Adorno

La Bossière, Camille R. (Ottawa): irony, paradox, (Herbert) Marshall McLuhan, Friedrich Wilhelm Nietzsche

Lacombe, Michèle (Trent): carnival

Latimer, Dan (Auburn): Paul de Man

Lawall, Sarah (Massachusetts): Geneva School, René Wellek

Lee, Alvin A. (McMaster): archetypal criticism, archetype, myth, Northrop Frye

Leenhardt, Jacques (EHESS): Lucien Goldmann

Le Grand, Eva (Québec, Montréal): kitsch, variation, Iurii Mikhailovich Lotman, Jan Mukařovský

Lehmann, Winfred P. (Texas): Ferdinand de Saussure

Leps, Marie-Christine (York): discourse

Loriggio, Francesco (Carleton): Emile Benveniste, Benedetto Croce

Loughlin, Marie H. (Queen's): bracketing, intention/intentionality, *Lebenswelt*, subject/object

McCallum, Pamela (Calgary): Walter Benjamin

McCance, Dawne (St. John's College): chora, genotext/phenotext, signifying practice, Julia Kristeva

McCracken, David (Washington): René Noel Girard

McGee, C.E. (St. Jerome's): performance criticism

Magnusson, A. Lynne (Waterloo): speech act theory

Merrill, Reed (Washington): M.H. Abrams, Henry James, Søren Aabye Kierkegaard,

Arthur Koestler, Mario Praz, Edmund Wilson

Moyal, Gabriel (McMaster): Michael Riffaterre

Moyes, Lianne (York): Sandra Mortola Gilbert and Susan David Gubar

Możejko, Edward (Alberta): constructivism, Hrvatsko filološko društvo [Croatian Philological Society], Nitra School, Polish structuralism

Murphy, Timothy S. (California, Los Angeles): Gilles Deleuze

Murray, Heather (Toronto): theory and pedagogy

Nielsen, Greg (York): communicative action, critical theory, Frankfurt School, literary institution

Noland, Richard W. (Massachusetts): Sigmund Freud

Nostbakken, Faith (Alberta): cultural materialism

O'Grady, Walter (Toronto): Percy Lubbock

O'Quinn, Daniel (York): episteme

O'Nan, Martha (SUNY): Jean Starobinski

Ouimette, Victor (McGill): José Ortega y Gasset

Paryas, Phyllis Margaret (Ottawa): character zones, double-voicing/dialogism, embedding, monologism, polyphony/dialogism

Paterson, Janet M. (Toronto): Tartu School

de Paul, Steven (Ottawa): phenomenological criticism

Perron, Paul (Toronto): A(lgirdas) J(ulien) Greimas

Prado, C.G. (Queen's): Richard Rorty

Radloff, Bernhard (Ottawa): hermeneutic circle, text, Martin Heidegger, Roman Ingarden

Ray, William (Reed College): affective stylistics, Stanley Fish, Georges Poulet

Rinehart, Hollis (York): pluralism, Elder Olson

Rivero, Maria-Luisa (Ottawa): competence/performance, Noam Avram Chomsky

Ross, Trevor (Dalhousie): aura, canon, literature

Ryan, Marie-Laure (California): code, narratee, narrative code, narratology (with Ernst van Alphen), narrator

Saim, Mirela (McGill): Georg Lukács

St. Jacques, Kelly (Ottawa): E(dward) M(organ) Forster

Savan, David (Toronto): C(harles) S(anders) Peirce

Schellenberg, Elizabeth (Simon Fraser): reader-response criticism

Seamon, Roger (UBC): Ernst Hans Josef Gombrich

Sexton, Melanie (Ottawa): code, self/other

Shea, Victor (York): New Historicism, Jonathan Dwight Culler

Siemerling, Winfried (Toronto): margin, praxis

Slethaug, Gordon E. (Waterloo): centre/de-centre, demythologizing, desire/lack, floating signifier, game theory, mirror stage (with Gregor Campbell), parody, theories of play/freeplay

Solecki, Sam (Toronto): ideology, David John Lodge, George Francis Steiner

Springer, Mary Doyle (St. Mary's College): Wayne C. Booth

Steele, James (Carleton): expressive devices, poetics of expressiveness, Tzvetan Todorov, Boris Andreevich Uspenskii, Alexander K. Zholkovskii

Stout, John (McMaster): semiotics

Straznicky, Marta (Queen's): authority, power

Thomson, Clive (Queen's): dialogical criticism (with Thierry Belleguic)

Thurston, John (Ottawa): hegemony, Ideological State Apparatuses (ISAs), overdetermination, problematic, social information, structural causality, symptomatic reading, Louis Althusser

Tomc, Sandra (UBC): Leslie A. Fiedler

Tötösy de Zepetnek, Steven (Alberta): Empirical Science of Literature (Constructivist Theory of Literature)

Trussler, Michael (Toronto): misprision

Turner, Hilary (McMaster): Maud Bodkin

Ungar, Steven (Iowa): Maurice Blanchot

Valdés, Mario J. (Toronto): aporia, binary opposition, concretization, intersubjectivity, reference/referent, Hans-Georg Gadamer, Jürgen Habermas

Vandendorpe, Christian (Ottawa): actant, classeme, isotopy, seme

Van de Pitte, Margaret (Alberta): Edmund Husserl

Vigneault, Robert (Ottawa): Gaston Bachelard

Vince, Ronald W. (McMaster): Neo-Aristotelian or Chicago School, R(onald) S(almon) Crane

Vulpe, Nicola (León): Pierre Félix Bourdieu, Galvano della Volpe

Walker, Victoria (Ottawa): Anglo-American feminist criticism (with Chris Weedon), Quebec feminist criticism

Wallace, Jo-Ann (Alberta): Elaine Showalter

Walton, Priscilla L. (Carleton): totalization

Waring, Wendy (University of Technology, Perth): essentialism

Weedon, Chris (Cardiff): Anglo-American feminist criticism (with Victoria Walker)

Contributors

Whiteside–St. Leger Lucas, Anna (McMaster):
   communication theory, hypogram, icon/
   iconology, index, sign
Wilson, Barrie A. (York): metacriticism
Woodbridge, Linda (Alberta): liminality (with
   Roland Anderson)
Zichy, Francis (Saskatchewan): pleasure/bliss,
   readerly/writerly text
Zitner, Sheldon P. (Toronto): universal

1

APPROACHES

Anglo-American feminist criticism: *see* Feminist criticism, Anglo-American

Archetypal criticism

Archetypal criticism focuses on the generic, recurring and conventional elements in *literature that cannot be explained as matters of historical influence or tradition. It studies each literary work as part of the whole of literature. This kind of criticism accepts as its informing principle that archetypes – typical images, characters, narrative designs, themes, and other literary phenomena – are present in all literature and so provide the basis for study of its interconnectedness. Sometimes called 'myth criticism,' archetypal literary criticism emerged in the 1930s, 1940s and 1950s in the work of *Maud Bodkin, Robert Graves, Joseph Campbell, G. Wilson Knight, Richard Chase, Francis Fergusson, Philip Wheelwright, *Northrop Frye, and others. It made extensive use of the ideas of social scientists, especially James G. Frazer and *Carl G. Jung. (See also *archetype, *myth.)

Frazer was one of the so-called Cambridge School of anthropologists, classicists and Middle East specialists. His massive 12-volume *The Golden Bough* (1890–1915) traces archetypal patterns of myth and ritual in the tales and ceremonies of diverse cultures. Importantly for literary criticism, Frazer tended to the view, a matter of controversy for many decades, that myth is an offshoot or projection of ritual, a narrative following or accompanying the ritual action. More recently *Claude Lévi-Strauss (1908) set aside the question of which comes first, ritual or myth. For him they were closely associated, with myth functioning on the conceptual level and ritual on the level of action. Frye went further and saw *The Golden Bough* as a 'kind of grammar of the human imagination,' 'a study of unconscious symbolism on its social side' complementing what *Sigmund Freud and Jung did with the private symbolism of dreams. For Frye the question of the origin of myth or ritual is unimportant; Frazer's work embodies an archetypal ritual from which the literary critic may logically but not chronologically derive the structural principles of naive drama. For the critic, ritual is the content not the source or origin of drama, because dramatists know that ritual is the best way of holding an audience's attention.

Archetypal criticism had a second extra-literary source in addition to cultural anthropology. It developed in part from Jung, particularly the Jungian idea of a 'collective unconscious' underlying the production of myths, visions, religious ideas, and certain kinds of dreams common to numerous cultures and periods of history. For Jung one major product of the unconscious is the hero myth, an exposition in the language of fairy tale of a child's development from infancy to adulthood. The details of this archetypal myth vary from culture to culture but the essentials are common. In Jung's writings the archetypes are not inherited by individual human beings. Rather what is passed on in the human species is a predisposition to fashion meaningful myths and symbols from the common experience of each individual life.

For Jung archetypal situations, figures, images, and ideas are thought to have powerful emotional meaning and to be expressions of typical human experience raised to a level of immense importance. In the 20 volumes of Jung's collected works numerous archetypes are mentioned or described but five have particular prominence. The archetypal mother and father figures, caused by the child's experience of parents, are paralleled by images underlying the individual's experience of the opposite sex. The *anima* is the name Jung gives to a man's image of a woman, the *animus* to a woman's image of a man. On one level these are simply personifications of erotic desire but, on another, they take on a wide range of connotations. Another archetypal figure, not clearly distinguished by Jung from the father figure but described as separate is the 'wise old man,' symbolizing intelligence, knowledge and superior insight. The 'shadow' archetype, never fully delineated in Jung, designates the negative or dark side of the individual human being, those grasping, mean, malicious, lustful, or even devilish aspects of the individual that are usually held in abeyance in mature, sane people but are given full scope in rituals, myths, religion, literature, and other art forms. The most important archetype for Jung is the '*self,' central to the process of individuation, which is his main contribution to analytic psychology and pertains to the second half of the individual's life, succeeding the 'hero myth' and its concerns with the way the individual establishes himself or herself in the world.

Jung placed the production of works of art on a lower level than the emergence of religious ideas and he was reluctant to apply his concepts to literature. Many others, who place a high value on art and literature, have made extensive use of the ideas of Jung, and Frazer as well, and have tried to show how archetypal myths lie behind all literature. Maud Bodkin, in *Archetypal Patterns in Poetry* (1934), interpreted Coleridge's *The Ancient Mariner* and *T.S. Eliot's *The Waste Land* as poems about the myth of rebirth. Robert Graves *(The White Goddess: A Historical Grammar of Poetic Myth* 1948 and *Greek Myths* 1958) attempted to demonstrate that many of the myths known to the modern world are misconstructions of pictures and sculptures of earlier myth and that an archetypal myth of a primordial Earth Mother served by males underlies all subsequent myths. Joseph Campbell, with a Jungian emphasis, considered the myth of the questing hero as the all-encompassing monomyth *(The Hero with a Thousand Faces* 1949). G. Wilson Knight, interpreter of Shakespeare and several other major English poets, made extensive use of myth, ritual and archetypal symbols. In *Fearful Symmetry* (1947) Northrop Frye interpreted Blake's poetic prophecies as coherent myths. In *The Quest for Myth* (1949) Richard Chase declared that 'myth is literature and must be considered as an aesthetic creation of the human imagination.' Francis Fergusson's *The Idea of a Theater* (1949) pointed to the rituals behind dramas from the classical Greeks until the 20th century. Philip Wheelwright used myth criticism to interpret the *Oresteia* of Aeschylus and Eliot's *The Waste Land* (*The Burning Fountain* 1954).

By the time of Frye's *Anatomy of Criticism: Four Essays* (1957) the theory and practice of archetypal criticism were well established and were capable of being placed in the context both of other schools of criticism and of a 'polysemous' theory of literary meaning. So far as Frye's account of archetypal criticism is concerned, it is important to recognize that he disengaged the concept of the literary archetype from its anthropological and psychological beginnings. For him Frazer's work is a study of the ritual basis of naive drama and Jung's work makes possible an understanding of the dream basis of naive romance. In learning from either of these pioneering thinkers, ac-

cording to Frye, the critic need not be concerned with ultimate sources in primitive ritual or a primordial unconscious, nor with questions of historical transmission. Archetypes are present in literature however they come to be there. The literary critic accepts this as a fact and goes on to use the archetypal perspective as one part of a comprehensive critical methodology.

The archetypal interconnectedness of literature has implications for considerations of an author's originality. The greatness in a literary work arises more often from the themes and images it shares with other texts than from the author's own originality. The first English poet known by name, Caedmon, was initiated, according to the Venerable Bede, into a Germanic 'word-hoard' and a biblical mythology, both of which existed prior to his career as a poet. Without both of these he had no significance as a poet. His new compositions were born into an already existing order of words. Because that order existed, his listeners understood and were deeply moved by the poems he fashioned. A new poem, from the perspective of archetypal criticism, manifests something that is already latent in the order of words. It communicates meaning because both poet and audience are members of a community in which that order already exists. Archetypal criticism, then, is concerned with texts as social facts, as involved in techniques that give imaginative focus to an existing community.

Archetypal criticism has been criticized as reductionist, as a reading of all literature in terms of a few monotonous patterns. It has also been judged negatively as blurring the boundaries between art and myth or between art and religion or philosophy. The most knowledgeable practitioners, however, like Frye, use archetypal concepts and methods as part of a larger critical and humanistic enterprise. So used, archetypal criticism is a valuable complement to other kinds of inquiry. It need not compete with historical criticism and its preoccupation with sources, influences and social context, or with biographical criticism's concern with the facts of a writer's life, because like these kinds of criticism it recognizes the importance of learned associations in literary experience. It may be of major assistance in the study of literary genres, which is based on analogies of form and proceeds on the hypothesis that whatever connections a literary work has with life, reality, the physical world, society, or philosophy for its content, it is not fashioned from these things. (See *genre criticism.) The literary work takes its form or shape or design from other literature, thus illustrating a central principle of archetypal criticism: works of literature imitate other works of literature.

Archetypal criticism complements close reading of texts as things in themselves, the special concern of the *New Criticism that developed from the 1920s. It sits, less easily, beside Leavisite evaluative criticism (see *F.R. Leavis) since archetypal criticism easily includes the popular and the naive as well as the complex sophisticated works of the traditional *canon. In a major sense, archetypal criticism, especially as articulated and practised by Frye, anticipates or prepares the way for *structuralism. When the work of the French structuralists emerged, saying that language in fact constructs our reality rather than reflects it, it had much in common with archetypal criticism. Similarly, the recognition in archetypal theory that the author does not control the whole meaning of his or her text prepared the way for what has come to be called *reader-response criticism, with its emphasis on the reader as a source of meaning-giving, a source conditioned by cultural experience, conscious or unconscious, by social and sexual roles, by ideological assumptions, and so on. Now, late in the 20th century, archetypal criticism is still widely used, especially in genre criticism and in those intertextual and comparative studies that include recognition and analysis of persistent, recurrent literary phenomena that cannot be adequately explained in terms of one particular historical tradition.

ALVIN A. LEE

Primary Sources

Bodkin, Maud. *Archetypal Patterns in Poetry: Psychological Studies of Imagination*. London: Oxford UP, 1934.

Campbell, Joseph. *The Hero with a Thousand Faces*. New York: Pantheon Books, 1949.

Chase, Richard. *The Quest for Myth*. Baton Rouge: Louisiana State UP, 1949.

Day, Martin S. *The Many Meanings of Myth*. Lanham, New York, London: University Presses of America, 1984.

Fergusson, Francis. *The Idea of a Theater, a Study of Ten Plays: The Art of Drama in Changing Perspective*. Princeton: Princeton UP, 1949.

Frazer, James G. *The Golden Bough: A Study in Magic and Religion*. 12 vols. London: Macmillan, 1890–1915. Abr. in 1 vol., 1954.

Frye, Northrop. *Anatomy of Criticism: Four Essays*. Princeton: Princeton UP, 1957.

– *Fearful Symmetry: A Study of William Blake*. Princeton: Princeton UP, 1947.

Graves, Robert. *Greek Myths*. London: Cassell, 1958.

– *The White Goddess: A Historical Grammar of Poetic Myths*. Amended and enl. ed. New York/London: Vintage Books/Faber and Faber, 1961.

Jung, Carl G. *Collected Works*. 20 vols. London: Routledge and Kegan Paul, 1953–79.

Knight, G. Wilson. *The Imperial Theme: Further Interpretations of Shakespeare's Tragedies, including the Roman Plays*. 3rd ed., repr. with minor corrections. London: Methuen, 1963.

– *The Starlit Dome: Studies in the Poetry of Vision*. London: Methuen, 1959.

– *The Wheel of Fire: Interpretations of Shakespearean Tragedy*. 4th rev. and enl. ed. London: Methuen, 1959.

Wheelwright, Philip. *The Burning Fountain: A Study in the Language of Symbolism*. New and rev. ed. Bloomington: Indiana UP, 1968.

Black criticism

Black criticism in its narrowest sense encompasses the study of African American literature, culture and theory, but in its broadest includes the study of certain post-colonial literatures and cultures (African and Caribbean) and overlaps with the feminist concerns of women of colour. (See *post-colonial theory, *feminist criticism, *literature.) Underlying all black criticism is the assumption that 'race' is a fundamental category of literary and cultural analysis (just as the broad range of feminisms takes gender to be a fundamental category of analysis). But exactly what constitutes race is not agreed upon; increasingly, it is viewed as less an essential or biological category than a social construct in which 'blackness' becomes a subject position in relation to the cultural dominant ('whiteness' or Euro-Americanism). Valerie Smith's definition of black feminist theory can usefully be adapted to define black theory: 'a way of reading inscriptions of race (particularly but not exclusively blackness) ... in modes of cultural expression' ('Black Feminist Theory' 39).

Origins and development

Black criticism, albeit without this title, has a fairly long tradition in American letters. Early examples include the work of the historian-sociologist W.E.B. Du Bois, whose concept of the 'double consciousness' of the African American remains influential today; Alain Locke (editor of the journal *The New Negro*) and the theorists of the Harlem Renaissance, who supported Pan-Africanism and saw art as a way of defining a black identity and fostering racial pride; Zora Neale Hurston, whose collecting and championing of black folklore when others were predicting its demise provided an invaluable service to American culture; and Ralph Ellison, whose *Shadow and Act* still elicits responses from more recent critics.

Black criticism as practised under that designation began to flourish in the 1960s 'along with the radicalization of the word "Black" and the emergence of the Black Power philosophy' (Henderson 'The Question of Form' 24). Since then, black criticism has taken a variety of forms, often grounding itself in other approaches but always revising them according to its own concerns and agendas. As *Henry Louis Gates, Jr., observes: 'The challenge of black literary criticism is to derive principles of literary criticism from the black tradition itself, as defined in the idiom of critical theory but also in the idiom which constitutes the "language of blackness" ... The sign of the successful negotiation of this precipice of indenture, of slavish imitation, is that the black critical essay refers to two contexts, two traditions – the Western and the black' (*Black Literature and Literary Theory* 8). To explore black cultural difference, critics must redefine 'theory' – which is not neutral – by turning to the black vernacular tradition for models (Gates 'Canon-Formation' 28). Barbara Christian argues that 'people of color have always theorized – but in forms quite different from the Western form of abstract logic. And I am inclined to say that our theorizing ... is often in narrative forms, in the stories we create, in riddles and proverbs, in the play with language' ('The Race for Theory' 226). (See *theories of play/free-play.)

Although the variety of African American criticism practised at any given time makes it difficult to trace a simple historical development, *Houston A. Baker, among others, has sketched broad 'generational shifts' in this criticism over the past 40 years (*Blues, Ideology* 68–112). The first stage, from the mid-1950s to the early 1960s, Baker labels a period of 'integrationist poetics,' characterized by a faith that recent landmark legislative and judicial decisions in the United States signalled the advent of social equality in America. In such a soon-to-be raceless, classless, pluralistic, democratic society, according to these optimistic critics, black American cultural forms would be integrated into the artistic mainstream; accordingly, any sense of a separate black tradition would rightly disappear, along with the belief that separate forms of cultural expression might call for separate standards of critical judgment. The proponents of 'integrationist poetics' included Richard Wright ('The Literature of the Negro in the United States'), Arthur P. Davis ('Integration and Race Literature') and Sterling Brown; even James Baldwin, no simple 'integrationist,' claimed at the time that black writers needed to appropriate the Western white cultural heritage in order to make their own romantic voyage of self-discovery.

The obvious failure of legal and political decisions and of the peaceful civil-rights movement in the American South to bring about meaningful social change resulted by the mid-1960s in the adoption of a much more militant stance against the dominant white *ideology and the development of a decidedly revolutionary, Afro-centred ideology known as 'Black Power.' As defined by Stokely Carmichael and Charles V. Hamilton, Black Power 'is a call for black people in this country to unite, to recognize their heritage, to build a sense of community. It is a call for black people to begin to define their own goals, to lead their own organizations and to support those organizations' (*Black Power* 44). The cultural wing of the Black Power movement was the Black Arts Movement, led by artists like Amiri Baraka (formerly LeRoi Jones) who founded the outdoor Harlem Black Arts Repertory Theater School in 1965 as a way of fostering and promoting the expressive forms, the art, of black Americans (jazz, blues, field hollers, work songs, spirituals, folk tales, and so on). Art, according to activists like Baraka, was to be used to further the social and political aims of African Americans. As Larry Neal states in his now-famous essay 'The Black Arts Movement': 'the Black Arts Movement proposes a radical reordering of the western cultural aesthetic. It proposes a separate symbolism, mythology, critique, and iconology' (*The Black Aesthetic* 272). Baraka's theatre school and Neal's rhetoric provided the model for revolutionary black cultural groups which sprang up across urban America and found outlets for their voices in such journals as *Black Scholar, Umbra, Black Dialogue,* and *Journal of Black Poetry.* The advent of wide interest in a distinctly black cultural heritage also gave rise to the establishment of Black Studies programs at many American universities in the late 1960s.

The theory of the Black Aesthetic reached a high point in Stephen Henderson's essay 'The Form of Things Unknown,' which claims that the 'commodity "blackness"' is most evident in black poetry and that such poetry can be truly appreciated only by a black-reference public or audience: 'the ultimate criteria for critical evaluation must be found in ... the Black Community itself' (66). Such 'folk,' by virtue of being in touch with their 'ethnic roots,' are fully immersed in and cognizant of the cultural codes (the 'Soul Field') necessary to comprehend and judge black poetry. These notions of cultural relativity, borrowed in part from anthropology, deny the existence of any 'universal' standards of literary judgment. (See *universal.)

Like its predecessor 'integrationist poetics,' the Black Aesthetic was overtaken by failure to achieve its own goals: despite the surge of interest in black history, culture and expressive forms, no separate black 'nation' came into being. The Black Arts Movement did not ultimately move audiences to revolutionary action and by the mid-1970s critics were accusing the movement of chauvinism, introspection and Marxist rhetoric. Neal himself was one of the first to recognize that art had failed to bring about social and political change. In a reassessment of the movement, 'The Black Contribution to American Letters,' he claims that the Black Aesthetic is a 'Marxist literary theory in which the concept of race is substituted for the Marxist idea of class.' (See *Marxist criticism.) He concludes that 'through propaganda alone the black writer can never perform the highest function of his art: that of revealing to man his most enduring human possibilities and limitations' (783–4). Neal had come full circle to Baldwin's romantic idealism; at the same time, he called for more rigorous attention to the uniqueness of expressive form in black art, a call later echoed by Stephen Henderson in 'The Question of Form and Judgement.'

After 1975 – ironically at the very time formalism in both its guises of *New Criticism and *structuralism was coming under attack in the academy – a concern with the 'literariness' or formal properties of African American writing achieved the ascendancy, as scholars sought a solid theoretical ground for black expressive culture. This shift coincided with the movement of much African American literary study out of interdisciplinary Black Studies programs (where it had been treated like history or sociology) into mainstream English departments, where its existence needed to be justified in formal terms and where, through the 1980s, it replaced black history as the dominant area of Black Studies. Scholars now examined the 'blackness' of texts through their uses of language; political and ideological concerns were deliberately subordinated to formalist issues, leading some radical scholars to view this move towards professionalism as a capitulation to the standards of white academia by an emerging black middle class more concerned with higher education than with revolutionary change. The 'reconstruction of instruction,' as it came to be called, was initiated by a number of significant conferences and resultant books. Three especially influential texts were *Minority Language and Literature* (1977), edited by Dexter Fisher, *Afro-American Literature: The Reconstruction of Instruction* (1979), edited by Dexter Fisher and Robert Stepto, and *English Literature: Opening Up the Canon* (1981), edited by *Leslie Fiedler and Houston Baker.

These books brought together the work of a new generation of scholars, including Mary Helen Washington, Generva Smitherman, Houston Baker, Robert Stepto, Kimberly Benston, Addison Gayle, Henry Louis Gates, Sherley Ann Williams, and Arnold Rampersad. All three volumes sought to revise the narrow *canon of American literature so as to make it more inclusive and representative of a pluralistic, multicultural society, while Addison Gayle's 'Blueprint for Black Criticism' called for the creation of 'positive' black characters who could combat 'the stereotypes of blacks' (44). The Fisher-Stepto collection also focused on 'a "literary" [formalist-structuralist] understanding of the literature' (vii). The Fiedler-Baker collection went a step further, however, by attacking the notion that the English language itself is a neutral container of cultural forms; language is marked as a political tool with ideological ramifications that need to be exposed and explicated, so that the study of black literature begins to move once more from a formalist to a poststructuralist stage sometimes referred to as a 'new black aesthetic' (Gates *PMLA* 21). (See *poststructuralism.*)

As Gates observes, in the work of these recent critics 'an initial phase of theorizing has given way to the generation of close readings that attend to the "social text" as well ... Black studies has functioned as a strategic site for autocritique within American studies itself. No longer, for example, are the concepts of "black" and "white" thought to be preconstituted; rather, they are mutually constitutive and socially produced' (*PMLA* 21). Gates himself has been at the forefront of promoting this type of criticism, both in his own work like *The Signifying Monkey* – which traces the relationship between African and African American vernacular traditions and cultural forms – and in his numerous editorial projects like *Black Literature and Literary Theory* and '*Race,' Writing, and Difference*. Gates raises such questions as the relationship between African cultural and Western mainstream cultural traditions, the relationship between the black vernacular and the black formal traditions, and the applicability of contemporary literary theory – particularly poststructuralism – to the reading of black texts.

The only other male critic to rival Gates' position of dominance in contemporary black criticism is Houston Baker who, while adopting strategies he finds useful from the 'reconstruction' project, nevertheless clings strongly to a neo-Marxist insistence on the contextualizing of literature. In *Blues, Ideology, and Afro-American Literature*, Baker builds what he calls an anthropology of art which insists 'that works of Afro-American expressive culture cannot be adequately understood unless they are contextualized within the interdependent systems of Afro-American culture' (109). *Modernism and the Harlem Renaissance* and *Afro-American Poetics* are further instalments in this project.

None of this theorizing would be possible, however, without the painstaking archaeological work that has, over the past decade, unearthed a host of 'lost' texts that now form the canon of African American literature. Examples – by no means exhaustive – of such recuperative projects include William L. Andrews' edi-

tions of African American autobiographies, especially slave narratives; *The Schomburg Library of 19th-Century Black Women Writers* (Oxford) series, under the general editorship of Henry Louis Gates, who is also the editor of G.K. Hall's *African American Women Writers* series, the director of Chadwyck-Healey's *Black Periodical Fiction* project, and the chief editor of the *Norton Anthology of Afro-American Literature*; and new editions of the works of many older black women writers, as well as more general anthologies, edited by feminist scholars like Mary Helen Washington (editor of *Black-Eyed Susans, Midnight Birds* and *Invented Lives*), Deborah E. McDowell (editor of the *Black Women Writers* series for Beacon Press), Gloria T. Hull (co-editor of *All the Women are White*), and Barbara Smith (editor of *Home Girls*). These projects – together with critical studies like Andrews' *To Tell a Free Story*, Bernard Bell's *The Afro-American Novel and Its Tradition*, and Barbara Christian's *Black Women Novelists* – have been instrumental in establishing alternative literary histories within American culture.

Black feminist criticism

One of the most active areas – some might claim the most active area – of recent black criticism is black feminist criticism, which has experienced an explosion of theory and practice over the past 20 years, and especially during the last decade, as a direct result of the growing critical acclaim for African American women writers such as Alice Walker, Toni Morrison and Gloria Naylor (who, between them, have won Pulitzer Prizes and National and American Book Awards), Paule Marshall, Gayl Jones, Ntozake Shange, Toni Cade Bambara, and Jamaica Kincaid, and the poets Gwendolyn Brooks, Nikki Giovanni, Audre Lorde, and Rita Dove. Black women writers have themselves played prominent roles in such criticism: Alice Walker has fought hard for the recuperation and recognition of a long tradition of black women writers within which she can discover a theory of black female creativity (*In Search of Our Mothers' Gardens*), while Audre Lorde – before it became widely accepted – remarked, in essays like 'The Master's Tools Will Never Dismantle the Master's House,' on the importance of developing and valorizing female language and emotional knowledge.

Black feminist criticism and theory emerged in the 1980s from the complex and conflicted relationship of black women to black men during the Black Power and civil-rights movement of the 1960s, and of women of colour to white women during the Women's Liberation Movement of the 1970s. Many black women recognized that while the Black Power movement was radically Afrocentric, it also remained powerfully androcentric, with the liberation of women within the group being subordinated to the aspirations of the group as a whole. The feminist movement seemed to offer some redress but women of colour increasingly saw that the concerns and standards of the movement were those of white, middle-class women who tended to ignore the different needs and desires of women of colour and Third World women. Powerful expressions of these arguments are found in bell hooks' *Ain't I a Woman: Black Women and Feminism* and Michelle Wallace's *Black Macho and the Myth of the Superwoman*. Perhaps the most influential – certainly the most galvanizing – work of black feminist criticism to date has been Barbara Smith's essay 'Toward a Black Feminist Criticism' (1977). Lamenting the fact that 'Black women's existence, experience and culture and the brutally complex systems of oppression which shape these are in the "real world" of white and/or male consciousness beneath consideration, invisible, unknown' (168), Smith proclaimed that 'a Black feminist approach to literature that embodies the realization that the politics of sex as well as the politics of race and class are crucially interlocking factors in the works of Black women writers is an absolute necessity' (170).

Despite the essentialist flaws in her argument – black feminist criticism is now practised by a number of critics who are neither female nor black – Smith's essay gave a name and a direction to this literary movement; it also championed the cause of black lesbian writing. Following Smith's lead, black feminist criticism has become increasingly theoretical and more sophisticated, although the whole question of theory versus practice remains a contentious one in black feminist circles. Barbara Christian, for example, in 'The Race for Theory' argues passionately against critical theory, which she claims now dominates the academy in hegemonic fashion: 'some of our most daring and potentially radical critics (and by *our* I mean black, women, Third World)

have been influenced, even co-opted, into speaking a language and defining their discussion in terms alien to and opposed to our needs and orientation' (226). Joyce A. Joyce has attacked Gates and Baker for moving into the sphere of ivy-league elitism, where the former is too influenced by *deconstruction (*Jacques Derrida and *Paul de Man) and the latter by poststructuralist Marxism (*Michel Foucault, *Jean Baudrillard, *Louis Althusser).

Still, some of the best recent black feminist criticism is what we would call highly theoretical; examples include the work of Hortense Spillers, Hazel Carby, Susan Willis, and Deborah McDowell. Warning against the simplifications of a linear historiography, Spillers challenges the notion of a unified, intertextual 'tradition' of African American women's writing, which she retheorizes as 'a matrix of literary discontinuities' (*Conjuring* 251). (See *intertextuality.) Similarly, Carby advocates that 'black feminist criticism be regarded as a problem, not a solution, as a sign that should be interrogated, a locus of contradictions' (*Reconstructing Womanhood* 15) in which the identity and experience of black womanhood must be seen as polyvalent, shifting, even self-contradictory. (See *sign.) She examines the material conditions under which black women intellectuals produced their work in order to explore how they represented the sexual ideologies of their times. McDowell also sees black women's *discourse as supremely dialogical, while Willis brings poststructuralist theories of *cultural materialism to bear in establishing historical contexts for black women's literature. (See also *double-voicing/dialogism.) As Valerie Smith points out, all of these approaches view black women's oppression as specific and complex and their methodologies examine the variables of race, gender and class without proclaiming the centrality of any one. At the same time, they challenge the traditional conceptions of literary study by making such questions important to literary analysis ('Black Feminist Theory' 46–7).

The significance of black/African American criticism and of black feminist criticism is manifold. As well as providing close readings of individual texts and the works of individual authors, black criticism has been instrumental in questioning the American canon and providing alternative lines of literary inheritance and literary tradition. Together with feminism, it has launched an assault on traditional ways of studying English and has thus repoliticized the 'institution' of English itself. Black feminist critics have also been in the vanguard of those challenging the totalizing tendencies of Western academic feminism (see *totalization). They have demonstrated that the very concept of woman is far more various than the mainstream may have thought and have presented black women's experience as an exemplary site both for rematerializing black critical theory and for examining the shifting positionality of the female subject. Finally, the acceptance of black literature and criticism as valid and important enterprises has paved the way for the introduction of a host of other ethnic and/or 'minority' literatures – Asian American, Chicano, Native American, gay, Third World – into the academy.

DONALD C. GOELLNICHT

Primary Sources

Andrews, William L. *To Tell a Free Story: The First Century of Afro-American Autobiography, 1760–1865.* Urbana: U of Illinois P, 1986.

Awkward, Michael. *Inspiriting Influences: Tradition, Revision, and Afro-American Women's Novels.* New York: Columbia UP, 1989.

Baker, Houston A., Jr. *Afro-American Poetics: Revisions of Harlem and the Black Aesthetic.* Madison: U of Wisconsin P, 1988.

– *Blues, Ideology, and Afro-American Literature: A Vernacular Theory.* Chicago and London: U of Chicago P, 1984.

– *The Journey Back: Issues in Black Literature and Criticism.* Chicago and London: U of Chicago P, 1980.

– *Modernism and the Harlem Renaissance.* Chicago and London: U of Chicago P, 1987.

– and Patricia Redmond. *Afro-American Literary Study in the 1990s.* Chicago and London: U of Chicago P, 1989.

Baldwin, James. *Nobody Knows My Name: More Notes of a Native Son.* New York: Delta, 1962.

– *Notes of a Native Son.* 1955. Boston: Beacon P, 1961.

Baraka, Amiri. 'The Myth of a "Negro Literature." ' In *Home: Social Essays.* New York: William Morrow, 1966.

– and Larry Neal, eds. *Black Fire: An Anthology of Afro-American Writing.* New York: William Morrow, 1968.

Bell, Bernard W. *The Afro-American Novel and Its Tradition.* Amherst: U of Massachusetts P, 1987.

Bell, Roseann P., Bettye J. Parker, and Beverly Guy-Sheftall, eds. *Sturdy Black Bridges: Visions of Black Women in Literature.* Garden City, NY: Anchor, 1979.

Black American Literature Forum (a journal).

Brown, Sterling, Arthur P. Davis, and Ulysses Lee, eds. *The Negro Caravan: Writings by American Negroes.* New York: Dryden P, 1941.

Cade, Toni, ed. *The Black Woman, An Anthology.* New York: Signet, 1970.

Callaloo (a journal).

Carby, Hazel V. *Reconstructing Womanhood: The Emergence of the Afro-American Woman Novelist.* New York: Oxford UP, 1987.

Carmichael, Stokely, and Charles V. Hamilton. *Black Power: The Politics of Liberation in America.* New York: Vintage, 1967.

Christian, Barbara. *Black Feminist Criticism.* New York: Pergamon P, 1985.

– *Black Women Novelists: The Development of a Tradition, 1892–1976.* Westport, Conn.: Greenwood P, 1980.

– 'The Race for Theory.' In *Gender and Theory: Dialogues on Feminist Criticism.* Ed. Linda Kauffman. Oxford: Basil Blackwell, 1989, 225–37.

Davis, Arthur P. 'Integration and Race Literature.' In *The American Negro Writer and His Roots.* New York: American Society of African Culture, 1960.

Du Bois, W.E.B. *The Souls of Black Folk: Essays and Sketches.* 1903. Greenwich, Conn.: Crest, 1965.

Ellison, Ralph. *Shadow and Act.* 1964. New York: Signet, 1966.

Evans, Mari. *Black Women Writers, 1950–1980: A Critical Evaluation.* New York: Anchor P, 1984.

Fiedler, Leslie, and Houston A. Baker, Jr., eds. *English Literature: Opening Up the Canon.* Baltimore: Johns Hopkins UP, 1981.

Fisher, Dexter, ed. *Minority Language and Literature: Retrospective and Perspective.* New York: MLA, 1977.

– and Robert B. Stepto, eds. *Afro-American Literature: The Reconstruction of Instruction.* New York: MLA, 1979.

Gates, Henry Louis, Jr. 'Canon-Formation and the Afro-American Tradition.' In *Afro-American Literary Study in the 1990s.* Ed. Houston A. Baker, Jr., and Patricia Redmond. Chicago and London: U of Chicago P, 1989, 14–39.

– *Figures in Black: Words, Signs, and the 'Racial' Self.* New York: Oxford UP, 1987.

– *The Signifying Monkey: A Theory of Afro-American Literary Criticism.* New York: Oxford UP, 1988.

– ed. *Black Literature and Literary Theory.* New York: Methuen, 1984.

– ed. *PLMA* 105 (Jan. 1990). Special issue on African and African American Literature.

– ed. *'Race,' Writing, and Difference.* Chicago and London: U of Chicago P, 1985–6.

– ed. *Reading Black, Reading Feminist: A Critical Anthology.* New York: Meridian, 1990.

Gayle, Addison, Jr. ed. 'Blueprint for Black Criticism.' *First World* (Jan.–Feb. 1977): 41–5.

– *The Black Aesthetic.* Garden City, NY: Doubleday, Anchor, 1972.

Henderson, Stephen. 'The Form of Things Unknown.' In *Understanding the New Black Poetry*. New York: William Morrow, 1973, 1–69.

– 'The Question of Form and Judgement in Contemporary Black American Poetry, 1962–1977.' In *A Dark and Sudden Beauty: Two Essays on Black American Poetry by George Kent and Stephen Henderson*. Ed. Houston A. Baker, Jr. Philadelphia: Afro-American Studies Program of the University of Pennsylvania, 1977.

Hernton, Calvin C. *The Sexual Mountain and Black Women Writers*. New York: Doubleday, Anchor, 1987.

hooks, bell. *Ain't I a Woman: Black Women and Feminism*. Boston: South End P, 1981.

Hughes, Langston. 'The Negro Artist and the Racial Mountain.' *Nation*, 23 June 1926, 692–4.

– and Arna Bontemps, eds. *The Book of Negro Folklore*. New York: Dodd, Mead, 1958.

Hull, Gloria T., Patricia Bell-Scott, and Barbara Smith, eds. *All the Women Are White, All the Blacks Are Men, But Some of Us Are Brave: Black Women's Studies*. Old Westbury, NY: Feminist P, 1982.

Hurston, Zora Neale. *Dust Tracks on a Road*. 1942. New York: Lippincott, 1971.

Joyce, Joyce A. ' "Who the Cap Fit": Unconsciousness and Unconscionableness in the Criticism of Houston A. Baker, Jr. and Henry Louis Gates, Jr.' *New Literary History* 18 (1987): 371–84.

Locke, Alain, ed. *The New Negro*. 1925. New York: Atheneum, 1968.

Lorde, Audre. 'The Master's Tools Will Never Dismantle the Master's House.' In *Sister Outsider*. Trumansburg, NY: Crossing P, 1984, 110–13.

McDowell, Deborah E. 'Boundaries: Or Distant Relations and Close Kin.' In *Afro-American Literary Study in the 1990s*. Ed. Houston A. Baker, Jr., and Patricia Redmond. Chicago and London: U of Chicago P, 1989, 51–70.

– 'New Directions for Black Feminist Criticism.' In *The New Feminist Criticism*. Ed. Elaine Showalter. New York: Pantheon, 1985, 186–99.

Neal, Larry. 'The Black Arts Movement.' In *The Black Aesthetic*. Ed. Addison Gayle, Jr. New York: Doubleday, 1971.

– 'The Black Contribution to American Letters: Part II, The Writer as Activist – 1960 and After.' In *The Black American Reference Book*. Ed. Mabel M. Smythe. Englewood Cliffs, NJ: Prentice-Hall, 1976, 781–4.

Smith, Barbara. 'Toward a Black Feminist Criticism.' 1977. In *The New Feminist Criticism*. Ed. Elaine Showalter. New York: Pantheon, 1985, 168–85.

– ed. *Home Girls: A Black Feminist Anthology*. New York: Kitchen Table/Women of Color P, 1983.

Smith, Valerie. 'Black Feminist Theory and the Representation of the "Other." ' In *Changing Our Own Words*. Ed. Cheryl A. Wall. New Brunswick and London: Rutgers UP, 1989, 38–57.

– *Self-Discovery and Authority in Afro-American Narrative*. Cambridge, Mass.: Harvard UP, 1987.

Soyinka, Wole. *Myth, Literature and the African World*. Cambridge: Cambridge UP, 1976.

Spillers, Hortense J., and Marjorie Pryse, eds. *Conjuring: Black Women, Fiction, and Literary Tradition*. Bloomington: Indiana UP, 1985.

Stepto, Robert B. *From Behind the Veil: A Study of Afro-American Narrative*. Urbana: U of Illinois P, 1979.

Tate, Claudia, ed. *Black Women Writers at Work*. New York: Continuum, 1983.

Walker, Alice. *In Search of Our Mothers' Gardens*. New York: Harcourt, Brace, Jovanovich, 1983.

Wall, Cheryl A., ed. *Changing Our Own Words: Essays on Criticism, Theory, and Writing by Black Women*. New Brunswick and London: Rutgers UP, 1989.

Wallace, Michelle. *Black Macho and the Myth of the Superwoman*. London: Calder, 1979.

Washington, Mary Helen, ed. *Black-Eyed Susans: Classic Stories by and about Black Women*. Garden City, NY: Doubleday, Anchor, 1975.

– *Invented Lives: Narratives of Black Women, 1860–1960*. Garden City, NY: Doubleday, 1987.

– *Midnight Birds: Stories of Contemporary Black Women Writers*. New York: Doubleday, Anchor, 1980.

Willis, Susan. *Specifying: Black Women Writing the American Experience*. Madison: U of Wisconsin P, 1987.

Wright, Richard. 'Blueprint for Negro Writing.' *New Challenge* 2 (Fall 1937): 53–65.

– 'The Literature of the Negro in the United States.' In *White Man, Listen!* Garden City, NY: Anchor, 1964, 69–105.

Chicago School: *see* Neo-Aristotelian or Chicago School

Communication theory

A vast subject, communication theory deals with systems and models of communication ranging from communications engineering to psycholinguistics and is related to a host of far-ranging fields (such as cybernetics, computer science, telemetry, *semiotics, neurology). The linguistic models are most relevant to literary theory.

Communication, as defined by the linguist John Lyons, is 'the intentional transmission of information by means of some established signalling-system.' All communications models account for the transmission of a signal or message between a sender and a receiver in some mutually decipherable *code. Shannon and Weaver's now classic model represents communication as a *signal transmitted* from a *source* by a *transmitter* through a *channel*. The signal is received by a *receiver* which relays it to its *destination*. The signal may be altered by 'noise' (defined as any information loss occurring in the channel of communication). In *Ferdinand de Saussure's model, the source is the brain, where the concept occurs before being translated into a sound image and transmitted by the voice. The ear is the receiver and the destination the brain, which decodes the signal into concepts. Transmitter and receiver may be far more complex. For example, an actor saying 'Is this a dagger which I see before me ...?' involves a transmitter which adds the conversion into a *text and the actor's articulation of it; the receiver is here expanded to include the deciphering of the written text. The ultimate destination in this case would be the audience or rather the mind of each spectator-listener. One might also add a further level of encoding and decoding to account for a producer's particular interpretation; lighting effects, make-up, costume, accent and inflexion, and sound effects would further add to the complexity of transmission, as would translation into another language. In the latter case the original sender (the author) and the ultimate receiver (the listener) do not share the same linguistic code.

The more levels of encoding and decoding added, the greater the possibility of 'noise' interfering with communication, since communication implies meaning for the sender and for the receiver (even if these meanings do not coincide). 'Noise' may be a gap, a distortion, creating confusion as to sound, code, context, or meaning. For example, communication in a novel may be temporarily suspended by a gap between chapters or a sudden switch in point of view, place or time, forcing the reader to deduce what is missing. In a thriller, conflicting versions may upset communication. Ambiguity or polyvalence may give rise to parallel levels of communication which may vie with or mutually enhance each other: an actress who says she is leaving, but signals by her movements or tone of voice that she is intent on staying, may first appear to defy the sense of the communication and, subsequently, to communicate that this departure is metaphysical rather than physical, that she does not mean what she says; in short, she may communicate, even if it is not the message we originally thought it was.

Despite interference, meaning may be retroactively restored. Thus a poem of seemingly unconnected sentences which at first fails to connect or communicate anything may, by the time we reach its end, communicate as the pieces fall into place in a recognizable pattern of meaning. Then, at last, we may see them as variants of the same matrix, as the expression of a *hypogram.

The model of linguistic communication most frequently used in literary analysis is probably *Roman Jakobson's. It comprises six elements: an *addresser* sending a *message* in a particular *code* and implying a *context*, to an *addressee* by means of some form of *contact*. For Jakobson meaning resides in the total act of communication. Otherwise, how do we know what deictics and shifters such as 'this,' 'here,' 'now,' 'then,' 'she,' 'it,' 'I,' refer to? How are we to interpret, for example, 'red'? Is it part of a traffic code addressed by a traffic operator to highway users, by sailors to show their port? Or is it part of a different code used in a different context to signify danger or passion? To account for all the factors which contribute to communication, Jakobson describes six functions corresponding to the six elements of his communication model: emotive, phatic, referential, metalinguistic, conative, poetic. The emotive function dominates when the addresser or implied 'I' expresses his emotions, as in a first-person narration or lyric poetry. If contact is being established, tested or maintained without there being any substance to the message, then the phatic function dominates. Such is the case when we say 'Hello,' 'How are you?,' or make comments about the weather: we are primarily establishing or maintaining contact, rather than wanting to communicate any message. Ionesco's cliché-ridden empty dialogue makes extensive use of the phatic function, showing how his characters are no longer capable of true communication. The referential function identifies the context so that, for example, we know that 'bat' refers in a given instance to a flying mouse-like animal and not to a baseball bat. The code is enhanced when the metalinguistic function comes to the fore, as it would if, for example, one wished to determine that 'bat' is an English word here, and not, say, French. If communication centres on the addressee, the conative (or vocative) function dominates, as in expressions like 'Look here,' 'Listen!' 'You there!' When communication accentuates the message, the poetic (or aesthetic) function is uppermost. This poetic function is paramount in literary texts and accounts for the special self-conscious quality of literary discourse, drawing attention to itself as form to further enhance the message, so that the form is the message. Verbal art, says Jakobson, is not a transparent window on the outside world, but is opaque and self-referential: it is its own subject. *Roland Barthes goes a step further by saying that form is the ultimate literary referent. (See *reference/referent.)

*Speech act theory is yet another aspect of communication theory, and deals primarily with speech production. In literary theory it accounts for the factors associated with discourse production, the way these are encoded in the text, the signs by which the receiver discerns them, and how they influence reception. (See *discourse, *sign.) *John L. Austin, *Emile Benveniste and Peter Strawson were among the first to show how speech act theory could be applied to textual analysis. *John Searle has developed their ideas.

Important aspects of speech act theory are the central role of 'I' (the utterer producing the utterance), the relationship between the utterer and (1) what he is talking about, and (2) the person to whom he is talking. Speech act theory takes into account situational (spatio-temporal) factors, mood and types of utterance. According to Austin these types are constative (statements) or performative (they accomplish an act: e.g. 'I promise'). Utterances can be serious or non-serious (fictional). Fictional utterances seem to have all the attributes of non-fictional ones, except for the understanding between writer and reader that the fictional utterance is a 'non-deceptive pseudo-performance,' to use Searle's expression. Within this framework, *Gérard Genette examines the relationship between different levels of fictional utterances, as when tales are told within tales and between their concomitant narrators and narratees. (See *narrator, narratee.)

Austin distinguishes three speech acts: (1) locutionary (the spoken act); (2) illocutionary (the act performed in saying something, e.g. asking, ordering, asserting); and (3) perlocutionary (the act performed indirectly by saying something; e.g. 'it's cold in here' could be a way of persuading someone to shut the door or turn up the heat).

French speech act theorists tend to represent relationships between utterer and utterance, utterer and receiver, receiver and utterance in terms of four concepts: (1) distance (the speaker may distance himself from his utterance by using the third person; e.g. 'He did it.'); (2) adherence (the utterer indicates his attitude by means of modalisors; e.g. 'doubtless,' 'horrifying,' 'it seemed ...,' 'perhaps,' and other indications of judgment); (3) transparency or opaqueness (the receiver's absence from or presence in the utterance – the more intimate the utterance [e.g. a letter to a friend] the more opaque it will be); and (4) tension (the dynamics between utterer and receiver).

Communication theory inevitably implies many related fields. Among these *structuralism, semiotics, poetics and *discourse analysis theory are some of the most obvious of interest to scholars of *literature.

ANNA WHITESIDE–ST. LEGER LUCAS

Primary Sources

Austin, John L. *How to Do Things with Words.* Cambridge, Mass.: Harvard UP, 1961.
Benveniste, Emile. *Problèmes de linguistique générale.* 2 vols. Paris: Gallimard, 1966, 1974.
Genette, Gérard. *Figures III.* Paris: Seuil, 1972.
Jakobson, Roman. 'Closing Statements.' In T.A. Sebeok, *Style and Language.* New York: Technology P of Massachusetts Institute of Technology and John Wiley and Sons, 1960.
Lyons, John. *Semantics.* 2 vols. Cambridge: Cambridge UP, 1977.
Searle, John. *Expression and Meaning.* Cambridge: Cambridge UP, 1979.
– *Speech Acts: An Essay in the Philosophy of Language.* Cambridge: Cambridge UP, 1969.
Strawson, Peter F. *Logico-Linguistic Papers.* London: Methuen, 1971.

Secondary Sources

Culler, Jonathan. *Structuralist Poetics. Structuralism, Linguistics and the Study of Literature.* Ithaca: Cornell UP, 1975.

Constance School of Reception Aesthetics [Reception Theory]

The Constance School is commonly used to designate a direction in literary criticism developed by professors and students at the University of Constance in West Germany during the late 1960s and early 1970s. In general the members of the Constance School turned to the reading and reception of literary texts instead of to traditional methods that emphasize the production of texts or a close examination of texts themselves. (See *text.) Their approach is therefore related to *reader-response criticism in the U.S.A., although for a time the Constance School was much more homogeneous in its theoretical presuppositions and general outlook than its American counterpart. Commonly known as reception theory or the aesthetics of reception (*Rezeptionsästhetik*), the approach developed by the Constance School dominated literary theory in Germany for about a decade but was not well known in the English-speaking world until around 1980, when the most seminal works were translated. *Hans Robert Jauss and *Wolfgang Iser are the two most original theorists of the school, although several of Jauss' students, among them Rainer Warning, Hans Ulrich Gumbrecht and Karlheinz Stierle, also made important contributions. In response to the writings of Jauss and Iser, scholars from the German Democratic Republic such as Robert Weimann, Manfred Naumann and Rita Schober raised objections to some propositions and suggested Marxist alternatives, with the result that the most productive East–West postwar dialogue in literary theory involved issues of reception and response. (See also *Marxist criticism.)

The Constance School arose at a time of great turbulence in West Germany society. At universities throughout the country the student movement agitated for educational reform and advocated a basic questioning of traditional methods and educational standards. The experimental University at Constance, founded in 1967, was at the forefront of educational reform and hence fostered an atmosphere in which new ideas in literary theory and aesthetics flourished.

Hans Robert Jauss and the aesthetics of reception

Reception theory dates from the 1967 inaugural lecture by Hans Robert Jauss, the newly appointed professor of Romance languages. His title echoed the famous inaugural essay by Friedrich Schiller at the University of Jena on the eve of the French Revolution. Schiller's 'Was heisst und zu welchem Ende studiert man Universalgeschichte?' ['What is and for what purpose does one study universal history?'] was modified by Jauss who substituted the word *Literatur* [literary] for 'Universal.' This alteration did not diminish the impact. Jauss suggests, as Schiller had in 1789, that the present age needed to restore vital links between the artefacts of the past and the concerns of the present. For literary scholarship and instruction such a connection can be established only if literary history is no longer relegated to the periphery of the discipline. The revised title of this lecture, 'Literaturgeschichte als Provokation der Literaturwissenschaft' ['Literary History as a Provocation to Literary Scholarship'], captures Jauss' innovative challenge.

The approach to literary texts outlined in his lecture became known as *Rezeptionsästhetik* and was an attempt to overcome what Jauss viewed as limitations in two important and putatively opposed literary theories: *formalism and Marxist criticism. In general, Marxism represents for him an outmoded approach to *literature related to an older positivist paradigm. Yet Jauss also recognizes in this body of criticism, especially in the writings of less orthodox Marxists like Werner Krauss, Roger Garaudy and Karel Kosík, a fundamentally correct concern with the historicity of literature. The formalists, on the other hand, are credited with introducing aesthetic perception as a theoretical tool for exploring literary works. However, Jauss also detects in their works the tendency to isolate art from its historical context, a *l'art pour l'art* aesthetics which supposedly values a 'timeless' formal organization over the historicity of the literary work. The task for a new literary history, therefore, becomes to merge the best qualities of Marxism and formalism. This can be accomplished by satisfying the Marxist demand for historical mediation while retaining the formalist advances in the realm of aesthetic perception.

The aesthetics of reception propose to do this by altering the perspective from which we normally interpret literary texts. Traditional literary histories were composed from the perspective of the producers of texts; Jauss proposes that we can truly understand literature as a process by recognizing the role of the consumer or reader. Interaction between author and public replaces literary biography as the basis for literary historiography. Thus Jauss meets the Marxist demand by situating literature in the larger continuum of events; he retains the formalist achievements by placing his concern with the perceiving consciousness at the centre. The historical significance of a work is not established by qualities of the work or by the genius of its author but by the chain of receptions from generation to generation. In terms of literary history Jauss thus envisions a historiography that will play a conscious, mediating role between past and present. The historian of literary reception is called upon to rethink continually the works of the canon in light of how they have affected, and are affected by, current conditions and events. Past meanings are understood as part of the prehistory of present experiencing.

The integration of history and aesthetics is to be accomplished largely by examining what Jauss refers to as the *horizon of expectation (Erwartungshorizont). This methodological centrepiece of Jauss' theory is an obvious adaptation of the notion of horizon (Horizont) found most prominently in the hermeneutic theory of Jauss' teacher *Hans-Georg Gadamer. (See *hermeneutics.) For Gadamer the horizon is a fundamental tenet for the hermeneutical situation. It refers primarily to our necessarily perspectival and limited worldview. Jauss' use of the term is slightly different. For him it denotes a system or structure of expectations that an individual brings to a text. Works are read against some horizon of expectation; indeed, certain types of texts – *parody, for example – intentionally foreground this horizon. The task of the literary scholar is to 'objectify' the horizon, so that we may evaluate the artistic character of the work. This is most readily accomplished when the work makes its horizon its theme. But even works whose horizon is less obvious can be examined with this method. Generic, literary and linguistic aspects of a work can be used to construct a probable horizon of expectation.

After establishing the horizon of expectation, the critic can then proceed to determine the artistic merit of a given work by measuring the distance between the work and the horizon. Basically Jauss employs a deviationist model: the aesthetic value of a text is seen as a function of its deviation from a given norm. If the expectations of a reader are not 'disappointed' or violated, then the text will be second-rate; if it breaks through the horizon, it will be high art, although a work may break its horizon of expectation and yet remain unrecognized as great. This poses no problems for Jauss. The first experience of disrupted expectations will almost invariably evoke strong negative responses which will disappear for later readers. In a later age the horizon changes and the work no longer ruptures expectations. Instead it may be recognized as a classic, that is, a work which has contributed to the establishment of a new horizon of expectation.

Wolfgang Iser and the phenomenology of reading

Jauss' historical approach to understanding literary works was complemented by Wolfgang Iser's examination of the interaction between reader and text. Like Jauss, Iser attracted attention with his inaugural lecture, but his theory is perhaps best represented in Der Akt des Lesens [The Act of Reading 1976]. What interests Iser is how and under what conditions a text has meaning for a reader. Whereas traditional interpretation has sought to elucidate hidden meanings, Iser wants to see meaning as the result of an interaction between text and reader, as an effect that is experienced, not a message that must be found. *Roman Ingarden provided a useful framework for his investigation. According to Ingarden the aesthetic object is constituted only through the reader's act of cognition. Adopting this precept from Ingarden, Iser thus switches focus from the text as an object to the text as potential, from the results to the act of reading.

To examine the interaction between text and reader Iser looks at those qualities in the text which make it readable or which influence our reading and at those features of the reading process essential for understanding the text. Particularly in his early work he adopts the term *implied reader to encompass both of these functions; it is at once textual structure and structured act. Later, depending more heavily on Ingarden's terminology, he distinguishes between the text, its *concretization, and the work of art. The first is the artistic aspect, what is placed there by the author for us to read, and it may be best conceived as a potential awaiting realization. Concretization, by contrast, refers to the product of our own productive activity; it is the realization of the text in the mind of the reader, accomplished by the filling in of blanks or gaps (*Leerstellen*) to eliminate *indeterminacy. Finally, the work of art is neither text nor concretization but something in between. It occurs at the point of convergence of text and reader, a point which can never be completely defined.

The work of art is characterized by its virtual nature and is constituted by various overlapping procedures. One of these involves the dialectic of protention and retention, two terms borrowed from the phenomenological theory of *Edmund Husserl. (See *phenomenological criticism.) Iser applies them to our activity in reading successive sentences. In confronting a text we continuously project expectations which may be fulfilled or disappointed; at the same time our reading is conditioned by foregoing sentences and concretizations. Because our reading is determined by this dialectic, it acquires the status of an event and can give us the impression of a real occurrence. If this is so, however, our interaction with texts must compel us to endow our concretizations with a degree of consistency – or at least as much consistency as we admit to reality. This involvement with the text is seen as a type of entanglement in which the foreign is grasped and assimilated. Iser's point is that the reader's activity is similar to actual experience. Although Iser distinguishes between perception (*Wahrnehmung*) and ideation (*Vorstellung*), structurally these two processes are identical. According to Iser, reading therefore temporarily eliminates the traditional subject-object dichotomy. (See *subject/object.) At the same time, however, the subject is compelled to split into two parts, one which undertakes the concretization and another which merges with the author or at least the constructed image of the author. Ultimately the reading process involves a dialectical process of self-realization and change. By filling in the gaps in the text, we simultaneously reconstruct ourselves, since our encounters with literature are part of a process of understanding others and ourselves more completely.

Continuations and criticisms

Iser's model of reading has been productively supplemented by the work or Karlheinz Stierle, the most incisive second-generation theorist from the Constance School during the 1970s. Stierle proceeds from Iser's contention that the formation of illusions and images is essential for the reading process and labels this level of reading 'quasi-pragmatic,' a designation that distinguishes it from the reception of non-fictional texts ('pragmatic reception'). While Iser seems to remain on this plane in his studies, Stierle suggests that the quasi-pragmatic reading must be supplemented with higher forms of reception capable of doing justice to the peculiarities of fiction. What distinguishes narrative fiction is pseudo-referentiality, which may be considered auto-referentially in the guise of referential forms. (See *reference/referent.) Fiction is self-referential, although it appears to be referential. What Stierle suggests, therefore, is an additional reflexive level of understanding in our encounter with literary texts.

The critics of the Constance School from the German Democratic Republic approached the accomplishments of reception theory from a somewhat different stance. Robert Weimann and Manfred Naumann are not as interested in the reading process outlined by Iser and Stierle as they are in the literary historiography developed by Jauss. Their objections to his theory are threefold. First they complain that reception theory has gone too far in emphasizing response. While Weimann and Naumann admit that this is an important aspect – perhaps downplayed somewhat in the Marxist tradition – Jauss and his colleagues, in positing reception as the sole criterion for a revitalization of literary history, destroy the dialectic of production and reception. Second, these Marxist critics detect a danger in the totally subjective apprehension of art and the resultant relativizing of literary history. The problem here is that if we follow Jauss (and Gadamer) in relinquishing all objective notions of the work of art then our access to history would seem to be completely arbitrary because it is ceaselessly changing. Finally, the Constance School model of reception theory provides scant sociological grounding for the reader who supposedly stands at the centre of its concerns. Scholars from the GDR found a general failure to link literary history with larger concerns. The reader in the reception theory of

Jauss and Iser, they claim, is conceived as an idealized individual, rather than as a social entity with political and ideological, as well as aesthetic, dimensions. (See *ideology.)

Jauss and Iser defended their positions against these and other objections in polemical rejoiners during the 1970s. They have also modified and refined their theoretical positions on the basis of this criticism. But the cost of correction has been a loss of the excitement surrounding the emergence of reception theory. Both Jauss and Iser subsequently took directions which depart from their most influential work. Increasingly Iser has concerned himself with the notions of the imaginary in fiction and literary anthropology. Jauss' magnum opus *Ästhetische Erfahrung und literarische Hermeneutik* [*Aesthetic Experience and Literary Hermeneutics* 1977 and 1982], develops a more differential notion of response, relinquishing the primarily deviationist model of the 'Provocation' essay. This work, however, has had a comparatively smaller impact on critical circles in Germany and its reception marked a diminishing of the influence of reception theory in the early 1980s. The Constance School, on the other hand, has survived the demise of its most important theoretical product by virtue of the personalities of its members and the biannual scholarly colloquia held there. The meetings of the group 'Poetik und Hermeneutik' ['Poetics and Hermeneutics'], so important for the advent of reception theory, continue to produce exciting contributions of literary, cultural and philosophical criticism in Germany.

ROBERT C. HOLUB

Primary Sources

Gumbrecht, Hans Ulrich. 'Konsequenzen der Rezeptionsästhetik oder Literaturwissenschaft als Kommunikationssoziologie.' *Poetica* 7 (1975): 388–413.

Iser, Wolfgang. *Der Akt des Lesens: Theorie Ästhetischer Wirkung*. Munich: Fink, 1976. *The Act of Reading: A Theory of Aesthetic Response*. Baltimore: Johns Hopkins UP, 1978.

– *Die Appellstruktur der Texte: Unbestimmtheit als Wirkungsbedingung literarischer Prosa*. Konstanz: G. Hess, 1970. 'Indeterminacy and the Reader's Response in Prose Fiction.' In *Aspects of Narrative: Selected Papers from the English Institute*. Ed. J. Hillis Miller. New York: Columbia UP, 1971, 1–45.

– 'The Current Situation of Literary Theory: Key Concepts and the Imaginary.' *New Literary History* 11 (1979): 1–20.

– *Der implizite Leser: Kommunikationsformen des Ro-*

mans von Bunyan bis Beckett. Munich: Fink, 1972. *The Implied Reader: Patterns of Communication in Prose Fiction from Bunyan to Beckett*. Baltimore: Johns Hopkins UP, 1974.

Jauss, Hans Robert. *Ästhetische Erfahrung und literarische Hermeneutik*. Munich: Fink, 1977. Rev. and exp. Frankfurt: Suhrkamp, 1982. *Aesthetic Experience and Literary Hermeneutics. Theory and History of Literature* 3. Minneapolis: U of Minnesota P, 1982.

– *Kleine Apologie der ästhetischer Erfahrung*. Konstanzer Universitätsreden 59. Konstanz: Universitätsverlag, 1972.

– *Literaturgeschichte als Provokation*. Frankfurt: Suhrkamp, 1970.

– 'Paradigmawechsel in der Literaturwissenschaft.' *Linguistische Berichte* 3 (1969): 44–56.

– *Toward an Aesthetic of Reception Theory and History of Literature* 2. Minneapolis: U of Minnesota P, 1982.

Naumann, Manfred. 'Das Dilemma der Rezeptionsästhetik.' *Poetica* 8 (1976): 451–66.

– et al. *Gesellschaft – Literatur – Lesen: Literaturrezeption in theoretischer Sicht*. Weimar: Aufbau, 1973.

Schober, Rita. *Abbild, Sinnbild, Wertung: Aufsätze zur Theorie und Praxis literarischer Kommunikation*. Berlin: Aufbau, 1982.

Stierle, Karlheinz. *Text als Handlung: Perspektiven einer systematischen Literaturwissenschaft*. Munich: Fink, 1975.

– 'Was heisst Rezeption bei fiktionalen Texten?' *Poetica* 7 (1975): 345–87. Abbr.: 'The Reading of Fictional Texts.' In *The Reader in the Text: Essays on Audience and Interpretation*. Ed. Susan R. Suleiman and Inge Crosman. Princeton: Princeton UP, 1980, 83–105.

Warning, Rainer, ed. *Rezeptionsästhetik: Theorie und Praxis*. Munich: Fink, 1975.

Weimann, Robert. ' "Rezeptionsästhetik" und die Krise der Literaturgeschichte: Zur Kritik einer neuen Strömung in der bürgerlichen Literaturwissenschaft.' *Weimarer Beiträge* 19.8 (1973): 5–33. ' "Reception Aesthetics" and the Crisis of Literary History.' *Clio* 5 (1975): 3–33.

– ' "Rezeptionsästhetik" oder das Ungenügen an der bürgerlichen Bildung: Zur Kritik einer Theorie literarischer Kommunikation.' In *Kunstensemble und Öffentlichkeit*. Ed. Robert Weimann. Halle-Leipzig: Mitteldeutscher Verlag, 1982, 85–133.

Weinrich, Harald. 'Für eine Literaturgeschichte des Lesers.' *Merkur* 21 (1967): 1026–38.

Secondary Sources

Burger, Peter. 'Probleme der Rezeptionsforschung.' *Poetica* 9 (1977): 446–71.

Fish, Stanley. 'Why No One's Afraid of Wolfgang Iser.' *Diacritics* 11.1 (1981): 2–13.

Fokkema, D.W., and Elrud Kunne-Ibisch. 'The Reception of Literature: Theory and Practice of "Rezeptionsästhetik." ' *Theories of Literature in the Twentieth Century.* New York: St. Martin's P, 1977, 136–64.

Grimm, Gunter. *Rezeptionsgeschichte: Grundlegung einer Theorie.* Munich: Fink, 1977.

Hohendahl, Peter Uwe, ed. *Sozialgeschichte und Wirkungsästhetik: Dokumente zur empirischen und marxistischen Rezeptionsforschung.* Frankfurt: Athenäum, 1974.

Holub, Robert C. *Reception Theory: A Critical Introduction.* London: Methuen, 1984.

Link, Hannelore. ' "Die Appellstruktur der Texte" und "ein Paradigmawechsel in der Literaturwissenschaft." ' *Jahrbuch der deutschen Schillergesellschaft* 7 (1973): 532–83.

Solms, Wilhelm, and Norbert Scholl. 'Rezeptionsästhetik.' In *Literaturwissenschaft heute.* Ed. Friedrich Nemec and Wilhelm Solms. Munich: Fink, 1979, 154–96.

Zimmermann, Bernhard. *Literaturrezeption im historischen Prozess: Zur Theorie einer Rezeptionsgeschichte der Literatur.* Munich: Beck, 1977.

Constructivism

Literary constructivism in Russia began with the *Literaturnyi tsentr konstruktivistov* [Literary Centre of Constructivists], established in 1923. The name derived from applied and visual arts such as sculpture, painting and film where it was used for the first time around 1920. The first official manifesto was published in the pages of *LEF* in 1924. The understanding of creative activity by literary constructivists differed considerably from that of their counterparts in other branches of art: they opposed blatantly utilitarian aesthetics and practical approaches to artistic creativity as represented, for example, by A. Gan in his book *Konstruktivizm* [Constructivism 1922]. Its main theoreticians were Ilia Sel'vinskii, Kornelii Zelinskii, Valentin Asmus, and Aleksandr Kviatkovskii. The group was strengthened in the mid-1920s by the poets Vera Inber, Vladimir Lugovskoi and Eduard Bagritskii.

Among the multiplicity of diverse artistic groupings of Soviet Russia in the 1920s, constructivists stressed that theirs was the *literature of the technological age, a kind of homologue to scientific discoveries of the 20th century. This is probably why constructivists were sometimes mistakenly viewed as not more than an offshoot of futurism and its early Soviet continuation – the Left Front of Art. While one cannot deny a certain degree of affinity between the two groups, it should be kept in mind that constructivists differed fundamentally from their predecessors on two accounts: they rejected the futurist principle of deformation in literature, that is, of radical artistic experimentation which destroyed the comprehensibility of content and opposed *LEF*'s postulate of documentary literature, the *literatura fakta* [literature of facts]. Instead, they defended the integrity of content and the necessity of delivering a message to the reader; at the same time they postulated invention as the basic principle which leads to the existence and specificity of imaginative literature.

In programmatic statements made in the late 1920s constructivists sometimes referred to themselves as modern heirs to the 19th-century 'Westernizers' who fought Russian backwardness and isolation from the rest of Europe. If proletarian writers claimed to represent the aspirations of the working class, constructivists expounded their own activity as an implementation of the aims and vision of the Russian intelligentsia.

Constructivism perceived culture as an all-embracing and comprehensive phenomenon, penetrating all spheres of human existence and activity. Hence, literary constructivists fostered the idea of creating not only literature but also its broad theoretical foundations.

Constructivists showed clear preference for the genre of poetry, followed by drama and then prose. Thematically, the literature of constructivism tended to raise issues related to the Revolution, the importance of technological progress, and the place of the intelligentsia in the process of industrial production. (See *theme.) While trying to create the image of a business-like protagonist, constructivists did not avoid moral questions and their assessment of the Revolution was not always credulous or flattering. The most prominent writer of this group was Ilia Sel'vinskii, author of the epic poem *Ulialaievshchina* [The Ulalayev's Revolt] and the play *Kamandarm-2* [The Army Commander-2]. Sel'vinskii also showed a strong interest in theoretical problems and formulated the concept of 'double realism': the manner in which an aesthetic idea is shaped, its material organized and perceived. Realism did not necessarily mean a 'truthful reflection of life' because it allowed the writer a subjective interpretation of the external world. Consequently, Selvinskii formulated double realism as a polychromatic, manifold representation of a transitional epoch in its contradicting aspirations. He clearly distanced himself from 19th-century realism with its developed 'sense of proportion' based on the aesthetic principle of *mimesis. If 19th-century realism was governed by the rule of *expediency*, then double realism would be founded on the precept of *purposefulness*. Double realism is neither a repetition of past artistic models nor a simple mimetic 'reflection of reality' as advocated by Marxists. The term assumes the fullest possible freedom of the writer's perception of the world that surrounds us and makes allowance for his or her whims, that is, it anticipates the use of artistic (creative) deformation.

Programmatic poetics and theory of literature occupied a large and important place in constructivist writings. Good literary practice rested on four basic principles: (1) the semantic dominant [*smyslovaia dominanta*]; (2) the assertion of the maximum 'weight' of meaning on the smallest possible textual unit; (3) the postulate of local semantics; and (4) the inclusion of epic narrative and artistic devices of prose in poetry. These principles were directed first of all against the modernist destruction of 'story-telling' literature so evident, for example, in the experimental devices of futurism. Constructivists opposed the formalist idea of 'artistic dominant' (formulated by *Roman Jakobson) to the concept of 'semantic dominant'; that is, each work of literature always expresses some prime ideological, philosophical, political, or ethical idea. (See *ideology.) Although a literary work of art evokes ambiguity and may provoke a multitude of interpretations, it remains subordinated to one organizing thought.

Constructivist writers aimed to achieve two first principles through rationality, succinctness, expediency, and clarity in their works; they held the belief that the shortest possible unit of literary text must bear the maximum 'weight' of meaning. The text must be 'loaded' with meaning and the theme exploited to the utmost. The concept of local semantics meant a particular interpretation of what is known in literature as 'local colour.' A theme, according to constructivist theoreticians, can be made homogeneous and artistically consistent if it avails itself of a store of words which is typical of its semantic field. Thus if a poet composes a poem about miners and their work, the poet ought to find the right words (for example, from their technical language) which would be most homologous to their professional occupation and way of thinking. The fourth principle calling for the introduction of epic elements into poetry followed the constructivist insistence

that artistic literature must deliver a message which can be accomplished through narrative and plot. (See *story/plot.)

On another theoretical level, constructivists presented their own definition of literature and the literary work of art. In *Poeziia kak smysl* [*Poetry as Sense*], Zelinskii argued for poetry as a fulfilment of both formal and semantic functions. The title of Zelinskii's treatise stood in clear contradiction to *Viktor Shklovskii's earlier statement of the formalist view. In 'Iskusstvo kak priem' ['Art as Technique'; also translated as 'Art as Device' 1917], Shklovskii argued that the evolution of literature means a continuous renewal of literary form and its artistic devices. (See also *formalism, Russian.) Zelinski did not dispute the assertion that poetry means an organization of form; in fact, the term 'organization' played a key role in constructivist theoretical thought, which claimed that every realm of human activity must be subjected to rational organization. However, Zelinskii rejected the formalist idea of treating literature as a technique only. For him, the most important, determinant factor in the evolution of literature remained *sense*, which he perceived as a manifestation of the dialectical relationship between the artist, the external world and the reader. The existence of poetry is conditioned by the constant struggle with sense. Poetry wants to subjugate life by endowing it with sense because there is an opposition between the sense of word and the sense of outer reality. Poetry does not 'reflect' life but creates sense. Whenever a writer tries to make poetry represent something, sh/e experiences constant disillusionment because sh/e is unable to express herself as adequately as initially intended but only in approximations. The contrasting forces that stand in the poet's way as impediments to expression are the outer world of objects and the word. Both these worlds stand in opposition not only to the writer but also in relation to each other. Consequently, the function of poetry consists of a continuous pursuit of sense.

Understandably, within such a concept of literature considerable attention is given to the 'word' as the main bearer of sense. Zelinskii differentiated between 'sense' and 'meaning' of the word: meaning is the more important, for it also functions as the bearer of 'sense.' When a writer wants to express something, he implements an inner orientation or intention to denote it. This process is accompanied by new forms which are conditioned by what Zelinskii calls a 'logical quantum.' The destruction of an old form does not have any logical justification; in fact, it is marked by a certain absurdity, a break or jump in logic. This break, that is, the destruction of the logic of old form together with the discovery of new innumerable designations and meanings, is defined by Zelinskii as the logical or verbal quantum. In this process 'word' plays a crucial role, but it is conditioned by various factors and cannot be recognized as a direct expression of what we want to say or designate.

Constructivists, above all Zelinskii, introduced the notion of sensing word [osmyslennnoe slovo]. If the function of thought is to designate singular units of sense, then the role of logic consists of linking these units into larger and purposeful entities. This process of 'constructing' such entities does not proceed without resistance. It is opposed by two forces: on the one hand, word is an unsteady value, constantly changing in its semantic quality because a word is a function of matter and whenever it is used it registers anew the relationship between man and nature; on the other hand, the semantic changeability of a word is opposed by its striving for stability, for semantic permanence derived from previous utterances. The word, then, is at the same time concrete, symbolic and ambiguous.

Unlike other groups or currents within modernism which often promoted ambiguity as their most important aesthetic principle, constructivists aimed at creating sense and precision. To achieve this, they proposed applying visual effects such as additional diacritical signs, diagrams, letters of the old Greek and Latin alphabets, and geometric figures. In the early experimental stages, they also used mathematical symbols such as square roots, placed at the end of or beside a poem, giving the synopsis and explanation of its content.

Experimentation was proposed on various levels of literary works of art, particularly poetry. Kviatkovskii, for example, emphasized the need for innovative changes in the Russian system of versification. He proposed the elimination of the existing systems of versification for the sake of introducing a new technique – the taktometr, which was intended to do away with the existing tonic metres (iamb, trochee, dactyl, and so on) and to introduce a more flexible poetic unit in order to reach a greater sense-capacity and bring poetry closer to music.

Constructivists did not have a chance to verify many of their experiments. Unfortunately, their most interesting theoretical statements of the late 1920s coincided with the growing bureaucratization and dogmatism of Soviet cultural life. In the spring of 1930 the most prominent constructivists (Zelinskii, Inber, Sel'vinskii) formed the *Brigade M 1* which was incorporated into the main organization of proletarian writers – RAPP (Russian Association of Proletarian Writers), a compromise which aimed to appease the most severe critics from the dogmatic Marxist camp. Under the umbrella of a proletarian organization, the constructivists hoped to survive, at least for a time. However, pressure grew and criticism remained unabated. Towards the end of 1930 the group ceased to exist, although its writers and critics continued to participate in Soviet literary life throughout the thirties, forties and fifties by accepting and practising the theoretical tenets of socialist realism. (See also *Marxist criticism.)

EDWARD MOŻEJKO

Primary Sources

Grübel, R.G. *Russicher Konstruktivismus*. Wiesbaden: Otto Harrassowitz, 1981.

Możejko, E. 'Russian Literary Constructivism: Towards a Theory of Poetic Language.' In *Canadian Contributions to the VIII International Congress of Slavists*. Ed. E. Heier, G. Luckyj, and G. Schaarschmidt. Ottawa: U of Ottawa P, 1978, 16–70.

Szymak, J. *Twúrczość Ilji Sielwinskiego na tle teorii konstruktywizmu*. Wrocław, Warsaw, Kraków: PAN, 1965.

Zelinskii, K. *Poeziia kak smysl*. Moskva: Federatsiia, 1929.

– and Sel'vinskii. *Biznes*. Moskva: Gosizdat, 1929.

– *Gosplan literatury*. Moskva: Krug, 1925.

– Zelinskii, K., A.N. Chicherin, and E.-K. Sel'vinskii. *Mena vsekh, Konstruktivisty poety*. Moskva, 1924.

Constructivist theory of literature: *see* Empirical Science of Literature

Croatian Philological Society: *see* Hrvatsko filološko društvo

Cultural materialism

Cultural materialism is an approach to *literature initiated in Britain in the late 1970s by the theoretical writings of *Raymond Williams. In the mid-1980s, Jonathan Dollimore and Alan Sinfield borrowed and redefined the term as they applied it to the study of Renaissance drama. Rooted in Marxism, cultural materialism stresses interaction between cultural creations such as literature and their historical context, including social, political and economic elements. (See also *Marxist criticism.)

Anthropological background

The term 'cultural materialism' first appeared in anthropological studies. Marvin Harris applied the name 'cultural materialism' to a scientific method of studying the interaction between social life and material conditions (*The Rise of Anthropological Theory* 1968). Influenced not only by Marxist thought but also by Darwinian evolutionary theory, cultural materialism explains 'cultural phenomena in terms of their place and their history in the material circumstances of specific people, and in the productive and reproductive demands of their environment' (Ross, xvi). Like classical Marxism, it sees material conditions as the primary influence on social life. Unlike Marxism, however, cultural materialism stresses an empirical rather than a dialectical stance. Consequently, studies give more attention to societal influences on economic production than to identifying class exploitation within a capitalist system. The interdependence of science and politics forms the primary assumption of this anthropological theory.

Raymond Williams

Raymond Williams appears to have coined the phrase 'cultural materialism' in *Marxism and Literature* (1977) independently of the parallel development in anthropology. Nevertheless, the two fields similarly emphasize material influences on cultural activities and the consequent need to ground culture in its historical context. Applying Marxist historical materialism to literary studies, Williams revises its central base/superstructure model. Classical Marxism identifies the economic base of material production as the sole determining factor of the superstructure encompassing communi-cation, art, human consciousness, and other cultural activities. Williams, however, adjusts both 'base' and 'superstructure' by describing the economic base as a process rather than a fixed state, by allowing superstructural aspects some autonomy from economic influences, and by indicating that the cultural superstructure is itself material. His understanding of materialism includes the cultural production of 'meanings and values' which use language as a material form that relies on 'specific technologies of writing' and 'mechanical and electronic communication systems' (*Problems in Materialism and Culture* 243). This theory of cultural materialism claims a 'constitutive' and 'constituting' relationship of activities at all levels of society as they mutually influence and determine one another.

Jonathan Dollimore and Alan Sinfield

In *Political Shakespeare: New Essays in Cultural Materialism* (1985), Jonathan Dollimore and Alan Sinfield brought Raymond Williams' theory to a study of Shakespearian drama and defined its parameters in their own terms. Noting the significance of 'cultural' and 'material,' they point out that the cultural aspect of the theory combines two meanings: the analytical term 'culture' referring to social systems studied in anthropology and the social sciences, and the evaluative term referring to art and literature as forms of 'high culture.' In addressing the materialist aspect of the theory, they reject two opposing views: idealism which asserts that art transcends society and time, and classical Marxism which assumes that culture is secondary to politics and economics. Suggesting that literary texts 'represent' rather than 'transcend' or 'reflect' material reality, Dollimore and Sinfield assert literature's potential both to interact with and to intervene in accepted practices and beliefs. This active role of literature they complement by explicitly identifying the political goals of cultural materialism itself, as a theory founded on 'commitment to the transformation of a social order which exploits people on grounds of race, gender and class' (*Political Shakespeare* vii–viii). Prefacing their collection of essays by indicating that cultural materialism involves 'historical context, theoretical method, political commitment and textual analysis' (viii), they see theory as broadly overlapping with and including studies of history, sociology, feminism,

Cultural materialism

Marxism, and *poststructuralism. (See also *sociocriticism, *materialist criticism, *feminist criticism.)

Ideology

A central concept in cultural materialism, '*ideology' has a complex background. From classical Marxism, it is a system of false beliefs founded on contradictions and inconsistencies that misrepresent social relationships. From the modified Marxism of theorists such as *Louis Althusser, it is the comprehensive system of ideas, beliefs and values that influences human behaviour in any society. Althusser describes all institutions, including educational systems, law, religion, and arts, as *Ideological State Apparatuses which represent and reproduce the myths or beliefs needed to maintain a society's existing mode of economic production (137). (See *myth.) Williams incorporates both the original and the modified Marxist views by placing ideology in a context of change comprising 'residual,' 'dominant' and 'emergent' elements in culture. At any historical moment, the dominant elements form the controlling ideology, while residual aspects of previous ideologies maintain some influence and emergent elements in the form of new ideas and values initiate change by challenging central beliefs. Dominant values 'misrepresent' by failing to acknowledge the complexity of social interaction, but marginal beliefs complete the ideological picture by accounting for historical change and cultural contradictions. In this understanding, ideology encompasses all social practices, including the production of literary texts which both evaluate and participate in contemporary values and beliefs. (See also *margin.)

Politics

Cultural materialists focus their study on literary representations of ideology as it is used to reinforce *power and *authority in the face of opposition. 'Consolidation,' '*subversion' and 'containment' are key words in this political interpretation. As Jonathan Dollimore explains, 'The first refers, typically, to the ideological means whereby a dominant order seeks to perpetuate itself; the second to the subversion of that order, the third to the containment of ostensibly subversive pressures' ('Introduction,' *Political Shakespeare* 10). Materialists view political power as a tenuous relationship between dominance and subversion. Their goal in textual analysis is to demystify the power described by pointing out that its legitimating ideas and values are merely chosen ideologies rather than sacred or inherently natural foundations of order. From a cultural materialist perspective, any dominant order restricts and falsifies human experience and literary texts play a politically subversive role by exposing the contradictions and inconsistencies which undermine domination.

Renaissance drama

Cultural materialism has significantly influenced the study of Renaissance drama, in which the interaction between politics and performance has been of particular interest in current literary criticism. (See *performance criticism.) Prior to identifying a name for the approach in *Political Shakespeare* (1985), Jonathan Dollimore applied its assumptions in *Radical Tragedy: Religion, Ideology and Power in the Drama of Shakespeare and His Contemporaries* (1984). His study incorporates two cultural materialist concerns: a political interpretation of texts and a challenge to modern essentialist views and criticism. (See *essentialism.) He portrays the Jacobean playwrights as political activists who, on the one hand, repeatedly question and subvert the ideological foundations of monarchical authority, but who, on the other hand, manifest adherence to some of the same contradictory beliefs because they lack ideological immunity to their own culture. In addressing modern assumptions and interpretations of Renaissance texts, Dollimore challenges essentialism, the view than human nature has inherent or universal qualities uniting readers and writers from one historical period to the next. To cultural materialists, individuals are not timeless and unchanging but historically and socially determined. This understanding has led scholars to study contextual influences on other Renaissance texts as well, from the political writings of Thomas More to the poetry of Edmund Spenser. (See also *universal.)

Textual reproduction and reception

Opposition to essentialism emerges in the cultural materialist attention to texts not only represented in their own cultural context but received and reproduced through history. Working on the assumption that literature serves political ends rather than capturing universal human values, materialists explore cultural practice in the 20th century to identify current literary adaptations and interpretations. Renaissance scholars such as Graham Holderness (1985), Jean Howard and Marion O'Connor (1987), and John Drakakis (1985) demonstrate an interest in historical, cultural change by evaluating contemporary television and film versions of Shakespeare's plays or by examining the image of Shakespeare fostered by the British educational system. They endeavour both to counter conservative views of early–Second World War theatres and academics and to raise awareness that all textual appropriation and analysis have a subjective, political dimension.

A concern with cultural self-consciousness and with literature and criticism as ideological practices provides the link between the popularity of cultural materialism in Renaissance studies and similar analytical methods applied to other historical periods and broader sociological topics. Jerome McGann's (1983) and Marjorie Levinson's (1986) focus on ideology and politics in Romantic poetry, Lee Patterson's (1987) re-evaluation of historical studies in medieval literature, Mary Poovey's (1988) study of material conditions affecting representations of women in Victorian society, and Alan Sinfield's *Literature, Politics and Culture in Postwar Britain* (1989) represent the broad scope of cultural materialist influences. The evident interest in textual reproduction and reception throughout literary studies is part of a much wider sociological discussion among writers such as Stuart Hall (1980), Terry Lovell (1980) and Janet Wolff (1981), who consider art as materialist practice and culture as social production. Similar critical assumptions and influences underlie this whole range of academic discourse whether or not the scholars deliberately identify themselves as practitioners of a cultural materialist approach.

Cultural materialism and old historicism

Cultural materialism objects to older historicist assumptions while sharing an interest in the relationship of literary texts to historical surroundings. Cultural materialists resist the distinction between history as static background and literature as foregrounded subject by seeing history more as subjective interpretation than as objectifiable fact and by including literature as an interactive part of history. They likewise assert cultural diversity, political instability and the interdependence of materialism and cultural expression to counter older historicist beliefs in a unified culture, a single political model and universal truths. In Renaissance studies, E.M.W. Tillyard's *The Elizabethan World Picture* (1948) provides the key historicist stance against which materialists define their position. Tillyard argues for a cosmic and hierarchical political order founded on universal acceptance of Providentialism. The same historical World Picture becomes in a cultural materialist interpretation the dominant ideology perpetuated by the monarchy but challenged by marginal political voices and emerging humanist developments.

Cultural materialism and *New Historicism

Cultural materialism shares its reaction to older approaches with New Historicism, a theory having a similar impact in the study of Renaissance texts and first attracting attention in Stephen Greenblatt's *Renaissance Self-Fashioning* (1980). The two practices are so closely related that critics adopting and discussing them often conflate the two or simply acknowledge the difficulty of delineating their differences. Both cultural materialism and New Historicism share a focus on power and ideology and a view that writers challenge political power by exploring its representations and exposing its inconsistencies. Dissolving the boundaries between literature and other disciplines, both likewise share the assumption that literature is completely integrated with political, social and economic forces.

Often understood as British and American counterparts of the same theory, cultural materialism and New Historicism can be distinguished partly by national differences. The British Marxist origins of cultural materialism link it to a tradition of oppositional politics, while New Historicism is influenced more directly by *Clifford Geertz's anthropology, *Michel Foucault's interest in power relations and *Jacques Derrida's *deconstruction theory than by American party politics. Marxist political background helps to account for the cultural materialist belief in freedom for social change through literary texts and analysis. Ties with deconstruction partly explain the

New Historicist view that individuals are self-fashioned but decentred, that they lack the psychological or emotional unity entailed in the political commitment advocated by cultural materialists. (See *centre/decentre.) Theoretical purpose is consequently more overtly expressed by the materialists.

The two also differ in their textual interpretation. Cultural materialists focus on the subversion of dominant ideologies and institutions represented in literature, while the New Historicists emphasize containment in asserting that the dominant is necessarily defined by the subversion it controls. Thus New Historicist studies frequently conclude with the inevitable and overwhelming presence of power, cultural materialists by asserting the contradictions that necessarily produce cultural change. In spite of their slightly different angles, the two approaches nevertheless remain closely aligned. Jonathan Dollimore and Alan Sinfield's inclusion of New Historicist articles in *Political Shakespeare: Essays on Cultural Materialism* and Stephen Greenblatt's recent preference for the term 'cultural poetics' rather than New Historicism (Greenblatt 1989; Felperin 1990) demonstrate the uncertain and shifting boundaries between the two theories.

Weaknesses and strengths

The political bias of cultural materialism is its most controversial aspect. With a deliberate Marxist orientation, its practitioners often choose texts that validate their own position or impose anachronistic values and perceptions on pre-Marxist periods. While the cultural materialists partly exonerate themselves by not pretending to cloak the political intentions of their analyses in any other terms, their goals nevertheless often lead to a narrow, predictable reading of texts or to a discussion of contemporary politics which overshadows focus on texts and history altogether. The political purpose also makes the scope of cultural materialism difficult to determine because some scholars who adopt similar analytical methods deliberately avoid identifying themselves with the approach to distance themselves from a polemical stance. With the collapse of communist regimes and accompanying attacks on the Left, Marxist influences in criticism show signs of becoming even less acceptable.

Scholars who do declare themselves cultural materialists have been criticized for being both too materialist and not materialist enough. Unintentionally, Raymond Williams undervalues materiality by asserting that it circumscribes every social practice, thereby leaving no non-materialist reality by which to identify the significance of the material. On the other hand, practitioners sometimes apply their assumptions to texts in such theoretical terms that they ignore historically and materially specific influences on writers, performers and publishers. Their assertion that textual production and reception are determined exclusively by external cultural forces can unsettle readers who recognize that their own appreciation of literature stems not solely from the need or desire to understand historical context but from pleasure in the story itself or identification with fictional experiences and personalities.

Cultural materialists have contributed to literary criticism in their re-evaluation of the relationship between present and past. They remind readers that texts do have a history and that knowing historical conditions can enrich one's understanding and appreciation of literature. While exposing monolithic interpretations which simplify and unify past periods, they call for a closer look at the complexities existing in any society by portraying culture more as a living organism that constantly changes than as a fixed entity than can be objectively described. They likewise emphasize that readers, scholars and critics deceive themselves if they think their own values and attitudes do not influence their understanding of literature, their own culture and the past.

FAITH NOSTBAKKEN

Primary Sources

Dollimore, Jonathan. 'Introduction: Shakespeare, Cultural Materialism and the New Historicism.' *Political Shakespeare: New Essays in Cultural Materialism.* Ed. Jonathan Dollimore and Alan Sinfield. Manchester: Manchester UP, 1985, 2–17.
– *Radical Tragedy: Religion, Ideology and Power in the Drama of Shakespeare and His Contemporaries.* Chicago: U of Chicago P, 1984.
– and Alan Sinfield, eds. *Political Shakespeare: New Essays in Cultural Materialism.* Manchester: Manchester UP, 1985.
Harris, Marvin. *The Rise of Anthropological Theory: A History of Theories of Culture.* New York: Thomas Y. Crowell Co., 1968.
Ross, Eric, ed. *Beyond the Myths of Culture: Essays in Cultural Materialism.* New York: Academic P, 1980.
Williams, Raymond. *Marxism and Literature.* Oxford: Oxford UP, 1977.

– *Problems in Materialism and Culture*. London: New Left Books, 1980.

Secondary Sources

Althusser, Louis. 'Ideology and Ideological State Apparatuses.' In *Lenin and Philosophy and Other Essays*. Trans. Ben Brewster. London: New Left Books, 1971, 121–73.

Drakakis, John, ed. *Alternative Shakespeares*. London: Routledge, 1985.

Felperin, Howard. ' "Cultural Poetics" versus "Cultural Materialism": The Two New Historicisms in Renaissance Studies.' In *The Uses of the Canon: Elizabethan Literature and Contemporary Theory*. Oxford: Clarendon P, 1990, 142–69.

Greenblatt, Stephen. 'Towards a Cultural Poetics.' In *The New Historicism*. Ed. H. Aram Veeser. New York: Routledge, 1989, 1–14.

– *Renaissance Self-Fashioning: From More to Shakespeare*. Chicago: U of Chicago P, 1980.

Hall, Stuart, ed. *Culture, Media, Language: Working Papers in Cultural Studies, 1972–79*. London: Hutchinson, 1980.

Holderness, Graham. *Shakespeare's History*. New York: St. Martin's, 1985.

Howard, Jean, 'The New Historicism in Renaissance Studies.' *English Literary Renaissance* 16 (1986): 13–43.

Howard, Jean, and Marion O'Connor, eds. *Shakespeare Reproduced: The Text in History and Ideology*. New York: Methuen, 1987.

Levinson, Marjorie. *Wordsworth's Great Period Poems*. Cambridge: Cambridge UP, 1986.

Lovell, Terry. *Pictures of Reality: Aesthetics, Politics, Pleasure*. London: British Film Institute Publishing, 1980.

McGann, Jerome J. *The Romantic Ideology: A Critical Investigation*. Chicago: U of Chicago P, 1983.

Montrose, Louis. 'Renaissance Literary Studies and the Subject of History.' *English Literary Renaissance* 16 (1986): 5–12.

Patterson, Lee. *Negotiating the Past: The Historical Understanding of Medieval Literature*. Madison: U of Wisconsin P, 1987.

Poovey, Mary. *Uneven Developments: The Ideological Work of Gender in Mid-Victorian England*. Chicago: U of Chicago P, 1988.

Sinfield, Alan. *Literature, Politics and Culture in Postwar Britain*. Oxford: Basil Blackwell, 1989.

Tillyard, E.M.W. *The Elizabethan World Picture*. London: Chatto and Windus, 1948.

Wolff, Janet. *The Social Production of Art*. London: Macmillan, 1981.

Cultural poetics: *see* New Historicism

Deconstruction

Deconstruction, a school of philosophy that originated in France in the late 1960s, has had an enormous impact on Anglo-American criticism. Largely the creation of its chief proponent *Jacques Derrida, deconstruction upends the Western metaphysical tradition. It represents a complex response to a variety of theoretical and philosophical movements of the 20th century, most notably Husserlian phenomenology, Saussurean and French *structuralism and Freudian and Lacanian psychoanalysis. Derrida's work represents both a continuation and a critique of *Heidegger's 'deconstruction' of philosophy and metaphysics and of *Nietzsche's polemic levelled at the same tradition of thought. (See *Edmund Husserl, *Ferdinand de Saussure, *Sigmund Freud, *Jacques Lacan, *psychoanalytic theory, *phenomenological criticism.)

For Derrida deconstruction's task is twofold: first, to expose the problematic nature of all 'centred' discourses, those which depend on concepts such as truth, presence, origin, or their equivalents; second, to overturn metaphysics by displacing its conceptual limits. Deconstruction seeks to inhabit the margins of traditional systems of thought in order to put pressure on their borders and to test their unexamined foundations. As an alternative to the strictures of the metaphysical tradition, the vestiges of which Derrida sees as still integral to both structuralism and phenomenology, deconstruction celebrates limitless interpretation and an unrestricted semantic play that is no longer anchored in any signified. This unrestricted play should not be taken to mean, however, that deconstruction naively advocates 'subjective' or 'free' interpretation. Derrida argues, rather, that the possibility of signification in general depends upon an irreducible effect of *dissémination*, on the fact that the wandering of meaning is the insurmountable condition of the production of meaning. (See *theories of play/freeplay, *discourse, *margin, *signified/signifier/signification.)

History

Although the influence of deconstruction was notable in the France of the late 1960s and early 1970s, it was most significant in the U.S.A. and grew throughout the 1970s and early 1980s. It became for a time the focus of considerable debate and controversy among literary critics and scholars, some of whom saw it as critical nihilism. In the United States, its most celebrated – and provocative – proponent was *Paul de Man, who along with *J. Hillis Miller, Barbara Johnson, *Geoffrey Hartman, *Harold Bloom, and others formed the 'Yale School.'

The impact of deconstruction can be understood partly in terms of its historical moment in the field of literary studies. At a time of intense intellectual crisis, it came to represent a powerful antihumanist scepticism regarding all the entrenched 'theological' securities of truth, *reference, meaning, *intention, unity of form, and content that still dominate historical, author-oriented, and formalist approaches to *literature. Indeed, its notoriety was such that it often became identified with the practice of literary theory per se. More recently it has been recognized and accepted as an important critical approach and to some extent can be regarded as the heir to *New Criticism, the school of interpretation against which its American practice seemed most pointedly directed. Logically for a movement of contestation and radical doubt, its own coming of age has been signalled by the fact that it is now the 'old' school currently challenged by other emergent programs, especially 'political' ones, such as *New Historicism.

Derrida's critique of metaphysics

Deconstruction as practised by Derrida should be carefully separated from the work of his American counterparts. Derrida's term *logocentrism describes the Western philosophical tradition as perpetuating a fundamental opposition between speech and writing. This tradition sees speech as possessing a vital immediacy, a 'presence,' as both the presence of its speaker and more important the presence of speech to consciousness. Writing disrupts this presence: through the advent of the graphic sign or written mark, the voice is alienated and falls into the realm of alterity, absence and death. Writing is traditionally viewed as exemplary of the 'absence' associated with the 'fallen' order of the *sign where the sign and the written sign in particular is understood only as 'the signifier of the signifier'; that is, as the merely secondary representation of a speech that is itself a representation, but one so approximate as to be thought of as virtually present to consciousness. According to Derrida, this inextricable link made between presence and the spoken word is the cornerstone of the metaphysical foundation and consequently is the most stubborn stone to dislodge, even in those discourses which most forcefully contest the metaphysical tradition, such as those of Sigmund Freud, Karl Marx, Ferdinand de Saussure, Edmund Husserl, Martin Heidegger, and Friedrich Nietzsche.

Derrida's first major work, *La Voix et le phénomène* [*Speech and Phenomena (and Other Essays on Husserl's Theory of Signs)* 1967], is a critique of Husserl's phenomenology, which for all its antimetaphysical intent Derrida exposes as still falling well within the strictest boundaries of metaphysical thinking. It is in this work that the terms *metaphysics of presence and logocentrism are first introduced. Derrida sees Husserl's work as ultimately founded on an assumption of presence and of a voice that is identifiable with the self-presence of consciousness, in opposition to the merely representational, exterior, 'fallen' mediation of the *grapheme* or written mark.

In 'La Structure, le signe, et le jeu' ('Structure, Sign, and Play,' *Writing and Difference* 1967) and more extensively in the opening section of *De la Grammatologie* [*Of Grammatology* 1967], Derrida undertakes an analogous critique of structuralism, to which phenomenology, in the philosophical tradition, is generally opposed. (See *grammatology.) Derrida makes explicit his debt to Saussure's understanding of language as a system of differences with no positive terms. But he insists on the need to free the structuralist conception of the sign from its deep-rooted metaphysical assumptions. In Saussure and his structuralist heirs, the pre-eminence of the signified over the signifier is the expression of the same metaphysical assumption concerning meaning as that of any system which posits as its foundation a transcendental signified or 'presence.' If language, however, is a system of relations exclusively defined by the difference between terms, then meaning can never be arrested but must perpetually be deferred among the signifiers in the network. Carrying Saussure's discovery to its logical conclusion, Derrida invents the neologism *différance* to describe, in the system of differences that is language, the production of both difference(s) and the deferral of the signified or 'presence' (see *différ-ance/différence*).

According to Derrida, Saussure also makes the same strategic move as Husserl when he rejects writing in favour of speech to serve as a suitable model of the sign in general. The decision is based on the same assumption of writing being merely a representation of speech and of the latter being present, or absolutely approximate, to consciousness. According to such a view, it is only subsequently that speech or the voice is alienated and exteriorized in the graphic mark, which simply represents it in its absence and in the absence of the speaker or intending subject.

Writing thus comes to play in metaphysical discourse the ambivalent role Derrida perceives it as occupying in Plato's *Phaedrus*. In 'La Pharmacie de Platon' (*La Dissémination* 1972), he shows how for Plato writing is the fatal contaminant which must be violently expelled from the vicinity of a responsible and reliable spoken word in order to protect the living, memorial power of consciousness; with writing comes the absence of a 'present' living subject and the dangerous distance produced by a representation that is exterior to consciousness, and thus the fatal wandering of meaning and memory from their source. As Derrida shows, however, the dangers associated with writing extend generally to the possibility of all signification in the first place, speech included. The subject – speaking or written – is divided in his or her very constitution by the act of signification since meaning always already depends upon a network of differential marks; such is the condition of the production of meaning from the beginning. This difference from itself is not something that befalls speech accidentally from the exterior and then must be corrected in order to preserve a 'proper' meaning. The *pharmakos*, Derrida notes, is always chosen from within the community and is then expelled to the outside, just as writing which is already 'proper' to speech as its inescapable condition is banished along with its inventor Thot by Thamus in Plato's fable in *Phaedrus*.

If the necessary condition of signification in general is a system of differential or classificatory marks, then we should no longer think of the subject's entry into the realm of language, signs and representation as an alienating catastrophe, as some sort of tragic expulsion from original identity into the exile of alterity, ab-

sense, death. For there is no conceivable identity or subject *before* there exists a signifying system in which differentiation is possible. In its very constitution, Derrida insists, the subject is a becoming – absent, cut adrift by difference and deferral. The idea of a self identical to itself in time is itself produced only within a network of signs in which distinction and therefore identity is possible in the first place. And yet, the desire for identity as self-presence is inherently frustrated precisely because the process by which meaning is conveyed is unlimited. Meaning is produced in such a system only by a perpetual displacement or deferral of the signified, the signified of the signifier being itself always already another signifier, ad infinitum. This is what Derrida means by writing as a differing and deferring movement which '*comprehends* language,' whereby 'the signified always already functions as a signifier. The secondarity that it seemed possible to ascribe to writing alone affects all signifieds in general, affects them always already, the moment they *enter the game*. There is not a single signified that escapes, even if recaptured, the play of signifying references that constitute language. The advent of writing is the advent of this play' (*Of Grammatology* 7).

The law of the proper

In Derrida's later writings, the term metaphysics of presence is eclipsed by a related term: the law of the proper. The advantage of this term lies in its own possibilities for dissemination. When Derrida uses the term, he exploits the various meanings of the French word *propre*, which include *sens propre* or literal meaning and *propreté* or cleanliness, as well as the family of terms and concepts that we also find in English: property and the proprietary, appropriation, expropriation, with all their related senses of ownership, appurtenance, and belonging, as well as of propriety, all of which he links further to the value of proximity (for example, the nearness of speech to consciousness, or of consciousness to its object, or of conceptions of truth as the approximation of representation to its object) and finally to presence or *parousia* itself. Finally, there is the fact that the phrase 'the law of the proper' or 'the law of the house,' as the science or administration of the proper, is a special translation of the Greek *oiko-nomia*, from which we get our word 'economy.' It thus signifies the restricted and circular 'economy' – in which the proper, as it were, is always returning to itself, to its proper place – which governs the metaphysics of presence in its most imperial scope. The shape of this philosophical project descends, it would seem, from the theological notion of fall and redemption: humanity is alienated from God (presence or origin of proper meaning) and enters the fallen dimension of history (the world of 'improper' representations and signs), for a period of wandering and error which results, finally, in a return to the proper place, the transcendent form of which is, in fact, an improvement on the original place of origin. A similar circularity of the 'proper' is at work in the totalizing ambition of philosophy, which would reappropriate everything to itself in the form of a unique knowledge, the whole dimension of human becoming, of history in its entirety, as that which, as a fallen order of 'aliases,' of alienated meaning, of alterity, must finally be resumed under a proper name and thus possess a unique, 'proper,' or literal meaning (*sens propre*). (See *white mythology, *totalization.)

This interest in the implications of the proper name and of *sens propre* lies behind Derrida's preoccupation with the *paradox of translation, the simultaneous necessity and impossibility of translation imposed by the irreducible plurality of languages and discourses. This dilemma represents a further case of the condition of signification in general as that of the unrestricted disseminal drifting of meaning, a drifting which is no longer to be conceived of as governed by any orientation away from or towards a unique, 'proper' source. (See also theories of *translation.)

The paradox of translation explains Derrida's fascination, for example in 'Des Tours de Babel,' with the story of Babel. The biblical fable tells of the loss of presence as a simultaneous 'fall' into history and into language as the loss of proper name(s) or proper meaning(s) – the confounding of one language into the confusion of languages, the loss of one name for humanity, one language, one meaning, and the exile into the plurality of languages, and into the negative necessity of translation. According to the same view, Apocalypse can be read as the story of the return or restoration of the proper name(s). In *La Carte postale: De Socrates à Freud et au-délà* [*The Post Card: From Socrates to Freud and Beyond* 1980] and else-

where, Derrida plays on the fact that the last book of the Bible is also a scene of writing, of dictation and letter-writing, a veritable postal scene of ordering, sending, and delegation, and therefore of potentially endless suspension, deferral and delay; it thus points to an undermining of the very 'truth' it purports to convey, the strictly circulated message that it purports to send without any damage to an identifiable 'proper' content or signified. For Derrida, any message is always already diverted from its proper destination by the disseminal condition of all signification. It is always a case, as he puts it in 'Le Facteur de la vérité' ['The Purveyor of Truth'] – an essay which contests Lacan's reading of Poe's 'The Purloined Letter' in 'Le Séminaire sur la lettre volée' ['Seminar on the Purloined Letter'] – of the no-possible return of the letter, of the signified; indeed, an implication of the disseminal dis-orientation of signification in general, as *écriture*, is that a letter – a proper meaning addressed by one subject to another – never arrives at its destination, that is, to its proper place.

Derrida's interest in the 'proper' finds perhaps its most intriguing manifestation in his fascination with the 'proper name' and its relation to the signature. There is, for example, his play in *Glas* (1974) on the name of Hegel and *aigle* and on Genet (in French, a homonym of the word for the flower 'broom'). Similarly, in *Signéponge/Signsponge* (1984), Derrida shows how Francis Ponge's proper name and its 'proper' meaning is methodically disseminated throughout his work. He exploits the added meaning in French of 'propre' as 'clean' in order to play on the idea of the impossible desire to efface the 'dirt' of difference, otherness, the irreducible plurality of 'aliases,' the metaphysical desire to reduce all difference to the purity of the unique, proper, literal, meaning, to a proper name which is the housing of a presence. Derrida's point is that the 'proper' is always already divided and disseminated in its very constitution. The 'proper name' with its presumed unique referent and irreplaceable subject is only possible because of a signature, and this dependency on a signature implies its reproducibility, its iterability as part of a differential and classificatory structure; thus, the subject as a unique referent is always already opened into an endless chain of copies and representations.

The implications for the study of *literature of what Derrida has to say about 'writing' have only begun to be fully explored. The notoriety of deconstruction has often distracted the scholarly community from an objective examination of that possible contribution. Literature, indeed, as a sort of 'open letter' to the world, would seem eminently to demonstrate the validity of Derrida's insistence on an endless 'wandering' of meaning as the very condition of interpretation. The history of interpretation alone points to the necessarily plural and disseminal character of signification.

Deconstruction in the United States

Although Derrida's work has held a prominent place in France, it has always been that of one voice among a clamorous many. Deconstruction has had its most significant impact in the United States. Initially, deconstruction was associated with a number of professors in the departments of comparative literature and English at Yale University, where Derrida taught a yearly seminar from 1975–85. The 'Yale School' was born in the early 1970s with Paul de Man's inaugural *Blindness and Insight* (1971) formulating the paradoxical critical position that interpretation is misinterpretation, that the only 'insight' comes through error, and that the only authentic path to knowledge about literary texts is through one's blindness: that is, through presuppositions which throw light on the object of interpretation only in obscuring it at the same time. (See *text.) Around de Man a loosely knit group formed, made up of colleagues and students at Yale. Harold Bloom's theory of poetic misprision or misreading as the source of imaginative power links his very different position to de Man's. J. Hillis Miller, whose critical position is closest to de Man's, still remains one of the most important champions of deconstruction. Geoffrey Hartman has been more an explicator of Derrida as an imaginative writer than an adherent to deconstruction. The publication of *Deconstruction and Criticism* (1979), a collection of essays by Derrida and the four above-mentioned critics, stands as the closest thing to a programmatic statement by the 'school.' Hartman and Bloom have never been, strictly speaking, proponents of deconstruction, and indeed represent a certain resistance to its main tenets. The charismatic de Man, on the other hand, remained closely associated with Derrida throughout his career and continued until his death in 1984 to offer his own brand of deconstruction, one which became known for the brilliance of its tenaciously close, often tortuous readings of the works of authors such as Rousseau, Nietzsche, Shelley, Proust, and Rilke.

The practice of deconstruction in America differs significantly from its French counterpart in many ways. Most obviously, it grafts an essentially philosophical program onto the reading and interpretation of literary texts. Although such a move is somewhat justified by Derrida's frequent choice of literary texts for analysis, it leads to a treatment of the literary object primarily as a philosophical statement, or as an indirect and often unwitting statement about what are essentially philosophical concerns (knowledge of reality, the foundation of truth and error) or strictly theoretical concerns (the absence of the referent).

De Man and others thus adapt Derrida's general view of signification as 'writing' or 'arche-writing' and turn it into a 'sceptical' method of reading aimed at challenging canonic or normative methods of interpretation. (See *canon.) If the absence of the subject is the condition of signification in general and if all discourse therefore shares with writing the liability of misinterpretation (traditionally understood as consequent on the absence of the speaker), then misinterpretation or misreading is the very condition of all discourse. Thus the correct or proper interpretation of literary texts according to established canons of intentionality, meaning and truth can only be upheld arbitrarily. There is no longer anything to prevent errors of reading, since error is the condition of language, and therefore at the heart of all our readings of literary texts there is an inevitable collapse of meaning.

De Man in *Allegories of Reading* (1979), *The Rhetoric of Romanticism* (1984), and *The Resistance to Theory* (1986), Miller in *The Linguistic Moment* (1985), and Johnson in *The Critical Difference* (1981) seek by their close attention to the language of the text to expose the inherently contradictory nature of the meaning we elaborate when we read. American deconstruction thus tends to ignore Derrida's affirmative interest in *écriture*, his name for the complex variety of effects produced by graphic signs. Chiefly adapted has been the means of dismantling any given discourse through a radical reading strategy. By close attention to some strategically chosen 'marginal' aspect of the text, the critic draws out the levels of meaning that threaten the text's global intelligibility. (See *centre/decentre.) By seeking out its contradictions, its inherent error regarding its own unexamined tenets, such readings demonstrate the impossibility of the text's saying anything or taking any position that it does not itself undermine. Such an approach discloses an epistemological concern; it is a form of reading as radical doubt or *aporia. Indeed, de Man regards the literary text as a privileged cognitive model: his interest is in what the text tells us about what we can and cannot know. Increasingly, de Man, Miller and Johnson focus on the figural or rhetorical language of the text to show how it escapes reduction to any proper meaning and how it relentlessly contests our capacity to make sense of its own metaphoric language. (See also *textuality.)

Influence and contestation of deconstruction

It is hard to gauge the extent of the impact of deconstruction, partly because of the school's notoriety, which has obscured the issues it has raised, partly because its influence has been diffuse – everyone has heard of deconstruction and knows a little about it – and partly because its influence is often inseparable from the other theoretical streams with which it is often associated. Deconstruction is one school that, along with a host of other theoretical developments represented by writers such as *Michel Foucault, Jacques Lacan, *Roland Barthes, *Jean-Francois Lyotard, *Julia Kristeva, and others, make up what is known as *poststructuralism. Deconstruction shares with all these discourses a profound 'suspicion' concerning traditional modes of understanding history, subjectivity and knowledge. On the other hand, deconstruction shares with the more conservative hermeneutical schools an interest in the interpretation of written texts (thus the label 'hermeneutical mafia' that detractors used for the 'Yale School' critics), even if the conclusions drawn by the two are at opposite poles: the meaning that the hermeneutical reader would reinstitute is that 'proper' meaning which Derrida and other deconstructionists declare is always already disseminated and irrecoverable. (See *hermeneutics.)

Deconstruction has met with a good deal of contestation and not only from traditional scholars. Derrida's work has, for example, been strongly challenged by Foucault and his adherents for its ahistorical and apolitical 'tex-

tualism,' its lack of awareness of critical historical distinctions, its treatment of the history of philosophy as one history and not as a series of discrete, discontinuous formations. In both France and North America, deconstruction has been similarly criticized by Marxist critics, who regard it as politically ineffective. Frank Lentricchia (*After the New Criticism* 1980) and others accuse it, especially in its American form, of being a mere rhetoric of contestation which does nothing to change the institutional structures. It is true that deconstructive critics tend to focus on canonic texts and have done little to challenge the shape of traditional literary history. It is also true that their readings tend to be like the New Critical (or in England, Leavisite) readings they so often contest, exclusively oriented to the isolated text or author, reflecting an apparent indifference to both social and literary history. Significantly enough, it is the importance of this historical context which has recently become the focus of the Foucault-inspired school of New Historicism. (See *Marxist criticism, *F.R. Leavis.)

It is hard to predict the future of deconstruction in North America. Based as it is on a general and not specifically literary theory of signification, the approach has largely become a method for reading texts as allegories of deconstruction itself, as the title of de Man's second book, *Allegories of Reading*, suggests. What began as a critique of methods and systems of reading can be legitimately accused of having succumbed to the normative methodization it criticized. The *reification and institutionalization of deconstruction has proved to be inevitable. Another one of de Man's titles, *The Rhetoric of Romanticism*, points to the other major limitation of American deconstruction: the focus on rhetorical structures betrays a tendency to identify literary meaning narrowly with the text's figural meaning. At the same time, the treatment of the literary text as a cognitive model that the verbal level contradicts could be perceived as reflecting a fundamental misunderstanding concerning the imaginative nature of literary vision. (See also *rhetorical criticism, *metacriticism.)

JOSEPH ADAMSON

Primary Sources

de Man, Paul. *Allegories of Reading: Figural Language in Rousseau, Nietzsche, Rilke, and Proust.* New Haven: Yale UP, 1979.
– *Blindness and Insight: Essays in the Rhetoric of Con-*

temporary Criticism. New York: Oxford UP, 1971.
- *The Resistance to Theory*. Minneapolis: U of Minnesota P, 1986.
- *The Rhetoric of Romanticism*. New York: Columbia UP, 1984.

Derrida, Jacques. *La Dissémination*. 1972. *Dissemination*. Trans. Barbara Johnson. Chicago: U of Chicago P, 1981.
- 'Le Facteur de la vérité.' In *The Post Card*, 411–96.
- *Glas*. Paris: Galilée, 1974.
- *Margins of Philosophy*. Trans. Alan Bass. Chicago: U of Chicago P, 1982.
- *Of Grammatology*. Trans. Gayatri Chakravorty Spivak. Baltimore: Johns Hopkins UP, 1977.
- *The Post Card: From Socrates to Freud and Beyond*. Trans. Alan Bass. Chicago: U of Chicago P, 1987.
- *Signéponge/Signsponge*. Trans. Richard Rand. New York: Columbia UP, 1984.
- *Speech and Phenomena (and Other Essays on Husserl's Theory of Signs)*. Trans. David B. Allison. Evanston: Northwestern UP, 1973.
- 'Structure, Sign, and Play.' In *Writing and Difference*, 278–93.
- 'Des Tours de Babel.' In *Difference in Translation*. Trans. and ed. Joseph F. Graham. Ithaca: Cornell UP, 1985, 165–248.
- *The Truth in Painting*. Trans. Geoff Bennington and Ian McLeod. Chicago: U of Chicago P, 1987.
- *Writing and Difference*. Trans. Alan Bass. Chicago: U of Chicago P, 1978.

Hartman, Geoffrey, ed. *Deconstruction and Criticism*. New York: Seabury, 1979.
Jacobs, Carol. *The Dissimulating Harmony: Images of Interpretation in Nietzsche, Rilke and Benjamin*. Baltimore: Johns Hopkins UP, 1978.
Johnson, Barbara. *The Critical Difference: Essays in the Contemporary Rhetoric of Reading*. Baltimore: Johns Hopkins UP, 1981.
- *Défigurations du langage poétique*. Paris: Flammarion, 1979.
Miller, J. Hillis. *Fiction and Repetition: Seven English Novels*. Cambridge: Harvard UP, 1982.
- *The Linguistic Moment: From Wordsworth to Stevens*. Princeton: Princeton UP, 1985.

Secondary Sources

Culler, Jonathan. *On Deconstruction: Theory and Criticism after Structuralism*. Ithaca: Cornell UP, 1982.
Hartman, Geoffrey H. *Saving the Text: Literature/Derrida/Philosophy*. Baltimore: Johns Hopkins UP, 1981.
Harvey, Irene. *Derrida and the Economy of Différance*. Bloomington: Indiana UP, 1986.
Lentricchia, Frank. *After the New Criticism*. Chicago: U of Chicago P, 1980.
Norris, Christopher. *Deconstruction: Theory and Practice*. London: Methuen, 1982.

Dialogical criticism

Dialogical criticism, covering a diverse set of critical practices that developed primarily in the last three decades of this century, is characterized by attention to two factors: the larger historical and critical context of a *text and, more specifically within the text proper, to a polyphonic heterogeneity. The work of *Mikhail Bakhtin is commonly considered its guiding inspiration. Martin Buber, Bakhtin's contemporary and also a highly original philosopher of 'dialogism' (*Ich und Du* 1923), and Francis Jacques (*Dialogiques* 1979), the philosopher, have not had the same widespread influence. The debate surrounding Bakhtin's politics (was he a Marxist or a liberal humanist?) carries over into the critical works in which his ideas have been extended or applied. Bakhtin's 'dialogism' can therefore be seen in the work of both apolitical and politicized critics. The discussion of dialogical criticism is restricted here to Bakhtin as dialogical critic and to criticism inspired by Bakhtin. (See *double-voicing/dialogism.)

Bakhtin as dialogical critic

Bakhtin's 'criticism' should be understood in a heuristic sense with an underlying ethical thrust and should not be reduced to a mere technique of formal analysis since it assumes an anthropological vision of the world. Such a vision informs the two most studied phases in Bakhtin's life: from 1924 to 1930, when he developed his ideas on *polyphony, utterance and 'double-voiced words' in the works of Dostoevsky; and between the early 1930s and 1950s when his attention focused on *discourse in the novel and the carnivalesque in the work of Rabelais. (See *carnival.) Generally speaking, Bakhtin's writings from the early 1920s and those from the last two decades of his life have played, to date, a limited role in the development of a dialogical criticism.

The dialogical approach appears for the first time in Bakhtin's *Problems of Dostoevsky's Poetics* (1929) as a means of characterizing Dostoevsky's tendency to create a textual space where several voices are literally heard, where they converse, answer one another, and yet where no voice dominates the others. In this study, Bakhtin sees Dostoevsky as 'the creator of the polyphonic novel': 'A plurality of independent and unmerged voices and consciousnesses, a genuine polyphony of fully valid voices is in fact the chief characteristic of Dostoevsky's novels' (6). Bakhtin contrasts the dialogical discourse of the Dostoevsky novel with the *monologism of traditional au thorial discourse in which one voice attempts to dominate all others. (See *polyphonic novel.)

Bakhtin's critical practice is doubly dialogical. First, he typically carries out a thorough critique of the different theoretical and ideological approaches to the topic that he wishes to explore. In both *Problems of Dostoevsky's Poetics* and *Rabelais and His World* (1965), for example, Bakhtin begins by instituting a dialogue between previous studies and his own commentaries. Such a method is characteristic of Bakhtinian thought, which sees itself as always taking place within the continuation of a larger historical and critical movement. By inserting his own analysis within the critical field he has carefully described, Bakhtin thus sees his own research as a temporary step that may soon be revised or rejected in the evolving continuum of critical theory. Second, Bakhtin's work is dialogical in so far as it reveals the polyphonic heterogeneity (that is, *dialogism*) of some of the major authors of world literature (Rabelais, Cervantes, Dostoevsky).

Bakhtin's approach is also dialogical in that it invokes different analytical disciplines in order to determine the object of its reflection. He derives his concepts from, among others, music (polyphony), the natural sciences (chronotope), psychology (*self/other) philosophy (value), anthropology (carnivalesque), and linguistics (utterance). The variety of these disciplines and their complementarity or their opposition prevent any monological (univocal) conclusions. Such a refusal of fixity can be observed in Bakhtin's criticism of the Russian formalist movement as well as of narrowly defined semiotic approaches, which, he claims, tend to view the text as a hermetic and self-signifying whole. (See *formalism, Russian; *semiotics.)

Bakhtin rejects an analysis that would ignore the context (sociohistorical, ideological) of production as well as the context of reception. Thus, in his introduction to *Rabelais and His World*, he attacks the studies on Rabelais that have not taken into account the cultural, popular and historical dimension of carnival.

Opposing dogmatism, which is necessarily

monological, Bakhtin raises questions and offers hypotheses, but his answers remain open and incomplete because he sees them as being intrinsically so: 'There is neither a first nor a last word and there are no limits to the dialogic context (it extends into the boundless past and the boundless future). Even past meanings, that is, those born in the dialogue of past centuries, can never be stable (finalized, ended once for all) – they will always change (be renewed) in the process of subsequent, future development of the dialogue' (*Speech Genres* 170). Bakhtin aims at thinking out the tensions of a text, at describing and analysing its dialogical dynamics, but not at resolving them, even dialectically, since dialectics is, in his eyes, the most elaborated and therefore the most pernicious form of monological thought.

However, in spite of himself, Bakhtin does not always resist the temptation of idealism, itself a form of monological thinking. In *Rabelais and His World*, he seems to propose a somewhat naive, 'optimistic' or utopian conception of the centrifugal (subversive) role of popular culture opposing the centripetal (stratifying) forces of official culture. Likewise in 'Toward a Methodology for the Human Sciences' (in *Speech Genres*), he adheres to the hypothesis of an eternal return of meaning that, like the phoenix, perpetually rises from its own ashes: 'Nothing is absolutely dead: every meaning will have its homecoming festival. The problem of great time' (historical time considered over long periods) (170). The ambiguity of this formulation has allowed some critics to situate Bakhtin as a metaphysical or transcendental thinker. Such a view is strongly opposed, however, by those who point out that when meanings (or interpretations) reappear through history, they are always in renewed and changed form.

Criticism inspired by Bakhtin

The key categories found in Bakhtin's work and most frequently brought into play in dialogical criticism are polyphony, the carnivalesque, alterity (self/other), genre, hybridization, monologism, context, and chronotope (an analytical category used to understand in a unified way the spatial and temporal dimensions of texts). Most critics have tended to choose one of these categories and to bring it to bear on an individual text (literary, anthropological, philosophical, etc.). Only a very few, such as *Tzvetan Todorov (France), Michael Holquist (United States), André Belleau (Canada), Ken Hirschkop (England), and some feminist critics (Patricia Yaegar, United States; Myriam Diaz-Diocaretz, Holland) have attempted to provide dialogical criticism with a broad conceptual framework. Although there is considerable disparity of opinion over what this approach entails as a precise methodology, most critics concur that Bakhtin's ideas have been crucial in encouraging interdisciplinary thinking.

Tzvetan Todorov

According to Todorov, the dialogical critic assumes that truth (in the sense of wisdom about a text) is attainable, although it may never be reached. The ideal relation between the critic and the text to be studied is seen as an encounter or dialogue between two separate voices neither of which is privileged over the other. The dialogical critic speaks *to* literary works, not *about* them. The text to be studied is a living discourse not an object to be mastered in light of some theory. If based on these principles, dialogical criticism avoids the traps of dogmatism (the assumption of privilege for the critic's voice) and relativism (all interpretations are equally valid). Todorov's *La Conquête de l'Amérique*, a study of the struggle between the colonizing voices of European explorers and the colonized voices of indigenous Amerindian peoples, is one example of dialogical criticism. (See also *post-colonial theory.)

Michael Holquist

Holquist's work provides dialogical criticism with a philosophical or, more specifically, epistemological basis. Bakhtin's dialogism is, in this view, primarily a meditation on language (a dialogue on dialogue) or a way of understanding human behaviour through the study of language. Dialogism and therefore dialogical criticism correspond to a new way of looking at the world, inspired, at the beginning of this century, by Einstein's theory of relativity. In dialogical criticism meaning is understood as relative or relational on two levels. First, the dialogical critic will never lose sight of the fact that his or her search for meaning is a tripartite phenomenon: there is the critic, the text to

be studied and the relation between the two. Second, the dialogical critic never looks for a single meaning in a text. Contesting meanings and the relations among them in the text are what the critic must describe. Katerina Clark and Michael Holquist's intellectual biography of Bakhtin (*Mikhail Bakhtin*) should be seen as an illustration of the dialogical approach: the relation between Bakhtin and the other important thinkers of his time is presented as a dialogue.

André Belleau

Belleau, a dialogical critic and theorist who has based his work in part on the concept of the carnivalesque as found in Bakhtin's study of Rabelais, also uses a sociological (or sociocritical) approach as well as tools from *narratology. (See also *sociocriticism.) Belleau sees both Quebec literature and Quebec society as profoundly imbued with carnivalesque elements: a conflictual mixture of the high or 'official' culture of France (or Europe more generally), the English-language culture of North America, and the indigenous 'popular' culture of Quebec. Belleau maintains that a dialogical criticism must avoid the pitfalls of positivism, binary thinking, ethnocentrism, *logocentrism, and idealism. His dialogical analyses of Quebec culture, society and language are always grounded, and insist on the open-ended, continually evolving character of social realities.

Ken Hirschkop

The basic tenet of Hirschkop's understanding of dialogical criticism is that the appropriation of Bakhtin's concepts, far from being neutral or arbitrary, is always political. An understanding of Bakhtin's dialogism can only be the 'sedimentation of past usages' (3) of the concept. Dialogism thus grounded in Marxism is not an abstract principle but rather a number of disparate critical practices (*parody, collage, stylization, etc.) as worked out by Bakhtin and subsequent critics. (See also *Marxist criticism.) Because of ambiguities in Bakhtin's own writing on dialogism, some appropriations of the concept have turned it into a transcendental principle of discourse. Hirschkop opposes this kind of 'theoreticism' (Bakhtin's term for a non-historical approach to cultural study). Dialogism is rather a critical practice whose objective is the unmasking of social languages. It will account for the conflicting pressures of the context in which socially conditioned utterances are produced.

Feminism

Most feminist critics who work from a dialogical perspective see Bakhtin's ideas as helpful in attacking patriarchal (or monological) myths about women and language. But because he neglected the category of gender (this has been called his misogyny or 'blind spot'), Bakhtin's concepts have to be adjusted to make them gender-sensitive. Feminist critics also have reservations about Bakhtin's utopian tendencies as expressed in the Rabelais book. Carnivalesque culture, rather than being characterized by a freeplay of discourses or voices (as Bakhtin sometimes suggests), is an unequal power struggle in which some voices will always try to control others. Critics like Patricia Yaeger and Myriam Diaz-Diocaretz have explored the notions of the carnivalesque, multivocality (the presence of several voices in a given language situation), the self/other, and hybridization (the bringing together of different literary genres in a given text) to forge an original version of dialogical criticism. (See *feminist criticism, *patriarchy, *theories of play/freeplay.)

Dialogical criticism is not an approach that can be easily defined or situated in relation to others. Dialogism has been said, however, to be more opposed to *deconstruction than to other approaches. In Bakhtin's work, the individual voice (with its own intonations and accents) is a fundamental category, whereas in deconstruction subjectivity is thoroughly problematized. Most dialogical critics seek to maintain a flexible and critical dialogue with other approaches. Although some commentators have seen the vagueness or ambiguity inherent in dialogism as a weakness, most feel that this is its greatest strength.

THIERRY BELLEGUIC and
CLIVE THOMSON

Primary Sources

Bakhtin, Mikhail. *The Dialogic Imagination: Four Essays by M.M. Bakhtin*. Ed. Michael Holquist. Trans. Caryl Emerson and Michael Holquist. Austin: U of Texas P, 1981.

- *Problems of Dostoevsky's Poetics*. Ed. and trans. Caryl Emerson. Minneapolis: U of Minneapolis P, 1984.
- *Rabelais and His World*. 1965. Trans. Hélène Iswolsky. MIT P, 1968; 2nd ed., Indiana UP, 1984.
- *Speech Genres and Other Late Essays*. Ed. Caryl Emerson and Michael Holquist. Trans. Vern W. McGee. Austin: U of Texas P, 1986.

Secondary Sources

Belleau, André. *Surprendre les voix: Essais*. Montreal: Boréal, 1986.
Clark, Katerina, and Michael Holquist. *Mikhail Bakhtin*. Cambridge: Harvard UP, 1984.
Diaz-Diocaretz, Myriam. 'Sieving the Matriheritage of the Sociotext.' In *The Difference Within: Feminism and Critical Theory*. Ed. Elizabeth Meese and Alice Parker. Amsterdam: John Benjamins, 1989, 115–47.
Hirschkop, Ken. 'Critical Work on the Bakhtin Circle: A Bibliographical Essay.' In *Bakhtin and Cultural Theory*. Ed. Ken Hirschkop and David Shepherd. Manchester: Manchester UP, 1989, 195–212.
Holquist, Michael. *Dialogism: Bakhtin and His World*. London: Routledge, 1990.
Todorov, Tzvetan. *Critique de la critique: Un roman d'apprentissage*. Paris: Seuil, 1984.
Yaeger, Patricia. *Honey-Mad Women: Emancipatory Strategies in Women's Writing*. New York: Columbia UP, 1988.
The following journals have published special issues on Bakhtin and dialogical criticism: *University of Ottawa Quarterly* 53.1 (1983); *Critical Inquiry* 10.2 (1983); *Etudes françaises* 20.1 (1984); *L'Immagine riflessa* 7.1/2 (1984); *Studies in Twentieth Century Literature* 9.1 (1984); *Critical Studies* 1.2 (1989), 2.1/2 (1990); *Bakhtin Newsletter* 1 (1983), 2 (1986), 3 (1991); *Discours social* 3.1/2 (1990), *Studies in the Literary Imagination* 23.1 (1990).

Discourse analysis theory

Discourse analysis is a cross-disciplinary method of inquiry which studies the structures of texts and considers both their linguistic and sociocultural dimensions in order to determine how meaning is constructed. (See *text.) In the Anglo-American context, discourse analysis concentrates on various forms of oral communication (everyday conversation, speech acts, 'talk') from an interactional and ethno-methodological perspective, and investigates how *power and *authority are distributed in verbal exchanges (Coulthard). The French stream of discourse analysis, following the works of *Michel Foucault, *Louis Althusser, Michel Pêcheux, and *Mikhail Bakhtin, constitutes its object very differently, concentrating largely, but not exclusively, on written material in its institutional, social and political contexts. Discourse analysis does not favour the 'high' cultural disciplines (*literature, philosophy, history); it employs methods developed in areas such as content analysis, *narratology, textual *semiotics, and Ideologiekritik to permit (if not favour) studies of all manifestations of *discourse in everyday life. Discourse analysis theory proposes that relations of power in our society affect and shape the way we both communicate with each other and create 'knowledge.'

Although *Ferdinand de Saussure's work on structural linguistics may have provoked or pre-empted interest in discourse analysis, Saussure was more interested in structures than in systems. More clearly a predecessor of contemporary discourse analysis is the linguist Zelig Harris who, in a book published in 1963, undertook to describe a 'method of seeking in any connected discrete linear material, whether language or language-like, which contains more than one elementary sentence, some global structure characterizing the whole discourse (the linear material), or large sections of it' (*Discourse Analysis Reprints* 7). Harris was interested in the ways in which segments of discourse (utterances, sentences, parts of sentences, words, parts of words) recur within a whole constituent or a sequence of constituents. Thus he concentrated upon the structure (the pattern or relations of meanings) in discourse which can be studied without reference to other information.

More recent work in discourse analysis relates studies in the structure of discourse to broader social and institutional phenomena and owes a significant debt to Foucault's work on enunciative analysis, the unities of discourse, and discursive formation set out in *L'Archéologie du savoir* [*Archaeology of Knowledge* 1969] and *L'Ordre du discours* ['Orders of Discourse' 1971], and to his many works which explore the articulation of knowledge and power in discourse: 'there is no power relation without the correlative constitution of a field of knowledge, nor any knowledge that does not presuppose and constitute at the same time power relations' (*Surveiller et punir; Disci-*

pline and Punish 1975; trans. 1977, 27). The work of Louis Althusser also contributes to the study of the way discourses are formed and of what institutional practices contribute to them. His 'Ideology and Ideological State Apparatuses' (1970) emphasizes that consciousness is constructed through ideologies and that 'ideologies are systems of meaning that install everybody in imaginary relations to the real relations in which they live' (McDonell 27). (See *Ideological State Apparatuses, *ideology, *ideological horizon.)

Discourse analysis contextualizes and formalizes studies in content analysis and thus generates questions concerning the production, reproduction, function, and effect of basic units of discourse within given ideological configurations and sociohistorical moments. These units are bound to their conditions of production and to the sociohistorical moment from which they emerge. Thus, discourse analysis is also a study of the rules, conventions and procedures which legitimate and to some degree determine a particular discursive practice. A thorough analysis of these areas of study covers a broad range of issues, beginning with the overriding problem of how to objectify the 'system' of a corpus, as well as the question of showing 'how the functional categories are realised by formal items' (Coulthard 8).

The French School of Discourse Analysis examines exchanges between several discourses (rather than any single practice). Marc Angenot, for example, defines social discourse as 'all that is said or written in a given state of society ... [or rather than] this empirical *whole*, ... the generic systems, the repertories of topics, the enunciative rules which, in a given society, organize the *sayable* – the narratable and the arguable – and insure the division of discursive labour' (1989, 13). Angenot et al. claim that within the compendium of social discourse, there emerge *patterns*, such as 'narrative and argumentional constructs, topical maxims, pragmatic markings, semantic paradigms, sociolectal markers and rhetorical figures that organize themselves into *social objects*' (Durkheim), and *facts* which, through usage, become powerful social forces which are neither strictly linguistic or gnoseological, and 'which *function independently* of particular usages and applications (1991, 3–4). By examining the relations between various kinds of texts (literary, political, scientific, religious, journalistic), discourse analysis both relies upon and develops research on *intertextuality (*Kristeva, *Riffaterre). Literature's once privileged place is abandoned in favour of a study of shared strategies of discourse which contribute to the general production of knowledge and power. Thus, for example, a study of 19th-century realism would focus not on 'a moment of literary history, but rather on *narrative realism* as ... [a] way of making sense of the world in various discourses – medical, sociological, criminological, in parliamentary debates, sermons, press reports' (Leps 232).

By concentrating upon the words and utterances of social discourse and by elucidating these rules, conventions, procedures, and facts, discourse analysis emphasizes the materiality of language, including that language which conveys the 'ideas,' 'mentalities,' 'values,' 'social imaginaries,' and 'representations' studied in fields such as the history of ideas. Such research also allows the study of broad political issues such as which *hegemony favours given discursive practices and what kinds of texts are preferred in particular sociodiscursive contexts. Discourse analysis is proving useful in many areas – sociology, history, anthropology – as a conceptual matrix to explore the social production of knowledges. (See also *sociocriticism.)

ROBERT F. BARSKY

Primary Sources

Althusser, Louis. 'Ideology and Ideological State Apparatuses (Notes towards an Investigation).' In *Lenin and Philosophy and Other Essays*. Trans. Ben Brewster. New York: Monthly Review P, 1971, 127–86.

Angenot, Marc. *Glossaire pratique de la critique contemporaine*. Montreal: Hurtubise, 1979.

– *1889: Un état du discours social*. Longueil, Que.: Le Préambule, 1989.

Angenot, Marc, Antonio Gomez-Moriana and Régine Robin. *Constitution: The Inter-University Centre for Discourse Analysis and Text Sociocriticism*. Trans. Nadia Khouri and Michelle Weinroth. Montreal: CIADEST, 1991.

Benzecri, J.P., ed. *Analyse des données: Leçons sur l'analyse factorielle et la reconnaissance de la forme, et travaux du laboratoire de statistique de l'Université de Paris VI*. Paris: Dunod, 1973.

Brown, G., and G. Yule. *Discourse Analysis*. Cambridge: Cambridge UP, 1983.

Coulthard, R.M. *Introduction to Discourse Analysis*. London: Longmans, 1977.

Foucault, Michel. *L'Archéologie du savoir*. Paris: Editions Gallimard, 1969. *The Archaeology of Knowledge*. Trans. A.M. Sheridan-Smith. New York/Hagerstown: Harper and Row, 1972.

– *L'Ordre du discours*. Inaugural lecture, Collège de France, 2 Dec. 1970. Paris: Editions Gallimard, 1971. 'Orders of Discourse.' Trans. Rupert Swyer. *Social Science Information* 10 (April 1971): 7–31. Repr. as 'Appendix: The Discourse on Language.' In *The Archaeology of Knowledge*. Trans. A.M. Sheridan-Smith. New York/Hagerstown: Harper and Row, 1972.

– *Surveiller et punir*. Paris: Editions Gallimard, 1975. *Discipline and Punish: The Birth of the Prison*. Trans. Alan Sheridan. New York: Pantheon, 1977.

Harris, Zelig. *Discourse Analysis Reprints*. The Hague: Mouton, 1963.

Leps, Marie-Christine. 'Discursive Displacements: The Example of 19th Century Realism.' *Proceedings of the 12th Congress of the International Comparative Literature Association* 5. Munich: Iudicium, 1988, 231–6.

McDonell, Diane. *Theories of Discourse: An Introduction*. Oxford: Basil Blackwell, 1986.

Stubbs, M. *Discourse Analysis: The Sociolinguistic Analysis of Natural Language*. Chicago: U of Chicago P. Oxford: Basil Blackwell, 1983.

Van Dijk, T.A., ed. *Handbook of Discourse Analysis*. 4 vols. London: Academic, 1985.

Empirical Science of Literature/Constructivist Theory of Literature

The Empirical Science of Literature (ESL) – or, alternatively, Constructivist Theory of Literature (CTL) – is a theoretical framework and methodology which was developed in the 1980s in the Federal Republic of Germany. In general terms, its theoretical, epistemological and methodological bases can be found in the sociology of *literature, in theories of communication, and in the more recent philosophical approach of constructivism. In addition to these three main areas, CTL can be traced back to the 19th-century notion of intellectual or cultural history and to the more ubiquitous notion of 'literary life.'

In its present state, CTL is best articulated in Siegfried J. Schmidt's *Grundriss der Empirischen Literaturwissenschaft* (1980–2; *Foundations for the Empirical Study of Literature* 1982). Its epistemological foundation, constructivism – only very remotely related to Russian *constructivism and developed from distinct philosophical and literary tenets – originated with, among others, the German thinker Hugo Dingler, who in turn developed it mainly from the works of Immanuel Kant. CTL's aim, to bridge the gap between the natural sciences and the humanities (cf. Butts and Brown, Foerster), and its concomitant focus on interdisciplinarity and team work has resulted in the fruitful cross-fertilization of ideas in literary scholarship with other disciplines such as the social sciences, psychology, philosophy, biology, neurology, mathematics, and physics. While the application and the development of the framework and methodology of a CTL has been steadily growing in the Western Hemisphere, in more recent years, centres or groups of literary scholars who subscribe to the theory and its methodology in a more focused manner have appeared in Germany, the Netherlands, the U.S.A., Hungary, Japan, and Canada. It has also attracted scholars interested in cognitive psychology and reading.

CTL is a systemic approach to literature. Its main purpose is to study what happens to literature and how it happens. The constructivist tenet that a subject largely construes its empirical world itself resulted in the recognition that literary interpretation and the strictly 'scientific' study of literature ought to be separate activities. It is important to note that the terms 'scientific' and 'empirical' are to be understood in the context of constructivism and not in their general context. 'Empirical' here means a non-positivist concept of empiricism, one that objectifies the literary *text; from this objectification it is developed into a procedural system of literature guided by rational argumentation (Schmidt in Foerster 150). The literary system of communicative interaction should be observed, not experienced. This postulate rests on two hypotheses. First, there is an aesthetic convention that is drawn from the convention of facts in the daily language of reference and, second, the literary system is based on a polyvalency convention that is different from the monovalency of the daily empirical world. These two hypotheses result in the study of literature by focusing not on the text per se but rather on the roles of social communicative interaction within the literary system, namely the production of the literary text, its distribution, its reception, and the processing of the text(s) (that is, criticism, scholarship, pedagogy, canonization, evaluation, and so forth) (van Gorp). ESL thus allows for the exploration of both the literary text and the socioliterary aspects of the literary system, thereby demon-

strating the social relevance of literature and of the study of literature. It also responds to the contemporary concern with marginality in and of certain types of literature while it maintains the locus of aesthetic value (Tötösy 1992).

The framework and methodology of CTL is related to other systemic approaches. These can be grouped into communication theories (including *semiotics) and the sociology of literature. Historically, the former includes the approaches of the Russian formalists, the *Prague School and the more recent *polysystem theory (Itamar Even-Zohar). (See also *formalism, Russian.) The sociology of literature group (e.g., Sarkany) includes the *champ littéraire* approach (*Pierre Bourdieu; cf. Bourdieu, van Rees, Schmidt and Verdaasdonk), *sociocriticism and the *école bibliologique* and the *l'institution littéraire* approach (Dubois). There are similarities between these systemic approaches and the various frameworks within cultural studies. However, these approaches and methodologies often become 'removed' from literature per se. In recent Anglo-American scholarship the works of Tony Bennett's *Outside Literature* (1990), Anthony Easthope's *Literary into Cultural Studies* (1991) and Jerome J. McGann's *The Textual Condition* (1991), for example, show sociological and system orientation.

More concretely, a specific branch of systemic theory groups, most clearly originating in the sociology of literature, are the French and Québécois-Canadian groups, which work with the concept of the *literary institution. This approach is most often associated with Dubois' *L'Institution de la littérature: Introduction à une sociologie* (1978), which also spawned a number of further studies (Moisan, Lemire and Lord, Nadeau, Robert).

Each of the systemic frameworks overlaps with other systemic theories. An early example of such overlapping occurs in K.E. Rosengren's *Sociological Aspects of the Literary System* (1968) and in P.E. Sørensen's *Elementare Literatursoziologie* (1976), which take both a systemic and an institutional view of literature. Also, polysystem theory, although in the first instance a communication/semiotic approach, contains many systemic components from the sociology of literature. For a range of similar works and approaches see Tötösy (1992).

While criticism of ESL has arisen in part because Anglo-American scholars frequently lack the German-language skills to become acquainted with the full context of the ESL/CTL framework, in general, systemic approaches encounter resistance among literary scholars because of the impression that the 'system' is imposed on literature. However, scholars working with systemic approaches insist that exactly because the literary system is a priori, literature should be studied within a systemic framework. Another frequent criticism occurs with reference to the terms 'empirical' and 'science,' as these beg the question whether either notion can or should be applied to literature. ESL/CTL scholars counter by pointing out that these terms should not be perceived in their traditional meanings but rather in the context of constructivism. Perhaps the most serious criticism of the framework is that its application results in trivialities (that is, in a confirmation of what was already known or intuited), that it is reductive, and that it is limited in its scope (for instance, to reader response instead of the study of the literary text). ESL/CTL scholars, however, contend that what are seen as trivialities often turn out to be assumptions rooted in scholarly conventions, traditions and desires. Thus empirical backing of these conventions and traditions is necessary because these assumptions often turn out to be just that, assumptions. Despite these criticisms, there is a growing corpus of works drawing upon the framework and methodology of ESL/CTL. (See also *communication theory, *reader-response criticism.)

STEVEN TÖTÖSY DE ZEPETNEK

Primary Sources

Bennett, T. *Outside Literature*. London and New York: Routledge, 1990.

Bourdieu, P. 'Questions of Method.' In *Empirical Studies of Literature: Proceedings of the Second IGEL-Conference, Amsterdam 1989*. Ed. E. Ibsch, D. Schram and G. Steen. Amsterdam/Atlanta, Ga: Rodopi, 1991, 19–36.

– K. van Rees, S.J. Schmidt, and H. Verdaasdonk. 'The Structure of the Literary Field and the Homogeneity of Cultural Choices.' In *Empirical Studies of Literature: Proceedings of the Second IGEL-Conference, Amsterdam 1989*. Ed. E. Ibsch, D. Schram and G. Steen Amsterdam/Atlanta, Ga: Rodopi, 1991, 427–43.

Butts, R.E., and J.R. Brown. *Constructivism and Science: Essays in Recent German Philosophy*. Dordrecht-Boston-London: Kluwer Academic, 1989.

Dubois, J. *L'Institution de la littérature: Introduction à une sociologie*. Paris: Nathan; Bruxelles: Labor, 1978.

– 'Institution littéraire.' In *Dictionnaire des littératures de langue française*. Ed. J.-P. de Beaumarchais, D. Couty, and A. Rey. Paris: Bordas, 1984, G–O: 1087–90.

Easthope, A. *Literary into Cultural Studies*. London and New York: Routledge, 1991.

Estivals, R. *Le Livre dans le monde*. Paris: RETZ, 1984.

– ed. *Le Livre en France*. Paris: RETZ, 1984.

Even-Zohar, I. *Polysystem Studies*. Special issue. *Poetics Today* 11.1 (Spring 1990).

Foerster, H. von, E. von Glasersfeld, P.M. Hejl, S.J. Schmidt, and P. Watzlawick. *Einführung in den Konstruktivismus*. Repr. München-Zürich: Piper, 1992.

Fokkema, D., and E. Ibsch. *Literatuurwetenschap & Cultuuroverdracht*. Muiderberg: Coutinho, 1992.

Gorp, H. van, et al. 'Empirische Literatuurwetenschap.' In *Lexicon van literaire termen*. 5th ed. Leuven: Wolters, 1991, 116–17.

Krohn, W., and G. Küppers. *Emergenz: Die Entstehung von Ordnung, Organisation und Bedeutung*. Frankfurt: Suhrkamp, 1992.

Lamonde, Y., éd. *L'Imprimé au Québec: Aspects historiques (18e–20e siècles)*. Quebec: Institut québécois de recherche sur la culture, 1983.

Lemire, M., and M. Lord, eds. *L'Institution littéraire*. Quebec: UP de Laval, 1986.

McGann, J.J. *The Textual Condition*. Princeton: Princeton UP, 1991.

Moisan, C. *Comparaison et raison: Essais sur l'histoire et l'institution des littératures canadienne et québécoise*. LaSalle: Hurtubise, 1987.

– *L'Histoire littéraire*. Paris: PUF, 1990.

– *Qu'est-ce que l'histoire littéraire?* Paris: PUF, 1987.

Nadeau, V. *Au commencement était le fascicule. Aux sources de l'édition québécoise contemporaine pour la masse*. Québec: Institut québécois de recherche sur la culture, 1984.

Robert, L. *Prolégomènes à une étude sur les transformations du marché du livre (1900–1940)*. Quebec: Institut québécois de recherche sur la culture, 1984.

– *L'Institution du littéraire au Québec*. Quebec: PU de Laval, 1989.

Rosengren, K.E. *Sociological Aspects of the Literary System*. Stockholm: Natur och Kultur, 1968.

Santerres-Sarkany, S. *Théorie de la littérature*. Paris: PUF, 1990.

Sarkany, S. *Québec Canada France: Le Canada littéraire à la croisée des cultures*. Aix-en-Provence: U de Provence, 1985.

Schmidt, S.J. *Grundriss der Empirischen Literaturwissenschaft*. Vol. 1: *Der gesellschaftliche Handlungsbereich Literatur*. Vol. 2: *Zur Rekonstruktion literaturwissenschaftlicher Fragestellungen in einer Empirischen Theorie der Literatur*. Braunschweig-Wiesbaden: Vieweg, 1980–2.

– *Foundations for the Empirical Study of Literature:*

The Components of a Basic Theory. Trans. R. de
Beaugrande. Hamburg: Buske, 1982.
– *Grundriss der Empirischen Literaturwissenschaft: Mit
einem Nachwort zur Taschenbuchausgabe.* Frankfurt:
Suhrkamp, 1991.
– 'Vom Text zum Literatursystem. Skizze einer kon-
struktivistischen (empirischen) Literaturwissen-
schaft.' In *Einführung in den Konstruktivismus.*
H. von Foerster, E. von Glasersfeld, P.M. Hejl,
S.J. Schmidt, and P. Watzlawick. Repr. München/
Zürich: Piper, 1992, 147–66.
Sørenson, P.E. *Elementare Literatursoziologie: Ein
Essay über literatursoziologische Grundprobleme.*
Trans. E. Meier and J. Glauser. Tübingen: Max
Niemeyer, 1976.
Tötösy de Zepetnek, S. 'The Empirical Science of
Literature and the Preface in the Nineteenth-Cen-
tury Canadian Novel: A Theoretical Framework
Applied.' *Canadian Review of Comparative Litera-
ture/Revue Canadienne de Littérature Comparée*
17.1–2 (1990): 68–84.
– 'The Empirical Science of Literature and the Nine-
teenth-Century Canadian Novel Preface: The Ap-
plication of a Literary Theory.' *SPIEL – Siegener
Periodicum zur Internationalen Empirischen Litera-
turwissenschaft* 9 (1990): 343–60.
– 'Systemic Approaches to Literature – An Introduction with Selected Bibliographies.' *Canadian Re-
view of Comparative Literature/Revue Canadienne
de Littérature Comparée* 19.1–2 (March/June 1992):
21–93.
Wilpert, G. von. 'Empirische Literaturwissenschaft.'
Sachwörterbuch der Literatur. 7th ed. Stuttgart:
Kröner, 1989, 233.
Würzbach, Natascha. 'Subjective Presentation of
Characters from the Perspective of Miriam's Expe-
rience in Dorothy Richardson's Novel *Pilgrimage*:
A Contribution to the Analysis of Constructivist
Narrative.' In *Modes of Narrative: Approaches to
American, Canadian and British Fiction.* Würzburg:
Königshausen and Neumann, 1990, 278–302.

Feminist criticism: *see* Feminist criticism, Anglo-American, French, Quebec

Feminist criticism, Anglo-American

Anglo-American feminist literary criticism
shares the same purpose as all feminist inquiry: that of exposing the mechanisms upon
which patriarchal society rests and by which it
is maintained, with the ultimate aim of transforming social relations. The object of feminist
criticism is therefore fundamentally 'political.'
Feminists advocate this transformational activity because they believe patriarchal society operates to the advantage of men and serves
men's interests above all others. A corollary of
this belief is the idea that patriarchal society
oppresses women. (See *patriarchy.)

There is no single, comprehensive definition
of feminism; feminism knows neither 'founding mothers' (cf. the respective 'fathers' of
Marxism and psychoanalysis, Marx and
*Freud) nor a distinctive methodology. At best,
we may speak of feminisms, all of which are
engaged in the transformational critical practice described above. These feminisms touch
many disciplines and are often interdisciplinary in approach; feminists tend to borrow
from other fields the methodological and conceptual tools that meet the needs of their
work. Feminist literary studies have touched
upon a vast array of critical problems, among
which are the following: the reconstruction of
women's history and of a female literary tradition; feminist historiography; canon formation;
black feminist criticism; the critique of representations of women in the visual arts and in
*literature; women and popular culture; the
debate over biological determinism versus the
social construction of gender; androgyny; lesbian culture and tradition; gendered reading;
the nature of women's writing and the conditions under which it is produced; autobiography and 'life-writing'; women and difference;
the question of a specifically 'female' language
and whether or not it exists; the *subversion
of patriarchal language; the problem of subjectivity and the constitution of gender identity;
post-colonialism and cultural imperialism; the
search for an alternative logic; the possibility
of a female epistemology. Feminists have been
able to engage a wide range of problems precisely because feminism is not grounded in an
integrated theory: diversity is the trademark of
feminist studies. (See also *canon, *subject/ob-
ject, *post-colonial theory.)

History

The Anglo-American world witnessed two major surges of feminism in the 20th century, the
first in connection with the fight for universal
suffrage (see Cott), the second arising out of
the widespread political movements of the
1960s as women came to realize that the goals
of the new left failed to take their aspirations

into account. The formation of women's groups and a growing interest in women's issues ensued, along with the call for the equality of the sexes and, in universities, for courses on women's literature. Anglo-American feminist literary studies have been marked by a number of general stages: early work focused on women's absence from the literary canon and strove to recover and promote a female literary tradition; the broad practice of critiquing or deconstructing representations of women in male-authored texts followed, then led to the business of finding 'accurate' representations of women which would allow for woman's 'reconstruction.' These studies helped extend feminist concerns to questions of class, race and sexual orientation. Finally, feminists have begun to engage in the critique of their own practices, a fact which indicates the positive development of a critical self-awareness.

Major practitioners

*Virginia Woolf (*A Room of One's Own* 1929) is widely recognized as an important forerunner of contemporary Anglo-American feminist thought. Early work on Woolf emphasized her role in modernism and in the Bloomsbury group; later, other scholars continued her attempts at charting a women's tradition in writing, based on the idea that women's difference was inscribed in their work (see Moers; Showalter 1977). More recent studies have related Woolf to the lesbian tradition. Mary Ellmann's *Thinking about Women* (1968), in which she posits the idea of 'modes' of writing (the masculine mode assuming a voice of *authority, the feminine taking a more playful approach) that are possible regardless of a writer's sex, was important in raising what has become a major issue of feminist criticism: the question whether women's writing is inherently different from men's, and, if so, how women's writing might be defined. Since the late 1970s and during the 1980s, this line of thought focused on theories of écriture féminine as developed by French feminists, notably *Hélène Cixous, *Luce Irigaray and *Julia Kristeva. (See *feminist criticism, French.) Other influential early work included Kate Millett's critique of 'femininity' and 'masculinity' in *Sexual Politics* (1970), which includes a study of the 'literary reflection' of women, according to patriarchal norms, in works by *D.H. Lawrence, Henry Miller and Norman Mailer. Millett describes

men's power over women as a form of coercive sexuality. Men's control is maintained through women's fear of rape and through the perpetuation of sex-role stereotypes that dictate, and thereby restrict, women's activity. Millett shows that sex roles are defined by cultural values which are in turn socially reproduced; hence, feminists speak of the 'social construction' of 'gender,' meaning that gender (unlike sex) is not biologically determined but is a product of social conditioning.

The critique of gender as a cultural construct proved a fruitful point of departure for subsequent feminist studies. Carolyn G. Heilbrun (1973) promoted the concept of androgyny in an effort to break the masculine/feminine dichotomy based on essentialist conceptions of gender. (See *essentialism.) Nancy Chodorow's theory of psychosexual development (1978) studied the role of mothering in reproducing psychological and gender differences which perpetuated the sexual division of labour and women's inferior position vis-à-vis men. (See *psychoanalytic theory.) Interest in sex roles and their representation in literary works led to a number of studies that attempted to deconstruct images of women in literature. *Sandra M. Gilbert and *Susan Gubar's study of female creativity in the 19th century, *The Madwoman in the Attic* (1979), was a rejoinder to *Harold Bloom's *The Anxiety of Influence* (1973). If, as Bloom suggests, male poets resorted to '*misprision' in reading the work of their predecessors to elude their crushing influence, women's creativity was doubly hindered by the prevailing myths which reserved artistic creativity to the masculine sphere. Gilbert and Gubar conclude that the very fact women dared to write – to take hold of the pen or 'metaphorical penis' – constituted a challenge to the roles that patriarchy had assigned. (See also *phallocentrism.) Other approaches focus more squarely on the historical dimension of women's writing and the practical project of recovering lost women writers. In describing the move away from 'revisionary' reading, Elaine Showalter coined the term 'gynocritics' for the study of women as writers, favouring textual interpretation over theory in an effort to explain the difference of women's writing.

Lesbian and black feminists

The women's movement had originally attempted to create a sense of female solidarity by emphasizing oppression common to all women united in their difference from men. But 'universal' womanhood was forced to give way to the plurality of women's experience and to recognize differences between women: early feminist criticism was faulted for racism (see B. Smith; hooks) and heterosexism (see Zimmerman). (See also *universal.) The revision of the literary canon undertaken by white, heterosexual women was broadened by lesbian and black feminists, who also overhauled the feminist agenda to include a more complex version of power relations. (See *Black criticism, *power.) Similarly, lesbian and black women's histories emerged and shed new light on women's past (see Faderman; Fox-Genovese). Adrienne Rich's work reversed the tendency to blame women's inequality on their reproductive potential by observing, in *Of Woman Born* (1976), that the fault lay not with biology but with the institution of heterosexuality, which had pressed motherhood into service for patriarchy. Rich redefined women's difference in positive terms. Her idea of a 'lesbian continuum' was not confined to sexual relationships between women; instead, it included a variety of 'woman-identified experience' which was to serve as the basis for women's bonding together in resistance to 'male tyranny' (1980). Rich also proposed a radical critique of literature in terms of a feminist 're-vision' which constituted 'an act of survival' (1979). Similarly, black women have had to write themselves into the canon. Hence, Alice Walker characterizes her activity as literally 'the saving of lives' (1983) as she works to resurrect the memory of her forebears. Some black feminists have also criticized feminism's growing concern with theory in recent years (see Christian 1989).

VICTORIA WALKER

Feminist materialists

Much of the impetus for feminist criticism came from critics familiar with Marxist cultural criticism. (See *cultural materialism, *Marxist criticism.) Marxism regards culture as a social and historical product marked by the economic and social relations of its time. Writing has an important role to play in the reproduction of the dominant *ideology. In the 1970s feminist theories and critics, particularly in Britain, sought to develop a Marxist feminism that could account for both the specificity of capitalism and patriarchy and the interrelation between the two. Examples of such work include Michèle Barrett's *Women's Oppression Today* (1980) and the work of the Women's Studies Group at the Centre for Contemporary Cultural Studies, particularly *Women Take Issue* (1978). This socialist-feminist tradition has continued in the journal *Feminist Review* (1979–). Marxism lacks a sophisticated theorization of subjectivity and, as Rosalind Coward and John Ellis' *Language and Materialism* (1977) illustrates, attempts to fill this gap led Marxists to turn to aspects of Lacanian psychoanalysis and the semiology of *Roland Barthes. Feminist critics have drawn, in particular, on the work of *Louis Althusser and *Pierre Macherey, both of whom use psychoanalytic analogies in their theories of ideology and the literary, and have supplemented this work with various other psychoanalytic and poststructuralist theories. (See *poststructuralism.) Feminist materialists, however, share a commitment both to historical and social specificity and to the need to look at gender in relation to class and race. For examples of more recent materialist feminist criticism see the work of Catherine Belsey and the anthology *Feminist Criticism and Social Change* edited by Judith Newton and Deborah Rosenfelt (1985).

Poststructuralist approaches

Poststructuralist feminism draws on the work of the influential French-language theorists *Ferdinand de Saussure, *Jacques Derrida, *Jacques Lacan, and *Michel Foucault together with the work of the French-based Bulgarian theorist Julia Kristeva. Concerned with two key areas, meaning and subjectivity, poststructuralism developed as a critique of Saussure's structural linguistics outlined in *Cours de linguistique générale* [*A Course in General Linguistics* 1967; 1974]. Saussure broke with theories that assume that language reflects a world outside itself. He argued that language constructs meaning. In Saussurean theory language consists of chains of signs composed of signifiers (sound images) and signifieds (concepts). Meaning is the product of the differences between signs rather than anything inherent in a particular *sign. (See *signified/signifier/signification.) 'Woman,' for example, acquires its meaning from its differences from 'man' and 'ran.' Poststructuralism reaffirms the Saussurean principle that meaning is an effect of difference but questions the simplicity of a fixed signified behind each signifier. Rather than signs, poststructuralism speaks of signifiers whose meaning is polysemic.

Starting from the principle that meaning is an effect of language and is never fixed but always deferred in an infinite web of *textuality, Derrida developed a theory of *deconstruction which has had a marked influence on Anglo-American criticism, both feminist and non-feminist. Deconstruction assumes that textuality creates hierarchical binary oppositions, for example, culture/nature and man/woman. (See *binary opposition.) The process of deconstruction unmasks these oppositions, showing how *discourse achieves its effects. Poststructuralist feminist critics have been particularly interested in deconstructing texts in order to make explicit the relations of power that structure discourse. These power relations, which structure the field of criticism itself, often have institutional bases, for example, in publishing, higher education and the press. Competing discourses – for example, *New Criticism, feminist criticism and Marxist criticism – constitute a discursive field, in this case cultural criticism. Critics read from positions within this discursive field and critical readings of texts produce particular versions of meaning, reaffirming particular social values.

Poststructuralism has also provided a critique of the rational, Enlightenment model of subjectivity in which the speaking subject is the source and guarantee of meaning. It has decentered the 'I,' the speaking subject of language, seeing it as an effect of language. (See *centre/decentre.) Feminists have used poststructuralist theory to analyse the construction of gendered subjectivity and power relations in cultural practices. In so doing they – like Althusser – reject all forms of essentialism, seeing subjectivity as socially and historically produced. Subjectivity encompasses individual consciousness, emotions and unconscious thoughts and desires. It is a process rather than a fixed identity, constituted by competing and often contradictory meanings, for example, meanings of femininity, individuality and the family. Literature, popular culture and film are some of the discursive practices in which gendered subjectivity is constructed.

This bringing to bear of poststructuralist theory on feminist concerns is characteristic of the work of many other critics. A particularly useful source for this work is the American feminist journal *Signs* which, under the editorship of Catherine Stimpson, has created a space for sophisticated theorized cultural analysis. Feminist poststructuralist critics, Teresa de Lauretis, for example, have written widely and influentially on film and cultural studies. Gayatri Chakravorty Spivak, translator of Derrida's *Of Grammatology* (1976), has brought together Marxism, deconstruction and perceptions of cultural difference which have placed cultural imperialism firmly on the feminist agenda (see *In Other Worlds* 1987). Similarly, Barbara Johnson (1987) has demonstrated how North American forms of deconstruction, which have tended towards a conservative formalism, can be used to ask political questions of interest to feminists. Catherine Belsey's work on Shakespeare and Renaissance drama, for example, *The Subject of Tragedy* (1985), marks a shift from a concern with the purely literary towards a broader conception of cultural history concerned with how an understanding of past gender relations can denaturalize the present. Linda Hutcheon has concentrated on the theory, practice and politics of postmodern cultural forms, drawing parallels between the project of *postmodernism and that of the various feminisms without collapsing the two.

CHRIS WEEDON

Implications, difficulties, drawbacks

Since the mid-1970s when Anglo-American feminism took a theoretical turn, feminist studies have proceeded along parallel lines of investigation: one more textually and historically inclined, the other favouring theoretical approaches. Ironically, this cleavage would appear to have reproduced the division between empiricism and phenomenology in the predominantly male philosophical tradition. (See *phenomonological criticism.) Textual-oriented critics are faulted for naive empiricism in failing to recognize the theoretical problems inherent in assuming that literary representations of women are 'true' reflections of women's condition; Marxist studies are scorned for ignoring the problem of subjectivity; critics who rely on the theory of the 'male masters' are criticized for retreating into the realms of abstraction at the expense of historical awareness and are seen to have betrayed the feminist agenda. Those who promote the pluralism of critical approaches are similarly accused of diluting the raison d'être of the feminist movement by contenting themselves with feminist readings that merely supplement those of humanist New Critics or purportedly neutral studies in reception, making feminism a choice rather than an imperative (see Benstock; Moi). The problem seems to be hierarchical in nature: which shall take precedence? the study of literature or the transformational practices of feminism? The most recent work in feminism is highly conscious of the problems resulting from the borrowing practices common to feminist studies and the nagging sense of compromise at having to use the conceptual tools produced by the very tradition that is being questioned (see Code et al.; Messer-Davidow). Other difficulties arise from the unclear, sometimes metaphorical use of terminology ('difference'; 'discourse'; 'sign'; 'ideology'). Some feminists have recognized the problems of reading French feminist thought in translation and the danger of abstracting intellectual developments from their social and political contexts (see Jardine 1985). Still others have faced the exacting task of subjecting contemporary theories to rigorous examination in an attempt to assess their implications for feminist studies (see Hekman; Meese and Parker). Anglo-American feminist thought has had an unmistakable effect on literary studies in the English-speaking world; present debates are proof of both its coming of age and its vitality.

V.W.

Primary Sources

Barrett, Michèle. Women's Oppression Today. London: Verso, 1980.

Belsey, Catherine. Critical Practice. London and New York: Methuen, 1980.

– The Subject of Tragedy. London and New York: Methuen, 1985.

Benstock, Shari, ed. Feminist Issues in Literary Scholarship. Bloomington: Indiana UP, 1987.

Carby, Hazel. Reconstructing Womanhood: The Emergence of the Afro-American Woman Novelist. New York: Oxford UP, 1987.

Chodorow, Nancy. The Reproduction of Mothering: Psychoanalysis and the Sociology of Gender. Berkeley: U of California P, 1978.

Christian, Barbara. Black Women Novelists: The Development of a Tradition 1892–1976. Westport, Conn.: Greenwood P, 1980.

– The Race for Theory.' Cultural Critique 6 (1987): 51–63. Repr. with some changes in Gender and Theory: Dialogues on Feminist Criticism. Ed. Linda Kauffman. Oxford: Blackwell, 1989.

Code, Lorraine, Sheila Mullet, and Christine Overall, eds. Feminist Perspectives: Philosophical Essays on Method and Morals. Toronto: U of Toronto P, 1988.

Cott, Nancy F. The Grounding of Modern Feminism. New Haven: Yale UP, 1987.

Coward, Rosalind. Female Desire: Women's Sexuality Today. London: Paladin, 1984. New York: Grove, 1985.

– and John Ellis. Language and Materialism: Developments in Semiology and the Theory of the Subject. London: Routledge and Kegan Paul, 1977.

Daly, Mary. Gyn/Ecology: The Metaethics of Radical Feminism. Boston: Beacon P, 1978.

de Lauretis, Teresa. Alice Doesn't: Feminism, Semiotics, Cinema. Bloomington: Indiana UP, 1984.

Eisenstein, Hester, and Alice Jardine, eds. The Future of Difference. Boston: G.K. Hall, 1980.

Ellmann, Mary. Thinking about Women. New York: Harcourt Brace Jovanovich, 1968.

Evans, Mari, ed. Black Women Writers (1950–1980): A Critical Evaluation. Garden City, NY: Anchor/Doubleday, 1984.

Faderman, Lillian. Surpassing the Love of Men: Romantic Friendship and Love Between Women from the Renaissance to the Present. New York: William Morrow, 1981.

Fox-Genovese, Elizabeth. Within the Plantation Household: Black and White Women of the Old South. Chapel Hill: U of North Carolina P, 1988.

Gallop, Jane. Feminism and Psychoanalysis: The Daughter's Seduction. Ithaca: Cornell UP, 1982.

Gilbert, Sandra M., and Susan Gubar. The Madwoman in the Attic: The Woman Writer and the Nineteenth-century Literary Imagination. New Haven: Yale UP, 1979.

Grahn, Judy. Another Mother Tongue: Gay Words, Gay Worlds. Boston: Beacon P, 1984.

Gubar, Susan. '"The Blank Page" and the Issues of Female Creativity.' Critical Inquiry 8 (1981): 243–63.

Heilbrun, Carolyn G. Toward a Recognition of Androgyny. New York: Alfred A. Knopf, 1973.

Hekman, Susan J. Gender and Knowledge: Elements of a Postmodern Feminism. Oxford: Polity P in association with Basil Blackwell, 1990.

hooks, bell. Ain't I A Woman: Black Women and Feminism. Boston: South End P, 1981.

Hutcheon, Linda. The Politics of Postmodernism. London and New York: Routledge, 1989.

Jacobus, Mary, ed. Reading Woman: Essays in Feminist Criticism. London and New York: Methuen, 1986.

– Women Writing and Writing about Women. London: Croom Helm, 1979.

Jardine, Alice. Gynesis: Configurations of Woman and Modernity. Ithaca: Cornell UP, 1985.

– and Paul Smith, eds. Men in Feminism. New York and London: Methuen, 1987.

Johnson, Barbara. A World of Difference. Baltimore and London: Johns Hopkins UP, 1987.

Kaplan, Cora. *Sea Changes: Essays on Culture and Feminism*. London: Verso, 1986.

Kaplan, E. Ann. *Women and Film: Both Sides of the Camera*. New York and London: Methuen, 1983.

Kitzinger, Celia. *The Social Construction of Lesbianism*. London: Sage, 1987.

Kroker, Arthur, Marilouise Kroker, Pamela Mc-Callum, and Mair Verthuy, eds. *Feminism Now – Theory and Practice*. Montreal: New World Perspectives, 1985.

Lorde, Audre. *Sister Outside*. Trumansburg, NY: The Crossing P, 1984.

McDowell, Deborah E. 'New Directions for Black Feminist Criticism.' *Black American Literature Forum* 14 (1980): 153–9.

Meese, Elizabeth, and Alice Parker, eds. *The Difference Within: Feminism and Critical Theory*. Amsterdam and Philadelphia: John Benjamins, 1989.

Messer-Davidow, Ellen. 'The Philosophical Bases of Feminist Literary Criticisms.' *New Literary History* 19 (1987): 64–103.

Millett, Kate. *Sexual Politics*. Garden City, NY: Doubleday, 1970.

Mitchell, Juliet. *Psychoanalysis and Feminism*. New York: Pantheon Books, 1974.

Moers, Ellen. *Literary Women*. Garden City, NY: Doubleday, 1976. London: Women's P, 1978.

Moi, Toril. *Sexual/Textual Politics: Feminist Literary Theory*. London and New York: Methuen, 1985.

Newton, Judith, and Deborah Rosenfelt, eds. *Feminist Criticism and Social Change: Sex, Class and Race in Literature and Culture*. New York and London: Methuen, 1985.

Rich, Adrienne. *Of Woman Born: Motherhood as Experience and Institution*. New York: Norton, 1976.

– *On Lies, Secrets, and Silence*. New York: Norton, 1979.

– 'Compulsory Heterosexuality and Lesbian Experience.' *Signs* 5 (1980): 631–60.

Robinson, Lillian. *Sex, Class, and Culture*. Bloomington: Indiana UP, 1978.

Rose, Jacqueline. *Sexuality in the Field of Vision*. London: Verso, 1986.

Showalter, Elaine. *A Literature of Their Own: Women Novelists from Brontë to Lessing*. Princeton: Princeton UP, 1977.

– ed. *The New Feminist Criticism*. New York: Pantheon Books, 1985.

– ed. *Speaking of Gender*. New York and London: Routledge, 1989.

Smith, Barbara. 'Toward a Black Feminist Criticism.' *Conditions Two* 1 (1977): 25–32. Repr. in *The New Feminist Criticism*. Ed. Elaine Showalter. New York: Pantheon Books, 1985.

Smith, Valerie. 'Gender and Afro-Americanist Literary Theory and Criticism.' In *Speaking of Gender*. Ed. Elaine Showalter. New York and London: Routledge, 1989.

Spivak, Gayatri Chakravorty. *In Other Worlds: Essays in Cultural Politics*. New York and London: Methuen, 1987.

Walker, Alice. *In Search of Our Mothers' Gardens*. San Diego: Harcourt Brace Jovanovich, 1983.

Weedon, Chris. *Feminist Practice and Poststructuralist Theory*. Oxford: Blackwell, 1987.

Women's Study Group, Centre for Contemporary Cultural Studies, University of Birmingham. *Women Take Issue*. London: Hutchinson, 1978.

Woolf, Virginia. *A Room of One's Own*. London: Hogarth P, 1929.

Wright, Elizabeth. *Psychoananlytic Criticism: Theory in Practice*. London and New York: Methuen, 1984.

Zimmerman, Bonnie. 'What Has Never Been: An Overview of Lesbian Feminist Literary Criticism.' *Feminist Studies* 7 (1981): 451–75.

Feminist criticism, French

French feminist criticism refers to the varied body of thought and the diverse theoretical works on woman and the feminine that appeared in France, Quebec and Belgium beginning in the late 1960s (the term 'French' includes theorists who wrote in French and who substantially share various preoccupations and approaches). (See also *feminist criticism, Quebec.) In the wake of political events in France and French Canada, intellectuals, mostly women, engaged in a re-evaluation of both the material position of women in society and the metaphysical status of the feminine in Continental thought. Despite national differences, these critics – philosophers, psychoanalysts, poets, novelists, linguists, journalists – were all educated in the modern European tradition and imbued with the French belief that all ideas are political. Their shared focus is women's relationship to language, in the broad sense of all the cultural discourses that woman speaks and that 'speak' woman. (See *discourse.) Most French intellectual feminists subscribe to the idea of sexual specificity or the existence of masculine and feminine attributes arising from ineradicable difference. They differ strongly, however, in their views of the nature and sources of sexual difference, resulting in the following conceptual tensions: locating difference between women and men rather than within each individual; using 'feminine' and 'masculine' literally (rather than metaphorically) to refer to real women and men, rather than to evoke philosophical concepts; giving primacy to cultural instead of psychobiological factors as constituting sexual difference; and subscribing to the idea of a specifically feminine writing or language rather than rejecting this belief as essentialist. (See *essentialism.) Psychoanalytically and philosophically oriented French feminists posit connections between the structures of the psyche and those of the material world. For that reason, these post-1968 'new feminists,' unlike their more reformist forerunners, seek to transform Western culture radically by changing its conceptualization of thought itself. (See *psychoanalytic theory.)

The feminist critiques of the key French thinkers, *Julia Kristeva, *Luce Irigaray, *Hélène Cixous, and Monique Wittig, have some roots in *Simone de Beauvoir's Le Deuxième sexe [The Second Sex 1949], although de Beauvoir's main influence was on Anglo-American feminism. Her elaboration of the construction of gender – of woman as a cultural product rather than a biological essence – as well as her focus on woman's fundamental altérité [otherness] in relation to the masculine sujet [self or subject] were crucial to subsequent feminist theories of sexual difference, material and metaphysical. (See *self/other, *feminist criticism, Anglo-American.)

Intellectual origins

The last 100 years of European thought and the experience of modernity that shook the foundations of Western humanism combined with the 20th-century crisis of two world wars to produce a number of writings formative for contemporary French feminist theory. Feminism's intellectual 'fathers' – Karl Marx, *Friedrich Nietzsche, *Ferdinand de Saussure, and *Sigmund Freud – and, especially, the postwar thinkers who reread and critiqued these earlier authors – the psychoanalyst *Jacques Lacan and the philosopher *Jacques Derrida – put in place the concepts that French feminists adopted and reinterpreted for their own analyses. Feminism's predecessors participated in the critique of traditional European metaphysics that attacked the latter's monolithic principles of absolute Truth, Authority, God, the Good, Capitalism, and the Self as a coherent entity. In place of the long-standing *metaphysics of presence – the belief that meaning is fully present in and has a one-to-one relationship to reality – modernist thinkers posited a dynamic view of reality-as-construction, as

ongoing process whose markers are ambiguity and absence. They developed a *problematic of alterity whose focus was the negated 'Other'; they sought to bring to light all the forces that Western *ideology has suppressed and deemed unknowable, untrue, unnatural, or unreal. Such heterogeneous concepts as the unconscious, the divided self, polytheism, and communism challenged the univocal premises of traditional Western epistemology and became central to feminist inquiry.

Negativity; *structuralism; difference

The areas in which the first critiques of phenomenological assumptions about reality and the place of the human *subject in it were carried were in philosophy, linguistics and psychoanalysis. (Phenomenology assumed that a transcendent human consciousness was capable of comprehending reality.) The 19th-century philosopher Nietzsche had exposed the hierarchies of *power underlying Western values or the negation of life essential to the affirmation of human mastery. His concept of negativity – the state of being 'other' and heterogeneous in relation to the dominant culture – became important for feminists who saw the feminine as both the life force most powerfully suppressed by *patriarchy and as a potential source of social and intellectual revolution. Marx's historical and materialist critique of Western economic systems provided feminists with several analytic tools: a dialectical view of the functioning of all cultural systems; an economic vocabulary for articulating human relationships; and a transcultural model of social and political struggle. Interpretations of woman's status as that of 'merchandise' exchanged in the dominant masculine economy derive from Marx's analysis of value. Saussure's Cours de linguistique générale [Course in General Linguistics 1906] established a structuralist vision of the functioning of language: rather than a static *code of words that directly imitates real phenomena, language for Saussure was a dynamic system of interrelationships among linguistic constituents. Structuralism's relational paradigm, in which meaning is generated by the interactions between and among different linguistic units, posited the central concept of difference: the opposition between binary terms, along with their interdependency, implied an ontology of 'absence,' in place of phenomenology's ontology of 'presence' or 'identity.' Subsequent theorists sexualized difference, associating binary terms metaphorically with the masculine (presence) and the feminine (absence). Feminist critics of the 1960s and 1970s further elucidated sexual difference as the cornerstone of women's material oppression and intellectual repression. Finally, Freud's early 20th-century work in psychoanalytic theory provided several key formulations for later feminist thought: that the human subject is fragmented and incoherent; that the psyche is an irreducibly 'other' domain that functions according to its own logic; that the unconscious exists in relation to and explains the workings of the conscious; and that sexual difference is both irremediable and constitutive of psychological and social development. (See also *phenomenological criticism, *Marxist criticism, *materialist criticism, *binary opposition.)

*Poststructuralism: phallogocentrism; *deconstruction

The next generation of intellectual 'fathers,' the poststructuralists, criticized structuralism's differential model: they claimed it masked what was in fact a hierarchical structure, since its adherence to a logic of opposition still privileged one term over the other. Derrida, the poststructuralist thinker who most strongly influenced French intellectual feminism through his writings *L'Ecriture et la différence* [*Writing and Difference* 1967], *De la Grammatologie* [*Of Grammatology* 1967], and *La Dissémination* [*Dissemination* 1972], coined the term '*logocentrism' (*logos* = the Word) to designate Western philosophy's grounding in mastery and in unitary, absolute principles. Rejecting oppositional systems as destructive of otherness, Derrida reconceptualized difference as that which exceeds binary structures: difference is the dissidence, the instability within entities, as well as among them. Derrida's concept of *différance* (from the verb 'différer,' to differ and to postpone) conveys the multiplicity underlying all unity, as well as the idea that meaning is never fully achieved, is always being constructed. From *différance*'s dislodging of fixed meanings arose Derrida's deconstructionist approach, in which the reading and writing of all cultural texts continually reverse and undo the order and hierarchy of terms. Two of French feminism's most important practitioners, Luce Irigaray and Hélène Cixous,

adopt a deconstructionist approach in their works. Since they view the utilization of conventional language (*le Nom du Père* or *Name-of-the-Father*), with its attendant order, logic and *authority, as part of the masculine discourse that has excluded woman, Irigaray and Cixous intentionally disrupt patriarchal (logical, sequential) language in their writing. In addition, Derrida's critique of Freud's phallocentric psychological model, or its positing of male sexual development as the norm against which female development is measured, became central to feminist redefinitions of women's sexuality. (See *phallocentrism.) Derrida's term phallogocentric, which feminist theorists took up, combines both philosophical and psychoanalytic paradigms to refer to the privileging of masculine desire in Western thought and representation. (See *desire/lack.)

The maternal; *jouissance*

Lacan's rereading of Freud, especially his application of the structuralist paradigm of absence (Lacan called it 'manque' or 'lack') to the workings of the unconscious, gave psychoanalytically oriented feminists further instruments with which to articulate sexual difference. From his works *Ecrits* (*Ecrits: A Selection* 1969) and *Séminaires* (conducted 1953–80) (some *Séminaires* are translated separately; several on women are collected in *Feminine Sexuality*), feminists retained the Lacanian model of parallel psychic and linguistic dynamics, in particular his categories of the imaginary (the mother-identified, pre-Oedipal and prelinguistic realm) and the symbolic (the paternal, Oedipal realm of language and signification). (See *imaginary/symbolic/real.) The movement within and between these sexualized imaginary and symbolic realms became for some theorists the bisexual configuration fundamental to all human subjects, for others, the origin of woman's alienation from masculine discourse. In addition, several feminists concentrated on Lacan's distinction between *jouissance* (feminine pleasure, which for Lacan is primal, contiguous and other) and desire (masculine and, for him, the primary sexual force), in order to affirm heretofore repressed female sexuality as the impetus for feminine creativity. Derrida's critique of Lacan's phallocentric fetishizing of the male Oedipal experience informed the feminist reclaiming of the repressed pre-Oedipal Mother.

Major feminist figures

Though intellectually formative for feminists, the male mentors, with the exception of Derrida, used 'woman' and 'the feminine' only metaphorically to refer to that which Western culture had always negated, and they were not at all concerned with women's social and political advancement. French feminism is therefore both critical and reconstructive: it faults previous theorists' lack of concern for the absent 'woman' and 'mother,' and it also reaffirms the feminine and the maternal as cultural forces. Further, suspicious of language and authorial mastery, the 'new' feminists produced self-conscious texts in which the traditional barriers between analysis and fiction, between the expository and the imaginative, break down.

Kristeva's *sujet en procès*

Julia Kristeva, a linguist and psychoanalyst, addresses in her works the politics of the speaking and writing subject, the producer of signification that for her is constantly in process (*le sujet en procès*). Rejecting the humanist fictions of a fixed self and a coherent language system, Kristeva examines the radical possibilities for the signifying subject to disrupt the symbolic or paternal order with what she calls 'poetic language.' In *La Révolution du langage poétique* [*Revolution in Poetic Language* 1974] and the essays collected in *Polylogue* (1977) (some translated in *Desire in Language*), she elaborates her central idea of the divided 'speaking subject,' or her view of sexual difference as lying within the individual bisexual psyche. For Kristeva, meaning is generated by the subject's constant traversal through and between the semiotic domain (the pre-Oedipal phase where no sexual difference exists and where preverbal 'pulsions' produce an infinite number of signifiers) and the symbolic domain (the socialized phase where the Law of the Father – the father's 'no!' – establishes sexual difference and where signification is limited as cultural discourse). (See *semiotics, *semiosis.) She grants the semiotic prestige as a liberating potential and sees the textual 'ruptures' in late-19th-century avant-garde *literature as markers of major cultural change (in *Revolution*). More recently, Kristeva has analysed (in *Pouvoirs de l'horreur; Powers of Horror* 1980) the poetics and politics of psychotic and fascist writers,

whose language also manifests eruptions of the semiotic in the cultural fabric. For Kristeva, the terms 'masculine' and 'feminine' are metaphorical designations for the subject's relation to the dominant culture. She develops her concept of 'femininity' most fully in *Des Chinoises* [*About Chinese Women* 1974], in some of the articles in *Polylogue*, and in 'Le temps des femmes' ['Women's Time' 1979]: femininity is a 'negativity,' or a force of *subversion which, to be effective, must remain marginal to the patriarchal order. (See *margin.) More recently, Kristeva has focused on the pre-Oedipal, bisexual Mother rather than Woman, to signal her wish to eradicate the destructive sexual categories 'woman' and 'man' decreed by the Law of the Father.

Luce Irigaray's *Speculum* and *parler-femme*

The psychoanalyst Luce Irigaray, who also holds doctorates in philosophy and linguistics, has contributed influential feminist critiques of Freudian and Lacanian psychoanalysis that situate psychoanalytic discourse within the broader context of Western thought in general. Like Kristeva, she sees the humanist *myth of a unified self as grounded in the phallogocentric ideology of a potent, unique masculine creator. But Irigaray's central concern is the construction of 'woman' by the masculine imagination that informs the entire philosophical tradition. She carries forward both Derrida's dictum that Western metaphysics has foreclosed 'woman-as-concept' and Lacan's formulation about the dynamics of absence: 'Woman does not exist.' In *Speculum de l'autre femme* [*Speculum of the Other Woman* 1974], Irigaray explores how male thinkers from Plato on have rendered woman passive through their elaborations of a *logique du propre* (logic of sameness/the same): in their philosophical speculations, the *subject merely reflects back on himself; all that is other than himself is negative, the unthinkable. The metaphor of the speculum suggests at once the problem of the 'invisibility' of female sexuality in Western thought, the masculine 'gaze' that has objectified woman, and the whole question of representation – of speaking and writing as pure reflection or imitation of the master discourse in place. (See *mimesis.) Irigaray's theoretical/poetic essays in *Ce sexe qui n'en est pas un* [*This Sex Which Is Not One* 1977] develop further her scrutiny of patriarchy's erasure of feminine difference, which for her exceeds and is outside of traditional sexual categories. She also goes on (in *This Sex Which Is Not One* and in the more recent poetic monologue *Passions élémentaires* 1982) to exalt long-repressed desire as the impulse for a specific *parler-femme* (woman's language or 'womanspeak'), a previously un-spoken and un-written discourse arising morphologically from the female body. Woman's genitals (multiple 'lips' that 'touch one another' in a gesture of unlimited *jouissance*) are Irigaray's image for feminine expression. She evokes, through her own writing, the fluid and playful quality of this potential woman's language. But, aware of the danger of biological essentialism, Irigaray refuses to codify a *parler-femme* and adopts a Derridean deconstructionist strategy in her texts, one that continually undoes fixed sexual designations and makes ambiguity the marker of her feminist re-evaluation. Like Kristeva, Irigaray has focused on the Mother in her more recent works (*Et l'une ne bouge pas sans l'autre*) ['And the One Doesn't Stir Without the Other' 1979] and *Le corps-à-corps avec la mère* [*Body to Body with the Mother* 1981]. She has emphasized the complicated mother-daughter bond of identification and separation that also characterizes all women's tangled relationship to symbolic discourse.

Hélène Cixous' *écriture féminine* and *bisexualité*

The philosopher, writer and university professor Hélène Cixous has been most involved with the inscription or marking of sexuality in literary texts. Like Kristeva, she began by analysing 'the poetics of creative doubt' in 19th- and 20th-century works that subvert their own meaning (*Prénoms de personne* 1974). Like Irigaray, Cixous then turned her attention both to criticizing the destruction of difference underlying logocentric ideology and to affirming a specific *écriture féminine* [woman's writing] grounded in female pleasure. Her critique of the *Empire du propre* (Empire of sameness/the same) fundamental to Western philosophy is expressed in detail in 'Sorties' ('Sorties Out and Out: Attacks / Ways Out / Forays'), her essay in *La Jeune née* [*Newly Born Woman* 1975]. Exposing the hierarchized oppositions (such as masculine/feminine, active/passive) upon which patriarchy rests, Cixous argues

that in these mythical 'couples,' the One in fact appropriates the Other. She locates this self-preserving repression of the feminine in the 'masculine libidinal economy,' a regime of desire based on the fear of castration ('Le Sexe ou la tête' ['Castration or Decapitation?' 1976]. Cixous' own prose reveals her deconstructive approach through its mimetic evocation of the multiple and incantatory articulation she projects that *l'écriture féminine* will be. Despite her refusal to reify this new language, Cixous comes close to describing it in her poetic manifestos, 'Le Rire de la Méduse' ['The Laugh of the Medusa' 1975] and 'La Venue à l'écriture' (in *La Venue à l'écriture* 1977): arising from feminine 'generosity' (*le don* or libidinal 'giving' that contrasts with the masculine *propre* or 'propietorship'), it will be irreducible, open-ended and limitless. In seeming contrast to her idea of a specifically feminine writing arising from women's psychic difference, Cixous also elaborates in 'The Laugh of the Medusa' and in 'Sorties' her concept of *bisexualité*: not what she deems the conventional notion of androgynous a-sexuality, Cixous' bisexuality locates repressed feminine components in both men and women. This 'other' bisexuality is a potential for plural sexualities that multiplies differences. According to Cixous, the imaginative liberation of the feminine in each individual will have the power to transform all of patriarchy's social and political arrangements.

Wittig's homosexuality and lesbianism

Monique Wittig is best known as the author of the experimental novels *L'Opoponax* (1964), *Les Guérillères* (1969), and *Virgile, non* (1985), and the poetic prose text *Le Corps lesbien* (1973), all of which challenge humanist literary conventions, in particular that of an individual hero who is the transcendental source of experience and language. Her fiction also puts into question language as a univocal medium. As theorist, Wittig has enlarged the feminist analytic framework by giving primacy to lesbianism, for her both a literal and figurative expansion of sexuality. She conceptualizes difference differently: unlike Kristeva, she rejects bisexuality as a concept; unlike Irigaray and Cixous, she refuses the feminine as specificity, replacing it with homosexuality. Heterosexuality, not the masculine, is the conceptual first principle Wittig seeks to dislodge; that which has been designated 'the unknown' and 'the unnameable' 'Other,' she argues, is lesbianism. Though materialist rather than psychoanalytic in her approach – she criticizes structuralist analyses of the unconscious as 'intellectual constructs' typical of 'straight thought' (*La Pensée straight*; 'The Straight Mind' 1979) – Wittig was nonetheless influenced by post-structuralist critiques of traditional phallogocentric models of sexuality. In 'Paradigm' (1979), she opens the concept of homosexuality beyond binary opposition to connote a Derridean-like desire which, in this case, 'exceeds' monolithic heterosexuality. She calls for new, multiple sexualities based on pleasure, not predetermined categories. In 'The Category of Sex' (1982), she blames the economic imperatives of reproduction for 'enslaving' women in compulsory heterosexuality. Trying to connect theoretical abstraction to a culture-based perspective, Wittig seeks to destroy the 'political' categories of 'women' and 'men' and thereby give women the semantic power to 'name' themselves (*'On ne naît pas femme'*; 'One Is Not Born a Woman' 1980). The essay's title, a reference to Beauvoir's *The Second Sex*, also suggests Wittig's belief that 'woman' is a universalizing cultural presupposition that heterosexism has naturalized. For her, as for Kristeva, Irigaray, and Cixous, the poetic and political are inextricable.

United States and England

Anglo-American scholars who have been influenced by French feminism exhibit varied objectives in their work: some seek to familiarize Anglo-Saxon feminists with French feminism's overall purpose (Duchen; Eisenstein and Jardine; Gelfand and Hules; Jardine; Marks and de Courtivron; Moi); some interpret for American and British readers the works of important French theorists, and several of these exegetes argue in favour of what they see as French feminism's more radical premises (Conley; Gallop; Jardine; Moi); and some expose patriarchal discursive strategies by analysing male canonical texts through a French feminist grid (Kamuf; Miller; Rabine; Schor). If French theorists have produced virtually no textual analyses, this last group of American critics has explored the ways literary works construct gender: they do 'symptomatic' readings that locate sexualized power and authority in the texts' language. (See also *text, *symptomatic reading.)

Relation to other approaches

French intellectual feminists generally focus on 'woman' and 'the feminine' as signifiers, not as referential terms for concrete female experience. (See *signified/signifier/signification.) Some even reject the term 'feminism' as another instance of the discourse of mastery. However, French feminists who are sceptical of philosophically and psychoanalytically oriented theories have criticized Kristeva, Irigaray and Cixous, saying their works are obscure and unverifiable and their views of psychic or linguistic specificity retrogressive. Instead, materialist feminist critics give precedence to analyses of the cultural arrangements that oppress women. Most American feminists, too, have expressed dissatisfaction with the abstract and ahistorical tendency of French inquiry, opting in their own work to study specific literary and social contexts and the representation of women in texts. American critics generally attend to a separate and authoritative female experience. The intellectual debate between (French) theoretical and (American) pragmatic modes has itself been a frequent topic of discussion. The attempt to reconcile French and Anglo-American perspectives has inspired much of American feminist literary scholarship of the 1980s: studies have appeared in which the Continental problematizing of language informs concrete textual interpretation, as well as collections incorporating international feminist approaches. For its defenders, French feminism, by questioning the ways gender has been constructed in all cultural 'texts,' revolutionizes the categories and methods of criticism itself.

ELISSA GELFAND

Primary Sources

Beauvoir, Simone de. *The Second Sex*. Trans. H.M. Parshley. New York: Knopf, 1952.
Cixous, Hélène. 'Castration or Decapitation?' Trans. Annette Kuhn. *Signs* 7.1 (Autumn 1981): 41–55.
– 'The Laugh of the Medusa.' Trans. Keith Cohen and Paula Cohen. *Signs* 1.4 (Summer 1976): 875–93.
– *Prénoms de personne*. Paris: Seuil, 1974.
– and Catherine Clément. *Newly Born Woman*.

Trans. Betsy Wing. Minneapolis: U of Minnesota P, 1986.
– Madeleine Gagnon, and Annie Leclerc. *La Venue à l'écriture*. Paris: UGE, 1977.
Derrida, Jacques. *Dissemination*. Trans. Barbara Johnson. Chicago: U of Chicago P, 1981.
– *Of Grammatology*. Trans. Gayatri Spivak. Baltimore: Johns Hopkins UP, 1974.
– *Writing and Difference*. Trans. Alan Bass. Chicago: U of Chicago P, 1978.
Irigaray, Luce. 'And the One Doesn't Stir Without the Other.' Trans. Hélène Vivienne Wenzel. *Signs* 7.1 (Autumn 1981): 60–7.
– *Le Corps-à-corps avec la mère*. Ottawa: Editions de la pleine lune, 1981.
– *Passions élémentaires*. Paris: Minuit, 1982.
– *Speculum of the Other Woman*. Trans. Gillian C. Gill. Ithaca: Cornell UP, 1985.
– *This Sex Which Is Not One*. Trans. Catherine Porter, with Carolyn Burke. Ithaca: Cornell UP, 1985.
Kristeva, Julia. *About Chinese Women*. Trans. Anita Barrows. New York: Urizen Books, 1977.
– *Desire in Language: A Semiotic Approach to Literature and Art*. Ed. Léon S. Roudiez. Trans. Alice Jardine, Thomas Gora, and Léon Roudiez. New York: Columbia UP, 1980.
– *A Kristeva Reader*. Ed. Toril Moi. Trans. Léon S. Roudiez, Séan Hand, et al. New York: Columbia UP, 1986.
– *Polylogue*. Paris: Seuil, 1977.
– *Powers of Horror: An Essay in Abjection*. Trans. Léon Roudiez. New York: Columbia UP, 1982.
– *Revolution in Poetic Language*. Trans. Margaret Waller. New York: Columbia UP, 1984.
– *Séméiótiké: Recherches pour une sémanalyse*. Paris: Seuil, 1969.
– 'Women's Time.' Trans. Alice Jardine and Harry Blake. *Signs* 7.1 (Autumn 1981): 13–35.
Lacan, Jacques. *Ecrits: A Selection*. Trans. Alan Sheridan. New York: Norton, 1977.
– *Encore: le Séminaire XX, 1972–73*. Paris: Seuil, 1975.
– *Feminine Sexuality: Jacques Lacan and the Ecole Freudienne*. Ed. Juliet Mitchell and Jacqueline Rose. Trans. Jacqueline Rose. New York: Norton, 1982.
– *The Four Fundamental Concepts of Psychoanalysis. Séminaire XI, 1964*. Ed. Jacques-Alain Miller. New York: Norton, 1978.
– *The Seminars of Jacques Lacan: The Theory of the Ego in Psychoanalytic Theory and Practice 1954–1955. Séminaire II*. Ed. Jacques-Alain Miller. New York: Norton, 1987.
Wittig, Monique. 'The Category of Sex.' *Feminist Issues* 2.2 (Fall 1982): 63–8.
– 'One Is Not Born a Woman.' *Feminist Issues* 4 (1981): 47–54.
– 'Paradigm.' Trans. George Stambolian. In *Homosexualities and French Literature*. Ed. George Stambolian and Elaine Marks. Ithaca: Cornell UP, 1979, 114–21.
– 'The Straight Mind.' *Feminist Issues* 1 (1980): 103–11.

Anglo-American Works (book-length studies):

Conley, Verena. *Hélène Cixous: Writing the Feminine*. Lincoln: U of Nebraska P, 1984.
Duchen, Claire. *Feminism in France: From May '68 to Mitterrand*. London: Routledge and Kegan Paul, 1986.
Eisenstein, Hester, and Alice Jardine, eds. *The Future of Difference*. Boston: G. K. Hall, 1980.
Gallop, Jane. *The Daughter's Seduction: Feminism and Psychoanalysis*. Ithaca: Cornell UP, 1982.
– *Reading Lacan*. Ithaca: Cornell UP, 1985.
Gelfand, Elissa, and Virginia Hules, eds. *French Feminist Criticism: Women, Language and Literature*. New York: Garland Publishing, 1985.
Jardine, Alice A. *Gynesis: Configurations of Woman and Modernity*. Ithaca: Cornell UP, 1985.
Kamuf, Peggy. *Fictions of Feminine Desire: Disclosures of Heloise*. Lincoln: U of Nebraska P, 1982.
Marks, Elaine, and Isabelle de Courtivron, eds. *New French Feminisms: An Anthology*. Amherst: U of Massachusettes P, 1980.
Miller, Nancy K. *The Heroine's Text: Readings in the French and English Novel, 1722–1782*. New York: Columbia UP, 1980.
Moi, Toril. *Sexual/Textual Politics: Feminist Literary Theory*. London and New York: Methuen, 1985.
– ed. *French Feminist Thought: A Reader*. Trans. Séan Hand, Roison Mallaghan, et al. Oxford: Blackwell, 1987.
Rabine, Leslie. *Reading the Romantic Heroine: Text, History, Ideology*. Ann Arbor: U of Michigan P, 1985.
Ruthven, K.K. *Feminist Literary Studies: An Introduction*. Cambridge: Cambridge UP, 1984.
Schor, Naomi. *Breaking the Chain: Women, Theory, and French Realist Fiction*. New York: Columbia UP, 1985.

Feminist criticism, Quebec

Quebec feminism owes its specificity to the political and social context in which it is rooted and to its particular adaptation of French and early American feminism: out of *l'écriture féminine* and social activism is born *'l'écriture au féminin.'* Building on the experimental writing of the 1960s and 1970s, Quebec feminist writings fuse the practices of writing and theorizing, thereby blurring the generic boundaries between poetry, prose, fiction, criticism, and theory. The result of this overlapping of critical and creative domains is a community of women readers and writers in dialogue. Likewise, the social is merged with the literary by a number of Quebec feminists who, addressing the question of subjectivity, self-consciously inscribe the *subject into the *text: the process of writing thus fixes women in history and lends them their materiality. The specificity of women's writing in Quebec lies in this inscription of the subject or referent rather than in its *deconstruction or fragmentation. (See *feminism, French, *Anglo-American; *reference, referent.)

Women's experience in Quebec society goes some way to explain the vitality of feminism since the late 1960s. Historically, representatives of the Catholic church and Quebec nationalists alike honoured francophone women as the guardians of *la race, la langue* and *la foi*; yet Quebec was the last province to grant women the right to vote, in 1940. Women's religious communities throve in the early 20th century, perhaps because married women were only granted the same rights as men in 1964 – 100 years after anglophone women (see Micheline Dumont et al.). Maurice Duplessis' government (1936–9; 1944–59) marked an era of repressive conservatism in Quebec. Once Liberal Jean Lesage came to power in 1960, the period known as the *Révolution tranquille*, or the Quiet Revolution, began, and women's situation improved. Secular and neo-nationalist, the period witnessed educational reform that introduced mixed classes and a single curriculum. By the late 1960s the nationalist movement had gained momentum. The *Front de libération des femmes du Québec* (FLF) was formed in 1970 with the aim of achieving women's liberation, the national liberation of Quebec and the social liberation of oppressed classes. Yet the FLF soon protested the neglect of women's concerns by nationalist and Marxist organizations, and women's groups became increasingly wary of political affiliation. An autonomous francophone women's movement emerged in 1975. (See *Marxist criticism.)

Influential early women's publications were *Québécoises deboutte!* (1971–4) and *Les Têtes de pioche* (1976–9), the latter radically feminist. Many endeavours were collective: the *Théâtre des Cuisines*, organized by housewives (1973); the *Librairie des femmes d'ici* (1975); publishers such as les Editions de la pleine lune (1975) and les Editions Remue-ménage (1976). Nineteen seventy-six saw the production of *La Nef des sorcières* (with Marthe Blackburn, Marie-Claire Blais, Nicole Brossard, Odette Gagnon,

Luce Guilbeault, Pol Pelletier, co-founder of the *Théâtre Expérimental des Femmes* in 1979, and France Théoret), composed of seven monologues reflecting on aspects of womanhood. A non-collective play that caused a scandal in 1978 for its challenge to the Catholic church's depiction of the Virgin Mary was Denise Boucher's *Les Fées ont soif*. Nicole Brossard, one of the most prolific and influential figures of Quebec feminism, was a co-founder of *La Barre du jour* (1965–77; then *La Nouvelle barre du jour*, 1977–90), a literary magazine of the avant-garde. Brossard's writing turned away from the formalist model in the mid-1970s, rejecting the autonomous modernist aesthetic for a more engaged mode of reading and writing; her later work exemplifies the merging of fiction, poetry and theory. Madeleine Gagnon has worked to collapse the opposition between theoretical and fictional writing, and to emphasize the role of the personal in political questions. The highly intimate writing of France Théoret also moves between theory and fiction. Théoret refuses to follow linear organization and formal integrity by exploiting the idea of the fragment, thereby accentuating the ephemeral voice of the female 'I.' Louky Bersianik, the author of Quebec's first feminist novel, *L'Euguélionne* (1976), takes a more myth-oriented, playfully subversive approach in her writings on the emergence of a new female culture. Critic Suzanne Lamy championed *la critique au féminin*, an approach defined by its subject-matter, contemporary women writers. Lamy's critical work does not take a feminist approach along the lines of the gender critique; instead, it links up with the project of inscribing the female subject by focusing on women who read and write in the present historical moment. Other important figures include Geneviève Amyot, Louise Cotnoir, Denise Desautels, Louise Dupré, Marie Laberge, Monique LaRue, Jovette Marchessault, Carole Massé, Michèle Mailhot, Madeleine Ouellette-Michalska, Suzanne Paradis, Marie Savard, and Yolande Villemaire. (See also *myth, *subversion.)

Like feminism elsewhere, feminism in Quebec has had to face divisions between heterosexuals and lesbians, radicals and liberals, and working-class and bourgeois women. The contradictory early alliance of feminism and nationalism was destined to give way to an autonomous feminist factor. Since then, *l'écriture au féminin* has continued to evolve and has had a considerable impact on the Quebec literary world, as evidenced by the space dedicated to feminist writers in critical publications and literary reviews. The 1980s saw the emergence of a second generation of writers and *l'écriture au féminin* now figures in the curricula of many colleges and universities.

VICTORIA WALKER

Primary Sources

Bersianik, Louky. 'Arbre de pertinence et utopie.' *L'Emergence d'une culture au feminin*. Ed. Marisa Zavalloni. Montreal: Saint-Martin, 1987, 117–32.
– *L'Euguélionne*. 1976. *The Euguélionne*. Trans. Gerry Denis, Alison Hewitt, Donna Murray, and Martha O'Brien. Victoria and Toronto: Press Porcépic, 1981.
– 'La Lanterne d'Aristote.' In *La Théorie, un dimanche*. Montreal: Remue-ménage, 1988, 81–106. 'Aristotle's Lantern: An Essay on Criticism.' Trans. A.J. Holden Verburg. In *A Mazing Space: Writing Canadian Women Writing*. Ed. Shirley Neuman and Smaro Kamboureli. Edmonton: Longspoon/ NeWest P, 1986, 39–48.
– 'Noli me tangere.' *La Barre du jour* 56–7 (1977): 148–64. 'Noli me tangere.' Trans. Barbara Godard. *Room of One's Own* 4.1 (1978): 98–110.
Brossard, Nicole. *L'Amer: ou le chapitre éffrité*. 1977. Montreal: L'Hexagone, 1988. *These Our Mothers or: The Disintegrating Chapter*. Trans. Barbara Godard. Toronto: Coach House Quebec Translations, 1983.
– 'Le Cortext exubérant.' *La Barre du jour* 44 (1974): 2–22.
– *La Lettre aérienne*. 1985. *The Aerial Letter*. Trans. Marlene Wildeman. Toronto: Women's P, 1988.
– 'La Tête qu'elle fait.' *La Barre du jour* 56–7 (1977): 83–92. 'The Face She Makes.' Trans. Josée M. LeBlond. *Room of One's Own* 4.1 (1978): 39–43.
– Boucher, Louise. *Les Fées ont soif*. 1979. *The Fairies Are Thirsty*. Trans. Alan Brown. Vancouver: Talonbooks, 1983.
Fremont, Gabrielle. 'Casse-texte.' *Etudes littéraires* 12 (1979): 315–30.
Gagnon, Madeleine. 'Mon corps dans l'écriture.' *La Venue à l'écriture*. Avec Hélène Cixous et Annie Leclerc. Paris: Union générale d'éditions, 1977, 63–116. 'My Body in Writing.' Trans. Wendy Johnston. In *Feminism in Canada: From Pressure to Politics*. Ed. Geraldine Finn and Angela Miles. Montreal: Black Rose Books, 1982, 269–82.
Guilbeault, Luce, et al. *La Nef des sorcières*. Montreal: Quinze, 1976. [*A Clash of Symbols*.]
Lamy, Suzanne. *d'elles*. Montreal: L'Hexagone, 1979.
– and Irène Pagès, eds. *Féminité, subversion, écriture*. Montreal: Remue-ménage, 1983.

Ouellette-Michalska, Madeleine. *L'Echappée du discours de l'oeil*. Montreal: Nouvelle Optique, 1981.
Québécoises deboutte! Montreal: Remue-ménage, 1982.
Les Têtes de pioche. Montreal: Remue-ménage, 1980.
Théoret, France. *Entre raison et déraison*. Montreal: Les Herbes rouges, 1987.
– 'Eloge de la mémoire des femmes.' In *La Théorie, un dimanche*. Montreal: Remue-ménage, 1988, 175–91.

Secondary Sources

Dumont, Micheline, Michèle Jean, Marie Lavigne, and Jennifer Stoddart. *L'Histoire des femmes au Québec depuis quatre siècles*. Montreal: Quinze, 1982.
Dupré, Louise. 'From Experimentation to Experience: Quebecois Modernity in the Feminine.' *A Mazing Space: Writing Canadian Women Writing*. Ed. Shirley Neuman and Smaro Kamboureli. Edmonton, Alta.: Longspoon/NeWest P, 1986, 355–60.
Dybikowske, Ann, et al., eds. *In the Feminine: Women and Words / Les Femmes et les mots: Conference Proceedings 1983*. Edmonton, Alta.: Longspoon P, 1985.
Forsyth, Louise. 'Nicole Brossard and the Emergence of Feminist Literary Theory in Quebec since 1970.' In *Gynocritics/Gynocritiques*. Ed. Barbara Godard. Oakville: ECW P, 1987, 211–21.
Godard, Barbara, ed. *Gynocritics/Gynocritiques*. Oakville: ECW P, 1987. Bibliography.
Gould, Karen. *Writing in the Feminine: Feminism and Experimental Writing in Quebec*. Carbondale and Edwardsville: Southern Illinois UP, 1990.

Special numbers of periodicals:

La Barre du jour: 50 *Femme et langage*; 56–7 *le corps les mots l'imaginaire* [9 of the texts included in numbers 56–7 are translated in *Room of One's Own* 4.1 (1978)].
La Nouvelle barre du jour: 90–1 *La Nouvelle écriture*; 157 *L'Ecriture comme lecture*; 172 *Le Forum des femmes*; 194 *L'Inframanifeste illimité*; 196 *Femmes scandales 1965–85*; 217 *Femmes de lettres*.
Etudes littéraires: 12 *Féminaire*.
Liberté: 106–7 *La Femme et l'écriture. Actes de la rencontre québécoise internationale des écrivains* (1975).

Formalism: *see* Formalism, Russian; New Criticism; structuralism

Formalism, Russian

Formalism emerged as a distinctly independent school in Russian literary scholarship in the second decade of the 20th century by focusing attention on the analysis of distinguishing features of *literature, as opposed to the prevailing tradition of studying literature in conjunction with other disciplines such as history, sociology or psychology.

It had two centres: the Moscow Linguistic Circle, founded in 1915 by *Roman Jakobson, Petr Bogatyrev and Grigorii Vinokur, and the Petrograd OPOIAZ (acronym for the Society for the Study of Poetic Language), formed in 1916 by *Viktor Shklovskii, *Boris Eikhenbaum, Lev Iakubinskii, Osip Brik, and others. The two groups maintained close contact, with their members travelling between the two cities to read and discuss their findings. They published three collections of articles: *Sborniki po teorii poeticheskogo iazyka* [*Studies on the Theory of Poetic Language* 1916, 1917] and *Poetika. Sborniki po teorii poeticheskogo iazyka* [*Poetics: Studies on the Theory of Poetic Language* 1919].

The Moscow Linguistic Circle was composed primarily of linguists who were developing new approaches to the study of language and regarded poetics as part of a broader discipline of linguistics. They were preoccupied with the question of the differences between poetic and practical language, drawing examples from contemporary Russian poetry and Russian folklore.

The members of OPOIAZ were mainly literary historians who viewed literature as a unique form of verbal art that had to be studied on its own without relying too heavily on linguistics. Concerned with the general principles which govern literature and transform extra-aesthetic material into a work of art, they turned their attention to the classics of Russian and European literature.

Despite the important differences between these two groups, they shared common concerns. First, they were united in their efforts to place the study of literature on a scientific footing by defining its object and establishing its own methods and procedures. Second, they aimed to undermine the theory that art is a reflection of reality by insisting that it is a unique aesthetic entity governed by its own internal laws.

Autonomy of literary scholarship

From the very beginning the formalists insisted on the autonomy of literary scholarship and criticized the prevailing approaches to literature for their tendency to substitute the study of literature for something else, most notably biography, sociology or psychoanalysis. Jakobson compared literary historians to the police who, when they wanted to find a culprit would arrest everyone and everything in an apartment including chance passers-by. Similarly, historians of literature felt they had to take in everything – everyday life, psychology, politics, philosophy. The formalists were particularly critical of the main approaches to literature practised in Russia at that time: the biographical, the sociohistorical and the philosophical.

The formalists insisted on isolating the object of literary studies from those of other disciplines by focusing solely on literary facts and not on the external conditions under which literature is created. In defining the object of the study of literature, however, they maintained that it is not literature as a whole but rather *literaturnost'* (literariness) that is the distinguishing feature of literature. In the words of Jakobson, 'the subject of literary science is not literature, but literariness, that is, that which makes a given work a literary work.' According to this view, it is not the *text itself which constitutes the field of literary analysis but certain techniques employed in the text.

Poetic versus practical language

In their first attempts to define 'literariness,' the formalists turned to poetry, focusing their attention on the differences between poetic and practical language. With the exception of one article, they devoted the entire two volumes of *Sborniki* to the question of poetic language, or more specifically to the study of the use of sounds in poetry. Concentrating on the analysis of the phonetic aspect of words, the OPOIAZ scholars advanced the theory of the supremacy of sound over meaning in poetry. In practical language, argued Iakubinskii in his article 'O zvukakh stikhotvornogo iazyka' ['On Sounds in Verse Language'], sounds do not have any independent value; they serve only as a vehicle for communication. In poetic language, they enter the field of consciousness and are deliberately experienced.

In a similar fashion, Jakobson differentiated between poetic and everyday language in his *Noveishaia russkaia poeziia* [*Recent Russian Poetry* 1921]. Everyday language aims at efficient communication through references to ideas and objects. Poetic language draws attention to its own texture rather than to objects or concepts which the words represent. 'Poetry,' concluded Jakobson, 'is simply an utterance oriented toward a mode of expression.' (See also *communication theory.)

In their early preoccupation with the phonetic aspect of poetry, the formalists were undoubtedly influenced by the Russian futurists who developed the theory of the self-valuable word and wrote trans-rational poetry based on sounds with a total disregard for meaning. The *zaum'* poetry of Velemir Khlebnikov and Aleksei Kruchenykh became the object of intensive studies by Shklovskii and Jakobson and left a strong impact on their respective theories of poetic language.

By the early 1920s, the formalists realized that poetry could not be reduced to its phonetic component and that meaning was no less essential to poetry than sound. They re-examined fundamental problems connected with the theory of verse: the problems of rhythm and its correlation with syntax and intonation, of verse sounds combined with articulation, and finally of vocabulary and semantics. This new approach to the study of poetry was evident in Osip Brik's 'Ritm i sintaksis' ['Rhythm and Syntax' 1927], Eikhenbaum's *Melodika russkogo liricheskogo stikha* [*Melody of Russian Lyric Verse* 1922], and above all *Iurii Tynianov's *Problema stikhotvornogo iazyka* [*The Problem of Verse Language* 1924], which incorporated the analysis of syntax and semantics and stressed the interdependence of various elements in a poetic text.

*Defamiliarization

After their initial preoccupation with poetry, the formalists turned their attention to the study of prose and the distinguishing features of literature in general. In the 1917 collection of *Sborniki* Shklovskii published his pioneering study 'Iskusstvo kak priem' ['Art as Device'], outlining the theory of *ostranenie* [defamiliarization] based on the opposition between a habitual response and a new perception, between a mechanical recognition and a new awareness of things. In everyday life, argued Shklovskii, we do not see things or their textures, we respond to them automatically. The purpose of art is to disrupt that automatic perception and to impart the sensation of things as they are perceived and not as they are known. Art operates through the device of 'defamiliarization' that makes objects unfamiliar and strange and increases the difficulty and length of perception because the process of perception is an aesthetic end in itself and must be prolonged.

Material/device

Having defined defamiliarization as a distinguishing feature of literature and separated it from other verbal modes, Shklovskii and his colleagues proceeded to investigate works of narrative fiction, aiming to establish the basic laws of narrative prose. They published numerous studies devoted to the analysis of individual texts and introducing theoretical pronouncements on the nature of the literary process such as Eikhenbaum's 'Kak sdelana "Shinel" Gogolia' ['How Gogol's "The Overcoat" Is Made' 1919], Shklovskii's *Tristram Shendi Sterna i teoriia romana* [*Sterne's Tristram Shandy and the Theory of Prose* 1921], and Tynianov's *Dostoevskii i Gogol': k teorii parodii* [*Dostoevsky and Gogol: Toward A Theory of Parody* 1921].

The formalist critics consistently changed their focus from the external conditions of the literary process to the internal organization of a literary work. They rejected the traditional dichotomy of form and content, arguing that it incorrectly implies the existence of two separable layers in a literary work. In imaginative literature, maintained Viktor Zhirmunskii, content appears only through a medium of form and therefore cannot be profitably discussed or indeed conceived of apart from its artistic embodiment.

In place of the notions of 'content' and 'form,' the formalist critics proposed the concepts of 'material' and 'device,' corresponding to the two phases of the creative process: preaesthetic and aesthetic. Thus 'material' was understood as the raw stuff of literature that a writer can use for his work: facts from everyday life, literary conventions, ideas. 'Device' was defined as the aesthetic principle that transforms material into a work of art. According to Shklovskii, art has its own organization which transforms its material into something artistically experienced. This organization is expressed in various compositional devices, rhythm, phonetics, and syntax, and the plot of the work. It is a device that transforms extra-aesthetic material into a work of art by providing it with form.

*Story/plot

While applying the concepts of 'material' and 'device' to fiction, the formalists distinguished between two aspects of the narrative: *fabula* [story] and *siuzhet* [plot]. Story was identified with a series of events linked together according to their temporal succession and their causality. Plot was the artistic rearrangement of the events in the text, in a different chronological order and without causal dependency. In addition to the temporal displacement and the lack of causality, the plot included all other elements of artistic structure, such as digressions and comments. 'The plot of *Eugene Onegin*,' wrote Shklovskii, 'is not Onegin's love affair with Tatiana, but the artistic treatment of the story, achieved by means of interpolating digressions.'

Considering plot the distinguishing element of narrative prose, the formalists turned their attention to the study of the devices which embody the internal laws of plot composition. Shklovskii isolated some typical categories of plot compositions such as the 'staircase,' the 'hook-like' construction and double-plotting. All of these constructions perform the same function: they splinter even apparently unified non-aesthetic material, distort and alter it, making it artistically perceptible.

In most literary works, argued Shklovskii, the devices of plot composition are motivated realistically, with the author providing valid reasons for their presence. But in some texts the devices are 'laid bare,' making the reader aware of their presence. For Shklovskii the best example of 'laying bare' the device was Laurence Sterne's novel *Tristram Shandy* with its continuous interruptions of the action, authorial digressions, displacement of chronology, transposition of chapters, and retardation. Shklovskii expressed a decided preference for unmotivated devices. He believed the writer should play with the expectations of the reader and deliberately destroy the illusion of reality.

Skaz

In contradistinction to Shklovskii's preoccupation with the devices of plot construction, Eikhenbaum investigated the role of the narrative voice as the organizing principle of fiction. In his essays 'Kak sdelana "Shinel" Gogolia,' 'Illiuziia *skaza*' ['The Illusion of *Skaz*' 1924], and 'Leskov i sovremennaia proza' ['Leskov and Modern Prose' 1925], he argued that in some literary works the focus is not on the plot and the interlocking of motifs but on the voice of the *narrator, forcing his way into the foreground by any means possible. Eikhenbaum defined this kind of narration as *skaz* and described it as a special type of *discourse oriented in its lexicon, syntax and intonation toward the oral speech of the narrator.

The critic distinguished two types of *skaz*: the 'narrating' *skaz*, relying on verbal jokes and semantic puns; and the 'reproducing' *skaz*, introducing elements of mimicry and gestures and inventing special comic articulation and phonetic puns. In Eikhenbaum's opinion, the best example of the first type was the 19th-century Russian writer Nikolai Leskov, who created a special kind of narration with the help of colloquial idioms, folk etymology and semantic puns. The best illustration of the second type was Nikolai Gogol, with his system of various mimical-articulatory gestures, creating a purely comical effect and a pathetic declamation conceived of as a contrasting aesthetic effect.

Two phases of formalism

Eikhenbaum's concept of *skaz*, Shklovskii's theory of defamiliarization and plot composition, and Jakobson's observations on the differences between poetic and practical language represent the first phase of the development of Russian formalism between the years 1916 and 1921. In the words of Eikhenbaum, these were the years of 'struggle and polemics,' when the young formalist scholars put forward many ideas that had value not only as scientific principles but also as slogans.

The most important achievements of that period were the separation of literary criticism from its dependence on other disciplines and the change of focus from the external conditions of the literary process to the internal organization of a literary work. Literature was viewed as a special type of verbal discourse governed by its own laws and developed in a unique fashion.

The inadequacies of the early formalists' approach to literature were threefold. Initially, their concept of a literary work was too mechanistic, reducing a text to a sum total of devices employed in it. Second, despite their theoretical insistence on the constant revitalization of literary forms, their actual analysis of literary works was ahistorical and geared toward the establishment of a static system of rules as they existed at one point in time. Third, there was a too strict separation of literature from life, based on their refusal to consider any possible interplay between literary and extraliterary phenomena.

Most of these inadequacies were eliminated in the second phase of formalism, between 1921 and 1926. Under the direction of Iurii Tynianov, formalism moved closer to *structuralism, broadening and deepening theoretical issues and redefining basic concepts. Thus, the static definition of a literary work was replaced by the concept of a dynamic structure in which the unity of elements was achieved not by equality and addition but by dynamic correlation and integration. The synchronic approach to literature gave way to a diachronic approach, addressing the question of historical change and the evolution of literary forms. Finally, a concession was made to the notion of the full autonomy of art by acknowledging the connections between art and reality.

Dynamic structure

The most important publication of the second phase of formalism was Tynianov's book *Problema stikhotvornogo iazyka* [*The Problem of Verse Language* 1924], not only outlining the internal laws of verse structure but also redefining some fundamental concepts of the early formalist theory. The most profound change involved the concept of literary form approached by Tynianov not as a static phenomenon but as a dynamic structure. A dynamic form, argued Tynianov, is generated not by means of combination and merger but by means of the interaction and integration of all components.

In each work of verbal art, there is a continuous struggle between all its components. The component which wins in that struggle becomes the 'constructive factor,' pushing itself forward and dominating all other components.

Thus each work of verbal art displays a hierarchy of elements. Only one of these elements can function as a 'constructive factor' and subordinate all other elements to itself. This process of subordination implies alteration and distortion of all subordinated elements according to the requirements of the 'constructive principle.'

The correlation between the constructive factor and the subordinated factors, stressed Tynianov, is always fluctuating. Only one of the elements can play the dominant role at any given time. It can be replaced, however, by another constructive factor in the course of the work. This continuous interaction and alteration of elements guarantees the artistic quality of a work. If this dynamic interaction disappears, a work ceases to function as a work of art. It becomes automatized.

Literary dynamics

The continuous process of transformation and alteration of all elements in response to the constructive factor was for Tynianov only one aspect of the dynamics of form. In addition to the interrelation of one element with the other elements within the same work, there was a simultaneous interrelation between elements of a given work and similar elements in other literary works and other systems.

Initially, Tynianov concentrated on the analysis of intraliterary relations by placing a text in the context of other literary texts and examining the interrelation between them. In 'O literaturnom fakte' ['On Literary Fact' 1924] he formulated the principle of literary dynamics, understood as a process of continuous renewal and revitalization of literary forms. He distinguished four steps in that process: the emergence of a new constructive principle in opposition to the automatized constructive principle; the application of that new principle in new works; the widespread use of that principle; and the automatization of that principle and the emergence of opposite constructive principles.

The idea of literary dynamics was central to Tynianov's theory of literature since he believed that only in evolution could we grasp the essence of the literary process. Literary facts of different periods, disparate in themselves, become related if they are placed within a concrete historical process and viewed according to the logic of that process.

Literary evolution

Tynianov returned to the question of literary evolution in his essay 'O literaturnoi evolutsii' ['On Literary Evolution' 1927]. He stressed that the very existence of a fact as literary depended on its interrelationship with both literary and extraliterary systems. In terms of the extraliterary connections, he advocated the study of literature first of all in relation to *byt* (social conventions). He argued that literature is related to social conventions in its verbal function. A writer has at his disposal different linguistic patterns which are part of social conventions. He selects some of them, foregrounds them and turns them into literary facts. Then the opposite process takes place: a literary fact becomes automatized, its literary function recedes and it turns into a social convention.

The study of literary evolution, concluded Tynianov, is possible only in relation to literature as a system interrelated with other systems and conditioned by them. Investigation must go from constructional function to literary function, from literary function to verbal function. The study of evolution must move from the literary system to the nearest correlated systems, not the distant even though major systems. In this way, the prime significance of major social factors was not discarded.

Tynianov recast his concept of relations between literary and extraliterary phenomena in the 1928 thesis 'Problemy izucheniia literatury i iazyka' ['Problems of the Study of Literature and Language'] written jointly with Jakobson. They conceived of literature as part of a complex network of systems all correlated with one another. Each system was governed by its own immanent laws and each was correlated to other systems through a set of specific structural laws. The task of the history of literature was to establish the structural laws of literature and to analyse the correlation between the literary and other historical systems. Only through the investigation of the correlation between literature and other systems could the process of literary evolution be established.

With its acknowledgment of the connections between literature and other systems, 'Problemy izucheniia literatury i iazyka' was a clear attempt to reconcile formalism with Marxism. But the formalist model of parallel, autonomous systems governed by their own structural laws was not acceptable to Marxist critics, who viewed literature as part of a superstructure dependent on and determined by the economic base. (See *Marxist criticism.)

Suppression of formalism

Throughout the 1920s, formalism was under constant attack by Marxist critics. In 1923 Leon Trotsky in his book *Literatura i revolutsiia* [*Literature and Revolution*] challenged the formalists to give up their idealistic premise of the autonomy of art and to accept the Marxist view of the dependency of literature on social and economic factors. He acknowledged the formalist search for the intrinsic laws of art, but urged them to go beyond their descriptive and semi-statistical analysis of literary devices to an in-depth investigation of the literary process and the interrelationship between literature and social factors.

In 1924 Anatolii Lunacharskii attacked formalism as a relic of old Russia, a product of the decadent and spiritually empty ruling class. The only type of art enjoyed by the bourgeoisie, argued Lunacharskii, in 'Formalizm v iskusstvovedenii' ['Formalism in the Theory of Art'], was non-objective and formal art. In order to meet this need, the bourgeois intelligentsia brought forth formalist artists as well as an auxilliary corps of formalist critics.

In 1928 another serious critique of formalism appeared, *Formal'nyi metod v literaturovedenii* [*The Formal Method in Literary Scholarship*], signed by Pavel Medvedev but now attributed to *Mikhail Bakhtin. The book criticized the formalists for their preoccupation with the theory of poetic language and their neglect of the social nature of literature. It advocated the necessity of elaborating 'sociological poetics,' combining the study of unique features of literature with an investigation of the relationship between literature and other fields of human activity.

By the end of the 1920s, the attacks intensified and the formalists were forced to abandon their theoretical explorations and switch to textual criticism. For more than 30 years, formalism was considered an anti-Marxist heresy in the Soviet Union and the word 'formalist' was a term of abuse applied to literary critics as well as to writers and artists in general. The situation changed only in the early 1960s when some of the earlier formalist studies were republished, stimulating interest in the intrinsic approach to literature and in structuralist poetics.

Formalism and other schools

Totally suppressed in the Soviet Union, formalism continued to exert influence on theoretical developments abroad, particularly in Czechoslovakia and Poland. There was a close link between Russian formalism and the *Prague School thanks to the personal involvement of Jakobson and Petr Bogatyrev, who both moved to Prague in 1921, and to the frequent visits by Tynianov and Grigorii Vinokur throughout the 1920s. The Prague scholars accepted the basic tenets of the formalist theory, including the insistence on the autonomy of literary studies, the importance of the dichotomy between poetic and practical language, and the reliance on a linguistic model. They redefined and redeveloped many of the formalist concepts such as dynamic structure, with its hierarchy of elements and a dominant factor, literary dynamics and evolution. But they placed these concepts into the framework of a coherent structuralist theory which defined both the immanent properties of literature as well as the correlation between literature and other social systems.

Russian formalism strongly influenced the development of the Polish 'integral' school in the 1930s. (See *structuralism, Polish.) The members of both the Warsaw and Wilno groups accepted the formalist plea for the autonomy of literary scholarship and advocated an 'integral' approach to literature, focusing on the intrinsic qualities of literature rather than the external conditions producing it. The Poles were particularly impressed with the formalist notion of the poetic language as a differentiating feature of literature and devoted many of their studies to the analysis of Polish prosody and stylistics.

Formalism did not exert any direct influence on the development of Anglo-American *New Criticism, although both shared a belief in the autonomy of literature and the necessity of focusing literary criticism on the verbal aspect of literature. Unlike the Russian scholars who submitted to the neopositivist *ideology and believed that literary criticism had to rely on empirical methods, the New Critics questioned the usefulness of positivism for literary science. They focused attention on the evocative and emotive function of literary discourse and interpreted the ambiguity of meaning in poetry.

Formalism did not have any appreciable impact on literary scholarship in the West until the publication of Viktor Erlich's monograph *Russian Formalism: History, Doctrine* (1955) and of *Tzvetan Todorov's anthology *Théorie de la littérature: Textes des formalistes russes, réunis, présentés et traduits par Tzvetan Todorov* (1965). These publications appeared at the time of the emergence in the West of structuralism and assisted the new movement with the awareness of the centrality of language and the importance of the linguistic model. Formalism had a particularly strong impact on French structuralism, stimulating the theoretical investigations of Todorov, *Roland Barthes and *Gérard Genette. The French structuralists shared with their Russian colleagues the conviction of the conventionality of art and the supremacy of language in literature. They exhibited the same tendency to reduce literary criticism to the study of language and to deny its moral and social relevance.

Formalism also played an important role in the development of structuralism in the Soviet Union in the 1960s. The scholars associated with the Tartu-Moscow group such as *Iurii Lotman, *Alexander Zholkovsky and *Boris Uspenskii openly acknowledged their debt to the formalists and accepted the formalist theory as the point of departure for their structuralist studies. (See *Tartu School.)

The influence exerted by formalism on literary scholarship in Czechoslovakia and Poland, France and the United States, and finally in the Soviet Union itself testifies to the extraordinary vitality and importance of the Russian school. The formalists transformed literary scholarship into a mature and scholarly discipline with its own methods and procedures. They replaced the impressionistic approach to literature by a rigorous investigation of the intrinsic laws of literature. They were the first to define literature as a form of verbal art and to concentrate on the analysis of poetic language as the distinguishing feature of literature. They developed the concepts of literary structure and literary dynamics which became the foundation of the structuralist approach.

The major inadequacy of formalism was its insistence on the autonomy of art and its refusal to consider any relationship between literature and other social systems. This resulted in a total disregard for the question of creative personality and the connections between literature and reality. Another weakness of formalist criticism was its one-sided preoccupation with artistic devices and its neglect of the thematics and the emotional content of literature. (See *theme.) Finally, its rejection of critical evaluation in literary criticism led to extreme relativism and failure to do justice to the aesthetic quality of literature.

NINA KOLESNIKOFF

Primary Sources

Brik, Osip. 'Ritm i sintaksis.' *Novyi lef* 3–6 (1927). Excerpts trans. as 'Contributions to the Study of Verse Language.' In *Readings in Russian Poetics: Formalist and Structuralist Views.* Ed. L. Matejka and K. Pomorska. Cambridge, Mass.: MIT Press, 1971, 117–25.
Eikhenbaum, Boris. 'Illiuziia skaza.' *Skvoz' literaturu.* Leningrad, 1924. 'The Illusion of "Skaz."' *Russian Literature Triquarterly* 12 (1975): 233–6.
– 'Kak sdelana "Shinel" Gogolia.' *Poetika. Sborniki po teorii poeticheskogo iazyka.* Petrograd, 1919, 151–65. 'How Gogol's "The Overcoat" Is Made.' *Russian Review* 20 (1963): 377–90.
– 'Leskov i sovremennaia proza.' *Literatura, teoriia, kritika, polemika.* Leningrad, 1927. 'Leskov and Modern Prose.' *Russian Literature Triquarterly* 11 (1975): 211–29.
– *Melodika russkogo liricheskogo stikha.* Leningrad, 1922.
Iakubinskii, Lev. 'O zvukakh stikhotvornogo iazyka.' *Poetika. Sborniki po teorii poeticheskogo iazyka.* Petrograd, 1916, 37–49.
Jakobson, Roman. *Noveishaia russkaia poeziia.* Prague, 1921.
– and Iu. Tynianov. 'Problemy izucheniia literatury i iazyka.' *Novyi lef* 12 (1928): 36–7. 'Problems in the Study of Literature and Language.' In *Readings in Russian Poetics,* 79–81.
Poetika. Sborniki po teorii poeticheskogo iazyka. Petrograd, 1919.
Sborniki po teorii poeticheskogo iazyka. I. Petersburg, 1916.
Sborniki po teorii poeticheskogo iazyka. II. Petersburg, 1917.
Shklovskii, Viktor. 'Iskusstvo kak priem.' In *Sborniki po teorii poeticheskogo iazyka.* II. Petrograd, 1917, 3–14. 'Art as Technique.' In *Russian Formalist Criticism: Four Essays.* Ed. L. Lemon and M.J. Reis. Lincoln: U of Nebraska P, 1965, 3–24.
– 'Sviaz' priemov siuzhetoslozheniia s obshchimi priemami stilia.' In *Poetika. Sborniki po teorii poeticheskogo iazyka.* Petrograd, 1919, 115–50. 'On the Connection Between Devices of Siuzhet and General Stylistic Devices.' In *Russian Formalism: A Collection of Articles and Texts in Translation.* Ed. S.

Bann and J. Bowlt. Edinburgh: Scottish Academic P, 1973, 48–72.
– *Tristram Shendi Sterna i teoriia romana.* Petrograd, 1921. 'Sterne's *Tristram Shandy* and the Theory of the Novel.' In *Russian Formalist Criticism: Four Essays,* 25–60.
Todorov, Tzvetan, ed. *Théorie de la littérature.* Paris: Editions du Seuil, 1965.
Tynianov, Iurii. *Dostoevskii i Gogol': k teorii parodii.* Petrograd, 1921.
– 'O literaturnoi evolutsii.' 4 (1927). 'On Literary Evolution.' In *Readings in Russian Poetics: Formalist and Structuralist Views.* Ed. L. Matejka and K. Pomorska. Cambridge, Mass.: MIT Press, 1971, 68–78.
– 'O literaturnom fakte.' *Lef* 2 (1924): 100–16.
– *Problema stikhotvornogo iazyka.* Leningrad, 1924. *The Problem of Verse Language.* Ann Arbor: Ardis, 1981.
– and R. Jakobson. 'Problemy izucheniia literatury i iazyka.' *Novyi lef* 12 (1928): 36–7. 'Problems in the Study of Literature and Language.' In *Readings in Russian Poetics,* 79–81.

Secondary Sources

Any, C. 'The Russian Formalist Tradition.' *Soviet Studies in Literature* 21.3–4 (1985): 5–28.
Bennett, Tony. *Formalism and Marxism.* London: Methuen, 1979.
Erlich, Viktor. 'Russian Formalism.' *Journal of the History of Ideas* 34.4 (1973): 627–38.
– *Russian Formalism: History, Doctrine.* The Hague: Mouton, 1955.
Greenfeld, Leah. 'Russian Formalist Sociology of Literature: A Sociological Perspective.' *Slavic Review* 46 (1987): 38–54.
Hansen–Love, Aage. *Der russische Formalismus.* Vienna: Academie der Wissenschaften, 1978.
Jackson, R.L., and S. Rudy, eds. *Russian Formalism: A Retrospective Glance. A Festschrift in Honour of Victor Erlich.* New Haven: Yale Centre for International and Area Studies, 1985.
Jameson, Frederic. *The Prison-House of Language: A Critical Account of Structuralism and Russian Formalism.* Princeton: Princeton UP, 1972.
Lunacharskii, A. 'Formalizm v iskusstvovdeenii.' *Pechat' i revolutsiia* 5 (1924).
Medvedev, Pavel. *Formal' nyi metod v literaturovedenii.* Leningrad, 1928. *The Formal Method in Literary Scholarship.* Baltimore: Johns Hopkins UP, 1978.
Pomorska, Krystyna. *Russian Formalist Theory and Its Poetic Ambiance.* The Hague: Mouton, 1968.
Selden, R. 'Russian Formalism: An Unconcluded Dialogue.' *Proceedings of the 1976 Conference on Literature, Society, and the Sociology of Literature.* U of Essex, 1977.

Frankfurt School

Steiner, Peter. 'Formalism and Structuralism: An Exercise in Metahistory.' *Russian Literature* 12 (1982): 299–330.
– *Russian Formalism: A Metapoetics.* Ithaca: Cornell UP, 1984.
– 'Three Metaphors of Russian Formalism.' *Poetics Today* 2 (1980–1): 58–116.
Striedter, Jurij. *Literary Structure, Evolution and Value: Russian Formalism and Czech Structuralism Reconsidered.* Cambridge: Harvard UP, 1989.
– 'The Russian Formalist Theory of Literary Evolution.' *PTL: A Journal for Descriptive Poetics and Theory of Literature* 3 (1978): 1–24.
– 'The Russian Formalist Theory of Prose.' *PTL: A Journal for Descriptive Poetics and Theory of Literature* 2 (1977): 429–70.
Thompson, Ewa. *Russian Formalism and Anglo-American New Criticism.* The Hague: Mouton, 1971.
Todorov, Tzvetan. 'L'Héritage méthodologique du Formalisme.' In *Poetique de la Prose.* Paris: Editions de Seuil, 1971, 9–31.
– 'Some Approaches to Russian Formalism.' In *Russian Formalism: A Collection of Articles and Texts in Translation.* Ed. S. Bann and J. Bowlt. Edinburgh: Scottish Academic P, 1973, 6–19.
Trotskii, Lev. *Literatura i revolutsiia.* Moskva, 1924. *Literature and Revolution.* Ann Arbor: U of Michigan P, 1960.

Frankfurt School

The Frankfurt Institute of Social Research was founded in 1923 as the result of an endowment established by an Austrian grain merchant, the father of the political scientist Felix Weil. The latter originally conceived the idea of a centre for the social sciences and humanities that would be autonomous of private and public financing even though it would be affiliated with the newly formed University of Frankfurt. This financial and political autonomy permitted the institute's members the freedom to embark on an exploration of a variety of subjects. Histories of the school, including Martin Jay's *The Dialectical Imagination* (1973), Rolph Wiggeshaus' *Die Frankfurt Schule* (1987) and *Fredric Jameson's book on *Adorno (1990) all argue that it was the first Western institute to be founded on principles of social democracy derived from Marxist and Weberian theory. Members of the institute challenged both the emerging orthodoxy of scientific Marxism from the Soviet bloc and compromised versions of state socialism evolving out of post–First World War Germany. (See *Marxist criticism.)

By 1932 philosopher Max Horkheimer assumed the direction of the institute and became the editor of its review *Zeitschrift für Sozialforschung* (1932–41). Under Horkheimer's direction an inner circle emerged that included Theodor Adorno, Leo Lowenthal and Herbert Marcuse. Their common interests in aesthetic and literary issues provided an informal bond across their varied projects. Though he did receive some financial support from the institute, *Walter Benjamin was not an official member; however, he played a seminal role in determining the parameters of debate concerning questions of aesthetics. After a stay in the U.S.A. following the outbreak of the Second World War, Horkheimer and Adorno returned to Frankfurt where new students were trained in the 1950s and 1960s who would ultimately carry on the tradition. These included two of the tradition's most prominent contemporary representatives, *Jürgen Habermas and Peter Bürger. The institute officially closed with the death of Horkheimer in 1973. Today, it is more appropriate to speak of the Frankfurt tradition rather than a school as such, since many continue to work in its heritage even though their philosophical and aesthetic positions often contradict the earlier ideas of the original members. The Frankfurt tradition continues to be felt in a variety of disciplines ranging from philosophical anthropology to political economy, psychoanalysis, aesthetics, and literary criticism.

Critical theory: three problem motifs

For almost 70 years the tradition has been both divided and held together over a debate concerning the definition of its central concept of *critical theory. Each generation has had to rework Nancy Fraser's question, 'What's Critical About Critical Theory?' Contemporary literary criticism employs the concept of 'critical theory' in too general a sense. Much of its critique would be defined by the Frankfurt tradition as either a form of *hermeneutics founded on the practical interests of interpretation and on the 'critique' or recovery of hidden or deferred meaning (*deconstruction, *reception theory), or a positivism founded on the technical interests of explanation (*semiotics, *narratology). The concept of 'critical theory,' as defined by the Frankfurt tradition is more specific. First developed by Horkheimer in the 1930s, the concept is offered as a rejection of

60

the purely immanent form of critique in traditional hermeneutics, best exemplified in the philosophy of *Wilhelm Dilthey. On the other hand, it also attacks scientific approaches that make claims of pure explanation based on objective experimental or statistical techniques of analysis. All knowledge is seen as being rooted in ideological interests. (See *ideology, *ideological horizon.) This position may be seen in three dominant frames of argument or problem motifs that each successive generation has reassessed.

The first of these is historical relativism. Horkheimer attacks this issue, that is, the view that all forms of knowledge including literary and aesthetic forms are related to specific interests, be they based on class, ethnicity or, we might today add, gender. This problem motif, which holds that no truth claims can be made that are universally valid, poses a philosophical and political dilemma to those who would claim *universal and thus metaphysical truths regarding the nature of fascism, for example, or more generally the nature of male violence against women. Horkheimer contrasts his approach to this problem with that of Karl Mannheim's theory of the sociology of knowledge. In *Ideology and Utopia* (1929), Mannheim argues that truth claims are ultimately bound to a distinct perspective. Knowledge can only be partial because it is founded in the social interest that gives rise to that perspective. Only déclassé intellectuals have the expertise and possibility of detachment from interests that would allow them to derive universal truth claims. Horkheimer argues against Mannheim, as does Adorno in *Prisms*, offering instead a neo-Marxian position that places the problem of truth claims in the realm of *praxis and a theory of social conflict that looks to explore the attempts of groups of social actors to achieve a state of emancipation. Both the concept of praxis, the emancipation or negation of the conditions of domination, and *Ideologiekritik*, the critique of the social interests that underlie systems of ideas or ideologies, are mined from Marx's work. Historical relativism is challenged by 'critical theory' within its other two problem motifs as well.

Posing the question of the condition in which knowledge is possible suggests the second problem motif for critical theory. It demonstrates the Kantian side of the Frankfurt tradition's definition of critique and its shifting reliance on transcendental reason as the means to access the critical interest of emancipation. But adapting the concept of reason from Hegel and Marx leads to two different definitions of reason. Universal reason is seen as a form of instrumental reason. It is a means to an end; yet universal reason can be subverted through critical reason. These are the two conditions in which knowledge is possible and they refer to two distinct processes. Instrumental reason seeks to protect its own interests. It is utilitarian and seeks an absolute identity with its truth referent. Critical reason seeks to dissolve the rigidity of the referent that is fixed in the immediate present or the actual by introducing negativity. Negation of instrumental reason opens the potentiality of the truth referent; that is, it opens the conditions of possibility in which *literature or art might come into being. (See *reference/referent.)

In this sense 'critical theory' must also be self-critical or reflexive. In the third problem motif, critical reason requires a sustained will to a self-reflection that allows it to overcome its own rigidity. Without this third problem motif, a properly existential one, 'critical theory' might not negate its own rigidity, nor could it claim an immanent critique of some other object. In order that the critical interest, the emancipatory interest, not collapse into an identity with its object, critique must oscillate between the transcendental position of its own place in the mass of possible approaches to the object and the immanent construction of the object itself, that is, the hermeneutic technique of understanding the object from its point of view. Unlike deconstruction, to which 'critical theory' is often inaccurately compared, the truth referent is defined both within and is external to the object. In this critical theory remains partially tied to a *metaphysics of presence. The referent to which the object refers is negated, but it is also constructed in the critical process through self-reflection, immanent critique and the appropriation of positive elements derived from other approaches to the same object.

Benjamin, Adorno, Horkheimer: aesthetic and literary debates

Aesthetic and literary questions were and are central to the Frankfurt idea of 'critical theory.' Several thinkers who were not part of the institute but had a wide-reaching impact on debates that divided the institute's members were Karl Mannheim, his teacher *Georg Lukács, Ernst Bloch and Bertolt Brecht. In their earlier years, Mannheim, Lukács and Bloch were frequent participants at the informal theory seminars on aesthetic and political issues held in the home of the sociologists Max and Marian Weber. Their influence on Benjamin eventually led to sharp differences between Benjamin and Adorno, differences which came to represent the two extremes that would be adopted within the circle and between which the members would oscillate.

To Lukács' approach to aesthetic questions, Benjamin adds Brecht's theory of political realism. This leads him to the concept of 'mediation.' For Benjamin, the evolution of art and literature is tied to the manner in which their reproduction is handed down. Art is no longer defined as a reflection of the social but as one mode of production among many and is mediated by the organizing and aesthetic practices that precede it. For example, in the case of the 'storyteller,' the oral means of reproduction depend on a social formation that has all but disappeared in the 'age of mechanical reproduction.' Yet, at the same time, art has its own specificity, which lends it a very specific beauty or *aura. In spite of Benjamin's theoretical break from Lukács and Brecht, there is still a strong sense in which a purely representational aesthetic theory informs his *problematic.

Adorno, in *Negative Dialectics* (1966), *Aesthetic Theory* (1970) and *Noten zur Literatur* (1981) develops the extreme version of a 'critical theory' of art in which the complete negation or refusal of the real is seen as the only means of achieving a valid artistic form. In sharp contrast to Benjamin's position, Adorno holds that the validity of art is not found in its identification with the social (as in Lukács' theory of realism) but in its autonomy and ultimately in its refusal of the social. Although Adorno accepts Benjamin's theory of mediation, he rejects his concept of correspondence as a thinly disguised reflection theory of art and literature. Instead, Adorno argues for a theory of *mimesis defined as the repetition of an autonomous artistic form that seeks an accidental rupture from its own past in the anticipation of an emancipated unknown future. For Adorno, the autonomy of artistic form makes it the negative knowledge of the actual or real. Adorno and Horkheimer's critique of Benjamin is primarily aimed at his belief in the inevita-

ble revolution of the proletariat and his conviction that art must ultimately take on a political identification.

In *Literature and the Image of Man* (1957) and *Literature, Popular Culture and Society* (1961), Leo Lowenthal helps develop a sociology of 'Great Literature' that Adorno and others put forth but he never has the commitment to the philosophy of pure critique, the absolute refusal to identify with the real in artistic representation that Adorno advocates. Similarly, Herbert Marcuse extends the implicit Adornian mood of pessimism in his critique of modern culture in *One-Dimensional Man*. But, in his last book, *The Aesthetic Dimension* (1977), he too holds back from Adorno's 'negative dialectics.' Horkheimer and Adorno's apocalyptic discussion of the culture industry in their *Dialectic of Enlightenment* (1944), a work heavily influenced by *Nietzsche and Adorno's *Introduction to the Sociology of Music* (trans. 1976), defines art as the negative knowledge of the real world. Only 'great works' have the capacity to overcome the commodification or *reification process henceforth technologically inherent in the modern culture industry. As Jameson points out, for Horkheimer and Adorno the reification process of the cultural industry is totalizing and has become so omnipresent that it transforms virtually every aspect of culture into 'mass mystification.' In the modern cultural apparatus all products are submitted to crushing rational models that require increasing standardization of reproduction techniques, a repetition of forms and contents that leaves no room for creativity. The culture industry creates a constant conformity, even regulating relations with the past: 'That which is new is the exclusion of everything that could be new.' (See *totalization.)

Habermas: agenda for a new critical theory

Almost 40 years after Horkheimer and Adorno's landmark work, Jürgen Habermas, an important contemporary member of the Frankfurt tradition, launched a blunt attack against their nihilism in 'The Entwinement of Myth and Enlightenment: Re-reading the Dialectic of Enlightenment' (1982). Habermas, an assistant to Adorno at the institute in the 1950s, claims to have been deeply influenced by his work. Like his predecessors, he was schooled in the tradition of German philosophy. However, he breaks in important ways from that tradition and becomes immersed in American pragmatism and contemporary language philosophy. Habermas argues that the work of his predecessors suggests an over-totalizing critique of modernity, a critique born in the epoch of the Enlightenment, which virtually eliminates the possibility of any kind of emancipation. He argues that their negation of rationalism and the idea that knowledge is inherently emancipatory, demonstrates the limits of a theoretical logic founded in historicism and a philosophy of consciousness, an approach that posits the will of the social actor as the determining force in the historical process. The elaboration of a 'New Critical Theory' which would go beyond these limits and recover the critical reason of the Enlightenment, he argues, must shift to a philosophy of language and a theory of communication. (See *communication theory.)

Although Habermas has never directly treated the question of the status of art and literature except through his commentary on the earlier members of the tradition, his controversial plea for a 'New Critical Theory' based in a philosophy of language has important consequences for the theory of aesthetics for which the tradition has been famous. Habermas develops his position in *The Theory of Communicative Action* (1984), adding four new fields previously ignored by the tradition. His main concept, *communicative action, is founded on his argument for a 'universal pragmatics' of speech and action, first outlined in *Communication and the Evolution of Society* (1977). He argues for a theory of transubjectivity that is developed from the rational logic of communicative action wherein the subject speaker is seen to share conjointly certain responsibilities with the listener.

Because utterances must be intelligible in order to make validity claims, Habermas argues for a second field of study in order to recapture the possibility of developing a normative theory of communicative action. The intelligibility of the utterance requires an apprenticeship in communicative competence. Emancipation of the subject occurs in the 'ideal speech situation,' where there are only attempts at understanding and where communication cannot be distorted. A maximum discourse can be expressed with a minimum set of constraints. But because the apprenticeship of communicative competence occurs as social systems move in and out of 'life-worlds,' colonizing primary cultures that seek to protect themselves from colonization by other competing 'life-worlds,' it is quite difficult to maintain an 'ideal speech act' outside of limited contexts. Studying the social system as a producer of objective knowledge is a third area Habermas addresses, particularly in *Legitimation Crisis* (1975). The fourth area he introduces, mostly in the second volume of *Theory of Communicative Action*, is the study of sociological theories of the evolution of the subject inside the life-world. (See *Lebenswelt.)

Peter Bürger: art and literature as institution

There is by no means any consensus regarding Habermas' plea for a 'New Critical Theory.' Many see his shift to the theory of communicative action as a shift away from the emancipatory interests of 'critical theory' toward the practical interests of hermeneutics. An important figure in contemporary *sociocriticism, and another member of this generation, Peter Bürger, continues to work through a 'critical theory' of literature and aesthetics, taking up some of the concepts and concerns first raised by Benjamin and Adorno. For the latter, the approach of 'critical theory' to cultural productions requires a split presupposition. Art and literature are seen as both institutional products and as institutions themselves. In *The Theory of the Avant-Garde* (1984), Bürger shows how in the 18th and 19th centuries autonomous art separated itself from day-to-day social life and as such created its own institution. He goes on to argue that the avant-garde movements of the 20th century must be interpreted as attacks against art and literature as institutions. Bürger's analysis privileges the social function of art as the primary object of analysis. Internally, the aesthetic practices of the institution work themselves out across the maze of discursive norms and codes that refer to the entire history of art and literature. (See *code.) In any period, art and literature as institution gives a definition to this discursive maze and thereby establishes a stratified scale of genres and subgenres. Narrative styles become the receptacles of social discourse itself. Aesthetic objects then both stratify and are stratified; they are both a social product and a social force. The ambiguity inherent in this proposition stems from an attempt, on the one hand, to privilege the potentiality of the aesthetic object (as in Benjamin, Adorno, Horkheimer) and, on the other, to explain how the process itself becomes objectified (as in Habermas).

This split assumption that posits art and literature as both products of social norms and as potentially emancipatory agencies refers directly to the organizing and regulating practices of social institutions in general. The Frankfurt tradition consistently defines these practices as being combined in the creation of a condition of production, and any discussion that holds them separate is seen to be purely analytical. At one pole, at least since Benjamin, the organizing practice is seen to bring together all the elements of the technical and discursive infrastructure of the institution, its systems of reproduction and distribution. At the other pole, from Adorno on, the imaginary negative knowledge of aesthetic practice brings together all the elements (codes, norms, themes, narrative) of the creative life-world. (See also *theme, *literary institution.) 'Critical theory' teaches that the judgments of the genius of aesthetic objects can only be derived from the specific reflections of immanent critique.

GREG NIELSEN

Primary Sources

Adorno, Theodor. *Aesthetic Theory.* Trans. C. Lenhardt. London: Routledge and Kegan Paul, 1984.
– *Introduction to the Sociology of Music.* New York: Seabury, 1976.
– *Negative Dialectics.* New York: Seabury, 1973.
– *Notzen zur Literatur.* Frankfurt: Suhrkamp, 1981.
– *Philosophy of Modern Music.* Trans. A. Mitchell and W. Bloomster. New York: Seabury, 1973.
– *Prisms.* Trans. Samuel and Shierry Weber. London: Neville Spearman, 1967.
Arato, Andrew, and Eike Gebhart, eds. *The Essential Frankfurt School Reader.* New York: Continuum, 1982.
Benjamin, Walter. *Charles Baudelaire: A Lyric Poet in the Era of High Capitalism.* Trans. H. Zohn. London: New Left Books, 1973.
– *Illuminations.* Trans. H. Zohn. New York: Harcourt, 1969.
– *The Origin of German Tragic Drama.* Trans. J. Osborne. London: New Left Books, 1977.
– *Understanding Brecht.* Trans. A. Bostack. London: New Left Books, 1973.
Bürger, Peter. 'The Institution of Art as a Category in the Sociology of Literature.' *Culture Critique* 2 (1985): 5–33.
– *The Theory of the Avant-Garde.* Minneapolis: U of Minnesota P, 1984.

Fraser, Nancy. 'What's Critical About Critical Theory? The Case of Habermas and Gender.' *New German Critique* 35 (1985): 97–131.
Guess, Raymond. *The Idea of Critical Theory: Habermas and the Frankfurt School.* London: Cambridge UP, 1981.
Habermas, Jürgen. *Communication and the Evolution of Society.* Trans. T. McCarthy. Boston: Beacon P, 1979.
– 'The Entwinement of Myth and Enlightenment: Rereading Dialectics of Enlightenment.' *New German Critique* 23 (1982): 14–29.
– *Legitimation Crisis.* Trans. T. McCarthy. Boston: Beacon P, 1975.
– *The Philosophical Discourse of Modernity.* Trans. F. Lawrence. Cambridge, Mass.: MIT P, 1987.
– *The Theory of Communicative Action: Vol. I, Reason and the Rationalisation of Society.* Trans. T. McCarthy. Boston: Beacon P, 1984.
– *Volume II: Lifeworld and System: A Critique of Functionalist Reason.* Boston: Beacon P, 1988.
Horkheimer, Max. *Critical Theory.* 1968. New York: Seabury, 1972.
– and T. Adorno. *Dialectic of Enlightenment.* Trans. J. Cunning. New York: Seabury, 1972.
Jay, Martin. *Adorno.* London: Fontana, 1984.
– *The Dialectical Imagination: A History of the Frankfurt School and the Institute for Social Research, 1923–1950.* Boston: Little Brown, 1973.
Jameson, Fredric. *Late Marxism: Adorno, or, the Persistence of the Dialectic.* New York: Verso, 1990.
Lowenthal, Leo. *Literature and the Image of Man.* Boston: Beacon P, 1957.
– *Literature, Popular Culture and Society.* Englewood Cliffs, NJ: Prentice-Hall, 1961.
Lukács, Georg. *Theory of the Novel.* Trans. A. Bostock. London: Merlin P, 1971.
Mannheim, Karl. *Ideology and Utopia.* New York: Harvest Books, 1975.
Marcuse, Herbert. *The Aesthetic Dimension: Toward a Critique of Marxist Aesthetics.* Boston: Beacon P, 1978.
– *One-Dimensional Man.* Boston: Beacon P, 1964.

French feminist criticism.
See feminist criticism, French

Game theory

Games have probably always been with us, and theories of them in the West go back to the classical Greeks. Heraclitus, Aristotle and Plato, for example, viewed games as valid contests of strength, power and wit. In ancient Greece games were part of public entertainment in the form not only of athletic contests but also of religious rites and related dramatic presentations, as well as debates among learned men and rhetoricians. Although the idea of game is often conflated with or confused with that of play, Plato, for one, in the *Phaedrus* separates the two. For him play (*paideia*) is unstructured and lacking in rules and goals, whereas game (*ludus*) has certain reasoned moves, rules and goals, and therefore provides activities and models for the young and diversions for adults. ('Ludic,' however, has become a fashionable academic term that stands for all play, whether or not formal game structures are involved.) Games, according to Plato, are less arbitrary and more considered than play, although both are subject to accident, chance, and the fated moves of the gods. (See theories of *play/freeplay*.)

Plato's distinction between game and play has been generally accepted and his attitude toward games has traditionally carried considerable authority, but in modern times it has come under review and, especially in the 20th century, under attack. Within the last 200 years, several philosophers and thinkers have presented alternative views of games. These include 18th-century German idealists (Kant and Schiller), later-19th-century thinkers (*Nietzsche) and 20th-century theoreticians (*Wittgenstein, *Heidegger, *Derrida, *Bakhtin, *Gadamer, Fink, and Axelos). Later writers who synthesize these theories and see their influence in culture at large include Huizinga, Callois, Ehrmann, and Spariosu. In addition, within the last decade a number of important discussions of game theory have appeared that link it not only with traditional areas of sport, theatre and religion but also with non-traditional fields such as *literature, political philosophy, economics, business management, and science.

Until the 18th century, most thinkers in the Western tradition tacitly consented to Plato's pronouncements. Even the 18th-century philosophers, mainly German, who considered the role of play and game, did not really revise the hierarchical preference of game over play, though they did reassess the value of play in human lives. In equating play and art and in liberating them from scientific observation and strict rational constraints, Immanuel Kant and Friedrich Schiller paved the way for later reassessments of the field, but they both followed Plato in accepting unfettered play as 'mere play' and play related to and regulated

by reason as a higher form. Kant in *The Critique of Pure Reason* and Schiller in *On the Aesthetic Education of Man in a Series of Letters* speak of the value of play as governed by the rules of reason – that is, as a sort of game. The principle of game, however, lacks the metaphysical connotations it later comes to assume; play and game for the 18th-century thinker are restricted to the liberation of art and aesthetic judgments from the utilitarian demands of representational *mimesis or scientific claims to truth.

A recent 20th-century thinker indebted to Kant's and Schiller's formulations is Hans-Georg Gadamer who in *Truth and Method* conceives of play as fundamental to art, both in the sense of art as a playful exercise and art as lacking final goals or necessary purposes. Both game and art are forms of play, though art differs from game insofar as it exists less for the play of forms than for the enjoyment of the audience or spectator. Art for Gadamer seems more complicated than game and ultimately of a higher order, yet Gadamer restores value to game in the relationship between art and the interpreter. A work of art exists within certain rules or boundaries circumscribed by cultural tradition and individual artistic creation; the interpreter, however, brings her or his own experiences into play. The interaction or contest of subject (interpreter) and object (artistic work) creates a game of a very high order. For Gadamer, then, game is part and parcel of the artistic process from creation to interpretation. It is infinitely repeatable but with new permutations each time it is played, for it is neither wholly restricted to one set of existing rules nor detached from guidelines, rules, standards, or structures in general. To use an analogy that arises from Gadamer himself, just as we are born into language and yet are able to use and command it and to develop individual styles, so the field of art creates possibilities for artists and interpreters, and yet it is changed by the background and activity of both creator and perceiver.

If Kant and Schiller restored the concept of play and game to the intellectual forum and Gadamer modified their discourse for modern *hermeneutics, it was Friedrich Nietzsche and Martin Heidegger who took the issue even further. For Nietzsche in *Ecce Homo*, *The Gay Science* and *The Birth of Tragedy*, play is not 'mere' play, but a kind of primal, arbitrary, unstructured, and anarchic activity stripped of reliance upon reason. Unconcerned with a conception of game as opposed to play, Nietzsche considers both as worthwhile in themselves and instrumental in disrupting traditional values and modes of operation within culture. As in the ancient contests, play and games can be used for combative strategies but their sites are ubiquitous and their subversive roles unending. Game is a strategy, a process and a goal.

Contemporary theories

Martin Heidegger further helps to restore the importance of game and in the process takes the concept beyond that of Nietzsche. In his view, everyone is involved in the great game of life and world play, although the rules and goals are shadowy at best. More than Nietzsche and much more than Kant and Schiller, Heidegger explores many different aspects of this game of being and establishes it as a concept that can be profitably explored philosophically and one that has relevance to every aspect of existence. He accepts Nietzsche's 'concept of the Will to Power, thus consolidating the latter's return to the prerational, archaic notion of power as *Weltspiel* – a violent, arbitrary, and ecstatic play of forces in which man is both player and plaything' (Spariosu, *Dionysus Reborn* 124). This agonistic game of *power, dependent upon and mediated and produced by language, gives rise to *deconstruction and the most influential views of game for literary criticism.

Affected by Heidegger's views of game as well as by the writings of Karl Marx, Mikhail Bakhtin in *Rabelais and His World* discusses how, in the late medieval and early Renaissance period, forms of social play and game such as carnivals and fairs became forums where the populace could, through disguised performances, protest against governmental and clerical policies. (See *carnival.) These were coded affairs, in which only certain members of the audience were expected fully to understand the allusions and *parody. This 'carnivalization' was a political act, one which helped to undermine received opinion and recognized *authority. Clearly, then, games can be acts of transgression and *subversion. This is, so to speak, Heidegger as read by Marx: the 'world play' must be subjected to parody in order to create new kinds of games. As a critic, Bakhtin has been warmly embraced by post-

modern artists who like to play with the sense of the past and imbed it in their works. (See *postmodernism.) This dialogue between past and present or fiction and non-fiction dismays some critics, but Bakhtin's view of carnival as transgression has had a significant impact upon the creation and interpretation of art.

Other 20th-century game theories, which are invariably linked to language, derive not only from Heidegger but also from Ludwig Wittgenstein and *Ferdinand de Saussure. In speaking of 'language-games,' Wittgenstein in *Philosophical Investigations* compares language to games insofar as both have resemblances or characteristic similarities that form a 'family.' These resemblances constitute their rules of expression, main structures and behaviour within eras and across periods. Saussure, too, talks about structures of language in *The Course in General Linguistics*, but his primary influence lies in his discussion of the relationship between signifiers and signifieds, which he assumes to be in stable linkage. Saussure's linguistic theories lead to conceptions of signs and of organized systems of signs like writing and society themselves. (See *signified/signifier/signification, *sign.)

Within literary criticism in the last two decades, Jacques Derrida's views of games have received considerable attention. They bear recognizable relationships to the metaphysics of Nietzsche and Heidegger and the investigations of Wittgenstein and Saussure. Like Nietzsche, Derrida in 'Structure, Sign, and Play in the Discourse of the Human Sciences' and *Of Grammatology* sees play and game as a means of disrupting hierarchies and privileged positions which have exercised power over individuals in Western society. He does, however, distinguish between play and game, preferring the notion of play, because it is less structured and has no particular goals; game gives patterns and structures to society, its myths and preferred forms of belief. While game is no less arbitrary than play, it carries with it socially determined, observed, and reified rules and goals. Play is the random disrupter, the leveller, the disseminator, whereas games are the privileged structures, meanings or signifieds that arise from the play. Consequently, for Derrida and other French poststructural theoreticians, game becomes descriptive of the way society organizes and approves certain kinds of behaviour and ideas; in keeping with the rhetoric of Heidegger, this is the 'game of the world' (*Of Grammatology* 50). (See *poststructuralism.)

Derrida and like-minded nonconformists and deconstructionists pitted against the conformists and constructionists see this game of the world as an all-pervasive contest for power. He assumes that playing to excess opens up the game of the world once more, so that new games or beliefs and modes of behaviour can rise to the surface and be moved from the margins to the centres of power. (See *margin.) Ultimately, there is a higher game of meaning and power in which play must be a fully functional part. While Derrida's critique of metaphysics may not immediately change the power structure, it has the potential for altering it over time or at least of making people aware of the privileged games of the past and the conditions for winning. (See *metaphysics of presence.)

*Roland Barthes and *Michel Foucault both suggest related deconstructive uses of game: for them games are the rules of society but ones which, when they exceed their own rules, open the field of play. In 'What Is an Author?' Foucault remarks that writing refers only to itself and 'is always testing the limits of its regularity, transgressing and reversing an order that it accepts and manipulates. Writing unfolds like a game that inevitably moves beyond its own rules and finally leaves them behind' (*Language* 116). Barthes explores related sign systems, including language and society, and similarly disputes their reputed stability. In recognizing that both are structured upon certain resemblances, he endeavours to be analytical and political: he wishes to destabilize the myths and games that govern social structures. He looks at ways to turn the structures (games) into open-ended discourses (play). (See *myth, *discourse.) For instance, in *S/Z* he maintains that all literature is a game and that particular aspects of it, such as metaphor, which have been given special privilege over time, actually work against themselves through excess. (See *metonymy/metaphor.) 'The excess of metaphor,' he says, 'is a game played by the discourse. The game, which is a regulated activity and always subject to return, consists then not in piling up words for mere verbal pleasure (logorrhea) but in multiplying one form of language (in this case comparison), as though in an attempt to exhaust the nonetheless infinite variety and inventiveness of synonyms, while repeating and varying the signifier, so as to affirm the plural existence of the text, its return' (58). (See *text.) Play opens up the texts (games) of the culture in such a way as to create new possibilities. Game theory for Foucault and Barthes, as for Derrida, deals with the conditions for human existence within particular societies and with ways to expose and alter those rules and significations.

Contemporary studies of games suggest that all of these theories have merit: game pervades our culture in more ways than we are at first likely to admit. Mathematicians began to talk about game theory or interest conflict as early as the 1920s, when Emile Borel identified a class of game theoretic problems and John von Neumann discussed one player's conflicts with another. The study of its pervasiveness for literature began in earnest with Johan Huizinga, who discovered elements of play not only in sports, board games, games of chance, and the theatre but, more unexpectedly, in religious practices, judicial proceedings, war, philosophy, poetry, and other 'serious' activities within the social and political forum. Huizinga's analysis, structural in nature, identifies important elements of these games including the field in which the game is played (the enclosed space, arena, sacred spot, or magic circle), the contest itself and its duration, governing rules and goals, ways in which those rules can be broken, and the contestants themselves. Huizinga is careful to separate game from work. On the one hand, says Huizinga, real or ordinary life is serious, involuntary and utilitarian, subject to duty and physical resources, and concerned with material interest and profit. Game, on the other hand, is playful, voluntary, usually non-utilitarian, and conducive to physical, emotional, and spiritual re-creation. This definition of games accounts for those which have visible, external structures but not for those that are invisible and internal; the latter obviously exist but are harder to define. (See also *performance criticism.)

Using some of Huizinga's observations about the nature of games and their appearance within culture, Roger Caillois classifies games according to four types: competition or *agon*, chance or *alea*, simulation or *mimicry*, and vertigo or *ilinx*. All of these are governed by certain common criteria: they are free, separate, uncertain, unproductive, rule-governed, and exist within the realm of make-believe. As a social critic, Caillois seeks to define the social meaning of games, but he also advocates a conception of games without rules, those games of 'as if,' which replace ordinary experience and observation and which are therefore not subject to the same kind of social control. Caillois continues to observe Huizinga's distinction between real life and play, but he sees more practical political and social uses for game than does Huizinga.

In some ways the most seminal and provocative works on game theory in the past few decades have been 'Game, Play, Literature,' a special 1968 issue of *Yale French Studies*, edited by Jacques Ehrmann, and a later *Festschrift* issue of *Yale French Studies, Inside Play Outside Game*, (1979), a memorial to Ehrmann edited by Michel Beaujour. These issues of *Yale French Studies* brought together some of the most prominent European and American thinkers on the issue of play and game and allowed Ehrmann himself a forum. Ehrmann assesses both Huizinga and Caillois, discovering in their treatments a certain duality that pits seriousness, usefulness and work against game, leisure, and gratuitousness. The duality Ehrmann perceives is reminiscent of the agonistic struggle that Nietzsche and Heidegger perceive; it is one that is endemic to Western cultures and one that should be overcome; Ehrmann advocates a culture in which boundaries disappear between play and the workaday world, one in which play, reality, and culture as terms, categories and functions would be inseparable, synonymous and interchangeable.

Other essays in the same volumes pick up similar refrains. Eugen Fink takes an existential, metaphorical and ontological view of games, as centred on themselves, with no apparent external purpose, but also serving as a metaphor of the ways in which reality is 'played' within culture. He senses that the same operative rules apply to game and life – both have players, play worlds, playthings, play atmospheres, and play communities – but play confronts all realities: 'it absorbs them by representing them. We play at being serious, we play truth, we play reality, we play work and struggle, we play love and death – and we even play play itself' (22). Another of the game critics, Kostas Axelos, accepts this view that play should not be set against other more

serious activities, for the nature of all activity is play. Indeed, he puts a Heideggerean and Derridean challenge before the reader – to read in every world-game every other game and to compose our own rules and goals: 'the Game of the World is the question. It is for men to play the game of questions and answers' (18). For Ehrmann, Fink and Axelos game is a metaludic pursuit undertaken at the heart of reality.

Another important volume on game theory is the 1985 issue on *Games and the Theories of Games* published by *The Canadian Review of Comparative Literature*, which brings together an extensive bibliography on the topic as well as several articles that highlight recent interpretations of game. Many of these articles by Canadian and American academics are especially indebted to distinctions between game and play made by Bernard Suits in *The Grasshopper: Games, Life and Utopia*.

Mihai Spariosu and R. Rawdon Wilson also deserve mention for their exhaustive and fair treatment of the subject of play and game. In *Dionysus Reborn*, Spariosu explores the difference between a prerational and a rational concept of play and game. The origin of prerational, agonistic games of power lies in pre-Socratic Greece and the rational games in post-Socratic Greece, but their manifestations can be found in most philosophies of play and in modern scientific discourses such as evolution (Spencer, Groos, Dawkins, Monod), psychoanalysis (*Freud, Erickson, Piaget, Bateson), biology (Thom), and physics (Planck, Einstein, Schrödinger, Heisenberg, Bohm, Capek). (See also *psychoanalytic theory.) Others who speak of the philosophy of science more generally as game include Vaihinger, Feyerabend and Kuhn.

More recently, R. Rawdon Wilson has identified eight categories or models of play and game which pertain not only to the larger sphere of human activities but specifically to the production of literary texts, the plots and activities of characters, and the use of language. These models include (1) educative play or *paideia*, which teaches children cultural perspectives, social values and patterns of responsibility; (2) ideational play, in which human beings realize their highest aspirations and fulfill their greatest potential; (3) psychic play, in which the unconscious manipulates the ego or conscious, assails the foundations of coherent rationality, and calls into question human language and textual activities predicated upon consciousness; (4) role-playing or role-simulation games, in which each person lives out various fantasies or wishes – in an everyday context or in a simulated environment that could include literary texts; (5) games as logical primitive activities that are governed by specific rules and that constitute the basis of all complex activities, including language; (6) games that are based upon mathematical and logical procedures and that can be mapped as 'trees,' based on analysis of choice, sequences of action, and plots; (7) games, such as those in fantasy, in which certain rules are laid down and observed within the particular context of a work but are not necessarily plausible or observable outside the text; and (8) the games of free play in which the parameters and rules of language, logic and culture are continually called into question. For Wilson the most important thinkers contributing to this understanding are Bakhtin, Gadamer and Derrida, though his book particularly explores Bakhtin's model of transgression and Bernard Suits' clarification of game features.

Wilson's predominant concern is to relate these models and theories to the study of narration. In so doing, he raises basic questions about the ways in which literature as a game differs from other forms of game. He argues that literature is self-contained, set apart from the workaday world, and consists of its own rhetoric of game. But, unlike other games, the conventions and strategies of literature are not enforceable and the goals not consistent.

The ideas of game and play obviously have a long and distinguished history; however, only within this century have so many authors written on the topic in such different ways and with such varied insights. Numerous critical analyses have been published which apply these insights to particular periods and forms of literature, but the field remains open to new players.

GORDON E. SLETHAUG

Primary Sources

Axelos, Kostas. 'Planetary Interlude.' *Yale French Studies* 41 (1968): 6–18.

Bakhtin, M.M. *Rabelais and His World*. Trans. Hélène Iswolsky. Cambridge, Mass: MIT P, 1968.

Barthes, Roland. *The Pleasure of the Text*. Trans. Richard Miller. New York: Hill and Wang, 1975.

– *S/Z*. Trans. Richard Miller. New York: Hill and Wang, 1974.

Beaujour, Michel, ed. *In Memory of Jacques Ehrmann: Inside Play Outside Game. Yale French Studies* 58 (1979): 1–237.

Caillois, Roger. *Man, Play and Games*. Trans. Meyer Burash. New York: Free P, 1961.

Derrida, Jacques. *Of Grammatology*. Trans. Gayatri Chakravorty Spivak. Baltimore/London: Johns Hopkins UP, 1976.

– 'Structure, Sign, and Play in the Discourse of the Human Sciences.' In *The Structuralist Controversy*, ed. Macksey and Donato, 247–72.

Ehrmann, Jacques, ed. *Game, Play, Literature. Yale French Studies* 41 (1968).

– 'Homo Ludens Revisited.' *Yale French Studies* 41 (1968): 31–57.

Fink, Eugen. 'The Oasis of Happiness: Toward an Ontology of Play.' *Yale French Studies* 41 (1968): 19–30.

– *Spiel als Weltsymbol*. Stuttgart: W. Kohlhammar, 1960.

Foucault, Michel. *The Archaeology of Knowledge*. Trans. A.M. Sheridan Smith. London/New York: Routledge, 1972.

– *Language, Counter-Memory, Practice: Selected Essays and Interviews*. Ed. Donald F. Bouchard. Ithaca: Cornell UP, 1977.

Gadamer, Hans-Georg. *Truth and Method*. Trans. Garrett Bardes and John Cumming. New York: Seabury P, 1975.

Game and the Theories of Game / Jeu et théories des jeux. Canadian Review of Comparative Literature 12 (June 1985): 177–370.

Heidegger, Martin. *Nietzsche*. 4 vols. Trans. Frank A. Capuzzi. New York: Harper and Row, 1982.

Huizinga, Johan. *Homo Ludens: A Study of the Play Element in Culture*. New York: Roy Publishers, 1950.

Macksey, Richard, and Eugenio Donato, eds. *The Structuralist Controversy: The Languages of Criticism and the Sciences of Man*. Baltimore/London: Johns Hopkins UP, 1972.

Marino, James A.G. 'An Annotated Bibliography of Play and Literature.' *Canadian Review of Comparative Literature* 12 (June 1985): 306–58.

Saussure, Ferdinand de. *Course in General Linguistics*. New York/Toronto: McGraw Hill, 1966.

Spariosu, Mihai I. *Dionysus Reborn: Play and the Aesthetic Dimension in Modern Philosophical and Scientific Discourse*. Ithaca/London: Cornell UP, 1989.

– *Literature, Mimesis, and Play: Essays in Literary Theory*. Tübingen: Gunter Narr Verlag, 1982.

Suits, Bernard. *The Grasshopper: Games, Life and Utopia*. Toronto/Buffalo: U of Toronto P, 1978.

Wilson, R. Rawdon. *In Palamedes' Shadow: Explorations in Play, Game, and Narrative Theory*. Boston: Northeastern UP, 1990.

Wittgenstein, Ludwig. *Philosophical Investigations*. Trans. G.E.M. Anscombe. New York: Macmillan, 1953.

Genetic criticism

Problems of literary genesis – the story behind the story – have been of interest to academic specialists for at least a century and to a wider public, writers included, for much longer. Since 1970, no doubt in part as a reaction against a structuralist orthodoxy that played down the role of both author and historical context in literary production, a new school of genetic studies has arisen. (See also *structuralism, *literature.) A recent survey (see *Texte* 7, 1988), while making no pretence of completeness, lists nearly 700 items.

Interest in the artistic process (as opposed to the finished product) may be traced at least as far back as the Romantic movement; more specifically, it may be linked to the way certain writers such as Coleridge and the Schlegels envisaged their craft: a common preoccupation with origins (whether of languages, cultures or institutions); a tendency to think of art as an organic process (rather than a well-made object); and a predilection for the *Gesamtkunstwerk*, a work synthesizing many genres and often, for the Romantics, spanning an entire career (such as Goethe's lifelong preoccupation with *Faust*, the successive versions of Hölderlin's *Death of Empedocles* and Wordworth's much-revised *Prelude*). Writers between 1770 and 1830 appear to have grown more aware of the dynamics of their craft because of a changing view of the role of the artist in post-Revolutionary society. If art is seen as a kind of religion – a commonplace of Romantic aesthetics – it was a logical step to value both the separate stages and the material traces of what was essentially, in Paul Bénichou's terminology, a sacred task.

Yet the Romantics never developed a poetics of composition to stand alongside their theories of the imagination. For this, a second form of self-consciousness was required, that of the artist as *bricoleur* or conscious craftsman, rather than divine messenger. Here Poe's celebrated account of the genesis of *The Raven* (1846) deserves pride of place in emphasizing the autonomous, generative power of poetic forms.

Modern literary genetics, as practised by 20th-century editors and critics, began life around the turn of the century and owes its existence to two parallel (but rarely convergent) revolutions in methodology: the appeal to psychology and more particularly to the notion of the unconscious in the study of artistic creativity; and the application of traditional editorial procedures to modern or near-contemporary authors. Only recently has the first acquired a solid theoretical basis, particularly in the work of Jean Bellemin-Noël. Long before *Sigmund Freud, however, journals such as *L'Année psychologique* discussed the psychological basis of the imagination; the translation and popularization of Freud's work in the 1920s built on a well-established tradition. Livingstone Lowes' *Road to Xanadu* (1927) was the most celebrated work in this psychological vein; while Pierre Audiat's *Biographie de l'oeuvre littéraire* (1924) anticipated many of the tenets of modern genetic studies by insisting on the need for a precise chronology of composition and recognizing that every act of literary creation involves both conscious decisions that may be recovered by posterity and unconscious impulses that may not. (See also *psychoanalytic theory.)

Despite these pioneering studies and the Freudian vogue among artists themselves in the 1920s, critics continued to concentrate on new readings of established texts rather than on the lessons to be drawn from the history of these texts. Thus *René Wellek and Austin Warren could still argue that 'drafts, rejections, exclusions and cuts ... are not necessary to an understanding of the finished work' (*Theory of Literature*). (See *text.)

The other essential precondition for any systematic study of literary genesis – the use of traditional bibliographical methods to edit modern and contemporary texts – enjoyed a steadier and relatively unproblematic growth. Initially focusing on 'national' poets (for instance, the Weimer edition of Goethe, the Imprimerie nationale edition of Hugo), these editorial projects now embrace near contemporaries like Brecht and *D.H. Lawrence and even entire national literatures (such as the *projet d'éditions critiques* in Quebec under the general editorship of J.-L. Major). While the principal aim is to produce a 'definitive' text, the tendency has been towards historical-critical editions providing the reader with a complete text-history.

Vigorously pursued in all major European literatures during the first half of the 20th century, the genetic studies derived from psychological criticism and textual editing have taken many forms, ranging from detailed examinations of evolving style to more general discussions of authorial revision, the most typical approach being, perhaps, the 'biography' of specific works. Yet despite their scope and sophistication, they have been pursued for the most part in a theoretical limbo, an area whose precise methological frontiers have yet to be drawn and which – at least in Anglo-American circles – is still without a name. *La critique génétique* has been current in France since the early 1970s and the cognate German, Italian and Spanish equivalents appear to be equally well established. As confusion with scientific usage, or with the genetic structuralism of *Lucien Goldmann, is unlikely, the adaptation of the English equivalent appears long overdue; the more so in that a clear distinction can now be drawn between *textual* criticism, the purpose of which is to produce an authoritative text, and *genetic* criticism, which uses preparatory material, variant textual states or any other evidence of the compositional process for purposes of interpretation and evaluation. Traditional textual scholarship has been based on the twin premises of faulty transmission and inadequate data. The modern literary geneticist's characteristic dilemma, however, is too much rather than too little textual evidence. Modern genetic scholars are usually more concerned with well-authenticated authorial changes than with anonymous textual deterioration; and in recent years, some of them have begun to cast serious doubts on the critical assumptions of their bibliographically trained predecessors, particularly with regard to the following questions.

(1) Value: traditional genetic criticism assumes the intrinsic critical value of preparatory material and variant states; to know the history of a text is to be better placed to understand it. That genetically minded critics, almost invariably specialists, have so rarely felt the need to explain *how* exactly such material enables us to read better, or differently, may account for their relative isolation and their modest impact on critics of other persuasions.

(2) Singularity: until recently scholars have clung to the idea of the literary text as a single object, despite the fact that evidence before them seems to point in the opposite direction, to a cluster of related texts, and that the nature of certain media, such as the theatre, runs contrary to the idea of a singular, fixed text. (See also *performance criticism.)

(3) Finality: the genetic study of literature has been overwhelmingly end-related. The telos may change from author to author or genre to genre but the basic assumption – that one textual state is interesting only in as far as it contrasts with, leads up to, or deviates from another – has remained constant, at least until the mid-1970s. Only gradually is it being recognized that the dynamics of textual growth may be interesting in itself, that preliminary sketches may follow poetic laws of their own.

(4) Authorial intention: every form of artistic composition occurs over a period of time and involves a multiplicity of choices. For traditional scholars, these choices are the result of individual acts of will; authors are seen as free agents; and studies of literary genesis have tended to rely heavily on biography, a bias which has brought scathing criticism from many quarters over the last two decades, particularly in France – with Gustave Lanson as the principal scapegoat. (See *intention/intentionality.)

These ideological battles of the late 1960s seem to have been inspired by a fundamental confusion about what textual scholars actually do, but their effect was to produce a new generation familiar with contemporary literary theory, who brought to the study of textual evolution concepts borrowed from other areas such as linguistics, *semiotics, Marxism, psychoanalysis, and feminism. (See also *Marxist criticism, *feminist criticism.) Much of the recent work in the field takes as its starting-point a new ontology of literary production. Authors are now seen as only a part of a larger communication network made up of printers, publishers, critics, and, above all, real as well as implied reading publics. (See *literary institution.) Stylistic changes, often highlighted by genetic evidence, are studied as the result of formal constraints, generic models or conditions of intelligibility, rather than mere reflections of authorial will. Conscious aesthetic decisions, of the kind so lucidly described in Flaubert's correspondence, Gide's diary and James' prefaces, once subjected to psychoanalytical scrutiny, may be shown to hide carefully concealed unconscious ones. (See *Henry James.) Above all, textual variation, the very stuff of genetic studies – as it is of so much medieval scholarship – is no longer subject to a predetermined hierarchy of values, with the author's first or last thoughts setting the standard by which all other readings are to be judged; variation as such may simply be the expression of polysemy or semantic latency.

In the light of these and other trends – such as the use of computers to sort out large (and formerly unmanageable) quantities of textual data – text-history and text-theory, far from being in opposition, seem to have entered a period of fruitful collaboration. Moreover, as currently practised, genetic studies tend to confirm what writers and literary sociologists have suggested in other contexts: that books, in one sense, write themselves; and that, in another, they are produced by the society that enjoys them.

GRAHAM FALCONER

Primary Sources

Audiat, P. *La Biographie de l'oeuvre littéraire: Esquisse d'une méthode critique.* Paris: Champion, 1924.

Biasi, P.-M. de. 'Vers une science de la littérature: L'Analyse des manuscrits et la genèse de l'oeuvre.' In *Encyclopedia universalis: Symposium.* Paris: Encyclopedia universalis, 1985, 466–76.

Cahiers de textologie. Paris: Minard, 1985–.

Editio: International yearbook of scholarly editing. Tübingen: Niemeyer, 1987–.

Espagne, M. 'Les Enjeux de la genèse.' *Etudes françaises* 20.2 (1984): 103–22.

Essais de critique génétique. Ed. L. Hay. Paris: Flammarion, 1979.

Falconer, G. 'Où en sont les études génétiques?' *Texte* 7 (1988): 267–86.

– and D.S. Sanderson. 'Bibliographie des études génétiques littéraires.' *Texte* 7 (1988): 287–325.

Langages no. 69. Ed. A. Gresillon and J.-L Lebrave. 'Manuscrits-écriture: Production linguistique.' 1983.

Leçons d'écriture: Ce que disent les manuscrits. Ed. A. Gresillon and M. Werner. Paris: Minard, 1985.

Madden, D., and R. Powers. *Writers' Revisions: An Annotated Bibliography of Articles and Books about Writers' Revisions and Their Comments on the Creative Process.* Metuchen, NJ, and London: Scarecrow P, 1981.

Martens, G., and H. Zeller, eds. *Texte und Varianten: Probleme ihrer Edition und Interpretation.* Munich: C.H. Beck, 1971.

Tadié, J.-Y. 'La Critique génétique.' In *La critique littéraire au XXème siècle.* Paris: Belfond, 1987, 275–93.

Text: Transactions of the Society for Textual Scholarship. New York: AMS Press, 1984–.

Texte (7): 'Ecriture – Réécriture: La Genèse du texte.' Toronto: Les Editions Trintexte, 1988.

Secondary Sources

Beach, J.W. *The Making of the Auden Canon.* Minneapolis: U of Minnesota P, 1957.

Bellemin-Noël, J. *Le Texte et l'avant-texte: Les Brouillons d'un poème de Milosz.* Paris: Larousse, 1972.

Bénichou, P. *Le Sacre de l'écrivain 1750–1830.* Paris: Corti, 1973.

Cerquiglini, B. *Eloge de la variante: Histoire critique de la philologie.* Paris: Seuil, 1989.

Dimoff, P. *La Genèse de 'Lorenzaccio,'* Paris: Droz, 1936.

Flaubert, G. *'Un Coeur simple': En appendice, édition diplomatique et génétique des manuscrits.* Ed. G. Bonaccorso et al. Paris: Les Belles Lettres, 1983.

Gardner, H. *The Composition of 'Four Quartets.'* London: Faber and Faber, 1978.

Hugo, V. *L'Ane.* Ed. P. Albouy. Paris: Flammarion, 1966.

Joyce, James. *'Ulysses': A Critical and Synoptic Edition.* Ed. H.W. Gabler et al. 3 vols. New York: Garland, 1984.

Lanson, G. *Etudes d'histoire littéraire réunies.* Paris: Champion, 1929.

Lowes, J. Livingstone. *The Road to Xanadu: A Study in the Ways of the Imagination.* Boston: Houghton Mifflin, 1927.

Major, Jean-Louis. *Projet d'éditions critiques.* 19 vols. Montreal: P de l'Université de Montréal. Bibliothèque du nouveau monde, 1986–.

McGann, J.J. *Textual Criticism and Literary Interpretation.* Chicago: U of Chicago P, 1985.

– *Social Values and Poetic Acts.* Cambridge, Mass.: Harvard UP, 1988.

McKenzie, D.F. *Bibliography and the Sociology of Texts.* The Panizzi Lectures. London: The British Library, 1985.

Nadal, O. *'La Jeune parque': Manuscrit autographe. Texte de l'édition de 1942. Etats successifs et brouillons inédits du poème.* Paris: Club du meilleur livre, 1984.

Parker, H. *Flawed Texts and Verbal Icons.* Evanston: Northwestern UP, 1984.

Pommier, J. *Créations en littérature.* Paris: Hachette, 1955.

Ponge, F. *La Fabrique du pré.* Geneva: Skira, 1971.

Ricatte, R. *La Création romanesque chez les Goncourt.* Paris: A. Colin, 1953.

Rudler, G. *Les Techniques de la critique et de l'histoire littéraires en littérature française moderne.* Oxford: Oxford UP, 1923.

Stallworthy, J. *Between the Lines: Yeats' Poetry in the Making.* Oxford: Clarendon P, 1963.

Geneva School

The Geneva School of literary criticism links a group of 20th-century critics who have varying ties to Geneva. Despite their different emphases, these critics share a general distaste for formalist or 'objective' methods and prefer a phenomenological approach that aims to reconstitute an author's world-view from literary language. (See *phenomenological criticism, *New Criticism.) Geneva critics pursue a hermeneutic strategy that awaits an interpretive 'signal' from the work; they seek an empathetic identification with the individual human experience or cogito as it is disclosed through words embodying structures of consciousness. (See *hermeneutics.) Marcel Raymond and Albert Béguin, the earliest Geneva School figures, and Raymond's students *Jean Starobinski and *Jean Rousset have all taught at the University of Geneva. *Georges Poulet, born in Belgium, was the first to offer a complete methodology representing the Geneva approach; Poulet was directly influenced by Raymond and later taught in Zurich, Switzerland, for many years. Jean-Pierre Richard, a Frenchman, and *J. Hillis Miller, an American, both recognize Poulet's influence on their work, although Miller has since rejected Geneva criticism in favour of *deconstruction. Work by Rousset, Richard and Starobinski moves beyond the focus on an individual author to include contexts in art history, psychoanalysis, intellectual history, and linguistics.

Origins

This Geneva School is often called the 'second' Geneva School in contrast to an earlier Geneva School of linguistic theory associated with *Ferdinand de Saussure, Charles Bally, and Albert Sechehaye. The later Geneva critics (especially Starobinski) have commented on Saussure's work but there is no real connection between the two schools. The relevant context for the 'second' Geneva School is to be found in phenomenological theory (see *Edmund Husserl and *Gaston Bachelard), in the Romantic literary tradition, in the thematic intellectual history of A.O. Lovejoy, and in Henri Bergson's analyses of perception of time.

The second Geneva School rejects 'objective' views of a work and believes that the literary

*text is more importantly organized by structures of consciousness. Authors project a series of imaginative worlds in order to comprehend their existential identity; readers adopt a text's mental universe in order to understand a human experience other than their own. A common analytic method is to extrapolate and correlate words showing perceptions of space and time, the two broad categories of physical experience. Recurrent patterns of space-time experience are examined throughout an author's work and also delineated as broader models in literary history. A basic metaphor is that of an inner space, an initial void from which consciousness emerges to plot the characteristic architecture of its experience. While Geneva critics reject aesthetic evaluation or any judgment from external criteria, in practice they prefer works demonstrating an existential authenticity in which patterns of consciousness are accepted, explored in all their contradictions, and given a coherent resolution.

Early figures

Although his work does not claim to present a philosophical method, Raymond was clearly influenced by phenomenological thought while teaching at the University of Leipzig. Lectures by colleague Hans Driesch taught him that 'consciousness always has an object' and that poetic experience could be considered a means of knowledge separate from rationality. Already sympathetic to an anticlassical literary tradition represented by Renaissance and baroque *literature, Raymond returned to France to prepare a book on modern French poetry that would examine the anticlassical 'genius' as a visionary search for reality through experiments with poetic form – his influential *De Baudelaire au surréalisme* [*From Baudelaire to Surrealism* 1933; trans. 1950], the first of the Geneva School studies. Béguin's work was more directly influenced by German literature, and his best-known book, *L'Ame romantique et le rêve* [*The Romantic Soul and Its Dream* 1937] is a comparative study of German Romantic and 19th/20th century French poetry. Analyses by Raymond and Béguin seize on passages that express a precritical or preconscious moment of awareness, that reveal a profound and undifferentiated experience which has yet to be structured at a conscious level. Raymond later developed his view of an antirational, anticlassical tradition pervading French literary history in his studies of baroque and Renaissance poetics, of Romantic and mystical authors, and of Jean-Jacques Rousseau, about whom he has written extensively. Béguin, always interested in an author's unifying or mythic vision, turned exclusively to religious themes after *Balzac visionnaire* [*Balzac the Visionary* 1946] and to Catholic poets and novelists.

Major theoretician

Georges Poulet retains some of the historical framework of Raymond and Béguin to which he has given more systematic development. The main figure in the modern Geneva School, Poulet is also the first to offer analytical coordinates for the representation of human experience in literature: the Kantian categories of space and time through which human beings perceive their existence in the world. He examines an author's complete work for examples of the way time and space are presented, accumulating and citing evidence out of context in a way that has outraged stylistic critics but follows logically from his idea of literature as a mode of existence given shape in words. He is not interested in the text as an aesthetic construct, or in the symbolism of individual images. For him, literary history is a history of the human consciousness and the most basic literary criticism is a *critique de la conscience* [criticism of consciousness]. As a historian, Poulet structures his *Etudes sur le temps humain* [*Studies in Human Time* 1949–68] very similarly to Lovejoy's *The Great Chain of Being* (1936), which described broad cultural shifts in metaphysical perception and value from the Greeks to Romanticism. The introduction to Poulet's first book describes, century by century, changes in the perception of time and divinity from the Middle Ages to the present. The second volume in the series, *La Distance intérieure* [*The Interior Distance* 1952; trans. 1959] emphasizes analogous changes in conceptions of space. These space/time analyses offer more than statistical observations. They are keys to concepts of being: to ideas of creation and continuity, of identity and difference, and to the human being's consciousness of existing in the world.

Similarly, Poulet's analysis of individual authors is different from the traditional literary-historical model. Essays on various writers are not chronological accounts of a life and work or critical analyses of a series of texts but efforts to imagine the author's spiritual identity, grasping the experience of the cogito as it projects various inner worlds to explore the sense of self. Everything an author has written offers evidence of an individual mental universe. Literary language is the richest source of information about the cogito, however, because it constitutes the most thoroughly worked-out network of phenomenological themes. There is always a generating core inside this mental universe, a *foyer* or starting-point (both terms borrowed from Charles Du Bos 1882–1939) that governs individual patterns of consciousness. Readers must try to identify with the cogito by an act of sympathetic imagination; they must place themselves in the mental space or interior distance of the world of the text. Poulet's criticism has also been called a *critique d'identification* [criticism of identification].

Works after the first two *Studies* build upon the notion of space and time as broad experiential patterns *(Les Métamorphoses du cercle, The Metamorphoses of the Circle* 1961 [trans. 1966]; *Le Point de départ, The Starting Point* 1964), or as individualized models for different authors (*L'Espace proustien, Proustian Space* 1963; *La Poésie éclatée, Exploding Poetry* [*Baudelaire and Rimbaud*], 1980). Critics too have discernible patterns of experience (*La Conscience critique, The Critical Consciousness* 1971). With *Le Point de départ*, Poulet briefly described the criticism of consciousness as a *genetic criticism: not in the New Critical sense of 'genetic' as a positivist belief in traceable causes, but as an attempt to show how the literary work is generated by and constituted of dispersed and fragmented moments of consciousness. In his most recent work, *La Pensée indéterminée* [*Indeterminate Thought* 1985–], Poulet returns to a broad historical framework while following the notion of 'indeterminate thought,' an intuitive mode of perception that he pursues as a general category over and above the study of individual writers. This latest enterprise no longer privileges literary works and replaces the extended study of individual authors with an openly metaphysical inquiry that is illustrated by a series of brief excerpts from a range of philosophers and religious writers.

Later figures

After Poulet, the chief European practitioners of the Geneva approach are Jean-Pierre Richard, Jean Rousset and Jean Starobinski, each of whom develops a separate area of inquiry.

Closest in many ways to Poulet's analyses of space and time are Jean-Pierre Richard's studies of interior landscapes. Where Poulet emphasizes the imagining subject, however, Richard concentrates on the materiality imagined by that subject. Like the philosopher Gaston Bachelard, who examines the symbolic life of 'intuitive' images like earth, air, water, and fire, and later develops a poetics of space and of reverie, Richard analyses the symbolic relationships created by objects as they appear and change inside a work's mental landscape. The way objects are presented in an author's work defines a specific way of perceiving the world, a 'sensuous logic' that structures the relationship between self and not-self at a preconscious level.

Object and landscapes in the text therefore symbolize larger attitudes towards reality and demonstrate a manner of being. The essays of *Littérature et sensation* [*Literature and Feeling* 1954 with a preface by Poulet] and *Poésie et profondeur* [*Poetry and Profundity* 1955] show how the material and metaphysical worlds of 19th-century novelists and poets are coordinated by various themes such as the proliferation of vegetal life, a sense of accessible or blocked-off space, the presence of precisely defined objects or of vague outlines, and categories of solidity or dispersion that juxtapose images of vapour, coagulation or stone. The notion of a significant interior landscape occurs throughout Richard's work, both in book-length studies like *L'Univers imaginaire de Mallarmé* [*Mallarmé's Imaginary Universe* 1961], *Paysage de Chateaubriand* [*Chateaubriand's Landscape* 1967], and *Proust et le monde sensible* [*Proust and the Perceptual World* 1974] and in collections of essays from *Onze Etudes sur la poésie moderne* [*Eleven Studies on Modern Poetry* 1964] through *Pages paysages: Microlectures II* [*Pages Landscapes: Microreadings II* 1984].

Richard's criticism has sometimes been called a thematic criticism, inasmuch as it organizes the literary representation of reality around themes and subthemes. These are not the formal themes of traditional objective criticism (for instance, the 'theme of love' or the 'Ulysses theme'), but what he calls 'internal' themes, categories of experience seen as forms of phenomenological perception. In earlier studies, such themes organize an author's personal struggle to resolve conflicting impulses and achieve full existential authenticity by testing out different manners of being. The two books on Mallarmé suggest a Freudian interpretation of many themes, and subsequent essays examine word sounds and clusters of phonemes for their subconscious associations. (See *Sigmund Freud.) After 1979, Richard prefers to work on a smaller 'myopic' scale that starts from individual texts to capture the 'grain' of a complex libidinal landscape. Here the thematic organization moves from details – motifs, images, scenes, individual words – to larger formal patterns and horizons of desire that participate in a continuous play of psycho-existential meaning. (See *theme.)

Jean Rousset is more specifically concerned with style than are other members of the Geneva School, although he too focuses on its existential impact and not on aesthetic evaluation. Rousset is particularly known for his studies of the baroque imagination both as a period concept (*La Littérature de l'âge baroque en France, The Literature of the Baroque Age in France* 1953) and as a poetic and theatrical tradition juxtaposing appearance and reality (*L'Intérieur et l'extérieur, Interior and Exterior* 1968). A key term is *foyer*, a focus or generating core that unites a cluster of related experiences: water is such a focal image for the baroque age because it represents both physical and metaphysical instability, reflection and metamorphosis. Rousset characteristically starts with a specific literary form: epistolary novels or Claudelian dramatic structure (*Forme et signification, Form and Meaning* 1962), variations in the first-person narrative (*Narcisse romancier, Narcissus as Novelist* 1973), a sequence of scenes describing falling in love which ultimately become a model of the reader's encounter with a text (*Les Yeux se rencontrèrent, Their Eyes Met* 1981). In each case, form becomes an agent of existential change. Writers do not merely express the variations of an underlying subjectivity in their works, but actually create their *moi profond* or core identity through the process of writing. Readers are engaged in a narrative situation that confirms or challenges their visualization of the world. While Rousset echoes Raymond and Poulet in the use of a literary-historical framework, he alone in the Geneva School draws such close connections between literary style and its impact on the individual imagination.

Jean Starobinski is the polymath of the Geneva School. Trained in medicine as well as in literature, he draws on art, literature, music, history, linguistics, and medical discourse to describe the processes of the creative imagination. The governing metaphor of his criticism is that of vision, of a *regard* [look, gaze] that never gains access to its object but instead establishes an intentional relationship between subject and object or between one subject and another. Montesquieu's rationalizing view of things is an attempt to control reality (*Montesquieu par lui-même, Montesquieu on Himself* 1967); Rousseau looks in vain for a human 'transparency' and tries to establish a viable self-identity between the opposite poles of seeming and being (*Jean-Jacques Rousseau, la transparence et l'obstacle; Jean-Jacques Rousseau, Transparency and Obstruction* 1957). Linked to this duality of seeming and being is the alienating condition of melancholia, whose history is written by Starobinski as physician (*Histoire du traitement de la mélancolie, History and Treatment of Melancholy* 1960), while as literary critic he analyses the masks and disguises of art (*Portrait de l'artiste en saltimbanque, Portrait of the Artist as Acrobat* 1970). Similar themes of alienation and expression occur in *L'Oeil vivant* [*The Living Eye* 1961], *La Relation critique* [*The Critical Relationship* 1970] and *Les Mots sous les mots: Les anagrammes de Ferdinand de Saussure* [*Words upon Words: The Anagrams of Ferdinand de Saussure* 1971]. Language here is not a means of naming but rather part of a sign system displaying codes of human perception; only literary language has any claim to authenticity, because it directly expresses human experience (understood as a structure of intentional relations). (See *sign, *code.)

Unlike other members of the Geneva School, Starobinski makes frequent use of broad interdisciplinary frameworks and pays considerable attention to historical evidence. In *La Relation critique* he describes, after Schleiermacher, a hermeneutical circle of understanding that correlates history, language and subjective experience. (See *hermeneutic circle.) In *L'Invention de la liberté* [*The Invention of Liberty* 1964] and *1789: Les Emblèmes de la raison* [*1789: The Emblems of Reason* 1973] his analysis draws on visual arts and social history

to portray a gradual liberation of cultural and intellectual vision around the time of the French Revolution. An account of medical discourse in the Renaissance supports his analysis of Montaigne's discovery of bodily (as opposed to rational) knowledge (*Montaigne en mouvement, Montaigne in Motion* 1982). Cultural history is not the end of Starobinski's criticism, however, for like other Geneva School thinkers he gives primary importance to the human subject interpreting a complex field of external and internal relationships.

J. Hillis Miller stands in a different relationship to the Geneva tradition. An American scholar coming out of New Criticism, he met Poulet and was influenced by him when the latter taught at Johns Hopkins. For over a decade, Miller described how an author's work displays a unique way of experiencing the world and how writers seek a 'true and viable identity' by exploring different imaginative universes. When examining the stages of Dickens' world-view (*Charles Dickens, The World of His Novels* 1958) or showing how reality is formulated differently by 19th- and 20th-century American poets (*The Disappearance of God* 1963; *Poets of Reality* 1965), Miller made use of different Geneva themes: the work's *foyer* or generating core, the author's quest for personal coherence or authenticity, the metaphysical opposition of alienation and harmony, and the framework of history of consciousness. Retaining a New Critical interest in the workings of literary language, he continued to discuss individual works and internal stylistic patterns. After *The Form of Victorian Fiction* (1968) and *Thomas Hardy, Distance and Desire* (1970), Miller abandoned the Geneva attempt to reconstruct totalizing models of individual consciousness and moved towards deconstruction as a language-oriented criticism emphasizing literature's 'heterogeneity.' Again, there is a some continuity with his earlier work. Studying seven English novels in *Fiction and Repetition* (1982), he focuses on the generating power of repetition and difference as two modes of conceiving the world inside an oppositional history of Western ideas about repetition. Where Geneva criticism valued existential authenticity, he seeks in *The Ethics of Reading* (1987) to identify an ethical moment of writing, reading, and criticism, and recommends 'good reading' as a cultural necessity which – since it focuses on the 'grain of language' – is best executed through rhetorical or deconstructionist theory. (See *rhetorical criticism.)

Influence

The Geneva School has broad recognition and influence but has not produced a generation of followers – appropriately enough, since this 'school' has no central doctrine or manifesto and its members pursue different lines of inquiry. Geneva books and essays are widely translated as individual studies and not as applications of a single approach. Even the most distinctive Geneva School activity – tracing a single consciousness throughout an author's entire work – is no longer common practice among its members. In the U.S.A, the most direct influence of the European school appears in J. Hillis Miller's early work. Other phenomenological analyses derive from a general tradition for which the Geneva School has given the most specific literary application. Citing Miller, Poulet, and Bachelard, Paul Brodtkorb examines the way the interwoven consciousness of materiality and time creates a world of meaning in *Ishmael's White World: A Phenomenological Reading of Moby Dick* (1965). David Halliburton alludes to the combined influence of Poulet, Bachelard, *Auerbach, and others in presenting *Edgar Allan Poe: A Phenomenological View* (1973), and Jean Mudge cites Miller, Bachelard and Gerard Manley Hopkins as sources for the inscape described in *Emily Dickinson and the Image of Home* (1973). The current impact of Geneva criticism also overlaps with other approaches: with the related hermeneutic approach of *reader-response criticism, or with forms of psychoanalytic criticism that emphasize reciprocal 'readings' inside a transference-countertransference relationship. (See *psychoanalytic theory.)

Relations and implications

Geneva critics are opposed to any form of 'objective' reading, since they examine structures of subjectivity. Unlike New Critics, they lift passages out of context and frequently from different books in order to reconstruct the picture of an underlying phenomenological ego. They are not interested in intrinsic aesthetic criticism or in the formal history of genres. Reader-response criticism is similar to Geneva criticism in that both explore the phenomenology of reading, but the former differs by emphasizing the text's formal structures as the source of reader response. (See *Wolfgang Iser, *Constance School of Reception Aesthetics, *genre criticism.)

Geneva critics also avoid analytic models that de-emphasize individual human consciousness. Their emphasis on the search for existential coherence allies them with humanistic tradition and sets them off from structuralist or poststructuralist approaches that employ a transindividual or decentred model. (See *structuralism, *poststructuralism.) While Geneva critics and structuralists both use thematic categories, in structuralism these categories derive meaning from the human sciences. (See *Claude Lévi-Strauss.) Poststructuralist or deconstructionist theories also reject the Geneva reliance on unified models of selfhood, and investigate instead the way patterns of experience become visible in the decentred systems of language. Finally, historically oriented theories such as Marxism, *New Historicism, reception theory or the various forms of cultural criticism would accuse Geneva criticism of minimizing the effect of economic, political, and gender-related forces in constituting the phenomenological ego. (See *Marxist criticism, *materialist criticism, *cultural materialism.)

Geneva criticism marks the first consistent attempt to derive formal analytic categories for the representation of experience in literature. Ranging from the subjective focus of the cogito to complex fields of relationship in art, music, literature, and history, Geneva critics propose diverse models of consciousness as ways to grasp the perceptual world projected by literary texts. The fact that they do not rely on aesthetic principles opens the way for anti-canonical applications in spite of their own emphasis on canonical works of the Western tradition. (See *canon.) From the point of view of objective or aesthetic criticism, however, they err by disregarding the formal structure of individual works in order to shape patterns of authorial consciousness. Indeed, Geneva criticism does not recognize texts as autonomous linguistic systems to be studied apart from a projected phenomenological ego. Later work by Geneva School members does expand their inquiry to include other modes of criticism. Unchanging, however, is an attachment to the analysis of patterns of consciousness and to the concept of literature as an intersubjective experience fully realized only in the act of reading.

SARAH LAWALL

Primary Sources

Béguin, Albert. *L'Ame romantique et le rêve. The Romantic Soul and the Dream.* Marseille: Cahiers du Sud, 1937.
– *Balzac lu et relu. Balzac Read and Reread.* Paris: Seuil, 1965.
– *Balzac visionnaire. Balzac the Visionary.* Geneva: Skira, 1946.
– *Poésie de la présence. Poetry of Presence.* Neuchâtel: Cahiers du Rhône, 1957.
Brodtkorb, Paul. *Ismael's White World: A Phenomenological Reading of 'Moby Dick'.* New Haven: Yale UP, 1965.
Halliburton, David. *Edgar Allan Poe: A Phenomenological View.* Princeton: Princeton UP, 1973.
Miller, J. Hillis. *Charles Dickens, The World of His Novels.* Cambridge: Harvard UP, 1958.
– *Ethics of Reading.* New York: Columbia UP, 1987.
– *The Form of Victorian Fiction.* Cambridge: Harvard UP, 1968.
– *Fiction and Repetition.* Cambridge: Harvard UP, 1982.
– *Poets of Reality.* Cambridge: Harvard UP, 1965.
– *Thomas Hardy, Distance and Desire.* Cambridge: Harvard UP, 1970.
– *The Disappearance of God.* Cambridge: Harvard UP, 1963.
Mudge, Jean. *Emily Dickinson and the Image of Home.* Amherst: U of Massachussetts P, 1975.
Poulet, Georges. *Études sur le temps human I–IV. Studies in Human Time.* 1949–68. Vols. I–III, Paris: Plon; vol. IV, Paris: Gallimard. Vol. I: *Studies in Human Time.* Trans. Elliott Coleman. Baltimore: Johns Hopkins UP, 1956. Vol. II: *The Interior Distance.* Trans. Elliott Coleman. Baltimore: Johns Hopkins UP, 1959. Vol. III: *The Metamorphoses of the Circle.* Trans. Carley Dawson and Elliott Coleman. Baltimore: Johns Hopkins UP, 1966.
– *L'Espace proustien.* 1963. *Proustian Space.* Trans. Elliott Coleman. Baltimore: Johns Hopkins UP, 1977.
– *La Conscience critique. The Critical Consciousness.* Paris: Corti, 1971.
– *Entre moi et moi: Essais critiques sur la conscience de soi. Between Me and Myself: Critical Essays on the Consciousness of Self.* Paris: Corti, 1976.
– *La Pensée indéterminée.* Paris: PUF, 1985.
– 'Phenomenology of Reading.' *New Literary History* 1 (Oct. 1969): 53–65.
– *La Poésie éclatée.* 1980. *Exploding Poetry, Baudelaire/Rimbaud.* Trans. Françoise Meltzer. Chicago: U of Chicago P, 1980.
– *Le Point de Départ.* Paris: Plon, 1964.

Raymond, Marcel. *De Baudelaire au surréalisme.* 1933. *From Baudelaire to Surrealism.* Trans. G.M. New York: Wittenborn, Schultz, 1950.
– *Jean-Jacques Rousseau: La Quête de soi et la rêverie. Jean-Jacques Rousseau: Reverie and the Search for the Self.* Paris: Corti, 1962.
Richard, Jean-Pierre. *Littérature et sensation. Literature and Feeling.* Paris: Seuil, 1954.
– *Microlectures I–II. Microreadings I–II.* Paris: Seuil, 1979–84.
– *Onze études sur la poésie moderne. Eleven Studies on Modern Poetry.* Paris: Seuil, 1964.
– *Paysage de Chateaubriand.* Paris: Seuil, 1967.
– *Poésie et profondeur. Poetry and Profundity.* Paris: Seuil, 1955.
– *Proust et le monde sensible. Proust and the Perceptual World.* Paris: Seuil, 1974.
– *L'Univers imaginaire de Mallarmé. Mallarmé's Imaginary Universe.* Paris: Seuil, 1961.
– 'Verlaine's Faded Quality.' 'Fadeur de Verlaine.' Trans. Sarah Lawall. *Denver Quarterly* 15.3 (Fall 1980): 27–43.
Rousset, Jean. *Forme et signification. Form and Meaning.* Paris: Corti, 1962.
– *L'Intérieur et l'extérieur.* Paris: Corti, 1968.
– *La Littérature de l'âge baroque en France. The Literature of the Baroque Age in France.* Paris: Corti, 1953.
– *Narcisse romancier.* Paris: Corti, 1973.
– *Les Yeux se rencontrèrent. Their Eyes Met.* Paris: Corti, 1981.
Starobinski, Jean. *1789: Les Emblèmes de la raison. 1789: The Emblems of Reason.* Paris: Flammarion, 1973.
– *Histoire du traitment de la mélancolie des origines à 1900.* Basle: Geigy, 1960.
– *L'Invention de la liberté, 1700–1789.* 1964. *The Invention of Liberty, 1700–1789.* Trans. Bernard C. Swift. Geneva: Skira, 1964.
– *Jean-Jacques Rousseau, la transparence et l'obstacle.* 1957; enl. ed. 1971. *Jean-Jacques Rousseau, Transparency and Obstruction.* Trans. Arthur Goldhammer. Chicago: U of Chicago P, 1988.
– *Montaigne en mouvement.* 1982. *Montaigne in Motion.* Trans. Arthur Goldhammer. Chicago: U of Chicago P, 1985.
– *Montesquieu par lui-même.* Paris: Seuil, 1967.
– *Les Mots sous les mots: Les Anagrammes de Ferdinand de Saussure.* 1971. *Words upon Words: The Anagrams of Ferdinand de Saussure.* Trans. Olivia Emmet. New Haven: Yale UP, 1979.
– *L'Oeil vivant. The Living Eye.* Paris: Gallimard, 1961.
– *L'Oeil vivant II: La Relation critique.* 1970. *The Living Eye.* Trans. Arthur Goldhammer. Cambridge: Harvard UP, 1989.
– *Portrait de l'artiste en saltimbanque.* Geneva: Skira, 1970.

Secondary Sources

Carrard, Philippe. 'Hybrid Hermeneutics: The Meta-criticism of Jean Starobinski.' *Stanford Literature Review* (Fall 1984): 241–63.

de Man, Paul. 'The Literary Self as Origin: The Work of Georges Poulet.' In *Blindness and Insight.* New York: Oxford UP, 1971, 79–101.

Derrida, Jacques. 'Force and Signification.' In *Writing and Difference.* Trans. Alan Bass. Chicago: U of Chicago P, 1978, 3–30.

Grotzer, Pierre, ed. *Albert Béguin et Marcel Raymond: Colloque de Cartigny sous la direction de Georges Poulet, Jean Rousset, Jean Starobinski, Pierre Grotzer.* Paris: Corti, 1979.

'Hommage à Georges Poulet.' *MNL* 97.5 (Dec. 1982): v–xii.

Lawall, S.N. *Critics of Consciousness: The Existential Structures of Literature.* Cambridge: Harvard UP, 1968.

Miller, J.H. 'The Geneva School.' In *Modern French Criticism.* Ed. J.K. Simon. Chicago: U of Chicago P, 1972.

Pour un temps / Jean Starobinski. Paris: Centre Georges Pompidou, 1985. Collection Cahiers pour un temps, dirigée par Jacques Bonnet.

Schwarz, Daniel R. 'The Fictional Theories of J. Hillis Miller: Humanism, Phenomenology, and Deconstruction in *The Form of Victorian Fiction and Fiction and Repetition'.* In *The Humanistic Heritage: Critical Theories of the English Novel from James to Hillis Miller.* Ed. Daniel R. Schwartz. Philadelphia: U of Pennsylvania P, 1986, 222–66.

Genre criticism

'Genre,' one of the most ancient theoretical concepts in the history of criticism, derives from the Latin *genus*, meaning 'kind' or 'sort.' As this etymology implies, genre criticism has traditionally concerned itself with (1) the classification and description of literary texts and (2) the evolution or development of literary forms. (See *text.) In modern genre theory these two concerns have often been supplemented or supplanted by other issues such as the question of a text's 'literariness' or the role of genre in framing the author's choices and the reader's responses.

Despite its long and impressive historical pedigree, the theory of genres is anything but a settled branch of criticism. The multiplicity of names that 'genre' has assumed in English – kind, species, type, mode, form – attests to the Babel-like confusion surrounding this critical *discourse. Indeed, because the concept of

genre raises fundamental questions about the nature and status of literary texts, there are perhaps as many definitions of 'genre' as there are theories of *literature. Beneath this bewildering variety of approaches, however, lurk a number of persistent questions. How many genres are there and where do they come from? Are genres to be regarded as descriptive or prescriptive categories? Are they to be understood as timeless, universal forms possessing some underlying essence or are they historically conditioned and subject to change? A number of 20th-century critical schools (the Russian formalists, structuralists, Neo-Aristotelians) and many individual theorists (*Benedetto Croce, *Northrop Frye, *E.D. Hirsch, Ralph Cohen, *Tzvetan Todorov, among others) have formulated responses to these questions. (See *Russian formalism, *structuralism, *Neo-Aristotelian or Chicago School.)

History of genre theory

Genre theory has been irrevocably shaped by Aristotle. The opening sentence of his *Poetics* announces the central aim of classical genre criticism: 'I propose to treat of Poetry in itself and of its various kinds, noting the essential quality of each.' In the third book of Plato's *Republic* Socrates had proposed a rudimentary taxonomy of three literary forms, based on the poet's manner of presentation: either a pure imitation of speech or dialogue (tragedy, comedy) or the recital of the poet's own words (dithyrambic poetry or choric hymn) or a mixture of the two (epic, in which narrative alternates with dramatic presentation). Accepting Plato's basic generic divisions, Aristotle introduces a more sophisticated method for discriminating among the three kinds, namely, by distinguishing in each instance 'the medium, the objects, [and] the manner or mode of presentation.'

Each of these has inspired its own distinct approach to the question of literary kinds, but the last criterion, that of 'manner' of imitation (impersonal narration, dramatic presentation or direct speech), has produced the most enduring of generic systems: the familiar triad of epic, drama and lyric. German writers and theorists from Hegel, Schiller and Goethe onwards have been especially influenced by these generic archetypes: Goethe declares them the three 'natural forms of poetry.' Many modern theorists, however, regard these large, amorphous categories as 'modes' or, as Frye puts it, 'radicals of presentation,' rather than specific genres. Unlike more narrowly defined genres, these 'modes' are common to all Western and many other literatures. Much disagreement remains about the definition of modes and their relation to genres.

Aristotle's other criteria for distinguishing genres have also greatly influenced subsequent theorists. Northrop Frye, for instance, has developed an elaborate theory of fictional modes from Aristotle's remarks about 'objects' of imitation: 'Since the objects of imitation are men in action ... it follows that we must represent men either as better than in real life, or as worse, or as they are.' From this Frye devises a five-fold classification of fictional works (mythic, romantic, high mimetic, low mimetic, ironic), based on 'the hero's power of action, which may be greater than ours, less, or roughly the same.' Perhaps the most conspicuous example of Aristotle's enduring influence is the Chicago or Neo-Aristotelian School of critics, whose reworking and expansion of ideas in the *Poetics* is described below. But equally telling is the widespread currency of other principles laid out by Aristotle. Thus, his theory of catharsis (his claim that tragedy produces pity and fear in the beholder) lays the basis for theories that distinguish genres according to their effects on the audience, and his insistence that tragedy should portray a single action offers a structural criterion for identifying genres.

Other classical writers who have contributed significantly to the exploration of genre include the rhetoricians (Cicero, Quintilian), whose elaborate rules for different kinds of oratory form the basis for Renaissance and 18th-century systems of genre classification, and the Roman poet Horace, whose poem *Art of Poetry* reformulated and popularized Aristotelian precepts. Though not himself an original thinker, Horace is important chiefly as a bridge between classical thought and the Renaissance. Much of the Renaissance restatement of classical genre theory is guided by Horace's urbane pronouncements. Thus, his emphasis on order and coherence in the work of art is echoed in the neoclassical doctrine of the unities (of time, place and action), and his idea of decorum, the insistence that each genre has a subject-matter, characters, language, and metre appropriate to it becomes a central doctrine in 17th- and 18th-century criticism.

Alexander Pope's witty justification of decorum in *An Essay on Criticism* (1711) highlights some key differences between neoclassical and modern genre theory. Pope's comparison of literary styles and genres to fashions of clothing implies a link between generic and social hierarchies and underscores the extent to which classical genre theory is 'regulative and prescriptive,' based, as Roger Fowler observes, 'on fixed assumptions about psychological and social differentiation.' Contemporary genre theory, by contrast, avoids such overt value judgments (about what are the best or most prestigious genres) and aims rather to describe genres and their interrelations.

Despite these differences, the theoretical awareness of many modern genre critics, including Rosalie Colie, Ralph Cohen and Alistair Fowler, has been shaped profoundly by the theory and practice of writers in earlier periods. Colie and Cohen, in particular, have shown that a great deal of experimentation with generic categories occurred, producing numerous mixed forms like the works of Rabelais, Burton and Swift. Their awareness of this flexibility has led them to a historically based understanding of genre and generic change. Colie argues that a genre-system offers the writer 'a set of interpretations, of "frames" or "fixes" on the world.' As changes occur in the ways that societies perceive and understand the world around them, corresponding changes take place in the genres employed by writers: literary kinds are connected with '*kinds* of knowledge and experience.' Cohen argues that in order to explain this process of literary change, we must think of genres as collocations of various features that shift in relative importance as literary purposes alter. Cohen suggests that such a genre theory (of mixed forms and shared generic features) can be used to elucidate the existence and character of postmodern literary genres. (See *postmodernism.)

Foundations of contemporary genre theory

The real departure point for modern genre theory is the Romantic rebellion against the perceived rigidity of traditional generic rules. With their emphasis on individuality and their insistence on the literary work as the expression of the author's sensibility, Romantic writers play down and sometimes even reject generic norms as tyrannical constraints upon individual feeling. At its most extreme this leads to

Benedetto Croce's nominalistic rejection of any generic categories whatsoever, with his insistence that each work is, in a real sense, a genre unto itself.

Croce's exasperation with the concept of genre can also be explained in part as a reaction to the 19th-century penchant for deterministic, pseudo-biological accounts of the evolution of genres, such as Ferdinand Brunetière's *L'Evolution des genres dans l'histoire de la littérature* (1890). Though Brunetière has been ridiculed for the reductiveness of his Darwinian biological analogy, his theoretical approach raises important questions about the ways in which genres change: the evolutionary model has remained, in one form or another, an attractive explanation for such historical change. Even Frye's theory of modes, which traces the displacement of European fiction over the last 15 centuries from *myth to greater and greater realism, implies a process of historical evolution (though Frye himself regards his scheme as cyclical, with the ironic mode signalling a return to myth).

In various ways these antigeneric tendencies have made themselves felt throughout the present century. The New Critical emphasis on the literary text as a 'linguistic fact,' centring the meaning of a poem on internal patterns of imagery, *metaphor, *paradox, and *irony, tends to devalue the generic features of a text as extrinsic to its essential literariness. (See *New Criticism.) Similarly, the concept of *textuality introduced by deconstructive theory, with its insistence on the *indeterminacy of textual meaning (texts being endless chains of signifiers), overthrows any interpretive privilege or literary *authority that the concept of genre may be said to have. (See *deconstruction.) Poststructuralist theory in general, with its focus on 'text,' '*écriture*,' and 'discourse,' leaves little room for generic classifications. (See also *signified/signifier/signification.)

But questions of genre have not disappeared from view altogether. *René Wellek and Austin Warren (1962), for instance, suggested a practical solution to the perennial problem of determining the criteria upon which a definition of genre should be based. Each genre must be defined in terms of its 'outer form' (specific metre or structure) and its 'inner form' (attitude, tone, purpose). This double scheme recognizes the detective novel as a genuine genre but rejects a category like the campus or university novel because the latter is differentiated on the basis of a 'purely sociological classification.' With its preference for intrinsic over extrinsic literary qualities, Wellek and Warren's approach to genre is marked by the then-prevailing theoretical bias towards formalism, but their insistence on two equally weighted criteria for determining genre points the way to a more inclusive, descriptive methodology in genre theory.

The Chicago or Neo-Aristotelian critics represent an important response to New Criticism. They argue that the revival and extension of an Aristotelian method in criticism will furnish a more comprehensive theory of literature than existing 'partial' criticisms: Aristotle is said to take into consideration a wide range of 'causes' of the work of art. Applying Aristotelian categories to the novel, *R.S. Crane develops a set of principles for studying prose fiction: the plot of a novel is a synthesis, in varying proportions, of the elements of action, character and thought, which has the power to affect the reader's emotions and opinions in certain ways. Crane's generic analysis attempts to show how the Aristotelian analysis of genre can be adapted to the study of a wide range of modern forms.

Formalist and structuralist approaches to genre

Reliance on a synchronic rather than a diachronic approach to genre has been most marked among formalist and structuralist critics. In particular, the Russian formalists and the French structuralists have each developed distinct, though related, views on genre. Both groups were influenced by the linguist *Ferdinand de Saussure, who argued that the rules governing language constitute a system in which the function or meaning of a given linguistic unit is determined by its relation to the other units in the overall system. Structuralists extended this idea, maintaining that meaning in a literary work arises from a structure that permits a sequence of words or sentences to have meaning. For them, genre is an important component of this structure.

The Russian formalists, however, sought to constitute literature as a genuinely autonomous science, a goal that entailed the exploration of 'literariness': those formal and linguistic qualities that distinguish literary works from other forms of discourse. The defining characteristic of a text's 'literariness' is its ability to defamiliarize or 'make strange' our normal habits of perception and the customary language we use to describe the world. (See *defamiliarization.) Thus, the study of literature is the study of those devices, forms and structures through which literary texts achieve the goal of defamiliarization. A new literary text will therefore employ formal mechanisms to lay bare or make strange the familiar conventions of the genre to which it belongs (such as the novel's continual reinvention of its formal realism). *Viktor Shklovskii's 'law of the canonization of the junior branch' outlines an important mechanism by which generic transformations occur: literature renews itself by drawing on the strategies and devices of previously marginal or subliterary forms such as ballads, farces or detective stories, and by incorporating them into existing, ossified genres as a means of revitalizing them. (See also *canon.)

Structuralist critics have pressed rigorously the view that literature, like language, has a 'grammar' or structure which enables it to communicate and generate meaning. Central to this structure are the conventions of genre, for without some shared conception of what a poem or a play is, writers would be unable to communicate with their readers. 'A genre,' maintains *Jonathan Culler, 'is a conventional function of language, a particular relation to the world which serves as norm or expectation to guide the reader in his encounter with the text.'

For the structuralists, genres are not systems of classification but codes of communication. (See *code, *communication theory.) The process by which strange texts are naturalized or made to correspond to familiar modes of order is called *vraisemblablisation* or naturalization. This occurs at various levels, the most simple being the text's assimilation to a conventional, 'commonsense' notion of reality. Another level of *vraisemblance* is that of genre, 'a set of literary norms to which texts may be related and by virtue of which they become meaningful and coherent' (Culler, *Structuralist Poetics* 145). At other levels of *vraisemblance*, the text may draw attention to its own conventionality or the text may *parody and repudiate certain generic conventions. These strategies complicate but do not foreclose the process of naturalization by which texts are rendered intelligible and made to communicate.

Tzvetan Todorov introduces those principles that he regards as axiomatic in genre studies by critiquing the generic system proposed by Northrop Frye. Todorov marks with approval the theoretical principles for the study of literature enumerated by Frye – criticism is a science whose object, literature, is a self-contained system – but he is critical of the various, overlapping schemes of classification laid out in Frye's *Anatomy of Criticism* (1957). Frye offers a cyclical system of archetypal forms or *mythoi* associated with the seasons: comedy (spring), romance (summer), tragedy (fall), and satire and irony (winter). Frye also extends the classic generic triad of drama, lyric, and epic with a fourth category, prose, consisting of works intended to be read (rather than performed or sung). Other classifications traced in *Anatomy of Criticism* include patterns of symbolism and imagery (apocalyptic, demonic and analogical), classifications of prose fiction (confession, romance, anatomy, and novel), and the broad division of thematic and fictional types of writing. All these categories interact in complex ways to produce a dizzying array of generic taxonomies. (See also *archetypal criticism.)

Todorov argues that Frye's classifications are logically incoherent, employing different criteria or categories of explanation in each case. As a consequence, Todorov notes, Frye's approach cannot go beyond taxonomy, however ingenious it may be. A proper theoretical basis must be found for the choice of categories on which generic distinctions are based: they must not be borrowed from non-literary sources like philosophy or psychology. Moreover, the structures that constitute genres cannot be located on the surface of texts, at the level of observable images (which is where Frye finds them); on the contrary, 'all the immediately observable elements of the literary universe [are] ... the manifestation of an abstract and isolated structure, a mental construction.' Todorov's own definition of the fantastic as a genre relies precisely on such an abstract construct, in this instance, the mental uncertainty between a naturalistic or supernatural explanation for an unusual event. Given the indispensability of structure and of genre's place in that structure, Todorov has a ready answer for those modern sceptics who doubt the continuing relevance of genre: an unwillingness to recognize the existence of genres amounts to a claim that a new work bears no relation to any existing literary work.

Claudio Guillén's assertion that 'a genre is an invitation to form' is another structuralist formulation. Guillén sees an intimate connection between theoretical 'restlessness' about genre and poetics in a given historical period and the writer's capacity to create a new work. In particular, theories of genre assist artists by opening up possibilities for writing – not so much in recommending a certain literary 'matter' or 'form,' as in suggesting a principle for matching the one to the other. Far from exerting a deadening, tyrannical influence, the idea of a genre is a necessary condition for artistic creation.

Hermeneutic and reader-oriented theories of genre

Hermeneuticists and reader-response critics emphasize those problems of genre most germane to their mode of inquiry: the function of genre as a hermeneutical frame of reference for the reader and the role genre plays in the changing 'horizon of expectations' that permits a text to be apprehended differently in successive historical periods. (See *hermeneutics, *horizon of expectation.) E.D. Hirsch, an exponent of the view that literary texts have a determinate meaning, places genre at the centre of his theory, arguing that the author's intention determines the essential meaning of any text. In order for this meaning to be communicable to an audience, however, it must be a 'type.' A type is a meaning that can be represented by more than one utterance; in a literary text the type that embraces the whole meaning of the utterance is the text's genre. The verbal meaning or type never changes but the significance of a text (what it means for us today) can and does change. The former is the object of interpretation, while the latter is the domain of criticism.

At the opposite end of the scale from Hirsch's antihistoricist insistence on the determinacy of literary meaning is the reader-oriented criticism of *Hans Robert Jauss, *Wolfgang Iser and others. Jauss argues that a literary text cannot be understood as a self-standing object that presents the same face to successive generations of readers. The text is an event rather than a fact and can be realized only through the continuing responses of readers. When a literary work appears, its audience brings to it a set of expectations that may be challenged and altered in the course of reading

the work. Generic assumptions play a key role in establishing this 'horizon of expectations.' The concept of genre is built up through the reception of a succession of related texts, each of which varies, corrects, alters, or simply reproduces the existing literary and generic expectations of its audience. Sometimes a work will break through the horizon of literary expectations so completely that an audience only gradually develops for it. Jauss rejects an 'essentialist' conception of genre: like the literary work itself, a genre must be grasped historically in the changing horizon of its successive manifestations. (See *reader-response criticism, *Constance School of Reception Aesthetics, *essentialism.)

New directions

Jauss' work contributes not only to a reader-centred theory of genre but also to a re-valuation of the relation between genre and literary history. As Barbara Lewalski points out, 'Recognition that generic codes change over time has engaged modern genre critics with issues of history, politics, gender, and audience expectation as well as with complex literary historical issues of mixed genre and generic transformations.' Feminist critics like *Sandra Gilbert and Susan Gubar have contended that traditional genres are the historical product of a patriarchal social order – forms devised by men to tell male stories about the world. (See *feminist criticism, *patriarchy.) Female writers have responded in various ways to the male-devised genres they have inherited, from the self-doubt that perceives the obverse of literary 'paternity' to be 'female literary sterility' and the self-denying acceptance of the lesser sphere of minor genres (journals, diaries, children's books), to a *subversion or deconstruction of patriarchal generic norms and a questioning of the male-dominated generic tradition. Similar expressions of doubt have come from other quarters, including writers from minority cultures and the Third World. (See *postcolonial theory.) By drawing attention to genres as historical and political constructs, these voices from the 'margins' have conferred new importance on theories of genre that explore such issues as the formation of genres, generic change and transformation, and the interrelation of forms. (See *margin.)

The work of *Mikhail Bakhtin has become increasingly influential in shaping critics' responses to these issues. His conception of genre is grounded in the view that language is thoroughly 'heteroglot': language is socially inscribed with the countless and contradictory intentions and usages of every conceivable socio-ideological group. Genres exist in everyday life as well as in literature and include such forms as private letters, shopping lists and telephone calls. In fact, without minimal, shared generic frameworks, communication itself would be impossible.

For Bakhtin, generic features are socially contextual constructs rather than components of an abstract, synchronic system; as such, they must be understood as a mediation between world and text and should be studied in the performance: 'Genre is reborn and renewed at every new stage in the development of literature and in every individual work of a given genre.' Bakhtin distinguishes sharply between poetry and prose, arguing that the language of poetry tends to be stratified and singular, as opposed to the 'dialogic' and 'heteroglot' character of prose language, especially in the novel. Bakhtin's conception of genre underscores his sense of literature's cultural importance and its grounding in specific social circumstance and ideological struggle. (See *ideology, *double-voicing/dialogism, *dialogic criticism.)

Marxist critic *Fredric Jameson, who also sees genre as a mediating concept, argues that genres undergo a process of 'sedimentation' over time. An emerging genre contains a more or less explicit ideological 'message,' which remains sedimented in the form when it is revived and 'refashioned' in a different social and cultural context. Consequently, literary texts are composed of heterogeneous and often contradictory generic strands and discourses. Jameson argues that this model of generic function (the inevitable layering and mixing of several genres in any text) obviates the 'typologizing abuses' of traditional genre theory.

The diachronic emphasis of these and other recent studies of genre offers the most promising new perspective on traditional problems in genre theory. With their respective commitments to dialogic and dialectical methodologies, for example, Bakhtin and Jameson have reoriented the focus of genre criticism – away from typologies and recurrent patterns, and towards generic models conceived in terms of process, interaction and change. Alistair Fowler's *Kinds of Literature* incorporates many of

these insights in a pragmatic synthesis that provides the practical critic with a working repertoire of definitions and distinctions. Thus, he suggests that representatives of a given genre are related in the Wittgensteinian sense of displaying 'family resemblances,' that is, 'making up a family whose septs and individual members are related in various ways, without necessarily having any single feature shared in common by all.' (See *Ludwig Wittgenstein.) Fowler's model leaves ample room for historical and cultural variations in a form without abandoning the continuities that link disparate writers and texts. Similarly, he clarifies the often muddled terminology of genre theory, distinguishing carefully between 'mode,' 'genre' and 'subgenre.'

Perhaps the greatest challenge that the concept of genre poses to contemporary theory is its refusal to disappear, its insistence on a rapprochement, rather than a rupture, between the old and the new in theoretical discourse. Though protean and endlessly variable, genre remains an irreducible characteristic of verbal art; as Fowler insists, literature 'cannot move away from genre altogether without ceasing to be literature.'

FRANS DE BRUYN

Primary Sources

Aristotle. *Poetics*. In *Criticism: The Major Texts*. Ed. Walter Jackson Bate. New York: Harcourt, Brace, Jovanovich, 1952.

Bakhtin, Mikhail M. *The Dialogic Imagination: Four Essays*. Ed. Michael Holquist. Trans. Caryl Emerson and Michael Holquist. Austin and London: U of Texas P, 1981.

– *Problems of Dostoevsky's Poetics*. Trans. Caryl Emerson. Minneapolis: U of Minnesota P, 1984.

Cohen, Ralph. 'Do Postmodern Genres Exist?' *Genre* 20 (1987): 241–58.

– *Historical Knowledge and Literary Understanding. Papers in Language and Literature* 14 (1978): 227–48.

Colie, Rosalie L. *The Resources of Kind*. Ed. Barbara K. Lewalski. Berkeley: U of California P, 1973.

Critics and Criticism. Ed. R.S. Crane. Chicago: U of Chicago P, 1952.

Culler, Jonathan. *Structuralist Poetics: Structuralism, Linguistics, and the Study of Literature*. Ithaca: Cornell UP, 1975.

Dubrow, Heather. *Genre*. London and New York: Methuen, 1982.

Fowler, Alistair. *Kinds of Literature: An Introduction to the Theory of Genres and Modes*. Cambridge: Harvard UP, 1982.

Frye, Northrop. *Anatomy of Criticism*. Princeton: Princeton UP, 1957.

Gilbert, Sandra M., and Susan Gubar. *The Madwoman in the Attic: The Woman Writer and the Nineteenth-century Literary Imagination*. New Haven and London: Yale UP, 1979.

Guillén, Claudio. *Literature as System: Essays toward the Theory of Literary History*. Princeton: Princeton UP, 1971.

Hernadi, Paul. *Beyond Genre: New Directions in Literary Classification*. Ithaca: Cornell UP, 1972.

Hirsch, E.D., Jr. *Validity in Interpretation*. New Haven and London: Yale UP, 1967.

Jameson, Fredric. *The Political Unconscious: Narrative as a Socially Symbolic Act*. Ithaca: Cornell UP, 1981.

Jauss, Hans Robert. *Toward an Aesthetic of Reception*. Trans. Timothy Bahti. Theory and History of Literature 2. Minneapolis: U of Minnesota P, 1982.

Renaissance Genres: Essays on Theory, History, and Interpretation. Ed. Barbara K. Lewalski. Harvard English Studies 14. Cambridge: Harvard UP, 1986.

Rosmarin, Adena. *The Power of Genre*. Minneapolis: U of Minnesota P, 1985.

Theories of Literary Genre. Ed. Joseph P. Strelka. Yearbook of Comparative Literature 8. University Park: Pennsylvania State UP, 1978.

Todorov, Tzvetan. *The Fantastic: A Structural Approach to a Literary Genre*. Trans. Richard Howard. Ithaca: Cornell UP, 1975.

– *Genres in Discourse*. Trans. Catherine Porter. Cambridge: Cambridge UP, 1990.

Wellek, René, and Austin Warren. *Theory of Literature*. 3rd ed. New York: Harcourt, Brace, and World, 1962.

Grotesque, theories of the

The idea of the 'grotesque' provides historical and verbal unity to a vast range of phenomena. Among these are the fantastic hybrid monsters of the ancient world, certain medieval sculpture, Raphaelite ornamentation, the works of Aretino and Rabelais, the commedia dell' arte, early opera, Gothic fiction, and modern *literature from Kafka and Joyce to Günter Grass and Thomas Pynchon. Efforts to find a 'universal' and abiding principle in the diverse production of the grotesque remain inconclusive. (See *universal.) Yet some theoretical consensus has been achieved: many agree that the grotesque is dual in its external features and in the response it evokes. It is a structure comprehending binary oppositions or a synthesis of contradictory ideas. (See *binary opposition.) Reader-response theorists note that the grotesque simultaneously attracts and repels, excites laughter and terror, invites pleasure and disgust. (See *reader-response criticism, *Constance School of Reception Aesthetics.) However, modern and postmodern theories divide over the psychological source, social purpose and philosophic meaning of the grotesque; questions remain over whether it is found only in the visual image or also in larger structures and fictional 'worlds.' In the first half of the 20th century, the grotesque was finally accepted as a meaningful aesthetic category, owing to the efforts of Wolfgang Kayser (1906–60). However, his emphasis on fearsome demonic aspects of grotesque is often modified in successor theories. *Mikhail Bakhtin, by contrast, emphasizes the comic aspect and restates grotesque dualities in terms of the carnival spirit as a positive awareness of natural degeneration and regeneration, destruction and renewal. Both theories have formed important bases for a current understanding of the grotesque and have made significant contributions to postmodern discussions of the subject. (See *postmodernism, *carnival.)

Origins of the grotesque

Although the grotesque does not enter theoretical discourse until the 18th century, the phenomena are ancient. Originating in religious festivals of early Western societies which celebrated fertility, death and resurrection, grotesque images occur in fabulous hybrid creatures such as monsters and the primitive deities of Mediterranean mythologies. Both comedic and tragic, the dualities of pagan revels survived in grotesque carnival-Lent games and other festivities of medieval Christian society, during which time official order was overturned and mocked for brief periods of holiday. Burlesque rituals were performed by disguised players and religious plays or mysteries, mingled with comic parodies, were presented by amateur groups. In the Renaissance, while masked dancing and riotous behaviour continued to mark holiday celebrations, professional acting groups turned festive play to profit, adopting carnival antics for improvised performances of commedia dell'arte which came to be known as 'grotesque-comedy.' These were licentious neoclassical parodies with clowns and buffoons and fantastic plays with magicians, demons and fairies. Much of the material was derived from popular communal activities which the first social historians identified as grotesque.

Early theories

For their fantastic parodies and anticlassical plots, commedia plays of the 17th century, called 'burlesque' or 'grotesque' by the French academicians led by Nicolas Boileau, met with increasing disapproval from religious and state institutions, abetted by neoclassical critics in 18th-century Europe. Early aesthetic theories were essentially polemics that placed social and moral values on the art forms. A rationalist or neoclassical school, exemplified by Edmund Burke, attempted to establish an aesthetic for heroic and learned matter that qualified as 'sublime' or 'beautiful,' while it disregarded or rejected the popular, creative grotesque. A theoretical understanding of the grotesque as a serious aesthetic category was as yet impossible given the dominance of such neoclassical views.

The grotesque of Augustan England was made synonymous with any inventive or 'irregular' representation and associated with the vulgar, the ridiculous, the bizarre, and the ugly from its reliance on disjunctive imagery of a comic-horrific nature and on chaotic scenarios that 'violated' classical forms. Commonplace in 18th-century commedia dell'arte was what the Germans called 'grotesque-comic' opera and drama in which a Harlequin figure almost always appeared. The populist school which opposed classicist views attempted to assert the validity of the 'grotesque-comic' using a socio-psychological viewpoint. In defence of this popular genre which many countries regulated and banned before the end of the 18th century, the German playwright Justus Möser, an admirer of Henry Fielding and William Hogarth, defended the entire corpus of 'grotesque-comic' literature which was under severe attack. Using Harlequin as his narrator, Möser objected to the narrowness of neoclassical categories of the comic and argued that many comic types of drama were possible, including burlesque, grotesque and farce, for the ancients themselves had embraced hybrids in their literary genres as well as in their visual arts. In the grotesque, specifically, Möser stressed its comic principle as an instinctive human necessity. (See also *genre criticism.)

The debate continued in Germany even after the popular grotesque-comic theatre was banned in 1770. The first history of popular grotesque culture, by the German scholar Karl Friedrich Flögel, was a further defence of the grotesque as a genre. Flögel examined manifestations of the grotesque in the low burlesque and farce of ancient literature and traced the dramatic form of 'grotesque-comedy' from the fantastic masks of Aristophanes' *Birds* to the character masks of commedia dell'arte in the 16th century and their French and German descendants in the 17th- and 18th-century theatre of improvisation. Like Bakhtin much later, he devoted a major portion of his work to medieval grotesque festivity, which he viewed as a joyous and creative force of the people. Although Flögel agreed with neoclassicist critics that the old French mystery plays were 'grotesque' because they were constructed without an orderly plan, defied Aristotelian unities and mingled folk devils with scriptural subjects, he was the first to memorialize the subliterary, popular festivities of the Middle Ages and Renaissance and to argue that popular culture would survive in spite of recurrent bans. (See *Neo-Aristotelian or Chicago School.) Finally, Flögel proposed as the grotesque's psychological source the popular 'tea-kettle' theory, which held that the subliterary grotesque expressed an essential need of mankind to find comic relief from the monotony of work by letting off steam through indulgence in the crude pleasures of carnival festivity.

Flögel's history, revised and republished throughout the 19th century, set the pattern for further studies. Like Flögel, Thomas Wright believed that the study of popular (grotesque) art and literature was the study of man and society and he traced its history from the 'beginnings' to 1800, finding ludicrous-horrific (ergo ugly) grotesque forms in ancient Egyptian, Greek, Roman, and later European cultures. Working in the intellectual idiom of his day, Wright was convinced that the production of the grotesque was a 'universal' human tendency, instinctive and enduring. In a special sense of the literary grotesque, Wright recognized Rabelais' extraordinary books of *Pantagruel* (1532) and *Gargantua* (1534) as new frontiers of achievement in the grotesque and acknowledged both comic and terrible aspects of the genre as descending from a long line of grotesque satire from ancient Egypt to the

Renaissance. In France Jules Fleury (Champfleury) fused concepts of distortion and exaggeration in caricature with the tensions of the comic-horrific grotesque; historically, he covered much the same ground as Flögel and Wright, from the antique satyr to the political caricatures of the French Revolution. John Addington Symonds, like Schneegans afterwards, saw the need to distinguish hybrid types of art from one another, but failed to see these comic genres in a serious philosophical light.

Psychological dualities of grotesque

A new conception of the grotesque emerged in the pre-Romantic and Romantic arts that was not derived from folk culture but from the anticlassical inclinations of individual artists. This new creative activity revived the chimerical qualities of earlier grotesque but introduced a subjective new emphasis on terror and nightmare. The external forms of grotesque produced by William Blake in England, Edgar Allan Poe in America, and Bonaventura in Germany exhibited an ironic laughter from the point of view of the devil who contemplates the destruction of mankind. (See *irony.) Along with this new literature, discussion of the psychological operation of ludicrous and fearsome dualities in the artist's mind began to emerge in 19th-century theory. Friedrich Schlegel, in *Gespräch über die Poesie* [*Discourse on Poetry* 1800] and various published fragments, responded to intrinsic oppositions of the grotesque which he described as a clash between contrasting form and content that produced both terrible and ludicrous emotional effects. And Jean Paul (Friedrich Richter) in *Vorschule der Ästhetik* [*Primer of Aesthetics* 1804] wrote of an annihilating idea of humour, that is, a type of 'destructive humour' that was comic and metaphysically painful at the same time because it turned the world into something alien. To Jean Paul this destructive humour pertained as much to medieval feasts of fools as to Rabelais and Shakespeare, while the positive aspect of this grotesque pertained to the freedom or release that occurred outside the work of art, after humour had annihilated all.

The key to these new theories was in the deployment of external features of grotesque to penetrate the artist's mind. In pre-Romantic German literature, as Lee Byron Jennings has explained, the coexistence of the comic and horrific in this period of grotesque had Freudian implications. Jennings defined the grotesque as a double image of fearsome primordial impressions which, arising in the demonic region of the artist's unconscious, are disarmed of their danger by their ludicrous aspect. Similarly, Thomas Cramer explained the grotesque in E.T.A. Hoffman as a feeling of anxiety over the confusion induced by extremes of the comic that is also annihilated by the comic. Grotesque dualities in Swift, Coleridge and Dickens were also the essence of Arthur Clayborough's Jungian-based theory, which proposed that the grotesque is most usually produced from a 'progressive-negative' or 'regressive-negative' state of mind, that is, from the artist's conscious or unconscious conflicts between his religious sense of the eternal and his perception of the real world. (See *Freud, *Jung, *psychoanalytic theory.)

Other approaches

A very different and important aesthetic theory of the grotesque was developed by John Ruskin, who examined the subject more formally than others had before and who laid the foundation for modern refinements of his ideas. In 'Grotesque Renaissance,' Ruskin examined certain sculptures of Venice, responding to their external features with a sense of the playful and the terrible; he was the first to admit the grotesque into serious aesthetic discourse. Making moral judgments of these works, he determined that the 'noble' and 'true' types of comic-demonic grotesque sculpture were those imperfectly carved out of sincere belief in the Middle Ages; the 'ignoble' or 'false' grotesques were usually Renaissance works, which he perceived as frivolous imitations, artificial, sensual, and base. In terms of its external qualities, the grotesque was a comic genre based on the juxtaposition of the ludicrous with the fearful, portrayed in varying degrees. But for Ruskin these external features depended on the internal state of the artist's mind, and were identified by four types of humanity which corresponded to the two grotesque species: artists who play wisely and produce the 'pure' grotesque; those who play of necessity and produce the fanciful and capricious grotesque; those who play inordinately and produce the sensual grotesque; and those who do not play, thereby producing the terrible grotesque. The significance of Ruskin's theory arises not from his penetration of the artistic psyche or moral condition but from his recognition of the grotesque as meaningful, artistic creation with metaphysical capabilities, and from his acknowledgment of its artistic individuality and of the artist's capacity to give external form to interior conflicts between the terrible and 'sportive' sides of his nature.

While Ruskin's definition of the grotesque gave significance to the genre in its sculptural form, the 19th century also introduced the grotesque to literary theory in an important genre study by Heinrich Schneegans, who defined it as a moral and satirical genre invented by Rabelais and distinct from caricature and burlesque. He described its generic form as an exaggeration beyond caricature, carried to fantastic extremes but with serious literary purpose.

Modern theory

Wolfgang Kayser undertook a new investigation of the subject, reacting against theories of 'grotesque-comedy.' He was the first in this century to attempt a new 'universal' theory, using the then-current methodology of structural analysis as well as the traditional historical review. Beginning his work in 1932 and completing it in 1957 with the publication of *Das Groteske* ..., Kayser drew his materials from his own reception of unsettling aspects of literature and art which he associated with the grotesque. He pointed out the serious, eerie qualities of Spanish painting and the strange fantasies of commedia dell'arte. Most of his study examined the metaphysical, demonic qualities of German Romantic and modern literature and art. Proceeding from this Gothic bias, Kayser formally defined the grotesque as a structure of the 'estranged world'; its playful element a game with the absurd that arises from that alienated world; its laughter 'involuntary and abysmal'; and its primary purpose 'to invoke and subdue the demonic aspects of the world' – a formulation better known as 'Gothic grotesque.' (See also *game theory.)

Kayser, believing that earlier aesthetic writers had failed to examine the intrinsic structure of the chimerical grotesque, sought to rescue it from trivialization. Taking hints from Jean Paul and other Romantics, he isolated the aspect of the 'nightmarish and ominously demonic' in the Romantic grotesque and located its philosophical depth in images of 'the world going to pieces.' With a sense of the grotesque

as artistic intention that coincided with reader responses of 'alienation' and confusion, Kayser linked the paintings of Bruegel, the fantastic world of commedia dell'arte, and the spirit of 'Sturm und Drang' to the realistic grotesque of the German romantics Keller, Vischer, Busch; to 20th-century writers in German – Wedekind, Schnitzler, Kafka, Mann; the surrealist painters Chirico, Dali, Ernst; and the fantastic grotesque art of Ensor, Kubin, and Weber, among others. In spite of his overemphasis on the fearsome, Kayser made an important contribution to modern theory for he was the first to demonstrate that the grotesque was a 'comprehensive structural principle' with meaningful implications for serious philosophical discourse.

Mikhail Bakhtin's study of Rabelaisian grotesque and medieval carnival (folk rites and festivities), completed as an unpublished dissertation in 1940 and revised for publication (1965; trans. 1968), falls within the same time frame as Kayser's work. Like Kayser, Bakhtin reacted to earlier aesthetic writers who had excluded the grotesque from the realm of art and aesthetics and had dismissed popular creative activity as vulgar manifestations of 'low' society. There were important differences between them, however. Kayser attempted to elevate the grotesque from low opinion by emphasizing its demonic, fearsome aspects and endowing them with metaphysical significance, so that the subject would be understood as a serious aesthetic category. Bakhtin elevated the grotesque by embracing its laughter and the 'low' comic aspect of popular culture. He endowed the comic principle of folk carnival with meaningful philosophical content that expresses utopian ideals of 'community, freedom, equality, and abundance.'

Bakhtin's concept of medieval grotesque was a system of material imagery, created by the 'culture of folk humour,' which found its fullest literary expression in Rabelais, Shakespeare and Cervantes. As had been noted in earlier histories, the medieval carnival world, in which grotesque imagery flourished, was usually permitted by church and civil authorities in the spirit of holiday. Bakhtin reinterpreted its entire social history (omitting antique and certain imitative Renaissance grotesques) and identified medieval carnival culture with a world that was diametrically opposed to the official, stultifying world of institutionalized authority, even including permissible festivity.

After the Renaissance, Bakhtin explained, carnival freedom was increasingly restricted by the state. The grotesque survived in later centuries in literary traditions, although divorced from folk culture.

Bakhtin's structuralist analysis of the Rabelaisian grotesque revealed its language and imagery in terms of the subliterary carnivalesque world of medieval popular culture. (See *structuralism.) Its images of feasts and the body (particularly the lower bodily stratum) were the literary exemplar of the positive, regenerating humour of folk grotesque. Although Bakhtin's study primarily examined the grotesque as the literary achievement of Rabelais, it also endowed medieval carnival culture with the positive philosophical significance of comic regeneration. The importance of Bakhtin's study, however, goes far beyond Rabelais in its social assumptions about class hierarchies, utopian ideals and aesthetics. For Bakhtin 'high' culture stifles creativity, 'low' culture renews and regenerates. His analysis of Rabelais and carnival challenged all 'finite' hierarchies and opened popular culture to serious discussion. (See also *dialogical criticism.)

Postmodern grotesque theory

Postmodern critics have usually chosen to deal with grotesque dualities in literature by creating syntheses of Kayser's and Bakhtin's theories or by rethinking older aesthetic systems. Thus Neil Rhodes found that a combination of Schneegans' and Bakhtin's concepts of grotesque realism explained Thomas Nashe's prose of the Elizabethan period. Michael D. Bristol employed Bakhtin's theoretical perspective to discuss the grotesque or carnivalesque in dramatic literature of the English Renaissance. Peter Stallybrass and Allon White applied Bakhtinian principles of grotesque to show how Augustan poets, searching for elevated discourse in the neoclassical mode, appropriated the 'low' grotesque in their attempts to restrain and reform it, but also became dependent on its inclusion in order to define the 'high' culture they wished to create. To analyse the work of Synge, Toni O'Brien Johnson combined Victor Hugo's 1827 aesthetic of the dualistic, antithetical structure of the grotesque with Philip Thompson's definition of grotesque as 'the unresolved clash of incompatibles in work and response,' and views from Kayser and Bakhtin. John Ruskin's systematization of

grotesque species also continues to attract postmodern scholars like G.G. Harpham, who reinterprets Ruskin's grotesque as artistic contradiction in Brontë, Poe, Mann, Conrad, and Flannery O'Connor. Most recently, Bernard McElroy returned to Ruskin for his theoretical system of a hybrid, sportive-terrible grotesque to analyse the fiction of Kafka, Joyce, Grass, and Pynchon.

FRANCES K. BARASCH

Primary Sources

Bakhtin, Mikhail. *Tvorchesto Fransua Rable*. Moscow, 1965. *Rabelais and His World*. Trans. Hélène Iswolsky. Cambridge, Mass.: MIT Press, 1968.

Barasch, Frances K. *The Grotesque: A Study of Meaning*. The Hague/Paris: Mouton, 1971.

Boileau-Despreaux, Nicholas. *L'Art poétique*. 1674. Trans. Sir William Soames. Rev. John Dryden. London 1710.

Bristol, Michael D. *Carnival and Theater: Plebeian Culture and the Structure of Authority in Renaissance England*. New York/London: Methuen, 1985.

Burke, Edmund. *Philosophical Inquiry into the Origin of Our Ideas of the Sublime and Beautiful* ... New York, 1863.

Clayborough, Arthur. *The Grotesque in English Literature*. Oxford: Clarendon, 1965.

Cramer, Thomas. *Das Groteske bei E.T.A. Hoffman*. Munich: W. Fink, 1966.

Fleury, Jules (Champfleury). *L'Histoire de la Caricature* ... 4 vols. 2nd ed. Paris: Dentu, 1872.

Flögel, Karl Friedrich. *Geschichte des Groteske-Komischen*. 4 vols. Liegnitz u. Leipzig, 1784–7. Repr. 1788. Rev. Friedrich W. Ebeling, 1862–. Rev. Max Brauer, 1914.

Harpham, G.G. *On the Grotesque*. Princeton: Princeton UP, 1982.

Hugo, Victor. *Cromwell*. Paris: Editions J. Hetzel, 1867.

Jennings, Lee Byron. *The Ludicrous Demon: Aspects of the Grotesque in German Post-Romantic Prose*. Berkeley: U of California P, 1963.

Johnson, Toni O'Brien. *Sygne: The Medieval and the Grotesque*. Totowa, NJ: Barnes and Noble, 1982.

Kayser, Wolfgang. *Das Groteske: Seine Gestaltung in Malerei und Dichtung*. Oldenburg: 1957. Trans. Ulrich Weisstein. Bloomington: Indiana UP, 1962.

McElroy, Bernard. *Fiction of the Modern Grotesque*. New York: St. Martin, 1989.

Möser, Justus. *Harlekin oder Verteidigung des Groteske-komischen*. 1761. In *Sämmtliche Werke*. 7 vols. Berlin, 1798. Trans. J.A.F. Warnecke. *Harlequin: or a defence of grotesque comic performances*. London, 1766.

Rhodes, Neil. *Elizabethan Grotesque*. London: Routledge and Kegan Paul, 1980.

Ruskin, John. *Stones of Venice*. Vol. 11 of *The Works*. Ed. Alexander Wedderburn and E.T. Cook. 31 vols. New York: 1871–1907.

Schneegans, Heinrich. *Geschichte der Grotesken Satire*. Strassburg, 1894.

Stallybrass, Peter, and Allon White. *The Politics and Poetics of Transgression*. Ithaca: Cornell UP, 1986.

Symonds, John Addington. *Caricature, the Fantastic, the Grotesque*. 1890. In *Essays Speculative and Suggestive*. 2 vols. London/New York: AMS P, 1970.

Thomson, Philip. *The Grotesque*. London: Methuen, 1972.

Wright, Thomas. *A History of Caricature and of Grotesque in Art and Literature*. 1865. Intro. Frances K. Barasch. New York: F. Ungar, 1968.

Hermeneutics

Traditionally hermeneutics is the theory or science of interpretation. The term hermeneutics goes back to the Greek *hermeneuein*: to interpret or translate into one's own idiom, to make clear and understandable, to give expression to. In Greek mythology, Hermes interprets the often cryptic messages of the gods to mortals. It is not surprising therefore that hermeneutics as a discipline began as scriptural exegesis and was closely allied to philology. The Reformation debate with the Catholic church's dogma that it alone had competence in the interpretation of Scripture was met by Protestant insistence on the self-sufficiency of the holy text and the determination to demonstrate the basic intelligibility of the Scriptures. (See *text.) The general body of theory and practice which resulted formed the basis of hermeneutics. The gradual systematization of this material into a methodology of textual interpretation developed in the late 19th century into a broader philosophical theory stressing the crucial importance of interpretation to most if not all aspects of human endeavour and culture. Through the impetus of the early work of *Martin Heidegger, hermeneutics deepened into a general philosophy of human understanding with implications for any discipline concerned with the interpretation of human language, action or artefacts.

The German theologian Friedrich Schleiermacher was the first scholar to seek a general theory of interpretation, one applicable not only to religious texts. Schleiermacher formulated what is known as the 'hermeneutic circle': a part of something is always understood in terms of the whole and vice versa. (See *hermeneutic circle.) The meaning of a word, for example, is determined by the sentence of which it is part and yet the sentence can only be understood through the words comprising it. Understanding occurs as a continual adjustment between these two. This circle, he claimed, is unavoidable in matters of understanding – a point of view that continues into 20th-century hermeneutics. On this basis Schleiermacher claimed that we are able to know a past author better than the author could know him- or herself because we can view the author within a broader historical context than was previously available.

Schleiermacher outlines both a grammatical hermeneutic concerned with the language and semantics of the text itself and a technical hermeneutic which goes beyond the language to the subjectivity of the author. In his later works, emphasis is placed on this technical or 'divinatory' character of the hermeneutic task.

The philological studies of Wilhelm von Humbolt are also a precursor to contemporary hermeneutics. By claiming that one's language shapes one's view of the world, Humbolt brought questions concerning the nature of language and interpretation to greater philosophical importance. But it is with another German, *Wilhelm Dilthey, that hermeneutics is worked into a broad philosophical position.

Dilthey saw that the human sciences all involve at a basic level the hermeneutical problem of interpreting human expressions. To understand human beings is to understand their cultural expressions – not merely texts but also the various forms of art and actions (historical culture in general). Unlike scientific investigation of the natural world, however, the investigators in the human sciences cannot exempt themselves from the equation. To understand the human, one must be human – another restatement of the hermeneutic circle. Dilthey saw this understanding as basically empathic, involving the projection of oneself into the mind of the other (the creator) through the reception of the cultural expressions. Such cultural expressions he called the 'objective mind.' We work back from the expression to the lived experience of the author. Hermeneutics thus becomes a form of speculative and intuitive psychology which seeks not merely what a text says but the genius of its creator. Dilthey is thus very much indebted to Schleiermacher's divinatory hermeneutics.

By the end of the 19th century, hermeneutics gained considerable respectability particularly in Germany as a philosophical discipline with relevance to all human studies, not simply to ancient texts. But Dilthey's approach was later seen as too romantic in its search for the soul of the author. He was accused of 'psychologism' because of his strong appeals to intentions, empathy and minds. To avoid this situation, some of Dilthey's inheritors concentrated on the text itself and the experience of reading rather than on the author or the problematic notion of authorial *intention. A text, it was claimed, can be read and understood even when its author is quite unknown. One need not even privilege the author's reading of his or her own text. The important subjectivity is the reader's, not the author's. (See also *reader-response criticism.)

Nineteenth-century hermeneutics was also accused of 'historicism': that we have no true objectivity in matters of textual interpretation because our interpretations are always restricted by our historical situation and the limits imposed by our concepts and practical concerns. These are still important problems, ones that have led to accusations of outright relativism. This is particularly true of the 20th-century phenomenological hermeneutics arising from the work of Martin Heidegger.

Heidegger has had an enormous influence on continental philosophy, from existentialism to contemporary hermeneutics and Derridean *deconstruction. (See *Jacques Derrida.) He was a student of *Edmund Husserl, the founder of phenomenology. (See *phenomenological criticism.) In his early seminal work *Being and Time* (1927), Heidegger instituted an anti-subjective form of hermeneutics that stresses our thorough locatedness in both history and language. The problem of understanding is completely separated from a scholarly inquiry into another person's mind. Instead, the emphasis is on our embeddedness in a temporal world whose meaning precedes us but of which we have a tacit understanding. We exist, says Heidegger, understandingly, and the aim of interpretation is to make explicit this pre-understanding that we already have of our being-in-the-world.

*Literature, on this Heideggerian model, is less the expression of an individual's thoughts or intentions than the raising to consciousness of a world or world-view. One experiences in literature a world portrayed by the author rather than particular and idiosyncratic mental states or intentions. Heidegger's later writings contain numerous reflections and insightful meditations on the works of various poets and on language, but they appear more mytho-poetic than methodological.

*Hans-Georg Gadamer, a student of Heidegger, is one of the most eminent exponents of philosophical hermeneutics. His work is dependent on his teacher's insights into language, temporality and understanding, but is more focused on traditional hermeneutic problems of textual interpretation. In his very influential *Truth and Method* (1960), Gadamer is primarily concerned with describing the act of understanding in its relation to our present practices and to tradition.

Gadamer accepts the Heideggerian position that the goal of textual interpretation is not authorial intentions but the text itself. The hermeneutic problem is one of overcoming alienating distanciation: how a work cut off from its original culture and historical circumstances communicates with or is understood by a contemporary audience. The problem recurs with all art works and in fact with all attempts to understand other cultures and other people. The goal of a hermeneutical understanding is not what an artefact meant to its original audience or author but what it can mean to us in the present, though this need not imply that we take liberties with the work. Hermeneutical understanding is the result of an authentic dialogue between the past and our present which occurs when there is a 'fusion of horizons' between the two. In the end this is an act of self-understanding, of understanding our own historical reality and its continuity with the past.

Contrary to a more scientific approach, Gadamer maintains that we can only understand because of our prejudices (historical and cultural conditioning), not by ridding ourselves of them. There can therefore be no final or definitive meaning to a work. A classic, for example, develops a history of meaning as it becomes interpreted differently and experienced differently in different centuries. The condition of the possibility for such understanding is tradition itself which is primarily embodied in art works, institutions and especially language. If our inherited prejudices do not come down to us from the same tradition as the work to be understood, then serious problems may arise with authentically understanding the work – it remains alien. Authentic understanding presupposes our taking on or belonging to the traditions and culture that surround us (much of which we passively absorb) and furthering those traditions by means of our own interpretative endeavours. There is initial interpretive philological, historical and biographical work to be done when a text fails to communicate across the distance that separates us from it.

Twentieth-century philosophical hermeneutics clearly has more than a mere antiquarian interest in texts. A text is fully realized only in the reading process, in which the world of the text and the world of the reader meet and fuse. The central ideas of Gadamer, as well as the works on literature by the phenomenologist *Roman Ingarden, have been of considerable importance for *reader-response theory and particularly for members of the *Constance School. Both *Hans-Robert Jauss and *Wolfgang Iser were students of Gadamer.

The other major figure in philosophical hermeneutics since Heidegger is the French philosopher *Paul Ricoeur. Ricoeur has written substantial works on hermeneutic methodology and the human sciences, *metaphor, Freud's psychoanalysis, and most recently on human temporality and its relation to narrative. (See *Sigmund Freud, *psychoanalytic theory.) *Hermeneutics and the Human Sciences* (1981) introduces Ricoeur's major themes. Ricoeur is in broad agreement with Gadamer regarding the aims of hermeneutics, though his work is more synthetic of 20th-century trends, particularly those of *structuralism, *semiotics and Anglo-American philosophy of language.

The goal of hermeneutics involves, for Ricoeur, not only a resolution to conflicts of interpretation but also the attainment of self-understanding. The self, a primary focus in Ricoeur's writings, cannot be understood by a form of Cartesian direct scrutiny, but only by way of a detour through cultural works, particularly works of art.

We can identify three basic stages to Ricoeur's hermeneutical understanding of literary works: (1) a more or less objective analysis of the text itself; this is the place of structural and semiotic analyses of the content and form of a work; (2) the reading process wherein the world of the text is actualized; reader-response theory is especially concerned with this level; finally, (3) the stage of existential and reflective appropriation of the meaning of the text to one's self. The second stage already prepares the third in that the *concretization of the world of the work is largely dependent upon implicit features of the reader's own world and own knowledge and personality. The work thus draws us into it, distancing us from ourselves, but only to deepen our self-understanding by reflecting aspects of and possibilities for ourselves that we might otherwise never encounter.

Ricoeur's recent work concerns the hermeneutical problem of how we come to define and understand ourselves in and through narratives and self-narration. Extending the Heideggerian analysis of human temporality, Ricoeur maintains that time becomes human time to the degree that it takes on a narrative form. Literature, both fictional and historical, contributes to this important configuring of time.

There is also a brand of contemporary hermeneutics that owes allegiance to romantic hermeneutics but opposes some key tenets of phenomenological hermeneutics. The Italian Emilio Betti published a number of important works in the 1950s and 1960s that detailed a supposedly more objective method for hermeneutics. The North American inheritor of Betti's work is the literary theorist *E.D. Hirsch.

Hirsch's widely read *Validity in Interpretation* (1967) draws a distinction between the meaning of a text and its significance, claiming that Heideggerian philosophical hermeneutics, along with the more radical trends in literary theory, overlook the distinction and deal one-sidedly with the latter aspect. Hirsch is not concerned with whether an interpretation is useful or personally enriching, but quite simply with whether it is the correct meaning of the text. He wants a criterion for validating interpretations that does not appeal to mere significance and his answer is the authorial intentions that produced the text. The goal of interpretation is, at least in principle, to reconstruct this authorial situation. Without this touchstone for truth, we have only a scepticism or relativism in which one interpretation could be just as defensible as another. There have, however, been numerous criticisms of Hirsch's phenomenologically inspired and somewhat idealistic theory of meaning.

The American critic *Stanley Fish exemplifies a more radical hermeneutics. For Fish there is no predetermined meaning to a text; its meaning is totally a product of how we interpret it. Any uniformity in our interpretations is simply a matter of our having shared interpretive strategies. Hirsch's appeal to authorial intentions is, for Fish, nothing more than one of many possible reading strategies.

Hirsch is often criticized for being too much on the side of the text, while Fish is criticized for emphasizing only the interpretive reading process. The philosophical theories of both Gadamer and Ricoeur can be seen to strike a middle path, denying autonomy to both the text and the reader and instead emphasizing their mutual enrichment.

A final development in hermeneutics that should be mentioned concerns the work of *Jürgen Habermas in critical social theory. (See also *sociocriticism.) While not exactly a self-professed hermeneute, Habermas has both absorbed the hermeneutic paradigm and developed important aspects of it. Most notable is his stress on the ideological distortions that prevent open communication between speakers and readers. Hermeneutics here takes a critical turn towards what has been called a 'hermeneutics of suspicion.' Tradition, a central and productive notion in Gadamer's work, becomes politicized and problematized, for it not only allows but may also systematically prevent authentic communication. Habermas' approach leads both hermeneutics and literary theory into the broader political arena where literature is one ideological instrument amongst numerous others. (See *ideology, *ideological horizon.)

Hermeneutics today is an important philosophical discipline predominantly committed to the belief that our reality is an interpreted reality mediated by both language and our historical situation. But hermeneutics is also a methodology concerned with the nature of interpretation and understanding and its results have had far-reaching effects not only on literary studies but also on comparative religion, anthropology and numerous other social and human sciences. The principal centres of research continue to be in Germany, the United States, Italy, and Canada.

ANTHONY KERBY

Primary Sources

Dilthey, Wilhelm. *Pattern and Meaning in History: Thoughts on History and Society.* Ed. H.P. Rickman. New York: Harper, 1961.
– *Selected Works.* Ed. Rudolf A. Makkreel and Fritjof Rodi. 6 vols. Princeton: Princeton UP, 1985.
– *Selected Writings.* Ed. H.P. Rickman. New York: Cambridge UP, 1976.
Fish, Stanley. *Is There a Text in This Class? The Authority of Interpretive Communities.* Cambridge, Mass.: Harvard UP, 1980.
– *Self-Consuming Artifacts: The Experience of 17th Century Literature.* Berkeley: U of California P, 1972.
– *Surprised by Sin: The Reader in 'Paradise Lost.'* New York: Macmillan, 1967.
Gadamer, H.-G. *Philosophical Hermeneutics.* Trans. David E. Linge. Berkeley: U of California P, 1976.
– *Wahrheit und Methode: Grundzüke einer philosophischen Hermeneutik.* Tübingen: J.C.B. Mohr, 1960; 2nd ed. 1965. Trans. Garret Barden and William G. Doerpel. *Truth and Method.* New York: Seabury, 1975.
Habermas, Jürgen. *Communication and the Evolution of Society.* Trans. T. McCarthy. Boston: Beacon P, 1979.
– *Knowledge and Human Interests.* Trans. J.J. Shapiro. Boston: Beacon P, 1975.
– *The Philosophical Discourse of Modernity.* Trans. Frederick Lawrence. Cambridge, Mass.: MIT P, 1987.
– *Theory and Practice.* Trans. J. Viertel. Boston: Beacon P, 1973.
Heidegger, Martin. *Beitrage zur Philosophie (Vom Ereignis).* Gesamtausgabe (GA), vol. 65. Frankfurt/Main: Klosterman, 1989.
– *Sein und Zeit.* Tübingen: Niemeyer, 1927. Trans. John Macquarrie and Edward Robinson. *Being and Time.* London: SCM, 1962.
Hirsch, E.D. *The Aims of Interpretation.* Chicago: U of Chicago P, 1976.
– *Validity in Interpretation.* New Haven: Yale UP, 1967.
Husserl, Edmund. *Cartesian Meditations. An Introduction to Phenomenology.* Trans. Dorion Cairns. New York: Humanities P, 1966.
– *The Idea of Phenomenology.* Trans. W.P. Alston and G. Nakhnikian. The Hague: Martinus Nijhoff, 1964.
– *Ideas Pertaining to a Pure Phenomenology and to a Phenomenological Philosophy.* 1st Book. Trans. F. Kersten. The Hague: Martinus Nijhoff, 1983.
Ingarden, Roman. *Das Literarisches Kunstwerk: Einer Untersuchung aus dem Grenzgebiet der Ontologie, Logik und Literaturwissenschaft.* Halle: Max Niemeyer, 1931. Trans. George G. Grabowicz. *The*

Literary Work of Art: An Investigation on the Border-lines of Ontology, Logic and the Theory of Literature. Evanston: Northwestern UP, 1973.

– *O poznawaniu dziela literackiego.* Lvov: Ossolo-neum, 1937. Trans. Ruth Ann Crowly and Kenneth R. Olson. *The Cognition of the Literary Work of Art.* Evanston: Northwestern UP, 1973.

Iser, Wolfgang. *Der Akt des Lesens: Theorie ästhetischen Wirkung.* Munich: Fink, 1976. *The Act of Reading: A Theory of Aesthetic Response.* Baltimore: Johns Hopkins UP, 1978.

– *Der implizite Leser: Kommunikationsformen des Romans von Bunyan bis Beckett.* Munich: Fink, 1972. *The Implied Reader: Patterns of Communication in Prose fiction from Bunyan to Beckett.* Baltimore: Johns Hopkins UP, 1974.

Jauss, Hans Robert. *Ästhetische Erfahrung und literarische Hermeneutik.* Munich: Fink, 1977. Rev. and exp. Frankfurt: Suhrkamp, 1982. *Aèsthetic Experience and Literary Hermeneutics.* Theory and History of Literature 3. Minneapolis: U of Minnesota P, 1982.

– *Literaturegeschichte als Provokation der Literaturwissenschaft.* [*Literary History as a Provocation to Literary Scholarship.*] Frankfurt: Suhrkamp, 1970.

– *Toward an Aesthetic of Reception.* Theory and History of Literature 2. Minneapolis: U of Minnesota P, 1982.

Ricoeur, Paul. *Hermeneutics and the Human Sciences.* Ed. and trans. John B. Thompson. Cambridge: Cambridge UP, 1981.

Hrvatsko filološko društvo [Croatian Philological Society]

Hrvatsko filološko društvo founded in 1951 by faculty members of the Philosophy Department at Zagreb University, initially aimed to promote research and develop new approaches to the study of philology in all its possible ramifications. In 1952 the Society split into smaller groups, two of the most prominent being the linguistic section (known since 1960 as the Zagreb Linguistic Circle) and the Section of Literary Theory and Methodology of Literary History.

Zdenko Škreb was the driving force behind the formation of the group which concentrated on questions of literary theory and history, influencing the Society's theoretical inquiries and its organizational, practical activity. In 1957 Škreb began to publish *Umjetnost riječi*, a quarterly devoted to the 'science of literature.' (See *literature.) As editor, he brought together a number of prominent Croatian scholars, such as Ivo Frangeš, Aleksandar Flaker, Radoslav Katičić, Svetozar Petrović, Krunoslav Pranjić, and Viktor Žmegač. From other parts of Yugoslavia the group was joined by Bratko Kreft, Stojan Subotin, Dragiša Živković, and others. The group's first concrete endeavor was *Pogledi 55* [*Views 55*], a collection of essays published in 1956. What they all had in common was a general conviction that literature is *umjetnost riječi* ('the art of the word'); hence the title of their journal.

The founder of the group, Škreb believed in the ontological objectivity of the literary work of art and its language in relation to the receiver. He insisted that the point of departure in the study of literature ought to be the reader's reaction to the text. While believing that the language of literature is a deviation from the standard language of communication, he carefully avoided using the word deviation as too general and vague; instead he defined poetic language as a linguistic (or stylistic) intensification.

In 'Sprachstil und Stilkomplex' ['Style of Language and Style Complex'] Škreb differentiated between 'style complex' and literary style period. The first is a higher stylistic unit which, reappearing in various literary periods, can play different functions in various works of literature. The synthetic term 'style' may designate either a literary current or a specific attribute of a certain style. In the latter case, Škreb seems to differentiate between the above-mentioned *Stilkomplex* [style complex] and *Stilzug*, that is, a single stylistic trait typical of a single literary work of art or of a writer and having no further artistic consequences for literary evolution.

The members of the Croatian Philological Society, at least in their initial period of activity, showed a preference for and an interest in a stylistic approach to literature, often drawing on the achievements of Italian and American theorists (e.g., Frangeš, Katičić). At the same time, however, they tried to establish an equilibrium between extrinsic and intrinsic approaches to literature. If E. Steiger, the well-known German theorist of stylistics (see Škreb) went too far in stressing the singularity and autonomy of the literary work of art, then *Marxist criticism was too strongly preoccupied with the external conditions of the existence of the literary work of art and literary process. For Škreb any explanation of the ontology of a literary work of art must avoid such one-sidedness or simplification and take into account the fact that imaginative literature is both dependent and autonomous: dependent because it is a product of history and autonomous because it is a work of art created by an individual. Contrary to the political conditions of the time, which favoured Marxist and sociological interpretations of literature and art, Zagreb's critics tried to re-establish or introduce equilibrium between the intrinsic and extrinsic methods of literary investigation.

The members of the group also shared the belief that literary theory constitutes an important base for the work of literary critics and historians and that it is particularly useful for a close reading of literary texts. In this, perhaps, they can be compared to the Anglo-American *New Criticism or the German analytical school, the difference being that as a group they never tried to work out any homogeneous theory or consistent terminology. They may be characterized by their openness to the achievements of international literary scholarship and by their attempt pragmatically and creatively to adapt its principles.

Theoretical contributions to *Umjetnost riječi,* especially those published in the 1970s and 1980s, are of structuralist inspiration, methodologically related to the 'discovery' of Russian *formalism, Czech *structuralism, Anglo-American New Criticism, and German *Literaturwissenschaft* inspired by phenomenological thought. (See also *Prague School, *phenomenological criticism.) Three basic theoretical presuppositions are representative of this periodical. Apart from Škreb's conviction about the ontological objectivity of the literary work of art and its language in relation to the receiver, two other views are evident. One emphasizes the gnostic-psychological relativization of the literary work of art in favour of the receiver and demonstrates the impossibility of mediating through language-constructs the specificity of the linguistic art-creation (Radoslav Katičić); the other emphasizes the paradoxical-dynamic structure of the relationship between the literary work and the reader, with the continual interplay between the two (Vladimir Biti).

These theoretical approaches to the relationship between the reader and the literary work of art are paralleled by a corresponding consideration of the relationship between the work of art and the ordinary language of communication. In the first case (Škreb's approach)

poetic language is understood as a deviation or 'intensification' of standard language; in the second (Katičić), language is nothing more than a 'medium'; and in the third (Biti), this relationship is interpreted as a creation of an intentional or possible 'world.' (See also *communication theory.)

The theoretical eclecticism of *Umjetnost riječi* was most probably dictated by the gradual decline of Marxist criticism in Yugoslavia and the need to fill the emerging vacuum. It also reflected a search for new ways of understanding literature. While the members of the Society demonstrated a preference for stylistic studies, they continued to maintain an openness towards other theories and methods of research.

EDWARD MOŻEJKO

Primary Sources

Pogledi 55. Zagreb: Naprijed, 1955.
Frangeš, Ivo. *Stilističke Studie.* Zagreb: Naprijed, 1959.
Škreb, Zdenko, ed. *The Art of the Word (Umjetnost riječi). Selected Studies 1957–1967.* Zagreb: JAZIU, 1969.
– *Umjetnost riječi.* Hrvatsko filološko društvo. Vols. 1–30. 1957–1987.

Marxist criticism

Marxist criticism is rooted in the critiques of *ideology and culture developed by Karl Marx and Friedrich Engels. While Marx and Engels themselves did not engage in extensive literary or cultural criticism, many of their followers did. Social Democrats like Franz Mehring wrote important studies of *literature and drama, while Lenin, Trotsky, Mao, and others wrote reflections on revolution, art and culture. But it was the so-called Western Marxists who made the most significant contributions to developing a Marxist criticism: theorists like *Georg Lukács, *Antonio Gramsci, *Walter Benjamin, *Louis Althusser, Ernst Bloch, *T.W. Adorno, *Jean-Paul Sartre, *Lucien Goldmann, and Herbert Marcuse.

More recently, *Pierre Macherey, *Terry Eagleton and Gayatri Chakravorty Spivak have combined Marxist analysis with *structuralism and/or poststructuralist schools like *deconstruction to develop new methods of textual analysis and cultural criticism. *Fredric

Jameson and other contemporary Marxist theorists, by contrast, have synthesized Marxism with Hegelian, Lukácsian and Sartrian approaches. (See *poststructuralism.)

Origins and genesis

In *The Holy Family*, Marx and Engels provide what later would be interpreted as an 'ideology critique' of Eugène Sue's novel *The Mysteries of Paris*. For Marx and Engels, cultural texts are permeated with ideology, with the ideas and values of the ruling class. (See *text.) Ideology legitimates ruling-class domination by making its ideas and norms appear natural, just and universal. (See *universal.) Certain cultural texts, like political treatises, contain ideologies which legitimate bourgeois institutions, ideas and practice. Marxist ideology critique discerns these ideologies and criticizes them, thus demystifying the ideological elements. Consequently, analysis of how texts advance class ideologies and viewpoints is an indispensable part of Marxist criticism. For example, Marx and Engels demonstrate how Sue utilizes bourgeois ideologies of love, suffering and pity to cover over the true sources of capitalist oppression and exploitation. Sue's novel holds out the hope that individual redemption can be won within bourgeois society itself. Such a representation of individualistic opportunity is read as an ideological legitimation of bourgeois society, suggesting that the society is capable of reform and improvement without structural transformation.

Yet Marx and Engels also saw cultural texts as sources of social knowledge; many later Marxist critics also take up this position. (See also *sociocriticism.) Marx wrote of British realist novelists (such as Dickens, Thackeray and Charlotte Brontë) that their 'eloquent and graphic portrayals of the world have revealed more political and social truths than all the professional politicians, publicists, and moralists put together.' Engels in turn observed that in Balzac 'there is the history of France from 1815–1848, far more than in the Valulabelles, Capefigues, Louis Blancs *et tutti quanti*. And what boldness! What a revolutionary dialectic in his poetical justice!'

Marx and Engels themselves set forth a realist conception of art which privileged art that accurately reproduced existing social reality. In a letter to Margaret Harkness, Engels rejects 'tendency literature' which conveys a political message in favour of realist texts which allow a correct political analysis. Engels continues to comment on Harkness' novel *City Girl*: 'if I have any criticism to make, it is perhaps that your novel is not quite realistic enough. Realism, to my mind, implies besides truth of detail, the truthful rendering of typical character under typical circumstances.'

Other contributions by Marx and Engels analyse culture in terms of its relationships to a mode of production and its specific *social formation. The mode of production consists of the forces and relations of production which constitute a particular social formation, that is, a specific type of society. Thus, for Marx and Engels, it is the capitalist relations of production which structure political, legal and cultural institutions of their time. Culture is a form of superstructure which articulates the interests and ideologies of those who control the economic base of society. Such a conception can lead to reductionism and economic determinism. Yet Marx and Engels allowed a relative autonomy to art. Marx comments in the *Grundrisse* that 'it is well known that some golden ages of art are quite disproportionate to the general development of society, hence also to the material foundation.' Greek art, for example, though bound up with obsolete forms of social development, continues to have a certain appeal to us today and thus is relatively free from its origins and social formation.

Other early contributions to aesthetic theory and criticism include Mehring's writings on literature and drama (1893) and Plekhanov's aesthetic theory (1912) which reduced art to the reflection of specific social conditions and the class viewpoint of its creator. While Lenin also maintained a rather narrow instrumental approach to art, calling for artists to serve the revolution's ideas, in practice he allowed a diversity of artistic production. The Russian revolution saw a dramatic proliferation of the arts during its first decade. Trotsky defended a broad range of styles and schools of art, though he criticized Russian formalists and championed proletarian literature (the so-called 'proletkult'). (See *formalism, Russian.) Stalin, by contrast, and his cultural commissar Zhdanov, enforced a narrow aesthetic of socialist realism, requiring artists to utilize realist techniques and to advance socialist ideology through idealizing the values, institutions and social system being developed in the Soviet Union.

Literary and cultural Marxist theory

Earlier 'classical' Marxist theoreticians and politicians did not really provide a comprehensive aesthetic theory or develop a fully elaborated Marxist criticism. These tasks were accomplished by 'Western' Marxists, who began developing Marxist criticism and aesthetic theory in the 1920s. 'Western Marxism' includes continental Marxists like Lukács, Brecht, Bloch, and the *Frankfurt School, as well as American and English Marxists. As Perry Anderson has noted, Western Marxists tended to emphasize the importance of culture and philosophy, topics often ignored by earlier generations of Marxists.

Combining approaches which theorize culture as modes of domination or liberation, Antonio Gramsci developed a theory of *hegemony, which distinguishes between overt, physical force and modes of inducing consent as two forms of social stability and reproduction. Bourgeois society, he argues, uses culture to induce consent. A Gramscian criticism thus analyses the specific modes of hegemony dominant in a given society: for Gramsci in Italy during the 1920s, it was religion, idealist philosophy, bourgeois 'common sense,' Machiavellian state politics, and new industrial developments of Fordism. In opposition to ruling-class hegemony, Gramsci proposed the need for subordinate classes to develop a revolutionary counter-hegemony.

Georg Lukács, by contrast, defended the tradition of bourgeois realism and argued with Marx and Engels that realist art reproduced the social totality, representing typical classes and their world-views, delineating the class struggle, and advancing progressive political positions. For Lukács, the historical novels of Sir Walter Scott, Balzac, Tolstoy, and others provided an important source of critical knowledge and progressive political enlightenment, delineating the class structures of their societies, depicting class oppression and inequality, and presenting critical visions of life in bourgeois society. Lukács also praised the works of realists like Thomas Mann and Solzhenitsyn, while attacking 'decadent' modernist art (German Expressionism, Kafka, Joyce, Beckett) which he believed presented mere fragments of a disintegrating bourgeois society. Such a society only produced cynicism and nihilism and not critical knowledge or progressive political insight.

Against Lukács, Brecht argued that genuinely revolutionary art must revolutionize form and content and produce new aesthetic forms for the new social conditions of contemporary life, and that modernist art was revolutionary in this sense. Ernst Bloch, in turn, defended the innovative techniques of expressionism and modernism, while Lukács retorted that modernism expressed a decaying and decadent bourgeois sensibility and was of no use for revolutionary cultural politics. From a related point of view, *Mikhail Bakhtin argued that some art provided a 'carnivalesque' overturning and subverting of ordinary consciousness and social order and thus could produce new perceptions and sensibility. (See *carnival.)

Other Marxist aesthetic debates questioned whether the mass media and new forms of mass culture provided progressive potentials for cultural revolution (Benjamin, Brecht, Enzensberger) or regressive forms of social control that provided the ruling class with powerful instruments of domination (the Frankfurt School). British Marxists like Christopher Caudwell and those associated with *The Left Review* theorized how art could serve revolutionary purposes, utilizing Marxian notions to interpret art. And American Marxists associated with the Communist party and its publications, as well as Trotskyist and non-party Marxists associated with *The Partisan Review* and other journals, analysed both high and popular culture from Marxian perspectives.

From the 1960s to the present, Marxist criticism of 'mass culture' has been extended from the Althusserian school's analysis of '*Ideological State Apparatuses' to a Marxist analysis and criticism of film, television, advertising, and other forms of mass culture. Fredric Jameson, for instance, proposes combining analysis of ideology and utopia in a 'double hermeneutic' which will criticize the ideological elements of popular culture while analysing their utopian projections of a better world whereby they attract an audience.

Influenced by Lukács, Lucien Goldmann developed a theory of homologies which analysed the relationship between an artist's class position, world-view, literary form, and ideological positions, encouraging a reading of cultural texts from Racine to Kant as expressions of social experience and ideology. For Goldmann the task of criticism was to reconstruct the historical context of the text and to situate the writer and text within the ideology of their class. With certain texts and writers, there are homologies between text, writer, and the 'trans-individual other' of their historical environment. For example, Goldmann reads Pascal and Racine as sharing Jansenist religious ideology, which articulates bourgeois disgust with the aristocracy and the renunciation of the world by a class denied *power. Literary criticism thus practised provides knowledge of history and diagnosis and critique of bourgeois ideologies.

Heller, Feher, Kolakowski, and other Eastern European Marxian theorists have often used Lukácsian positions to defend so-called bourgeois thinkers and artists against the Marxian social realist orthodoxy that ruled the Soviet bloc countries until the late 1980s, when Gorbachev's policy of glasnost opened new possibilities for cultural expression and experimentation and Communist party domination of culture in Eastern Europe ended with the collapse of the communist regimes in this area. Kolakowski's early work attempted to develop a Marxist humanism which championed certain bourgeois philosophers and writers as contributing to the liberation of human beings – a project that he argued was also the task of socialism (1968).

Several Marxist theoreticians have indeed seen art as an essential component of liberation. Bloch argued that art contained a utopian dimension in which humanity's most deeply rooted desires for a better world were encoded. Marcuse too argued that art projects images of a better world and upholds deeply rooted human desires for freedom and happiness. Following Friedrich Schiller, he claimed that education of the senses and freely emergent play were crucial to human happiness. Marcuse stressed the importance of developing a 'new sensibility' as a force of socio-political change and championed a cultural revolution in which art would transform life. (See also *play/freeplay, theories of.)

For Marcuse, Adorno and other members of the Frankfurt School, it is primarily 'authentic art' which serves as a vehicle of emancipation. Adorno praised the heroes of high modernism (Schönberg, Kafka and Beckett) who systematically negated bourgeois ideology, radicalized the form of art, and provided complex, aesthetic texts which helped produce more critical and complex views of the world. Brecht, Benjamin and others by contrast thought that popular forms of art too could have progressive

effects. In particular, they believed that the new media of radio and film could be used to enlighten the working class concerning its oppression and could be positive forces in a revolutionary project. Adorno and his other colleagues in the Frankfurt School disagreed completely, seeing mass culture primarily as an instrument of domination and social control.

The Althusserian aesthetic position proposes to develop a scientific set of concepts to do literary analysis and ideology critique (Eagleton 1976) and to develop sets of categories and analyses which show how ideologies exhibited in texts often fail, deconstruct or unwittingly present social criticism even when they attempt to celebrate the existing society (Macherey 1968 and Sprinker 1987). For Althusser, art falls between science and ideology and can describe the lived experience of dominant ideologies, as well as subverting or undermining them. For Macherey, it is the task of the critic to articulate the limits and gaps of bourgeois ideologies which art exhibits. In his early work, Eagleton (1976) argues that art primarily reproduces ideological discourses, though texts also can rework, exhibit and possibly disturb. ideologies; thus, criticism objectively describes how ideologies work, how they are textually produced, and how they affect readers.

While Eagleton later criticized this 'scientism,' Sprinker believes that Althusser's concepts combined with *Jacques Derrida's method of deconstruction provide the basis for a science of criticism. Sprinker attempts to develop a scientific Marxian aesthetic theory that will theorize the semi-autonomy of art and will establish aesthetic theory as a discipline grounded in scientific concepts. This requires breaking with all narrative, teleological and humanist theories of history and producing a materialist theory of historical artefacts. (See *materialist criticism.)

Contemporary developments

Contemporary Marxist critics develop and apply these earlier theoretical positions, combining them in unique ways. There is really no one unitary conception of Marxist criticism; rather there is a wide variety. For example, Jameson advocated Marxism as the most comprehensive horizon of all interpretation because it provides a pre-eminently contextualizing and historicizing method which both interprets texts in terms of their context and also grasps historical contexts through the reading of texts. (See *ideological horizon.)

*Raymond Williams has presented a systematic delineation of Marxist cultural perspectives, providing an inventory and explication of key concepts of Marxist criticism (1977), complemented by new concepts of his own. For Williams, culture constitutes a continuum of artefacts, ranging from television programs to opera, that are worthy of a materialist analysis that focuses on production, on the codes and other socio-cultural constituents of the text, and on reception. This conception influenced Stuart Hall and other British cultural Marxists associated with the Birmingham School of cultural studies. (See *cultural materialism, *code.)

Against this 'humanist' Marxian tradition, more 'scientific' and structuralist tendencies have emerged. Consequently, there are important debates within the Marxian tradition as well as between Marxists and other traditions. Most structuralist Marxists, for instance, tend to see culture as a form of domination, while the humanist Marxists see it as a potential vehicle for emancipation. In terms of textual analysis, humanist Marxists are more interested in the meaning and ideological content of texts and employ hermeneutical methods, while more structuralist Marxists are concerned with analysing how texts work and produce meaning and ideology through an analysis of their formal elements and operations. Further, structuralists and poststructuralists focus on the contradictions and fissures of the text and the way that ideology reveals itself (Macherey, Spivak), while the Frankfurt School and others focus attention on the ways that ideology functions and on the text's 'strategies of containment' (Jameson).

In addition, many contemporary Marxist critics have combined classical Marxian ideology critique with Freudian theory, feminism, poststructuralism, *hermeneutics, and other contemporary approaches – just as those working in each of these areas have also been drawing on Marxist criticism. Gayatri Spivak, for instance, combines Derridean deconstruction with Marxism, feminism and the analysis of 'other voices' in Third World, marginal or minority groups. (See *psychoanalytic theory, *feminist criticism, *post-colonial theory.)

This variety raises the question of whether such eclectic Marxist criticism falls prey to liberal *pluralism and loses its specific identity. Eagleton (1983) answers by insisting that genuine Marxist criticism retains its identity primarily in terms of its political commitments. Thus, he combines a diversity of theoretical methods with what he calls a 'political criticism' that is the key criterion for a Marxist approach.

Most recently, Marxist criticism has intervened in the debate over *postmodernism. Jameson utilizes the Marxist critique of capitalism to interpret postmodernism as 'the cultural logic of late capital' (1984). He argues that Marxist theory provides the best framework for interpreting contemporary culture and has conducted a wide variety of studies to validate this claim.

Other Marxist critics, such as Stuart Hall and his colleagues in the Birmingham School of Cultural Studies, however, have criticized elements of postmodernism while attempting to incorporate its progressive elements, such as its intense focus on popular culture and its criticism of modernism and modernity. Some Marxist theorists incorporate elements from the postmodern theories of *Jean Baudrillard, *Jean-François Lyotard, *Michel Foucault, and others into a revitalized Marxist criticism, while others, like *Jürgen Habermas, attack postmodernity as a form of bourgeois ideology.

Marxist criticism continues to be a vital force in the contemporary scene, although many have argued against the excessive focus on class in favour of expanded focus on race, gender, ethnicity, and other 'subject positions.' Most Marxist criticism today does indeed carry out a multidimensional critique of ideology and continues to attempt to incorporate new theoretical developments into the Marxian theory. This leads on the one hand to increasing eclecticism and diversity among Marxist criticism, while on the other it produces a more open and supple theory.

DOUGLAS KELLNER

Primary Sources

Classical Marxism

Baxandall, Lee. *Marxism and Aesthetics: A Selective Annotated Bibliography.* New York: Humanities P, 1968.
– and Stefan Morawski, eds. *Marx and Engels on Literature and Art.* St. Louis: Telos P, 1973.

Lenin, V.I. *On Literature and Art.* Moscow: Progress Publishers, 1967.

Lifshitz, Mikhail. *The Philosophy of Art of Karl Marx.* London: Pluto P, 1973.

Mehring, Franz. *The Lessing Legend.* New York: 1938; abridgment of 1893 text.

Trotsky, Leon. *Literature and Revolution.* Ann Arbor: U of Michigan P.

Plekhanov, G.V. *Art and Social Life.* 1912. New York: Critic's Group, 1936.

Solomon, Maynard, ed. *Marxism and Art.* New York: Knopf, 1973.

Macherey, Pierre. *A Theory of Literary Production.* London: Routledge and Kegan Paul, 1978.

Marcuse, Herbert. *Eros and Civilization.* Boston: Beacon P, 1955.

Spivak, Gayatri. *In Other Worlds.* New York: Metheun, 1987.

Sprinker, Michael. *Imaginary Relations.* London: Verse, 1987.

Wald, Alan. *The New York Intellectuals.* New York: 1983.

Williams, Raymond. *Marxism and Literature.* New York: Oxford UP, 1977.

Western Marxism

Althusser, Louis. *Lenin and Ideology.* New York: Monthly Review P, 1971.

Anderson, Perry. *Considerations on Western Marxism.* London: New Left Books, 1983.

Bakhtin, Mikhail. *Rabelais and His World.* Cambridge: MIT P, 1968.

Benjamin, Walter. *Illuminations.* New York: Schocken, 1968.

Bloch, Ernst. *The Principle of Hope.* 3 vols. Cambridge, Mass.: MIT P, 1986.

– et al. *Aesthetics and Politics.* London: New Left Books, 1977.

Brecht, Bertolt. *Brecht on Theater.* New York: Hill and Wang, 1964.

Caudwell, Christopher. *Illusion and Reality.* London: Lawrence and Wishart, 1937.

Eagleton, Terry. *Criticism and Ideology.* London: New Left Books, 1976.

– *Walter Benjamin or Towards a Revolutionary Criticism.* London: New Left Books, 1981.

Enzensberger, Hans-Magnus. *The Consciousness Industry.* New York: Seabury, 1974.

Goldmann, Lucien. *The Hidden God.* London: Routledge and Kegan Paul, 1984.

Gramsci, Antonio. *Prison Notebooks.* New York: International Publishers, 1971.

Habermas, Jürgen. *The Philosophical Discourse of Modernity.* Cambridge, Mass.: MIT P, 1987.

Hall, Stuart. 'Gramsci's Relevance for the Study of Race and Ethnicity' and 'The Problem of Ideology

– Marxism without Guarantees.' *Journal of Communication Inquiry* 10.2 (1986): 5–27.

Jameson, Fredric. *Marxism and Form.* Princeton: Princeton UP, 1971.

– *The Political Unconscious.* Ithaca: Cornell UP, 1981.

– 'Postmodernism, or, the Cultural Logic of Late Capital.' *New Left Review* 174 (1984): 53–92.

Kolakowski, Leszek. *Toward a Marxist Humanism.* New York: Grove P, 1968.

Lukács, Georg. *The Historical Novel.* Boston: Beacon P, 1963.

– *Realism in Our Time.* New York: Harper and Row, 1964.

Materialist criticism

Like many important critical terms, 'materialism' is often used as a code-word. In contemporary theory it is sometimes used to denote any critical practice that seeks to understand the *text as a 'process.' Sometimes it is used as a code-word for Marxism. Most often 'materialism' implies a combination of meanings: a sense of process, an acknowledgment of historical implication, and an *authority grounded in something called 'the material.' (See also *Marxist criticism, *cultural materialism.)

Any argument for a particular definition of materialism must deal with the complex and sometimes contradictory ways in which the term has historically been defined. *Raymond Williams identifies three main historical meanings for 'materialism': (1) the proposition that matter is 'the primary substance of all living and non-living things, including human beings'; (2) a related 'highly various set of explanations and judgements of mental, moral and social activities' based on the idea of the primacy of matter; and (3) the derogatory sense of 'an overriding or primary concern with the production or acquisition of things and money.' A complex pattern of interaction can be traced between these three senses, with those opposed to (1) and (2) often taking advantage of the negative associations of sense (3) (Williams 163).

The roots of the modern term are found in the old distinction between the material and the ideal. Materialist inquiries explain phenomena in terms of natural laws and reject theological or metaphysical explanations. The extension of materialist explanations into the spheres of society and morality has had a strong impact on thought since the 18th century. One extreme result of this can be found in 19th-century 'naturalist' fiction, which assumes that the lives of human beings are entirely determined by natural laws.

Marx's intervention into materialist inquiry still underlies most contemporary attempts to define a 'materialist criticism.' What is difficult about the Marxist 'materialist theory of history' is that it is constructed by way of a double polemic. On the one hand, Marx rejects traditional materialism, particularly as it is played out in the economics of Adam Smith, on the grounds that such analyses naturalize the present (capitalistic) relations of production. On the other hand, he also rejects criticisms of materialism that are intended to maintain metaphysical or idealist explanations. The double polemic sets Marxism against both idealism and what could be called 'vulgar,' 'mechanical,' or 'undialectical' materialism. From this point of view, materialism resists both poles of the 'objectivist/subjectivist' dichotomy. So in Marx, for instance, the concept of 'mode of production' sometimes invokes a quasi-metaphysical 'real' (an underlying structure that explains the 'real' lives of 'real' individuals) and sometimes insists on historical relativity (the succession of modes described in the *German Ideology* is intended to call into question the 'naturalness' of the capitalistic mode of production).

The complexity of the materialist project can be hinted at by two different readings of Marx's famous epigrammatic definition of historical materialism in the preface to *A Contribution to the Critique of Political Economy*: 'In the social production of their life, men enter into definite relations that are indispensable and independent of their will, relations of production which correspond to a definite stage of development of their material productive forces. The sum total of these relations of production constitutes the economic structure of society, the real foundation, on which rises a legal and political superstructure and to which correspond definite forms of social consciousness. The mode of production of material life conditions the social, political and intellectual life process in general. It is not the consciousness of men that determines their being, but, on the contrary, their social being that determines their consciousness' ('Preface' 4).

One reading of this passage assumes a determinism in which the historical 'real' is an expression of the economic 'mode of production.' From this point of view, the 'material' is closely related to the 'physical,' to the raw materials and products of economic production, the unequal distribution of which determines the class structure of society. Yet the passage itself suggests a second reading, one which emphasizes the importance of 'the relations of production' as much as the economic or material base. For most contemporary Marxists a dialectical relationship exists between the relations of production and the economic base, so that each, in a sense, determines the other. *Louis Althusser tries to account for this mutual determination by arguing that the *social formation is an 'overdetermined structure in dominance,' in which the superstructural elements have a 'relative autonomy' from, and effect a reciprocal action on, the economic base (*Lenin and Philosophy* 130). (See *overdetermination.)

Attempts to define a materialist literary criticism have followed both readings of this passage. Classical Marxist literary theory was constructed almost uniformly on the first interpretation, according to which literary texts were seen as passive embodiments of the historical or material conditions in which they were produced. This led to a version of materialist criticism, in writers like Christopher Caudwell and the early Raymond Williams, that was very close to a sociology of literature. (See *sociocriticism.) Also associated with early materialist criticism is the theory of 'reflection' most often associated with *Georg Lukács. Reflection theory established criteria for the analysis and evaluation of texts on the basis of their 'correspondence with the immanent meaningfulness of historical life' (Frow 13). Though Etienne Balibar and *Pierre Macherey have tried to recuperate 'reflection' by reference to its original complexity (see Balibar and Macherey 82–3), the concept remains an essentialist one, dependent on a mechanical materialist interpretation of the base/superstructure model. (See also *Frankfurt School, *essentialism.)

Most contemporary attempts to define materialist criticism have tried to go beyond reflection theory. In so doing, they build on the implications of the second reading of Marx's passage. One way to summarize these readings is by noting that contemporary materialist criticism seeks to understand the text as a 'historical process,' with all the connotations of that phrase. As a *historical* process, the text is the product of a specific social formation and is marked in some fashion by this formation; as a historical *process*, the text is not a simple expression of an outside 'real' economic base, but is rather part of an on-going production, a production that – like the historical transformation of modes of production – is never complete.

Materialist criticism, then, grapples with two impulses derived from Marx's double polemic: it seeks to root the text in history, but also to understand the text as an on-going process. The second of these approaches challenges the possibility of the first, yet also implies its necessity. Rather than settling for one approach or the other, materialist criticism works positionally, adopting its own form in response to what it is working against. It also makes the existence of the different, sometimes contradictory approaches into itself an object of analysis. In this way materialist criticism becomes dialectical. As defined by *Fredric Jameson, dialectical thought aims 'not so much at solving the particular dilemmas in question, as at converting those problems into their own solutions on a higher level, and making the fact and the existence of the problem itself the starting point for new research' (*Marxism and Form* 307).

Finally, materialists accept the responsibility and limits of taking a position. The demands of materialist analysis suggest that the study of literature must be non-reductive – that is, it must attend to the specificity of literary structures and systems; yet it also maintains that literary texts cannot and should not be separated from ordinary political struggle. Materialist analysis is always part of the wider practice defined by Marx in the 11th thesis on Feuerbach: 'The philosophers have only *interpreted* the world, in various ways; the point, however, is to *change* it.'

With the advent of post-Saussurean linguistics, the term 'materialist' is now also commonly applied to analyses that accept the poststructuralist assertion of the primacy of the signifier. (See also *Ferdinand de Sausssure, *signified/signifier/signification, *structuralism, *poststructuralism.) In this use, the signifier is understood to embody the 'materiality' of language, the graphematic or 'written' quality described by *Jacques Derrida, and the effects of the signifier's primacy – the undecideability of meaning, and so on – are taken to be 'materialist' effects. Aligned with this is an argument for the close interpene-

tration of language and history, so that, for instance, the psychoanalysis of *Jacques Lacan is taken as a 'materialist' (that is, as a social and historical) description of the human subject because it describes the construction of the subject in language. (See *psychoanalytic theory.) Although poststructuralist analysis is not incompatible with many aspects of materialism, there are dangers in such a use of 'materialist.' There is, for instance, the danger of returning to a vulgar materialist position that substitutes the 'signifier' for the 'physical,' and the mirror opposite of the signifier's untranslatability for the physical's empirical certainty. More important, the use tends to efface the political consequences of what it means to be historically implicated. In literary production, 'taking a position' means in part to 'actively politicize the text,' as Tony Bennett argues (168), but also – perhaps more important – to acknowledge the already political context in which all reading takes place. (See also *ideology, *ideological horizon.)

JAMIE DOPP

Primary Sources

Althusser, Louis. *Lenin and Philosophy and Other Essays*. Trans. Ben Brewster. London: New Left Books, 1971.
Balibar, Etienne, and Pierre Macherey. 'On Literature as an Ideological Form.' In *Untying the Text: A Post-Structuralist Reader*. Ed. Robert Young. London: Routledge & Kegan Paul, 1981.
Bennett, Tony. *Marxism and Formalism*. London: Methuen, 1979.
Bottomore, Tom, et al. *A Dictionary of Marxist Thought*. Cambridge: Harvard UP, 1983.
Frow, John. *Marxism and Literary History*. Cambridge: Harvard UP, 1986.
Jameson, Fredric. *Marxism and Form*. Princeton: Princeton UP, 1971.
Marx, Karl. *A Contribution to the Critique of Political Economy*. Moscow: Progress Publishers, 1970.
Williams, Raymond. *Keywords: A Vocabulary of Culture and Society*. London: Fontana, 1976.

Metacriticism

The study of criticism, metacriticism examines theories or critical approaches to textual meaning, author-text-reader relationships, and the criteria by which texts and other cultural artefacts should be judged. Metacriticism is sometimes referred to as *hermeneutics (although hermeneutics can also refer to a specific approach to metacriticism) or as meta-interpretation since issues of interpretation play a major role in metacriticism.

Issues: Micro levels of study

In illustrating metacriticism, it is helpful to distinguish between micro and macro levels of study, for each raises a distinctive set of issues. At the micro level, metacriticism focuses on issues involved in the interpretation of a *text: (a) an author produces (b) a text (c) within a context and with a specific audience in mind which is then subsequently read by (d) a reader or interpreter who (e) stands within his or her own context and who (f) offers an interpretation of that text (g) either for himself or herself or some other audience.

ISSUES INVOLVING THE AUTHOR

For texts for which the author is known, metacriticism considers the theoretical role which information about the author should play in interpretation. Should an interpreter, for instance, attempt to discern in texts such as Dante's *The Divine Comedy* the author's intended meaning and give it primacy over other considerations? Using this approach, an interpreter would attempt to find in the text, or in an author's preface, or in articles written by the author what the author intended to communicate to the audience via the text.

Alternatively, perhaps an interpreter should just take into account some details about the author. In this view, information about the author would play a lesser role in ascertaining the meaning of the text: it would simply be one datum amongst many.

Some texts such as myths and epics do not have an author in the usual sense and their historical origins are often difficult to pin down. How would a metacritical approach that favours a definitive role for the author handle an interpretive situation such as this? Or does this situation favour the view that authors are relatively unimportant, at least for this sort of text? (See *myth, *archetypal criticism.)

Some texts, moreover, have several distinct authors at different times: for example, the parables of Jesus were first uttered by Jesus but edited in the form we now have them by the early Christian community 40–70 years after his death. What, then, is being inter-

preted: the words of Jesus or the views of first-generation Christianity? Even more difficult is the metacritical question: can one 'go beyond' the editing to the words of the original author?

What, moreover, is 'an author'? Is the author *as a person* what is significant about authorship? Or does reference to 'the author' stand as a surrogate for historical and cultural dating, as a convenient way of pinning the text down to a time and place?

Some texts, moreover, have disputed authorship. Is *Henry VIII* Shakespeare's or Shakespeare's and John Fletcher's text? Different responses suggest different interpretive conclusions. In other cases, we know very little about the authors – such as Hesiod (*Theogony, Works and Days*) and Homer (*Iliad, Odyssey*). What, then, in these cases, is the significance of authorship? And, in general, just because an author wrote the work, does the author have any privileged metacritical position with respect to the work he or she has produced? (See also *authority.)

ISSUES INVOLVING THE TEXT

Should different kinds of texts be interpreted differently? Specifically, do the same principles apply when making sense of literary, philosophical, legal, and religious texts? Do the differences between these fields of inquiry suggest that their texts receive different kinds of considerations? Is there one metacritical approach that would apply to all texts? Or are there a variety of metacritical approaches, depending on the field?

What role does the text's genre play in making sense of a text? (See *genre criticism.) In what sense should the fact that Shakespeare's plays are plays influence their interpretation? What role should the dialogue format of Plato's writings play in making sense of what Plato means? What, moreover, is genre? Is genre, for instance, a textual characteristic (something inherent perhaps in its form or structure) or is genre classification imposed on the text by the interpreter? Indeed, are genre criteria sufficiently precise to be of use? It is one thing to describe Shakespeare's plays as plays, but for other works the appropriate genre classification is far from clear. The Book of Job, for instance, has been variously classified as a tragedy, epic, lament, meditation, and even comedy, with quite different interpretive results.

A few genres pose special problems. For example, some of Jesus' utterances are called 'parables.' But what does this tell us about their appropriate mode of interpretation? Are they to be interpreted allegorically, morally or in some other way – perhaps as provocations? Are Jesus' 'parables' similar in genre to Plato's 'parables'? When contemporary works are described as 'parables' of the modern predicament – for instance, T.S. Eliot's *The Waste Land*, Albert Camus' *Le Mythe de Sisyphe* or Samuel Beckett's *Waiting for Godot* – are these parables in the same sense as Jesus' or Plato's parables?

ISSUES INVOLVING ORIGINAL CONTEXT/
AUDIENCE

Of what metacritical significance is the text's original environment? What does it say about how the text should be understood? This raises the question what meaning to them/there/then has to do with meaning to us/here/now.

If the original context is of some metacritical significance, what interpretive difficulties are there likely to be when the context of the original text is not now known? In addition, how extensive is 'context'? What, for instance, is the context of Shakespeare's *Hamlet*? Is it the circumstances of Shakespeare's composing the play? The events of 1600/1601? The revenge-play tradition? An earlier English play about Hamlet (about which we now know nothing), volume 5 of François de Belleforest's *Histoires tragiques* (1576) or Saxo Grammaticus' account of Amleth in the 12th-century *Historiae Danicae*?

ISSUES INVOLVING READER/HEARER/
INTERPRETER

An interpreter is, in some sense, 'an activator' of textual meaning. But how influential is the interpreter? Does he or she, for instance, discern and articulate the meaning that lies inherent in the text? In this view, meaning would be something a text possesses, and it would be the reader's task to discover, uncover or recover it.

Or should the interpreter be viewed as someone who attributes to the text whatever it represents to him? In this view, meaning would be something *imputed* or *attributed* to a text. At its extreme it would allow the widest possible range of meaning suggested by a text (for example, Sophocles' *Oedipus Tyrannus* is

about the plight of the Inuit in Canada today). A more moderate view would place limits on the extent of what can be attributed to a text by way of meaning (for example, Sophocles' play is about pride, the price paid for inquiry or the supremacy of fate, but is not about the Inuit).

Or should meaning be viewed quite differently, perhaps as the result of a creative interaction or transaction between text and interpreter? What role do the interpreter's interests play? If the interpreter has an interest in art, religion or psychology, what role does this play in how that person makes sense of a text? What role, moreover, does the interpreter's attitude play? Are hostile or perverse interpretations of a work any less reliable than sympathetic or friendly ones? Can there be 'neutral' interpretations? And, if so, are these more reliable?

What role does the interpreter's ideological stance play? Does it function, for instance, as a hindrance, blocking out what the text is saying? Or does *ideology operate as a means of liberation, enabling the interpreter to see meaning within the text that the casual reader may not perceive?

Closely related to this issue is the 'tribal' aspect of interpretation: a group of interpreters frequently shares a communality of outlook as a result of shared methodology (for example, Freudian, Jungian, deconstructionist), shared ideology (for example, Marxist, feminist), shared philosophy (for example, Platonic, Aristotelian, Thomistic, Lockean, Humean) or shared religious stance (for example, fundamentalist, liberal Protestant, modernist, New Age). If the same text receives differing interpretations by different tribes of interpreters, what possibility is there of inter-tribal sharing of meaning? Or is all interpretation tribal by nature and unshareable by those outside the commitments and convictions of the group? (See *Sigmund Freud, *psychoanalytic theory, *Carl G. Jung, *deconstruction, *Marxist criticism, *feminist criticism, *reader-response criticism.)

If interpretation is largely shaped by shared beliefs, then this would argue for a view of interpretation that attributes a large measure of control to the interpreter of the text. In this case, the interpreter's presuppositions and convictions would play a major role in ascertaining the meaning of a work. If this is so, then what role does the author or the text play? Another metacritical issue has to do with the legitimacy of giving older texts readings reflective of contemporary stances. For instance, is it legitimate to give Shakespeare's *Macbeth* a Freudian, Marxist or feminist interpretation when its composition clearly predates these movements?

ISSUES INVOLVING THE INTERPRETER'S CONTEXT

Even broader than the interpreter are metacritical issues involving the environment in which the reader makes sense of a text. What, for instance, is the interpreter's context? In one sense, this question may be construed as asking what the interpreter's purpose is in interpreting the work. Is it to write a scholarly study? to give a lecture? a sermon? to prepare an essay for a course? to interest a friend in reading the work? to challenge the author's view? to learn more about the topic under discussion? to provoke someone? In another sense, the question may have to do with the forum in which the interpretation will appear. Is it 'private,' for one's own pleasure only. Or is it 'public,' in which challenge and debate are likely to ensue? The context of academic scholarship invites discussion, as do contexts such as sermons and theological defences, legal proceedings and constitutional debates, and clinical psychological interpretations of behaviour.

ISSUES INVOLVING THE INTERPRETATION

What is an interpretation? Is everything said about a text an 'interpretation' of that text? What criteria must an interpretation satisfy in order to be considered an interpretation of a text? Must it, for example, be 'faithful' to the original? Must it have the same vitality and impact that the original had? Must it 'mean' the same? Can it be 'applied' differently and still be 'an interpretation'?

What adjectives are correctly applied to interpretation? Is 'correct' one of them? Does it make sense to speak of 'correct' interpretations? What about 'plausible,' 'well-founded,' 'rich,' 'insightful,' or 'acceptable'?

Should texts be viewed as having one and only one correct interpretation? Throughout the history of metacriticism, correctness of biblical interpretation has been important for the foundation of church doctrines. If so, how is

this one and only one correct interpretation to be ascertained? If not, what are the epistemological implications for metacriticism as a field of study? Is metacriticism the sort of discipline that yields 'knowledge'?

On the other hand, perhaps texts can be viewed as having a variety of interpretations. If so, are all interpretations of a work equally good? Or are some better than others? If so, how does one tell? If not, what is the purpose of interpretation?

What is to be made of differing interpretations of the same work? Are they simply the result of the tribal nature of metacriticism? or of differing interpretive purposes, interests or attitudes? Are there perhaps different 'levels' of interpretation so that interpretations differ in terms of degree of insight or depth of understanding?

While many interpretations may differ in emphasis, there are some instances of incompatible interpretations of the same work. This represents the more difficult form of interpretive diversity. Sophocles' *Oedipus Tyrannus*, for instance, has been interpreted as urging a return to traditional Olympian religion or as advocating the new humanism which opposed traditional Olympian religion. Are the grounds for such hard cases inherent in the original work or is this to be attributed to the influence of the interpreter upon the work?

Some texts themselves present incompatible positions. What, then, should the interpretation favour? Genesis, for example, contains two accounts of creation (Genesis 1:1–2:25, the transition from one account to the other occurring in the middle of 2:4), and some details are incompatible (for example, the role of woman is equal to man's in Genesis 1, but is derivative in Genesis 2). Furthermore, the New Testament Gospels, themselves highly edited documents of a pre-existing and creative oral tradition, present quite different pictures of the teachings of Jesus. Three of them (Mark, Matthew, Luke) present Jesus putting forth, largely in the form of parables, teachings concerning the Kingdom of God; by contrast, John portrays Jesus as speaking chiefly about himself ('I') in terms of complex images (Son of Man, Son of God, Bread of Life, Light of the World, Good Shepherd, the Resurrection, the True Vine), largely in monologue form.

For whom is the interpretation intended? Often it is the reader himself or herself, making sense of a work for enjoyment or enrichment. The recipient, however, could be an audience assembled for the purpose of hearing an interpretation: students, the scholarly community, a law court, or a congregation. To what extent does the knowledge level of the audience impose constraints upon the interpretation of the work that is offered? To what extent is an interpretation 'adapted' to a particular audience?

Macro levels of study

Metacriticism at the macro level is concerned with broader issues than the theoretical ones involved in the interpretation of a text, although much of the discussion is interconnected. (See *polysystem theory, *Empirical Science of Literature.) Several general issues have received widespread attention and these are illustrated here. As with micro issues, the way in which these controversies are posed is contentious.

Some metacritical issues at the macro level focus on methodology. Is there a metacritical method (or methods)? Is there a way (or, are there ways) of arriving at textual meaning? If the goal of metacriticism is regarded as textual understanding, is understanding an activity that is appropriately viewed as susceptible to methodological pursuit?

Do the humanities (broadly conceived of as including *literature, philosophy, law, religion, history), which employ metacritical methods, have a methodology? Is it a distinctive methodology? Or is it similar in some respects to the methodology used in the natural and social sciences? Even more radically, is the whole notion of a metacritical methodology appropriate to an understanding of the humanities? Perhaps the notion of methodology reveals a scientific perspective imposing itself upon the humanities?

If the humanities do not employ a methodology, what then is textual understanding or insight? A number of metacritical discussions focus on understanding *understanding*. How is understanding to be characterized? What would distinguish understanding from little understanding or no understanding at all?

Does objective understanding exist? Or is all understanding at least reflective (if not indicative) of the interpreter's ideology, gender, race, class, and position within history? Is all interpretation 'personal'? Or 'tribal'? Closely related to these controversies are issues concerning the worth, purpose and value of the humanities. Is the objective of the humanities, like that of the sciences, to yield knowledge? If so, what would characterize the humanities' kind of knowledge? On the other hand, the purpose of the humanities may simply be to share insights. Or perhaps the humanities should be construed as activities aimed at personal enjoyment, enrichment or enlightenment. From a metacritical perspective, how should the humanities be understood?

In addition, metacriticism seen from a macro perspective also considers the range of metacritical application. Can a theory of interpretation apply to other human-produced cultural artefacts than just written texts? Is there a generalized metacritical theory that would cut across a wide swath of fields? For instance, should one metacritical theory of interpretation apply to texts, dreams, works of art, music, gestures, actions, and expressions of people? Or must there be separate metacritical theories for each separate field of inquiry?

None of the issues of metacriticism, at either the macro or micro level, is settled and the literature that emanates from literary, philosophical, legal, religious, and psychological perspectives reflects considerable debate and dissension.

Metacriticism originated in ancient Greek thought, primarily at a time when traditional Olympian religion (and its supporting texts – Hesiod's and Homer's poems, various works by the dramatists) were being called into question by a more sophisticated audience. The question arose, 'How should ancient, gory but nonetheless sacred texts be understood'?

Greek thinkers gave various answers. In the *Republic*, Plato rejected much of classical Greek literature (Hesiod, Homer and 'the poets') primarily on the grounds that it failed to do justice to the nature of the gods (portraying them as weak or immoral) and that such literature influenced young impressionable children in negative ways (that is, making them fearful or irresponsible). Such works, he contended, should be banned from his ideal society, which would focus instead on truer representations of reality. In an earlier work, however, the *Ion*, Plato had advanced a quite different view, that poetry is the result of being possessed by the god; thus, while it does not yield knowledge, it embodies divine inspiration (and so presumably has value).

In the *Poetics*, Aristotle proposed looking at literary works chiefly in terms of their genre, structure and especially their impact on the reader. In this connection Aristotle highlighted the importance of an effect he called 'catharsis.'

THE ALLEGORICAL APPROACH

The answer that found widespread acceptance, however, was that originally proposed by the Stoics, who developed the concept of allegorical (hidden or deeper) meanings. The gods, they claimed, do not represent personal supernatural beings but forces of nature, and interactions between gods represent interactions between earthly forces. This approach permitted texts to be enjoyed at their superficial (literal) level while allowing those with more sophistication to appreciate their insights into the workings of nature.

The allegorical approach was extensively developed with the arrival of both Judaism and Christianity on the Roman scene. Within Judaism, for instance, Philo extensively used the allegorical approach to present the meanings of the Hebrew Bible (Old Testament) to a sophisticated Roman and Jewish audience. On the Christian side, Origen proposed a threefold allegorical approach, corresponding to his anthropology. At the most superficial level a text has the bodily (or literal) sense; for those more advanced, the moral sense; and for audiences mature in faith and understanding, the spiritual (or allegorical) sense.

Augustine and Cassian proposed a four-fold allegorical approach, with levels that corresponded to different levels of reader sophistication. For Augustine, these levels were identified as follows: the historical (or literal level, including metaphor) which was written or done; the aetiological level, which is that for which something has been said or done; the analogical level, or that which reflects a congruence of the Old and New Testaments; and finally, the allegorical level, which is its figurative sense as it pertains to Christ or the general body of Christian teaching. Augustine's model of meaning was widely adopted as standard biblical metacritical methodology.

However, there were some dissenters from the allegorical model of metacriticism. Theodore of Mopsuestia and the Nestorians, whose metacritical writings have not survived, are known to have adopted a differing model, one that favoured the literal historical meaning. In addition, they are known to have developed a metacritical theory of typology: an event in the Old Testament (such as the passage out of Egypt through water) may prefigure or foreshadow an event in the New Testament (such as baptism). Unlike allegory, which is a theory of meaning, typology represents a theory of events within history.

The allegorical approach represented a congenial approach to metacritical considerations. It allowed a plurality of interpretations and applications, accounted for different levels of understanding brought to texts by readers, and preserved the integrity of the text which, on face value, might seem unsuitable for a sophisticated and enlightened audience.

This approach, however, ignored historical circumstances of the text's composition, a matter which was not judged critical in the early Middle Ages, which favoured a more Platonic view that relegated reality to a timeless, eternal heaven and left history as part of the changing, temporal world. The approach also led to a proliferation of meanings – many more than the four of Augustine – and to what some later metacritical theorists deemed fanciful and far-fetched interpretations. In the early 16th century, for instance, Tyndale vigorously attacked allegorical interpretation, contending that it nullified textual meaning and arguing that Scripture should be viewed as having but one interpretation, namely the literal historical sense.

Aquinas in the 13th century, while upholding the model favoured by Augustine, nevertheless suggested that higher (deeper) levels of meaning should be congruent with the literal historical meaning. This served to orient metacriticism much more closely to the importance of history.

THE REFORMATION APPROACH

By the time of the Reformers, much more was known about the ancient languages (Greek, Hebrew, Aramaic) and the process of textual transmission of ancient literary remains (often Greek or Hebrew/Aramaic into Syriac, then Arabic, then Latin). In addition, the view of history changed. Contemporary metaphysics, shifting from Platonism and neo-Platonism to Aristotelianism, seemed poised to value more highly the changing world in which history plays a major role.

By and large, the classical 16th-century Protestant reformers (Luther, Calvin, Knox) favoured a metacritical approach that would result in one and only one interpretation of a passage, namely that based on the literal historical meaning (unless clearly metaphorical or allegorical in the original). This metacritical approach grew out of a theological concern, for it was essential that texts speak to readers unambiguously if true doctrine was to be discerned on the basis of one authoritative text.

An 18th-century Protestant thinker, Ernesti, made modifications to the Reformation model, suggesting that there was occasional justification for a plurality of meanings for a text when the literal historical sense of the original clearly allowed for a diversity of meanings.

In practice, while a community could hold to the view that the sacred text had one and only one correct interpretation, those who held contrary views as to the text's meaning often had to form their own community. Thus, with the Protestant approach to criticism, rival communities with differing views begin to emerge, and criticism becomes 'denominational.' This development served to highlight the 'tribal' nature of metacriticism.

ROMANTICIST APPROACH

In all of the models advanced hitherto, the role of the author had been ignored. In the early 19th century, Friedrich Schleiermacher proposed that understanding occurs when an interpreter 'goes through' the text to comprehend the author's thought, in a sense communing with the author about the matter under discussion. As Schleiermacher portrayed it, every act of understanding is the obverse of the act of *discourse: the interpreter must come to grasp the thought which was at the base of the discourse.

CONTEMPORARY APPROACHES

Contemporary metacriticism begins with the late-19th-century seminal work of *Wilhelm Dilthey who attempted to lay the foundations for a comprehensive theory of the humanities (*Geisteswissenschaften*) based on a methodology differing from that of the natural sciences. At times he called the methodology of the humanities 'understanding' (*Verstehen*). His objective was to portray the distinctiveness and value of the humanities in an era in which these were under attack. Critics of Dilthey, however, contend that by focusing on method he was already employing the mindset of the natural sciences.

The products of the humanities – 'the Mind-affected World' or 'cultural achievements' – included, for Dilthey, such human productions as works of art, social movements, political ideologies, ideas, texts, dances, constitutions, and laws, political forms, languages, religions, and mythologies, customs and traditions. In sum, cultural achievements included all the human creations and expressions that comprise the humanities. By focusing on 'understanding,' Dilthey attempted to develop the foundations of the humanities, trying to give them a basis for being treated as a serious academic enterprise worthy of inclusion into the curriculum of a modern university. It was Dilthey's significance that he raised the foundations of the humanities as a serious hermeneutical problem with wide-sweeping implications. These questions have preoccupied 20th-century scholarship.

Since Dilthey, metacriticism has been explored from a number of critical perspectives – hermeneutic, structuralist, positivistic, and 'other' – and by scholars working in a number of different fields – biblical and classical studies, literary theory, various psychological approaches, legal theorists, and philosophers of analytic, positivistic and phenomenological persuasions. (See *structuralism, *phenomenological criticism.)

Positivism gained considerable prominence in the 1930s and 1940s in Europe, Britain, Canada, and the U.S.A. It contended that the works of the humanities were cognitively meaningless and, as such, contributed nothing that was true (unlike the sciences). Rudolf Carnap, A.J. Ayer, Otto Neurath, and others led the assault on scholarship in the humanities, challenging academics, literary critics and religious thinkers to articulate statements that were capable of being either true or false. The movement caused considerable excitement but eventually floundered because of the difficulties of formulating a criterion of meaningfulness.

Hermeneutics has been developed by theorists such as *Hans-Georg Gadamer, Emilio Betti, *Jürgen Habermas, *Paul Ricoeur, Rudolf Bultmann, and many others who, in a variety of ways, have attempted to uncover the presuppositions of criticism. Building upon the philosophical contributions of *Martin Heidegger, Gadamer in particular stresses the role that presuppositions ('prejudice') play within criticism, along with tradition (and community), and the interpreter's historicity and horizon. (See *horizon of expectation.) Acknowledging the interpreter's historicity recognizes the historical situatedness of all beings and the role this plays in understanding works from the humanities. This is clearly illustrated in Bultmann's widely adopted hermeneutic procedure that he called 'de-mythologizing.' (See *demythologizing.) In order to acknowledge the differing historicities of the interpreter and ancient texts, Bultmann proposed using the 'mythology' (pattern of thought) of the original text to uncover its 'kerygma' (message), then abandoning the original mythology in favour of embedding the kerygma in a more current mythological format. Thus meaning is preserved (same kerygma) while accommodating the differing historicities of author and interpreter (kerygma is 'de-' and 're-mythologized').

In general, a hermeneutical approach to metacriticism favours an approach that emphasizes the plurality of interpretations for interpreters, and for the historical epoch in which they live, and stresses a strong interaction between text and interpreter. One exception is *E.D. Hirsch, Jr., who contends that the author's intended meaning is the meaning of a text. As a metacritic and as an interpreter who has studied the Romantic poets and Blake extensively, Hirsch is perhaps the major exponent today in literary metacriticism of the 'single sense' approach to hermeneutics, with fundamentalist scholars representing a similar approach in religious metacriticism.

There are many metacritical approaches that favour focusing on the structure of the work. Form-critical and text-critical approaches within religious studies consider stylistic and structural considerations to ascertain meaning. Such approaches, for instance, consider the metacritical impact of four literary strands (J,E,P, and D) within the Pentateuch (Torah),

isolating the different emphases and traditions within the edited text, and using this to give the text an interpretation. Similarly, the structure of the Book of Job (which consists of a Prologue, Dialogue, Monologue of Elihu, Monologue of Yahweh, and Epilogue) has been used in interpretation, although here the metacritical situation is more complex depending on whether all or only some of the five structural units are judged 'authentic.'

Another emphasis on structure has developed out of structuralist research into the nature of language. Often this research has been anthropological (Claude *Lévi-Strauss) or linguistic (*Ferdinand de Saussure) in nature, and this has had some impact on literary approaches to metacriticism. Structuralist approaches focus on the universe of discourse created by a set of signs, and attempt to understand this universe in all its distinctiveness. (See *sign.) Structuralist metacritics would then focus on 'the language of Sartre,' or 'the language of the Book of Job.' In a way, *Northrop Frye's metacritical stance in *The Great Code* is 'structuralist' in practice in the sense that his archetypal analysis focuses on 'the language of the Bible' in all its unique patterns.

For structuralists like *Roland Barthes, moreover, language is made up of signs which have two components: the signifier and signified. (See *signifed/signifier/signification.) Other metacritical approaches (such as the hermeneutic approach of Ricoeur) would contend that a third component of language is the referent. (See *reference/referent.) The debate over the components of language raises a metacritical issue concerning that about which a text speaks. For Ricoeur, discourse is the vital movement of the components of language towards the world. For Barthes it is the organization of the signifiers much more than the signified which is of metacritical interest. Thus for Barthes literary criticism becomes the making sense of a coherent system of signs.

Alongside the development of hermeneutics and structuralism is the approach called '*New Criticism,' which originated in the early 1940s with Robert Penn Warren, *Cleanth Brooks, Allen Tate and John Crowe Ransom. This approach focused on 'the text,' contending that literature should be viewed as a separate and self-contained entity. This metacritical focus set the New Critics apart both from those metacritics who emphasized the role of the author and from those who contended that the role of the reader/interpreter is not so transparent or self-effacing. The latter would include historicist, Marxist and psychoanalytical metacritics who emphasized the role of the critic's perspective. (See also *New Historicism, *materialist criticism.)

A more recent approach is deconstruction, which questions canonicity (that certain works, for whatever reason, have more importance or significance than others, or should have more dominance in study than others). (See *canon.) Accordingly, a text may be pop cultural, mythological, historical, or philosophical. Ashtrays, Saturday-morning cartoons, operas, and pieces of prose are all 'text.' On another level, deconstruction attempts to discern the suppressed voice struggling for articulation within the dominant voice. *J. Hillis Miller, *Paul de Man and *Harold Bloom have championed deconstruction in the U.S. during the last 15 years. Similarly, feminists such as *Hélène Cixous, *Julia Kristeva, Alice A. Jardine and *Luce Irigaray have begun to deconstruct text and language, rejecting centuries of white, male, patriarchal domination. In order to bring an end to masculine discourse, Cixous and Jardine both began to remake language.

Metacritical approaches since Dilthey have not resolved the micro and macro issues with which metacriticism is concerned. Theorists are still deeply divided about the relationships between author, text (language, structure, genre, historicity), reader/interpreter (including tradition, affinities), interpretation (meaning, application) and audience (for whom the interpretation is rendered).

BARRIE A. WILSON

Primary Sources

Beardsley, Monroe C. *The Possibility of Criticism*. Detroit: Wayne State UP, 1970.
Bultmann, Rudolf. *Essays Philosophical and Theological*. London: SCM, 1955.
– *Jesus Christ and Mythology*. New York: Charles Scribner and Sons, 1958.
– *Kerygma and Myth, I*. Ed. W.Bartsch. London: SPCK, 1964.
Crossan, John Dominic. *In Parables*. New York: Harper and Row, 1973.
Dilthey, Wilhelm. *Pattern and Meaning in History*. Ed. H.P. Rickman. New York: Harper and Row, 1961.
– *Selected Works*. Ed. Rudolf A. Makkreel and Fritjof Rodi. 6 vols. Princeton: Princeton UP, 1985.
– *Selected Writings*. Ed. H.P. Rickman. New York: Cambridge UP, 1976.
Gadamer, H.-G. *Wahrheit und Methode: Grundzuke einer philosophischen Hermeneutik*. Tübingen: J.C.B. Mohr, 1960. 2nd ed. 1965. 2nd ed., trans. and ed. Garrett Barden and John Cumming. *Truth and Method*. New York: Seabury, 1975.
– *Philosophical Hermeneutics*. Trans. David E. Linge. Berkeley: U of California P, 1976.
Grant, Robert M., John T. McNeill, Samuel Terrien. 'History of the Interpretation of the Bible.' In *The Interpreter's Bible*. Vol. 1. New York: Abingdon-Cokesbury, 1952, 718–24.
Hirsch, E.D. *The Aims of Interpretation*. Chicago: U of Chicago P, 1976.
– *Validity in Interpretation*. New Haven: Yale UP, 1967.
Margolis, Joseph. *The Language of Art and Art Criticism*. Detroit: Wayne State UP, 1965.
Palmer, Richard E. *Hermeneutics*. Evanston, Ill.: Northwestern UP, 1969.
Perrin, Norman. *Jesus and the Language of the Kingdom*. Philadelphia: Fortress, 1967.
Weitz, Morris. *Hamlet and the Philosophy of Literary Criticism*. Chicago: U of Chicago P, 1964.
Wilson, Barrie. *About Interpretation: From Plato to Dilthey – A Hermeneutic Anthology*. New York: Peter Lang, 1989.
– *Interpretation, Meta-Interpretation*. Berkeley: Center for Hermeneutical Studies, 1980.

Narratology

Narratology is the set of general statements on narrative genres, on the systematics of narrating (telling a story) and on the structure of plot. (See *story/plot.) The history of narratology can be divided into three periods: prestructuralist (until 1960); structuralist (1960–80); and poststructuralist (including not only further developments of structuralist ideas such as *deconstruction but also the recent development of narratology into an interdisciplinary pursuit). (See *structuralism, *genre criticism, *poststructuralism.)

Origins

In the third chapter of the *Poetics* Aristotle makes a distinction, still a starting-point in narratology, between representing an object (a 'history') by a *narrator and by characters. In the first case the history is told (*diegesis) and the text is narrative; in the second, the history is shown (*mimesis) and the *text is dramatic. The diegetic representation of the narrative text may, however, embed mimetic elements as the narrator lets the story be told by the dialogues and monologues of characters. (See *embedding.)

Aristotle's remarks fuelled an aesthetic debate among novelists of the late 19th and early 20th century. The concept of mimesis, wrongly interpreted as 'imitation' ('representation' is the better translation), became the standard of reliable narrative. For realist and naturalist authors, the mode of narration was determined by the demands of le vraisemblable (appearance of truth, credible representation). Some thought that an objective narrator was the best guarantee for a reliable, realistic representation (Zola); others, that the narrator had to be invisible, that only the characters could give a perspective on the events (Flaubert). In one of the first treatises on narrative technique (1921), *Percy Lubbock argued against narratorial intervention and proclaimed the aesthetic superiority of a mode of narration which lets characters reveal themselves through their behaviour and perceptions. This position, also endorsed by *Henry James (1900), led to an increasing use of the 'free indirect style,' by which the thoughts of a character could be represented seemingly without mediation. The ideal of objectivity thus paradoxically motivated subjective modes of narration.

The theory of narrative technique and modes of narration was systematized in the U.S.A. by *Wayne C. Booth (1961) and the Chicago School and in Europe by Franz Stanzel (1971, 1984) and Eberhardt Lämmert (1955). (See *Neo-Aristotelian or Chicago School.) Booth refined the concept of narrator, distinguishing this speaking instance from the historical author as well as from the implied author who embodies the whole of meanings, norms and values transferred by the text. Because the narrator and the implied author can be in contradiction with each other, this distinction contributed to insights into the phenomena of *irony and of unreliable narration.

In the area of narrative semantics, early contributions include the distinction by novelist *E.M. Forster (1927) between round and flat characters. The first are complex and dynamic, the second are simple and static. Forster also raised the question of minimal conditions of narrativity: 'the king died and then the queen died' is a plot, but '... and then the queen dies of grief' is a story. The systematic study of the structure of plot was pioneered by a Russian

formalist, *Vladimir Propp, in Morphology of the Folktale (1928). (See *formalism, Russian.) Whereas folklorists formerly classified fairy tales according to concrete motifs – horses, witches, princesses – Propp proposed a taxonomy based on the more abstract concepts of role and function. Roles such as hero, villain, helper, and desired object define the mode of participation of characters in the plot independently of their individuating features; functions such as reward, mission or test capture the strategic significance of events for the story as a whole independently of the particular nature of these events. The same role can be performed by a frog or an old man, the same function fulfilled by cleaning stables or slaying a dragon.

Another pioneering contribution to the study of plot is the work of *Viktor Shklovskii (1929). Breaking away from the 19th-century view that plots reflect socio-economic and religious institutions in folklore, and mostly biographical data in literature, he argued that narrative forms are the product of 'special laws of plot formation still unknown to us' (Theory of Prose 18). His studies of plot construction focused on such devices as repetition, parallelism, framing, embedding, juxtaposition, and the emplotment of puns and riddles, evaluating them in terms of their contribution to what he regarded as the global purpose of the textual machinery: the aesthetic effect of *defamiliarization.

In a more formal domain of semantics – the logic of literary communication – the early work of Käthe Hamburger (1957) foresaw the preoccupations of the 1980s with definitions of fictionality and illocutionary approaches to narrative, though her position challenged, rather than supported, contemporary uses of a communicative model of narration.

Structuralist period

The theoretical foundations of contemporary narratology were laid down in France in the 1960s by scholars with a common allegiance to Russian formalism and Saussurean linguistics whose impact can be seen in the designation of units: narremes, mythemes, functions, roles, modalities, types of events. These units are combined in a temporal sequence according to the rules of a narrative syntax. (See *Ferdinand de Saussure.)

Structuralist narratology moved in two directions, following the Russian formalist distinction between story and *discourse (*fabula* and *siuzhet*, in the terminology of *Boris Tomashevskii [1925]). *Claude Bremond (1973) defines story as a semantic structure independent of any medium, while discourse is the verbal or visual presentation of this structure. The main contributions of structuralism to the theorizing of story include the following.

1. *Claude Lévi-Strauss' 'structural analysis of myth' (1958): the segmentation of myths into basic units of signification (mythemes) and the rearrangement of these units into a matrix which brings together the deep meaning of the myth and the diachronic unfolding of the plot. (See *myth, *signified/signifier/ signification.)

2. *Tzvetan Todorov's (1969) narrative grammar in which narrative elements function as syntactic categories: actions are assimilated to verbs, characters to nouns, and their attributes to adjectives. The most original part of the system is a catalogue of operators inspired by the verbal modes of language: 'optative,' 'obligative,' 'conditional,' and 'prescriptive' (as well as the unmarked case of 'indicative'). Through these operators which modify the verb, the system is able to take unactualized events into consideration and to describe the status of these events in the minds of characters. The introduction of the virtual as a semantic dimension of narrative events represented a significant advance over Propp's model, which limited the plot to a sequence of objectively realized facts.

3. Bremond's (1973) characterization of narrative logic as a series of choices between alternatives and his elaboration of a semantic system to code narrative action. The elements of this system include the roles fulfilled by the participants (agent, patient, beneficiary, victim, adjuvant, opponent, and so on); the process taking place among the participants (protection, punishment, trap, revelation); the phase of accomplishment (planned, under way, completed); and the voluntary status of the process (voluntary/inadvertent).

4. *A.J. Greimas' distinction between surface structures and deep structures, his use of the 'semiotic square' to describe the latter and his system of narrative *actants (the last derived from Propp's concept of role). (See *semiotics, *semiosis.) In this model, characters are classified according to their function in the fabula. The subject or main character pursues a certain goal or object; meets with resistance from an opponent and receives help from a helper; a decisive power (*destinateur*) sends the subject on the mission. The project benefits a receiver (*destinataire*) (1970, 1971, 1976).

5. *Roland Barthes' concept of narrative codes (1970) and his classification of narrative events into kernels and satellites (1966). (See *code, *narrative code.) Kernels are logically necessary to the plot and cannot be deleted without leaving a gap in its causal structure. Satellites fill in the narrative structure, adding vividness to the representation of the narrative world but without moving the plot significantly forward.

6. In the area of discourse, structuralist narratology is dominated by the painstaking taxonomic work of *Gérard Genette (1973). The terminology elaborated in his book *Figures III* has become the lingua franca of the field. Genette studies such topics as order of presentation (disruptions of chronology through analepses [flash back] and prolepses [flash forward]; duration of representation (distinction between scene and summary; relations between narrated time and time of narration); mode of representation (the interplay of mimesis and diegesis); narration (who speaks? how does the narrator relate to the narrated events?); focalization (who sees?); narrative levels created by stories within stories; and the concept of *narratee as communicative partner of the narrator.

Contemporary trends

The poststructuralist era has been characterized by an increase of interest in non-literary narratives and by an influx of ideas from other disciplines. In the literary domain narratology reflects the critical trends of the period: deconstruction, feminism and psychoanalysis. (See *feminist criticism, *psychoanalytic theory.)

The tradition of close scrutiny of discourse initiated by Genette continued and his repertory of analytical concepts underwent further refinements. Seymour Chatman (1978) widened the investigation of narrative discourse to visual media. Under the influence of *Mikhail Bakhtin, the narrative text came to be regarded as a polyvocal utterance and the question 'who speaks' opened into an investigation of such phenomena as quotation, *parody, *intertextuality, narrative embedding, the hierarchy of narrative voices, and narrative *authority

(Sternberg 1982, Bal 1985, McHale 1978, Martínez-Bonati 1981, Lanser 1981, Doležel 1980). Working in the framework of Chomskyan linguistics, Ann Banfield (1982) developed a theory of the representation of thought and perception which systematized earlier work on free indirect discourse and stream of consciousness (Lips 1926, Humphrey 1954, Pascal 1977, Cohn 1978), and challenged communicative models of narration. (See *Noam Chomsky.)

Under the influence of *Jacques Derrida, proponents of deconstruction read plots as allegories of all things textual, paying particular attention to *mise-en-abyme*, an emblematic form of self-reference (Dällenbach 1977). In deconstructive readings of narrative texts, Cynthia Chase (1978) and *Jonathan Culler (1981) challenged the traditional view of the hierarchy between story (fabula) and discourse, arguing that discourse does not follow or repeat the fabula but that the fabula is produced by discourse.

New critical developments were set in motion by an integration of narratology with psychoanalysis. Peter Brooks' *Reading for the Plot* (1984) focuses on the 'motor' or drive behind plotting. Ross Chambers (1984), challenging the cognitive status of narrative as well as of narratology, argued that the authority of the storyteller, undermined in modern fiction, is replaced by the *power and authority of the story itself, thus bridging the gap between psychoanalytic and deconstructive narratology. In general, as Silverman (1988) demonstrated, the psychoanalytic focus on the formation and functioning of the subjects intersects with the interests of a subject-oriented narratology. Bal's later work (1986) explored this intersection systematically.

Feminist studies, especially of film (de Lauretis 1988, Silverman 1988), demonstrated the complicity between narrative form and Oedipal *ideology as well as the possibility for alternative forms of storytelling. Bal and then Susan Sniader Lanser (1986) argued in favour of a feminist narratology, attributing the same theoretical importance to the category 'gender of narrator' as to narrative point of view or to the distinction between first-person and third-person narration.

The rise of Chomskyan linguistics inspired literary theorists to adapt the model of transformational/generative grammar to the case of narrative. Thomas Pavel (1976), *Gerald Prince (1973) and Teun van Dijk (1972) defined the conditions of narrativity by means of generative rules which map stories on tree-shaped diagrams. Transformational rules were proposed to account for differences between the logical structure of the story and its textual realization.

Narrative grammars and systems of plot units were also proposed by cognitive psychologists attempting to capture processes of memorization, summary and information retrieval (Rumelhart 1975, Mandler and Johnson 1977). In Artificial Intelligence (AI), formal models of plot are designed as part of the simulation of the mental operations involved in understanding stories (Lehnert 1981, Dyer 1983). The AI concepts of 'script' and 'plan' (Schank 1977) were integrated into a semantics of narrative action (van Dijk 1976, Bruce and Newman 1978). Pavel (1985) invoked *game theory in developing the concept of 'narrative move.'

As psychologists investigate the cognitive processing of the narrative text, representatives of the humanities raise the converse issue of the cognitive value of narrative structures. Historian *Hayden White (1980), critic Peter Brooks (1984), and philosopher *Paul Ricoeur (1982) stressed the importance of narrativity in shaping our experience of reality and in coming to terms with temporality.

As the scope of linguistic analysis widened from the sentence to texts and to discourse, linguists became interested in narrative data collected in the field: conversational anecdotes (Polanyi 1979, 1981; Sacks 1977), narratives of personal experience (Labov and Waletzky 1967), tall tales (Bauman 1986). These studies added a pragmatic component to narratology by raising such issues as the relations between narrative and its context, narrative 'points' and narrative 'tellability,' audience participation, strategies for gaining and keeping the floor, and techniques for highlighting and topicalizing narrative information. Inspired by this work, literary theorists turned their attention to the pragmatics of literary communication (Pratt 1977) and to narrative contracts between audience and storyteller (Chambers 1984).

Under the influence of philosophy of language and *speech act theory, the issues of narrativity and fictionality were separated. Increasing attention was devoted to the formal definition of fiction and to the question of the truth-functionality of fictional utterances (Lewis 1978, Woods 1974, Howell 1979, Walton

1990). The structuralist doctrine of the non-referentiality of literary language was challenged by the view that reference does not presuppose actual existence or truth in the real world. Philosophers and literary theorists raised the question of the illocutionary status of 'the act of producing fiction.' Some regarded it as an autonomous speech act (Ohmann 1971, Currie 1985), others (Banfield 1982, Kuroda 1976, responding to Hamburger's position) considered fictional storytelling to stand outside of the speech act system; still others regarded narrative fiction as a collection of non-seriously performed speech acts (*Searle 1975), or as the artificial imitation of 'natural' genres (Pratt 1977, Smith 1978).

Another major influence on narrative semantics was modal logic and the theory of possible worlds. The concept of possible world was used in addressing the problem of truth in fiction (Lewis 1978), in assessing the autonomy and dependency of narrative universes with respect to reality (Maître 1983), in describing the configuration of the narrative system of reality and its partition into distinct ontological regions (Doležel 1976, Pavel 1986), in modelling the interplay of actual and virtual events in a plot (*Eco 1979), and in resolving the question of the relations between real individuals and their fictional counterparts (the real Napoleon vs. the Napoleon of *War and Peace*).

For lack of a unifying model, the theory of characters lags somewhat behind other aspects of narrative semantics. Two opposite views dominate this domain. The classical structuralist/semiotic position regards characters as aggregates of semantic features subsumed by a name. Proponents of the theory of possible worlds invoke a game of make-believe which enables readers to relate to characters as if they were real persons with an autonomous existence. At stake is the problem of ontological completeness: do characters possess only those features specified by the text (Doležel 1988) or are unspecified features to be treated as missing information (Martínez-Bonati 1980)? Whatever the answer, the theory of characters still faces the task of explaining the semantic and phenomenological differences between flat and round characters.

MARIE-LAURE RYAN and
ERNST VAN ALPHEN

Primary Sources

van Alphen, Ernst. 'Reading Visually.' *Style* 22.2 (1988): 219–29.

Aristotle. 'Poetics.' *The Basic Works of Aristotle*. Ed. R. McKeon. New York: Random House, 1941.

Bakhtin, Mikhail. *The Dialogic Imagination*. Trans. Caryl Emerson and Michael Holquist. Austin: U of Texas P, 1981.

Bal, Mieke. *Femmes imaginaires: L'Ancien testament au risque d'une narratologie critique*. Paris: Nizet, 1986.

– *Narratology: Introduction to the Theory of Narrative*. Trans. Christine Van Boheemen. Toronto, Buffalo, and London: U of Toronto P, 1985.

Banfield, Ann. *Unspeakable Sentences: Narration and Representation in the Language of Fiction*. London: Routledge, 1982.

Barthes, Roland. 'An Introduction to the Structural Analysis of Narrative.' 1966. *New Literary History* 6 (1975): 237–62.

– *S/Z*. Paris: Seuil, 1970.

Bauman, Richard. *Story, Performance, and Event: Contextual Studies of Oral Narrative*. Cambridge and New York: Cambridge UP, 1986.

de Beaugrande, Robert, and Benjamin N. Colby. 'Narrative Models of Action and Interaction.' *Cognitive Science* 3 (1979): 43–66.

Booth, Wayne. *The Rhetoric of Fiction*. Chicago: U of Chicago P, 1961.

Bremond, Claude. *Logique du récit*. Paris: Seuil, 1973.

Brooks, Peter. *Reading for the Plot: Design and Intention in Narrative*. New York: Random House, 1984.

Bruce, Bertram, and Dennis Newman. 'Interacting Plans.' *Cognitive Science* 3 (1978): 195–233.

Chambers, Ross. *Story and Situation: Narrative Seduction and the Power of Fiction*. Minneapolis: U of Minnesota P, 1984.

Chase, Cynthia. 'The Decomposition of the Elephants: Double Reading of *Daniel Deronda*.' *PMLA* 93.3 (1978): 215–27.

Chatman, Seymour. *Story and Discourse*. Ithaca: Cornell UP, 1978.

Cohn, Dorrit. *Transparent Minds: Narrative Modes for Presenting Consciousness in Fiction*. Princeton: Princeton UP, 1978.

Culler, Jonathan. 'Story and Discourse in the Analysis of Narrative.' In *The Pursuit of Signs*. Ithaca and London: Cornell UP, 1981.

– *Structuralist Poetics*. Ithaca: Cornell UP, 1975.

Currie, Gregory. 'What is Fiction?' *Journal of Aesthetics and Art Criticism* 43.4 (1985): 385–92.

Dällenbach, Lucien. *Le Récit spéculaire: Essai sur la mise-en-abyme*. Paris: Seuil, 1977.

de Lauretis, Teresa. *Technologies of Gender*. Bloomington: Indiana UP, 1988.

van Dijk, Teun A. 'Philosophy of Action and Theory of Narrative.' *Poetics* 5 (1976): 287–338.

- *Some Aspects of Text Grammars*. The Hague: Mouton, 1972.
Doležel, Lubomír. 'Mimesis and Possible Worlds.' *Poetics Today* 9.3 (1988): 475–96.
- 'Narrative Modalities.' *Journal of Literary Semantics* 5.1 (1976): 5–14.
- 'Truth and Authenticity in Narrative.' *Poetics Today* 1.3 (1980): 7–25.
Dyer, Michael G. *In-depth Understanding: A Computer Model of Integrated Processing for Narrative Comprehension*. Cambridge, Mass.: MIT P, 1983.
Eco, Umberto. *The Role of the Reader: Explorations in the Semiotics of Texts*. Bloomington: Indiana UP, 1979.
Forster, E.M. *Aspects of the Novel*. London: Arnold, 1927.
Fowler, Roger. *Linguistics and the Novel*. London: Methuen, 1977.
Garvey, James. 'Characterization in Narrative.' *Poetics* 7 (1978): 63–78.
Genette, Gérard. *Figures III*. Paris: Seuil, 1973. *Narrative Discourse*. Trans. J. Lewin. Ithaca and London: Cornell UP, 1980.
- *Nouveau discours du récit*. Paris: Seuil, 1982.
Greimas, Algirdas Julien. *De Sens: Essais sémiotiques*. Paris: Seuil, 1970.
- *Maupassant: La Sémiotique du texte. Exercices pratiques*. Paris: Seuil, 1976.
- 'Narrative Grammar: Units and Levels.' *MLN* 86 (1971): 795–806.
Hamburger, Käthe. *Die Logik der Dichtung*. Stuttgart: Klett, 1957. *The Logic of Literature*. Bloomington: Indiana UP, 1973.
Hamon, Philippe. 'Pour un status sémiologique du personnage.' *Littérature* 6 (1972): 86–110.
Howell, Robert. 'Fictional Objects: How They Are, and How They Aren't.' *Poetics* 8 (1979): 129–178.
Humphrey, Robert. *Stream of Consciousness in the Modern Novel*. Berkeley and Los Angeles: U of California P, 1954.
James, Henry. 'The Art of Fiction.' 1890. In *The Future of the Novel: Essays on the Art of Fiction*. Ed. Leon Edel. New York: Vintage, 1956.
Kuroda, S.Y. 'Reflections on the Foundations of Narrative Theory.' In *Pragmatics of Language and Literature*. Ed. Teun A. van Dijk. Amsterdam: North Holland, 1976, 107–40.
Labov, William, and Joshua Waletzky. 'Narrative Analysis: Oral Versions of Personal Experience.' In *Essays on the Verbal and Visual Arts: Proceedings of the 1966 Spring Meeting*. Ed. June Helm. Seattle: U of Washington P, 1967, 12–44.
Lanser, Susan Sniader. *The Narrative Act*. Princeton: Princeton UP, 1981.
- 'Toward a Feminist Narratology.' *Style* 20.3 (1986): 341–63.
Lämmert, Eberhardt. *Bauformen des Erzählens*. Stuttgart: J.B. Metzlersche Verlag, 1955.
Lehnert, Wendy. 'Plot Units and Narrative Summarization.' *Cognitive Science* 4 (1981): 293–332.

Leitch, Thomas M. *What Stories Are: Narrative Theory and Interpretation*. University Park: Pennsylvania UP, 1986.
Lévi-Strauss, Claude. *Anthropologie structurale*. Paris: Plon, 1958.
Lewis, David. 'Truth in Fiction.' *American Philosophical Quarterly* 5 (1978): 37–46.
Lips, Marguerite. *Le Style indirect libre*. Paris: Payot, 1926.
Lubbock, Percy. *The Craft of Fiction*. London: Cape, 1921.
Maître, Doreen. *Literature and Possible Worlds*. Middlesex: Polytechnic P, 1983.
Mandler, Jean, and Nancy Johnson. 'Remembrance of Things Parsed: Story Structure and Recall.' *Cognitive Psychology* 9 (1977): 111–51.
Margolin, Uri. 'Characterization in Narrative: Some Theoretical Prologomena.' *Neophilologicus* 67 (1983): 1–14.
- 'The Doer and the Deed: Action Basis for Characterization in Narrative.' *Poetics Today* 7.2 (1986): 205–26.
Martin, Wallace. *Recent Theories of Narrative*. Ithaca and London: Cornell UP, 1986.
Martínez-Bonati, Félix. 'The Act of Writing Fiction.' *New Literary History* 11.3 (1980): 425–34.
- *Fictive Discourse and the Structures of Literature*. Ithaca: Cornell UP, 1981.
- 'Towards a Formal Ontology of Fictional Worlds.' *Philosophy and Literature* 7 (1983): 182–95.
McHale, Brian. 'Free Indirect Discourse: A Survey of Recent Accounts.' *PTL* 3 (1978): 249–87.
Ohmann, Richard. 'Speech Acts and the Definition of Literature.' *Philosophy and Rhetoric* 4 (1971): 1–19.
Pascal, Roy. *The Dual Voice: Free Indirect Speech and Its Functioning in the 19th Century European Novel*. Manchester UP, 1977.
Pavel, Thomas. *Fictional Worlds*. Cambridge: Harvard UP, 1986.
- *The Poetics of Plot: The Case of English Renaissance Drama*. Minneapolis: U of Minnesota P, 1985.
- *La Syntaxe narrative des tragédies de Corneille*. Paris: Klincksieck, 1976.
Polanyi, Livia. 'So What's the Point? *Semiotica* 25.3/4 (1979): 207–41.
- 'What Stories Can Tell Us about Their Teller's World.' *Poetics Today* 2.2 (1981): 97–112.
Pratt, Mary Louise. *Towards a Speech Act Theory of Literary Discourse*. Bloomington: Indiana UP, 1977.
Prince, Gerald. *Dictionary of Narratology*. Lincoln: U of Nebraska P, 1987.
- *A Grammar of Stories*. The Hague: Mouton, 1973.
- *Narratology*. The Hague: Mouton, 1982.
Propp, Vladimir. *Morphology of the Folktale*. 1928. Trans. Laurence Scott. Austin: U of Texas P, 1968.
Ricoeur, Paul. *Temps et récit I, II, III*. Paris: Seuil, 1982, 1984, 1985.

Rimmon-Kenan, Shlomith. *Narrative Fiction: Contemporary Poetics*. London: Methuen, 1980.

Rumelhart, David. 'Notes on a Schema for Stories.' In *Representation and Understanding: Studies in Cognitive Science*. Ed. D.G. Bobrow and M. Collins. New York: Academic P, 1975, 211–35.

Ryan, Marie-Laure. *Possible Worlds: Artificial Intelligence and Narrative Theory*. Bloomington: Indiana UP, 1991.

Sacks, Harvey. 'An Analysis of the Course of a Joke's Telling in Conversation.' In *Explorations in the Ethnography of Speaking*. Ed. Richard Bauman and Joel Sherzer. London and New York: Cambridge UP, 1977, 337–53.

Schank, Roger, and R. Abelson. *Scripts, Plans, Goals and Understanding*. Hillsdale, NJ: Lawrence Erlbaum, 1977.

Scholes, Robert. *Structuralism in Literature: An Introduction*. New Haven and London: Yale UP, 1974.

– and Robert Kellogg. *The Nature of the Narrative*. New York: Oxford UP, 1966.

Searle, John. 'The Logical Status of Fictional Discourse.' *New Literary History* 6 (1975): 319–32.

– *Speech Acts*. London: Cambridge UP, 1969.

Shklovsky, Viktor. *Theory of Prose*. 1925. Trans. Benjamin Scher. Elmwood Park, Ill.: Dalkey Archive P, 1990.

Silverman, Kaja. *The Acoustic Mirror*. Bloomington: Indiana UP, 1988.

Smith, Barbara Herrnstein. *On the Margins of Discourse*. Chicago: U of Chicago P, 1978.

Stanzel, Franz. *Typische Formen des Romans*. Göttingen: Vandenhoek & Ruprecht, 1964. *Narrative Situations in the Novel*. Bloomington: Indiana UP, 1971.

– *A Theory of Narrative*. Trans. C. Goedsche. Cambridge: Cambridge UP, 1984.

Sternberg, Meir. 'Proteus in Quotation-Land.' *Poetic* 3.2 (1982): 107–56.

Todorov, Tzvetan. *Grammaire du Décameron*. The Hague: Mouton, 1969.

Tomashevskii, Boris. *Teoriia Literatury*. Leningrad, 1924. (The relevant segment, 'Thematics,' is reprinted in *Russian Formalist Criticism: Four Essays*. Ed. Lee Lemon and Marion Reis. Lincoln: U of Nebraska P, 1965, 61–95.)

Walton, Kendall. *Mimesis as Make-Believe*. Cambridge: Harvard UP, 1990.

White, Hayden. 'The Value of Narrativity in the Representation of Reality.' In *On Narrative*. Ed. W.J.T. Mitchell. Chicago: U of Chicago P, 1980, 1–24.

Woods, John. *The Logic of Fiction*. The Hague: Mouton, 1974.

Young, Katharine Galloway. *Taleworlds and Storyrealms: The Phenomenology of Narrative*. Dordrecht: Martinus Nijhoff, 1987.

Neo-Aristotelian or Chicago School

Neo-Aristotelian is a designation applied to a group of scholars and academic critics associated as students or teachers with the University of Chicago. Active since the 1930s and 1940s, the group established its credentials and group identity in *Critics and Criticism: Ancient and Modern* (1952), a collection of essays. The contributors were *Ronald S. Crane, W.R. Keast, Norman Maclean, *Elder Olson, Bernard Weinberg and Richard McKeon. The first four were professors of English; Weinberg was a professor of Romance languages and literatures; and McKeon was professor of Greek and philosophy. Although both Weinberg and McKeon have considerable reputations as scholars and intellectual historians, the two principal theoretical apologists for the Chicago critics were Crane and Olson. A younger colleague, also at the University of Chicago, *Wayne C. Booth, sometimes identifies himself with the group.

Origins

The Chicago Aristotelians should be seen in the context of the debate among college teachers between 1935 and 1955 concerning the relative emphasis in literary studies of scholarship and criticism, and of the emergence of the *New Criticism in departments of *literature in the U.S.A. Although the Chicago critics consistently denied that they comprised a 'school,' the several members shared a scholarly interest in the history of literary criticism and theory, a deep distrust of New Criticism, especially of the notion that language was the distinguishing characteristic of literature and the sole cause of poetry, and an appreciation of Aristotle's *Poetics* as providing a methodology and a terminology, albeit in outline only, for dealing most appropriately with the multiple causes of poetic wholes.

Crane had initially defended the need for a theoretical and philosophical basis for literary criticism in 'History versus Criticism in the Study of Literature' (1935), but the Chicago critics did not identify Aristotle specifically as the locus for that basis until the 1940s, and even then Aristotle was seen as a starting-point, not as the ultimate authority. The Chi-

cago critics, though never mindlessly doctri-
naire, were unremitting in their attacks on critical orthodoxy in the American academy. They
found their perspective in Aristotle's four
causes of a work of literary art: the efficient
cause (the poet), the final cause (the effect on
the reader), the material cause (the language),
and the formal cause (the mimetic content).
They castigated the New Criticism for its 'critical monism,' for isolating the material cause as
the sole *differentia* for poetry: hence Crane's
seemingly harsh references to *I.A. Richards'
'Pavlovian mythology concerning the behavior
of words,' and to *Cleanth Brooks' 'materialist
monism.' Similar in approach is Keast's dia-
tribe on Robert Heilman's analysis of *King Lear*
which, he argues, makes of the play 'an inferior philosophic dialogue' and reduces it to 'an
epistemological discourse in dialogue form.'
(See *discourse.) Given McKeon's and Weinberg's predilection for dissertations on ancient
and Renaissance philosophy and theories of
poetic and rhetoric and Crane's nearly impene-
trable prose style, it can be argued that the influence of the Chicago Aristotelians derived in
large part from the notoriety of their attacks
on the New Criticism.

Languages of criticism

The Chicago critics agreed that contemporary
literary criticism was a Tower of Babel, lacking
a common vocabulary and devoid of a valid
philosophical basis. They traced this critical
dysfunction to the historical breakdown of an
Aristotelian method which differentiates
among poetic causes in the face of a Platonic
dialectic which employs a single, subsuming
integral cause and conceives of literature in its
relation to other modes of discourse. After
Longinus' work on the sublime, the distinction
between poetics and rhetoric broke down and
poetry, rather than being considered as a class
of mimetic art, became simply another mode
of discourse to be treated in terms extrinsic to
its formal structure. (See *mimesis.) Although
both Aristotelian poetics and Platonic dialectic
are comprehensive systems seeking to account
in a complete way for literature, modern criticism, argued the New Aristotelians, is usually
partial in that one of several causes is assumed
to be the only explanatory cause of poetry. Literary criticism therefore failed to assert itself as
a discipline and became instead a collection of
distinct languages, each dependent upon a

uniquely conceptualized subject-matter and a
particularly determined mode of reasoning. It
follows that the statements made in these various languages often appear to be in contradiction.

The Chicago Aristotelians agree in general
with the classification of criticism into dialectical and literal. Dialectical criticism originated
with Plato, who analysed art in terms of the
object of imitation, the imitation itself, the execution of the imitation, and the correspondence of each to the ideal (a dialectic of things).
Dialectical criticism later shifted to a dialectic
of knowledge and later yet to a dialectic of
processes and relations, where communication
or expression replaces imitation. Opposed to
dialectical criticism are the several modes of
literal criticism, which is concerned with the
causes of a literary work conceived as the
product of the poet's art and genius, as the
producer of certain effects of pleasure or instruction in the reader or audience, or as a formal structure analysable in terms of its parts.

Since the purposes and methods of the various modes of criticism differ so radically,
there should be no surprise to find that statements using similar terminology are often at
odds with one another, or that statements
apparently opposed can at times be in agreement. McKeon summarizes: 'There is doubtless
but one truth in aesthetics as in other disciplines, but many statements of it are found to
be adequate, more are partially satisfactory,
and even more have been defended' (Crane,
ed., *Critics and Criticism* 473).

*Pluralism

The Chicago Aristotelians postulated a solution
to the seemingly contradictory languages of
criticism in the idea of pluralism. They deliberately considered and rejected other possible responses such as radical scepticism, historical
relativism, dogmatism, and synthesisism (syn-
creticism). Pluralism recognized that apparently inconsistent or contradictory positions
may simply represent different answers to different questions. Systems may be compared in
terms of their scope, flexibility, and powers of
explanation, but in an imperfect world a universally satisfactory system is unlikely to be
found. Systems are 'instruments of inquiry and
analysis,' not doctrinal absolutes, and the
choice of system is a practical decision dependent upon the critic's purposes.

The new Aristotelianism

Their conception of pluralism notwithstanding, the Chicago critics were united in their 'strictly pragmatic and non-exclusive commitment' to the methods of Aristotle. They found in Aristotle a spirit of disinterested inquiry and the most flexible and comprehensive method of critical analysis, a method which allowed them to isolate problems peculiar to literature.

All poetic theory, they believed, is a form of causal explanation and such explanation, if it is to be complete and adequate, must take all the causes of poetic structure into account. Nevertheless, it is the structure and form of literary works of art that characterize them, in Aristotelian terms, as the result of 'productive' science, artefacts valued over and above the particular actions that produce them. It is therefore the causes of the formal characteristics of literature that are the proper concerns of poetics. Poetics are concerned specifically with what a poet does as a poet and with the things that distinguish this activity from what the poet might incidentally do as a psychological organism, a moral being, a philosopher, a member of society, and so on. Such issues are more properly treated by other disciplines: the poet's thought and the reader's response are the concerns of psychology; the means and the medium of poetic expression are the concerns of rhetoric; the moral and political implications of literature are the concerns of the 'practical' sciences of ethics and politics. (See *psychoanalytic criticism, *reader-response criticism, *rhetorical theory.) Neo-Aristotelian poetics considers these matters accidental causes of poetic variation and concentrates instead on the internal shaping causes of the poem as made art.

Crane also argued that the literary work thus analysed and defined might be put into its historical setting and a history of literature developed which would trace the interaction of artistic and extra-artistic causes. He outlined this possibility in 'Critical and Historical Principles of Literary History' (reprinted in *The Idea of Humanities* 2: 45–156).

Imitation

Central to the critical thought of the Chicago Aristotelians is the concept of poems as concrete wholes of various kinds. Although they distinguish between imitative (mimetic) and non-imitative (didactic) poetry, recognizing that different principles of construction are involved in each, they follow Aristotle in concentrating almost exclusively on the idea of literary works as imitations of human actions, passions, thought, and characters. Aristotelian mimesis, however, is interpreted in a more sophisticated sense than crude realism. On a practical level, imitation is seen as an artistic analogue of a natural process or form and is, consequently, 'an empirically verifiable hypothesis for distinguishing objects of art from natural things' (*Critics and Criticism* 18). For Crane in particular mimesis is integral to the internal causes of a poem that are central to a proper poetic. In *The Languages of Criticism and the Structure of Poetry* he defines mimesis as 'the internal relationship of form and matter characteristic of the class of objects to which poems, or rather some of them, belong' (81).

Critical procedure

The critic proceeds inductively from the particular concrete whole and infers from its nature the necessary and sufficient internal artistic causes of its form, structure, and effect, that is, infers the process that constitutes poetic art. It is assumed that the aim of the poet's activity is the successful execution of the poem within its confines. We derive pleasure from recognizing and appreciating the poet's success in solving the artistic problems in the making of the work. We comprehend the poem's structure in terms of the problems faced and the reasons for the particular solution employed. Since the critic is confined to the evidence of the poetic work itself, the method can lead to a kind of critical merry-go-round in which the poem's generic kind is defined by the poem itself and therefore the critic is required to assume that the form has been perfectly realized. (See *genre criticism.) In other words, there is no standard by which the critic can judge the poem. The language that Crane uses to discuss this process does little to clarify the problem. He refers to 'the hypothesized form of a poetic work' (*Languages* 182) against which the work itself can presumably be measured, and to the poet's 'primary intuition of form' (*Languages* 146); but he does not make clear exactly how the critic is to comprehend the ideal form except by equating it with the completed poem.

Influence

Historically, the Chicago Aristotelians were among the earliest, most philosophically sophisticated, scholarly, and perceptively analytic of the opponents of the New Criticism. They led the way in attacking the notion of the centrality of language as literary *differentia* and refocused attention on plot and genre. Their critical methodology, however, has had little direct effect on subsequent critical thought. Ironically, the Chicago critics are themselves sometimes seen as practitioners of the New Criticism they deplored. This is especially true of Olson's famous piece on Yeats' 'Sailing to Byzantium.' Crane's essay on *Tom Jones*, on the other hand, expands the Aristotelian idea of plot to make it the controlling factor in a hierarchy of elements that relegates diction to the bottom. Olson's books on tragedy and comedy are learned, acute and commonsensical; but they wisely reflect Aristotle in a general not a specific way. Wayne C. Booth is the only well-known critic to acknowledge the influence of the Chicago Aristotelians, particularly in his *Critical Understanding* (1979), but his work in general suggests that the influence does not extend far. With the waning of the New Criticism, the raison d'être of the Chicago critics disappeared. Their Aristotelianism has been subsumed in other methodologies, although the school's broad influence might be detected in the work of a second generation of scholars including Robert Marsh, Homer B. Goldberg, Walter Davis, Richard Levin, and Austin M. Wright, as well as in the journal *Critical Inquiry*.

RONALD W. VINCE

Primary Sources

Booth, Wayne C. *Critical Understanding: The Powers and Limits of Pluralism*. Chicago: U of Chicago P, 1979.
Crane, R.S., ed. *Critics and Criticism: Ancient and Modern*. Chicago: U of Chicago P, 1952. [Essays by R.S. Crane, W.R. Keast, Norman Maclean, Richard McKeon, Elder Olson, and Bernard Weinberg]
– 'History versus Criticism in the Study of Literature.' *English Journal* 24 (1935): 645–67. Repr. in *The Idea of the Humanities and Other Essays*. Vol. 2. Chicago: U of Chicago P, 1967.
– *The Idea of the Humanities and Other Essays*. 2 vols. Chicago: U of Chicago P, 1967.
– *The Languages of Criticism and the Structure of Poetry*. Toronto: U of Toronto P, 1953.
McKeon, Richard. 'Rhetoric and Poetic in the Philosophy of Aristotle.' In *Aristotle's Poetics and English Literature*. Ed. Elder Olson. Chicago: U of Chicago P, 1965.
Olson, Elder. *On Value Judgments in the Arts and Other Essays*. Chicago: U of Chicago P, 1976.
– 'An Outline of Poetic Theory.' In *Critics and Criticism: Ancient and Modern*. Ed. R.S. Crane. Chicago: U of Chicago P, 1952.
– 'The Poetic Method of Aristotle: Its Powers and Limitations.' In *English Institute Essays, 1952*. New York: Columbia UP, 1952. Repr. in *Aristotle's Poetics and English Literature*. Ed. Elder Olson. Chicago: U of Chicago P, 1965.
– '"Sailing to Byzantium": Prolegomena to a Poetics of the Lyric.' *The University Review* 8 (1942): 209–19.
– *The Theory of Comedy*. Bloomington: Indiana UP, 1968.
– *Tragedy and the Theory of Drama*. Detroit: Wayne State UP, 1961.
Ransom, John Crowe. 'Humanism at Chicago.' *Kenyon Review* 14 (1952): 647–59. Repr. in *Poems and Essays*. New York: Random House, 1955.
Vivas, Eliseo. 'The Neo–Aristotelians of Chicago.' *Sewanee Review* 61 (1953): 136–19. Repr. in *The Artistic Transaction and Essays on the Theory of Literature*. Ed. Eliseo Vivas. Columbus: Ohio State UP, 1963.
Weinberg, Bernard. 'From Aristotle to Pseudo-Aristotle.' In *Aristotle's Poetics and English Literature*. Ed. Elder Olson. Chicago: U of Chicago P, 1965.
– *A History of Literary Criticism in the Italian Renaissance*. 2 vols. Chicago: U of Chicago P, 1961.
Wimsatt, William K. 'The Chicago Critics: The Fallacy of Neoclassic Species.' In *The Verbal Icon: Studies in the Meaning of Poetry*. Ed. William K. Wimsatt. Lexington: U of Kentucky P, 1954.

Secondary Sources

Holloway, John. 'The New and Newer Critics.' In *The Charted Mirror: Literary and Critical Essays*. Ed. John Holloway. London: Routledge and Paul, 1960.
Krieger, Murray. *The New Apologists for Poetry*. Bloomington: Indiana UP, 1956.
Lemon, Lee T. *The Partial Critics*. New York: Oxford UP, 1965.
Wellek, René. *A History of Modern Criticism 1750–1950. Vol. VI: American Criticism, 1900–1950*. New Haven and London: Yale UP, 1986.
– 'Literary Scholarship.' In *American Scholarship in the 20th Century*. Ed. Merle Curti. Cambridge, Mass.: Harvard UP, 1953.

New Criticism

Never a formal school, New Criticism is an approach to *literature extrapolated from the often discrete literary theories and critical practices of British literary critics such as *I.A. Richards, *William Empson and *F.R. Leavis, and American literary critics such as *Cleanth Brooks, *W.K. Wimsatt, Jr., Allen Tate, Richard Palmer Blackmur, Robert Penn Warren, and John Crowe Ransom, whose book, *The New Criticism* (1941), provided the name for the movement. The New Critical sensibility first received articulation in the 1920s in the essays of the Anglo-American poet and critic *T.S. Eliot, and subsequently flourished in the pedagogy of North American and British teachers of English literature. (See also *theory and pedagogy.)

Origin

In half a dozen essays published between 1919 and 1923 – from 'Tradition and the Individual Talent' to 'The Function of Criticism' – Eliot gave voice to a provocative combination of modernist principle and prejudice that was to ground most of the New Critical theory and practice developed during the next 30 years. Against the Romantic celebration of the poem as a record of an exceptional person's personality, Eliot argued that 'honest criticism and sensitive appreciation is directed not upon the poet but upon the poetry' (*Selected Essays* 17). Similarly, against Walter Pater's impressionism, he argued that attention ought to be directed solely upon the poem, and not upon the critic. In short, he disallowed genetic and affective accounts of the work of art (to become known as the intentional and affective fallacies, respectively) because they compromised the integrity of the work of art *as* art. (See *genetic criticism.)

Responding to scientific positivism's claim that science alone produces knowledge, Eliot argued that the study of literature ought to strive towards scientific objectivity. Reacting against positivism, however, he claimed that literature contains a unique knowledge not available to science – a knowledge born of the multiple perspectives on experience that the juxtaposition of words in a work of art allows. By marking such an antiscientific use of language as a fact, and by agreeing that knowledge is a matter of facts, Eliot effected an uneasy rapprochement between positivism and literary criticism.

Beginning with Richards' important works of the 1920s (*The Principles of Literary Criticism, Science and Poetry* and *Practical Criticism*), New Critics developed these arguments into major axioms about the autonomy of the work of art, its resistance to paraphrase, its organic unity, its inevitably ironic use of language, and its welcoming of close reading.

Autonomy of literature

Like the Russian formalists – largely unknown to New Critics before René Wellek's *Theory of Literature* (1949) – New Critics rejected the prevailing tendency to substitute another discipline for the study of literature itself. (See *formalism, Russian.) Richards, one of the first and most influential of the critics associated with New Criticism, warns in *Practical Criticism* (1929) that readers ought to refrain from applying to a poem the external standards of the chemist, the moralist, the logician, or the professor. The poem is an autonomous verbal artefact. What matters, suggests Cleanth Brooks in *The Well Wrought Urn* (1947), is 'what the poem says as a poem' (ix). (New Critics generally regard 'poem' as a synonym for 'literature.')

W.K. Wimsatt, Jr., and Monroe C. Beardsley, in 'The Intentional Fallacy' (1946), argue that the meaning of a poem is internal, determined by what is public linguistic fact – grammar, semantics, syntax – and not by what poets might reveal in conversation, letters or journals concerning their intentions (often the focus of traditional positivistic or historical scholarship). Even the 'I' speaking in a lyric poem is a creation of the poem, they insist, and ought to be regarded as a dramatic persona, and not as the poet. Developing Allen Tate's interest in 'Literature as Knowledge' (1941) in the ontology of a poem, Wimsatt and Beardsley suggest that poetry's obligation is not just to convey knowledge but also to *be* knowledge. Even earlier, in *The World's Body* (1938), John Crowe Ransom argues that meaning is always a function of the poem's full linguistic being, for it exists in a tension between its paraphrasable core and its lively local details – the latter being capable of subverting the former – and so the poem can never be reduced to a static and lifeless concept or intention.

Heresy of paraphrase

Like all New Critics since, Richards recognized
the threat to the autonomy and integrity of the
poem contained in the habit of reducing the
poem to just such a concept or intention – the
habit of paraphrase. In *New Bearings in English
Poetry* (1932), his student F.R. Leavis depre-
ciates the limitation of a poem's self-sufficiency
represented in the shifting of focus away
from the poem to something outside it. Yet
it was Brooks who most notoriously raised the
warning about paraphrase by labelling it a
'heresy.' Brooks acknowledges that paraphrase
is useful as a shorthand in describing a poem
or pointing to certain aspects of it, but he will
not allow that it can ever represent the essential meaning of the poem. It is like a scaffolding that can be erected around a building but
which ought never to be mistaken for the
structure within. For Brooks, as for Ransom,
the structure of the poem is a 'pattern of resolved stresses' (203). This resolution is not a
matter of finding a mean between extremes (a
process that might well lend itself to paraphrase) but rather a dramatic balancing and
harmonizing of attitudes, feelings, ideas, denotations, and connotations. The analogy between drama and poetry is deliberate: conflict
is built into the being of each such that they
become action instead of a *statement about* action. To paraphrase the poem as a statement
about its action, therefore, is to refer to something outside it and so to deny its autonomy.
In its extreme form, the argument against paraphrase leads to R.P. Blackmur's conclusion in
The Double Agent (1935) that, beyond paraphrase, 'the rest, whatever it is, can only be
known, not talked about' (300).

Organic unity

For New Critics, what is known but difficult to
talk about is the experience of the poem as a
unified whole. In this experience, the reader
perceives the poem as a 'total meaning' – a
blending of many meanings and several language tasks simultaneously (*Practical Criticism*
180). Borrowing both from Eliot's concept of
the poet as always forming new wholes and
from Samuel Taylor Coleridge's concept of the
imagination as a vital 'esemplastic' power,
Richards, in *The Principles of Literary Criticism*
(1924), defines the poem as an intricate and
exquisite reconciliation of experience. The

poem, then, is not only an autonomous being,
but also – given that this reconciliation is vital
and dynamic – an organic being, complete
with both internal tensions and structural unity. Each word is a part of the context of interrelated meanings that are fused together as the
poem, and the poem's complex totality also
infuses the individual words and phrases. In
short, the part is a determiner of the meaning
as a whole and the meaning as a whole determines the precise meaning of each part. According to Brooks, then, one appreciates a
poem's significance not just by reading the
poem as a poem, but also by reading 'the
poem ... as a whole' (194).

*Irony

Poetry depends for its being upon irony. A
word used by New Critics in several ways,
irony may be understood as represented by a
continuum of definitions ranged between
'irony is the tendency of any word, but particularly words combined as poetry, to suggest
more than one meaning' and 'irony is the
tendency of a good poem to include a significant number and subtle variety of factors at
odds with what is apparently being said in the
poem.' In 'Pure and Impure Poetry' (1942),
Robert Penn Warren claims that the poet
'proves his vision by submitting it to the fires
of irony – to the drama of his structure' (29).
In other words, as a dramatic tension – as a
balancing and reconciliation – of opposite or
discordant qualities, a poem is ironic in structure. The poem is defined by the ironic competition of meanings within it – the inevitably
ironic aspect of language having been wrought
up to a very high degree in poetry, in which a
structural harmony amongst competing meanings is achieved. 'Irony,' explains Brooks, 'is
the most general term that we have for the
kind of qualification which the various elements in a context receive from the context'
(209).

New Critics are unanimous in celebrating
irony as the essence of poetry. For Ransom,
the effect of the qualification of the poem's
various elements by its context is a construction that is a simulacrum of democracy –
poetry and democracy allowing free exercise
to individual words and citizens, respectively.
For Tate, poetry is a more general simulacrum
of reality: a construction of reality (whatever
it be) in language that, as poetry, is a more

complete mode of utterance than scientific language. For Brooks, the good poem is a simulacrum of the oneness of reality and so the poet's task is 'to unify experience' (212). The instrument for the latter is *paradox – for Brooks, a rhetorical strategy that claims to unify opposites. The instrument for representing the manifold variety in reality is ambiguity, the poet's tribute to the diversity in human experience. The particularly democratic consequence of the irony within the poem is contradiction, the celebration of dissension among the words of a poem as the instrument of a complex whole.

Close reading

Richards' definition in *Practical Criticism* of the four different kinds of meaning possible in a poem (sense, feeling, tone, and intention) invited a new kind of reading: 'All respectable poetry invites close reading' (203). Every New Critic acknowledges the importance of close reading, for the concomitant of New Critical praise of irony, paradox, ambiguity, and complexity in general is the requirement that each word of a poem be scrutinized in detail with regard to all relevant denotations and connotations. Attention to detail is necessary if the whole both depends upon accurate perception of the many-sided parts and also reveals in the parts unsuspected sides illuminated only retrospectively by the whole.

In Britain, notable close readers were F.R. Leavis and William Empson. The name of Leavis' literary magazine, *Scrutiny* (founded 1932), implies the line-by-line examination of literature that he favoured. Empson's *Seven Types of Ambiguity* (1930) demonstrates that word-by-word analysis of poems is necessary in order to appreciate the inevitability and meaningful productivity of ambiguity's omnipresence in poetry. His definition of ambiguity as 'any verbal nuance, however slight, which gives room for alternative reactions to the same piece of language' was very influential upon American New Critics in general, but particularly so upon Cleanth Brooks (1).

Influence

The element of New Critical practice that has established itself most ineradicably is this habit of close reading. Few, if any, contemporary approaches to literature can forgo the careful reading for irony, paradox, ambiguity, and contradiction that New Critics offered as the sine qua non of literary study. The ahistorical element implicit in this relatively exclusive focus upon the poem, its individual words, and their manifold meanings recommended New Criticism to many university teachers of English literature during the 1940s, 1950s, and 1960s, for as universities expanded and gathered within their walls a student population more variously educated than ever before in the history of the university, teachers found it possible to avoid the potentially extensive remedial instruction in history and philosophy that (before the advent of New Criticism) had been assumed to be necessary as preparation for reading literature, for they now had New Criticism's assurance that knowledge of the poem's language and a good dictionary were the only prerequisites for literary study.

Relation to other schools

For the most part, New Criticism enjoyed an antipathetic relation to other schools. It arose as a reaction to Romantic 'great man' theories of poetry, impressionism and similar affective accounts of literature (such as contemporary *reader-response criticism), old historicism (including the history of ideas), Marxism, psychoanalysis, *archetypal criticism – whatever represented the status quo in literary criticism in the early years of the 20th century or whatever offered itself as the rival method of the future. (See also *Marxist criticism, *psychoanalytic theory.)

New Criticism's closest neighbour – though no relation – was Russian formalism. Both approaches to literature celebrate the autonomy of the work, the distinction between poetic and practical language, and the dynamic structure of the poem. Similarly, although unrelated to *structuralism, New Criticism (as well as Russian formalism) shares with this approach to literature a conviction that meaning is determined by a structure within the *text. Richards, by distinguishing between the emotive and the referential function of language, and by defining the latter as irrelevant to poetry, comes closest to the structuralist's lack of interest in the referential function of language. New Criticism, structuralism and Russian formalism are also similar in their ahistorical dimensions, denying, ignoring or de-emphasizing a poem's involvement in the ideological

projects of its place and time. (See also
*ideology.)

*Harold Bloom, in *The Anxiety of Influence*,
implies a debt to New Criticism in his book's
dedication to W.K. Wimsatt, Jr. His use of
Freud's theory of the family romance to focus
attention upon the life-cycle of 'the poet-as-
poet' simultaneously echoes New Criticism's
interest in the poem as poem and subverts
Wimsatt's own attempt to sever the poet from
the poem in 'The Intentional Fallacy' (7). (See
*Sigmund Freud, *anxiety of influence.) Apart
from the intrusion of Freud, Bloom's theories
of anxiety are New Critical in the close reading that enables them and in the assertion of
the autonomy of literature (an enlarging of
New Criticism's assertion of the autonomy of
the poem) that circumscribes them.

New Criticism shares with *deconstruction
in particular and *poststructuralism in general
a determination to expose the falseness of the
calm often presented by the surface of a text.
Each is antipositivistic, happy to acknowledge
the death of the author and alert to the play in
literary language. Yet there is a great gulf fixed
between New Criticism's logocentric claim that
there is nothing outside the text (which functions as a repository of meaning) and deconstruction's non-logocentric claim that there is
nothing outside text (which functions as a de-
ferrer of meaning). (See *logocentrism.)

Implications, difficulties, drawbacks

New Criticism has been under sustained attack
from the beginning, and especially since the
1960s, for a variety of real and/or apparent in-
discretions.

The New Critics' insistence on referring to
literature as poetry immediately prompted the
complaint that New Criticism's theories and
methods were relevant primarily to poetry,
secondarily to drama, and perhaps not at all
to prose fiction. Brooks, increasingly turning
his attention after the triumph of *The Well
Wrought Urn* to New Critical analysis of modern fiction, tacitly concedes the force of such
an objection by implying that a novel's cultural setting (unlike a poem's cultural setting)
is relevant to the study of such a work of art
as a work of art.

Hermeneutic critics complain that New Criticism failed to maintain its antipositivistic
impulse, lapsing into an 'increasingly technological' perspective (Palmer 6). (See *hermeneu-

tics.) In the hands of later practitioners it became too matter-of-fact and down-to-business
in its quest for objectivity – unwittingly realizing the other than humane possibilities implicit in the title of Ransom's early essay about
New Criticism's goals, 'Criticism, Inc.' (*The
World's Body*). *Paul de Man identifies New
Criticism's difficulties in this respect as deriving from its disqualification of intention as
relevant to the analysis of poetry. (See *inten-
tion/intentionality.) The poem begins to look
like a natural object – the thing studied by
science – as opposed to the structurally intentional phenomenon of human consciousness
(the focus of humanistic concern) when the
latter is thrown out with the object of legitimate New Critical suspicion: the *contingent* intention (the poet's state of mind).

Politically, New Criticism is suspect on several counts. Formalisms like New Criticism are
accused of ignoring or denying the political
implications of literature, but they are not regarded as politically innocent themselves. One
can detect in New Criticism's respect for the
unity expressed in a poem a thinly disguised
apology for liberal pluralism, for its 'formalist
interpretation subtends the larger ideology,
satisfying within a narrower domain of practice the longing for consensus, for a metaphysics of the same' (Guillory 194). For Marxists
and feminists, among others, New Criticism's
respect for unity in the poem beyond paraphrase is 'a recipe for political inertia' (Eagleton 50). (See *feminist criticism.) For many,
the academy's embrace of New Criticism's
quest for objectivity in literary study is 'one
more symptom of the university's capitulation
to the capitalist-military-industrial-technologi-
cal complex' (Graff 129).

To review New Criticism's theories and
practices from the point of view of the pragmatic strategies motivating them, however,
rather than from the point of view of the contradictory or inadequate epistemologies and
metaphysics extrapolated from them retrospectively, is to see that New Criticism was neither
the ultimate good nor the ultimate evil that it
was sometimes thought to be. The attention of
New Critics to close reading was not just an
attempt to imitate science's attention to facts,
but also an attempt to counter the academy's
acquiescence in scientific positivism's refusal to
accept the study of literature as a legitimate
way of acquiring knowledge. The objectivity
that New Critics sought was not an empirical

objectivity in league with the technological will to dominate being, but rather a more phenomenological objectivity that would let the poem be what it is. In fact, it is possible to argue that, despite its positivistic and empirical elements, New Criticism participates in the revolt against positivism and empiricism that has characterized 19th- and 20th-century intellectual development and that continues to be a factor in the contemporary theories that oppose New Criticism (Graff 137). (See also *phenomenological criticism.)

DONALD J. CHILDS

Primary Sources

Blackmur, R.P. *The Double Agent.* 1935. Repr. Gloucester, Mass.: Peter Smith, 1962.
Brooks, Cleanth. *The Well Wrought Urn.* New York: Harcourt, Brace, 1947.
Eliot, T.S. *Selected Essays.* 1932. 3rd. enl. ed. London: Faber, 1951.
Empson, William. *Seven Types of Ambiguity.* 1930. 3rd ed. London: Hogarth, 1984.
Leavis, F.R. *New Bearings in English Poetry.* London: Chatto & Windus, 1932.
Ransom, John Crowe. *The New Criticism.* 1941. Repr. Westport, Conn.: Greenwood P, 1979.
– *The World's Body.* 1938. Repr. Baton Rouge: Louisiana State UP, 1968.
Richards, I.A. *Practical Criticism.* 1929. Repr. London: Routledge and Kegan Paul, 1964.
– *The Principles of Literary Criticism.* 1924. Repr. New York: Harcourt, Brace, 1959.
– *Science and Poetry.* New York: Norton, 1926.
Tate, Allen. 'Literature as Knowledge.' In *Reason in Madness.* New York: Putnam, 1941.
Warren, Robert Penn. 'Pure and Impure Poetry.' In *Selected Essays.* New York: Random House, 1958.
Wimsatt, W.K., Jr., and Monroe C. Beardsley. 'The Intentional Fallacy.' In *The Verbal Icon.* Lexington: UP of Kentucky, 1954.

Secondary Sources

Adams, Hazard. *Critical Theory Since Plato.* New York: Harcourt, Brace, Jovanovich, 1971.
Bloom, Harold. *The Anxiety of Influence.* Oxford: Oxford UP, 1973.
Coleridge, Samuel Taylor. *The Collected Works of Samuel Taylor Coleridge 7: Biographia Literaria 1.* Princeton: Princeton UP, 1983.
de Man, Paul. 'Form and Intent in the American New Criticism.' In *Blindness and Insight.* 1971. 2nd rev. ed. Minneapolis: U of Minnesota P, 1983.
Eagleton, Terry. *Literary Theory.* London: Blackwell, 1983.
Graff, Gerald. *Literature Against Itself.* Chicago: U of Chicago P, 1979.
Guillory, John. 'The Ideology of Canon-Formation: T.S. Eliot and Cleanth Brooks.' *Critical Inquiry* 10 (Sept. 1983): 173–98.
Krieger, Murray. *The New Apologists for Poetry.* Minneapolis: U of Minnesota P, 1956.
Lentricchia, Frank. *After the New Criticism.* Chicago: U of Chicago P, 1980.
Palmer, Richard E. *Hermeneutics.* Evanston, Ill.: Northwestern UP, 1969.
Robey, David. 'Anglo-American New Criticism.' In *Modern Literary Theory.* Ed. Ann Jefferson and David Robey. 2nd ed. London: Batsford, 1986.
Thompson, Ewa M. *Russian Formalism and Anglo-American New Criticism.* The Hague: Mouton, 1971.

New Historicism

Emerging in the 1980s in the field of Renaissance studies, 'New Historicism' designates a variety of heterogeneous writing practices shared among its proponents: opposition to the compartmentalization of disciplines; attention to the economic and historical contexts of culture; self-reflexiveness about the critic's implication in the act of writing about culture; and concern with the *intertextuality of texts and discourses. Opposed to orthodox scholarship, New Historicism reconstructs literary texts as historical objects by considering documents and methods previously excluded from traditional literary and aesthetic study. (See also *text, *discourse, *literature.)

As a term for literary and aesthetic analysis, 'New Historicism' was used in 1972 by Wesley Morris to designate a mode of literary criticism derived from German historicists such as Leopold von Ranke and *Wilhelm Dilthey, and American historians such as Vernon L. Parrington and Van Wyck Brooks. Michael McCanles employed the term in 1980 in reference to Renaissance culture, arguing that *semiotics 'may well be on its way to becoming a new historicism' (85). Now in widespread use, 'New Historicism' was most closely associated with Stephen Greenblatt and his associates at the University of California at Berkeley. In the introduction to a special issue of *Genre* in 1982 he remarks: 'The new historicism erodes the firm ground of both criticism and literature. It tends to ask questions about its own methodological assumptions and those of others' (3).

Although Greenblatt has distanced himself from the term (in 1980 he used 'cultural poetics,' a term to which he returned in 1988 and 1989), 'New Historicism' continues to designate identifiable scholarly methods. Its institutional centre is the journal *Representations* (1983–), first edited by Greenblatt with Joel Fineman, Catherine Gallagher, Walter Benn Michaels, and others. Other scholars associated with New Historicism include Jonathan Goldberg, Lisa Jardine, Alan Liu, Arthur Marotti, Louis A. Montrose, and Stephen Orgel.

New Historicists do not form a single school nor do they share an agreed-upon theoretical program: 'crisis not consensus surrounds the New Historicist project'; it is not 'a doctrine' but a consolidation of 'themes, preoccupations, and attitudes' (Veeser xv, xiii). New Historicism simultaneously criticizes and incorporates aspects of traditional and contemporary theory, and in doing so 'offends against a number of orthodoxies in both literary and historical studies' (White 'Comment' 294). While it recoils from the formalism of *New Criticism – with its privileged literary text as a self-contained vessel of immanent meaning – it retains some of the techniques of New Critical close reading. Similarly, while it opposes the ahistorical tendencies of *structuralism and *deconstruction, New Historicism nevertheless uses both to read systems of representation as texts. Structuralism facilitates the analysis of the signifying practices of literary and historical texts as systems, while deconstruction locates the gaps, absences and silences which constitute the traces of the metaphysical assumptions of such textual systems. New Historicists deploy structuralist and deconstructive strategies, particularly those of *Michel Foucault and *Paul de Man, to read human agency as subjectivity established as a text within historically specific sets of social relations. (See *signifying practice.)

New Historicism also positions itself against at least two forms of writing history. First, it rejects the base-superstructure model of vulgar Marxism because of its economism and its unilinear explanation of historical determinations (Williams, 'Base'); nevertheless, it retains the Marxist notion that human beings and their artefacts are 'constructed by social and historical forces' (Howard, 'New Historicism' 15). (See *Marxist criticism.) Second, while not relinquishing notions of periodicity, New Histori-

cism repudiates the history-of-ideas approaches to Renaissance studies of such earlier humanist scholars as Douglas Bush, *C.S. Lewis and E.M.W.Tillyard, who are criticized for their monological and homogeneous constructions of a historical period. (See *totalization, *essentialism.)

Many New Historicists have focused on Tillyard's *The Elizabethan World Picture* as a sustained object of attack and as a locus for establishing the dimensions of their emerging methodologies (Dollimore, 'Introduction'; Howard, 'New Historicism'; Liu, 'Power'; McCanles; Montrose, 'Renaissance'; and Wayne). They criticize at least five aspects of the relations between literature and history in Tillyard's position: (1) the presentation of history as a 'picture,' a 'background order' (Tillyard 8) that is ontologically separated from literature; (2) the view of social reality as a 'collective mind' (Tillyard 17) that is expressed in canonical literary works; (3) the derivation of the 'collective mind' from a notion of unchanging, universal human nature, a human nature that finds its most privileged articulation in the literary *canon, particularly in Shakespeare; (4) the reflection or expression of essentialized aspects of a historical period by these literary masterworks; (5) the assumption that the universal human nature expressed in these masterworks enables them to transcend the 'world picture,' the historical moment of literary production with its complex political implications. (See *universal.)

Opposing such relations between literature and history, New Historicists have elaborated alternative reading practices. They argue that forms of discourse, artistic or documentary, popular or elitist, interact with and are determined by other discourses and institutional practices in a specific historical moment. (See *discourse analysis theory.) They also emphasize rhetoric by relating literary theories of text to the constitution of historical objects as well as to the reading of them. That is, they presuppose both 'the historicity of texts' and 'the textuality of history' (Montrose, 'Renaissance' 8). (See *rhetorical criticism.)

Different emphasis is given to 'historicity' and '*textuality' by each New Historicist. For instance, Montrose stresses 'historicity' in his writing when he examines the convention of Elizabethan pastoral in relation to the landholding practices and the hierarchical relations of the Elizabethan court. The pastoral 'is ubiquitous not only in established literary and pictorial genres, but also in religious, political, and didactic texts ... [It is] a symbolic formation which has been selected and abstracted from a whole way of life that is materially pastoral ... in which animal husbandry is a primary means of production' ('Gentlemen' 420–1). Greenblatt emphasizes 'textuality' when in *Renaissance Self-Fashioning* the '*self' is a literary construct of the text: historical personages are inscribed in documents as textual systems. Whatever the emphasis, however, a New Historicist position does not privilege 'historicity' or 'textuality' to the exclusion of either. Instead, the mediations and interactions between the two are the focus of New Historicist practice. New Historicism, as Greenblatt says, shifts the emphasis from 'the level of reflection' to 'engage questions of dynamic exchange,' exchanges between the context and the text, between the content and the form (*Negotiations* 11). That is, New Historicists relate dialectical tensions between systems of historical referentiality and of literary representation, between a contextual emphasis on literary 'historicity' and a mimetic emphasis on historical 'textuality.' (See *mimesis.)

Refusing to confer literature any transhistorical status, New Historicists read a literary text first as constituted within historically specific literary institutions. (See *literary institution.) Literary texts are related to other texts produced within other historically specific institutions. So Greenblatt writes of the Elizabethan theatre: 'each play is bound up with the theatre's long-term institutional strategy ... An individual play mediates between the mode of theatre, understood in its historical specificity, and elements of society out of which that theatre has been differentiated' (*Negotiations* 14). 'Society,' constructed as a text of interrelated institutions, becomes a system of circulation in which its 'elements' are differentiated between a dominant order and subversive forces. New Historicists construct order as both a literary and political principle, so that correspondences can be drawn between the aesthetic conventions inscribed in the literary text and the hegemonic political forces of society. The drawing of such correspondences emphasizes silenced or marginalized positions that are always contained by the literary and social order; hence the dominant position, conventionally read as a transcendental natural

order, is opened to question: it is taken from the privileged realm of aesthetics and is repoliticized in a new kind of 'play.' The text is made a 'drama' of conflicting forces 'whose "paradigms" dramatize the world as all a Representation of struggle between subversives and dominants' (Liu, 'Local' 96). (See *centre/decentre, *hegemony, *margin, theories of *play/freeplay.)

Different paradigms, drawn by New Historicists from the social sciences but mediated in their adaptation and usage by cultural critics, function to represent these 'struggles,' to establish the mediations and interactions that link the literary to the historical, the textual system to social effect. New Historicists rely on Foucault's 'power,' or 'episteme,' *Raymond Williams' 'culture,' *Louis Althusser's 'ideology,' and *Clifford Geertz's 'thick description' to establish these relations. By choosing one of these paradigms, or by using them in combination, New Historicists specify the historical context in which the literary text is to be read. (See *power, *episteme, *ideology.)

New Historicists typically relate the 'historicity' and 'textuality' of their own subject position by making various self-reflexive, first-person gestures. (Montrose, 'Elizabethan' 323; Greenblatt *Negotiations* 39). In doing so, the writer is placed in a problematic relation to the historical object being written about, since our 'analyses and our understandings necessarily proceed from our own historically, socially and institutionally shaped vantage points; ... the histories we reconstruct are the textual constructs of critics who are, ourselves, historical subjects' (Montrose, 'Poetics' 23). The instability of these relations between past and present is played out in the act of writing: to Montrose, this act of writing the past is an intervention in 'an increasingly technocratic and commodified academy and society' (ibid. 25); it is also the occasion for acute epistemological anxiety, psychologized as a 'desire' to speak with the dead (Greenblatt, *Negotiations* 1–20). Traditional scholarly apparatuses that have facilitated the popular and academic writing of history, together with the metaphysical assumptions that, New Historicists claim, hide both critic and historian behind a mask of objectivity, are thrown open to question by these self-reflexive gestures. But since reading and writing practices are necessarily limited to such apparatuses, they must be used by the New

Historicist, despite their limitations and enforced alignments.

While using these systems of reading and writing, a New Historicist actively works to undermine them. Thus, Princeton's *Collected Coleridge*, for instance, described as 'a magisterial product of the modern critical institution,' 'does not memorially enclose a Romantic Coleridge so much as open up the phenomenon of English Romanticism to the strategies of cultural contention that first composed its complex "history"' (Klancher 86). Similarly, the traditional scholarly conventions of the reference book or the introductory textbook can be opened up 'to the strategies of cultural contention.' This entry on 'New Historicism,' for example, could be read, up until now, as such 'a magisterial product.' Its 'scholarly' apparatus, with its 'neutral' tone, 'objective' presentation of factual history contained in a linear narrative moving from origin to definition and application, and its assumption of mastery over a field of knowledge assumed to be limited, is a convention of knowledge production in 'the modern critical institution.' In rewriting such an entry to question these conventions, a New Historicist would relate the reference book or introductory textbook as historically constituted genres: such epistemological projects are derived from the Enlightenment; they give an articulated order to knowledge, as outlined with respect to taxonomies and classification by Foucault in *The Order of Things*. The rewritten entry would historicize its own textuality by relating the Enlightenment paradigm to specific institutional moments of the objectification of knowledge, such as the compilation of dictionaries and encyclopedias (for example, in Diderot's *Encyclopédie* [1751–80], Johnson's *Dictionary* [1755], and the *Britannica* [1771]).

A New Historicist rewriting of this entry would also self-consciously situate the position of the writer using the conventions of objective knowledge within a highly diverse field of knowledge production at a particular historic conjuncture. Denying the possibility of any such objectivity, a New Historicist constructs such mastery as a rhetorical vantage point which functions to displace any attention towards how that field of knowledge is constituted, in the process closing off areas of contestation. A New Historicist would read the pedagogical need and commercial marketability for this introduction to 'Contemporary Theory,' representing diverse critical practices as

objective information, in terms of closure and legitimation. Such collapsing of points of difference into authoritative definition constitutes a containment of subversive critical strategies and a silencing of diverse theoretical positions within the North American academy. But the necessary use of institutional conventions implicates the writer of an entry on 'New Historicism' in a double bind in the institutional practices of mastery, where the use of scholarly conventions is simultaneously legitimated and undermined.

Opponents of New Historicism have directed their attacks upon its apparent lack of interest in the history of its constituting label, as well as on its evasion of or implication in an overt political agenda. As for the first issue, a focus upon the configuration 'New' and 'Historicism' brings charges of 'unacknowledged debt' (Thomas 'New Historicism' 192) against the New Historicists, charges that are related to the failure to ground their concepts historically. In marking out their differences with their intellectual predecessors, New Historicists have tended to concentrate on post-structuralist methodologies, ignoring connections with previous traditions of historiography. (See *poststructuralism.) Predecessors of New Historicism include members of the Warburg-Courtauld Institutes in London (such as *E.H. Gombrich, Erwin Panofsky and Frances Yates) who influenced scholars such as Roy Strong and Stephen Orgel in examining the relations between culture and power. 'Historicism' is a 19th- and early-20th-century German concept 'based on the assumption that past events and situations are unique and non-repeatable and therefore cannot be understood in universal terms but only in terms of their own particular contexts' (Ritter 183). A failure to acknowledge these relations and explore their implications has led Brook Thomas to dispute 'the new historicism's claim to newness' ('New Historicism' 188).

In its 'newness,' the New Historicism may also be related to the 'New History,' a historiography associated in America with James Harvey Robinson and Charles Beard. Since the 1960s the New History has been associated with certain progressive historians in the U.S.A., as well as with the Annales school in France and certain Marxist historians in Britain. The New History is opposed to orthodox historiography because of its concentration on political and diplomatic events, and its reliance on narrative as the essential means of articulating the past. To construct their New History, these historians have derived both their subjects and their methodologies from the social sciences (Gross, Himmelfarb). Indicating problems of documentation and, more important, 'the profound problems posed by the notion of the historical "event,"' Leeds Barroll has argued that 'some of the confusions plaguing the new historicism' are related to their failure to consider 'the concerns raised – to cite only a few examples – by Fernand Braudel as long ago as his 1950 survey of the state of post-Rankean historiography, or more recently by Lawrence Stone' (464, 441, 462). Furthermore, he questions the assertion of some New Historicists that literature may be politically subversive in specific historical moments. Examining the nature of the evidence they adduce, he cites three instances where 'the epistemic problems posed by the question of "historical evidence" are so great ... that there is no way that we can know the "true" story' (453). Finally, he criticizes their 'pre-Marxian dependence on the historical roles of dominant personalities' such as Elizabeth I and James I (463). Another critic, David Harris Sacks criticizes the 'language of "subversion" and "containment"' of some New Historicists as being an 'overtly mechanistic interpretation of cultural politics,' one 'now commonplace in literary studies' (477–8).

In the second place, critics of New Historicism launch their attacks upon its politics from both the political left and right. Attacks from the left level several charges. The self-conscious positioning of the writer often collapses onto a psychological category of 'desire,' converting the political contestation of intertextual systems into a personal drama of anxiety and fulfilment (Gallagher). (See *desire.) The New Historicist pragmatism, a refusal to systematize theoretical presuppositions, is an evasion of an explicit political position, 'nothing but a breast-beating' (Spivak 285). New Historicists are particularly open to such attacks when their evasion is compared to *cultural materialism. British cultural materialism, while sharing many of the presuppositions of New Historicism, has consistently directed its theoretical agenda in accord with a leftist political agenda. While New Historicism tends to remain within the problematic of representation, cultural materialists move from systems of representation

to specific historical referents and their political effects as a way of grounding their own political position (Belsey; Dollimore, 1984; Dollimore and Sinfield; Sinfield 1982; Wayne). Furthermore, the New Historicists have also been criticized for not acknowledging their debt – theoretical and methodological – to feminists (Newton 153). (See *feminist criticism.)

'New Historicism' is often used by the political right within the American academy, and frequently by the mass media and government agencies, as a stalking-horse for attacks on poststructuralist and politically explicit methodologies in the humanities (Brooks; D'Souza; Lehman; Pechter). In these attacks, some of New Historicism's methodological borrowings from the left, particularly from Marxism, allow polemicists of the right to revive 'Red-scare' tactics (Veeser xi) and 'cold war rhetoric' (Thomas New Historicism vi) to attack positions and practices which to them threaten to undermine traditionalist conceptions of history and literature. 'New Historicism' has functioned in the popular press as a means of crudely bashing the political left for 'the study of books not because of their moral or esthetic value but because they permit the professor to advance a political, often Marxist agenda' (Lehman 62). Such attacks in both the academy and the press have prompted many responses (Gallagher 45; Holstun 203–7; Montrose 'Poetics' 15–17; Porter 743–51).

Despite these attacks, the popularity of the New Historicism has grown throughout the academy. Although it originated in Renaissance studies, its methods and practices are increasingly employed in almost every period of literary studies from the 16th century to the present in North American departments of English, History, Anthropology, and Art History, and in other disciplinary and interdisciplinary fields. This rapid spread has signalled the increasing acceptance of its methods and presuppositions. Such success also signals a certain irony: the increasing acceptance of New Historicism is at once a mark of its accommodation to the conventions of the academy and an undermining of its foundational gesture of opposing academic orthodoxies. (See also *materialist criticism.)

VICTOR SHEA

Primary Sources

Althusser, Louis. 'Ideology and Ideological State Apparatuses.' In *Lenin and Philosophy and Other Essays*. Trans. Ben Brewster. London: Monthly Review P, 1971, 127–86.

Barroll, Leeds. 'A New History for Shakespeare and His Time.' *Shakespeare Quarterly* 39 (1988): 441–64.

Belsey, Catherine. *The Subject of Tragedy: Identity and Difference in Renaissance Drama.* London: Methuen, 1985.

Brooks, David. 'From Western Lit to Westerns as Lit.' *Wall Street Journal* 2 Feb. 1988: 24.

Cohen, Walter. 'Political Criticism of Shakespeare.' In *Shakespeare Reproduced: The Text in History and Ideology*. Ed. J.E. Howard and M.F. O'Connor. New York: Methuen, 1987, 18–46.

Dollimore, Jonathan. 'Introduction: Shakespeare, Cultural Materialism and the New Historicism.' In *Political Shakespeare: New Essays in Cultural Materialism*, 2–18 (see below).

– *Radical Tragedy: Religion, Ideology, and Power in the Drama of Shakespeare and His Contemporaries.* U of Chicago P, 1984.

– and Alan Sinfield, eds. *Political Shakespeare: New Essays in Cultural Materialism*. Ed. J. Dollimore and A. Sinfield. Ithaca: Cornell UP, 1985.

Drakakis, John, ed. *Alternative Shakespeares.* London: Methuen, 1985.

D'Souza, Dinesh. 'Illiberal Education.' *The Atlantic* March 1991: 51–79.

Fineman, Joel. *Shakespeare's Perjured Eye: The Function of Poetic Subjectivity in the Sonnets.* Berkeley: U of California P, 1986.

Foucault, Michel. *The Order of Things: An Archaeology of the Human Sciences.* New York: Vintage, 1973.

Gallagher, Catherine. 'Marxism and the New Historicism.' In *The New Historicism*. Ed. H. Aram Veeser. New York: Routledge, 1989, 37–48.

Geertz, Clifford. *The Interpretation of Cultures.* New York: Basic Books, 1973.

– *Local Knowledge: Further Essays in Interpretive Anthropology.* New York: Basic Books, 1983.

Goldberg, Jonathan. *James I and the Politics of Literature: Jonson, Shakespeare, Donne, and Their Contemporaries.* Baltimore: Johns Hopkins UP, 1983.

– 'The Politics of Renaissance Literature: A Review Essay.' *English Literary History* 49 (1982): 514–42.

Greenblatt, Stephen. 'The Forms of Power and the Power of Forms in the Renaissance.' *Genre* (1982): 1–4.

– 'Murdering Peasants: Status, Genre, and the Representation of Rebellion.' *Representations* 1 (1983): 1–29.

– *Renaissance Self-Fashioning: From More to Shakespeare.* Chicago: U of Chicago P, 1980.

– *Shakespearean Negotiations: The Circulation of Social Energy in Renaissance England.* Berkeley: U of California P, 1988.

– 'Towards a Poetics of Culture.' In *The New Historicism*. Ed. H. Aram Veeser. New York: Routledge, 1989, 1–14.

Gross, David. '"The New History": A Note of Reappraisal.' *History and Theory* 12 (1974): 53–8.

Hawkes, Terence. 'Shakespeare and New Critical Approaches.' In *The Cambridge Companion to Shakespeare Studies.* Cambridge: Cambridge UP, 1986.

Himmelfarb, Gertrude. *The New History and the Old.* Cambridge, Mass.: Harvard UP, 1987.

Holstun, James. 'Ranting at the New Historicism.' *English Literary Renaissance* 19 (1989): 189–226.

Howard, Jean. 'The New Historicism in Renaissance Studies.' *English Literary Renaissance* 16 (1986): 13–43.

– and Marion O'Connor, eds. *Shakespeare Reproduced: The Text in History and Ideology.* New York: Methuen, 1987.

Iggers, Georg G. *The German Conception of History: The National Tradition of Historical Thought from Herder to the Present.* Middletown, Conn.: Wesleyan UP, 1968.

Jardine, Lisa. *Still Harping on Daughters: Women and Drama in the Age of Shakespeare.* Brighton: Harvester, 1983.

Klancher, John. 'English Romanticism and Cultural Production.' In *The New Historicism*. Ed. H. Aram Veeser. New York: Routledge, 1989, 77–88.

LaCapra, Dominic. *History and Criticism.* Ithaca: Cornell UP, 1985.

– 'Ideology and Critique in Dickens's *Bleak House*.' *Representations* 6 (1984): 116–23.

– *Rethinking Intellectual History: Texts, Contexts, Language.* Ithaca: Cornell UP, 1983.

Lehman, David. 'Deconstructing de Man's Life: An Academic Idol Falls into Disgrace.' *Newsweek* 15 Feb. 1988: 62.

Levinson, Marjorie. *Wordsworth's Great Period Poems: Four Essays.* Cambridge: Cambridge UP, 1986.

Litvak, Joseph. 'Back to the Future: A Review-Article on the New Historicism, Deconstruction, and the 19th Century.' *Texas Studies in Literature and Language* 30 (1988): 120–49.

Liu, Alan. 'Local Transcendence: Cultural Criticism, Postmodernism, and the Romanticism of Detail.' *Representations* 32 (1990): 75–113.

– 'The Power of Formalism: The New Historicism.' *English Literary History* 56 (1989): 721–72.

– *Wordsworth: The Sense of History.* Stanford: Stanford UP, 1989.

– 'Wordsworth and Subversion, 1793–1804.' *Yale Journal of Criticism* 2 (1989): 55–100.

Marotti, Arthur F. *John Donne, Coterie Poet.* Madison: U of Wisconsin P, 1986.

McCanles, Michael. 'The Authentic Discourse of the Renaissance.' *Diacritics* 10 (1980): 77–87.

Michaels, Walter Benn. *Gold Standard and the Logic of Naturalism: American Literature at the Turn of the Century.* Berkeley: U of California P, 1987.

Miller, D.A. 'Discipline in Different Voices: Bureaucracy, Police, Family, and *Bleak House.*' *Representations* 1 (1983): 58–9.

– 'Under Capricorn.' *Representations* 6 (1984): 123–9.

Montrose, Louis Adrian. 'Celebration and Insinuation: Sir Philip Sidney and the Motives of Elizabethan Courtship.' *Renaissance Drama* n.s. 8 (1977): 3–35.

– '"Eliza, Queen of Shepheardes," and the Pastoral of Power.' *English Literary Renaissance* 10 (1980): 153–82.

– 'The Elizabethan Subject and the Spenserian Text.' *Literary Theory/Renaissance Texts.* Ed. Patricia Parker and David Quint. Baltimore: Johns Hopkins UP, 1986.

– 'Gifts and Reasons: The Contexts of Peele's *Araygnement of Paris.*' *English Literary History* 47 (1980): 433–61.

– 'Of Gentlemen and Shepherds: The Politics of Elizabethan Pastoral Form.' *English Literary History* 50 (1983): 415–59.

– '"The Place of a Brother" in *As You Like It*: Social Process and Comic Form.' *Shakespeare Quarterly* 32 (1981): 28–54.

– 'The Poetics and Politics of Culture.' In *The New Historicism.* Ed. H. Aram Veeser. New York: Routledge, 1989, 15–37.

– 'The Purpose of Playing: Reflections on a Shakespearean Anthropology.' *Helios* 7 (1980): 51–74.

– 'Renaissance in Literary Studies and the Subject of History.' *English Literary Renaissance* 16 (1986): 5–12.

– '"Shaping Fantasies": Figurations of Gender and Power in Elizabethan Culture.' *Representations* 2 (1983): 61–94.

Morris, Wesley. *Towards a New Historicism.* Princeton: Princeton UP, 1972.

Mullaney, Stephen. *The Place of the Stage: License, Play, and Power in Renaissance England.* Chicago: U of Chicago P, 1988.

Newton, Judith Lowder. 'History as Usual? Feminism and the "New Historicism."' In *The New Historicism.* Ed. H. Aram Veeser. New York: Routledge, 1989, 152–67.

Orgel, Stephen. *The Illusion of Power: Political Theater in the English Renaissance.* Berkeley: U of California P, 1975.

Parker, Patricia, and Geoffrey Hartman, eds. *Shakespeare and the Question of Theory.* New York: Methuen, 1985.

Pechter, Edward. 'The New Historicism and Its Discontents: Politicizing Renaissance Drama.' *PMLA* 102 (1987): 292–303.

Porter, Carolyn. 'Are We Being Historical Yet?' *South Atlantic Quarterly* 87 (1988): 743–86.

Ritter, Harry. 'Historicism, Historism.' In *Dictionary of Concepts in History.* New York: Greenwood, 1986, 183–8.

Sacks, David Harris. 'Searching for "Culture" in the English Renaissance.' *Shakespeare Quarterly* 39 (1988): 465–88.

Simpson, David. *Wordsworth's Historical Imagination: The Poetry of Displacement.* New York: Methuen, 1987.

Sinfield, Alan. *Literature in Protestant England 1560–1660.* London: Methuen, 1982.

– 'Power and Ideology: An Outline Theory and Sidney's *Arcadia.*' *English Literary History* 52 (1985): 259–77.

Spivak, Gayatri Chakravorti. 'The New Historicism: Political Commitment and the Postmodern Critic.' In *The New Historicism.* Ed. H. Aram Veeser. New York: Routledge, 1989, 227–93.

Thomas, Brook. 'The New Historicism and Other Old-fashioned Topics.' In *The New Historicism.* Ed. H. Aram Veeser. New York: Routledge, 1989, 182–204.

– *The New Historicism and Other Old-fashioned Topics.* Princeton: Princeton UP, 1991.

Tillyard, E.M.W. *The Elizabethan World Picture.* London: Cox and Wyman, 1943.

Veeser, H. Aram, ed. *The New Historicism.* New York: Routledge, 1989.

Wayne, Don E. 'Power, Politics, and the Shakespearean Text: Recent Criticism in Britain and the United States.' In *Shakespeare Reproduced.* Ed. J.E. Howard and M.F. O'Connor, 47–67.

White, Hayden. *The Content of the Form: Narrative Discourse and Historical Representation.* Baltimore: Johns Hopkins UP, 1987.

– 'Historicism, History, and the Figurative Imagination.' *History and Theory* 14 (1975): 48–67.

– *Metahistory: The Historical Imagination in 19th Century Europe.* Baltimore: Johns Hopkins UP, 1973.

– 'New Historicism: A Comment.' In *The New Historicism.* Ed. H. Aram Veeser. New York: Routledge, 1989, 293–303.

– *Tropics of Discourse.* Baltimore: Johns Hopkins UP, 1978.

Williams, Raymond. 'Base and Superstructure in Marxist Cultural Theory.' In *Problems in Materialism and Culture.* London: New Left Books, 1980, 31–50.

– *Marxism and Literature.* Oxford: Oxford UP, 1977.

Nitra School

Theoretical research which led to the establishment of the Nitra School of Literary Criticism can be traced back to the pre-war structuralist activity of some Slovak scholars and critics in the 1930s and early 1940s, the most prominent of whom were Mikuláš Bakoš, Igor

Hrušovsky, Milan Pišut, Michal Považan, and Jaroslav Dubnický. Some Russian emigrés such as Alexander Isachenko and Peter Bogatyrev were also part of the group. Its centre was Bratislava, the capital of Slovakia. Although representatives of Slovak *structuralism worked in the shadow of their more prominent Czech colleagues, their achievements were significant to the discipline. Before the Second World War, the Prague and Bratislava groups remained in close cooperation until they were both repressed by the Marxist orthodoxy imposed on Czechoslovakian intellectuals after the communist takeover in 1948. (See also *Prague School, *Marxist criticism.)

The revival of the structuralist tradition in Slovakia in the early 1960s thanks primarily to the research conducted by František Miko and, somewhat later, by Anton Popovič, and was institutionalized in 1967 by the establishment of the Cabinet of Literary Communication and Experimental Methodology at the Pedagogical Faculty in Nitra, a small town in south-western Slovakia. Apart from Miko and Popovič, other scholars (Jan Kopal, Peter Zajac, Peter Liba, Imrich Deneš, Viliam Obert, and Tibor Zsilka) made important contributions to the development of this theoretical literary centre. The Soviet invasion of 1968 and the subsequent ideological squeeze compelled the group to introduce some tactical concessions in order to satisfy the new regime: it declared that its theory was based on Marxism and constituted a concrete implementation of Marxist ideas in modern literary scholarship.

Nitra critics begin with the assumption that *literature is a specific process of communication which contains two basic aspects: the literary work of art (Miko) and its reception (Popovič). A literary work is always rooted in a given social and historical situation; it grows out of a certain literary climate and inherits in its structure a diversity of past literary experience and the richness of cultural tradition in general. Thus, a literary work of art is the result of a number of factors which remain in constant interaction. At the same time, the work functions as an author's message to readers and, as such, generates metacommunication (messages about the message).

The strategic principle of literary communication is based on the balancing advantage of production over reception. (See *communication theory.) If the level of both partners of communication were equal, communication would be unnecessary; the receiver would know as much as the author and consequently the information would be redundant. But the advantage of the producer (author) over the receiver cannot be too great because the literary work of art would become incomprehensible and lose its communicative power. However, such a situation may arise. It usually happens when a new literary current defies and tries to break old aesthetic conventions of a preceding and 'automatized' period or when a single writer is far ahead of his contemporaries in what he or she writes. For example, some early texts of the 20th century literary avant-garde were rejected by the reading public as 'incomprehensible' but later accepted as significant. Theoreticians from Nitra defined the 'incomprehensible' texts as texts which were 'prematurely' realized. (See also *text.)

The system of literary communication is based on two intersecting axes: communicative and contextual. The immediate purpose of the first is to transmit information: it has a practical, 'operative' task to perform and therefore Miko calls it 'communicative operativity' or simply 'operativity.' Operativity functions on the horizontal level of author-text-receiver and can be defined as the global communicative relation between the performer (in this case the author) and the receiver of the text. The contextual axis reveals a vertical correlation between tradition (both national and international), text and external reality and contains everything that can be defined as expression, image or 'iconicity.' Miko defines iconicity as the most general global relation between the text and the referential reality. It is in iconicity that the structure of the literary work resides.

The literary work of art

Miko defines the nature of the literary work by referring to two concepts: style and expressive system (or expressive categories). Style is the expression of the author's perception of depicted reality, a realization of his or her artistic attitudes and his or her image of the world. It lends a functional and semiotic unity to the text. (See *semiotics, *semiosis.) Style always exists as *the* style of the text's content. While content is the founding category, as its formal expression style constitutes the text's existential aspect: content exists as a result of style. Consequently, style has a system of expressive categories whose occurrence in the literary work is constant but their marked aesthetic function varies from one text to another because they remain in a dynamic correlation, depending on the role they are 'assigned' to play in a given text. A text is not generated but 'programmed'; Miko calls his model of expressive categories not a generator but a 'programme' of the text. All expressive categories specified by Miko are concentrated along the two basic axes of operativity and iconicity and each has two major opposing poles: if operativity is implemented through the struggle of its two aspects called 'subjectivity' and 'sociativity,' then iconicity is characterized by the contrast between 'conceptuality' and 'experientiality.' Subjectivity implies the aspect of the performer (the author) who promotes his own world-view; sociativity represents the attitude of the recipient who is conditioned by a social context and may or may not resist the realization of the sender's communicative aim. The process of communication rests on the tension between these two opposites. In the realm of iconicity the difference between conceptuality and experientiality is the difference between literary expression (experientiality) and technical, scientific expression (conceptuality). Experiential expression presupposes a reference to reality. Conceptual expression is aimed at generalization, elimination of the concrete and unique aspect; it is directed at formulating concepts, definitions and theories. (See Miko's *The Programme of the Text* 1978.)

The act of reception: the process of literary metacommunication

Once the literary work of art is published it assumes a life of its own and undergoes a multiplicity of transformations. Popovič discovered this 'law' by investigating the essence of artistic translation. (See *translation, theories of.) Each translation has a preceding text written in another language. Whenever a translator renders a text into a new language she or he performs a metatextual operation which provides a particular interpretation of the original. Such an operation is even more distinctly at work in a review, which serves both to explain and to interpret. Thus, metacommunication always involves two texts: 'prototext' and 'secondary' texts.

A text can relate to another, preceding text in a number of ways: (1) a metatext is linked to one concrete prototext; (2) a metatext is linked to a group of prototexts in a rigorous (in relation, for example, to the preceding epoch) or liberal (towards texts of older periods) way; and (3) intertextual relations can be neutralizing when the prototext produces very similar metatextual variants, as is particularly true of folklore's oral poetry. (See *intertextuality.)

The application of the concept of metatexts is particularly useful in the analysis of literary tradition. Basically, metatexts relate to the past in a twofold way: they project either affirmative or controversial (neglecting, rejecting) attitudes of artists, the latter proving to be the most innovative and generating new aesthetic values.

Metatextual activity does not happen in a vacuum but occurs in a certain literary environment. Metacommunication or metatexts originating from the primary communication can be arranged in a particular system which Nitra scholars call the 'system of literary education.' Literary communication does not confine itself only to spontaneous and direct contact between the reader and the text; it may be regulated by intermediary texts that sometimes serve as substitutes for the original (for example, a reader reads a digest of the *Odyssey* and not the *Odyssey* itself). There are four principal functions of literary education: (1) instructional: the system of literary education serves the reader as the only definite source of ideological, cultural, social, and literary norms; (2) supervisory: the receiver masters the *code of 'the original,' becomes acquainted with original works through the popularizing role of the texts which belong to the system of literary education, thus controlling, through the agency of literary education, the quality of reception of original texts; (3) didactic: the readers are prepared for the reception of 'high' art; and (4) equalizing: the system of literary education serves as a regulatory factor, becoming 'an intermediary language' between 'high' and 'popular' literature; it functions whenever there is a need to equalize existing 'gulfs' between them.

On the whole, the theory of literary communication as formulated by Nitra scholars displays a close affinity with the Polish theoretical postulates and is considered by some scholars (for example, Walter Kroll) to be an offshoot of Warsaw structuralism. (See *structuralism, Polish.) However, it should be mentioned that Nitra theoreticians are, to a great extent, also indebted to the theoretical studies of the late Czech structuralist Jiři Levý, particularly in the area of translation theory and literary communication.

EDWARD MOŻEJKO

Primary Sources

Miko, F. *Estetika vyrazu: Teoria vyrazu a styl.* Bratislava: SPN, 1969.
– *Od epiky k lyrike.* Bratislava: Tatran, 1973.
– *The Programme of the Text.* Nitra: Pedagogická Fakulta, 1978.
– and Popovič, A. *Tvorba a recepcia.* Bratislava: Tatran, 1978.
Popovic, A. *Dictionary for the Analysis of Literary Translation.* Edmonton: Department of Comparative Literature, U of Alberta P, 1976.
– *Teória umeleckého prekladu.* Bratislava: Tatran, 1970.
– *Štrukturalizmus v slovenskej vede.* Martin: Matica slovenska, 1970.
– *Teória metatextov.* Nitra: Pedagogická Fakulta, 1974.

Secondary Sources

Doležel, L. *Occidental Poetics. Tradition and Progress.* Lincoln/London: U of Nebraska P, 1990.
Levý, J. *Die Literarische Übersetzung: Theorie einer Kunstgattung.* Frankfurt a/M: Athenäum, 1969.
– 'Teorie informace a literarni proces.' In *Česká literatura* 11 (1963): 281–308.
Kroll, W. 'Poljska znanost o književnosti u kontekstu novije književnoteorijske diskusije.' In *Umjetnost riječi. Književna komunikacija. Antologija poljske znanosti o književnosti* 2–4 (1974): 95–122. The entire issue of this periodical is devoted to the question of literary communication as developed by Polish theoreticians.
Możejko, E. 'Slovak Theory of Literary Communication: Notes on the Nitra School of Literary Criticism.' In *PTL: A Journal for Descriptive Poetics and Theory of Literature* 4 (1979): 371–84.

Performance criticism

Performance criticism treats the written *text of a play as a script to be realized in performance. As a method of analysis, performance criticism is based on the assumption that plays were meant to be performed; consequently they ought to be studied in the light of the theatrical conditions for which they were originally written and in which they have been or are currently staged. Taking into consideration the work of contemporary theatre professionals and informed by their own experience as producers, directors, and actors of plays, critics such as *Raymond Williams, John L. Styan, Bernard Beckerman, and John Russell Brown set forth the key points of performance criticism as a distinctive approach to the analysis of plays, and thereby set in motion an ongoing debate about its theory and practice.

Historical developments

If modern performance criticism can be said to have a symbolic birthplace, it would be William Poel's production in 1881 of the first quarto of *Hamlet* in 'Elizabethan' dress on a bare 'Elizabethan' stage and with the lines delivered in the quickly paced 'Elizabethan' rhythms. This experimental production reveals directly how important historical research is to performance criticism. Indirectly, the antiquarian character of Poel's work suggests the further need to study plays as translated into the stage idioms of other periods, including those of the present.

Moments of performance criticism can be found throughout the history of literary criticism. In the *Ion* (ca. 390 BC), Plato's Socrates plays the part of the performance critic when he focuses attention on the two essentials of the theatre: a performer (the rhapsodist, Ion) and an audience. Socrates asks Ion to recall what happens during a successful performance in order to confirm that just as the muse inspires or possesses the poet with a particular sequence of emotions, so the poet's work inspires those emotions in the rhapsodist, and the rhapsodist prompts them in the audience. In Plato's *Republic* (ca. 370 BC), Socrates argues a similar case. Because dramatic poets foster emotion rather than reason in their audiences, they are to be banned from the ideal republic. Plato's use of performance is noteworthy in two respects. First, Plato turns to performances to clinch some philosophical arguments, and thus implies that texts can be performed in only one way. (In part this view may flow from the high degree of stylization in classical Greek drama.) Second, Plato reveals an antitheatrical prejudice. He argues that manipulative and financially self-serving imitative poets debase the tastes and character of their audiences by providing transitory and unwarranted emotional experiences rather than stimulating the authentic responses of philo-sophical logic.

Aristotle shares some aspects of Plato's prej-udices and develops them in a particularly im-portant way in the *Poetics* (335–322 BC) when he judges 'spectacle' to be the least significant element of tragedy, for 'it is the least artistic [part], and connected least with the art of po-etry. For the power of Tragedy, we may be sure, is felt even apart from representation and actors. Besides, the production of spectacular effects depends more on the art of the stage machinist than on that of the poet' (Kaplan 29). As the actors and technicians who collab-orate in a production of a play are denigrated (in part on social grounds), so the 'literary' ele-ments of a play – plot, character, ideas, diction – are celebrated as the essentials of the play-wright's craft. What is crucial here is the affir-mation that the essence of a play exists prior to and independent of its performance. How-ever, Aristotle is far more attentive than Plato to the performance aspects of plays, as his dis-cussion of the history of Greek theatre, his ac-count of the constituent parts of tragedy as staged, and his theory of the cathartic effect of drama on audiences suggest. His theory of tragedy draws on a knowledge of the plays as performed; indeed he confirms key points of his argument by reference to performance, as when he defends Euripides' plot by saying, 'The best proof is that on the stage and in dra-matic competition, such plays, if well worked out, are the most tragic in effect' (Kaplan 34).

The derogation of performance recurs again and again in the history of criticism: for exam-ple, in the Renaissance, Sir Philip Sidney at-tends to staging in order to expose the absurdity of English plays in performance; in the 19th century, Charles Lamb concluded that *King Lear* was 'essentially impossible to be rep-resented on a stage;' in the 20th century, some advocates of the *New Criticism subordinated the performative aspects of a script to the ver-bal elements of the text. Modern performance criticism is in part a refutation of this abiding antitheatrical prejudice, which is also chal-lenged by broader cultural developments, such as the quest for a national theatre in England, the growth of amateur theatre groups, the in-stitutionalization of the study of theatre arts in programs at colleges and universities, and the radical reconsideration of the art of theatre by influential playwrights from Henrik Ibsen to Harold Pinter.

Performance critics regularly situate them-selves in opposition to the dominant critical methodology of the mid-20th century, the New Criticism. The page versus the stage; readers versus seers; the text versus the script; silent solitude versus public hearing; readerly considerations versus actorly ones; 'slit-eyed analysis' versus 'wide-eyed playgoing' – such dichotomies reveal how heavily performance criticism has depended upon New Criticism in order to distinguish itself from New Criticism. Appropriating drama as a literary form, the New Criticism treated plays as if they were elaborate poems, verbal icons of which all the elements could be perceived simultaneously. Verbal subtleties, patterns of imagery, ironic structures, themes and their variations – the means by which a play was thought to gener-ate its meanings – were judged to be the legiti-mate basis for understanding drama. But the same forces that dislodged the Aristotelian de-valuation of performance also challenged the adequacy of New Critical methods as applied to plays. Increasingly scholars, literary critics and theorists not only saw professional pro-ductions of plays but also produced, directed or acted, especially within the universities. Such experiences confirmed for them the accu-racy of what Raymond Williams observed in *Drama in Performance*: 'In much contemporary thinking, a separation between literature and theatre is constantly assumed; yet the drama is, or can be, both literature and theatre, not the one at the expense of the other, but each *because* of the other' (4). (See also *literature.)

Major concepts and concerns

Radical forms of performance criticism assume that plays exist only in performance. In the main, however, the theory and practice of performance criticism still involves an investi-gation of text/performance relations. Perform-ance, not literary criticism, it is argued, is in-dispensable as the means by which to 'ap-preciate fully' the 'true nature' of a play, to bring a dead text to life, or to get, as John L. Styan affirms in *The Shakespeare Revolution*, 'the genuine Shakespeare experience' (1). This argument, taken in a slightly different direc-tion, makes the performance of plays the only sure way of testing and controlling the inter-pretations of them: what's playable is what's valid. These uses of performance assume that plays, by definition, are written to be performed – to be spoken aloud by actors, to be given visual form in theatres and to progress though time in front of audiences.

Attending to performance is the rule rather than the exception in the criticism of contemporary drama. Studies of individual authors draw on the experience of seeing many productions of the playwright's works. To this research (playgoing) are added interviews with directors, designers, actors, and technicians; conversations with the playwright; study of the script(s) for cuts, additions, and rearrangements of material, or annotations by any member of the company; examination of theatres, stages, sets, costumes, props, lighting, scores, and sound effects. Critics can take advantage of the opportunity to act as 'observers' of the rehearsal process. Some track the development of a production as it goes through reading and rehearsal, into 'previews,' 'tryouts,' or 'showcasing,' and then into its run, during which its reception by reviewers and audiences becomes an important consideration. Given the accessibility of many of the people who collaborate in the production of a play, given also the availability of the material effects of their work, performance criticism of contemporary theatre makes the process by which a play takes shape in a theatre and produces its impact upon an audience, rather than the product, the central concern of the critical enquiry.

To study plays in this way is to study them in light of the theatrical conditions for which they were written. Performance criticism of plays of earlier periods strives to do the same. This endeavour, exemplified by Bernard Beckerman's *Shakespeare at the Globe*, depends upon various kinds of historical research: studies of the composition and the tastes of audiences, of their behaviour when at the theatre, even of their physical disposition in the playhouse; studies of actors and acting styles, of the organization and operation of professional companies and of the conventions governing the production of speech, gesture, comportment, and movement on stage; studies of the theatrical spaces – playhouses and their stages – which allowed for the realization in performance of some of the possibilities of the script while precluding the staging of others. The discovery in 1989 of the foundations of the Rose Theatre provides a good illustration of the importance of such historical research. The discovery prompted intense excitement among performance critics, who saw in the wooden piles, erosion lines and hazelnuts hard data by which to test hypothetical performances. Such knowledge of theatrical conditions provides the basis for one basic form of performance criticism, that of readers whose work with plays involves a deliberate, sustained act of the imagination to envision the play, a verbal construct, vocalized and enacted on a stage and in the presence of an audience. But many performance critics go beyond a reading of this sort, however informed, sensitive and imaginative it may be. 'Reconstructing' the stage for which a play was first written or 'workshopping' a script under contemporary conditions, they use performance as a method of research; teachers and students at the University of Toronto have regularly explored early English drama in this way, building 'medieval' pageant wagons for the York Cycle in 1977 and producing *The Castle of Perseverance* 'in the round' in accordance with the contemporary manuscript stage diagram.

Because a play's investigation of its own premises as a play establishes one of the theatrical conditions governing its writing and production, metatheatre or metadrama are important concerns of performance criticism. Metadrama, 'theatre pieces about life seen as already theatricalized' (Abel 60), blurs the sharp borderline between 'real' life and the 'artificial' representation of life within the form of the play. This self-reflexivity becomes apparent when the action includes a play within the play, or characters in search of an author, or a character who plays a part with an awareness that he or she is playing a part. Metadramatic works may go further, self-consciously exploring language and speech, genres and theatrical conventions, or the ways in which dramatic art is understood to relate to truth and social order. The metadramatic concerns may influence the whole performance style of a production because metadrama challenges naturalistic representation on stage. Instead, such plays, by devices such as ritualized forms of action, sparse sets, or audience members situated so that they can see others in the audience, establish that the experience of theatre is an experience of artifice. Metadramatic elements of a play may provide specific help to an actor who, playing the part of a character who knows that he or she is playing a part, may learn how to play that part.

Acting is a central concern of performance

criticism. For example, John Russell Brown, in *Discovering Shakespeare*, made 'the art of the actor' the very basis of 'this new guide to Shakespeare's plays' (2). The script is of course crucial to the actor's art but an actor (or an actorly performance critic) has to work with it in ways different from those of a literary critic. Many of the topics that appear in 'literary' criticism of the drama – for example, diction and metaphor, versification and syntax, rhythms and structures of entire speeches – reappear in performance criticism but in the latter these elements are noteworthy as clues to breathing, stress, tempo, gesture, and physical comportment. The language directs the actor whose speeches – more important, whose speaking – and whose physical activity create character. Critics who take the actor's art as the basis of dramatic analysis also address themselves to the 'subtext' of a role, so called by the actor-director-teacher Konstantin Sergeivich Stanislavsky, and referring to the 'inner vision' or 'inner essence' (quoted in Thompson and Thompson 79) of a character. This inner life, often understood in terms of psychological background, unconscious motives, or unstated thoughts, finds expression in and through the words, the speaking, the bodily presence, and physical activity of the actor. Enacting the plays, observing rehearsals and interviewing actors about their roles have become well-established ways by which performance critics try to appreciate the actor's art.

Performance critics regularly scrutinize the text of a play for whatever directives it gives about what is to be seen on stage. This may include the presence and the movement of the actors, along with many other features of a show, such as stylization, decor, sets, properties, costumes, lighting, blocking, and 'special effects.' The study of explicit stage directions is obviously a part of this enterprise; many indications of stage business, however, are implicit, embedded in the speeches or in the interplay among characters. Students of drama, seeing a play for the first time, often comment on how the performance clarified the text through some bit of business. Matching deeds to words is only one way – and that the simplest and most prescriptive – of understanding the relation of action and script. Building characters in collaboration with others on stage may require responses to the text or interpretations of it that take the form of action, action for which there are no precise directives in the script. What is seen on stage has also been considered to be important as 'stage imagery.' To think of the visual effects of a production in this way is to link physical features of a performance to verbal patterns in the text, as halting Jack Falstaff's walk becomes a part of the disease imagery of *2 Henry IV* or Prospero's costume changes become part of patterns of clothing imagery in *The Tempest*.

Attending to what's said, done and seen as an actor might or for an imaginary performance throws into relief conspicuously absent words, actions or visual effects. A good deal of work has been done on such moments in plays, especially on the silences required of actors. The silence may be that of an observer, whose presence is nevertheless seen and felt, and, as a result, complicates the impact of the scene on the audience. Even more important are silences that occur when a verbal reaction would seem to be in order; Isabella's failure to reply to the Duke's marriage proposal in the finale of *Measure for Measure* is a famous instance. For performance criticism, such moments – dramatic cruces – are important because they reveal the openness of the script, its richness of playable possibilities. While a silence may allow for many coherent performances, each cast producing the moment has to make a decision about how to perform that moment. Whatever decision is made will be revealing, shedding light on the actor's conception of the character, the cast's understanding of the interaction among characters at that moment, and the whole production's interpretation of the play. Silences are but one kind of dramatic crux; other elements of the script may be no less crucial. Performance depends upon myriad decisions: in what sense is a word to be taken? to whom is a line to be directed? with what import is an action to be performed? For example, did Gertrude in the finale of *Hamlet* commit suicide and, if so, how must all her earlier scenes be played to establish a through-line to that ultimate decision?

That dramatic scripts are tractable and contain a rich variety of performance possibilities becomes clear when critics study either the performance history of a particular work or many modern productions of it. Playgoing alerts performance critics to opportunities inherent in a text of a play that they may have failed to see in their imaginative study of it. The study of productions of a play in different historical periods and different cultural milieux sheds light both on the peculiar signifying details of each production and on the cultural pressures shaping each one. In performance criticism of Shakespeare and to a lesser degree in that of other 'canonized' playwrights, performance history serves an additional purpose – to establish the authenticity of their plays. John Styan describes criticism that checks text against performance and vice versa as a process by which criticism adjusts and corrects itself. Criticism can accommodate the new qualities of a play, new qualities demonstrated in a new performance, 'until at some unseen vanishing point the focus is felt to be exact and the play defined' (Styan 1977, 72). More recent performance critics address themselves to the same issue but without Styan's sense of some ultimate definition. As Marvin and Ruth Thompson explain, authenticity is a condition not of being but of becoming: 'As is true of a cantata or major choral work by Bach, so with a play by Shakespeare: one is never quite finished with it. Such a work has its own organic, living growth, and as each age interprets it, successive performances of a play take us a bit closer to the larger – if forever elusive – authentic'(15).

Impact and influence

Performance criticism has had a major impact upon the editing of texts of plays. This is especially clear in Shakespeare studies, almost every aspect of which has felt the effects of performance criticism so that 'Shakespeare the Poet' has been dislodged by 'Shakespeare the Playwright.' More specifically, editors of scholarly texts have increasingly followed the advice of Harley Granville Barker, that it is 'unwise to decide upon any disputed passage without seeing it *in action*, without canvassing all its dramatic possibilities' (1921). The metamorphosis of editions of Shakespeare's plays reveals how strong an impact performance criticism has made: 19th-century texts were overwhelmed by scholarly annotation, much of it of a philological character; contemporary texts set forth cleanly the lines of the play (sometimes – witness the Oxford University Press *William Shakespeare: A Textual Companion* – relegating the scholarly apparatus to a separate volume) and employ annotations to direct attention to performances, past and possible. A performance history has become a standard

part of the introduction or the general commentary in an edition of a play. Analogous developments have occurred in the study of every period in the history of drama, so that 'performance texts' of works from *Everyman* to *Equus* are now available. Indeed, in the study of contemporary drama, performances often produce the texts, because previews, tryouts, or the run itself may result in major revisions to the script with which the company worked at the outset.

Performance criticism, because of its emphasis upon acting as a physiological process, also represents a challenge to some other critical approaches, such as *speech act theory and *semiotics. As an utterance, a dramatic speech act is produced by a human body and it is to be heard by an audience even in the farthest reaches of a theatre. Similarly, the body of an actor, even one perfectly still and silent on stage, remains one of the signifying elements of a play in performance. From the perspective of performance criticism, to disembody the 'voice,' to treat the actor's body as a vortex of signs, or to remove speech acts from the physiological processes by which they are made is to oversimplify. Fundamental to an anatomy of performance criticism is the criticism of anatomy.

Difficulties and directions

As research, performance criticism has serious difficulties because of the evanescence of plays and the subjectivity of audiences. For many productions, documentary evidence is simply not available; this is obviously the case for plays of other historical periods but, given the understandable indifference of theatre professionals to the development and maintenance of archives, this is also true for many contemporary shows. For many other productions, the kinds of resources of information that are extant are limited in their usefulness: photographs of productions are often 'staged' for publicity purposes and do not capture a moment in the actual performance; promptbooks record masses of peripheral to-ing and fro-ing but often fail to register the revealing look or gesture or stage business; and published reviews or archival videotapes usually record the performance on one day and from one point or view. But no two performances are quite the same, nor are any two audiences, so that the experience of the reviewer (on whose work the performance critic relies) or of the play-going critic may well be conditioned by the excitement of an opening night, the energy of a warm audience, or the torpor of a cold one. Apart from the need for raw data about performances and for great care in the analysis of that data, performance criticism needs a psychology of audience response if the 'wide-eyed playgoer' is to be trusted as the arbiter of what a play, a play that only reveals fully its true essence in performance, means.

As writing, performance criticism is bedevilled by the difficulty of writing about dramatic moments. To note how a line in a Shakespearean play requires an action is simple enough. To describe the interplay among actors in performance, actors who speak of the process as one in which the effort of each one to be 'honest,' 'truthful' or 'generous' vitalizes their performances, is a task of an altogether different order. The problem of how to write about a moment in a performance is compounded when one takes into consideration other signifying elements: mise en scène, lighting, costume, stylization, music, rehearsal techniques, the place of the moment in the overall rhythm of the work, and the audience tastes and reactions. Richard Schechner defines 'performance' as 'the whole constellation of events, most of them passing unnoticed, that take place in/among both performers and audience from the time the first spectator enters the field of the performance – the precinct where the theater takes place – to the time the last spectator leaves' (72). Clearly, to develop a *discourse to come to terms with so many elements, in so many possible complex relationships to one another, is a tall order.

As theory, performance criticism faces a number of challenges. As performance critics need to situate themselves historically and ideologically, so the rise to power of performance criticism as an approach needs to be studied as a part of modern and postmodern culture. (See *postmodernism.) Performance criticism also needs to move beyond the impasse created by the text/performance dichotomies, as William Worthen and Harry Berger have suggested and tried to do. Such oppositions privilege either the written play or the performed play by affirming that one or the other represents the 'true nature' of the work. To argue that the performed play has this status requires that acting be de-historicized so that the essence of a work be accessible to modern actors as it

was to the original performers of the script. As Worthen argues, 'Our access to the text is always through its performance, a performance continually taking place offstage – as reading, education, advertising, criticism, and so on – before any stage performance is conceived' (455). This points to the need of performance critics to attend to the status and the use of theatre as a body of signifying practices that confirms ideologically prescribed ideas of character, realism and significance.

C.E. McGEE

Primary Sources

Abel, Lionel. *Metatheatre: A New View of Dramatic Form*. New York: Hill and Wang, 1963.

Beckerman, Bernard. *Dynamics of Drama: Theory and Method of Analysis*. New York: Knopf, 1970.

– *Shakespeare at the Globe, 1599–1609*. New York: Macmillan, 1962.

Berger, Harry, Jr. *Imaginary Audition: Shakespeare on Stage and Page*. Berkeley, Los Angeles, and London: U of California P, 1989.

Bradbrook, M.C. *Elizabethan Stage Conditions: A Study of Their Place in the Interpretation of Shakespeare's Plays*. Cambridge: Cambridge UP, 1932.

Brook, Peter. *The Empty Space*. London: MacGibbon and Kee, 1968; Harmondsworth: Penguin, 1979.

Brown, John Russell. *Discovering Shakespeare: A New Guide to the Plays*. New York: Columbia UP, 1981.

– *Shakespeare's Plays in Performance*. New York: Edward Arnold, 1967.

Craig, Gordon. *On the Art of the Theatre*. London: Mercury Books, 1962.

Dawson, Anthony B. 'The Impasse over the Stage.' *English Literary Renaissance* 21 (Autumn 1991): 309–27.

– *Indirections: Shakespeare and the Art of Illusion*. Toronto, Buffalo, London: U of Toronto P, 1978.

– *Watching Shakespeare: A Playgoers' Guide*. New York: St. Martin's P, 1988.

Dessen, Alan C. *Elizabethan Stage Conventions and Modern Interpreters*. Cambridge: Cambridge UP, 1984.

Goetsch, Paul, ed. *English Dramatic Theories: 20th Century*. English Texts Series 13. Ed. Theo Stemmler. Tübingen: Max Niemeyer Verlag, 1972.

Goldman, Michael. *Acting and Action in Shakespearean Tragedy*. Princeton: Princeton UP, 1985.

– *The Actor's Freedom: Toward a Theory of Drama*. New York: Viking P, 1975.

Granville-Barker, Harley. *Prefaces to Shakespeare*. 2 vols. Princeton: Princeton UP, 1946–7.

– 'Shakespeare: A Standard Text.' *The Times Literary Supplement* 996 (17 Feb. 1921), 107.

Hobgood, Burnet M., ed. *Master Teachers of Theatre: Observations on Teaching Theatre by Nine American Masters*. Carbondale: Southern Illinois UP, 1988.

Howard, Jean. E. *Shakespeare's Art of Orchestration: Stage Technique and Audience Response.* Urbana and Chicago: U of Illinois P, 1984.

Innes, C.D. *Holy Theatre: Ritual and the Avant-Garde.* Cambridge: Cambridge UP, 1981.

– ed. *Directors in Perspective* (series). Cambridge: Cambridge UP, 1982–91.

Kaplan, Charles, and William Anderson, eds. *Criticism: Major Statements.* 3rd ed. New York: St. Martin's P, 1991.

Lamb, Charles. 'On the Tragedies of Shakespeare, Considered in Reference to their Fitness for Stage Representation.' 1818. In *The Works of Charles and Mary Lamb.* Ed. E.V. Lucas. 7 vols. London: Methuen, 1903–5. Vol. 1: *Miscellaneous Prose 1798–1834* (1903), 97, 111.

Lusardi, James, and June Schlueter. *Reading Shakespeare in Performance: King Lear.* London and Toronto: Associated UPs, 1991.

Mazer, Cary M. *Shakespeare Refashioned: Elizabethean Plays on Edwardian Stages.* Theatre and Dramatic Studies 5. Ann Arbor: UMI Research P, 1981.

McGuire, Philip C. *Speechless Dialect: Shakespeare's Open Silences.* Berkeley: U of California P, 1985.

Schechner, Richard. *Performance Theory.* Rev. and exp. ed. New York and London: Routledge, 1988.

Slater, Ann Pasternak. *Shakespeare the Director.* Totawa, NJ: Barnes and Noble Books, 1982.

Styan, J.L. *Drama, Stage, and Audience.* London: Cambridge UP, 1975.

– *Modern Drama in Theory and Practice.* 3 vols. Cambridge: Cambridge UP, 1981.

– *The Shakespeare Revolution: Criticism and Performance in the 20th Century.* Cambridge: Cambridge UP, 1977.

Szondi, Peter. *Theory of the Modern Drama: A Critical Edition.* Ed. and trans. Michael Hays. Theory and History of Literature 29. Minneapolis: U of Minnesota P, 1987.

Taylor, Gary. *Moment by Moment by Shakespeare.* London and Basingstoke: Macmillan, 1985.

Thompson, Marvin, and Ruth Thompson. *Shakespeare and the Sense of Performance: Essays in the Tradition of Performance Criticism in Honor of Bernard Beckerman.* London and Toronto: Associated UPs, 1989.

Wickham, Glynne. *Early English Stages, 1300–1600.* 3 vols. London: Routledge and Kegan Paul, 1959–81.

Williams, Raymond. *Drama in Performance.* Rev. and exp. ed. Harmondsworth: Penguin, 1972.

– *Drama in a Dramatised Society: An Inaugural Lecture.* Cambridge: Cambridge UP, 1975.

Worthen, W.B. 'Deeper Meanings and Theatrical Technique: The Rhetoric of Performance Criticism.' *Shakespeare Quarterly* 40 (Winter 1989): 441–55.

Phenomenological criticism

Phenomenology, a philosophical method founded by *Edmund Husserl in the first two decades of the 20th century, seeks to provide a descriptive analysis of the objective world as it appears to the subject. Rather than engaging in metaphysical questions, phenomenology describes 'phenomena,' in the Greek sense of the term, as the appearance of things. Central to this philosophy is the notion that the world of appearing things is governed, ordered and given meaning by consciousness itself. Later students of Husserl's thought, notably *Martin Heidegger and *Maurice Merleau-Ponty, extended the phenomenological method to other contexts.

A critical application of phenomenology to *literature was developed early in the 20th century by *Roman Ingarden. In addition, the literary criticism of the *Geneva School, of American critics such as the early *J. Hillis Miller, and of Paul Brodtkorb applies the phenomenological method to the study of individual works.

Philosophical origins

While Hegel and Kant used the term 'phenomenology,' Edmund Husserl is the architect of the phenomenological movement in *Logische Untersuchungen* [*Logical Investigations* 1900], *Ideen zur einer reinen Phänomenologie und phänomenologischen Philosophie* [*Ideas: General Introduction to Pure Phenomenology* 1913], and *Die Krisis der europäischen Wissenschaften und die transzendentale Phänomenologie* [*The Crisis of European Sciences and Transcendental Phenomenology* 1936].

Husserl's phenomenology distinguishes consciousness (a faculty of the thinking and perceiving subject) from the world 'out there.' In phenomenology the interrelationship of subject and object constitutes consciousness itself. Thus, there is no such thing as an act of consciousness without an object, nor can there be an object without a subject to apprehend it. (See *subject/object.)

Husserl believed that early-20th-century thought had reached an impasse. The science of the day naively neglected the role of the perceiving subject's influence on his knowledge of the world. On the other hand, the risk of subjectivity could lead to a psychologistic study of mental processes. Husserl's alternative was a philosophy that attempted to reconcile thought and world through a description of the transcendental structures of human consciousness. Husserl contended that phenomenology should be a science of consciousness, a programmatic description of how self and world interact. Because of this emphasis on immediate experience, the phenomenologist generally avoids metaphysical issues.

Concept of the life-world

Husserl's phenomenology favours an analysis of the constructs of everyday consciousness, the *Lebenswelt* [life-world] of the perceiving subject. The life-world is the frame of subjectivity through which the individual apprehends and interprets the external world. But such a description requires that the 'natural attitude' by which we confront daily experience be suspended in the face of a heightened reflection that opens the way for a true philosophy of human experience. Locked into the natural attitude, we remain unaware of the structures of consciousness which underlie day-to-day existence.

To reveal those structures of consciousness, Husserl proposes another level of reflection called 'phenomenological reduction.' Without undermining the natural attitude, phenomenological reduction 'brackets' it, leaving intact all of its attributes, throwing into relief both consciousness itself and the object it apprehends. In short, the common-sense realities of the natural attitude are placed in abeyance to make way for an analysis of the 'givenness' to consciousness of those realities. Rather than merely assuming that the world exists for us in the ways that it does, we now confront the world 'as-meant,' as intended by the structures of consciousness.

This revelation of 'essences' of consciousness Husserl terms 'eidetic reduction.' By essences, Husserl does not mean any entity above and beyond our experience of the world. Rather, the structures of consciousness are universal, irrespective of historical epoch or cultural boundaries which might otherwise divide consciousness into relative and variant properties. Phenomenological reduction turns our attention away from the social, historical and cultural determinants of the ego to a transcendental domain of consciousness.

Intentionality

Another tenet of Husserl's phenomenology is intentionality. (See *intention/intentionality.) Though phenomenological reduction emphasizes the essence of consciousness, the objects of the world are also aspects given to consciousness by the experience of the world. The phenomenologist considers intentional things as they appear; they are resident *in* and constituted *by* consciousness. It is important here to distinguish Husserl's use of the term 'phenomena' from Kant's. The phenomenologist does not suggest that phenomena are mere appearances as opposed to things as they 'really' are. Husserl regards phenomena as real insofar as they are intended by consciousness and are aspects of the world. In short, phenomena are always apprehended 'as-meant' by the subject perceiving them. Intentionality is a central doctrine in phenomenology for it situates philosophy in the 'lived experience' of the individual subject.

By advancing these concepts, Husserl believed that he was breaking away from classical idealism and basing philosophical inquiry on reliable knowledge of the world. Yet he also avoided the positivism that he disdained by demanding that phenomenology be a description of subjectivity, rather than a structure of metaphysical judgments.

Some argue, however, that the method of Husserlian phenomenology belies its theory and that it is an analysis fraught with jargon and classifications which obscure the simplistic quality of both his analysis of consciousness and the philosophy of experience. Others have concluded that Husserlian phenomenology gives the subject side of consciousness priority over the world of objects 'as-meant.' Such critics have asked whether subjectivity, according to Husserl's analysis, does not merely impose itself on the world without due regard for the effect of those objects on the subject.

Heidegger's 'existential' phenomenology

The philosophy of Martin Heidegger is a response to Husserl. Dedicated to Husserl, *Sein und Zeit* [*Being and Time* 1927], Heidegger's most comprehensive work, is an ambitious attempt to define existence from a human perspective. Heidegger's later period, characterized by works such as *Einfuhrung in die*

Metaphysik [*An Introduction to Metaphysics* 1935], *Der Ursprung des Kunstwerkes* [*The Origin of the Work of Art* 1935] and 'Die Frage nach der Technik' ['The Question Concerning Technology' 1954], shows the philosopher's turn from a description of how man inhabits the world of experience to a difficult description of the phenomenological and existential ground of art, language and technology.

Heidegger shares with Husserl an antimetaphysical bias. For both, the task of philosophy is to understand reality as it confronts the self in the context of experience. For both, the starting-point of phenomenological investigation is the world as it shows itself to us within the confines of our knowledge. Unlike Husserl, Heidegger denies that philosophy can be totally without presupposition.

Husserl's phenomenology is 'essentialist,' since the foundations of his method of inquiry are those 'essences' which render consciousness universal. (See *essentialism, *universal.) By contrast, Heidegger's 'existentialist' direction attempts to place subject and object in the experience of human existence. He resists the temptation to view the world in abstract mental images. For Heidegger, the world is not so much a set of entities 'out there' as part of a complex of our own existence, a living existence that we can never fully objectify. At the same time, he accedes that the world is not passively absorbed into our own endeavours in life. Rather, he acknowledges that the world resists our attempts to interpret and master it, despite the fact that it constitutes our subjective existence.

For Heidegger phenomenology is a method that emerges from *Befindlichkeit* [attunement]. Husserl, by contrast, aims for a philosophy founded on a 'presuppositionless' description of consciousness, irrespective of whatever position we might take in the natural attitude.

Dasein

Heidegger also differs from Husserl in focusing on the quiddities of the individual's 'being-open,' making Being rather than consciousness the pivotal event of philosophical investigation. Yet his phenomenological method retains some of Husserl's analysis of the *Lebenswelt*. Everydayness is that condition of habit and convention in which we move to accomplish the mundane tasks of life. If Husserl looked to

phenomenology as a non-metaphysical inquiry, Heidegger attempted to historicize existence by locating modern thought in a *post*-metaphysical epoch. For Heidegger the aim of phenomenology is the recovery of this dwelling with Being through the experiential and temporal character of *Dasein*.

Dasein [being-there] is a uniquely human existence which is engaged in the rest of the world in the way that, for example, the existence of trees, animals and rocks is not. *Dasein* projects itself forward in time to a point of possibility. An individual is never a finished product: human existence is, by definition, open-ended. Another property of *Dasein* is its 'thrownness,' by which Heidegger means that existence for every individual involves being thrown into a world whose structure had long since been established. This condition forces us to come to terms with the origins of a tradition of which we are already a part. The meaning of our existence is tied, to some extent at least, to the objective meaning of that tradition. These are the circumstances out of which *Dasein* projects itself into a future.

Heidegger asserts that the individual must seize the possibility for self-fulfilment and engagement in the world both with and against the thrownness that defines the origins of its existence. Language is one domain in which this destiny is accomplished. For Heidegger, language is more than the mere instrument of human communication. It is the very dimension of existence. In effect, it is language that brings the world to the existent. Heidegger imbues language with a high degree of historicality, often using etymological word-play to reinforce his point that *Dasein* is part of that tradition extending back to the pre-Socratics. His view of language also restates his antimetaphysical bias. Metaphysics is itself an imperious language which has obscured the relationship between the individual and Being. Heidegger's own words convey the concreteness with which he views language: 'Language is the house of Being. In its home man dwells. Those who think and those who create with words are the guardians of this house.' Language, like the tradition into which man is born, pre-exists the individual person. It is the site where Truth 'unconceals' itself. In Heidegger's phenomenology, truth is the aletheia or unconcealment of Being.

Later in his career in writings concerning the

Phenomenological criticism

nature of art, such as *The Origin of the Work of Art* and parts of *An Introduction to Metaphysics*, Heidegger connects un-concealment with the endeavours of the poet and even with the poetic creations of the natural world. *Poiesis* is a bringing forth, or a creation of the world in a primordial event of language. Heidegger calls the thought of the pre-Socratic philosophers, Parmenides and Heraclitus particularly, 'poetic thinking.' All true art, like all authentic thinking, is for Heidegger more than mere communication; it is, rather, an 'opening up' of the artist to origins. Some commentators think that Heidegger's concern with *poiesis* in these later works is not phenomenological at all. Through his career, the focus in his writing shifts from the human experience of Being to the revelation of Being in historical language.

Merleau-Ponty's phenomenology

The concern with the placement of the subject in a historical language carries over from Heidegger to Maurice Merleau-Ponty. His major works include *Sens et non-sens* (1948), *Phénoménologie de la perception* (1945), *Le visible et l'invisible* (1964), and *Signes* (1960). Merleau-Ponty's philosophy asserts a radical interconnection of the subject and object in a redefinition of Husserl's notion of intentionality. All consciousness according to this definition is a unified subject-object relation. Merleau-Ponty's phenomenology, while respecting the import of Husserl's phenomenological reduction, has none of Husserl's classifications.

Less abstract than Husserl's precise categories of consciousness, Merleau-Ponty's philosophy is more closely related to the tactile experience of the world. Reminiscent of Heidegger, Merleau-Ponty sees the subject as a nexus of historical language and self-identity rather than as a centre of consciousness. He poses questions concerning the origins of history in human consciousness and, like the later Heidegger, he asserts that man inhabits the fields of language and history. Both are aspects of human consciousness. Language in Merleau-Ponty's phenomenology is an intentional act. The word is more than a conveyor of meaning; it is an incarnation of meaning in a kind of flesh, or tissue. The symbolic quality of Merleau-Ponty's own language demonstrates the gestural quality he attributes to

words which point not to mental images but to the world itself. Merleau-Ponty therefore rejects the notion that language is a prison, a system of images referring only to other images.

For Merleau-Ponty the boundary between the body and the world is an ambiguous one. Consequently, his restatement of the phenomenological interpenetration of subject and object leads him to reject the idea that another person beyond the subject is a mere object. For Merleau-Ponty, 'the other-person-as-object is nothing but an insincere modality of others, just as absolute subjectivity is nothing but an abstract notion of myself.'

Influences on literary criticism

Several key concepts of phenomenology have been applied to literary theory and practice. As might be expected, the literary applications are as diverse as their philosophical origins.

Roman Ingarden in his *Das literarische Kunstwerk* [*The Literary Work of Art* 1965] undertakes a description of the literary work of art in theoretical terms. Ingarden applies Husserlian principles to a programmatic analysis of the ways that we experience literature as a unique event in consciousness. Just as Husserl seeks to throw into relief the universal essences of consciousness, so Ingarden attempts to reveal the universal, 'essential anatomy' of the work that underlies our experience of reading. Starting from a stance resembling Husserl's natural attitude, Ingarden's method brackets what we take for granted in the reading experience. Ingarden contends that if we do not assume a phenomenological attitude toward the texts we read, we are bound to confront in them only what we already know. (See *text.)

Husserl resists idealism on the one hand and empiricism on the other. Similarly, Ingarden resists an understanding of the work as either a purely ideal object and merely a physical entity. The alternative to this dualism is to treat the literary work of art as an intentional object, constituted in consciousness through the act of reading.

The result is Ingarden's distinction of four interrelated 'strata' which constitute the literary work of art as an 'imaginational object' in the consciousness of the reader. These are (1) word sounds and phonetic formation; (2)

meaning units of various orders; (3) multiple aspects of the world as seen from various points of view; and (4) represented objects in the literary work. Through the interplay of these strata, the work is concretized in consciousness. Such *concretization breaks down the traditional split between the subjectivity of our interpretation of a work of literature and the objectivity of the book's existence in the form of printed marks and pages.

Geneva School

While Roman Ingarden is highly abstract, the Geneva School, a group of European literary critics, has put phenomenological principles into critical practice. Generally included in the Geneva School are Marcel Raymond, Albert Beguin, *Georges Poulet, Jean-Pierre Richard, and *Jean Starobinski. Though not homogeneous, the Geneva School works from common assumptions regarding the ontology of the literary work of art. True to the phenomenologist's aim of founding a science of consciousness, Geneva School critics seek to describe the precise ways in which the world is given to the consciousness of reader and writer through the agency of literary language.

Geneva School criticism also draws on the phenomenological assertion that the world, as it presents itself to the consciousness observing it, engenders philosophical inquiry. Generally, these critics address the 'experiential patterns' of the author *in* the work, and suspend consideration of cultural, biographical and historical influences. In essence, phenomenological literary criticism explicates the relationship between the world depicted in the text and the writer's imagination. The experiential patterns that concern the phenomenological critic emerge in the texture of literary language and in its special capacity for structuring the self-world relationship that is unique to the author.

Of prime concern to the Geneva critic is not so much which contents of the artist's world are reconstituted in the literary text, but how such a reconstitution of objects is accomplished by the phenomenological ego constructed by the text. Another distinctive feature of the Geneva School is the working assumption that the entire corpus – not a single text – must be examined in order to trace the development of the author's characteristic self-world relationship.

The experiential patterns given over to, and enlivened by, the specialized language of literature assume various forms in phenomenological criticism. Georges Poulet's emphasis on practical criticism is evident in his *Etudes sur le temps humain* (1953), where he discusses the self-world relationship unique to each author. In accordance with Geneva School methodology, Poulet rarely analyses the writer behind the art; instead, his subject is the literary language that is the fabric of the writer's phenomenological ego. In lieu of the historical or social reality of people, Poulet strives for the signatures of selfhood inscribed on the literary work.

American practitioners

American phenomenological critics preserve the Geneva school's respect for the subjectivity of the artist as manifest in the work of art. In his phenomenological phase, J. Hillis Miller wrote *Charles Dickens: The World of His Novels* (1958), portraying the author's imagination as a consolidated subjectivity whose consistent view of the world transcends the diversity of individual novels.

Paul Brodtkorb, in *Ismael's White World: A Phenomenological Reading of 'Moby Dick'* (1965), regards phenomenology as the one critical approach which interprets in the arrangements of letters on the page states of being and, subsequently, states of mind. Brodtkorb thus sees in phenomenology a discipline that can be adapted for the comprehension of subjectivity emergent in Melville's novel. In what might be considered a practical manifestation of Ingarden's stratum of the multiple aspects of the world represented in a literary text, Brodtkorb examines the phenomenological registering upon the 'Ishmaelean consciousness' of the four elements: earth, air, fire, and water.

Relationship to approaches

Regardless of its philosophical transformations and of its literary applications, phenomenology is ultimately a description of aspects of human consciousness as they register the outside world in meaningful ways. Compared with other 20th-century literary theories that question the validity of interpretation, phenomenology asserts that coherent meaning is both possible in theory and reliable in practice.

Yet, unlike more traditional modes of Anglo-American criticism, phenomenological criticism disregards the boundaries that distinguish one text from another. The phenomenological ego of the writer that is mapped into poetic language from the actualities of the writer's life, while subject to changes and contradictory motivations at various points, is itself a transcendental entity. As such, it can be studied as a unified object.

With its focus on the structures of meaning in consciousness as it appears in the literary work, phenomenology is closely related to *hermeneutics, the study of the interpretation of texts. *Hans-Georg Gadamer in *Wahrheit und Methode* [*Truth and Method* 1960] rejects the notion of an objective reading of historical texts, on the grounds that the acts of both reading and interpretation are phenomenologically grounded in the experience of the reader, just as the act of literary creation is grounded in the historical epoch of the writer. Hence universal criteria for the judgment of texts from various epochs are not attainable. This position is derived from the phenomenological assertion that the subject and the object – in the case of hermeneutics, the reading subject and the object that is read – are inseparable.

Unlike the structuralist, the phenomenologist generally sees the formation and maintenance of meaning as attributes of human consciousness rather than of the autonomous grid of language existing outside the subject. The same charge of ahistorical perspective has been levied at both phenomenology and *structuralism. According to their critics, both approaches have neglected to consider the role of historical change in their description of meaning.

Phenomenology must also be distinguished from poststructuralist theories of language and literature that throw into question the centrality of the perceiving subject and the knowledge of the self. (See *poststructuralism.) Phenomenology rests on the belief that subjectivity *is* in practice a reliable centre of human knowledge, contrary to *deconstruction, for example, which argues that the positing of the self as the centre of meaning is metaphysically arbitrary. Yet, both the poststructuralist and the phenomenologist assert the end of metaphysics. For phenomenology, knowledge can be verified to the extent that consciousness itself is the only register of reality. The literary, theoretical and critical applications of this philosophical method transfer the burden of

consciousness to the self-world relation established in and by literary texts; thus the mandate of literary consciousness is reconstitution, not deconstruction.

STEPHEN DE PAUL

Primary Sources

Brodtkorb, Paul. *Ishmael's White World: A Phenomenological Reading of 'Moby Dick.'* New Haven: Yale UP, 1965.

Gadamer, Hans-Georg. *Truth and Method.* New York: Crossroad, 1982.

Heidegger, Martin. *Basic Writings.* Ed. David Farrell Krell. New York: Harper and Row, 1977.

– *Being and Time.* Trans. John Macquarrie. New York: Harper and Row, 1962.

Husserl, Edmund. *The Crisis of European Sciences and Transcendental Phenomenology: An Introduction to Phenomenological Philosophy.* Trans. David Carr. Evanston: Northwestern UP, 1970.

– *Ideas: General Introduction to Pure Phenomenology.* Trans. W.R. Boyce Gibson. New York: Macmillan, 1931.

– *Logical Investigations.* Trans. J.N. Findlay. 2 vols. New York: Humanities P, 1970.

Ingarden, Roman. *The Literary Work of Art: An Investigation on the Borderlines of Ontology, Logic, and Theory of Literature.* Trans. George G. Grabowicz. Evanston, Ill.: Northwestern UP, 1973.

Merleau-Ponty, Maurice. *In Praise of Philosophy.* Trans. John Wild and James M. Edie. Evanston, Ill.: Northwestern UP, 1963.

– *Phenomenology of Perception.* Trans. Colin Smith. London: Routledge and Kegan Paul, 1962.

– *Sens et non-sens.* Paris: Nagel, 1948.

– *Signs.* Trans. Richard C. McCleary. Evanston, Ill.: Northwestern UP, 1964.

– *The Visible and the Invisible.* Trans. Alphonso Lingis. Evanston, Ill.: Northwestern UP, 1968.

Miller, J. Hillis. *Charles Dickens: The World of His Novels.* Cambridge, Mass.: Harvard UP, 1958.

Poulet, Georges. *Studies in Human Time.* Trans. Elliott Coleman. New York: Harper, 1956.

Secondary Sources

Magliola, Robert. *Phenomenology and Literature: An Introduction.* West Lafayette, Ind.: Purdue UP, 1977.

Palmer, Robert E. *Hermeneutics: Interpretation Theory in Schleiermacher, Dilthey, Heidegger and Gadamer.* Evanston, Ill.: Northwestern UP, 1969.

Spiegelberg, Herbert. *The Phenomenological Movement: A Historical Introduction.* 2 vols. 2nd. ed. The Hague: Nijhoff, 1965.

Play/freeplay, theories of

(See *game theory.) In recent years, several articles and books have been published that consider play not only as 'theoretical discourse' but also as 'scientific research, gradually spreading in our century to ... biology, ethology, zoology, anthropology, sociology, psychology, education, economics, political science, modern warfare, cybernetics, statistics, physics, mathematics, and philosophy of science' (Spariosu, *Dionysus Reborn* 1). (See *discourse.) Of course, play is not a new concept, but these studies crystallize a growing trend during the last 200 years to see play as influencing adult human activity and thought in a positive way.

While the range of meanings and uses of the word 'play' is not infinite, Spariosu's list suggests the degree to which the concept applies to literary theory while going well beyond it. In short, while play as a term may seem straightforward, its definition and perceived function depend upon historical periods under consideration as well as particular writers and their disciplines.

Historical background

The earliest concepts of play for adults probably involved athletic contests and those of war as well as the perceived struggle of the elements and divine forces. Pre-Socratic thinkers such as Heraclitus formulated conceptions of play based upon physical contests of human and divine strength (*agon* and *athlon*), 'warring, impersonal forces' (*eris, polemos*), and rational contests revealing 'the arbitrary will of the gods to which men must submit' (Spariosu, *Dionysus Reborn* 15). Plato and Aristotle, on the other hand, considered play from a more rationalistic perspective as consisting of performativeness, imitation, role-playing, and child-like entertainment. In the *Phaedrus*, Plato compares play (*paideia*) unfavourably to game (*ludus*). For him play is a wholly unstructured activity, whereas games are structured activities with guidelines, rules, and goals. Games, in Plato's eyes, provide models for children and adolescents, while mere play is frivolous.

Plato's view remained largely uncontested for centuries and not until 18th- and 19th-century philosophers such as Kant, Schiller and *Nietzsche provided corrective models

was play considered useful in itself and appropriate for literary theory.

The work of Immanuel Kant is often taken as the critical turning-point in the conceptualization of play, for he linked aesthetic judgment and art to play and considered them independent of cognition and scientific claims to truth. As a form of play, art is spontaneous, free and pleasurable in itself, liberated from the necessity of having to be about reality, of having to be representational, or of having to say anything at all; it could assert its independence from, and play with, various conceptions of reality without being bound by a specific content. As to method, however, Kant prefers art with order and balance and based upon reason rather than art which appeals to sensation: play, then, should be used to create a certain kind of art.

One of the first to take advantage of the position taken by Kant was Friedrich Schiller. In his *On the Aesthetic Education of Man in a Series of Letters*, he hypothesized that play, itself a spontaneous drive, maintains an equipoise between the other two major drives – the empirical (material and sensuous) and rational or ideational (formal and abstract). He accorded play a position of considerable importance, not only in its relation to art but especially in its effect on personality development, for it allowed people to realize their full potentialities. For Schiller play is an indispensable feature of humanity, especially effective, like art, as self-conscious illusion, when governed by reason. By giving play such a prominent role in human development, Schiller set 'the pattern for all modern discussions of play, which will always involve a polarity of play and seriousness, ... in which one term will invariably take precedence over the other' (Spariosu, *Dionysus Reborn* 59). Schiller's concept also highlights the 'two irreducible and often conflicting senses' of play: 'free voluntary action' and 'random motion' (Wilson 66).

If Kant and Schiller redefined play in such a way as to make it a useful concept for moderns, it was Friedrich Nietzsche who freed it from the constraints of reason. In his writings, including *Ecce Homo, The Gay Science* and *The Birth of Tragedy*, Nietzsche pitted himself against idealism and traditional morality, preferring instead to associate himself with the repressed Dionysian spirit and its various disruptions. While he always stressed a duality in human behaviour – Apollonian and Dionysian, idealism and materialism, and so forth – he believed that the most effective way to unsettle given cultural priorities and hierarchies is through the spirit of play. Play as transgressive unreason and absurdity serves to correct the imbalance in culture and thought, and art, like play, standing apart from privileged modes of reason in culture, works to promote the spirit of unrest and misrule, challenging and directing its audience to new conceptions of reality.

Contemporary theories

Within contemporary literary theory, three conceptions of play have achieved prominence: political (*Bakhtin), hermeneutic (*Gadamer) and deconstructive (*Derrida, *Lacan, *Foucault, *Barthes, and *Kristeva). (See *hermeneutics, *deconstruction.)

The political theory of play is best represented by Mikhail Bakhtin, whose ideas about texts and the imagination are heavily indebted to Marx and Nietzsche. (See *text.) Like Nietzsche, Bakhtin assumes play to be disruptive of established forms of social thought and behaviour. By playing with privileged ideas and imagining and espousing their opposites, a thinker can turn a game of 'what if' into a direct means of social change. Bakhtin, however, is not just a metaphysician (or, as he prefers to call himself, a metalinguist), but a social revisionist, and is interested in the way play affects society in a more than hypothetical sense. Using medieval and Renaissance carnivals and fairs as illustration, he explores how play was capable of exposing privileged forms of behaviour and abuses within the social system, of providing a corrective through laughter, and of thus effecting social change. Play structured as public entertainment is capable of transgression, disruption and social revolution. *Literature, too, can accomplish such results directed at political and social ills: wit and comedy ('carnivalization') can be used to play with and reveal unjust practices in such a way as to suggest specific cures. Carnivalization is part of literary transgression, in which a specific social ill is parodied, carried to excess and laughed out of existence. Transgressive play is simultaneously an effective agent of social change and social change itself. (See *parody, *carnival.)

Hans-Georg Gadamer's position on play is far less political. For Gadamer play is a natural activity and, like nature itself, 'without pur-

pose or intention' (95). It can lead, however, to other activities like games and art, which do have purposes and structures. Play, characterized by self-representation and self-movement, is carried to its highest form in art, which deals with conceptions of truth and in which the object (the art or game) and the subject (the audience, interpreters, or players) engage in a dynamic relationship that is comprehensible only through language: the 'hermeneutical principle of the artwork' is 'an ongoing interplay of tradition and interpreter' (Spariosu, *Dionysus Reborn* 140).

By far the most prominent theories of play are those of the deconstructionists, who link them to theories of signification. Important figures in this area include Jacques Derrida, Michel Foucault, Roland Barthes, Jacques Lacan, Julia Kristeva, and Jacques Ehrmann. To some extent their view of play is apolitical, but they would argue that, through an understanding of culture, conditions for individual social and political action are created that can lead to change. The primary spokesperson for this position has been Derrida, whose *Of Grammatology, Writing and Difference* and *Dissemination* were among the first works to treat the topic extensively. Derrida announces that meaning is impossible except through signs and that the limitlessness of play is equated with 'the absence of the transcendental signified' (*Of Grammatology* 50). For him explorations of signs begun by linguists and philosophers such as *Ferdinand de Saussure, Louis Hjelmslev and *C.S. Peirce confirm that language and sign-making are akin to and coexistent with play. (See *sign.)

'Freeplay' (*jeu libre*), a term frequently used by deconstructionists, was initially popularized by Derrida, who, in 'Structure, Sign, and Play in the Discourse of the Human Sciences,' identifies language and all meaning as a field of freeplay. In his opinion society attempts to organize and structure freeplay – of language, ideas, and social practices – to form hierarchies, to give certain forms of expression privilege over others, and to regard some ideas as being self-evident, having transcendency or 'presence.' (See *metaphysics of presence.) Derrida assumes that all organizing principles are socially constructed, one principle being intrinsically no better than another, even though accorded a superior status. His way of approaching the problem of these hierarchies or centres is to demonstrate that threads of language, logic and understanding, though woven together, can, through patient unravelling, be decentred. By demonstrating that what has been perceived as 'natural' or 'as it should be' is really cultural and formed according to behaviour and practice within a given context, Derrida exposes 'gaps,' lacunae or aporias – splits, ruptures and discontinuities – in otherwise carefully structured arguments; he 'decentres' the normative processes of argumentation and meaning, forces the reader to recognize the falseness of unified and totalized wholes, and allows the free play of alternatives to resume. 'Freeplay is,' Derrida asserts, 'the disruption of presence' or transcendent structure (*Structure* 263). (See *aporia, *centre/decentre.)

One of the first gaps that Derrida exposes is the Platonic preference for games over play and, in a related sense, for speech over writing. In 'Outwork' and 'Play: From the Pharmakon to the Letter and from Blindness to the Supplement' he argues that Plato, who represents an origin in the philosophy of language, represses play in favour of game; Plato prefers games because they have a seriousness of intention and unity of purpose, whereas play depends upon accident and chance. Similarly, Plato regards spoken language as natural, honest, serious, and unplayful, but views written language as unnatural, artificial, and subject to fooling and play. As a consequence, Derrida devotes *Dissemination* to a consideration of how Plato has given privilege to speech and why it is necessary to decentre this notion and award writing equal status. Derrida undertakes this decentring, not to give writing a privileged place but to recognize its value as play, to repudiate through arbitrariness, excessiveness and indirectness, the 'untruth' of writing, and to deny the rules, intuited logic, simplicity, directness, structures, and 'truth' of speech. Derrida knows that he cannot reverse his culture's attitudes to play and writing but he hopes at least to call them to his readers' attention or put them under erasure. One method he uses to call speech into question and to validate writing is to highlight the use of analogy. Analogy, he says, is dependent upon certain forms of repetition and he demonstrates that since both speaking and writing use analogy, and since both extensively use repetition (as do games), the way to decentre language and

games is through excessive use of analogy and repetition: this is the 'play of dissemination' in which anything may finally undermine itself by excess.

By calling into question or decentring privileged meanings, transcendent significations, or 'presences,' Derrida creates the possibility of 'a field of infinite substitutions.' To acknowledge this field is, he says in *Of Grammatology*, to destroy 'onto-theology and the metaphysics of presence' and to affirm 'absence' or the endless play of possible meanings (50). Derrida plays with language and the reader, often making his essays difficult to follow, in order to bring home forcefully that the privileged structures of discourse – including grammar, standardized vocabulary, and framework – can be, and need to be, undone to let the play of alternatives emerge. He destabilizes or designifies meaning so that meaning is scattered or dispersed throughout a chain of signifiers. (See *signified/signifier/signification.)

Derrida acknowledges his indebtedness to Jacques Lacan on several occasions and it seems quite clear that Lacan's view of the instability of the signifier is one of those debts. Lacan has taken the Saussurean notion of the arbitrariness of language as a means of undermining Saussure's own ideas about the stability of the relationship between the signifier and the signified. Whereas Saussure sees sound and concept (signifier and signified) as inextricably tied together and therefore stable, Lacan sees language as much more elusive, slippery and playful. In interrogating language, Lacan begins with his view of the *self as consisting of the conscious and the unconscious. The conscious is the part of the personality that affects our public personae, that is, our ability to understand and participate in the various social structures, including language and other social discourses. The unconscious is the more impulsive and antisocial part of the personality and, Lacan speculates, has a language of its own; it is, moreover, constituted like a language. The language of the unconscious is, however, not available to the conscious except through parapraxis – dreams, slips of the tongue and other non-rational and uncontrollable activities. In the midst of a conscious activity comes an unbidden unconscious one: the language of the unconscious inserts itself into the conscious. The self, then, is divided or split, and language is neither coherent nor under control. Lacan uses this view to suggest that the meaning of words is always elusive; there is never a firm relationship between signifier and signified. Language is finally without predictable pattern and is open to chance, accident and chaos; it is a form of play. For Lacan play is a basic form of human activity, and its recognition is basic to an understanding of both language and the self.

Although Michel Foucault is not always associated with the theory of play, his works decidedly address the issue. Like Derrida and Lacan, he often approaches the issues of play through a theory of language. For him, language is not transcendent and involves no sacred purposes or results. Spoken language is based on the play of signs and written language upon a 'play of representations' (*Language* 120); that is, our alphabetical written language represents nothing beyond the limited domain of spoken language. All concepts – of history, for example – exist only insofar as they are structured by language and discursive practices; language, the dissemination of knowledge, and *power itself are not matters of transcendent rights but rather of arbitrary modes of expression, circumstances and opportunities. As such, language, power and knowledge are the results of forces at play as well as creators of them. For Foucault, then, all reality results from 'the play of surfaces' (*Language* 168), 'the interplay of differences' (*Archaeology* 13), or the 'play of dominations' (*Language* 150). Lacking in presence, transcendency and unity, or what Foucault identifies as the world, self and God (the sphere, circle and centre), reality has no deep structure but consists only in ludic manoeuvrings through 'the scandalous, the ugly, the impossible' (*Order* 300). Concepts that are wrongly taken to be normative, rational and ideal can, then, best be put back into the arena of freeplay by subjecting them to interruptions, transgressing their limitations, and exposing their gaps. These mechanisms will disrupt their network of discourses, the coherency of their arguments and the solidity of their paradoxes. Foucault 'sets the free play of his own discourse over against *all* authority. He aspires to a discourse that is free in a radical sense, a discourse that dissolves its own authority, a discourse that opens upon a 'silence' in which only 'things' exist in their irreducible Difference, resisting every impulse to find a Sameness uniting them all in any order whatsoever' (White 85–6). In Foucault's own words, he would 'pervert good sense and al-low thought to play outside the ordered table of resemblances' (*Language* 183). (See *authority, *différance/différence.)

Holding many of the same views as Derrida, Lacan and Foucault about the play of signification, Roland Barthes and Julia Kristeva are perhaps the most vocal champions of literature as play and the most ludic of writers themselves. Barthes takes for granted that 'the *play* of signifiers can be endless,' but he goes on to say that, since Homer, writers and readers have understood literature to be 'an unfulfilled technique of meaning' and the literary sign to be immutable (*Essays* 268–9). As a sign, literature pretends to replicate or double reality, but, since it is never known as reality, its significations are always unfulfilled or unclosed. Insofar as Barthes queries literature per se and thinks of all his own writings as literary, he plays with his style so as to render his ideas and assertions as discontinuous and uncertain as possible. The work which best exemplifies this tendency is *The Pleasure of the Text*, in which Barthes blurs the significations of the works/texts and their *pleasure/bliss so as not to privilege any form or meaning. Julia Kristeva, too, speaks of the play of writing but centres on the play of *intertextuality and dual, transgressive voices. For her the internal rules and ideas of a text constitute a certain field of play, which can be transferred in part or in total to another work so that the whole field of literature is contaminated by the interplay of language and forms. All of literature becomes a dialogue between present and past or between one voice and another, in short, a field of play with artists and readers playing with and recognizing the interplay of signs. One text always transgresses another and, in so doing, creates new possibilities.

Others take this view even further. Jacques Ehrmann, for example, who edited several important issues of *Yale French Studies* and was responsible for the influential 1968 issue on game theory, speaks of 'the world's play at the level of its decentering' (*Tragic* 17, 30). This rhetoric is drawn from *Heidegger and Derrida and suggests that all reality is an assemblage of agreed-upon meanings; consequently, there is nothing in human perception that is intrinsically natural and there is nothing in the world that is supernatural. All reality is constituted upon arbitrary signifiers and significations, which can be endlessly disrupted and decentred.

Examples of contemporary writing that have been greatly influenced by theories of play include postmodern, metafictive and experimental works, all of which emphasize performative and self-reflexive aspects, antirealist perspectives, and linguistic play. These writings often pit themselves against normative conventions of writing or against conventional views of politics and society: they sometimes affect ideological innocence and neutrality and sometimes anti-authoritarian and antibourgeois sentiments. The freeplay of fiction and social values is, then, usually antihegemonic and pluralistic, at the same time using and refuting traditional societal values. (See *hegemony, *performance theory, *postmodernism.)

GORDON E. SLETHAUG

Primary Sources

Barthes, Roland. *Critical Essays.* Trans. Richard Howard. Evanston, Ill.: Northwestern UP, 1972.
– *The Pleasure of the Text.* Trans. Richard Miller. New York: Hill and Wang, 1975.
Beaujour, Michel, ed. *In Memory of Jacques Ehrmann: Inside Play Outside Game. Yale French Studies* 58 (1979): 1–237.
Derrida, Jacques. *Dissemination.* Trans. Barbara Johnson. Chicago: U of Chicago P, 1981.
– *Of Grammatology.* Trans. Gayatri Chakravorty Spivak. Baltimore/London: Johns Hopkins UP, 1976.
– *Positions.* Trans. Alan Bass. Chicago: U of Chicago P, 1981.
– 'Structure, Sign, and Play in the Discourse of the Human Sciences.' In *The Structuralist Controversy,* ed. Macksey and Donato, 247–72.
Ehrmann, Jacques. 'The Tragic/Utopian Meaning of History.' *Yale French Studies* 58 (1979): 15–30.
– ed. *Game, Play, Literature. Yale French Studies* 41 (1968).
Foucault, Michel. *The Archaeology of Knowledge.* Trans. A.M. Sheridan Smith. London/New York: Routledge, 1972.
– *Language, Counter-Memory, Practice: Selected Essays and Interviews.* Ed. Donald F. Bouchard. Ithaca: Cornell UP, 1977.
– *The Order of Things: An Archaeology of the Human Sciences.* New York: Pantheon Books, 1970.
Gadamer, Hans-Georg. *Truth and Method.* Trans. Garrett Bardes and John Cumming. New York: Seabury, 1975.
'Game and the Theories of Game / Jeu et théories des jeux.' *Canadian Review of Comparative Literature* 12 (1985): 177–370.
Kristeva, Julia. *Séméiôtikè: Recherches pour une sémanalyse.* Paris: Editions du Seuil, 1969.
Lacan, Jacques. 'Of Structure as an Inmixing of an Otherness Prerequisite to Any Subject Whatever.'

In *The Structuralist Controversy,* ed. Macksey and Donato, 186–200.
Macksey, Richard, and Eugenio Donato, eds. *The Structuralist Controversy: The Languages of Criticism and the Sciences of Man.* Baltimore/London: Johns Hopkins UP, 1970.
Spariosu, Mihai I. *Dionysus Reborn: Play and the Aesthetic Dimension in Modern Philosophical and Scientific Discourse.* Ithaca/London: Cornell UP, 1989.
– *Literature, Mimesis, and Play: Essays in Literary Theory.* Tübingen: Gunter Narr Verlag, 1982.
White, Hayden. 'Michel Foucault.' In *Structuralism and Since.* Ed. John Sturrock. Oxford/New York: Oxford UP, 1979.
Wilson, R. Rawdon. *In Palamedes' Shadow: Explorations in Play, Game, and Narrative Theory.* Boston: Northeastern UP, 1990.

Poetics of expressiveness

The poetics of expressiveness is a theory of literary structure advanced by *Alexander K. Zholkovsky and Yuri Shcheglov. While it is partly based on certain insights of Sergei Eisenstein, its main components are rigorously defined notions of 'theme,' 'deep design,' 'deep structure,' 'surface structure,' and 'text,' together with a set of *expressive devices that serve to organize the expressive components of the model. (See *theme, *text.) The theory is essentially a *metalanguage for the analytical description of the expressive transformations by which a non-expressive theme becomes – through its expressive deep design, deep structure and surface structure – an engagingly expressive text. An analytical description of a work, which is referred to in the theory as a 'derivation,' thus consists of a hierarchy of expressive transformations linking theme to text.

The poetics of expressiveness is based on the assumption that 'a literary text is an expressive embodiment of ... a nonexpressive theme,' where 'theme' is defined as 'the invariant of all the components of a particular text' (Zholkovsky, *Themes* 19). When analysing the expressive structure of a particular work, the first task of the critic is to give an explicit and precise formulation to its theme, bearing in mind that it may be either a referential message about the world (a 'Class I' theme) or a stylistic message about a work's own means of expression or *code (a 'Class II' theme). In either case, the theme is typically an idea that runs implicitly through the whole of the text and subsumes all of its parts. The next task is to explain how an expressive text may be derived from its non-expressive theme through certain transformations. This is done by postulating three intermediate constructs or levels-of-representation, each organized in an increasingly concrete way by one or more expressive devices. These intermediate levels consist of (1) a highly abstract 'deep design' incorporating the expressive element that is fundamental to the organization of the text under inspection; and (2) a less abstract 'deep structure' specifying the expressive form that is close to the structure of the text itself. The expressive devices that serve to organize these intermediate levels of the model consist of ten theme-preserving, expressiveness-enhancing types of transformation: *concretization, augmentation, repetition, *variation, division, contrast, preparation, combination, concord, and reduction.

While expressive devices constitute the 'grammar' or expressive syntax of the model, the analogous 'lexicon' component (that is, the basic material that is organized by this grammar) is a hypothetical 'dictionary of reality' – or 'the writers' and readers' shared knowledge of and experience with "life" and "letters" that makes possible their literary intercourse.' The dictionary of reality, which is an 'ideal point of reference,' consists of the referential and code spheres. It also 'contains all the specific concretizations, augmentations and contrasts, and some of the other ED [expressive-device] rules for each thematic entity listed in it' (Zholkovsky, *Themes* 275–6).

A 'theme-text' analysis is designed to elucidate the ideal artistic logic inherent in a completed work and not the writer's process of composition. Nevertheless, the poetics of expressiveness does not make possible the description of an author's 'poetic world' – or the system linking all themes of an author (Zholkovsky, *Themes* 277).

Zholkovsky has suggested that the poetics of expressiveness is a 'pre-post-structuralist' kind of literary theory. (See *poststructuralism.) While its critical metalanguage can be used to describe different readings of a text as well as various kinds of play among both signifiers and signifieds, it nevertheless stipulates that a unified derivation be elaborated for any given interpretation of a work. (See theories of *play/freeplay, *signified/signifier/signification.)

Zholkovsky and Shcheglov have demonstrated that the theory can be used to describe the aesthetic organization of works by such authors as Anna Akhmatova, Ovid, Sherlock Holmes, Boris Pasternak, Alexander Pushkin, Jean-Baptiste Molière, François de La Rochefoucauld, and Leo Tolstoy. Zholkovsky has also used the theory to elucidate the expressive structure of such diverse things as folktales, proverbs, epigrams, puns, maxims, and a cookie-wrapper.

JAMES STEELE

Primary Sources

Shcheglov, Yuri, and A.K. Zholkovsky. 'Generating the Literary Text.' *Russian Poetics in Translation* 1 (1975): 1–77.
– 'Poetics as a Theory of Expressiveness: Towards a "Theme-Expressiveness Devices-Text" Model of Literary Structure.' *Poetics* 5 (1976): 207–46.
– *Poetics of Expressiveness: A Theory and Applications*. Linguistic and Literary Studies in Eastern Europe 18. Amsterdam/Philadelphia: John Benjamins, 1987.
Zholkovsky, A.K. 'Levels, Domains, Invariants: A Format for the Analysis of Poems.' *Proceedings of the 8th Annual Meeting of the Semiotic Society of America*. Bloomington: Indiana UP, 1984.
– 'On Three Analogies between Linguistics and Poetics (semantic invariance, obligatoriness of grammatical meanings, competence vs. performance).' *Poetics* 6 (1977): 77–106.
– *Themes and Texts: Toward a Poetics of Expressiveness*. Trans. from the Russian by the author. Ed. Kathleen Parthé. Ithaca/London: Cornell UP, 1984.
– and Yuri Shchlegov. 'Structural Poetics Is a Generative Poetics.' In *Soviet Semiotics*. Ed. D. Lucid. Baltimore: Johns Hopkins UP, 1978, 175–192.

Secondary Sources

Seyffert, Peter. *Literary Structuralism: Background Debate Issues*. Columbus, Ohio: Slavica, 1985.
Steele, James. 'Re-constructing Structuralism: The Theme-Text Model of Literary Language and F.R. Scott's "Lakeshore."' In *Future Indicative: Literary Theory and Canadian Literature*. Ed. John Moss. Ottawa: U of Ottawa P, 1987, 153–67.

Polish structuralism: *see* Structuralism, Polish

Polysystem Theory

Since the late 1960s the Polysystem Theory (PST) has been developed by Itamar Even-Zohar and later by Gideon Toury, Zohar Shavit, Shelly Yahalom, and other collaborators of the Porter Institute for Poetics and Semiotics at Tel Aviv University in Israel, on the basis of previous work by the Russian formalists. (See *formalism, Russian; *semiotics.) Elements of the theory also elaborated ideas presented by members of the *Prague School of structuralism and Central and East European and Soviet semioticians, particularly *Iurii Lotman (for these roots see Even-Zohar *Polysystem Studies* 1–7; Dimić and Garstin 'The Polysystem Theory'). The theory itself and the praxis inspired by it are largely compatible with, and often parallel to, those contemporary sociological approaches to *literature which systemically study 'the field of literature' (*le champ littéraire*) as a partially autonomous institution (*l'institution littéraire*) (see, for example, publications by *Pierre Bourdieu and Jacques Dubois). The Polysystem (PS) also anticipates certain ideas emanating from the approach known as the *Empirical Science of Literature, developed in the 1980s in Germany by Siegfried J. Schmidt and other scholars, and is able to use a broad range of pragmatic reception studies.

These approaches differ in their roots: formalism, Prague structuralism and the PST evolved from linguistically and semiotically oriented studies of literature and culture, the others from the sociology of culture and certain philosophical and psychological assumptions about the radical construction of meaning. Nevertheless, they all define the area of their study and its specificity in homologous terms: they consider a similar range of phenomena as interrelated and therefore designated for description and interpretation (that is, the whole field of 'literary life' or of 'the literary communication situation'); they postulate heuristic models (explicatory hypotheses) indebted to semiotics and the modern sociology of literature and are firmly based on concepts of dynamic and functional systems; and they profess a strong preference for empirical observation and verification, instead of speculation and metaphorical description. In the broadest sense they belong to those socially oriented schools which do not define literary and artistic works as aesthetic, free and unpredictable creations of inspired or gifted individuals, works which carry their permanent intrinsic values and meanings in themselves, but that accept them as products, with relative merits and functions which depend on many changing factors of social practices. (See also *sociocriticism.)

In its present state, the PST is most authoritatively expressed in Itamar Even-Zohar's *Polysystem Studies* (1990), which expands and refines previous versions of the theory, discusses some of the critical reactions to it, and gives additional prominence to the institutional aspect of literature. The PST, sometimes combined with other systemic and socially oriented approaches to literature, has become part of the international debate in the humanities, and has found applications especially in Israel and Belgium, and a more tentative following by individuals or research teams in the Netherlands, Canada, the U.S.A, India, and other countries. So far, the best results have been obtained in the study of genres and their hierarchies (e.g., Shavit, D'hulst), and even more impressively in the study of translations (e.g., Toury, Lambert). (See theories of *translation, *genre criticism.) Nevertheless, the impact of PST and that of its Russian and Czech predecessors on literary historiography has been somewhat restricted both because of suspicions about totalizing theories and because of the continuing interest in *hermeneutics. (See *totalization.) Resistance is sometimes based on popular misunderstandings about the polysystem theory and present systemic concepts in general, but also on different epistemological and ideological postulates (such as those of *deconstruction, for instance). Another difficulty has arisen from the fact that most inquiries conducted on the basis of the principles of these schools, and the examples used to illustrate their methods, have been limited to languages and literatures that are not well known in the West, for example Russian, Czech and Hebrew.

The PST understands literature as a dynamic, functional, stratified, open semiotic system which is perceived as having the form of an institution. The model of the system in question is similar to *Roman Jakobson's schema of linguistic activity, published in his 'Linguistics and Poetics' (*Linguistics and Style*). The factors inalienably involved in verbal communication, and by analogy in poetics, were represented by Jakobson and adapted by Even-Zohar (*Polysystem Theory* 31) as follows: producer (addresser in Jacobson or 'writer' in common parlance), institution (context), repertoire (*code), market (contact/channel), product (message or 'work'), and consumer (addressee or 'reader'). A communication act is a multi-dimensional situation, bearing upon the relation of the *text to the language that it uses, to the speaker, to the audience, and to the world. (See also *communication theory.) The PST provides a complex but very clear set of inter-related hypotheses about these factors, which influence each other in an active and hierarchical fashion. The theory has developed a number of heuristic constructs such as 'canonized' and 'non-canonized' texts, 'model,' 'repertoire,' 'primary' and 'secondary' systems, 'periphery' and 'centre,' 'intra-' and 'inter-relations,' 'stability' and 'instability' of the system. Many of these terms are shared with other contemporary forms of literary scholarship. The PST also accounts for phenomena such as contact and interference among literary, artistic and other symbolic systems that co-exist within a designated macro system, and it has made particularly useful contributions to the theory and historical study of translations, including the distinction between 'acceptable' and 'adequate' translations. (See *canon, *centre/decentre.)

In this context, *literary institution is not understood to mean only an establishment, organization, or association instituted for the promotion of some object, but also to include the sense of an established and structured pattern of behaviour or of relationships that is accepted as a fundamental part of a culture. Sociologists of culture generally employ the concept of the institution to cover the entire range of factors involved in the production, transmission and consumption of the 'artefacts' of literature, the visual arts, cinema, music, and other cultural activities. These factors include both institutions in the narrow sense, such as publishing houses, the media, schools, and universities, and the broader institution, that is, the system (network, *champ*) in which they participate, dynamically and functionally. The study of the literary institution can be pursued therefore both in fairly narrow sociological and economic terms and in the wider context of the literary PS or as part of the Empirical Science of Literature. The particularity of the PST is that it uses the study of the social conditioning and manipulation of texts to describe and explain the evolution and functioning of literature, as well as its regularities ('laws'), instead of taking literature only as one of the elements of society or even as simple illustration of social mechanisms.

The hypothesis of a system – or rather PS, because semiotic systems are by necessity heterogeneous, open structures – is based on the notion not of the existence of elements, but of their function; it permits the explanation of the structure, the stratification and the evolution of literature. One does not look, therefore, for a static model of a text according to a given historical period, but rather for the shifts in models in terms of relations within the period, and also relational shifts outside the individual period. Synchrony and diachrony are admitted as systemic factors, and one arrives at heterogeneity by viewing the system not as static synchrony, but as dynamic polychrony.

The PST, like its Russian and Czech predecessors, makes allowance for the insertion of phenomena usually relegated to the periphery or even excluded from scholarly scrutiny, such as oral literature, literature of the masses and paraliterature, and their diachronic and synchronic interactions with the 'mainstream.' In terms of the PS, the tension between the official and unofficial cultural strata may be seen as the stratificational opposition between canonized and non-canonized literature. At any given time and place, literature may have more than one canon and centre, and the subsystems can be classified as primary and secondary. Unlike the notion of canonization versus non-canonization, the primary versus the secondary is a historical-typological notion. A conservative system will have an established repertoire with predictable products, while an innovatory system draws on a new repertoire: 'primary' activity is presumed to be the activity which creates new models for the repertoire, while 'secondary' is conceived of as a derivatory, conservatory and simplificatory activity. Primary activity, which consists of new procedures, usually takes place within a canon, in order to create new models of reality or to illuminate the canonized information in such a way as to bring about de-automatization (excessive reader familiarity with devices and contents of works).

Since the PS is a network of multi-relations,

it deals with many texts, often through sampling methods. Hence, the importance of the idea of repertoire and model in terms of function. The model is a potential combination selected from a given repertoire upon which certain textual relations have already been imposed. The individual text would be discussed as a manifestation of a certain model, whether conservative or innovatory. The importance of a text for the PS is not that of a closed linguistic system but is largely determined by the position it might occupy in the process of model creation and/or preservation. In studying historical periods and specific categories of texts, other distinctions can be elaborated, such as the following: which are the dominant and marginalized norms and models, and which is their hierarchy; which phenomena (writers, works, styles, codes, contact channels, institutions, and readers) occupy a central or peripheral position; what is the role of metatexts (for example, literary criticism) compared to the primary texts (the works themselves); what is the function of primary (innovative) texts compared to that of secondary (traditional, conservative and epigonal) texts? The evolution, success, and prestige of genres is relevant to the establishment of norms, both positive and negative. (See *margin, *metacriticism, *metalanguage.)

In a way which is very useful to comparative literature as a discipline, the PS deals with contacts and interferences with adjacent systems. These are either other literatures or cultures, or other symbolic representational systems, such as the other arts. The starting point is compatible with the 'system of culture' notion postulated by the *Tartu School of cultural semiotics. Within the PST these ideas have been defined, in particular, in terms of literature by Itamar Even-Zohar (see, for example, 'Literary Dynamics' and *Polysystem Theory*), in the area of literary translation by Gideon Toury, José Lambert and others, and, in relation to literature and other systems, by Shelly Yahalom and Zohar Shavit. Even-Zohar defines interference as a relationship where a source literature may become a resource for direct or indirect loans to the other, target literature. Usually such interferences occur in two situations: when there are synchronic or diachronic ruptures in the PS, and in the case of a PS's insufficiency (for example, the situation of emerging literary systems).

In interliterary interferences translations play major functions. In cases of 'crises,' instead of acceptable translations, which adapt the text from the source system (SS) to the conventions of the target system (TS), the translation is adequate to the original and therefore to some extent 'alien.' Under normal circumstances, translated literature occupies a secondary position in the 'importing system' and is subjected to the requirements of the TS's models and canons, so that the result is 'acceptable' rather than 'adequate' translations. While traditional translation studies use normative approaches or the theory of semiotic 'equivalence,' the PST favours descriptive studies of actual translations and their critical understanding.

The notion of interference is also used to relate literature to the other arts and systems of culture. For example, within the framework of the PST one might designate as a macro system to be studied the set of systems of literature, the visual arts and music, using the notion of interference as a methodological linkage. While not yet arriving at a semiotic language which is common to all the arts, such an approach would, nonetheless, point out the veritable relations between the arts and the way in which elements from one of them may be used and re-functionalized in another. (See also *semiosis.)

By its very nature, the PST is an open, heuristic (explanatory) theory, oriented towards praxis, that is, towards its own verification and emendation in the process of historical studies, rather than towards continuous theorizing and the logical but abstract refinement of its hypotheses. Because of this orientation and the special nature of its conceptualization, this theory promises to be particularly useful in studying emerging literatures and multilingual societies such as those of Canada or India. (See *post-colonial theory.) This approach also addresses the problem of the relationship between periphery and centre, and allows for the contextualization and placement of so-called marginal forms or genres. Without embracing the priorities of such theories of literature which take as their task the identification and deconstruction of ideology, the PST inevitably contributes to the clearer perception of the forces which validate and shape literature, the other arts and culture. The notion of contacts and interferences with adjacent literary and artistic systems, or with other cultural systems, is also significant for modern literary scholarship, and has already changed translation studies.

MILAN V. DIMIĆ

Primary Sources

Dimić, Milan V., and Marguerite K. Garstin. 'The Polysystem Theory: A Brief Introduction, with Bibliography.' In *Problems of Literary Reception/ Problèmes de réception littéraire.* Ed. E.D. Blodgett and A.G. Purdy. Edmonton: Research Institute for Comparative Literature, University of Alberta, 1988, 177–96.

Even-Zohar, Itamar. 'The Function of the Literary Polysystem in the History of Literature.' In *Communication, Symposium on the Theory of Literary History.* Tel Aviv, 1970. Repr. in *Papers in Historical Poetics.* Ed. I. Even-Zohar and B. Hrushovski. Tel Aviv: Porter Institute, 1978, 11–13.

– 'Funktionswandel und Sinnentlehrung.' *Zeitschrift für Semiotik* 5 (1983): 220–7.

– 'An Introduction to a Theory of Literary Translation.' Ph.D. diss. Tel Aviv University, 1971. [In Hebrew; English summary: i–xx.]

– 'Literary Dynamics,' 'Literary Interference,' 'Literary System.' [Under 'Literature.'] *Encyclopedic Dictionary of Semiotics.* Vol. 1. Approaches to Semiotics, 73. Ed. Thomas A. Sebeok et al. Berlin-New York-Amsterdam: Mouton de Gruyter, 1986, 459–66.

– *Papers in Historical Poetics.* Papers on Poetics and Semiotics, 8. Tel Aviv: Porter Institute, 1978.

– *Polysystem Studies.* Special issue. *Poetics Today* 11.1 (Spring 1990).

– 'Polysystem Theory.' *Poetics Today* 1:1–2 (1979): 287–310.

– 'The Position of Translated Literature Within the Literary Polysystem.' In *Literature and Translation: New Perspectives in Literary Studies.* Ed. J.S. Holmes, J. Lambert and R. Van den Broeck. Leuven: Acco, 1978, 117–27.

– 'The Quest for Laws and Its Implication for the Future of the Science of Literature.' In *The Future of Literary Scholarship.* Ed. György M. Vajda and Janos Riesz. Frankfurt-New York: Peter Lang, 1986, 75–9.

– 'Translation Theory Today: A Call for Transfer Theory.' *Poetics Today* 3:4 (1981): 1–7.

– 'Universals of Literary Contacts.' In *Functional Studies in Language and Literature.* Ed. F. Coppieters and D. Goyvaerts. Ghent: Story-Scientia, 1978, 5–15. [Also in *Papers in Historical Poetics.*]

– and Gideon Toury, eds. 'Translation Theory and Intercultural Relations.' Topical issue. *Poetics Today* 3:4 (Summer/Autumn 1981).

D'hulst, Lieven. *L'Evolution de la poésie en France* (1780–1830): Introduction à une analyse des interférences systématiques. Symbolae, series D, Litteraria 1. Leuven: Leuven UP, 1987.

Lambert, José. 'L'Eternelle question des frontières: Littératures nationales et systèmes littéraires.' In *Langue, Dialecte, Littérature: Etudes romanes à la mémoire de Hugo Plomteux.* Ed. C. Angelet et al. Leuven: Leuven UP, 1983, 355–70.

– 'Plaidoyer pour un programme des études comparatistes: Littérature comparée et théorie du polysystème.' *Actes du XVIe Congrès de la Société française de Littérature générale et comparée.* Montpellier: U de Montpellier, 1984.

– 'Production, traduction et importation: Une clef pour la description de la littérature et de la littérature en traduction.' *Canadian Review of Comparative Literature/Revue Canadienne de Littérature Comparée* 7 (1980): 246–52.

– 'Les Relations littéraires internationales comme problème de réception.' *Oeuvres et Critiques* 11.2 (1986): 173–89.

– 'La Traduction.' In *Théorie littéraire, problèmes et perspectives.* Ed. M. Angenot et al. Paris: PUF, 1989, 151–9.

– *Un Modèle descriptif pour l'étude de la littérature: La littérature comme polysystème.* Katholieke Universiteit Leuven, paper 29. Leuven: Universiteit, 1983.

Shavit, Zohar. 'The Entrance of a New Model into the System: The Law of Transformation.' In *Issues in Slavic Literary and Cultural Theory.* Ed. K. Eimermacher, P. Grzybek, G. Witte. Bochum: Brockmeyer, 1989, 593–600.

Sheffy, Rakefet. 'The Concept of Canonicity in Polysystem Theory.' *Poetics Today* 11 (Fall 1990): 511–22.

Tötösy de Zepetnek, Steven. 'Systematic Approaches to Literature – An Introduction with Selected Bibliographies.' *Canadian Review of Comparative Literature/Revue Canadienne de Littérature Comparée* 19.1–2 (1992): 21–93.

Toury, Gideon. 'A Rationale for Descriptive Translation Studies.' *Dispositio* 6 (1982): 19–23. Also in *The Manipulation of Literature: Studies in Literary Translation.* Ed. Theo Hermans. London-Sydney: Croom Helm, 1985, 16–41.

– 'Aspects of Translating into Minority Languages, from the Point of View of Translation Studies.' *Multilingua* 4.1 (1985): 3–10.

– *In Search of a Theory of Translation.* Tel Aviv: Porter Institute, 1980.

– 'Translation: A Cultural Semiotic Perspective.' In *Encyclopedic Dictionary of Semiotics.* Approaches to Semiotics, 73. Vol. 2. Ed. Thomas A. Sebeok et al. Berlin-New York-Amsterdam: Mouton de Gruyter, 1986, 1111–24.

– 'Translation, Literary Translation and Pseudotranslation.' In *Comparative Criticism.* Ed. E.S. Schaffer. Cambridge: Cambridge UP, 1984, 73–85.

Yahalom, Shelly. 'Le Comportement d'un polysystème littéraire en cas de crise: Contacts intersystémiques et comportement traductionnel.' *Poetics Today* 2:4 (1984): 143–60.

- 'Du non-littéraire au littéraire.' *Poétique* 44 (1980): 406–21.
- 'Problèmes d'interférences de systèmes sémiotiques.' In *Semiotics Unfolding: Proceedings of the 2nd Congress of the International Association for Semiotic Studies*. Ed. Tasso Barbé. Berlin: Mouton, 1983, 671–8.

Post-colonial theory

Post-colonial theory is a term for a collection of theoretical and critical strategies used to examine the culture (*literature, politics, history, and so forth) of former colonies of the European empires, and their relation to the rest of the world. While it embraces no single method or school, post-colonial theory – or, more accurately, theories – share many assumptions: they question the salutary effects of empire (visible in phrases such as 'the gift of civilization,' 'the British literary heritage' or even 'the Renaissance') and raise such issues as racism and exploitation. Central to all, although not always presented in such terms, is the position of the colonial or post-colonial subject. (See *subject/object.) Post-colonial criticism offers a counter-narrative to the long tradition of European imperial narratives yet its 'post' prefix is not always easily worn. Whereas historically these cultures are after the colony, many theorists would present the post-colonial, often without a hyphen, as like *poststructuralism and *postmodernism, a word best seen as presenting an almost completely different state of consciousness from the antecedent enclosed.

Methods

Post-colonial theorists use a variety of methods and theories, and the *bricolage* so often evident is usually presented as a positive move away from totalizing European traditions. (See *totalization.) Many aspects of the development of post-colonial theory can be particularly compared to the rise of cultural studies, feminist studies and to the more political versions of comparative literature. (See also *deconstruction, *feminist criticism, *psychoanalytic theory, *Marxist criticism, *cultural materialism, *New Historicism, *materialist criticism.)

Major figures and history

As one of the leading practitioners of post-colonial theory, *Edward Said, has shown elsewhere, it is always difficult to find beginnings. Presumably post-colonial theory could be said to begin with the first colonial who discussed his or her state. However, most present-day commentators begin with Frantz Fanon's *Black Skin, White Masks* and *The Wretched of the Earth*. Fanon's major contribution was his focus on the colonial subject as colonized and as subject, and his use of a psychoanalytic framework. His depiction of the colonized as always situated as other and unable to assume the necessary role as self has provided the central terms for the post-colonial debate. (See *self/other.)

In the Anglo-American critical tradition, the colonial subject becomes prominent with the publication of Said's *Orientalism* in 1978. Still very influential, this work looks at European representations of the Middle East to consider how a mind-set of orientalism shaped academic study. The political import of the work lies in claiming that while the portraits of the culture did not represent reality, their contours were a product of real conditions of imperialism and racism. After Said, the most important theorists are probably Gayatri Chakravorty Spivak and Homi K. Bhabha. While Said has made much use of Foucauldian theories, he remains in opposition to many of their elements. (See *Michel Foucault.) On the other hand, Spivak has creatively extended her own combination of Althusserian Marxism and Derridean deconstruction, while Bhabha has taken up the work of those associated with British *Screen* magazine on *semiotics and representation. (See also *Louis Althusser.)

Recently a number of major European theorists have devoted attention to colonial problems. *Jacques Derrida and *Tzvetan Todorov, originally from Algeria and Bulgaria respectively, have become pillars of the French intelligentsia. Their emphasis has not been on their own backgrounds, however, but in the case of Derrida's 'Racism's Last Word,' South Africa, and in Todorov's *The Conquest of America*, Latin America.

Any consideration of post-colonial theory as a general study must recognize the post-colonial critical traditions in each nation and region. Definition of what is post-colonial is a problem here. For example, in 'Cadence, Country, Silence: Writing in Colonial Space,' Dennis Lee, a Canadian, examines the difficulty of overcoming colonialism to find an original voice, when he studies a settler culture overlaid by an English tradition. The Canadian experience also must take into account the fact that the French were the first major colonizers. This fact has always complicated constitutional and cultural debate in Canada. Canada is officially bilingual, a political and economic construction of two of the most potent European powers, France and Britain. The increasingly multicultural nature of the country also complicates the relation between indigenous and settler countries. In the francophone cultures of Africa, various statements on negritude by Aimé Cesaire can be seen as post-colonial. It is also too often the case that literary critics in Western Europe and North America have overlooked Russian, Japanese, Chinese and other colonizations and their cultural consequences.

Since at least the early 1960s the field of English literature has recognized a subset called 'Commonwealth Literature,' often associated with two scholars, William Walsh, of the University of Leeds, and Joseph Jones, of the University of Texas. For the most part Commonwealth literature has consisted of studies of individual national literatures, but there has always been some comparative work. Both early and notable is J.P. Matthews' *Tradition in Exile*, an examination of Australian and Canadian poetry. For the individual regions, the first major commentators were probably creative writers from the Caribbean – George Lamming and Wilson Harris – and from Africa – Chinua Achebe, Wole Soyinka and Ngugi wa Thiongo. As well, a great many lesser known scholars have laboured to preserve and develop their national literatures. Most working on their national literatures have done so with some awareness of the larger issues of Commonwealth literature, although this has generally been less true in Canada.

While all the cultures which were colonies of European nations can be treated as post-colonial there are many special cases and exceptions. For example, Ireland is seldom considered in this context, nor is the United States. Latin American literatures, at least partly because of the language of writing, are usually considered only in their own context,

with little connection to the post-colonial cultures in English or French, although critics like Earl Fitz have produced comparative studies of 'American' literatures. On the other hand, at least until the recent burgeoning interest in the Indian subcontinent spurred by Spivak, Bhabha and their colleagues, the majority of Anglo-American concern has been with African literatures. The same has been true of French and German scholars. A particular emphasis has been found in the United States, where much of African studies has been connected to the roots of African American culture. (See *Black criticism.) Recently, however, an exploration of various aspects of what has been termed the Third World, most notably through the work of Chandra Mohanty and Trinh T. Minh-ha, has become central to American post-colonial scholarship.

Issues

The Empire Writes Back: Theory and Practice in Post-Colonial Literatures by Bill Ashcroft, Gareth Griffiths and Helen Tiffin demonstrates the agenda for post-colonial studies in English. This book is of particular interest in that the authors are all representative of the younger generation of scholars of 'Commonwealth literature,' the descendants of Walsh and Jones. However, unlike their forebears they are highly conversant with the work of Spivak and Bhabha and the poststructuralists in general. Their approach represents a major change from the past, in which figures such as Spivak showed little interest in the critical traditions of Commonwealth literature and the Commonwealth literature scholars even less in poststructuralist theory.

The Empire Writes Back takes its title from Salman Rushdie's polemical piece, 'The Empire Strikes Back With a Vengeance,' a phrase representative of the *ideology of the book. Said, Spivak and Bhabha have pursued colonial critique, an oppositional dissection of imperialist views of the colonial texts which are themselves anti-colonial, the product of authors such as Rushdie. *The Empire Writes Back* emphasizes what it terms 'hybridization,' through which indigenous traditions combine with imperial remnants to create something newly post-colonial in a language which *Empire* calls english, a lower-case blend in contrast to the upper-case English which the empire sent.

Points of debate with *Empire* demonstrate primary problems of the field in general. *Empire* presents little support for authors, such as Ngugi wa Thiongo, who write in an indigenous language and reject english as but part of English. Second, *Empire* seems to have rather less interest in a text which speaks for the indigenous than that which speaks against the imperial. Third, its desire to establish the importance of the post-colonial statement leads to some questionable emphases and evaluations, as in the claim that Wilson Harris came to the same conclusions before Derrida or the statement that what appears to be postmodern in contemporary texts from the post-colonial world is just post-colonial.

It is difficult to subsume post-colonial theory under any one topic but the question of subject positions comes closest. This is at least the constant subtext of Robert Young's *White Mythologies: Writing History and the West*, to date the best excursion through the central theorists and central concepts in the debate, from Hegel and Marx to Bhabha and Spivak. A consideration of the titles of some recent central texts is revealing of preoccupations: Trinh's *Woman, Native, Other*, Spivak's *In Other Worlds*, and two collections, Bhabha's *Nation and Narration* and *Third World Women and the Politics of Feminism*, edited by Mohanty et al. The issue of subject positions, in all their manifestations, has led post-colonial scholars to make significant use of African American critics, especially bell hooks and *Henry Louis Gates, Jr.

Since the early 1990s post-colonial studies seem to be growing rapidly. (For significant comments since 1990 besides the above, in a wide variety of methods and regions, see Benitez-Rojo, Fitz and Miller.) Many major scholars who work primarily in other areas have recently turned to or made comments on colonialism, such as *Terry Eagleton and *Fredric Jameson. With this turn comes a variety of important new insights but also a variety of dangers. A number of commentators have claimed that 'post-colonialism' threatens to become one more totalizing method. The Commonwealth is often seen as a political anachronism, a view which in part explains the gradual shift in the universities of the former British realm from courses in 'Commonwealth' to courses in 'post-colonial.' Yet the post-colonial seems simply to regroup under a different heading. A

difficulty in the work of those like Ashcroft, Griffiths and Tiffin, especially when most imaginative and creative, as in the work of Stephen Slemon, is that disparate cultures such as India and Canada begin to look alike, both exemplars of the post-colonial imagination. Moreover, cultures such as the indigenous peoples of Canada, New Zealand and Australia are designated post-colonial while still colonies within settler nations (Narogin, Goldie). However, some indigenous writers, such as Thomas King, have deemed settler cultures colonial, because indigenous peoples of all the colonized nations had their own developed cultures before their encounter with Europeans. Divergent views on these topics, as on other theoretical problems, are likely to persist (see Hart).

JONATHAN HART and TERRY GOLDIE

Primary Sources

Achebe, Chinua. *Morning Yet on Creation Day*. New York: Doubleday, 1975.

Ashcroft, Bill, Gareth Griffiths, and Helen Tiffin. *The Empire Writes Back: Theory and Practice in Post-Colonial Literatures*. London: Routledge, 1989.

Benitez-Rojo, Antonio. *The Repeating Island: The Carribean and the Postmodern Perspective*. Trans. James Maraniss. Durham: Duke UP, 1992.

Bhabha, Homi K. 'Difference, Discrimination and the Discourse of Colonialism.' In *The Politics of Theory*. Colchester: U of Essex, 1983.

– 'The Other Question.' *Screen* 24:6 (1983), 18–35.

– ed. *Nation and Narration*. London: Routledge, 1990.

Cesaire, Aimé. *Cahier d'un retour du pays natale*. Paris: Présence Africaine, 1971.

Derrida, Jacques. 'Racism's Last Word.' Trans. Peggy Kamuf. *Critical Inquiry* 12.1 (1985): 290–9.

Eagleton, Terry. *Nationalism, Colonialism and Literature*. Derry: Field Day Pamphlets, 1988.

Fanon, Frantz. *Black Skin, White Masks*. Trans. Charles Lam Markman. New York: Grove P, 1967.

– *The Wretched of the Earth*. Trans. Constance Farrington. New York: Grove, 1968.

Fitz, Earl E. *Rediscovering the New World: Inter-American Literature in a Comparative Context*. Iowa City: U of Iowa P, 1990.

Gates, Henry Louis, Jr. *The Signifying Monkey: A Theory of Afro-American Literary Criticism*. New York: Oxford UP, 1989.

Goldie, Terry. *Fear and Temptation: The Image of the Indigene in Canadian, Australian and New Zealand Literatures*. Montreal: McGill-Queen's UP, 1989.

Harris, Wilson. *Exploration: A Selection of Talks and Articles 1966–1981*. Ed. Hena Maes-Jelinek. Aarhus, Denmark: Dangaroo, 1981.

– *The Womb of Space: The Cross-Cultural Imagination*. Westport, Conn.: Greenwood, 1983.

Hart, Jonathan. 'A Comparative Pluralism: The Heterogeneity of Methods and the Case of Fictional Worlds.' *Canadian Review of Comparative Literature/Revue Canadienne de Littérature Comparée* 14 (1988): 320–45.

hooks, bell. *Feminist Theory: From Margin to Center*. Boston: South End P, 1984.

Jameson, Fredric. 'Third-World Literature in the Era of Multi-national Capitalism.' *Social Text* 15 (1986): 67–87.

King, Thomas. 'Godzilla vs Post-Colonial.' *World Literature Written in English* 30 (1990): 10–16.

Lamming, George. *The Pleasures of Exile*. London: Michael Joseph, 1960.

Lee, Dennis. 'Cadence, Country, Silence: Writing in Colonial Space.' *boundary 2* 3:1 (Fall 1974): 151–68.

Matthews, J.P. *Tradition in Exile*. Toronto: U of Toronto P, 1962.

Miller, Christopher L. *Theories of Africans: Francophone Literature and Anthropology in Africa*. Chicago: U of Chicago P, 1990.

Minh-ha, Trinh T. *Women, Native Other*. Bloomington: Indiana UP, 1989.

Mohanty, Chandra Talpade, Ann Russo and Lourdes Torres. *Third World Women and the Politics of Feminism*. Bloomington: Indiana UP, 1991.

Narogin, Mudrooroo. *Writing from the Fringe: A Study of Modern Aboriginal Literature*. Melbourne: Hyland House, 1990.

Ngugi wa Thiongo. *Decolonising the Mind: The Politics of Language in African Literature*. London: Currey, 1986.

Rushdie, Salman. 'The Empire Strikes Back with a Vengeance.' *The Times* (London) 3 July 1982.

Said, Edward. *Beginnings: Intention and Method*. New York: Columbia UP, 1975.

– *Orientalism*. London: Routledge and Kegan Paul, 1978.

Slemon, Stephen. 'Monuments of Empire: Allegory/Counter-discourse/Post-colonial Writing.' *Kunapipi* 9.3 (1987): 1–16.

Soyinka, Wole. *Myth, Literature and the African World*. Cambridge: Cambridge UP, 1976.

Spivak, Gayatri Chakravorty. *In Other Worlds: Essays in Cultural Politics*. New York: Methuen, 1987.

Todorov, Tzvetan. *La Conquête de l'Amérique*. Paris: Seuil, 1982. Trans. as *The Conquest of America*. Trans. Richard Howard. New York: Harper, 1984.

Young, Robert. *White Mythologies: Writing History and the West*. London: Routledge, 1990.

Poststructuralism

The term 'poststructuralism' entered critical theoretical usage in the 1970s, together with *postmodernism (*Jean Baudrillard, *Jean-François Lyotard), 'postcriticism' (*Fredric Jameson) and *deconstruction (*Jacques Derrida). Poststructuralism is not a unified school of thought or even a movement; the term is most prominent in the external discourse of criticism. Authors most frequently labelled by the word (Jacques Derrida, *Michel Foucault and *Roland Barthes) seldom characterize their work as such, and confess to no shared doctrine or commitment to a single method. Nevertheless, a sceptical even subversive attitude to the heritage and 'project of modernity' (*Jürgen Habermas 'Modernity') does bring into an uneasy family of relations works of such conflicting politics and interests as Derrida's critique of metaphysics, Foucault's inquiries into the formations of *power and *episteme, or the radical feminist critique of *phallocentrism (*Luce Irigaray, *Hélène Cixous). (See also *discourse.)

Poststructuralism and postmodernism are terms often used interchangeably, signalling, besides an excess of labels, that the 'post' turn of theory is often seen as a symptom of the very malaise it illuminates: 'the post modern condition' (Lyotard *Condition*), 'the age of the simulacra,' the crisis, indeed, 'the immense process of the destruction of meaning' (Baudrillard 'On Nihilism') witnessed in the social domain. This confusion of life and theory, domains hitherto considered distinct if not discontinuous, often generates another domain for criticism if not for theory: whether to read 'post'-theory as a diagnosis of an epoch (with social reality serving as its referent) or as a radical turn (against representation, the referent) by theory. This confusion is further aggravated when students of postmodern culture (Ihab Hassan, Hal Foster, Arthur Kroker) discover the same spirit of *subversion at work in avant-garde painting, cinema, music, and narrative, thus exposing their artifices of illusion and transgressing yet another distinction – that of medium and message. (See *reference/referent.)

Art also takes the 'theoretic turn' and joins the assault on reality already in progress by theory and culture in the postmodern age. While this weakening of the 'real' (an original, authentic, stable referent, experience, and meaning) is both a topic and an effect of poststructuralist inquiries, this 'confusion' of different domains – signifier and signified, event and concept – is perhaps the strongest mark of poststructuralism. (See *signified/signifier/signification.) Erasure, or at least a weakening of divisions (between signifier/signified, reading/writing, literature/criticism) sustaining distinct identities, is the sign of theory at work in the postmodern age. (See also *literature, *text, *sign.)

The prefix 'post' in its many usages testifies to the significance the past (*Nietzsche, *Heidegger and *Freud; Western metaphysics and *structuralism) has for poststructuralist theory. Derrida, Lyotard, Barthes repeatedly turn to this question and emphatically reject any suggestion of inquiry denouncing or aspiring to surpass its predecessors. The notions of a fresh beginning, of overcoming and of progress speak to the 'heroic mode' (Lyotard Condition) of modernity and are the very ideas the 'post' hopes to displace. Inquiry functions as 'anamnesis' of the past, as dislocation and as rupture of a discursive system (Derrida L'Ecriture). Barthes, who having worked his way through structuralism is perhaps the only true post-structuralist, puts the 'fissuring of the very representation of meaning' ('Interview' 271) on the theoretical agenda. Lyotard, who describes poststructuralism as the re-writing of modernity, cautions that today 'a work can become modern only if it is first postmodern' (Condition 79). Paradoxically, the 'post' enterprise is concerned only with the present.

Structuralism had an impact in two fields: linguistics (*Ferdinand de Saussure) and anthropology (*Claude Lévi-Strauss), although the latter developed by pursuing a science analogous in its form to linguistics. Saussure gave a synchronic grounding to the science of language by presenting it with a new object and unit of analysis, the sign and sign system. A structure composed of a signifier and a signified separated by a bar, the sign postulates an arbitrary relation between the material sign (letter or sound) and the immaterial concept (signified). As structuralist linguistics shifts the concern away from meaning to organization, meaning ceases to be intrinsic to the signifying element. The meaning of signs emerges only in relation to (that is, as difference from) other signs and thus exists in the form, not the substance, of language.

Structuralism creates a fundamental disruption in the discourse of modernity in two respects. First, structure, a 'simulacrum' of a function (Barthes 'Structuralist Activity'), regulates all appearances – the concrete, the particular, the historical. It postulates a 'profit' in excess of the empirical and the historical. Since it regulates history, structure transcends history. Structure thus immobilizes time, 'empties' modernity's heroic conception of history (as revival, renewal, renaissance, progress). As Derrida's critique (L'Ecriture) shows, structure as a closed field admits no secret place (inside) and no limit (outside). Second, the science of language (as opposed to individual utterance or parole) separates meaning from sign and reconstitutes the former as the effect of the play of structure. It thus displaces the speaking subject from its position in discourse as a figure which confers and authorizes meaning. (See *langue/parole, theories of *play/freeplay.)

Yet as Foucault ('Structuralism') points out, structuralism nevertheless preserves one last illusion: it attempts to present the world to consciousness as if it were made to be read by man. It may have realized the death of the speaking subject but not the death of subject-centred discourse. (See *subject/object.) The unsettling of this last illusion is the task poststructuralist theory in its various forms takes upon itself. While literally made possible by structuralist notions of difference and of language as a social contract, poststructuralism thus also goes beyond the perceived limits of Saussurean thought.

Intellectual precursors to poststructuralism include Nietzsche's 'genealogy,' Georges Bataille's part maudite (accursed share) and Marcel Mauss' work on 'gift,' all of which are examples of theory disrupting an order and an economy by turning its concepts against its own discourse. Generally, Derrida is credited with launching one phase of poststructuralism. In De la Grammatologie and L'Ecriture et la différence he turns to the founding texts (of Saussure and Lévi-Strauss) in order to subject the notion of structure and sign as stable and unified structures to a method he introduces as deconstruction.

Deconstruction discovers in the discourse of structuralist linguistics the founding concepts of a philosophy that has always sought to posit a contingent, superficial exteriority of language to articulated thought. The sign legislates the order which had permitted philosophy from its very beginning to treat its own writing as unproblematic: to speak of the signified (thought) as producing itself spontaneously and from within the self, to treat its text as a window to thought and consciousness, and to treat meaning as stable, immediately accessible and anchored in the text.

Derrida's early work (*L'Ecriture, Grammatologie, Marges*) is dedicated to the rereading of philosophy and writing and to examining the relationship between philosophy and linguistics. Concepts of *supplément* and *différance* exploit the Saussurean notion of difference in order to dislocate the metaphysical concept of presence inscribed in the sign. Derrida reformulates absence (for Saussure a sheer negativity) as the *trace of an absent presence. (See *supplementarity, *différance/différence.) The signifier is thus a supplement of the absent referent which it does not present but whose empty place it occupies. Signification always involves the silent play of deferral; representation never presents, it only delays/defers the presence of the signified. Signification, for Saussure a play of binary opposites, is reformulated as an endless play of *différance* (deferral of presence in space and time) which is never anchored and never comes to rest. (See *binary opposition.)

Derrida's critique of the sign opens the way to a new mode of textual criticism – a change not of content but of 'tampering with language itself.' It leads to a criticial re-examination throughout the humanities of the relation between language on the one hand and truth, error, knowledge, power, reason, *desire, and the speaking subject on the other. Not surprisingly, deconstruction has had a profound influence on literary criticism, shifting its entire field and blurring the division between fiction and theory (Malcolm Bowie), literature and philosophy (Jacques Derrida), reading and writing, the critic and the writer (*Geoffrey Hartman). Together with the *psychoanalytic theory of *Jacques Lacan, deconstruction has inspired a new category of writing: a reading – of Lacan reading Freud (Gallop *Reading Lacan*), of Derrida reading Plato (Hartman *Saving the Text*) and Rousseau (*Paul de Man *Blindness*), of Cixous reading Lispector (*Reading*), or Barthes reading Balzac (*S/Z*) – which situates itself as yet another moment in a complex intertextual chain. (See *intertextuality.)

In the fields of social thought and philosophy of science Michel Foucault inaugurates 'genealogy' as a work and method analogous in its effects to deconstruction. An inquiry into discursive regimes and formations, 'genealogy' does not simply replace but functions to displace history as written by the modern subject. *Histoire de la folie*, the first in a series, rewrites the history of reason as it comes to gain knowledge of its 'object,' madness, as a history of silencing and suppressing the voice of unreason in language. In his subsequent writings Foucault develops his methodology (from archaeology to genealogy) and works out its implications for the subject of knowledge across a diversity of different domains: the sciences and epistemology (*Les Mots et les choses, L'Archéologie du savoir*), medicine (*Naissance de la clinique*), punishment (*Surveiller et punir*), ethics, sexuality, technologies of the self (*Histoire de la sexualité*). These histories examine the complex relation between discourses and their objects (the body, disease, sexuality, order, truth, knowledge) in order to write a genealogy of the modern subject. Ultimately, these inquiries find that discourse functions both as regime and as object. As regime, it is implicated in relations of power – the production and control of its 'objects'; as object it is subject to its own regime of discursive operations.

In certain essays ('What is Enlightenment?' and 'Nietzsche, Genealogy, History' in Rabinow), Foucault explores the limits genealogy places on the discourse of inquiry itself. He examines the overlapping relations of power, knowledge and truth, not as objects external to discourse nor as abstract concepts constructed by discourse, but as operations by, events in, and effects of, discourse.

Roland Barthes' writings trace the turn theory takes in various areas from structuralism to poststructuralism, shifting the object of inquiry from work to text (Barthes 'Structuralist'), from the *énoncé* (statement) to *énonciation* (the act of enunciation) (Metz *Significant*, Foucault *L'Archéologie*), from *histoire* (story) to *discours* (discourse) (Metz, ibid.) and *dispositif* (apparatus) (Jean-Louis Comolli, Jean-Louis Baudry) to a set of discursive operations at work. (See *énoncé/énonciation.)

If the work is a stable and closed structure, identical with itself and organized by a logic of narrative transcendental to several texts (so that Lévi-Strauss' *Mythologies* is itself a sort of mythology), then the text is a site of productivity (Kristeva *Sémiótiké*), dissemination (Derrida *Dissemination*), a field of encounter in which even the author is a mere visitor (Barthes 'Work') or a function of writing (Foucault *Souci*) without any privileged access to meaning. 'Everything signifies ceaselessly and several times, but without being delegated to a great final ensemble, to an ultimate structure' (Barthes, ibid: 12).

A similar shift is effected from *énoncé* to *énonciation*; (literary or filmic) text labouring to create the illusion of pure content or (his)story (spoken by no one, coming from no where) is questioned as a field of operations. Inquiry (Foucault *L'Archéologie*) abandons the analysis of meanings concealed in the text in favour of studying operations whereby language regulates the order of its discursive formations. Film theory (Jean-Louis Baudry, Jean-Louis Comolli, Teresa de Lauretis) can thus question the filmic text as the work of an apparatus (of *ideology and the cinema) which anticipates, plans and positions the spectator, 'suturing' her or him into its own seamless text. The spectator, hitherto confused with the empirical subject, is reformulated as a cinematic construct: a position in the text, a function (of reading) and an effect of meaning.

Freud's 'unconscious' is the most influential historical example of a theoretic strategy that unsettles an economy of discourse by reinserting its order's repressed and excluded voice. This stratagem is common to a diverse body of poststructuralist writing in different disciplines: Michel Serres' *Parasite* and *Hermes* take this stratagem as their topic, showing that the parasite, the noise, and the excluded third voice are essential for the functioning of a certain kind of economy: the dialogue, communication and exchange. Foucault in *Les Mots et les choses* sets out to reveal the 'positive unconscious of knowledge' (xi) and, in *Histoire de la folie*, the suppressed voice of unreason. Both these operations dislocate the 'host' discourses of science and reason. However, several writers acknowledge the difficulty inherent in this enterprise: the repressed, not simply present elsewhere, cannot be represented in writing. Foucault's history of madness is thus an 'archaeology of silence.' Derrida, too, cautions that radical alterity will never make an appearance 'in person' but speaks only through proxies and delegates.

Jacques Lacan's theoretical apparatus – his tripartite structure of *l'imaginaire* (the imaginary), *le symbolique* (the symbolic) and *le réel*

(the real) – articulates this impossibility: the real is that absent object (referent) to which neither theory nor subject can regain access. The price of subjecthood, of being in language, is that loss: a permanently mediated (delayed/deferred) relation to the 'real.' (See *imaginary/symbolic/real.)

This difficulty is faced perhaps most urgently and painfully by feminist theory, which has embarked on the task of recovering the excluded feminine from the dominant discourses of philosophy, criticism and narrative (in fiction and cinema). Influenced by psychoanalysis and deconstruction – though painfully aware of the gender of this inheritance (Gallop) – poststructuralist feminism is a quest for this excluded voice in the sciences, in philosophy and other arts, and in feminist writing itself. This quest involves the dual task of criticism and representation. Feminist criticism reads representations of the feminine doubly as mirror: while these discourses reflect women as suffering from a lack (the phallus), this negative image also functions as the very mirror in which the male subject recognizes itself as whole (Silverman). As far as this critique fails to provide the feminine with a positive identity, it shows the difficulty feminist theory has in finding and writing a discursive position from which the feminine can articulate itself (Cixous *Reading*). (See *feminist criticism.)

In deconstruction, genealogy, psychoanalysis, and feminism, poststructuralist theory takes the 'linguistic turn': it renounces its privileged position in language and over its object. When theory confesses to being without a *metalanguage capable of describing another object in language, it also renounces the quest for a cause, an author, scientific 'objectivity,' or a grounding institution behind what the text is saying. The text (its meaning) is no longer thinkable as an originary or unified mode of presence. Everything begins with, and is already, a reproduction: meaning is always already reconstituted by deferral and delay.

ZSUZSA BAROSS

Primary Sources

Barthes, R. 'Changer l'objet lui-même.' *Esprit* 4 (1971): 603–17.
– 'From Work to Text.' In *Image, Music, Text*. Trans. Stephen Heath. New York: Hill and Wang, 1977.

- 'Interview with Raymond Bellour.' In *Le Livre des Autes*. Paris: L'Herne, 1971.
- 'The Structuralist Activity.' In *The Structuralists: From Marx to Lévi-Strauss*. Ed. R.T. and F.M. de George. New York: Anchor Books, 1972.
- *S/Z*. Paris: Seuil, 1970. Trans. R. Miller. New York: Hill and Wang, 1974.
Bataille, G. *La Part maudite*. Paris: Editions de Minuit, 1967. *The Accursed Share: An Essay on General Economy*. Trans. Robert Hurley. New York: Zone Books, 1988.
Baudrillard, J. 'The Ecstasy of Communication.' In *The Anti-Aesthetic*. Ed. Hal Foster. Washington: Bay P, 1983.
- 'On Nihilism.' *On the Beach* 6 (1984): 38–49.
Baudry, J-P. 'The Apparatus: Metapsychological Approaches to the Impression of Reality in the Cinema.' In *Narrative, Apparatus, Ideology*. Ed. Philip Rosen. New York: Columbia UP, 1986.
Bowie, M. *Freud, Proust and Lacan: Theory as Fiction*. Cambridge: Cambridge UP, 1987.
Cixous, H. *Reading with Clarice Lispector*. Trans. Verena A. Conley. Minneapolis: U of Minnesota P, 1990.
- and C. Clement. *La Jeune née*. Paris: Union General, 1975. *The Newly Born Woman*. Trans. B. Wing. Manchester UP, 1986.
Comolli, J-L. 'Machines of the Visible.' In *The Cinematic Apparatus*. Ed. Teresa de Lauretis and Stephen Heath. Basingstoke: Macmillan, 1978.
Derrida, J. *La Carte postale: De Socrate à Freud et au-delà*. Paris: Flammarion, 1980. *The Post Card*. Trans. Alan Bass. Chicago: U of Chicago P, 1987.
- *De la Grammatologie*. Paris: Editions de Minuit, 1967. *Of Grammatology*. Trans. Gayatri Spivak. Baltimore: Johns Hopkins UP, 1974.
- *Dissemination*. Trans. Barbara Johnson. Chicago: U of Chicago P, 1981.
- *L'Ecriture et la différence*. Paris: Seuil, 1967. *Writing and Difference*. Trans. A. Bass. Chicago: U of Chicago P, 1978.
- *Glas*. Paris: Galilée, 1974. Trans. John P. Leavey and R. Rand. Lincoln: U of Nebraska P, 1986.
- *Marges de la philosophie*. Paris: Editions de Minuit, 1972. *Margins of Philosophy*. Trans. A. Bass. Chicago: U of Chicago P, 1982.
- 'The Supplement of Copula: Philosophy before Linguistics.' In *Margins of Philosophy*, 175–207.
Foster, H. *The Anti-aesthetic: Essays in Postmodern Culture*. Washington: Bay P, 1983.
Foucault, M. *L'Archéologie du savoir*. Paris: Gallimard, 1969. *The Archaeology of Knowledge*. Trans. A.M. Sheridan Smith. Pantheon Books, 1972.
- *Histoire de la folie*. Librairie Plon, 1961. *Madness and Civilization*. Trans. R. Howard. London: Tavistock, 1965.
- *Les Mots et les choses*. Paris: Editions Gallimard, 1966. *The Order of Things*. New York: Vintage Books, 1973.
- *Naissance de la clinique*. PUF, 1963. *The Birth of the Clinic: An Archaeology of Medical Perceptions*. Trans. A.M. Sheridan Smith. New York: Vintage Books, 1973.
- *Le Souci de soi*. Paris: Gallimard, 1984. *The Care of the Self. History of Sexuality*, vol. 3. Trans. R. Hurley. New York: Random House, 1986.
- 'Structuralism and Post-structuralism: An Interview with Michel Foucault,' with Gerard Raulet. *Telos* 55 (1983): 195–211.
- *Surveiller et punir: Naissance de la prison*. Paris: Gallimard, 1975. *Discipline and Punish: The Birth of the Prison*. Trans. A.M. Sheridan Smith. New York: Vintage Books, 1977.
- *L'Usage des plaisirs*. Paris: Gallimard, 1984. *The Uses of Pleasure. History of Sexuality*, vol. 2. Trans. R. Hurley. New York: Random House, 1985.
- *La Volonté de savoir*. Paris: Gallimard, 1976. *History of Sexuality, I: An Introduction*. Trans. R. Hurley. New York: Random House, 1978.
Gallop, J. *The Daughter's Seduction: Feminism and Psychoanalysis*. Basingstoke: Macmillan, 1982.
- *Reading Lacan*. Ithaca: Cornell UP, 1985.
Habermas, J. 'Modernity versus Postmodernity.' *New German Critique* 22 (1981): 3–14.
Hartman, G. *Criticism in the Wilderness: The Study of Literature Today*. New Haven: Yale UP, 1980.
- *Saving the Text: Literature, Derrida, Philosophy*. Baltimore: Johns Hopkins UP, 1981.
Hassan, I. *The Postmodern Turn: Essays in Postmodern Theory and Culture*. Columbus: Ohio State UP, 1987.
Irigaray, L. *Ce sexe qui n'est pas un*. Paris: Editions de Minuit, 1977. *This Sex Which Is Not One*. Trans. C. Porter. Ithaca: Cornell UP, 1985.
Kristeva, J. *Sémiôtiké: Recherches pour une sémanalyse*. Paris: Seuil, 1969.
Kroker, A., and D. Cook. *The Postmodern Scene: Excremental Culture and Hyper Aesthetics*. New York: St. Martin P, 1986.
Lacan, J. *Ecrits*. Paris: Seuil, 1966. *Ecrits*. Trans. A.M. Sheridan. New York: W.W. Norton, 1977.
de Lauretis, T. *Alice Doesn't*. Bloomington: Indiana UP, 1984.
Lyotard, J.-F. *La Condition postmoderne: Rapport sur le savoir*. Paris: Editions de Minuit, 1979. *The Postmodern Condition: A Report on Knowledge*. Trans. G. Bennington and B. Massumi. Minneapolis: U of Minnesota P, 1984.
- 'Re-writing Modernity.' *Substance* 54 (1987): 3–10.
de Man, P. *Blindness and Insight: Essays in the Rhetoric of Contemporary Criticism*. Minneapolis: U of Minnesota P, 1971.
Metz, C. *Le Signifiant imaginaire*. Paris: Union Générale d'Editions, 1977. *The Imaginary Signifier*. Trans. Celia Britton. Bloomington: Indiana UP, 1982.
Rabinow, P., ed. *Foucault Reader*. New York: Random House, 1984.

Serres, M. *Hermes: Literature, Science, Philosophy.*
  Baltimore: Johns Hopkins UP, 1982.
– *The Parasite.* Trans. Lawrence Schehr. Baltimore:
  Johns Hopkins UP, 1982.
Silverman, K. *Acoustic Mirror.* Bloomington: Indiana
  UP, 1988.

Secondary Sources

Harari, J.V., ed. *Textual Strategies: Perspectives in
  Post-structural* Criticism. London: Methuen, 1979.
Young, R., ed. *Untying the Text.* Boston: Routledge
  and Kegan Paul, 1981.

Prague School: *see* Semiotic Poetics of the Prague School

Psychoanalytic theory

Psychoanalysis, a clinical and interpretive science founded by *Sigmund Freud (1886–1939), offers a genetic theory of the evolution of the human mind as 'psychic apparatus.' Central to Freud's theory is his concept of the unconscious mind, in which the body and the sexual history of the human subject persist in all productions of the conscious mind. For Freud the concept of sexuality is not one of mere biology or genital urge but is rather the complex of bodily and mental desire which manifests itself in earliest infancy as well as adult life (*New Introductory Lectures on Psychoanalysis* 1933). Contemporary theorists such as *Jacques Lacan, *Norman Holland and *Harold Bloom draw upon Freud for their theories of language, reading and literary influence.

Clinical origins of psychoanalysis

Freud's experiments with hypnosis while working with Jean Martin Charcot in the 1880s led him to formulate his discovery that the unconscious mind reveals itself in actions, words and mental images, the meaning of which is barred from conscious knowledge because of repression, the process of psychic censorship which consists in simply turning away and keeping something at a distance from consciousness ('Repression' 1915). Through his early work with hysterical patients, Freud theorized that the contents of the unconscious mind ultimately derive from the sexual body

and are driven by a dynamic energy which strives to bring them into consciousness (*Studies in Hysteria*, with Josef Breuer, 1893–5). The force of repression, however, demands that any release of unconscious material assume a disguised character. Hence, it is in physical symptoms, dreams, jokes, parapraxes ('Freudian slips'), and accidental gestures that the unconscious reveals itself, disguised, in everyday life (*The Psychopathology of Everyday Life* 1904). By the same token, however, Freud insists that the artist, by virtue of his openness to the power of fantasy in the production of his work, has always had a privileged relation to the unconscious.

Though originally a therapeutic method, the psychological theory which evolved from Freud's clinical discoveries is deeply indebted to the insights he gained from the study of *literature and culture. Chief among these is his discovery of the Oedipus complex, named after Sophocles' tragedy *Oedipus Rex* (*Three Essays on the Theory of Sexuality* 1905). Throughout his career, Freud turned to literature to verify his clinical findings. Though many of Freud's intellectual progeny neglected the place of creative production in psychoanalytic research and method, recent theorists have returned to the relationship between psychoanalysis and cultural critique.

Metapsychology

Freud's theory of the mind answers metaphysics with a metapsychology which leads behind consciousness, seeing much philosophical and mythical foundations as projections of unconscious properties onto external reality. Over the course of his career, Freud defined three major models of the psychic apparatus: the dynamic, the economic and the topographical. The dynamic model describes the conflict within the mind between unconscious drives, which strive for release, and the equally powerful forces of repression, which strive to keep unconscious urges from surfacing. From this struggle emerge derivatives of the repressed material which satisfy both forces: it is these 'compromise formations' – the clusters of mental images, actions and words – which reveal themselves as symptoms.

The economic model considers the distribution and circulation of the psychic energy or excitation which is attached to certain ideas, objects, bodily parts, and so on. This concept Freud calls 'cathexis'; it captures the scientific presuppositions of his training in the neurophysiology of his day, while it also derives from his clinical findings, particularly with hysterics. Within the human subject, there is a certain quantifiable amount of instinctual energy which must be variously distributed among objects, the body and mental content in order to maintain psychic equilibrium. The economic hypothesis leads to Freud's crucial notions of 'displacement' and 'condensation,' both modes of functioning in the unconscious by which ideas are separated from affects. With displacement, the intensity of affect once connected with a certain idea or image is detached from it and passed onto other ideas or images which hold only an associative connection to the original idea. Condensation, on the other hand, occurs when one idea comes to represent a cluster of associated affects. Both mechanisms find their clearest exposition in Freud's *Interpretation of Dreams* (1900).

The topographical theory divides the psychical apparatus into various subsystems according to a spatial metaphor. Freud devised two different topographies in his career, the first dividing the mind into three systems: the conscious, preconscious and unconscious. The conscious is the realm of perceptions, sensory apprehension of the external world; the preconscious, the realm which can be called up by consciousness, is usually associated with memory and that which can be accessed through language; the unconscious is the realm of the censored – that which is barred from conscious and preconscious knowledge. The second topology (also called the structural model), introduced later by Freud in *The Ego and the Id* (1923), divides the mind into three agencies: the id (the centre of instinctual drives), the ego (the agency which represents the subject's identifications and mediations with external reality), and the superego (which represents internalized parental and social injunctions, or the conscience).

Psychosexuality

Freud's conception of psychosexuality depends on his understanding of 'libido' or the available sexual energy which directs both human development and human action. His notion of sexuality, however, must be understood to encompass the entire range of human experiences directed by the drive to achieve bodily and mental satisfaction, or the 'pleasure principle.' Freud's postulation of infantile sexuality depends on this conception of the human infant's organization into erogenous zones which variously dominate at different stages in the child's development. Freud identifies three major stages in this organization: the 'oral' stage, in which the infant derives most pleasure from the mouth's sucking and biting; the 'anal' stage, in which the infant is preoccupied with the anus and its products; and the 'phallic' stage, in which genital primacy throws the child into the Oedipus complex. The opposition of the sexes is experienced as representations of phallic and castrated positions ('Some Psychical Consequences of the Anatomic Distinctions Between the Sexes' 1923). In its simplest formulation, the positive Oedipus complex identifies the child's desire for the parent of the opposite sex and a consequent rivalry with the parent of the same sex; in its negative form, the parent of the same sex is loved, while the parent of the opposite sex is identified as the rival. Freud's discovery of human bisexuality allows for the manifestation of both versions of the Oedipus complex occurring in the development of the child, with its resolution being the crucial determinant in structuring of the personality and sexual orientation.

The psychoanalytic process

The child's movement away from purely narcissistic investment in his or her own body to the family cluster is the central crisis in human development; its resolution is only partially achieved and it remains the centre of neurotic conflict. In the psychoanalytic process, the Oedipal conflict is relived through the 'transference' whereby the analysis becomes, by dint of the analyst's position as a parental substitute, the opportunity to 're-work' the original crisis, this time with clinical insight. Psychoanalysis, as a therapeutic procedure, operates by foregrounding those features of a patient's 'free associations' (uncensored repetition in a patient's speech of whatever is in his or her mind) which the analyst comes to understand as the revelation of the unconscious in fantasies, spontaneous associations and dreams. The analytic encounter becomes, in short, the incremental unfurling of the analysand's subjectivity. The analyst's own unconscious reaction to the material brought by the patient Freud terms 'countertransference.'

Classical psychoanalytical literary criticism

Since Freud's primary interest is in the psyche and its productions, he traces art to the dream; he generally approaches dream work as the 'royal road' to the unconscious. Early applications of psychoanalysis to the literary arts tend to the biographical: the *text and its creator fall on the side of the analysand, the critic on the side of the analyst. The reductionism of this approach, however, which became the hallmark of Freudian criticism never, in fact, limited Freud's own explorations of creativity. His writings on art include 'Creative Writers and Day-dreaming' (1908), *Jokes and Their Relation to the Unconscious* (1905), *Delusions and Dreams in Jensen's 'Gradiva'* (1907), and 'Leonardo de Vinci and a Memory of His Childhood' (1910). Here Freud extends his analysis to the strategies whereby the artist (like the dreamer) creates 'compromise formations' by which an unacceptable wish becomes, through the construction of an acceptable form, not only conscious but a highly pleasing work of art. He considers the readers' implication in the creator's devices, analysing the effect of the work on its viewer. Though these questions of artistic strategies and their impacts were taken up by later psychoanalytic critics such as *Lionel Trilling and Norman Holland, the first generation of Freudian critics were almost entirely concerned with the psychoanalysis of the creator.

The early contributors to the journal of applied psychoanalysis *Imago* (1912–37, now published in America as *American Imago*) were interested in finding in culture evidence to exemplify recent psychoanalytic findings. The classic example of such psychobiography of the artist is Marie Bonaparte's *Edgar Poe: Etude psychanalytique* (1933). Relying on many of the techniques formulated in *The Interpretation of Dreams*, the early Freudian critics approach the work of art as it revealed a pattern of unconscious figures – imagos – which represent memories and parental personas. As with the dream, the surface or manifest content of the work contains within it a latent meaning which can be deciphered through interpretation. The symbolism of art, like the dream, reveals unconscious content in a relatively consistent relationship between symbol and unconscious 'meaning.' Key also to classical applied psychoanalysis is the theory of sublimation, whereby an original sexual instinct is said to be diverted into neutralized activity with the aim of a socially valued, creative production. This, according to Freud, is the central civilizing mechanism of the psyche (*Civilization and Its Discontents* 1930).

*Archetypal criticism

Where Freud's theory of symbolic meaning centred on the individual within his cultural context, Freud's colleague *Carl Gustav Jung diverged from this emphasis to develop a theory of 'universal symbols.' For Jung the individual unconscious participates in its images and fantasies in a 'collective unconscious' which cuts across all time and culture to contain the inheritance of the entire human race. Certain primordial images issue from this collective unconscious to the individual's psyche; these Jung calls archetypes, because he can find them consistently appearing in legends and myths worldwide (*Two Essays on Analytical Psychology* 1972; *Man and His Symbols* 1964). (See *archetype.) Resisting Freud's identification of art with neurosis, Jung postulates that creative energy in the artistic process follows an autonomous course through the individual consciousness but ultimately derives from the collective unconscious. This process makes the true artist a vehicle for a universal language. The chief practitioner of Jungian criticism is *Maud Bodkin, whose *Archetypal Patterns in Poetry* (1934) stresses the subjective reality of the communal human experience articulated by the writer and responded to in the reader. Bodkin recognizes recurring emotional patterns and psychic figurations as archetypal patterns in art throughout the ages. She attempts to classify works of art according to a universal system of mythic structures which themselves derive from a universal nature; the artist is the progenitive agency of expression for this nature. (See *myth.)

Ego-psychology

Freud's typological theory of the psyche posits the ego as a force derived from the id, a force responsible for assessing external reality and discerning the appropriate release for the libidinal and aggressive drives of the id. Later followers of Freud, most notably Heinz Hartmann, Ernst Kris, Freud's daughter Anna Freud, and the American analyst Erik Erikson, postulate the existence of an 'autonomous ego' which is neither derived from nor bound up with the id-conflict. Drawing on Freud's second topographical structure of the psyche, ego-psychology stresses that certain ego-functions such as intellectual and creative activity, which in Freud's scheme were performed by the sublimation of libido, take their force from neutralized energy from the ego.

Kris' influential *Psychoanalytic Explorations in Art* (1952) postulates that in creative production the ego is master; the unconscious is controlled by the operations of the conscious and preconscious strategies of the artist. The important contributions ego-psychology has made in the field of literary criticism stem from its realigning the artist in a position of control over his production. 'Regression in the Service of the Ego' describes the ego-psychologists' understanding that the complexities and ambiguities which manifest themselves in a work of art are safely under the domination of the artist' ego. Prominent literary critics who helped bring ego-psychology into the mainstream of literary criticism by allying its insights with the *New Criticism include such figures as *William Empson in his *Seven Types of Ambiguity* (1930) and Lionel Trilling in his essays 'Art and Neurosis' (1945) and 'Freud and Literature' (1947). The emphasis on ego-mastery and the creation of socially acceptable forms takes the focus away from the pathology of the artist, thrusting it onto the formal features of the creative work itself.

Ego-psychology has also seized upon the dynamic of the reader's response to the work of art. (See *reader-response criticism.) Simon O. Lesser in *Fiction and the Unconscious* (1957) draws attention to the ego-psychologist's analysis of the wish-fulfilling fantasy shared by both author and reader and of the necessity of formal disguise of that fantasy in the language of art. The place of the reader in the application of ego-psychology to literary criticism receives elaborate systematization in Norman Holland's *The Dynamics of Literary Response* (1968). Holland offers a 'dictionary of fantasy' in which the 'core fantasies' shared by author and reader can be correlated to the stages of infantile development. The literary text is decoded to reveal how disguise and adaptation into socially acceptable language serve to make unconscious wishes accessible to the reader through creative transformation. It is this last point which Holland takes up in his transactive theory of reading (*Five Readers Reading* 1975; 'Recovering the "Purloined Letter"' 1980). By this account, the text only obtains meaning in the act of reading; it is therefore to the reader that psychoanalytic criticism should turn, seeing in the act of reading the re-creation of the reader's 'core' self.

Harold Bloom also sets the reader at the centre of his theory of texts, but for Bloom all reading and all writing is 'transferential.' Bloom's *The Anxiety of Influence: A Theory of Poetry* (1975) sets the reader of the text and the author in an ancient rivalry. (See *anxiety of influence.) The reader Bloom has in mind is the poet/critic who reads in order to write and to surpass the anxious influence of past greatness. The spell cast upon the son by the father instils 'castration anxiety' and the need to obliterate the progenitor. All reading is therefore fraught with idealization, envy and strife; all reading is transferential because it beckons the poet/critic to repeat the same pattern of rivalry which has historically inspired and permitted sons to surpass their fathers. All reading is therefore a 'misreading,' a troping which Bloom relates to both classical rhetorical figures as well as to Anna Freud's system of psychic 'defense mechanisms,' presented in her *Ego and the Mechanisms of Defense* (1936).

Object-relations theory

Object-relations theory concerns itself less with the intrapsychic relationship between the ego and the id than with the relationship between the 'self' and its related 'objects.' 'Object' in this context takes on a specialized, non-pejorative meaning in psychoanalysis, including all persons to whom instinctual energy is directed. Object-relations theory stresses, therefore, the interaction between the self and the Other. (See *self/other.) The subject is constituted by his objects just as he constitutes the object world outside himself. Melanie Klein and D.W. Winnicott are perhaps the most influential theorists in their stress on, in particular, the crucial role of the mother-infant dyad in human development. Klein's seminal case studies from her psychoanalysis of children are collected in

Love, Guilt and Reparation and Other Works 1921–1945 (1977). She identifies in the developing child an active fantasy life, filled with imagos of 'good' and 'bad' objects which derive from both the infant's introjection of gratification and frustration and from his projection of his own libidinal and aggressive instincts. The infant fragments the external world, in particular the mother's body, into part-objects which are invested with the love and hate felt for the whole person. The child will, in the course of development, assume two major positions toward the mother. It will move from the early 'paranoid-schizoid' position in which the 'good-breast' and the 'bad-breast' characterize its fragmented perception, to the 'depressive' position in which the infant begins to see its mother as a whole person and to achieve a separate sense of self through the fantasy of making reparation for the imagined injuries of the first period. D.W. Winnicott also emphasizes the earliest mother-infant dynamic; his key contribution to psychoanalytic thought lies in his notion of the transitional object. In 'Transitional Objects and Transitional Phenomena' (1953), Winnicott outlines the normal transitional phase experienced by the infant in which it relies on a material object (such as a blanket corner) to enable its movement from oral dependence on the mother to a true 'object relationship.' The 'transitional object' takes on importance to literary critics because it occupies the space of illusion in adult creativity. The transitional phenomena occupy an intermediate area of experience, halfway between subjective and objective reality, half-perceived and half-created: it is this space which belongs to art, religion and all human creativity.

Structural psychoanalysis: Jacques Lacan

Jacques Lacan's now famous dictum that the 'unconscious is structured like a language' provides an inlet into structural psychoanalytic theory. Before Lacan, applications of psychoanalytic theory to the arts considered the psychology of the person: whether artist, character or audience. For Lacan the text itself as a linguistic structure has its own 'psyche.' Borrowing from linguistic philosophers *Ferdinand de Saussure and *Roman Jakobson, Lacan puts language at the centre of psychoanalysis, even as language structures and mediates human existence in the world. Lacan posits the existence of what he calls three 'orders'

in human experience: the imaginary, the symbolic and the real. (See *imaginary/symbolic/real.) If classically the unconscious is understood to be the prelinguistic locality which contains instinctual representatives, then for Lacan the unconscious is the *effect* of the human subject's entry into the linguistic order. For Lacan, the human subject (a term used to avoid the concept of 'self' with its connotations of a stable identity) is born into a linguistic system with societal imperatives built in: this system he calls the symbolic order. (See *subject/object.) Lacan answers traditional psychoanalytic theories of development in his theory of the *mirror stage in which the human infant, while in a state of helplessness and uncoordination, experiences an imaginary state of mastery and bodily unity. This fantasy of original unity is represented concretely by the child's reflection of itself in the mirror: the infant makes an imaginary identification with its reflection and takes this as a model for its interaction with the external world and especially the mother. The child's entry into the symbolic order breaks this imaginary unity and its fantasy of mastery by demanding that all impulse and desire be mediated through signification. It is this repression of desire by the signifying imperative which effects the split between conscious and unconscious knowledge.

Lacan diverges from Saussure's equation of the signifier and the signified to expose the unstable relation between the two, illustrating not only that the signifier 'slides' over the field from which the signified is represented, but also that, beyond any sign system (symbolic) or infantile fantasy (imaginary), there exists a real which defies and yet demands representation. (See *signified/signifier/signification, *sign.) The real is beyond all signification and yet can only be accessed through the signifier available to us through language. Lacan's formulation of the subject's constitution in language leads him again to revise Freud's unconscious mechanisms of condensation and displacement according to Roman Jakobson's tropes of metonymy and metaphor as the two fundamental poles of all language. (See *metonymy/metaphor.) If the unconscious is structured like a language, then its mechanisms can best be described by rhetorical tropes. (See *trope.) Metonymy, like displacement, functions according to contiguity, while metaphor, like condensation, functions according to similarity. The unconscious, with its store of memories, words and images moves along a chain of signifiers which can mistake one signifier for another similar to it and substitute that signifier. Or it can find one signifier to be proximate to another and so provide an associative link. The crucial point for Lacan is that the processes of symbolization effect a cut, a castration, which shatters the illusion of unity with the desire of the Other while at the same time promising a substitution in representing desire in language. The substitution is, of course, never complete and never satisfying. Language acts like the '*Name-of-the-Father' in the human subject, separating the subject from the mother while inserting the subject into the social order of names. This constitutes the subject's fundamental 'lack.' (See *desire/ lack.) Naming destroys the imaginary wholeness of the prelinguistic, pre-Oedipal state. Lacan is, in this regard, highly dismissive of the ego-psychologists and object-relationists who see the autonomous ego as whole and stable, an entity with its own energies and aims.

Lacan's work has implications for literary criticism which are, finally, wider than the classical 'applications' of psychoanalytic theory to a given work of art. Lacan emphasizes that language *structures* the human subject; it not only mediates all relations to the other and the real but defines it. Lacan makes the analysis of language and its productions in culture *the* central task of the critic and analyst.

Relation to other schools/approaches

Lacan's well-known 'Seminar on "The Purloined Letter"' takes Edgar Allan Poe's tale of sexual and political intrigue as a kind of metaphor of the subject caught in a web of signifiers. Lacan punningly recognizes that the incriminating, circulating 'letter' in the Poe story acts 'like' the signifier in language exchange which contains, represents and determines the vicissitudes of human desire. Lacan's essay has been exposed by *Jacques Derrida for what he calls the phallogocentrism in his theory. Derrida's 'The Purveyor of Truth' (1975) asserts that Lacan inserts the signifier as supreme in the constitution of the subject and so totalizes and idealizes it in a phallic dominance. (See *totalization, *phallocentrism.) The unconscious for Derrida is not structured like a language, does not come into being with the accession to the symbolic. In-

stead, the unconscious is *before* language, *in* language and *beyond* language. Derrida's principles of *deconstruction seek to dethrone the dominant signifier, to discover 'traces' of the unconscious in all *discourse, and to dismantle the repressive power held by the 'Name-of-the-Father' over the subject. (See *trace.) Derrida's deconstruction of texts exposes the repression of desire in all language, while it also demonstrates that desire is revealed in unconscious traces which are always already inscribed in the text and in the reader, who is himself written into in a culturally shared discourse.

Structuralist and poststructuralist schools of psychoanalytic criticism undermine the classical reader/author distinction because both are implicated in the grid of language and caught up in the transferential structures implied in the acts of reading and writing. (See *structuralism, *poststructuralism.) *Roland Barthes collapses the distinction between critic and author in his *S/Z* (1970), a critical rewriting of Balzac's *Sarrasine*. In *The Pleasure of the Text* (1973) and *Lover's Discourse* (1977), Barthes exposes the reader's collusion with the author's fantasies as inscribed in the conventions and discourse of love. The author-ity of the text is pronounced dead by Barthes; the text lives only in the reader's experience of it. (See *authority.)

Psychoanalysis and cultural criticism

Many of the most prominent contemporary theories of cultural discourse derive from fundamental psychoanalytic concepts. Though by no means sympathetic to classical psychoanalysis, contemporary critiques of the discourses of history, sexuality and *power rely on psychoanalytic theories of the unconscious and its mechanisms. *Michel Foucault has systematically drawn attention to power relations within society and history in *The History of Sexuality* (1976). He posits a continually fluctuating, cultural unconscious which directs and determines class distinctions, truth value, gender relations, and the nature of all knowledge. It is in uncovering the unformulated and therefore unrecognized rules which govern this unconscious that Foucault finds the necessary *subversion of the power structures served by these cultural assumptions. Foucault's analysis of the discourse of power is generative of much contemporary discussion of *ideology. His theories are heavily indebted to psychoanalytic notions of unconscious determination and schemes of unconscious mechanisms.

Feminist, Marxist and New Historicist schools of literary and cultural criticism are all similarly indebted to and directed by psychoanalytic assumptions about the ways in which the human subject experiences the world and the body through language. (See *feminist criticism, *New Historicism, *cultural materialism.) Between feminism and psychoanalysis especially there exists a peculiar mutual implication. Feminist theory has traditionally identified psychoanalysis with rigid patriarchal assumptions which are made doubly dangerous by being rooted in a 'biology' of human development. Early feminists such as *Simone de Beauvoir exposed how Freud's infamous and bastardized concepts such as 'penis envy' and 'anatomy is destiny' have been used to validate sexual, economic and political oppression of women as a class. But following Juliet Mitchell's highly influential *Psychoanalysis and Feminism* and then her publication, along with Jacqueline Rose, of Lacan's papers on *Feminine Sexuality*, the trend among feminist theorists has been to recognize the value of psychoanalytic insights into the unconscious structures of language and culture to any feminist critique. By reconsidering Freud's theory of the unconscious in light of Lacan's theory of signification as 'lack,' feminist theorists have found a vocabulary with which to critique the very phallocentric order which traditionally structures the discourse of psychoanalysis. Drawing from clinical and theoretical research as well as from contemporary *semiotics, writers as diverse as *Julia Kristeva, *Luce Irigaray, Nancy Chodorow, and Jane Gallop have each drawn on revisionary psychoanalytic concepts to develop theories of the gendered subject. Feminist theory places the ineluctable material and maternal body at the centre of human experience anterior to symbolic language and so critiques the primacy of the phallus in the formation of human subjectivity.

It is some measure of the power of psychoanalytic theory that many of its central precepts are now themselves part of what Foucault has termed the unconscious of the culture. In this regard, psychoanalysis itself, especially the American models of therapeutic analysis, is now repeatedly subjected to scrutiny as an institution. Here the contemporary connection between psychoanalysis and theories of language and culture have brought to the 'Freudian field' the kind of self-analysis upon which Freud's science and art depends.

VERA J. CAMDEN

Primary Sources

Barthes, Roland. *Fragments d'un discours amoureux.* Paris, 1977. *A Lover's Discourse.* New York: Hill and Wang, 1979.
– *Le Plaisir du texte.* Paris, 1973. *The Pleasure of the Text.* London: Jonathan Cape, 1976.
– *S/Z.* Paris, 1970. Trans. R. Miller. London: Jonathan Cape, 1975.
Bloom, Harold. *The Anxiety of Influence: Theory of Poetry.* London: Oxford UP, 1975.
Bodkin, Maud. *Archetypal Patterns in Poetry.* London: Oxford UP, 1934.
Bonaparte, Marie. *Edgar Poe: Etude psychoanalytique.* Paris, 1933. *The Life and Works of Edgar Allan Poe: A Psycho-Analytic Interpretation.* London: Imago, 1949.
Chodorow, Nancy. *The Reproduction of Mothering: Psychoanalysis and the Sociology of Gender.* Berkeley: U of California P, 1978.
Derrida, Jacques. 'The Purveyor of Truth.' *Yale French Studies* 52 (1975): 31–113. 'Le Facteur de la verité.' *Poetique* 21 (1975): 96–147.
Empson, William. *Seven Types of Ambiguity.* London: Chatto and Windus, 1930.
Erikson, Erik. *Childhood and Society.* 1950. New York: W.W. Norton, 1963.
Felman, Shoshana. 'Turning the Screw of Interpretation.' *Yale French Studies* 55–6 (1977): 94–207.
Foucault, Michel. *La Volonté de savoir.* Paris, 1976. Trans. as *The History of Sexuality, I: An Introduction.* Harmondsworth: Penguin, 1981.
– *Les Mots et les choses.* Paris, 1966. *The Order of Things: An Archaeology of the Human Sciences.* London: Tavistock Publications, 1974.
Freud, Anna. *Das Ich und die Abwehrmechanismen.* Vienna, 1936. *The Ego and the Mechanisms of Defenses.* New York: International Universities P, 1966.
Freud, Sigmund. *Gesammelte Werke,* vols 1–18. London and Frankfurt, 1940–68. *The Standard Edition of the Complete Psychological Works.* 24 vols. London: Hogarth P and Institute of Psychoanalysis, 1953.
Gallop, Jane. *The Daughter's Seduction: Feminism and Psychoanalysis.* Ithaca: Cornell UP, 1974.
Hartmann, Heinz. 'Notes on the Theory of Sublimation.' In *Essays in Ego-Psychology.* New York: International Universities P, 1964, 215–40.
Holland, Norman N. *The Dynamics of Literary Response.* New York: Oxford UP, 1968.
– *Five Readers Reading.* New Haven: Yale UP, 1975.
– 'Recovering "The Purloined Letter": Reading as a Personal Transaction.' In *The Purloined Poe: Lacan, Derrida, and Psychoanalytic Reading.* Ed. John P.

Miller and William J. Richardson. Baltimore: Johns Hopkins UP, 1988, 307–22.

Irigaray, Luce. *Speculum de l'autre femme*. Paris: Editions de Minuit, 1974. *Speculum of the Other Woman*. Ithaca: Cornell UP, 1985.

Jakobson, Roman, and Morris Halle. *Fundamentals of Language*. The Hague: Mouton, 1956, 76–82.

Jung. *Man and His Symbols*. New York: Doubleday, 1964.

– *Über die Psychogie dem Unbewussten* (Zürich, 1943) and *Die Beziehungen zwischen dem Ich und dem Unbewussten* (Zürich, 1928). *Two Essays on Analytical Psychology*. New Jersey: Princeton UP, 1972.

Klein, Melanie. 'The Importance of Symbol Formation in the Development of the Ego.' In *Love, Guilt and Reparation and Other Works, 1921–1945*. London: Hogarth P, 1977, 219–32.

Kris, Ernst. *Psychoanalytic Explorations in Art*. 1952. New York: Schocken Books, 1964.

Kristeva, Julia. *Desire in Language*. New York: Columbia UP, 1980.

Lacan, Jacques. *Ecrits: A Selection*. London: Tavistock Publications, 1970.

– *Le Séminaire de Jacques Lacan*, Livre 11, 'Les Quatre concepts fondamentaux de la psychanalyse.' Paris, 1973. *The Four Fundamental Concepts of Psychoanalysis*. London: Hogarth P, 1977.

Lesser, Simon O. *Fiction and the Unconscious*. Chicago: U of Chicago P, 1957.

Mitchell, Juliet. *Psychoanalysis and Feminism: Freud, Reich, Laing, and Women*. New York: Vintage Books, 1975.

Mitchell, Juliet, and Jacqueline Rose. *Feminine Sexuality: Jacques Lacan and the Ecole Freudienne*. London: Macmillan, 1982.

de Saussure, Ferdinand. *Cours de linguistique générale*. 1915. *Course in General Linguistics*. Ed. Charles Bally and Albert Sechehaye. London: Fontana and Collins, 1977.

Trilling, Lionel. 'Art and Neurosis' and 'Freud and Literature.' In *The Liberal Imagination*. London: Heinemann, 1964, 160–80 and 34–57.

Winnicott, D.W. *Piggle: An Account of the Psychoanalytic Treatment of a Little Girl*. Harmondsworth: Penguin, 1974.

– *Playing and Reality*. Harmondsworth: Penguin, 1974.

– 'Transitional Objects and Transitional Phenomena.' *International Journal of Psycho-Analysis* 34 (1953): 89–97.

Secondary Sources

Laplanche, Jean, and Pontalis, Jean-Baptiste. *Vocabulaire de psychanalyse*. Paris, 1967. *The Language of Psychoanalysis*. London: Hogarth P, 1973.

Wright, Elizabeth. *Psychoanalytic Criticism: Theory in Practice*. London and New York: Methuen, 1984.

Quebec feminist criticism: *see* Feminist criticism, Quebec

Reader-response criticism

Reader-response criticism designates a cluster of critical theories and practices prominent in the late 1960s and 1970s in North America. The work of a disparate group of theorists, reader-response criticism nevertheless shares an emphasis upon the role of the reader or the act of reading in the interpretation of texts. (See *text.) Its primary impulse is one of reaction to the Anglo-American *New Criticism's treatment of the literary text as an object that could and should be interpreted in dissociation from the reader's experience of it. In the self-reflexive philosophical climate of the later 20th century, with its consciousness of the observer's influence upon the observed and its suspicion of any discourse's claim of transparent signification, each of the theories thus concerns itself centrally with issues of *hermeneutics. Interpretation is explained as a subjective construction of knowledge, while relativism is avoided by situating reading within the bounds of either the text or an interpretive community. Theorists associated with reader-response criticism include *Jonathan Culler, *Stanley Fish, *E.D. Hirsch, Jr., *David Bleich, and *Norman Holland, as well as the German *Wolfgang Iser, whose work as a reception theorist is compatible with the American response approach. (See *Constance School of Reception Aesthetics.)

In seeking a corrective to the *reification of the literary object, reader-response criticism draws principally upon *structuralism, *rhetorical criticism, psychoanalysis, and phenomenology. (See *psychoanalytic theory, *phenomenological criticism.) Early reader-response criticism emphasizes the reader over the text in an attempt to correct the imbalance of the formalist text-reader relation. Under pressure of the poststructuralist rejection of the very subject-object *binary opposition upon which a privileging of reader over text depends, subsequent reader-response approaches describe the interpretive act as a process of communication which to some degree blurs the distinction between text and reader, yet retains a basis for *authority. (See *poststructuralism, *subject/object.) In the past decade, reader response has diverged into either *deconstruction, which subsumes both text and reader in the notion of *discourse, or theories affirming the primacy of the perceiving subject. The impetus for this divergence is generated largely by the mutual critiques of reader-response theorists themselves.

Jonathan Culler and the structuralist approach

In *Structuralist Poetics* (1975) Jonathan Culler attempts to 'free' criticism from its interpretive role under the New Criticism by developing a poetics that defines the conditions of interpretation. Using the model of structuralist linguistics, Culler describes *literature as a 'second-order' semiotic system that uses language to produce and govern literary meaning. Authors, texts, and readers are thus all inscriptions within a literary system of signification. (See *semiotics, *signified/signifier/signification.)

The conditions of meaning are most easily examined as the enabling assumptions of the reader. Culler's readers embody the structuralist notion of literary competence, or mastery of texts, that allows them to determine meaning, to 'naturalize' texts by bringing the apparently strange within a discursive order. (See *competence/performance.) While such a notion of interpretation suggests that 'we can ... make anything signify' (*Structuralist Poetics* 138), Culler limits interpretive possibility through his description of the *ideal reader as one whose readings are at once produced by, and affirm, the activities of the *literary institution. Admittedly, such interpretations are ideologically determined, but since all meaning is governed by cultural conventions, a poetics can only aspire to a fuller understanding of signifying systems, rather than attempting to move beyond *ideology and system. In later works Culler withdraws the term 'ideal reader' as ahistorical; nevertheless, his readers are able to use the system which produces them as a means to self-knowledge and cultural transcendence.

Stanley Fish and the rhetorical approach

Stanley Fish's theory of reader response first moves from a rhetorical to a structuralist position. The rhetorical method is generalized in 'Literature in the Reader' (1970). In opposition to the New Critical notion of the Affective Fal-

lacy, Fish argues that any literary artefact 'means' as an event rather than an object. Criticism must therefore produce a temporal analysis of the reader's developing responses, which follow the pattern of succeeding insights that continually prove preceding conclusions to be false, so that the text becomes a 'self-consuming' artefact. To this point, as the highly self-conscious Fish points out, the model is monistic in that it allows a text only one meaning, albeit an experiential meaning that is a complex of many constituents. The 'informed' reader involved in the creation of this meaning is like Culler's reader, competent; real readers who inform themselves as fully as possible and therefore recognize and control their own subjectivity can approach such competence.

E.D. Hirsch, Jr., and the ethical hermeneutics approach

In *Validity in Interpretation* (1967) and *The Aims of Interpretation* (1976), E.D. Hirsch, Jr., proposes a hermeneutical resolution to the issues of interpretation, as a response to what he calls the 'dogmatic relativism' of theorists such as Fish. Hirsch argues in support of the New Critical focus on a text's meaning, while reintroducing intentionality as the only authority for determining that meaning. (See *intention/intentionality.) Using *Edmund Husserl and the Italian Emilio Betti as the source of his hermeneutics, Hirsch argues that the recovery of authorial intention is a valid goal because cultural subjectivity is not determinate: an individual is capable of adopting an indefinite number of cultural systems of interpretation. Although readers can never be sure that the meaning they assign to a text is that intended, they are nevertheless ethically obliged to try to reconstruct authorial intent.

Hirsch distinguishes between meaning and significance as successive components of the reading act. Because the verbal meaning of the text, that which the interpreter takes it to represent, precedes the act of interpretation itself, it is not subject to alteration by the reader's choice of the interpretive approach. The significance of a text, on the other hand, is its textual meaning in relation to a larger context – for example, a literary, linguistic or psychoanalytic one. Meaning is thus a stable quality which gives the text its self-identity over time for the reader who is interpreting it, while significance (or meaningfulness) changes according to context. Critics such as David Bleich have questioned the validity of Hirsch's meaning-significance distinction and rejected his commitment to intentionality as incompatible with contemporary understandings of personal and cultural subjectivity.

David Bleich and subjective criticism

David Bleich resolves the conflict of authority between text and reader on the side of the reader in his theory of subjective criticism. *Readings and Feelings* (1975) and *Subjective Criticism* (1978) are the principal texts in which he outlines his belief that the perception and indeed the composition of the literary work is entirely a function of the reader's personality. The reading subject's initial perception of, or response to, the textual object is its symbolization, while the subsequent interpretation and public presentation of that response is its 'resymbolization.' This continuity of response and interpretation is intended to overcome the objectivist tendency to dissociate the response of the subject from valid interpretation of a work. The reader negotiates his or her resymbolization with the community of individuals who share a common interest and thereby contributes to a collective response.

Bleich's theoretical starting-point is the subjective paradigm, which he traces historically as arising in physics, psychoanalysis and phenomenology out of a rejection of the objective doctrines of Western thought. Associated particularly with Edmund Husserl, the subjective paradigm maintains that self-transcendence is impossible and seeks to overcome as contradictory the subject-object distinction of Western thought. Nevertheless, the replacement of the objective by the subjective paradigm has been seen by Bleich's critics as a continuation of this dichotomy.

Norman Holland and the psychoanalytic approach

In a series of writings ranging from *The Dynamics of Literary Response* (1968) to 'The New Paradigm: Subjective or Transactive?' (1976), Norman Holland has elaborated and revised a psychoanalytic model of reader response. He claims that the reading experience follows a generalized pattern designed to re-create the reader's own identity theme, or personal style, through her or his response to textual elements. The reader moves from locating, in the work's form, defence structures which will help control its anxiety potential, to projecting a pleasure-giving fantasy onto the work's content, to transforming that fantasy into a more acceptable 'sense' of the text. This model of reading assumes a text that displays an organic unity, 'a central or nuclear fantasy' (*Dynamics* 310).

In his subsequent work, however, Holland shifts his emphasis from the text to the reader as the locus of fantasy, as the 'literent' who 'creates meaning and feeling in one continuous and indivisible transaction.' Concern about consensus in interpretation thus gives way to an invitation to 'use human differences to add response to response, to multiply possibilities, and to enrich the whole experience' ('Recovering "The Purloined Letter"' 367, 370). Holland's work has been criticized for its transfer of the traditional value of textual unity to a philosophically similar unity of a self with a fixed identity. Indeed, in his recent work Holland has responded to deconstructive textualizations of the subject by subsuming the literary text into the general category of experience upon which the subject's unique identity acts.

Wolfgang Iser and the phenomenology of reception

Wolfgang Iser's work as a member of the Constance School of Reception Aesthetics has been made accessible to an English-speaking audience in a series of works beginning with 'Indeterminacy and the Reader's Response in Prose Fiction' (1971) and including *The Act of Reading* (1978). Drawing on the phenomenology of Edmund Husserl and *Roman Ingarden, Iser describes the individual reading act as the *concretization or realization of the text as a literary work. Because the literary work has no objective reference outside of itself, it must create its own object through the provision of numerous perspectives of that object. These determinate perspectives are incomplete, however, leaving gaps that are filled in during the act of reading. Gaps (or blanks) can occur at numerous levels of the text – semantic, plot or narrative, for example – and together form the *indeterminacy which invites the reader's response. (See also *story/plot.)

The literary work is therefore a dynamic entity: the reader selects and relates the text's perspectives in order to form a viewpoint that is itself continually shifting or wandering. This wandering viewpoint of the reader is both free to choose between potential meaning patterns and limited by boundaries to possible interpretations that are imposed by the text. However, Iser's attempt to use phenomenology to replace the opposition between objective text and subjective reader with the virtual work and the implied reader, a dyad formed by the text and the reader's realizing act, is significantly undermined by his simultaneous treatments of the text as authoritative and of the reader as formulating meaning and transcending culture. Critics therefore see Iser's theory as ultimately founded upon the formalist and New Critical principles it professes to correct. Furthermore, as Stanley Fish, among others, has pointed out, the distinction between determinate and indeterminate elements of the text is subject to the criticism that it is simply arbitrary and conventional.

Conclusion

Jane P. Tompkins argues that reader-response criticism has merely revised formalism, since 'although New Critics and reader-oriented critics do not locate meaning in the same place, both schools assume that to specify meaning is criticism's ultimate goal' (201). Under pressure of this kind of critique, reader response has lost its theoretical force. In *On Deconstruction* (1982), his 'sequel' to *Structuralist Poetics*, Culler uses deconstruction's notion of difference and deferral to explain the contradictions between the actual and the competent reader, between subjective and texual authority, which have been criticized in his own and other theories of reading. (See *différance/différence*.) By positing a division in the notion of reading, Culler claims to retain both the experience of the reader as a subject and the notion of that experience as an interpretive construct which asserts both the reader's and the text's dominance as necessary fictions.

Having posited a gap similar to that of Culler between reading and criticism, Fish also deconstructs his model of reading in the essay 'Interpreting the *Variorum*,' originally published in 1976 and later presented as the conversion point in his autobiography as a theorist. Fish abandons his binary opposition of the text and the reader, dismissing the first as the vestige of the formalist reification of

the text holding subjectivity at bay, and the second as an essentialist affirmation of the free self. (See *essentialism.) Instead, Fish subsumes author, text and reader in the category of interpretive communities. The critic becomes an 'utterer' who communicates the meaning-making conventions of the community to others and therefore need not be 'right' but only 'interesting.' Fish subsequently modifies this relativistic claim with the limitation that 'within a community, however, a standard of right (and wrong) can always be invoked because it will be invoked against the background of a prior understanding as to what counts as fact, what is hearable as an argument, what will be recognized as a purpose, and so on' (*Is There a Text?* 174). (See *discourse analysis theory.)

Despite its theoretical eclipse, however, reader-response criticism continues to exert a significant practical influence, in part because its allowance for communal interpretation affirms the activity of the literary institution and in part because the language of criticism has found no satisfactory substitute for the assumption of a reader-text dichotomy. More positively, many proponents of reader response have made classroom application integral to their work; theorists advocating the engagement of criticism in broader cultural discourses have been influenced by the new centrality of the reading subject. By these means, reader-response theory has helped to effect change in pedagogical and critical practice.

ELIZABETH SCHELLENBERG

Primary Sources

Bleich, David. *Readings and Feelings: An Introduction to Subjective Criticism.* Urbana, Ill.: National Council of Teachers of English, 1975.
- *Subjective Criticism.* Baltimore: Johns Hopkins UP, 1978.
Culler, Jonathan. *On Deconstruction: Theory and Criticism after Structuralism.* Ithaca: Cornell UP, 1982.
- 'Prolegomena to a Theory of Reading.' In *The Reader in the Text: Essays on Audience and Interpretation.* Ed. Susan R. Suleiman and Inge Crosman. Princeton: Princeton UP, 1980, 46–66.
- *Structuralist Poetics: Structuralism, Linguistics and the Study of Literature.* London: Routledge, 1975.
Fish, Stanley. 'Interpreting the *Variorum*.' *Critical Inquiry* 2 (1976): 465–85.
- *Is There a Text in This Class? The Authority of Interpretive Communities.* Cambridge, Mass.: Harvard UP, 1980.

- 'Literature in the Reader: Affective Stylistics.' *New Literary History* 2 (1970): 123–62.
- *Self-Consuming Artifacts: The Experience of 17th Century Literature*. Berkeley: U of California P, 1972.
- *Surprised by Sin: The Reader in 'Paradise Lost.'* London: Macmillan; New York: St. Martin's, 1967.
Hirsch, E.D., Jr. *Validity in Interpretation*. New Haven: Yale UP, 1967.
- *The Aims of Interpretation*. Chicago: U of Chicago P, 1976.
Holland, Norman N. *The Dynamics of Literary Response*. New York: Oxford UP, 1968.
- *Five Readers Reading*. New Haven: Yale UP, 1975.
- *Poems in Persons: An Introduction to the Psychoanalysis of Literature*. New York: Norton, 1973.
- 'Re-Covering "The Purloined Letter": Reading as Personal Transaction.' In *The Reader in the Text: Essays on Audience and Interpretation*. Ed. Susan R. Suleiman and Inge Crosman. Princeton: Princeton UP, 1980, 350–70.
- 'UNITY IDENTITY TEXT SELF.' *PMLA* 90 (1975): 813–22.
- 'The New Paradigm: Subjective or Transactive?' *New Literary History* 7 (1976): 335–46.
Iser, Wolfgang. *Der Akt des Lesens: Theorie ästhetischer Wirkung*. Munich: Fink, 1976. *The Act of Reading: A Theory of Aesthetic Response*. Baltimore: Johns Hopkins UP, 1978.
- *Der implizite Leser: Kommunikationsformen des Romans von Bunyan bis Beckett*. Munich: Fink, 1972. *The Implied Reader: Patterns of Communication in Prose Fiction from Bunyan to Beckett*. Baltimore: Johns Hopkins UP, 1974.
- 'Indeterminacy and the Reader's Response in Prose Fiction.' In *Aspects of Narrative: Selected Papers from the English Institute*. Ed. J. Hillis Miller. New York: Columbia UP, 1971, 1–45.
- 'Interaction between Text and Reader.' In *The Reader in the Text: Essays on Audience and Interpretation*. Ed. Susan R. Suleiman and Inge Crosman. Princeton: Princeton UP, 1980, 106–19.
- 'The Reading Process: A Phenomenological Approach.' *New Literary History* 3 (1972): 279–99.
Suleiman, Susan R., and Inge Crosman, eds. *The Reader in the Text: Essays on Audience and Interpretation*. Princeton: Princeton UP, 1980.
Tompkins, Jane P., ed. *Reader-Response Criticism: From Formalism to Poststructuralism*. Baltimore: Johns Hopkins UP, 1980.

Secondary Sources

Barthes, Roland. *S/Z*. Paris: Seuil, 1970. *S/Z*. New York: Hill and Wang, 1974.
Booth, Wayne. *The Rhetoric of Fiction*. Chicago: U of Chicago P, 1961.
Fish Stanley. 'Why No One's Afraid of Wolfgang Iser.' *Diacritics* 11.3 (1981): 2–13.
Freund, Elizabeth. *The Return of the Reader: Reader-Response Criticism*. London: Methuen, 1987.
Holland, Norman N. 'Stanley Fish, Stanley Fish.' *Genre* 10 (1977): 433–41.
Holub, Robert C. *Reception Theory: A Critical Introduction*. New York: Methuen, 1984.
Horton, Susan R. 'The Experience of Stanley Fish's Prose or The Critic as Self-Creating, Self-Consuming Artificer.' *Genre* 10 (1977): 443–53.
Iser, Wolfgang. *Prospecting: From Reader Response to Literary Anthropology*. Baltimore: Johns Hopkins UP, 1989.
Jauss, Hans Robert. *Towards an Aesthetic of Reception*. Trans. Timothy Bahti. Minneapolis: U of Minnesota P, 1982.
Mailloux, Steven. 'Reader-Response Criticism?' *Genre* 10 (1977): 413–31.
Poulet, Georges. 'Phenomenology of Reading.' *New Literary History* 1 (1969): 53–68.
Prince, Gerald. 'Introduction à l'étude du narrataire.' *Poétique* 14 (1973) 178–96. 'Introduction to the Study of the Narratee.' In *Reader-Response Criticism: From Formalism to Poststructuralism*. Ed. Jane P. Tompkins. Baltimore: Johns Hopkins UP, 1980, 7–25.
Riffaterre, Michael. 'Describing Poetic Structures: Two Approaches to Baudelaire's "Les Chats."' *Yale French Studies* 36–7 (1966) 200–42.
- *The Semiotics of Poetry*. Bloomington: Indiana UP, 1978.
Rosenblatt, Louise. 'The Poem as Event.' *College English* 26 (1964): 123–8.
Steig, Michael. *Stories of Reading: Subjectivity and Literary Understanding*. Baltimore: Johns Hopkins P, 1989.
Slatoff, Walter. *With Respect to Readers: Dimensions of Literary Response*. Ithaca: Cornell UP, 1970.
Tompkins, Jane P. 'The Reader in History: The Changing Shape of Literary Response.' In *Reader-Response Criticism: From Formalism to Poststructuralism*. Ed. Jane P. Tompkins. Baltimore: Johns Hopkins UP, 1980.

Reception theory: *see* Constance School of Reception Aesthetics

Rhetorical criticism

Rhetorical criticism is not a single method nor do its practitioners constitute one school of analysis or interpretation. Developed primarily within the 20th-century American academy, rhetorical criticism refers to a collection of critical approaches or points of view united by a single general assumption: that a communicator's intentional use of language or other symbols, a receiver's response and the situation or context in which communication takes place all interact to change human thought, feelings, behaviour, and action. The triadic relation of speaker/writer, discourse/text and environment (including the audience/reader) generates the diverse approaches available to rhetorical critics: some focus primarily on the *discourse or *text and its role in persuading an audience; some on the role of the communicator; some on the communication context; others on the audience itself. Various 'ratios' or combinations of focus produce a complex set of critical goals and methodologies. (See also *communication theory.)

Goals

The general goals of rhetorical criticism are, first, to understand how discourse works to initiate and sustain changes within the communicator, the receiver or the communication environment at large, and second to improve the conduct of such discourse. (See also *discourse analysis theory.) To achieve the first goal, rhetorical criticism proceeds from and contributes to rhetorical theory: a systematic body of general principles applicable to specific rhetorical transactions. The variety of rhetorical theories currently available to critics – from Aristotle's concept of logical, ethical and emotional proofs to *Kenneth Burke's dramatic pentad – accounts for the multiplicity of ways in which rhetorical critics understand discourse. To achieve the second goal of improving persuasive discourse, rhetorical criticism employs and generates the tools required of practical arts: techniques of analysis, a core of commonly cited cases and criteria for assessing the success or failure of persuasive communication.

Methods

Methods vary with the definitions of rhetorical criticism. Some critics define rhetorical criticism as the analysis of rhetorical discourse and others as the rhetorical analysis of all discourse. The former analyses texts that are intentionally persuasive and traditionally rhetorical such as sermons, courtroom speeches and controversial essays. This definition locates persuasion within the conventions of discourse and the intentions of the communicator, and employs methods of analysis associated with historical, neo-Aristotelian and formalist criti-

cism. The second definition, however, allows for the analysis of a wider range of communication: the rhetorical dimensions of all discourse, including critical discourse itself. Following this definition, rhetorical critics borrow widely from the methodologies of almost all critical schools and approaches, including *New Criticism, *structuralism, reader response, *speech act theory, and *deconstruction, as well as from other disciplines: psychology, sociology, anthropology, linguistics, and aesthetics. Separating rhetorical criticism from all other schools and disciplines is the emphasis placed on the interaction among and resulting changes within the rhetorical triad of communicator, discourse and communication environment. (See also *psychoanalytic theory, *Constance School of Reception Aesthetics, Russian *formalism, *Neo-Aristotelian or Chicago School.)

History: major figures and concepts

The 20th century has seen significant and ongoing changes in the definitions, theories and methodologies shaping rhetorical criticism. Many current definitions now include the rhetorical analysis of all discourse, not just texts that are distinctly and intentionally persuasive. The traditional neo-Aristotelian theories, concerned primarily with the structure and effect of argument, have been expanded or replaced by the plurality of methodologies generated by most major current approaches and schools of literary and social criticism.

The history of rhetorical criticism in this century falls into three phases – the traditional, the transitional and the contemporary. The traditional approach is best represented by Herbert Wicheln's landmark essay 'The Literary Criticism of Oratory' (1925) and Lester Thonssen and Craig Baird's *Speech Criticism* (1948). The traditional approach is primarily historical in three senses. First, traditionalists often prefer to analyse past discourse, often oral communication; second, they focus on the communicator's biography and the history of the times shaping and shaped by the discourse; and third, they look back to classical precepts, especially Aristotle's *Rhetoric*, for theoretical principles.

Traditionalists define rhetorical criticism as the study of intentionally persuasive discourse. For this reason, they analyse well-established rhetorical genres and models – such as public addresses – the purpose and effect of which can be reviewed and assessed historically. They give the communicator primacy within the rhetorical triad. When considering the communication environment, they examine the communicator's ability to reflect and influence 'the times.' When considering the discourse, they study the communicator's ability to select the right appeals, order the argument, and express ideas using appropriate language. They assume that Aristotle's distinctions between the three kinds of appeals (logical, ethical, emotional), the two kinds of proof (artistic and inartistic), and the fourfold division of rhetoric (invention, arrangement, style, and delivery) provide the most theoretically sound and practical methodology for analysing and judging persuasive discourse.

The transitionalists attack and share many of the fundamental tenets of the traditionalists. Both Edwin B. Black's *Rhetorical Criticism* (1965) and Donald C. Bryant's *Rhetorical Dimensions in Criticism* (1973) criticize the neo-Aristotelian emphasis on the speaker and the assumption that rhetorical criticism must overlook the critic's response in favour of the original or intended audience's reaction to a persuasive speech. Both agree that the critic must look at written as well as oral communication and that the critic's insights are an essential component of rhetorical criticism. To this end, Black calls for a 're-creative criticism' to replace the traditionalists' emphasis on 'historical reconstruction.'

Black and Bryant attempt to replace neo-Aristotelian theories of rhetoric – interested chiefly in argument and the speaker's ability to move an audience – with a transactional model. According to this model, the function of the critic is to penetrate the transactions among the rhetorical situation (the world influencing the reception of discourse), the rhetorical strategies (features of the discourse) and the rhetorical effects (audience response). Good critics discover and describe the elements, forms and dynamics of rhetorical art.

'Rhetorical art,' however, turns out to be any discourse that seeks to persuade. So while the transitionalists are more interested in the intention than the effect of discourse, they share the traditionalists' assumption that rhetorical criticism treats discourse that self-consciously attempts to influence an audience. As well, they share with the traditionalists a lack

of an original methodology. Neither Black nor Bryant provides any techniques of analysis that can help others to systematically judge or understand rhetorical transactions.

There is no single, unified contemporary approach to rhetorical criticism. Contemporary approaches fall into two general groups: those that accept *pluralism as a feature of rhetorical criticism and those that assume the possibility of a single, systematic definition of, and methodology for, rhetorical criticism. A third approach, drawing from the other two, focuses on very large-scale units of rhetorical criticism: genre and historical-social movements. (See *genre criticism.)

Wayne Booth's *Rhetoric of Fiction* (1961) and *Rhetoric of Irony* (1974), and Edward P.J. Corbett's *Rhetorical Analyses of Literary Works* (1969), and Mark Klyn's essay 'Toward a Pluralistic Rhetorical Criticism' (1968) provide a foundation for pluralism by defining rhetorical criticism as an interest in the product, the process and the effect of linguistic activity. (See *Wayne C. Booth, *irony.) Using this definition, a critic considers a work to be rhetorical not because of its intrinsic quality but because of the interpretive stance of the rhetorical critic, who chooses to view discourse primarily as a communicative act. This stance is not itself a method but a framework of rhetorical interpretation that guides the critic's development, adaptation and application of critical methodologies. Other, equally valid stances are available to critics, but only those who attend to the intention, process and effect of discourse together can be considered 'rhetorical critics.'

Those contemporary rhetorical critics who advocate or presuppose a pluralistic approach – such as Lawrence W. Rosenfield in his theoretical essay 'The Anatomy of Critical Discourse' (1968), Wayne Brockriede in 'Dimensions of the Concept of Rhetoric' (1968) and Ernest Bormann in 'Fantasy and Rhetorical Vision' (1972) – all share a number of fundamental assumptions: first, that reality is a social construction and as such is constantly changing and being changed by language; second, that all discourse reveals the presence of rhetorical interactions conditioned by socio-political-economic forces; third, that the critic rather than rhetorical theory is central to the critical act and that theories must evolve to reflect the insights of, rather than dictate to, rhetorical critics; and fourth, that because reality –

and the theoretical accounts of it – are always changing, no predetermined method can prescribe to rhetorical critics how or what to analyse. Discourse, according to these critics, must always be studied afresh, requiring the integration of new insights taken from media studies, political science, economics, and psychology into the critical act.

Those contemporary approaches which challenge the ideals of pluralism – multiple methodologies and the priority of the critic over theory – look for a unified theory and method in a non-Aristotelian system. Some take their inspiration from language-action approaches pioneered by Richard Weaver in *The Ethics of Rhetoric* (1953), *I.A. Richards in *The Philosophy of Rhetoric* (1936), the work of the General Semanticists, such as Alfred Korzybski, and more recently, the speech act theories of *J.L. Austin and *John Searle, all of which attempt to establish a systematic way of explaining the relationship between patterns of language and human interaction. Examples of rhetorical criticism applying language-action theories include John Sommerville's 'Language and the Cold War' (1966) and Hermann Stelzer's '"War Message"' (1966).

Other contemporary rhetorical critics look to Kenneth Burke's notion of dramatism expressed in such articles and books as 'Dramatism' (1968), 'Rhetoric, Poetics, and Philosophy' (1978), and *Language as Symbolic Action* (1966). Dramatism – the concept that rhetoric is a performance enacting identification and division and that a rhetorical performance (act) involves someone (agent) using symbolic means (agency) within a context (scene) to achieve some end (purpose) – has provided psychologists, sociologists, political scientists, journalists, and literary scholars with a body of theoretical assumptions out of which a unified, interdisciplinary methodology may emerge. Examples of rhetorical criticism that both apply and develop these concepts include Jeanne Y. Fisher's 'A Burkean Analysis' (1974) and Carol Berthold's 'Kenneth Burke's Cluster-Agon Method' (1976).

Genre and movements approaches are less interested in specific rhetorical transactions and theories than in developing broad distinctions useful to all rhetorical critics. *Genre criticism asks the questions: 'Is there a systematic way to classify rhetorical acts'?; 'What can a classification system show us about rhetorical

interactions'?; 'What does genre tell us about the nature of criticism itself'? *Form and Genre* (1978), edited by Karolyn Kohrs Campbell and Kathleen Hall Jamieson, as well as Jackson Harell and Wil A. Linkugel's 'On Rhetorical Genre' (1978), set out to develop a theoretical framework capable of answering these questions. The movements approach looks at patterns of historical and social change, especially revolutionary and reform movements, that shape communication and action. Leland Griffin combines Burkean analysis with the movements approach in 'A Dramatistic Theory of the Rhetoric of Movements' (1969), and Robert S. Cathcart outlines a distinctly 'rhetorical' definition of movements in his essay 'New Approaches to the Study of Movements' (1971).

Limitations

No single paradigmatic methodology has emerged from the contemporary approaches to rhetorical criticism. Traditionalist, transitionalist, pluralistic, and non-pluralistic approaches all coexist, borrowing from and contributing to each other. If rhetorical criticism is paradigmatic, then, the unifying force is the rhetorical stance itself: the rhetorical critic's concern with the social nature of reality and, specifically, with the interrelationship between language and human action. Rhetorical critics look to whatever theories and methodologies can explain and evaluate the motivations of speakers, the responses of audiences, the structures of discourse, and the changes in a communication environment.

The relation of rhetorical to literary criticism

Traditionally, rhetorical criticism has been distinguished from literary criticism in three ways. First, rhetorical criticism analyses and interprets a wider range of communication, including any form of public discourse such as lawsuits, political speeches, lectures, sermons, and pamphlets. Second, literary texts lend themselves to rhetorical criticism, but are analysed not for what they are but for what they do, namely, how they change the world outside the work. Third, rhetorical critics use distinctions belonging solely to classical and modern rhetorical theory, as does, for example, the traditional five-part division of an oration into the *exordium* (introduction), *narratio* (history, summary), *partitio* (division of topic), *confirmatio* (arguments for), *refutatio* (arguments against), and *peroratio* (conclusion).

A better way to define the differences between rhetorical and literary criticism is to invoke the rhetorical stance. New Criticism, for instance, resembles rhetorical criticism in its emphasis on close reading and the form of discourse, but differs in its rejection of questions important to the rhetorical stance: what motivates the speaker? how does this discourse affect the audience? Similarly, certain elements of structuralism and deconstruction resemble rhetorical criticism: the first, in its focus on signs, linguistic structure and the possibilities of interpretation; the second, in its examination of all discourse, not just literary works, for their assumptions and logic. The differences separating structuralism and deconstruction from rhetorical criticism, however, are significant. Unlike structuralists, rhetorical critics are interested in the symbolic, communicative aspects of language, and examine the extralingual questions of audience response and authorial *intention. And unlike deconstructionists, rhetorical critics assume and affirm the adequacy of language to communicate intentions and change human behaviour.

DAVID GOODWIN

Primary Sources

Arnold, Carroll C. *Criticism of Oral Rhetoric.* Columbus: Charles E. Merrill, 1974.

Aristotle. *Rhetoric.* Trans. W. Rhys Roberts. In *Aristotle.* New York: Modern Library, 1954.

Berthold, Carol A. 'Kenneth Burke's Cluster-Agon Method: Its Development and Application.' *Central States Speech Journal* 27 (1976): 302–9.

Bitzer, Lloyd F., and Edwin Black, eds. *The Prospect of Rhetoric.* New York: Prentice-Hall, 1971.

Black, Edwin B. *Rhetorical Criticism: A Study in Method.* New York: Macmillan, 1965.

Booth, Wayne C. *The Rhetoric of Fiction.* Chicago: U of Chicago P, 1961.

– *The Rhetoric of Irony.* Chicago: U of Chicago P, 1974.

Bormann, Ernest. 'Fantasy and Rhetorical Vision: The Rhetorical Criticism of Social Reality.' *Quarterly Journal of Speech* 58 (1972): 396–407.

Brockriede, Wayne. 'Dimensions of the Concept of Rhetoric.' *Quarterly Journal of Speech* 54 (1968): 1–12.

Bryant, Donald C., ed. *Rhetorical Dimensions in Criticism.* Baton Rouge: Louisiana State UP, 1973.

Burke, Kenneth. 'Dramatism.' *International Encyclopedia of the Social Sciences.* Ed. David L. Sills. Vol. 7. New York: Macmillan/Free P, 1968, 445–52.

– *Language as Symbolic Action: Essays on Life, Literature and Method.* Berkeley: U of California P, 1966.

– 'Rhetoric, Poetics, and Philosophy.' In *Rhetoric, Philosophy, and Literature: An Exploration.* Ed. Don M. Burks. West Lafayette: Purdue UP, 1978, 15–33

Campell, Karlyn Kohrs, and Kathleen Hall Jamieson, eds. *Form and Genre: Shaping Rhetorical Action.* Falls Church, Va.: Speech Communication Association, 1978.

Cathcart, Robert S. 'New Approaches to the Study of Movements: Defining Movements Rhetorically.' *Western Speech* 36 (1972): 82–7.

Corbett, Edward P.J. *Rhetorical Analyses of Literary Works.* New York: Oxford UP, 1969.

Fisher, Jeanne Y. 'A Burkean Analysis of the Rhetorical Dimensions of a Multiple Murder and Suicide.' *Quarterly Journal of Speech* 60.2 (1974): 175–89.

Griffin, Leland. 'A Dramatistic Theory of the Rhetoric of Movements.' In *Critical Responses to Kenneth Burke, 1924–1966.* Ed. William H. Rueckert. Minneapolis: U of Minneapolis P, 1969.

Harrell, Jackson, and Wil A. Linkugel. 'Rhetorical Genre: An Organizing Perspective.' *Philosophy and Rhetoric* 2 (1978): 262–81.

Klyn, Mark. 'Towards a Pluralistic Rhetorical Criticism.' In *Essays on Rhetorical Criticism.* Ed. Thomas R. Nilsen. New York: Random House, 1968.

Mohrmann, G. P., Charles J. Stewart, and Donovan Ochs, eds. *Explorations in Rhetorical Criticism.* Pennsylvania State UP, 1973.

Nichols, Marie Hochmuth. *Rhetoric and Criticism.* Baton Rouge: Louisiana State UP, 1963.

Nilsen, Thomas R., ed. *Essays on Rhetorical Criticism.* New York: Random House, 1968.

Richards, I.A. *The Philosophy of Rhetoric.* New York: Oxford UP, 1936.

Rosenfield, Lawrence W. 'The Anatomy of Critical Discourse.' *Speech Monographs* 25 (1968): 50–69.

Scott, Robert, and Bernard L. Brock. *Methods of Rhetorical Criticism.* Detroit: Wayne State UP, 1980.

Sommerville, John. 'Language and the Cold War.' *Review of General Semantics* 23.4 (1966): 425–34.

Stelzner, Hermann G. '"War Message": December 8, 1941, An Approach to Language.' *Speech Monographs* 33 (1966): 419–37.

Thonssen, Lester, and Craig Baird. *Speech Criticism: The Development of Standards for Rhetorical Appraisal.* New York: Ronald P, 1948.

Weaver, Richard. *The Ethics of Rhetoric.* Chicago: Henry Regnery, 1953.

Wichelns, Herbert. 'The Literary Criticism of Oratory.' *Studies in Rhetoric and Public Speaking in Honor of James A. Winans.* Ed. A.M. Drummond. New York: Century, 1925.

Russian formalism: *see* Formalism, Russian

Semiotic poetics of the Prague School (Prague School)

Twentieth-century *semiotics and *structuralism emerged simultaneously from the same source: the post-positivistic model originated by *Ferdinand de Saussure and *formalism, Russian. Semiotic structuralism replaced the organic model which had dominated the 19th-century social and human sciences. Semiotic thinking conceives of the entire domain of culture as a realm of signs, with *literature assuming its own, special position. (See *sign.) The first systematic formulation of semiotic structuralism came from a group of scholars gathered in and around the Prague Linguistic Circle, now known as the Prague School. Its system of thought is a heritage of the blossoming of Central-European culture in the first three decades of the 20th century; during this relatively short period Central Europe gave us several theoretical systems which were to dominate the 20th century's intellectual climate: phenomenology (*Husserl, *Ingarden), psychoanalysis (*Freud, Rank), neopositivism (the Vienna Circle), Gestalt-psychology (Wertheimer, Kohler, Koffka), symbolic logic (Leśniewski, Tarski), and, last but not least, structuralism (the Prague School). (See also *phenomenological criticism, *psychoanalytic theory.)

History

The Prague Linguistic Circle was inaugurated in 1926 by Vilém Mathesius (director of the English seminar at Charles University) and his colleagues *Roman Jakobson, Bohuslav Havránek, Bohumil Trnka, and Jan Rypka. Mathesius gave the group not only an organized form but also a clear theoretical direction. The Circle quickly grew into an international association with about 50 members, including such prominent scholars as *Jan Mukařovský, Nikolai V. Trubetskoi, Sergei Kartsevskii, Petr Bogatyrjov, and Dmitrii Chyzhevskii. Russian scholars, most of them former members of the formalist groupings, represented a substantial contingent in the Prague Linguistic Circle. In

the 1930s, younger scholars joined the Circle, among them *René Wellek, Felix Vodička, Jiří Veltruský, Jaroslav Průšek, and Josef Vachek. Initially, papers presented at the regular meetings were concerned with theoretical linguistics, but questions of poetics soon became an equally important topic of discussion. Many foreign scholars (including such luminaries as Husserl, Carnap, *Tomashevskii, and *Benveniste) came to Prague to discuss their ideas in the Circle.

The Circle's international scholarly series *Travaux du Cercle linguistique de Prague (TCLP)* contains in eight volumes (1929–39) pivotal contributions of members and 'fellow travellers,' written in English, French and German. In 1928 the Prague participants of the First International Congress of linguists in The Hague drafted jointly with the *Geneva School scholars a document outlining the principles of the new, structural linguistics. The programmatic 'Thèses du Cercle linguistique de Prague' (published in *TCLP* I, 1929) set out the structural theory of language, literary language and poetic language. In the same year, Jakobson coined the term 'structuralism' to designate the 'leading idea' of contemporary science and the epistemological stance of the Prague Linguistic Circle. In 1932, in the documents of the Third International Congress of Phonetic Sciences in Amsterdam, the label 'L'Ecole de Prague' was first used in a narrow application to refer to the innovative phonology of the Prague Linguistic Circle linguists.

In the 1930s the Circle emerged as a strong cultural force on the domestic scene. Its first important Czech publication was a tribute to the philosopher president of the Czechoslovak republic T.G. Masaryk (on the occasion of his 80th birthday), *Masaryk a řeč [Masaryk and Language* 1930], with papers by Mukařovský and Jakobson. The volume *Spisovná čeština a jazyková kultura* [Standard Czech and Language Culture, 1932] resulted from a lively polemic with conservative linguistic purists; in alliance with avant-garde writers and poets, the Prague Linguistic Circle formulated principles of language culture and planning which have retained their significance to the present day. In 1935 the Circle launched its Czech journal *Slovo a slovesnost [The Word and Verbal Art]*, exploiting in its title the happy etymological link which in Slavic languages exists between the terms for language and for literature. Three widely read collections reaffirmed the Prague Linguistic Circle's eminent position in the rapidly changing political conditions: a jubilee volume, *Torso a tajemství Máchova díla* [*Torso and Mystery of Macha's Work* 1939]; a popularizing work, *Čtení o jazyce a poesii* [*Readings on Language and Poetry* 1942]; and a cycle of radio broadcasts, *O básnickém jazyce* [*On Poetic Language* 1947].

As the Prague Linguistic Circle's influence grew, so did the voices of the critics, coming both from the right – the traditional academics – and from the left – the Marxists. The polite but polemical exchange between the Prague School scholars and the Marxist publicists (1930–4), is probably the first confrontation between structuralism and Marxism in the 20th century. (See *Marxist criticism.)

In the final years of Czechoslovak independence and even during the German occupation, the Prague School scholars continued their theoretical endeavours and published their best works in literary analysis. When Czech universities were closed by the Nazis in November 1939, the meetings of the Circle continued in private homes and apartments. Public activities were resumed in June 1945. A few leaders were lost, either to natural death (Trubetskoi, Mathesius) or to exile (Jakobson, Wellek); on the other hand, many Prague Linguistic Circle members found themselves in key positions in Czechoslovak universities and in the newly established Czechoslovak Academy of Sciences. In fact, the brief spell of democracy in postwar Czechoslovakia (May 1945 – February 1948) was a most productive time for the Prague School. In 1946 Mukařovský visited Paris and presented a lecture at the Institute d'Etudes slaves, which offered the most concise explanation of Prague School structuralism; however, the lecture was never published in French and had no impact on the Parisian intellectual scene. Nineteen forty-eight saw the publication of the standard, three-volume edition of Mukařovský's selected works, *Kapitoly z české poetiky* [*Chapters from Czech Poetics*], as well as of the last representative work of Prague School poetics, Vodička's monograph *Počátky krásné prózy novočeské* [*The Beginnings of Czech Artistic Prose*]. Shortly afterwards, in December 1948, the last lecture in the Circle took place. After more than 40 years, the Prague Linguistic Circle resumed its activities in February 1990.

Principles

The crux of Prague semiotic thinking is the functional view which, according to Mukařovský, 'permits us to conceive of things as events without denying their materiality. It shows the world simultaneously as motion and as a fixed basis of human activity' (*Kapitoly*). The Prague School put great emphasis on the pluri- or polyfunctionality of sign systems. Taxonomies of functions and 'functional languages,' the differentiation of dominant and secondary functions, and the idea of historical shifts in functional hierarchies are the lasting inheritance of Prague School functionalism. Among the functions of semiotic activities, the aesthetic function received prominent attention. It warranted the autonomy of the arts, differentiating them from practical activities (such as economy, politics, propaganda). However, the Prague School scholars did not consider the aesthetic function to be ludic or self-directed. Art is not created for its own sake but is an expression and fulfilment of a basic human need – making us 'again and again aware of the many-sidedness and diversity of reality' (*Kapitoly*).

Prague School semiotics was focused on language, not only because of its crucial role in human culture but also because linguistic structuralism provided the impetus for semiotic thinking. Prague School linguistic theory and its most important achievements – phonology, morphonemics, semantics of grammatical categories, functional syntax, and structural stylistics – have been integrated into modern linguistics. Despite the prominence of linguistics, the Prague School did not subsume culture under the linguistic model. The culture systems are different in their material bases, formal structures, modes of signification, and social channels of communication; therefore, semiotic study requires diverse models and methods appropriate for each system. This principle was implemented by the development of special semiotics of material culture, architecture, visual arts, cinema, music, the theater, and, first and foremost, literature.

Semiotics of literature (semiotic poetics)

In the functional perspective of the Prague School, literature is a form of verbal communication dominated by the aesthetic function. This function which literature shares with the other arts determines the specific features in the production, structure and reception of literary works. The semiotics of the producer (authorial subject) is a critique of all forms of determinism – biographical, psychological, sociological. The literary work signifies the poet's life, his personality structure and the social circumstances of its genesis in many different ways, direct as well as figurative (Mukařovský, *Studie z estetiky*). (See also *genetic criticism.) To be sure, the individual creative act is constrained by historically changing objective factors (literary norms), but it is the author who is ultimately responsible for the uniqueness of his work. He imprints on it his 'semantic gesture,' a global regularity which can be recognized both in the work's overall organization and in each minute detail (*Kapitoly*). By making the poet's characteristic 'gesture' responsible for the semantic characteristics of the literary work, Mukařovský promotes the authorial subject to the main factor of aesthetic structuration.

For the study of the literary structure, the Prague School poeticians developed an advanced model on two basic levels – verbal structure (sounds and meanings) and thematic structure (motifs, thematic planes, fictional world). Language and themes enter the work from outside literature as 'material,' to become its constituents only through aesthetic organization ('form'). In later modifications of the model the difference between material and form is relativized and all constituents of the literary work become 'vehicles of meaning.' The literary sign produces meaning in a dynamic, bi-directional process of semantic accumulation. (See also *theme.)

Turning to the receiving subject's activity, Mukařovský accepts the self-evident fact that the responses of different readers of one and the same literary work are not identical. But semiotic thinking is concerned with 'the *conditions* for inducing this state, conditions which are given equally for all receiving individuals and are objectively identifiable in the structure of the work' (*Studie z poetiky*). Thanks to the supra-individual status of the literary work, the idiosyncratic mental states of the readers 'always have something in common' and therefore 'a generally valid judgment about the

value and the sense of a work is possible' (*Kapitoly*).

Literary history

Literary theory tends to focus on the synchronous aspects of literature. In Prague, this tendency was reinforced by the influence of Saussure who installed the synchronic structure of language as a legitimate subject of scientific investigation. While Saussure's differentiation between synchrony and diachrony was accepted in Prague, his ideas about linguistic evolution were critically re-examined. The Prague scholars proceeded from the assumption (accepted in social sciences) that 'the concepts of a system and its change are not only compatible but indissolubly tied' (Jakobson *Dialogues* 58). The dialectic of stability and change and the idea of a systemic evolution stimulated an original theory of literary history. Its early formulation is Mukařovský's study of the historical significance of a 19th-century Czech descriptive poem (Polák's *Sublimity of Nature* 1934). In *TCLP* (1936), Wellek published a penetrating but rather neglected essay, 'The Theory of Literary History.' The most significant contributions to literary history were made by Vodička in two papers ('Problematika,' 'Literárni historie') and in his book (*Počátky*).

Prague School scholars were unanimous in postulating a close connection between literary theory (poetics) and literary history: a new understanding of literary evolution is possible only on the foundations of a structural and semiotic theory of literature. Mukařovský derived the dynamism of literature from the inherent tensions within the structural whole. Wellek, who spelled out the new epistemology of literary history in contrast to the traditional trends of English literary scholarship, demands a history focused on the 'internal development' of 'art in literature.' In a similar vein, Vodička assigned to literary history the task of studying all texts displaying the aesthetic function; the shifting domain of this function is itself a literary historical problem.

In the Prague School semiotic framework, literary history necessarily becomes a three-pronged study: the history of production (genesis), the history of literary structure and the history of reception. But production history, concerned with the relationship between the individual creative acts and the supra-individual aesthetic norms (tradition), is absorbed into the history of the literary structure.

The positivistic literary historians sought the 'causes' of literary change outside literature; in contrast, structuralism emphasizes 'self-motion,' the immanent evolution of the literary series. The impact of external factors (*ideology, politics, economy, science) is not denied. But if literature is treated as a commentary on social, political, economic, or other historical events, then it has no historical continuity. The most powerful immanent factor of evolution is the principle of contrast (in the Hegelian sense), evident in such sequences as classicism-romanticism-realism. But Vodička warned against reducing the complex literary process to a simple teleological schema; literary history is never a straightforward transformation of one structure into another but a chain of 'attempts, failures and half-successes.' In reconstructing the evolving series, the literary historian discovers evolutionary tendencies and this provides a ground for assessing the historical value of individual works. Historical value is not identical with the work's aesthetic value; the former is given by the work's participation and success in implementing the tendencies of the literary process, the latter is oriented towards the work's reception.

The foundations of reception history were laid by Vodička. As a sign, the literary work is destined for the 'community of readers,' to be perceived aesthetically, interpreted and evaluated. The dynamism of reception and the diversity of interpretations arise from two factors – the aesthetic properties of the literary text and the changing attitudes of the reading public. Vodička's reception history is an empirical study of the post-genesis fortunes of literary works as attested in recorded concretizations (diaries, memoirs, letters, critical reviews, and essays). His study of the reception of the 19th-century Czech poet Jan Neruda is concerned exclusively with critical texts. Literary criticism is of special interest for the literary historian because the critics' concretizations are representative of a particular historical stage of reception. (See also *reader-response criticism, *Constance School of Reception Aesthetics.)

Vodička started the development of his reception theory from the premise that a literary work is an 'aesthetic sign.' He concluded it with the trenchant observation that reception itself is an aesthetic process: 'Just as automatised devices in poetic language lose their aesthetic effectiveness, which motivates the search for the new, aesthetically actualised devices, so a new *concretization of a work or author emerges not only because literary norms change but also because older concretizations lose their convincingness through constant repetition. A new concretization always means a regeneration of the work; the work is introduced into literature with a fresh appearance, while the fact that an old concretization is repeated (in schools, for example) and no new concretizations arise is evidence that the work has ceased to be a living part of literature' (1941). Vodička thus reaffirmed the basic principle of Prague School poetics: all literary phenomena, from minute poetic devices to literary history spanning centuries, are the products of unceasing human aesthetic activity.

LUBOMÍR DOLEŽEL

Primary Sources

Bogatyrjov, Petr. *The Functions of Folk Costume in Moravian Slovakia*. Trans. Richard G. Crum. The Hague: Mouton, 1971.

Červenka, Miroslav. 'O Vodičkově metodologii literárnich dějin.' ['On Vodička's Methodology of Literary History.'] Postscript to Vodička, 1966, 329–50.

Garvin, Paul L., ed. and trans. *A Prague School Reader on Esthetics, Literary Structure and Style*. Washington: Georgetown UP, 1964.

Jakobson, Roman. *The Framework of Language*. Ann Arbor: Michigan Studies in the Humanities, 1980.

– *Language in Literature*. Ed. Krystyna Pomorska and Stephen Rudy. Cambridge, Mass.: Harvard UP, 1987.

– *Selected Writings*. 8 vols. The Hague: Mouton, 1966–88.

– and Krystyna Pomorska. *Dialogues*. Cambridge, Mass.: MIT P, 1983.

Matejka, Ladislav, and Irwin R. Titunik, eds. *Semiotics of Art: Prague School Contributions*. Cambridge, Mass.: MIT P, 1976.

Mukařovský, Jan. *Aesthetic Function, Norm and Value as Social Facts*. 1936. Trans. Mark E. Suino. Ann Arbor: Michigan Slavic Publications, 1970.

– *Kapitoly z české poetiky*. [Chapters from Czech Poetics.] 3 vols. Prague: Svoboda, 1948. Eng. trans. in part in Mukařovský 1977.

– *Structure, Sign and Function: Selected Essays by Jan Mukařovský*. Ed. and trans. Peter Steiner and John Burbank. New Haven: Yale UP, 1978.

- *Studie z estetiky*. [*Studies from Aesthetics*.] Prague: Odeon, 1966. Eng. trans. in part in Mukařovský 1978.
- *Studie z poetiky*. [*Studies from Poetics*.] Prague: Odeon, 1982.

Steiner, Peter, ed. *The Prague School: Selected Writings, 1929–1946*. Austin: U of Texas P, 1982.

Vachek, Josef, ed. *A Prague School Reader in Linguistics*. Bloomington: Indiana UP, 1964.

Vachek, Josef, and Libuše Dušková, eds. *Praguiana: Some Basic and Less Known Aspects of the Prague Linguistics*. Amsterdam: Benjamins, 1983.

Veltruský, Jiří, *Drama as Literature*. Lisse: de Ridder, 1977.

Vodička, Felix. 'Literárni historie. Jeji problémy a úkoly.' ['Literary History: Its Problems and Tasks.'] In *Čteni o jazyce a poesii*. Ed. B. Havránek and J. Mukařovský. Prague: Družstevni práce, 1942, 309–400. Repr. in Vodička 1966. Eng. trans. in part in Matejka and Titunik, eds. 1976.
- *Počatky krásné prózy novočeské*. [*The Beginnings of Czech Artistic Prose*.] Prague: Melantrich, 1948.
- 'Problematika ohlasu Nerudova dila.' ['Problems of the Echo of Neruda's work'.] *Slovo a slovesnost* 7 (1941): 113–32. Repr. in Vodička 1966. Eng. trans. in Steiner, ed. 1982.
- *Struktura vývoje*. [*Structure of Evolution*.] Prague: Odeon, 1966.

Wellek, René. 'The Theory of Literary History.' In *Travaux du Cercle linguistique de Prague*. Vol. 6. Prague: Cercle linguistique de Prague, 1936, 173–91.

Secondary Sources

Armstrong, Daniel, and C.H. van Schooneveld, eds. *Roman Jakobson: Echoes of His Scholarship*. Lisse: de Ridder, 1977.

Bojtár, Endre. *Slavic Structuralism*. Amsterdam: Benjamins, 1985.

Broekman, Jan. *Structuralism: Moscow – Prague – Paris*. Dordrecht: Reidel, 1974.

Červenka, Miroslav. 'Semantic Contexts'. *Poetics* 4 (1972): 91–108.

Chvatík, Květoslav. 'Semiotics of a Literary Work of Art. Dedicated to the 90th Birthday of Jan Mukařovský (1891–1975).' *Semiotica* 37 (1981): 193–214.

Doležel, Lubomír. *Occidental Poetics: Tradition and Progess*. Lincoln: U of Nebraska P, 1990.

Erlich, Victor. *Russian Formalism: History-Doctrine*. 2nd ed. The Hague: Mouton, 1965.

Fokkema, D.W., and Elrud Kunne-Ibsch. *Theories of Literature in the Twentieth Century*. London: Hurst, 1977.

Galan, F.W. *Historic Structures: The Prague School Project, 1928–1946*. Austin: U of Texas P, 1984.

Holenstein, Elmar. *Roman Jakobson's Approach to Language: Phenomenological Structuralism*. Bloomington: Indiana UP, 1976.

Jankovič, Milan. 'Perspectives of Semantic Gesture'. *Poetics* 4 (1972): 16–27.

Jefferson, Ann, and David Robey, eds. *Modern Literary Theory: A Comparative Introduction*. London: Batsford, 1982.

Matejka, Ladislav. *Crossroads of Sound and Meaning*. Lisse: de Ridder, 1975.
- ed. *Sound, Sign and Meaning: Quinquagenary of the Prague Linguistic Circle*. Ann Arbor: Michigan Slavic Publications, 1978.

Merquior, J.G. *From Prague to Paris: A Critique of Structuralist and Poststructuralist Thought*. London: Verso, 1986.

Odmark, John, ed. *Language, Literature and Meaning I: Problems of Literary Theory*. Amsterdam: Benjamins, 1979.

van Peer, Willie. *Stylistics and Psychology: Investigations on Foregrounding*. London: Croom Helm, 1986.

Steiner, Peter, M. Červenka, and R. Vroon, eds. *The Structure of the Literary Process: Studies Dedicated to the Memory of Felix Vodička*. Amsterdam: Benjamins, 1982.

Striedter, Jurij. *Literary Structure, Evolution and Value: Russian Formalism and Czech Structuralism Reconsidered*. Cambridge, Mass.: Harvard UP, 1989.

Tobin, Yishai, ed. *The Prague School and Its Legacy*. Amsterdam: Benjamins, 1988.

Vachek, Josef. *The Linguistic School of Prague*. Bloomington: Indiana UP, 1966.

Veltruský, Jiří. 'Jan Mukařovský's Structural Poetics and Esthetics'. *Poetics Today* 2 (1980–1): 117–57.

Vodička, Felix. 'The Integrity of the Literary Process: Notes on the Development of Theoretical Thought in J. Mukařovský's Work'. *Poetics* 4 (1972): 5–15.

Wellek, René. *The Literary Theory and Aesthetics of the Prague School*. Ann Arbor: Michigan Slavic Publications, 1969; repr. in *Discriminations: Further Concepts of Criticism*. New Haven: Yale UP, 1970, 275–303.

Semiotics

Semiotics is the systematic study of all the factors involved in the production and interpretation of signs or in the process of signification. (See *signified/signifier/signification.) A multidisciplinary field, semiotics is concerned with issues of communication and meaning as they occur in various sign systems. The term 'semiotics' (or 'semiology,' as some, especially French, practitioners prefer to call it) is derived from the Greek root work *semeîon*, meaning 'sign.' (See *sign.) Although the roots of semiotic thought extend as far back in history as ancient Greece, contemporary semiotics has developed primarily from two sources: the work of the Swiss linguist *Ferdinand de Saus-sure and the writings of the American logician *Charles Sanders Peirce. In the early 20th century these two thinkers independently formulated theories of signs and their functioning which, several decades later, came to serve as a basis for the research of major specialists in numerous disciplines (literary studies, sociology, anthropology, the visual arts, film studies, and others). Semiotics is too heterogeneous in its methods and in its goals to be considered a unified discipline; rather, it is generally seen as an interdisciplinary field motivated by different approaches to, and different philosophical definitions of, its particular object. The object of semiotic research is anything (for example, architecture, fashion, a literary *text, a *myth, a painting, a film) that can be studied as a system of signs organized according to cultural codes and conventions or signification processes. (See *code.)

Historical background

Rich and varied traditions of thought concerning the nature and function of signs, signification and communication emerge in Western writings on philosophy, logic, grammar, epistemology, and other fields from early Greek thought forward. However, Western contributions to sign theory prior to the work of Saussure and Peirce cannot be considered semiotics in today's sense of the term. The same must be said of Indian, Chinese, Japanese, and Arabic reflections upon signs, although all of these earlier traditions of sign theory remain indispensable for the construction of a history of semiotics. The thinkers before Saussure and Peirce whose work is generally considered crucial to the history of semiotics are Aristotle, the Stoics, St. Augustine, Poinsot, and Locke. Aristotle developed an important theory of signs in his writings on poetics, rhetoric and logic. Stoicism was founded in Athens by Zeno of Citium. The Stoics wrote extensively on the theory of signs within the context of their discussions of the *logos* or reason which governs the cosmos in their world-view. Augustine created a major synthesis of the thinking on signs before and during his time. He discussed them in relation to knowledge and produced a classification of signs that strongly influenced the philosophy of language of the later Middle Ages. John Poinsot (1589–1644)

produced what is often viewed as the first systematic semiotic treatise with his *Tractatus de Signis* [*Treatise on Signs* 1632]. The term 'semiotic' was first used by John Locke (1632–1704) in his *Essay Concerning Human Understanding* (1690). Locke proposed the elaboration of a theory called 'semiotic' concerned with the relation between ideas and signs. From its beginnings, semiotics has implied a preoccupation with epistemological questions.

Saussure's semiology

Between 1907 and 1911 Saussure delivered the lectures presenting his unprecedented theories of language and communication. After his death, his students Bally and Sechehaye compiled the *Cours de linguistique générale* [*Course in General Linguistics* 1916] using notes taken during three of Saussure's linguistics courses as well as fragments of his own notes covering the period 1891–1912. The *Cours de linguistique générale* has become one of the seminal books of this century. Saussure's theory of language and of the linguistic sign and his proposal for a new science to be called semiology have decisively influenced the methodologies, the terminology and the goals of numerous disciplines in the humanities and the social sciences.

Saussure's definition of language and of the linguistic signs that constitute it provides the basis of his thought. He begins with distinctions between *langue* (language considered as a self-regulating, abstract system) and *parole* (actual utterances, including the personal speech traits of the speaker). (See *langue/parole.*) Saussurean linguistics studies *langue*, language as abstract form, rather than the concrete utterances that constitute *parole*. In a famous metaphor Saussure likens language, as *langue*, to the rules necessary for playing chess, in contrast to any actual games of chess played; the games actually played correspond to language as *parole*. Langue is an impersonal system functioning independently of any individual's will or choices. What *langue* includes and how it operates are determined by social convention. Thus, language is institutional in character, a formal network of signs.

Saussure defines the linguistic sign as a double entity divided into an acoustic image, or signifier, and the concept, or signified, that is correlated to the signifier. Neither the signifier nor the signified is a sign in and of itself; they become a sign only through their structural relationship to each other. The connection between a given signifier and its corresponding signified is radically arbitrary in Saussure's view; no natural motivation unites them. The French word *'cheval,'* the English word 'horse,' and the German word *'Pferd'* all refer to the same concept. The particular sound-image that we associate with the concept in each case proves arbitrary. The signifier and signified coexist like the two sides of a piece of paper: connected yet separate.

Another innovation of Saussure's conception of language is his insistence that in language there are only differences, without positive terms. In other words, no linguistic sign has meaning in itself; it acquires meaning by contrasts between itself and other signs within the system. From the point of view of phonology (the branch of linguistics studying sounds as a system organized by differences) 'cat' becomes meaningful only by contrast with 'cap' or 'bat.' Saussure generalizes this principle of difference central to phonology in order to characterize the workings of language in general. From a Saussurean perspective – one which will prove decisive for later semiotics – individual units of a system become meaningful solely through oppositions and differences. Meaning is entirely a product of the relations between the elements within the system.

A further vital aspect of Saussure's thought involves the distinction between the syntagmatic and paradigmatic axes of language. The syntagmatic axis consists of the linear juxtapositions of linguistic units, their combination in series. The paradigmatic axis consists of the linguistic units not chosen but substitutable for the signs chosen in a particular utterance by virtue of their similar meaning to that of the signs chosen. By making the distinction between paradigmatic and syntagmatic axes central to his conception of language, he heightens his readers' awareness of two distinct forms of mental activity fundamental to language use: first, the combining of elements in linear fashion in which each element acquires meaning through contrasts with preceding and subsequent elements (*in praesentia*); second, the possible substitution of one element for another, absent element on the basis of associations which the two elements share (*in absentia*). Saussure's definitions of the syn-

tagmatic and paradigmatic axes have influenced later studies of metonymy and metaphor. (See *metonymy/metaphor.)

Saussure also differentiates between synchrony and diachrony. He sets aside the diachronic study of language – that is, the study of language on the basis of developments over time. He favours a synchronic view, in which one considers the functional relation of signs in a given system at a given time. This distinction has strongly influenced later work in semiotics. Taking synchrony, rather than diachrony, as the framework for understanding and analysis allows him to distance his work from that of earlier linguistics, which had relied on a perspective Saussure considers narrowly historical to chart the evolution of languages over time. The advantage of a synchronic view is its foregrounding of structural relationships and functions considered as an independently functioning system.

Saussure's emphasis on the fundamentally arbitrary character of language and on its differential functioning constitute his most significant contributions to subsequent semiotic thought.

Peirce's semiotic

Charles Sanders Peirce formulated definitions of the sign different from Saussure's in several respects. Initially, Saussurean concepts tended to dominate semiotic studies. In more recent years, the influence of Peirce's ideas has broadened in semiotic circles, rivalling – to some extent even displacing – the importance previously accorded to the ideas of Saussure. Peirce's thought is idiosyncratic and difficult; for a long time it was available only in part. However, a new edition of Peirce's philosophical works, to comprise roughly two dozen volumes of 600 pages each, is currently being published and is extending the influence of his thought.

As a logician, Peirce is interested in signs primarily in relation to knowledge and abstract thought. He regards *semiosis (the process of the production and interpretation of signs) as fundamental to all of reality, as coextensive with life itself. Saussure had defined the sign as dyadic, as the structural relationship between two terms. Peirce proposes another view; for him, a sign is triadic. The Peircean sign is constituted through its connection to both its *object* (the thing to which it refers) and to its *interpretant* (roughly, the idea which the sign produces). Peirce's concept of the interpretant distinguishes his thinking on signs from that of others. The interpretant, as the mental effect or thought generated by the relation between the sign and object, is itself a sign. Moreover, it produces a further sign – a further interpretant – through the process of understanding and interpretation. Peirce calls this successive, perpetual production of new interpretants that defines the formal structure of intelligence 'unlimited semiosis.' Peirce's conception of the sign partakes of both substitution and interpretation. The sign stands for something other than itself. Each sign, each successive interpretant, furthers knowledge.

In addition to providing definitions of signs, Peirce devises a system for classifying them: through their primary qualities as signs, through their relationship to their object, and through their relationship to their interpretant. He also distinguishes between three modes of being in his classification of signs: firstness, secondness and thirdness. Firstness characterizes the qualities of things in and of themselves (for example, the redness of a red object). Secondness pertains to actual events, unlike the inherent qualities Peirce calls 'firsts.' A 'second' exists relative to, or in reaction with, something else. Thirdness, a more complex mode of being, characterizes general conceptions or laws that bring firsts and seconds into relation with each other. Among the groupings of signs classified by Peirce, the trichotomy of *icon, *index and symbol has received the most attention from later theorists and practitioners of semiotics. The icon is a sign which resembles its object. A portrait, which resembles the person it represents, would be an icon. The index relates to its object by physical proximity. The relationship between smoke and the fire it indicates would be indexical. The symbol relates to its object by some convention or law. The linguistic sign, which by convention stands for a particular concept, would be a symbol. Peirce cautions that there are few pure instances of icon, index and symbol. In fact, these types of sign supplement one another.

Peirce's triadic view of signs and his explanation of semiosis by means of the interpretant have proven most influential for 20th-century semiotics.

Influence of semiotics on literary critical method

The impact of semiotics on literary studies has entailed critics focusing on structures and relations within texts rather than on a mere naming of 'themes.' (See *theme.) Whereas much earlier literary criticism is concerned primarily with the meaning of texts, semiotics highlights how meaning is produced in texts by patterns of interrelating signs. The influence of semiotics has arguably produced a more systematic and rigorous, more 'scientific,' literary criticism and reflects a new preoccupation with methodologies in the humanities. Also, because semiotics considers meaning as constructed, as a product of codes and conventions rather than as a natural event, there has been increasing criticism of reading a literary text as the expression of an individual author's unique, personal psyche or imaginary world.

Semiotics and poetry

The work of the Soviet theorist *Iurii Lotman and of the French-born American critic *Michael Riffaterre have provided important critical models for the analysis of poetry. Lotman, the founder and leading theorist of the *Tartu School of semiotics, has inherited and developed the ideas and methods of the Russian formalists. (See Russian *formalism.) His books *Struktura khudozhestvennogo teksta* [The Structure of the Artistic Text 1970] and *Analiz poeticheskogo teksta: struktura stikha* [The Analysis of the Poetic Text: The Structure of Poetry 1972] constitute one of the major expositions of Soviet literary semiotics. Lotman regards a poetic text as a complex, hierarchical system, each of whose elements is correlated with the others. Every literary text involves several systems (such as rhyme, metre, lexical elements). The clashes and tensions between these various systems generate the text's effects on the reader. Lotman has developed a method of 'contrast-comparison' for isolating recurrent elements and thereby determining the underlying organization of a text. He seeks to articulate the rule system operative in a text, then to isolate various deviations from the rules. The occurrence of such deviations provides a challenge to reader perception. This process of challenging established literary conventions by deviating from them seems to Lotman to be a fundamental aspect of the evolution of *literature.

Riffaterre's *Semiotics of Poetry* (1978) distinguishes between two levels of the poetic text: that of *mimesis (the text as a representation of reality, a string of successive information units) and that of significance (the text as a unique semantic unit, constituted by interpretation). To grasp the text at the level of semiosis – and literariness – necessitates the reader's passage from the mimetic level, where certain elements fail to make sense if read referentially, to the level of significance, where meaning expresses itself by indirection and allusiveness. In order to move from the mimetic level to the level of significance, the reader must succeed in recognizing and manipulating a semantic matrix which Riffaterre calls the *hypogram (a word, cliché, sentence, or group of conventional associations). The hypogram is both located outside the text itself and generates the text. The hypogram does not correspond to the meaning of the text but it is necessary for its discovery. As the reader traces semes (minimal units of meaning) and presuppositions which words from the text suggest, he or she may discover the hidden network of associations that form the hypogram. In the first few chapters of *Semiotics of Poetry*, Riffaterre repeatedly demonstrates how this process occurs. (See *seme.)

Semiotics and narrative

The semiotic study of narrative – or *narratology – begins with the Russian formalists' efforts during the 1920s to formulate typologies of the basic plot–functions of narrative. *Vladimir Propp's 1928 study *Morfologiia skazki* [*Morphology of the Folktale*] has proved especially influential for subsequent narrative semiotics. Theorists of the *Prague School (between 1926 and 1948) continued and expanded the work in narrative semiotics begun by the Russian formalists. During the 1960s and 1970s, narratology flourished in France and produced important theoretical and critical studies by *Roland Barthes, *Tzvetan Todorov, *Gérard Genette, and *A.J. Greimas.

Barthes' 1966 article on the structural analysis of narrative, 'L'Analyse structurale des récits' ['The Structural Analysis of Narratives'], has greatly influenced work in narratology, though Barthes himself later modified his

methods and presuppositions. He proposes the critical transformation of the narrative text into distinct structural units: functions and indices (indicators of character, atmosphere and so on). By means of this process, Barthes attempted to posit a structural model of analysis applicable to narrative texts in general. In a later work, *S/Z* (1970), a study of Balzac's tale *Sarrasine*, Barthes abandoned his 1966 approach of breaking a text down into fixed structural units. Rather, he insisted on the text's polysemy and on the multilevel dynamic play of meaning. (See theories of *play/freeplay.)

In *Sémantique structurale* [*Structural Semantics* 1966], *Du Sens* [*On Meaning* 1970] and *Maupassant: La sémiotique du texte* [*Maupassant: Textual Semiotics* 1976], Greimas distils a grammar of plot from narrative texts using concepts from structural linguistics. (See *story/plot.) Basically, Greimas seeks a deep structure underlying all narrative texts. His 'actantial model' results from the application of the analysis of syntax to the analysis of plot, in the tradition of Propp's analyses of narrative. (See *actant.) Any given plot, in Greimas' view, can be reduced to the paired actantial functions of subject and object, sender and receiver, helper and adversary. Greimas uses the Saussurean and Jakobsonian concept of binary oppositions as producers of meaning to construct a theoretical model that, he argues, accounts for the elementary structure of signification. (See *binary opposition.) He has applied a four-term homology which he calls the 'semiotic square' to narratives in order to express their fundamental semantic structure. It is formed by oppositions and contrasts between such terms as life and death, together with their alternative terms, non-life and non-death. Through their interplay, the terms supposedly encompass all the possible actions for a particular narrative.

Semiotics and theatre

The application of a semiotic perspective to the study of theatre began with the work of the Prague School in the 1930s. In their writings, Prague School theorists address such issues as the specificity of the theatrical sign, the identification and classification of theatrical signs, and the precise nature of their functioning on stage.

In an important essay of 1968 the Polish scholar Tadeusz Kowzan proposes a classification of the 13 systems of signs that interact during a theatrical performance and questions the adequacy of the linguistic model to account for the complexity and heterogeneity of theatre as a sign system. In general, there has been a movement away from the application of semiotic methods to the study of the dramatic text in favour of the study of the theatrical 'spectacle' of 'performance-text' as the object of semiotic theatre studies. (See also *performance criticism.) The work of Patrice Pavis – to name only one of several significant recent semioticians of theatre – has been of particular interest. His book *Problèmes de sémiologie théâtrale* [*Problems in the Semiology of Theatre* 1976] articulates the main issues posed by this approach to the theatre.

The relationship of semiotics to other schools and approaches

Many Marxist critics denounce semiotics as formalist, ahistorical, reactionary, and in complicity with bourgeois *ideology because semioticians tend to approach literary texts synchronically, as impersonal systems whose interpretation depends on a deciphering of the internal structural hierarchies and interrelations of textual signs. (See *Marxist criticism, *materialist criticism.) Certain Marxist critics accuse semioticians who follow Saussure and Peirce in this regard of denying the importance of history by excluding the referent (the social world to which language refers) from their analyses. (See *reference/referent.) Nevertheless, other Marxist thinkers, notably *Louis Althusser, attempt to combine a Marxist-oriented concern with social relations and *ideology with a semiotic approach to language and textuality.

Feminist critics respond to semiotics with both caution and enthusiasm. Because semiotics studies formal structures within supposedly impersonal systems, some feminists suspect semiotics of disguising the point of view of a male subject behind a falsely neutral system. Other feminist critics welcome the emphasis in semiotics on meaning as socially constructed and culturally determined; semiotics potentially fosters the feminist assertion that meanings are neither natural nor God-given. (See *feminist criticism.)

A significant critique of semiotics has been articulated by the philosopher *Jacques Derrida. Derrida's *De la Grammatologie* [*On Grammatology* 1967] presents the basic ideas and terms of his critical position known as *deconstruction. Derrida uses his arguments against Saussure's conception of language and of the linguistic sign as the point of departure for a new view of language and textuality. He commends Saussure for defining language as form rather than substance and for characterizing the relationship between signifier and signified along with that between sign and referent as arbitrary. Nevertheless, Derrida still finds that Saussure privileges spoken language and the materiality of the signifier. By this bias, he makes writing secondary, merely a derivative of spoken language; furthermore, he manifests a tendency toward a *metaphysics of presence which, in Derrida's view, besets Western thought in general. Derrida argues that in the Western tradition, spoken language, with its illusions of immediacy and presence, is consistently taken to represent the essence of language itself. Thus, Western thought allows itself to fall victim to mistaken notions regarding the ability of language to express being, to capture the fullness of an individual's thought as writing, and so on. In Derrida's opinion, Saussure is correct in insisting that in language there are no positive terms, only oppositional differences; however, Saussure fails to pursue this insight to its logical conclusion. Derrida replaces the Saussurean notion of difference as the principal feature of language with *différance*. (See *différance/différence.) The concept of *différance* indicates that language operates by constant differings and deferrings of meaning that leave only linguistic traces in their wake. (See *trace.) These traces do not represent fullness and presence, as Saussure's linguistic signs still do, according to Derrida. Instead, they demarcate a movement toward meaning that cannot end. Derrida's conception of writing as constituted negatively by absence and deferral radically alters the way in which literary critics understand *textuality, in addition to altering how they read Saussure and other semiotic thinkers.

The psychiatrist and critic *Jacques Lacan effects an important fusion of Freudian psychoanalytic thought and post-Saussurean linguistics in his work. (See *psychoanalytic theory.) He argues that language determines human subjectivity much as the unconscious does in Freudian theory. Language, like

the unconscious, is an impersonal system outside the subject's control – a system from
which the subject is irrevocably alienated. By
asserting that psychosexual processes operate
in fundamentally linguistic ways, Lacan alters
the Freudian model. (See *Sigmund Freud.) He
asserts not only that linguistic acts of communication and signification are closely related to
the workings of the unconscious but also that
the unconscious itself is structured like language. He modifies Saussure's figure for the
relationship between signifier and signified in
order to incorporate Freud's theory of processes of repression into the functioning of
language itself. The bar separating signifier
and signified comes to represent in Lacanian
thought a gap or fissure (a *béance*) that stands
both for the differential functioning of language in which signifier and signified can
never coincide and for an inescapable gap at
the centre of subjectivity. In certain respects,
Lacan's sense of *desire in language resembles
Derrida's concept of writing as *différance*; Lacan, too, denounces as illusory all assumptions
that language can give access to presence and
unmediated knowledge. For Lacan, perhaps
the crucial moment in the constitution of subjectivity takes place as the subject passes from
the imaginary (a preverbal realm of phantasies
and illusions of totality) into the symbolic.
(See *imaginary/symbolic/real.) Entry into the
symbolic entails the subject's recognition of
the distancing and alienating effects of language, which cannot make present a fullness
of meaning, as well as the subject's awareness
of castration and of the impossibility of ever
satisfying desire.

The intense activity that characterizes current semiotic theorizing and the innumerable
applications of semiotic methods to the analysis of a wide range of objects of research in
this century suggest a continuing expansion
and refinement of the concepts and methods
developed by semiotics in all fields. Some observers, nonetheless, predict a waning of the
influence of semiotics in years to come.

JOHN STOUT

Primary Sources

Barthes, Roland. *Elements of Semiology.* Trans. An-
nette Lavers and Colin Smith. New York: Hill and
Wang, 1967.
– 'Introduction to the Structural Analysis of Narra-
tive.' In *Image, Music, Text.* New York: Hill and
Wang, 1977, 74–124.

– *S/Z* Trans. R. Miller. New York: Hill and Wang,
1974.
Derrida, Jacques. *Of Grammatology.* Trans. Gayatri
Chakravorty Spivak. Baltimore: Johns Hopkins
UP, 1976.
Garvin, Paul, ed. *A Prague School Reader on Esthetics,
Literary Structure and Style.* Washington: George-
town UP, 1964.
Greimas, Algirdas Julien. *On Meaning: Selected Writ-
ings in Semiotic Theory.* Trans. Paul J. Perron and
Frank H. Collins. Minneapolis: U of Minnesota P,
1987.
Jakobson, Roman. *Language in Literature.* Ed. Krys-
tyna Pomorska and Stephen Rudy. Cambridge:
Harvard UP, 1987.
Lacan, Jacques. *Ecrits: A Selection.* Trans. Alan Sheri-
dan. New York: Norton, 1977.
Lotman, Yury. *Analysis of the Poetic Text.* Ed. and
trans. D. Barton Johnson. Ann Arbor: Ardis, 1976.
– *The Structure of the Artistic Text.* Trans. Ronald
Vroon. Ann Arbor: U of Michigan P, 1977.
Pavis, Patrice. *Problèmes de sémiologie théâtrale.*
Problems in the Semiology of Theatre. Montreal:
U of Quebec P, 1976.
Peirce, Charles Sanders. *Collected Papers.* Cambridge:
Harvard UP, 1931–58.
Riffaterre, Michael. *Semiotics of Poetry.* Bloomington:
Indiana UP, 1978.
Saussure, Ferdinand de. *Course in General Linguistics.*
Ed. Charles Bally and Albert Sechehaye. Trans.
Roy Harris. La Salle, Ill.: Open Court, 1986.

Secondary Sources

Eagleton, Terry. 'Structuralism and Semiotics.' In *Lit-
erary Theory: An Introduction.* Minneapolis: U of
Minnesota P, 1983.
Eco, Umberto. *A Theory of Semiotics.* Bloomington:
Indiana UP, 1976.
Innis, Robert E., ed. *Semiotics: An Introductory An-
thology.* Bloomington: Indiana UP, 1985.
Sebeok, Thomas A., ed. *Encyclopedic Dictionary of
Semiotics.* Berlin: Mouton de Gruyter, 1986.

Sociocriticism

Sociocriticism originated in France, where it
was born of the momentum of the *New Criticism and by analogy with the concept of psychocriticism, introduced by *Charles Mauron.
Championed first by Edmond Cros, Claude
Duchet and later Pierre V. Zima, sociocriticism
developed in many directions during the
1970s, although common guiding principles
underlie the various approaches. These were
articulated for the first time in a 1971 issue of
the periodical *Littérature*, edited by Claude

Duchet, and which proposed a sociology of the *text which would contribute to the development of *Marxist criticism.

History and major practitioners

*Georg Lukács and *Lucien Goldmann undoubtedly exerted the strongest influence on the field of sociocriticism. Lukács is considered by many the father of the sociology of *literature and Goldmann his most faithful disciple. Goldmann was at the centre of the debate in France which opposed traditional to modern criticism; his most important work, *The Hidden God* (1955), explores the connections between the structure of meaning in Racine's tragedies and an encompassing structure – that is, the world-view held by the *noblesse de robe* of 17th-century France. The meaning and value of a literary work are thus ascribed to a social group and, more generally, to a historically determined social structure. Goldmann's theory thus differs from traditional criticism on two counts. First, it considers meaning in literature to be based on extratextual factors rather than on literature itself. Second, it rejects dependence on the concept of 'author' for evaluating this extratextuality.

Although they reject formalism and the cult of the author, sociocritics nonetheless do not fully accept Goldmann's deterministic orientation. Forced to deal with *Wilhelm Dilthey's dichotomy (*Erklären/Verstehen*), sociocriticism tends toward the second option and refuses, without really acknowledging it, to *explain* the literary text in light of social, historical and economic conditions. Instead, its primary goal is to develop a type of criticism whose investigations are wholeheartedly dedicated to the form of literary texts, and thereby to free Marxist aesthetics from the fetters of analysis of content. The *Frankfurt School, *Mikhail Bakhtin and, to a lesser degree, the *Prague School developed research models which gave weight to both polysemy and the social semantics functioning within texts.

*Julia Kristeva was one of the first to develop this new tendency in criticism. Among other things, she was one of the first in France to read Mikhail Bakhtin, from whom she borrowed the crucial concept of dialogism, which she translated by the neologism '*intertextuality.' (See *double-voicing/dialogism.) Working with *Roland Barthes and others, she also applied new findings from *semiotics to a social

reading of works considered to have departed from ordinary language.

Virtually the entire field of sociocriticism has appropriated the concept of intertextuality, considering it an essential conceptual tool for understanding the interrelationship of the social and the textual. Despite its insistence from its beginnings on *materialist criticism, sociocriticism nonetheless inherited one of the main postulates of New Criticism, namely, that the social – like the unconscious for *Jacques Lacan – is structured like a language: society is no longer a thing, a material structure, but rather a text. In other words, it is taken for granted that if there is a social unconscious in the text, as Claude Duchet maintained, there is also (as odd as it may sound) a textual unconscious in society.

Accordingly, it is impossible to speak of extratextuality since non-literary interferences are apparent in and through the text. Well aware of this problem, Claude Duchet suggested the concept of the *sociogram* as mediator between literature and society: 'a vague, unstable, dissonant collection of partial representations, revolving and interacting with one another around a central theme.' (See *theme, *textuality.) The concept of the sociogram marks a considerable evolution from the Marxist concept of *ideology, since instead of false beliefs and homogeneous doctrines (such as progress, nationalism, anti-Semitism) it emphasizes heterogeneous representations gathered around a strong central theme.

Like Claude Duchet, Edmond Cros re-evaluates in *Theory and Practice of Sociocriticism* the contributions of Goldmann's genetic *structuralism and replaces his world-view with a concept that takes into account the ideological locus of text enunciation, as well as the mesh of representations upon which a text is built, without introducing the idea of a consciousness (collective or individual). (See *énonciation/énoncé.) He calls this concept the *idéosème*. First posing the question of the relationship between social and textual practice, this form of sociocriticism studies the process of semantization which, in the semiotic functioning of texts, gives rise to relationships with the world which are neither perceived nor perceptible in the context of day-to-day experience. The ideoseme thus makes it possible to associate textual forms with a materialized ideology (in the Althusserian sense, ideology can exist only on the material level and under specific conditions). (See *Louis Althusser.) The ideoseme is 'conceived as a connection which is both semiotic, since it builds systems of iconic, gestural or linguistic signs based on the representations to which all social practices can be reduced, and discursive, since it plays a structural role when transferred to the text.' (See *sign.)

Pierre V. Zima, author of the *Manual of Sociocriticism* and numerous works on the French and European novel, sought to reconcile contributions from semiotics with the theories of *Jan Mukařovský, *Theodor Adorno and Lucien Goldmann. His sociology of the text shifts social problems (such as commercialization, ideological struggles) to the linguistic level, as proposed by Edmond Cros and Claude Duchet. Zima maintains that literary texts are located at the crossroads between two major traditions: literature and social languages. In *L'Ambivalence romanesque: Proust, Kafka, Musil [Ambivalence in Novels: Proust, Kafka, Musil]*, he points out that Proust, for example, incorporates and criticizes several contemporary *sociolects* in his work, including that of the leisure class.

In the 1970s several French critics claiming allegiance to sociology studied the formal aspect of text without, however, fully recognizing the validity of sociocriticism. Included among these researchers were Michel Zeraffa, Jacques Leenhardt, *Charles Grivel, Henri Mitterand, *Pierre Macherey, and Pierre Barbéris. Also influenced by sociocriticism during this period were two important movements which had oscillating relations with it: the sociology of the *literary institution and discourse analysis. (See *discourse, *discourse analysis theory.)

The concept of the literary institution was developed by Jacques Dubois, following the earlier work of *Pierre Bourdieu on the concept of literary field. While attributing to the expression 'literary institution' more sociological significance by analogy with other social institutions (such as military, medical, educational, legal), Jacques Dubois sought to establish the link between institution and text, while insisting upon one of sociocriticism's principal and, in his view, neglected goals, namely, the consideration of the material conditions of a text. Dubois' approach reveals what is undoubtedly the most frequent reproach levelled at sociocriticism, that it resolutely concentrates on the text in an effort to

escape the reductionism associated with traditional literary sociology and hence makes only partial contributions to materialist research. The sociology of the literary institution resembles sociocriticism to the extent that it also considers the text as a subject for investigation: its literary status, its genre, its context, its thematic content, and its rhetorical style are all textual components that are functions of the institution's historical structure. (See *genre criticism, *rhetorical criticism.) It is important to note, however, the emphasis on a sociology of texts as a whole, rather than of a single text in isolation. From such a perspective, the main contribution made by the sociology of the literary institution was to provide literary history with a structure and to have revealed the underlying logic of textual groups (schools, movements, the avant-garde, and so forth).

The analysis of social discourse, as practised since the 1980s by Marc Angenot and Régine Robin, begins by accepting the basic premise of sociocriticism: a social reading of a text is possible only if literary form and social realities are considered on equal terms. Aware of the overly 'text-centred' approach often encountered in sociocritical studies, both authors first declare sociocriticism's need for a theory of text as well as a social theory. 'Social discourse' is proposed as a basis for this approach and is presented as the focal point for the main social influences on literary texts.

While institutional sociology, like the semiotics of ideology, considers society to be a collection of institutionalized practices, the analysis of social discourse apprehends things in light of the points of view from which they are spoken, and the *words* chosen to describe and, indeed, modify reality. Social discourse includes 'everything that is said and written in a state of society; everything that is printed, everything that is stated in public or distributed today by the electronic media' (Angenot). Taking into account the increasing eclecticism of social approaches to textology, Angenot proposes a redefinition of the general heuristic framework, allowing us to grasp the tension that gives rise to sociocriticism. Sociocriticism refuses to grant an autonomous status to its subject of study, although it observes, and often affirms, an original approach that hallows the text in its uniqueness.

In Angenot's analysis of the year 1889 in France, Belgium and Switzerland, literature is integrated in the whole of social discourse and thus is subject to the same grammars, axioms and thematic networks as other forms of discourse (scientific, legal, medical, philosophical, and so forth). In his view, there is therefore co-intelligibility of literary discourse with the various methods of narration and argumentation used by society at a given time. To avoid excessive relativism, this iconoclastic conception of the text is based upon a double assumption: the general interaction of utterances (taken from Bakhtin) and a degree of discursive *hegemony. Angenot argues that a period's language patterns are both limited and hierarchical and, as a result, can be apprehended in their totality as well as in their diversity. Sociocriticism must take into account interdiscursive hegemony and the degree of acceptability of utterances – in short, the general rules governing that which it is permissible to say and write in a given society – to chart a sort of topographical distribution of utterances in their distinctiveness.

Influence

Although similar in many ways to contemporary literary criticism, sociocriticism is actually a tributary of better-established approaches (such as Marxism, semiotics, *narratology), which have had a direct impact on the social sciences and on literary studies in particular.

The field most conspicuously marked by sociocriticism is undoubtedly literary historiography. For example, *Histoire littéraire de la France* (begun in 1965) sought to place the French literary tradition in the framework of social evolution, as its co-editors Pierre Barbéris and Claude Duchet observed (foreword, vol. 4). The conditions and mediations of literary production form the basis of this new approach to historiography.

Relation to other approaches

Sociocritism did not simply borrow methodological tools from the fields of linguistics, rhetoric, poetry, or narratology. It embraced and adapted immanent or formal functional theories and contributed to their renewal. For example, in their development of a new rhetorical criticism, the Mu Group in Liège includes in its discussion of tropes several social components inherent in specific figures of speech. Working from this basis, Pierre Popović

and Michel Biron have recently focused on the elaboration of a definition of a sociocriticism of poetry, a genre previously neglected by literary sociology, which focused almost exclusively on the novel. In a similar vein, the concept of pragmatic utterances in Spanish writing, elaborated by Antonio Gomez-Moriana, demonstrates the profound correlation between sociocriticism and theories of enunciation. A social viewpoint has thus often become indispensable for any theoretical consideration of the formal mechanisms of literary texts, and is becoming increasingly predominant in the field of contemporary criticism.

Implications, difficulties, drawbacks

The heyday enjoyed by the field of sociocriticism from 1970 to 1985 did not last. Today, several theoreticians tend to disclaim sociocriticism, asserting that it encompasses views that are too varied and that it breeds theoretical incompatibilities within its own field. Claude Duchet's early insistence on the text as the focal point of social investigation now appears exaggerated or even redundant, despite the tendency among current researchers to take this methodology for granted. Sociocriticism has evolved in the eyes of some into social *hermeneutics, regardless of the critical developments it allows. However, while sociocriticism is no longer seen as providing a unified theoretical approach and seems to have been replaced by other approaches with more rigorous methodologies (such as *genetic criticism, pragmatics, narratology), it is not alone in its confusion. Rather, its disarray stems from a generalized crisis currently affecting all theories of culture, since culture itself has been shaken by the loss of fundamental ideological reference points.

MICHEL BIRON

Primary Sources

Cros, Edmond. *Théorie et pratique sociocritique.* 1983. *Theory and Practice of Sociocriticism.* Trans. Jerome Schwartz. Minneapolis: U of Minnesota P, 1988.

Duchet, Claude. 'Pour une sociocritique'. *Littérature* 1 (1971): 5–14.

– ed. *Sociocritique.* Paris: Nathan, 1979.

Zima, Pierre V. *Manuel de sociocritique.* Paris: Picard, 1985.

– *Pour une sociologie du texte littéraire.* Paris: UGE, 1978.

Secondary Sources

Angenot, Marc. *1889. Un Etat du discours social*. Longueuil: Le Préambule, 1989.

Auerbach, Erich. *Mimesis*. Trans. W.R. Trask. Princeton: Princeton UP, 1953.

Bakhtin, Mikhail. *Esthétique et théorie du roman*. Paris: Gallimard, 1978.

– *Rabelais and His World*. Trans. Hélène Iswolsky. Cambridge, Mass.: MIT P, 1968.

Benjamin, Walter. *Charles Baudelaire: A Lyric Poet in the Era of High Capitalism*. London, 1973.

Chambers, Ross. *Mélancolie et opposition. Les Débuts du modernisme en France*. Paris: José Corti, 1987.

Dubois, Jacques. *L'Assommoir de Zola. Société, discours, idéologie*. Paris, Larousse, 1973.

– *L'Institution de la littérature*. Paris/Bruxelles: Nathan/Labor, 1978, 1983.

Falconer, G., and H. Mitterand. *La Lecture sociocritique du texte romanesque*. Toronto: S. Stevens Hakkert, 1975.

Goldmann, Lucien. *Le Dieu caché. Etude sur la vision tragique dans les Pensées et dans le théâtre de Racine*. 1955. *The Hidden God*. New York: Humanities P, 1964.

Jameson, Fredric. *The Political Unconscious*. Ithaca: Cornell UP, 1981.

Kristeva, Julia. *La Révolution du langage poétique*. 1974. *Revolution in poetic language*. Trans. Margaret Waller. New York: Columbia UP, 1984.

Leenhardt, Jacques. *Lecture politique du roman. La Jalousie d'Alain Robbe-Grillet*. Paris: Minuit, 1973.

Lukács, Georg. *Balzac et le réalisme français*. Paris: Maspero, 1967.

– *La Théorie du roman*. Paris: Gonthier, 1963. *Theory of the Novel*. Trans. Anna Bostok. Merlin, 1971.

Marcotte, Gilles. *Littérature et circonstances*. Montreal: L'Hexagone, 1989.

– *Le Roman à l'imparfait*. Montreal: La Presse, 1976.

– 'Sociocritique de la poésie.' *Etudes françaises* 27.1 (1991).

Speech act theory

Speech act theory, which took shape between 1939 and 1959 in the lectures and addresses of *John L. Austin, a prominent Oxford philosopher of ordinary language, focuses on how speech utterances themselves perform deeds in particular contexts. The fullest statement of Austin's views appears in *How to Do Things with Words*, first published posthumously in 1962, a work in which he also states that he leaves to others the pleasure of working out the implications and uses of his theory. Taking up the challenge, other philosophers revised and extended Austin's work, chief and most prolific among them the American thinker *John R. Searle. Work by H. Paul Grice on implied meanings generated in conversation also strongly influenced the direction in which speech act theory developed.

The speech act model of language offers insight into contextual use and meaning and situates speech behaviour amidst the social and institutional circumstances in which it arises. In the early 1970s this model seemed to answer emerging needs in many disciplines, and uses or adaptations of it developed quickly in linguistics, sociology, social anthropology, cognitive psychology, speech communication, and literary criticism. Works by such figures as Richard Ohmann, Mary Louise Pratt, *Stanley Fish, and Keir Elam exemplify the wide diversity of uses found for it in literary theory and criticism.

Philosophical origins: Austin

For John L. Austin, ordinary language embedded in everyday contexts was neither an impediment to nor a distraction from the work of philosophy. Instead, he regarded the elucidation of its resources as his chief work. That words can themselves be deeds, the basic premise of Austin's theory, is an observation easily available to common sense. Hence to say that Austin invented speech act theory requires us to notice the context in which it could be regarded as novel or surprising. All intellectual disciplines rest on a bedrock of presuppositions and Austin worked in a discipline that operated usually with a propositional model of language. Speech act theory could be viewed as surprising partly because it interrupted this model of language. For the class and conception of utterance given preferred attention in philosophy Austin coined the term 'constative,' that is, an utterance conceived as describing a situation or stating a fact and assessed as true or false. He pointed to the implausibility of conceiving some everyday utterances in this way: sayings like 'I christen thee Mary Jane' or 'With this ring I thee wed' or 'I promise to repay this debt.' With such sayings, speakers do not state facts; instead, given appropriate circumstances, speakers actually perform conventional actions with their words. This class of utterances, initially conceived as a fairly limited class, Austin called 'performatives.' Not truth or falsity but 'happiness' or 'unhappiness' (elsewhere termed 'felicity' or 'infelicity') he took to be the most suitable criterion for assessing performatives. Austin proposed four main felicity conditions, requirements that must obtain for the happy performance of an action in words: first, that there be an accepted procedure governing the performance of the conventional verbal action under consideration; second, that the procedure be executed correctly and, third, completely; and, fourth, that whatever undertaking is made be made sincerely.

Austin developed his concepts by means of a rigorous process of definition and testing. Finding his preliminary distinction between performatives (utterances that do) and constatives (utterances that say) wanting, he considered whether performatives are not, in some sense, subject to truth conditions and whether constatives are not, in some sense, subject to felicity conditions. His findings about statements are particularly interesting. Statements can indeed be subject to sincerity conditions, he shows, in that a statement like 'The cat is on the mat' implies the speaker's belief that the cat is on the mat. Similarly, the felicity requirement that for a performative action there be an accepted procedure is not unlike logical presupposition, the requirement for propositional reference that what is referred to exists. Constatives start to look like performatives, in that they satisfy requirements applicable to performatives. 'Stating' starts to look like a performative act on a level with 'warning,' 'arguing,' 'promising,' and other performatives. Furthermore, Austin calls into question the straightforwardness of the distinction between truth and falsity, asking whether the truth or falsity of a proposition is not dependent on the act being performed with the words of a statement and on the specific circumstances, or context, in which the statement is being made. (In his example, it may be true for a general that France is hexagonal, but not for a geographer.) Finally, through the elegant reversal of his reasoning, Austin concludes that constatives and performatives are not separate classes of utterances. He replaces his initial constative/performative distinction with the locutionary/illocutionary distinction, suggesting that all utterances are speech acts, having both meaning and force, performing both locutionary and illocutionary acts, though in particular instances one may be dominant over the other. He divides the speech act into three: the *locutionary act*, or the act of uttering a sentence with meaning, that is, the act of saying something; the *illocutionary act*, or the act performed in saying the words, the force of the utterance; and the *perlocutionary act*, or the act, whether intended or not, occasioned by saying the words (often their effect on the listener).

Having isolated the illocutionary act as the focus of his inquiry, Austin concludes by offering five rough classes of deed performed in word. 'Verdictives' pertain to the giving of verdicts, 'exercitives' to the exercise of power, 'commissives' to what we promise or undertake, 'behabitives' to our social behaviour, and 'expositives' to the force of our words in spoken or written *discourse.

Extending the theory: Searle and Grice

John R. Searle continued the task of fine-tuning the speech act model in *Speech Acts* (1969) and in a series of articles later collected as *Expression and Meaning* (1979). While Austin had articulated appropriateness conditions for such ritualized performatives as marrying and christening, Searle worked out corresponding rules for those speech acts less rigidly tied to set scripts and ceremonial circumstances – everyday speech events like promising, requesting, stating, ordering. He considered it important to establish the status of these rules: they are not 'regulative' but 'constitutive.' That is, they do not make prescriptions about the conduct of pre-existent forms of behaviour but instead define behaviour that has no existence apart from its constitutive rules. For the promise, he works out a specific 'propositional content rule' (a future act of the speaker must be predicated), 'preparatory rules' (the speaker must believe the promisee wishes the act performed, and it must not be obvious that the speaker would perform the act anyway), a 'sincerity rule' (the speaker must intend to perform the act), and an 'essential rule' (uttering the words counts as an undertaking to perform the act). The general analytic framework used here for the promise Searle adapts to descriptions of requests, questions and other speech acts.

Searle questions the adequacy of Austin's classification of illocutionary acts and offers an alternative ('representatives,' 'directives,' 'commissives,' 'expressives,' and 'declarations'). He also joins with P.F. Strawson in finding Austin's locutionary/illocutionary distinction problematic; Searle prefers to speak instead of a proposition and a function-indicating device.

Searle opens the important issue of indirection in ordinary language use, when he treats indirect speech acts. It is easy to see how a listener might construe the primary illocution 'Please pass the salt' as roughly equivalent to the explicit 'I request that you pass the salt.' More interesting is the matter of how formulations like 'The potatoes could use some salt' or 'Are you going to pass the salt?' come to be construed (given the right contexts) as having the same force. Searle tries to adapt his rules for constituting speech acts to an account of indirect speech acts, suggesting, for example, that one can make an indirect directive by stating that the sincerity condition obtains ('I would like you to pass the salt') or by asking whether the preparatory rule obtains ('Can you pass the salt?'). This inquiry into indirect speech acts alerts us to neglected complexities in everyday speech production and reception.

In his influential article 'Logic and Conversation' (1975), H. Paul Grice also takes up the topic of indirection in ordinary language. His concern is to elucidate the implicit or indirect meanings generated in talk, which he calls 'conversational implicatures,' in order to establish that ordinary conversation has its own rigorous logic. While Austin and Searle enunciate appropriateness conditions governing the production and recognition of particular speech acts, Grice enunciates a generalized 'Cooperative Principle' (CP) governing the production and interpretation of conversational implicatures. He suggests that conversationalists, without calling the CP to consciousness, nonetheless govern their speech behaviour by this internalized principle: 'Make your conversational contribution such as is required, at the stage at which it occurs, by the accepted purpose or direction of the talk exchange in which you are engaged' (45). Furthermore, he lays out four attendant maxims: of quantity (loosely – be as informative as required but not more so); of quality (be truthful); of relation (be relevant); and of manner (be perspicuous). Despite the imperative usage here, Grice's interest in listing these maxims is not to prescribe rules for the polite conduct of conversation. Instead his interest is in the listener's practice of inference when any one of these maxims is not fulfilled. If, for example, an English professor is asked whether or not a student is qualified to

teach writing and she replies that the student is good-natured, the listener may infer from the failure of relation a negative answer. The listener in such a circumstance endeavours, according to Grice, to reconcile the non-fulfilment of a particular maxim with the assumption that the overall CP is being observed. He or she does so by 'filling in' a missing logical step, in much the same way that a New Critical reader of a poem would fill in a gap or discontinuity on the assumption that poems present coherent wholes. (See *New Criticism.) Grice offers four possible ways that a speaker might fail to fulfil one of the conversational maxims: (1) by unobtrusively violating it; (2) by opting out of the maxim and overall CP; (3) by confronting a clash with another maxim; and (4) by deliberately flouting the maxim.

Influence on literary theory and critical practice

Applications of speech act theory to literary theory and critical practice are various. Indeed, those regarding it as a useful resource for redefining *literature develop arguments that pull in opposite directions. Richard Ohmann, in 'Speech Acts and the Definition of Literature' (1971) and other articles, uses speech act theory to refine the familiar distinction between literary texts and everyday discourse, between fiction and reality, literary and ordinary language. In *Toward a Speech Act Theory of Literary Discourse* (1977), Mary Louise Pratt, by contrast, uses speech act theory to challenge the formalist opposition between literary and ordinary language, and in 'How to Do Things with Austin and Searle' (1976), Stanley Fish takes this challenge in a different direction to break down the opposition between fiction and reality. (See also *text.)

Definitions of literature and fiction

Speech act theories of literature or fiction take their cue from Austin's own casual glimpses at stage-acting, poetry, lies, and other forms of pretence as exceptional cases: 'a performative utterance will ... be *in a peculiar way* hollow or void if said by an actor on the stage, or if introduced in a poem ... Language in such circumstances is in special ways – intelligibly – used not seriously, but in ways *parasitic* upon its normal use – ways which fall under the doctrine of the *etiolations* of language' (22). Richard Ohmann develops the suggestion into a definition of literature, arguing that he can draw a clear line between literary and other discourses with the help of speech act theory. In literary works, he remarks on the occurrence of words or sentences which, produced in non-literary contexts, would constitute such illocutionary acts as stating, ordering or promising. Yet, when Donne, for example, writes 'For God's sake hold your tongue,' he issues no order, and when Shelley writes, 'I met a traveler from an antique land,' he makes no assertion. Their words don't count as illocutionary acts in the normal way; they lack illocutionary force, because they are abstracted from the situations and circumstances in which such acts could be constituted. A literary work, according to Ohmann, is a discourse without normal illocutionary force or a discourse whose *'illocutionary force is* mimetic' ('Speech Acts' 14).

Ohmann puts his point about imitation speech acts another way that has implications for *reader-response criticism, when he asserts that 'literary mimesis reverses the usual direction of inference for the reader' ('Speech, Literature' 369). (See *mimesis.) In non-literary discourse, when we recognize or decipher an act performed in words, we do so by testing the match between situation and sentence, between world and words. In the case of literary discourse, the situation does not pre-exist the sentence nor the world the words. In non-literary discourse, the recipient infers from the situation the force of the utterance; in literary discourse, the reader infers from the utterance an imagined situation in which the utterance can have illocutionary force. The reader of a literary work does make use of his or her tacit knowledge of speech act rules but uses them in a special way: to construct a world answerable to the pseudo-speech acts of the literary text.

Ohmann's theory appears in a number of versions with different emphases, but he usually tries to connect his speech act model to some understanding of the social value of literature. In 'Literature as Act' (1973), for example, he suggests that the reader's action in inferring the social circumstances and world to fit an illocution implicates her or him in the ethos of the society so created. To read, then, is not to withdraw from social and moral responsibility but instead to negotiate risky ethical predicaments. In 'Speech, Literature and the Space Between' (1972), on the other hand, Ohmann argues that in literature, as in television commercials, the attenuation of the normal illocutionary force obtaining in the face-to-face transactions of talk corresponds to an attenuation of the writer's and the reader's social responsibility. Ohmann's positions on this matter are not consistent; instead, his various formulations are tentative efforts to find literary applications of speech act theory.

Others have developed arguments related to Ohmann's speech act definition of literature. In 'The Logical Status of Fictional Discourse' (1975), John Searle uses speech act theory to distinguish fictional from serious discourse. Stanley Fish deconstructs Searle's distinction in 'How to Do Things with Austin and Searle,' arguing that the 'serious' world is not more than the 'standard story,' with its 'truths' only shared pretences like the shared agreements that make conventional speech acts possible. In 'The Poem as Act' (1975), Charles Altieri adapts Ohmann's model to poetry: he argues that a speech act theory of poetry can reconcile presentational views (stressing the poem as action unfolding in the reader's experience) and mimetic views (stressing the poem as imitation of the external world).

Questioning the poetic/ordinary language dichotomy

While Ohmann dwells on distinctions between literary and ordinary language, Mary Louise Pratt's effort in *Toward a Speech Act Theory of Literary Discourse* is to show what literary and other discourses have in common, and so to bring the disciplines of poetics and linguistics closer together. In 'How Ordinary Is Ordinary Language?' (1973), Stanley Fish had offered a similar argument, asserting that the privileging of literary language that is part of a formalist or New Critical legitimation of literary study is accomplished by trivializing other discourse. One way to see how extraordinary 'ordinary' language is, according to Fish, is simply to note the presence in 'ordinary' texts of the various special features, uses or functions attributed to poetic language. Pratt makes a similar point by showing how an analysis of extraliterary 'oral narratives of personal experience' (conducted by William Labov, an American sociolinguist) produces a structural description of everyday storytelling equally applicable to the novel. In considering why the subtlety and interest of ordinary language eluded those committed to a special status for poetic language, Pratt suggests that the structural emphasis dominant in linguistics through the 1950s and 1960s played a role. Linguists described the phonology, morphology and syntax of a language, bracketing off from treatment matters of meaning and context. A structural grammar or morphology will not yield characterizations of the load of implicit meaning an utterance bears or of its rhetorical figuration or of its power to change minds or of the action it performs in a specific context. This is so not because everyday discourses lack these features or other special features attributed to poetic discourses but because structural grammars do not concern these features. The fact that linguists and poeticians looked differently at language, Pratt suggests, contributed to the assumption that they looked at different languages.

With speech act theory and the wider discipline of discourse analysis in which speech act theory is finding a place, linguistics is shifting its attention to the suprasentential and interactive organizations of discourses and to their social contexts. (See *discourse analysis theory.) In these developments Pratt sees promise for an integrated description of literary and extraliterary discourse. She turns first to the emerging vocabulary for conversational analysis for help in characterizing the literary speech situation. Conversational analysis – with its emphasis on turn-taking, topic and speaker selection, sequencing, repair mechanisms – regards even small talk as rule-governed behaviour of some sophistication. A usual and obvious feature of conversation is speaker change. Pratt investigates the anomalous situation of audience non-participation in literary discourse, not in order to class literature as sui generis but instead to examine its relation to other speech situations (for example, classroom lectures) where potential speakers waive access to speaking turns.

Next Pratt turns to Grice's Cooperative Principle and theory of conversational implicature and finds in it a model for literary interpretation. Of the four possible ways that a speaker might fail to fulfil a conversational maxim (violating, opting out, confronting a clash, flouting), Pratt focuses on flouting as the method of producing contextual and implicit meaning

most characteristic of literature. Jane Austen in her famous opening of *Pride and Prejudice*, for example, is said to be flouting the maxim of Quality. Pratt's speech act model for literature also has implications for genre theory: she suggests that the contextual knowledge constituting the genre of a literary work is analogous to the appropriateness conditions governing particular speech acts in everyday discourse. Pratt uses the new resources of speech act theory and discourse analysis eclectically to advance her claim that a language model that accounts adequately for the uses of language outside literature will also account for literary discourse. But her enthusiasm for speech act theory is qualified: 'no such [adequate] apparatus exists at present' (xiii). (See *genre criticism.)

Other literary applications

A few other efforts to apply speech act theory deserve mention – among them a concept of drama and a concept of style. Keir Elam, in *Shakespeare's Universe of Discourse* (1984), looks to it for a way to re-evaluate the status of language in drama, or to redefine dramatic action. Whereas the Aristotelian tradition ranks 'diction' as a minor component of the drama and privileges action over verbal expression, Austin's theory, suggests Elam, should invite us to construe dramatic language as itself action. Any effort to view dramatic action as an unfolding series of speech acts must, however, recognize that the actions conducted in words are not all embraced in Austin's concept of the illocutionary act, the conventional speech act with which the theory is most centrally concerned. Elam finally finds the speech act model too restrictive for his purposes.

Practitioners of stylistics have looked for ways to adapt speech act theory, with Richard Ohmann in 'Instrumental Style' (1972) again offering one of the earliest versions. Most definitions of verbal style oppose it to 'content' or 'meaning': Ohmann makes an effort to identify the meaning/style distinction with Austin's locutionary/illocutionary distinction. This latter distinction is itself criticized by later philosophers and linguists interested in contextual meaning and Stanley Fish is surely right to regard Ohmann's notion of illocutionary style as spurious ('How to Do Things' 230).

Objections and directions

Speech act theory has generated criticism both from outside and from within its own ranks. With its insistence on the adequate resources of everyday language for negotiating conventional actions and for communicating complex meanings, this practical Anglo-American approach to language is at odds with the sceptical approach of French *deconstruction. Indeed, *Jacques Derrida chose to contest Austin's theory in 'Signature Event Context' (1972). Derrida characterizes Austin as proposing – like himself – an alternative to the traditional view of communication as transference of thought content. By conceptualizing utterances as performatives or as illocutionary acts, Austin displaces the traditional conception of speech and writing in terms of an idea/sign relation, and Derrida regards this displacement as innovative. (See *sign.) However, Derrida criticizes (1) Austin's retention of speaker intention as a category for assessing utterances, (2) his assumption that contexts are determinable (and so determinative of sense or illocutionary force), and (3) his exemption from consideration of a class of non-serious uses – or mentions – of performatives (for example, in words spoken on stage or in poems). In a characteristic manoeuvre, Derrida insists on the priority of Austin's excepted class and puts forward his own concept of citation or iterability as a defining, rather than peripheral, feature of speech and writing. Derrida continues the controversy with Searle, republishing and extending his own collected contributions as *Limited Inc* (1988).

From within, even some of the strongest advocates for its utility to literary criticism, like Mary Louise Pratt and Keir Elam, have found the speech act model not entirely adequate to the uses they imagine for it. Stanley Fish articulates the most thoroughgoing critique of efforts to adapt it to literary criticism in the essay 'How to Do Things with Austin and Searle,' in which he also articulates and critiques his own speech-act reading of *Coriolanus*. In literary applications, the highly technical vocabulary of speech act theory has been, at best, cumbersome. Fish's critique dwells in part on terminological slippages, as in Ohmann's comments about the 'infelicity' of King Lear's speech acts at the start of Shakespeare's play, when he is really talking about the negative social and moral consequences of

Lear's action and not about a mismatch of utterance and circumstance that constitutes failure to execute a conventional illocutionary act. Fish points out that while speech act theory draws attention to the existence of perlocutionary effects, that is, to the impact of a speaker's words on an audience (and hence the province of rhetoric), it gives no special help in analysing them. (See *rhetorical criticism.) Speech act theory offers only a partial account of what draws many literary critics to it – that is, only a partial view of how our language use is grounded in social interaction and cultural circumstances.

From its beginnings in Austin's own probative formulations and restatements, speech act theory has been a theory in evolution. It is now taking its place as a foundation piece in the broader interdisciplinary study of discourse analysis or pragmatics. Newly developing exchanges between discourse analysis and literary studies hold promise of a fruitful interaction.

A. LYNNE MAGNUSSON

Primary Sources

Altieri, Charles. 'The Poem as Act: A Way to Reconcile Presentational and Mimetic Theories.' *Iowa Review* 6.3–4 (1975): 103–24.

Austin, J.L. *How to Do Things with Words.* 1962. Ed. J.O. Urmson and Marina Sbisà. 2nd ed. Cambridge, Mass.: Harvard UP, 1975.

Derrida, Jacques. 'Signature Event Context.' 1972. Trans. Samuel Weber and Jeffrey Mehlman. *Glyph* 1 (1977): 172–97. Repr. in *Limited Inc.* Evanston, Ill.: Northwestern UP, 1988, 1–23.

Elam, Keir. *Shakespeare's Universe of Discourse: Language-Games in the Comedies.* Cambridge: Cambridge UP, 1984.

Fish, Stanley E. 'How Ordinary Is Ordinary Language?' *New Literary History* 5 (1973): 41–54. Repr. in *Is There a Text in This Class?* 97–111.

– 'How to Do Things with Austin and Searle: Speech-Act Theory and Literary Criticism.' *Modern Language Notes* 91 (1976): 983–1025. Repr. in *Is There a Text in This Class?* 197–245.

– *Is There a Text in This Class? The Authority of Interpretive Communities.* Cambridge, Mass./London: Harvard UP, 1980.

Grice, H.P. 'Logic and Conversation.' In *Speech Acts.* Ed. Peter Cole and Jerry L. Morgan. Vol. 3 of *Syntax and Semantics.* New York: Academic P, 1975, 41–58.

Ohmann, Richard. 'Instrumental Style: Notes on the Theory of Speech Action.' In *Current Trends in Stylistics.* Ed. Braj B. Kachru and Herbert F.W.

Stahlke. Edmonton: Linguistic Research, Inc., 1972, 115–41.

– 'Literature as Act.' In *Approaches to Poetics*. Ed. Seymour Chatman. New York/London: Columbia UP, 1973, 81–107.

– 'Speech, Action, and Style.' In *Literary Style: A Symposium*. Ed. Seymour Chatman. London/New York: Oxford UP, 1971, 241–54.

– 'Speech Acts and the Definition of Literature.' *Philosophy and Rhetoric* 4 (1971): 1–19.

– 'Speech, Literature and the Space Between.' *New Literary History* 4 (1972): 47–64. Repr. in *Essays in Modern Stylistics*. Ed. Donald C. Freeman. London/New York: Methuen, 1981, 361–76.

Pratt, Mary Louise. *Toward a Speech Act Theory of Literary Discourse*. Bloomington: Indiana UP, 1977.

Searle, John R. *Expression and Meaning: Studies in the Theory of Speech Acts*. Cambridge: Cambridge UP, 1979.

– 'Indirect Speech Acts.' In *Speech Acts*. Ed. Peter Cole and Jerry L. Morgan. Vol. 3 of *Syntax and Semantics*. New York: Academic P, 1975, 59–82. Repr. in *Expression and Meaning*, 30–57.

– 'The Logical Status of Fictional Discourse.' *New Literary History* 6 (1975): 319–32. Repr. in *Expression and Meaning*, 58–75.

– 'Reiterating the Differences: A Reply to Derrida.' *Glyph* 1 (1977): 198–208.

– *Speech Acts: An Essay in the Philosophy of Language*. Cambridge: Cambridge UP, 1969.

– 'A Taxonomy of Illocutionary Acts.' In *Language, Mind, and Knowledge*. Ed. Keith Gunderson. Vol. 7 of *Minnesota Studies in the Philosophy of Science*. Minneapolis: U of Minnesota P, 1975, 344–69. Repr. in *Expression and Meaning*, 1–29.

– 'What Is a Speech Act?' In *Philosophy in America*. Ed. Max Black. Ithaca: Cornell UP, 1965, 221–39.

Strawson, P.F. 'Austin and "Locutionary Meaning."' In *Essays on J.L. Austin*. Ed. G.J. Warnock. Oxford: Oxford UP, 1973, 46–68.

Secondary Sources

Coulthard, Malcolm. *An Introduction to Discourse Analysis*. 2nd ed. London and New York: Longman, 1985.

Petrey, Sandy. *Speech Acts and Literary Theory*. New York and London: Routledge, 1990.

Structuralism

Structuralism generally refers to the French thought of the 1960s associated with such thinkers as *Claude Lévi-Strauss, *Roland Barthes, *Michel Foucault, *Gérard Genette, *Louis Althusser, *Jacques Lacan, *Algirdas J. Greimas, and Jean Piaget. As Piaget repeats throughout *Structuralism*, 'structuralism is a method, not a doctrine' (142). Though closely related to Russian *formalism and offshoots such as the *Prague School and *Polish structuralism, French structuralism is distinguished by its variety and interdisciplinary vigour. A step beyond humanism and phenomenology, structuralism is concerned with the immanent relations constituting language and all symbolic or discursive systems. (See also *phenomenological criticism.)

Twentieth-century structuralism as such begins with a series of lectures delivered by the Swiss linguist *Ferdinand de Saussure at the University of Geneva, published after his death from lecture notes as *Course in General Linguistics* (1916). Saussure's breakthrough consisted in a new definition for the object of linguistics. What we refer to imprecisely as 'language' is separated by Saussure into two distinct manifestations: *langue* (language) and *parole* (speech or utterance). (See *langue/parole*.) As a result of this separation, language exists apart from speech as 'outside the individual who can never create nor modify it by himself' (14). The space of language is a self-authenticating system that is not determined by the world of things, since all that is required of language is that it connect a meaning to a particular sound-image. What remains remarkable in hindsight is that Saussure was aware of the potential consequences of his discovery: '*A science that studies the life of signs within society* is conceivable; it would be part of social psychology and consequently of general psychology; I shall call it *semiology* (from Greek *semeîon* "sign")' (16).

Along with the American philosopher *C.S. Peirce, Saussure can be considered a founder of *semiotics. Saussure's notion of the linguistic *sign has been highly influential within French structuralism. Whereas for Peirce a 'sign stands for something, its *object*' ('Logic as Semiotic' 5), Saussure's theory of the sign is not concerned with a sign's ultimate referent. (See *reference/referent.) For Saussure, the linguistic sign has only two essential parts, the signifier and the signified. (See *signified/signifier/signification.) By dispensing with the necessity of a third term (a referent or object), Saussure's theory affords itself a remarkable degree of autonomy since 'the bond between the signifier and the signified is arbitrary' (*Course* 67). Although the bond is arbitrary from the point of view of representation, the meaning of any particular signifier is assured by its place within language as a whole. This is Saussure's major structuralist insight. Language is a system of differences that generates meaning through its own internal mechanisms. The signifier 'dog' signifies simply because we know how to place it within the English language as a whole; a signifier such as 'zog' has no place in the system. Saussure's understanding of language as a system of signs has some important consequences. Because signs are meaningful only in their totality, the question of language as having an origin can no longer be asked. Language can only appear in the form we now experience it. (*Wittgenstein's arguments in the *Philosophical Investigations* against the possibility of a private language offer a helpful counterpoint to Saussure: language always belongs to a community.) To distinguish between the evolution of a particular language, possible in part *because* the bond between signifier and signified is arbitrary, and the unchanging systematic qualities of a language, Saussure posited *diachronic* and *synchronic linguistics*. Although many subsequent critics have attacked structuralism for its disavowal of temporality, Saussure at least makes the synchronic/diachronic distinction basic to his methodology. Synchronic linguistics reconstructs the perspective of individual speakers who operate only within the possibilities that exist for a language in a given moment. By reconstructing linguistic change through time, diachronic linguistics offers a perspective on language that is unavailable to actual speakers.

Structuralism enters the French intellectual scene of the 1960s largely through the ethnography of Claude Lévi-Strauss. Work in structural linguistics since Saussure gave Lévi-Strauss confidence that 'for the first time, a social science is able to formulate necessary relationships' (*Structural Anthropology* 33). The principles underlying these 'necessary relationships' are fourfold: (1) conscious laws may be reduced to their unconscious assumptions; (2) no term of the analysis will be meaningful apart from its binary opposite, in other words every social fact is embedded in relationships; (3) the concept of system is justified on a methodological level as something more than the result of any particular configuration; and (4) the move to posit general laws is justified by the underlying systematic assumptions of 1–3 (*Structural Anthropology* 33). (See *binary opposition.) Thus in the introduction to *The

Raw and the Cooked, Lévi-Strauss is confident that 'certain categorical opposites drawn from everyday experience with the most basic sorts of things – e.g. "raw" and "cooked," "fresh" and "rotten," "moist" and "parched," and others – can serve a people as conceptual tools for the formation of abstract notions and for combining these into propositions' ('Overture to *Le Cru et le cuit*' 31). By breaking cultural study down into basic binary oppositions, Lévi-Strauss can then reconstruct complex social and cultural formations from the ground up. The effect of this kind of analysis is a leveling of cultural institutions: the laws governing table manners in a particular *social formation are commensurable with the conceptual system of ideas found in that culture's religion. The concept of structure itself implies a remarkable consistency among otherwise dissimilar institutions. For structuralist methodology as a whole, this implies 'transformations, whereby equivalences in divergent materials can be explicated' and makes 'possible the prediction of how modifications in one element will alter the model as a whole' (Giddens 19).

Lévi-Strauss' most famous single analysis has been directed towards *myth, where the underlying question is no less than the role of *literature and imagination in society as a whole. 'Myth, like the rest of language, is made up of constituent units' (*Structural Anthropology* 210), but the meaning of myth is to be found not in any particular unit but in how the units as a whole are combined. The problem of how to find these units (exactly how many are there? how does one recognize and isolate them?) is solved by the principle that 'the true constituent units of a myth are not the isolated relations but *bundles of such relations*' (211). In concrete analysis of the Oedipus myth, Lévi-Strauss' inventory of bundles looks for principles of recurrence whereby acts of violence belong to a bundle that is distinct from a grouping of acts in violation of kinship prohibitions. When all the elements have been isolated and sorted into their respective bundles, the myth seems to interpret itself as a series of internal oppositions. In what is essentially a functionalist interpretation, Lévi-Strauss sees in the Oedipus myth a crisis of origin: are we born of nature or of culture? If the actual synchronic interpretation of the myth as dealing with basic oppositions is disappointing, the diachronic realization that the myth consists of 'all its versions,' including

Freud's, suggests the extent of Lévi-Strauss' achievement. (See *Sigmund Freud.) By removing myth from its reified isolation within culture, Lévi-Strauss makes it even more interesting from a theoretical point of view.

Lévi-Strauss' collaboration with linguist *Roman Jakobson (see 'Les Chats of Charles Baudelaire') demonstrates the former's reliance on linguistics and highlights the latter's importance for all of the French structuralists. In his seminal essay 'Closing Statement: Linguistics and Poetics,' Jakobson set out principles that would enable the structural analysis of literary texts. Beginning with the question of 'what makes a verbal message a work of art?' (147), Jakobson went on to work out a theory that could account for the many levels of functions at work in linguistic communication. Whenever an addresser sends a message to an addressee, the message refers to some context; in order to be sent it must be put into a *code and sent via 'a physical channel and psychological connection between the addresser and the addressee' (150) or contact. 'Focus on the message for its own sake is the poetic function of language' (153). For Jakobson (and it is consistent with Saussure's linguistics), the production of a message implies 'two basic modes of arrangement' in relation to the pre-existing code: selection and combination. Works of art are generated by a change in our relation with the code: 'The poetic function projects the principle of equivalence from the axis of selection into the axis of combination' (155). This implies that while communication needs a context, the literary work is in some primary sense self-referential.

More than any other French structuralist, Roland Barthes popularized the structural analysis of literature, although the concerns of his work are very diverse. In 11 books and over 152 articles, Barthes originated what we now call cultural criticism. Ranging from the semiology of fashion (The Fashion System) and the mythology of wrestling ('The World of Wrestling' in Mythologies) to the pleasure of reading (The Pleasure of the Text) and the value of criticism itself (Criticism and Truth), Barthes' work resists the simple classification 'structuralist.' It is possible, however, to read much of his work as examples of structuralist methodology. S/Z, for example, is a paradigm of an actual structuralist reading of fiction. Barthes divides Balzac's novella Sarrasine into 561 'lexias' and proceeds to analyse them one by one.

A Lévi-Straussian grouping into bundles is replaced by five codes: (1) 'the hermeneutic code ... by which an enigma can be distinguished, suggested, formulated, held in suspense, and finally disclosed'; (2) a realm of symbols that 'we shall refrain from structuring'; (3) a proairetic code concerning the rational sequence of actions; (4) a non-rational, empirical sequence of actions that is unstructured; and (5) culturally given codes that refer to existing bodies of knowledge ('physical, physiological, medical, literary, historical, etc.') [19–20]. (See *narrative code.) The major difference between the myth analysis of Lévi-Strauss and the semiology of S/Z is the polyvalent notion of *text that Barthes introduced in the essay 'From Work to Text': 'It is the space in which no one language has a hold over any other, in which all language circulates freely' (80). Thus in S/Z the proliferation of codes does not imply hierarchy so much as circulation and exchange – an economy of signs and a continual expansion of meaning. At the beginning of S/Z Barthes speaks of the 'writerly' text, which he values 'because the goal of literary work ... is to make the reader no longer a consumer, but a producer of the text' (4). The 'writerly' text stands in binary opposition to its 'counter-value,' the readerly or 'classic text.' The writerly text cannot be found because it is the structure of structure: 'poetry without the poem' (5). (See *readerly/writerly text.) Barthes' later work is marked by many such poststructuralist moments. In the middle of S/Z, for example, he wonders if the reconstruction of cultural codes is worth the effort considering its limited results. What can structuralist analysis ultimately hope for? Barthes answers the concern by setting structuralism up as the inescapable, endless logic of *textuality. Once we have created a cultural code, we must watch it disappear since 'the function of writing' is 'to make ridiculous, to annul the power (the intimidation) of one language over another, to dissolve any metalanguage as soon as it is constituted' (98). (See *metalanguage.) While battling the reductive tendencies of structuralism, Barthes seems also to be commenting on the restless variety of his own career.

In the influential essay 'Introduction to the Structural Analysis of Narratives,' Barthes can be seen as an orthodox structuralist. The influence of both Saussure and Russian formalists such as *Vladimir Propp, who isolated 31 individual narrative functions that remain constant in folktales, is apparent. A theory of narrative is possible if it can be shown that all narratives share common structures. Barthes moves in this direction by positing three levels of description in narrative *discourse: functions, actions and narration (88). The isolation of functions – which requires the complex theoretical distinction of 'indices' concerning characters from 'informants' concerning time and space – results in the possibility of a narrative syntax. (See also *index.)

The difficulty inherent in structuralist *narratology is readily apparent in the work of Algirdas Greimas, which is distinguished by its mathematical rigour, precision of definition and overall systematic complexity. Greimasian semiotics does not waver from the position that structure *precedes* meaning: 'the generation of meaning does not first take the form of the production of utterances and their combination in discourse; it is relayed, in the course of its trajectory, by narrative structures and it is these that produce meaningful discourse articulated in utterances' ('Elements of a Narrative Grammar' 64–5). This position is the utter reverse of *speech act theory and most subject-centred theories of language. (See *subject/object.) Even in Saussure, there is a sense of isolated subjects whose speech behaviour is generated by choosing from existing language structures. In a step beyond Barthes' notion that sentences themselves are narratives, Greimas isolates 'narrative structures as an *autonomous instance* within the general economy of semiotics' (65). The role of free agents or characters within narrative shrinks in Greimasian narratology with the introduction of the term *actant*, which as the subject in narrative grammar can be a person or thing (the 'actantial model' actually consists of six actants: subject, object, sender, receiver, helper, and opponent, following Propp and Etienne Souriau [see *Prince 1–2]). Greimas is able to generate a 'deep grammar' of narrative that is capable of fully situating narrative in linguistic terminology. Thus narrative is, in a sense, tamed and made the possible object of knowledge. The structural study of narrative is certainly not the only approach available to narratology, but the very isolation of narrative as an object is a legacy of structuralism and formalism.

The extent of structuralism as an intellectual movement can be measured by Jacques Lacan's return to Freud and Louis Althusser's return to Marx. Lacan *is* a structuralist, even though a certain radical quality in his thought opens a door to *poststructuralism. For Lacan, and it remains a constant of his thought, 'the unconscious is structured ... like a language' (*Ecrits* 234). Lacan's debt to Saussure is explicit in the essay 'The Agency of the Letter in the Unconscious.' Lacan interprets Saussure's theory of the linguistic sign to mean that 'no signification can be sustained other than by reference to another signification' (150); he goes on to suggest that the horizontal chain of signifiers – the relation of signifiers to each other above and beyond what they signify – constitutes the subject. If we recall Jakobson's distinction between selection and combination, then Lacan's claim that the relation between signifiers forms a 'metonymic structure' approaches intelligibility. It is a Lacanian axiom that the arbitrary relation between signifier and signified inscribes a lack at the core of human desire thus 'man's desire is a metonymy' (175). (See *desire/lack.) With metaphor roughly equivalent to selection and metonymy to combination, Lacan's theory of the unconscious can be reconstructed by following Jakobson's logic of similarity and contiguity (see 'Two Aspects of Language and Two Types of Aphasic Disturbances'). (See *metonymy/metaphor.) Lacan derives from Freud the discovery of 'the self's radical ex-centricity to itself' (171) but shifts this displacement to the contiguous realm of signifiers. As tropes, metaphor and metonymy no longer indicate a deviation from correct usage (or an unassailable signifier/signified bond): 'one word for another' – Lacan's definition of metaphor – establishes the semantic logic of psychoanalysis. (See also *trope, *psychoanalytic theory.)

Althusser's structural Marxism occurs within the context of French Communist politics as a need to clarify some basic Marxist principles. (See *Marxist theory.) In a relatively early essay, 'Marxism and Humanism,' Althusser questioned the tendency to see Marxism as a humanism that argues for an unchanging, human essence. Althusser argues for a post-1845 break with humanism in Marx with his theory of *ideology, which robs humanism of its '*theoretical* pretentions.' Althusser's major achievement, however, was to produce a fully structuralist theory of ideology that allows for no independent or neutral position outside of ideological systems. In 'Ideology and Ideological State Apparatuses,' Althusser convincingly describes how ideology functions within the institutions of modern societies, including the education system, the media and the culture industry. (See *Ideological State Apparatuses.) His actual definition of ideology has a decidedly Lacanian focus, not just in the thesis that 'ideology represents the imaginary relationship of individuals to their real conditions of existence' (162), but in the anti-humanist assertion that *all ideology has the function (which defines it) of "constituting" concrete individuals as subjects'* (171). Barthes argues for a similar position in his notion of the 'reality effect' (see Culler 193–4), the ability of discourse to assert its claim as accurate representation by hiding evidence to the contrary. Althusser's unpopularity among literary theorists for the past ten years or so, attests, perhaps, to the lingering persistence of humanist notions as the source of resistance to the wholesale appropriation of structuralist methods.

Michel Foucault denied being a structuralist throughout his career, but commentators have not taken him at his word. In two major theoretical works, *The Order of Things* and *The Archaeology of Knowledge* (which were later superseded by a comprehensive theory of *power), Foucault suggested that signifying practices 'systematically form the objects of which they speak' (*Archaeology* 49). (See *signifying practice.) *The Order of Things* traces the historical trajectory or archaeology of negotiations that have occurred between words and things in large epistemological groupings known as *epistemes*. (See *episteme.) Although the regularity of any particular episteme permits a structural or linguistic analysis, Foucault wants to emphasize that his reinvention of the history of science and ideas does not operate on a homogeneous object; he gives high priority to the very concepts that threaten his approach: 'discontinuity, rupture, threshold, limit, series, and transformation' (*Archaeology* 21). In speaking of the tension in his work between the structuralism he himself deploys against his own objections, Foucault occupies a curious position: he is the structuralist against structuralism. Lacan and Althusser avoid this position by linking themselves to Freud and Marx respectively, while Foucault hopes for perpetual renewal through what he calls 'a decentring that leaves no privilege to any centre' (*Archaeology* 205). (See *centre/decentre.)

Foucault's move into poststructuralism occurs with his shift to a theory of power that carries a large debt to *Friedrich Nietzsche and his critique of German idealism. Although it has been influential, its ultimate philosophical value is open to question (see *Habermas 266–93). The shift in France from structuralism to poststructuralism can be understood either as a repudiation of or reaction to structuralism or as structuralism's final triumph. Foucault (and perhaps Lacan) illustrate the latter view, while the work of *Jacques Derrida can be seen as oppositional and a genuine step beyond Saussurean linguistics. After Derrida delivered his paper 'Structure, Sign, and Play in the Discourse of the Human Sciences' at a 1966 conference in the U.S.A., the international prestige of structuralism was very much reduced. In the essay, Derrida attacked the 'structurality of structure,' the whole spatial metaphor of organization around a single centre that is implied by structural analysis. (See *spatial form.) Derrida argues that the notion of centre used by linguists and structuralists is incapable of organizing the complexity of discourse when the history of philosophical concepts is examined from a linguistic point of view. Derrida, who takes the notion of text seriously as a philosophical problem brought to light by structuralism, demonstrates that the primacy of language in structuralism carries with it some questionable metaphysical presuppositions, in particular the notion of a structure's immediate presence. (See *metaphysics of presence.) For Derrida, presence is no more that the lost dream of humanism, the hope of recovering some absolute point of origin as a 'reassuring foundation.' In light of Derrida's criticism, it seems clear that his infamous notion of textuality – 'there is nothing outside the text' – pulls structure back into the text and is actually a serious claim to make in the wake of structuralism and its metalinguistic pretentions.

GREGOR CAMPBELL

Primary Sources

Althusser, Louis. 'Ideology and Ideological State Apparatuses.' In *Lenin and Philosophy and Other Essays*. Trans. Ben Brewster. New York: Monthly Review P, 1971.
– 'Marxism and Humanism.' In *For Marx*. Trans. Ben Brewster. London: Verso, 1979.
– and Etienne Balibar. *Reading Capital*. Trans. Ben Brewster. London: Verso, 1979.
Barthes, Roland. *Criticism and Truth*. Trans. and ed.

Katrine Pilcher Keuneman. Minneapolis: U of Minnesota P, 1987.
- *The Fashion System*. Trans. Matthew Ward and Richard Howard. Berkeley: U of California P, 1990.
- 'From Work to Text.' In *Textual Strategies: Perspectives in Post-Structuralist Criticism*. Ed. Josué V. Harari. Ithaca: Cornell UP, 1979.
- 'Introduction to the Structural Analysis of Narrative.' In *Image-Music-Text*. Trans. Stephen Heath. New York: Hill and Wang, 1977.
- *Mythologies*. Trans. Annette Lavers. St. Albans, GB: Paladin, 1976.
- 'The Reality Effect.' In *The Rustle of Language*. Trans. Richard Howard. Berkeley: U of California P, 1986.
- *The Rustle of Language*. Trans. Richard Howard. Berkeley: U of California P, 1986.
- *S/Z*. Trans. Richard Miller. New York: Hill and Wang, 1974.
Benveniste, Emile. *Problems in General Linguistics*. Trans. Mary Elizabeth Meek. Coral Gables: U of Miami P, 1971.
Foucault, Michel. *The Archaeology of Knowledge*. Trans. A.M. Sheridan Smith. New York: Pantheon, 1972.
- *The Order of Things: An Archaeology of the Human Sciences*. New York: Vintage, 1970.
Greimas, Algiras Julien. 'Elements of a Narrative Grammar.' In *On Meaning*. Trans. Paul J. Perron and Frank H. Collins. Minneapolis: U of Minnesota P, 1987.
- *The Social Sciences: A Semiotic View*. Trans. Paul Perron and Frank H. Collins. Minneapolis: U of Minnesota P, 1990.
Jakobson, Roman. 'Closing Statement: Linguistics and Poetics.' In *Semiotics: An Introductory Anthology*. Ed. Robert E. Innes. Bloomington: Indiana UP, 1985.
- 'Two Aspects of Language and Two Types of Aphasic Disturbances.' In *Language and Literature*. Ed. Krystyna Pomorska and Stephen Rudy. Cambridge, Mass.: Harvard UP, 1987.
- and Claude Lévi-Strauss. 'Les Chats of Charles Baudelaire.' Trans. F.M. De George in *The Structuralists: From Marx to Lévi-Strauss*. Ed. Richard T. De George and Fernande M. De George. New York: Doubleday, 1972.
Lacan, Jacques. 'The Agency of the Letter on the Unconscious.' In *Ecrits*. Trans. Alan Sheridan. New York: Norton, 1977.
- *Ecrits*. Trans. Alan Sheridan. New York: Norton, 1977.
Lévi-Strauss, Claude. 'Overture to *Le Cru et le cuit*.' In *Structuralism*. Ed. Jacques Ehrmann. New York: Anchor, 1970.
- *The Raw and the Cooked*. New York: Harper and Row, 1969.
- *Structural Anthropology*. Trans. Claire Jacobson and Brooke Grundfest Schoepf. New York: Basic Books, 1963.

Peirce, Charles S. 'Logic as Semiotic: The Theory of Signs.' In *Semiotics: An Introductory Anthology*. Ed. Robert E. Innes. Bloomington: Indiana UP, 1985.
Piaget, Jean. *Structuralism*. Trans. Chaninah Maschler. London: Routledge and Kegan Paul, 1971.
Saussure, Ferdinand de. *Course in General Linguistics*. Ed. Charles Bally and Albert Sechehaye in collaboration with Albert Riedlinger. Trans. Wade Baskin. New York: McGraw-Hill, 1959.

Secondary Sources

Bennett, Tony. *Formalism and Marxism*. London: Methuen, 1979.
Caws, Peter. *Structuralism: The Art of the Intelligible*. Atlantic Highlands, NJ: Humanities P, 1988.
Culler, Jonathan. *Structuralist Poetics*. London: Routledge and Kegan Paul, 1975.
Derrida, Jacques. 'Structure, Sign, and Play in the Discourse of the Human Sciences.' In *The Structuralist Controversy: The Languages of Criticism and the Sciences of Man*. Ed. Richard Macksey and Eugenio Donato. Baltimore: Johns Hopkins UP, 1972.
Giddens, Anthony. *Central Problems in Social Theory: Action, Structure and Contradiction in Social Analysis*. London: Macmillan, 1979.
Jameson, Fredric. *The Prison-House of Language: A Critical Account of Structuralism and Russian Formalism*. Princeton, NJ: Princeton UP, 1972.
Habermas, Jürgen. *The Philosophical Discourse of Modernity*. Trans. Frederick Lawrence. Cambridge, Mass.: MIT P, 1987.
Harland, Richard. *Superstructuralism: The Philosophy of Structuralism and Post-Structuralism*. London: Methuen, 1987.
Hawkes, Terence. *Structuralism and Semiotics*. Berkeley: U of California P, 1977.
Prince, Gerald. *Dictionary of Narratology*. Lincoln: U of Nebraska P, 1987.
Scholes, Robert. *Structuralism in Literature: An Introduction*. New Haven: Yale UP, 1974.
Seung, T.K. *Structuralism and Hermeneutics*. New York: Columbia UP, 1982.
Sturrock, John. *Structuralism*. London: Paladin, 1986.
Wittgenstein, Ludwig. *Philosophical Investigations*. Trans. G.E.M. Anscombe. Oxford: Basil Blackwell, 1963.

Structuralism, Polish

The origins of Polish structuralism are associated with Kazimierz Wóycicki and his literary stylistics. In 1914 Wóycicki published two important studies: 'Historia literatury i poetyka' ['History of Literature and Poetics'] and 'Jedność stylowa utworu poetyckiego' ['The

Stylistic Unity of the Literary Work of Art']. In the first, he proposed to divide the history of *literature into (1) the external history of literature (the relation of belles-lettres and poetic works to reality) and (2) the internal literary history which could supplement the former by analysing the aesthetic value of literature or, in other words, create a history of poetic art (a 'historical poetics'). In addition, Wóycicki proposed that poetics should also include two subcategories: (1) psychological poetics (to discover the laws of the creative process and the experience of the reader); and (2) aesthetic or 'objective' poetics (to explore the structure of the poetic work as a 'verbal [lexical] aesthetic creation'). In 'The Stylistic Unity of the Literary Work of Art,' Wóycicki observed that each element in a work acquires a proper sense and significance, lives in an appropriate manner, and acts only in relationship with other elements. Thanks to this interdependence, all constituents of the work are united in a common aim. A literary work of art is not the sum total of static formal devices but is an entity of dynamically correlated elements. Wóycicki's article appeared almost 15 years before the publication of *Iurii Tynianov and *Roman Jakobson's 'Problems in the Study of Literature and Language,' considered the 'manifesto' of structuralist poetics, and thus predates their notion of literature as a dynamically evolving phenomenon. (See *structuralism.)

Other Polish scholars developed new formalist approaches to literature as well. Thus, in the early 1920s Zygmunt Łempicki showed a close affinity with the phenomenological understanding of literature (later substantiated by *Roman Ingarden) and came close to formulating a semiotic theory of literature and art. Manfred Kridl followed the line of Russian formalists and insisted that the most important, distinct feature of imaginative literature is its fictionality. (See also *phenomenological criticism, *semiotics, Russian *formalism.)

Out of these early theoretical inquiries emerged two major centres of literary studies: the Wilno (today Vilnius) group, under the theoretical guidance of Kridl, and the Warsaw Circle, inspired by Wóycicki's studies and known as Koło Polonistów Uniwersytetu Warszawskiego [The University of Warsaw Polonists' Circle]. The latter determined to a great extent the evolution of structuralism in Poland after the Second World War. The early stage of its development is marked by the publica-

tion of *Prace ofiarowane Kazimierzowi Wóyckiemu* [*Essays in Honor of Kazimierz Wóycicki* 1937]. The participation of Jakobson and Nikolai Trubetzkoi in this volume was not only a sign of Polish literary scholarship leaving the confines of traditional interests but also a proof of the existing ties with both Russian formalism and the *Prague School. The outbreak of the Second World War brought the evolution of Polish structuralism to a standstill. Some of its representatives died or perished in concentration camps.

The immediate postwar period did not foster any structuralist revival because of the imposition of Marxism as an offical doctrine and theoretical direction in all spheres of cultural life. Still, in 1946, under the editorship of Kazimierz Budzyk, *Stylistyka teoretyczna w Polsce* [*Theoretical Stylistics in Poland*] appeared, containing some structuralist essays. (See *Marxist criticism.)

Generally speaking, Kazimierz Budzyk was the scholar who revived literary structuralism in Poland, although he did so under the banner of stylistics: in the postwar climate this term offered protection from the watchdogs of Marxist ideological 'purity' for whom the word 'structuralism' was anathema. In his early studies such as 'Z zagadnień stylistyki' ['The Problems of Stylistics'], 'Gwara a utwór literacki' ['Dialect and the Literary Work of Art'], 'Sprawa neologizmów w literaturze' ['The Question of Neologisms in Literature'], Budzyk stressed the fact that literature is first of all a linguistic phenomenon but is governed by specific laws of composition (or 'structure'). Narrative prose is characterized by complex structural units and cannot be reduced to purely linguistic analysis. Thus he differentiated four major structural segments in narrative prose: narration, description, dialogue, and monologue. (See also *narratology.)

In the late 1950s structuralism began a spectacular recovery and reached its full bloom in the second half of the 1960s and throughout the 1970s, challenging Marxist literary scholarship. This happened mainly thanks to the theoretical activities of Janusz Sławinski and Michal Głowiński, both students and followers of Budzyk.

There are three currents of Polish structuralism: (1) one that concentrates on the structure of literary texts and poetics (Maria Renata Mayenowa, Lucylla Pszczolowska, Anna Wierzbicka, Jerzy Faryno); (2) one that situates the literary work within a wider integrating context of anthropological, semiological and social perspectives which can be understood as knowledge about literary culture (Stefan Żół-kiewski, Janusz Lalewicz, Wincenty Grajewski, and Kamila Rudzińska); and (3) one interested in literary entities of a 'higher' and more complex order (for example, 'group *code' or 'compound poetics') than in the questions of *text or the pragmatics of the socio-anthropological, semiological approach (J. Sławiński, M. Gło-wiński, Kazimierz Bartoszyński, E. Balcerzan, and Alexandra Okopień-Sławińska). (See also *narrative code.)

Polish structuralists' wide-ranging theoretical inquiries led to the development of a comprehensive theory of literary communication understood as both a communication between structural constituents of imaginative literature itself and as communication on the axis author-text-receiver, taking place in the external (that is, outside strictly literary matters) reality. (See also *communication theory.)

While easily grouped into three divisions, members of one group often encroached on the 'territory' of another. This is particularly true of Sławiński-Głowiński's line of theoretical reflection. Diversity of interests is evident in Sławiński's important book Dzieło. Język. Tradycja [The Literary Work. Language. Tradition 1974] in which he delineated his areas of theoretical investigation as historical poetics, sociology of literature (or literary communication), and linguistic poetics. Sławiński's methodological point of departure is based on three fundamental premises: (1) one should not confuse the consideration of the structure of the literary work of art with the analysis of the literary process; (2) one should not confound the structure of the literary work of art with the analysis of literature's communicative situation; and (3) the characterization of the literary work's structure requires an application of a twofold terminology – one in relation to its linguistic stratum and another in relation to the 'represented objects.' The totality of this theoretical approach is clearly at work in an article on the semantics of narrative discourse (1967), addressing the question of differentiation between poetry and prose. According to Sławiński, the existing distinction between poetry and prose is incorrect because it is founded on inconsistent criteria. While poetry is viewed as 'intra-lexical' reality in which the 'content' is generated by verbal relationships

and operations (syntax, intonation, metaphors, similes, and so on), the ontological status of prose is usually determined by its referential value, by what is (re)presented in it as an 'extra-lexical' reality. Sławiński does not question the common claim that in poetry the cognitive (or referential) function of the word is weaker than in prose. What he objects to is the treatment of prose as the exclusive result of extraliterary conditions. Like poetry, the novel or any subgenre of literary prose is composed of words, but they are used differently than in a poetic utterance. Still, both are built of lexical fabric. It is exactly the commonness of this main feature that compels us to treat prose in terms of poetics. At the same time, through the mediation of prose's specificity (the word has stronger cognitive value than in poetry) arises the opportunity to enrich the discipline of poetics by the inclusion of literary semantics to its range of issues.

'Synchronia i diachronia w procesie history-czno-literackim' ['Synchrony and Diachrony in the Historico-Literary Process' 1967], Sławiń-ski's theoretical credo, aims to overcome a strictly synchronic approach which treats the literary work of art as a correlate of literary norms and aims to reconcile it with a diachronic analysis; the latter makes us aware that the 'structure' of each literary work is at the same time part and parcel of the historico-literary process. Hence the interest in historical poetics. In short, Sławiński points out the necessity of reconciling the category of structure with the category of evolutionary process. Literary works cannot be treated as 'illustrative' material only but as active participants in a system. Literary utterance (or *discourse) is the 'application (or "use") of tradition.' The relation between the supra-individual (general) system and its individual 'use' (or application) is always of a functional nature. To make this relationship clearer, Sławiński introduced the concepts of 'fenotype' and 'genotype,' also known in other disciplines of the humanities. 'Fenotype' is an explicit structure of a given literary work of art; 'genotype,' the implicit structure of literary norms which remain at work in shaping an individual work of art. Tradition 'enters' into each work. At the same time, however, a simple work of literature becomes part of the tradition to the degree to which it is able to interiorize the literary heritage. Sławiński's formulation of literary tradition (which has its roots in the work of

*Mikhail Bakhtin) is similar to that of *intertextuality, popularized by *Julia Kristeva and known in Lubomír Doležel's terminology as literary transduction (*Occidental Poetics* 1990); it also shares some affinity with *T.S. Eliot's ideas ('Tradition and the Individual Talent').

Głowiński's theoretical contribution intersects at many points with that of Sławiński's studies, with one essential difference: he combines theoretical reflection with a more pragmatic attitude and a concrete literary analysis. In Głowiński's work three or four areas receive particular attention: narratology (particularly the question of the *narrator), the theory of reception, tradition and literary periods, and genres (especially the novel.) (See also *Constance School of Reception Aesthetics, *genre criticism.) Although Głowiński's theoretical and critical interests are versatile he is preoccupied with literary communication, which he divides into two categories – 'internal' and 'external': the literary work constitutes a communicative act which is always addressed to unknown readers ('external' communication). The reader, however, constitutes part of the signifying structure and yet cannot be identified with a real person, existing outside the text and actually reading the text. Each text contains an 'embedded' or *implied reader whom he calls a 'virtual receiver' ('internal' communication). The existence of *wirtualny czytelnik* [the virtual reader] who is determined by the structure of the text prompts the latter to be read in a particular way. A writer can opt for a variety of strategies to address the virtual reader (for example, directly or indirectly) who is delineated not only by the structure of the individual work (the text) but also by the nature of a given literary convention. (See also *embedding.)

Thanks to Sławiński's and Głowiński's theoretical contributions, Polish structuralism was most influential in literary communication and historical poetics. Less visible were its achievements in the theory of literary texts because of the legacy of Ingarden's theory which, dating from the early 1930s, exerted pressure on the way structuralism and literary theory in general evolved in Poland. Polish structuralists simply filled spaces left 'empty' or insufficiently developed by Ingarden's theory. Still, M.R. Mayenowa made significant contributions to the theory of literary texts in *Poetyka teoretyczna. Zagadnienia języka* [*Theoretical Poetics. Problems of Language* 1974]. Instead of the strati-

fication of the artistic text, Mayenowa speaks of its cohesion (*spójność*). Mayenowa does not subscribe to the *Tartu School's view that poetic language, a secondary modelling system, grew primarily out of and above natural language. Artistic texts are creations of the language sensu stricto. Each poetic text contains some additional transformational rules which impose new limitations on it because it enters into different relations with other systems and structures (for example, versification system); there exists yet another, non-linguistic sign system which also transmits essential meanings contained in the text. To discover secondary modelling systems which function in various texts is, according to Mayenowa, the most difficult and least formalized task of literary scholarship. (See also *sign.)

The concentration of 'structuralist activity' in postwar Warsaw gave scholars such as W. Kroll the inducement to speak of a Warsaw School of Structuralism. If indeed such a school ever existed, it never achieved any theoretical homogeneity; rather it was methodologically and analytically diverse. Unlike Russian and Czech theory, in which one approach to literary studies was dominant, modern Polish literary theory was characterized by theoretical polarization and an almost simultaneous rise of three major tendencies: structuralism (Wóycicki in Warsaw); phenomenology (Ingarden in Lwów); and formalism (Kridl in Wilno). Although Warsaw structuralism gained the upper hand in the 1960s and 1970s, it too reflected a diversity of theoretical attitudes, assimilating concepts and ideas of both formalism and phenomenology.

Outside of Warsaw two scholars from Łódz and Kraków respectively made significant contributions to the development of Polish literary scholarship: Stefania Skwarczyńska and Henryk Markiewicz. Thanks to its dynamic evolution in the 1960s and 1970s, Polish structuralism provided a kind of intellectual shelter for those who could not accept the imposition of Marxist philosophy, possibly because of the milder political conditions in Poland than those existing, for example, in the Soviet Union or East Germany. At the same time Polish structuralism managed to exercise considerable impact on theoretical discussions in Central Europe, particularly in Slovakia and Yugoslavia, and in Israel and West Germany.

EDWARD MOŻEJKO

Primary Sources

Bartoszyński, K. 'Glosa o współczesnym literaturoz-
nawstwie w Polsce.' In *Teksty drugie* 1.2 (1990):
99–112.
Budzyk, K. 'Z zagadnień stylistyki.' In *Prace ofiaro-
wane Kazimierzowi Wóycickiemu*. Wilno-Warszawa:
PZDI, 1937.
Głowiński, M. *Gry powieściowe. Szkice z teorii i histo-
rii form narracyjnych*. Warszawa: PWN, 1973.
– *Porządek. Chaos. Znaczenie*. Warszawa: PWN, 1968.
– *Style odbioru. Szkice o komunikacji literackiej*. Kra-
ków: Wydawnictwo Literackie, 1977.
Markiewicz, H. *Główne problemy wiedzy o litera-
turze*. Kraków: Wydawnictwo Literackie, 1965.
– *Teoria badań literackich w Polsce*. Vol. 1–2. Kra-
ków: Wydawnictwo Literackie, 1960.
Mayenowa, M.R. *Poetyka teoretyczna. Zagadnienia ję-
zyka*. Wrocław: Zakład im. Ossolinskich, 1974.
Sławiński, J. *Dzieło. Język. Tradycja*. Warszawa:
PWN, 1974.
– *Koncepcja jezyka poetyckiego awangardy krakowskiej*.
Wrocław: Ossolineum, 1965.
– 'Synchronia i diachronia w procesie historyczno-
literackim.' In *Proces historyczny w literaturze i
sztuce*. Ed. M. Janion and A. Piorunowa. War-
szawa: IBL, 1967.
– *Teksty i teksty*. Warszawa: PEN, 1990.
– *Próby teoretyczno literackie*. Warszawa: PEN, 1992.
Wóycicki, K. *Historia literatury i poetyka*. Warsaw,
1914. Repr. in *Teoria badań literackich w Polsce*.
Vol. I. Ed. H. Markiewicz. Kraków: Wydawnictwo
Literackie, 1960.
– 'Jedność stylowa utworu poetyckiego.' Repr. in
Teoria badań literackich w Polsce. Vol. I.
– *Prace ofiarowane Kazimierzowi Wóycickiemu*. Wilno-
Warszawa: PZDI, 1937.

Secondary Sources

Doležel, L. *Occidental Poetics: Tradition and Progress*.
Lincoln: U of Nebraska P, 1990.
Eliot. T.S. 'Tradition and the Individual Talent.' In
The Selected Prose of T.S. Eliot. Ed. Frank Kermode.
London: Faber and Faber, 1975.
Fieguth, R. 'Semantik und literarische Tradition. Ein
strukturalistisches Gesamtkonzept der Literaturwissenschaft.' In J. Sławiński, *Literatur als System
und Prozess*. Munich: Nymphenburger Verlags-
handlung, 1975.
Głowiński, M. 'Polish Structuralism.' *Books Abroad*
49.2 (1975): 238–43.
Kroll, W., ed. *Književna komunikacija. Antologija
poljske znanosti o književnosti. Umjetnost riječi*
(Zagreb) 28.2–4 (1974). The entire issue of this periodical is devoted to the question of literary communication as developed by Polish theoreticians.
Popovič, A., ed. *Slovo. Vyznam. Dieló. Antologia
pol'skej literárnej vedy*. Bratislava: Slovenský spisovatel', 1972.

Tartu School

Founded in the summer of 1964 at the University of Tartu in Estonia by *Iurii Lotman, the
Tartu School of Semiotics provided a forum
for discussions and publications in the discipline of *semiotics. Among the numerous contributors to the school are Viacheslav V. Ivanov, Iu.I. Levin, A.M. Piatigorskii, I.I. Revzin,
D.M. Segal, Yuri K. Shcheglov, Vladimir N.
Toporov, *A.K. Zholkovsky, and *Boris Uspenskii. Developing the research of the Russian formalists and the Prague structuralists
(see *Prague School, Russian *formalism), the
semiotic movement attracted scholars from a
wide range of disciplines (mathematics, mythology, etymology, folklore, Oriental studies,
music, visual arts, cinema, and so on) whose
common ground was an interest in modern
theories of communication, cybernetics, machine translation, and linguistics. (See *communication theory.) Instrumental in establishing the new discipline of semiotics was a symposium held in Moscow in 1962 on the topic
of 'The Structural Study of Sign Systems.' (See
also *sign.)

The Tartu School rapidly became a centre
for the field of semiotics through its biennial
conferences and series of publications. The
summer meetings attracted scholars not only
from Russia but also from abroad, such as *Julia Kristeva and Thomas Sebeok. Of particular
importance and influence within the school
was the publication of Lotman's work on the
poetics of *literature in *Lektsii po struktural'noi
poetike* [*Lectures on Structural Poetics* 1964].

Until 1970 the school concentrated on the
analysis of particular modelling systems such
as literature, religion, *myth, and folklore.
Later, its goals were expanded to include a semiotics of culture, the school's main area of
experimentation. The school was also characterized by its extensive publications program
(more than 2000 items), which included important works of the past such as *Mikhail
Bakhtin's *Tvorchestvo Fransua Rable i narodnaia
kul'tura srednevekov'ia i Renessansa* [1965;
trans. 1968 as *Rabelais and His World*] and Lev
Vigotskii's *Psikhologiia iskusstva* [*Psychology of
Art* 1965; trans. 1971]. Although writings in
the area of cultural semiotics proliferated in
the late 1970s and early 1980s, the activities of
the school ceased with the emigration of many

Tartu scholars to the West and with the lack of government support.

Approach and concepts

In *The Structure of the Artistic Text*, Lotman provides a theoretical framework for the notion that art is a language which communicates. In creating and perceiving works of art, humans receive and transmit a particular kind of information which can be called a language because it is an organized system of communication which uses signs. In postulating that art is a language, Lotman also suggests that the work of art is a *text which communicates artistic information in a way that is unlike any other form of communication. One of the distinctive features of artistic language is a high information content (the consequence of the fact that elements in a work of art function simultaneously in several systems) coupled with a low economy of means.

For Lotman, as for other semioticians of the Tartu School, the concept of text is not an absolute but a dynamic entity. Three principles underlie Lotman's textual poetics: meaning is paramount, content is determined by immanent analysis of the text, but extratextual systems must not be ignored. After an initial synchronic analysis, the work of art should be related to other modelling systems and situated within a historical and social context.

According to Lotman, the artistic text holds many characteristic features. It belongs to the realm of *parole* rather than *langue*; it is a system composed of many systems; and it is 'multiplanar' because a given element fits into several structures, thus acquiring different meanings. Within the complex hierarchical system of multi-relations, there is always a deviation, conflict or rupture. (See *langue/parole*.) This deviation produces the dynamism of the text, or as Lotman calls it, its 'energy.' The conflict can be internal (semantic versus syntactic) or external (when a given text functions in opposition to certain norms and constraints).

In Uspenskii's *A Poetics of Composition*, the concept of text is approached from the notion of 'point of view.' While identifying the different points of view that structure a literary work, Uspenskii also embraces the area of pragmatics by establishing a relationship between author, work and assumed reader.

Many pioneering studies written by other members of the Tartu group examine various aspects of the literary text. For example, frequency lists combined with semantic classification are used by Z.G. Mints and Levin to compare different texts by one or several authors or to illustrate how formal distribution governs the creation of themes and images. A theory of 'generative poetics,' essentially a model to show the formulation of a text from a *theme or semantic kernel, is developed by Shcheglov and Zholkovsky. This theory differs from *A.J. Greimas' narrative grammar in formulating the theme in terms of *expressive devices (repetition, division, variation, contrast, combination) rather than in basic binary oppositions. (See *binary opposition.) Numerous original studies attempt to define various genres such as the folk song, the detective story and the limerick (Revzin, Toporov) or to describe the logic of tropes (Levin). (See *genre criticism, *trope, *poetics of expressiveness.)

Secondary modelling systems

The concept of 'secondary modelling system,' a key notion of the Tartu School, represents a conceptual framework for the analysis of various forms of art. 'Secondary' refers to the idea that while all art is founded on the primary system of natural language, it also acquires a supplementary structure. Thus myth, folklore, fine arts, and ritual are secondary because they are built onto the linguistic system of primary language. Verbal language, for example, has been taken as a model for visual arts in some of Uspenskii's writings and for musical composition in some of the work of Boris M. Gasparov. 'Modelling' suggests that the secondary system of art represents a structure of elements and rules for combining them that is analogous to the entire sphere of an object of knowledge and insight. Finally, 'system' posits that art uses signs which are organized into a system of communication. The concept of 'secondary modelling systems' has been employed extensively by semioticians of the Tartu School to study a variety of cultural systems such as cinema, music, myth, and folklore.

Cultural semiotics

Although art is perceived by the Tartu School as a special kind of semiotic system governed by internal rules, its signifying capacity is also determined by a wider cultural context. In

1973 several Tartu scholars (Lotman, Uspenskii, Ivanov, Toporov, and Piatigorskii) defined
the semiotics of culture as 'the study of the
functional correlation of different sign systems'
('Theses on the Semiotic Study of Culture').
Thus, the theory of literature was placed within the context of the study of culture and of
the function of relationships of literary texts to
other systems. Accordingly, increasing attention was given to the semiotics of non-literary
cultural systems. Within this larger diachronic,
historical and social perspective, many questions were examined, notably the processes by
which a culture evolves.

The attempt to perceive a work of art within
a larger context was further extended by an
effort to view all of the artistic activities of a
certain period as a comprehensive semiotic
system. Within these systems, artistic practices
were perceived in terms of mutual influence
and interdependence.

In addition, Tartu semioticians have attempted to develop cultural typologies. Lotman, for instance, has distinguished between
cultures oriented towards beginnings and those
oriented towards ends; ones that are sign-
oriented (medieval culture) and those that are
oriented against the sign (the Enlightenment);
cultures that are 'text-oriented' and those that
are 'code-oriented'; and, finally, cultures oriented towards myth and ones toward science
(Shukman 'Lotman'). The works published by
Tartu semioticians since 1970 stress the importance of historical and social relativism in the
context of a general theory of culture. (See
also *code.)

Influence

It is difficult and perhaps premature to assess
the influence of the Tartu School of Semiotics,
although it is generally perceived as a leader
in cultural semiotics. The emigration of several
of its members to the West, together with the
growing number of translations available in
English and French of their work, will probably enhance North American and European
interest in the school's work. The writings of
Lotman specifically have been influential in literary criticism in France and North America.
His best known work, *The Structure of the Artistic Text*, is often cited in a variety of contexts
and has been the object of scrutiny both in
Europe and in North America.

Other schools and approaches

In spite of its interest in immanent artistic
structures and in poetic language, especially
in the material published before 1970, Tartu
semiotics must be distinguished from Russian
formalism and Prague *structuralism. Unlike
these two schools, the Tartu group perceives
the cultural framework of modelling systems
as determining their poetic function. In addition, the goals of the Tartu semioticians differ
from those of their predecessors in that they
seek to develop a total theory of culture. Tartu
semiotics also differs from certain Western semiotic approaches because it views art as a socially functioning and historically continuing
semiotic phenomenon. Unlike Greimas' synchronic immanent approach, for example,
Tartu semiotics takes into account broader
areas of culture, history and society. Generally
speaking, Tartu semiotics also differs from
other approaches, such as *C.S. Peirce's, because most of its writings constitute applied
semiotics, analysis rather than theory, with an
emphasis on empirical evidence instead of abstract constructs.

However, certain similarities can be perceived with some semiotic practices in France,
notably in *Roland Barthes' work in which semiotic investigation was expanded to integrate
questions of pragmatics and culture.

Limitations

The major criticism levelled at the Tartu
School has been conceptual. Although Tartu
scholars attempted to develop a scientific approach to cultural semiotics, their frequent dependence upon a metaphoric language was
regarded as imprecise and unscientific. Western scholars have also attacked the central
tenet of the Tartu School, the 'secondary modelling system', arguing that natural language
does not necessarily provide the primary
model for all other cultural systems. Pettit
(1975), for example, claimed that the linguistic
model fails to be explanatory outside of the
realm of language. Other critics have questioned the relationship of the linguistic model
to music and visual arts. This problem has
been attenuated to a certain extent in the past
few years because, in their writings on cultural
semiotics, Tartu scholars no longer stress the
relationship between linguistic and other

models of communication. In fact, Ivanov has suggested that some sign systems are structured quite differently from natural language.

However, in spite of these drawbacks, the research of the Tartu School in various cultural phenomena has been seminal in developing, on a world scale, the field of cultural semiotics and thus in expanding the boundaries of all semiotic inquiry.

JANET M. PATERSON

Primary Sources

Baran, Henryk, ed. *Semiotics and Structuralism: Readings from the Soviet Union.* New York: International Arts and Sciences P, 1976.
Lotman, Jurij. *Analysis of the Poetic Text.* Trans. D. Barton Johnson. Ann Arbor: Ardis, 1976.
– *Lektsi po struktural' noi poetike.* Tartu: Tartu State U, 1964. Repr. Providence: Brown UP, 1968.
– *Semiotics of Cinema.* Trans. Mark E. Suino. Ann Arbor: Michigan Slavic Publications, 1976.
– *The Structure of the Artistic Text.* Trans. Ronald Vroon. Ann Arbor: Michigan Slavic Contributions, 1977.
– and Boris Uspenskij. *The Semiotics of Russian Culture.* Ed. and trans. Ann Shukman. Ann Arbor: Michigan Slavic Contributions, 1984.
Lucid, Daniel P., ed. and trans. *Soviet Semiotics: An Anthology.* Baltimore and London: The Johns Hopkins UP, 1977.
Nakhimovsky, Alexander D., and Alice Stone Nakhimovsky, eds. *The Semiotics of Russian Cultural History.* Ithaca: Cornell UP, 1985.
Soviet Semiotics and Criticism: An Anthology. Special issue of *New Literary History* 9.2 (1978).
Soviet Semiotics of Literature and Culture. Special issue of *PTL: A Journal for Descriptive Poetics and Theory of Literature* 3.3 (1978).
Uspenskij, Boris. *A Poetics of Composition.* Trans. Valentina Zavarin and Susan Witting. Berkeley: U of California P, 1973.
– V.V. Ivanov, V.N. Toporov, A.M. Pjatigorskij, and Ju. M. Lotman. 'Theses on the Semiotic Study of Culture.' In *Structure of Texts and Semiotics of Culture.* Ed. Jan van der Eng and Mojmír Grygar. Paris/The Hague: Mouton, 1973.

Secondary Sources

Eirmermacher, Karl, and Serge Shishkoff. *Subject Bibliography of Soviet Semiotics: The Moscow-Tartu School.* Ann Arbor: Michigan Slavic Publications, 1977.
Meletinsky, Eleazar M., and Dimitri M. Segal. 'Structuralism and Semiotics in the USSR.' *Diogenes* 73 (1971): 88–125.
Pettit, Phillip. *The Concept of Structuralism: A Critical Analysis.* Berkeley: U of California P, 1975.
Segal, Dimitri M. *Aspects of Structuralism in Soviet Philology.* Tel Aviv: Porter Institute for Poetics and Semiotics, 1974.
Seyffert, Peter. *Soviet Literary Structuralism.* Columbus: Slavica, 1985.
Shukman, Ann. *Literature and Semiotics: A Study of the Writings of Yu. M. Lotman.* Amsterdam: North Holland Publishing, 1977.
– 'Lotman: The Dialectic of a Semiotician.' In *The Sign: Semiotics around the World.* Ann Arbor: Michigan Slavic Contributions, 1978, 194–206.

Thematic criticism: *see* Theme

Translation, theories of

There is no universally accepted theory of translation. While agreeing that translation is a use of language, translation theorists differ over the subject of a theory of translation and over the goal of translation, but come to some agreement on its definition.

The subject of a theory of translation depends both on what one thinks language is and on the discipline from which one comes. Rival theorists of language fall between the extremes of Platonism and Aristotelianism. In its modern form, linguistic Platonism goes back to the Romantics, who endowed languages with a creative energy which moulded cognition. All languages were taken to draw their creative energy from what the poet Hölderlin called *reine Sprache* [Pure Speech], a distilled essence of meaning of the same order as the Platonist forms, creative, self-sufficient and, in a certain sense, divine. Individual languages not only interpret the world but the categories they impose are also taken to be the bases of cognition (Steiner 81). The human being is therefore a creature of his language. Language is, in *Heidegger's phrase, 'the House of Being'; and in the true Platonic sense, one resides in that House by contemplation: in this Platonist world the linguistic *sign generates what it signifies and the Saussurean division between signifier and signified is at best a misleading construct. (See *Ferdinand de Saussure, *signified/signifier/signification.) The Aristotelian approach to language is exemplified by Lewis Carroll's Humpty Dumpty who had complete control of the words he used. Even if such linguistic Aristotelianism takes signifier and signified as inseparable, they are completely distinct. Because the distinction between signifier and signified depends on the principle that a *sign cannot be what it signifies, the connection between signifier and signified is therefore arbitrary. Thus, the sign has meaning only in relation to what it signifies and is not in any sense a creator of reality. Both *C.S. Pierce and Saussure and the translation theorists influenced by them repeat the classical Aristotelian model of the sign with some elaborations.

Lying between these extremes are schemas like that of Michael Halliday, who distinguishes between 'language as knowledge,' 'language as behaviour', and 'language as art,' the first being the handmaiden to the other two. 'Language as knowledge' is our grasp of the lexical, grammatical and discourse systems of a language. (See *discourse.) 'Language as behaviour' is our use of 'language as knowledge' as a way of communicating with ourselves and others. Under this aspect language has not only existence but also functions. For translation theory the most influential typology of language functions has been that of Karl Buhler, who distinguishes between language as information, as self-expression and as persuasion (Newmark 'Approach'). The most typical manifestation of 'language as art' is *literature. While fitting into a complex historical creative and behavioural matrix (its 'polysystem'), literature treats language not merely as a vehicle for communication but also as an object in its own right. (See *polysystem theory, *communication theory.)

Traditionally the objects of theories of translation have been based on Halliday's 'language as knowledge.' This is not only knowledge of the items and structures that make up a language but also easy participation in its characteristic ways of creating and expressing meaning. Though largely unacknowledged, *Ernst Cassirer's categorization of Man as 'the animal which creates symbols' has had a deep influence on many thinkers about language and translation. To some extent this had already been taken up by Martin Buber, for whom a language is a dynamic system kept in constant tension by its speakers' experiencing of self and of the world around them. (See *self/other.) Thus, as bodies of experience differ, so do languages. In two essays which

follow his version of *Hamlet* (1962), Yves Bonnefoy, drawing from symbolist and structuralist theories of language, seeks to explain why French has no version of Shakespeare to rival the great German one by Schlegel and Tieck. (See *structuralism.) He claims that French and English are ruled by two contrary metaphysics. Thus, while the English word, tending towards the concrete, is *ouverture*, that is, it bears transferred meaning easily and is a very evocative of the reality it signifies, the French word is a Leibnitzian construct tending towards the abstract. It is *fermeture*, that is, it excludes all that is not specifically designated and it filters the reality it signifies through intellectual priorities. Therefore, the intellectual mediation by which the systems of the two languages were formed in their speakers force upon them contrary ways of organizing reality, one sensorial, the other intellectual. While Shakespeare's plays evoke the human condition, the great French classical dramatists, like Corneille and Racine, evoke an ideal Platonist world. Bonnefoy accuses all the French translators of Shakespeare, including himself, of producing a French Shakespeare with the Platonist overtones of Racine.

Bonnefoy's discussion of translation arrives at an extreme form of the Sapir-Whorf hypothesis, which postulates that each language has a different perception, even a different reality, and crucially different behaviours and types of symbolization. He has some kinship with Karl Vossler, who had reversed the priorities between language and translation: seeing that the natural state of language is communication, a translation act is at the root of all language behaviour, as a person using language has to translate his interlocutor's meaning into his own (Vossler 181).

The subjects of a theory of translation are disposed along a similar continuum. Those influenced by the Platonist view of language concentrate on its formal properties: language is a way of creating a set of symbols by which one defines oneself in relation to the world. Any other use, especially translation, is derived from that. In its most extreme form, that preached by *Walter Benjamin, the Platonist 'language' is the Platonist *pneuma*, which breathes through the phonic and lexical material of speech, and translation is the attempt to reproduce this in another language: the presence of a reader or listener is of no consequence. There is an almost universal rejection of the idea of 'meaning', arising partly from a well-founded scepticism about modern semantic theory, partly from the flight from signification towards form characteristic of arts like painting and music during the middle years of the 20th century. Hence, there is a strong insistence on literality because the shape of the sign is meaning in all its energy. The other continuum is represented by theorists influenced particularly by linguistics, who view the meaning of a *text as paramount and who take it for granted that the arbitrary nature of the link between meaning and sign demands functional, rather than closely literal, translation: an Aristotelian implicitly denies that a translator seeks or utilizes any universals in language. (See *universal.)

Most of this century has been dominated by *hermeneutics, the discovery of the values of the text. For the English-speaking world its most important proponent is *George Steiner, who distinguished four 'hermeneutic movements' (*After Babel* 296–301). 'Trust' is the assumption that there is something worth translating in the text. The translator gets it out by 'aggression,' an image of interpretation taken from Hegel. 'Incorporation' means bringing the source text into the translator's language, and society and 'restitution' is repairing the damage the translator's Hegelian violence has done the source text.

These issues raise the question of difference. At extremes of difference translation is impossible. One attempt at arguing this traditional case was Quine's 'indeterminacy hypothesis,' according to which translation is impossible because so much depends on the second-language receptor's interpretative reactions, which could not be predicted. Benjamin and those influenced by him see the reader as irrelevant. If 'Truth' is to be attained in translation, Benjamin demands reproduction of the essential differences between languages themselves as essential to translation; Bonnefoy sees it as a regrettable consequence. Among those influenced by *Jacques Derrida and deconstructionist theory the object of translation theory is made to revolve around 'differences' in content, perception and in language structure itself. (See *deconstruction, *différance/différence.) Beneath the surface unity of a text the deconstructionist seeks the contradictions and paradoxes which uncover the underlying motives, frustrations and desires of the author. (See *paradox.) In passing from one language

to the other translation brings about an interpretative rupture which represents a certain assumption of *power over one's original and an attitude towards difference, either acceptance or rejection. This rupture is not unlike Steiner's aggression. Like *New Criticism, to which it bears a certain resemblance, deconstructionist theory takes the text by itself, for itself, and in isolation from all external factors.

Ancillary to these concerns are theories governing translation operations, the linguistic tools by which one attains 'equivalence.' Translators have always had to contend with Jakobson's principle that languages differ in what they *must* do, not in what they *can* do; and most see the problems arising in terms of what one *cannot* do in the target language and the consequent effect on the content of the text. Following on from the Völkerpsychologie of the late 19th century, Charles Bally categorized the different ways French and German see universal categories like number, time and modality. From his mentalistic grammatical categories his colleagues and followers developed *stylistique comparée*, which drew up ways of comparing lexicon, grammatical structure and discourse habits. There are strong parallels with contemporary work in contrastive linguistics from the *Prague School and other Eastern European groups. For both of these schools translation involves a shift of vision – a major one in the case of literary texts, a less radical one in the case of technical work. From the anti-mentalist viewpoints on American structuralism and Firthian linguistics, Eugene Nida and John Catford isolated certain constants in translator behaviour *before* differences in syntagmatic and paradigmatic structure between source and target languages.

Right from the beginning of theoretical statements on translation, discussion of technique has focused on lexicon and discourse: it was not really until Bally and the Prague School that grammatical analysis was thought relevant to the translation specialist.

Traditionally the confrontation between source and target languages has divided the lexicon into three types of words: those that are completely translateable, those that are untranslateable, and those, the vast majority, that are partially translateable. The discussion of this issue by the Bible translator George Campbell in his *Four Gospels* (1789) is still relevant and often unconsciously reproduced. Campbell demands that one translate according to the 'scope' of the word. This takes in not only semantic factors in word meaning but also the pragmatic and social. The completely translateable is of little theoretical interest: it can be dealt with either by 'literal translation,' what Nida (1964) calls 'formal equivalence,' or by borrowing the foreign word. The other types of vocabulary are dealt with by 'dynamic equivalence,' which for both Nida and Catford depend on the reaction of the reader. Before the completely untranslateable one uses 'adaptation,' which is the substitution of a target-language concept for the untranslateable source-language concept; and before the partially translateable one uses 'modulation,' which is a change in point of view, usually categorized as a type of metaphor, *synecdoche, or metonymy, 'languages' often denoting the same reality through different types of conceptualization. (See *metaphor/metonymy.) Though the terms come from the Geneva tradition of Bally, they have been widely adopted. (See *Geneva School.) To cover both of these terms Nida sums these up under the rubric 'adjustments of language to experience.'

'Transposition' first appears as a technique in grammar in Charles Sechehaye, *Structure logique de la phrase* (1926). It depends on the fact that any idea can be expressed by a range of grammatical categories and constructions. Transposition therefore is a change in morphological or syntactic category. In Catford's terms it consists of 'shifts' at various grammatical levels. (See Kelly 133.) It has long been clear that contrastive grammar is not a sufficient explanation for transposition. The final argument for adopting a particular grammatical shape in the target text is always pragmatic: the needs of the discourse will always dictate the form of the grammar, whether in prose or in verse.

Discourse 'techniques,' that is, the ordering of information within the sentence and paragraph, have not been isolated by scholars. Adding to the poetic translator's traditional worries about reproducing the original form in the target language, there is a growing body of discussion taking in matters like the Prague School's 'functional sentence perspective' or the 'naturalness' of a translated text. Difference in discourse revolves around two issues which bedevil all theorists: whether it is possible to translate in the target text certain types of information and attitude peculiar to the source culture and whether stylistic behaviour pecul-

iar to one culture always has its counterpart in a given target language. Both are problems of behaviour: Michael Grant's discussion of Pliny's panegyric of Trajan highlights both the difficulty of translating fulsome flattery of a ruler into our more low-key 20th-century English and the difficulty of finding a modern English equivalent for densely woven Latin prose.

Particularly in the light of Cassirer and Bonnefoy, the question of equivalence is certainly only partially semantic – it is also behavioural and pragmatic. One promising way out of the impasse between the radically different views is the model proposed by William Frawley. He takes translation to be recoding – a secondary semiotic process. His model assumes that one passes from the 'matrix code' (the translation) to another code. The subject then of a theory of translation is explaining how the information to be translated passes from the source text and is restated according to the parameters of the target texts in the 'new code.' (See *code.) Frawley treats the question of synonymy between the words of source and target texts as contingent – if some type of synonymy does occur that is all to the good; if not, that in no way impugns the validity of the translation.

The word 'code' takes into account not only the relationship between signifier and signified within the linguistic sign but also the purpose of translation as communication, the social background of the text, and to a large extent the tradition and history of both source and target languages. Consideration of the communicative function of the text is vital. To this end Buhler's theory of language function was taken up by Newmark ('*Approach*') and further developed by Kelly (*Interpreter*) as a basis for a theory of translation bridging linguistic and literary approaches, making the contest between partisans of 'literal' and 'free' translation irrelevant and also providing a thread unifying the multiplicity of translation types. Clearly, the subject of a theory of translation remains ill-defined.

The second element in a theory of translation is its purpose. We can distinguish goals within text and goals outside text. The first have been emmeshed in the problem of fidelity and truth. This double-barrelled concept was not well enough defined to be part of theory until George Steiner (*After Babel* 303), who makes fidelity the restoration of the 'balance of forces, the integral presence which his [the translator's] appropriative comprehension has disrupted.' Kelly (ibid., 207) links Steiner's attitude to the Horatian commonplace, the *lex operis*: the conventions governing the work mean both communicative purpose and Steiner's balance between matter and form, a functional equivalence. In general theorists show confusion between dynamic and formal equivalence – Frawley's remark that 'synonymy' between texts is contingent is a case in point and a refusal to accord translations the range of communicative function recognized in original texts. The most extended statements on the goals of translation have come from literary theorists and they have varied according to the theory of literature adopted. For genres of translation outside literature the answer has always been unambiguous – the purpose of a translated text is to bring the sense of the source text into the new language. In the light of Buhler's typology of language function one would expect technical translators to be Aristotelians and religious translators to mix large doses of Platonism with their Aristotelianism. Technical writing subordinates language to the information it vehicles and religious documents mix the objectivity of technical writing with persuasive elements designed to affect belief and behaviour. In literary translation the position is not so clear. Literary writing has all three of the Buhler functions or, to put it another way, it is Halliday's language as art in which categorizations of purpose, handy divisions between signifier and signified, and even the distinction drawn between Aristotelian and Platonist attitudes are often no more than flags of convenience.

Since the Romantics theories of literary translation have been Platonist. If translation entails the continuation of the life of the text, 'communication' is not necessarily the goal of creation, neither is 'transfer of meaning.' Indeed, at one extreme Walter Benjamin hoped that language will eventually free itself from the bondage of meaning as usually understood in order to reach down to the 'Pure Language.' Just as the first Jewish translators of the Bible did, theorists of this persuasion enjoin complete literality on translators so that the 'energies of meaning,' as Steiner puts it, can operate as efficiently in the target text as in the source (Buber 'Verdeutschung').

To draw on this type of argument, theorists did not necessarily have to swallow it whole.

Ezra Pound claims that every idea has its own rhythm, no matter the language, and his own translation follows this principle assiduously. However, he also argues that a translator must 'make it new' in that he is presenting a text to a new society with its own 'mental baggage,' and recasting it in a new language with its own norms. In essence, the translator is a creator. Pound agrees with *Roman Jakobson that languages differ in what they must say, not in what they can. Thus, in countering the resistance a new language and tradition puts up to the target text, translation becomes a criticism of the original; it 'casts light' on it.

This is the attitude of Yves Bonnefoy. Working from a more linguistic perspective, he argues that while the goal of translation is creation, translation puts language at war with itself. Through the different norms of experience, of conceptualization, of signification inherent in the target language translation becomes a test of the work's qualities. One gets the impression that Bonnefoy would like to be able to produce something equivalent. What he does opt for is something approximate within a different cultural and linguistic structure.

As a goal of translation, equivalence is a thorny business. It has long been taken for granted that equivalence of textual units must be nuanced by other factors, taking in the target culture and the expectations of the reader of the translation. Where the linguistic theorists speak about pragmatics, Roman Jakobson speaks about loyalty to 'values' in the target text. Approaches to the problem lie between the unquestioning acceptance of 'dynamic equivalence' in much of the work of the Summer Institute of Linguistics to the equally unquestioning acceptance of strangeness by the spiritual descendants of Walter Benjamin. Much of the battle has settled around the question of whether one will reproduce the poetic form native to the source text in the target. The battle has settled on the artistic and metaphysical values of poetic form in source and target language; and the problems of creating the same 'values' in the target language with a form deemed equivalent.

This is but one aspect of another question: the way in which languages differ in the way they organize information into discourse structures. If the goal of translation is communication of information, this could have a radical effect on the way one will acclimatize information in order to make it acceptable to the reader, or not to give false impressions. In technical translation circles this theoretical question has become one of the responsibilities of translator to client to produce a text that will do the same job in the target language as in the source. In literary circles the debate settled around the problems of transferring a work from one literary polysystem to another (Even-Zohar). The problem of difference, accidental in this sort of theory, becomes crucial in theorists following Derrida. Here translation becomes the exercise of power over the text and the aim of responsible translation becomes the demonstration of the individuality, the 'otherness,' of the source text, rather than Steiner's appropriation.

The goals external to the text all revolve around the effect the translation is meant to have on the receptor culture. From the Romans onward, translation has been meant to transform the receptor, to break its mould by introducing new elements. These new elements can be methods of composition – as they were in Rome, Renaissance Europe and in the Romantic period – or types of new literature and sensibility. These 'external goals' of introducing new experience depend on the type of fidelity one expects in the act of translation, and on the 'internal goals' and the risks entailed to the integrity of the work in adaptation to the host polysystem. Hence the debates revolving around 'difference,' assimilation and power structures in translation.

While the goal assigned to translation depends upon the assumptions about the nature of language and the purpose of the text, on our third point, the definition of translation, there seems to be relative agreement. Dr. Johnson's *Dictionary* defines it as 'to change into another language retaining the sense,' a definition not at all out of line with what most people take translation to be. Similarly *The Concise Oxford Dictionary* defines translation as 'the action or process of turning from one to another.' This definition reflects both the etymology of the word, the Low Latin *translatare*, a frequentative of the classical *transferre*, and the metaphor of turning into, traditional in both Latin and English. Because translation was defined long before theories grew, definitions of both types have had their influence on theory.

Because the legal and ecclesiastical senses of 'translate' have kept something like the etymo-

logical sense of transference and change alive, since at least the 16th century translation has been attested in the sense of rendering anything in another form. Hence the otherwise surprising generality of the definition of translation by Roman Jakobson: '1. Intralingual translation or *rewording* is an interpretation of verbal signs by means of other signs of the same language; 2. Interlingual translation or *translation proper* is an interpretation of verbal signs by means of some other language; 3. Intersemiotic translation or *transmutation* is an interpretation of verbal signs by means of signs of non-verbal sign-systems' ('Linguistic' 428). These linguistically oriented 'definitions' can only be fully understood in the context of Jakobson's theories on poetics and verbal behaviour. As a member of the Prague School, Jakobson was deeply influenced by its vision of language as a structure which itself fits into a structure of behaviour. He paid a certain attention to Buhler's categorization of language functions, taking the central act of translation to be communication; thus, the communicative intent of the original no matter what was reflected, if not reproduced, in the translation.

Obviously the Platonists fit into Buhler's typology, albeit badly, in that translation becomes an expressive use of language. In this connection Bonnefoy represents a fusion of Platonism and Aristotelianism: he envisages the translator as passing from one active type of symbolization to another, rather than from one set of fixed symbols to another. Because translation questions the very way in which we create meaning, Bonnefoy sees it as a struggle of a language with both itself and the target language. Language is therefore the prime object of the translator's activity and its human aspects are subordinated to the formal aspects of language.

Though the above definitions are verbally oriented, they are normally interpreted or rephrased as context- or content-oriented definitions. Steiner (*After Babel* 45) hyphenates the word 'trans-lation' in the manner of followers of Heidegger and defines it as 'a vertical or horizontal transfer of significance,' placing it squarely in the centre of the communicative act. For Steiner as for Frawley translation is essentially understanding encoded in another language. For a large part of this century the emphasis in defining translation has been the Romantic one of hermeneutics, inspired directly by the application of biblical criticism techniques to translations by Ernst Schleiermacher and developed in the 20th century, particularly by German translators. The basic issues are made succinctly by Ezra Pound in his critical writings: the act of interpretation that underlies translation has to do with both vehicle and content, with both language and meaning. Kelly (*Interpreter* 67–99) argues that the balance between vehicle and content depends upon the communicative purposes of the text and that any hermeneutic movement must take into account the writer's purpose.

One important aspect of the hermeneutics is the creativity entailed in shared experience. For Martin Buber such sharing is part of effective communication, and therefore translation is essentially communication through participation in experience. This is an essential element of translation for a large number of literary translators. Day Lewis, for instance, speaks of the drive which sent him to translate Virgil's *Georgics* during the Second World War as he felt a strong kinship between his own passion for the English countryside and Virgil's love of Roman Italy. This viewpoint has had its counterpart in the countless descriptions of translation as friendships, imitation, and portraiture that can be found as early as the Romans.

It is commonplace to say that translation is 'an art based on a science.' The major difficulty is 'What science?' Translation is a use of language whose theory can only arise from an interdisciplinary appeal to all the sciences that deal with language. For no adequate theory of translation can exist until one passes from consideration of sentences to consideration of texts, supplements description of translation aspirations by examination of techniques, and elucidates formal criteria by functional. We still have a long way to go.

LOUIS G. KELLY

Primary Sources

Bally, Charles. *Linguistique générale et linguistique française*. 3rd ed. Bern: Franck, 1944.

Benjamin, Walter. 'Die Aufgabe des Übersetzens.' 1923. In *Das Problem des Übersetzens*. Ed. H.J. Störig. Stuttgart: Govert, 1962, 182–95.

Bonnefoy, Yves. *Hamlet*. Paris: Mercure de France, 1962.

Buber, Martin. *I and Thou*. 1923. Trans. R.G. Smith. Edinburgh: T. & T. Clark, 1937.

– 'Zu einer neuen Verdeutschung der Schrift.' 1954.

In *Das Problem des Übersetzens*. Ed. H.J. Störig. Stuttgart: Govert, 1962, 348–88.

Catford, J.C. *A Linguistic Theory of Translation*. Oxford: Oxford UP, 1961.

Day Lewis, C. 'On Translating Poetry.' In *Essays by Divers Hands*. Ed. J. Richardson. London: Royal Society of Literature, 1963, 18–36.

Even-Zohar, Itamar. 'The Position of Translated Literature within the Literary Polysystem.' In *Literature and Translation*. Ed. James S. Holmes et al. Leuven: Acco, 1978, 117–27.

Frawley, William, ed. *Translation, Literary, Linguistic and Philosophical Perspectives*. Newark: U of Delaware P, 1984.

Graham, Joseph, ed. *Difference in Translation*. Ithaca and London: Cornell UP, 1985.

Grant, Michael. 'Translating Latin Prose.' In *The Translator's Art. Essays in Honour of Betty Radice*. Ed. William Radice and Barbara Reynolds. Harmondsworth: Penguin, 1987, 81–91.

Green, Peter. 'Metre, Fidelity and Sex: The Problems Confronting a Translator of Ovid's Love Poetry.' In *The Translator's Art. Essays in Honor of Betty Radice*. Ed. William Radice and Barbara Reynolds. Harmondsworth: Penguin, 1987, 92–111.

Heidegger, M. *Der Satz vom Grund*. 1957. In *Das Problem des Übersetzens*. Ed. H.J. Störig. Stuttgart: Govert, 1962, 395–409.

Holmes, James S. 'The Future of Translation Theory.' In *Translated! Papers on Literary Translation and Translation Studies*. Amsterdam: Rodopi, 1988, 98–102.

Jakobson, Roman. 'On Linguistic Aspects of Translation.' 1959. In *Language in Literature*. Ed. Krystyna Pomorska and Stephen Rudy. Cambridge, Mass./London: Belknap P, 1987, 428–35.

Kelly, L.G. *The True Interpreter*. Oxford: Blackwells, 1979.

Newmark, Peter. 'An Approach to Translation.' *Babel* 19 (1973): 3–18.

Nida, Eugene A. *Toward a Theory of Translating*. Leiden: Brill, 1964.

Pound, Ezra. *Literary Essays of Ezra Pound*. Ed. T.S. Eliot. New York: Faber, 1954.

Quine, Willard V. *Word and Object*. Cambridge, Mass.: MIT P, 1960.

Schleiermacher, Ernst. 'Über die verschiedenen Methoden des Übersetzens.' 1813. In *Das Problem des Übersetzens*. Ed. H.J. Störig. Stuttgart: Govert, 1962, 38–70.

Steiner, George. *After Babel*. Oxford: Oxford UP, 1975.

Toury, Gideon. *In Search of a Theory of Translation*. Tel Aviv: Porter Institute, 1980.

Vossler, Karl. 'Sprachgemeinschaft als Gesinnungsgemeinschaft.' 1925. *Das Problem des Übersetzens*. Ed. H.J. Störig. Stuttgart: Govert, 1962, 196–219.

Theory and Pedagogy

The advent of literary theory to the academy in its first form – through what was initially perceived by many as an 'importation' of European structuralist and poststructuralist ideas – posed an immediate challenge to the premises upon which common pedagogic practices rested. (See *structuralism, *poststructuralism.) The connections between 'literature' and 'life' of a Leavisite criticism were broken by the rethinking of both signification and representation following from the work of *Ferdinand de Saussure; at the same time, *New Criticism's assumption of the self-containment of the art object and of a complementarity of form and content were queried, respectively, by a structuralist contextualization of literary with social codes and by the rhetorical practices of *deconstruction. Since, as *Jonathan Culler notes, it has been commonly held that 'the test of any critical activity is whether it helps us to produce richer, more compelling interpretations' (13), this new and often non-interpretational work seemed at odds with the very purpose of literary studies. In turn, however, questions were raised about theory's utility and teachability. (See also *literature, *F.R. Leavis, *code.)

Paradoxically, therefore, 'theory' has appeared extraneous to literary studies while raising questions absolutely central to the discipline. Issues of literary *canon and quality, of how we read and why we study, of the aesthetic principles and institutional organization of literary inquiry, are all at stake. Yet there has been curiously little direct treatment, either analytic or practical, of the pedagogic complexities of this new work. It may be helpful, therefore, to place the entry of theory into the academy against the more general context of literary-studies pedagogy, taking the example of English, which is the most thoroughly examined of the literary disciplines.

The teaching of English

'Theory' is not new to literary scholarship or to the classroom. All scholarship has critical procedures and presuppositions; recent theoretical work has contributed much by making explicit the underpinnings of even the most 'natural, ' neutral' or 'objective' readings. As well, literary study often has a social or moral

raison d'être, as demonstrated by a variety of mission statements, polemics and programs. In England, literary study was seen to play a special role in the culturing and acculturation of colonial agents, in both the home and the 'host' country; and it was further hoped (by Matthew Arnold, most prominently) that shared sensibilities could heal or stablilize social and class divisions. Literacy and literature were central to the education of the European-origin citizenry of Canada and the U.S.A., and rhetorical and language skills were considered a prerequisite for participation in public life. (Conversely, enforced illiteracy and political disenfranchisement were closely linked, most notably in the slave states.) In the 20th century, the history of English studies has been the history of its success – or failure – to carry the humanist ideals of the university. And, in an argument first elaborated by William Wordsworth but repeated regularly ever since, the reading and study of literature can provide compensation for lost commonalities (religion for Arnold, an 'organic sensibility' for F.R. Leavis) or a counterbalance to mass culture or media. (*I.A. Richards, for example, held that training in literature provided protection against advertising, propaganda and radio programming.) Deeply implicated not only with state and *social formation but also with populist movements (including women's education), 'English' continues to provide a focal point for discussions of humanities education and 'culture' more generally. The 1970s call for Canadian materials in the curriculum, for example, centred on the teaching of 'CanLit'; while contemporary demands for a non-Eurocentric system are frequently rebutted from a 'Great Books' perspective. Literary questions and social issues are inextricably linked through the educational.

Key statements

A series of key statements gives a broad outline of important developments in English-studies pedagogy at the university level (although national and regional differences abound). W.J. Alexander's 1889 inaugural address on his appointment to the University of Toronto marks the moment at which literary study replaces rhetorical or philological instruction and takes on a form that would be familiar to us 100 years later. Alexander advocates a 'natural method' (25) of study which will result in the formation of 'a complete image of the thought of an age' (30). Reading of selected literary works is then followed by the study of literary history and intellectual context; only when this has been completed may the student make 'profitable use' of criticism (26). Alexander also places such study at the heart of the curriculum, since 'in all departments of study, written authorities must be submitted to the crucible of higher criticism' (9). While the concentration on (indisputably great) works was intended by Alexander and his contemporaries to provide a historical understanding, it could and did as easily lead to a more belletristic 'appreciation'; *Practical Criticism* (1929) is I.A. Richards' reaction to such critical impressionism. Although the term 'practical criticism' is now used to denote applied criticism, or instruction in poetry-reading skills, Richards himself was concerned with more general questions of how interpretation and communication do and do not occur. Undertaking this 'fieldwork in comparative ideology' (6), Richards collected student readings of poems and used these 'protocols' to generate a typology of readerly error. The source of misreading was seen to lie in an inability to differentiate sense, feeling, tone, and intention, in turn symptomatic of immaturity or confusion; but better reading skills, he concluded, would also result in improved mental and moral adjustment. (See *ideology, *ideological horizon.)

While Richards' concern is not with the literary per se but with how reading is accomplished, his demand for close reading would influence and underpin the work of other 20th-century critics. F.R. Leavis was to deplore how 'practical criticism' had come to mean 'a specialized kind of gymnastic skill to be cultivated and practiced as something apart'; the task of Leavis and his followers was to develop a more vital and engaged 'criticism in practice' (*Living* 19). The pedagogic ramifications of this are worked out in the journals *Scrutiny* and *English in Schools*. A succinct statement is found in Leavis' own thesis in *Education and the University* that the goal of literary study is nothing less than training in 'the sensitive and scrupulous use of intelligence' (*Education* 71). Indicative, too, is the title of another of his books, *The Living Principle: English as a Discipline of Thought*.

Leavisite criticism remained influential in the English academy and its emphasis on the thematics of a 'great tradition' inclined it in large measure to the study of dramatic and prose works. The New Criticism which was to predominate in the U.S.A., on the other hand, favoured poetry; of numerous statements, the 'Letter to the Teacher' written by *Cleanth Brooks and Robert Penn Warren as a preface to *Understanding Poetry* (1938) is inaugural. Historical and biographical study are only substitutes for insight into 'the poem in itself'; further, the elements of the poem must be studied in terms of *'the total intention'* of the work (emphasis theirs) (iv). Brooks and Warren's attention to classroom techniques and their arrangement of the book in terms of 'pedagogical expediency' (xi) helped to ensure the academic incorporation of New Criticism as both theory and method.

Teaching as a theoretical genre

It is far easier to trace the political and philosophic history of English than its pedagogic development. Increasing specialization in literary study and occasionally a separation of research and teaching skills (and often, staff) have meant that work on pedagogy, both current and historical, is more thoroughly undertaken for lower educational levels. When English is defined as the study of selected canonical works, discussions of content overrule considerations of method; when English pedagogy takes the form of a display of professorial reading skills, interpretation appears a matter of personal sensibilities or insights rather than shared presuppositions or acquired skills. This situation is compounded by the characteristic time lag between 'theory' and 'pedagogy' – for what appears in books and conference papers does not necessarily surface in the classroom.

Yet the classroom situation itself raises a number of interesting theoretical questions (some of which were first taken up in the important issue of *Yale French Studies* titled 'The Pedagogical Imperative: Teaching as a Literary Genre'). Validity (and plurality) of interpretation; 'authority' in its most literal sense, involving assessment of assignments and adjudication of discussion; the relationship between the realm of canonical texts and the world of real readers – all are issues staged in the classroom on a daily basis. 'Theory' brought to this situation some answers and many new questions. (See *authority.)

A number of critics have addressed themselves directly to the debate over the utility or applicability of theory. In some cases, the question of the relationship between theory and pedagogy is referred directly to the classroom context. Robert Scholes' *Textual Power: Literary Theory and the Teaching of English* (1985) asserts the practicality of theory in the college classroom; much of the book is designed to demonstrate how certain structuralist and semiotic principles can elucidate a short story. The various writers of *Writing and Reading Differently: Deconstruction and the Teaching of Composition and Literature* (Douglas and Johnson 1985) attempt to join a type of theory often considered inapplicable (deconstruction) to a subject area denigrated as untheoretical (composition). (See *semiotics.) The articles commonly consider the relationship between 'writing' and 'reading' on which deconstruction has been productive. In *Theory in the Classroom* (1986), edited by Cary Nelson, the contributors – whether from feminist, Marxist or psychoanalytic perspectives – explore the transactions between the pedagogic and theoretical; how one would teach in a certain mode but also how the 'scene of instruction' poses theoretically significant questions about *power and expertise. Jeffrey Robinson's *Radical Literary Education* develops a pedagogic program combining genre study, textual study, biography, and literary history, and aiming to 'develop and exercise an historical imagination' (3). Such considerations have occasioned design of new texts and teaching materials, notably – in a series of interrelated projects – *Reading Texts: Reading, Responding, Writing* (K. McCormick et al.); *The Lexington Introduction to Literature* (G. Waller et al.) and its accompanying *Instructor's Guide* (L. Fowler et al.), which bring to the literary classroom theoretical materials developed in the areas of reader-response and the 'new rhetoric.' (See *feminist criticism, *Marxist criticism, *psychoanalytic theory, *genre criticism, *reader-response criticism, *rhetorical criticism.)

While the compatability of theory and teaching is apparent to some, in many places the 'resistance to theory' has been long-lived and stubborn, occasioning a turn to study of the institutions within which criticism and pedagogic practices are formed. (On this problem the examinations of *Jacques Derrida and Sam-

uel Weber, analysing the intersections of philosophic and literary interpretation and institutions, are proving increasingly influential.) *Re-Reading English*, edited by Peter Widdowson, was early and consequential. Writing in the moment of a perceived 'crisis in English studies,' the contributors conclude that the complex connection between 'English' and programs for national education as well as a residual Leavisism hinder disciplinary change. (Here the construction of 'Shakespeare' is crucial as examined in another context in Alan Sinfield's article 'Give an Account of Shakespeare and Education ...') The short-lived but influential journal *Literature/Teaching/Politics* offered analyses of specific habits and practices such as 'A' level examination questions, funding policies, and teacher training. Related later volumes include *Rewriting English: Cultural Politics of Gender and Class* (Batsleer et al.) which devotes special attention to the relationship between literacy and literature education Brian Doyle's *English and Englishness*, which extends his *Re-Reading* analysis of English education as national education; and the anthology *Dialogue and Difference: English into the Nineties* (Brooker and Humm), which details experiments in curricular change. *Literary Studies in Action*, designed by Alan Durant and Nigel Fabb, is a workbook for undergraduates based on such inquiry.

While such 're-reading' work has been influential in Canada as well as England, Wales, Scotland, and Ireland, it appears to have had little impact in the U.S. academy. Far more important in that context has been the work of Gerald Graff, with the disciplinary history *Professing Literature*, and the supporting documents published as *The Origins of Literary Studies in America* (Graff and Warner). Both volumes demonstrate that disciplinary upheaval is nothing new, since disciplinary formation has always occurred through critical conflict. Graff has suggested that the solution to curricular impasse (whether in 'theory' or the humanities more generally) is to make critical conflict itself the course subject, through team teaching and the staging of public debate ('How to Deal ...'). Gregory Ulmer, in the ingenious *Applied Grammatology*, also assumes that the classroom can be used for theoretical staging – in this case, of deconstructionist text-reading practices. Other writers, however, believe that literary studies require a more thorough restructuring. The contributors to

Reorientations: Critical Theories and Pedagogies (Henricksen and Morgan) draw on educational reformists such as *Pierre Bourdieu, Paolo Freire and Henry Giroux in developing their critiques of curriculum, canonicity and received practices, and push English in the direction of cultural studies and cultural criticism. (See also *cultural materialism.) Other writers also pay greater attention to the institutional determinants of classroom study and to the power relations embedded in pedagogic relations: this concern occupies the contributors to *Theory/Pedagogy/Politics* (Morton and Zavardazeh).

While all the above writers find some sort of fit between 'theory' and 'pedagogy,' it should not be assumed that these concerns are necessarily synonymous. The work of Richard Ohmann, while in some respects 'anti-theoretical,' is pedagogically aware and politically attuned; at the same time, as Gayatri Chakravorty Spivak warns, much theoretical work can be pedagogically and politically oblivious. By this point, however, it may be observed that pedagogic questions enter into a wide variety of materials that do not address the topic directly; similarly, pedagogic issues, such as choice of materials and approaches, stand revealed as basically theoretical. Whether or not 'theory' does or will provide a superior teaching method, it has occasioned a new legitimization and a recharging of pedagogic issues. (See also *metacriticism.)

HEATHER MURRAY

Primary Sources

Alexander, W.J. *The Study of Literature: Inaugural Lecture Delivered in the Convocation Hall. October 12th, 1889.* Toronto: Rowsell and Hutchison, 1889.

Atkins, G. Douglas, and Michael L. Johnson. *Writing and Reading Differently: Deconstruction and the Teaching of Composition and Literature.* Lawrence: U of Kansas P, 1985.

Batsleer, Janet, et al., eds. *Rewriting English: Politics of Gender and Class.* London: Methuen, 1985.

Bourdieu, Pierre, and Jean-Claude Passeron. *Reproduction in Education, Society and Culture.* Trans. Richard Nice. London: Sage, 1977.

Brooker, Peter, and Peter Humm, eds. *Dialogue and Difference: English into the Nineties.* London: Routledge, 1989.

Brooks, Cleanth, Jr., and Robert Penn Warren. *Understanding Poetry: An Anthology for College Students.* New York: Henry Holt, 1938.

Culler, Jonathan. *Framing the Sign: Criticism and Its Institutions.* Norman: U of Oklahoma P, 1988.

Derrida, Jacques. 'Où commence et comment finit un corps enseignant.' In *Politiques de la philosophie.* Ed. Dominique Grisoni. Paris: Bernard Grasset, 1976, 55–98.

Doyle, Brian. *English and Englishness.* London: Routledge, 1989.

Durant, Alan, and Nigel Fabb. *Literary Studies in America.* London: Routledge, 1990.

Fowler, Lois Josephs, Kathleen McCormick, and Gary Waller. *Instructor's Guide to 'The Lexington Introduction to Literature.'* Lexington, Mass.: D.C. Heath, 1987.

Freire, Paolo. *Pedagogy of the Oppressed.* Trans. Myra Bergman Ramos. New York: Continuum, 1985.

Giroux, Henry. *Ideology, Culture, and the Process of Schooling.* Philadelphia: Temple UP, 1981.

Graff, Gerald. 'How to Deal with the Humanities Crisis: Organize It.' *ADE* [Association of Departments of English] *Bulletin* 95 (Spring 1990): 4–10.

– *Professing Literature: An Institutional History.* Chicago: U of Chicago P, 1987.

– and Michael Warner, eds. *The Origins of Literary Studies in America: A Documentary Anthology.* New York: Routledge, 1989.

Henricksen, Bruce, and Thaïs E. Morgan. *Reorientations: Critical Theories and Pedagogies.* Urbana, Ill.: U of Illinois P, 1990.

Leavis, F.R. *Education and the University.* Cambridge: Cambridge UP, 1979.

– *The Living Principle: English as a Discipline of Thought.* London: Chatto and Windus, 1975.

McCormick, Kathleen, Gary Waller, and Linda Flower. *Reading Texts: Reading, Responding, Writing.* Lexington, Mass.: D.C. Heath, 1987.

Morton, Donald, and Mas'ud Zavarzadeh, eds. *Theory/Pedagogy/Politics: Texts for Change.* Urbana, Ill.: U of Illinois P, 1991.

Nelson, Cary, ed. *Theory in the Classroom.* Urbana, Ill.: U of Illinois P, 1986.

Ohmann, Richard. *English in America: A Radical View of the Profession.* New York: Oxford UP, 1976.

– *Politics of Letters.* Middletown, Conn.: Wesleyan UP, 1987.

The Pedagogical Imperative: Teaching as a Literary Genre. Special issue of *Yale French Studies* 63 (1981).

Richards, I.A. *Practical Criticism: A Study of Literary Judgement.* New York: Harcourt, Brace and World, n.d.

Robinson, Jeffrey C. *Radical Literary Education: A Classroom Experiment with Wordsworth's 'Ode'.* Madison: U of Wisconsin P, 1987.

Scholes, Robert. *Textual Power: Literary Theory and the Teaching of English.* New Haven: Yale UP, 1985.

Sinfield, Alan. 'Give an Account of Shakespeare and Education, Showing Why You Think They Are Effective and What You Have Appreciated About Them. Support Your Comments With Precise References.' In *Political Shakespeare: New Essays in Cultural Materialism*. Ed. Jonathan Dollimore and Alan Sinfield. Ithaca: Cornell UP, 1985, 134–57.

Spivak, Gayatri Chakravorty. 'French Feminism in an International Frame.' In *In Other Worlds: Essays in Cultural Politics*. New York: Routledge, 1988, 134–53.

Ulmer, Gregory L. *Applied Grammatology: Post(e)-Pedagogy from Jacques Derrida to Joseph Beuys*. Baltimore: Johns Hopkins UP, 1985.

Waller, Gary, Kathleen McCormick, and Lois Fowler, eds. *The Lexington Introduction to Literature: Read-ing and Responding to Texts*. Lexington, Mass.: D.C. Heath, 1987.

Weber, Samuel. *Demarcating the Disciplines: Philosophy, Literature, Art*. Minneapolis: U of Minnesota P, 1988.

– ed. *Institution and Interpretation*. Minneapolis: U of Minnesota P, 1987.

Widdowson, Peter, ed. *Re-Reading English*. London: Methuen, 1982.

2

SCHOLARS

Abrams, M.H.

(b. U.S.A., 1912–) Literary critic, cultural historian, critical philosopher, and editor. Meyer H. Abrams received his B.A. from Harvard (1934), studied at Cambridge University (1934–5), and earned his M.A. (1937) and Ph.D. (1940) also from Harvard. In 1945 he began a long association with Cornell University, becoming Whiton Professor (1961–73) and Class of 1916 Professor (1963–present). Although he has been called 'our pre-eminent historian and interpreter of English Romanticism,' his range extends far beyond the confines of Romanticism to the history of ideas, criticism and theory. Abrams' influence on American letters has been especially dominant in his editorship of the standard texts for English literature studies, *The Norton Anthology of English Literature*, in the two-volume edition, and *The Norton Anthology of English Literature, Major Authors*, one-volume edition. His best-known contribution to literary history and the history of ideas remains *The Mirror and the Lamp: Romantic Theory and the Critical Tradition*, which has been translated into many languages and is considered a major work on the background to Romantic theory and on English Romanticism in particular. (See *literature.)

His first book, *The Milk of Paradise* (1934), written as a senior thesis when Abrams was an undergraduate at Harvard, is a brief but useful study of the effects of opium on the writings of Coleridge, De Quincey, Crabbe, and Thompson. *The Mirror and the Lamp* (1953) begins with a brief history of 'expressive' and 'objective' theories of literary imitation and is followed by a discussion of expressive theory, with particular emphasis on Longinus, a precursor of formalism. The balance of the book concerns the 'varieties of romantic theory' from Coleridge and Wordsworth to *I.A. Richard's idea of 'statements'and 'pseudo-statements' and modern views of the schism between science and the humanities, fact and fiction. *The Mirror and the Lamp* is atypical of much American literary criticism of its time because of its emphasis on the connections of history, traditional philosophy, humanism and the humanities, and their intimate relation to literary analysis and creation. The book combines discussions of the meaning of *mimesis (imitation theory) in a tradition from Aristotle and Plato to the 19th

century and serves as a useful guide in English to this background. (See also *metacriticism.)

Abrams' *A Glossary of Literary Terms* (1988), originally published in 1971, contains a new section, 'Modern Theories of Literature and Criticism,' that does much to organize the plethora of current literary theories. This reference work is typical of Abrams' effort to synthesize and systematize critical concepts and terminologies for the widest possible audience.

Natural Supernaturalism (1971) is an extension of *The Mirror and the Lamp*, but with an emphasis on 19th-century philosophers and poets who 'conceived themselves as elected spokesmen for the Western tradition in a time of profound cultural crisis.' In Abrams' view Wordsworth was the 'great and exemplary poet of his age.'

While each of the essays in *The Correspondent Breeze* (1984) and *Doing Things with Texts* (1989) has been previously published in a variety of periodicals, both are significant collections and display well Abrams' breadth of knowledge as well as his grasp of contemporary issues in criticism and their relation to the humanistic tradition. Two essays address the current popularity of *deconstruction and its relative values as a critical tool. 'The Deconstructive Angel' is a response to a tendency in contemporary American criticism toward ideological monism as well as to deprecating the usefulness of knowledge of the intellectual tradition of East and West (the so-called *canon) and questioning the virtues of pluralistic humanism. It is also a defence of traditional criticism and the principles of moral philosophy. (See *pluralism.)

Other essays, most notably 'Behaviorism and Deconstruction,' 'Constructing and Deconstructing,' and 'A Colloquy on Recent Critical Theories' summarize current issues in Anglo-American literary theory and criticism, largely the confrontation of the tradition and its values with a variety of ideologies. (See *ideology.) In spite of the current theories, Abrams continues to be a firm advocate of humanism, openness and affirmation in literary *discourse.

REED MERRILL

Primary Sources

Abrams, Meyer H. *The Correspondent Breeze: Essays on English Romanticism*. New York: W.W. Norton, 1984.

- *Doing Things with Texts: Essays in Criticism and Critical Theory.* New York: W.W. Norton, 1989.
- *A Glossary of Literary Terms.* Based on the original version by Dan S. Norton and Peter Rushton. 5th ed. New York: W.W. Norton, 1988.
- *The Milk of Paradise: The Effect of Opium Visions on the Works of De Quincey, Crabbe, Francis Thompson, and Coleridge.* New York: Octagon Books, 1971.
- *The Mirror and the Lamp: Romantic Theory and the Critical Tradition.* New York: Oxford UP, 1953, 1960, 1971.
- *Natural Supernaturalism: Tradition and Revolution in Romantic Literature.* New York: W.W. Norton, 1971.
- and Jonathan Wordsworth and Stephen Gill. *William Wordsworth: The Prelude: 1799, 1805, 1850.* New York and London: W.W. Norton, 1979.
- ed. *English Romantic Poets: Modern Essays in Criticism.* New York: Oxford UP, 1960.
- ed. *Literature and Belief.* English Institute Essays. New York: Columbia UP, 1958.
- ed. *The Poetry of Pope: A Selection.* New York: Appleton-Century Crofts, 1954.
- ed. *Wordsworth: A Collection of Critical Essays.* Twentieth-Century Views series. Englewood Cliffs, NJ: Prentice-Hall, 1972.
- general ed. *The Norton Anthology of English Literature.* Major Authors Edition. 3rd edition. New York: W.W. Norton, 1975.
- general ed. *The Norton Anthology of English Literature.* 2 vols. 5th ed. New York: W.W. Norton, 1986.

Secondary Sources

Lipking, Lawrence, ed. *High Romantic Argument: Essays for M.H. Abrams.* Ithaca, NY: Cornell UP, 1981. Includes a bibliography of Abrams' publications compiled by Stuart A. Ende.

Theodor W. Adorno

(b. Germany 1900–d. 1969) Philosopher, social theorist, music critic. In 1924 Adorno received his Ph.D. in philosophy from J.W. Goethe University in Frankfurt. His study of *Husserl was later rewritten and published in 1956 as *Zur Metakritik der Erkenntnistheorie.* After receiving his Ph.D., Adorno spent two years in Vienna studying with Alban Berg. In 1923 he became acquainted with *Walter Benjamin and Max Horkheimer, with whom he formed his most important intellectual relationships. After completing his habilitation in 1931 (published in 1933 as *Kierkegaard: Konstruktion des Ästhetischen*) Adorno was ap-

pointed to the philosophy department of J.W. Goethe University. Shortly thereafter, he joined Horkheimer's Institute for Social Research [Institut für Sozialforschung], which was designed to carry out empirical social research guided by Marxian and Freudian theory. (See *Freud, *Marxist criticism, *materialist criticism.) In 1938 Adorno left Nazi Germany, spending a short time in Oxford before finally emigrating to the United States where he rejoined Horkheimer and the relocated Institute. During the war, he and Horkheimer wrote their famous book, *Dialektik der Aufklärung* (published in 1944). In 1953, Adorno returned to Germany to take up his old position at J.W. Goethe University and, along with Horkheimer, co-directed the re-established Institute for Social Research. (See *Frankfurt School.)

Along with *Jürgen Habermas, Adorno is the best-known exponent of Frankfurt School *critical theory. Unlike his successor's, Adorno's thought shares much with that of the leading figures of French *poststructuralism, *Jacques Derrida and *Michel Foucault. Adorno's view of modernity and his analysis of the 'administered world' anticipated Foucault's analysis of the panoptic and disciplinary society. In his interpretive practice, in his choice of themes, and in his conception of philosophy emphasizing the question of its *presentation*, Adorno anticipated Derrida. (See *theme.) Opposed to the adherents of logical positivism, one of the most prominent philosophical schools of his time, Adorno did not believe philosophical practice could be reduced to the methods of formal logic, or to logical analysis of any kind. Philosophy, for Adorno, meant the mutual interpenetration of apparently non-cognitive phenomena and the schemata of cognition. The outcome of this activity took on forms which might best be described as trans-discursive. Adorno referred to them as *constellations*. Like Foucault and Derrida, he was most concerned with the grammar of particularity; that is to say, with the structure of excluded or marginalized practices on the one hand, and with the significance of non-subsumable or *non-identical* meaning on the other. (See *margin.)

Displaying his Nietzschean allergy to philosophical systems, Adorno's work does not reside in a systematically developed set of propositions. Rather, it depends on a systematically employed interpretive practice tied to the formation and the elaboration of corresponding interpretive categories: *mimesis, constellation, nonidentity, construction, expression, instrumental rationality, truth-content, determinate negation, force-field, mediation, and monad. The relation between these categories is deliberately non-hierarchical. Therefore the best way to approach Adorno's work is to weave one's way into it, acquiring a sense of the whole by taking up and connecting the categories of his conceptual vocabulary one at a time; above all, in the contexts of their use. While Adorno's categories emerge with a relatively stable semantic core, their frame of meaning undergoes constant revision. Each time they are injected into different interpretive contexts they reappear in a somewhat transformed, sometimes even contradictory, shape. This categorial flexibility and plasticity is normative to Adorno's interpretive practice.

At the same time, Adorno's interpretive practice bound itself to the principle of disclosing the object of interpretation from the inside. To this end he insisted, following Hegel, on the *priority of the object* [Vorrang des Objekts]. Correlative to the priority of the object is the subject's capacity to experience, perceptually and conceptually, the object's *truth-content* [Wahrheitsgehalt]. (See *subject/object.) This capacity is one of the two necessary conditions of Adorno's model of interpretive critique. The object's truth-content is not to be construed as an ahistorically valid essence, but rather as a nonintentional meaning locked in a specifically historical shape. (See *intention/intentionality.) And, following Hegel once again, Adorno insisted that there is an internal relation of co-dependence between the form of the presentation [Darstellung] and its truth-content. In answering the challenge of presenting truth in a form appropriate to its specific content, we fulfil the second of the necessary conditions of Adorno's model of interpretive critique. Constructing a form of presentation correlative to and disclosive of truth was understood to be a decidedly cognitive achievement. But Adorno would not prescribe what specific form presentation should take; he only asserted that truth's most adequate form was a consciously constructed act of cognition circumscribed by the cognitive potential available to a particular sociohistorical configuration.

In his treatment of philosophical texts, as in his treatment of works of art, Adorno strove ceaselessly to demonstrate the illusionary na-

ture of any objectively binding or unifying context of meaning (Sinnzusammenhang). Like deconstructive critique, Adorno's interpretive practice, his method of immanent critique, or more precisely, *determinate negation*, is based on the premise that texts, artworks, social and cultural practices, and so forth are vulnerable to and display an internal logic of disintegration. (See *deconstruction.) This logic of disintegration comes about from a dialectical reversal of the basic impulses of modern rationality. The objectifying, totalizing and self-preserving character of modern rationality encounters the outcome of its interventions in the world as a series of catastrophes. (See *totalization.) Human subjects experience their rational activity, including their own self-formation, as a process in which they become their own oppressors and their own victims at one and the same time. Adorno and Horkheimer put forward the controversial thesis that modernity is constituted by a world-historical process, stretching back to the beginnings of hominization, in which each stage of the evolution of the species exhibits an inextricable structural transformation that is equally progressive and regressive. They interpreted the forms of mythic thought and modern rationality as structurally homologous expressions of the same basic compulsion: the mastery and domination of inner and outer nature. With bittersweet irony they referred to this process as the 'dialectic of enlightenment,' a process in which *myth is as fatefully entwined with enlightenment as enlightenment is with myth.

Adorno's model of interpretive critique was designed to rescue the disfigured and mutilated traces of this dialectic; to bring to light the buried semantic contents of a disintegrative process in whose remnants the possibility of a symmetrical *reconciliation* between reason and nature, subject and object, was waiting to be deciphered – but not a false reconciliation, not one in which the differences between them was subsumed by an imposed identity. In keeping with this view, Adorno's interpretive analyses tended to focus on the *membra disjecta* of modernity; on the nonintentional or non-linguistic aspects of thought and action, which enjoyed only a subordinate status within the human sciences, and to which he referred with the designation *concrete particular*.

It was one of the assumptions of Adorno's

philosophy of history that a symmetrical, non-subsumptive, reconciliation of differences was the regulative ideal of critical thought, exemplarily embodied in certain works of modern art. Among the categories of Adorno's conceptual vocabulary it is *mimesis* which best captures the normative content of this notion of reconciliation. Right from the start, however, what Adorno understands by mimesis should be disassociated from both Aristotelian and Platonic construals of mimesis. For Adorno, the interpretation of mimesis as representation only captures its derivative, secondary features. While Adorno's interpretation of mimesis shares something with that of *René Girard's, in so far as they both emphasize its anthropological and psychological dimensions, he differs sharply with Girard as to its meaning. Adorno's version of mimesis is more comprehensive, encompassing the largely negative meaning it has for Girard while remaining a plenipotentiary of utopian content and energy.

Most of all, Adorno is interested in restoring the primary meaning of mimesis which he defines as a mode of behaviour [*Verhaltensweise*] with a complementary attitude [*Stellung*] toward the world. Mimesis can be construed as a bio-anthropological, epistemological, a social-psychological, and an aesthetic category. Bio-anthropologically, it refers to the continuity between the phenomenon of mimicry in nature and mimetic modes of behaviour specific to human societies. Epistemologically, it refers to the most primitive – that is, genetically earliest – relation of knowing between subject and object based on attunement and empathy. Social-psychologically, it refers to a domination-free relation between societal subjects – at least in its utopian sense. It can also refer to a pathological variant which is linked to victimization. (For example, see the analysis of anti-Semitism in *Dialectic of Enlightenment*.) Aesthetically, it refers both to the nature of the relation between the individual elements of a work of art and to the corresponding relation between those elements and the totality of the artwork.

In Adorno's view, modern art distinguishes itself from all other artistic epochs by virtue of an unprecedented transformation in the structure of works of art. Whereas in pre-modern art the individual elements occupied a hierarchically regulated position in the overall structure of the work, the constitutive feature of modern art consisted in the individuation of elements pushed to the point where each particular element occupied a place equidistant from the centre. That means there is no privileged position in the totality of the work of art. The mimetic behaviour of modern works of art, ambiguously transformed by modern rationality, undoes this very notion of totality. In the transient autonomy of their semblance [*Schein*], works of art are able to articulate and preserve the epistemological dimension of mimesis without regressing to archaic modes of cognition, thereby closing the distance between subject and object opened up by abstract knowledge. And in the non-hierarchical organization of their elements, authentic works of modern art, that is, those works of art that achieve this condition, offer themselves as models of domination-free intersubjectivity. Naturally, the possibility of reconciliation between reason and nature, subject and object, can be experienced but not actualized in our interaction with works of art. Aesthetic experience offers only a semblance of reconciliation. The structural contradictions and antagonisms of modernity are actual.

In spite of his view of the *instrumental* character of modern rationality, Adorno maintained that this truncated form of rationality could be overcome only in and through the medium of reason itself. His oft-cited remark in the opening pages of *Negative Dialectics* that the self-transcendence of the *concept* – Adorno's Hegelian moniker for rationality – was only possible by means of the concept, should be understood in this light. The restrictiveness, the deforming character of rationality, its compulsion to master and subsume, cannot be circumvented by appealing to something outside of conceptual reflection. Adorno remained resolute in his belief that reason, understood in its most comprehensive sense, was an irreplaceable and unavoidable medium of cognition and of emancipation. Unlike Nietzsche, Adorno could conceive the 'other' of reason only dialectically, as an excluded moment of reason that had to be recuperated in historical time. (See *self/other.) The identifying feature of Adorno's thought might, in fact, lie in the tension between his proto-poststructuralism and his cognitive-constructivism; between his Nietzschean historicism and his confidence in the objectivity of critique; and between his antifoundationalism and his emphatic (largely Hegelian) conception of truth.

Adorno's *Aesthetic Theory*, arguably the last

great systematic contribution to aesthetics, is systematically built upon the tensions between its Nietzschean and Hegelian components. The antisystematic organization of the *text only disguises Adorno's highly reflective, self-conscious and persistent treatment of the incommensurable yet interdependent components of his aesthetics. His aesthetic theory is both Nietzschean and anti-Nietzschean, Hegelian and anti-Hegelian. The Nietzschean component stresses the experience of art as the locus of an excluded 'other' of reason. But, unlike Nietzsche, Adorno did not view the experience of art as reducible to one of the basic manifestations of an arational 'will to power.' The Hegelian dimension stresses the cognitive element of art as a reflectively accessible medium of truth. But, unlike Hegel, Adorno did not accept that the truth of art has been fully comprehended, and therefore superseded, by the conceptual power of philosophical thought. Both art and philosophy remain caught in the struggle to complete themselves, a struggle which cannot be carried out successfully without the mutual interaction of their respective, but partial, truths.

The significant exchange of letters that took place in the 1930s between Adorno and Walter Benjamin is too often reduced to a debate about who was the better Marxist theorist, or to the question of who best understood the limitations or potential of mass culture. Adorno's criticisms of Benjamin's studies of Baudelaire and the Paris of the 19th century had to do with a much deeper issue: whether the form of the presentation of insights should be intuitively or reflectively directed. Adorno's and Benjamin's quite different approaches to this issue reflected their investment in two distinct methods (derived from art rather than from philosophy) of presentation; Benjamin's in *montage* (associated with surrealism) and Adorno's in *construction* (associated with 12-tone music). Benjamin's method of montage proceeded intuitively, seeking to generate sudden unexpected flashes of illumination; Adorno's method of construction proceeded by conceptual labour on a resistant object requiring a convertible act of critical reception and interpretation. Adorno believed that the montage procedures of surrealism unchained the nonintentional aspects of meaning at the price of becoming unreflectively absorbed in them. Against surrealism, Adorno insisted on a cog-

nitive relation to the historically sedimented layers of nonintentional meaning.

Consistent with the thesis of the 'dialectic of enlightenment,' Adorno was very wary of Benjamin's claims for the emancipatory possibilities of new media and cultural forms. In Adorno's theory the internal structure of every technical advance carries with it the possibility of a dialectically reserved regression. While some of Adorno's critics argue that his critique of popular culture is conservative and élitist, they fail to do justice to his equally pessimistic critique of high culture. The theory of the culture industry – that mass enlightenment is a mass deception – is, in fact, extended to both 'high' and 'low' dimensions of culture. In one of his exchanges with Benjamin, Adorno described the division of culture into 'high' and 'low' as the torn halves of an integral freedom which had to be regained in another form.

Unlike conservative cultural critics to whom Adorno is sometimes – not altogether wrongly – compared, and unlike certain strains of contemporary criticism, Adorno neither mourned nor celebrated the disunity of modern experience. He was too dialectical a thinker to get caught on either side of this debate. What remained crucial to Adorno was the preservation of the capacity for experiencing emancipatory possibilities within the multiple horizons of modernity. It was only from the well of possibilities not yet realized – perhaps unrealizable – that the interpretive practice he espoused could draw its power of critical disclosure.

Two decades before it was dramatized in the poststructuralist Paris of the 1960s, Adorno had already, one might say, foreseen the 'death of the subject.' 'For many people it is already an impertinence to say I' (*Minima Moralia* #29). But Adorno understood the consequences of this phenomenon in a manner which set him apart from poststructuralists. For him, to speak of the 'death of the subject' was far too premature. The freedom of subjectivity selected by Hegel as *the* accomplishment of modernity was, in Adorno's eyes, equally premature. Yet, he persistently held on to the hope of its authentic realization.

Since the early 1980s the critical reception of Adorno's work, particularly in Germany, has been determined by the cogent and persuasive arguments put forward by Habermas and Albrecht Wellmer. As the evaluation of Adorno's work intensifies, it will have to contend with these two strong readings of his philosophical program. Habermas puts into serious question Adorno's views of rationality and modernity by undercutting the premises of Adorno's philosophy of history and by criticizing Adorno's continued, albeit ambivalent, reliance on the subject/object model of traditional epistemology. From the perspective of Habermas' criticisms the *necessity* Adorno ascribed to the paradoxes of enlightenment seems to dissolve. Wellmer follows Habermas in portraying the narrowness of Adorno's construal of rationality, as well as the shortcomings of his philosophy of language, but he goes one step further by trying to rescue the insights of Adorno's aesthetic theory, setting them within a more comprehensive and capacious model of rationality and language.

NIKOLAS KOMPRIDIS

Primary Sources

Adorno, T.W. *Aesthetic Theory.* Trans. C. Lenhardt. London: Routledge and Kegan Paul, 1984.
– *Against Epistemology: A Metacritique.* Trans. W. Domingo. Cambridge, Mass.: MIT P, 1982.
– *Drei Studien zu Hegel.* Frankfurt: Suhrkamp Verlag, 1963.
– *In Search of Wagner.* Trans. Rodney Livingstone. London: New Left Books, 1981.
– *Kierkegaard: Construction of the Aesthetic.* Trans. R. Hullot-Kentor. Minneapolis: U of Minnesota P, 1989.
– *Minima Moralia.* Trans. E. Jephcott. London: Verso, 1978.
– *Die Musikalische Monographien.* Frankfurt: Suhrkamp, 1971.
– *Negative Dialectics.* Trans. E.B. Ashton. New York: Continuum, 1973.
– *Noten zur Literatur.* Frankfurt: Suhrkamp, 1971.
– *Philosophy of Modern Music.* Trans. A. Mitchell and W. Blomster. New York: Continuum, 1973.
– and Max Horkheimer. *Dialectic of Enlightenment.* Trans. John Cumming. New York: Continuum, 1972.

Secondary Sources

Buck-Morss, S. *The Origin of Negative Dialectics.* New York: Free P, 1977.
Dews, Peter. *The Logics of Disintegration.* London: Verso, 1987.
Habermas, J. *The Philosophical Discourse of Modernity.* Trans. F. Lawrence. Cambridge, Mass.: MIT P, 1987.
– and L. von Friedeburg, eds. *Adorno-Konferenz 1983.* Frankfurt: Suhrkamp, 1983.
Menke, Christoph. *Die Souveränität der Kunst.* Frankfurt: Suhrkamp, 1991.

Rose, G. *The Melancholy Science.* London: Macmillan, 1978.
Wellmer, Albrecht. *The Persistence of Modernity.* Trans. D. Midgley. Cambridge, Mass.: MIT P, 1991.

Althusser, Louis

(b. Algeria, 1918–d. France, 1990) Marxist philosopher. Called up for military service in 1939, Louis Althusser was captured in 1940 and spent the rest of the war in a prison camp in Germany. Supervised by *Gaston Bachelard at l'Ecole Normale Supérieure he completed a thesis on Hegel in 1948. He remained on the faculty at the school and joined the Parti Communiste de France (PCF), which he never left. Plagued by manic depression since the war, in 1980 he strangled his wife. Although he confessed to the murder, the case was declared a nonsuit owing to insanity. He remained under supervisory psychiatric treatment until his death from heart failure. Althusser's work has been influential in anthropology, sociology, political economy, philosophy, history, and literary theory.

Althusser's major essays began to appear in 1960, attracting attention when they were collected in *Pour Marx* [*For Marx* 1965; trans. 1969]. This and *Lire le Capital* [*Reading Capital* 1965; abr. trans. 1970] written with Etienne Balibar inaugurated 'structural Marxism,' rejecting the Hegelianism dominating Western Marxist thought from *Georg Lukács to *Jean-Paul Sartre. Well received in England, Althusser's theories were amalgamated with the psychoanalytic theories of *Jacques Lacan and with *semiotics. By the later 1960s there was an identifiable 'Althusserian school.' But Althusser's pronouncements on the strikes and demonstrations of May 1968 in France contributed to a reaction against him, and *poststructuralism and 'post-Marxism' have been viewed as supersessions of his work. (See also *Marxist criticism, *psychoanalytic theory, *structuralism.)

Althusser worked in the context of the humanist Marxism (which places Marx in the mainstream of Western bourgeois thought) established by the 20th Congress of the Communist Party of the Soviet Union (1956), and in the context of the Sino-Soviet split over its political correlates of peaceful coexistence and democratic transition to socialism. He implicitly criticized the 'humanism' of the Soviet and Western Communist parties from a Chinese perspective.

Althusser considers the young Marx to have been bound by the ideological *problematic of German idealism with which he broke to establish 'a new scientific discipline' (For Marx 85). He defines a science as a type of 'theoretical practice' (167). (A practice is any process through which raw material is transformed by human labour into a product.) A scientific theoretical practice is born when it makes an 'epistemological break' – a concept borrowed from Bachelard – with its ideological prehistory. Scientific theoretical practice elaborates 'its own scientific facts through a critique of the ideological "facts" elaborated by an earlier ideological theoretical practice' (184). Althusser circumvents the traditional epistemological dilemma of how a subject appropriates an object by asserting that 'the process of theoretical practice ... all takes place "within knowledge"' (185). Theoretical practice deals with 'the concrete-in-thought;' 'the concrete-reality' survives untouched by the production of knowledge which appropriates it for thought (186). By assuming that essential truths lie behind phenomenal appearances, empiricism, Althusser claims, collapses the distinction between 'the object of knowledge and the real object' (Reading Capital 40). Empiricism seeks guarantees in the correspondence between its truths and the external world, but theoretical practice is 'its own criterion' which validates 'the quality of its product' (59) through 'the systematicity of the system' (68).

Althusser criticizes the orthodox Marxist contradiction between capital and labour as simple, abstract and Hegelian, and develops the concept of *overdetermination to account for the complexity of social contradictions which he finds in Marx. In this 'new conception of the relation between determinant instances in the structure-superstructure complex' (For Marx 111) the economic base is determinant in the last instance, while the political and intellectual superstructures retain a relative autonomy. Althusser insists that Marx treats society as a 'complex whole [which] has the unity of a structure articulated in dominance' (202). The contradictions of any *social formation exist within a hierarchical structure in which principal and secondary contradictions, which may change positions of priority, provide mutual conditions of possibility.

Althusser's concept of the social formation requires a new concept of causality. Historicism has only two types of causality. One, 'a transitive mechanical causality,' is suited to a 'homogenous planar space' (Reading Capital 182) and cannot 'think the effectivity of a whole on its elements' (186); the other, 'expressive causality' (187), reduces the social totality to an unstructured 'inner essence' whose elements are 'no more than the phenomenal forms of [its] expression' (186). Marx needed a type of causality which would allow for the relative independence of the various levels and would yet bind them together in a totality. This third type of causality, the only one adequate to its object, is 'structural causality' (186). (See *structural causality.) Emphasis on the 'structural nature' (180) of the social totality obviates the requirement to posit history as a "human" phenomenon' (139). Individuals occupy 'places and functions' determined for them by 'the relations of production (and political and ideological social relations)' (180). These relations which define and distribute individuals provide the content of social and historical study: 'history is a process without a subject' (Lenin and Philosophy 122)

According to Althusser, Marx rejected any 'essence of man' as ideological; 'theoretical anti-humanism' was the precondition for his science of society (For Marx 229). But a science does not dissipate the reality of the *ideology which is its prehistory. Ideology is not the false shadow of science but 'is distinguished from science in that in it the practico-social function is more important than the theoretical function' (231). Ideology is necessary to every society because it is through ideology that 'men are ... formed, transformed and equipped to respond to the demands of their conditions of existence' (235). Ideology is 'the "lived" relation between men and the world' (233).

Althusser's most important text after For Marx and Reading Capital is 'Idéologie et appareils idéologique d'état (Notes pour une recherche)' (1970, Lenin and Philosophy 127–86) in which he develops his concepts of *interpellation and *Ideological State Apparatuses (ISAs). Distinct from specific ideologies, ideology in general has 'a structure and a functioning ... present in the same form throughout ... history' (161). In a formula borrowing from Lacan, he states that 'ideology represents the imaginary relationship of individuals to their real conditions of existence' (162). Althusser's 'central thesis' depends on *'the category of the subject'* (170): *'ideology has the function ... of "constituting" concrete individuals as subjects'* (171). It constitutes subjects through *'interpellation or hailing'* (174); we recognize ourselves as subjects by acknowledging our interpellation by ideology. '[A] Unique and central Other Subject' (178) hails us as its subjects through ideology, but this Subject in turn only exists through our acceptance of subjection. Thus the structure of ideology is *'speculary*, i.e. a mirror-structure ... [w]hich means that all ideology is *centred*, that the Absolute Subject occupies the unique place of the Centre' (180). Both subjects and Subject are imaginary, however, and the misrecognition implied conceals real conditions of existence. Nonetheless, the 'quadruple system of interpellation as subjects, of subjection to the Subject, of universal recognition and of absolute guarantee' ensures that 'subjects work all right "all by themselves"' (181). Through 'the ambiguity of the term *subject*' we are given the illusion of 'free subjectivity' in order that we will *'submit freely to the commandments of the Subject'* (182). We (mis)recognize social conditions as a natural order and so ideology ensures the reproduction of society. (See *centre/decentre.)

We are all 'always-already' subjects of ideology; only through 'scientific knowledge' is it even possible to say 'I am in ideology' (175). Althusser lists *literature and art under 'the cultural ISA' (143), but elsewhere grants art a privileged status almost equivalent to science: *'I do not rank real art among the ideologies'* (*Lenin and Philosophy* 221). Without providing distinguishing criteria, he claims that 'authentic art,' as opposed to 'mediocre' works, lets us see 'the *ideology* from which it is born.' The perception which art provides 'presupposes ... an *internal distantiation*' from ideology (222). Art and science 'give us the same object in quite different ways: art in the form of "seeing" and "perceiving" or "feeling," science in the form of *knowledge*' (223). Criticism should 'produce an adequate (scientific) *knowledge* of the processes which produce the "aesthetic effect"' (225).

This theory of literature's production of, yet detachment from, ideology, and its attendant methodology of *symptomatic reading, has most influenced literary theory, beginning with *Pierre Macherey's *Pour une théorie de la production littéraire* [*A Theory of Literary Production* 1966; trans. 1978] and *Terry Eagleton's

correctives in *Criticism and Ideology* (1976). Eagleton retains the view that criticism can become scientific by breaking with its ideological prehistory, although in subsequent texts he rejects the privileging of both literature and science. Where literature sits among the social practices continues to occupy critics influenced by Althusser. In *Critical Practice* (1980) Catherine Belsey credits him along with Lacan, *Jacques Derrida and *Roland Barthes with decentring humanist assumptions about subjectivity, history and authorship, and uses Althusser and Macherey to define an interrogative narrative, the conditions of which are contradiction and ideological critique. *Fredric Jameson's *The Political Unconscious* (1981), the one major American text by a literary theorist seriously to appropriate Althusser, employs the concepts of social formation and structural causality. Althusser's emphasis on the constitution of subjectivity through ideology and designation of the family as an ISA have also influenced socialist feminist literary theory. (See *feminist criticism.)

Althusser's theory of ideology remains the most viable part of his work, occupying a pivotal position in Eagleton's *Ideology: An Introduction* (1991) and Christopher Norris' *Spinoza and the Origins of Modern Critical Theory* (1991). But the all-encompassing nature of ideology in Althusser has been criticized for, on the one hand, vitiating any oppositional critique and on the other, requiring an idealism of science. He has been both damned and praised for cross-breeding Marxism with structuralism, Spinozism and Freudianism; his rejection of most Marxist thinkers except Marx, Lenin and Mao has been both credited as part of the first attempt to establish the principles of Marxist philosophy and bemoaned as leading to post-Marxism. His concepts (conjuncture, problematic, overdetermination, and interpellation) have become part of critical vocabulary. His conception of the social formation with its relatively autonomous levels has justified many regional studies and underwritten politically committed intellectual work. His characterization of theory as a theoretical practice with its own mode of production retains its force and has been extended to such areas as literary and semiotic practice. While his critiques of Hegelianism, humanism, empiricism, and historicism are too indiscriminate to be useful in their details, they still retain many salient points. Althusser ranks with Lukács and *Antonio Gramsci as among this century's most important Marxist philosophers. (See also *Sigmund Freud.)

JOHN THURSTON

Primary Sources

Althusser, Louis. *Essays in Self-Criticism*. Trans. Grahame Lock. London: New Left Books, 1976.
– *For Marx*. Trans. Ben Brewster. London: New Left Books, 1977.
– *Lenin and Philosophy and Other Essays*. Trans. Ben Brewster. New York: Monthly Review P, 1971.
– *Philosophy and the Spontaneous Philosophy of the Scientists and Other Essays*. Ed. Gregory Elliott. Trans. Ben Brewster, James H. Kavanagh, Thomas E. Lewis, Grahame Lock, and Warren Montag. London: Verso, 1990.
– *Politics and History: Montesquieu, Rousseau, Marx*. Trans. Ben Brewster. London: New Left Books, 1972.
– and Etienne Balibar. *Reading Capital*. Trans. Ben Brewster. London: New Left Books, 1970.

Secondary Sources

Benton, Ted. *The Rise and Fall of Structural Marxism: Althusser and His Influence*. London: Macmillan, 1984.
Callinicos, Alex. *Althusser's Marxism*. London: Pluto P, 1976.
Eagleton, Terry. *Criticism and Ideology*. London: Verso, 1976.
– *Ideology: An Introduction*. London: Verso, 1991.
Elliott, Gregory. *Althusser: The Detour of Theory*. London: Verso, 1987.
Geras, Norman. 'Althusser's Marxism: An Account and an Assessment.' *New Left Review* 71 (1972): 57–86.
Macherey, Pierre. *A Theory of Literary Production*. 1966. Trans. Geoffrey Wall. London: Routledge and Kegan Paul, 1978.
Norris, Christopher. *Spinoza and the Origins of Modern Critical Theory*. Oxford: Basil Blackwell, 1991.

Auerbach, Erich

(b. Germany, 1892–d. U.S.A., 1957) Romance philologist. Auerbach originally trained as a lawyer, taking his doctorate at Heidelberg in 1913. After serving in the German army throughout the First World War, he entered the University of Griefswald and took a doctorate in Romance philology with a thesis on the technique of the early Renaissance *novelle* in France and Italy (1921). From 1923–9 he continued work on Romance philology while in the employ of the Prussian State Library. The most significant productions of this period were his German translation of Giambattista Vico's *Scienza nuova* [*The New Science* 1924] and *Dante als Dichter der Irdischen Welt* [*Dante: Poet of the Secular World* 1929]. Following the publication of this second book he succeeded Leo Spitzer in the Chair of Romance Philology at Marburg. After being removed in 1935 by the Nazis, he went to the State University of Istanbul where he taught Romance philology. While in Istanbul, in spite of poor library resources, he wrote his most important work, *Mimesis* (1946), as well as an elementary manual of Romance philology, *Introduction aux études de philologie romane* [*Introduction to Romance Languages and Literature* 1949]. After a visit to the U.S.A. in 1947 he accepted several short-term appointments there and in 1950 went to Yale where he was named Sterling Professor of Romance Philology in 1956. (See also *mimesis.)

The most comprehensive account Auerbach gives of his intellectual credo is in the opening of *Literatursprache und Publikum in der lateinischen Spätantike und im Mittelalter* [*Literary Language and Its Public in Late Latin Antiquity and the Middle Ages* 1958]. There he traces his intellectual roots to the German tradition in Romance philology. Because this tradition takes philology as the meeting-point of all the human sciences, the term 'philology' covers both the better-known comparative and historical linguistics and the interpretative *herme-neutics pioneered by Johann Gottfried Herder (1744–1803) and his Romantic successors. They reflected the political turmoil of their times in a historicism committed to analysing the development of the *Volksgeist* [Spirit of the People] of individual ethnic and cultural groups in Europe; but where the Romantics themselves from Herder onwards had been mostly concerned with the German soul and indeed fostered the development of a German national consciousness through *literature, 18th-century German classical and Romance philologists had worked within a pan-European perspective dictated by Europe's Latin background and Christian civilization. Though he nowhere treats the issue specifically, Auerbach takes for granted the Romantic view that language is at base a numinous set of universals governing human creativity, cognition and expression. (See *universal.) Shaped by the experiences of both individuals and cultural groups, individual languages are separate realizations of the potentialities the 'pure language' offers the human spirit. In essence this is a literary version of the Sapir-Whorf (see *structuralism) hypothesis, which had also been developed from Romantic speculation but through the Viennese school, which laid the groundwork in the early years of the 20th century.

For Auerbach as for the Romantics, the basic language act is creating a literary work and the central facet of literature is poetry. Given this emphasis on language as creation, it is therefore significant that Auerbach's own account of himself makes much of the mid-18th-century reaction against the Enlightenment by Herder and his contemporaries, hurdles the creative pedantry of the German 19th century and pays tribute to his great contemporaries Vossler, Curtius and Spitzer. Not that Auerbach was unskilled in the 19th-century tradition: his introduction to Romance philology for his Istanbul students is an excellent example of that type of linguistic scholarship at its best.

In developing the German tradition, he took Vico as his intellectual godfather: under Vico's inspiration, Auerbach had 'complemented and moulded' the ideas developed by German historicism. Beginning with the principle that we can only know what we have made, Vico had stated that history can be known to us because it is our artefact. For all of our acts, past, present, and future, are within the potentialities, or as Vico puts it, the *modificazioni*, of the human mind, a word recalling the Aristotelian and Scholastic *motus* [change, process, movement]. Working from this, Auerbach refines the balance Herder saw between the universal and the particular in culture and builds into his theory of historical criticism the 'observer's paradox.' For the presence of an observer will affect the data and the interpreter's experience will shape what he sees in a work of art. In consequence, Auerbach makes a strong distinction between 'philosophy,' which is objective, and 'philology,' which is not. There is even a Platonist tinge here: one's judgment depends upon one's ability to 'rediscover' the facts of the matter in one's own mind. Consequently, for Auerbach as for his Romantic forebears the boundary between art and criticism is tenuous: one is reminded of the Romantic translators' constant sense that translation was at one and the same time criticism and creation. (See *translation, theories of.)

Thus Auerbach's criticism follows both the Romantics and Vico in equating the historical with the human. He begins from Vico's principle that Man has no other nature but his history and that all history begins in forms of expression. Like the great late-18th-century classicist Christian Gottlob Heyne, Auerbach treats philology as the high road to understanding the modern world: his experiences with the Nazis had amply confirmed the point common to Vico and the Romantics, that language has the power to create societies and shape human beings. Auerbach's philological history therefore sees political and social evolution through the history of thought, expression and culture. Thus a work of literature cannot be properly approached or criticized independently of its cultural matrix. The kinship between this and the Sapir-Whorf hypothesis is only to be expected.

Auerbach casts his critical net extremely wide. The authors discussed in *Mimesis* range from Homer to Virginia Woolf, and the background against which he puts them shows a deep acquaintance with the historical development of all facets of European life and a strong sense of how human beings react. His thesis, the essential unity of European culture, is balanced against variations within that unity. The major evolutionary force has been the result of an increasing sense of history. The Renaissance and 17th century set in train what he calls 'historicism,' that is, transcending the classical ideologies that assume a Golden Age, sensing the relativity of history and placing a value on one's own place in history without devaluing the past.

This was the first of the consequences of Auerbach's melding of the German tradition and Vico. The second was taking European literature as a whole in itself reflecting the wholeness of culture. Therefore, the European cultural matrix can be effectively characterized through a proper description of one salient feature, in Auerbach's case the styles of literary works. Auerbach's criticism moves constantly between examination of content and an analysis of the language in which it is couched. Though this is the *res et verba* approach of the ancient Roman rhetoricians, it also lies deep in the German tradition; outstanding precursors of Auerbach's ideas range from Luther's language-bound theology to

Schlegel's translation and criticism. It is within this balance between *res* and *verba* that one can place his peculiarly evocative treatment of *figura*, a medieval commonplace based solidly on the classical *figura rerum*, but passed through the religious sensibility of the Christian Fathers to become central to their understanding of the dealings between God and Man. Given the importance of such symbolism in the language of the Bible, in the Talmudic tradition rising from it, and in the habitual use of parts of the Bible like the Book of Psalms in prayer, Auerbach's Jewish upbringing seems to have had an important influence in creating sensitivity to this basically religious use of words as multilevel *figurae*.

In an absolute sense there is little new in what Auerbach writes about *figura*: any theologian who knows his Aquinas or medieval mystics will still find no surprises in Auerbach's exposition, except that Auerbach's wholesale application of the idea to literature, and to Dante in particular, would take him aback. The *figura* is a figure of thought, not a figure of speech, which is properly called a 'trope.' (See*trope.) Hence every *figura* is something real that is to be read on two levels when circumstances are right. In its own time it has only its apparent meaning. But when it is 'fulfilled' in the sense common in the Bible, later generations look back to an event in the past as a *figura* prefiguring events in their own time without losing its role as history. To illustrate, Auerbach cites the Old Testament, the history of the Jewish people, which in the Christian dispensation is read as anticipating the story of salvation in the New; or coming closer to home, the medieval persecution of the Jews prefigures the modern. His analyses of certain puzzling passages in Dante show that a *figura* could enjoy 'polysemy,' that is, it could take on several meanings, depending on the passage it occurred in.

Auerbach's philological bent shows in the care given to interpreting individual words for critical ends. His article on *figura*, for instance, begins with the derivation and history of the word itself; and then passes to a careful exegesis of how it is used as a technical term from Cicero to the medieval theologians. We find the same care in minor details: words like *passio, public, cour* are all accorded a similar historical exegesis when a critical point has to be made.

Apart from delineating the internal economy of a work, 'criticism' also means delineating the relationship between a work of art and its public. From this follows another task, showing how this relationship has evolved through the balance between the universally human and the culturally relative. Because style portrays a view of reality, the 'movement' or change in literary styles between periods is an index of changes in aesthetic and social realities. Hence the ground-plan of *Mimesis*, in essence a series of *lectures expliquées* of favourite passages ranging from discussions of individual words to analyses of character delineation, all set within a matrix of cultural history. It is a style of criticism which entails entering into the skin of the author, tracing his techniques of creation and assessing his public. In this way Auerbach shows that one of the turning-points in European literature coincided with the realization that classical and Renaissance longing for a Golden Age had to be outgrown if literature was to match reality. Auerbach's remarks on the rise of historicism in literature during the 16th century are balanced by his very scathing attitude toward the *New Criticism, in which he sees a serious threat to scholarship and even to culture.

Auerbach's work is unified by its goal of showing the evolution of European culture and the way in which literature expresses reality. He thought of himself as a historian in an age losing the sense of history. There is a sense of urgency and pessimism about his work. He was convinced that time was running out for both philology and European civilization and he remarks that books like *Mimesis* would have been untimely in earlier generations, and will become impossible in later ones.

LOUIS G. KELLY

Primary Sources

Auerbach, Erich. *Dante als Dichter der Irdischen Welt.* Berlin/Leipzig: de Gruyter, 1929. *Dante: Poet of the Secular World.* Trans. Ralph Manheim. Chicago: U of Chicago P, 1961.

– *Gesammelte Aufsätze romanischen Philologie.* Ed. Frank Schalk. Bern: Francke, 1967.

– *Introduction aux études de philologie romane.* Frankfurt: Klostermann, 1949. *Introduction to Romance Languages and Literature.* Trans. Guy Daniels. New York: Capricorn Books, 1961.

– *Literatursprache und Publikum in der lateinischen Spätantike und im Mittelalter.* Bern: Francke, 1958. *Literary Language and Its Public in Late Latin Antiquity and the Middle Ages.* Trans. Ralph Man-

heim. New York: Bollingen Foundation, 1965.
- *Mimesis. Dargestelle Wirklichkeit in der abendlän-dischen Literatur.* Bern: Francke, 1946; 2nd ed. 1959. *Mimesis. The Representation of Reality in Western Literature.* Trans. W.R. Trask. Princeton: Princeton UP, 1953; repr. Doubleday, 1957.
- *Scenes from the Drama of European Literature.* New York: Meridian Books, 1959.
- *Zur Technik der Früherenaissancenovelle in Italien und Frankreich.* Heidelberg: Winter, 1921. Griefs-wald doctoral thesis.
- trans. Vico, *Die neue Wissenschaft über die gemein-schaftliche Natur der Völker.* Munich: Algemeine Verlagsanstalt, 1925.

Secondary Sources

De Pietro, Thomas M. 'Literary Criticism as History: The Example of Auerbach's *Mimesis.' Clio* 8 (1979): 377–87.
Fergusson, F. 'Two Perspectives on European Litera-ture.' *Hudson Review* 7 (1954–5): 119–27.
Fleishmann, W.B. 'Auerbach's Critical Theory and Practice.' In *Velocities of Change: Critical Essays from MLN.* Ed. R.A. Macksey. Baltimore: Johns Hopkins UP, 1974, 230–6.
Green, Geoffrey. *Literary Criticism and the Structures of History: Erich Auerbach and Leo Spitzer.* Preface by Robert Scholes. Lincoln and London: U of Ne-braska P, 1982.

Austin, J(ohn) L(angshaw)

(b. England, 1911–d. 1960) Philosopher. J.L. Austin, White's Professor of Moral Philosophy at Oxford University from 1953 until his death in 1960, was a major player in the 'ordinary language' movement in Anglo-American ana-lytical philosophy. According to this move-ment, ordinary language offers a rich accumu-lation of discriminations and distinctions that generations of people have felt worth making. If one examines the assumptions and impli-cations of these distinctions, one can often dissolve, if not solve, the pseudo-problems generated by the woolly word-spinning of traditional philosophy.

It was only after his death that theorists and critics 'discovered' *How to Do Things with Words*, a book that was constructed from the William James Lectures Austin delivered at Harvard University in 1955. Since that discov-ery, Austin's distinction between constative and performative utterances has been part of the repertoire of advanced critical theory. *Speech act theory, the name for the version

of ordinary-language philosophy that ema-nates from *How to Do Things with Words*, is still flourishing and is associated in philosophy with *John Searle, H.P. Grice and Stanley Cavell, and in *literature with Richard Ohmann, *Wolfgang Iser, Mary Louise Pratt and Shoshana Felman. The theory has also spawned deconstructive critiques from *Jacques Derrida and *Jonathan Culler. (See *decon-struction, *Constance School of Reception Aes-thetics.)

The central premise of speech act theory is laid out explicitly by John Searle. 'All linguistic communication,' he writes, 'involves linguistic acts. The unit of linguistic communication is not, as has been generally supposed, the sym-bol, word, or sentence, but rather the produc-tion or issuance of the symbol, word, or sentence in the performance of a speech act' (*Speech Acts* 16). A theory of language is part of a theory of action, for speech acts are not simply sentences; they are modes of linguistic behaviour that take place in a situational con-text and that depend on conventions and pro-cedures which are valid for both addresser and addressee. Speech act theory views language as use-oriented and context-dependent. Its basic emphasis is on what an utterer (U) means by his or her utterance (X) rather than on what X means in a language (L). Meaning therefore is a kind of intending and the ad-dressee's recognition that U means something by X is part of the meaning of X. In contrast to the assumptions of *structuralism (a theory that privileges *langue*, the system, over *parole*, the particular speech act), speech act theory holds that the investigation of structure always presupposes something about intention, be-haviour, usage, and context. (See *langue/parole*.)

In *How to Do Things with Words*, Austin commences by enunciating a clear-cut distinc-tion between constative and performative utterances. An utterance is constative if it describes or reports some state of affairs such that one could say its correspondence with the facts is either true or false. That is, constative utterances have truth value and are the para-digm case for the analysis of propositions in traditional philosophy. Performative utter-ances, on the other hand, do not describe or report some state of affairs and thus have no truth value. The uttering of a performative is or is part of the doing of an action. Marrying, promising, betting, bequeathing, christening, knighting, blessing, firing, baptizing, and so forth involve performatives. Whereas the constative utterance is true or false, the performative utterance is felicitous or infelicitous, sincere or insincere authentic or inauthentic, well invoked or misinvoked. A solemnly pronounced 'I do' at a marriage ceremony is void, insincere and misinvoked if the utterer is already married and has no intention of abiding by the conditions of the contract. The situational context and the conventions and procedures that surround it are equally if not more important than the meaning of the sentences deployed and the truth value that they may or may not possess. Already, then, the sharpness of the distinction between constative and performative is beginning to erode.

Austin further divides the linguistic act into three components. First, there is the locutionary act, 'the act of "saying something"' (94). Second, there is the illocutionary act, 'the performance of an act *in* saying something as opposed to the performance of an act *of* saying something' (99). Third, there is the perlocutionary act, for 'saying something will often, or even normally, produce certain consequential effects upon the feeling, thought, and actions of the audience, or of the speaker, or of other persons: and it may be done with the design, intention, or purpose of producing them' (101). In other words, a locutionary act has meaning – that is, sense and reference. It is the act of producing a recognizable and understandable utterance in a given language. An illocutionary act has force. It is informed with a certain tone, attitude, feeling, motive, or intention. A perlocutionary act has consequence. It has an effect upon the addresser, the addressee or other persons. By describing an imminently dangerous situation (locutionary component) in a tone that is designed to have the force of a warning (illocutionary component), the addresser may actually frighten the addressee into moving (perlocutionary component). Or, to give another example, 'he said x=y' is locutionary; here the constative dimension is primary because the sentence foregrounds the truth value of 'x=y.' 'He argued that x=y' is illocutionary; here the performative dimension is primary because the sentence foregrounds the force of his utterance. 'He convinced me that x=y' is perlocutionary; here the conative dimension is primary because the sentence foregrounds the consequence of his utterance. Yet even this simple example is not without

complexity. From my point of view as addressee, I have to assume that if U said x=y and if U is not deliberately trying to deceive, then the illocutionary force of the utterance is that U believes x=y. Moreover, if U argues that x=y, then I have to assume not only that U believes x=y but also that he would be prepared to make a factual utterance constating x=y to be the case. Third, for me to be convinced that x=y, I have to assume not only that U is sincere (though, strictly speaking, it is possible for me to be convinced that x=y even while suspecting U's motives) but also that x=y is true. Hence even in a simple example, the components overlap. The more complex the speech act, the more the components interfuse. None of this, Austin maintains, is particularly surprising. 'That the giving of straightforward information produces almost always consequential effects upon action is no more surprising than the converse, that the doing of an action (including the uttering of a performative) has regularly the consequence of making ourselves and others aware of facts. To do any act in a perceptible or detectable way is to afford ourselves and generally others also the opportunity to know both (a) that we did it, and further (b) many other facts as to our motives, our character or what not which may be inferred from our having done it' (110n).

Originally, then, to recapitulate, Austin contrasts the performative with the constative utterance, saying that 'the performative should be doing something as opposed to just saying something' and that 'the performative is happy or unhappy as opposed to true or false' (132). Yet he comes to the conclusion that constating something is doing something and is likely to be happy or unhappy as well. It would be unhappy, for example, if my describing a dangerous situation to you did not have the force of a warning and the consequence of frightening you into moving. As Austin points out, 'once we realize that what we have to study is not the sentence but the issuing of an utterance in a speech situation, there can hardly be any longer a possibility of not seeing that stating is performing an act' (138). His conclusion is that 'the familiar contrast of "normative or evaluative" as opposed to the factual is in need, like so many dichotomies, of elimination' (148). We must rid ourselves of both 'the true-false fetish' and 'the fact-value fetish' (150). The constative and the performative then are not categorically separable even though they can do useful conceptual work as relative terms. Such self-deconstruction from a philosopher who in *Sense and Sensibilia* declares war on 'the deeply ingrained worship of tidy-looking dichotomies' (3) is not surprising.

Both Austin and Searle exclude literary language from their analysis of speech acts. As Austin puts it, 'a performative utterance will ... be *in a peculiar way* hollow or void if said by an actor on the stage, or if introduced in a poem, or spoken in soliloquy ... Language in such circumstances is in special ways – intelligibly – used not seriously, but in ways *parasitic* upon its normal use – ways which fall under the doctrine of the *etiolations* of language. All this we are *excluding* from consideration. Our performative utterances, felicitous or not, are to be understood as issued in ordinary circumstances' (22). This distinction between the literary and the ordinary, the parasitic and the normal, the non-serious and the serious, has generated different responses from different literary theorists.

As Mary Louise Pratt observes, the first attempt to apply speech act theory to the literary speech situation was made by Richard Ohmann in his 1971 article, 'Speech Acts and the Definition of Literature.' According to Ohmann, literary utterances are 'quasi-speech-acts' because they do not have any illocutionary force. 'The writer *pretends* to report discourse and the reader accepts the pretense. Specifically, the reader constructs (imagines) a speaker and a set of circumstances to accompany the quasi-speech-act, and makes it felicitous (or infelicitous – for there are unreliable narrators, etc.) ... *A literary work is a discourse whose sentences lack the illocutionary forces that would normally attach to them. Its illocutionary force is mimetic ... A literary work purportedly imitates* (or reports) a series of speech acts, which in fact have no other existence. By so doing, it leads the reader to imagine a speaker, a situation, a set of ancillary events, and so on' (14). Ohmann goes on to say that 'since the quasi-speech-acts of literature are not carrying on the world's business – describing, urging, contracting, etc. – the reader may well attend to them in a non-pragmatic way, and thus allow them to realize their emotive potential. In other words, the suspension of normal illocutionary forces tends to shift a reader's attention to the locutionary acts themselves and to their perlocutionary effects' (17). In a similar vein, Wolfgang Iser maintains that fictional

language 'deals with conventions in a different way from ordinary performative utterances ... It depragmatizes the conventions it has selected (*The Act of Reading* 60–1). Both Ohmann and Iser, then, accept Austin's distinction between the literary and the ordinary, the parasitic and the normal, the non-serious and the serious. But as Pratt points out, this distinction can 'only stand if it were true that all and only the fictive utterances in a language were literature' (*Toward a Speech Act Theory of Literary Discourse* 91).

Derrida and Culler also attack Austin's distinction but for more subversive reasons. Whereas they applaud Austin's reversal of the constative/performative hierarchy and his valorizing of the marginal term – the performative – they feel that by distinguishing between the literary and the ordinary, the parasitic and the normal, the non-serious and the serious, and by privileging the latter term in each case, Austin has reintroduced the 'logocentric' premises that his work puts into question. (See *logocentrism.) That is, although Austin makes the performative the paradigm case and thereby overturns the assumptions of traditional philosophy, he also makes the ordinary, the normal and the serious the paradigm case and thereby reintroduces those very assumptions at a different level.

As the above examples attest, speech act theory has had considerable influence upon contemporary criticism and theory. Austin's characteristic irony and modesty notwithstanding, his own meditations on 'ordinary language' have served to complicate the critical agenda in a fertile way. (See also *discourse, *discourse analysis theory.)

GREIG HENDERSON

Primary Sources

Austin, J.L. *How to Do Things with Words.* 2nd ed. Oxford: Oxford UP, 1975.
– *Philosophical Papers.* 3rd ed. Oxford: Oxford UP, 1979.
– *Sense and Sensibilia.* Oxford: Oxford UP, 1962.

Secondary Sources

Berlin, Isaiah, et al. *Essays on J. L. Austin.* Oxford: Clarendon P, 1973.
Cavell, Stanley. *Must We Mean What We Say?* New York, 1967.
Cole, Peter, and Jerry Morgan, eds. *Syntax and Se-*

mantics, Vol. III: Speech Acts. New York: Academic P, 1975.

Culler, Jonathan. On Deconstruction: Theory and Criticism after Structuralism. Ithaca, NY: Cornell UP, 1982.

Derrida, Jacques. 'Signature Event Context.' Glyph 1 (1977): 172–97.

Fann, K.T., ed. Symposium on J.L. Austin. New York: Humanities P, 1969.

Felman, Shoshana. The Literary Speech Act: Don Juan with J.L. Austin, or Seduction in Two Languages. Trans. Catherine Porter. Ithaca, NY: Cornell UP, 1983.

Furberg, Mats. Saying and Meaning: A Main Theme in J.L. Austin's Philosophy. Totowa, NJ: Rowan and Littlefield, 1971.

Graham, Keith. J.L. Austin: A Critique of Ordinary Language Philosophy. Hassocks: Harvester P, 1977.

Grice, H. Paul. Excerpt from Logic and Conversation. Unpub. ms., 1967. In Cole and Morgan, eds, Syntax and Semantics.

Iser, Wolfgang. The Act of Reading: A Theory of Aesthetic Response. Baltimore and London: Johns Hopkins UP, 1978.

Ohmann, Richard. 'Speech Acts and the Definition of Literature.' Philosophy and Rhetoric 4 (1971): 1–19.

Pratt, Mary Louise. Toward a Speech Act Theory of Literary Discourse. Bloomington: Indiana UP, 1977.

Searle, John. 'Reiterating the Differences: A Reply to Derrida.' Glyph 1 (1977): 198–208.

– Speech Acts: An Essay in the Philosophy of Language. Cambridge: Cambridge UP, 1969.

Bachelard, Gaston

(b. France, 1884–d. 1962) Philosopher, phenomenologist of the imagination. After beginning his career in the French postal service (1903–13), Bachelard took undergraduate degrees in mathematics and philosophy. In 1922, he qualified as a teacher of philosophy and taught this subject as well as physics and chemistry at the Collège de Bar-sur-Aube. In 1927 he obtained his doctorate with a thesis entitled 'Essai sur la connaissance approchée,' in which he proposed a new epistemology. He was professor of philosophy in the Faculty of Arts at Dijon University (1930–40) and held the chair in the history and philosophy of science at the Sorbonne (1940–54). Bachelard's multidisciplinary training can be seen in the characteristic duality of his work: a major part of his writing is dedicated to the philosophy of science but his epistemological research led him to become interested in the field of the imagination. His works on the imagination of matter revolution-

ized the field of French literary criticism. They gave rise during the 1950s to a criticism based on the study of images, or 'thematic' criticism, springing from this 'new' or interpretative criticism on the fringes of traditional university criticism, which had focused on such elements as literary history, biographies, sources, and influences. (See *theme.)

Bachelard chose earth, water, air, and fire as the methodological context for his research on images. These traditional four elements, considered the principal constituents of all matter by ancient chemists and alchemists, were redefined by Bachelard as 'the hormones of the imagination.' He assembled thick files of literary images on each of them. An intertextual approach, naturally drawing from the work of many writers in many languages, Bachelard's rich harvest of images is stored in his books on the elements: La Psychanalyse du feu [The Psychoanalysis of Fire 1938], L'Eau et les rêves [Water and Dreams 1942], L'Air et les songes [Air and Dreams 1943], La Terre et les rêveries de la volonté [Earth and Reveries of Will 1948], La Terre et les rêveries du repos (1948). The three books to follow brought more clarity and depth to Bachelard's approach to the world of the imagination: La Poétique de l'espace [The Poetics of Space 1957], La Poétique de la rêverie [The Poetics of Reverie 1960], and La Flamme d'une chandelle (1961).

Not a critic, or a semiotician, Bachelard firmly opposes the very concept of a science of *literature. He has frequently contrasted his approach to literature with approaches based on psychology, Freudian psychoanalysis and biography, all more or less reductionist, given their methodological principles. (See also *Sigmund Freud, *psychoanalytic theory.) His goal was to study the imagination as a basic form of consciousness. This began when he undertook to expose, through his work on epistemology and in The Psychoanalysis of Fire, what he calls 'epistemological obstacles.' Images are not part of the world of scientific and conceptual thought; they must be 'suppressed' soundly by means of 'dialectical sublimation,' an idea explored in The Psychoanalysis of Fire. Conversely, with a poetics of reverie, one must surrender completely to the imaginary, which then entirely regains its positivity. Excluding neither study nor reverie, Bachelard always sought to distinguish between these two psychic activities. Both science and poetry are essential and meaningful, therefore the scholar of epistemology justifiably pursues the study of the imagination and attempts to identify constants and rules. Within the unlimited, yet suggestive and operational, context of the elements (in accordance with his materialist principles), Bachelard succeeded in proposing a structure of images rich enough to engender a 'new literary spirit' (*La Terre et les rêveries du repos* 176) – one of the driving forces behind the *New Criticism.

Bachelard realized that the study of images could be approached in two ways. The first, based on rationalism and the search for explanations, is the path of biographers, psychologists, psychoanalysts, and critics who feel that the image can be 'explained' or 'understood' only if reduced to a past and to other concepts. In other words, they must go beyond the image. Inspired by the discoveries of the Freudian school, Bachelard gradually moved away from this inevitably negative approach to images, which were thus viewed as camouflage or lies, symbolizing something else, namely sexual concepts. Bachelard preferred Jung's approach, focusing on the suggestive realm of archetypes or paradigms in a series of images. He became more and more aware of the need to study images from a positive perspective, to avoid immobilizing images by explaining them. Instead, wishing to experience them, 'visit' them, to capture their dynamism to the maximum, he sought a more appropriate method, one more in keeping with the very nature of the imagination. His approach to images is that of a phenomenologist – that is, one who partakes in the life of the image from the moment it enters the consciousness of each individual reader until the image reverberates in the reader's entire being. However, it is not until the *Poétiques* that Bachelard adheres to the principle of phenomenological resonance and accepts the creative movement of images defined as phenomenology. (See also *Carl Gustav Jung, *archetype, *archetypal criticism, *phenomenological criticism.)

In short, Bachelard sought to study the dynamics of the imagination. He collected samples of images from the works of many poets of diverse cultures to bring up to date the universals of the imagination: dreams of the house, fireside, trees, childhood, birds flying, reflections in the water, the flame of a candle, and so forth. (See *universal.) According to Bachelard, it is not necessary to study the structure of the works as a whole – that is, to undertake literary criticism. That entails a study of images from a 'distance,' which is precisely what he wanted to avoid. A philosopher turned essayist (or phenomenologist) of the literary imagination, Bachelard attempted to examine the themes and variations of images in order to propose 'a general theory of the imagination' (*The Poetics of Space* 62). Evidence of his influence can be found in critical essays by Jean-Pierre Richard, *Jean Starobinski, *Jean Rousset, *Georges Poulet, and countless others who were led by Bachelard to believe that better dreaming is the key to better reading.

ROBERT VIGNEAULT

Primary Sources

Bachelard, Gaston. *L'Air et les songes. Essai sur l'imagination du mouvement.* Paris: José Corti, 1943, 1965.
– *L'Eau et les rêves. Essai sur l'imagination de la matière.* Paris: José Corti, 1942, 1964, 1965.
– *La Flamme d'une chandelle.* Paris: PUF, 1961, 1964.
– *Lautréamont.* Paris: José Corti, 1939. New exp. ed. Paris: José Corti, 1956, 1963.
– *La Poétique de l'espace.* Paris: PUF, 1957, 1964, 1989.
– *La Poétique de la rêverie.* Paris: PUF, 1960, 1965.
– *La Psychanalyse du feu.* Paris: Gallimard, 1938, 1949, 1965.
– *La Terre et les rêveries du repos. Essai sur les images de l'intimité.* Paris: José Corti, 1948, 1965, 1971.
– *La Terre et les rêveries de la volonté. Essai sur l'imagination des forces.* Paris: José Corti, 1948, 1965.

Secondary Sources

Bachelard. Colloque de Cerisy 1970. Paris: Union générale d'éditions, '10–18,' 1974.
Bachelard, L'Arc 42 (1970).
Dagognet, François. *Gaston Bachelard.* Paris: PUF, 1965.
Gaston Bachelard. L'Homme du poème et du théorème. Dijon: Editions Dijon U, 1984.
Ginestier, Paul. *Pour connaître la pensée de Bachelard.* Paris: Bordas, 1968.
Mansuy, Michel. *Gaston Bachelard et les éléments.* Paris: José Corti, 1967.
Margolin, Jean-Claude. *Bachelard.* Paris: Seuil, 'Ecrivains de toujours,' 1974.
Naud, Julien. *Structure et sens du symbole. L'imaginaire chez Gaston Bachelard.* Tournai and Montreal: Desclée et Bellarmin, 1971.
Quillet, Pierre. *Bachelard.* Paris: Seghers, 1964.
Richard, Jean-Pierre. 'Quelques aspects nouveaux de la critique littéraire en France.' *Le Français dans le monde* 15 (1963): 2–9.

Tuzet, Hélène. 'Les Voies ouvertes par Gaston Bachelard à la critique littéraire.' In *Les Chemins actuels
de la critique*. Ed. Georges Poulet. Paris: Plon,
1967, 359–71. 'Discussion,' 381–92.

Vigneault, Robert. 'Lecture et critique. Essai.' In *Littératures*. Montreal: Hurtubise HMH, 1971, 257–63.

Baker, Houston A., Jr.

(b. U.S.A., 1943–) Critic, theorist, editor, and
poet. Houston A. Baker, Jr. received a B.A.
from Howard University in 1965 and a Ph.D.
from UCLA in 1968 with a dissertation entitled
'The Idea of Aestheticism,' which argued that
Victorian aestheticism was a form of social activism. He taught at Yale in 1968–9 and at the
Center for Advanced Studies, University of
Virginia, as an associate professor (1970–3). In
1974 he moved to the University of Pennsylvania as director of Afro-American Studies; he
is currently professor of English and the Albert
M. Greenfield Professor of Human Relations at
Pennsylvania, where he also directs the Center
for the Study of Black Literature and Culture.

Baker, whom Henry Louis Gates has called
'the leading and most prolific theorist of Afro-
American literature,' has undergone a number
of changes in his theoretical/critical outlook.
Trained in New Critical methodology as a
student, Baker was soon strongly influenced
by the political activism of the Black Power
movement of the late 1960s. (See *New Criticism.) He turned from Victorian studies to the
study of Black American literature and culture,
at the same time rejecting purely formal criticism in favour of sociological, historical and
biographical concerns; as a self-conscious
theorist of the Black Aesthetic in the late
1960s – albeit a more academic and ambivalent one than Stephen Henderson or Larry
Neal – he attempted to define the 'soul' of
black literature and culture, the 'ineffable
"something" that made black American creativity *Not-Art*' (*Afro-American Poetics* 13). (See
*Black Criticism, *literature.)

By the mid-1970s Baker had moved beyond
the Black Aesthetic – with its overtly nationalistic, utopian concerns – to concentrate on developing a broad theory of black expressive
culture: *Reading Black* marks this transition. He
became involved in the 'reconstruction of instruction' project, which sought to revise the
narrow *canon of American literature so as to
make it more inclusive and representative of

pluralistic, multicultural society and to provide
a more formal theoretical base for black literary study. Unlike the purely 'literary' and linguistic (formalist-structuralist) concerns of
many 'reconstructionist' critics, however, Baker's project – as exemplified in a collection of
essays edited with *Leslie Fiedler – attacked
the notion that the English language itself is a
neutral container of cultural forms; language is
marked as a political tool with ideological
ramifications that need to be exposed and explicated. Baker also called for criticism to pay
'requisite attention to the vernacular – to
everyday social and political realities' (*Afro-
American Poetics* 88) such as black music (especially blues and jazz) and black religious oratory, rather than exclusively to literary texts.
(See *text.) He employs the rhythm of the
blues – combined with the material conditions
of black American life – as an exemplum of a
sophisticated, reflexive and subversive black
semiotic system, a Blues Poetics, that can be
used to read literary texts as well. Thus, while
adopting strategies he finds useful from the
'reconstruction' project, Baker nevertheless
clings strongly to a neo-Marxist insistence on
the contextualizing of literature. In *Blues, Ideology, and Afro-American Literature* he states: 'it
is the attempt to understand the coextensive-
ness of language as a social institution and literature as a system within it that constitutes a
defining project of literary-theoretical study in
our day' (100). (See also *structuralism, *semiotics, *Marxist criticism, *subversion, *materialist criticism.)

Beginning with *The Journey Back* (1980),
Baker has been building what he calls an 'anthropology of art' (*Journey* xvi) which insists
'that works of Afro-American expressive culture cannot be adequately understood unless
they are contextualized within the interdependent systems of Afro-American culture' (*Blues,
Ideology* 109). He has appropriated 'an array
of "standard" disciplines [linguistics, history,
anthropology, psychology, philosophy] to
the task of building a vernacular theory of
Afro-American expressive culture' (*Afro-American Poetics* 90). *Modernism and the Harlem
Renaissance* – which reinterprets the Harlem
Renaissance as a success through redefining
modernism in its African American incarnation
– and *Afro-American Poetics* are instalments in
this anthropological/historical enterprise, with
the latter also reflecting Baker's increasing
sense that criticism is a personal rather than

an objective mode; hence his interest in auto-biography as a critical genre. (See *genre criticism.)

Finally, Baker has become one of the champions of black women's writing, which he views as the most important 'spirit work' of the last decade. Himself influenced by semiotic, poststructural, neo-Marxist, and feminist theory, he has profoundly influenced theoretical issues of *ideology, gender, genre, and literary history within African American studies. (See also *feminist criticism, *poststructuralism.)

DONALD C. GOELLNICHT

Primary Sources

Baker, Houston A., Jr. *Afro-American Poetics: Revisions of Harlem and the Black Aesthetic.* Madison: U of Wisconsin P, 1990.
– *Blues, Ideology, and Afro-American Literature: A Vernacular Theory.* Chicago and London: U of Chicago P, 1984.
– *The Journey Back: Issues in Black Literature and Criticism.* Chicago and London: U of Chicago P, 1980.
– *Long Black Song: Essays in Black American Literature and Culture.* Virginia UP, 1990.
– *Modernism and the Harlem Renaissance.* Chicago and London: U of Chicago P, 1987.
– *Singers of Daybreak: Studies in Black American Literature.* Washington: Howard UP, 1974.
– *Three American Literatures: Essays in Chicano, Native American and Asian American Literature for Teachers of American Literature.* New York: MLA, 1982.
– *Workings of the Spirit: The Poetics of Afro-American Women's Writing.* Chicago and London: Chicago UP, 1990.
– ed. *A Dark and Sudden Beauty: Two Essays in Black American Poetry.* Philadelphia: U of Pennsylvania P, 1977.
– ed. *Narrative of the Life of Frederick Douglass, an American Slave.* Harmondsworth: Penguin, 1982.
– ed. *Reading Black: Essays in the Criticism of African, Caribbean and Black American Literature.* Africana Studies and Research Center Series no. 4, 1976.
– and Leslie Fiedler, eds. *English Literature: Opening Up the Canon.* Baltimore: Johns Hopkins UP, 1981.
– and Patricia Redmond, eds. *Afro-American Literary Study in the 1990s.* Chicago and London: Chicago UP, 1989.
– and Joe Weixlmann, eds. *Black Feminist Criticism and Critical Theory.* Greenwood, Fl.: Penkevill Publishing, 1988.

Bakhtin, Mikhail Mikhailovich

(b. Russia, 1895–d. 1975) Philosopher of language, literary scholar and theorist. After a comfortable childhood in Vilnius and Odessa, Bakhtin earned a degree in classics and philology at the University of Petrograd during the war years (1913–18). Upon graduation, hoping to escape the terrible privations in the capital, he moved to the small town of Nevel, and later to Vitebsk, in western Russia. There he worked as a schoolteacher and participated in study circles devoted to philosophy, *literature and ethics (other members included his friends, the Marxist scholars and critics Valentin Voloshinov and Pavel Medvedev). During the early 1920s, Bakhtin wrote a massive treatise on the nature of moral responsibility and aesthetics (translated as 'Toward a Philosophy of the Act,' 'Author and Hero in Aesthetic Activity'), in spirit quite opposed to both neo-Kantianism and Marxism. (See *Marxist criticism.)

In part because of this lack of political credentials under the new regime and in part owing to his health (a bone disease that left him often bedridden and resulted in the amputation of his right leg in 1938), Bakhtin did not succeed in finding permanent work during the 1920s. In 1929 he was arrested. The particular charge concerned alleged activity in the underground Russian Orthodox church, although evidence for this activity is circumstantial. He was sentenced to ten years on the Solovetsky Islands, a death camp in the Soviet Far North. Thanks to the intervention of influential friends and because of his precarious health, Bakhtin's sentence was commuted to six years' internal exile in Kazakhstan. During the 1930s, while working as a bookkeeper on a collective farm and at other odd jobs in exile, Bakhtin wrote his most famous essays on the theory of the novel. He also researched a major work on Rabelais which he submitted as his doctoral dissertation in 1941 to the Gorky Institute of World Literature in Moscow.

In 1936 Bakhtin took up a professorship at the remote Mordovia Pedagogical Institute in the town of Saransk, east of Moscow. With some interruptions, he taught (and eventually chaired) Russian and world literature at that institution until 1961. During this time of mass political repression and re-arrest of intellectuals, Bakhtin's relative obscurity and low profile in print might well have saved his life.

Bakhtin's final years are the story of rediscovery and rising fame. In the 1950s, on the other side of the Stalinist night, a group of Moscow graduate students who had read Bakhtin's 1929 book on Dostoevsky learned, to their astonishment, that its author was still alive. As literary studies were rethought in the post-Stalinist period, Bakhtin became an emblem of an earlier and freer intellectual climate, a survivor from a past that was long believed lost. 'Pilgrimages' to Saransk began and Bakhtin was persuaded to rework the Dostoevsky book for a second edition. Once this book was reapproved for print (1963), other long-delayed manuscripts were published ('Discourse in the Novel,' 'Epic and Novel,' the essay on the chronotope, *Rabelais and His World*). His advice was sought by both the structuralist semioticians of the *Tartu School and the more conservative Marxist-Leninist humanists of the Soviet establishment. Bakhtin became a 'classic,' although his legacy and politics remained ambivalent. Was he a Marxist, a phenomenologist, a carnival clown, a Russian Orthodox Christian, a revisionist formalist, a deconstructionist before the name? His thought has been appropriated by all of those positions. (See *phenomenological criticism, *carnival, *deconstruction, *semiotics, *structuralism.)

Part of the confusion stems from the fact that Bakhtin shared with his Marxist associates an opposition to certain ideological trends then current (formalist, Freudian, structuralist-linguistic). (See also *Sigmund Freud, *psychoanalytic theory.) But available evidence indicates that Bakhtin himself was not a Marxist and could not create effectively within that *ideology. This question is of some importance because the case has been made (although not persuasively) that Bakhtin in fact authored three quite remarkable and indisputably Marxist texts published under the names of two associates in his circle: Voloshinov's *Freudianism: A Critical Sketch* (1927) and *Marxism and the Philosophy of Language* – the latter book also being a fine sociological study in the semiotics of language; and Medvedev's polemic, *The Formal Method in Literary Scholarship* (1928). Bakhtin's disciples in the Soviet Union first attributed these texts to him in 1970.

A careful reading of the disputed texts suggests that the attribution is unfounded. Bakhtin's own critique of the formalists, 'The Problem of Content, Material, and Form in Verbal Art' (1924; first published 1975, trans. in *Art and Answerability* 1990), is cast in abstract Kantian categories quite different from Medvedev's more practical criticism aimed at the early 'mechanical' formalists. Bakhtin's polemic with Freudian-style thinking in his early writings is both more philosophical and less politically opportunistic than Voloshinov's. And the seminal idea of *polyphony, as outlined in Bakhtin's first major published work, *Problems of Dostoevsky's Poetics* (1929), owes nothing to Marxism or to semiotics. Despite widespread confusion on this point, literary 'polyphony' is not the same as 'heteroglossia,' social diversity or stratification, and it does not investigate issues of social coding or decoding. Bakhtin's polyphony is an approach to the creative process that speculates on possible multiple positions for the author in a text and on modes of sharing 'authorial surplus' with heroes in the construction of a non-Aristotelian plot. (See *heteroglossia, *code.)

In contrast to Bakhtin, Voloshinov's and Medvedev's works of the late 1920s are sincerely sociological and Marxist: that is, they take Bakhtin's concepts of dialogism and radical individual responsibility for events and incorporate them into a dialectical system based on the ideas of class and 'choral support.' Confronted with a sophisticated sociological version of his own ideas, Bakhtin appears to have responded in the 1930s with theories of language and literature that were sociological without being Marxist, dialectical or 'systematizing.'

In retrospect, Bakhtin's intellectual development appears to coalesce around three major ideas and divide into four periods. These three 'global concepts' are prosaics, dialogue and unfinalizability. 'Prosaics' refers to that deep preference Bakhtin had for the obligations and complexities of prose as opposed to the regularities of a poetics (and of poetry generally); it also privileges particular concrete events over the abstract or the systematic. By 'dialogue' Bakhtin meant a model of creativity which assumed that the interaction of at least two embodied voices or personalities was the sine qua non for genuine consciousness. Dialogue need not be exclusively verbal interaction, although Bakhtin came to investigate dialogue largely in terms of the word. The final concept, 'unfinalizability,' refers to Bakhtin's conviction that the messy potential of prosaics and the interactive energies of dialogue, taken together, make the world an open place where real creativity is an ongoing and everyday event.

These three global concepts emerged at different times, sometimes complementing, sometimes contradicting, one another. In Bakhtin's first period, the 'word' as such was not yet central. True to his neo-Kantian origins, what concerned him were ethical and aesthetic acts. In the second period (1924–30), his discovery of the potential of the word led to a redefinition of language – not as understood by structural linguists or Russian futurists but as uttered *discourse. In the Dostoevsky book (1st ed. 1929), attempting to match the poetic rigour of the formalists, Bakhtin produces a 'prosaic' typology of 'double-voiced words' (words serving more than one voice-centre). (See *double-voicing.)

The discovery of the dialogic word made possible a third period, lasting from the early 1930s until the 1950s, in which the novel itself becomes the hero. Two related but distinct lines of thought can be said to issue from the Dostoevsky book. In the first, the double-voiced word and the 'word with a loophole' become traits of all truly novelistic prose. Here, Bakhtin also speculates provocatively on the history of 'novelistic consciousness' in terms of changing ideas about time, space and the concomitant understanding of human agency (what he calls the 'chronotope,' his term for that matrix of presumptions about the workings of time and space that underlies every narrative text). Bakhtin then succumbs to exaggerating and idealizing 'novelization,' however, in a second line of thought that reached its peak during the 1930s and 1940s. Taking one of his global concepts, 'unfinalizability,' to an extreme (even to the point where it contradicts the other two), Bakhtin celebrates the 'joyously ambivalent carnivalesque' in his book on Rabelais. For all its current vogue and critical productivity, carnival – with its indifference to dialogue, its fascination with violence without pain and its absorption of human particularity in a common immortal body – is arguably one of Bakhtin's weaker formulations. It is no surprise that, during these years of High Stalinism, maximalist rhetoric, political terror, and widespread sentimentalization of the battlefield, one type of rebellious and aggressively code-breaking novel becomes for Bakhtin the essence of novels in general, and

that the virtues of such novels are glorified to the detriment of all other genres. Carnival utopia is linked to the imperialism of the novel. (See *polyphonic novel.)

Bakhtin's fourth and final period, stretching from the early 1950s until his death, was a time of recapitulation and a return to the earlier ethical themes of the 1920s. His last essay concerned the role of the humanities in contemporary culture. Bakhtin is peculiar among literary theorists today in that he is an opponent of both system and 'relativism' – that is, he resists the idea that in literary as well as in real-life structures either there is system or there is nothing. All lasting value is generated in the 'middle space' of subtly voiced and negotiated human exchanges; the proper development of a personality is analogous to the experience of a novel. (See *dialogical criticism, *character zones, *embedding, *monologism.)

CARYL EMERSON

Primary Sources

Bakhtin, M.M. *Art and Answerability: Early Philosophical Essays.* Ed. Michael Holquist and Vadim Liapunov. Trans. and notes by Vadim Liapunov. Supplement trans. Kenneth Brostrom. Austin: U of Texas P, 1990.
– 'Author and Hero in Aesthetic Activity.' In *Estetika slovesnogo tvorchestva* [*Aesthetics of Verbal Creation.*] Ed. Sergei G. Bacharov. Moscow: Iskusstvo, 1979.
– *The Dialogic Imagination: Four Essays by M.M. Bakhtin.* Ed. Michael Holquist. Trans. Caryl Emerson and Michael Holquist. Austin: U of Texas P, 1981.
– *Problems of Dostoevsky's Poetics.* Ed. and trans. Caryl Emerson. Minneapolis: U of Minnesota P, 1984.
– *Rabelais and His World.* Trans. Hélène Iswolsky. Cambridge, Mass.: MIT P, 1968. 2nd ed. Bloomington: Indiana UP, 1984.
– *Speech Genres and Other Late Essays.* Trans. Vern W. McGee. Ed. Caryl Emerson and Michael Holquist. Austin: U of Texas P, 1986.

Secondary Sources

Clark, Katerina, and Michael Holquist. *Mikhail Bakhtin.* Cambridge, Mass.: Harvard UP, 1984.
Hirschkop, Ken, and David Shepherd. *Bakhtin and Cultural Theory.* Manchester: Manchester UP; New York: St. Martin's P, 1989.
Morson, Gary Saul, ed. *Bakhtin: Essays and Dialogues on His Work.* Chicago: U of Chicago P, 1986.

– *Mikhail Bakhtin: Creation of a Prosaics*. Stanford: Stanford UP, 1990.
– and Caryl Emerson. *Rethinking Bakhtin: Extensions and Challenges*. Evanston: Northwestern UP, 1989.

Barthes, Roland

(b. France, 1915–d. 1980) Literary critic and semiotician. Roland Barthes was educated at the Sorbonne, taught at universities in Romania and Egypt, and for seven years did research in lexicology and sociology at the Centre National de la Recherche Scientifique (1952–9). He taught in Paris at the Ecole Pratique des Hautes Etudes from 1960 until his death. In 1976 a chair in literary semiology was created especially for him at the Collège de France. One of the first critics to apply the structuralist ideas developed by *Ferdinand de Saussure in linguistics to the study of *literature, Barthes was a prime mover in the revolt against academic historical and biographical criticism and, in the last phase of his career, became particularly concerned with the personal, subjective response of the reader to the *text. (See *reader-response criticism, *semiotics, *structuralism.)

In the first phase of his published work, Barthes was concerned with how ideologies or value-systems become encoded in language and in social usages, and thus appear 'natural' – ideas subsequently developed by F. Rossi-Landi (*Linguistics and Economics* 1975). (See *ideology.) For example, a child in France in 1925 might feel that it was 'natural' for a man to go out to work, while his wife stayed home to take care of the children. It might also seem 'natural' in the previous sentence, to name the man first, and to make the wife linguistically 'his' possession. But there is nothing natural in these arrangements; Barthes might have said that they reflect a pattern based on a stereotype, which is passed on through a particular culture. He called assumptions such as these 'mythologies,' and in his celebrated book of that name showed how they permeated French life. (See *myth.) For Barthes language is a powerful determining influence on the way individuals and societies see the world around them. In a view he shared with B.L. Whorf (*Language, Thought, and Reality: Selected Writings* 1969), Barthes believed that language is never transparent; it partly creates and gives a structure to the world which the individual encounters. So French-speakers and English-speakers live in different worlds, as do people such as Christians and Freudians who use different vocabularies. Barthes considered it part of a thinker's moral responsibility to be aware that language is never innocent or free of ideology. Sensitive to subtle forms of domination, and particularly those which occur through the agency of language, Barthes was anti-authoritarian and put great energy into challenging (and deconstructing) institutions and languages which allow one group of people to dominate another. In his thinking about literature, this led him to the idea of 'the death of the author' – that is, the belief that the author does not have a privileged position in determining the meaning of his or her work. This view, presented in *Critique et vérité* [*Criticism and Truth* 1966], caused a celebrated conflict between Barthes and some more conservative professors of literature who gave primacy to the author's meaning.

During his second period Barthes was inspired by the methods of structural linguistics and the light they could shed on other 'signifying systems,' such as those of narration or of fashion. Barthes was one of the leading exponents of structuralism as it developed in the 1960s and he felt the excitement of the possibility of developing a science of culture. During this period he had close connections with other structuralists such as *Claude Lévi-Strauss and *Michel Foucault. Two important texts of this period are *Eléments de sémiologie* and 'Introduction à l'analyse structurale des récits' [*Elements of Semiology* 1968 and 'Introduction to the Structural Analysis of Narrative' 1966]. Barthes delighted in systems of classification and binary oppositions such as Saussure's distinction between synchrony and diachrony. (See *binary opposition.) In *Le Plaisir du texte* [*The Pleasure of the Text* 1973] he evolves a contrast between two responses to literature, 'pleasure' (which is steady and fairly predictable) and '*jouissance*,' which can be translated as 'bliss' or 'orgasm.' (*Jouissance* is sudden, unpredictable and shocking.) Barthes took a festive attitude toward ideas and contrasts such as these, and seemed to feel them almost physically. 'Abstraction,' he said, 'is not in the least contrary to sensuality.' (See *pleasure/bliss.)

In his third phase, disillusioned with his own scientific ideal, Barthes expressed sympathy with *Nietzsche's statement that 'we are scientists because we lack subtlety.' Taking part in the development of *poststructuralism in the 1970s, Barthes laid great emphasis on the physical experience of the body and on sexuality. His works emphasized subjective experience, the nature of the subject (see *Lacan) and the undoing of systems of classification (see *deconstruction, *subject/object). Autobiographical elements in his later works attest to subjective realities which might have escaped the attention of Barthes the structuralist.

Barthes' influence spread quickly to North America in the 1970s. His influence was partly due to his unusual ability to develop distinctions and typologies which are highly revealing and widely applicable. His work was also attractive because he did not want to become the leader of a critical school. In spite of his attempts to reduce his own authority, he inspired reverence and affection in both students and readers.

STEPHEN BONNYCASTLE

Primary Sources

Barthes, Roland. *Critique et vérité*. Paris: Seuil, 1966. *Criticism and Truth*. Trans. Katrine Pilcher Keuneman. Minneapolis: U of Minnesota P, 1987.
– *Le Degré zéro de l'écriture*. Paris: Seuil, 1953. *Le Degré zéro de l'écriture et Elements de sémiologie*. Paris: Seuil, 1964. *Writing Degree Zero*. Trans. Annette Lavers and Colin Smith. New York: Hill and Wang, 1972. *Elements of Semiology*. Trans. Annette Lavers and Colin Smith. New York: Hill and Wang, 1968.
– *Le Grain de la voix: Entretiens*. Paris: Seuil, 1981. *The Grain of the Voice*. Trans. Linda Coverdale. New York: Hill and Wang, 1985.
– 'Introduction à l'analyse structurale des récits.' *Communications* 8 (Nov. 1966). 'Introduction to the Structural Analysis of Narrative.' In *Image Music Text*. Trans. Stephen Heath. New York: Hill and Wang, 1977.
– *Leçon*. Paris: Seuil, 1978. (Inaugural Lecture, Collège de France.) In *A Barthes Reader*. Trans. Richard Howard. New York: Hill and Wang, 1982.
– *Mythologies*. Paris: Seuil, 1957. *Mythologies*. Trans. Annette Lavers. New York: Hill and Wang, 1972.
– *Le Plaisir du texte*. Paris: Seuil, 1973. *The Pleasure of the Text*. Trans. Richard Miller. New York: Hill and Wang, 1976.
– *Roland Barthes par Roland Barthes*. Paris: Seuil, 1975. *Roland Barthes by Roland Barthes*. Trans. Richard Howard. New York: Hill and Wang, 1977.

– *Système de la mode*. Paris: Seuil, 1967. *The Fashion System*. Trans. M. Ward and R. Howard. New York: Hill and Wang, 1983.
– *S/Z*. 1970. *S/Z*. Trans. Richard Miller. New York: Hill and Wang, 1975.

Secondary Sources

Culler, Jonathan. *Barthes*. London: Collins, 1982.
Lavers, Annette. *Roland Barthes: Structuralism and After*. London: Methuen, 1982.
Rossi-Landi, F. *Linguistics and Economics*. The Hague: Mouton, 1975.
Sontag, Susan. 'Introduction' to *A Barthes Reader*. New York: Hill and Wang, 1982.
Thody, Philip. *Roland Barthes: A Conservative Estimate*. London: Macmillan, 1977.
Ungar, Steven. *Roland Barthes: The Professor of Desire*. Lincoln: U of Nebraska P, 1983.
Whorf, B.L. *Language, Thought, and Reality: Selected Writings*. Cambridge: Technology Press of MIT, 1958. Trans. as *Linguistique et anthropologie*. Trans. Claude Carme. Paris: Denoël, 1969.

Baudrillard, Jean

(b. France, 1929–) Sociologist and cultural critic. In contemporary cultural criticism, Jean Baudrillard is best known for his claims that Western societies have entered a new period of history, a postmodernity that emerges with the disappearance of the fundamental structures and referents of modern society because of the impact of mass media and informational systems. (See *postmodernism.)

As a sociologist at Nanterre writing during the intellectual and political upheavals of the 1960s, Baudrillard was well acquainted with American and French theories of consumer society and his first books attempted to put forth a systematic analysis and critique of advanced capitalism. Baudrillard's assumption, shared by other French theorists such as Henri Lefebvre and Guy Debord, was that the key dynamics of capitalism had shifted from production to consumption, and that, in *Antonio Gramsci's words, culture had become a site of *hegemony.

Like these theorists, Baudrillard sees consumption as a new form of alienation and social control. In his first three books, *Le Système des objets* (1968), *La Société de consummation* (1970) and *For a Critique of the Political Economy of the Sign* (1972; trans. 1981), he theorizes the process whereby needs are produced, desires are managed and individuals are integrated into a differential system of objects and signs. His detailed descriptions of art and architecture, fashion and design, domestic environments, and commodities of all kinds present the 'new field of everyday life,' the 'new environment,' and the new form of 'hypercivilization' created by consumer/media/informational society.

This early work synthesizes a number of critical perspectives (including those of *Lukács and the *Frankfurt School) and engages Marxian theories. (See *Marxist criticism.) Baudrillard's key thematic is already established: analysis of the new field of media, information, and the proliferating field of objects which constitute and transform the subject. *For a Critique of the Political Economy of the Sign* proposes that the Marxian critique of political economy needs to be supplemented with a theory of the semiotic aspects of commodities. (See *semiotics.) Where Marxism analyses the modes of production and distribution of commodities, semiology analyses the symbolic meanings of objects, the social prestige they confer upon the consumer. Hence, Baudrillard proposes that the Marxian theory of use and exchange value needs to be supplemented with a new theory of 'sign value.'

What Baudrillard here theorizes as the relative autonomy of the *sign from political economy became a full autonomy in his subsequent works. After the *Critique*, he privileges codes and signs over social practices, institutions and political economy. The break with Marxism in *The Mirror of Production* (1973; trans. 1975) presents Marxism as a 'conceptual imperialism' that extends to all history economic categories which apply, at best, only to the early stage of industrial capitalism. (See *code.)

Influenced by the theories of Marcel Mauss and Georges Bataille, Baudrillard interprets all precapitalist societies as being governed by a logic of 'symbolic exchange': objects are exchanged in rituals that value waste and expenditure and are indifferent to human 'needs' and social rationality. Baudrillard interprets capitalism not from the Marxian point of view as a revolution in social classes, instantiating the capital/wage labour relation, but rather as a 'semiological revolution' that reduces symbolic practices to the quantitative nexus of (use and exchange) 'value.' In a deconstructive critique, Baudrillard analyses Marxism as a

pseudo-revolutionary 'alibi' of capitalism that is locked into the repressive instrumental logic of modernity. (See *deconstruction.) Renouncing Marxist political strategies, Baudrillard proposes a rupture with all functionalist and utilitarian imperatives through a return to symbolic exchange – a transgression of production and instrumental rationality. This is to be accomplished by the micropolitical action of students, women and blacks, groups who, unlike the working class, stand outside the productivist 'code' of modernity and are therefore not already absorbed into the logic of the system.

After breaking with Marxism and its Enlightenment presuppositions, Baudrillard proceeds to break with modernity *tout court*. In *L'Echange symbolique et la mort* (1976), the key study of which is published in *Simulations* (1983), he develops his theories of postmodernism and postmodernity, claiming that we have entered another radically new historical era – postmodernity – passing from a 'metallurgic' into a 'semiurgic' society. The disenchanted world of industrial production, based on incessant growth, energy output, transformation, and differentiation, comes to an end with the rise of media and high technology and the proliferation of cultural images and signs. These forces negate meaning in a white noise of 'information,' dissolve individuals and social classes into a homogenous mass, and collapse the distinction between reality and unreality.

The postmodern, abstract, electronically processed world is thus constituted not by political economy and class conflict but by codes, signs, information, computerization, and cybernetic systems that completely dominate all individuals. (See *communication theory.) As an epochal break in history, postmodernity results in a cancellation and liquidation of every key modernist referent: truth, society, meaning, *power, history, and reality itself. To use Baudrillard's key terms, there is an 'implosion' of all classical oppositions, leading to a 'hyper-reality' dominated by an indeterminant play of 'simulations.' Under these conditions, the boundaries between reality and unreality blur, the 'artificial' becomes 'realer' than the 'real' itself, and 'reality' as simulacrum is produced as an effect from the models and codes that precede it.

After 1976, Baudrillard disavows the potency of any political strategy, including his

Baudrillard

own 'politics' of symbolic exchange which, from his later perspective, represents a nostalgic longing for lost origins and an impossible escape from the No-Exit world of cybernetic control. Since the late 1970s, Baudrillard has aimed his guns at his own contemporaries, at feminism and at the French Left. (See *feminist criticism.) Beginning with *Forget Foucault* (1977; trans. 1987), Baudrillard shifts toward increasingly cynical, nihilistic positions, turning away from developing postmodern theories and declaring himself a metaphysician (Kellner 1989). His 'metaphysical' texts are characterized by speculative abstractions and essentialist categories relying on binary oppositions such as seduction/production, masculine/feminine and subject/object. (See *totalization, *binary opposition, *essentialism.) He describes a universe where everything is connected and predestined. Unlike previous metaphysical theories in Western philosophy, however, Baudrillard's metaphysics is informed by the 'pataphysics' of Alfred Jarry and is ironic rather than serious, fragmentary rather than systematic, and abandons the belief in an objective, representational reality.

While Baudrillard has reconstituted many of his previous positions, he still pursues his *idée fixe* – the ever-proliferating world of objects and its hegemony over the subject. (See *subject/object.) In *Fatal Strategies*, Baudrillard substitutes a metaphysics of the object for that of the subject. He describes an object world that is now totally out of control, metastasizing like cancer. The *reification described by Lukács has become complete, as subjects and objects switch roles: the subject is reduced to inert passivity, the object plays out its ruses and social relations are nowhere in sight. In this 'transpolitical' world there are no secrets or hermeneutic depths, only the play of appearances and the full transparency of objects, the 'ecstasy' and 'obscenity' of a fully liberated objectivity. History has come to an end as all events become inconsequential.

In successive works such as *The Ecstasy of Communication* (1987; trans. 1988), *America* (1986; trans. 1988) and *Cool Memories* (1987; trans. 1990), Baudrillard turns to a more fragmentary and aphoristic style of writing and gives up theorizing in favour of travel reports, memoirs and pastiches of previous works, seemingly comfortable in his role as cultural 'critic' attached to and fascinated by the postmodern object world. Where *America* provides

an example of an idealist cultural analysis that limits itself to signs and appearances, promoting the U.S.A. as a 'utopia achieved,' *Cool Memories* reveals what many see as Baudrillard's sexism, racism and contempt for the handicapped and elderly.

An interpreter of our contemporary world, a theorist of the 'modes of disappearance' of Western realities, a self-proclaimed intellectual terrorist, Baudrillard has challenged existing theories of society and culture and argued that sign systems, media and information have radically changed our world. While some have found his ideas extreme or exaggerated, Baudrillard dramatically points to new social and cultural phenomena that require attention and analysis.

STEVEN BEST

Primary Sources

Baudrillard, Jean. *America*. Trans. Chris Turner. London: Verso, 1988.
– *Cool Memories*. Trans. Chris Turner. London: Verso, 1990.
– *L'Echange symbolique et la mort*. Paris: Gallimard, 1976.
– *The Ecstasy of Communication*. Trans. B. and C. Schutze. New York: Semiotext(e), 1988.
– *Fatal Strategies*. Trans. Philip Beitchman and W.G.J. Niesluchowski. New York: Semiotext(e), 1990.
– *For a Critique of the Political Economy of the Sign*. Trans. Charles Levin. St. Louis: Telos P, 1981.
– *Forget Foucault*. New York: Semiotext(e), 1987.
– *In the Shadow of the Silent Majorities*. New York: Semiotext(e), 1983.
– *The Mirror of Production*. Trans. Mark Poster. St. Louis: Telos P, 1975.
– *Seduction*. Trans. Brian Singer. New York and London: St. Martin's P and Macmillan, 1990.
– *Simulations*. New York: Semiotext(e), 1983.
– *La Société de consommation*. Paris: Gallimard, 1970.
– *Le Système des objets*. Paris: Denoël-Gonthier, 1968.

Secondary Sources

Best, Steven. 'The Commodification of Reality and the Reality of Commodification.' *Current Perspectives in Social Theory* 9 (1989): 23–51.
– and Douglas Kellner. *Postmodern Theory: Critical Interrogations*. New York: Macmillan and Guilford P, 1991.
Kellner, Douglas. *Jean Baudrillard: From Marxism to Postmodernism and Beyond*. Oxford: Polity, 1989.

Benjamin, Walter

(b. Germany, 1892–d. 1940) Literary critic. Benjamin came from an upper-middle-class assimilated German Jewish family. He completed a doctoral dissertation on *Der Begriff der Kunstkritik in der deutschen Romantik* [*The Concept of Art Criticism in the German Romantics*] in 1919 and in 1925 submitted *Ursprung des deutschen Trauerspiels* [*The Origin of German Tragic Drama*] as his *Habilitationsschrift*. Such a higher qualification was required for a full-time appointment in the German academy. However, the *Trauerspiel* study was found unacceptable by Benjamin's examiners and he was compelled to support himself as a freelance critic and translator. After the Nazi seizure of power in 1933 Benjamin left Germany for exile in Paris; he committed suicide in 1940 while attempting to escape from occupied France. Just a short time before his death he had finished his influential 'Über den Begriff der Geschichte' ['Theses on the Philosophy of History']. He made a posthumous reputation in several areas: as a literary critic who interpreted baroque and modern allegory; as an essayist who wrote on Goethe, Proust and Kafka; as a critic of mass culture who explored the disappearance of traditional aesthetic *aura in a world of mechanical reproduction and machine technology.

In his study of baroque *Trauerspiel* and other works Benjamin tries to develop a philological technique that begins with the marginal or seemingly trivial details of the *text. As he writes, 'truth-content is only to be grasped through an immersion in the most minute details of subject-matter' (*Origin* 29). Much of his literary criticism is characterized by this philological and historical approach: his account of the *Trauerspiel* is a firmly grounded historical description and analysis of 17th-century German baroque drama; his investigation of Baudelaire's poetry and Second Empire Paris (the unfinished *Arcades* project) is carried out with the greatest attention to the smallest historical detail; his essay 'The Work of Art in the Age of Mechanical Reproduction' (in *Illuminations*) exhibits a great density of historical cross-reference; his 'Theses On the Philosophy of History' insist that the aesthetic object must be read and apprehended in terms of the historical context which conditioned it.

For Benjamin the task of literary criticism is not to elaborate universal classificatory schemas which efface the particularity of artistic innovations. On the contrary, the critic 'looks for that which is exemplary, even if this exemplary character can be admitted only in respect of the merest fragment' (*Origin* 44). For unless the exemplary ideas or monads are constructed out of the transitory fragments of empirical reality there can be no theoretically satisfactory formal definition of a work of art. Benjamin's conception of the aesthetic object as a determinate particularity assumes that the critic fabricates monadic ideas whose internal structure is determined by the empirical individuality of the immediate data themselves. Only in and by virtue of the apparently insignificant detail can the aesthetic object be grasped in a complex and differentiated way. As Benjamin remarks, 'Without at least an intuitive grasp of the life of the detail in the structure, all love of beauty is no more than empty dreaming' (*Origin* 182). The difficulty in conventional literary criticism was that it proceeded by a typologizing and classifying analysis that did not do justice to the particular uniqueness of the aesthetic object. The purpose of Benjamin's critical method is to put into question categorizing, universalizing reading habits which subsume diverse phenomena under overgeneralized classificatory schemas. Still, it is important to remember that the singular empirical phenomenon must be elevated to the level of an objective interpretation through its insertion into what Benjamin called 'constellations.' Otherwise, textual readings would offer little more than a celebration of dispersal and fragmentation. Stated somewhat differently, the discrete details have to be placed in relation to a conceptually accessible historical whole or concrete totality that redeems the transitory empirical data.

In the 1920s and 1930s Benjamin was peripherally associated with the *Frankfurt School or Institut für Sozialforschung (Max Horkheimer, *Theodor Adorno and others). Like other Institut members he attempted to bring out the relationship between the aesthetic text and the wider sociohistorical context. But his philological-critical method differed in several ways from the Institut's theoretical orientation. Thus, it was hardly surprising that his friend Adorno raised a number of theoretical objections to the empirical and positivistic features of Benjamin's work. From Adorno's perspective Benjamin's microscopic gaze failed to construct an interpretive model which might articulate the disparate data and factual information that he had assembled. Nowhere were the immediately given 'facts' located in a larger system of relationships within which the critic might understand them; nowhere was the documentary evidence 'mediated through the total social process' as a whole (*Aesthetics and Politics*, ed. Anderson, 129). Thus, in Adorno's view the historical and documentary material was not theoretically deciphered in its mediated relationship to the social totality. Benjamin in his reply argued that it was the absence of detailed analyses which encouraged the forced systematizations of classificatory procedures. In his strong emphasis on the minutiae, on the seemingly unimportant details, he wanted to counter the stasis and abstraction which characterized closed theoretical systems. It is worth observing in this context that Adorno himself acknowledged the suggestive power of this philosophy of fragmentation when he later wrote that Benjamin's thought 'protected itself from the "success" of unbroken cohesion by making the fragmentary its guiding principle' (*Prisms* 239). This antisystematic systematization, by Adorno's own admission, is what is new in Benjamin's literary criticism.

Another crucial relationship in Benjamin's career was his close friendship with the poet and dramatist Bertolt Brecht. During the 1930s Benjamin frequently visited Brecht in his Danish exile and subsequently wrote a series of critical essays on his poetry and theatre. Two common themes which coincide in Benjamin and Brecht's oeuvre deserve to be mentioned: an intense preoccupation with modernist art and with left-wing avant-garde politics. Both preferred a modernistic and stylized art over the older organic model; both broke with the established social democratic parties of their time and moved towards an explicit Marxism. There can be no doubt that conversations with Brecht inspired essays such as 'The Author as Producer' or 'What Is Epic Theatre?' Moreover, it seems very likely that Brecht's more implacable politicization of art influenced Benjamin's views on the possibility of a genuine political aesthetic. One noticeable difference between Benjamin and Brecht was their theoretical assessment of Kafka's writings. For example, Brecht argued that certain mystical elements in Benjamin's essay on Kafka promoted an obscurantism which served reactionary social forces. The whole of Brecht's efforts were dedicated to the cognitive or scientific perspectives of historical materialism. He ascribed a priority to rationalist cognition over against Benjamin's religious empathy. From Brecht's point of view Benjamin's more esoteric theological mode of speculation in the Kafka essay was mystical, unpolitical and irrational. This is the basis for the often-repeated accusation that Benjamin transposed the themes and motifs of the Jewish mystical tradition into the conceptual framework of historical materialism. These complaints foreground the limitations of Benjamin's interpretive model. But it remains true that Brecht's strong preference for a materialist critical practice became a major constitutive principle of Benjamin's later work. (See *Marxist criticism, *materialist criticism.)

What Benjamin sought to retrieve in the smallest details of past art forms was an opening onto the future itself. For it is clear that his critical method re-evokes the dispersed and fragmentary traces of the past so as to rescue those repressed meanings which could serve to anticipate an emancipated future. Of course, it is obvious that a fondness for the objects of the distant past can lapse into dreamy reminiscences and sterile nostalgia (what he called 'homogeneous and empty time,' *Illuminations* 264). But this conception of history must be sharply distinguished from Benjamin's 'time of the now' (*Jetztzeit*) which demands a lucid identification of those broken fragments and traces still holding the hope of a new future. As he puts it, 'History is the subject of a structure whose site is not homogeneous, empty time, but time filled by the presence of the now' (*Illuminations* 261). Nothing conveys more eloquently than this succinct formulation Benjamin's 'hope in the past.'

PAMELA McCALLUM

Primary Sources

Benjamin, Walter. *Gesammelte Schriften*. Ed. Rolf Tiedemann and Hermann Schweppenhauser. Frankfurt: Suhrkamp Verlag, 1972.
- *Charles Baudelaire: A Lyric Poet in the Era of High Capitalism*. Trans. H. Zohn. London: New Left Books, 1973.
- *Der Begriff der Kunstkritik in der deutschen Romantik*. Berlin: Buchdruckerei A. Scholem, 1920.
- *Illuminations*. Trans. H. Zohn. New York: Schocken Books, 1969.
- *One-Way Street*. Trans. E. Jephcott and K. Shorter. London: New Left Books, 1979.

- 'A Reply.' In *Aesthetics and Politics*. Ed. P. Anderson et al. London: New Left Books, 1977.
- 'A Short History of Photography.' *Screen* 13.1 (Spring 1972).
- 'Über den Begriff der Geschichte.' In *Neue Rundschau* 61.3 (1950).
- *Ursprung des deutschen Trauerspiels*. Berlin: E. Rowohlt, 1928. Trans. as *The Origin of German Tragic Drama*. Trans. J. Osborne. London: New Left Books, 1977.
- *Understanding Brecht*. Trans. A. Bostock. London: New Left Books, 1973.

Secondary Sources

Adorno, Theodor. 'A Portrait of Walter Benjamin.' In *Prisms*. London: Spearman, 1967.

Allen, Richard W. 'The Aesthetic Experience of Modernity: Benjamin, Adorno, and Contemporary Film Theory.' *New German Critique* 40 (1987): 225–40.

Anderson, Perry, et al., eds. *Aesthetics and Politics*. London: New Left Books, 1977.

Buck-Morss, Susan. *The Origin of Negative Dialectics: Theodor W. Adorno, Walter Benjamin and the Frankfurt Institute*. New York: Free P, 1977.

Cowan, Bainard. 'Walter Benjamin's Theory of Allegory.' *New German Critique* 22 (1981): 109–22.

Eagleton, Terry. *Walter Benjamin, or Towards a Revolutionary Criticism*. London: New Left Books, 1981.

Hansen, Miriam. 'Benjamin, Cinema and Experience.' *New German Critique* 40 (1987): 179–224.

Jacobs, Carol. *The Dissimulating Harmony: The Image of Interpretation in Nietzsche, Rilke, Artaud, and Benjamin*. Baltimore: Johns Hopkins UP, 1978.

Jameson, Fredric. 'Walter Benjamin; or, Nostalgia.' In *Marxism and Form*. Princeton: Princeton UP, 1971.

Jennings, Michael. *Dialectical Images: Walter Benjamin's Theory of Literary Criticism*. Ithaca: Cornell UP, 1987.

Lunn, Eugene. *Marxism and Modernism: An Historical Study of Lukács, Brecht, Benjamin and Adorno*. Berkeley: U of California P, 1982.

Roberts, Julian. *Walter Benjamin*. London: Macmillan, 1982.

Wolin, Richard. *Walter Benjamin: An Aesthetic of Redemption*. New York: Columbia UP, 1982.

The following special issues have been devoted to Walter Benjamin: *New German Critique* 17 (1979), 34 (1985), 39 (1986), 48 (1989) and *The Philosophical Forum* 15.1–2 (1983–4).

Benveniste, Emile

(b. Syria, 1902–d. France, 1976) Linguist. Brilliantly precocious, Emile Benveniste, as a young man, met the great Antoine Meillet, who initiated him into linguistics. By the time Benveniste was 25 years old, he succeeded his teacher and mentor at the Ecole des Hautes Etudes. By 1937 he was already a member of the prestigious Collège de France – the highest achievement in France – remaining there for the rest of his life but for the German occupation during the Second World War (when he fled the country to avoid persecution) and the period from the late 1960s to the mid-1970s, when he was incapacitated by the illness that eventually led to his death.

The meteoric ascent, however, explains only part – and not necessarily the most compelling part – of the appeal of Benveniste's career. What is striking about his work is its mixture. Non-linguists associate Benveniste with the articles in *Problèmes de linguistique générale* (1966; trans. 1971) and in its sequel *Problèmes de linguistique générale II* (1974). Yet most of the 18 volumes, 297 articles and the many reviews and notes he wrote deal with topics recondite and esoteric to all but the specialist: Middle Eastern languages and Indo-European grammar. Together with the two volumes of *Problèmes*, a list of his most significant publications would have to include at least the early *Essai de grammaire sogdienne: Morphologie, syntaxe et glossaire* (1923), a reconstruction of Ogdian, an extinct Iranian language that Benveniste deduced from very limited materials; *The Persian Religion According to the Chief Greek Texts*, a collection of lectures published in English in 1929; *Origines de la formation des noms en indo-européen* (1935); and the monumental *Vocabulaire des institutions indo-européenes [Indo-European Language and Society* 1969; trans. 1973].

Although various theoretical camps have recently claimed him for their own, it is clear that Benveniste's roots extend from the same ground as critics such as Leo Spitzer, Ernst Robert Curtius and *Erich Auerbach – a ground in which linguistics is indistinguishable from philology, etymology or stylistics. Like his major contemporaries, Benveniste was very much attracted by the play of form and rules, by the view that the linguist must study systems, discover laws and simplify. Already in the 1930s, he attended several sessions of the structuralist-oriented *Prague School. (See *structuralism.) At the same time, he never lost sight of the pluralities which everyday communication implies. Thus, the importance of Benveniste's work lies in the fact that it exemplifies and confronts tensions basic not just to linguistics but to the humanities as such.

A central issue of his works is the relation between language and the category of the person. In some now classic analyses of French verbs and French pronouns (1966), Benveniste was able to show that while language is composed of a system of rules, actual enunciation occurs when the speaker assumes the role of the subject. (See *énonciation/énoncé.*) For there to be speech, someone must say 'I,' must, that is, organize his or her utterance starting from his or her spatial, temporal and evaluative perspective. The structure of language in action (*discours*) emanates from the here and now of the speaker: it is by way of their connection with this present and this space that references to past and future events or to other places and other persons acquire meaning. To eliminate the 'I' is to enter other realms of language and, in particular, to engage in narrative (*histoire*), a type of expression which records events, and in which places and persons exist independently of the subject or of the instance of discourse that is recounting them. Not by coincidence, the tense used for narration in French is the simple past, and, Benveniste points out, it is not used in oral communication (*Problèmes* 1966: 243). (See *discourse, *discourse analysis theory.)

Toward the end of his life, Benveniste turned his attention more and more toward the consequences of his grammatical and syntactical analyses. The temporal and spatial adverbs, the pronouns or adjectives that situate the 'I' or the instance of speech are empty forms, forms that can be enunciated by always different speakers and be adapted to always different circumstances. But precisely for that reason – because they are the apparatus by which language can be converted into speech – they have always different referents and an always specific significance. (See *reference/referent.) Contrary to signs, which need only be recognized, utterances, texts, instances of discourse need to be understood, to be interpreted, and this is a contingent, local affair, an operation always permeated by and steeped in history and culture. (See *sign, *text.) For language as a system of distinct units, the approach advocated by *Ferdinand de Saussure will do. Enunciation, instead, presupposes the 'structure du dialogue' (1974: 85) and hence entails new rules, new procedures. From the province of linguistics proper, the study of discourse, of speech thrusts us into the still-to-be-defined disciplines of translinguistics.

The literary criticism most directly indebted to the essays of *Problèmes* has up to now focused primarily on the two notions of *discourse* and *histoire*. This is perhaps not surprising, given that Benveniste did not manage to expand the intimations arising from his writings on general linguistics to their full potential. Moreover, the articles on *discours* do provide literary critics authoritative material with which to ponder the impact of language on the construction of self and of subjectivity. And, as *Gérard Genette has suggested ('Frontiers' 138), the dichotomy with *histoire* parallels oppositions that have occupied literary theory from Plato and Aristotle on; it is a variation on the controversy about the role of *diegesis and *mimesis, of telling and showing in narration.

Benveniste's conclusions bring to mind above all *Mikhail Bakhtin's work, which also calls for the development of a translinguistics. With its insistence on the uniqueness, the unrepeatability, the historicity of each utterance, the dialogism of the Russian thinker acts as a corrective to Benveniste's still somewhat confident allegiance to formalist analysis. (See *double-voicing, *dialogical criticism.) Since instances of discourse entail dialogue, and dialogue the interaction between individuals, there is a dimension of discourse that escapes the ken of any perspective concerned only with linguistic matters. On the other hand, Benveniste's descriptions of the functioning of pronouns, adverbs and other deictics can balance any excessively philosophical version of dialogue. How Benveniste would have resolved the contradictions in his argument – how, that is, he would have reconciled the linguistics with the translinguistic – we do not know. We can only say that his difficulty is also ours, that his essays remain important reading for anyone interested in learning about the state of current reflection on *literature.

FRANCESCO LORIGGIO

Primary Sources

Benveniste, E. 'The Correlation of Tense in the French Verb.' In *Problems in General Linguistics.* Trans. M.E. Meek. Coral Gables: U of Miami P, 1971, 205–15.
– *Essai de grammaire sogdienne. Deuxième partie: Morphologie, syntaxe et glossaire.* Paris: P. Geuthner, 1929.
– *Les Mages dans l'ancien Iran.* Paris: G.P. Maisonneuve, 1938.

- 'The Nature of Pronouns.' In *Problems in General Linguistics*, 217–22.
- *Noms d'agent et noms d'action en indo-européen*. Paris: A. Maisonneuve, 1948.
- *Origines de la formation des noms en indo-européen*. Paris: A. Maisonneuve, 1935.
- *The Persian Religion According to the Chief Greek Texts*. Paris: P. Geuthner, 1929.
- *Problèmes de linguistique générale*. Paris: Gallimard, 1966. *Problems in General Linguistics*. Trans. Mary Elizabeth Meek. Coral Gables: U of Miami P, 1971.
- *Problèmes de linguistique générale II*. Paris: Gallimard, 1974.
- 'Relationship of Person in the Verb.' In *Problems in General Linguistics*, 195–204.
- 'The Semiology of Language.' In *Polyphonic Linguistics: The Many Voices of Emile Benveniste*. *Semiotica*. Special Suppl. (1981): 5–23.
- 'Subjectivity in Language.' In *Problems in General Linguistics*, 223–30.
- *Titres et noms propres en iranien ancien*. Paris: Klincksieck, 1966.
- *Le Vocabulaire des institutions indo-européenes*. Vols. 1, 2. Paris: Editions de Minuit, 1969. *Indo-European Language and Society*. Trans. Elizabeth Palmer. London: Faber and Faber, 1973.
- *Vrtra et VrOragna. Etude de mythologie indo-iranienne*. Paris: Cahiers de la Société Asiatique, 1934.

Secondary Sources

Barthes, Roland. 'On Emile Benveniste.' In *Polyphonic Linguistics: The Many Voices of Emile Benveniste*. *Semiotica*. Special suppl. (1981).
- 'Pourquoi j'aime Benveniste.' In *Le Bruissement de la langue*. Paris: Editions du Seuil, 1984, 191–6.
Genette, Gérard. 'Frontiers of Narrative.' In *Figures of Literary Discourse*. Trans. A. Sheridan. New York: Columbia UP, 1982, 127–44.
Hagège, C. 'Benveniste et la linguistique de la parole.' In *E. Benveniste aujourd'hui*. Ed. G. Serbat. Paris: Société pour l'information grammaticale, 1984, 104–17.
Kristeva, Julia. 'La Fonction prédicative et le sujet parlant.' In *Langue Discours Société*. Ed. J. Kristeva, J-C. Milner, N. Ruwet. Paris: Editions du Seuil, 1975, 229–59.
MacCabe, C. 'On Discourse.' In *The Talking Cure*. Ed. C. MacCabe. London: Macmillan, 1981, 188–217.
Malkiel, Y. 'Lexis and Grammar – Necrological Essay on Emile Benveniste.' *Romance Philology* 34.2 (1980): 160–94.
Watkins, C. 'L'Apport d'Emile Benveniste à la grammaire comparée.' In *E. Benveniste aujourd'hui*. Ed. G. Serbat. Paris: Société pour l'information grammaticale, 1984, 3–11.

Blanchot, Maurice

(b. France, 1907–) Essayist, literary critic and novelist. Maurice Blanchot studied in the late 1920s at the University of Strasbourg, where he also began a lifelong friendship with the philosopher and writer Emmanuel Lévinas. Between 1931 and 1935, he published a number of articles in the *Journal des débats*, *La Revue française* and *La Revue universelle*. In 1936 and 1937, he wrote over 70 articles in the *Combat* and *L'Insurgé*. Little is known concerning Blanchot's activities between 1938 and the liberation of France in 1944. During the occupation, he contributed dozens of short reviews and articles to the *Journal des débats* while publishing novels (*Thomas l'obscur* 1941 and *Aminadab* 1942) and a volume of collected essays (*Faux pas* 1943). After the war, he served on the first editorial board of *Critique*, the monthly founded in 1946 by Georges Bataille. The following 20 years were a period of high activity, resulting in essays collected in *L'Espace littéraire* (1955), *Le Livre à venir* (1959), *L'Entretien infini* (1969), and *L'Amitié* (1971). Between 1954 and 1968, Blanchot was the major literary critic at the *Nouvelle revue française*. He was also reputed to have been a moving force behind the 1960 'Manifesto of the 121' that called for active public protest among writers and other intellectuals opposed to French policies in Algeria. Since the early 1960s, Blanchot's work has straddled fiction and the essay. *Le Pas au-delà* (1973) and *L'Ecriture du désastre* (1980) were composed as extended series of fragments, combining terse modular passages on writing and language with longer reflections on the interwar and wartime pasts. The latter added a historical dimension to what otherwise resembled a personal account of the periods in question. *La Folie du jour* (1973) was more cohesive and – possibly – even confessional. Its allegorical tone recalled the short narratives of the 1930s published first in 1951 under the title *Le Ressassement éternel* and again in 1983 with a closing afterword under the title of *Après-coup*. Since the 1970s, Blanchot has also written short occasional pieces on figures ranging from *Michel Foucault and *Martin Heidegger to Samuel Beckett and Nelson Mandela.

The conception of *literature associated with Blanchot's postwar writings derives in large part from Stéphane Mallarmé. For Blanchot as for Mallarmé, literature is less of a practice or an institution than a realm or space in which language produces meaning in the absence of the object it designates. Literary space becomes the place where language negates the world in order to preserve it as a fictional whole, as that imaginary point 'where the world can be seen in its entirety' (*Gaze of Orpheus* 57). Blanchot's postwar theorizing also responds to the question 'Comment la littérature est-elle possible?' ['How is Literature Possible?'] in the title of his 1942 response to the views set forth by Jean Paulhan in *Les fleurs de tarbes ou la terreur dans les lettres* [*The Flowers of Tarbes or Terror in Literature* 1941]. For Paulhan, terror is a consequence of a belief that literature invariably betrays the purity of thought prior to language. A desire to return to this pure origin underlies his deep suspicion of literature – equated with language and rhetoric. This suspicion of language as detrimental to 'pure' thought is a prime doctrine of the conception of literature whose evolution since the late 18th century Paulhan studies. As in the 1793–4 revolutionary period from which its name derives, literary terror persists in attempts to restore the priority of thought over language against a condition of unbridled expression that seemingly threatens its health. But where Paulhan makes terror into the negative moment of a future rhetoric of communication and consensus, Blanchot extends terror by asserting what he sees as the unique capacity of literature to negate the world in order to recreate it as language. This overlapping between negation and assertion remains central to Blanchot's conception. It extends to the interplay between the work (*oeuvre*) and the book (*livre*) beyond authorial intention and within an austere impersonal realm of 'unworking' (*désoeuvrement*). It also suggests that Blanchot's misgivings about the progression from terror to communication in Paulhan's *Fleurs* may explain the extent to which the transposition of terror from politics to literature in his own writings is never fully completed.

The sum and scope Blanchot's critical essays amount to an encyclopedia of 20th-century literary modernity. Beginning with *La Part du feu*, Blanchot extends the thematics of crisis, loss and death associated with Mallarmé and French symbolism to their variants in the writings of Arthur Rimbaud, Lautréamont, Paul Valéry, and Marcel Proust. German and central European figures – from Friedrich Hölderlin and Franz Kafka to Rainer Maria Rilke, Robert Musil and Hermann Broch – are also prominent. Debts to *Friedrich Nietzsche openly inform the views on nihilism and the fragment in *L'Entretien infini*, while Martin Heidegger's vision of being-in-the-world and being-unto-death appears both in the postwar narratives (*L'Arrêt de mort*) and the essays ('La Littérature et le droit à la mort') that inform Blanchot's literary vision.

Blanchot also writes at length on his contemporaries *Jean-Paul Sartre, René Char, Michel Leiris, and Georges Bataille. The crucial link with Bataille is marked by a common interest in transgression, as in *Lautréamont et Sade* (1949). It is also at work in the sensibility that leads Blanchot to assert the dynamism of interpretation as accompaniment, repetition and dialogue. Recurring references to Orpheus at the hands of the Furies and the identification of literature with the experience of death in his criticism through *L'Espace littéraire* and *Le Livre à venir* are transposed in Blanchot's more recent work into terms of difference and deferral associated with *Jacques Derrida's conception of writing as *différance*. (See *différance/différence*.) Along with Heidegger, Blanchot remains a key forebear of *deconstruction in Derridean and other modes. Evidence also points to the importance of Blanchot's early political essays as a possible point of reference for conceptions of writing and literature associated with nonconformist politics (neither right nor left) whose place in interwar French modernity is only now being explored. Such evidence and the inquiries it has spawned suggest that the challenge to reading uttered by the narrator at the end of Blanchot's *L'Arrêt de mort* as 'Noli me legere' remains unmet and is open to further disclosure.

STEVEN UNGAR

Primary Sources

Blanchot, Maurice. *L'Amitié*. Paris: Gallimard, 1971.
– *L'Arrêt de mort*. Paris: Gallimard, 1948.
– *Après-coup précédé par 'Le Ressassement éternel.' Vicious Circles: Two Fictions and 'After the Fact.'* Trans. Paul Auster. Barrytown, NY: Station Hill, 1985.
– *L'Attente l'oubli*. Paris: Gallimard, 1962.
– *Comment la littérature est-elle possible?* Paris: Corti, 1942. [Repr. in *Faux pas*.]

- *La Communauté inavouable.* Paris: Minuit, 1983. *The Unavowable Community.* Barrytown, NY: Station Hill, 1988.
- *L'Ecriture du désastre.* Paris: Gallimard, 1980. *The Writing of the Disaster.* Trans. Ann Smock. Lincoln: U of Nebraska P, 1986.
- *L'Entretien infini.* Paris: Gallimard, 1969.
- *L'Espace littéraire.* Paris: Gallimard, 1955. *The Space of Literature.* Trans. Ann Smock. Lincoln: U of Nebraska P, 1982.
- *Faux pas.* Paris: Gallimard, 1943.
- *La Folie du jour.* Montpellier: Fata Morgana, 1973. *The Madness of the Day.* Trans. Lydia Davis. Barrytown, NY: Station Hill, 1985.
- *The Gaze of Orpheus and Other Literary Essays.* Trans. Lydia Davis. Barrytown, NY: Station Hill, 1981. [Selected essays, 1949–69.]
- *Lautréamont et Sade.* Paris: Minuit, 1949.
- *Le Livre à venir.* Paris: Gallimard, 1959.
- *Michel Foucault tel que je l'imagine.* Montpellier: Fata Morgana, 1986. 'Michel Foucault as I Imagine Him.' In *Foucault/Blanchot.* Trans. Jeffrey Mehlman and Brian Massumi. New York: Zone Books, 1987.
- *La Part du feu.* Paris: Gallimard, 1949.
- *Le Pas au-delà.* Paris: Gallimard, 1973.
- *Le Ressassement éternel.* Paris: Minuit, 1951. See *Après-coup.*
- *The Sirens' Song.* Ed. Gabriel Josipovici. Trans. Sacha Rabinovitch. Bloomington: Indiana UP, 1982. [Selected essays, 1949–69.]

Secondary Sources

Collin, Françoise. *Maurice Blanchot ou la question de l'écriture.* Paris: Gallimard, 1971.
de Man, Paul. 'Impersonality in the Criticism of Maurice Blanchot.' In *Blindness and Insight.* Rev. ed. Minneapolis: U of Minnesota P, 1985.
Derrida, Jacques. *Parages.* Paris: Galilée, 1986.
Hartman, Geoffrey. 'Maurice Blanchot: Philosopher-Novelist.' In *Beyond Formalism: Literary Essays, 1958–1970.* New Haven: Yale UP, 1970.
Lawall, Sarah N. 'The Negative Consciousness: Maurice Blanchot.' In *Critics of Consciousness: The Existential Structures of Literature.* Cambridge: Harvard UP, 1968.
Lévinas, Emmanuel. *Sur Maurice Blanchot.* Montpellier: Fata Morgana, 1975.
Mehlman, Jeffrey. *Legacies: Of Antisemitism in France.* Minneapolis: U of Minnesota P, 1983.
– 'Orphée scripteur.' *Poétique* 20 (1974): 458–82.
Oxenhandler, Neal. 'Paradox and Negation in the Criticism of Maurice Blanchot.' *Symposium* 16 (1962).
Stoekl, Allan. 'Blanchot and the Silence of Specificity.' In *Politics, Mutilation, Writing: The Cases of Bataille, Blanchot, Leiris, and Ponge.* Minneapolis: U of Minnesota P, 1986.
Strauss, Walter A. *Descent and Return: The Orphic Theme in Modern Literature.* Cambridge: Harvard UP, 1971.
Syrotinski, Michael. 'How is Literature Possible?' In Denis Hollier, ed. *A New History of French Literature.* Cambridge: Harvard UP, 1989.
Ungar, Steven. 'Parts and Holes: Heraclitus, Nietzsche, Blanchot.' *Sub-Stance* 14 (1976): 126–41.

Bleich, David

(b. U.S.A., 1940–) Literary critic. David Bleich studied humanities and physics at the Massachusetts Institute of Technology for his B.S. and then English literature at New York University, where he gained his M.A. and Ph.D. After teaching for many years at the University of Indiana, he moved to the University of Rochester, where he is now teaching both in the Department of English and the Graduate School of Education and Human Development. Bleich has specialized in research on reader response to literature. (See *reader-response criticism.) As an undergraduate at NYU, Bleich studied with *Norman Holland and then later, as a graduate student, with Leon Edel, whom he credits with teaching him about 'subjectivity' from discussions on 'the subjective novel.' To describe his own approach to criticism, Bleich coined the term 'subjective criticism.' His theoretical approach grows out of the studies of Louise Rosenblatt (*Literature as Exploration* 1938), Simon Lesser (*Fiction and the Unconscious* 1957), as well as his independent readings in psychology and his four years of psychoanalytic therapy (1962–6).

Bleich works from the Romantic belief that the so-called objective world is in large part a construct of human perceptions and values. In *Subjective Criticism* (1978), he notes that what is commonly regarded as an objective literary work (out there in the world) comes into full being only when someone reads the words on the page and interprets the *text as *literature. For Bleich, readers compose the literary work as a response to their discrete psychological and social backgrounds.

To counter the belief that the literary work is an objective entity, Bleich maintains that readers need to become aware of their primary psychological responses to the text. To this end, he encourages readers to develop their initial responses through free association, a technique which parallels the Freudian exercise of free association used to unravel the meaning of a dream. (See *Freud, *psychoanalytic theory.) Once the reader has given a full subjective and associative response to the text, an interpretation of the work can then be offered. With this ordering of response and interpretation, readers use their psychological responses as the grounding for their interpretations. Also, readers can 'negotiate' their interpretations of a text with other readers to arrive at the meaning for their particular community of readers. For Bleich, however, this negotiated meaning of a text should not be thought of as an objective meaning, rather as knowledge about the community's feelings and values at a particular time and place.

In *The Double Perspective* (1988), Bleich widens his concerns to argue that knowledge demands a 'double perspective' if we are to appreciate both its objective and its subjective nature. In the past, such a double perspective seemed unnecessary, since people assumed that everyone belonged to a homogeneous society which investigated an objective world that was somehow set over and against the individual. The questioning by marginalized groups, such as blacks and women, has shown that knowledge can never be objective but always relates to a group interest. (See *feminist criticism, *black criticism, *margin.)

Opposing the tenets of the Derridean school of literary *deconstruction and modifying the insights of *Edmund Husserl, Bleich argues that it remains important to begin not with texts but with individual consciousness. (See also *Jacques Derrida.) He does not re-establish the ontic priority of the individual, the individual who pretends to spin the world out of his own subjectivity; instead, he proposes a view of intersubjectivity, a double perspective, in which the individual develops as a participant in the communality of human life.

Bleich's epistemological views also possess practical consequences for classroom teaching. Literacy for Bleich always remains literacy in one culture among many. To treat literacy as a trainable skill involves acquiescing to the logic of corporate business, which sees individuals as workers in, and consumers of, their world of values – that world being deemed objectively given. Bleich argues that the universities should make students aware of the relationship between differing language styles and the resulting constructions of reality. To achieve this awareness of the connection between subjectivity and objectivity, Bleich believes it essential to change the classroom: do away with grades and the hierarchical structure in which the teacher possesses authority and independent knowledge. The student must no longer treat the classroom as a preparation for a later objective world but must become aware of how group interaction creates different worlds.

Although most of Bleich's articles and books develop ideas of reader response, in 1984 he published *Utopia: The Psychology of a Cultural Fantasy*. Here Bleich posits a psychoanalytic model in which the work of art acts as a defence for a motivating fantasy. A revision of his earlier 1968 dissertation, *Utopia* investigates the relation of the utopian novel to the utopian fantasy, the child's desire to merge with the world or to possess total control over it, a desire which is later mobilized by undisciplined adolescent energy. In this work, one can see the origins of Bleich's belief that contemporary literature and teaching bases itself in the subjective character of all social forms.

RONALD B. HATCH

Primary Sources

Bleich, David. 'Academic Ideology and the Teaching of Writing.' In *Gender, Culture, Institutions, Feminism*. Ed. Debra Holdstein. New York: MLA, 1992.
– 'Do We Need Sacred Texts and Great Men?' In *(Inter)views: Cross-Disciplinary Perspectives on Rhetoric and Composition*. Ed. Gary Olson and Irene Gale. Carbondale: South Illinois P, 1991, 1–24.
– *The Double Perspective: Language, Literacy, and Social Relations*. New York: Oxford UP, 1988.
– 'Gender Interests in Reading and Language.' In *Gender and Reading: Essays on Readers, Texts, and Contexts*. Ed. Elizabeth Flynn and Patrocinio Schweickart. Baltimore: Johns Hopkins UP, 1986, 234–66.
– 'The Identity of Pedagogy and Research in the Study of Response to Literature.' In *Researching Response to Literature and the Teaching of Literature: Points of Departure*. Ed. Charles Cooper. Norwood, NJ: Ablex, 1985, 253–72.
– 'Negotiated Knowledge of Language and Literature.' In *American Critics at Work: Examinations of Contemporary Literature*. Ed. Victor Kramer. Troy, NY: Whitson, 1984, 226–50.
– *Readings and Feelings: An Introduction to Subjective Criticism*. Urbana, Ill.: National Council of Teachers of English, 1975.
– *Subjective Criticism*. Baltimore: Johns Hopkins UP, 1978.

– *Utopia: The Psychology of a Cultural Fantasy.* Ann Arbor, Mich.: UMI Research P, 1984.
– et al., eds. *Writing With: New Directions in Collaborative Teaching and Research.* Albany: State U of New York P, 1992.
Lesser, Simon. *Fiction and the Unconscious.* Boston: Beacon P, 1957.
Rosenblatt, Louise. *Literature as Exploration.* New York: D. Appleton-Century, 1938.

Secondary Sources

Cooper, Charles R., ed. *Researching Response to Literature and the Teaching of Literature: Points of Departure.* Norwood, NJ: Ablex, 1985.
Freund, Elizabeth. *The Return of the Reader.* London and New York: Methuen, 1987.
Suleiman, S.R., and I. Crosman, eds. *The Reader in the Text: Essays on Audience and Interpretation.* Princeton: Princeton UP, 1980.
Tompkins, Jane P. *Reader-Response Criticism: From Formalism to Post-Structuralism.* Baltimore: Johns Hopkins UP, 1980.

Bloom, Harold

(b. U.S.A., 1930–) Literary critic and critical theorist. After undergraduate studies at Cornell, Bloom continued his graduate work at Yale, earning his Ph.D. in 1955 with a dissertation on Shelley. Since his graduation he has taught at Yale, where he is now Sterling Professor of the Humanities. During his formative graduate years – years coinciding with the institutionalization of *New Criticism – Bloom saw New Critical ideals displace English Romanticism, and in particular Shelley, from the literary *canon. In such an atmosphere, his study of Shelley was controversial; this polemical and revisionist stance has from the outset inspired Bloom's writings on poetic influence, English Romanticism and the American Romantic tradition.

In his first study, *Shelley's Mythmaking* (1959), Bloom borrowed the theologian Martin Buber's distinction between I-Thou and I-It relationships – between visionary and alienated modes of perception – to celebrate Shelley's imagination and its mythopoeic, visionary creations. Bloom addressed the major Romantic poets in *The Visionary Company* (1961) and two years later focused on another champion of the creative imagination, William Blake, in *Blake's Apocalypse* (1963). The struggle of the Romantic imagination in its efforts to evade both solipsism and the seductions of nature constituted for Bloom a unique and heroic drama.

Noting the enduring presence of Romanticism as a dynamic and vital force, Bloom proceeded to revise conventional readings of literary history. Romanticism was not a brief, blinding light that had exhausted itself with Byron; it was transplanted to America, he maintained, through its influence on Emerson. It was reformulated, however, through a uniquely American matrix of concerns. According to Bloom the American Romantic tradition sought to herald not simply – like its English predecessor – a sense of revolutionary rebirth but an even more radical 'self-begetting.' In *Yeats* (1970) Bloom similarly extended the currency of Romanticism into the 20th century. The New Critics had long championed modernism as a corrective to the excesses of Romanticism; the mature Yeats had in particular – with his metrical virtuosity and chiselled, lapidary vocabulary – proven amenable to New Critical aesthetics. But by highlighting the Romanticism of Yeats, Bloom moved once more to consolidate the legacy of the visionary imagination as a living tradition.

Already latent in Bloom's early studies of the 'visionary company' was a concern with the psychic economy of the imagination; it was perhaps predictable that he would find psychoanalytical models more and more congenial. The important essay 'The Internalization of Quest Romance' (1968) in the 1971 collection *The Ringers in the Tower* directly engaged Freud, but it was not until *The Anxiety of Influence* (1973) that Bloom's interests crystallized in his very own revisionist psychoanalytic literary theory. (See *Sigmund Freud.) According to Freud, the son perceives the father as a dangerous rival; by translating this complex into literary theory, Bloom revolutionized the study of poetic influence. A powerful *anxiety of influence renders *literature the scene of an Oedipal struggle; the *ephebe*, or 'beginning poet,' manoeuvres to repress, through creative acts of misreading or *misprision, the crippling influence of powerful 'forefathers.' In particular, Bloom argued, the strategies of misprision could be reduced to an elaborate taxonomy or map of six 'revisionary ratios'; he classified these misreadings which resembled both Freudian defences and traditional rhetorical tropes *clinamen, tessera, kenosis, daemonisation, askesis,* and *apophrades.* Over the course of an important tetralogy, *The Anxiety of Influence, A Map of Misreading* (1975), *Kabbalah and Criticism* (1975), and *Poetry and Repression* (1976), Bloom consolidated and enriched this model with references to Gnosticism, Vico, *Nietzsche, Blake, and Emerson. Although the exotic terminology is largely muted, his study of Wallace Stevens, *The Poems of Our Climate* (1977), represents the culmination of this method, detailing Stevens' anxious engagement with the American and English Romantic traditions.

Bloom combines the *archetypal criticism of *Northrop Frye with a psychoanalytic approach to poetic influence; Frye's self-enclosed literary universe, a benign, cooperative realm in which literature refers only to itself, is invaded by themes of contestation. Bloom's work has been commended as an attempt to save literary history from the levelling and ahistorical formalisms of both New Criticism and *deconstruction. But because of his exclusive focus upon the *literariness* of literary history, Bloom has been challenged by Marxist or sociohistorical critics seeking to re-introduce extraliterary formations into literary study. (See *Marxist criticism). Although accused of exaggerating the powers of the imagination, of placing it in a transcendental space sheltered from historical contingency, Bloom's early studies, along with those of *Geoffrey Hartman, represented an advance upon the received accounts of Romanticism. Romanticism had been thought by many a response to an epistemological crisis: it was a struggle to heal the division between subject and object, self and nature opened up by the scepticism of British empiricism. (See *subject/object.) Bloom detected subtler and more sensitive strains in this response; he stressed the dangers posed by nature – as a kind of seductive distraction – to the creative imagination, while also recognizing the crippling solipsism always nestling within imaginative activity.

As a member in the late 1970s of the so-called Yale School of Deconstruction, Bloom was associated with *Paul de Man, Geoffrey Hartman, *Jacques Derrida, and *J. Hillis Miller. Indeed, Bloom's thesis that all reading amounted to *mis*-reading, to the inability to uncover an underlying, 'objective' meaning, was perfectly compatible with the deconstructive notion of the ungrounded, indeterminate *text. Through his typology of six 'revisionary ratios,' however, Bloom sought to delimit the free play or radical *indeterminacy of the signifier. Bloom has denied affiliations with both deconstruction and psychoanalytic criticism. His identification with any single critical school would be misleading; the act of reading is for Bloom always a highly personal and solitary undertaking. (See also theories of *play/freeplay, *psychoanalytic theory, *signified/signifier/signification.)

PAUL ENDO

Primary Sources

Bloom, Harold. *Agon: Towards a Theory of Revisionism*. New York: Oxford UP, 1982.
– *The Anxiety of Influence: A Theory of Poetry*. New York: Oxford UP, 1973.
– *Blake's Apocalypse: A Study in Poetic Argument*. Garden City, NY: Doubleday, 1963.
– *Kabbalah and Criticism*. New York: Seabury P, 1975.
– *A Map of Misreading*. New York: Oxford UP, 1975.
– *Poetry and Repression: Revisionism from Blake to Stevens*. New Haven: Yale UP, 1976.
– *The Ringers in the Tower: Studies in Romantic Tradition*. Chicago: U of Chicago P, 1971.
– *Shelley's Mythmaking*. New Haven: Yale UP, 1959.
– *The Visionary Company: A Reading of English Romantic Poetry*. Rev. ed. Ithaca: Cornell UP, 1971.
– *Wallace Stevens: The Poems of Our Climate*. Ithaca: Cornell UP, 1977.
– *Yeats*. New York: Oxford UP, 1970.

Secondary Sources

De Bolla, Peter. *Harold Bloom: Towards Historical Rhetorics*. London: Routledge, 1988.
Fite, David. *Harold Bloom: The Rhetoric of Romantic Vision*. Amherst: U of Massachusetts P, 1985.

Bodkin, Maud

(b. England, 1875–d. 1967) Scholar and critic. The daughter of a free-thinking doctor and of an active member of the Congregationalist church, Maud Bodkin once suggested that her life's work could be explained as an attempt to reconcile these opposing parental influences. Bodkin received her M.A. from the University College of Wales and was employed for 11 years as a lecturer in psychology at a teachers' training college in Cambridge. Failing in health, she took early retirement and dedicated herself to a study of the works of *Carl Gustav Jung. Though neither a trained psychoanalyst nor an academic critic, she was among the first to apply systematically the Jungian idea of the collective unconscious to the study of *literature. *Archetypal Patterns in Poetry* (1934) tests Jung's hypothesis that the emotional effects of literature are owing to its activation in the reader of 'primordial images' or archetypes, recognizable through the accumulations of racial memory. (See *archetype, *archetypal criticism.) Bodkin's critical method was both to explore subjective responses (her own and those of other readers and critics) to specific archetypal patterns in the works of classical and modern writers; and, in the second place, to compare versions of selected archetypes as they appear in various authors and cultural periods. Rather than regarding the artist's use of archetypal images as material upon which to exercise the techniques of psychoanalysis, Bodkin's intention in her first book was to supply specifically literary data to 'the philospher seeking to systematize the most general truths of existence' (327). Her later works, however, are more religious than literary in emphasis. (See *psychoanalytic theory.)

Bodkin's originality consists in the balanced and wide-ranging character of her investigations and her avoidance of the dogmas of academic psychology. Her references to *Benedetto Croce, *T.S. Eliot, Jessie L. Weston, Emile Durkheim, George Santayana, Samuel Alexander, *I.A. Richards, and *William Empson suggest that her strength as a critic lies in a well-informed eclecticism. She resembles several of these writers in her willingness to consider the symbolism of the Gospels within the context of ritual and mythology, but she is unusual for her time in applying the insights of psychology to questions of gender difference in literature and art. *Archetypal Patterns in Poetry* speculates about the presence in women writers' works of images of men 're-lated to the distinctive inner life of a woman in the same way as an image of woman appearing in poetry shows relation to the emotional life of man' (299). Both in the emphasis she places upon the literary responses of the individual reader and in her inquiry into gender images, Bodkin may be seen to anticipate some of the concerns of academic criticism after 1960.

Bodkin's work has received relatively little attention in either Britain or North America; an exception is Stanley Edgar Hyman, who admires her work for focusing 'not on the art

as a disguised fulfillment of repressed wishes, but on *how* a work of art is emotionally satisfying' (166). Walter Sutton regards her as 'an important channel' (176) for psychoanalytic criticism, and numbers Robert Penn Warren and *Leslie Fiedler among her American counterparts.

HILARY TURNER

Primary Sources

Bodkin, Maud. *Archetypal Patterns in Poetry: Psychological Studies of Imagination.* London: Oxford UP, 1934.
– 'Literary Criticism and the Study of the Unconscious.' *The Monist* 37 (1927): 445–68.
– 'Literature and the Individual Reader.' *Literature and Psychology* 10.2 (1960): 39–44.
– *The Quest for Salvation in an Ancient and a Modern Play.* London: Oxford UP, 1941.
– *Studies of Type-Images in Poetry, Religion, and Philosophy.* London and New York: Oxford UP, 1951.

Secondary Sources

Hyman, Stanley Edgar. *The Armed Vision: A Study in the Methods of Modern Literary Criticism.* New York: Knopf, 1948.
van Meurs, Jos. *Jungian Literary Criticism, 1920–1980: An Annotated Critical Bibliography of Works in English.* Metuchen, NJ.: Scarecrow, 1986.
Sutton, Walter. *Modern American Criticism.* Englewood Cliffs, NJ: Prentice-Hall, 1963.

Booth, Wayne C.

(b. U.S.A., 1921–) Rhetorician, formalist, ethicist, and philosopher of education. Wayne C. Booth received his B.A. from Brigham Young University (1944), and his M.A. (1947) and Ph.D. (1950) from the University of Chicago. He taught at Haverford and Earlham Colleges and, since 1962, at the University of Chicago, where he served until retirement as George M. Pullman Professor of English and Distinguished Service Professor. With Sheldon Sacks, Booth was one of the founding editors of *Critical Inquiry.* His critical interests are partly revealed by his contributions to that journal and by his membership on the boards of *Novel, Philosophy and Rhetoric, Scholia Satyrica, Rhetorica,* and *Philosophy and Literature.* Booth is a Fellow of the American Academy of Arts and Sciences. In 1982 he was president of the Modern Language Association.

Booth

A wide-ranging scholar, Booth's interests encompass neo-Aristotelian formalism, rhetoric, philosophy of education, and ethical criticism. (See *Neo-Aristotelian or Chicago School, *rhetorical criticism.) In graduate school he was a student of *R.S. Crane at the height of the Aristotelian movement at Chicago, as it was being defined by Crane, *Elder Olson, Richard McKeon, and other members of the Chicago faculty. A study of some of their major theoretical essays, collected and edited by R.S. Crane in *Critics and Criticism: Ancient and Modern* (1952) reveals the distinctions that existed between the Neo-Aristotelian school and the *New Criticism. Neo-Aristotelians objected to the narrowness of the New Criticism's attempt to discuss form in *literature mainly through a study of language, including its ambiguities, an approach which can be seen to have led the way to the relative scepticism of such contemporary movements as *deconstruction.

Booth's critical work is influenced from first to last by the Aristotelian idea that the power of a literary work results from the wholeness with which all its parts – not just language but language constructs such as narrative manner, character and plot – work together to achieve an effect. However, from his earliest work in *The Rhetoric of Fiction* (1961) Booth is restive with any formalism which seems to ignore the rhetorical effects of fiction upon the reader and thus the world outside the book. *The Rhetoric of Fiction* has become a much-translated international classic in the study of narration and point of view in fiction and contains terms now so universally employed that they have been absorbed into the language of fiction studies, usually without citation: for instance, the 'implied author' as distinguished from the *narrator and the actual author, the reliable and 'unreliable narrator' (the one whose point of view and judgments of events cannot be trusted by the reader).

In the augmented new edition of the book published in 1983, Booth acknowledges that *The Rhetoric of Fiction* is concerned not only with the narrative manner employed by authors to address and influence readers but also with the influence of fiction itself conceived as a rhetorical act. Author and reader are caused to meet on crucial moral grounds that reveal the one and influence the other. Thus the 'implied author,' a literary construct who arises from what the actual author does, is of pro-

found interest not merely to a discussion of form but also to the potential influence of the work on an '*implied reader' (a term employed by *Wolfgang Iser and quite surely derived from Booth's 'implied author'). Along this path, Booth moves quite naturally from form and rhetoric to the ethics of fiction as it affects real life ('Would I want the implied author of this book for a friend?').

In their chronology Booth's seemingly extremely varied writings are thus perceptible as a continuity. Formalism, rhetoric of narrative manner, *irony and *metaphor, the rhetoric by which we are led to assent to dogma, the metacritical plea for critical *pluralism, the collected essays on the vocation of a teacher (not modes of instruction but the calling of the teacher and what that implies), and the crowning work on the ethics of fiction – all are related by a thread of moral concern (see *metacriticism). In Booth's view, formalism needs some attention to its rhetorical effects (*The Rhetoric of Fiction*); rhetoric should look to its potential gaps in communication and evaluation ('Metaphor as Rhetoric' 1978 and *A Rhetoric of Irony* 1974); there are dangers to the human spirit not only in 'unstable irony but in the stability of dogma' (*Modern Dogma and the Rhetoric of Assent* 1974); the war of the critics needs to recognize the limitations of each critical school and to undertake a more fruitful *discourse among the differences (*Critical Understanding* 1979). It follows readily for a humanist like Booth that one must pay attention not only to abstract critical studies but also to the potential victims of our failures in those studies: students in the classrooms of teachers who have not understood their own rhetorical effect (*The Vocation of a Teacher* 1989). Finally, to care about students of literature is to care about the company they keep, about the ethical effects of what they read (*The Company We Keep* 1988).

Booth's contribution to contemporary criticism may be seen as a career-long demonstration that a social and ethical concern for the context of a literary work may be enhanced by a formalist study of the internal workings of the *text in its various literary devices. His practice implies the critical pluralism he preaches: the improvement of each pair of critical eyeglasses by looking also through other and different ones, thus advancing pluralism to an ethical principle.

MARY DOYLE SPRINGER

Primary Sources

Booth, Wayne. *The Company We Keep: An Ethics of Fiction*. Berkeley: U of California P, 1988.
– *Critical Understanding: The Powers and Limits of Pluralism*. Chicago: U of Chicago P, 1979.
– 'Freedom of Interpretation: Bakhtin and the Challenge of Feminist Criticism.' *Critical Inquiry* 9 (Sept 1982): 45–76.
– 'Metaphor as Rhetoric: The Problem of Evaluation.' *Critical Inquiry* 5 (Autumn 1978): 49–72. Repr. in *On Metaphor*. Ed. Sheldon Sacks. Chicago: U of Chicago P, 1979.
– *Modern Dogma and the Rhetoric of Assent*. Notre Dame: Notre Dame UP, 1974.
– *Now Don't Try to Reason with Me: Essays and Ironies for a Credulous Age*. Chicago: U of Chicago P, 1970.
– *The Rhetoric of Fiction*. Chicago: U of Chicago P, 1961. Augmented ed., 1983.
– *A Rhetoric of Irony*. Chicago: U of Chicago P, 1974.
– *The Vocation of a Teacher: Rhetorical Occasions*. Chicago: U of Chicago P, 1989.
– 'The Way I Loved George Eliot': Friendship with Books as a Neglected Critical Metaphor.' *Kenyon Review*, new series 2 (Spring 1981): 4–27.

Bourdieu, Pierre Félix

(b. France, 1930–) Sociologist. Pierre Bourdieu studied at the Faculté de lettres de Paris and at the prestigious Ecole Normale Supérieure before passing the *agrégation* and working, from 1955 to 1958, as a professor of philosophy at a *lycée* in Moulins. From 1958 to 1960, during some of the most critical moments of the Algerian war, he was an assistant at the Faculté de lettres d'Alger. In 1960 he took another assistantship, at the Faculté de lettres de Paris, staying only one year before obtaining a position as *maître de conférences* in Lille. He became director of studies at the Ecole Pratique des Hautes Etudes in Paris in 1964 and has held the chair in sociology at the Collège de France since 1981.

Since the mid-1960s Bourdieu has been a polemic figure. Though trained as a philosopher, from the start Bourdieu distanced himself from traditional philosophical *discourse, both in the style of his writing and in the orientation of his research. He undertook ethnosociological studies of the Basque country and Algeria, publishing *Sociologie de l'Algéria* in 1961, *Travail et travailleurs en Algérie* in 1963 (abridged as *Algérie 60* in 1977), and *Esquisse*

d'une théorie de la pratique, précédée de trois études d'éthnologie kabyle in 1972. However, it was *Les Héritiers*, written in collaboration with the sociologist J.C. Passeron and published in 1964, that first earned Bourdieu his notoriety and set the tone for his future work. He and Passeron scandalized France by proposing that, contrary to official doctrine, the French school system was first of all an instrument not for reducing economic and cultural differences but for reinforcing class barriers and maintaining a status quo that excludes all but a small élite from positions of political and economic power.

Most of Bourdieu's subsequent work has focused on the same question: the manner in which the dominant group in (French) society employs culture to maintain its exclusivity and power; and on the problem of method in the social sciences. His work reveals the influence of Marxist theory and the works of the sociologists Emile Durkheim, Marcel Mauss, Max Weber, and Karl Mannheim. (See *Marxist criticism, *sociocriticism.) Staunchly antipositivist, Bourdieu nonetheless insists upon the scientificity of sociology. Equally critical of phenomenology, he has nonetheless adapted concepts from *Edmund Husserl, *Martin Heidegger and *Maurice Merleau-Ponty, focusing his research on the pre-objective contact between subject and object (Bourdieu and Wacquant 27) and cautioning that 'the humblest workings of science are only worth the theoretical and epistemological awareness that accompanies them' ('Postface' 167) and that a 'reflection on the instruments of analysis is ... a condition of any scientific understanding of the object' (*Distinction* 103). (See *subject/object, *phenomenological criticism.) Attempting to go beyond objectivist theories, which 'identify social classes ... with discrete groups' and subjectivist theories, which 'reduce "the social order" to a sort of collective classing ... where the classers class themselves and others' (563), Bourdieu proposes a genetic and reflexive sociology and a theory of practice. Sociological phenomena can only be examined and explained as elements belonging to and occurring in specific temporal and class – both economic and cultural – contexts. They exist and can only be understood *relationally*, that is, as they occur in diachronic and synchronic relation to other sociological phenomena – including the examiner's own position. Notions of good taste in clothes, for example, are a product of the social position of the person who holds the beliefs or, more exactly, who practices a certain way of dressing, and of their relation to other beliefs and practices that are consciously or unconsciously aspired to or rejected as strategies in a struggle for recognition and acceptance in a particular place and role in society; these notions and practices can only be understood if all such relations are taken into account.

Bourdieu's most important book of 'aesthetics' to date is *La Distinction* (1979). Subtitled *Critique sociale du jugement* [*A Social Critique of Taste*] and including as its final chapter a 'vulgar critique' of Kantian aesthetics, *La Distinction* immediately drew criticism from the intelligentsia because it does not discuss art in the usual sense (Châtelet, Deguy). Rather, Bourdieu proposes that 'in opposition to the ideology of charisma, which maintains that taste in cultural matters is a gift of nature, scientific observation shows that cultural needs are the product of education' (*Distinction* i).

Breaking with traditional distinctions between art and non-art, Bourdieu applies to contemporary society the concept of *habitus* developed by Erwin Panovsky: 'This *habitus* could be defined, by analogy with Noam Chomsky's "generative grammar," as a system of interiorized schemata that allow all the thoughts, perceptions and actions of a culture, and these only' ('Postface' 152). (See *Chomsky.) Society is divided chiefly by two types of capital: economic and cultural. What is generally considered art and good taste is primarily the *habitus* of those who have had the economic and cultural capital, and hence power, long enough to define their way of life and their tastes as legitimate: the distinction between legitimate and illegitimate (or popular) culture is tacitly accepted even by those who are excluded from legitimate culture and is one of the principal means used by the dominant classes to maintain their exclusivity and economic and cultural dominance.

Whatever their political orientations, by their *habitus* artists belong to the dominant class, though to a dominated fraction of this class; they are materially dependent upon those with economic capital and are politically powerless ('Disposition' 1357). Challenges to artistic conventions do not show the relations and the struggles behind notions of art, culture and taste but simply oppose 'a dominated culture ... to a dominant culture' and 'take on thus the

role, for all eternity, of a cultural avant-garde which, by its very existence, contributes to the functioning of the cultural game' (*Distinction* 280n). All cultural habits within the dominant class are part of this game, not of demystification but of struggles for legitimacy – acceptance by those above in the social hierarchy – and distinction – demarcation from those below, especially from the dominated class, which is not even in the running. (See also *game theory.)

Paradoxically, but in concordance with his thesis that not only artistic but also intellectual activity is inseparable from struggles for legitimacy, Bourdieu's merciless demystification of cultural habits has earned him a prominent position in French intellectual circles – a fact his critics have noted on several occasions, as they have also noted that, though his writing is consciously antiphilosophical, Bourdieu's books demand the kind of intellectual training available almost exclusively to those whose exclusivity he attacks. Similarly, scrupulously 'scientific,' Bourdieu restricts his research and his discussions to French society at a specific moment in its development, a fact which has limited its appeal outside France, except for sociologists. Nevertheless, and though many philosophers and critics have categorically refused to accept his theses – as he has refused theirs – Bourdieu's work has made a mark on French intellectual and political life. Both at home and abroad, *La Distinction* has become a 'classic' of contemporary sociology, influencing sociologists, such as those publishing *Theory, Culture and Society* in Britain, and literary critics like *Terry Eagleton, whose *Ideology of the Aesthetic* owes much to Bourdieu.

NICOLA VULPE

Primary Sources

Bourdieu, Pierre. 'Champ du pouvoir, champ intellectuel et habitus de classe.' *Scolies* 1971: 7–26.
– *Ce que parler veut dire: L'Économie des échanges linguistiques*. Paris: Fayard, 1982.
– 'Disposition esthétique et compétence artistique.' *Les Temps modernes* 26.295–7 (1971): 1345–78.
– *La Distinction: Critique sociale du jugement*. Minuit, 1979. *Distinction: A Social Critique of the Judgement of Taste*. Trans. R. Nice. Cambridge, Mass.: Harvard UP, 1984, 1987.
– *Esquisse d'une théorie de la pratique, précédée de trois études d'ethnologie kabyle*. Geneva: Droz, 1972. *Outline of a Theory of Practice*. Cambridge: Cambridge UP, 1977.

- *Homo academicus.* Paris: Minuit, 1984. *Homo Academicus.* Trans. P. Collier. Stanford: Stanford UP, 1988.
- *Leçon sur la leçon.* Paris: Minuit, 1982.
- *La Noblesse d'Etat.* Paris: Minuit, 1989.
- *L'Ontologie politique de Martin Heidegger.* Paris: Minuit, 1988. *Die politische Ontologie Martin Heideggers.* Frankfurt/M: Syndicat, 1970. *La Ontologia politica de Martin Heidegger.* Trans. C. de la Mezsa. Barcelona: Paidos, 1991.
- 'Postface'. In *Architecture gothique et pensée scolastique.* By Erwin Panovsky. Paris: Minuit, 1967, 135–67.
- *Questions de sociologie.* Paris: Minuit, 1980.
- *Le Sens pratique.* Paris: Minuit, 1980.
- *Sociologie de l'Algérie.* Paris: PUF, 1961. *The Algerians.* Boston: Beacon P, 1962.
- and J-C. Passeron. *Les Etudiants et leurs études.* Paris: Mouton, 1964.
- and J-C. Passeron. *Les Héritiers.* Paris: Minuit, 1964. *The Inheritors.* Chicago: U of Chicago P, 1979.
- and J-C. Passeron. *La Reproduction.* Paris: Minuit, 1970. 2nd ed. 1971.
- and A. Sayard. *Le Déracinement.* Paris: Minuit, 1964.
- A. Darbel and D. Schnapper. *L'Amour de l'art: Les Musées d'art européens et leur public.* Paris: Minuit, 1966.
- J-C. Passeron and J-C. Chamboredon. *Le Métier de sociologue.* Paris: Mouton/Bordas, 1968.
- L. Boltanski, R. Castel and J-C. Chamboredon. *Un art moyen: Les Usages sociaux de la photographie.* Paris: Minuit, 1965.
- A. Darbel, R. Castel and J-C. Chamboredon. *Travail et travailleurs en Algérie.* Paris: Mouton, 1963. Abr.: *Algérie 60.* Paris: Minuit, 1977. *Algeria 1960.* Cambridge: Cambridge UP, 1979.
- and Loïc J.D. Wacquant. *Réponses.* Paris: Seuil, 1992. Includes a complete bibliography of Bourdieu's publications to date, and an extensive bibliography of studies of his work.

Secondary Sources

Calhoun, Craig J. 'Putting the Sociologist in the Sociology of Culture: The Self-Reflexive Scholarship of Pierre Bourdieu and Raymond Williams.' *Contemporary Sociology* 19.4 (1990): 500–5.
Châtelet, François. 'Où est-il question de l'art?' *Le Monde,* 12 Oct. 1979.
Deguy, Michel. 'La Haine de la philosophie.' *Le Temps de la réflexion.* Paris: Gallimard, 1980.
Eagleton, Terry. *The Ideology of the Aesthetic.* Oxford: Basil Blackwell, 1990.
Harker, Richard K., et al, eds. *An Introduction to the Work of Pierre Bourdieu: The Practice of Theory.* London: Macmillan, 1990.
Honneth, Axel, et al. 'The Struggle for Symbolic Order: An Interview with Pierre Bourdieu.'

Theory, Culture and Society 3 (1986): 35–51.
Jameson, Fredric. *Postmodernism or The Cultural Logic of Late Capitalism.* Durham: Duke UP, 1990.
Lash, Scott. 'Modernization and Postmodernization in the Work of Pierre Bourdieu.' In *Sociology of Postmodernism.* London: Routledge, 1990, 237–65.

Bremond, Claude

(b. France, 1929–) Literary theorist. Claude Bremond has undergraduate and postgraduate degrees in philosophy, and was granted a doctorate in sociology in 1972. He began his career at the Ecole des Hautes Etudes en Sciences Sociales in 1960, successively holding the positions of project head in 1962, *maître assistant* in 1973, and finally *directeur d'études* in 1980. His first works, written in the the 1960s in the context of *structuralism and semiology, dealt with the logic of the narrative; these formally continued *Vladimir Propp's studies. Since 1980, however, Bremond's studies have dealt with content and themes. (See *semiotics, *theme.)

Bremond's research on the logic of the narrative has extended over ten years. His first article, 'Le Message narratif' (1964), is a concise critique of Propp's *Morphology of the Folktale* (1928). In it, Bremond states that the fundamental invariants of the narrative have yet to be discovered. By expanding the field of study to all narratives rather than limiting himself, as Propp did, to the Russian tale, Bremond laid the foundation for a semiology independent of the story, separate and apart from the *discourse that uses it. (See *story/plot.)

While this article develops the outline of a logical model of the narrative, 'La Logique des possibles narratifs' (1966), presents Bremond's more developed model. Still in search of the laws of the narrated world, Bremond conserves Propp's basic unit: the function which, when applied to actions and events, creates a story as a set of sequences. All sequences are composed of three functions: the first introduces a potentiality, the second carries out this potentiality as an event, and the last ends the process in the form of the result achieved. A model of the logical possibilities of the story is then constructed, based on the primary sequences of improvement and degradation from which stem numerous other sequences that act as the means for realizing the primary sequence.

In *Logique du récit* (1973), Bremond presents a kind of treatise on the principal narrative roles, seeking to explain the entire network of options available to the narrator in order that he or she may, at some point in the narrative, be able to continue the story already begun. Still seeking to trace a logical and universal structure of the narrative, he proposes a model that is much less complex and less linear than his earlier one, based on a new distinction – that of actors and those acted upon as fundamental narrative roles.

Today, *narratology is still divided into two branches. On the one hand are the studies of narrative content which do not take into consideration their relation to discourse; on the other are works that postulate the impossibility of studying these contents outside of their discursive modalization. *Gérard Genette is undoubtedly the proponent of the latter: a narratology of narrative discourse. To the study of the former, narrative content or what Genette calls 'thematic' or 'deep' narratology, Bremond has made the greatest contribution. Opposing the postulates of *A.J. Greimas' school of thought, Bremond rejects the theory that the surface or discursive elements are subordinated by the elements of the deep structure and, indeed, proposes the opposite.

Since the 1980s, Bremond's interests have shifted toward a study of content and, in particular, toward the methodological problems posed by the conceptualization of themes. His most recent work shows that in order to attain meaning a combination of both the synchronic study of the system of themes and motives and the diachronic study of their evolution is needed. The 1988 issue of the periodical *Communications* entitled 'Variations sur le thème' shows this line of thinking. Moreover, this approach is also applied to the great narrative traditions that passed from the Orient to the West during the medieval era through *The Thousand and One Nights*. (See also *variation.)

Bremond's contribution to the logic of the narrative remains of great importance still today. His work has raised Propp's cultural or generic models to a higher level of abstraction and generalization. However, it is undoubtedly the great power of the model that has diverted Bremond from his proper subject, narrative, and led other researchers, such as *Gerald Prince and Mieke Bal, to redefine narrative itself on new foundations.

PIERRE HÉBERT

Primary Sources

Bremond, Claude. 'La Logique des possibles narratifs.' *Communications* 8 (1966): 60–76.
– *Logique du récit.* Paris: Seuil, 1973.
– 'Le Message narratif.' *Communications* 4 (1964): 4–32.
– and Thomas G. Pavel. 'La Fin d'un anathème.' *Communications* 47 (1988): 209–20.
– and Thomas G. Pavel, eds. 'Variations sur le thème.' *Communications* 47 (1988).

Brooks, Cleanth

(b. U.S.A., 1906–) Literary critic. Educated at Vanderbilt, Tulane and Oxford, Brooks began teaching at Louisiana State University in 1932, moving to Yale University in 1947, where he held the Gray professorship, and later became Emeritus Professor of Rhetoric. He received numerous honorary degrees from universities in England and the United States, served as cultural attaché at the American Embassy in London, and continued to be an active lecturer and scholar well into his eighties.

Described as 'the quintessential New Critic' (Robert Con Davis), Brooks incorporated some of the critical concepts of Coleridge, *T.S. Eliot, *William Empson, John Crowe Ransom, and others into a critical methodology: exegesis through close reading. Brooks was concerned with the literary work as a self-contained entity. The structure was regarded as a tension of relationships of image and language, independent of such externals as the author's intention or the effect it might have on the reader. With *René Wellek, Robert Penn Warren and *W.K. Wimsatt, Jr., Brooks made Yale an active centre for the practice of criticism in the immediate post–Second World War period, integrating as critical practice some of the precepts drawn from those creative figures of the two decades preceding that have subsequently become known as the Modernists. As an academically centred activity, *New Criticism represented a new direction, displacing historical and textual scholarship as the reigning activity of literature departments in American universities and paving the way for the acceptance of critical theory as an academic discipline in the 1960s and after.

In 1935, when most university-centred publications were philological in nature, Brooks and Robert Penn Warren founded and co-edited *The Southern Review* at Louisiana State University. Both critical and creative in its concerns, it was a literary magazine that purposefully reflected the views of the so-called Southern Fugitives or Agrarians which had originated earlier at Vanderbilt University where Brooks had studied under John Crowe Ransom. Traditional and conservative in their social views, the Agrarians as a group took a primarily aesthetic approach in their criticism. They were concerned with linguisitic analysis less from a historical interest than from a concern with the nuances of meanings and the implications of the language of a given work. In this respect, Brooks represented the movement in his conception of the work as a poem by nature, regardless of its content.

Unlike others of his group, such as Ransom, Warren and Allen Tate, Brooks was not a writer of original poetry or fiction; however, his major work in the 1930s and 1940s became an immensely influential body of applied criticism, much of it in the form of textbooks that routinely applied the methodology of New Criticism to each of the literary genres. (See *genre criticism.) Books such as *Understanding Poetry* (1938), *Understanding Fiction* (1942) and *Understanding Drama* (1948) changed the way an entire generation of serious readers came to look at English *literature from the Renaissance to the mid-20th century. (Although Brooks had co-authors in each case, Robert Penn Warren for the first two, and Robert B. Heilman for the third, the controlling voice is that of Brooks'.)

Brooks' theory is abstract in nature but precise in terminology and application. His basic conception of the proper critical approach is expressed in the Introduction to *A Shaping Joy* (1971), where he tells the reader that there are three areas of emphasis: 'criticism focused on the reader, on the writing, and on the writer.' The first stresses the reader's own reactions to a poem and gives us an impressionistic criticism. The second 'views the work with an eye to what it may reveal about its creator and about the culture which produced him and it.' These are the two fallacies that W.K. Wimsatt entitled, respectively, 'the affective fallacy' and the 'intentional fallacy.' Brooks rejects both of them. The critic who concerns himself with the writing itself, however, stresses 'the meaning of the work as developed through its form and structure.' Here stands the New Critic, in Brooks' view. Some of the key words that are

consistently applied in Brooks' theory are '*paradox,' '*irony' and 'tension.' (R.P. Blackmur has added to that list the words 'ambiguity,' 'attitude,' 'tone,' and 'belief' as significant elements in Brooks' criticism.)

While the effect of a work on any particular reader is rejected by Brooks as capricious and unrelated to the intrinsic character of a poem, careful analytical reading itself is at the core of his technique. Ransom, whose 1941 book *The New Criticism* provided a name for this group of like-minded critics, characterized Brooks as 'our best living reader' in a compliment that is virtually synonymous with the approach. The living nature of language accessible to the expert reader is very different from that uncovered in casual reading. (For some sceptics the very approach seems to subordinate emotional evocation in favour of an intellectual form that is too rarified to represent a common value.) 'The Language of Paradox,' the introductory chapter in his *The Well -Wrought Urn* (1942), describes the poem's ability to hold contradictory ideas, images or feelings in meaningful balance. The relationships of paradox, the balance of contradictions, represents a tension which correspondingly achieves the irony that Brooks regards as central to the meaning of a poem. Having little to do with the popular term, Brooks' irony is that positive charge of meaning that comes from the quality and co-existence of apparently opposing elements achieving simultaneous validity. Such reconciliation comes about without the discarding of either contradictory view. It follows that absolute or specific meaning is not possible (or desirable), for it relates the poem to an external value, a limited contingency, while the poem – as poem – must be a self-contained unit, integral and coherent, made up of its parts in relation to each other. All of this leads to structure, the totality of the multiple relationships of metaphor, image and language. Thus, structure in its multiform identity is the poem. Perhaps inevitably, though inaccurately, this has sometimes led to Brooks being labelled as a formalist.

Influenced in part by *I.A. Richards' distinction between scientific and emotive language, Brooks identified the presence of paradox as the signal element of poetry, since the poem is built on metaphor and fully creates itself through connotations and extended meanings carefully placed in relationship to achieve their complex but integral totality. Thus there is a crucial 'language of poetry.' Conversely, there is, too, what Brooks calls the 'heresy of paraphrase': a poem is never in its living quality represented by any prose statement that paraphrases it, since logically that statement in itself has no need of any poetic element to transmit the information that it represents. Accordingly, the poem is properly regarded as an aesthetic complex, the extended reverberation of interrelationships of meaning that are realized in the process of close reading, the elaboration of which comes about as exegesis.

Given his view of poetry as autonomous, Brooks sees the rediscovery of meaning through close reading as applicable to the poetry of any age; exegesis results in the revitalization and recovery of the past. He has followed T.S. Eliot in the belief that a distinct intellectual tradition lives in the poetry of Western culture (*Modern Poetry and the Tradition* 1942). On the whole, his applied criticism has been of considerable influence with respect to the poetry of the Metaphysicals and such 20th-century figures as Yeats and Eliot, writers whose work can be convincingly interpreted structurally and intellectually. The correspondence between two such apparently dissimilar poets as Donne and Milton has been established by Brooks through applying similar reading techniques to each and finding similar paradox and balance in their language. The importance of image prevails in such comparisons and reinforces Brooks' rejection of historical detail as relevant.

On the other hand, his criticism of the Augustans and Romantics as writers tied to extraliterary concerns has invited heavy attack from critics such as *R.S. Crane and others who see Brooks and the New Critics generally as exclusionary. William Empson, whose ambiguities fit well into Brooks' own critical techniques, sees Brooks as affirming successful technique rather than testing it, since – Empson feels – Brooks does not have a sufficiently defined value system. Another criticism made against Brooks is that his critical parameters are made to order for certain kinds of writing but not for others. Although Brooks clearly refers to 'the poem' as an artistic structure, a criticism that was quickly applied to him was that the techniques of New Criticism were inappropriate to prose fiction. Perhaps in reaction, Brooks as early as 1942 turned his attention to modern fiction and, in books such as *The Hidden God* (1963) and *A Shaping Joy*

(1971), explored the art of prose writers from Poe and *Henry James up through Hemingway and Faulkner. In his later writings Brooks himself has brought in much material that might be considered ancillary to the autonomous poem. To do him justice, Brooks has long protested that every reader must bring an educated consciousness to the task of criticism, a view that lets in at least a glint of both 'the intentional fallacy' and 'the affective fallacy,' those two capital sins to the New Criticism.

From the early 1960s on, Brooks has, in fact, moved farther into prose fiction, particularly the writings of William Faulkner. Deeply responsive to the cultural setting of the southern novelist's Mississippi, Brooks' two-volume study of Faulkner's work, *William Faulkner: The Yoknapatawpha Country* (1963) and *William Faulkner: To Yoknapatawpha and Beyond* (1974) was created, as were most of Brooks' volumes, of chapters that first were crafted as individual studies, reflecting his purposeful concern with a narrow question.

Since the 1960s and the rapid growth of particular theoretical schools of literary criticism in an academic setting, New Criticism – and Cleanth Brooks in particular – have been under sustained attack for real and alleged indifference to social relevance, historicism and psychology, as well as for belief in a non-subjective meaning at the core of each successful poem. Nonetheless, the critical writings of Brooks remain seminal and it seems evident that his modes of explication have become a permanent part of the literary heritage.

ROBERT G. COLLINS

Primary Sources

Brooks, Cleanth. *The Hidden God: Studies in Hemingway, Faulkner, Yeats, Eliot and Warren.* New Haven: Yale UP, 1963.
– *The Language of Poetry.* Princeton: Princeton UP, 1942.
– *Modern Poetry and the Tradition.* Chapel Hill: U of North Carolina P, 1939.
– *The Poetry of Tension.* St. John's, Nfld.: Memorial UP, 1972.
– *A Shaping Joy: Studies in the Writer's Craft.* London: Methuen, 1971.
– *The Well Wrought Urn.* New York: Harcourt, Brace and World, 1947.
– *William Faulkner: The Yoknapatawpha Country.* New Haven: Yale UP, 1963.
– *William Faulkner: Towards Yoknapatawpha and Beyond.* New Haven: Yale UP, 1974.

- and R.B. Heilman. *Understanding Drama*. New York: H. Holt, 1948.
- and R.P. Warren. *Understanding Fiction*. New York: F.S. Crofts, 1943.
- and R.P. Warren. *Understanding Poetry*. New York: Holt, Rinehart and Winston, 1938.
- and W.K. Wimsatt, Jr. *Literary Criticism: A Short History*. New York: Alfred A. Knopf, 1957.

Secondary Sources

Blackmur, R.P. *New Criticism in the United States*. New York: Ridgeway Books, 1959.
Crane, R.S., ed. *Critics and Criticism: Ancient and Modern*. Chicago: U of Chicago P, 1952.
Graff, Gerald. *Poetic Statement and Critical Dogma*. Chicago: U of Chicago P, 1970.
Pulos, C.E. *New Critics and the Language of Poetry*. U of Nebraska Studies, n.s. 19. Lincoln: U of Nebraska P, 1958.
Ransom, John Crowe. *The New Criticism*. Norfolk, Conn.: New Directions, 1941.
Rubin, Louis D., and Robert D. Jacobs, eds. *Southern Renascence: The Literature of the Modern South*. Baltimore: Johns Hopkins UP, 1953.
Simpson, Lewis P., ed. *The Possibilities of Order: Cleanth Brooks and His Work*. Baton Rouge: Louisiana State UP, 1976.
Sutton, Walter. *Modern American Criticism*. Englewood Cliffs, NJ: Prentice-Hall, 1963.

Burke, Kenneth Duva

(b. U.S.A., 1897–) Literary theorist and critic. Burke was a student at Ohio State University (1916–17) and at Columbia University the following year. Early in his career, he served as music critic for *The Dial* and *The Nation*. He has taught literary criticism and theory at the New School for Social Research, the University of Chicago, Bennington College, Princeton University, Kenyon College, Indiana University, and Pennsylvania State University. In 1929 he received The Dial Award for distinguished service to American letters and he has been a Fellow at the Princeton Institute for Advanced Study and the Stanford Center for Advanced Study in the Behavioral Sciences. He was elected to the National Institute of Arts and Letters in 1946 and won the National Medal for Literature in 1981.

Though his ideas have made an impact on sociology, rhetoric, discourse theory, and speech act theory, Burke's influence is most strongly felt in the field of literary criticism and theory. (See *sociocriticism, *rhetorical criticism, *discourse analysis theory.) Never an endorser of the *New Criticism, a school which flourished in the U.S.A. from the 1940s to the 1970s, Burke persistently argues against the New Critical tendency to conceive of the *text as an autonomous object. Throughout his writings, Burke refuses to essentialize literary *discourse by making it a unique kind of language and is always attuned to the dialectical relationship between literary productions and their sociohistorical contexts. (See *essentialism.)

That 'the ultimate metaphor for discussing the universe and man's relation to it must be the poetic or dramatic metaphor' (*Permanence and Change* 263) is the animating idea of Burke's criticism and theory. According to Burke, 'dramatism' is a method of linguistic and conceptual analysis that treats language and thought primarily as modes of action rather than means of conveying information. All verbal acts are to be considered as symbolic action and dramatism is built about the systematic view of language and *literature as species of symbolic action. Poetry, then, which in Burke's extended sense comprises 'any work of critical or imaginative cast' (*The Philosophy of Literary Form* 1), 'is to be considered as "symbolic action,"' and symbolic action is to be considered as having at least three levels.

First, on the level of dream ('the unconscious or subconscious factors in a poem' [*The Philosophy of Literary Form* 5]), symbolic action is symptomatic action and plays a compensatory or therapeutic role. It has an author-regarding element and is expressive either directly or indirectly of his or her psyche.

Second, on the level of prayer ('the communicative functions of a poem' [*The Philosophy of Literary Form* 5]), symbolic action has a rhetorical dimension or audience-regarding element and induces attitudes and actions. Rhetoric deals with the arousal and fulfilment of expectations. Form, Burke argues, is 'the psychology of the audience ... the creation of an appetite in the mind of the auditor, and the adequate satisfying of that appetite' (*Counter-Statement* 31).

Third, on the level of chart ('the realistic sizing-up of situations that is sometimes explicit, sometimes implicit, in poetic strategies' [*The Philosophy of Literary Form* 6]), symbolic action has a reality-regarding element. 'The Symbol is the verbal parallel to a pattern of experience' (*Counter-Statement* 152) and has realistic content insofar as it encompasses the situation it represents. The encompassment is necessarily imperfect because human beings have no non-symbolic or non-linguistic access to the structure of reality.

In later writings, Burke elaborates the dream/prayer/chart triad into a more sophisticated scheme: grammar (which corresponds to chart), rhetoric (which corresponds to prayer) and symbolic (which corresponds to dream).

Burke has a grammar in the Aristotelian sense of a set of verbal terms or categories by means of which a discourse can be analysed. His dramatistic grammar centres on observations of this sort: for there to be an act, there must be an agent. Similarly, there must be a scene in which the agent acts. To act in a scene, the agent must employ some means or agency and there cannot be an act, in the full sense of the term, unless there is a purpose. These five terms – act, agent, scene, agency, purpose – Burke labels the dramatistic pentad. His aim in *A Grammar of Motives* is to show how the functions which they designate operate in the imputing of motives.

The grammatical is a series of blanks to be filled out when one imputes motive to action. Any statement of motives involves the dramatistic pentad of act (what was done), agent (who did the act and under what subjective conditions), scene (the environment in which the act took place, the extrinsic factors that determined it), agency (how the act was done, what instruments were used), and purpose (why the act was done, its ultimate motive or final cause). The grammatical blanks offer opportunities for '*dis*-position and *trans*-position' (*A Grammar of Motives* 402) and dialectic explores the combinatory possibilities. Different philosophical systems emphasize different parts of the pentad: realism emphasizes act, idealism emphasizes agent, materialism emphasizes scene, pragmatism emphasizes agency, and mysticism emphasizes purpose.

What Burke was doing in 1945 has a decidedly contemporary ring, especially his view of the subject or agent as the function of a system. As a method of discourse analysis, *A Grammar of Motives* is protostructuralist to the extent that structure in all kinds of texts can be accounted for by five key terms. It is antistructuralist, however, to the extent that Burke recognizes that every grammar of motives implies a rhetoric of motives. Since every dialectic transposes and disposes the terms of the dramatistic pentad in a uniquely constitutive fashion and with a uniquely exhortative attitude, every dialectic implies a rhetoric of action. Though a Marxist might see the historical and economic scene as determinative of the acts and attitudes that agents engage in, his 'scenic' grammar implies a program of social change that urges the strategic deployment of linguistic and political agency for the purpose or revolution. (See *structuralism, *Marxist criticism.) 'The dramatistic view of language, in terms of symbolic action,' Burke writes, 'is exercised about the necessarily *suasive* nature of even the most unemotional scientific nomenclatures' (*Language as Symbolic Action* 45).

In contrast to grammar's 'exploration of verbal forms, Burke sees rhetoric's function as the overcoming of estrangement. Human beings are alienated from each other by differences of ethnic and social background, level of education, race, sex, age, economic class. When language is used to overcome these differences, to foster cooperation and establish community, we are in the realm of rhetoric – and since all language use to varying degrees involves this end, all language use has a rhetorical dimension' (Crusius, 'A Case for Kenneth Burke's Dialectic and Rhetoric' 24).

To the classical notion of rhetoric as persuasion, Burke adds the dramatistic notion of rhetoric as identification, by which he means the inducement to identify one's own substance with something larger and more comprehensive. He also adds unconscious factors of appeal, especially as they pertain to the subliminal and suasive function of imagery. As Crusius points out, for Burke dialectic and rhetoric 'are counterparts because to identify is to share substance with something or someone, the study of substance (or motivational essence) being the affair of dialectic [or grammar], the study of tactics for achieving identification (or consubstantiality) being the affair of rhetoric' (31). Although rhetoric involves the formation of identity and the establishment and maintenance of affiliation and community, it is predicated upon division and difference. If identification and consubstantiality were really possible, there would be no need to induce them.

The symbolic, which Burke associates with poetics per se, is grounded in the proposition that 'a work is composed of implicit or explicit "equations" (assumptions of "what equals what"), in any work considered as one particular structure of terms, or symbol system' (*The Philosophy of Literary Form* 8). Along with identifications or equations (what equals what), there are also dissociations or agons (what versus what). And this apposition and opposition of terms unfolds in a certain way, making for dramatic resolution and dialectical transformation (what leads to what). The symbolic, then, should take at least three factors into account: associative clusters, dramatic alignments and narrative progressions.

All told, then, there is symbolic action as designation (the grammatical), as communication (the rhetorical) and as expression (the symbolical). For Burke, however, the various levels of symbolic action are interdependent. 'Since the work of art is a synthesis, summing up a myriad of social and personal factors at once, an analysis of it necessarily radiates in all directions at once' (*Attitudes Toward History* 199). This is why he admits that his 'general approach to the poem might be called "pragmatic" in this sense: it assumes that a poem's structure is to be described most accurately by thinking always of the poem's function. It assumes that we can make the most relevant observations about its design by considering the poem as the embodiment of this act' (*The Philosophy of Literary Form* 89–90).

A case in point is Burke's 'The Rhetoric of Hitler's Battle,' an essay in which he brings his critical arsenal to bear on *Mein Kampf*. Burke sees Nazism with its projective device of the scapegoat ('the "curative" unification by a fictitious devil-function' [*The Philosophy of Literary Form* 218]) and its ritual of rebirth (the compensatory doctrine of inborn superiority whereby Aryans are born again into the purity of their ancestral blood) as the materialization and perversion of a religious pattern. He examines Hitler's use of sexual symbolism, of the imagery of blood, pollution and disease, and of the rhetoric of identification and dissociation, focusing on the dialectical relationship between the literary strategy and the extra-literary situation. *Mein Kampf* provides 'a non-economic interpretation of economic ills' (*The Philosophy of Literary Form* 204). The cause of Germany's malaise, which was in reality a product of the Versailles Treaty and the Weimar Republic, Hitler derives from his racial theory. This interpretation appeals because it supplies 'a "world-view" for people who had previously seen the world but piecemeal' and is thus 'the *bad* filling of a good need' (*The*

Philosophy of Literary Form 218). Rejecting both the formalism of an intrinsic approach, which regards literature as a self-enclosed universe of discourse, and the determinism of an extrinsic approach, which regards literature as reducible to some other frame of reference such as Freudianism or Marxism, Burke demonstrates how the formal unfolding and internal coherence of a work – its iterative imagery, recurrent symbolism, associative clusters, dramatic alignments, and narrative progressions – are part of its rhetorical force. The intrinsic and extrinsic aspects are mutually dependent. (See *Sigmund Freud.)

Burke's insistence on the necessity of an integrative point of view is an attempt to bring literary criticism and theory back into the mainstream of social life and his essay on Hitler gives us an idea of what that sort of criticism involves. Words, for Burke, are agents of power; they are value-laden, ideologically motivated, and morally and emotionally weighted instruments of persuasion, purpose and representation. As a form of symbolic action in the world, literature is inextricably linked to society – it is not a privileged form of language that exists in its own sphere. An interdisciplinary maverick and unrepentant synthesist working in a world of professional specialists, Burke was for the greater part of his career relegated to the margins of academic scholarship but is now beginning to receive widespread recognition.

GREIG HENDERSON

Primary Sources

Burke, Kenneth. *Attitudes Toward History*. Berkeley/Los Angeles: U of California P, 1937.
– *Counter-Statement*. Berkeley/Los Angeles: U of California P, 1931.
– *Dramatism and Development*. Barre, Mass.: Clark UP, 1972.
– *A Grammar of Motives*. Berkeley/Los Angeles: U of California P, 1945.
– *Language as Symbolic Action. Essays on Life, Literature and Method*. Berkeley/Los Angeles: U of California P, 1966.
– *On Symbols and Society*. Ed. Joseph R. Gusfield. Chicago: U of Chicago P, 1989.
– *Permanence and Change: An Anatomy of Purpose*. Berkeley/Los Angeles: U of California P, 1935.
– *Perspectives by Incongruity*. Ed. Stanley Edgar Hyman. Bloomington: Indiana UP, 1964.
– *The Philosophy of Literary Form: Studies in Symbolic Action*. Berkeley/Los Angeles: U of California P, 1941.

- *A Rhetoric of Motives*. Berkeley/Los Angeles: U of California P, 1950.
- *The Rhetoric of Religion: Studies in Logology*. Berkeley/Los Angeles: U of California P, 1961.
- *Terms for Order*. Ed. Stanley Edgar Hyman. Bloomington: Indiana UP, 1964.

Secondary Sources

Booth, Wayne. *Critical Understanding: The Powers and Limits of Pluralism*. Chicago/London: U of Chicago P, 1979.

Brown, Merle Elliot. *Kenneth Burke*. Minneapolis: U of Minnesota P, 1969.

Crusius, Timothy. 'A Case for Kenneth Burke's Dialectic and Rhetoric.' *Philosophy and Rhetoric* 19.1 (1986): 23–37.

Frank, Armin Paul. *Kenneth Burke*. New York: Twayne Publishers, 1969.

Heath, Robert. *Realism and Relativism: A Perspective on Kenneth Burke*. Macon, Ga.: Mercer UP, 1986.

Henderson, Greig. *Kenneth Burke: Literature and Language as Symbolic Action*. Athens/London: U of Georgia P, 1988.

The Legacy of Kenneth Burke. Ed. Herbert W. Simons and Trevor Melia, 1989. Madison: U of Wisconsin P, 1989.

Lentricchia, Frank. *Criticism and Social Change*. Chicago: U of Chicago P, 1983.

Rueckert, William H. *Kenneth Burke and the Drama of Human Relations*. 2nd. ed. Berkeley/Los Angeles: U of California P, 1982.

– ed. *Critical Responses to Kenneth Burke, 1924–1966*. Minneapolis: U of Minnesota P, 1969.

Southwell, Samuel B. *Kenneth Burke and Martin Heidegger – With a Note Against Deconstruction*. Gainesville: U of Florida P, 1987.

White, Hayden, and Margaret Brose. *Representing Kenneth Burke*. Baltimore and London: Johns Hopkins UP, 1982.

Cassirer, Ernst Alfred

(b. Silesia, 1874–d. 1945) Philosopher and historian of philosophy. Ernst Cassirer was identified with the so-called Marburg School of neo-Kantian philosophy as a student of Hermann Cohen, and he became the most prominent interpreter and exponent of Kantian critical philosophy in the 20th century. He was professor of philosophy and later rector of Hamburg University before, as a Jew, he was forced to leave Germany with his family in 1933. What he called the 'odyssey' of his later life took him from Oxford, England (1933–5), to Göteborg, Sweden (1935–41), to Yale University (1941–4); he died as a visiting professor at Columbia University in New York. The hallmarks of his writings are his range of ideas and scope of reference. For students of *literature he is valuable as a historian of ideas and theorist of symbolic forms.

Cassirer made his mark with the first two of four comprehensive volumes on the history of scientific thought (*The Problem of Knowledge* 1906–7); the subject of science dominates his early writings, but as Cassirer describes earlier philosophers' views of concept formation in the sciences here and in *Substance and Function* (1910), he anticipates his own distinctive contribution to the study of human culture. The orientation to science which evolves in the modern period offers an insight into the forms of culture: the objective worlds of science and culture can be known only as they are differentiated and ordered by a priori principles.

This argument is first explored with respect to German intellectual history in *Freiheit und Form* [*Freedom and Form* 1916; pub. 1961] and it receives its fullest exposition in Cassirer's magnum opus, the three published volumes of *The Philosophy of Symbolic Forms* (1923–9). Of the principal works written just before and during Cassirer's years of exile, the most notable and influential focus on historical periods and figures representative of this argument: *The Philosophy of the Enlightenment* (1932), *The Platonic Renaissance in England* (1932), the fourth volume of *The Problem of Knowledge* (written about 1940), *The Logic of the Humanities* (1942), and *The Myth of the State* (1942). A short compendium of Cassirer's philosophy, *An Essay on Man*, written and first published in English in 1944, has been translated into at least eight languages. The large corpus of Cassirer's writings (over 30 books and over 100 articles and reviews) continues to grow through collections of essays, such as *Symbol, Myth, and Culture* (1979) and new translations, such as the English version of his Kant biography (1981). A current project, the publication of the fourth volume of *The Philosophy of Symbolic Forms* from Cassirer's manuscript notes, will expand his reputation among students of literature, as it will elaborate his philosophy of art.

Two distinct traditions in the critical reception of Cassirer's work reflect the pattern of his own career: German or, more broadly, Continental commentary has focused on his neo-Kantian epistemology, while in the Anglo-American context he is regarded mainly as a historian of ideas. Literary theorists indebted to Cassirer incorporate various aspects of his philosophy. *Language and Myth* (1925), translated in 1946 by Susanne Langer, was influential on mytho-critical approaches to literary texts in the 1950s and 1960s. (See *myth, *archetypal criticism.) For his way of writing history, Cassirer has also been credited as a protostructuralist, and his theory of language is related to *C.S. Pierce's by contemporary semioticians. (See *structuralism, *semiotics.) His interpretive bias is contextual and holistic and, although he most often uses the analysis of literary texts to display their philosophical content, he also demonstrates the value of genre-concepts in literary studies. (See *genre criticism.)

WALTER EGGERS

Primary Sources

Cassirer, Ernst. *An Essay on Man: An Introduction to a Philosophy of Human Culture.* New Haven: Yale UP, 1944.
– *Freiheit und Form.* Darmstadt: Wissenschaftliche Buchgesellschaft, 1961.
– *Language and Myth.* 1925. Trans. Susanne K. Langer. New York: Harper and Brothers, 1946.
– *The Logic of the Humanities.* 1942. Trans. Clarence Smith Howe. New Haven: Yale UP, 1961.
– *The Myth of the State.* New Haven: Yale UP, 1946.
– *The Philosophy of the Enlightenment.* 1932. Trans. Fritz C.A. Koelln and James P. Pettegrove. Princeton: Princeton UP, 1951.
– *The Philosophy of Symbolic Forms.* 1923–9. Trans. Ralph Manheim. 3 vols. New Haven: Yale UP, 1953, 1955, 1957.
– *The Platonic Renaissance in England.* 1932. Trans. J.P. Pettegrove. Austin: Texas UP, 1953.
– *The Problem of Knowledge: Philosophy, Science, and History since Hegel.* 1902–40. Trans. from the German manuscript. William H. Woglom and Charles W. Hendel. New Haven: Yale UP, 1950.
– *Substance and Function* (1910) *and Einstein's Theory of Relativity* (1921). Trans. William Curtis Swabey and Marie Collins Swabey. Chicago: The Open Court, 1923.
– *Symbol, Myth, and Culture: Essays and Lectures of Ernst Cassirer 1935–1945.* Ed. Donald Phillip Verene. New Haven: Yale UP, 1979.

Secondary Sources

Eggers, Walter, and Sigrid Mayer. *Ernst Cassirer: An Annotated Bibliography.* New York: Garland, 1988.
Hamburg, Carl H. *Symbol and Reality: Studies in the Philosophy of Ernst Cassirer.* The Hague: Martinus Nijhoff, 1956.

Itzkoff, Seymour W. *Ernst Cassirer: Scientific Knowledge and the Concept of Man.* Notre Dame: Notre Dame UP, 1971.
Krois, John Michael. *Cassirer: Symbolic Forms and History.* New Haven: Yale UP, 1987.
Lipton, David R. *Ernst Cassirer: The Dilemma of a Liberal Intellectual in Germany 1914–1933.* Toronto: U of Toronto P, 1978.
Schilpp, Paul Arthur, ed. *The Philosophy of Ernst Cassirer.* Evanston, Ill.: The Library of Living Philosophers, 1949.

Chomsky, Noam Avram

(b. U.S.A., 1928–) Linguist, political writer and activist. The son of the Hebrew scholar and historical linguist William Chomsky, Noam Chomsky studied mathematics, philosophy and linguistics, and specialized in the last discipline, working under the direction of the American distributionalist Zelig S. Harris at the University of Pennsylvania. He wrote a Master's thesis called 'Morphophonemics of Modern Hebrew,' and began publishing articles on the logical structure of language in 1951. His Ph.D. thesis, 'Transformational Analysis,' is contained in *The Logical Structure of Linguistic Theory,* written in 1955 on the basis of research done at the Society of Fellows at Harvard University and published in part in 1975. Chomsky joined the Massachusetts Institute of Technology in 1955 and has been Ferrari Ward Professor of Modern Languages and Linguistics since 1966 and Institute Professor since 1976.

Chomsky is the founder of transformational generative grammar, the major trend in linguistics in the second half of this century. His proposals, first published in *Syntactic Structures* (1957), revolutionized the development of linguistics. His work has been profoundly influential in psychology, philosophy and cognitive science, and has had repercussions in mathematics, anthropology and literary theory. He has also achieved eminence as a political writer and activist, vigorously opposing the foreign policies of the United States and aspects of the American social and political system tied to the military-industrial complex.

According to Chomsky, the goals of a generative grammar are (1) to render explicit the implicit system of knowledge, or competence, of an adult speaker or hearer and (2) to account for the growth and attainment of that

Chomsky

knowledge with an explanatory theory where general principles are viewed as properties of a biologically given innate structure or Universal Grammar (the Innateness Hypothesis). (See *competence/performance.) From such a perspective, linguistics can be considered a branch of cognitive psychology within the rationalist tradition. Early 20th-century linguistics was concerned with cataloguing the facts of language. By contrast, Chomsky proposes to concentrate on the mental properties which underlie human linguistic abilities. Linguistic competence constitutes an autonomous system whose properties are not derivable from the society, culture or personality of the speaker or hearer, and includes the ability to produce and understand novel utterances, and to recognize ambiguities and deviations. Competence is one of the many components that interact to determine performance, that is, the actual use of language in concrete situations.

In developing the above position, Chomsky employed ideas already voiced by the rationalist philosophers and grammarians of the 17th and 18th centuries. He provided incisive criticisms of behaviouristic, empiricist and taxonomic theories of language dominant in the European structuralist schools (*Prague School, glossomatics) and among the American structuralists, also known as distributionalists – followers of Leonard Bloomfield (1887–1949) in the second quarter of the century. He was instrumental in reviving rationalism, as opposed to logical empiricism (W.V. Quine in philosophy) and behaviourism (B.F. Skinner in psychology), and in reopening the debate on innate ideas in philosophy and psychology alike.

An explicit characterization of linguistic competence is a formalized theory or a generative grammar. Such a grammar comprises a syntactic component which is central, a semantic component which assigns meaning to the structures generated – that is, explicitly enumerated – by the syntax, and a phonological component providing phonetic interpretation. The syntactic component has two different levels of representation known as 'deep structure' and 'surface structure,' and these are related by the transformational rules. Phrase-structure rules specify the hierarchical structure of the sentences of a language and generate deep structures in conjunction with the lexicon, which contains information about

lexical items. The deep-structure phrase-markers are mapped by the transformations onto surface-structure phrase-markers. Speaking informally, the surface structure corresponding to 'What book will John think that we bought?' is derived from a deep structure resembling 'John will think that we bought what book' by the application of two transformations: (1) 'What book' is moved to the first position of the sentence in surface structure, and (2) 'will' is moved to the second position. The two transformations are subcases of the more general rule 'Move alpha,' with properties defined by the innate faculty of language or Universal Grammar.

Since its inception, generative grammar has gone through several phases of development and elaboration. The first stage corresponds to *Syntactic Structures* (1957). The second phase, the Standard Theory or the Aspects-model is presented in *Aspects of the Theory of Syntax* (1965). The revised or Extended Standard Theory resulted from debates on the connection between the levels of representation in syntax and the semantic component, as partially reflected in *Studies on Semantics in Generative Grammar* (1972). The more recent Government and Binding or GB model, also known as the Principles-and-Parameters approach, begins with *Lectures on Government and Binding* (1981).

Chomskyan linguistics held out the promise of a collaboration between linguists and literary scholars in analysing the grammatical base of a literary work in its historical context. More specifically, generative grammar has influenced literary criticism in stylistics and poetics, as reflected in the studies collected by D.C. Freeman in *Linguistics and Literary Style* (1970) and in *Essays in Modern Stylistics* (1981). The principles of generative phonology are applied to metrics in M. Halle and S.J. Keyser's *English Stress* (1971). Also, *Jonathan Culler has extended Chomsky's notion of competence to 'literary competence': the mastery of literary conventions required (in addition to linguistic competence) for an understanding of *literature.

From a philosophical perspective, alternative views to Chomsky's proposals can be found in the essays by H. Putman, W.V. Quine and J. Searle in *On Noam Chomsky: Critical Essays*, ed. Harman (1974). *Language and Learning: The Debate between Jean Piaget and Noam Chomsky,* ed. Piattelli-Palmarini (1980) reflects psychological positions alternative to those of Chomsky. (See also *discourse analysis theory, *structuralism, *speech act theory.)

MARIA-LUISA RIVERO

Primary Sources

Chomsky, N. *Aspects of the Theory of Syntax.* Cambridge, Mass.: MIT P, 1965.
– *Barriers.* Cambridge, Mass.: MIT P, 1986.
– *Cartesian Linguistics.* The Hague: Mouton, 1966.
– *Current Issues in Linguistic Theory.* The Hague: Mouton, 1964.
– *Essays on Form and Interpretation.* Amsterdam: North-Holland, 1977.
– *Knowledge of Language: Its Nature, Origin, and Use.* New York: Praeger, 1986.
– *Language and Mind.* Enl. ed. New York: Harcourt Brace Jovanovich, 1972.
– *Language and Problems of Knowledge: The Nicaraguan Lectures.* Cambridge, Mass.: MIT P, 1988.
– *Lectures on Government and Binding.* Dordrecht: Foris, 1981.
– *The Logical Structure of Linguistic Theory.* New York: Plenum, 1975.
– *Reflections on Language.* London: Fontana, 1976.
– *Rules and Representations.* Oxford: Blackwell, 1980.
– *Some Concepts and Consequences of the Theory of Government and Binding.* Cambridge, Mass.: MIT P, 1982.
– *Studies on Semantics in Generative Grammar.* The Hague: Mouton, 1972.
– *Syntactic Structures.* The Hague: Mouton, 1957.
– *Topics in the Theory of Generative Grammar.* The Hague: Mouton, 1966.

Secondary Sources

Cook, V. *Chomsky's Universal Grammar.* London: Blackwell, 1988.
Culler, Jonathan. *Structuralist Poetics.* Ithaca: Cornell UP, 1975.
D'Agostino, F. *Chomsky's System of Ideas.* Oxford: Oxford UP, 1985.
Freeman, D.C., ed. *Essays in Modern Stylistics.* New York: Methuen, 1981.
– *Linguistics and Literary Style.* New York: Holt, Rinehart and Winston, 1970.
Greene, J. *Psycholinguistics: Chomsky and Psychology.* London: Penguin, 1972.
Halle, M., and S.J. Keyser. *English Stress: Its Form, Its Growth, and Its Role in Verse.* New York: Harper and Row, 1971.
Harman, G. ed. *On Noam Chomsky: Critical Essays.* New York: Doubleday, 1974.
Lyons, J. *Chomsky.* Rev. ed. by Frank Kermode. London: Fontana, 1977.

Newmeyer, F.J. *Linguistic Theory in America: the First Quarter-Century of Transformational Generative Grammar.* New York: Academic P, 1980.
Piattelli-Palmarini, M., ed. *Language and Learning: The Debate between Jean Piaget and Noam Chomsky.* London: Routledge and Kegan Paul, 1980.
Radford, A. *Transformational Grammar: A First Course.* Cambridge: Cambridge UP, 1988.
Smith, N.V., and D. Wilson. *Modern Linguistics: The Results of Chomsky's Revolution.* Harmondsworth: Penguin, 1979.

Cixous, Hélène

(b. Algeria, 1937–) Feminist theorist, literary critic, novelist, playwright. In 1959, Hélène Cixous passed the *agrégation* in English, beginning her teaching career in the French university system as an *assistante* at the University of Bordeaux (1962), then *maître assistante* at the Sorbonne (1965–7) and *maître de conférence* at Nanterre (1967). In 1968 she was awarded the Doctorat d'Etat ès lettres for *L'Exil de James Joyce ou l'art du remplacement*, a poststructuralist study of Joyce and the decentring of subjectivity. (See *poststructuralism, *centre/decentre.) In 1969, she won the Prix Médicis for her fiction. She also started the influential literary theory review *Poétique* (with *Tzvetan Todorov and *Gérard Genette). Named *chargé de mission* to found the experimental Université de Paris VIII at Vincennes, now at Saint-Denis, on its establishment in the autumn of 1968 she was appointed Professor of English Literature. Here in 1974 Cixous founded the Centre de recherches en études féminines of which she is director. Her graduate research seminar is offered at the Collège Internationale de Philosophie. (See also *feminist criticism, French.)

To make a distinction between Cixous' 'creative' and 'critical' texts is problematic in the light of her insistence on the interrelatedness of reading and writing. Engagement with a *text involves one in the 'process of creation' ('Conversations' 148), encounter with the other and self-creation reaching a 'poetically beyond' (ibid. 145). (See *self/other.) Her aim, like that of *Jacques Derrida, is to blur boundaries, undo limits between genres and between subjects, not by pushing logic to its limits in the demonstrative movement of philosophy, but by responding to the call of an other, poetically exploring the in-between that is the one-within-the-other. (See *subject/object, *genre criticism.)

While a number of Cixous' most recent 'theoretical' texts are explicit exercises in reading attentively, such as *Reading with Clarice Lispector* (1990), many of her 'creative' texts are meditations on or 'interventions' in the text of another writer/theorist. Her play *Portrait de Dora* (1976), stages *Sigmund Freud's analytic narrative in order to expose his own counter-transference. Her 'fiction' *Illa* (1980), resonates with *Martin Heidegger's 'il y a,' 'es gibt' ('De la scène' 22), as rewritten by Derrida (*il y a cent blancs*), and raises questions of giving, investing and divesting in relation to writing and to the Orphic *myth so as to displace its social contract predicated on the sight and death of a woman. Such works are related to Cixous' attempts to write the '*présent absolu*' through the fragment or 'infinite detail' (*Reading* 227). This aim situates Cixous in the 'heretic hermeneutic' of the Rabbinic tradition which, on the basis of 'principles of multiple meaning and endless interpretability,' maintains that interpretation and text are inseparable, not hierarchized according to degrees of 'originality' (Handelman xiv). (See *hermeneutics, *metacriticism.)

The narrative of a woman 'coming to writing' with its displacement of death and mourning in a revolutionary (Utopian) going 'beyond' is closely associated with her first fictional work, *Dedans* (1969). Here Cixous attempts to escape from her dead, hence idealized, father, an effort which continues to be part of the trajectory of her writing as she articulates it in 'De la scène de l'Inconscient à la scène de l'Histoire' ['From the Scene of the Unconscious to the Scene of History' 1990; trans. 1989]. Informed by the Oedipal myth, the scene of writing for Cixous is an attempt to go beyond the absent Father, to escape from the Law, the Symbolic. (See *imaginary/symbolic/real, *Name-of-the-Father.) Rather than remembering, writing entails a movement of getting beyond the ego in a dispossession through loss, mourning, an encounter with the undescribable, the radically other, a reciprocal pouring out as a gift to those others who make us strangers to ourself ('De la scène' 23–4). Rewriting the Hegelian *Aufhebung*, with its dialectics of appropriation and specularization, Cixous, unlike *Simone de Beauvoir, aims not for transcendence of the feminine and equality

with men but for the exploration of the possibilities of difference. The attention she accords the other subverts the Hegelian model of subjectivity, desire, knowledge, where the other is mastered by the subject. Writing is always writing 'from' not to a point of synthesis: from something given by the other (*Coming to Writing* 43), moving away from 'Death, our double mother, through writing' (ibid. 38), writing as 'search,' in the fullness of life's 'terrible power of invention' (ibid. 41). These are qualities she responds to in the texts she admires and reads 'critically': Shakespeare, Joyce, Kafka, Tsvetaeva, Kleist, Mandelshtam, and Lispector. Many are Jewish writers: the figure of 'juifemme' ('De la scène' 27) frames Cixous' concern with what she calls the 'modern tragedy' of banishment, exclusion and heterogeneity ('A Propos de *Manne*' 220). Conscious of the contradiction in exile, she wants it to be productive and focuses on the going beyond entailed in the symbolic, verbal assumption of loss. This involves a shift in focus in the Nietzschean paradigm from the orgies of dismemberment and suffering of the son to Demeter's joy in beginnings. (See *Nietzsche.)

Unlike *Luce Irigaray, who uses *irony to expose the effect of the sacrifical social contract, or *Julia Kristeva, who analyses the aberrant subjectivities produced when women are forced into the contract against their will, Cixous explores the possibilities for transformation this breach opens. This 'denationalization' is a 'deterritorialization' like Kafka's '*littérature mineure*,' the invention of a singular or 'nomadic' writing forged in the exile's condition of multiple languages (Deleuze). Her theory of translation as dialogic encounter recalls that of German Romanticism (Berman) and of *Mikhail Bakhtin's theory of *heteroglossia. (See theories of *translation, *polyphony/dialogism.) It is this narrative of 'coming to writing' through the heterogeneity of her 'mother tongue' that informs Cixous' feminist theoretical/autobiographical texts of the 1970s in both their 'jewessness' ('jewoman'; *La Jeune née* 101) and their '*jouissance*' (orgasmic pleasure, textual freeplay; ibid. 90). It also shapes her reading of James Joyce, whose writing, she shows, in the shadow of Thoth's *Book of the Dead*, involves a disintegration of the subject which he goes beyond to make of language his 'reality.' There are, nonetheless, for Cixous, different modes (genres) of interrelating reading and writing – the 'critical' work more attentive to the text of the other than is the creative – which have to do with their different work on time.

Like Irigaray's, Cixous' theoretical contribution is a strategy and ethics of *symptomatic reading. However, her mode of reading is not that of ventriloquism, of quoting in a new context – displacement through repetition – but of inundation, of overwhelming a fragmentary quotation in the flow of her quasi-automatic writing or improvisational performance – of displacement through dissolution, of modulation. Her constant strategy is to work upon the signifier, making it 'vibrate' or slip from one phoneme to a homophone, developing a web of meanings through sound rather than semantics ('A Propos de *Manne*' 220), 'Soundsense' (*Coming to Writing* 58). '*Voler*,' writing as 'stealing,' making signifiers 'fly' in new contexts (ibid. 46). (See *signified/signifier/signification.)

Cixous wishes to expose the workings, and to move beyond the logic, of the proper, the principle of identity and *mimesis in the order of the Selfsame, which has limited the concept of difference in European thought exclusively to gendered difference, restricted to the maternal, which is figured as castration and death. This critical/theoretical work may be divided into three moments: Cixous' poststructuralist readings of English and German classics, her 'feminist' critiques of the Symbolic with its Law and retentive libidinal economy, and the readings of Lispector.

Cixous' critical narrative of escape through exile and reinvention in languages structures her first book, *L'Exil de James Joyce ou l'art du déplacement* [*The Exile of James Joyce* 1968; trans. 1972]. Here Cixous delineates the textual unconscious in an approach that stresses the affinity between Joyce's work and the theory of *textuality and the decentred subject emerging as poststructuralism in Paris. There is no *metalanguage, no application of theory to Joyce's text. Rather the text reads the theory and is read by it at the same time. Within Joyce criticism, Cixous innovates. Instead of explicating Joyce's texts in light of the earlier 'realistic' *Dubliners*, she confronts their unreadability to look at the textual mechanisms of infinite productivity in light of the *deconstruction of representation in *Finnegan's Wake*.

Prénoms de personne (1974) is an anagram of *père* as *per*, *pré* that dismembers the paternal in a proliferation of first names. Such multiplying of the subject is undermined by the polysemy of '*personne*' as nobody, as well as somebody. The title outlines Cixous' critical approach to reading as the process of loss of one's own name, the divisibility of the subject, and the merging of the I/you, as she engages in dialogue with texts from her personal *canon: Freud, Kleist, Joyce, Hoffman, Poe. Cixous like many other poststructuralists challenges the reigning paradigm of the subject and desire in the Hegelian master/slave dialectic (appropriation by the master and closure [death] to the slave other) in favour of a dispersed and mobile subjectivity, organized by the drives of the unconscious that produce transformation. Cixous also critiques Freud and *Jacques Lacan on the subject of desire born of lack, veil, separation, and death: she sees fiction (phantasm) as 'an action, having an efficacy' (Conley 16), opening new possibilities for life. In particular, she is concerned with elaborating an economy of exchange, of abundance, of limitlessness, as space of opening, possibility, change. (See *desire/lack.)

Cixous began writing of symbolic exchange and libidinal economies, of a need in contemporary society for an economy of dissolution of the subject, of the *subversion of property, of the *propre*, law, logic, order, meaning. *Literature in an economy of *dépense* (expenditure) or loss would connect with the subversion of the German Romantics, Cixous writes, to destroy the bastions of 'logocentrism and idealism, theology, all supports of society, the structure of political and of subjective economy, the pillars of property,' the entire 're-pressive machine' (*Prénoms* 10). (See *logo-centrism.) Passion is political, the political is libidinal. In adapting this general deconstructive program, however, Cixous makes a distinction between masculine and feminine libidinal economies, the latter characterized as economies of loss, of contradiction and limitlessness because of the political constraints that have socialized and metaphorized the feminine as lack. This difference foregrounds the *paradox of feminist deconstruction: the decentring of the Subject has a different meaning and political effect for those who have never been positioned as subject in mastery, who are always already other.

The oscillation between deferral and affirmation is a contradiction Cixous makes productive especially in her autobiographical feminist texts of the 1970s. Here, the valorization of laughter and the irrational as an economy of subversion and transformation receives its most extended development in what has become known as *'écriture féminine'* or 'writing the body' (Jones) for its work upon the improper (the excessive body) as *trace and the maternal metaphor in the institutions of philosophy and literature. Cixous herself uses the terminology *'écriture dite féminine'* ('writing said to be feminine': *Limonade* 147, 148) to describe her writing *from* the body: 'Life becomes text starting out from my body. I am already text. History, love, violence, time, work, desire inscribe it in my body' (*Coming to Writing* 52). It is a contingency of a materially specific instance of enunciation. (See *énonciation/énoncé.*) Such traces of bodily inscription are frequent in autobiographical texts such as 'Coming to Writing' in which she refers to writing as menstrual blood or as mother's milk. While these signifiers have most frequently been read by critics within a network of biological signifiers, they should also be read within a network of textual signifiers, as Cixous suggests, for they are reworked quotations of Symbolist poets (ibid. 52). Concretized in 'Coming to Writing' as women giving birth to themselves in writing, images of white ink echo their use in *La Jeune née* [*The Newly Born Woman* 1975; trans. 1986], in which Cixous exposes the work of the maternal metaphor in Symbolist poetics through her puns. These are also allusions to Derrida's account of metaphor effaced but active within a text. Foregrounding or 'disseminating' the metaphor, as Cixous does, is 'blanching' (whitening). Through the self-reflexive deployment of the maternal metaphor, Cixous raises the question whether the literal can be divorced from the figurative, the sensible from the intelligible, the proper from the improper. The metaphor is contaminated by the referent of the female body. Indeed, the metaphor is not a metaphor, but a metonymy. (See *metonymy/metaphor.*) Like Irigaray's, Cixous' exploration of a different libidinal economy is staged through work on the axis of contiguity, metonymy, not that of substitution or metaphor (Binhammer). This decipherable libidinal economy can be read in the texts of a male or a female, of Shakespeare or Lispector. In a historical moment when the masculine is the sole reigning *power over discourse, Cixous aims to subvert its *authority by putting the feminine into circulation, what has been called 'gynesis' (Jardine). (See *gynesis.*)

This theoretical aim is articulated in Cixous' work of the 1970s in different phases. 'Sorties,' her section of *La Jeune née* which includes much of 'Le Rire de la Méduse' ['The Laugh of the Medusa' 1975; trans. 1976] and 'Le Sexe ou la tête?' ['Castration or Decapitation?' 1976; trans. 1981], developed from Hegel and Bataille to focus on the moments of rupture, of break-out as the title 'Out and Out: Attacks/Ways Out/Forays' suggests. Beyond *phallocentrism, where women are constrained between Medusa and the abyss, she writes into the unknown, writing herself away from woman as object of desire, inventing the feminine future where subjectivity would be reciprocal desire without the exclusion or closure objectifying an other. (See *closure/disclosure.*)

La Venue à l'écriture [*Coming to Writing* 1977; trans. 1991] develops the work on the maternal metaphor in an autobiographical text to expose an original difference at work in her 'mother tongue,' *'ma lalemande'* (22), an interlanguage of German crossed with French. This narrative unfolds the story of the one who, known as *'das Kind,'* of neutral gender, tries unsuccessfully to make herself into 'a proper woman' in French according to the principle of non-contradiction. She is unable to do so because of the split, the foreignness of her relation to the French language, always used fraudulently since she had no 'ownership,' no 'mastery' over it. Throwing herself into *'languelait'* (English, milk tongue) complicates the attempt to develop an 'object-language' by placing her at the 'intersection of languages.' Becoming the search, she risks all, moving from the abyss, through laughter, to music beyond.

The engagement with the other, with alterity in language(s), is staged in *Vivre l'orange* (1979), as the autobiographical trajectory of a Jewish-woman-in-a-Spanish-and-German-speaking-household-in-an-Arab-speaking-French-colony who 'does languages' as she 'makes languages' ('Je fais des langues': 21) to engage with a Brazilian writer, Clarice Lispector (a 'flash' of light), author of a text 'The Apple in the Dark' that produces the call of the other to which Cixous must respond. But 'in the translation of the apple (into orange) I denounce myself' (*Vive l'orange* 40). As a Jewish woman from Europe, writing in the Portuguese of Brazil, Lispector's hybridity matches that of Cixous. More specifically, however, in Lispector Cixous has found Kafka as a woman, a writer of a 'minor literature,' an artist of the minimal whose generosity and respect for objects she celebrates. Since this discovery of the Brazilian writer, Cixous has focused her research and teaching on Lispector's writing. This has taken the form of extended oral meditations on details of Lispector's texts which have recently come into print, sometimes accompanied by seminar papers of students on Cixous' or other writers' texts, as in *Writing Differences: Readings from the Seminars of Hélène Cixous* (1988). Cixous works on a number of questions related to an economy of loss such as poverty, innocence, the valorization of nothing, of silence in the scene of writing, non-possibility, unreadability.

This format of presentation introduces additional questions of pedagogy, since the critical scene is that of the classroom. The dialogic nature of the presentation of Cixous' critical texts underlines what has been her common practice since the 1970s, exchanges with other women. While Cixous has extensively theorized the exploded or heterogeneous subject, other within the self in both national and gendered identifications as the *'plus-je'* ('L'Essor de Plus-je' 1973), she has also worked to produce the 'feminine plural' (*Coming to Writing* 48) in her editorial practices. *The Newly Born Woman* is composed of two essays and a debate involving Cixous and Catherine Clément; *La Jeune née* contains meditations/manifestos on gender and language by Madeleine Gagnon and Annie Leclerc as well as Cixous; *Vivre l'orange* is both a reading of Lispector's texts introducing her language and an exercise in collaborative translation with two anglophones, Ann Liddle and Sarah Cornell. This practice of multiplying authors and languages within the boundaries of a book is a strategy of overwhelming the economy of the book, not by the 'death of the author' and the rise of *discourse and the text, as *Michel Foucault and *Roland Barthes would have it, but by reinforcing the 'arguments' of the texts against sublimation, appropriation, fetishization, of a language-object, a process furthered by the active engagement of the reader on the textual surfaces. The performative and dialogic are extended in Cixous' theatrical work.

The response to Cixous' work has been sharply polarized. On the one hand, there are critics, mostly outside France, who have embraced her mode of empathetic reading 'with' the texts of writers and responding in a poetic,

rather than demonstrative, mode. Cixous' influence in Quebec has been considerable, not confined to her collaboration with Madeleine Gagnon, but extending to a whole generation of writers whose predilection for the exploration of desire was stimulated by Cixous' teaching at the Université de Montréal in the early 1970s. While writers such as Nicole Brossard, France Théoret and Louise Cotnoir have adapted the theories of work on the Symbolic, exploded subjectivity and work on the signifier to develop a textuality demanding the reader's interaction, they have rejected the psychoanalytic theory underpinning Cixous' project, accepting only its deconstructionism. (See *feminist criticism, Quebec.)

Cixous' opponents are equally forceful in manifesting their objections. This opposition was first clearly articulated in France in the context of the struggles within the women's movement over positions taken by *Psych et Po*. Cixous was grouped with *Psych et Po*, Irigaray, Kristeva and others working with psychoanalysis as 'cultural feminism,' feminism of 'difference' – and was denounced as 'neo-feminine' by 'radical' (materialist) feminists in the founding manifesto of *Questions féministes*. (See *materialist criticism.) Cixous' utopian aim of inventing a transformed imaginary is in question, though she acknowledges the historical determination of the imaginary by the discourses of the present mode of domination, she does not enquire into the material history of the workings of discourse, but attempts to reach beyond to invent the future. Cixous is caught in the very contradiction she locates at the heart of Joyce's work: there is freedom only outside a culture in which one is imprisoned, though her texts have tried to acknowledge their contradictory nature by the multiplication of the possibilities of languages and meanings.

The contradiction foregrounded in Cixous' work between psychoanalysis and politics or between poetics and politics has been the key point critics address, whether they view positively creative potentials of excess and rupture in her 'exorbitant texts' (Duren) or find this contradiction an impasse for the 'engaged' critic who wishes her theorizing to produce political action for social change. A contradiction between the writerly and the social is perceived in Cixous' work by materialist critics like Leslie Rabine, who notes how what is written is exceeded (contradicted) through metaphors of the scene of writing. (See *readerly/writerly text.) Substituted for the phallic metaphor of the book-fetish in Cixous' textual economy is a metaphor of the text as weaving, not the Freudian veiling producing the *Unheimliche*, but a non-fetishistic, non-representational textuality which binds women together in the unconscious.

The Anglo-American rejection of the premises of French feminism has been so effective that one recent critic, referring to 'the decline of Cixous' version of "feminine" writing,' uses her as an exemplary case for 'assessing the difficulties ... of an oppositional reading of culture,' the (im)possibility of engaging in critique of dominant cultural practices in order to change the prevailing order (Davis 267). (See *feminist criticism, Anglo-American.) This is a more general dilemma, he suggests, for the socially engaged intellectual who wants his or her discourse to effect change, when the rupture is neutralized and appropriated by the dominant discourse as 'opposition' (275). That this may be a premature elegy is indicated by recent work on Cixous appearing in England. Barbara Freeman tackles the problem of *essentialism by attributing it to the 'presuppositions' of Cixous' critics who are caught up in the very problem of the Cartesian mind/body split Cixous challenges. Their vocabulary is based on the assumption that the body and the text, the sensible and the intelligible, are inevitably separate (Freeman 59–60). The body never has a referential status independent of linguistic or textual mediation in Cixous' work: feminine sexuality is always an effect of its inscription or representation (Freeman 64). Cixous' constant concern is with the mediation of the body through representations of literature and psychoanalysis in the context of political issues, 'the relation between categories of thought and structures of oppression' (Shiach 1989, 155). (See *psychoanalytic theory.) To shift attention away from Cixous' work as a 'feminine aesthetic' (155), Morag Shiach delineates the philosophical underpinnings of Cixous' concern with the Symbolic as the source of power and the generator of categories, narrative structures, 'that provide both the rationale for, and the means of, the oppression of women' (ibid. 154). Shiach reads the possibilities for a stategic alliance between the 'feminine' (textualized representations) and 'women' (historically situated agents) as best

actualized in theatrical writing, which allows for a complex *intertexuality and temporality that questions the 'natural' bases for 'character' and 'identity' (ibid. 162–3). Interweaving 'theory' and 'theatre' as modes of 'spectacle,' this practice bridges the opposition between abstraction and action, between philosophy and politics which Cixous' critics have decried.

BARBARA GODARD

Primary Sources

Cixous, Hélène. *Coming to Writing and Other Essays.* Ed. Deborah Jenson. Cambridge: Harvard UP, 1991.
- 'Conversations.' In *Readings from the Seminar of Hélène Cixous.* Ed. Susan Sellers. Milton Keynes: Open UP; New York: St. Martin's P, 1988, 141–54.
- *Dedans.* Paris: Grasset, 1969.
- *Entre l'écriture.* Paris: des femmes, 1986.
- 'L'Essor de Plus-je.' *L'Arc* 54 (1973): 46–52.
- 'An Exchange.' In *Hélène Cixous: Writing the Feminine* by Verena Andermatt Conley. Lincoln: U of Nebraska P, 1984, 129–65.
- *L'Exil de James Joyce ou l'art du remplacement.* 1968. *The Exil of James Joyce.* Trans. Sally Purcell. New York: David Lewis, 1972.
- *L'Heure de Clarice Lispector.* Paris: des femmes, 1989.
- *Illa.* Paris: des femmes, 1980.
- 'Joyce, la ruse de l'écriture.' *Poétique* 4 (1970). 'Joyce: The (R)use of Writing.' Trans. Judith Still. In *Post-Structuralist Joyce: Essays from the French.* Ed. Derek Attridge and Daniel Ferrer. Cambridge: Cambridge UP, 1984, 15–30.
- *Limonade tout était si infini.* Paris: des femmes, 1982.
- *Portrait de Dora.* Paris: des femmes, 1976.
- *Prénoms de personne.* Paris: Seuil, 1974.
- 'A Propos de *Manne.*' In *Hélène Cixous, chemins d'une écriture.* Ed. Françoise van Rossum-Guyon and Myriam Diaz-Diacoretz. Amsterdam: Rodopi; Paris: PU Vincennes, 1990, 213–34.
- *Reading with Clarice Lispector.* Ed. and trans. Verena Conley. Minneapolis: U of Minnesota P, 1990.
- 'Le Rire de la Méduse.' *L'Arc* 61 (1975): 39–54. 'The Laugh of the Medusa.' Trans. Keith and Paula Cohen. *Signs* 1.4 (1976): 875–93. Repr. in *New French Feminisms.* Ed. Elaine Marks and Isabelle de Courtivron. Amherst: U of Massachusetts P, 1980, 245–64.
- 'De la scène de l'Inconscient à la scène de l'Histoire. Chemins d'une écriture.' In *Hélène Cixous, chemins d'une écriture.* Ed. Françoise van Rossum-Guyon and Myriam Diaz-Diacoretz. Amsterdam: Rodopi; Paris: PU Vincennes, 1990, 15–34. 'From the Scene of the Unconscious to the Scene of His-

tory.' Trans. Deborah Carpenter. In *The Future of Literary Theory*. Ed. Ralph Cohen. New York: Routledge, 1989, 1–18.

– 'Le Sexe ou la tête?' *Cahiers du GRIF* 13 (Oct. 1976): 5–15. 'Castration or Decapitation?' Trans. Annette Kuhn. *Signs* 7.2 (1981): 41–55.

– *Vivre l'orange*. Bilingual ed. Trans. Hélène Cixous with Ann Liddle and Sarah Cornell. Paris: des femmes, 1979.

– with Catherine Clément. *La Jeune née*. 1975. *The Newly Born Woman*. Trans. Betsy Wing. Minneapolis: U of Minnesota P, 1986.

– with Madeleine Gagnon and Annie Leclerc. *La Venue à l'écriture*. Paris: UGE 10/18, 1977. 'Coming to Writing.' Trans. and ed. Deborah Jenson. In *Coming to Writing and Other Essays*. Cambridge: Harvard UP, 1991, 1–58.

Secondary Sources

Attridge, Derek, and Daniel Ferrer. *Post-Structuralist Joyce: Essays from the French*. Cambridge: Cambridge UP, 1984.

Binhammer, Katherine. 'Metaphor or Metonymy? The Question of Essentialism in Cixous.' *Tessera* 10 (Summer 1991): 65–79.

Conley, Verena Andermatt. *Hélène Cixous: Writing the Feminine*. Lincoln: U of Nebraska P, 1984.

Davis, Robert Con. 'Woman as Oppositional Reader: Cixous on Discourse.' *Papers on Language and Literature* 24.3 (Summer 1988): 265–82.

Deleuze, Gilles, and Felix Guattari. *Kafka: Pour une littérature mineure*. Paris: Minuit, 1975.

Duren, Brian. 'Cixous' Exorbitant Texts.' *Sub-Stance* 32 (1981): 30–51.

Freeman, Barbara. '"Plus corps donc plus écriture": Hélène Cixous and the Mind-Body Problem.' *Paragraph* 11.1 (March 1988): 58–70.

Handelman, Susan. *The Slayers of Moses: The Emergence of Rabbinic Interpretation in Modern Literary Theory*. Albany: SUNY P, 1982.

Jardine, Alice. *Gynesis: Configurations of Woman and Modernity*. Ithaca: Cornell UP, 1985.

Marks, Elaine, and Isabelle de Courtivron, eds. *New French Feminisms*. Amherst: U of Massachusetts P, 1980.

Rabine, Leslie W. 'Ecriture Féminine as Metaphor.' *Cultural Critique* 8 (Winter 1987–8): 19–44.

Rossum-Guyon, Françoise van, and Myriam Diaz-Diacoretz, eds. *Hélène Cixous, chemins d'une écriture*. Amsterdam: Rodopi; Paris: PU Vincennes, 1990.

Shiach, Morag. *Hélène Cixous: A Politics of Writing*. London and New York: Routledge, 1991.

– '"Their 'Symbolic' Exists, It Holds Power – We, the Sowers of Disorder, Know It Only Too Well."' In *Between Feminism and Psychoanalysis*. Ed. Teresa Brennan. London: Routledge, 1989, 153–67.

Questions féministes Collective. 'Variations on Common Themes.' *Questions féministes* 1 (Nov. 1977). Trans. Yvonne Rochette-Ozello. In *New French Feminisms*. Ed. Elaine Marks and Isabelle de Courtivron. Amherst: U of Massachussetts P, 1980, 212–30.

Wilcox, Helen, Keith McWatters, Ann Thompson and Linda R. Williams, eds. *The Body and the Text: Helen Cixous, Reading and Teaching*. Hemel Hempstead: Harvester Wheatsheaf, 1990.

Crane, R(onald) S(almon)

(b. U.S.A., 1886–d. 1967) Literary scholar and critic. A 1908 graduate of the University of Michigan, R.S. Crane (as he preferred to be known) earned his Ph.D. from the University of Pennsylvania in 1911 with a dissertation on 'The Vogue of Medieval Chivalric Romance during the English Renaissance.' Between 1911 and 1924 he taught at Northwestern University. He then moved to the University of Chicago, where he remained until his retirement in 1951. Crane subsequently taught as Visiting Professor at the University of Toronto (1952), at Cornell University (1952–3 and 1957), at Carleton College (1954–5), and at Indiana University (1955–6).

Crane is best known as the leader of the Neo-Aristotelian School centred at the University of Chicago, but for the first 25 years of his academic career he busied himself with more conventional literary scholarship and teaching. (See *Neo-Aristotelian or Chicago Schoo.) He continued his work on the vogue of the medieval romance and developed a continuing interest in the *literature of the 18th century. Much of this work involved the history of ideas and bibliography. He wrote and edited textbooks and anthologies and published his doctoral dissertation and several articles. In 1926 he contributed the first of six annual bibliographies on the 18th century to *Philological Quarterly*. So impressive was this bibliographical work that the bibliography continued to feature Crane's name long after his active participation had ceased. In 1930 he assumed the editorship of *Modern Philology*, a position he held until 1952. It was from this matrix of literary history, scholarly precision, teaching responsibilities, and professional activities that Crane emerged in 1935 as an advocate of literary criticism and as a significant critical theorist.

Crane's 'History versus Criticism in the Study of Literature' (1935) was his contribution to a controversy initiated by John Livingston Lowes who, as president of the Modern Language Association, had in 1933 formally advocated criticism as the goal of literary study. Lowes' address prompted a response from Howard Mumford Jones, who argued with equal vigour that the true concerns of literary scholarship were historical, not aesthetic. Crane unhesitatingly and – given his work up to this time – surprisingly favoured literary explication and aesthetics. Oddly too, Crane published little else on critical theory before the appearance of 'The Critical Monism of Cleanth Brooks' (1947–8) and 'I.A. Richards on the Art of Interpretation' (1949), both of which were reprinted in *Critics and Criticism: Ancient and Modern* (1952), the manifesto of the Neo-Aristotelians. (See *Cleanth Brooks, *I.A. Richards.) Crane edited the volume and outlined in his introduction the critical tenets of the group. A more elaborate statement of his critical theory was presented in the Alexander Lectures at the University of Toronto in 1952, published the next year as *The Languages of Criticism and the Structure of Poetry*, Crane's only book on the subject. Several previously unpublished papers on literary theory were printed in the eclectic collection *The Idea of the Humanities* (1967).

Crane rightly perceived that literary criticism proceeds under a great variety of banners, with a variety of seemingly contradictory purposes and methods, and that some systematic response to these multitudinous approaches is necessary if criticism is to have an epistemological basis. He rejected both scepticism and dogmatism and postulated instead a critical *pluralism, which recognizes that different questions demand different frames of reference. A given critical system is an instrument of inquiry, valid in its own terms, and represents a choice the critic makes in response to the questions he chooses to ask. Since principles and terms function only within the context of a given *discourse, there can be no ultimate critical synthesis. Crane suggested in 'Questions and Answers on the Teaching of Literary Texts,' delivered in 1953 but not published until 1967, that there are five 'major distinguishable aspects' of a literary work which might serve as the bases of critical pluralism: the verbal composition, the structure or

form, the traits of substance and expression, the historical circumstances of composition, and the function and value of the work. It is not difficult to see here a reflection of Aristotle's four causes; indeed, Crane and the Chicago critics followed the lead of their colleague Richard McKeon in finding in the Greek philosopher the most flexible and comprehensive method of critical analysis, a method, they believed, that was best able to take into account all the causes of poetic structure. As a theorist of criticism, then, Crane was a pluralist; as a critic he chose Aristotelianism. As a theorist he recognized that his Aristotelianism was one language among many; in practice he often wrote as though it were the only valid language.

Crane's influence beyond his immediate colleagues and students has not been great. Neo-Aristotelianism was itself a short-lived phenomenon. The critical Tower of Babel that Crane and his colleagues confronted is still with us, the languages more numerous and diverse than ever.

RONALD W. VINCE

Primary Sources

Crane, R.S., ed. *Critics and Criticism: Ancient and Modern*. Chicago: U of Chicago P, 1952.
– *The Idea of the Humanities and Other Essays*. 2 vols. Chicago: U of Chicago P, 1967.
– *The Language of Criticism and the Structure of Poetry*. Toronto: U of Toronto P, 1953.

Secondary Sources

Bashford, Bruce W. 'The Humanistic Criticism of R.S. Crane.' Northwestern University dissertation. 1971.
Booth, Wayne C. *Critical Understanding: The Powers and Limits of Pluralism*. Chicago: U of Chicago P, 1979.
Davis, Walter A. 'Theories of Form in Modern Criticism: An Examination of the Theories of Kenneth Burke and R.S. Crane.' University of Chicago dissertation. 1969.
Denham, Robert D. 'R.S. Crane's Critical Method and Theory of Poetic Form.' *Connecticut Review* 5.2 (1972): 46–56.
Keast, W.R. 'R.S. Crane, Editor of *Modern Philology*, 1930–1952.' *Modern Philology* 50 (1952): 1–4.
Lipking, Lawrence. 'R.S. Crane and the Idea of the Humanities.' *Philological Quarterly* 47 (1968): 455–71.
Sherwood, John C. *R.S. Crane: An Annotated Bibliography*. New York and London: Garland, 1984.

Croce, Benedetto

(b. Italy, 1866–d. 1952) Philosopher. From about 1910 to 1950 – that is, for most of his adult life – Benedetto Croce was one of the dominant intellectual figures in Italy. A philosopher by training and vocation, he engaged in and gave direction to many aspects of the culture of his country. His writings on history and historiography, on *literature and literary criticism, on political, autobiographical and journalistic matters influenced Italian scholarship in an unprecedented way. Equally important, he was for many decades a public, visible presence. He served as minister of education in the years immediately following the First World War. Although he initially did not oppose Mussolini's ascent to power, he quickly became the rallying symbol of disaffection with Fascism and Fascist policies for those Italians who did not find leftist dissent either appealing or possible. So extensive and so acknowledged was Croce's authority that he played a major role in negotiating the conditions of the return to peace in Italy when the Second World War was over. He also was instrumental in determining the mode of government that replaced Fascism.

Croce's philosophical program was a very ambitious one, amounting to no less than the complete reassessment and revision of 19th-century idealism. From 1900 to about 1910, in such works as Estetica come scienza dell'espressione e linguistica generale [Aesthetics as Science of Expression and General Linguistic], Filosofia della pratica: Economia ed etica [Philosophy of the Practical: Economy and Ethics], Logica come scienza del concetto puro [Logic as the Science of the Pure Concept], Croce outlined the amendments he would bring to the philosophy of spirit, the term he preferred to employ. Basically, these consisted in identifying more precisely the field upon which philosophy was to exercise itself, in describing its components and their place in the system. For Croce the manifestations of the spirit were of two kinds: theoretical (or cognitive) and practical (or volitional). Each manifestation could in turn be subdivided into moments or categories, best summarized by the discipline they give rise to, aesthetics and logic for the theoretical, economy and ethics for the practical domain. In addition, the categories and the disciplines followed an order of priority: aesthetics precedes and is presupposed by the other three.

This move is in many ways typically end-of-the-century. By putting aesthetics first, Croce reversed positivist views and rejected those criteria which had reduced art to an after-effect of milieu or biography, hence to an enterprise valid only as a field of study and to the extent that it made itself available to the procedures and the perspectives of the natural sciences. Indeed, in Aesthetics as Science of Expression and General Linguistic it is the most unscientific of qualities – intuition – that guarantees the privilege of aesthetics. Writers, painters and other creators of artistic works express feelings in an intuitive synthesis of content and form. Thus, for Croce intuition was a kind of knowledge, albeit a kind different from that afforded by general concepts. And it is knowledge that can exist without or in spite of logic or economics and ethics. The latter, instead, will not even come into being without some compelling, imaginative impulse and are, therefore, permeated by intuition.

But Croce went further than his contemporaries. His practice as a militant critic (for four decades he was editor of La Critica, a journal he founded in 1903) forced him to confront and to reflect upon the more specific issues his philosophical allegiance entailed. Over the years he appended a number of corollaries and caveats to his original affirmation of the primacy of intuition. A lecture of 1908, 'L'Intuizione pura e il carattere lirico dell'arte' ['Pure Intuition and the Lyrical Character of Art'], already identifies art with lyricism. Establishing the equivalence was to lead Croce to envisage longer pieces of literature as strings of lyrical moments held together by devices which in themselves belonged to the practical rather than to the aesthetic realm. On the other hand, by lyricism Croce did not mean autobiographical, confessional outpouring. The intuitive character of art, he maintained, accords well with a classicist outlook. As he pointed out in 'Il Carattere di totalità dell'espressione artistica' ['The Totality of Artistic Expression' 1918], if intuition is intuition of particular entities (of this tree, this face), great works of art are nonetheless endowed with universality, for in the concrete, particular images that compose them lie 'human destiny' (263), and 'the breath of the cosmos' (265). (See *universal.)

The peculiar ingredients that went into the making of Croce's definition of the aesthetic could not, evidently, be without strictly critical consequences. How does one accost items which, while they may be about ethical or economic issues, are impervious to all proddings from the practical dimension and which, in so far as they are intuitively constituted, are at once universal in scope and adamantly unique? Croce had a simple answer: one admits that much of the 'toolery' criticism usually deploys in its attempt to deal with art – the concepts of genre, movement, period, for example – satisfy practical needs, but one realizes that distinctions, rubrics and other abstract pigeon-holing provide little insight into the aesthetic reality of art. (See *genre criticism.) That reality – always singular, unrepeatable – can be apprehended only by remaining firmly anchored to the work. In Croce's own criticism, perhaps best illustrated by the essays in *Ariosto, Shakespeare e Corneille* [*Ariosto, Shakespeare, and Corneille*], the ultimate aim is to uncover the complex of images that recapitulate the text's unity. When the focus is a set of texts, an entire corpus, the critic's task is to portray properly what Croce called the author's poetic personality – the particular, individual, unshared feeling or state of mind that the works embody. (See *text.)

All of this – the definitions of art, the critical strategy – resonates ambiguously in the history of the later decades of the century. Among the array of schools and movements, the most receptive to Croce was probably Anglo-American *New Criticism. *I.A. Richards and John Crowe Ramsom pay homage to him at several instances; *René Wellek, *W.K. Wimsatt Jr. and *Cleanth Brooks devoted articles to his aesthetics. Even then, the sympathy (which involved primarily the argument in favour of the autonomy of art) was more than matched by the incompatibilities. Croce did not have much faith in the study of formal structures and, just as he decried the increasing premium that the age seemed to lay on method, he would have questioned the value of the close reading or of the professionalization of criticism his British or American counterparts championed. His insistence on the priority of intuition, his idea that art is a synthesis of form and content, and therefore not accessible to technical know-how alone, still separate him from the greater portion of our present. Yet, in spite of the apparent anachronism, many of the challenges he voiced remain. The postulate of the singularity of texts continues to be a theoretical embarrassment in an age which denies singularity; and, given the decline of formalist approaches,

we have become less certain that acquiring a methodology is the most crucial requisite for appreciating or for understanding literature. For this and other reasons, it is not surprising that some are now beginning to predict a 'return' of Croce. (See also *Jacques Maritain.)

FRANCESCO LORIGGIO

Primary Sources

Croce, Benedetto. 'Aesthetics.' *Encyclopaedia Britannica.* 14th ed. 1929, 263–5.
– *Ariosto, Shakespeare e Corneille.* Bari: Laterza, 1920. *Ariosto, Shakespeare, and Corneille.* Trans. D. Ainslie. New York: Russell and Russell, 1966.
– 'Il Carattere di totalità dell'espressione artistica.' *La Critica* 16 (1918): 129–40. Repr. in *Filosofia, poesia, storia.* Milano-Napoli: Ricciardi, 1951, 236–47.
– *Estetica come scienza dell'espressione e linguistica generale.* 1902. 10th ed. Bari: Laterza, 1958. *Aesthetics as Science of Expression and General Linguistic.* Trans. D. Ainslie. London: Macmillan and Co., 1909.
– *Filosofia della pratica: Economia ed etica.* 1909. 8th ed. Bari: Laterza, 1957.
– 'L'Intuizione pura e il carattere lirico dell'arte.' In *Problemi di estetica e contributi alla storia dell'estetica italiana.* 1910. 5th ed. Bari: Laterza, 3–30.
– *Logica come scienza del concetto puro.* 1909. 9th ed. Bari: Laterza, 1963. *Logic as the Science of the Pure Concept.* Trans. D. Ainslie. London: Macmillan, 1917.
– *Philosophy, Poetry, History.* Trans. C. Sprigge. London: Oxford UP, 1966.
– 'The Totality of Artistic Expression.' In *Philosophy, Poetry, History.* Trans. C. Sprigge. London: Oxford UP, 1966, 261–73.

Secondary Sources

Moss, M.E. *Benedetto Croce Reconsidered.* Hanover and London: UP of New England, 1987.
Orsini, Gian N.G. *Benedetto Croce: Philosopher of Art and Literary Critic.* Carbondale: Southern Illinois UP, 1961.
Ransom, J.C. 'Humanism at Chicago.' In *Poems and Essays.* New York: Vintage Books, 1955.
Richards, I.A. *Principles of Criticism.* 1925. New York: Harcourt, Brace and World, n.d.
Tessitore, F., ed. *L'Eredità di Croce.* Napoli: Guida, 1985.
Wellek, René. *Four Critics: Croce, Valéry, Lukács, and Ingarden.* Seattle: U of Washington P, 1981.
Wimsatt, W.K., Jr., and Cleanth Brooks. 'Expressionism: Benedetto Croce.' In *Literary Criticism: A Short History.* New York: Vintage Books, 1957, 499–521.

Culler, Jonathan Dwight

(b. U.S.A. 1944–) Literary critic. Culler received his B.A. at Harvard (1966), then went to St. John's College, Oxford, where he received his B.Phil. in comparative literature (1968) and his D.Phil. in modern languages (1972). He has taught at Selwyn College, Cambridge (1973), and and at Brasenose College, Oxford (1974–7). Since 1977 he has been professor of English and comparative literature and director of the Society for the Humanities at Cornell University. Throughout his writings he has argued 'against interpretation': against the proliferation of readings of individual literary texts that mark the procedures of *New Criticism. Instead, he has attempted to articulate 'the conditions of meaning,' to systematize the conventions and institutional operations which enable textual 'intelligibility.' He is particularly known for introducing contemporary French theory to the American academy and for his abilities to elucidate its complex ideas and arguments in lucid and economical prose. Both *Saussure* (1976) and *Barthes* (1983) demonstrate this ability. (See *Ferdinand de Saussure, *Roland Barthes, *text.)

Flaubert: The Uses of Uncertainty (1974) utilizes contemporary French theory in a discussion of the works of one writer to call 'into question the notion that made literature a communication between author and reader' (13). (See *literature.) One year later, Culler published his best-known work, one which is credited as having 'practically single-handedly mediated (and constituted) our understanding of structuralism' (Lentricchia 104) in the American academy. (See *structuralism.) *Structuralist Poetics: Structuralism, Linguistics, and the Study of Literature* (1975), awarded the prestigious James Russell Lowell Prize by the Modern Language Association in 1976, is divided into three parts. The first section introduces 'the linguistic model' by surveying the work of *Claude Lévi-Strauss, *Roman Jakobson, *A.J. Greimas, *Vladimir Propp, and particularly Roland Barthes. Throughout this section, Culler draws attention to the theoretical limitations of each of these thinkers, limitations that he expands upon in the second and longest section of the book. Here he attempts to synthesize 'the linguistic model' deriving from European *semiotics and structuralism of the 1960s, especially Saussure's concept of *langue*. He then articulates a structuralist 'poetics,' an effective

model for reading literature whose 'task' it would be 'to make explicit the underlying system which makes literary effects possible' (118). This 'poetics' is predicated upon a notion of 'literary competence,' an extension of linguistic competence first formulated by *Noam Chomsky. (See *competence/performance.) Culler's 'literary competence' is the possession or 'mastery' of the literary conventions which are required, in addition to linguistic competence, for either the writing or reading of literature. The last section consists of an attack on 'the theorists associated with the review *Tel Quel*,' particularly *Jacques Derrida and *Julia Kristeva. In particular, Culler reacts against poststructuralist procedures that produce meaning as open-ended and limitless: 'without restrictive rules there would be no meaning whatsoever ... Whatever type of freedom the members of the *Tel Quel* group secure for themselves will be based on convention and will consist of a set of interpretive procedures. There is a crucial difference between the production of meaning and arbitrary assignment of meaning, between plausible development and random association' (252). These assertions became the grounds of subsequent attacks on Culler. (See *poststructuralism.)

Since *Structuralist Poetics*, Culler has incorporated poststructuralist perspectives into his work as he continues to attempt to analyse 'the conditions of meaning.' *The Pursuit of Signs* (1981) is a collection of essays that explores relations between semiotics and *deconstruction. As a sustained attempt simultaneously to introduce and to criticize deconstruction, *On Deconstruction* (1982) is described by the publisher as 'a sequel' to *Structuralist Poetics*. In it, Culler carefully positions himself in relation to 'deconstructive criticism,' defining it not as 'the application of philosophical lessons to literary studies but [as] an exploration of textual logic in texts called literary' (227).

Culler's critics point out that his lucid and economical expository introductions are often simplistic reductions. He has been attacked for treating theoretical positions with little or no concern for the historical mediations that produce and inform them. Referring to *Structuralist Poetics*, *Terry Eagleton has written of the 'violent depoliticization' of French theory in Culler's project of rendering 'Parisian radicalism safe for the Free World' (52). In the most

de Beauvoir

sustained and important of these criticisms, Frank Lentricchia argues that Culler does this by collapsing structuralism onto the presuppositions of New Criticism, a collapse made possible 'because his mediation rests on intellectual principles easily recognizable and very dear to the traditionalist American critical mind' (104).

Culler's most recent work, explicitly connecting 'the Reagan administration' with the study of 'canonical authors' (*Framing the Sign* 33), suggests that he is moving to incorporate the historical and the political in more direct ways. (See *canon.)

VICTOR SHEA

Primary Sources

Culler, Jonathan. *Barthes*. Glasgow: Fontana, 1983.
– *On Deconstruction: Theory and Criticism after Structuralism*. Ithaca: Cornell UP, 1982.
– *Flaubert: The Uses of Uncertainty*. Ithaca: Cornell UP, 1974.
– *Framing the Sign: Criticism and Its Institutions*. Norman: U of Oklahoma P, 1988.
– *The Pursuit of Signs: Semiotics, Literature, Deconstruction*. Ithaca: Cornell UP, 1981.
– *Saussure*. Glasgow: Fontana, 1976. Rev. ed. *Ferdinand de Saussure*. Ithaca: Cornell UP, 1986.
– *Structuralist Poetics: Structuralism, Linguistics and the Study of Literature*. Ithaca: Cornell UP, 1975.

Secondary Sources

Bertonneau, Thomas F. 'An Interview with Jonathan Culler.' *Paroles Jelées: UCLA French Studies* 6 (1988): 1–14.
Campa, Roman de la. 'Mainstreaming Poststructuralist and Feminist Thought: Jonathan Culler's Poetics.' *The Journal of the Midwest Modern Language Association* 18 (1985): 20–7.
Eagleton, Terry. 'The Idealism of American Criticism.' In *Against the Grain*. London: Verso, 1986.
Finney, Kathe Davis. 'Crazy Jane Talks with Jonathan Culler: Using Structuralism to Teach Lyric Poetry.' *CEA Critic: An Official Journal of the College English Association* 43 (1981): 29–36.
Lentricchia, Frank. *After the New Criticism*. Chicago: U of Chicago P, 1980.
Ray, William. *Literary Meaning: From Phenomenology to Deconstruction*. Oxford: Blackwell, 1984.

de Beauvoir, Simone

(b. France, 1908–d. 1986) Feminist, writer and philosopher. Simone de Beauvoir was born into a bourgeois Catholic family of a devoutly religious mother and an unbelieving, socially ambitious father. Her comfortable childhood was unsettled at adolescence by her family's financial misfortunes; she, however, took her future into her own hands by eagerly pursuing her studies and eventually succeeding, in 1929, at the Sorbonne's *agrégation de philosophie*. De Beauvoir then taught philosophy until 1944, when she resigned from teaching and devoted the remainder of her professional life to writing, travel and political activism (she was most energetic in her opposition to the French colonial presence in Algeria and in her attempts to liberalize French abortion laws). In addition to many works in philosophical, literary and political analysis, de Beauvoir's publications include fiction, drama, autobiography, travel writing, journals, and letters; her influence is also pervasive in the writings of *Jean-Paul Sartre, who became her lifetime companion after they met at the Sorbonne in 1929.

All of de Beauvoir's works are in some sense a reflection of her continual engagement with existentialist philosophy. The fiction depicts the ways in which philosophical problems involving freedom, choice and responsibility take complex forms in individual lives. *She Came to Stay* (1943) – based partly on the troubled relationships of de Beauvoir, Sartre and Olga Kosakiewicz, the young woman they 'adopted' from the provinces – recounts a woman's decision to murder her sexual rival; the act is presented as an existentialist triumph, an accomplishment by the protagonist of her own will. *The Blood of Others* (1945), set during the Second World War, dramatizes the ethical crisis of a French Resistance fighter when contemplating the German policy of killing civilians in retaliation for Resistance activities; the thinking behind his anguished decision can be summed up in the book's epigraph from Dostoevsky's *Brothers Karamazov*: 'everyone is responsible for everything.' In *All Men Are Mortal* (1946) a 13th-century Italian drinks an elixir that makes him immortal. Surviving for seven centuries, he finds himself increasingly indifferent to those around him. Here the philosophical question involves the moral status of indifference, which is finally viewed as an active denial of freedom to others.

The later fiction continues to examine philosophical problems but contextualizes them in more fully detailed social worlds and explores them more specifically in the context of gender. *The Mandarins* (1954) depicts the intellectual and political confusion that marked the years immediately following the Second World War. The novel also explores some of the basic ideas in *The Second Sex* by comparing two pairs of lovers: in one pairing, the woman sacrifices all for her lover, who eventually leaves her; in the other pairing, the woman, knowing her present pleasures to be temporary and illusory, walks away from a love affair in order to return to her marriage and professional life. *Les Belles images* (1966) examines a woman's life played out in the social world of a capitalist consumer economy in which 'images' replace all concerns about moral responsibility. *The Woman Destroyed* (1968) is a collection of three stories outlining, as in *The Mandarins*, the cost to women of buying into a romantic ideal of love: emotional dependence on men leads in de Beauvoir's fiction, as in her analysis of gender relations more generally, to loss and alienation.

De Beauvoir is best known for her treatise on sexual difference, *The Second Sex* (1949). A thorough analysis of the position of women in Western culture, it rejects a priori definitions of sexuality and challenges in particular the naturalness of femininity: 'the "true woman" is an artificial product that civilization makes, as formerly eunuchs were made' (*The Second Sex* 408). Woman's basic difficulty, according to de Beauvoir, is that she is 'a free and autonomous being' who 'nevertheless finds herself living in a world where men compel her to assume the status of the Other' (xxix). As man's Other, woman is doomed to immanence, while man is allowed – both in the sexual act and in life – the possibility of transcendence. This means that man is potentially more free than woman, who is constricted by the contingencies that accompany the position of the Other. (See *self/other.) Rejecting *Freud for his 'sexual monism' and Engels for his 'economic monism,' de Beauvoir insists on 'an existentialist foundation' for her analysis of gender because it alone 'enables us to understand in its unity that particular form of being which we call human life' (*The Second Sex* 60). She thus concludes her study with a call for the 'free woman' who is 'just being born' and who will be educated to achieve intellectual, economic and emotional independence. This woman, according to de Beauvoir, will secure precisely the freedom that already belongs to men: 'it will be through attaining the same situation as

theirs that she will find emancipation' (*The Second Sex* 715).

The autobiographical writings, which began to appear after de Beauvoir was an established novelist and thinker, use her own life to document and explore the practical and philosophical problems described in her fiction and in *The Second Sex*. De Beauvoir also produced a range of other works in various genres, including a drama, *Les Bouches inutiles*, first performed in 1945.

De Beauvoir wrote two short philosophical treatises: *Pyrrhus and Cinéas* (1944), in defending existentialism, argues for the possibility within particular situations of making free and responsible choices; *The Ethics of Ambiguity* (1947), which presents a series of portraits of ethical types, summarizes the basic tenets of existentialism. There is also a collection, *Existentialism and the Wisdom of Nations* (1948), which reprints four essays that first appeared in *Les Temps modernes*, a journal founded by de Beauvoir and Sartre in 1945. In addition to the accounts of travel that appear in the autobiographical volumes, de Beauvoir wrote two travel books: *America Day by Day* (1948), a harsh criticism in diary form of American culture, and *The Long March* (1957), an attempt to make China understandable to a resistant West. An essay on Marat de Sade ('Must We Burn Sade?' 1950–51) considers de Sade's sexual practices as an existential choice and a defiance of bourgeois values; in 1955, it was collected, along with two other essays ('What the Right Is Thinking Today' and 'Merleau-Ponty and Pseudo-Sartrism') in a book entitled *Privilèges*. (See *Merleau-Ponty.) Another essay, *Brigitte Bardot and the Lolita Syndrome* (1960), celebrates the French actress for her forthright expression of female sexuality, while *Djamila Boupacha* (1962) is an exposé, focusing on the case of one girl, of torture in Algeria.

In de Beauvoir's later years, both her autobiographical and her analytical writings focused on the predicament of the elderly and on the past. Employing the organizational structure and the thoroughness that had characterized *The Second Sex*, *Old Age* (1970) documents the situation of old people in Western culture. Coming after de Beauvoir's commitment to Marxism, however, *Old Age* dwells much more than her earlier analysis on economic contingencies. (See *Marxist criticism.) After the death of Sartre in 1980, de Beauvoir wrote *Adieux: Farewell to Sartre* (1981), an account of the philosopher's last years. She also edited a two-volume edition of Sartre's letters, *Letters to Castor and Others* (1983). Since de Beauvoir's own death in 1986, two further volumes of her writings have been published: *War Journal* (1990) and *Letters to Sartre* (1990).

The legacy of Simone de Beauvoir is rich but problematic. As an existentialist philosopher, she tends to be subordinated to Sartre. As a writer of fiction and autobiography, she is respected, but with the virtual displacement of existentialism by *structuralism and *poststructuralism, the interest in many of her writings has diminished. As a feminist, however, de Beauvoir continues to inspire admiration and controversy. Valued for a feminist stance that was bold and even revolutionary in 1949, she is now seen as representing contradictory positions: while anticipating poststructuralism by viewing gender as a social construction, she also clings to essentialist interpretations of woman as 'a "hysterical" body' with 'no distance between the psychic life and its physiological realization' (*The Second Sex* 332); while offering a valuable critique of Freud's theory of penis envy, she presents no rationale for her rejection of the important theory of the unconscious, except that it interferes with the existentialist notion of freedom; while asserting repeatedly that 'in human society nothing is natural' (*The Second Sex* 725), she insists on the naturalness of the heterosexual relationship and views the lesbian as 'a castrate' who is 'unfulfilled as a woman' and 'impotent as a man' (*The Second Sex* 412); while strongly criticizing man's position in Western society, she urges women to assume that same position, thus reinforcing the very tenets of bourgeois individualism that had originally placed them in the position of Other. The indisputable fact, however, is that the thinking and the presence of Simone de Beauvoir have profoundly affected the development of the feminist movement in the 20th century. (See *feminist criticism, *essentialism.)

KRISTIN BRADY

Primary Sources

de Beauvoir, Simone. *L'Amérique au jour le jour*. Paris: Morihien, 1948. *America Day by Day*. Trans. Patrick Dudley. London: Gerald Duckworth, 1952.
– *Les Belles images*. Paris: Gallimard, 1966. *Les Belles images*. Trans. Patrick O'Brian. London: Fontana, 1969.

– *Les Bouches inutiles*. Paris: Gallimard, 1945. *Who Shall Die?* Trans. Claude Francis and Fernande Gontier. Florissant, Miss.: River P, 1983.
– *Brigitte Bardot and the Lolita Syndrome*. London: Deutsch, Weidenfeld and Nicolson, 1960.
– *La Cérémonie des adieux* suivi de *Entretiens avec Jean-Paul Sartre*. Paris: Gallimard, 1981. *Adieux: A Farewell to Sartre*. Trans. Patrick O'Brian. London: Deutsch, Weidenfeld and Nicolson, 1984.
– *Le Deuxième sexe*. Paris: Gallimard, 1949. *The Second Sex*. Trans. and ed. H.M. Parshley. New York: Knopf, 1953.
– *L'Existentialisme et la sagesse des nations*. Paris: Nagel, 1948.
– 'Faut-il brûler de Sade?' *Les Temps modernes*. Dec. 1950 and Jan. 1951. *Must We Burn Sade?* Trans. Annette Michelson. London: Peter Nevill, 1953.
– *La Femme rompue*. Paris: Gallimard, 1968. *The Woman Destroyed*. Trans. Patrick O'Brian. London: Collins, 1969.
– *La Force de l'âge*. Paris: Gallimard, 1960. *The Prime of Life*. Trans. Peter Green. London: Deutsch, Weidenfeld and Nicolson, 1962.
– *La Force des choses*. Paris: Gallimard, 1963. *Force of Circumstance*. Trans. Richard Howard. London: Deutsch, Weidenfeld and Nicolson, 1965.
– *L'Invitée*. Paris: Gallimard, 1943. *She Came to Stay*. Trans. Yvonne Moyse and Roger Senhouse. London: Penguin, 1966.
– *Journal de guerre*. Ed. Sylvie Le Bon de Beauvoir. Paris: Gallimard, 1990.
– *Lettres à Sartre*. Ed. Sylvie Le Bon de Beauvoir. 2 vols. Paris: Gallimard, 1990.
– *La Longue marche*. Paris: Gallimard, 1957. *The Long March*. Trans. Austryn Wainhouse. London: Deutsch, Weidenfeld and Nicolson, 1958.
– *Les Mandarins*. Paris: Gallimard, 1954. *The Mandarins*. Trans. Leonard M. Friedman. London: Collins, 1957.
– *Mémoires d'une jeune fille rangée*. Paris: Gallimard, 1958. *Memoirs of a Dutiful Daughter*. Trans. James Kirkup. London: Deutsch, Weidenfeld and Nicolson, 1959.
– *Une Mort très douce*. Paris: Gallimard, 1964. *A Very Easy Death*. Trans. Patrick O'Brian. London: Deutsch, Weidenfeld and Nicolson, 1966.
– *Pour une morale de l'ambiguïté*. Paris: Gallimard, 1947. *The Ethics of Ambiguity*. Trans. Bernard Frechtman. New York: Philosophical Library, 1948.
– *Privilèges*. Paris: Gallimard, 1955.
– *Pyrrhus et Cinéas*. Paris: Gallimard, 1944. 'Pyrrhus and Cineas.' Selections. Trans. Christopher Freemantle. *Partisan Review* 13 (1946): 330–7.
– *Quand prime le spirituel*. Paris: Gallimard, 1979. *When Things of the Spirit Come First*. Trans. Patrick O'Brian. London: Deutsch, Weidenfeld and Nicolson, 1982.
– *Le Sang des autres*. Paris: Gallimard, 1945. *The Blood of Others*. Trans. Yvonne Moyse and Roger

Senhouse. London: Secker and Warburg, 1948.
- *Tous les hommes sont mortels*. Paris: Gallimard, 1946. *All Men Are Mortal*. Trans. Leonard M. Friedman. Cleveland: World Publishing, 1955.
- *Tout compte fait*. Paris: Gallimard, 1972. *All Said and Done*. Trans. Patrick O'Brian. London: Deutsch, Weidenfeld and Nicolson, 1974.
- *La Vieillesse*. Paris: Gallimard, 1970. *Old Age*. Trans. Patrick O'Brian. London: Deutsch, Weidenfeld and Nicolson, 1972.
- in collaboration with Gisèle Halimi. *Djamila Boupacha*. Paris: Gallimard, 1962. *Djamila Boupacha*. Trans. Gisèle Halimi. New York: Macmillan, 1962.
- ed. *Lettres au Castor et à quelques autres*. By Jean-Paul Sartre. 2 vols. Paris: Gallimard, 1983.

Secondary Sources

Appignanesi, Lisa. *Simone de Beauvoir*. Harmondsworth: Penguin, 1988.
Ascher, Carol. *Simone de Beauvoir: A Life of Freedom*. Boston: Beacon, 1981.
Bair, Deirdre. 'In Summation: The Question of Conscious Feminism or Unconscious Misogyny in *The Second Sex*.' *Simone de Beauvoir Studies* 1 (1983): 56–67.
- *Simone de Beauvoir: A Biography*. New York: Summit, 1990.
Bennett, Joy, and Gabriela Hochmann. *Simone de Beauvoir: An Annotated Bibliography*. New York: Garland, 1988.
Bieber, Konrad. *Simone de Beauvoir*. Boston: Hall, 1979.
Cayron, Claire. *La Nature chez Simone de Beauvoir*. Paris: Gallimard, 1973.
Cottrell, Robert D. *Simone de Beauvoir*. New York: Ungar, 1975.
Dijkstra, Sandra. 'Simone de Beauvoir and Betty Friedan: The Politics of Omission.' *Feminist Studies* 6 (1980): 290–303.
le Doeuff, Michèle. 'Simone de Beauvoir and Existentialism.' *Feminist Studies* 6 (1980): 227–89.
Evans, Mary. *Simone de Beauvoir: A Feminist Mandarin*. London: Tavistock, 1985.
Fallaize, Elizabeth. *The Novels of Simone de Beauvoir*. London: Routledge, 1988.
Felstiner, Mary Lowenthal. 'Seeing *The Second Sex* Through the Second Wave.' *Feminist Studies* 6 (1980): 249–76.
Fitch, Brian T. *Le Sentiment d'étrangeté chez Malraux, Sartre, Camus et Simone de Beauvoir*. Paris: Minard, 1964.
Fuchs, Jo-Ann. 'Female Eroticism in *The Second Sex*.' *Feminist Studies* 6 (1980): 304–13.
Gagnebin, Laurent. *Simone de Beauvoir ou le refus de l'indifférence*. Paris: Editions Fischbacher, 1968.
Gennari, Geneviève. *Simone de Beauvoir*. Paris: Editions Universitaires, 1958.
Girard, René. 'Memoirs of a Dutiful Existentialist.' *Yale French Studies* 27 (1961): 41–6.

Jardine, Alice. 'Interview with Simone de Beauvoir.' *Signs* 5 (1979): 224–36.
Jeanson, Francis. *Simone de Beauvoir ou l'entreprise de vivre (suivi de deux entretiens avec Simone de Beauvoir)*. Paris: Editions du Seuil, 1966.
Julienne-Caffié, Serge. *Simone de Beauvoir*. Paris: Gallimard, 1966.
Kaufmann McCall, Dorothy. 'Simone de Beauvoir, *The Second Sex*, and Jean-Paul Sartre.' *Signs* 5 (1979): 209–23.
Keefe, Terry. *Simone de Beauvoir: A Study of Her Writings*. London: Harrap, 1983.
Lasocki, Anne-Marie. *Simone de Beauvoir ou l'Entreprise d'écrire*. The Hague: Nijhoff, 1971.
Leighton, Jean. *Simone de Beauvoir on Woman*. London: Associated UP, 1975.
Lloyd, Genevieve. 'Masters, Slaves and Others.' *Radical Philosophy* 34 (1983): 2–9.
Madsen, Axel. *Hearts and Minds: The Common Journey of Simone de Beauvoir and Jean-Paul Sartre*. New York: Morrow, 1977.
Marks, Elaine. *Critical Essays on Simone de Beauvoir*. Boston: Hall, 1987.
- *Simone de Beauvoir: Encounters with Death*. New Brunswick, NJ: Rutgers UP, 1973.
Merleau-Ponty, Maurice. 'Le Roman et la métaphysique.' In *Sens et non-sens*. Paris: Nagel, 1948, 45–71.
Moi, Toril. *Feminist Theory and Simone de Beauvoir*. Oxford: Blackwell, 1990.
Moorehead, Caroline. 'A Talk with Simone de Beauvoir.' *New York Magazine*, 2 June 1974, 16–34.
Moubachir, Chantal. *Simone de Beauvoir ou le souci de différence*. Paris: Seghers, 1972.
Nahas, Hélène. *La Femme dans la littérature existentielle*. Paris: PUF, 1957.
O'Brien, Mary. *The Politics of Reproduction*. London: Routledge, 1981.
Patterson, Yolanda. *Simone de Beauvoir and the Demystification of Motherhood*. Ann Arbor: UMI Research P, 1989.
Radford, C.B. 'The Authenticity of Simone de Beauvoir.' *Nottingham French Studies* 4 (1965): 91–104.
- 'Simone de Beauvoir: Feminism's Friend or Foe?' Part 1. *Nottingham French Studies* 6 (1967): 87–102; Part 2. *Nottingham French Studies* 7 (1968): 39–53.
Schwarzer, Alice. *Simone de Beauvoir Today: Conversations 1972–1982*. Trans. Marianne Howarth. London: Chatto and Windus, 1984.
Simons, Margaret A. 'The Silencing of Simone de Beauvoir: Guess What's Missing from *The Second Sex*.' *Women's Studies International Forum* 6 (1983): 559–64.
- and Jessica Benjamin. 'Simone de Beauvoir: An Interview.' *Feminist Studies* 5 (1979): 330–45.
Walters, Margaret. 'The Rights and Wrongs of Women: Mary Wollstonecraft, Harriet Martineau and Simone de Beauvoir.' In *The Rights and*

Deleuze

Wrongs of Women. Ed. Ann Oakley and Juliet
Mitchell. Harmondsworth: Penguin, 1976.
Wenzel, Hélène, ed. Simone de Beauvoir: Witness to a
Century. New Haven: Yale UP, 1987.
Whitmarsh, Anne. Simone de Beauvoir and the Limits
of Commitment. Cambridge: Cambridge UP, 1981.
Zéphir, Pierre. Le Néo-feminisme de Simone de Beau-
voir. Paris: Denoël Gonthier, 1982.

Deleuze, Gilles

(b. France, 1925–) Deleuze was trained in
philosophy at the Sorbonne under Georges
Canguilhem and Jean Hyppolite, passing his
agrégation examination in 1948. He has taught
philosophy at the Sorbonne, the University
of Lyon and the University of Paris VIII-
Vincennes/St. Denis, from which he retired in
1987. Along with his younger contemporary
*Jacques Derrida, Deleuze is the most influen-
tial proponent of the philosophy of 'difference'
that, in the form of a critique of *essentialism,
challenged Hegelian Marxism and *structuralism in the 1960s. (See *Marxist criticism, *dif-
férance/différence.) Deleuze's first book, a
study of Hume's empiricism entitled Empirisme
et subjectivité [Empiricism and Subjectivity
1953], inaugurated the first phase of his development, characterized by a focus on philosophers out of the mainstream of postwar
Marxist phenomenology. (See *phenomenological criticism.) Studies of Bergson (1966) and
Spinoza (1968 and 1970) followed, as well as
an introduction to Kant's critical philosophy
(1963) and a polemic against Platonism (1967),
but the most important was his second book,
Nietzsche et la philosophie [Nietzsche and Philosophy 1962]. In this influential work, one of the
first in contemporary France to take *Nietzsche
seriously as a thinker, Deleuze presents the
concerns of his own philosophical itinerary in
the course of a systematic explication of
Nietzsche's rebuttal of the Hegelian dialectic.
Deleuze's Nietzsche, like Deleuze himself, criticizes the reductive tyranny of the dialectic's
polarized oppositions and the triumphant negation that synthesizes them, offering as non-
dialectical alternatives to these mechanisms the
subtler differences/displacements of the will to
*power and the affirmative linking of necessity
and chance in the eternal return, not of the
same, but of difference. Already present here
are analyses of the unconscious as a process of
production and of universal history as process

of inscription that anticipate the critiques of
*Freud and Marx underpinning L'Anti-Oedipe
[Anti-Oedipus 1972].

In addition to these philosophical monographs, Deleuze also wrote two literary studies
during this period. Marcel Proust et les signes
[Marcel Proust and Signs 1964] develops the
premise that A la recherche du temps perdu is a
novel about Marcel's relation to and education
in the interpretation of signs, while Présentation de Sacher-Masoch (1967; Masochism 1971)
argues through a close reading of Venus in
Furs that masochism is not inverted sadism but
operates by another logic that allows the ma-
sochist to escape the traps of Oedipalized subjectivity. This argument prefigures the break
with Freudian and Lacanian psychoanalytic
theory that will be elaborated in l'Anti-Oedipe.
(See *Lacan, *psychoanalytic theory, *sign.)

Deleuze's thought entered a new phase with
the publication of his principal doctoral thesis,
Différence et répétition [Difference and Repetition
1968], a survey of the conceptions of differ-
ence-in-itself and repetition-for-itself in the
history of philosophy, a survey that leads to
the method of 'transcendental empiricism'
which would allow a critical examination and
'disordering' of the a priori Kantian faculties.
In it, Deleuze develops his alternative to the
Platonic model of repetition (copies that refer
to an original model or Form): the repetition of
simulacra, without model or ideal, that causes
a non-conceptual, non-representational idea of
difference to emerge. This thesis was followed
by Logique du sens [The Logic of Sense 1969], a
set of 'series' or parallel meditations on the
paradoxical foundations of linguistic meaning
and subjectivity. Through analyses of Antonin
Artaud, Lewis Carroll and the Stoic philosophers, Deleuze formulates a model of self and
signification as restricted cases of delirium and
nonsense, the ceaselessly shifting play of
phantasmatic surface effects over the physical
bodies of words and things. Linguistic meaning, like subjectivity, is founded in the double
articulation of two series, signifier and signified, through a paradoxical element similar to
Lacan's point de capiton. (See *self/other, *paradox, *signified/signifier/signification.)

The third and most influential phase of Deleuze's career began after his meeting in 1969
with the psychoanalyst and political activist
*Félix Guattari. Their intellectual partnership
lasted through the 1970s and resulted in three
books: L'Anti-Oedipe: Capitalisme et schizo-

288

phrénie [*Anti-Oedipus: Capitalism and Schizo-phrenia* 1972], *Kafka: Pour une littérature mineure* [*Kafka: Towards a Minor Literature* 1975] and *Mille Plateaux: Capitalisme et schizophrénie 2* [*A Thousand Plateaus: Capitalism and Schizophrenia 2* 1980]. Initially conceived as an investigation of the French Communist party's failure to support the May 1968 student revolt in Paris, *L'Anti-Oedipe* became in execution a far-ranging critique of the Oedipal myth and the *ideology of lack in psychoanalysis, as well as a reinterpretation of the Marxist struggle against capitalist exploitation. To psychoanalysis' 'holy trinity' of the law's prohibition, castration's lack and the signifier's structured absence in the production of subjectivity, Deleuze and Guattari oppose the line of flight out of repression, the productivity of desire conceived as affirmation rather than lack, and the immanent relation of words and things that split the subject into multiplicities, a task they call 'schizoanalysis' in *L'Anti-Oedipe* and 'nomadology' in *Mille Plateaux*. (See *desire/lack.) Deleuzean desire (in the form of 'desiring-machines,' modelled after Melanie Klein's part-objects and Freudian/Lacanian partial drives, operating through the Oedipally unorganized 'body without organs' that is opposed to the humanist subject) invests objects directly, rather than becoming enmeshed in forms of ideology and representation. Its affirmative and relational character attests to its origin in Nietzsche's will to power. This desire flows from a machinic unconscious, which is productive like a factory, rather than from a linguistic unconscious like Freud's and Lacan's, which is representational like a theatre. Deleuze's and Guattari's formulation, endorsed and later expanded by *Michel Foucault in his *History of Sexuality*, provides a perspective on the connection of desire to the social system that is similar in many ways to Wilhelm Reich's materialist psychiatry. The Oedipal stage codes and reduces the multiplicity of desiring-machines into a subject that is based on socially exploitable genital sexuality and that mirrors the authoritarian form of the State, but the decoding tendency of capitalism constantly opens new markets of desire that capitalism must rigidly control in order to survive. Deleuze's and Guattari's strategy is to push the capitalist process further, to remove the limits capitalism places on this decoding or 'deterritorialization' which will free the desiring-machines and dismantle the subject and the State;

Kafka's writing, they insist, is an important example of this decoding operation, rather than the desperate mysticism it is often taken to be. *Mille Plateaux* takes the completion of this task (deterritorialization, the scrambling of all codes, which subsumes the *deconstruction of metaphysics that Derrida undertakes) as its starting point, and proceeds to create concepts for a world free of hierarchy and dialectical opposition. Like the work of *Jean-François Lyotard, that of Deleuze and Guattari seeks an ethics for a postmodern, deconstructed society. (See *code, *postmodernism.)

Since 1980 Deleuze has refused to confine himself to academic philosophy, preferring to create concepts for the understanding and practice of politics and the arts. He published a study of British painter Francis Bacon (1981), and produced the two volumes of a study of cinematic 'images' that relies on further Bergsonian meditations (1983, 1985). In the late 1980s he returned to the writing of monographs on individual philosophers, beginning with *Foucault* (1986). Deleuze sees Foucault as a philosopher and not as a historian because of what he considers to be Foucault's radical revision of the historian's task: Foucault's studies treat a two-fold object, the articulable and the visible (words and things, or statements and non-discursive objects of institutions), which interrelate to form the rigid historical strata or epistemes that constitute the apparatus of knowledge, the archive. (See *episteme.) Power, Foucault's often misunderstood preoccupation, becomes for Deleuze the fluid, strategic counterpart of knowledge that is manifested diagrammatically (as in the panopticism of *Discipline and Punish*). Deleuze's reading of this theory of power, which is often considered to be the most pessimistic facet of Foucault's work, stresses the dispersion of power throughout social space, a dispersion which can give rise to positioned subjects who resist centralized forms of domination. Thus Deleuze's Foucault, like his Nietzsche, becomes a figure of affirmation, as Deleuze himself has always been.

TIMOTHY S. MURPHY

Primary Sources

Deleuze. Gilles. *Le Bergsonisme*. Paris: PUF, 1966.
  Bergsonism. Trans. Hugh Tomlinson and Barbara Habberjam. New York: Zone, 1988.

- *Cinema 1: L'Image-Mouvement.* Paris: Editions de Minuit, 1983. *Cinema 1: The Movement-Image.* Trans. Hugh Tomlinson and Barbara Habberjam. Minneapolis: U of Minnesota P, 1986.
- *Cinema 2: L'Image-Temps.* Paris: Editions de Minuit, 1985. *Cinema 2: The Time-Image.* Trans. Hugh Tomlinson and Robert Galeta. Minneapolis: U of Minnesota P, 1989.
- *Différence et répétition.* Paris: PUF, 1968.
- *Empirisme et subjectivité.* Paris: PUF, 1953. *Empiricism and Subjectivity.* Trans. Constantin V. Boundas. New York: Columbia UP, 1991.
- *Foucault.* Paris: Editions de Minuit, 1986. *Foucault.* Trans. and ed. Sean Hand. Minneapolis: U of Minnesota P, 1988.
- *Francis Bacon: Logique de la sensation.* Paris: Editions de la Différance, 1981.
- *Logique du sens.* Paris: Editions de Minuit, 1969. *The Logic of Sense.* Trans. Mark Lester with Charles Stivale. New York: Columbia UP, 1990.
- *Marcel Proust et les signes.* Paris: PUF, 1964. *Proust and Signs.* Trans. Richard Howard. New York: George Braziller, 1972.
- *Nietzsche et la philosophie.* Paris: PUF, 1962. *Nietzsche and Philosophy.* Trans. Hugh Tomlinson. New York: Columbia UP, 1983.
- *Périclès et Verdi: La Philosophie de François Châtelet.* Paris: Editions de Minuit, 1988.
- *La Philosophie critique de Kant.* Paris: PUF, 1963. *Kant's Critical Philosophy.* Trans. Hugh Tomlinson and Barbara Habberjam. Minneapolis: U of Minnesota P, 1984.
- *Le Pli: Leibniz et le Baroque.* Paris: Editions de Minuit, 1988.
- *Pourparlers 1972–1990.* Paris: Editions de Minuit, 1990.
- *Présentation de Sacher-Masoch.* Paris: Editions de Minuit, 1967. *Masochism.* New York: George Braziller, 1971; Zone, 1989.
- 'Renverser le Platonisme.' In *Revue de Métaphysique et de Morale* 1967. 'Plato and the Simulacrum.' In *The Logic of Sense.* Trans. Mark Lester and Charles Stivale. New York: Columbia UP, 1990.
- *Spinoza: Philosophie pratique.* Paris: PUF, 1970. Rev. ed. Editions de Minuit, 1981. *Spinoza: Practical Philosophy.* Trans. Robert Hurley. San Francisco: City Lights, 1988.
- *Spinoza et le problème de l'expression.* Paris: Editions de Minuit, 1968. *Expressionism in Philosophy: Spinoza.* Trans. Martin Joughlin. New York: Zone, 1990.
- and Carmelo Bene. *Superpositions.* Paris: Editions de Minuit, 1979.
- and Michel Foucault. 'Les Intellectuels et le pouvoir.' In *L'Arc* 49 (1972). 'Intellectuals and Power.' In Foucault, *Language, Counter-Memory, Practice.* Trans. Donald F. Bouchard and Sherry Simon. Ithaca: Cornell UP, 1977.

- and Félix Guattari. *Capitalisme et schizophrénie 1: L'Anti-Oedipe.* Paris: Editions de Minuit, 1972. *Anti-Oedipus.* Trans. Robert Hurley, Mark Seem and Helen R. Lane. New York: Viking, 1977; Minneapolis: U of Minnesota P, 1983.
- and Félix Guattari. *Capitalisme et schizophrénie 2: Milles plateaux.* Paris: Editions de Minuit, 1980. *A Thousand Plateaus.* Trans. Brian Massumi. Minneapolis: U of Minnesota P, 1987.
- and Félix Guattari. *Kafka: Pour une littérature mineure.* Paris: Editions de Minuit, 1975. *Kafka: Toward a Minor Literature.* Trans. Dana Polan. Minneapolis: U of Minnesota P, 1986.
- and Félix Guattari. *Politique et psychanalyse.* Alençon: des mots perdus, 1977. Partial Eng. trans. in Paul Foss and Meaghan Morris, eds., *Language, Sexuality and Subversion.* Trans. Paul Foss and Meaghan Morris. Darlington, Australia: Feral P, 1978.
- and Félix Guattari. *Qu'est que-ce la philosophie?* Paris: Editions de Minuit, 1991.
- and Félix Guattari. *Rhizome.* Paris: Editions de Minuit, 1976. 'Rhizome.' Trans. John Johnston. In *On the Line.* By Gilles Deleuze and Félix Guattari. New York: Semiotext(e), 1983.
- and Claire Parnet. *Dialogues.* Paris: Flammarion, 1977. *Dialogues.* Trans. Hugh Tomlinson and Barbara Habberjam. New York: Columbia UP, 1987.

Secondary Sources

L'Arc 49 (1972, rev. 1980). Special Deleuze issue.

Baudrillard, Jean. *Oublier Foucault.* Paris: Galilée, 1977. *Forget Foucault.* Trans. Nicole Dufresne. New York: Semiotext(e), 1987.

Bogue, Ronald. *Deleuze and Guattari.* New York: Routledge, 1989.

Buydens, Mireille. *Sahara: L'Esthétique de Gilles Deleuze.* Paris: Vrin, 1990.

Chassaguet-Smirgel, Janine, ed. *Les Chemins de l'Anti-Oedipe.* Toulouse: Privat, 1974.

Cressole, Michel. *Deleuze.* Paris: Editions Universitaires, 1973.

Descombes, Vincent. *Le Même et l'autre.* Paris: Editions de Minuit, 1979. *Modern French Philosophy.* Trans. L. Scott-Fox and J.M. Harding. Cambridge: Cambridge UP, 1980, ch. 5–6.

Foucault, Michel. 'Theatrum Philosophicum.' 1970. In Foucault, *Language, Counter-Memory, Practice.* Trans. Donald F. Bouchard and Sherry Simon. Ithaca: Cornell UP, 1977.

Frank, Manfred. *Was ist Neostrukturalismus?* Frankfurt: Suhrkamp, 1984. Lectures 20–25. *What is Neostructuralism?* Trans. Sabine Wilke and Richard T. Gray. Minneapolis: U of Minnesota P, 1989.

Girard, René. 'Système du délire.' 1972. 'Delirium as System.' In Girard, *'To double business bound': Essays on Literature, Mimesis, and Anthropology.*

Trans. Paisley N. Livingston and Tobin Siebers. Baltimore: Johns Hopkins UP, 1978.

Guilmette, Armand. *Gilles Deleuze et la modernité*. Trois Rivières, Qué.: Éditions du Zéphyr, 1984.

Laruelle, François. *Les Philosophies de la différence*. Paris: PUF, 1986.

Lecercle, Jean-Jacques. *Philosophy Through the Looking Glass*. La Salle: Open Court, 1985.

Lendemains 14.52 (1989). Special Deleuze issue.

Lyotard, Jean-François. 'Capitalism énergumène.' 1972. 'Energumen Capitalism.' Trans. James Leigh. *Semiotext(e)* 2.3 (1977).

Magazine littéraire 257 (Sept. 1988). Special Deleuze issue.

Massumi, Brian. *User's Guide to Capitalism and Schizophrenia: Deviations from Deleuze and Guattari*. Cambridge: MIT P, 1992.

Perez, Rolando. *On An(archy) and Schizoanalysis*. Brooklyn: Autonomedia, 1990.

Semiotext(e) 2.3 (1977). Special *Anti-Oedipus* issue.

Sub-Stance 8.3–4 (1984) and 20.3 (1991). Special Deleuze issues.

della Volpe, Galvano

(b. Italy, 1895–d. 1968) Philosopher. Born into an aristocratic family of modest means, Galvano della Volpe served as a junior officer in the First World War, then earned a degree from the University of Bologna in 1920. From 1925 to 1938 he taught history and philosphy at a *liceo* in Ravenna, then at Bologna. He also taught history of philosophy at the University of Bologna from 1929 until 1938, when he obtained the chair of history of philosophy at the University of Messina. He worked there until his retirement in 1965. Della Volpe joined the Italian Communist party after the liberation of Sicily and, when the publication of *Logica come scienza positiva* [Logic as Positive Science 1950] brought him out of relative obscurity, he helped define its cultural policies, becoming an important contributor to party journals like *Società*. During the late 1950s and early 1960s he was the focal point of a loosely knit group of Marxist intellectuals. (See *Marxist criticism.)

Della Volpe was briefly associated with the Hegelian philosopher Giovanni Gentile, whose *attualismo* (which stresses the truth-value of spontaneous acts) was central to Fascist philosophy and *ideology, but soon became an ardent and effective critic of both Gentile and the Hegelian *Benedetto Croce. Della Volpe's opposition to the two most powerful figures

in Italian philosophy between the wars was confirmed by *Hegel romantico e mistico* [Hegel the Romantic and Mystic 1929], *La Filosofia dell'experienza di David Hume* (2 vols., 1933–5) and by his more explicit critique of Romanticism: *Critica dei principii logici* (1942). It was as a Marxist philosopher, however, during the 1940s and expecially after Stalin's death, that Della Volpe did his most original and influential work.

Until the publication of *Logica come scienza positiva* (the definitive edition published posthumously as *Logica come scienza storica*) Italian Marxist thought was dominated by historicism. Rejecting the Hegelian tendencies in Marxism as well as 'dia-mat,' the vulgarized dialectical materialism of Stalinist theoreticians, della Volpe retrieved from obscurity Marx's now famous 1857 *Introduction* to *A Contribution to the Critique of Political Economy*. Arguing against what he considered a contamination by Romanticism and idealism, he noted that starting with the *Critique of Hegel's Philosophy of Law* Marx had begun a radical epistemological break with Hegel, and suggested that Marxism was both a form of historicism and a positive science. In opposition to the generic abstractions of idealism, della Volpe proposed determinate abstractions derived from empirical inquiry and a methodology (found in embryo in the 1857 *Introduction* but having an important precedent in Galileo's hypothetico-deductive method) that moves from concrete to abstract to concrete. In *Rousseau e Marx* (1957; final edition 1964) della Volpe applied his method in an attempt to show how socialism is the only road by which humankind can realize both the civil liberty of Locke and Kant and the egalitarian liberty of Rousseau, and that 'only by proceeding from a gnoseological [cognitive], experimental-historical criterion is it possible to transform the world' (99).

Della Volpe's aesthetics and poetics complemented his work in epistemology, representing both a development of his theses and a testing ground for them. (See *Crisi dell'estetica romantica* [1941], *Poetica del Cinquecento* [1954] and *Il Verosimile filmico e altri scritti di estetica* [1954]). The final section of *Critica dell'ideologia contemporanea* (1967) has some important remarks on aesthetics and, with *Schizzo di una storia del gusto estetica* (1971), presents the final development of della Volpe's thought. His best known and most influential work on aesthetics, *Critica del gusto* (1960) is typically anti-Romantic and materialist. Though it is in part a response to Crocean idealism, it is also and more explicitly a critique of Georgii V. Plekhanov and especially *Georg Lukács. Though della Volpe agreed with the Marxian emphasis on the sociohistorical contextuality of art and was principally concerned with the relation of art to its social and historical 'humus,' stating that the greater the poetry the more it demands a concrete, sociological account of its style (46), he considered the use in aesthetics of sociopolitical criteria – criteria external to the work of art – as unjustified. The resulting choices, such as Lukács' preference for Thomas Mann over Franz Kafka, are artificial because 'authentic poetry is always realist (sociological) truth' (243).

Della Volpe insisted on the concrete reality of *parole*, the subjective speech-act, and *langue*, the historical and social institution without which communication would be impossible. (See *langue/parole*.) He drew on Saussurean linguistics and Hjelmslev's glossomatics (empirical and deductive linguistics rather than grammar and phonology), affirming that the linguistic *sign is arbitrary with respect to the signified and that it is made up of pleremes, which contain meaning and thought, and cenemes, which do not. (See *Ferdinand de Saussure.) Contrary to the Romantic and post-Romantic theories espoused by many Marxists, della Volpe considered that '"form" ... is to be identified with thought or concept, and not with ... abstract or mystical "images" ... which lack meaning,' while 'content' is to be identified 'with matter and multiplicity' (22). There is a 'gnoseological distinction between "form" as instrument and means of knowledge ... and form-end, or thought, of expressed value,' and it is necessary to give back 'its full gnoseological and philosophical meaning – synonymous with *thought* – to the term (poetic) *form*' (*Critica dell'ideologia* 136).

In poetry as in science, thought is the end and language always the means. Poetry has a semantic-formal rigour different from but in no way inferior to scientific language. Both stand in opposition to ordinary language: the latter is equivocal, while scientific discourse is univocal and poetry is polysemic. Della Volpe's theory of the autonomy of poetic *discourse has its basis in the plurality of its meanings, which are indissociable from a determinate context; it is therefore a semantic and scientifically verifiable autonomy rather than a metaphysical one (124). But poetry has an artistic as well as a scientific specificity; this specificity is the essence of a historical phenomenon, but is concrete and characteristic rather than simply what is most common at a given historical moment. The differences between scientific and poetic discourse neither contradict their equal cognitive value nor affirm the traditional dichotomy between reason and feeling. There is no such thing as the ineffable, and all poetry worthy of the name is translatable. (See theories of *translation.)

In the last section of *Critica del gusto*, 'Laocoonte 1960,' della Volpe expands his inquiry to the other arts. Like Lessing before him, he maintains (against Horace) the plurality of means of expression and '*the peaceful co-existence of the arts* on equal terms' (230). He also argues for the separation of the artistic genres, whose structural differences mean that one genre cannot be translated into another. (See *genre criticism.) In light of della Volpe's views on the arbitrary nature of the linguistic sign and the rational essence, and hence translatability, of poetry these affirmations present difficulties which have been noted by some of his critics. Della Volpe's discussion of films made from literary works is generally convincing, but music especially presents problems which he did not fully resolve though he returned to the question several times before his death. He also left unresolved some confusions concerning the linguistic sign and its counterparts in the other arts.

Della Volpe's theories have been variously criticized and praised for their perceived positivist or structuralist tendencies, positions which he explicitly rejected. Though his influence waned after the closing of *Società* in 1962 and no 'school' continued to explore the specific lines of inquiry he had initiated, della Volpe's work was important for (especially but not exclusively) Marxian philosophy and aesthetics in and beyond Italy. His return to the 1857 *Introduction* proved decisive in the development of materialist epistemology. In 1974, for example, Colletti remarked that when he read *Louis Althusser's *For Marx* he found a 'convergence with classical theses of the della Volpean current in Italian Marxism' ('Interview'), while the methodology of the *Introduction* has been central to Lucien Sève's defence of dialectical materialism in France. Della Volpe's aesthetics represented a reappraisal and critique of the dominant trends in Marxian thought, helping distance Marxian aesthetics from Zhdanovist dogmatism and providing a materialist alternative to formalism and *structuralism. (See also *materialist criticism.)

NICOLA VULPE

Primary Sources

della Volpe, Galvano. *Opere*. Ed. Ignazio Ambrogio. 6 vols. Rome: Editori Riuniti, 1972–3.
– *Crisi dell'estetica romantica*. Messina: D'Anna, 1941.
– *Critica del gusto*. 1960. 5th ed. Milan: Feltrinelli, 1979. *Critique of Taste*. Trans. M. Caesar. London: NLB, 1978.
– *Critica dell'ideologia contemporanea: Saggi di teoria dialettica*. Rome: Editori Riuniti, 1967. *Critique de l'idéologie contemporaine: Essais de théorie dialectique*. Trans. P. Méthais. Paris: PUF, 1976.
– *Critica dei principii logici*. Messina: G. d'Anna, 1942.
– 'Discorso poetico e discorso scientifico.' In *Marxismo e critica letteraria in Italia*. Ed. F. Bettini and M. Bevilacqua. Rome: Editori Riuniti, 1975.
– *La Filosofia dell'experienza di David Hume*. Firenze: G.C. Sansoni, 1933–5.
– *Hegel romantico e mistico*. Firenze: Le Monnier, 1929.
– *Logica come scienza positiva*. Messina: 6 d'Anno, 1950. *Logic as Positive Science*. Trans. J. Rothschild. London: NLB, 1980. *La Logique comme science historique*. Trans. P. Methays. Brussels: Editions Complexe, 1977.
– *Poetica del Cinquecento*. Bari: Laterza, 1954.
– *Rousseau e Marx e altri saggi di critica materialistica*. Rome: Editori Riuniti, 1964. *Rousseau and Marx and Other Writings*. Trans. J. Fraser. Atlantic Highlands, NJ: Humanities, 1979. *Rousseau et Marx et autres essais de critique matérialiste*. Trans. R. Paris. Paris: Bernard Grasset, 1974.
– *Schizzo di una storia del gusto estetica*. Rome: Editori Riuniti, 1971.
– *Il Verosimile filmico e altri scritti di estetica*. Rome: Filmcritica, 1954.

Secondary Sources

Ambrogio, Ignazio. 'Per un teoria letteraria marxista: Galvano della Volpe.' In *Ideologie e techniche letterarie*. Rome: Editori Riuniti, 1974, 183–208.
Bettini, Filipo, et al., eds. *Marxismo e structuralismo nella critica letteraria italiana*. Rome: Savelli, 1974.
Bettini, Filipo, and Mirko Bevilacqua, eds. *Marxismo e critica letteraria in Italia*. Rome: Editori Riuniti, 1975.
Colletti, Lucio. 'A Political and Philosophical Interview.' *New Left Review* 86 (1974): 3–28.

Fraser, John. *Introduction to the Thought of Galvano Della Volpe*. London: Lawrence and Wishart, 1977.
Guiducci, Armanda. *Dallo zdanovismo allo strutturalismo*. Milan: Feltrinelli, 1967.
Howard, D., and K.E. Klare, eds. *The Unknown Dimension*. New York: Basic Books, 1972.
'Introduction to Della Volpe.' *New Left Review* 59 (1970): 97–100.
Montano, Mario. 'On the Methodology of Determinate Abstraction: Essay on Galvano della Volpe.' *Telos* 7 (1971): 30–49.
Musolino, Rocco. *Marxismo ed estetica in Italia*. Rome: Editori Riuniti, 1971.
Rossi, Mario. 'Galvano della Volpe: Dalla gnoseologia critica alla logica storica.' *Critica Marxista* 4–5 (1968): 165–201 and 6 (1968): 89–124.
Quaderni dell'Istituto Galvano della Volpe. Messina: La Libra, 1978–83.
Tosel, André. *Praxis*. Paris: Editions sociales, 1984.
Vacca, Giuseppe. *Scienza stato e critica di classe: Galvano Della Volpe e il marxismo*. Bari: De Donato, 1970.

de Man, Paul

(b. Belgium, 1919–d. 1983) Philologist and literary critic. Paul de Man was born in Antwerp in 1919 into an upper-middle-class Fleming family already intellectually and politically prominent. As a student of engineering at the Université Libre de Bruxelles, he wrote his first articles for two journals of the socialist Cercle du Libre Examen, dedicated to democratic free-thinking and hostile to dogmatism, Fascism and the clergy (*Responses* xii). In this spirit, he opposed war and opposed Hitlerism as an 'intra-European colonization,' the ultimate defeat of which, though desirable, would be useless without the rectification of the economic and social debacle which gave rise to Fascism in the first place (*Wartime Journalism* 8, 13).

The invasion of Belgium by Germany (May 1940) brought publishing under the control of the Military Occupation's Propaganda Department. De Man continued to review books, lectures and musical occasions for *Le Soir*, Belgium's largest newspaper. These articles, discovered and reprinted only after his death, have given rise to charges of collaboration and anti-Semitism. In fact, de Man shows from the first perhaps an excessive confidence in a strategy of cooperative disrespect or solemn insolence (Derrida, 'Like the Sound' 602, 628) with regard to the censor. He urges upon his readers the example of Till Eulenspiegel, who victimized authority figures by pretending stupidity; his best weapons were 'mystification and language,' not arms (*Wartime Journalism* 232). The article from 4 March 1941, which some have found unequivocally anti-Semitic, claims that Jewish writers, because of their utter mediocrity, have had no pernicious effect on modern *literature at all (references to such 'perniciousness' were a commonplace of Nazi propaganda at the time). The same article celebrates Franz Kafka, a Jew, as a modern master of psychological realism. The piece also attacks 'vulgar anti-Semitism' as a conception that could lead to 'quite dangerous consequences' (*Wartime Journalism* 45).

The second phase of de Man's literary career began after the war with his emigration to the U.S.A. in 1948. In 1952 he enrolled at Harvard to study comparative literature. His literary work from the period centres on the notion of 'inwardness,' a contemplative inwardness dissimilar to the anti-intellectual, ahistorical nihilism of writers like Jünger, Malraux and Hemingway (*Critical Writings* 14, 16). Any positive inwardness must be a meditation on history as process and becoming (*le devenir* in *Critical Writings* 66). Positive inwardness embraces the consciousness of struggle (33) and accepts the painful dialectic of desire and sacrifice (85). Historical action, though always a defeat, and often degrading, is not in vain (*The Rhetoric of Romanticism* 36). Such defeat can be 'temporally productive,' allowing for the 'language of reflection to constitute itself' (ibid. 57). The moment that action is seen as error, interpretive reflection can begin. So 'the coming-to-consciousness is in arrears vis-à-vis the actual act' (58). Titanic excess, after failure, turns back upon itself to be transformed into language (57, 63), into self-recollection (45), and thought 'whose law is that of an incessantly heightened concentration and rigor' (*Critical Writings* 75). Heroes of this pulsation to inwardness, of consciousness as mediated apprehension of being (*The Rhetoric of Romanticism* 40), are Wordsworth as disillusioned Girondist, the mature Hölderlin and his character Hyperion, as well as Goethe's Faust. The publication of *Blindness and Insight* (1971) represents the principal monument of this second phase of de Man's work.

The third and last phase is both better known and more obscure, involving an affiliation with Yale University (after 1970), a friend-ship with *Jacques Derrida (since 1966), and the controversial American extrapolation of *deconstruction, a continental philosophical practice deriving from *Martin Heidegger. The group of writers designated as the Yale Critics – including, aside from de Man, *Harold Bloom, *Geoffrey Hartman and *J. Hillis Miller – had primarily their university in common, but nevertheless achieved a certain critical hegemony between 1975 and de Man's death in 1983. The group's unfamiliar, 'un-American' vocabulary, as well as a gleeful vertiginousness of interpretation, aroused both widespread hostility as well as admiration.

This part of de Man's production, culminating in the publication of *Allegories of Reading* (1979), is marked by increasingly radical meditations on the relationship of language to reality. If a tragic encounter with history was the starting-point of reflection in de Man's Hölderlin period, reflection and the texts it generates now seem to be the starting-point of history. Not that reflection itself is an unproblematic process; it is never entirely under the control of the will. There is an intent to mean, to reflect in a certain way, but because we reflect in language, our meaning is subject to linguistic properties that are not subject to us, properties, devices that at times function in a purely mechanical way. Consequently, the effort made by Rousseau to make sense of his defamation of the servant Marion, an unbearable episode which he says motivated the entire *Confessions*, cannot obscure the fact that his false accusation of Marion has no rational connection to the interpersonal dynamics in the Comte de la Roque's household and nothing to do with either the play of desire or Rousseau's perverse need for self-exposure. Marion was simply 'the first object that offered itself'; her subsequent fate, and Rousseau's, are the random results of anacoluthia, non-sequentiality (*Allegories of Reading* 289; Latimer 115). The disjunction between Rousseau's interests and his accusation could not be more complete. Similarly, in his *Essay on the Origin of Language*, Rousseau traces (in de Man's account) the very possibility of human society from two metaphoric distortions masquerading as straightforwardly literal moments of denomination (naming). When primitive man first encounters a fellow human, he designates the other as 'giant,' displacing his own inner fear, which then becomes the outward property of the other. Fear, the expression of a comparison between two entities, is figural, but when fear becomes the name 'giant,' hypothesis becomes definite and fiction is passed off as fact. Later, when primitive first impressions are modified by experience and 'giant' becomes 'man,' the new denomination relies on a numerical illusion of identity (the other is after all only one person of my own size) to obscure ontic difference (size and number have nothing to do with relative danger). (See *self/other.) But the circuitous invention of this word 'man' engenders 'men' and ultimately 'the sameness within difference of civil society' (*Allegories of Reading* 155; Sprinker 253). Passionate error is followed by deliberate error to provide the quaking foundation of the social contract. 'The political destiny of man ... is derived from a linguistic model' (*Allegories of Reading* 159). Such application of linguistic reality to natural reality is as inevitable as it is erroneous. When it happens, the aesthetic realm oversteps its proper bounds into natural life, into matters of ethics, into the empirical world. And 'nothing can be more destructive' (158). Language is referential, but its actual referent remains problematic (160).

Because of these difficulties and dangers, we must try to assert some control over language's technical problems (*The Resistance to Theory* 121). Vigilant reading will discover the dangerous asymmetry between *text and world and refuse to suppress a text's discontinuities to produce illusory coherence or yield to the dissimulating harmony of the aesthetic (*Critical Writings* 222). It is de Man's persistent emphasis on the epistemological as against the rhetorical properties of language (Norris 71, 203) that associates his work with *Ideologiekritik* (*The Resistance to Theory* 121; Norris 155; Culler 130–5). For de Man, *ideology, or the pervasive intellectual ambiance in which we live our lives, would certainly include all tendencies on the part of the educational apparatus of universities and their professors to see the teaching of literature as a lesson on how to live properly or how to be a good citizen (*The Resistance to Theory* 24). What literature in such instances becomes is a solicitation or *interpellation by a given social order, the seduction or absorption of the student by his or her culture through *Erziehung* (*The Resistance to Theory* 24). De Man associates the aesthetic with precisely this attempt to manipulate others, to deprive them of their freedom through the machinery of persuasion and the luxuri-

ance of rhetoric. As an antidote to the aesthetic, de Man prescribes 'literariness' (*The Resistance to Theory* 9). Literariness breaks the Cratylian 'secular myth' (the belief in the coincidence of names and essences, in motivated signs) that the union of sound and meaning found in aesthetic objects, with their fusion of the sensuous and conceptual, the phenomenal and intelligible, can be anything more than a rhetorical effect, or can provide any warrant for responsible pronouncements about the nature of the world. The relationship between word and thing, says de Man, is purely conventional, not at all phenomenal. To forget this lesson of the literary is to fall into the trap of the aesthetic, to participate in an imaginative choreography which disguises its coercion and violence as 'the gracefulness of a dance' (*The Rhetoric of Romanticism* 290).

Hostility to theory derives in part from theory's role in exposing ideological mystifications involved in the teaching of literature. It is not certain, says de Man, that literature is a reliable source of information about anything but its own language (*The Resistance to Theory* 11). Furthermore, despite all vigilance, the randomness of linguistic operations can at times transcend the powers of the human will. The structures and tensions of language are independent of our intent to mean. Language 'does things ... so radically out of our control' that we must not say, as Schiller does, that language defines the human. Indeed, it cannot be said with confidence that language is a human thing at all (*The Resistance to Theory* 87, 101).

DAN LATIMER

Primary Sources

de Man, Paul. *Allegories of Reading: Figural Language in Rousseau, Nietzsche, Rilke, and Proust.* New Haven/London: Yale UP, 1979.
– *Blindness and Insight: Essays in the Rhetoric of Contemporary Criticism.* 1971. 2nd ed., rev., intro. by Wlad Godzich. Minneapolis: U of Minnesota P, 1983.
– *Critical Writings, 1953–1978.* Ed. and intro. by Lindsay Waters. Minneapolis: U of Minnesota P, 1989.
– *The Resistance to Theory.* Foreword by Wlad Godzich. Minneapolis: U of Minnesota P, 1986.
– *The Rhetoric of Romanticism.* New York: Columbia UP, 1984.
– *Wartime Journalism, 1939–1943.* Ed. Werner Hamacher, Neil Hertz and Thomas Keenan. Lincoln/London: U of Nebraska P, 1988.

Derrida

Secondary Sources

Arac, Jonathan, Wlad Godzich and Wallace Martin, eds. *The Yale Critics: Deconstruction in America*. Minneapolis: U of Minnesota P, 1983.

Brooks, Peter, Shoshana Felman and J. Hillis Miller, eds. 'The Lesson of Paul de Man,' *Yale French Studies* 69 (1985): 132.

Culler, Jonathan. 'De Man's Rhetoric,' In *Framing the Sign: Criticism and Its Institutions*. Oxford: Basil Blackwell, 1988, 107–35.

Derrida, Jacques. 'Biodegradables: Seven Diary Fragments.' Trans. Peggy Kamuf. *Critical Inquiry* 15 (Summer 1989): 812–73.

– 'Like the Sound of the Sea Deep within a Shell: Paul de Man's War.' Trans. Peggy Kamuf. *Critical Inquiry* 14 (Spring 1988): 590–652.

– *Mémoires: For Paul de Man*. New York: Columbia UP, 1986.

Hamacher, Werner, Neil Hertz and Thomas Keenan, eds. *Responses: On Paul de Man's Wartime Journalism*. Lincoln/London: U of Nebraska P, 1989.

Latimer, Dan. 'Anxieties of Reading: Paul de Man and the Purloined Ribbon.' In *Comparative Poetics*. Ed. Claudio Guillén. New York: Garland, 1985, 113–20.

Lentricchia, Frank. *After the New Criticism*. Chicago: U of Chicago P, 1980.

Norris, Christopher. *Paul de Man: Deconstruction and the Critique of Aesthetic Ideology*. New York/London: Routledge, 1988.

Sprinker, Michael. *Imaginary Relations: Aesthetics and Ideology in the Theory of Historical Materialism*. London/New York: Verso, 1987.

Waters, Lindsay, and Wlad Godzich, eds. *Reading de Man Reading*. Minneapolis: U of Minnesota P, 1989.

Derrida, Jacques

(b. Algeria, 1930–) Philosopher. Derrida studied at the Ecole Normale Supérieure (Paris), taught philosophy at the Sorbonne (1960–4) and from 1965 was professor of philosophy at the Ecole Normale Supérieure. Founding director of the Collège International de Philosophie in Paris, he is now *directeur d'études* at the Ecole des Hautes Etudes en Sciences Sociales in Paris. For over a decade beginning in 1975 Derrida taught a yearly seminar at Yale University and now has visiting appointments at the University of California at Irvine and Cornell University.

A radical philosophical thinker, Derrida joins a polemic of tradition directed against metaphysics that extends from *Nietzsche to *Heidegger. His critique of metaphysics and of the 'presence' of consciousness owes much to *Freud's discovery of the unconscious and theory of unconscious memory. His challenging of idealist conceptions of language is an extension of principles laid down by *Ferdinand de Saussure and his structuralist heirs. Derrida has, as well, French precursors, most notably *Maurice Blanchot who, like Derrida, celebrates the *trace of writing or *écriture* as the originary play of presence and absence. (See *metaphysics of presence, *structuralism, *text, *textuality.)

Derrida's writings critique the Western metaphysical tradition, which he sees as dominated by a discourse of 'presence' in the assumption, for example, that truth is a function of the presence of consciousness to itself and to its object; or in the assumption that time is oriented to its end – the destruction of history – as the advent of *parousia* or of a transcendental signified. (See *signified/signifier/signification.) Derrida links such assumptions to the *logocentrism of the Western metaphysical tradition in which faith in 'presence' conspires with the privilege bestowed upon the spoken word or voice as opposed to the graphic sign or writing. He maintains that in the history of Western thought writing or graphic representation has been consistently devalued in favour of the proximity (or 'presence') of the voice or speech to thought and consciousness.

The early part of Derrida's career was devoted to a demonstration of the dominance of these metaphysical presuppositions through the treatment of a great variety of writers and thinkers. What Derrida calls *deconstruction consists in an analysis which overturns these tenacious metaphysical foundations. But Derrida also showed an interest in those texts which 'deconstruct' their own traditional frameworks, which manage to test and force the logocentric boundaries within which they must operate: hence his interest in Nietzsche, Artaud, Bataille, Genet, Ponge, Célan, and others. This double focus forms a pattern throughout Derrida's career.

Just as important is Derrida's strategy of reading in the 'margins,' which strongly influenced the development of deconstruction in North America as a method for the analysis of literary texts. An apparently marginal aspect of the text, often located in a key word or series of cognate words, is isolated as the locus of a doubleness and contradiction undermining the text's coherence and intelligibility, a coherence and intelligibility that traditional interpretation has only been able to uphold by an act of suppression. A set of such double words (the supplement, the pharmakon, the hymen, the 'parergon') might be seen as intellectual milestones in Derrida's career. (See *margin, *supplementarity.)

For Derrida, what all these effects have in common is their relationship to writing. They are images of writing and of its ambivalent doubleness in the history of metaphysics. On the negative side, writing appears as that which is merely secondary, external, a necessary but dangerous supplement to speech. Writing represents and reproduces a natural, living 'presence' only at the price of the becoming-absent and death of the subject and its meaning. The other face of writing is the one that the metaphysical tradition has been unable to consistently suppress, a general or 'arche-writing' which is the condition of signification in the first place. Derrida does not simply repeat the metaphysical opposition by championing writing in opposition to speech but attempts to show how both speech and writing share precisely the same features. The absence of the subject and the referent is a consequence of the possibility of signification in general, since the intelligibility of any *sign, whether spoken or written, depends on a differential network of signifiers. The subject is thus divided in its very constitution by the institution of the sign. By the same token the deferral of the signified or 'proper meaning' is endless. (See *subject/object, *reference/referent.)

Derrida's most programmatic statement can be found in *De la Grammatologie* [Of Grammatology 1967], the book for which he is best known in North America and one which resumes many of his central concerns. Equally seminal are a handful of early essays, such as 'La Pharmacie de Platon' ('Plato's Pharmacy' 1968), 'La Mythologie blanche' ('White Mythology' 1971) and 'Le Facteur de la vérité' (1975), as well as the essay devoted to the one term by which Derrida is perhaps best known: 'La Différance' (1968). (See *white mythology, *différance/différence, *grammatology.)

Derrida's greatest influence has been in the U.S.A., where his work inspired a new critical scepticism initially associated with the so-called Yale School of deconstruction. This influence, especially as it concerns the reading strategy that he developed to deconstruct texts,

is prominent in the work of *Paul de Man, *J. Hillis Miller and Barbara Johnson, among others. Derrida's work has proven, in spite of the great controversy that has surrounded it, to be both remarkably consistent in the development of its original tenets and surprisingly various in its applications.

JOSEPH ADAMSON

Primary Sources

Derrida, Jacques. *The Archaeology of the Frivolous: Reading Condillac.* Pittsburgh: Duquesne UP, 1981.
– *Dissemination.* Trans. Barbara Johnson. Chicago: U of Chicago P, 1981.
– *The Ear of the Other: Otobiography, Transference, Translation.* Ed. Christie McDonald. Lincoln: U of Nebraska P, 1988.
– *Glas.* Paris: Galilée, 1974.
– *Margins of Philosophy.* Trans. Alan Bass. Chicago: U of Chicago P, 1982.
– *Of Grammatology.* Trans. Gayatri Chakravorty Spivak. Baltimore: Johns Hopkins UP, 1977.
– *The Post Card: From Socrates to Freud and Beyond.* Trans. Alan Bass. Chicago: U of Chicago P, 1987.
– *Signéponge/Signsponge.* Trans. Richard Rand. New York: Columbia UP, 1984.
– *Speech and Phenomena.* Trans. David B. Allison. Evanston: Northwestern UP, 1973.
– *Spurs.* Trans. Alan Bass. Chicago: U of Chicago P, 1979.
– *D'un ton apocalyptique adopté naguère en philosophie.* Paris: Galilée, 1983.
– *The Truth in Painting.* Trans. Geoff Bennington and Ian McLeod. Chicago: U of Chicago P, 1987.
– *Writing and Difference.* Trans. Alan Bass. Chicago: U of Chicago P, 1978.

Secondary Sources

Culler, Jonathan. *On Deconstruction: Theory and Criticism after Structuralism.* Ithaca: Cornell UP, 1982.
Hartman, Geoffey H. *Saving the Text: Literature/Derrida/Philosophy.* Baltimore: Johns Hopkins UP, 1981.
Harvey, Irene. *Derrida and the Economy of Différance.* Bloomington: Indiana UP, 1986.
Norris, Christopher. *Deconstruction: Theory and Practice.* London: Methuen, 1982.

Dilthey, Wilhelm

(b. Germany, 1833–d. 1911) Philosopher. After briefly studying theology, Dilthey transferred his interest to philosophy and history, receiving a doctorate from Berlin (1864) and becoming *Privat-Dozent* in philosophy the next year. His outwardly uneventful life was marked by series of professorships: Basel (1867), Kiel (1868), Breslau (1871), and Berlin (1882). After retiring from teaching in 1905, he devoted himself to working on what was to have been his magnum opus, a Kantian 'Critique of Historical Reason.' Though prolific, he published in his lifetime only three books; the fact that two of these were initial parts of larger projects (never completed) led to the label 'Mann der ersten Bände' – a man of first volumes. But after his death, his study yielded many thousands of manuscript pages of works promised and previously unknown, now published as *Gesammelte Schriften*. Until recently his work was virtually unknown by English readers. A useful one-volume selection was published in 1976 and in 1985 a projected 6-volume edition of major texts began to appear. Dilthey holds a pivotal position in the continuing debate over *hermeneutics and his work is an important influence in the thought of *Martin Heidegger, *Hans-Georg Gadamer and *Paul Ricoeur.

As a philosopher Dilthey was indebted to both the Hegelians and neo-Kantians and also to British empiricism and French positivism. By rejecting the metaphysical apriorism of the former, however, and the bloodless mechanism of the latter, he elaborated a philosophy in which life is understood from the experience of life itself. Investigative methods based on mathematics and appropriate to the natural sciences *(Naturwissenschaften)*, he argued, ignore the affective and volitional aspects of human experience and reduce knowledge – as Locke, Hume, Kant, and their various followers had done – to the a priori edicts of a legislative Reason. For Dilthey experience and cognition depend upon the complex interrelations of thought, feeling and will as these are revealed in life itself and in those records of life preserved (for example) in history and *literature. His enterprise therefore was to distinguish from the natural sciences and their methods a group of disciplines which he called the 'human studies' *(Geisteswissenschaften)*. These comprise essentially what we would call the humanities and social sciences. Personal interest led Dilthey to explore especially psychology, history, literature, and music.

The essence of Dilthey's epistemology may be summarized in the definition of two terms: lived experience *(Erlebnis)* and understanding

(Verstehen). An *Erlebnis* is a coherent unit of immediate experience in which elements of feeling, will and desire are unified in a common meaning and rescued from temporal flux. Several trips to a gallery to view a particular painting, for example, form a single lived experience. Such *Erlebnisse* (plural) are prelogical and constitute the empirical ground on which consciousness is built, and it is axiomatic with the antimetaphysical Dilthey that human consciousness cannot go behind itself, that is to say, that *Erlebnisse*, its basic units, constitute the irreducible root of knowledge. Dilthey, then, is a psychological empiricist and relativist; but he is not a solipsist. While personal awareness is the primary reality, mental life also depends on the vicarious apprehension of the lived experiences of other minds. It is understanding *(Verstehen)* which makes possible a dynamic involvement in the not-self and Dilthey defines it as a rediscovery of the I in the Thou *(das Verstehen ist ein Wiederfinden des Ich im Du)*. To understand is to relive or to reconstruct another's experience, to make his *Erlebnis* my own, and this is possible because human beings share the same mental structure. Understanding, then, which is fundamental to the *Geisteswissenschaften*, provides access to the human world beyond the parochial self. History and literature, for example, both demand imaginative participation in worlds outside the self – a dynamic interaction that involves a projection of I into the Thou and an assimilation of Thou to the I. They thus give breadth and depth (as well as objectivity) to experience and, since understanding implies self-discovery, they actualize the self's latent potential. In this way art and history, no less than science, are vehicles of truth.

Central to Dilthey's method in the 'human studies' is his adaptation of the scheme for a general hermeneutics proposed by Friedrich D.E. Schleiermacher (1768–1834), the subject of Dilthey's first major publication, *Leben Schleiermachers* (1870). In his *Hermeneutik* (1836) Schleiermacher distinguished between a grammatical (philological) and a psychological understanding of a text, the object of the latter being to reconstruct the living idea in an author's mind, of which his *text was the expression. Hermeneutics as an *art* of understanding (not a *science* of explanation) and Schleiermacher's 'divinatory' recovery of an author through his writings offered the possibility, as Dilthey saw, of employing psychology as the universal basis and theoretical, methodological vindication of the *Geisteswissenschaften* as a group. The interpretation of art furnished an analogy for the interpretation of life itself. As a poem or play (the educts of experiential imagination or *Erlebnisphantasie)* is an objectification of lived experience that mediates the living mind of the author himself and his *Weltanschauung,* so historical acts or even the gestures and facial expressions of those around us open outward and inward, through interpretive and reconstructive understanding, both to discovery and self-discovery. But as Ricoeur has pointed out, 'the counterpart of a hermeneutical theory founded on psychology is that psychology remains its ultimate justification' (51); and the central *aporia of Dilthey's method is that it deflects understanding away from the *text itself and onto the author, so that the text loses its autonomy and becomes, in fact, a pretext. After Dilthey, interest shifts from epistemology to ontology in the work of Heidegger and Gadamer and the presuppositions of psychological hermeneutics become themselves the object of investigation. Instead of asking 'How do I know?', the question of philosophic hermeneutics is 'What are the ontological conditions of my knowing?' – an approach with its own methodological difficulties and frustrations.

JOHN SPENCER HILL

Primary Sources

Dilthey, Wilhelm. *Hermeneutics: The Handwritten Manuscripts of F.D.E. Schleiermacher.* Ed. Heinz Kimmerle. Trans. James Duke and Jack Forstman. Missoula, Mont.: Scholars P, 1977.
– *Leben Schleiermachers.* Vols. 13 and 14. In *Gesammelte Schriften,* 17 vols. (1914–74). Vols. 1–12, Stuttgart: B.G. Teubner. Vols. 13–17, Göttingen: Vandenhoeck and Ruprecht.
– *Pattern and Meaning in History: Thoughts on History and Society.* Ed. H.P. Rickman. London: Allen and Unwin, 1961; New York: Harper and Row, 1962.
– *Selected Works.* Ed. Rudolf A. Makkreel and Frithjof Rodi. 6 vols. Princeton: Princeton UP, 1985.
– *Selected Writings.* Ed. H.P. Rickman. Cambridge: Cambridge UP, 1976.

Secondary Sources

Emarth, Michael. *Wilhelm Dilthey: The Critique of Historical Reason.* Chicago: U of Chicago P, 1978.
Hodges, Herbert Arthur. *The Philosophy of Wilhelm Dilthey.* London: Routledge and Kegan Paul, 1952. Repr. Westport, Conn.: Greenwood P, 1974.
– *Wilhelm Dilthey: An Introduction.* London: Routledge and Kegan Paul, 1944. Repr. New York: Howard Fertig, 1969.
Makkreel, Rudolf A. *Dilthey: Philosopher of the Human Studies.* Princeton: Princeton UP, 1975.
Mueller-Vollmer, Kurt, ed. *The Hermeneutics Reader: Texts of the German Tradition from the Enlightenment to the Present.* New York: Continuum, 1985.
Palmer, Richard E. *Hermeneutics: Interpretation Theory in Schleiermacher, Dilthey, Heidegger, and Gadamer.* Evanston, Ill.: Northwestern UP, 1969.
Plantinga, Theodore. *Historical Understanding in the Thought of Wilhelm Dilthey.* Toronto: U of Toronto P, 1980.
Rickman, H.P. *Wilhelm Dilthey: Pioneer of the Human Studies.* Berkeley: U of California P, 1979.
Ricoeur, Paul. 'The Task of Hermeneutics.' (1975). In *Hermeneutics and the Human Sciences.* Ed. John B. Thompson. Cambridge: Cambridge UP, 1981, 43–62.

Ducrot, Oswald

(b. France, 1930–) Linguist and philosopher. Oswald Ducrot received his formal education in philosophy at the Ecole Normale Supérieure, Sorbonne. After teaching philosophy at various institutes of higher learning, he became a member of the Centre Nationale de Recherche Scientifique and now teaches at the Ecole des Hautes Etudes en Sciences Sociales, Paris, where he has been director since 1968. He has been honoured by the Université de Génève with a doctorate honoris causa for his work on the history of linguistics, the notion of enunciation and for his study of the marks and structures of argumentation in language. (See *enonciation/énoncé.*)

Ducrot first concentrated on the history of linguistics and particularly that of *structuralism. He then turned to semantics and, together with Jean-Claude Anscombre, developed the linguistic current known as *Nouvelle Linguistique.* His theory moves beyond a narrow consideration of elements belonging to the language *code and integrates the concept of enunciation proceeding from English analytical philosophy (Peter Strawson, Bertrand Russell, *John Austin, and *John Searle) into linguistics. Ducrot understands *énonciation,* or 'enunciation,' as a sequence of sentences that is actualized, assumed by a particular speaker and hearer (called the interlocutor) in specific temporal and spatial circumstances. By taking into account the specific circumstances of linguistic production, Ducrot institutes an opposition between language and logic that neither reduces one into the other nor proposes radically heterogeneous categories. He feels that the logic inherent in language cannot be enclosed within the syllogistic logic of formal, philosophical systems. While a formal logic seeks to prove a hypothesis, ordinary language by nature seeks to persuade or convince through argument.

Nouvelle Linguistique examines integrated rhetoric or argumentation parting from this new logic of language and moves semantics beyond a study that is limited to the enunciation's explicitly transmitted information to include a consideration of its levels of implicit meaning as well. Ducrot's study of the relation between the explicit and implicit aspects of *discourse has shown that enunciations express different directions of argument as well as varying degrees of persuasive force. An enunciation can indicate (suggest, imply, promote, or presuppose) a conclusion which, although not explicitly stated, a speaker wants her or his partner in a dialogue to draw. An enunciation's argumentative 'direction' toward this implied conclusion does not depend only on the explicitly transmitted information. It also depends on words with a grammatical function or morphemes such as 'and,' 'or,' 'no,' or 'but.' When presenting two propositions coordinated by 'but,' for example, the first proposition may suggest a conclusion that is invalidated by the second. This second proposition, then, opposes the first in its direction or orientation of argument. In addition to the argumentative direction, enunciations carry different degrees of argumentative force. Once again the force of argument does not depend only on explicitly transmitted information but also on morphemes such as 'no' or 'but.' In the example cited above, the proposition following 'but' would carry greater force because it can invalidate the conclusion suggested by the proposition preceding it. Ducrot proposes a hierarchy or gradation of levels of force brought to bear in arguing a point. In this way certain enunciations can be characterized in terms of both their orientation and force on a graduated scale, that is, by the type of conclusions they suggest and by the weight they are given.

For Ducrot an enunciation's sense must be understood as both this reflective commentary on the saying itself and as an allusion to the historical event of its appearance. The sense (what is said) lies between the nature of the saying and the relationships that arise among the participants in discourse. Rather than one 'speaking subject,' Ducrot proposes polyphonic levels that bring the interaction and antagonism of different 'voices' to the fore. One can speak of an addresser or *locuteur* and an utterer or *énonciateur* as well as of an addressee or *allocutaire* and an utteree or *destinataire*, depending on the multiple relationships possible between speaker and audience. In the case of a political speech, for example, the *allocutaires* would be all those who listen; while the *destinataire* are those particular members of the public that can be regarded as the object of the illocutionary act. Thus, Ducrot's concept of polyphonic levels points to an area of discourse where what is said by an enunciation (the sense) reflects a plurality of subjects.

Ducrot's study of enunciations' implicit and explicit aspects, together with the ever-changing role of the participants in discourse, is consequential not only for current linguistic theory but also for contemporary philosophy and literary criticism. Philosophical positions such as that represented by Chaim Perelman's *Nouvelle rhétorique* can find a significant complement in Ducrot's analysis of argumentative morphemes. Ducrot's elucidation of argumentative direction and force also enhances literary theories that examine the reader's role of interpreting implicit meaning from a text's explicit indications. Thus, by examining the relation between participants, discourse and context, Ducrot's *Nouvelle Linguistique* moves beyond the concept of a 'self-sufficient' sentence to offer an important perspective from which to explore the interaction of philosophy, language and *literature.

DANIEL CHAMBERLAIN

Primary Sources

Anscombre, Jean-Claude, and Oswald Ducrot. *L'Argumentation dans la langue*. Bruxelles: P Mardaga, 1983.
Ducrot, Oswald. *Le Dire et le dit*. Paris: Minuit, 1984.
– *Dire et ne pas dire: Principes de sémantique linguistique*. Paris: Hermann, 1972.
– *Les Echelles argumentatives*. Paris: Minuit, 1980.
– *Logique, structure, énonciation: Lectures sur le langage*. Paris: Minuit, 1989.

- *Les Mots du discours.* Paris: Minuit, 1980.
- *La Preuve et le dire: Langage et logique.* Paris: Mame, 1973.

Secondary Sources

Meyer, Michel. *Logique, langage et argumentation.* Paris: Hachette, 1982.
Ducrot, Oswald, et Tzvetan Todorov. *Dictionnaire encyclopédique des sciences du langage.* Paris: Seuil, 1972.

Eagleton, Terry

(b. England, 1943–) Literary critic. Educated at De La Salle College, Pendleton, and Trinity College, Cambridge, where he studied under *Raymond Williams, in 1964 Terry Eagleton became a Fellow in English at Jesus College, Cambridge, and since 1969 a Fellow and Tutor at Wadham College, Oxford. Eagleton was one of the founders of the Catholic left journal *Slant* in the 1960s and his early work included a number of books and essays on the political theology of the 'Catholic left.'

Eagleton's critical writings fall into three distinct categories: theoretical studies, practical criticism and 'popularizing' works. The latter two kinds grow directly out of the former because, as he argues in *The Function of Criticism,* one of the primary tasks of the socialist intellectual is to work toward the creation of a 'counterpublic sphere' – socialist institutions of intellectual and mass culture. This goal is to be achieved in part through 'the resolute popularization of complex ideas ... [in] works which make socialist theory intelligible to a mass audience' (113). Thus, some of Eagleton's writings are significantly more concrete and less complex than others, though they are all united by a cluster of recurring themes and theoretical concerns. One of these is the complex relation between *literature and *ideology. Eagleton rejects the 'vulgar Marxist' notion that literary works, as an element in the 'superstructure' of society, are simply a passive reflection of the economic 'base.' Drawing on but also modifying theories developed by *Louis Althusser and *Pierre Macherey, he argues in *Criticism and Ideology* that the literary *text is neither a slavish expression of a dominant ideology nor a wholly autonomous element. The text displays its precise relation to the ideology it 'produces' by the

degree of internal dissonance, displacement or self-contradiction that it yields up. Literature constitutes the most revealing mode of experiential access to ideology available, more immediate than science (by which Eagleton means a 'Marxist science' capable of revealing ideological distortion) and more coherent than lived experience.

Eagleton's conception of the critic's role follows logically from his analysis of literature's relation to ideology. The critic must break through the literary work's seeming unity and naturalness to reveal its hidden knowledge – the conditions and contradictions of its making that it cannot itself express. He or she must seek out the source of the work's conflict of meanings, a conflict produced by the work's problematic relation to ideology, which reduces the work at certain points to silence. To do this, criticism must situate itself outside the text and its enveloping ideology, bringing to bear its 'scientific' knowledge of ideologies, their modes of operation and their relation to history. Implicit in this critical program is a view of literary form that emphasizes the text as 'open' – a locus of conflicting languages, symbols and genres – rather than 'closed,' resolved or completed. (See *genre criticism.) Here Eagleton rejects *Lukács, whom he regards as overemphasizing art's capacity to draw together the contradictions and alienations of daily life in an overarching totality, embracing instead Brecht's modernist conception of art as a relentlessly dislocating, demystifying force *(Walter Benjamin* 81–93). (See *totalization, *defamiliarization.)

In his more recent work, Eagleton has questioned the institution of literary criticism as a whole. (See *literary institution.) He argues in *The Function of Criticism* that criticism today lacks any real social function. Employing as his guiding concept *Jürgen Habermas' notion of the 'public sphere' *(Structural Transformation of the Public Sphere* 1962), he maintains that modern criticism's beginnings in the early 18th century served a genuine social and political need for a cultural *discourse independent of the absolutist state. Contemporary criticism, by contrast, has become marginalized by its loss of a sense of purpose and audience. Eagleton seeks to recall criticism to what he regards as its traditional cultural role, namely, a concern with the symbolic processes of social life through which political power is deployed, reinforced and resisted. Through its renewed participation in public discourse, particularly the 'counterpublic sphere' which is emerging out of the women's movement and other previously repressed voices, criticism can revive itself as a culturally and politically relevant voice.

One of criticism's important tasks, according to Eagleton, is to question the existence and purpose of the institutions that organize our lives and knowledge. In his most popular book, *Literary Theory: An Introduction,* he questions the academic institutionalization of literature as a discrete field of study and confronts the recent emergence of literary theory as a new subdiscipline. After surveying virtually all major critical approaches of this century – from *New Criticism and phenomenology to *poststructuralism and psychoanalysis – Eagleton concludes that neither literature nor literary theory really exists as an unalterable object or method of inquiry. (See *phenomenological criticism, *psychoanalytic theory.) Literature is simply those writings that are highly valued by a particular dominant culture at a particular time; yet the academic appropriation of literature as a field of study has cripplingly narrowed the range of texts previously considered literary. Literary theory, for its part, fails to achieve intellectual coherence, whether one attempts to define it in terms of its evanescent object (literature) or in terms of its methods, which are various and have more in common with other intellectual disciplines than with each other. Eagleton does not advocate that literary theory be abandoned but that its insights be harnessed in the service of a new enterprise, namely, the cultural politics and discourse theory that he also argues for in *The Function of Criticism* – theory as a politicized rhetorical study, which would consider 'the various sign-systems and signifying practices in our own society, all the way from *Moby Dick* to the Muppet show, from Dryden and Jean-Luc Godard to the portrayal of women in advertisements and the rhetorical techniques of government reports' (207). The rationale for this systematic investigation of discursive practices is the recognition that all texts are 'interested,' grounded in a particular ideology. (See also *discourse analysis theory, *rhetorical criticism, *signifying practice.)

Eagleton's more recent *Walter Benjamin: or, Towards a Revolutionary Criticism* represents in part a movement away from the abstractions of Althusserian theory and towards a more experiential and political approach to literary texts which involves such concerns as feminism, humour, the 'carnivalesque,' the body, and cultural practices. (See *feminist criticism, *carnival.) He argues that *Benjamin prefigures some of the central developments in poststructuralist theory, a claim that is designed not so much to make him 'relevant' to present-day readers as to prevent his work from being co-opted and domesticated by the mainstream critical establishment. Indeed, Eagleton sees Benjamin's texts as a battleground of rival interpretive strategies, a field of contention in which *deconstruction appears as the latest challenger. The tone of his critical encounter with Benjamin, highly partisan and polemical, is representative of his approach to theory generally and exemplifies his sense of the kind of 'engagement' that a literary critic should practise.

FRANS DE BRUYN

Primary Sources

Eagleton, Terry. *Against the Grain: Selected Essays 1975–1985.* London: Verso/New Left Books, 1986.
– *The Body as Language: Outline of a 'New Left' Theology.* London and Sydney: Sheed and Ward, 1970.
– *Criticism and Ideology: A Study in Marxist Literary.* London: Verso/New Left Books, 1976.
– *Exiles and Emigres: Studies in Modern Literature.* New York: Schocken Books, 1970.
– *The Function of Criticism: From the Spectator to Post-Structuralism.* London: Verso/New Left Books, 1984.
– *The Ideology of the Aesthetic.* Oxford: Basil Blackwell, 1990.
– *Literary Theory: An Introduction.* Oxford: Blackwell; Minneapolis: U of Minnesota P, 1983.
– *Marxism and Literary Criticism.* Berkeley and Los Angeles: U of California P, 1976.
– *Myths of Power: A Marxist Study of the Brontës.* London: Macmillan; New York: Barnes and Noble, 1975.
– 'Nationalism: Irony and Commitment.' In *Nationalism, Colonialism, and Literature.* Minneapolis: U of Minnesota P, 1990, 23–39.
– *The Rape of Clarissa: Writing, Sexuality and Class Struggle in Samuel Richardson.* Minneapolis: U of Minnesota P, 1982.
– *Walter Benjamin or, Towards a Revolutionary Criticism.* London and New York: Verso, 1981.

Secondary Sources

Bennett, Tony. *Formalism and Marxism.* London: Methuen, 1979.

Burns, Wayne. 'Marxism, Criticism, and the Disappearing Individual.' *Recovering Literature* 12 (1984): 7–28.

Craib, Ian. 'Criticism and Ideology: Theory and Experience.' *Contemporary Literature* 22 (1981): 489–509.

Frow, John. 'Marxism after Structuralism.' *Southern Review: Literary and Interdisciplinary Essays* 17 (1984): 33–50.

– *Marxism and Literary History.* Cambridge, Mass.: Harvard UP, 1986, passim.

– 'Structuralist Marxism.' *Southern Review: Literary and Interdisciplinary Essays* 15 (1982): 208–17.

Norris, Christopher. 'Image and Parable: Readings of Walter Benjamin.' *Philosophy and Literature* 7 (1983): 15–31.

Poole, Roger. 'Generating Believable Entities: Post-Marxism as a Theological Enterprise.' *Comparative Criticism* 7 (1985): 49–71.

Eco, Umberto

(b. Italy, 1932–). Professor of *semiotics, critic, novelist, journalist. Son of a railway worker, Umberto Eco attended the University of Turin, where in 1954 he completed a doctoral thesis on the aesthetics of St. Thomas Aquinas. Before joining the editorial staff of the Bompiani Publishing House in 1959 he worked for the RAI (the Italian national TV) and began collaborating with some of the most prestigious journals and newspapers (both academic and popular) in Italy. The journalistic activities promoted and intensified his interests in modern culture, mass media, communication, and semiotics. In 1963 Eco played a key role in the formation (and in the later dissolution) of the 'Gruppo 63' – Italian neo-avant-garde writers and critics who shared some views with their French counterpart, the Tel Quel group. Eco's academic career began in the early 1960s at the University of Florence. He later taught at the universities of Turin and Milan and, from 1966, abroad in Sao Paulo, Brazil, at NYU and Northwestern, and at many other American and Canadian universities. From 1971 he has been teaching semiotics at the University of Bologna and currently edits the international semiotic journal *VS*.

The fundamental influence of the Middle Ages on Eco dates back to his doctoral dissertation and is particularly apparent in his novel *The Name of the Rose* (1980), as well as in *The Aesthetics of Thomas Aquinas, Art and Beauty in the Middle Ages* (1956), and *The Aesthetics of Chaosmos: The Middle Ages of James Joyce* (1982). *The Aesthetics of Thomas Aquinas*, an exposition of Aquinas' notions of allegory and of the meaning of beauty related to goodness, wholeness, proportion, and splendour, also documents the way diachronic linguistic and semiotic preoccupations are at the centre of Eco's studies.

Opera aperta [*The Open Work* 1962], which gave Eco instant popularity, became the primary work with which, for many years, critics associated him. Eco revised his poetic of the 'open work' four times as he developed and modified his theories on the intentionally ambiguous and plurivocal meanings in texts and on the multiple (but not endless) interpretations that the reader may derive from them. (See *text.) The shifts in his theory of texts, meaning, readers, and interpretation can be charted from *The Open Work* to *La Struttura assente* [*The Absent Structure*], *The Role of the Reader*, and *The Limits of Interpretation*, as structuralist theories in vogue in the 1960s give way to reader response and theories of interpretation of the 1970s and 1980s, particularly *hermeneutics and *deconstruction. (See *structuralism, *reader-response criticism.) Eco constantly affirmed that meaning and interpretation have contextual, historical and sociological roots; moreover, in the act of writing, the author foresees the role of the reader as 'model,' 'ideal' or 'real'. Thus, the reader indirectly plays a collaborative role in the writing of the text in so far as he or she is one of the textual strategies planned by the author. In the same way the author plans 'inferential walks' and intertextual allusions which take the reader outside the text in order to draw on his verbal, textual and extratextual experiences – in short, on his cultural competence – for interpretation. In *The Limits of Interpretation*, Eco insists on a distinction between interpreting and using a literary text (open or closed) by showing why there must be some limits to the power of an interpreter/reader. In essence, one can make an intentionally ambiguous text say many things, but one cannot (should not?) make a text say what it was not meant to say. *The Limits of Interpretation* does not negate or contradict *The Open Work*, rather it confirms the dangers of unlimited *intertextuality and interpretation.

In addition to such questions, *kitsch, high and pop culture, and the role of mass media have interested Eco from the early 1960s, as illustrated by his numerous essays and journalistic writings (a selection appears in *Travels in Hyper Reality*) on such topics as James Joyce, J. Luis Borges, Superman, Michelangelo Antonioni, Woody Allen, popular movies, TV serials, Disney characters, and comic books. These essays indicate how Eco the semiotician and critic is never divorced from Eco the observer of cultural phenomena, or from the novelist. Often showing affinities with the writings of *Leslie A. Fiedler, *Roland Barthes and *Marshall McLuhan, Eco prefers a postmodern 'integrated' writer/intellectual to an 'apocalyptic' one who, with his elite notions of art, snubs mass media and popular culture. (See *postmodernism.)

Eco's semiotic works show the same type of development and revisions which accompany his theoretical studies on constructing, reading and interpreting texts. Beginning with *Il Segno* and moving on to the larger studies *La Struttura assente* (1968), *A Theory of Semiotics* (1979) and *Semiotics and the Philosophy of Language* (1984), Eco's fascination grows with *Charles S. Peirce's theories on signs and unlimited *semiosis and with his own overall view of semiotics as a science pertaining to communication and to the reading and interpreting of all social and cultural aspects of life. From Saussurean notions of *langue/parole* and Jakobsonian concerns with the relations of sender-signs-codes-messages-receiver/interpreter, Eco has moved to a wider area of the production and interpretation of signs: to the encyclopedia of culture – where all signs (information) and meaning can ultimately be interconnected through networks of rhizomes, depending on the level of verbal and general cultural competence of both the sender and the receiver of messages. (See *Saussure, *Jakobson, *communication theory, *code, *sign.)

His novels presented Eco with international fame. *The Name of the Rose* sold over 8 million copies throughout the world and was made into a popular film; and the more difficult *Foucault's Pendulum* at times resembles a small encyclopedia of esoteric literature. Amusing and instructive, both novels are well engineered pastiches of intertextual allusions which send readers to both Eco's and other authors' texts (particularly to those of C.S. Peirce, Karl Popper, *Michel Foucault, and *Harold Bloom).

ROCCO CAPOZZI

Primary Sources

Eco, Umberto. *The Aesthetics of Chaosmos: The Middle Ages of James Joyce*. 1965. Tulsa, Okla.: U of Tulsa, 1982.
- *The Aesthetics of Thomas Aquinas*. 1956; 1970. Cambridge, Mass.: Harvard UP, 1988.
- *Apocalittici e integrati*. Milano: Bompiani, 1964.
- *Art and Beauty in the Middle Ages*. New Haven: Yale UP, 1986.
- *Il Costume di casa*. Milano: Bompiani, 1973.
- *Dalla periferia all'impero*. Milano: Bompiani, 1977.
- *La Definizione dell'arte*. Milano: Mursia, 1973.
- *Diario minimo*. Milano: Mondadori, 1963; 1990.
- *Diario minimo II*. Milano: Bompiani, 1992.
- *Le Forme del contenuto*. Milano: Bompiani, 1971.
- *Foucault's Pendulum*. 1988. San Diego: Harcourt Brace Jovanovich, 1989.
- *The Limits of Interpretation*. Bloomington: Indiana UP, 1990.
- *The Name of the Rose*. 1980. San Diego: Harcourt Brace Jovanovich, 1983.
- *The Open Work*. 1962; 1966; 1971; 1976. Cambridge, Mass.: Harvard UP 1989.
- *Postscript to the Name of the Rose*. San Diego: Harcourt Brace Jovanovich, 1984.
- *The Role of the Reader*. Bloomington: Indiana UP, 1979.
- *Il Segno*. Milano: Isedi, 1973.
- *Semiotics and the Philosophy of Language*. Bloomington: Indiana UP, 1984.
- *Sette anni di desiderio*. Milano: Bompiani, 1983.
- *La Struttura assente*. Milano: Bompiani, 1968.
- *Sugli specchi e altri saggi*. Milano: Bompiani, 1985.
- *Il Superuomo di massa*. Milano: Cooperativa scrittori, 1976; 1978.
- *A Theory of Semiotics*. Bloomington: Indiana UP, 1976.
- *Travels in Hyper Reality: Essays*. San Diego: Harcourt Brace Jovanovich, 1986.

Secondary Sources

Cannon, JoAnn. *Postmodern Italian Fiction*. Rutherford, NJ: Fairleigh Dickinson P, 1989.
Capozzi, Rocco. 'Palimpsests and Laughter: The Dialogical Pleasure of Unlimited Semiosis in *The Name of the Rose*.' *Italica* (Winter 1989): 412–28.
Coletti, Theresa. *Naming the Rose*. Jackson: U Presses of Mississippi, 1988.
de Lauretis, Teresa. *Umberto Eco*. Firenze: La Nuova Italia, 1981.
Giovannoli, Renato, ed. *Saggi sul Nome della rosa*. Milano: Bompiani, 1985.
Inge, Thomas M. *Naming the Rose: Essays on The Name of the Rose*. Jackson: U Presses of Mississippi, 1988.
Robey, David. 'Umberto Eco.' In *Writers and Society in Contemporary Italy*. Ed. Michel Caesar and Peter Hainsworth. Warwickshire: Berg Publishers, 1984.

Stauder, Thomas. *Umberto Ecos 'Der Name der Rose.'* Erlangen: Palm and Enke, 1989.
'Umberto Eco. Du Sémiologue au romancier.' Monographic issue of *Magazine littéraire* 262 (Feb. 1989).

Eikhenbaum, Boris Mikhailovich

(b. Russia, 1886–d. 1959) Russian formalist scholar. After studying at the Military Medical Academy, Eikhenbaum switched to the Faculty of Philology of St. Petersburg University. Graduating in 1912, he taught in a private gymnasium, and from 1918 to 1949 he was a professor at Leningrad University. He joined OPOIAZ (acronym for the Society for the Study of Poetic Language) and became a spokesman for the formalists at all important debates and discussions in the early 1920s. 'Teoriia "formalnogo metoda"' ['The Theory of the Formal Method' 1926] is a classic exposition. Following the suppression of formalism, Eikhenbaum concentrated on the problems of literary history, writing numerous studies on Mikhail Lermontov and Leo Tolstoy. In 1949 he was dismissed from the university for his 'eclecticism and cosmopolitanism.' Reinstated in 1956 at the Institute of Russian Literature, he published two more monographs on Lermontov and Tolstoy. (See *formalism, Russian.)

Eikhenbaum, one of the most productive formalist scholars (he published more than 300 works), focused on the questions of narrative fiction and poetics. In both areas he combined theoretical analysis with literary history. His most important contribution to the theory of prose was his concept of *skaz*, developed in 'Kak sdelana "Shinel" Gogolia' ['How Gogol's "The Overcoat" Is Made' 1919], 'Illiuziia skaza' ['The Illusion of Skaz' 1924] and 'Leskov i sovremennaia proza' ['Leskov and Modern Prose' 1925]. Eikhenbaum defined *skaz* as a special type of written *discourse oriented toward the oral speech of the *narrator and demonstrated its importance in the works of such writers as Gogol, Leskov, Remizov, and Zoshchenko.

Eikhenbaum's major statement was his monograph *Melodika russkogo liricheskogo stikha* [*Melody of Russian Lyric Verse* 1922] on the importance of phrase melody in Russian lyric poetry. In it he introduced the concept of

the *dominanta*, a focusing element, which orders all other components of the literary work and guarantees the integrity of its structure. The *dominanta* of lyric poetry, according to Eikhenbaum, is intonation since it deforms all other aspects, including syntax, word order and verse division.

Among formalists, Eikhenbaum was unique in his keen interest in literary history and the interaction between *literature and milieu. While not disputing the notion of the uniqueness of literature, he always maintained that literature should not be studied in isolation from other spheres of life. His most explicit argument for this approach was 'Literaturnyi byt' ['Literary Environment' 1927], against a narrow formalism that excluded the possibility of interaction between literature and life and against vulgar sociology that tried to explain literary phenomena exclusively in terms of socio-economic factors.

Eikhenbaum successfully applied his theory in his own studies of Lermontov and Tolstoy, analysing their literary evolution against the background of historical and social changes. His recognition of the importance of extraliterary factors in the development of literature brought him closer to the Soviet ideological mainstream and saved him from losing his job in the 1930s. As a professor at the Leningrad University, he taught several generations of Soviet scholars, among them G.A. Bialyi and B.S. Meilakh. He also played an important role in stimulating research in poetics carried out by scholars associated with the Tartu-Moscow School. (See *Tartu School.)

NINA KOLESNIKOFF

Primary Sources

Eikhenbaum, B.M. 'Illiuziia skaza.' *Skvoz' literatury*. Leningrad, 1924. 'The Illusion of "Skaz."' *Russian Literature Triquarterly* 12 (1977): 233–6.
– 'Kak sdelana "Shinel" Gogolia.' *Poetika. Sborniki po teorii poeticheskogo iazyka*. Petrograd, 1919, 151–65. 'How Gogol's "The Overcoat" Is Made.' *Russian Review* 20 (1963): 377–99.
– 'Leskov i sovremennaia proza.' *Literatura, teoriia, kritika, polemika*. Leningrad, 1927. 'Leskov and Modern Prose.' *Russian Literature Triquarterly* 11 (1975): 211–29.
– 'Literatura i literaturnyi byt.' *Na literaturnom postu* 9 (1927): 47–52. 'Literary Environment.' In *Readings in Russian Poetics: Formalist and Structuralist Views*. Ed. L. Matejka and K. Pomorska. Cambridge, Mass: MIT P, 1971, 56–65.

- *Melodika russkogo liricheskogo stikha.* Leningrad, 1922.
- 'Teoriia formal'nogo metoda.' *Chervonii shliakh* 7–8 (1926). 'The Theory of the Formal Method.' In *Russian Formalist Criticism: Four Essays.* Ed. L. Lemon and M. Reis. Lincoln: U of Nebraska P, 1965, 91–144.

Secondary Sources

Any, C. 'Boris Eikhenbaum in OPOIAZ: Testing the Limits of the Work-Centered Poetics.' *Slavic Review* 49.3 (1990): 409–26.

Jakobson, R. 'Boris Mikhailovich Eikhenbaum.' *International Journal of Slavic Linguistics and Poetics* 6 (1963): 160–7.

Rice, M. 'On "Skaz."' *Russian Literature Triquarterly* 12 (1975): 409–24.

Steiner, P. *Russian Formalism: A Metapoetics.* Ithaca: Cornell UP, 1984.

Striedter, J. 'The Russian Formalist Theory of Prose.' *PTL: A Journal for Descriptive Poetics and Theory of Literature* 2 (1977): 429–70.

Eliade, Mircea

(b. Romania, 1907–d. U.S.A., 1986) Historian of religions, phenomenologist of religion, novelist. Mircea Eliade obtained his master's degree at the University of Bucharest in philosophy (1928) with a thesis on Italian Renaissance philosophy. He studied for three years in India under Surendranath Dasgupta and returned to Bucharest, completing a doctoral dissertation on a comparative history of techniques of yoga (1933). During the 1930s, Eliade gained fame as an influential and controversial literary figure in his native Romania. He was a member of the faculty of the University of Bucharest until he became a cultural attaché with the Royal Legation of Romania in London (1940) and Lisbon (1941–5). In the decade following the war, while living in Paris, Eliade established his international scholarly reputation as a historian of religions. He became a permanent member of the faculty at the University of Chicago in 1957, where he taught history of religions until his retirement in 1983. (See *phenomenological criticism.)

A prolific writer, Eliade had a remarkable career, first as a major literary figure in Romania, especially following the publication of his hugely successful novel *Maitreyi* (1933), and later as a historian and phenomenologist of religion, starting with the publication of

Traité d'histoire des religions [Patterns in Comparative Religion] and *Le Mythe de l'éternel retour [The Myth of the Eternal Return* and *Cosmos and History* 1949] and continuing through *Le Chamanisme [Shamanism]* and *Le Yoga [Yoga* 1954]. Romanian was his literary language, while his major scholarly works, culminating with the three-volume *Histoire des croyances et des idées religieuses [A History of Religious Ideas,* 1976, 1978, 1983; trans. 1979, 1982, 1985], were written in French. Approximately 35 of his books have been published in English.

It is difficult to place Eliade's works because he was a generalist, comparativist and synthesizer, drawing on texts reflecting spiritual and cultural experiences from the entire history of humankind. Especially influenced by his encounter with Indian spirituality, which revealed to him much of his understanding of symbol and *myth and of the nature of religious experience, he often focused on 'archaic spirituality,' privileging an 'archaic ontology' with its nonhistorical, nontemporal, repetitive, eternal, archetypal structures of meaning, and on an antihistorical, nature-oriented 'cosmic religiosity' of Romanian and other peasants. (See *archetype, *archetypal criticism.)

Often citing Goethe as his literary and scholarly model, Eliade was critical of many modern, post-Enlightenment scholarly assumptions and approaches: an overemphasis on the conceptual and rational, faith in scientific progress, historicism, and secular reductionism of spiritual meanings. Much closer to a tradition of German Romanticism and metaphysical idealism in his interpretation of meaning, Eliade may be placed within a structural, synchronic, hermeneutical, and phenomenological tradition, going back at least to Schleiermacher and sharing many characteristics with more recent existential phenomenologists, such as *Maurice Merleau-Ponty, and hermeneutical phenomenologists, such as *Paul Ricoeur. (See *structuralism, *hermeneutics.)

Eliade often discusses his 'dual vocation' as fiction writer and scholar. At times, he emphasizes that each is autonomous and separate; at others, he emphasizes that literary and scholarly concerns are complementary, necessary for his 'spiritual equilibrium,' separate but interdependent parts of the same universal cultural creativity. The basic assumptions, methods and concerns defining his scholarly work in the history and phenomenology of religion also define his attitude and approach to *literature. Eliade views literature as an autonomous creation of the literary imagination, interpreted on its 'own plane of reference,' with its own structures and meanings, and not devalued or reduced to any one of its 'elements' or to any secular, scientific, rational, economic, psychological, or historical perspective. Such claims for the autonomy of the literary might seem to identify Eliade with the New Critics; however, he invariably reduces the literary to some religious plane of reference. (See *New Criticism.)

According to Eliade, literature, through the universal structure of the 'dialectic of the sacred' and through nonhistorical mythic and symbolic structures, is capable of revealing the sacred – permanent, universal, dynamic structures of transcendence, expressing what is transhistorical, paradigmatic, meaningful. The sacred is always mediated in a 'paradoxical' manner, not contained within the secular but expressed through that which is ordinarily finite, limited, temporal, natural, historical, 'profane.' (See *paradox.). Especially in modern, Western, secular culture, the sacred, as a structure of human consciousness, as a 'mode of being,' is 'camouflaged' and 'concealed': the transhistorical is 'hidden' and 'unrecognized' in the historical, the extraordinary in the ordinary, the fantastic and supernatural in the banal and mundane. Literature, through the creative functioning of the imagination, discovers camouflaged sacred dimensions of reality, inexhaustible 'ciphers' and hidden languages and meanings, 'polyvalent' structures capable of being 'revalorized' and reconstituted as new literary creations.

Eliade emphasizes the importance of narrative, sometimes submitting that narrative is constitutive of 'the human condition,' and he views both oral and written literature as an offspring of mythology and fulfilling the same mythic functions. Literature plays an essential role in a desperately needed 'cultural renewal' and 'new humanism,' in which we overcome our 'provincialism' and begin to define ourselves as planetary beings.

Various literary critics and theorists use Eliade routinely, often in a phenomenological vein. For the most part, Eliade's influence on literary criticism is thematic rather than methodological or theoretical, with the adoption of certain Eliadean ideas such as the 'sacred and the profane,' the 'myth of the eternal return,'

and the 'nostalgia for a mythic paradise' (or premodern ahistorical time when the sacred was more humanly accessible). (See *theme.)

Although Eliade was sometimes described as the most popular and influential contemporary historian of religions and as the foremost interpreter of myth and symbol, he was controversial and not without his critics. Many felt that he was an 'old-fashioned' generalist, who was methodologically uncritical, arbitrary and subjective, 'read' all sorts of 'profound' nonhistorical meanings into his documents, and ignored the historical and cultural boundaries and specificity of his texts.

DOUGLAS ALLEN

Primary Sources

Eliade, Mircea. *Autobiography. Vol. 1: 1907–1937.* Trans. M.L. Ricketts. New York: Harper and Row, 1981; *Autobiography. Vol. 2: 1937–1960.* Trans. M.L. Ricketts. New York: Harper and Row; Chicago: U of Chicago P, 1988.
– *The Forbidden Forest.* Trans. M.L. Ricketts and M.P. Stevenson. Notre Dame: Notre Dame UP, 1978.
– *The History of Religions: Essays in Methodology.* Ed. with J. Kitagawa. Chicago: U of Chicago P, 1959.
– *Journal I, 1945–1955.* Trans. M.L. Ricketts. Chicago: U of Chicago P, 1990; *No Souvenirs: Journal 1957–1969.* Trans. F.H. Johnson. New York: Harper and Row, 1977 (also pub. as *Journal II, 1957–1969.* U of Chicago P); *Journal III, 1970–1978.* Trans. T.L. Fagan. Chicago: U of Chicago P, 1989; *Journal IV, 1979–1985.* Trans. M.L. Ricketts. Chicago: U of Chicago P, 1990.
– *The Myth of the Eternal Return.* Trans. W.R. Trask. New York: Pantheon Books, 1954. (Pub. as *Cosmos and History,* Harper Torchbook ed., and by Princeton UP.)
– *Ordeal by Labyrinth: Conversations with Claude-Henri Rocquet.* Trans. D. Coltman. Chicago: U of Chicago P, 1982.
– *Patterns in Comparative Religion.* Trans. R. Sheed. New York: Sheed and Ward, 1958.
– *The Sacred and the Profane.* Trans. W.R. Trask. New York: Harcourt, Brace and Co., 1959.
– *Symbolism, the Sacred, and the Arts.* New York: Crossroad, 1986.

Secondary Sources

Allen. D. *Structure and Creativity in Religion.* The Hague: Mouton, 1978.
Allen, D., and D. Doeing. *Mircea Eliade: An Annotated Bibliography.* New York: Garland, 1980.
Girardot, N.J., and M.L. Ricketts, eds. *Imagination*

and Meaning: The Scholarly and Literary Worlds of Mircea Eliade. New York: Seabury, 1982.

Kitagawa, J., and C. Long, eds. Myths and Symbols: Studies in Honor of Mircea Eliade. Chicago: U of Chicago P, 1969.

Marino, A. L'Herméneutique de Mircea Eliade. Paris: Gallimard, 1981.

Tacou, C., ed. Mircea Eliade. Paris: L'Herne, 1978.

Eliot, T(homas) S(tearns)

(b. U.S.A., 1888–d. England, 1965) Poet, playwright and literary critic. T.S. Eliot entered Harvard University in 1906 and studied languages and *literature – especially Elizabethan literature, metaphysical poetry and literature of the Italian Renaissance. He also studied philosophy under George Santayana. Emerging with an M.A. (1910), he travelled to the University of Paris and attended the lectures of Henri Bergson. Returning to Harvard in 1911, he studied Sanskrit and Oriental philosophy. In 1914 he went abroad again, studying philosophy for a year at Oxford and eventually completing his doctoral dissertation on the philosophy of F.H. Bradley. In 1925 he began a long association with the publishing company now known as Faber and Faber, eventually becoming one of its directors. In 1927 he was confirmed in the Church of England and became a British subject. From that point on, he described himself as 'a royalist in politics, a classicist in literature, and an Anglo-Catholic in religion.' Throughout his productive career, he published a substantial amount of poetry, seven plays and innumerable essays. He was awarded the Nobel Prize for Literature in 1948.

Eliot's ideas of tradition, impersonality and objectivity – along with his Coleridgean insistence that the literary work be regarded as 'autotelic,' as an autonomous and unified object that contains its purpose within itself – set the agenda for British critics such as *F.R. Leavis as well as for American New Critics such as John Crowe Ransom, *Cleanth Brooks and Allen Tate. (See *New Criticism.)

'Tradition and the Individual Talent' (1919) is Eliot's earliest articulation of his position. Rebelling against the Romantic cult of originality and novelty, Eliot argues in favour of tradition. 'The historical sense,' he maintains, 'involves a perception, not only of the pastness of the past, but of its presence; the histor-

ical sense compels a man to write not merely with his own generation in his bones, but with a feeling that the whole of the literature of Europe from Homer and within it the whole of the literature of his own country has a simultaneous existence and composes a simultaneous order ... The existing monuments form an ideal order among themselves, which is modified by the introduction of the new (the really new) work of art among them. The existing order is complete before the new work arrives; for order to persist after the supervention of novelty, the whole existing order must be, if ever so slightly, altered' (Selected Prose of T.S. Eliot 38). For Eliot then the significance and value of writers must be appreciated and understood in terms of their relation to the past. One cannot value writers alone.

Aligned with this idea of tradition is a deliberately anti-Romantic conception of the poetic personality. According to Eliot's impersonal theory of poetry, 'the more perfect the artist, the more completely separate in him will be the man who suffers and the mind which creates ... The poet has not a 'personality' to express, but a particular medium ... in which impressions and experiences combine in peculiar and unexpected ways ... Poetry is not a turning loose of emotion, but an escape from emotion; it is not the expression of personality, but an escape from personality' (Selected Prose 41–3). It follows from this that 'the only way of expressing emotion in the form of art is by finding an "objective correlative"; in other words, a set of objects, a situation, a chain of events which shall be the formula of that particular emotion; such that when the external facts, which must terminate in sensory experience, are given, the emotion is immediately evoked' (Selected Prose 48). This notion of the objective correlative comes from Eliot's famous essay on why Hamlet is a failure. According to Eliot, Hamlet's intensely subjective feelings – and, by extension, Shakespeare's – are not objectified in the play. Because these feelings are in excess of anything that the play can concretely dramatize, they lack an adequate objective correlative; consequently the play fails to communicate any particular emotion. For Eliot, artistic integrity, the sense of inevitability that a formally perfect work of art enshrines, 'lies in this complete adequacy of the external to the emotion' (Selected Prose 48). Significant emotion, he maintains, has its life in the work of art and not in the history of the artist.

Eliot's ideas were part of a larger strategy for revising the *canon of English literature. The revaluation of 17th–century metaphysical poetry and the accompanying devaluation of Milton, Dryden, Pope, and the Romantics, however temporary, were in large measure due to the persuasive power of Eliot's authoritative rhetoric and to its impact on F.R. Leavis, *I.A. Richards, *William Empson, the American New Critics, and others (which is not to say that any of these critics accepted Eliot's judgments en masse). In 'The Metaphysical Poets' (1921), Eliot sets out his reasons for this revaluation. He commends these poets for their elaboration of a figure of speech to the end of the line, their telescoping of images, their multiplied associations, and their ability to compel a heterogeneity of material into unity. 'When a poet's mind is perfectly equipped for its work, it is constantly amalgamating disparate experience ... The poets of the 17th century, the successors of the dramatists of the 17th, possessed a mechanism of sensibility which could devour any kind of experience ... In the 17th century a dissociation of sensibility set in, from which we have never recovered' (Selected Prose 64). According to Eliot, then, the 17th-century poets who escaped being influenced by Milton – poets such as Donne, Crashaw, Vaughan, Herbert, and Marvell – had unified sensibilities; they found objective correlatives for their subjective thoughts and feelings, thereby transmuting their ideas into sensations. Since the time of Milton, however, thought has been divorced from feeling and as the former became more refined and subtle, the latter became cruder. The Romantics were no better; they merely exalted feeling at the expense of thought. Eliot believes that this dissociation of sensibility is a linguistic and cultural malaise from which English literature and society have never recovered. In order to combat this dissociation, the modern poet 'must become more and more comprehensive, more allusive, more indirect, in order to force, to dislocate if necessary, language into his meaning' (Selected Prose 65). Thus, Eliot's critical theory is a rationalization not only of his own poetic practice but also of literary modernism in general. Tradition, it would seem, is always tradition-making, a way of understanding the past that makes room for oneself in the present. 'Manipulating a continuous parallel between contemporaneity and antiquity,' Eliot writes, 'is simply a way of controlling, of or-

dering, of giving a shape and a significance to the immense panorama of futility and anarchy which is contemporary history' (Selected Prose 177).

Eliot brought to modern literary criticism an attitude of imperious objectivity. Vehemently opposed to any sort of impressionistic criticism that seeks to convey what the critic subjectively feels and thinks about a work of art, Eliot argues that the perfect critic seeks to transcend his personal impressions and to make objective statements about the work, using the tools of comparison, contrast and analysis. Criticism, he writes, is 'the disinterested exercise of intelligence' (Selected Prose 56), not 'the satisfaction of a suppressed creative urge' (Selected Prose 53); it should devote itself to 'the elucidation of works of art and the correction of taste ... the common pursuit of true judgment' (Selected Prose 69). The difference between objective classicism and subjective romanticism is the difference between 'the complete and the fragmentary, the adult and the immature, the orderly and chaotic' (Selected Prose 70). After his conversion to Anglo-Catholicism Eliot tended more and more to identify classicism with 'unquestioned spiritual authority outside the individual' and romanticism with the 'inner voice' (Selected Prose 70).

In his later literary criticism and in his social and religious criticism, Eliot contends that valid criticism must be solidly anchored in ethical, political and theological doctrine. The doctrine expressed in these later works, especially in such works as After Strange Gods: A Primer of Modern Heresy (1934) and The Idea of a Christian Society (1939), is conservative if not reactionary, ethnocentric if not racist. Eliot's ideas of a homogeneous Christian culture and society purged of religious and racial impurities, along with his hysterical animadversions against such allegedly heretical writers such as *D.H. Lawrence, were in sinister congruence with the fascist and totalitarian tendencies of the times. And this, finally, is the *paradox of T.S. Eliot – eloquent champion of the radical innovations of literary modernism, dogmatic defender of the reactionary politics of ultraconservativism and Christian orthodoxy.

Despite the above Eliot has influenced *postmodernism. Eliot's literary strategies – juxtaposition of images without explanation, eliminination of logical transitions, manipulation of a continuous parallel between contemporaneity and antiquity, allusion, quotation, *parody, pastiche, indirection, dislocation, *irony, and so forth – are as much a part of the postmodernist arsenal as they were of the modernist arsenal. Also, there is enough inconsistency in Eliot's criticism to justify the claim that he not only inspires New Critical formalism but also anticipates the antiformalism that was to replace it. For all of his insistence that the literary work is a self-sufficient and autotelic object, Eliot sees all of literature as having a simultaneous existence and as composing a simultaneous order. Works do not signify in a vacuum; they are part of a system of relations and cannot acquire their complete meaning alone. True, Eliot is committed to the idea of canonicity – his ideal order consists of classical male texts – but we also see an adumbration of what *Julia Kristeva calls *intertextuality, the sum of knowledge that makes it possible for texts to have meaning. For both Eliot and Kristeva, a text can be read only in relation to other texts. In a similar vein, *Harold Bloom's notion of the *anxiety of influence – his claim that strong writers make literary history by misreading and misinterpreting their predecessors so as to clear imaginative space for themselves – is an anxiety-ridden post-Romantic counterpart to Eliot's benign classical view of literary influence. Although Bloom's theory of the genesis of poems has a self-admitted pyschoanalytical resonance, Freud's Oedipal scenario being used as an analogy for the relationship between poet and predecessor, both he and Eliot, their severe ideological incompatibility notwithstanding, are akin in their assumption that every text is a response to and interpretation of other texts. (See *Freud, *psychoanalytic theory.) Since 1980 readers of Eliot's dissertation ('Knowledge and Experience') such as Bechler, Michaels and Shusterman have highlighted the semiotic and antimetaphysical dimensions of his early work in philosophy and are re-examining his poetry and criticism as an unacknowledged 'discourse of difference' prescient of the poststructural world. (See *semiotics, *semiosis, *poststructuralism, *discourse.)

It is clear that Eliot does not now have the pre-eminence he once had in the first half of this century. But whether one sees his work as an integral part of the theory and practice of modernism and *formalism, or as a cautionary tale about the dangers and temptations of reactionary politics, or as a precursor of postmodernist strategies and ideas, or as a com-bination of all three, one cannot escape the lingering presence of his influence.

GREIG HENDERSON

Primary Sources

Eliot, T.S. *After Strange Gods: A Primer of Modern Heresy*. London: Faber and Faber, 1934.
– *The Classics and the Man of Letters*. London: Oxford UP, 1942.
– *Dante*. London: Faber and Faber, 1931.
– *Elizabethan Essays*. London: Faber and Faber, 1934.
– *Essays Ancient and Modern*. London: Faber and Faber, 1936.
– *For Lancelot Andrewes: Essays on Style and Order*. London: Faber and Gwyer, 1928.
– *Homage to John Dryden: Three Essays on the Poetry of the 17th Century*. London: Hogarth P, 1924.
– *The Idea of a Christian Society*. London: Faber and Faber, 1939.
– *John Dryden. The Poet. The Dramatist. The Critic*. New York: Terence and Elsa Holliday, 1932.
– *Milton*. London: Oxford UP, 1947.
– *The Music of Poetry*. Glasgow: Jackson, 1942.
– *Notes toward the Definition of Culture*. London: Faber and Faber, 1948.
– *On Poetry and Poets*. London: Faber and Faber, 1957.
– *Poetry and Drama*. London: Faber and Faber, 1951.
– *The Sacred Wood: Essays on Poetry and Criticism*. London: Methuen, 1920.
– *Selected Essays*. New York: Harcourt Brace, 1932. A new edition containing the author's choice among all the prose he wrote since 1917 was published by Faber in 1951.
– *Selected Prose of T.S. Eliot*. Ed. Frank Kermode. London: Faber and Faber, 1975.
– *Shakespeare and the Stoicism of Seneca*. London: Oxford UP, 1927.
– *The Three Voices of Poetry*. Cambridge: Cambridge UP, 1953.
– *To Criticize the Critic*. London: Faber and Faber, 1965.
– *The Use of Poetry and The Use of Criticism*. London: Faber and Faber, 1933.
– *What Is a Classic?* London: Faber and Faber, 1945.

Secondary Sources

Ackroyd, Peter. *T.S. Eliot*. London: Hamilton, 1984.
Bechler, Michael. *T.S. Eliot, Wallace Stevens, and the Discourses of Difference*. Baton Rouge: Louisiana State UP, 1987.
Bergonzi, Bernard. *T.S. Eliot*. New York: Macmillan, 1972.
Chace, William M. *The Political Identities of Ezra Pound and T.S. Eliot*. Stanford: Stanford UP, 1973.
Dale, Alzina Stone. *The Philosopher Poet*. Wheaton, Ill.: H. Shaw, 1988.

Ellmann, Maud. *The Poetics of Impersonality: T.S. Eliot and Ezra Pound.* Cambridge: Harvard UP, 1987.

Gardner, Helen. *The Art of T.S. Eliot.* London: Cresset P, 1949.

Gordon, Lyndall. *Eliot's Early Years.* Oxford and New York: 1977.

– *Eliot's New Life.* New York: Farrar, Straus, Giroux, 1988.

Jay, Gregory. *T.S. Eliot and the Poetics of Literary History.* Baton Rouge: Louisiana State UP, 1983.

Litz, A. Walton, ed. *Eliot in His Time: Essays on the Occasion of the 50th Anniversary of the 'Waste Land.'* Princeton: Princeton UP, 1973.

Lucy, Sean. *T.S. Eliot and the Idea of a Tradition.* London: Cohen and West, 1960.

Martin, Graham, ed. *Eliot in Perspective.* London: Macmillan, 1970.

Menand, Louis. *Discovering Modernism: T.S. Eliot and His Context.* New York: Oxford UP, 1987.

Michaels, Walter Benn. 'Philosophy in KinKanja: Eliot's Pragmatism.' *Glyph* 8: 170–202.

Newton-de Molina, David, ed. *The Literary Criticism of T.S. Eliot: New Essays.* London: Athlone P, 1977.

Rajan, B., ed. *T.S. Eliot: A Study of His Writings by Several Hands.* New York: Haskell House, 1964.

Ricks, Christopher B. *T.S. Eliot and Prejudice.* London: Faber, 1988.

Shusterman, Richard. *T.S. Eliot and the Philosophy of Criticism.* London: Duckworth, 1988.

Tamplin, Ronald. *A Preface to T.S. Eliot.* London: Longman, 1988.

Tate, Allen, ed. *Eliot: The Man and His Work.* Harmondsworth: Penguin, 1971.

Empson, (Sir) William

(b. England, 1906–d. 1984) Poet and literary critic. Born into the landed gentry in Yorkshire, Empson went to preparatory school in Folkestone, then entered Winchester College (1920) and Cambridge (1925), where he first studied mathematics, then English. He began to publish his poems at Cambridge and became co-editor of the literary magazine *Experiment*. His *Seven Types of Ambiguity*, which began as an essay for his tutor *I.A. Richards, appeared in 1930 when Empson was only 24. In 1931 he was appointed professor of English literature at the Tokyo University of Literature and Science. Empson returned to England in 1934 and his *Poems* and *Some Versions of Pastoral* appeared in 1935. In 1937 he became a professor at Peking National University. Returning to England in 1940, Empson worked during the war for the BBC's Far Eastern sec-

tion, where one of his colleagues was George Orwell. After another four years at Peking National University, Empson returned permanently to England in 1952. He became professor of English *literature in 1953 at Sheffield University, where he worked until his retirement in 1971. He was knighted in 1978.

Empson's importance in Anglo-American literary criticism during the middle decades of the 20th century lies in his introduction of methods for analysing and attempting to classify ambiguities in literary works. This work, presented in *Seven Types of Ambiguity*, became important in the close analysis of texts undertaken by scholars using the *New Criticism, though it must be remembered that Empson never accepted the 'intentional fallacy' to which he always referred disdainfully as 'the Wimsatt Law' *(Using Biography* 225). (See *W.K. Wimsatt, Jr.) *The Royal Beasts* (1986) contains an outline discovered among Empson's papers (now in Harvard's Houghton Library): 'The seven classes of ambiguity. 1. Mere richness; (a metaphor valid from many points of view). 2. Two different meanings conveying the same point. 3. Two unconnected meanings, both wanted but not illuminating one another. 4. Irony: two apparently opposite meanings combined into a judgment. 5. Transition of meaning; (a metaphor applying halfway between two comparisons). 6. Tautology or contradiction, allowing of a variety of guesses as to its meaning. 7. Two meanings that are the two opposites created by the context' (113–14). Apart from items 4 and 5, these definitions agree quite closely with the sentence-long definitions that Empson offers on the 'Contents' pages of the book. (See also *metonymy/metaphor, *irony.)

In his Preface to the Second Edition (1961) Empson admits that some critics have viewed *Seven Types of Ambiguity* as 'an awful warning against taking verbal analysis too far' (vii). Empson's analysis of ambiguity proceeds from the assumption that 'good poetry is usually written from a background of conflict' (xiii). Therefore, 'the machinations of ambiguity are among the very roots of poetry' (3). The usefulness of literary criticism for Empson is that 'the more one understands one's own reactions the less one is at their mercy' (15). Attempting to describe the book's method in conclusion, Empson argues: 'I have continually employed a method of analysis which jumps the gap between two ways of thinking; which produces a possible set of alternative meanings with some ingenuity, and then says it is grasped in the preconsciousness of the reader by a native effort of the mind' (239). Empson's most controversial analyses are of Shakespeare's Sonnet 73, Hopkins' 'The Windhover' and George Herbert's 'The Sacrifice.' His emphasis on the importance of perceiving ambiguity in literary works is clearly original and in 1930 was ground-breaking. What is less satisfactory is the pseudo-scientific attempt at classification into types that proceeds, perhaps, from his training in mathematics.

Some Versions of Pastoral (1935) is essentially a discussion of the pastoral mode undertaken from a Marxist and, in the final chapter on *Alice in Wonderland*, from a Freudian standpoint. (See *Marxist criticism, *Sigmund Freud, *psychoanalytic theory.) Empson seeks 'to show, roughly in historical order, the ways in which the pastoral process of putting the complex into the simple ... and the resulting social ideas have been used in English literature' (25). The introductory chapter, 'Proletarian Literature,' appeared originally in Leavis' *Scrutiny*. (See *F.R. Leavis.) Empson's interest in double plots leads him to explore the juxtaposition of heroic and pastoral which he sees as attempting to maintain the social bond in a divided society. Empson's first collection of poems appeared in the same year. While poems like 'To an Old Lady,' 'Villanelle' and 'Arachne' are deeply moving, some of the more obscure pieces constitute an eighth type of ambiguity.

The Structure of Complex Words (1951) returns to the analysis of language that characterized *Seven Types of Ambiguity*. Here Empson located his work 'on the borderland of linguistics and literary criticism' (1). His central argument, that words have implications beyond their literal meanings that are determined by their context, is persuasive. Less convincing is the use of equations and formulae derived again, perhaps, from Empson's early work in mathematics. As before, Empson is preoccupied with what he calls 'literary double meanings.' Particularly impressive is his consideration of the change in meaning of the word 'sense' through works as widely different in time and in kind as *Measure for Measure, Sense and Sensibility* and *The Prelude*.

Milton's God (1961) is a different sort of study of literary ambiguity, in this case of Milton's failure to 'justify the ways of God to men.' For Empson, whose anti-'neo-Christian' polemic grew into an obsession in his later career, it is impossible to justify the Christian God. Empson shares Blake's and Shelley's view that 'the reason why the poem is so good is that it makes God so bad' (13, 275). He argues that 'the picture of God in the poem, including perhaps even the high moments when he speaks of the end, is astonishingly like Uncle Joe Stalin' (146).

Although Empson did not publish another book of criticism in his lifetime, it is a measure of his importance as a critic as well as of his continuous activity that four books of criticism have appeared since his death: *Using Biography* (1984), *Essays on Shakespeare* (1986), *Faustus and the Censor: The English Faust-book and Marlowe's Doctor Faustus* (1987), and *Argufying: Essays on Literature and Culture* (1987). A further book of essays on Renaissance literature is anticipated. These posthumously published books illustrate the depth and range of Empson's critical engagement.

Using Biography, which gathers essays written between 1958 and 1982, reveals Empson's distance from 'the Wimsatt Law' and the strength of his commitment to literary history. His work on Marvell shows his capacity for scholarly speculation, which is also evident in *Faustus and the Censor* and in his work on the Globe Theatre in *Essays on Shakespeare*. *Argufying*, which gathers Empson's reviews and previously uncollected pieces, reveals the vigour of his less formal writing as well as the diversity of his critical interests. The title, 'argufying,' a favourite term of Empson's, captures well his life-long engagement in critical dispute.

In his introduction to *Argufying* (1987), John Haffenden argues that Empson's 'career has popularly been reckoned to fall into roughly two halves, the first ending with *The Structure of Complex Words* (1951), the second appearing to forsake semantic interests in favour of chastising the aberrant morality of what Empson himself styled the "Neo-Christian school of critics"' (3). Empson's chief targets apart from the Neo-Christian school were imagism, symbolism and the intentional fallacy. The Neo-Christian school (spearheaded by *T.S. Eliot) provided in Empson's view a falsely medieval emphasis in Renaissance studies, succumbed too readily to Milton's theology and presented falsely Christian readings of modern authors like Joyce. Counting himself a son of 'the free-thinking Enlightenment' (Essays on Shakespeare 243) and a Benthamite rationalist, Empson found imagism and symbolism full of mystification. Works of literature, he believed, were for the most part capable of rational explanation. The idea posited by Wimsatt's intentional fallacy, that we could never know an author's intent, Empson also resisted. He argued in favour of 'the old custom of placing a poem in its milieu, and remembering the circumstances in which it was written. This does seem a basic need; having some grasp of the mind of the author is more of a luxury though I don't believe you can have real criticism without it' (Argufying 58).

Empson's importance in modern literary criticism will always be connected with his development of the work I.A. Richards in Seven Types of Ambiguity, a book that contributed to the New Criticism. Despite his mathematical background and his penchant for classifications and equations he did not have a strong interest in theory. 'The English have not the American theoretical drive,' he wrote, 'but this does not keep them pure' (Using Biography 34). An old-fashioned liberal, Empson believed that the purpose of studying literature was to increase our awareness of others and our understanding of ourselves. On more than one occasion he wrote that 'the central function of imaginative literature is to make you realize that other people act on moral convictions different from your own' (Milton's God 261; Using Biography 142). Critical judgment was of final importance to him. He believed that 'as the author claims to be judging a real situation, important to himself, the critic is committed to judging it too' (Milton's God 328). With Henry Fielding he believed that we should be 'prepared in literature as in life, to handle and judge any situation' (Using Biography 157). Empson's early work, especially Seven Types of Ambiguity, was regarded as important and original. It has even been argued recently that he is a herald of *deconstruction. His later work, however, especially his anti-'neo-Christian' polemic, has been viewed as obsessive and as a falling-off (Haffenden, Argufying 50, 29).

JOHN FERNS

Primary Sources

Empson, William. Argufying: Essays on Literature and Culture. Ed. John Haffenden. Iowa City: U of Iowa P, 1987.
– Collected Poems. London: Chatto and Windus, 1962.
– Essays on Shakespeare. Ed. David B. Pirie. Cambridge: Cambridge UP, 1986.
– Faustus and the Censor: The English Faust-book and Marlowe's Doctor Faustus. Ed. John Henry Jones. Oxford: Basil Blackwell, 1987.
– The Gathering Storm. London: Faber and Faber, 1940.
– Milton's God. London: Chatto and Windus, 1961.
– Poems. London: Chatto and Windus, 1935.
– The Royal Beasts and Other Works. Ed. John Haffenden. London: Chatto and Windus, 1986.
– Seven Types of Ambiguity. London: Chatto and Windus, 1930.
– Some Versions of Pastoral. London: Chatto and Windus, 1935.
– The Structure of Complex Words. London: Chatto and Windus, 1951.
– Using Biography. London: Chatto and Windus, 1984.
– and David B. Pirie. Coleridge's Verse: A Selection. London: Faber and Faber, 1972.

Secondary Sources

Day Frank. Sir William Empson: An Annotated Bibliography. New York and London: Garland, 1984.
Fry, Paul H. William Empson: Prophet Against Sacrifice. London and New York: Routledge, 1991.
Gardner, Philip, and Averil Gardener. The God Approached: A Commentary on the Poems of William Empson. London: Chatto and Windus, 1978.
Gill, Roma, Ed. William Empson: The Man and His Work. London and Boston: Routledge and Kegan Paul, 1974.
Norris, Christopher. William Empson and the Philosophy of Literary Criticism. London: Athlone P, 1978.
The Review: A Magazine of Poetry and Criticism. Special issue devoted to Empson. June 1963.
Willis, J.H., Jr. William Empson. New York and London: Columbia UP, 1969.

Fiedler, Leslie A.

(b. U.S.A., 1917–) Literary and social critic, novelist, storywriter, poet. Leslie A. Fiedler received his Ph.D. from the University of Wisconsin, taught in the English department at Montana State University from 1941 to 1965, then moved to the State University of New York at Buffalo.

As a literary critic, Fiedler attained recognition, first, for his indictments of the *New Criticism of *I.A. Richards and *Cleanth Brooks; second, for his studies of the way in which marginal groups (Negro, native Indian, Jewish, and homosexual) are represented in American *literature; and third, for his promotion of the study of popular or what he calls 'majority' texts. His most important theoretical essays, 'Archetype and Signature' (1952) and 'In the Beginning was the Word: *Logos* or *Mythos?*' (1958), refute the New Critical notion of the literary *text as aesthetic mechanism and argue instead for its status as a tissue of universal myths. (See *myth.)

Fiedler's interest in literature as a purveyor of archetypes is at the heart of his 'Come Back to the Raft Ag'in, Huck Honey]' (1948), though his emphasis here is on specific cultural rather than universal mythologies. (See *archetype.) Still known for its daring thesis, this essay argues outright that the interracial friendships of Huck and Jim in Mark Twain's *Huckleberry Finn*, Ishmael and Queequeg in Herman Melville's *Moby Dick* and Natty Bumppo and Chingachgook in James Fenimore Cooper's Leatherstocking Tales are innocent displays of homoerotic desire. That such friendships are a feature of America's most cherished novels suggests to Fiedler a sentimental need on the part of the white American male to be accepted by the minorities whom he regularly offends and exploits.

In Fiedler's most famous work of criticism, *Love and Death in the American Novel* (1960, 1966), this thesis is expanded to account for what Fiedler sees as the American novel's 'obsession with violence and embarrassment before love': its rejection of domestic forms and figures and its preference instead for the gothic. White America's guilt over the exploitation of its land and native people, over its treatment of the Negro, over its own perpetually revolutionary flight from civilization, have produced a literature preoccupied with death and psychological horror. In this study, as elsewhere, Fiedler's method, referred to by many as 'anthropological,' involves the reading of popular as well as 'high-brow' literatures, a strategy which leads him in his later work to argue for the expansion of the American *canon. *What Was Literature?* (1982) under-

stands the domestic American novel, beginning with Harriet Beecher Stowe's *Uncle Tom's Cabin*, as part of a national counter-tradition, a feminine obverse to the homocentric culture Fiedler had explored in *Love and Death*.

In its tendency to understand American literary history in terms of the paradigms of psychosexual conflict, Fiedler's criticism owes much to the work of *Sigmund Freud. His studies may also be understood as part of a larger mid-20th-century attempt to describe and define the uniquely American author as an 'outsider' and the uniquely American novel as essentially gothic, antirealistic, antihistorical, and antifeminine. Such ideas have been challenged by American feminist and New Historicist critics but even among these Fiedler remains important for his abiding emphasis on the role of minorities and 'minor' literatures in the development of a white American consciousness. (See *feminist criticism, *New Historicism.)

SANDRA TOMC

Primary Sources

Fiedler, Leslie. 'Archetype and Signature.' In *No! in Thunder: Essays on Myth and Literature*. Boston: Beacon P, 1960, 309–28.
– 'Come Back to the Raft Ag'in, Huck Honey!' *Partisan Review* 15 (1948): 664–71.
– 'In the Beginning Was the Word: *Logos* or *Mythos?*' In *No! in Thunder: Essays on Myth and Literature*, 295–308.
– *Love and Death in the American Novel*. New York: Criterion Books, 1960. Rev. ed. New York: Stein and Day, 1966.
– *What Was Literature? Class Culture and Mass Society*. New York: Simon and Schuster, 1982.

Fish, Stanley

(b. U.S.A., 1938–) Literary critic and theoretician. Fish received his B.A. (1959) from the University of Pennsylvania and his M.A. (1960) and Ph.D. (1962) from Yale University. He has taught at the University of California, Berkeley (1962–74), the Johns Hopkins University (1974–84), and Duke University (1984–). Fish first attained prominence as a leading American practitioner of *reader-response criticism and as the originator of *affective stylistics. Later he gained notoriety for his view that meaning is determined entirely by the interpretive strategies which regulate its perception by readers rather than by any formal architecture within texts. Although he develops his theories for the most part independently of continental philosophy, Fish's concept of reading as a dialectical experience of reversals, as well as his scepticism with respect to the possibility of objective meaning or formal autonomy, place him in the tradition of *poststructuralism.

The critical practice of 'affective stylistics' for which Fish initially gained prominence grew out of his innovative readings of 17th-century English *literature. In *Surprised by Sin: The Reader in 'Paradise Lost'* (1967) and *Self-Consuming Artifacts: The Experience of 17th Century Literature* (1972), Fish argued that the meaning of works from this period was not to be found in their formal configuration or in any objective reality to which they referred but in the experience of the reader attempting to make sense of them. According to Fish these works tempt their readers into various erroneous conclusions, poor judgments and ill-conceived analytical partitions, thereby compelling them to abandon their discursive, reason-based ways of thinking and acknowledge the primacy of divine revelation. Because this transcendence of discursive selfhood also involves a transcendence of the literary *discourse which occasions it, Fish refers to the works he treats in this period as 'self-consuming artifacts.'

During a second period, in a series of articles commencing with 'Literature in the Reader: Affective Stylistics' (1970) and collected in *Is There a Text in This Class?* (1980), Fish shifted his emphasis from practice to theory and from the experiences which texts elicit in their readers – from what texts 'do' to the reader – to the way in which readers shape texts and textual meaning through their interpretive conventions. (See *text.) Reversing his own earlier tendency to portray the textual units as modulating the reading experience, he postulated that readers actually shape texts. Fish argued that literary meaning, like 'ordinary' linguistic meaning more generally, derives from the practical context of its production. Even the most fundamental determination of meaning is always already informed by its historical situation, which includes the motives, cultural background, belief system, and disciplinary allegiances of the perceiver. What

is 'in' the text is therefore not intrinsic to the text but is the product of the reader's unconscious interpretive decisions. These decisions are in turn regulated by collective standards and beliefs which limit the range of what the text can mean. Thus, while the meaning of texts may change over time, some meanings will always appear more 'obvious' or 'literal' than others. This accounts for critical consensus.

In his most recent collection of essays, *Doing What Comes Naturally* (1989), Fish extends his analysis to the debates surrounding poststructural theoreticians and their adversaries in literary and legal studies. He argues that theorizing, like any professional activity, entails interpretive decisions which always reflect the belief systems and current protocols of a profession and are therefore both self-interested and political yet constrained in their range. Thus, the hope that theory could provide a disinterested understanding of meaning apart from its instantiation in a particular case is, Fish argues, as deluded as the fear that theory could somehow subvert the discipline. Similarly, he demonstrates that attacks on professionalism during the 1980s are based on the untenable assumption that there could be viable academic behaviour that was not contingent on and enabled by disciplinary protocols. Ultimately Fish's work leads to an understanding of literary criticism as a series of shifting beliefs and practices in an ongoing process of change, the mechanisms of which provide an insight into the structure of history itself.

WILLIAM RAY

Primary Sources

Fish, Stanley. *Doing What Comes Naturally: Change, Rhetoric, and the Practice of Theory in Literary and Legal Studies.* Durham: Duke UP, 1989.
– *Is There a Text in This Class? The Authority of Interpretive Communities.* Cambridge, Mass.: Harvard UP, 1980.
– *John Skelton's Poetry.* New Haven: Yale UP, 1965.
– *The Living Temple: George Herbert and Catechizing.* Berkeley: U of California P, 1978.
– *Self-Consuming Artifacts: The Experience of 17th-Century Literature.* Berkeley: U of California P, 1972.
– *Surprised by Sin: The Reader in 'Paradise Lost.'* New York: Macmillan, 1967.

Secondary Sources

Culler, Jonathan. 'Stanley Fish and the Righting of the Reader.' In *The Pursuit of Signs*. Ithaca: Cornell UP, 1981.

Dasenbrock, Reed Way. 'Accounting for the Changing Certainties of Interpretive Communities.' *MLN* 101.5 (1986): 1022–41.

Goodheart, Eugene. *The Skeptic Disposition in Contemporary Criticism*. Princeton: Princeton UP, 1984.

Mailloux, Steven. 'Learning to Read: Interpretation and Reader-Response Criticism.' In Victor A. Kramer, ed. *American Critics at Work: Examinations of Contemporary Literary Theory*. Troy, NY: Whitston, 1984, 296–315.

Ray, William. 'Stanley Fish: Supersession and Transcendence.' In *Literary Meaning: From Phenomenology to Deconstruction*. Oxford: Basil Blackwell, 1984, 152–69.

Forster, E(dward) M(organ)

(b. England, 1879–d. 1970) Novelist and critic. After his father's early death, E.M. Forster was raised from infancy by his mother and his paternal aunts. Though the time he spent as a day-boy at Tonbridge School, Kent, was not happy and was the basis for much of his later criticism of the English public school system, Forster was fortunate enough to receive an inheritance which made it possible for him to attend King's College, Cambridge, an institution that liberated his spirit, freeing him to follow his own intellectual inclinations. Financial security also meant that Forster could devote his life to his writing. His three-year sojourn in Egypt during the First World War and his early visits to India were of great importance in the development of his writing career. Between 1905 and 1924 he achieved renown as a novelist; however, his fifth novel, *A Passage to India* (1924), was to be the last published during his lifetime. After *A Passage* he continued to be known and respected as an essayist and as a spokesman for the committed intellectuals of the period. In 1946 his former college gave him an honorary fellowship, and he became one of the most celebrated figures at the university.

Forster contributed over 500 articles to periodicals and newspapers during a career that spanned half a century. Three anthologies contain the best of these: *Pharos and Pharillon* (1923), *Abinger Harvest* (1936) and *Two Cheers for Democracy* (1951). He was a liberal humanist, who felt as well that he was something of an anachronism, belonging as he did to an era that had been overwhelmed by modernism, an era that 'practised benevolence and philanthropy, was humane and intellectually curious, upheld free speech, had little colour-prejudice, believed that individuals are and should be different, and entertained a sincere faith in the progress of society' (*Two Cheers for Democracy* 54).

By far the most important of Forster's writings of literary criticism is *Aspects of the Novel* (1927). The chapters making up this book were originally delivered as a part of Cambridge University's Clark Lectures series, perhaps the best-known of all such series in the field of English *literature. Forster was the first novelist to be honoured with an invitation to deliver the lectures. *Aspects* is divided into chapters (originally individual lectures) on story, people, plot, fantasy, prophecy, and pattern and rhythm. (See *story/plot, *narratology.) Though it does not articulate what would now be considered a complete theory of the novel, it addresses the questions of form, point of view and the relationship of art and life that are crucial in discussions of literature today. After its publication it was for a quarter of a century the most widely read English critical work on the novel.

Central to *Aspects of the Novel* is Forster's notion that 'there are in the novel two forces: human beings and a bundle of various things not human beings, and it is the novelist's business to adjust these two forces and conciliate their claims' (73). Forster believes in the primacy of people over form, of life over art, in the novel (indeed 'people' is the only subject to which Forster devotes two chapters in *Aspects*). He consistently praises novels which convey a sense of the 'inner life' and the 'unseen,' those elements of life which resist attempts to describe them in words. For Forster, the novelist's task is 'to reveal the hidden life at its source' (31).

In his introductory chapter Forster insists on an ahistorical or synchronic approach which conceives of all English novelists 'writing their novels at once' (8). Forster's approach, which favours comparison over analysis, freed him to look at the novel from a perspective unencumbered by considerations of tradition and influence, and likely contributed to the general tendency towards studying the novel in terms divorced from traditional theories of literary history.

Aspects was conceived at least in part as a response to *Percy Lubbock's *The Craft of Fiction,* a study of form in the novels of *Henry James, which argues for the primacy of point of view in the novel. While Lubbock fears that readers and writers will disregard the novel's art and examine it solely as a representation of life, Forster is concerned that they might focus on the artistry to the extent that life is forgotten. Point of view is discussed in Forster's second chapter on 'people' only as a secondary 'aspect' of the novel. For Forster, the question of the novelist's method is resolved not in the question of point of view but in 'the power of the writer to bounce the reader into accepting what he says' (54). By discussing point of view so briefly, Forster attempts to right the balance which he feels is upset by critics' 'overstressing' the problem in the interest of discovering concerns peculiar to the novel. For Forster, point of view is not as important as 'a proper mixture of characters' (55).

This interest in the proper mixture of characters is behind what has become Forster's most important contribution to the aesthetic of the novel: the distinction between 'flat' and 'round' characters. Flat characters are 'constructed round a single idea or quality' (47) and can be expressed in a single sentence; round characters are multi-faceted and unpredictable. For Forster, the 'test of a round character is whether it is capable of surprising in a convincing way' (54). Both flat and round characters can coexist in the same novel. While 'it is only round people who are fit to perform tragically for any length of time and can move us to any feelings except humour and appropriateness' (50–1), flat characters have the advantage of being easily recognized and convenient for their creators. The use of volume to describe character may derive from the criticism of *Charles Mauron, the modern French aesthetician to whom *Aspects* is dedicated. Mauron's essay 'Beauty in Literature,' which Forster could easily have read before it was published, attempts to show how post-impressionist aesthetic theory can be used to discuss literary beauty and suggests how post-impressionism may have influenced Forster in the writing of *Aspects of the Novel.* Forster's distinction between flat and round characters is still important because it demonstrates that art and life do not operate on the same principles and that elements of the novel need not necessarily be 'lifelike' to be effective.

Aspects examines as well the distinction between story and plot and emphasizes the importance of temporality in the novel, thereby moving novel criticism away from James' conception of *spatial form. Forster's discussion of endings as nearly always 'feeble' anticipates later work on the subject. (See *closure/disclosure.) Subsequent chapters on fantasy, prophecy, and pattern and rhythm introduce subjects that show Forster refusing to restrict himself to what can easily be analysed in the novel and give credence to the place of imagination and creativity in criticism.

Forster's most important work of literary criticism has what would now be seen as serious shortcomings. He is not entirely clear and consistent in his use of terms (*Virginia Woolf, for example, had serious reservations about Forster's use of 'life' in a novel as an indicator of its merit). He does not examine form and technique in enough detail and does not consider language or ideas at all. At times Forster's evaluations of writers are little more than eccentric and highly personal statements of his own likes and dislikes. However, the artistry of *Aspects of the Novel* itself and the power of its most memorable discussions have ensured its place in the criticism of the English novel.

KELLY ST-JACQUES

Primary Sources

Forster, E.M. *Aspects of the Novel.* 1927. Repub. as *Aspects of the Novel and Related Writings.* Ed. Oliver Stallybrass. Abinger edition. London: Edward Arnold, 1974.
– *Two Cheers for Democracy.* 1951. Ed. Oliver Stallybrass. Abinger ed. London: Edward Arnold, 1972.

Secondary Sources

Advani, Rukun. *E.M. Forster as Critic.* London: Croom Helm, 1984.
Brander, Laurence. *E.M. Forster: A Critical Study.* Lewisburg: Bucknell UP, 1970.
Gardner, Philip, ed. *E.M. Forster: The Critical Heritage.* London and Boston: Routledge and Kegan Paul, 1973.
Herz, Judith Scherer, and Robert K. Martin, eds. *E.M. Forster: Centenary Revaluations.* Toronto and Buffalo: U of Toronto P, 1982.
Kirkpatrick, B.J. *A Bibliography of E.M. Forster.* London: Rupert Hart-Davis, 1965. 2nd ed. 1968. The Soho Bibliographies XIX.

Lubbock, Percy. *The Craft of Fiction.* London: Cape, 1921.

McDowell, Frederick P.W. *E.M. Forster.* TEAS 89. Boston: Twayne, 1982.

Schwarz, Daniel R. 'The Importance of E.M. Forster's *Aspects of the Novel.*' *South Atlantic Quarterly* 82.2 (1983): 189–205.

Stallybrass, Oliver, ed. *Aspects of E.M. Forster: Essays and Recollections Written for his Ninetieth Birthday 1st January 1969.* London: Edward Arnold, 1969.

Stone, Wilfred. *The Cave and the Mountain: A Study of E.M. Forster.* Stanford: Stanford UP, 1966.

Foucault, Michel

(b. France, 1926–d. 1984) Historian and philosopher. The son of a medical professor and prominent surgeon, Paul-Michel Foucault began his education in Poitiers but soon left for Paris, where he studied philosophy with Jean Hyppolite at the Lycée Henri IV. He entered the Ecole Normale Supérieure in 1946 and after receiving degrees there in philosophy and psychology, he was awarded the Diplôme de psycho-pathologie from the Institut de Psychologie of Paris in 1952. Foucault taught at the ENS and the Université de Lille for several years but he left France in 1955 to teach in Sweden, Poland and then Germany. In 1961 he returned to France for a postion at the University of Clermont-Ferrand. Following the social and political turmoil of 1968, Foucault became head of the department of philosophy at the new experimental campus of the Université de Paris at Vincennes. The next year he was elected to the Collège de France, where he remained until his death.

Shortly before his death, Michel Foucault observed that his earliest personal memories were all associated with the political turmoil in France during the 1930s and this connection between public and private experience interested him throughout his career. His earliest books dealt with the history of medical knowledge and practice. *Folie et déraison* [*Madness and Civilization* 1961] described changes in the concept and treatment of madness from the Middle Ages through the 19th century. *Naissance de la clinique* [*Birth of the Clinic* 1963] traced the emergence of clinical medicine at the end of the 18th century. The importance of these works lies in Foucault's claim that madness and disease are not simple, empirical facts but are always conceived in relation to the

social norms and specific forms of *discourse current at particular historical moments.

In his next book, *Les Mots et les choses* [*The Order of Things* 1966], Foucault described the combination of discourses, assumptions and values that distinguish historical periods as the 'episteme' or epistemological paradigm governing what is considered truth or knowledge at the time. (See *episteme.) In his conclusion, he claimed that one of the most important truths of the 19th-century episteme, the philosophical concept of 'Man,' was being replaced by language in the modern human sciences. This elevation of language over 'mind' or 'consciousness' as the determining principle of human experience resembled the priority granted to linguistic analysis in *structuralism, but it was Foucault's prediction of the 'death of Man' that most directly challenged the traditions of Western humanism and generated a bitter controversy about his work. His 'anti-humanism' was condemned as a deterministic system that discounted the role of human agency in the discovery and dissemination of knowledge, and historians objected that the concept of the episteme could not account for changes from one period to another.

As Foucault continued to explore the link between language and society, his emphasis shifted from the abstract structural parallels of the episteme to the specific social rituals that determine who gets to say what to whom. The analysis of language at this concrete, material level of discourse was termed 'archaeology,' and in *L'Archéolgie du savoir* [*Archaeology of Knowledge* 1969] and 'L'Ordre du discours' ['*The Discourse on Language*' 1971], Foucault described the array of institutional constraints and political practices that regulate different forms of discourse. Those regulations join the production of knowledge in the discourse of a particular field to the exercise of *power in society as a whole. This link between power and knowledge, Foucault claimed, characterizes the 'disciplinary' character of all modern political organizations.

In *Surveiller et punir: Naissance de la prison* [*Discipline and Punish* 1975], Foucault argued that the disciplinary techniques underlying the development of the modern prison pervade contemporary society and govern even the minute details of everyday life. This 'microphysics of power' reaches past the limits of law and repression actually to produce the individual as a subject in, as well as subject to, the disciplinary mechanisms of the state. Power thus regulates not only speech but also the most intimate recesses of the speaker's 'self.' (See *self/other.) Rather than being something that one group possesses or uses over individuals, however, power is for Foucault a network of relations that encompasses the rulers as well as those they rule in a vast web of discrete, local conflicts. So while Foucault rejected the notion of a single, centralized 'Power' in the hands of a few, he also concluded that there is no 'outside' of power, no disengaged point from which power can be exercised or even studied without implicating the subject in the very forces he or she would escape.

Once again, Foucault's critics attacked the deterministic and monolithic character of his social model, claiming that such a pervasive notion of power left no room for freedom or even resistance to oppressive practices of the State. But Foucault insisted that relations constituted through the exercise of power 'define innumerable points of confrontation, forces of instability, each of which has its own risks of conflict, of struggles, and of an at least temporary inversion of the power relations' (Discipline 27). Possibilities for resistance therefore inhere in every exercise of power. So instead of trying to escape into some abstract realm of scholarly objectivity or academic freedom, Foucault argued that it was the job of the 'specific intellectual' to struggle against power on the very site that he or she occupies in its network, using the specificity of that site to challenge 'the politics of truth in our societies.'

The notion that power produces knowledge rather than merely repressing behaviour enabled Foucault to extend his analysis of discipline across the border that separates private experience from public regulation. In the introductory volume to his Histoire de la sexualité, La Volonté de savoir [History of Sexuality I: An Introduction 1976], Foucault explored the disciplinary structure of the private sphere through what he called 'technologies of the self,' the various techniques through which human beings come to know who they are and what they should do. Rather than repressing some hidden 'truth' of sex, Foucault says, institutional rituals such as the confessional and psychoanalysis constitute an administrative 'apparatus.' This apparatus produces sexuality as a form of discourse in which the 'will to know' one's desires serves as the primary

mechanism through which individuals are subjected to control in the disciplinary state of the modern age. The second and third volumes of the Histoire, L'Usage des plaisirs [The Use of Pleasure 1984] and Le Souci de soi [The Care of the Self 1984], focus on the complex social hierarchies and moral discriminations that regulated sexual behaviour in ancient Greece and Rome. At the time of his death Foucault was working on a fourth volume devoted to sexual ethics in the context of Christian theology.

With the publication of Les Mots et les choses, Foucault emerged as one of the prominent intellectuals in France. Because of his profound scepticism towards many concepts and values of Western culture, Foucault's work was often linked with that of *Jacques Derrida, *Jacques Lacan, *Louis Althusser, and *Roland Barthes in what later became known as *poststructuralism. Foucault's attacks on such humanist shibboleths as Reason, the individual, Truth, and freedom were not based on general philosophical principles, however. They usually grew out of detailed historical analyses of a range of texts. His work attracted readers from the fields of intellectual history, the history of medicine, psychiatry, law, the social or 'human' sciences, and literary studies, where his work on discursive regulation eventually served as the basis for the *New Historicism. Despite the often arcane nature of Foucault's scholarship and despite attacks on his generalizing and poetic style, his works aspired to a broader political critique of contemporary social practices that immediately appealed to a wide audience. With the regular translation of his books, essays and even interviews into English and most other European languages, Foucault's impact had extended throughout Europe and North America by the early 1970s, and 20 years later he remains an influential writer of our time. (See also *psychoanalytic theory.)

MICHAEL CLARK

Primary Sources

Foucault, Michel. L'Archéologie du savoir. Paris: Editions Gallimard, 1969. Trans. A.M. Sheridan-Smith. The Archaeology of Knowledge. New York: Pantheon, 1972.
– Folie et déraison: Histoire de la folie à l'âge classique. Paris: Plon, 1961. Trans. Richard Howard. Madness and Civilization: A History of Insanity in the Age of Reason. New York: Pantheon, 1965; London: Tavistock, 1967.

- *The Foucault Reader.* Ed. Paul Rabinow. New York: Random House, 1984.
- *Histoire de la sexualité, I: La Volonté de savoir.* 1976. Trans. Robert Hurley. *The History of Sexuality, I: An Introduction.* New York: Pantheon, 1978; London: Tavistock, 1979.
- *Histoire de la sexualité, II: L'Usage des plaisirs.* Paris: Editions Gallimard, 1984. Trans. Robert Hurley. *The Use of Pleasure.* New York: Random House, 1985.
- *Histoire de la sexualité, III: Le Souci de soi.* Paris: Editions Gallimard, 1984. Trans. Robert Hurley. *The Care of the Self.* New York: Random House, 1986.
- *Language, Counter-Memory, Practice: Selected Essays and Interviews.* Ed. Donald F. Bouchard. Trans. Bouchard and Sherry Simon. Ithaca: Cornell UP, 1977.
- *Les Mots et les choses: Une Archéologie des sciences humaines.* Paris: Editions Gallimard, 1966. Trans. anon. *The Order of Things: An Archaeology of the Human Sciences.* New York: Pantheon, 1970.
- *Naissance de la clinique: Une Archéologie du regard médical.* Paris: PUF, 1963. Trans. A.M. Sheridan-Smith. *The Birth of the Clinic: An Archaeology of Medical Perception.* New York: Vintage, 1973.
- *L'Ordre du discours: Leçon inaugurale au Collège de France.* 1971. Trans. A.M. Sheridan-Smith. 'The Discourse on Language.' In *The Archaeology of Knowledge.*
- *Politics, Philosophy, Culture: Interviews and Other Writings, 1977–1984.* Ed. Lawrence D. Kritzman. Trans. Alan Sheridan et al. New York and London: Routledge, 1988.
- *Power/Knowledge: Selected Interviews and Other Writings, 1972–1977.* Ed. Colin Gordon. New York: Pantheon, 1980.
- *Surveiller et punir: Naissance de la prison.* Paris: Editions Gallimard, 1975. Trans. Alan Sheridan. *Discipline and Punish: The Birth of the Prison.* New York: Vintage, 1977.

Secondary Sources

Baudrillard, Jean. *Oublier Foucault.* Paris: Gallimard, 1977. Trans. Nicole Dufresne. 'Forgetting Foucault.' *Humanities in Society* 3 (Winter 1980): 87–111.
Carroll, David. *Paraesthetics: Foucault, Lyotard, Derrida.* New York: Methuen, 1987.
Clark, Michael. *Michel Foucault, An Annotated Bibliography: Tool Kit from a New Age.* New York: Garland Publishing, 1983.
Deleuze, Gilles. *Foucault.* Paris: Editions de Minuit, 1986. Trans. Séan Hand. *Foucault.* Minneapolis: U of Minnesota P, 1988.
Dreyfus, Hubert L. *Michel Foucault, Beyond Structuralism and Hermeneutics.* Chicago: U of Chicago P, 1982.
Eribon, Didier. *Michel Foucault.* Paris: Flammarion,

1989. Trans. Betsy Wing. *Michel Foucault.* Cambridge: Harvard UP, 1991.
Lemert, Charles C., and Garth Gillan. *Michel Foucault: Social Theory as Transgression.* New York: Columbia UP, 1982.
Lentricchia, Frank. *Ariel and the Police: Michel Foucault, William James, Wallace Stevens.* Madison: U of Wisconsin P, 1988.
Poster, Mark. *Foucault, Marxism, and History.* Cambridge: Polity P, 1984.
Racevskis, Karlis. *Michel Foucault and the Subversion of Intellect.* Ithaca: Cornell UP, 1983.
Rajchman, John. *Michel Foucault: The Freedom of Philosophy.* New York: Columbia UP, 1985.
Sheridan, Alan. *Michel Foucault: The Will to Truth.* London: Tavistock, 1980.
Smart, Barry. *Foucault, Marxism, and Critique.* London: Routledge and Kegan Paul, 1983.

Freud, Sigmund

(b. Moravia, 1856–d. England, 1939) Founder of psychoanalysis. After graduation from gymnasium in Vienna at the head of his class, Freud began his medical studies in 1873 at the University of Vienna, where he was influenced by the physiologist Ernst Brücke. In Brücke's laboratory he absorbed thoroughly the view that all human thought and action could be understood by an analysis of chemical and physical forces. The need to make a living and to afford marriage compelled him to abandon his plans for a career in research, to complete his medical studies (1881) and to train for private practice at the General Hospital in Vienna. In 1886 he began private practice as a neurologist. As early as 1882, he had heard from his older friend Josef Breuer, the physician, of the patient later to be called Anna O. In 1885–6 he worked in Paris with Jean-Martin Charcot. Both of these events aroused his interest in hysteria.

During the 1890s, he gradually developed the basic ideas of psychoanalysis. This development involved a gradual shift from physiological to psychological explanations of the mind and can be seen in *Studies on Hysteria* (1895), co-published with Breuer. From 1897 to 1900, when Freud combined his own self-analysis with the continuing treatment of neurotic patients, psychoanalysis as a new term and a new science of the mind emerged. *The Interpretation of Dreams* (1900), *The Psychopathology of Everyday Life* (1901), *Three Essays on the Theory of Sexuality* (1905), *Jokes and*

Their Relation to the Unconscious (1905), and 'Fragment of an Analysis of a Case of Hysteria' (1905) established the basic principles of psychoanalysis, which include the idea of repressed unconscious mental processes, the meaning of dreams, the significance of infantile sexuality (especially the Oedipus complex) in normal and neurotic human experience, and the role of transference in the therapeutic process – that is, the patient's unconscious projection onto the analyst of feelings and fantasies derived from other, usually childhood, relationships. (See *psychoanalytic theory.)

Up to 1923, Freud worked with the 'topographical' model of the mind involving three levels of mental experience – conscious, preconscious (unconscious but not repressed) and repressed unconscious. In his view the repressed unconscious was inaccessible to consciousness except indirectly through parapraxes (slips of the tongue or pen, errors of memory and so on), dreams, neurotic symptoms, and jokes. He understood each of these mental phenomena as a compromise formation between an unconscious impulse or desire and a conscious or unconscious attempt to defend against, to deny that impulse. (See also *desire/lack.) His therapeutic goal in the case of neurosis was to infer the unconscious impulse through the process of free association (uncensored talking) on the part of the patient, to interpret this impulse to the patient, and thereby to make it conscious. In this way, neurotic symptoms could be cured.

The Ego and the Id (1923) set forth a structural model of psychic process – a modification of the earlier layered model – and introduced a new set of terms – ego, id, superego – into psychoanalysis. It focused on the way in which the conscious and unconscious (defensive) ego mediates among the demands of external reality, the id (the repressed unconscious) and the superego (conscience). Freud's therapeutic goal became not merely the uncovering of repressed unconscious material but the extension of the control of the ego over the id. With this new view there developed out of Freud's later psychoanalytic theory an ego psychology which was to emphasize ego defence and ego adaptation as a central concern of psychoanalysis and which received definitive expression in Anna Freud's *The Ego and the Mechanisms of Defense* (1936) and Heinz Hartmann's *Ego Psychology and the Problem of Adaptation* (1939).

The development of psychoanalytic criticism parallels this two-stage evolution of Freud's work. Like psychoanalysis, psychoanalytic criticism begins with Freud. Freud wrote most of his essays on art during the period when the topographical model dominated his thought (1900–23), with the one exception, 'Dostoevsky and Parricide' (1928). His aesthetic ideas reflect his primary interest in the interpretation of dreams and other forms of unconscious fantasy life and in the significance of infantile sexuality (especially the Oedipus complex) in human experience and human neurosis. In his comments on Sophocles' *Oedipus the King* in *The Interpretation of Dreams*, he sees the unconscious Oedipal fantasy rather than the conscious intellectual themes as the central fact. The literary *text – like the dream – is a compromise formation between unconscious and conscious intent. The unconscious fantasy, moreover, exists not only in the text but also in the author's and the reader's mind – a view which opens the way to psychobiography and to reader-response theory. (See *reader-response criticism.) In such works as 'Delusions and Dream's in Jensen's *Gradiva*' (1907), 'Creative Writers and Day-Dreaming' (1908) and *Leonardo Da Vinci and a Memory of His Childhood* (1910), Freud further discusses his views on the relationship between fantasy and creativity, the unconscious content of literary works, and the importance of unconscious infantile experience in adult creativity.

Though they were primarily concerned with illustrating his theories, Freud's essays and comments on art strongly affected the initial development of psychoanalytic criticism, as Claudia C. Morrison (1968) has shown. From F.C. Prescott's *Poetry and Dreams* (1912) to Maud Bodkin's 'Literary Criticism and the Study of the Unconscious' (1927), two theoretical issues were central: first, the neurosis of the artist; and second, the relationship between art and dream. (See *Maud Bodkin.) The first led to the psychobiography, as in Marie Bonaparte's *Edgar Poe* (1933), the second to textual criticism, as in Ernest Jones' *Hamlet and Oedipus* (1949).

Freud's structural theory changed psychoanalytic criticism. Its emphasis on ego defence and adaptation allowed critics to rethink the nature of the artist. Instead of being dominated by the unconscious, the artist was understood as endowed with an ability to use unconscious material for artistic purposes.

Moreover, critics now had a theoretical basis with which to appreciate the role of artistic form (largely neglected in the earlier phase) as an aspect of the defensive and adaptive function of art. In this respect, Freud's *Jokes and Their Relation to the Unconscious* received renewed study as a disguised treatise on aesthetics because of his emphasis on the role of the ego in shaping unconscious material into the communicable form of the joke, or, as *E.H. Gombrich (1966) would say, the work of art. By 1952 in *Psychoanalytic Explorations in Art*, Ernst Kris was able to add to the already established view of the work of art as the expression of disguised unconscious fantasy the idea of the defensive function of the ego in controlling and shaping repressed unconscious material into art. Two literary critics – Simon O. Lesser in *Fiction and the Unconscious* (1957) and *Norman N. Holland in *The Dynamics of Literary Response* (1968) – elaborated the related ideas of the repressed unconscious as the source of literary meaning and the defensive ego as the source of literary form into full-scale psychoanalytic theories of *literature. In *The Literary Use of the Psychoanalytic Process* (1981), Meredith Anne Skura has provided a valuable study of the several psychoanalytic approaches to literature – as case history, fantasy, dream, and transference experience.

In the last twenty years, both psychoanalysis and psychoanalytic criticism have continued to develop. Psychoanalysis has produced a number of models of the mind in addition to Freud's: self psychology (Heinz Kohut), object relations theory (Melanie Klein and D.W. Winnicott) and Lacanian theory. (See *Jacques Lacan). Each has influenced psychoanalytic criticism, as have also feminist theory and cognitive psychology (Holland 1990). (See *feminist criticism.) Although these developments have roots in Freud's thought, they are not directly related to his life and work. They belong to the ongoing history of psychoanalysis.

For Freud, applied psychoanalysis was a field that could and should take all of culture as its province. Thus in *Totem and Taboo* (1913), he studied the origin of society, religion and human morality. In *Group Psychology and the Analysis of the Ego* (1921), he examined group psychology as an extension of individual psychology. In *Civilization and Its Discontents* (1930), he undertook an analysis of the nature of aggression and its effect on civilization. And in *The Future of an Illusion* (1927)

and *Moses and Monotheism* (1939), he turned again to the study of religion.

Freud and psychoanalysis have always attracted controversy and criticism. In particular, Freud has been accused of an overemphasis on sexuality, of an overly mechanistic and deterministic view of the importance of early experience in shaping adult character, and of creating an unscientific, speculative and untestable system of psychology. Feminist work in the humanities has incorporated psychoanalytic ideas, though often ambivalently. His insistence that sexuality and aggression were the two basic instincts which influence human motivation has always been rejected by psychologists who believe in no inherited human predispositions. Psychoanalytic criticism has always had critics who have accused it of reducing literary texts to two or three unconscious, usually infantile, themes (such as the Oedipus complex). (See *theme.)

Yet, with all the criticism, Freud's influence in the 20th century is pervasive. His goals for psychoanalysis – that it develop as a medical technique for the treatment of the neuroses; that it make important contributions to general psychology; and that it reach beyond psychology to other disciplines – have all been met. Psychoanalysis is central to dynamic psychiatry and clinical psychology, and it has also remained as a separate professional area in its own right. Many of its ideas (such as the dynamic unconscious, the importance of infantile experience, the nature of ego defence mechanisms, and the structure of inner conflict) have entered into general psychology. Beyond these two areas, psychoanalysis has touched almost every aspect of modern culture – painting, drama, poetry, film, biography, and fiction, as well as history, philosophy, anthropology, and the social sciences in general. James Joyce, *D.H. Lawrence, Thomas Mann, *Virginia Woolf, William Faulkner, and W.H. Auden are only a few of the numerous modern writers who have been directly influenced by Freud. Among literary critics, psychoanalytic criticism has become one of the essential elements of modern critical theory and practice. The range and continuity of this influence, combined with the prevalence of Freud's name and ideas at all levels of contemporary society, indicate that he is one of the supreme makers of the modern mind.

RICHARD W. NOLAND

Primary Sources

Note: All references to Freud are to *The Standard Edition of the Complete Psychological Works of Sigmund Freud*. Trans. from German under the general editorship of James Strachey.

Freud, Sigmund. *Civilization and Its Discontents*. 1930. *Standard Edition* 21: 64–145. London: Hogarth P, 1961.

– 'Creative Writers and Day-Dreaming.' 1908. *Standard Edition* 9: 141–53. London: Hogarth P, 1957.

– 'Delusions and Dreams in Jensen's *Gradiva*.' 1907. *Standard Edition* 9: 3–95. London: Hogarth P, 1959.

– 'Dostoevsky and Parricide.' 1928. *Standard Edition* 21: 175–96. London: Hogarth P, 1961.

– *The Ego and the Id*. 1923. *Standard Edition* 19: 12–66. London: Hogarth P, 1961.

– 'Fragment of an Analysis of a Case of Hysteria.' 1905. *Standard Edition* 7: 7–122. London: Hogarth P, 1953.

– *The Future of an Illusion*. 1927. *Standard Edition* 21: 5–56. London: Hogarth P, 1961.

– *Group Psychology and the Analysis of the Ego*. 1921. *Standard Edition* 18: 69–143. London: Hogarth P, 1955.

– *Interpretation of Dreams*. 1900. *Standard Edition* 4 and 5. London: Hogarth P, 1953.

– *Jokes and Their Relation to the Unconscious*. 1905. *Standard Edition* 8. London: Hogarth P, 1960.

– *Leonardo Da Vinci and a Memory of His Childhood*. 1910. *Standard Edition* 11: 59–137. London: Hogarth P, 1957.

– *Moses and Monotheism*. 1939. *Standard Edition* 23: 7–137. London: Hogarth P, 1964.

– *The Psychopathology of Everyday Life*. 1901. *Standard Edition* 6. London: Hogarth P, 1960.

– *Three Essays on the Theory of Sexuality*. 1905. *Standard Edition* 9: 125–243. London: Hogarth P, 1953.

– *Totem and Taboo*. 1913. *Standard Edition* 13: 1–161. London: Hogarth P, 1953.

Secondary Sources

Bocock, Robert. *Freud and Modern Society*. New York: Holmes and Meier Publishers, 1978.

Bodkin, Maud. 'Literary Criticism and the Study of the Unconscious.' *The Monist* 37 (July 1927): 445–68.

Bonaparte, Marie. *Edgar Poe, étude psychoanalytique*. Paris: Denoël and Steele, 1933.

Eagle, Morris N. *Recent Developments in Psychoanalysis: A Critical Evaluation*. New York: McGraw-Hill, 1984.

Ehrenzweig, Anton. *The Hidden Order of Art*. Berkeley and Los Angeles: U of California P, 1971.

Ellenberger, Henri. *The Discovery of the Unconscious: The History and Development of Dynamic Psychiatry*. New York: Basic Books, 1970.

Fine, Reuben. *The Development of Freud's Thought*. New York: Jacob Aronson, 1973.

– *A History of Psychoanalysis*. New York: Columbia UP, 1979.

Freud, Anna. *The Ego and the Mechanisms of Defense*. Rev. ed. NY: International Universities P, 1966.

Gay, Peter. *Freud: A Life for Our Time*. New York: W.W. Norton and Company, 1988.

Gombrich, E.H. 'Freud's Aesthetics,' *Encounter* 26 (Jan. 1966): 30–40.

Hartmann, Heinz. *Ego Psychology and the Problem of Adaptation*. New York: International Universities P, 1958.

Holland, Norman N. *The Dynamics of Literary Response*. New York: Oxford UP, 1968.

– *Holland's Guide to Psychoanalytic Psychology and Literature-and-Psychology*. New York: Oxford UP, 1990.

Jones, Ernest. *Hamlet and Oedipus*. New York: W.W. Norton, 1976.

Kris, Ernst. *Psychoanalytic Explorations in Art*. New York: Schocken Books, 1952.

Kurzweil, Edith. *The Freudians: A Comparative Perspective*. New Haven and London: Yale UP, 1989.

Lesser, Simon O. *Fiction and the Unconscious*. New York: Vintage Books, 1962.

McGrath, William J. *Freud's Discovery of Psychoanalysis: The Politics of Hysteria*. Ithaca and London: Cornell UP, 1986.

Morrison, Claudia C. *Freud and the Critic: The Early Use of Depth Psychology in Literary Criticism*. Chapel Hill: U of North Carolina P, 1968.

Munroe, Ruth L. *Schools of Psychoanalytic Thought*. New York: Henry Holt and Company, 1955.

Nelson, Benjamin, ed. *Freud and the 20th Century*. New York: Meridian Books, 1957.

Prescott, Frederick C. 'Poetry and Dreams.' *The Journal of Abnormal Psychology* 7 (April–May 1912): 17–46; (June–July 1912): 104–43.

Ragland-Sullivan, Ellie. *Jacques Lacan and the Philosophy of Psychoanalysis*. Urbana and Chicago: U of Illinois P, 1986.

Rieff, Philip. *Freud: The Mind of the Moralist*. Garden City, NY: Doubleday and Company, 1961.

Roazen, Paul. *Freud: Political and Social Thought*. New York: Alfred A. Knopf, 1968.

– *Freud and His Followers*. New York: New American Library, 1971.

Rothenberg, Albert. *Creativity and Madness: New Findings and Old Stereotypes*. Baltimore and London: Johns Hopkins UP, 1990.

Rothstein, Arnold, ed. *Models of the Mind: Their Relationships to Clinical Work*. New York: International Universities P, 1985.

Rycroft, Charles. *Psychoanalysis and Beyond*. Chicago: U of Chicago P, 1985.

Skura, Meredith Anne. *The Literary Use of the Psychoanalytic Process*. New Haven and London: Yale UP, 1981.

Frye

Spector, Jack J. *The Aesthetics of Freud: A Study in Psychoanalysis and Art*. New York: McGraw-Hill, 1972.
Wallace, Edwin R. *Freud and Anthropology: A History and a Reappraisal*. New York: International Universities P, 1985.
Wollheim, Richard. *Sigmund Freud*. New York: Viking, 1971.

Frye, Northrop

(b. Canada, 1912–d. 1991) Literary critic and theoretician. Frye grew up in a Methodist family, studied philosophy and English at Victoria College, the Bible and Protestant theology at Emmanuel College (both in the University of Toronto) and English at Merton College, Oxford. Although ordained a minister in the United Church of Canada (1936), aside from one summer's work as a student pastor in rural Saskatchewan, he never held a pastoral charge. In his early years Frye was strongly influenced by Blake, *Jung, Spengler, *Freud, and Frazer. Especially important influences on him later were Ruskin, Graves and Vico.

From 1939 for more than 50 years Frye taught in the Department of English, Victoria College, University of Toronto. From this Canadian base, he wrote and lectured for both national and international publics on the whole range of *literature in the English language and on European and world literature. His major concern was with the theory and practice of literary criticism and with the role of the creative imagination in human culture.

Frye postulated the whole realm of literature as a self-contained verbal universe, a massive, complex and intricate product of human imagining which is a kind of 'second nature.' This imagined order of words constantly grows and expands through new works of literature even as it continues to use its essential archetypes. (See *archetype, *archetypal criticism.) Since in Frye's view literature develops from literature, criticism should be based upon 'what the whole of literature actually does' (*Anatomy* 6). According to Frye, literature projects an organized *myth of human experience. Human beings encounter the world through their imaginations, shaping and reshaping that world in accord with their desires and anxieties or confronting it dispassionately and objectively in a multitude of attempts to describe it clearly. The verbal expression of this whole encounter is the domain of literature, both fictional and non-fictional.

The resultant universe of words is describable by criticism, provided that critics are not determined by non-literary questions (historical, biographical, psychological, political, ideological, religious) and concentrate on what literature is and does. Such concentration implies an attitude in the critic that will permit criticism to develop some of the characteristics of a science, that is, a kind of study that facilitates scrutiny of literature as an object of study not as a subject and that proceeds systematically to describe what is there, in a manner similar to what is done in any science that progressively builds an expanding body of knowledge.

Frye's prodigious output includes two books on the Bible, four on Shakespeare's plays, one on Milton's epics, and one on *T.S. Eliot, as well as books on English Romanticism, the structure of romance, the social uses of literature and criticism, and Canadian literature and culture. Most of this output and something of the response to it are recorded in the 2500 entries of Robert D. Denham, *Northrop Frye: An Annotated Bibliography* (1987).

Much of Frye's work is concerned with constructing a taxonomy or anatomy of literature. It is the encyclopedic *Anatomy of Criticism: Four Essays* (1957) that sets out most fully Frye's theoretical account of the whole of literature. The 'First Essay' of *Anatomy* characterizes literary works by focusing on the relative powers of action of the protagonist. From this perspective there emerge five primary modes (mythical, romantic, high mimetic, low mimetic, and ironic) all of which take both thematic and fictional forms. The thematic forms are either encyclopedic or episodic, the fictional ones tragic or comic, giving a total of 20 broad categories. Frye demonstrates that, historically, Western literature has constantly used the same narrative structural principles but, through the centuries, has moved from undisplaced myth toward realism. The 'Second Essay' is an analysis of symbolic meaning in terms of five phases (literal, descriptive, formal, mythic, and anagogic), each involving a particular kind of literary work and inviting a particular kind of critical analysis: the literal level is best understood by rhetorical or textural analysis, the techniques of *New Criticism. The descriptive level lends itself to historical and biographical criticism, the formal to allegorical commentary, and the mythic and anagogic levels to archetypal criticism. The 'Third Essay' of *Anatomy* is an account of the structure of archetypal imagery considered both as meaning *(dianoia)* and narrative *(mythos)* and gives extended analyses of the four basic narrative patterns (romance, comedy, tragedy, and satire and *irony), each of these having six distinguishable phases. The 'Fourth Essay' defines four genres (drama, *epos,* fiction, and lyric) according to their forms and rhythms, but differentiates a wide range of variants within each genre. (See *genre criticism.)

Anatomy is widely viewed as a significant and influential work of Anglo-American critical theory. It has been recognized and used by many as a clear introduction to the structural principles of literature and as a defence or justification of criticism as a systematic and coherent body of knowledge. It has provided critical terms and vocabulary for much of the literary discourse of recent decades and in its dominance took the place of the pronouncements made by Eliot, Pound and *Richards in the 1920s and 1930s. *Anatomy* has been extensively admired and criticized for its attempt to remove matters of taste and value judgment from the structure of criticism. It has been seen as overly theoretical and schematic, as engaging in terminological buccaneering and 'as a work of criticism that has turned into literature' (Kermode 323). At once formidably theoretical and securely rooted in a wide-ranging literary experience and knowledge, *Anatomy* should be seen in the context of Frye's total production where it has many companion volumes and essays of practical criticism.

In addition to *Anatomy,* three other books by Frye loom especially large in his total output: *Fearful Symmetry: A Study of William Blake* (1947); *The Great Code: The Bible and Literature* (1982); and *Words with Power, Being a Second Study of the Bible and Literature* (1990). In the book on Blake, Frye articulated his conception of the human imagination which underlies all his own theoretical formulations. The imagination is the 'creative force in the mind' from which comes 'everything that we call culture and civilization. It is the power of transforming a sub-human physical world into a world with a human shape and meaning' ('The Imaginative and the Imaginary' 152).

The Great Code, translated into more than 20 languages, is about the Bible in its 'centripetal' or internal aspect: its language, myths, meta-

phors, and typology. (See also *metonymy/ metaphor.) The unity of 'this huge, sprawling, tactless book' that sits 'inscrutably' *(The Great Code* xviii) in the middle of our culture proceeds through seven phases of revelation – Creation, Exodus, Law, Wisdom, Prophecy, Gospel, and Apocalypse – each phase being the type or partially concealed form of the following phase and also the antitype or realized form of the preceding one. This progressive revelation, moving vertically as well as horizontally, assumes creative, imaginative or revolutionary forms according to the principle expressed in the text 'Behold I make all things new,' and has the energy and power to invoke the kind of human imaginative responses that we find in literature and the arts, where language is purely imaginative and hence hypothetical, 'where the limit is the conceivable and not the actual' *(The Great Code* 232).

Words with Power has an outward or 'centrifugal' reference and is meant to show 'the extent to which the canonical unity of the Bible indicates or symbolizes a much wider imaginative unity in secular European literature' *(Words with Power* x). Like *The Great Code, Words with Power* is entirely free of faith or doctrine as these terms are usually understood. It is not primarily a book about religion, however many implications it has for Bible-based religions and for other religions and ideologies. Its main intended readership is students of literature, including literary theorists and critics. The first half sets out, in a kind of Viconian sequence in reverse, the different idioms of linguistic expression – descriptive, conceptual, ideological, imaginative – and approaches the question, 'what is the basis of the poet's authority, if he has any?' (ibid., xx). This leads to a restatement of Frye's lifelong fundamental idea, developed here with the help of four major metaphorical images (the mountain, the garden, the cave, and the furnace), that mythological thinking, with its language of myth and metaphor, is 'the framework and context for all thinking' (ibid., xvi). Every human society possesses a mythology (the Bible in the Western world) which is inherited, transmitted and diversified by literature. The central structural principles of literature are derived from myth and it is these that 'give literature its communicating power across the centuries through all ideological changes' (ibid., xiii).

ALVIN A. LEE

Primary Sources

Denham, Robert D., ed. *Northrop Frye on Culture and Literature: A Collection of Review Essays.* Chicago: U of Chicago P, 1978.

Frye, H. Northrop. *Anatomy of Criticism: Four Essays.* Princeton, NJ: Princeton UP, 1957.

– *The Bush Garden: Essays on the Canadian Imagination.* Toronto: Anansi, 1971.

– *Creation and Recreation.* Toronto: U of Toronto P, 1980.

– *The Critical Path: An Essay on the Social Context of Literary Criticism.* Bloomington: Indiana UP, 1971.

– *The Double Vision.* Toronto: U of Toronto P, 1991.

– *The Educated Imagination.* Toronto: Canadian Broadcasting Corporation, 1963.

– *T.S. Eliot.* Edinburgh: Oliver and Boyd, 1963.

– *Fables of Identity: Studies in Poetic Mythology.* New York: Harcourt, Brace and World, 1963.

– *Fearful Symmetry: A Study of William Blake.* Princeton, NJ: Princeton UP, 1947.

– *Fools of Time: Studies in Shakespearean Tragedy.* Toronto: U of Toronto P, 1967.

– *The Great Code: The Bible and Literature.* New York: Harcourt Brace Jovanovich, 1982.

– 'The Imaginative and the Imaginary.' In *Fables of Identity: Studies in Poetic Mythology.*

– *The Modern Century: The Whidden Lectures at McMaster University 1967.* Toronto: Oxford UP, 1967.

– *The Myth of Deliverance: Reflections on Shakespeare's Problem Comedies.* Toronto: U of Toronto P, 1983.

– *A Natural Perspective: The Development of Shakespearean Comedy and Romance.* New York: Columbia UP, 1965.

– *The Return of Eden: Five Essays on Milton's Epics.* Toronto: U of Toronto P, 1965.

– *The Secular Scripture: A Study of the Structure of Romance.* Cambridge, Mass.: Harvard UP, 1976.

– *Spiritus Mundi: Essays on Literature, Myth, and Society.* Bloomington: Indiana UP, 1976.

– *The Stubborn Structure: Essays on Criticism and Society.* Ithaca, NY: Cornell UP, 1970.

– *A Study of English Romanticism.* New York: Random House, 1968.

– *The Well-Tempered Critic.* Bloomington: Indiana UP, 1963.

– *Words with Power, Being a Second Study of the Bible and Literature.* Markham, Ont.: Penguin Books Canada; New York: Harcourt Brace Jovanovich, 1990.

– Sheridan Baker and George W. Perkins. *The Harper Handbook to Literature.* New York: Harper and Row, 1985.

Kermode, Frank. [Review of *Anatomy of Criticism.*] *Review of English Studies* 10 (1959): 317–23.

Polk, James, ed. *Divisions on a Ground: Essays on Canadian Culture.* Toronto: Anansi, 1982.

Sandler, Robert, ed. *Northrop Frye on Shakespeare.* Markham, Ont.: Fitzhenry and Whiteside, 1986.

Secondary Sources

Arye, John. *Northrop Frye: A Biography.* Toronto: Random House, 1989.

Bate, Walter Jackson. 'Northrop Frye.' In *Criticism: The Major Texts.* New York: Harcourt Brace Jovanovich, 1970, 597–601, 609, 615–17.

Cook, Eleanor, Chaviva Hošek, Jay Macpherson, Patricia Parker and Julian Patrick, eds. *Centre and Labyrinth: Essays in Honour of Northrop Frye.* Toronto: U of Toronto P, 1983.

Denham, Robert D. *Northrop Frye: An Annotated Bibliography of Primary and Secondary Sources.* Toronto: U of Toronto P, 1987.

Hamilton, A.C. *Northrop Frye: Anatomy of His Criticism.* Toronto: U of Toronto P, 1990.

Krieger, Murray, ed. *Northrop Frye in Modern Criticism: Selected Papers from the English Institute.* Incl. a checklist by John E. Grant of writings by and about Frye. New York: Columbia UP, 1966.

Gadamer, Hans-Georg

(b. Germany, 1900–) Philosopher. Gadamer studied philosophy and classics in Marburg. Awarded the doctorate at the age of 22, he did not begin teaching until he was 29. Named professor in 1937, he taught at Leipzig (1938–47) and at Frankfurt (1947–9). From 1949 until his retirement in 1968 he was professor at Heidelberg. Gadamer enjoyed a lifelong friendship with *Martin Heidegger, especially from 1923 when Heidegger was named professor at Marburg until 1928 when Heidegger left Marburg to take up *Edmund Husserl's chair of philosophy at Freiburg. From the outset of his career Gadamer combined his interests in *literature and poetry with philosophy.

Gadamer's role in the development of *hermeneutics in the poststructuralist era cannot be overestimated. (See *poststructuralism.) Not only has his work been the starting-point of reader-response theory and *phenomenological criticism, but his major work *Truth and Method* (1960) has brought about a phenomenological development of hermeneutics. (See *reader-response criticism.) Gadamer took Heidegger's brilliant but often cryptic and hermetic thought, expanded it, and gave a new ground to the human sciences. In his own work he responded to the major philosophers of his tradition: Heidegger, Husserl, *Dilthey, and Bultmann. He also eagerly engaged in dialogue and debate with the next generation of philosophers: *Paul Ricoeur, *Jürgen Habermas and *Jacques Derrida.

Five major areas of Gadamer's thought are subjectivity, play, interpretation, tradition, and truth. *Truth and Method* reconsiders Dilthey's impasse in the subject-object dualism of knowing the world. (See *subject/object.) The question of how we know the world is examined through the phenomenology of Heidegger's *Sein und Zeit* [Being and Time 1927]. In brief, Gadamer insists that the entire problem of how the subject can know the object is the result of a metaphysical error of Western philosophy since Descartes. Before the knowing subject is aware of subjectivity, before the subject can encounter objects, before there is a knowing consciousness of self-identity, the subject already belongs to the language-speaking community to which the subject by chance was born. Participation precedes awareness of one's self and of others; thus all problems of communication and of knowing the world are aspects of the self's participation within the language community. Similarly, Gadamer insists that all language usage is laden with values and value judgments. The idea of objectivity or an objective use of language is nothing more that an artificial abstraction which can be functionally expedient but is possible only because it is surrounded by real intersubjective communication. Thus prejudgments are an essential part of all natural language usage. When a writer or a speaker attempts to hide his or her prejudice, the context will make the prejudices even more pronounced because they have been suppressed.

Gadamer explains communication through the paradigm of dialogue. The dialogical situation is explained as *Spiel* [play], as in the sense of putting an idea in play or playing a position in a game like football or playing one's part in an activity. Dialogue is the interaction between players in a rule-governed activity, but it is above all the interaction of language, that is, participation in communication. Language usage, Gadamer argues, demands that certain rules be observed but allows for individual expression in the creative use of the system; furthermore, just as in a real game, in language use, especially in the dialogical situation, the outcome is not and cannot be anti-cipated. The outcome is the result of playing the game following the rules but playing creatively as well. Two teams meet to play a game of hockey and they both must abide by the rules; both teams are made up of various players, each of whom has an identical style of playing; neither team, however, can know how the game will turn out until it is played. Also, as in a game, in the dialogical situation there is an element of risk. The more the individual puts into the playing the more there will be at stake. This explanation of dialogue can be expanded to cover all modes of communication wherein language is the game, dialogue is playing and a gain in meaning for the individual is the outcome of participation. (See theories of *play/freeplay and *game theory.)

Gadamer describes the interpretation of texts through another striking metaphor: the fusion of horizons. (See *metonymy/metaphor.) The *text is always historical, that is, it was written by someone at a given time in a specific language. Thus the historicity of the text is an essential part of any consideration of it. But the reader who is interpreting the text is also grounded in his or her own historicity. The historical vantage point from which the reader approaches the text is a significant part of all interpretation. As the reader engages the text, the difference and distance between the two historicities is at its greatest at the outset. The reading experience is an engagement of the two poles. The text, which is the work of another person and reflects this historicity, resists attempts by the reader to make it over into something more familiar to his or her perspective. The breakthrough in interpretation comes when the two historicities are transcended in the fusion of the two different viewpoints into one experience. The text as human composition projects purpose as meaningful action; it has intentionality but so does the reader have his or her own historical projection and his or her own values to maintain. (See *intention/intentionality.) When these two viewpoints come together in the encounter of reading there can be a fusion of these two horizons which creates meaning. This meaning does not belong either to the text or to the reader but is the outcome of the interaction between the two. Distance therefore can become the bridge rather than the barrier to understanding. (See also *horizon of expectation, *ideological horizon.)

One of the most controversial aspects of

Gadamer's thought is his insistence on participation within a tradition – a target of criticism by German Marxist thinkers, especially Jürgen Habermas and Karl-Otto Apel. (See *Marxist criticism.) Habermas' review of *Truth and Method* and Gadamer's response have become a classical debate on the ideological distortions of communication. Gadamer insists that interpretation is always situated within a community of readers; significantly, this community is not limited to the contemporary readership of the interpreter/critic, but is a historically constituted community, that is, a tradition of commentators. To speak of a tradition of literary authors is commonplace, but Gadamer argues that authors are the landmarks and not the full scope, for surrounding texts from the past is a tradition of commentary that constantly renews the works of the past as present. Habermas claims that there can be no free engagement in the dialogical situation as long as readers are unknowingly prisoners of ideologies, that they cannot openly interact with texts because of the uncritical acceptance of the institutional bias of vested interests. The system of beliefs that are the institutional means of maintaining political power precludes all dialogical engagement until the reader can learn to cut through these screens. Gadamer responds that critical reflection cannot lead to any clear view free of prejudice; he argues that because we have our basis in language usage, which is subjective and intersubjective, and there are no universal norms, we cannot overthrow tradition; we must debate within it. (See *universals, *ideology.)

Some critics of *Truth and Method* claim with some justification that it is ironic that in a book about truth there is no systematic development of a theory of truth but only numerous statements equating truth with self-knowledge. An explanation for this apparent lacuna is that Gadamer has ruled out any univeral and coherent theory of truth as untenable because of the nature of the linguistic make-up of man as belonging to a community. A further response to such critics as *Richard Rorty is that there is no specific discussion of truth because the entire book is about truth as self-knowledge. Gadamer argues that, because we are what we have made of ourselves within the linguistically constituted world to which we belong, what we know in the last analysis is ourselves. Gadamer presents the self as participating in the Being-in-the-world

that can be understood and that being is language. (See *self/other.) Falsehood to Gadamer is self-deception, muddled thought about who we are and a non-reflective acceptance of the social order of the world, and truth is the revelation that the human sciences can offer us about how we have constituted our world and our place in it and how we participate in it. The human sciences are a dialogue in which the participants must always presuppose some shared meaning and concern if they are to engage in it. Speaking in this dialogue is playing the language game of world-making wherein the outcome of the game is knowing ourselves as players and knowing how we play the game.

MARIO J. VALDÉS

Primary Sources

Gadamer, Hans-Georg. *Dialogue and Dialectic: Eight Hermeneutical Studies on Plato*. Trans. Christopher Smith. New Haven: Yale UP, 1980.
- *Hegel's Dialectic. Five Hermeneutical Studies*. Trans. Christopher Smith. New Haven: Yale UP, 1976.
- 'Hermeneutik.' In *Historisches Wörterbuch der Philosophie*. Vol. 3. Ed. J. Ritter. Darmstadt: Wissenshaftl. Buchgesellschaft, 1974, 1061–73.
- *Kleine Schriften*. 3 vols. 1: *Philosophie und Hermeneutik*. 2: *Interpretationen*. 3: *Idee und Sprache*. Tübingen: J.C.B. Mohr, 1967–72.
- 'On the Scope and Function of Hermeneutical Reflection.' Trans. G.B. Hess and R.E. Palmer. In *Hermeneutics and Modern Philosophy*. Ed. Brice R. Wachterhauser. Albany: SUNY P, 1986, 277–99.
- *Philosophical Apprenticeships*. Trans. Robert G. Sullivan. Cambridge, Mass.: MIT P, 1985.
- *Philosophical Hermeneutics*. Trans. David E. Linge. Berkeley: U of California P, 1976.
- *Poetica: Ausgewählte Essays*. Frankfurt: Insel, 1977.
- *Reason in the Age of Science*. Trans. Frederick G. Lawrence. Cambridge, Mass.: MIT P, 1981.
- 'Text and Interpretation.' Trans. Dennis J. Schmidt. In *Hermeneutics and Modern Philosophy*. Ed. Brice R. Wachterhauser. Albany: SUNY P, 1986, 377–96.
- *Text und Interpretät* (with a response by Jacques Derrida). Munich: Fink Verlag, 1984.
- *Theorie Diskussion: Hermeneutik und Ideologierkritik*. (Discussion with Jürgen Habermas.) Frankfurt: Suhrkamp, 1971.
- *Truth and Method*. Trans. Garret Barden and William G. Doerpel. New York: Seabury, 1975. *Wahrheit und Methode: Grundzüke einer philosophischen Hermeneutik*. Tübingen: J.C.B. Mohr, 1960; 2nd ed. 1965.

Secondary Sources

Apel, Karl-Otto. *Understanding and Explanation: A Transcendental Pragmatic Perspective.* Trans. Georgia Warnke. Cambridge, Mass.: MIT P, 1985.

Bernstein, Richard J. 'What Is the Difference that Makes a Difference? Gadamer, Habermas and Rorty.' In *Hermeneutics and Modern Philosophy.* Ed. Brice R. Wachterhauser. Albany: SUNY P, 1986, 343–76.

Bliecher, Josef. *Contemporary Hermeneutics.* London: Routledge and Kegan Paul, 1980.

Dallmayr, Fred R. 'Hermeneutics and Deconstruction: Gadamer and Derrida in Dialogue.' In *Critical Encounters.* Notre Dame, Ind.: U of Notre Dame P, 1987.

Habermas, Jürgen. 'A Review of Gadamer's *Truth and Method.*' In *Hermeneutics and Modern Philosophy.* Ed. Brice R. Wachterhauser. Albany: SUNY P, 1986, 243–76.

Hans, James S. 'Hans-Georg Gadamer and Hermeneutic Phenomenology.' *Philosophy Today* 22 (1978): 3–19.

Haw, Alan R. 'Dialogue as Productive Limitation in Social Theory: The Habermas-Gadamer Debate.' *Journal of the British Society of Phenomenology* 11 (1980): 131–43.

Hirsch, E.D., Jr. *Validity in Interpretation.* New Haven: Yale UP, 1967.

Howard, Roy T. *Three Faces of Hermeneutics: An Introduction to Current Theories of Understanding.* Berkeley: U of California P, 1982.

Hoy, David Couzens. *The Critical Circle: Literature and History in Contemporary Hermeneutics.* Berkeley: U of California P, 1978.

Jay, Martin. 'Should Intellectual History Take a Linguistic Turn? Reflections on the Habermas-Gadamer Debate.' In *Modern European Intellectual History.* Ed. Dominick LaCapra and Stephen L. Kaplan. Ithaca: Cornell UP, 1982.

Johnson, Patricia. 'The Task of the Philosopher: Kierkegaard, Heidegger, Gadamer.' *Philosophy Today* 28 (1984): 3–19.

Kisiel, Theodore. 'The Happening of Tradition: The Hermeneutics of Gadamer and Heidegger.' *Man and World* 2 (1969): 358–85.

Knapke, Margaret Lee. 'The Hermeneutical Focus of Heidegger and Gadamer: The Nullity of Understanding.' *Kinesis* 12 (1981): 3–18.

Mueller-Vollmer, Kurt. 'Introduction.' In *The Hermeneutics Reader.* Ed. K. Mueller-Vollmer. New York: Continuum, 1985, 1–53.

Palmer, Richard. *Hermeneutics: Interpretation Theory in Schleiermacher, Dilthey, Heidegger and Gadamer.* Evanston: Northwestern UP, 1969.

Ricoeur, Paul. 'The Hermeneutical Function of Distanciation.' In *Paul Ricoeur: Hermeneutics and the Human Sciences.* Ed. and trans. John B. Thompson. Cambridge: Cambridge UP, 1981, 131–44.

– 'Hermeneutics and the Critique of Ideology.' In *Paul Ricoeur: Hermeneutics and the Human Sciences,* 67–100.

– 'The Task of Hermeneutics.' In *Paul Ricoeur: Hermeneutics and the Human Sciences,* 43–62.

Wachterhauser, Brice R. 'Must We Be What We Say? Gadamer on Truth in the Human Sciences.' In *Hermeneutics and Modern Philosophy.* Ed. Brice R. Wachterhauser. Albany: SUNY P, 1986, 219–42.

Warnke, Georgia. *Gadamer: Hermeneutics, Tradition and Reason.* Stanford: Stanford UP, 1987.

Weinsheimer, Joel C. *Gadamer's Hermeneutics.* New Haven: Yale UP, 1985.

Westphal, Merold. 'Hegel and Gadamer.' In *Hermeneutics and Modern Philosophy.* Ed. Brice R. Wachterhauser. Albany: SUNY P, 1986, 65–86.

Wright, Kathleen. 'Gadamer: The Speculative Structure of Language.' In *Hermeneutics and Modern Philosophy.* Ed. Brice R. Wachterhauser. Albany: SUNY P, 1986, 193–218.

Gates, Henry Louis, Jr.

(b. U.S.A., 1950–) Critic, theorist and editor. Henry Louis Gates, Jr., graduated with a B.A. in history from Yale in 1973 and then entered Clare College, Cambridge (on a Mellon Fellowship), where friendship with Nobel Laureate Wole Soyinka resulted in a switch to African American *literature. He received his Ph.D. from Cambridge in 1979 with a thesis on the critical reception of black literature during the Enlightenment. Returning to Yale as assistant professor of English and Afro-American Studies, in 1981 Gates was one of the first recipients of a MacArthur Foundation fellowship for 'exceptionally talented individuals.' In 1985 he became a full professor at Cornell, where an endowed chair, the W.E.B. Du Bois Professorship of Literature, was created for him. In 1990 Gates moved to Duke, to become John Spencer Bassett Professor of English, and in 1991 to Harvard University.

As an editor Gates has been at the forefront of the reconstruction of a *canon of African American literature. In 1982 he 'rediscovered' the first novel published by a black American, *Our Nig*, written by Harriet E. Wilson in 1859. Other significant projects he has edited include the 30-volume *Schomburg Library of 19th-Century Black Women Writers*; the Black Periodical Fiction Project, of which he is director and which has unearthed thousands of short sto-

329

ries, poems, book reviews, and notices published between 1827 and 1940; *The Works of Zora Neale Hurston;* and the *Norton Anthology of Afro-American Literature.* All of these projects constitute part of Gates' attempt to de-centre the humanities by revising and expanding the literary/intellectual canon to include works by members of non-European ethnic minorities and by women. (See *centre/de-centre.) He has fought hard to have African and African American culture included in university curricula by insisting both on the legitimacy of black studies programs and on the necessity for such programs to be closely linked to traditional departments.

Gates has also edited a number of important collections of essays, including *Black Literature and Literary Theory* (1984), *'Race,' Writing, and Difference* (1985–6), *Reading Black, Reading Feminist* (1990), and the first special issue of *PMLA* on African and African American literature (1990). Again, his insistence on the importance of race and gender to academic inquiry is apparent, along with his raising of such important questions as the relationship between African cultural traditions and Western/mainstream cultural traditions, the relationship between the black vernacular tradition and the black formal tradition, and the applicability of contemporary literary theory – particularly *poststructuralism – to the reading of black texts. (See *text.) Gates claims that 'the challenge of black literary criticism is to derive principles of literary criticism from the black tradition itself, as defined in the idiom of critical theory but also in the idiom which constitutes the "language of blackness" ... The sign of the successful negotiation of this precipice of indenture, of slavish imitation, is that the black critical essay refers to two contexts, two traditions – the Western and the black' (*Black Literature and Literary Theory* 8). To explore black cultural difference, critics must redefine 'theory' – which is not colour-blind or neutral – by turning to the black vernacular tradition for models. This contentious relationship has been a major preoccupation of Gates' three books, which he views as a trilogy. The first, *Figures in Black* (1987), makes 'use of contemporary criticism to read black texts [from the 18th century to the present], but [is] a use designed to critique the theory implicitly' (xxix). The second, *The Signifying Monkey* (1988), traces the relationship between African and African American vernacular traditions and

cultural forms, focusing on the practice of 'signifyin(g),' a subversive rhetorical strategy and a figure for black intertexual revision, what Gates calls the African American tradition's 'trope of tropes.' (See *trope, *intertextuality.) He thus builds a theory of black literature from within the tradition itself. The third book, *Black Letters in the Enlightenment*, is a study of the history of the reception of black texts during the first 100 years of the tradition; it critiques the Eurocentric bias of such criticism and demonstrates its effect on subsequent black writers.

Gates has moved from being a staunch 're-constructionist' – a member of a group of critics who, in the mid-1970s, attacked the dominant notion that black literature must be approached as social realism, calling instead for attention to the formal elements, the language, of black texts – to being a theorist/critic who balances emphasis on close reading of formal figures and tropes with attention 'to the "social text" as well ... the larger dynamics of subjection and incorporation through which the subject is produced' (*PMLA* 21). He has championed the concept that 'race' is a social construct (with 'blackness' as a subject position in relation to the cultural dominant) rather than a biological or essential category. His theoretical, critical and editorial work has had great influence on issues of race, gender, literary history, and canon formation in African American studies. (See also *black criticism.)

DONALD C. GOELLNICHT

Primary Sources

Gates, Henry Louis, Jr. *Figures in Black: Words, Signs and the 'Racial' Self.* New York: Oxford UP, 1987.
– *The Signifying Monkey: A Theory of Afro-American Literary Criticism.* New York: Oxford UP, 1988.
– ed. *Black Literature and Literary Theory.* New York: Methuen, 1984.
– ed. *Black Literature, 1827–1940.* Alexandria, Va.: Chadwyck-Healey, 1990.
– ed. *The Classic Slave Narratives.* New York: NAL, 1987.
– ed. *In the House of Osubgo: Critical Essays on Wole Soyinka.* New York: Oxford UP, 1989.
– ed. *Our Nig,* by Harriet E. Wilson. New York: Random House, 1983.
– ed. *PMLA* 105 (Jan. 1990). Special issue on African and African American Literature.
– ed. *'Race,' Writing, and Difference.* Chicago and London: U of Chicago P, 1985–6.
– ed. *Reading Black, Reading Feminist: A Critical Anthology.* New York: Meridian, 1990.

– ed. *The Schomburg Library of 19th Century Black Women Writers*. 30 vols. New York: Oxford UP, 1988.
– ed. *Three Classic African-American Novels*. New York: Random House, 1990.

Geertz, Clifford

(b. U.S.A., 1926–) Cultural anthropologist. Geertz is a leading authority on Bali, Java and Morocco and is best known outside his own discipline as the foremost theorist of cultural or interpretive anthropology. He has sought to transform ethnographic study by proceeding from a semiotic concept of culture, thus making cultural analysis 'not an experimental science in search of law but an interpretive one in search of meaning' (*Interpretation of Cultures* 5). (See *semiotics.)

Geertz received his Ph.D. from Harvard University and carried out most of his fieldwork in Bali and Java during the 1950s. During his decade at the University of Chicago (1960–70) he pioneered what became known as the 'symbolic anthropology' movement, serving as professor of anthropology and later chairman of the Committee for the Comparative Study of New Nations. These were also the years of most of his fieldwork in Morocco. Since 1970 he has been professor of social science at the Institute for Advanced Study in Princeton, New Jersey.

Geertz's semiotic approach to ethnographic analysis construes culture as a *text, something to be read and interpreted. Also present in this rendering of social action as a document is the primordial meaning of 'text' as something woven, the idea of culture as an intricate 'fabric of meaning' (*Interpretation of Cultures* 145). Continuing with this analogy, culture as a whole consists of interwoven strands of various symbol systems, defined according to general issues such as aesthetics, religion, law, or even common sense. Each symbol system is in turn composed of individual symbolic forms or signs, meaning 'any object, act, event, quality, or relation which serves as a vehicle for conception' *Interpretation of Cultures* 91). (See *sign.)

Culture, as the accumulated body of symbolic forms and systems, is socially constituted and historically transmitted. It enables individuals not only to comprehend and interpret their experience but also to express themselves and direct their behaviour on the basis of such judgments. As a theory of human subjectivity, Geertz's concept of culture is thus a dialectical one: culture is both 'a [historically evolving] product and a determinant of social interaction' (*Interpretation of Cultures* 250). In relation specifically to aesthetic theory, this dialectical definition of culture emphasizes the interactive rather than the mimetic aspect of art forms, which are understood to function as 'positive agents in the creation and maintenance of [cultural sensibilities]' (*Interpretation of Cultures* 451). (See *mimesis.)

A common interest in semiotics would initially appear to align Geertz with the structural anthropologist *Claude Lévi-Strauss, who first applied semiotic theory to anthropological analysis. However, Geertz situates his work firmly in opposition to *structuralism and other brands of *formalism, whose laws and static paradigms run the risk of reifying cultures and of obstructing the analysis of change within a given society. Geertz insists that culture is above all a public rather than a merely conceptual phenomenon. It is therefore most accurately understood through the various symbolic forms by which people make interpretive sense of themselves to themselves.

Geertz has designated the practice of 'thick description' as the methodology of cultural analysis and hence the essence of ethnography. His essay 'Deep Play: Notes on the Balinese Cockfight' (*Interpretation of Cultures*) remains the best-known demonstration of this practice. Thick description often begins with what might be called 'thin' description, the detailed but essentially superficial presentation of a specific cultural artefact: perhaps an anecdote, a local custom, an incident, an institution, or a historical episode. This description is 'thickened' when it gives way to analysis and interpretation, when the cultural artefact becomes a text to be read. In an elaborately meticulous fashion the ethnographer proceeds to 'unpack' this text by examining the symbol systems that inform it, working through the layers of conceptual structures, social institutions, local conventions, and individual motives which make that isolated artefact – now viewed as a text – meaningful. In short, the ethnographer endeavours to set particular events within the circumstances of their significance, the contexts which give them resonance. Notwithstanding such analytical scrutiny, Geertz willingly acknowledges that all cultural interpretation is 'essentially contestable,' not only because such analysis is 'intrinsically incomplete' (*Interpretation of Cultures* 29), but also because meaning and interpretation are themselves indeterminate.

Although the intimate encounter with a cultural artefact and its specific contexts, what Geertz calls 'local knowledge,' receives particular attention in his essays, he emphasizes that thick description should also yield a more comprehensive view of the culture under study. His overall method of analysis is therefore a version of the *hermeneutic circle: in his words, 'a continuous dialectical tacking between the most local of local detail and the most global of global structure in such a way as to bring them into simultaneous view ... [and to turn them] into explications of one another' (*Local Knowledge* 69). Finally, Geertz believes that the most productive generalizations are those which provide a new vocabulary or conceptual framework for interpreting the symbol systems of any culture. The guiding objective of his theoretical work has been to articulate such a vocabulary, to move 'toward an interpretive theory of culture' (*Interpretation of Cultures* 3).

Geertz's theoretical formulations are more often scattered throughout his work rather than systematized in individual essays. The most important of these are collected in *The Interpretation of Cultures* and *Local Knowledge*. His work has been open to challenge for its lack of historical content and inattentiveness to social change, and some critics have observed his reluctance to acknowledge the subjectivity of the ethnographer as an important element in cultural interpretation. Nonetheless, within the social sciences the impact of his hermeneutic approach to cultural analysis has been great; while in the first collection of essays he labours to make a case for interpretive anthropology, the later book reveals his methodology as fully established. (See *hermeneutics.) Geertz's concept of culture and his practice of thick description have influenced work in fields as diverse as literary criticism, social and political theory, intellectual history, and the history of art. In literary criticism, Geertz's work has been most frequently cited and employed by New Historicists, who apply his 'thick description' in their study of literature and culture. Intent on dissolving the boundaries between literature and other, especially

historical, discourses, New Historicists presuppose both 'the historicity of texts' and 'the textuality of history' (Montrose 8). Like Geertz, they move dialectically between the 'local' and the 'general,' although their work has been subject to many of the same criticisms as those levelled at Geertz himself. (See *New Historicism, *discourse.)

JULIA M. GARRETT

Primary Sources

Geertz, Clifford. *Agricultural Involution: The Process of Ecological Change in Indonesia*. Berkeley: U of California P, 1963.
– *The Interpretation of Cultures*. New York: Basic Books, 1973.
– *Islam Observed: Religious Development in Morocco and Indonesia*. New Haven: Yale UP, 1968.
– *Local Knowledge: Further Essays in Interpretive Anthropology*. New York: Basic Books, 1983.
– *Negara: The Theater State in 19th Century Bali*. Princeton: Princeton UP, 1980.
– *Peddlers and Princes: Social Change and Economic Modernization in Two Indonesian Towns*. Chicago: U of Chicago P, 1963.
– *The Religion of Java*. New York: Free Press/Macmillan, 1960. Chicago: U of Chicago P, 1976.
– *The Social History of an Indonesian Town*. Cambridge: MIT P, 1965.
– *Works and Lives: The Anthropologist as Author*. Stanford: Stanford UP, 1988.

Secondary Sources

Geertz, Clifford, Hildred Geertz and Lawrence Rosen. *Meaning and Order in Moroccan Society: Three Essays in Cultural Analysis*. New York: Cambridge UP, 1979.
Geertz, Clifford, ed. and introd. *Myth, Symbol and Culture*. New York: Norton, 1971.
– ed. *Old Societies and New States: The Quest for Modernity in Asia and Africa*. New York: Free Press/Macmillan, 1963.
Geertz, Hildred, and Clifford Geertz. *Kinship in Bali*. Chicago: U of Chicago P, 1975.
Gunn, Giles. 'The Semiotics of Culture and the Diagnostics of Criticism: Clifford Geertz and the Moral Imagination.' In *The Culture of Criticism and the Criticism of Culture*. New York: Oxford UP, 1987, 93–115.
Lieberson, Jonathan. 'Interpreting the Interpreter.' Rev. of *Local Knowledge*, by Clifford Geertz. *New York Review of Books* 15 Mar. 1984: 39–46.
Montrose, Louis. 'Renaissance Literary Studies and the Subject of History.' *English Literary Renaissance* 16 (1986): 5–12.
Morgan, John H., ed. *Understanding Religion and Culture: Anthropological and Theological Perspec-*

tives. Washington: UP of America, 1979 [essays in honour of Clifford Geertz].

Peacock, James. 'The Third Stream: Weber, Parsons, and Geertz.' *Journal of the Anthropological Society of Oxford* 12 (1981): 122–9.

Pecora, Vincent P. 'The Limits of Local Knowledge.' In *The New Historicism.* Ed. H. Aram Veeser. New York: Routledge, 1989, 243–76.

Rice, Kenneth A. *Geertz and Culture.* Ann Arbor: U of Michigan P, 1980.

Roseberry, William. 'Balinese Cockfights and the Seduction of Anthropology.' *Social Research* 49 (1982): 1013–28.

Shankman, Paul. 'The Thick and the Thin: On the Interpretive Theoretical Program of Clifford Geertz' [with *Current Anthropology* comment]. *Current Anthropology* 25 (1984): 261–79.

Walters, Ronald G. 'Signs of the Times: Clifford Geertz and the Historians.' *Social Research* 47 (1980): 537–56.

Genette, Gérard

(b. France 1930–) Literary theoretician and structuralist critic. Gérard Genette studied at the Ecole Normale Supérieure in Paris. He taught at lycées in Amiens and du Mans, at the Sorbonne (1963–7), and since then has directed a seminar on poetics and aesthetics at the Ecole des Hautes Etudes en Sciences Sociales (Paris). Although renowned for his studies on narrative *discourse, which provided the foundations of *narratology, Genette's ongoing interest in poetics and rhetoric characterizes all of his works. His most recent studies, less narratological in focus, deal with *genre criticism, forms of *textuality, mimologism, and literariness. (See also *structuralism, *rhetorical criticism.)

Genette's earliest books, *Figures I* (1966) and *Figures II* (1969) are collections of essays with a structuralist, semiotic and linguistic orientation, dealing with a variety of literary and theoretical issues. (See *semiotics.) Despite their diversity in subject and scope, these essays can be grouped together in terms of several common themes. Certain essays present a discussion of critical works, such as Richard's *Univers imaginaire de Mallarmé*, Matoré's *L'Espace humain*, Cohen's *Structure du langage poétique*, and *Mauron's theories on the psychology of reading. While certain articles focus on specific authors (such as Robbe-Grillet and Valéry) and their works, a number of essays study baroque poetry and prose to elucidate particular characteristics of the baroque imagination and universe by means of an emphasis on rhetorical figures such as antithesis, the oxymoron and catachresis. Other studies deal with methods of literary criticism, some of which feature early work on the structure of narrative discourse, introducing distinctions which will be systematized and elaborated in *Figures III.*

In his influential 'Discours du récit,' *Figures III* [Narrative Discourse 1972; trans. 1980], Genette describes the major forms and characteristics of narrative discourse, distinctions which have determined all subsequent research in narratology. Some of these categories are discussed and developed further in *Nouveau discours du récit* [Narrative Discourse Revisited 1983; trans. 1988], in which Genette responds to the comments of other narratological critics (Cohn; Bal; Prince; Lintvelt; Rimmon-Kenan). 'Discours du récit' is not merely a discourse on narrative and an erudite study of the poetics of narrative discourse, but it is also an intricate analysis of Proust's *A la recherche du temps perdu* and how it exemplifies and transforms basic narrative categories. Genette begins the study by distinguishing between story (*histoire* – the set of narrated events, or narrative content), narrative (*récit* – the narrative *text itself) and narrating (*narration* – the act of narrative *énonciation* which produces the text). (See *énonciation/énoncé.) The remainder of the essay is an analysis of the various relationships existing between these three concepts and is based on the premise that a narrative is a linguistic production, the expansion of a verb. Drawing upon the grammatical categories of the verb, Genette describes three major classes relevant to the study of narrative discourse: tense, which deals with temporal relations between narrative and story; mood, or the types of discourse used by the *narrator to recount the story, and the forms and degrees (modalities) of narrative representation; and voice, which refers to the relationships between narrating and narrative, and narrating and story. (See also *story/plot.)

Order, the first subcategory of tense, deals with the relations between the temporal succession of events in the story and their actual arrangement in the narrative: here, two types of discordance are noted (analepsis, or the narration of an event at a point in the story after more recent events have already been recounted, and prolepsis, or the narration of an event at a point in the text prior to the narration of earlier events). A second temporal category, duration, which Genette later proposes to rebaptize as 'speed' (*Nouveau discours du récit* 23), pertains to the pace of narrative events, that is, the relationship between the duration of events in the story and the length of text devoted to narrating these events. The four different types of duration outlined, in terms of increasing acceleration, are the pause, the scene, the summary, and the ellipsis. The final temporal category is frequency, related to the verbal aspect, which studies the relationship between the number of times an event takes place in the story and the number of times this event is narrated in the text: an event may occur x times and be narrated the same number of times (singulative frequency); an event may only occur once but be narrated several times (repetitive) or an event may occur many times but be recounted only once (iterative).

In his discussion of mood, Genette distinguishes between narrative perspective (who 'sees' the story) and narrative voice (who recounts the story), claiming that only the latter belongs to the category of voice. The category of mood is thus restricted to problems of distance (which involves various types of discourse in the narrative of events and the narrative of words or dialogue), and perspective or point of view: here, Genette develops his theory of the forms of narrative focalization in terms of the narrator's versus the characters' vision and knowledge of events, and the variations of these focalizations.

The final category, voice, deals with the act of narrating and the traces it has imprinted in the narrative, in terms of the time of this act (subsequent, prior, simultaneous, or interpolated) in relation to the events depicted; narrative levels (extra-, intra- and metadiegetic); and person, that is, the relationships between the narrator, the *narratee, and the story. In the subcategory of person, Genette distinguishes between the heterodiegetic narrator, who is absent from the story she recounts, and the homodiegetic narrator, who is present as a character in her own story. In *Nouveau discours du récit*, Genette develops the category of person further, adding more detailed commentary on the use of the present tense, examining the correlations between mood and voice in terms of narrative situation, and elaborating on the notion of the narratee in response to the

work of *Gerald Prince (1973). (See also *diegesis.)

In his next work, *Mimologiques: Voyage en Cratylie [Mimologies: Voyage to Cratylus 1976]*, Genette draws upon an extensive interdisciplinary corpus of Western texts (from the history of ideas, the philosophy of language, linguistics, and so on) to trace the history, forms and transformation of a persistent desire that has characterized discourse concerning the origin and nature of language throughout the centuries: the reverie of mimologism. Using Plato's *Cratylus* as the founding instance of this debate, Genette notes two opposing positions, as outlined by Cratylus and Hermogenes. While Cratylus advocates the mimetic, mimological thesis that proposes a motivated, natural relationship of analogy or imitation between word and thing (hence the appropriateness of the word chosen), the Hermogenist doctrine outlines an artificial, arbitrary correspondence between a thing and its name: here, the accuracy of the name is a matter of agreement and convention between speakers. Mimological theories frequently include the doctrine of a natural, universal language, and an emphasis on its onomatopoeic nature and origins, eliminate the social dimension of language, and privilege the power of naming. Genette distinguishes between phonic mimologism (as in Augustine's *De origine verbi* and Nodier's notion of correspondence between the vocal organs, sounds, colours, and objects) and graphic mimologism, as in *Ferdinand de Saussure's anagrams and Ponge's writings. *Mimologiques*, with its thorough treatment of graphic cratylism, could well be read as a companion to *Jacques Derrida's *deconstruction of phonocentrism. (See also *logocentrism.)

In his *Introduction à l'architexte [Architext 1979]*, Genette undertakes a detailed history of the theory of genres, demonstrating the historical error of attributing the three fundamental genres (lyric, epic and dramatic) to Plato and Aristotle, and examining the roles of *mimesis, representation, thematic content, and modes of *énonciation* in the classificiation of genres over the centuries. (See also *theme.) This study concludes with a consideration of archigenres, complex categories in which the intersection of thematic classes and modal/submodal classes determines a considerable number of existing or possible genres. Architextuality refers to the relation of inclusion uniting all texts in terms of generic, formal and thematic features and is, for Genette, the true subject of poetics, as it constitutes the literariness of literature.

The notion of textuality, introduced at the conclusion of *Introduction à l'architexte*, is further developed in Genette's encyclopedic *Palimpsestes* (1982), which presents five different types of transtextuality or textual transcendence (that is, 'everything which puts the text in explicit or implicit relationship with other texts') (7). These forms are discussed in terms of an increasing degree of abstraction and globality. The first such form, *intertextuality, is defined in a narrower manner than is *Michael Riffaterre's understanding of the concept: for Genette, intertextuality is 'the demonstrable presence of one text within another' (8) and its forms include citation, plagiarism and allusion. The following two forms of transtextuality are paratextuality (investigated in *Seuils* 1987) and metatextuality, or the relationship of commentary or discussion that one text may have with another, the most obvious example being that of literary criticism. While the fifth, most abstract and implicit form of textuality, architextuality, was discussed in *Introduction à l'architexte*, it is the fourth form, hypertextuality, which constitutes the subject of *Palimpsestes*. Hypertextuality denotes any relationship, excluding that of commentary, that links a later text (a hypertext) with an earlier text (its hypotext). Using the image of the palimpsest, where one text is superimposed upon another that it does not completely conceal, Genette embarks upon a massive study of hypertextual genres, producing a detailed, formal categorization. The two major types of hypertextual derivations noted are the transformation of a text according to a particular formal constraint or semantic intention; and imitation, which necessitates a model of the imitated text in order to produce the hypertext (89–90). Genette's thorough discussion of transformative hypertextual practices (which includes the burlesque travesty, translation, versification, and prosification, among many other forms) is best known for its study of literary *parody, which has made *Palimpsestes* a canonical text on this genre (see also Hutcheon; Rose; Thomson and Pagès). Genette defines parody structurally, as a minimal transformation of a text (33), focuses on short texts (such as puns, titles, proverbs, and the lipograms of the Oulipo group), denying the possibility of the parody of a genre. As for imitative hypertextual practices, Genette cites the pastiche (a ludic genre), the satirical pastiche or *charge* (with the principal function of mockery), and forgery or serious imitation, which serves to extend or continue a previous literary work in one of several ways.

Paratextuality, Genette's second major category of transtextuality as introduced in *Palimpsestes*, is the subject of *Seuils* (1987), which is a study of the auxiliary texts (such as the title, preface or epigraph) accompanying or surrounding the main body of a text. These shorter texts introduce, frame and present a text, may lengthen and comment upon it, and ensure and affect its reception. The paratext forms an indistinct threshold between the inside and outside (the discourse of the world on the text) of the text and is a transitional zone without strict boundaries. The two types of paratexts in terms of spatial categories are the peritext, located within the same volume as the main text (such as the indication of the text's genre, the preface, dedication, epigraph, footnotes, chapter titles, and the author's name), and the epitext, which refers to all messages concerning the text that are located outside of the text itself (such as interviews, colloquia, debates, advance publication notices, and private communication, as, for example, diaries, correspondence and verbal commentary regarding the text).

Genette's most recent work, *Fiction et diction* (1991), focuses on the criteria of literariness, the pragmatic status of fiction, and the forms of factual versus fictive narration. The influence of Genette's extensive contributions to narratology, poetics, textuality, and various other areas of literary theory cannot be overestimated. Countless analyses of particular literary texts (for example, Bishop; Concalon; De Vos; Hébert; Reid) have been based on Genette's narratological theories; and numerous studies of cinematographic texts and narration in the cinema (see Gaudreault; Gaudreault and Jost; Jost; Simon) have featured the development, modification and application of Genette's theories to the medium of film. While certain analyses of *A la recherche du temps perdu* (de Man 57–78; Wimmers 89–120) have responded to Genette's detailed study of Proust's work (in *Figures III*), other studies have made use of Genette's work on intertextality (Morgan 239–79), paratextuality (Calin), and mimology (Cappello).

BARBARA HAVERCROFT

Primary Sources

Genette, Gérard. *Fiction et diction*. Paris: Editions du Seuil, 1991.

– *Figures I*. Paris: Editions du Seuil, 1966.

– *Figures II*. Paris: Editions du Seuil, 1969.

– *Figures III*. Paris: Editions du Seuil, 1972.

– *Figures of Literary Discourse*. [Selections from *Figures* 1966–72]. Trans. Alan Sheridan. New York: Columbia UP, 1982.

– *Introduction à l'architexte*. Paris: Editions du Seuil, 1979.

– *Mimologiques: Voyage en Cratylie*. Paris: Editions du Seuil, 1976.

– 'Modern Mimology: The Dream of a Poetic Language.' [Translation of excerpt of ch. 12, *Mimologiques*]. Trans. Thaïs E. Morgan. *PMLA* 104.2 (March 1989): 202–14.

– *Narrative Discourse*. [Translation of 'Discours du récit,' *Figures* III]. Trans. Jane E. Lewin. Ithaca: Cornell UP, 1980.

– *Nouveau discours du récit*. Paris: Editions du Seuil, 1983. *Narrative Discourse Revisited*. Trans. Jane E. Lewin. Ithaca: Cornell UP, 1988.

– *Palimpsestes: La littérature au second degré*. Paris: Editions du Seuil, 1982.

– *Seuils*. Paris: Editions du Seuil, 1987.

– Hans Robert Jauss, et al. *Théorie des genres*. Paris: Éditions du Seuil, 1986.

Secondary Sources

Bal, Mieke. 'The Laughing Mice or: On Focalization.' *Poetics Today* 2.2 (Winter 1981): 202–10.

– *Narratologie*. Paris: Klincksieck, 1977.

Bishop, Neil B. 'Distance, point de vue, voix et idéologie dans *Les Fous de Bassan* d'Anne Hébert.' *Voix et Images* 9.2 (1984): 113–29.

Calin, Françoise. 'Une Occultation révélatrice: Le Paratexte de *Paludes*.' *Australian Journal of French Studies* 25.3 (1988): 247–60.

Cappello, Sergio. 'Onomatopées fictionnelles.' *Francofonia* 7.12 (Spring 1987): 85–94.

Cohn, Dorrit. 'The Encirclement of Narrative: on Franz Stanzel's *Theorie des Erzählens*.' *Poetics Today* 2.2 (Winter 1981): 157–82.

– *Transparent Minds: Narrative Modes for Presenting Consciousness in Fiction*. Princeton: Princeton UP, 1978.

Concalon, Elaine D. '*La Porte étroite*: Ou le triomphe du métadiégétique.' *French Literature Series* 17 (1990): 69–78.

– (intro.) and Gerald Prince (comment). 'Gide à la lumière de Genette.' *Bulletin des Amis d'André Gide* 13 [18].68 (1985): 11–55.

de Man, Paul. *Allegories of Reading*. New Haven: Yale UP, 1979.

De Vos, Wim. 'La Narration est-elle un acte libre? Le Métalepse dans *Jacques le Fataliste*.' *Les Lettres Romanes* 44.1–2 (1990): 3–13.

Gaudreault, André. *Du littéraire au filmique. Système du récit*. Quebec: Les Presses de l'Université Laval; Paris: Klincksieck, 1988.

– and François Jost. *Le Récit cinématographique*. Paris: Nathan, 1980.

Hébert, Pierre. 'La Technique du "retour en arrière" dans le nouveau roman au Québec et en France.' *Neohelicon* 12.2 (1985): 265–86.

– 'Vers une typologie des analepses.' *Voix et Images* 8.1 (1982): 97–109.

Hutcheon, Linda. *A Theory of Parody*. New York and London: Methuen, 1985.

Jost, François. 'Narration(s): En deça et au-delà.' *Communications* 38 (1983): 192–212.

Lintvelt, Jaap. *Essai de typologie narrative: Le point de vue*. Paris: Corti, 1981.

Morgan, Thaïs. 'The Space of Intertextuality.' In *Intertextuality and Contemporary American Fiction*. Ed. Patrick O'Donnell and Robert Con Davies. Baltimore: Johns Hopkins UP, 1989, 239–79.

Prince, Gerald. 'Introduction à l'étude du narrataire.' *Poétique* 14 (avril 1973): 178–96.

– *Narratology: The Form and Function of Narrative*. The Hague: Mouton, 1982.

Reid, Ian. 'The Death of the Implied Author? Voice, Sequence, and Control in Flaubert's *Trois Contes*.' *Australian Journal of French Studies* 23.2 (1986): 195–211.

Rimmon-Kenan, Shlomith. 'A Comprehensive Theory of Narrative: G. Genette's *Figures III* and the Structuralist Study of Fiction.' *PTL: A Journal for Descriptive Poetics and Theory of Literature* 1.1 (January 1976): 33–62.

– *Narrative Fiction: Contemporary Poetics*. London and New York: Methuen, 1983.

– 'Problems of Voice in V. Nabokov's *The Real Life of Sebastian Knight*.' *PTL: A Journal for Descriptive Poetics and Theory of Literature* 1.3 (Oct. 1976): 489–512.

Rose, Margaret. *Parody/Metafiction*. London: Croom Helm, 1979.

Simon, Jean-Paul. 'Enonciation et narration. Gnarus, auctor et Protée.' *Communications* 38 (1983): 155–91.

Thomson, Clive, and Alain Pagès, eds. *Dire la parodie*. New York and Bern: Peter Lang, 1989.

Wimmers, Inge Crosman. *Poetics of Reading: Approaches to the Novel*. Princeton: Princeton UP, 1988.

Gilbert, Sandra Mortola, and Susan David Gubar

(Gilbert b. U.S.A., 1936–; Gubar b. U.S.A., 1944–) Feminist literary critics. Sandra Gilbert studied at Columbia University and received her Ph.D. in 1968; her thesis, '"Acts of Attention": The Major Poems of D.H. Lawrence,' was published in 1973. (See *D.H. Lawrence.) She taught English at Hayward, St. Mary's College, Moraga, Indiana University, Bloomington, and the University of California, Davis; in 1985 she took up the position she currently holds in the Department of English at Princeton University. In addition to her work in literary criticism, she has published four books of poetry and contributed poems to a number of anthologies. Susan Gubar studied at the University of Iowa and in 1972 gained her Ph.D. with a thesis entitled 'Tudor Romance and 18th Century Fiction.' She taught English at the University of Illinois, Chicago, before taking up her current post in the Department of English at Indiana, Bloomington, in 1973. Gilbert and Gubar began their collaborative work at Indiana in 1974 when they co-taught a course in *literature by women.

Gilbert and Gubar helped bring about the shift in Anglo-American feminism from 'images of women' criticism to what has been called a 'woman-centred' approach. (See *feminist criticism, Anglo-American.) In the former practice, images of women in texts by men and women are judged on the basis of their fidelity to the reality of women's lives and their capacity to provide positive role models. In the latter approach, the critic reads texts by women for patterns that define a distinctive feminine literary imagination and that aim to provide the historical continuity that the writers themselves were denied. Towards these ends Gilbert and Gubar co-edited *The Norton Anthology of Literature by Women* (1985), a text that has shaped the curricula of women's studies in literature. In addition to publishing widely as individuals in such major American journals as *Critical Inquiry, New Literary History* and *Signs*, Gilbert and Gubar have provided opportunities for collaborative work by women critics in such collections as *Shakespeare's Sisters: Feminist Essays on Women Poets* (1979) and *The Female Imagination and the Modernist Aesthetic*, a special issue of *Women's Studies* (1986).

In *The Madwoman in the Attic* (1979), Gilbert and Gubar analyse the implications for women writers of the metaphor of literary paternity – 'the notion that the writer "fathers" his text just as God fathered the world' (*Madwoman* 4). (See *metonymy/metaphor.) According to the logic of this metaphor, a woman who writes defies the bounds of nature; she is a figure of montrous unwomanliness. Gilbert and Gubar suggest that this monstrous unwomanliness lies beneath the veneer of social convention and lurks behind the 'proper' ladies of texts by 19th-century women writers. Palimpsestic texts, hidden madwomen and other doublings allow these writers to achieve 'true female authority by simultaneously conforming to and subverting patriarchal literary standards' (73). (See *authority.)

Gilbert and Gubar take *Harold Bloom's theory of the '*anxiety of influence' both as an example of the patrilinearity of literary history and as a point of departure for a theory of women's literary creativity. Bloom suggests that each writer stands in the shadow of his predecessor/father and faces the anxiety of not being the origin of his words. The 'strong' writer overcomes his anxiety by creatively misreading his predecessor and assimilating that work to his own. Gilbert and Gubar find Bloom's model useful as a way of understanding the intertextual and revisionary relation of women's writing to the writing that precedes it. (See *intertextuality.) However, they note that the 19th-century woman writer needs to find her female predecessors rather than do battle with them; anxiety here is more an issue of legitimizing claims to authorship than one of influence. Gilbert and Gubar go on to argue in *No Man's Land* (1988, 1990), a multivolume study of women writers and modernism, that the case of the 20th-century woman writer differs even more significantly from Bloom's model. She has a multiplicity of affiliative possibilities: matrilineal inheritance, patrilineal inheritance or alienation from both and a turning to other contemporary women writers – as in the case of lesbian expatriates in early 20th-century Paris.

No Man's Land emphasizes the interrelations of social history and literary history more than does *Madwoman*. Gilbert and Gubar take issue with poststructuralist theorists who 'claim that all accounts of history are arbitrary fictions' or who 'deny the reality of the author,' insisting instead that 'texts are as marked by the maker's gender as they are by the historical moment in which they were produced' (1:xiv). (See *poststructuralism.) They analyse this gender difference through the metaphor of the battle of the sexes and claim that modernist writers divide along gender lines on such issues as the languages writers imagine for themselves and the representation of women's entry into the public sphere. Gilbert and Gubar argue that whereas men seek to mystify or usurp the power of ordinary language – the 'mother tongue' – women dream of languages that predate the patronymics of culture, that play with puns, verb tenses, neologisms, archaisms, and nonsense, and that celebrate the role of the mother in the process of language acquisition. Such languages, Gilbert and Gubar believe, answer the 'female need to achieve a command over language' (1:237).

Gilbert and Gubar's approach differs from French feminist approaches in its unproblematized use of the oppositional male-female sex identities and in its view of the writer as a coherent subject capable of controlling meaning in a text. (See *feminist criticism, French.) Their approach has been criticized along these lines in the Anglo-American context. *Toril Moi suggests that rather than simply replacing God the father/author with the woman author, Gilbert and Gubar need to question the critical practice that relies on the author as guarantor of meaning. Mary Jacobus calls for greater recognition of the discontinuities between writer and text and of the complex relation between dominant text and feminist revision. And Janet Todd insists that any search for a continuous 'female tradition' must not lose sight of the particular historical moment in which each woman writes. Gilbert and Gubar's work is nevertheless important for its attention to the ways in which gender inflects the dominant tropes of literary production and to the ways in which women writers creatively misread these tropes. (See *trope.)

LIANNE MOYES

Primary Sources

Gilbert, Sandra M., and Susan D. Gubar. *The Madwoman in the Attic: The Woman Writer and the 19th-Century Literary Imagination.* New Haven: Yale UP, 1979.
– *No Man's Land: The Place of the Woman Writer in the 20th Century.* 2 vols. to date. New Haven: Yale UP, 1988, 1989.
– eds. *The Female Imagination and the Modernist Aesthetic.* Special issue of *Women's Studies: An Interdisciplinary Journal* 13.1–2 (1986).
– eds. *The Norton Anthology of Literature by Women.* New York: Norton and Co., 1985.
– eds. *Shakespeare's Sisters: Feminist Essays on Women Poets.* Bloomington: Indiana UP, 1979.

Secondary Sources

Jacobus, Mary. 'Review of *The Madwoman in the Attic.*' *Signs* 6.3 (1981): 517–23.
Moi, Toril. *Sexual/Textual Politics: Feminist Literary Theory.* New York: Methuen, 1985.
Todd, Janet. *Feminist Literary History.* London: Routledge, 1988.

Girard, René Noel

(b. France, 1923–) Cultural theoretician. René Girard studied archival sciences and paleography at the Ecole Nationale des Chartes. He received a Ph.D. from Indiana University in 1950 and held teaching positions at Indiana, Duke, Bryn Mawr, SUNY Buffalo, and Johns Hopkins. Since 1981, he has been Professor of French Language, Literature and Civilization at Stanford. Although most of Girard's professional career has been spent in the U.S.A., where he is a citizen, many of his books were originally published in France and later translated into English and other languages.

In the early part of his career, Girard published literary studies of Cervantes, Dostoevsky, Stendhal, and others. Already in these works he displayed broad, extraliterary interests in psychology and theology. *Mensonge romantique et vérité romanesque [Deceit, Desire, and the Novel* 1961] examines the lie or self-deceit – the romantic's belief that his or her desire is original and creative, whereas in fact the desire springs from a wish to appropriate something that is already desired by another. The romantic lie stands in contrast to the truth (*vérité romanesque*) of what Girard later comes to call 'mimetic desire,' a desire that is based on rivalry, appropriation and violence. According to Girard, the truth about desire is revealed in the works of great writers like Dostoevsky and Shakespeare, the subject of Girard's recent works. (For Girard, the literary *canon is a useful embodiment of a non-Platonic, because acquisitive, *mimesis: the canon contains representations of mimetic desire as the hidden motor of violence and the greatest literary works are agents of demystification that bear on what is hidden in human interactions.) Girard calls desire 'triangular' because there is no straight line between the desire of a subject for an object; one desires only what is given value by an other, who becomes part of the process of mimetic rivalry as both rival and double of the subject. This mimetic desire leads to violence, which, as Girard explains in *La Violence et le sacré* [Violence and the Sacred 1972], may be traced anthropologically to the *scapegoat mechanism* – originally the murder of an innocent victim sacrificed ('made sacred') to establish order and community. Violence is thus double-faced; it destroys but it also gives significance to human events and institutions. From this founding event, civilization is marked by a cycle of order, desire or antagonistic mimesis, crisis, the all-against-one of collective violence, and the temporary re-establishment of order. In *De Choses cachées depuis la fondation du monde* [*Things Hidden since the Foundation of the World* 1978] Girard most clearly discusses the alternative to this cycle – a logic of love revealed in a non-sacrificial interpretation of Biblical texts.

Girard is sometimes criticized for a reductionism through which all violence is traced to the scapegoat mechanism, or all *literature viewed as a revelation of – or a false concealing of – mimetic desire. Some criticize Girard for arguing that Christian symbolism alone is *universal, and others for adopting a too secular, materialist view of the sacred or a too restricted view of the Gospel as a exposé of sacrificial violence, without need for ritual or grace. Girard has also excited opposition through his frequent critiques of Freudianism, of various postmodern theorists like *Claude Lévi-Strauss, *Gilles Deleuze and *Félix Guattari, and of some varieties of *deconstruction. (See *Sigmund Freud, *postmodernism, *materialist criticism, *psychoanalytic theory.) He argues that failure of all dogmatic methodologies, when fully acknowledged, will lead not to a cognitive nihilism, which is erroneous, but to a new scientific knowledge not tied to empirical evidence or to intuition but to verification of hypotheses through a wide variety of data, including the anthropological and literary data of his studies. In Girard's system the *skandalon* (or 'stumbling-block') is the obstacle and model of mimetic rivalry; it is a scandal or offence that seductively stands in the way of the truth by sowing rivalry and violence. Girard's aim is to move the reader and society 'beyond scandal' to a recognition of victims and to the elimination of violence. But his ideas themselves and his spirited analyses of his opponents' positions sometimes themselves prove to be scandalous, evoking an energetic opposition from widely diverse positions.

Nonetheless, even his opponents often concede the power of his analysis of desire and violence, and his readings of texts and social phenomena – including Biblical narratives, African and Greek myths, and medieval anti-Semitism – are admired by many who do not wholly adopt what Girard considers to be a scientifically based system. His ideas have wide-ranging implications well beyond literary or anthropological studies. Jean-Michel Oughourlian has, for example, applied some of Girard's ideas to the field of psychotherapy, Paul Dumouchel and Jean-Pierre Dupuy to economics, and Raymund Schwager to theology. (See also *myth, *text, *desire/lack.)

DAVID McCRACKEN

Primary Sources

Girard, René. *Le Bouc émissaire*. Paris: Grasset, 1982. *The Scapegoat*. Trans. Yvonne Freccero. Baltimore: Johns Hopkins UP, 1986.
– *De Choses cachées depuis la fondation du monde*. Paris: Grasset, 1978. *Things Hidden since the Foundation of the World*. Stanford: Stanford UP, 1987.
– *Critique dans un souterrain*. Lausanne: L'Age d'Homme, 1976.
– *Dostoievski: Du double à l'unité*. Paris: Plon, 1963.
– *Mensonge romantique et vérité romanesque*. Paris: Grasset, 1961. *Deceit, Desire, and the Novel: Self and Other in Literary Structure*. Trans. Yvonne Freccero. Baltimore and London: Johns Hopkins UP, 1965.
– *La Route antique des hommes pervers*. Paris: Grasset, 1985. *Job: The Victim of His People*. Trans. Yvonne Freccero. Stanford: Stanford UP, 1987.
– *A Theater of Envy: William Shakespeare*. New York: Oxford UP, 1991.
– 'Theory and Its Terrors.' In *The Limits of Theory*. Ed. Thomas M. Kavanagh. Stanford: Stanford UP, 1989, 225–54.
– '*To double business bound': Essays on Literature, Mimesis, and Anthropology*. Baltimore: Johns Hopkins UP, 1978. [Some of these essays also publ. in *Critique dans un souterrain*.]
– *La Violence et le sacré*. Paris: Grasset, 1972. *Violence and the Sacred*. Trans. Patrick Gregory. Baltimore and London: Johns Hopkins UP, 1977.
– Walter Burkert and Jonathan Z. Smith. *Violent Origins: On Ritual Killing and Cultural Formation*. Ed. Robert G. Hamerton-Kelly. Stanford: Stanford UP, 1987.

Secondary Sources

Chirpaz, François. *Enjeux de la violence: Essais sur René Girard*. Paris: Cerf, 1980.
Deguy, Michel, and Jean-Pierre Dupuy, eds. *René*

Girard et le problème du mal. Paris: Grasset, 1982.

Dumouchel, Paul, and Jean-Pierre Dupuy. *L'Enfer des choses: René Girard et la logique de l'économie*. Paris: Seuil, 1979.

Dumouchel, Paul, ed. *Violence et vérité: Autour de René Girard*. Paris: Grasset, 1985. Selections publ. in *Violence and Truth: On the Work of René Girard*. Stanford: Stanford UP, 1988.

Johnsen, William. 'Myth, Ritual, and Literature after Girard.' In *Literary Theory's Future(s)*. Ed. Joseph Natoli. Urbana and Chicago: U of Illinois P, 1989, 116–48.

Orsini, Christine. *La Pensée de René Girard*. Paris: Retz, 1986.

Oughourlian, Jean-Michel. *Un Mime nommé désir*. Paris: Grasset, 1982. *The Puppet of Desire: The Psychology of Hysteria, Possession and Hypnosis*. Trans. Eugene Webb. Stanford: Stanford UP, 1991.

'René Girard and Biblical Studies.' *Semeia* 33 (1985). Special issue.

Schwager, Raymund. *Brauchen Wir Einen Sündenbock?* Munich: Kösel, 1978. *Must There Be Scapegoats? Violence and Redemption in the Bible*. Trans. Maria L. Assad. San Francisco: Harper and Row, 1987.

Special Issue on the Work of René Girard. *Diacritics* 8 (Spring 1978).

To Honor René Girard. Stanford French and Italian Studies. Saratoga, Calif.: Anma Libri, 1986. (Also publ. as *Stanford French Review* 10 [1986].)

Webb, Eugene. *Philosophers of Consciousness*. Seattle and London: U of Washington P, 1988, 183–225.

Goldmann, Lucien

(b. Romania 1913–d. France, 1970) Philosopher and literary sociologist. Lucien Goldmann studied in Bucharest, Vienna and Paris. Driven from France by the war, he worked with Piaget in Geneva before returning to Paris to work at the CNRS until 1959, when he was elected director of studies at the VIth section of the Ecole Pratique des Hautes Etudes. He founded the Centre de Sociologie de la Littérature at the Free University of Brussels in 1961.

Goldmann's work, which develops a sociology of thought based upon the teachings of Kant, Marx and *Lukács, covers the epistemology of the social sciences as well as *literature. His work on the relationship between philosophy, seen as a coherent system, and sociology, which he regarded as the science of social dynamics, led him to formulate what he called *genetic structuralism*. (See also *structuralism,

*genetic criticism.) This theoretical and methodological approach is based on the idea that all thought tends systematically to create a link between the person as the thinking subject, the world and the absolute. Yet Goldmann insisted that such formulations are insufficient for the framing of what he termed a *world-view* unless they arise from a social force (such as a group or class). Therefore the philosopher or artist cannot but supply the most adequate form to a thought, since its structure is necessarily tied to the coherence of the practices of a social group and is thus beyond the individual's capacity to formulate it.

Goldmann simultaneously studied the positions of these groups in the evolution of societies and the peculiarities, conceptual (in the case of philosophy) and textual (in the case of literature), within the framework of a global theory which facilitates an interpretation of the coherence of literary works and their explanation by examining the context of the social dynamics in which they were written.

Goldmann developed his theory in *Le Dieu caché* [*The Hidden God*], a work which analyses Pascal's *Pensées* and Racine's tragedies in light of the ideological evolution of the French Jansenists and the *noblesse de robe* of 17th-century France. Here he demonstrates how the concept of a tragic world-view can only be understood in light of the loss of *power by this segment of nobility, which occurred when Louis XIV reorganized the State.

It is important to note, however, that what Goldmann calls world-view constitutes as a form a historically determined process of crystallization of structural principles which are in turn independent of the vagaries of history. The influence of Piaget's constructivist epistemology is evident here, along with a certain Kantianism of a priori forms of human thought, though reformulated according to the dialectical tradition inherited from Hegel and Marx. (See *constructivism.)

Sciences humaines et philosophie (1952) and *Recherches dialectiques* (1959) established the theoretical groundwork for the genetic-structuralist method, which Goldmann had started to explore in his *Mensch, Gemeinschaft und Welt in der Philosophie Immanuel Kants* (1945).

Goldmann always stressed his indebtedness to Georg Lukács who greatly influenced all his works, particularly *Pour une sociologie du roman* (1964). In that work, Goldmann explains the evolution of the romanesque form from

Malraux to the *nouveau* roman by the homologous structure: between the position of the romanesque character in terms of values and the position of the individual subject in a society producing for the market. Although based upon a more deterministic theory than *Le Dieu caché*, this very influential and suggestive work occasioned much debate. Undoubtedly because of his gradual loss of faith in the leading role of the proletariat, already evident in the late 1950s, Goldmann abandoned his theory of culture as an expression of the state of social consciousness, replacing it with a theory based on homologous structure, in which the economic infrastructure played a key role. Later, he would return, in part, to his earlier views.

Marginalized by academic institutions, as well as by the rigidity of the Marxism espoused by the French communist movement in the 1950s and 1960s, Goldmann was closer to Austrian-Marxism and to the *Frankfurt School (especially *Theodor Adorno and Herbert Marcuse), although he did not fully share in the pessimism of the latter group. Goldmann contributed precision and intellectual rigour to the social analysis of intellectual and artistic phenomena. His studies on Lumière, Valéry, Robbe-Grillet and Genet attempted to define the social role of an artistic creation on the premise that an important work of art does not reflect the actual state of social consciousness but rather its potential development of it – called possible consciousness – within the framework of an evolutionary view of thought and society. (See *sociocriticism, *Marxist criticism.)

JACQUES LEENHARDT

Primary Sources

Goldmann, Lucien. *La Création culturelle dans la société moderne*. Paris: Denoël, 1971.
– *Le Dieu caché. Etude sur la vision tragique dans les Pensées de Pascal et dans le théâtre de Racine*. Paris: Gallimard, 1955, 1976.
– *Epistémologie et philosophie politique*. Paris: Denoël, 1979.
– *Lukács et Heidegger: Fragments posthumes établis et présentés par Youssef Ishaghpour*. Paris: Denoël, 1973.
– *Marxisme et sciences humaines*. Paris: Gallimard, 1970.
– *Mensch, Gemeinschaft und Welt in der Philosophie Immanuel Kants. Studien zur Geschichte der Dialektik*. Zurich/New York: Europa Verlag, 1945.
– *Pour une sociologie du roman*. Paris: Gallimard, 1964, 1965, 1986.
– *Recherches dialectiques*. Paris: Gallimard, 1959.
– *Sciences humaines et philosophie*. Paris: PUF, 1952, 1966, 1971.
– *Structures mentales et création culturelle*. Paris: Anthropos, 1970.

Gombrich, (Sir) Ernst Hans Josef

(b. Austria, 1909–) Art historian and theorist. E.H. Gombrich studied with Julius von Schlosser, Emil Reich and Emanuel Loewy at Vienna University (1928–33) where he received his Ph.D. In 1936 Gombrich left Austria and settled in England in order to work on the papers of Aby Warburg. He later became the director of the Warburg Institute. During the Second World War he worked for the Monitoring Service of the BBC. Gombrich has held numerous chairs; he has been Durning Lawrence Professor at University College (London), Slade Professor of Fine Art (Oxford and Cambridge) and Andrew D. White Professor (Cornell). He was knighted in 1972 and received the Order of Merit in 1988.

Gombrich's concern with theory arose from problems in art history, particularly the question of why representation is always within a style. (See also *mimesis.) *Art and Illusion*, his most important work, 'is largely concerned with the reason for the collapse of a theory of art which concentrated on the need to copy the phenomenal world' (*The Image and the Eye* 164) and thus implicitly denied the inevitable presence of style in all representation. The copy theory of representation was at the centre of the 'Greek revolution' in visual art (*Art and Illusion* ch. 4), a revolution which was revived in the Renaissance and continued to dominate the course of art history through the 19th century. Gombrich's theoretical work is best viewed as an effort to criticize this theory and at the same time to protect the notion of representation itself from radical relativism – the belief that no way of representing the world is cognitively better than any other. Gombrich tries to accomplish this task by substituting the idea of visual discovery for the idea of accuracy in his theory of visual illusion. This substitution permits him to conceive of the history of art as a series of experiments (conducted in pictures) whose aim is 'the discovery of new aspects of the outer and inner world' (*Tributes* 206). Gombrich compares these visual experiments to the efforts of scientists to improve their theories of the natural world by testing hypotheses.

At the centre of Gombrich's theories about how to write the history of representational art is a contrast between 'conceptual' and 'illusionistic' images. (It should be made clear that Gombrich does not identify art with either representation or expression; witness *The Sense of Order*, his monumental study of decorative art.) He claims that 'the wish to turn the beholder into an imaginary eyewitness of the mythical events' (*The Image and the Eye* 220) initiated the revolution in image-making which made a history of art possible. Conceptual images do not make eyewitnesses of viewers and thus do not encourage audiences to scan the image for forms of coherence appropriate to our perception of the actual world. A modern tourist map and a medieval picture of a town are conceptual images to which we do not apply illusionistic criteria. But once artists began to make images which tried to mimic our ordinary perception they revolutionized image-making. Now artist and audience were not only using images for some purpose but were also exploring the nature of the image and thus the nature of visual effects. It is this exploration, Gombrich argues, that makes a history of art possible. 'Images may indeed teach us to recognize and specify a visual and emotional effect which has always been present in our experience. The search for these effects is much older than the science of psychology. It is known as the history of art' (*The Image and the Eye* 214).

As this passage implies, Gombrich also adapts his theory of visual discovery to the concept of expression, for the artist inherits an expressive as well as a representational vocabulary. Just as Gombrich criticizes the copy theory for its claim to unmediated access to the outer world, so he criticizes the theory of self-expression which is, in effect, the 'inner' version of the copy theory. Expression, like representation, depends upon conventions (*Art and Illusion* 310–20) and the artist, like the person, learns what is expressive through feedback (*Tributes* 196–200).

Most versions of the mimetic and expressive theories of art, which until recently dominated aesthetics, hold that the true artist should free himself from habit, convention and tradition in order to see with an 'innocent eye' (Ruskin's phrase) or express an unmediated self. Gom-

brich agrees with the sceptics that this is not possible and he introduces the notion of the 'schema' in order to explain what does in fact happen. He claims that an artist starts with an inherited or 'found' schema (it can even be his own doodle) which he then modifies as he tests it against the 'motif,' that is, the actual scene to be portrayed. This is what Gombrich calls 'making' and 'matching.' He later alters 'making and matching' to 'recall and recognition' (*The Image and the Eye* 12) because instead of matching the image against some motif the artist and his audience test its adequacy as a coded translation of what an eyewitness might see. To say that one picture is more realistic than another does not mean that it better matches some external reality but that it meets this test.

The presence of a schema in all representation means that there can be no 'neutral naturalism' (*Art and Illusion* 75), for the schema always leaves its traces. That is why style is an inevitable aspect of image-making. The concern with the image is closely tied to the development of distinctive skills and the ability to conceive experiments in image-making that are rooted in tradition. The idea that artists always build on traditions which they modify and criticize is based on Karl Popper's theory that accepted scientific ideas are not to be understood as true statements about the world but as unfalsified hypotheses that remain in place until they are shown to be wrong. Gombrich repeatedly compares this notion of science to what occurs in perception. What we see is not what is simply there nor is it something which we conjure out of mere sense data. It is a guess, a hypothesis, about what the world out there is really like and it can be disconfirmed. In ordinary life our perceptual guesses are almost always adequate because they have biological foundations (*The Sense of Order* 1–4) but there are moments when our visual hypotheses are stymied and that is when we become aware that perception is an interpretive process.

The way that perceptual habits and expectations based upon knowledge of the actual world influence how we read images Gombrich calls 'the beholder's share.' He emphasizes the role of the beholder in the making of images, since what the artist does is dependent upon what he (the first beholder) perceives as he confronts what he does. The issue here is how much of what we see is the contribution of our knowledge and habits and how much is due to what is 'really' there. What we see is often determined by what we know, what we expect and by the potent force of what psychologists call 'constancy,' 'our relative imperviousness to the dizzy variations that go on in the world around us' (*Art and Illusion* 47). We automatically correct for foreshortening so that a hand thrust toward us from a few feet away does not appear weirdly large, as it does in a photograph. The crucial role of constancy in perception rules out both the copy theory (because we *actively* keep the world constant) and relativism (since the need for constancy implies a real world).

In *Art and Illusion* Gombrich tries to establish the theoretical basis for the existence of a history of art which will understand image-making as a critical process. He opposes this view to many contemporary intellectual currents but principally to the Hegelian 'historicism' (Popper's term) that he believes wrongly governed much writing in art history. Hegelian 'exegesis' assumes that artists, as well as all others, are not self-conscious and critical persons, but vehicles for the expression of world-historical eras (*Ideals and Idols* 24–59). At the same time Gombrich opposes the 'empiricism' of an art history which ignores theory and confines itself to cataloguing the archive.

Gombrich's ideas have been discussed primarily by philosophers interested in the 'controversy over conventionalism' (Blinder) but also by literary critics who have taken up his views on representation, perception and, especially, the 'beholder's share.' (See *horizon of expectation.) Gombrich's view of perception as a form of interpretation and his concern with the viewer's role in the 'reading' of images is closely related to reader-response theory, and F.W. Bateson's notion of the semantic gap (a good poem challenges our capacity to interpret but does not defeat it) is not unlike Gombrich's claim that 'we must ultimately be able to account for the most basic fact of aesthetic experience, the fact that delight lies somewhere between boredom and confusion' (*The Sense of Order* 9). (See *reader-response criticism.)

Gombrich's reputation is built upon a union of great erudition, a talent for theory and a lucid style that makes his work available to the educated public. He has developed a cognitive, biologically grounded theory of the visual arts that has unusual scope and power and can be extended to other arts as well. Gombrich is also an eloquent spokesman for the tradition of liberal humanism to which the theory is a major contribution. Often expressing a debt to Popper's ideas about society, Gombrich has repeatedly stated his commitment to critical reason, which he believes should be at the core of intellectual, artistic and political life.

ROGER SEAMON

Primary Sources

Gombrich, E.H. *Art and Illusion: A Study in the Psychology of Pictorial Representation*. Oxford: Phaidon P, 1960. 5th ed. 1977.
– *The Heritage of Appelles: Studies in the Art of the Renaissance*. Oxford: Phaidon P, 1978.
– *Ideals and Idols: Essays on Values in History and in Art*. Oxford: Phaidon P, 1979.
– *The Image and the Eye: Further Studies in the Psychology of Pictorial Representation*. Ithaca: Cornell UP, 1982.
– *Means and Ends: Reflections on the History of Frescoe Painting*. London: Thames and Hudson, 1976.
– *Meditations on a Hobby Horse and Other Essays on the Theory of Art*. London: Phaidon P, 1963.
– *New Light on Old Masters*. Oxford: Phaidon P, 1986.
– *Reflections on the History of Art: Views and Reviews*. Ed. Richard Woodfield. Oxford: Phaidon P, 1987.
– *The Sense of Order: A Study in the Psychology of Decorative Art*. London: Phaidon P, 1979.
– *The Story of Art*. Oxford: Phaidon P, 1950. 15th ed. 1984.
– *Symbolic Images: Studies in the Art of the Renaissance*. Oxford: Phaidon P, 1978.
– *Tributes: Interpretations of Our Cultural Tradition*. Oxford: Phaidon P, 1984.

Secondary Sources

Blinder, David. 'The Controversy over Conventionalism.' *Journal of Aesthetics and Art Criticism* 41 (1983): 253–64.
Bryson, Norman. *Vision and Painting: The Logic of the Gaze*. New Haven and London: Yale UP, 1983.
Carrier, David. 'Gombrich on Art Historical Explanations.' *Leonardo* 16 (1983): 91–6.
– 'Perspective as a Convention: On the Views of Nelson Goodman and Ernst Gombrich.' *Leonardo* 13 (1980): 283–7.
– 'Theoretical Perspectives on the Arts, Science and Technology. Part I: An Introduction to the Semiotic Theory of Art.' *Leonardo* 17 (1984): 288–94.
Donnell-Kotroza, Carol. 'Representation and Expression: A False Antinomy.' *Journal of Aesthetics and Art Criticism* 34 (1980): 161–73.

Gablick, Suzi. 'On the Logic of Artistic Discovery: Art as Mimetic Conjecture.' *Studio* 186 (1973): 65–8. Reply: John Stezaker, 'Towards Nihilism.' 169–70.

Hansen, Robert. 'This Curving World: Hyperbolic Linear Perspective.' *Journal of Aesthetics and Art Criticism* 32 (1973): 147–61.

Lycan, William G. 'Gombrich, Wittgenstein, and the Dick-Rabbit.' *Journal of Aesthetics and Art Criticism* 30 (1971): 229–37.

Mitchell, W.J.T. *Iconology: Image, Text, Ideology*. Chicago and London: U of Chicago P, 1986.

Novitz, David. 'Conventions and the Growth of Pictorial Style.' *British Journal of Aesthetics* 16 (1976): 324–37.

Wilkinson, Terence. 'Representation, Illusion and Aspects.' *British Journal of Aesthetics* 18 (1978): 45–58.

Wollheim, Richard. 'Art and Illusion.' In *Aesthetics in the Modern World*. Ed. Harold Osborne. New York: Weybright and Talley, 1968, 235–63.

Gramsci, Antonio

(b. Italy 1891–d. 1937) Marxist critic. Antonio Gramsci studied in Turin, where he became active within the Socialist party, and was one of the founders of the journal *L'Ordine Nuovo* [The New Order]. He left the party to help found the Italian Communist party (1921), of which he became leader in 1924, and was subsequently elected to parliament. Gramsci was arrested by Mussolini's Fascists in 1926 and condemned, in 1928, to over 20 years of prison. While in prison he maintained a voluminous correspondence (mostly with his wife's sister, Tatiana Schucht) and filled 32 notebooks with 2848 pages of writings; these constitute the basis of his reputation today as the 'greatest Marxist writer of the twentieth century' (Joll). Gramsci was given conditional liberty in 1937 as the result of an international campaign (led by French writers Romain Rolland and Henri Barbusse and Cambridge economist Piero Sraffa), but he died in that year, his health having been destroyed. His major contribution to Marxist thought was his notion of the 'materiality' of ideas, his theorizing of the role of the intellectual within political *praxis*, and his development of the concept of *hegemony. His contemporary influence is felt throughout the field of cultural studies. (See *materialist criticism, *Marxist criticism, *cultural materialism.)

As a *meridionale* – a Southerner – Gramsci was acutely aware of the way in which the industrial North of Italy had colonized the agrarian and impoverished South, and this led him to formulate a theory of politics which modified Marx's notion of class struggle with that of the confrontation between centre and *margin. (See also *post-colonial theory.)

Like *Ferdinand de Saussure, Gramsci insisted on the material importance of language as a social constructor, as he suggests in his most sustained piece of literary criticism (most of these pieces being short ones, often written for journals), on the tenth canto of Dante's *Inferno*. He may also be linked to *Mikhail Bakhtin in his insistence on language as a dramatic, active agent of social relations, as well as in his belief that language comprises the social and political history of a people.

The core of Gramsci's thought concerns the material role which ideas play within social relations, and this constitutes his major contribution to Marxist thought, which had tended to grant prime consideration to the material and economic bases of society and to see the superstructure (ideas) as products of these forces. For Gramsci, however, history could be influenced by ideas, and by individuals; it was not preordained. This position also represented his debt to and distance from the major Italian intellectual of his time, *Benedetto Croce, for whom history was the working out of certain universal ideas. Gramsci, however, materialized these ideas in place and time.

The major concept in Gramsci's writing is hegemony, which represents the set of values and beliefs through which the ruling class exercises its *power over the masses, including religion, education and the media (cf. *ideology). In elaborating this concept, he follows Lenin's emphasis on the consent of subordinate groups to the leadership or hegemony of the proletariat. Hegemonic ideas are the 'common sense' or 'myths' (in *Roland Barthes' sense of the term) that govern a society and to which the masses freely consent; this consent would likewise have to be accorded to any new ruling group. (See also *myth.) Hegemony thus defined is a dynamic process, since the hegemonic group must continually make compromises in order to incorporate as many elements of society as possible.

Power for Gramsci is relational, in that social relations are also relations of power. Thus power is present everywhere in society and not just in the state. Revolution would thus have to extend throughout society, and could not be achieved simply by seizing control of the apparatus of state power (as the Fascists had done). Gramsci had hoped to develop a theory of power for his own (fascist) times along the lines of those developed by Machiavelli in the Renaissance, though where Machiavelli posited the Prince, Gramsci placed the collectivity. His central insight was that power was exercised not only economically and physically but also through ideas, and that ideas were not purely products of economic forces. Thus, a revolution in which the holders of power simply changed hands was insufficient, since power would still be indirectly applied hegemonically – indeed, Gramsci constructed a theory of 'passive revolution,' in which reforms were carried out while hegemony remained intact among the ruling elite. As well, the working (or subaltern) class need no longer be theorized as the sole agent of revolution; subalternity was seen to exist elsewhere (for example, among women, people of colour and gays).

Given that ideas were themselves the sites of power relations (knowledge as a function of power), the intellectual, for Gramsci, took on an important role as a political organizer (as opposed to the more traditional roles of writer and academic, for example). Thus pedagogy emerged as a major aspect of Gramsci's 'revolutionary' thought: only if subaltern groups had an awareness of how they were repressed hegemonically could they react to that repression by constructing their own systems of ideas, their agency being enacted through intellectual leadership. The role of cultural studies becomes the exposition of these repressive myths of hegemony (cf. *Walter Benjamin).

RICHARD CAVELL

Primary Sources

Adamson, Walter L. *Hegemony and Revolution: A Study of Antonio Gramsci's Political and Cultural Theory*. Berkeley: U of California P, 1980.
Fiori, Giuseppe. *Antonio Gramsci: Life of a Revolutionary*. Trans. T. Nairn. London: Verso, 1990 [1965].
Gramsci, Antonio. *The Modern Prince and Other Writings*. Trans. L. Marks. New York: International Publishers, 1957.
– *Lettere dal carcere*. Ed. S. Caprioglio and E. Fubini. Torino: Einaudi, 1965.
– *Letters from Prison*. Trans. L. Lawner. New York: Harper and Row, 1973.
– *Quaderni del carcere*. 4 vols. Ed. V. Gerratana. Torino: Einaudi, 1975.
– *Selections from Cultural Writings*. Ed. D. Forgacs and G. Nowell-Smith. Trans. W. Boelhower. Cambridge: Harvard UP, 1985.
– *Selections from Political Writings, 1910–1920*. Ed. J. Mathews and Q. Hoare. New York: International Publishers, 1978.
– *Selections from Political Writings, 1921–1926*. Ed. and trans. Q. Hoare. New York: International Publishers, 1978.
– *Selections from the Prison Notebooks*. Ed. and trans. Q. Hoare and G. Nowell-Smith. New York: International Publishers, 1971.
Joll, James. *Gramsci*. London: Fontana/Collins, 1977.
Laclau, Ernesto, and Chantal Mouffe. *Hegemony and Socialist Strategy: Towards a Radical Democratic Politics*. Trans. W. Moore and P. Cammack. London: Verso, 1985.
Landy, Marcia. 'Culture and Politics in the Work of Antonio Gramsci.' *boundary 2* [Special Gramsci issue] 14.3 (Spring 1986): 49–70.
Mouffe, Chantal, ed. *Gramsci and Marxist Theory*. London: Routledge and Kegan Paul, 1979.
Special Gramsci issue. *boundary 2* 14.3 (Spring 1986).

Secondary Sources

Bocock, Robert. *Hegemony*. London: Tavistock, 1986.
Eley, G. 'Reading Gramsci in English: Observations on the Reception of Antonio Gramsci in the English-Speaking World 1957–1982.' *European History Quarterly* 14 (1984): 441–78.
Hobsbawm, Eric. 'The Great Gramsci.' *New York Review of Books*, 4 April 1974, 39–44.
Mauro, Walter. *Invito alla lettura di Gramsci*. Milano: Mursia, 1981.
Morera, Esteve. *Gramsci's Historicism: A Realist Interpretation*. London: Routledge, 1990.
Simon, Roger. *Gramsci's Political Thought: An Introduction*. London: Lawrence and Wishart, 1982.

Greimas, A(lgirdas) J(ulien)

(b. Russia, 1917–d. France, 1992) Semiotician. After his baccalauréat (1934), A.J. Greimas studied law in Kaunas (Lithuania) before enrolling at the University of Grenoble, France, where, from 1936 to 1939, he developed an interest in the language and *literature of the Middle Ages. He obtained the degree of licence ès lettres with a specialization in Franco-Provençal dialectology. After he returned to Lithuania for his military service, his country was invaded, first by the Soviets (1940), then the Germans (1941), and was finally occupied again by the Soviets (1944). Greimas escaped to France where he obtained his doctorat d'état in 1948 with a primary thesis on fashion in 1830, a lexicological study of the vocabulary of dress according to the journals of the times, and a secondary thesis, based on a synchronic model of analysis, on various aspects of social life in 1830. Greimas began his university career teaching the history of the French language at Alexandria, Egypt, where he met *Roland Barthes. He abandoned lexicology, which he considered inadequate to describe semantic fields and in 1958 he took up the chair of French language and grammar at the University of Ankara, Turkey. After appointments at the Universities of Istanbul and Poitiers, he was elected in 1965 to the Ecole Pratique des Hautes Etudes in Paris, where he directed a seminar in *semiotics that attracted a large number of students and professors from France and abroad, subsequently evolving into the Paris school of semiotics.

Greimas' semiotics must be understood within the intellectual context of the structuralist and poststructuralist movements that flourished in the latter half of this century (at one time or other in their training, *Julia Kristeva, *Tzvetan Todorov and *Oswald Ducrot were his assistants). (See *structuralism, *poststructuralism.) Greimas was influenced by pioneering work undertaken in anthropology (*Claude Lévi-Strauss), folklore (*Vladimir Propp), linguistics (*Ferdinand de Saussure and especially Louis Hjelmslev), mythology (Georges Dumézil), and phenomenology (*Maurice Merleau-Ponty), as well as by research in the social sciences and humanities stemming directly from Saussurean advances in theoretical linguistics, which focused on the synchronic (the state of language at a given moment in time) rather than the diachronic (elements of the system belonging to different states of development) dimension of language (Roland Barthes, *Emile Benveniste, *Michel Foucault, *Roman Jakobson, *Jacques Lacan, and Hans Reichenbach). (See *phenomenological criticism.) All of these had an impact on the methodological and theoretical reframing of Greimas' work after the late 1950s. In this context Greimas envisaged his project of establishing semiotics on a 'scientific' or at least systematic basis (The Social Sciences: A Semiotic View 1970).

The concept of a semantic universe, borrowed from Hjelmslev and the Danish School of Glossomatics, and defined as the sum of all possible significations that can be produced by the systems of values that are co-extensive with the entire culture of an ethnolinguistic community, is fundamental to Greimas' semiotics (Structural Semantics 1966). However, since the semantic universe cannot be conceived of in its entirety, Greimas had to introduce the concepts of semantic micro-universe and discourse universe. The semantic micro-universe, which can be grasped only if it is deployed at its most abstract level by semantic categories such as life/death (the individual universe) or nature/culture (the collective universe), appears in the form of the discourse universe that it generates. The notion of discourse universe that has its origin in logic contains both syntactic implications and presuppositions, whereas that of micro-universe contains only the semantic component of discourse. The semantic micro-universe can be established by reconstituting isotopies (recurring semantic features) and basic axiologies (value systems); it is self-contained, whereas the discourse universe includes references to the 'exterior' world (Semiotics and Language 1979). (See *isotopy.) From this perspective, literary *discourse is defined as a specific realization of the discourse universe and thus of the semantic micro-universe that brings together and deploys the semiotics of language and of the natural world, which are considered as vast reservoirs of signs themselves containing numerous sign systems. (See *sign.) Although scientific or philosophical discourses also interrelate with both of these semiotic domains, what distinguishes them from literary discourse is that the latter is figurative in nature, as opposed to the former which is not (Semiotics and Language).

For Greimas a literary *text can be considered as a specific actualization of literary discourse encompassing several semiotic systems (linguistic, natural and rhythmic). To analyse such a text one has, first of all, to consider it as the result of a presupposed act of enunciation (speech act) and show how it incorporates the various sign systems constituting it by establishing descriptive procedures and constructing a *metalanguage (an artificial language using the same terms as the natural language it describes, that is, grammatical language). (See *énonciation/énoncé.) Hence, to come to grips with the problem of signification or the production of meaning in a literary text, one must transpose one level of language (the text) into a different level of language (the metalanguage) and work out adequate techniques of transposition (*On Meaning* 1970). The next step is to work out a rigorous descriptive language containing its own rules and constituting a semiotic system made up of a hierarchy of definitions. (See Greimas' 280-page *Maupassant* [1976], which analyses a 6-page short story.) In addition, the concepts making up the system are established as postulates and are integrated into a network of inter-definitions, thereby ensuring its internal coherence. (See *signified/signifier/signification.)

The notion of narrativity and the descriptive procedures of *narratology are at the very core of Greimassian semiotics. In much the same way, Benveniste and *Gérard Genette identified two autonomous discursive levels: narrative, what is related, and discourse, the way of narrating the narrative. Greimas adopted similar distinctions: the discursive level that is part of enunciation (speech act) and the narrative level corresponding to the utterance (the state resulting from enunciation). Narrative analyses undertaken by Propp, Dumézil and Lévi-Strauss made it possible to analyse texts by describing the transformations of connected actions. Under the appearance of figurative narratives, these also attest to the existence of abstract and deep (semio-narrative) structures that govern the production and reading of this kind of discourse. The concept of narrativity, which is the transformation of the semio-narrative structures identified in the first instance as figurative discourse, was extended and considered as the organizing principle of all other types of discourse, whether narrative or non-narrative.

In working out his theoretical model Greimas took the 31 functions that were initially developed by Propp to account for the structure of the folktale and reformulated them in terms of actants, defined as beings or things that participate in processes in any form whatsoever (*subject/object, sender/receiver), actantial structures (subject → object; sender → object → receiver) and a canonical narrative schema. This schema is a formal framework made up of three successive sequences in which two communication sequences (a mandate sequence [how the sender manipulates the subject either pragmatically or cognitively] and an evaluation sequence [passing judgment on self or others]) encompass an action sequence (how competence is acquired to carry

out performance). (See *competence/performance.) The narrative schema is considered as recording 'life meaning' through its three essential domains: the qualification of the subject (mandate sequence), which introduces it into life; its realization by means of which it acts (action sequence); and finally the sanction (evaluation sequence) – at one and the same time retribution and recognition – which alone confirms the meaning of its actions and installs it as a subject (*Semiotics and Language*).

The next step was to construct a narrative grammar and work out a syntax of narrative programs in which subjects are joined up with, or separated from, objects of value (desire), for example, wealth, a loved one or goodness, and thereby transformed. The subjects' changes of state are accounted for by simple operations such as conjunctions, disjunctions and transformations. The principle of confrontation between two subjects is interpreted as an elementary polemico-contractual relation. Whether engaged in conversation or in argumentation or actually fighting, the subjects in question are involved in a relation either of trust or of conflict. A series of modalizations is then postulated, two virtualizing (wanting and having to virtualize the process) and two actualizing ones (being able and knowing how to actualize it) that account for the subjects' modal competence, existence and performance, thereby establishing a semiotic syntax freed from Proppian constraints. This modal semiotics, concerned with defining the manipulating and sanctioning subject, is developed, opening the way to a semiotics of passions that studies both how passions modify pragmatic and cognitive performances and how epistemic categories, such as knowing and believing, modify the subject's competence and performance (*Greimassian Semiotics* 1989; 'Cognitive Dimension'). In short, Greimassian semiotics evolves from a semiotics of actions to a semiotics of cognition and passions and the challenge ahead lies in working out adequate and necessary descriptive procedures not only of the modal but also of the aspectual features of discourse: for example, aspects such as inchoativity (the beginning of an action), durativity (the unravelling of an action) and terminativity (the end of an action), that allow for the representation of temporalization as processes in texts. To analyse texts in this way is to construct models that can account, on the one hand, for the trajectory of the lives of subjects (the canonical narrative schema) and, on the other, come to grips with both the problem of objects of value sought after by subjects and the organization of values into specific axiological discourse sequences.

Generally, critics who disagree with Greimas' theory have either rejected the whole by denying the possibility of any theory in the human and social sciences ever attaining 'scientificity' or have attempted to demonstrate its internal insufficiencies and incoherences by examining problems related to semiotic and narratological modelling (the relationship between explanation and comprehension); and questions of immanence (the bracketing off of the referent), conversion (the relationship between the semiotic square, which is logically oriented – actional – and the cognitive and passional dimension of texts), stratificational models in general, and the generative trajectory (that is, should one proceed from deep structures to surface or the other way around). (See also *reference/referent.)

PAUL PERRON

Primary Sources

Greimas, A.J. 'The Cognitive Dimension of Narrative Discourse.' Trans. Michael Rengstorf. *New Literary History* 7 (1976): 433–47.
– *Greimassian Semiotics.* Trans. and ed. P. Perron and F. Collins. *New Literary History* 20.3 (1989).
– 'The Interpretation of Myth: Theory and Practice.' 1971. Trans. Kipnis Clougher. In *Structural Analysis of Oral Tradition.* Ed. Pierre Maranda and Elli K. Maranda. Philadelphia: U of Pennsylvania P, 1971, 81–121. 'Eléments pour une théorie du récit mythique.' *Communications* 8 (1966): 28–59.
– *Maupassant. The Semiotics of Text: Practical Exercises.* Trans. P. Perron. Amsterdam and Philadelphia: John Benjamins, 1988. *La Sémiotique du texte: Exercise Pratiques.* Paris: Seuil, 1976.
– 'Narrative Grammar: Units and Levels.' Trans. Phillip Bodrock. In *Modern Language Notes* 86 (1971): 793–807. 'Eléments d'une grammaire narrative.' In *Du Sens.* Paris: Seuil, 1970, 157–83.
– *On Gods and Men.* Trans. Milda Newman. Bloomington: Indiana UP, 1992. *Des Dieux et des hommes.* Paris: PUF, 1985.
– *On Imperfection.* Trans. Teresa Keane. Amsterdam and Philadelphia: John Benjamins, 1992. *De L'Imperfection.* Périgueux: Pierre Fanlac, 1987.
– *On Meaning: Selected Writings in Semiotic Theory.* Trans. P. Perron and F. Collins. Minneapolis: U of Minnesota P, 1987. Texts from *Du Sens* and *Du Sens 2.* Paris: Seuil, 1970, 1983.
– *The Social Sciences: A Semiotic View.* Trans. P. Perron and F. Collins. Minneapolis: U of Minnesota P, 1989. Texts from *Du Sens, Du Sens 2* and *Sémiotique et sciences sociales.* Paris: Seuil, 1970, 1976, 1983.
– *Structural Semantics: An Attempt at a Method.* Trans. A. Velie, D. McDowell, and R. Schleifer. Lincoln: U of Nebraska P, 1983. *Sémantique structurale.* Paris: Larousse, 1966.
– and J. Courtés. *Semiotics and Language: An Analytical Dictionary.* Trans. L. Crist, D. Patte et al. Bloomington: Indiana UP, 1982. *Sémiotique: Dictionnaire raisonné de la théorie du langage.* Paris: Hachette, 1979.
– and J. Fontanille. *The Semiotics of Passions.* Trans. P. Perron and F. Collins. Minneapolis: U of Minnesota P, 1992. *Sémiotique des passions.* Paris: Seuil, 1991.
– and François Rastier. 'The Interaction of Semiotic Constraints.' *Yale French Studies* (1968): 86–105. In *Du Sens.* Paris: Seuil, 1970, 135–55.

Secondary Sources

Calloud, J. *Structural Analysis of Narrative.* Philadelphia: Fortress P, 1976.
Collins, F. 'More on Greimas in the Realm of Arthur.' *Structuralist Review* 2.2 (1981): 61–7.
Culler, J. *Structural Poetics.* London: Routledge and Kegan Paul, 1975.
Fabbri, P., and P. Perron. Foreword to *The Social Sciences: A Semiotic View.* Minneapolis: U of Minnesota P, 1989.
– Foreword to *The Semiotics of Passions.* Minneapolis: U of Minnesota P, 1992.
Hawkes, T. *Structuralism and Semiotics.* Berkeley: U of California P, 1977.
Jameson, F. *The Prison-House of Language.* Princeton: Princeton UP, 1972.
– Foreword to *On Meaning: Selected Writings in Semiotic Theory.* Minneapolis: U of Minnesota P, 1987.
Maddox, D. *The Semiotics of Deceit: The Pathelin Era.* London and Toronto: Bucknell UP, 1984.
Parret, H. *Discussing Language.* The Hague: Mouton, 1974.
– Introduction to *Paris School Semiotics I: Theory.* Ed. P. Perron and F. Collins. Amsterdam and Philadelphia: John Benjamins, 1989.
Patte, D., and A. Patte. *Structural Exegesis: From Theory to Practice.* Philadelphia: Fortress P, 1978.
Perron, P. Introduction to *On Meaning: Selected Writings in Semiotic Theory.* Minneapolis: U of Minnesota P, 1987.
– Foreword to *Maupassant. The Semiotics of Text: Practical Exercises.* Amsterdam/Philadelphia: John Benjamins, 1988.
– Introduction to *Greimassian Semiotics. New Literary History* 20.3 (1989).

– and F. Collins, eds. *Paris School Semiotics: I Theory, II Practice*. Amsterdam and Philadelphia: John Benjamins, 1989.

Schleifer, R. *A.J. Greimas and the Nature of Meaning*. Lincoln: U of Nebraska P, 1987.

Grivel, Charles

(b. Switzerland, 1936–) Literary critic and theorist. After completing his undergraduate studies in *literature and philosophy (1960) at the University of Geneva under Marcel Raymond, *Jean Rousset and *Jean Starobinski, Charles Grivel continued his multidisciplinary studies at Dakar (Sénégal) in anthropology and the history of art. Returning to Europe in 1961, Grivel became assistant professor in Giessen (Germany) where he had close contact with *Hans Robert Jauss. Since then he has held a number of academic posts in the Netherlands and in Germany.

Grivel's major work, *Production de l'intérêt romanesque* (1973), is based on a theory of texts which is linked to cultural *communication theory. Other theoretical publications explore the manifold directions opened up by this book and lead him to analyse different types of discourses ranging from print media to photography. (See *sociocriticism, *discourse analysis theory, *text, *discourse.)

Grivel's theory focuses on the novel, the textual effect of which he regards as a chain of significations themselves displaced by manifold readings in an evolving ideological framework. (See *signified/signifier/signification.) Aspects of Kristevan research (*Le Texte du roman*) and of Derridean '*trace' (*Of Grammatology*) reappear in his theory, especially in its preoccupation with *intertextuality, the absence of beginnings and the problem of authenticity. (See *Julia Kristeva, *Jacques Derrida.) Given the inherent *indeterminacy of the novel as a form of discourse within a sociological ensemble (a General Textual Ideological Ensemble), its intention to stability and identity necessarily remains unrealized ('Thèses préparatoires sur les intertextes' 1983).

The cardinal fact for Grivel is that every novel is written in conformity to its context – sociological, ideological, psychological, cultural. This leads him to speculate that a particular text or group of texts generates thematic or material differences which are inscribed in the general ideological production of the novel. (See *theme, *materialist criticism.) Thus the narrative series perpetuates the chain of signifiers and masks its contradictions. The unveiling of the contradictions inherent in the diffusion of the novel (or of any broad and disseminated type of discourse) would ultimately rest on a theory which analyses both the production of meanings and readings in context, and which reveals the contradictions of the self-perpetuation of ideological universals ('Les Universaux du texte' 1978). (See *universal.)

Like *A.J. Greimas, Grivel analyses narrative structures as series of actions connected on the surface level but resting, at a deeper level, on a semantic paradigm congruent with the traditional square of contradiction. Narrative necessarily transforms because, as Greimas argues, it normally concludes with an inversion of its initial semantic content. The novel's norm, though, is stability, which is realized in a semantic redundancy justifying the established cultural order. Thus, in these conclusions linked to a dialectical and somewhat Marxian perspective on the production of texts, Grivel, while inspired by the method of *Vladimir Propp and Greimas, is on the whole deeply opposed to their conclusions, be it only because they view the text of the novel as generating ahistoricity, a kind of eternal return of immutable 'nature': 'The tactic of the novel consists in imitating the overturning of the rule in order to reaffirm its final invulnerability' (*Production de l'intérêt romanesque* 201). Grivel thus demonstrates that the narrative in the novel produces affirmation through negation and arouses interest by temporarily suspending 'archetypal' significations. (See also *Marxist criticism, *archetype.)

Grivel's global ideological research, which uncovers the dynamics of process, allows him to go beyond the framework of his narrow historical data (1870–80) and to enter into both general and precise considerations about the relationship between *margin and centre, literature and society. (See *centre/decentre.) The novel and every literary endeavour, except that which is (at a certain period) considered unreadable (but which will become readable later, thanks to its forced inclusion into an acceptable series), obscure daily contradictions and reduce class conflicts to individual and personal psychological problems: 'The novel renders unreal a conflict already silenced' (*Production de l'intérêt romanesque* 227).

Analysing the main argumentative networks of the novel seen as an infinite series included in the General Text and also the framework of the constant recourse to fiction, Grivel underlines the fact that 'this is never it,' that one never reads what one thinks one reads. He shares this point of view with writers like Edmond Jabès (*Du Désert au livre*) who refers to a particular Jewish tradition (Midrash) of producing significations. This conception, with its far-reaching impact for hermeneutic criticism, is directly opposed to the generalized literary 'stock of beliefs' (*fonds de créance*) concerning the origin, stability, and authenticity of texts and concerning the possibility of establishing definitive interpretations. (See *hermeneutics.)

Grivel's exploration of types of argumentation goes well beyond the novel and opens into the 'Société des textes' (*Littérature* 63) linked to a semiotic-sociology of the *sign. (See *semiotics.) The different types of discourses and their arguments intermingle in various intertextual tactics and strategic games temporarily displacing paradigmatic categories (interior/exterior, heterogene/homogene, centre/margin), but always in order to reassert the same permanent archetypal discursive order. (See *game theory.) In all his writings Grivel considers the ways in which the building of closed narrative structures from a series of cultural/semantic elements is linked to a clashing of epistemologies. This violence in turn is linked to the imposition of beliefs in the return of the same in a cycle which a French writer like Philippe Sollers tries to deconstruct in his fictions (*Femme* and *Paradis*). (See *deconstruction.) Grivel, also a writer of fiction, participates in this endeavour in texts such as *Précipité d'une fouille* and *Le Grand et le petit Albert*. This is why he regularly participates with other theoreticians and writers, like Toma Pavel, in the Noesis Foundation in Calaceite (Spain), dedicated to the exploration of the numerous aspects of fictionality.

PATRICK IMBERT

Primary Sources

Grivel, Charles. 'L'Appareil de représentation naturaliste, ce qu'il s'y marque. Le corps, le nu.' In *Le naturalisme* 10–18: 197–228.
– 'Appareils et machines à représentation: J'introduis aux machines.' *MANA* 8 (1989): 11–17.
– 'La Communication de texte. Cadrage sémiotique de la théorie de l'information.' *Neohelicon*, IV 3–4 (1970): 29–64.
– 'Déjets. La Poussée sur le cadre.' In *Texte-Image. Bild-Text*. Ed. Sybil Dümchen and Michael Nerlich. Colloquium Berlin 2–4. XII, 1988, TU Berlin, 55–69.
– 'Le Discours du sexe.' (Fin de siècle en littérature). In *Die Modernisierung des Ich*. Ed. M. Pfister. Passau: Wissenschaftverlag R. Rothe, 1989, 96–107.
– 'Esquisse d'une théorie des systèmes doxiques.' *Degrés* 24–25 (1980–1): d1–d23.
– *Le Fantastique*. MANA 1 (1989).
– 'Idée du texte.' *Romantische Zeitschrift für Literaturgeschichte / Cahiers d'histoire des littératures romanes* 1–2 (1985): 162–80.
– 'Inscription des codes, mesure de l'information textuelle, degrés d'actes de correspondance: Le compliment, la lettre.' Universita di Urbino, Centro Internazionale di Semiotica e di Linguistica, Documents de travail 52, mars 1976.
– *Production de l'intérêt romanesque. Un Etat du texte (1870–1880). Un Essai de constitution de sa théorie*. La Haye-Paris: Mouton, 1973.
– *Production de l'intérêt romanesque*. Vol. complémentaire. Hoofddorp-Amstelveen. Hoekstra Offset, 1973.
– 'Le Retournement parodique des discours à leurres constants.' In *Dire la parodie*. Colloque de Cerisy. Ed. Clive Thomson and Alain Pagès. New York: Lang, 1989. *American University Studies II* 16: 1–34.
– 'Sémiotique des représentations.' In *Sémiotique en jeu*. Ed. Michel Arrivé and Jean-Claude Coquet. Hades-Benjamins, 1987, 193–211.
– 'La Société des textes. Médiation médiatique en 13 points.' *Littérature* 63 (1986): 3–23. For a more complete version see *Degrés* 46–7 (1986): e.1–e.2g.
– 'The Society of Texts. A Mediation on Media in 13 Points.' *Sociocriticism* 1 (1985): 153–78.
– 'Le Sujet de l'école et de la littérature.' In *Littérature, enseignement, société. Revue de l'Institut de sociologie*. Ed. R. Heyndels. Bruxelles: Université libre de Bruxelles, nos. 3–4, 461–79.
– 'Thèses préparatoires sur les intertextes.' In *Dialogizität*. Herausgegeben von Renate Lachmann. München, Fink, 1983, 237–48. (Actes du Symposium *Dialogizität in Prozessen der literarischen Kommunikation*, 8–11 juillet 1980, Université de Constance).
– 'Les Universaux de texte.' *Littérature* 30 (1978): 25–50.
– 'Vingt-deux thèses préparatoires sur la doxa, le réel et le vrai.' *Revue des sciences humaines* 201 (1986): 49–55.
Spivak, Gayatri C. 'Reading the World: Literary Studies in the 1980s.' In *Writing and Reading Differently*. Ed. G. Douglas Atkins and Michael L. Johnson. Lawrence: UP of Kansas, 1985.

Guattari, (Pierre) Félix

(b. France, 1930–) Psychoanalyst, political activist and theorist. Educated in philosophy and pharmacy, Félix Guattari has since 1953 been an analyst at the Clinique de la Bord à Cour-Cheverny, where he has engaged in alternative psychoanalytic praxis. The Clinique de la Borde has been a key institution in the so-called antipsychiatric movement inspired in part by the *psychoanalytic theory of *Jacques Lacan. In the 1950s and 1960s Guattari attended Lacan's seminars, underwent analysis with Lacan from 1962 to 1969 and in 1969 joined Lacan's Ecole Freudienne. From the mid-1950s Guattari published essays in psychoanalytic theory and practice, especially on the issues of the institution and the group. These essays were collected in *Psychanalyse et transversalité [Psychoanalysis and Transversality* 1972]. However, Guattari was also engaged in Marxist politics, at first in a strained relationship with the French Communist party, and later completely outside the party, which he increasingly came to see as restrictive and reactionary. He founded or was a member of numerous political and research groups and took an active role in the events of May 1968. In 1969 he met the philosopher *Gilles Deleuze and they began to work together. (See also *Marxist criticism.)

Guattari is known for his collaborations with Deleuze, especially for his work on the two volumes of *Capitalisme et schizophrénie [Capitalism and Schizophrenia], L'Anti-Oedipe [Anti-Oedipus* 1972] and *Mille plateaux [A Thousand Plateaus* 1980]. *L'Anti-Oedipe* is a critique of the capitalist era as a time when the tyrannical state and the oedipalized individual have been fostered by political and psychiatric institutions to the detriment of the more liberatory group and 'sub-individual' (the human as a body of variant and unorganized desires). *Mille plateaux* uses the terms of this critique to extend the analysis into various pre-capitalist pasts and a post-capitalist future, thereby working to displace and marginalize the present capitalist and oedipalized era. Although it is impossible to separate the contributions of the two men to this project, the two key terms of the work, capitalism and schizophrenia, indicate an alignment with the basic interests of Guattari's work from the 1950s onwards: the critique of capitalism and of institutional psychiatric practice. Guattari's own work, however, is much

less concerned than Deleuze's with a reading of sympathetic literary and philosophical figures of the Western tradition, such as Spinoza, *Nietzsche and Proust.

Guattari has produced a substantial body of work independent of Deleuze as well as in collaboration with a number of others, including Jean Oury (the founder of the Clinique de la Borde), the Italian Marxist Toni Negri and the Brazilian psychoanalyst Suely Rolnik. An elaboration and application of earlier concepts developed with Deleuze such as schizoanalysis, the micropolitics of desire, molecular revolution, and the importance of understanding human activity as machinic, these works reveal Guattari's search for 'new spaces of freedom' outside of the restrictions of Western capitalism and East Bloc socialism.

Guattari's reconfiguration of psychoanalysis and Marxism, especially in his work with Deleuze, has yet to receive adequate evaluation, which would work through its many insights and limitations. Although the specifically literary is not Guattari's overriding concern, his work could be made use of in any politically or psychoanalytically informed literary theory, critique or practice, and has influenced, for instance, the writings of German dramatist and theorist Heiner Müller.

MARK FORTIER

Primary Sources

Guattari, Félix. *Les Années d'hiver: 1980–1985*. Paris: Barrault, 1986.
– *Cartographies schizoanalytiques*. Paris: Galilée, 1989.
– *L'Inconscient machinique: Essais de schizo-analyse*. Paris: Recherches, 1979.
– *Psychanalyse et transversalité*. Paris: Maspero, 1972.
– *La Révolution moléculaire*. Paris: Recherches, 1977. *Molecular Revolution: Psychiatry and Politics*. Trans. Rosemary Sheed. New York: Penguin, 1984.
– *Les Trois écologies*. Paris: Galilée, 1989.
– and Gilles Deleuze. *Capitalisme et schizophrénie 1. L'Anti-Oedipe*. Paris: Minuit, 1972. *Anti-Oedipus*. Trans. Robert Hurley, Mark Seem and Helen R. Lane. New York: Viking, 1977.
– and Gilles Deleuze. *Kafka: Pour une littérature mineur*. Paris: Minuit, 1975. *Kafka: For a Minor Literature*. Trans. Dana Polan. Minneapolis: U of Minnesota P, 1986.
– and Gilles Deleuze. *Capitalisme et schizophrénie 2: Mille Plateaux*. Paris: Minuit, 1980. *A Thousand Plateaus: Capitalism and Schizophrenia*. Trans. Brian

Massumi. Minneapolis: U of Minnesota P, 1987.
- Eugenio Miccini and Luigi Serravalli. *Sarenco.* Paris: Veyrier H., 1988.
- and Toni Negri. *Les Nouveaux espaces de liberté.* Paris: Dominique Bedou, 1985. *Communists Like Us: New Spaces of Liberty, New Lines of Alliance.* Trans. Michael Ryan. New York: Semiotext(e), 1990.
- Jean Oury and Jean Tosquelles. *Pratique de l'institutionnel et politique.* Paris: Matrice, 1986.
- and Suely Rolnik. *Micropolitica: Cartografias do Desejo.* Petropolis, Brazil: Vozes, 1986.

Gubar, Susan David: *see* Gilbert, Sandra Mortola, and Susan David Gubar.

Habermas, Jürgen

(b. Germany, 1929–) Philosopher. Having received his doctorate at the University of Bonn, Habermas worked as an assistant to *Theodor Adorno and Max Horkheimer at the Institute for Social Research in Frankfurt. (See *Frankfurt School.) In 1961 he received the *Habilitation* degree from the University of Mainz and began teaching in Heidelberg where he was a colleague of *Hans-Georg Gadamer. Three years later he was named professor of philosophy at Frankfurt. His stay there was cut short when he was censured for having supported the German student protests of 1967–9. Since 1971 Habermas has been a member of the Max Planck Institute in Starnberg, where he is now co-director and visiting professor in Frankfurt. His first important book was *Communication and the Evolution of Society* (1962). *Knowledge and Human Interests,* his first philosophical work (1968), marked the beginning of his still growing influence in the English-speaking world. In these two books he displays a mastery of and participation in the hermeneutic tradition. His work, together with that of *Paul Ricoeur, has been influential in bringing together humanities and social sciences under the scrutiny of a philosophical interpretation. (See *hermeneutics.)

To understand Habermas' complex philosophy of communication one must begin with his fundamental premise that the two essential types of human action are work and communication. Work is the purposeful, rational use of tools for the satisfaction of human needs; communication is interaction through which

the knowing subject comes to know himself or herself through the eyes of others. The separation is essential since it is commonplace to be liberated from material want and still be enslaved in the ideological prison of institutional language.

The major contribution Habermas has made to hermeneutics must be put into the context of his debate with Gadamer, which begins with his 1967 review of *Truth and Method* but continues through his constant re-elaboration of his own work in response to Gadamer's powerful argument. The differences between the two thinkers come down to one essential point: Gadamer holds that there are no privileged positions which can be construed as being outside of history since there can be no interpreter without language. The aim of phenomenological hermeneutics is not to bring a certain aspect of the world under theoretical control or to clear away institutional propaganda of vested interests through a critique of *ideology. (See also *phenomenological criticism.) Rather, phenomenological hermeneutics hopes to arrive at understanding through dialogue, first with others in one's own culture but also with others from other cultures and from the past. Habermas retorts that it is impossible to have a dialogue with someone who is trapped in the ideological webs of social institutions and whose only function is self-aggrandizement. In order to have a dialogue both partners must be free of institutional ideology in the domain of communication. To pursue the challenge posed by Gadamerian hermeneutics, Habermas developed an ever more comprehensive and ambitious program of ideological critique, his Universal Pragmatics. This program has five main points: (1) that the very act of dialogue implicitly makes truth-claims; (2) that all speakers who are communicatively competent operate on the basis of pragmatic universals; (3) that in order to study communication the philosopher has to construct an ideal speech situation but that this construct is present in everyday speech as a pragmatic assumption; (4) that truth is a truth-claim which can be rationally judged to have validity in the *discourse of the ideal speech situation; and (5) that human vested interests when institutionalized become social belief systems or ideologies which preclude social interaction. (See universal.)

A closer look at these five basic points brings out the fundamental agreement and disagreement between Gadamer and Habermas and reveals the grounds for Ricoeur's mediation in the debate. The first point about the implicit truth-claims of speaking to another person in dialogue can be summed up this way. When two persons have a successful spoken interchange, it is because a relation has been established in which they have come to an understanding about something. This relationship can be explained only through the recognition that some things have been said as implicit truth-claims and that these have been recognized by both partners. The fundamental assumption is that understanding is the basic aim of communication. The second aim of Habermas' program is that of the pragmatic universals of dialogue. Habermas argues that for two persons to engage in dialogue both speakers must be aware of each other as subjects, must be aware of the world around them and, third, must be able to distinguish between the two. The two speakers draw upon the linguistic tools available to establish this recognition and distinction. Habermas claims that these are universals of communication which are pragmatically established. A third aim is the establishment of the ideal speech situation. Dialogue assumes that it is possible and desirable for the two speakers to come to some agreement. To come to an agreement does not mean that one speaker overpowers or intimidates the other but that the agreement is based exclusively on reason. This ideal situation, however, is impossible if there are any external or internal constraints such as fear, timidity or ignorance. The aim of the ideal situation is to serve as a goal toward which a systematic critique might strive. The fourth aim is to establish truth. The truth-claim, which can be explicit or implicit, must be judged as to its validity on the basis of a rational consensus among all the speakers. This consensus can only be arrived at through free dialogue. The fifth aim is to establish a systematic critique of ideology that would enhance the possibilities of speakers to solve human problems and differences through dialogue.

Gadamer insists that there is no philosophical justification for the assertion that by means of a systematic critique it is possible to combat the effects of ideology. Since all speakers can only speak through language which is made through the values and value systems of the community of speakers, any critique does not rise above ideology; it revises, supplants and adjusts ideologies. Habermas' response is that

Gadamer has not considered the institutional formation of ideology which supports the vested economic and political interests of these institutions. Not personal belief systems but institutionally devised ones are the impediment to communication. Therefore, a systematic study of social communication must be aimed at removing the barriers of ideology operating under the pretence of truth.

In literary theory Habermas' philosophy provides a powerful attack on what *Fredric Jameson has called the 'political unconscious'; Habermas' argument also conforms with Ricoeur's view that the final aim of interpretation is to redescribe the world of action of both critic and readers. (See also *speech act theory, *communication theory.)

MARIO J. VALDÉS

Primary Sources

Habermas, Jürgen. *Communication and the Evolution of Society*. Trans. T. McCarthy. Boston: Beacon P, 1979.
– 'Habermas Talking: An Interview.' By Boris Frankel. In *Theory and Society* 1 (1974): 37–5.
– *Knowledge and Human Interests*. Trans. J.J. Shapiro. Boston: Beacon P, 1975.
– *Legitimation Crisis*. Trans. T. McCarthy. Boston: Beacon P, 1975.
– *The Philosophical Discourse of Modernity*. Trans. Frederick Lawrence. Cambridge, Mass.: MIT P, 1987.
– 'A Review of Gadamer's *Truth and Method*.' 1967. In *Understanding and Social Inquiry*. Ed. F. Dallmayr and T. McCarthy. Notre Dame, Ind.: Notre Dame UP, 1977, 335–63.
– *Theory and Practice*. Trans. J. Viertel. Boston: Beacon P, 1973.
– *Toward a Rational Society: Student Protests, Science and Politics*. Trans. J.J. Shapiro. Boston: Beacon P, 1970.

Secondary Sources

Bernstein, Richard. *The Restructuring of Social and Political Thought*. Oxford: Basil Blackwell, 1976.
Giddens, Anthony. *New Rules of Sociological Method: A Positive Critique of Interpretive Sociologies*. London: Hutchinson, 1976.
Guess, Raymond. *The Idea of a Critical Theory: Habermas and the Frankfurt School*. Cambridge UP, 1981.
Held, David. *Introduction to Critical Theory: Horkheimer to Habermas*. London: Hutchinson, 1980.
McCarthy, Thomas. *The Critical Theory of Jürgen Habermas*. Cambridge, Mass.: MIT P, 1978.

O'Neil, John, ed. *On Critical Theory*. New York: Seabury, 1976.

Ricoeur, Paul. 'Hermeneutics and the Critique of Ideology.' In *Hermeneutics and the Human Sciences*. Ed. and trans. John B. Thompson. Cambridge: Cambridge UP, 1981, 63–100.

– *Lectures on Ideology and Utopia*. Ed. George H. Taylor. New York: Columbia UP, 1986, 216–53.

Thompson, John B. *Critical Hermeneutics*. Cambridge: Cambridge UP, 1981.

– and David Held. *Habermas: Critical Debates*. Cambridge, Mass.: MIT P, 1982.

Hartman, Geoffrey H.

(b. Germany, 1929–) Author, editor, literary critic, and educator. The Karl Young Professor of English and Comparative Literature at Yale University, where he received his Ph.D., Hartman has published widely on biblical texts, contemporary *literature, cultural criticism, and Holocaust studies, though his chief contributions to criticism have been in the areas of Romanticism and literary theory. Since the publication of his first book, *The Unmediated Vision* (1954), Hartman has been known best for his work on the poetry of William Wordsworth.

At the centre of Hartman's approach to the study of literature is his conception of the interpreter or reader who stands not in a subservient relation to the literary work, merely illuminating or explicating it, but who rather engages the *text in a dialogue that also reveals the creativity of the reader. Interpretive commentary itself thus becomes a text that legitimately can be regarded as a form of creative writing. While Hartman is a close reader of texts, he is never content with merely local explication, but rather always seeks to make his reading address larger issues of literary history, genre, the nature of literary language, or the practice of criticism itself.

For Hartman, conventional academic prose style needs to be liberated to offer the critic the same range of rhetorical and stylistic freedoms that the literary author possesses. Specifically, this more adventurous style of Hartman's results in a greater degree of playfulness, punning and rhetorical brilliance than is traditionally found in Anglo-American literary criticism. Hartman's method tends to operate on the level of the signifier, exercising the associative, echoic or sylleptic resources of language. (See *signified/signifier/signification.) Yet stabilizing the verbal ingenuity is the ground of scholarly argument, the close reading thoroughly informed by literary history or by the implicit acknowledgment of critical decorum.

As a comparatist, Hartman has always been attuned to traditions and developments in Continental criticism and theory. His approach has shifted from phenomenological modes of criticism in the 1950s and 1960s toward the more linguistically oriented methodologies of the 1970s and 1980s, finding a genial spirit in the emergence of *Jacques Derrida and *poststructuralism, and producing some of his best essays in response to the new wave of theory. (See *phenomenological criticism.)

Despite his close association with *deconstruction and the 'Yale School' of criticism, Hartman was never dogmatic in his adoption of poststructuralist principles, never truly an adherent, maintaining rather a Blakean scepticism of systems. There were, however, many aspects of poststructuralism in general and deconstruction in particular that attracted Hartman: greater interpretive freedom for commentary and the commentator, legitimation of a creative critical style, new techniques for understanding literary language and, perhaps above all, the necessity of theory itself. Though Hartman's interest in theory predates the rise of poststructuralism – even his earliest works reveal considerable theoretical preoccupations – there is no doubt that the rise of theory as a discipline was felt by Hartman as both necessary and liberating in the history of literary studies.

In *Wordsworth's Poetry 1787–1814* (1964), which won the Christian Gauss Award, Hartman presents an influential reading of Wordsworth in which Nature and Imagination engage each other in a 'drama of consciousness.' Proceeding from the definition that Wordsworthian imagination is 'consciousness of self raised to apocalyptic pitch,' Hartman traces the development of Wordsworth's fearful understanding that Nature would lead the poet beyond Nature; the drama that is played out in Wordsworth's poetry thus necessitates what Hartman calls the 'humanizing of imagination,' the conversion of a mighty apocalyptic vision into a poetry of earth. Yet the struggle of conversion, as Hartman demonstrates, is problematic and never completely successful; Wordsworth's visionary imagination remains in conflict with and in excess of any exquisite fitting to the world.

Hartman's book introduced a new level of theoretical sophistication to Wordsworth studies and made the 'apocalyptic' Wordsworth the centre of critical discussion for decades. It also argued for placing Wordsworth and Romanticism in the larger context of classical, Renaissance and 18th-century literary traditions. Though Hartman did not emphasize theory itself in *Wordsworth's Poetry*, preferring instead to subordinate psychology and phenomenology to his close reading of the theme of consciousness, he prepared the way for Romantic literature and Wordsworth especially to emerge as a proving ground for newer theories. His recent book *The Unremarkable Wordsworth* (1987), a collection of his essays on Wordsworth written since the appearance of *Wordsworth's Poetry* in 1964, demonstrates a number of such theoretical approaches to the study of Wordsworth, including *structuralism, psychoanalysis, deconstruction, and *semiotics. (See also *psychoanalytic theory.)

The one element that has informed all of Hartman's work from the beginning, first as a mode of thought, and more recently as an explicit *theme, is his interest in Judaic studies, particularly Holocaust education and the practice of Midrash, a form of interpretation of sacred Jewish texts that focuses on narrative gaps or discontinuities. As cofounder and director of the Video Archive for Holocaust Testimonies at Yale University, Hartman has acted as adviser to many projects on Holocaust education and remembrance, including the United States Holocaust Memorial Council. He has also written essays and edited volumes on social and political aspects of the Holocaust and on Midrashic readings of biblical and other literary texts.

J. DOUGLAS KNEALE

Primary Sources

Hartman, Geoffrey H. *André Malraux*. London: Bowes and Bowes; New York: Hilary House, 1960.
- *Beyond Formalism: Literary Essays 1958–1970*. New Haven: Yale UP, 1970.
- *Criticism in the Wilderness: The Study of Literature Today*. Yale UP, 1980.
- *Easy Pieces*. New York: Columbia UP, 1985.
- *The Fate of Reading and Other Essays*. Chicago: U of Chicago P, 1975.
- *Minor Prophecies: The Literary Essay in the Culture Wars*. Cambridge: Harvard UP, 1991.

- *Saving the Text: Literature/Derrida/Philosophy*. Baltimore: Johns Hopkins UP, 1981.
- *The Unmediated Vision. An Interpretation of Wordsworth, Hopkins, Rilke and Valéry*. New Haven: Yale UP, 1954.
- *The Unremarkable Wordsworth*. Minneapolis: U of Minnesota P, 1987.
- *Wordsworth's Poetry 1787–1814*. New Haven: Yale UP, 1964; 2nd ed. 1967; 3rd ed. 1971; Harvard Paperbound, 1987.
- *Bitburg in Moral and Political Perspective*. Bloomington: Indiana UP, 1986.
- *Canon and Commentary*. With Moshe Idel. New Haven: Yale UP, 1992.
- *Hopkins: A Selection of Critical Essays*. Prentice-Hall, 1966.
- *Midrash and Literature*. With Sanford Budick. New Haven: Yale UP, 1986.
- *New Perspectives on Coleridge and Wordsworth*. New York: Columbia UP, 1972.
- *Psychoanalysis and the Question of the Text*. Baltimore: Johns Hopkins UP, 1978.
- *Romanticism: Vistas, Instances, Continuities*. With David Thorburn. Ithaca: Cornell UP, 1973.
- *Shakespeare and the Question of Theory*. With Patricia Parker. London: Methuen, 1985.
- *Shapes of Memory*. London: Blackwell, 1992.
- *Wordsworth: Selected Poetry and Prose*. New York: Signet, 1970.

Heidegger, Martin

(b. Germany, 1889–d. 1976) Philosopher. A student of *Edmund Husserl, Martin Heidegger emerged from and transformed the phenomenological movement and the hermeneutic tradition of continental philosophy. He taught at Marburg (1923–8) and Freiburg im Breisgau (1928–44) and was briefly rector of Freiburg University (1933–4). Heidegger's work has influenced much contemporary thought: existentialists (*Jean-Paul Sartre), Marxists and poststructuralists (*Jacques Derrida, *Jean Baudrillard) have taken up his critique of modern society, technology and the '*logocentrism' of metaphysics. Ontological *hermeneutics (*Hans-Georg Gadamer, *Paul Ricoeur) owes much to Heidegger's understanding of language and history. (See also *phenomenological criticism, *Marxist criticism, *poststructuralism.)

Heidegger's first studies were theological and through many transformations the question of the relation of the logos to the divine remained central to all his work. By his own account, the central question of Heidegger's thought is the question of being: what does it mean to say that a human being, a thing, a work is, each in its own way, in being? Heidegger's investigation of this question – which is both 'systematic' and 'historical' – calls for the radical dismantling and recovery on a more primordial ground of the entire metaphysical tradition, from its Greek beginnings to its consummation in and dissolution into the technological practices and metadiscourses of our time. The question of art, in turn, is implicated in the being-question and Heidegger thus calls for the abandonment of the metaphysical premises of aesthetics.

One may distinguish at least six major phases in his thought directly or indirectly pertinent to an exploration of the arts: (1) *Sein und Zeit* [*Being and Time* 1927] and the lectures on mood – *Die Grundbegriffe der Metaphysik* (1929–30) – the first remains the starting point for any reflection on a 'Heideggerian' literary theory; (2) 'The Origin of the Work of Art' (1936) and the *Beiträge zur Philosophie* (*Vom Ereignis* 1936–8), its systematic context; (3) the Hölderlin lectures (volumes 39, 52 and 53 in the complete edition); (4) Heidegger's recovery of *Friedrich Nietzsche's aesthetics (The Will to Power as Art* 1936–7); (5) the late essays on language and poetry collected in *On the Way to Language* (1959); (6) essays on technology and the fate of art and thought in the technological era (*Discourse on Thinking* 1959; 'The Question Concerning Technology' 1953). The question of art as it is posed within the horizon of technology is the essential source of Heidegger's reflection on art. The arts, in Heidegger's estimation, have the potential of bringing to light and 'in-corporating' the dynamic event of the arrival and departure of beings into being in the face of a technological modelling of all that is as static, 'finished' products on line and on call.

Sein und Zeit (1927), Heidegger's first major work, has as its goal the analysis of the structure of human being taken as a clue to the investigation of the meaning – the different possible senses – of being. Human being, or *Da-sein*, is understood as openness-to-being: *Dasein* is the site where beings manifest themselves. The analysis of language, truth and 'emotion' carried out in this work, while far removed from the specific concerns of literary theory, nonetheless offers the basis for a radical reappraisal of *literature (Corngold; Marshall). The language of poetry has traditionally

been regarded as being without 'truth value.' In the formulation of *I.A. Richards, it is composed of 'pseudo-statements' which are parasitical (*J.L. Austin) upon 'normal' language use: given that poetic devices have a merely decorative function without cognitive insight, the chief 'value' of poetry finally resolves itself into its ability to communicate sincerely the emotion of the speaker. This account rests on the assumptions that the pre-eminent form of language use is the propositional schema of the statement and that truth is a property of the proposition.

In deconstructing this metaphysical doctrine, Heidegger allows that the origin of truth is not the proposition but the disclosure of the things themselves. (See *deconstruction.) For in order for a statement to say truely or falsely about something, thus corresponding or failing to correspond to it, the things must already be manifest. Truth as the openness of manifestation, as the 'unhiddenness' of beings (the Greek *aletheia*), is the condition of the 'truth' of the statement. The statement, moreover, is just one, derivative way in which things can be disclosed and thus become meaningful. What Heidegger calls *discourse (die Rede) – understood as the articulation or 'jointedness' of the meaningfulness of *Dasein*'s being in the world – articulates itself more primordially in other forms of disclosure – for example, in action, in silence and in art works. The power of literature to disclose, therefore, cannot be judged by the criterion of the proposition. The truth of the artwork ultimately rests on its power to found a structure of meaning or 'world.' Propositional language-use makes statements about aspects of the already founded and is in this sense less primordial than the linguistic work.

Inasmuch as Heidegger deconstructs the metaphysics of subjectivity he also distances himself from the long-standing aesthetic problems associated with the concept of 'aesthetic emotions' and attempts to ground the nature of 'emotion' in the fundamental structure of *Dasein*. Human being is always open – and at the same time closed – to beings; we are always already prereflectively disposed to our being in the world as a whole. Disposition (*die Befindlichkeit*), which opens the whole of what is to us to disclose and conceal our world, expresses itself through different ways of being attuned (*die Stimmung*) to and at one with things. Emotions arise out of our being-attuned, out of the rhythm of our involvement with things. Heidegger argues that the 'subject' in its self-consciousness and the 'objective' world of 'facts' are equally derivative abstractions from the unitary structure of a given rhythm. In Heidegger's estimation, literary works (as well as other art forms) play an essential role in communicating attunements or moods. The work discloses the meaningful whole of a set of relations. In effect, it manifests the possibilities for being of a fictional world by giving expression to the governing moods which modulate the work to attune the different modes of being presented in it – the being of humans, of nature, of the divinities – to each other. The *modes* of attunement of the 'chain of being,' as presented in a literary work, would correspond in some respect to the traditional plot forms which developed in the course of literary history. By the same measure, tropes articulate the interconnectedness and mutual sympathy of different modes of being on the microlevel of the work: hence, Dylan Thomas' 'the force that through the green fuse drives the flower,/ Drives my green age' gathers the human, organic and inorganic into one articulated whole.

In later works (in his Hölderlin lectures), Heidegger argues that artworks have the potential to inaugurate, as well as to structure and communicate, fundamental attunements; their disclosive power is therefore more primordial than that of rational discourse, for reason always operates within a horizon of disclosure opened up by an attunement. Every attunement is historical, not merely in that a certain 'Zeitgeist' agitates an era, but that the basic, prereflective understanding inherent in an attunement establishes the rhythm of the interrelatedness of beings, the how of their manifestation, and that this rhythm of manifestation inaugurates what we call a 'period' of history. 'Renaissance melancholy,' 'Romantic agony,' and the stylistic periods of art history, for example, may thus be read as conceptualizations of an attunement to beings as a whole. The same goes for current attempts to define *postmodernism by describing its characteristic mood (is it boredom? or panic?).

Heidegger's 'The Origin of the Work of Art' (1936), his first major essay dedicated entirely to the question of art, is central to his development of the question of being, *die Seinsfrage*. While the 'Origin' does not deal with the issue of the meaning of technology, it is within the horizon of this question that the essay has to be understood to be made fruitful for us. Two key questions are posed: (1) Why art? What necessity for this kind of event and this kind of being in the technological epoch?; (2) Why the artwork? What 'originates' the work and in what sense is the work itself an origin?

In his analysis of 'world' in *Sein und Zeit*, Heidegger begins with a consideration of equipment and its use. The being of equipment, of a tool such as a hammer, for example, is circumscribed by its servicability and fulfils this being when it unobtrusively 'disappears' into the work-context where it is serviceable. The particular world, moreover, which gives the use of the tool in its immediate work-context its 'rationale,' also withdraws from view as long as tools function without breakdown. As Heidegger's late discussions of technology will propose, the smooth frictionless functioning of equipment totalities is the *telos* of the technological ordering of the modern 'world.' By 'world,' however, Heidegger ultimately understands the *event*, the open horizon of meaningfulness which constitutes the wherefore and why of technological mastery. 'World' in this dynamic sense is dissimulated by the functioning of the system of production because it aims at presenting all that is as available (or unavailable) stock. Whereas equipment disappears into its functioning, and becomes the function of an equipmental context, art has the power to 'save' the phenomena by allowing each thing to come into its own and shine forth as that which it is. The artwork acts as a kind of midwife to manifestation, which is to say, to the emergence of truth; its truth-potential is greater than that of equipment in the rank order of beings because it allows the things to be – to come into their own – more fully. In the late essays collected in *On the Way to Language* Heidegger allows that it is ultimately the essence of language as 'saying' (*die Sage*) which calls upon things to show, to 'own' themselves as that which they are. The structure of the artwork, moreover, manifests the world-as-event, bringing it out of the concealment into which it is cast by the opacity of technological functioning. In this way, by bringing a world to light, and by saving the phenomena from becoming transparent functions and weightless simulacra of themselves, art becomes necessary to the manifestation of the being of beings.

The art*work* comprehends the structure of an event which includes the artist (who comes into being through the work) and the 'audience' (*die Bewahrenden* – the 'preservers') – which 'preserves' the work by letting the work happen, put itself to work, in their lives. Only in a derivative sense, therefore, is the work an object of aesthetic contemplation defined by its formal qualities. In Heidegger's estimation, the object-being of art, which is inscribed by cultural critique, institutionalization and the economics of the art industry, is a relatively static representation and derivation of its work-being. But neither is the literary work, for example, a '*text*' understood as a subsystem of signifiers fading away at the edges, as it were, into the context of 'writing in general.' (See *signified/signifier/signification.) The work has its own, unique self-subsistence and shines forth within the limits set by its form. The self-subsistence of the work, which withdraws it from the grasp of conceptuality, is what Heidegger calls 'earth.' The work unites in a fruitful strife the intelligibility of a world and the self-seclusion and withdrawal of earth. The way in which a historical earth and world are attuned to each other gives the work its unique structure. It is precisely as *this* unique 'thing' that the work *works* and it works by enacting and incorporating the event of the emergence of beings. But emergence into manifestation is itself the primordial sense of 'truth.' Hence the origin of the work is the happening of truth, inasmuch as it incorporates itself in a being. With this incorporation, the work itself becomes an origin: for just as a sculpture, one of Henry Moore's 'Reclining Figures' for example, creates its *own* space, so the work opens up a new site, and new possibilities for being emerge from the rhythm it establishes in the midst of beings. The work 'legislates' by setting the measure for beings by overthrowing conventional ways of seeing to found a new law.

Broadly speaking, Heidegger's explication and 'mystical' reflections on Hölderlin may be considered as a more concrete working out of the conditions of authentic community and historicity first broached in *Being in Time*. The lectures devoted to this poet mark a crucial turning in Heidegger's thought: for example, the potential of art will be unrealized and the work remain a truncated fragment as long as the earth does not become a homeland (*Heimat*) to its peoples. The homeland has nothing to do with the modern nation-state, for this collective entity is conditioned by the metaphysical tradition beyond which Heidegger seeks to go. The homeland rather *is* as the healing whole of the mutual attunement of a people and their earth. This attunement realizes itself in the festival when the wholeness of the homeland sends itself to humanity in the guise of the messengers (the gods) of the holy. The poet receives these messengers and incorporates their message in the work ('Hölderlin and the Essence of Poetry').

The seemingly hermetic character of Heidegger's encounter with Hölderlin apparently offers no way, no methodology, which might guide us toward the 'same' goal or insight. Hence the frustration of many commentators (de Man, Fynsk). Yet Heidegger would argue that his approach to Hölderlin is as rigorously phenomenological (although in a transformed sense) as his description of *Dasein* in *Sein und Zeit*. In fact, it can be argued that Heidegger's *way* to the things themselves, including the poem, cannot be a methodology. In section 77 of the *Beiträge*, entitled 'Sätze über "die Wissenschaft"' ('Statements concerning "Science"'), Heidegger takes issue with the premises of the modern sciences (*die Wissenschaft* includes the human as well as the natural sciences). Heidegger does not consider science – and thus also literary theory and criticism to the extent they aspire to formulate a methodology and become systematic – as a form of knowledge, but rather as the derivative institutionalization of a knowledge of the truth (the manifestation) of beings. Hence every attempt to formulate a methodological approach to poetry would exclude itself from the *truth* of poetry (which does not mean that a methodology could not ascertain much that is *correct*). Literary theory predetermines the totality of its object area or field as already known in advance. Its investigations amount to determinations of the correctness or incorrectness of statements within the field of the given. It is precisely this presupposition, that poetry belongs to the already-given, which Heidegger questions (poetry is rather the radical overthrow of the given if it 'is' – in being [as origin] – at all). Confirmed in its object-being, on the other hand, poetry ceases to be poetry and becomes 'literature'; but with the progressive triumph and pre-eminence of methodology ('theory') over its subject area, even the object-being of the work implodes – it becomes 'text.' Defined as a cultural object or an ideological structure, as an expression of the artist or a formal system, the work is not in being *as* a work but merely makes itself available in some derivative objectification or function of itself and the general economy which circumscribes it. A 'reform' of method, moreover, cannot change this state of affairs, because what counts methodologically is the production of results, not the essential truth of its subject. A turn in our relation to poetry, Heidegger maintains, is only possible within the horizon of a fundamentally new attunement to the whole of what is: only when we cease to think primarily in categories of production and consumption can poetry come into its own again. While we cannot *will* such a turn to come about, a turn in our attunement to beings can 'overcome' us insofar as we are open to the mystery of the withdrawal of beings – which postmodernism experiences as the implosion of phenomena – from the vice-grip of technological calculation.

BERNHARD RADLOFF

Primary Sources

Heidegger, Martin. *Beiträge zur Philosophie (Vom Ereignis).* Gesamtausgabe (GA), vol. 65. Frankfurt/Main: Klostermann, 1989.
– 'Das Ende der Philosophie und die Aufgabe des Denkens.' In *Zur Sache des Denkens.* Tübingen: Niemeyer, 1969. Trans. 'The End of Philosophy and the Task of Thinking.' In *Basic Writings.* Ed. David Farrell Knell. New York: Harper, 1977, 369–92.
– 'Die Frage nach der Technik.' In *Vorträge und Aufsätze.* Pfullingen: Neske, 1954. Trans. 'The Question Concerning Technology.' In *Basic Writings,* 283–317.
– *Gelassenheit.* Pfullingen: Neske, 1959. Trans. John M. Anderson, E.H. Freund. *Discourse on Thinking.* New York: Harper, 1966, 43–57.
– *Die Grundbegriffe der Metaphysik. Welt-Endlichkeit-Einsamkeit.* GA vols. 29–30, 1983.
– 'Die Herkunft der Kunst und die Bestimmung des Denkens.' In *Denkerfahrungen.* Frankfurt/Main: Klostermann, 1983.
– *Hölderlins Hymne 'Andenken.'* GA vol. 52, 1982.
– *Hölderlins Hymnen 'Germanien' und 'Der Rhein.'* GA vol. 39, 1980.
– *Hölderlins Hymne 'Der Ister.'* GA vols. 53, 1984.
– 'Hölderlin und das Wesen der Dichtung.' In *Erlauterungen zu Höderlins Dichtung.* GA vols. 4, 33–49. Trans. Douglas Scott. 'Hölderlin and the Essence

of Poetry.' In *Existence and Being.* Ed. Werner Brock. Chicago: Regnery, 1949, 291–315.
– *Nietzsche I: Der Wille zur Macht als Kunst.* Pfullingen: Neske, 1961. Trans. David Farrell Krell. *Nietzsche I: The Will to Power as Art.* New York: Harper, 1979.
– *Sein und Zeit.* Tübingen: Niemeyer, 1927. Trans. John Macquarrie, Edward Robinson. *Being in Time.* London: SCM, 1962.
– *Unterwegs zur Sprache.* Tübingen: Neske, 1959. Trans. Peter D. Hertz. *On the Way to Language.* New York: Harper, 1971.
– 'Der Ursprung des Kunstwerkes.' In *Holzwege.* Frankfurt/Main: Klostermann, 1950. Trans. Albert Hofstadler. 'The Origin of the Work of Art.' In *Poetry, Language, Thought.* New York: Harper, 1971, 17–87.
– 'Wozu Dichter.' In *Holzwege,* 265–316. Trans. Albert Hofstadler. 'What Are Poets For?' In *Poetry, Language, Thought,* 89–142.

Secondary Works

Bruns, Gerald L. *Heidegger's Estrangements. Language, Truth and Poetry in the Later Writings.* New Haven: Yale UP, 1989.
Corngold, Stanley. '*Sein und Zeit*: Implications for Poetics.' *boundary* 2 4 (Winter 1976): 439–55.
Fynsk, Christopher. *Heidegger: Thought and Historicity.* Ithaca: Cornell, 1986.
Gadamer, Hans-Georg. *Philosophical Hermeneutics.* Trans. David E. Linge. Berkeley: U of California P, 1976.
Haar, Michel. 'Le Primat de la *Stimmung* sur la corporéité du *Dasein.*' *Heidegger Studies* 2 (1986): 67–79.
Halliburton, David. *Poetic Thinking: An Approach to Heidegger.* Chicago: U of Chicago P, 1981.
von Herrmann, F.W. *Heideggers Philosophie der Kunst.* Frankfurt/Main: Klostermann, 1980.
Kockelmans, Joseph J. *Heidegger and Science.* Washington: UP of America, 1985.
– *Heidegger on Art and Art Works.* Dordrecht: Martinus Nijhoff, 1985.
Levin, David Michael. 'Logos and Psyche: A Hermeneutics of Breathing.' *Research in Phenomenology* 14 (1984): 121–47.
de Man, Paul. 'Heidegger's Exegesis of Hölderlin.' Trans. Wlad Godzich. In *Blindness and Insight.* Minneapolis: U of Minnesota P, 1983, 246–66.
Marshall, Donald. 'The Ontology of the Literary Sign: Notes Toward a Heideggerian Revision of Semiology.' In *Martin Heidegger and the Question of Literature.* Ed. William V. Spanos. Bloomington: Indiana UP, 1979.
McCormick, Peter. *Heidegger and the Language of the World.* Ottawa: U of Ottawa P, 1976.
Metha, J.L. *The Philosophy of Martin Heidegger.* New York: Harper, 1971.

Palmier, Jean Michel. *Les Ecrits politiques de Heidegger*. Paris: Editions de l'Herne, 1968.

Vycinas, Vincent. *Earth and Gods: An Introduction to the Philosophy of Martin Heidegger*. The Hague: Martinus Nijhoff, 1969.

Hirsch, E(ric) D(onald), Jr.

(b. U.S.A., 1928–) Literary critic, educator. Educated at Cornell (B.A. 1950) and Yale (M.A. 1953; Ph.D. 1957), E.D. Hirsch taught in the English departments of Yale (1956–60) and the University of Virginia (1966–) where he was named William R. Kenan Professor in 1973. Although he has written substantial works on a variety of topics, including Wordsworth, Blake and the principles of teaching composition, his two major contributions are both ultimately hermeneutical in the broad sense of that term. (See *hermeneutics.) The first, with which Hirsch's name was primarily identified from the moment 'Objective Interpretation' appeared until the publication of *Cultural Literacy* (1987), is the argument for the possibility and, in general, the necessity of reconstructing an author's intended meaning ('Objective Interpretation' 1960). The second, presented in *Cultural Literacy*, is that to understand even simple texts the reader must necessarily possess a minimum knowledge of the culture – the knowledge that authors assume to be shared by their intended readers. (See *text.)

'Objective Interpretation' is a direct challenge to two approaches to the interpretation of *literature that were powerful at the time of writing. First, it denies what was widely understood to be an essential dogma of *New Criticism, that literary texts are to be understood without regard to authorial intention, the historical circumstances surrounding their composition, or biographical information about the author. Second, Hirsch's essay denies the doctrine of the school of hermeneutics (deriving primarily from *Hans-Georg Gadamer) that it is impossible to recover the historical situation of a text sufficiently to understand the author's intended meaning.

Hirsch's thesis is elaborated in *Validity in Interpretation* (1967) in which he distinguishes between 'verbal meaning'– the object of 'understanding' – and 'significance' – the object of 'criticism.' 'Verbal meaning is whatever someone has willed to convey by a particular sequence of linguistic signs and which can be conveyed (shared) by means of those linguistic signs' (31). (See *sign.) 'Understanding' is the reader's construction of verbal meaning, that is, of the author's intention as embodied in the text. 'Interpretation' is the explanation of such meaning. 'Significance' results from the reader's judgment about the text's relationship to his or her view of the world, theoretical assumptions, individual interests, and personal experience. The meaning of a work is always synonymous with the author's intention; significance alters with historical change and personal predilection. The argument is not that one can be certain of an author's intended meaning as it is embodied in the text, but rather that nothing forbids the possibility of a correct understanding. 'It is a logical mistake to confuse the impossibility of certainty in understanding with the impossibility of understanding' (17). In other words, a reader's understanding can never be more than probable, but careful attention to genre, authorship, date of composition, external context, and internal structure can greatly increase the probability. (See also *genre criticism, *genetic criticism.) 'Validation' of an interpreation is achieved by demonstrating that one's construction of the meaning is the most probable in the light of all one can discover. Hirsch never denies that criticism, the seeking of significance, is valuable and indeed often the primary source of our interest in literature. However, he insists that understanding of the author's intended meaning is logically and psychologically prior to consideration of significance.

The Aims of Interpretation (1976) clarifies and develops these positions, while taking into account the assertions of Continental philosophy concerning the *indeterminacy of textual meaning and the separation of the text from the question of authorial intention. (See *intention/intentionality.) *The Aims of Interpretation* is therefore directed against *Martin Heidegger and *Jacques Derrida as much as against the New Critics. Here Hirsch pursues the concept of understanding and interpretation as based on 'corrigible schema' (a phrase from Jean Piaget) as an alternative to that of the *hermeneutic circle. He reiterates more fully that literary studies, and the humanities generally, provide both knowledge through understanding and the valuable application of that knowledge through criticism.

Turning from the interpretation of literature

to addressing writing skills in *The Philosophy of Composition* (1977), Hirsch surveys the results of various types of research into the relation between oral and written language, changes in the English language in recent centuries, and the ease with which various syntactic and semantic choices are understood. He develops an argument for emphasizing 'relative readability' or 'intrinsic effectiveness' in composition instruction. Hirsch's *Cultural Literacy: What Every American Needs to Know* focuses on the problem of competence in reading. (See *competence/performance.) In particular it stresses the importance of a basic level of shared knowledge of historical, scientific and aesthetic meanings, allusions to which the educated reader is expected to understand. Readers who do not share common, basic information are able neither to understand texts nor to participate adequately as members of society. The first half of *Cultural Literacy* makes the argument, the second consists of a list of 5000 names and words illustrating the kind of knowledge readers are expected to have.

Cultural Literacy was followed in 1988 by *The Dictionary of Cultural Literacy*, edited by Hirsch, Joseph F. Kett (professor of history), and James Trefil (professor of physics), and in 1989 by *A First Dictionary of Cultural Literacy*, edited by Hirsch, William G. Rowland, Jr., and Michael Stanford as associated editors. All these works have been the subjects of substantial controversy. The concepts of cultural literacy and of lists have been attacked for: (1) favouring mainstream rather than minority cultures, the bourgeoisie rather than the proletariat; (2) including much more than can be reasonably taught in the average high school; and (3) omitting too much that the educated reader should know and encouraging superficial knowledge.

The central responses of those who agree with Hirsch's position are that we actually don't know how much solid information students can absorb and relate since many schools no longer try very hard to impart more than bare mechanical literacy; that the acquisition of new knowledge requires a minimum base of existing knowledge; and that to deny students from disadvantaged and minority backgrounds access to central cultural traditions and basic scientific knowledge is to deny them a substantial portion of what is needed to achieve equality in our society.

In order to further the kind of educational reform for which *Cultural Literacy* calls, Hirsch has created the Cultural Literacy Foundation in Charlottesville, Virginia. To encourage the teaching of a core of general knowledge, the Foundation has prepared General Knowledge Lists and Cultural Literacy Tests judged appropriate for various primary and secondary grades. (See also *theory and pedagogy.)

WENDELL V. HARRIS

Primary Sources

Hirsch, E.D. *The Aims of Interpretation*. Chicago: U of Chicago P, 1976.
– 'Cultural Literacy.' *The American Scholar* 52 (Spring 1983): 159–69.
– *Innocence and Experience: An Introduction to Blake*. New Haven: Yale UP, 1964.
– 'Meaning and Significance Reinterpreted.' *Critical Inquiry* 11 (Dec. 1984): 202–24.
– 'Objective Criticism.' *PMLA* 75 (Sept. 1960): 463–79. Repr. with slight changes as Appendix I in *Validity in Interpretation*.
– 'Past Intentions and Present Significance.' *Essays in Criticism* 33 (April 1983): 79–98.
– *The Philosophy of Composition*. Chicago: U of Chicago P, 1977.
– 'Truth and Method in Interpretation.' *The Review of Metaphysics* 18 (March 1965): 488–507. Repr. as Appendix 2: 'Gadamer's Theory of Interpretation.' In *Validity in Interpretation*.
– *Validity in Interpretation*. New Haven: Yale UP, 1967.
– 'What Isn't Literature?' In *What is Literature?* Ed. Paul Hernadi. Bloomington: Indiana UP, 1978.
– *Wordsworth and Schelling: A Typological Study of Romanticism*. New Haven: Yale UP, 1960.
– Joseph Kett and James Trefil. *Cultural Literacy: What Every American Needs to Know*. Boston: Houghton Mifflin, 1987.
– with Joseph Kett and James Trefil. *The Dictionary of Cultural Literacy*. Boston: Houghton Mifflin, 1988.
– with William G. Rowland, Jr., and Michael Stanford. *A First Dictionary of Cultural Literacy: What Our Children Need to Know*. Boston: Houghton Mifflin, 1989.

Secondary Sources

Cain, William E. 'Authority, "Cognitive Atheism," and the Aims of Interpretation.' *College English* 39 (1977). Repr. in *The Crisis in Criticism*. Baltimore: Johns Hopkins UP, 1984.
Caraher, Brian G. 'E.D. Hirsch, Jr.' In *Dictionary of Literary Biography* 67. Detroit: Gale, 1988, 151–61.
Lentricchia, Frank. 'E.D. Hirsch: The Hermeneutics of Innocence.' In *After the New Criticism*. Chicago: U of Chicago P, 1980.

Holland, Norman N.

(b. U.S.A., 1927–) Literary theorist. Currently Milbauer Professor of English at the University of Florida, Norman N. Holland founded the Institute for Psychological Study of the Arts at the State University of New York, Buffalo, in 1970. After publishing two books on Shakespeare and developing an interest is psychoanalysis, Holland produced a major theoretical work, *The Dynamics of Literary Response*, in 1968. The central question Holland poses is 'What is our emotional response to a literary work?' Psychoanalysis offers him a theoretical tool for comprehending the role of the unconscious as a determining factor in the way we read texts and what we find in them. (See *text.) He is thus one of the founders of *reader-response criticism. As an orthodox Freudian, Holland generates a five-level pattern of fantasy affecting writers and readers: oral, anal, urethral, phallic, and Oedipal. (See *Sigmund Freud.) Realists, he argues, such as Ben Jonson, 'tend to be anal writers' (40) while 'most of the greatest literature – *Oedipus Rex, Hamlet, The Brothers Karamazov* and the like – builds from an Oedipal phantasy' (47). In the first section of the book, Holland develops a *psychoanalytic theory of meaning; in the second section, he applies it to a wide range of literary texts.

In *Poems in Persons* (1973) and *5 Readers Reading* (1975), Holland modified much of his earlier thinking in response to actual case studies of how readers read. By looking closely at the American poet H.D.'s account of her analysis with Freud and at the way his own students actually read literary texts, Holland concluded that readers, not texts, produce meaning. His subsequent work has focused more and more on the individuality of human subjectivity and the complexity of transactions between reader and text. In 'UNITY IDENTITY TEXT SELF' (1975) and 'Human Identity' (1978), Holland began to explore the importance of a reader's personal identity *theme as a force at work in the act of reading. In *The I* (1985), Holland has produced an entire theory of subjectivity. The book is divided into four long sections: 'The Aesthetics of I,' 'A Psychology of I,' 'A History of I,' and 'A Science of I.' Just as reading is a transaction between reader and text, so subjectivity for Holland suggests a reciprocity between self as originating agent and self as consequence of determining, external facts. (See *self/other.) The shift into language is mediated by a number of psychoanalytic factors, including expectation, defence, fantasy, and representation, though by this stage in his career Holland has left behind the orthodoxies of the American psychoanalytic establishment, 'moving psychoanalytic criticism in the opposite direction from that in which psychoanalysis itself is moving – toward the ego instead of toward the id' (Kaplan and Kloss 274).

Strictly speaking, *The I* is not a work of literary theory, except insofar as poststructuralist theories of subjectivity have come to dominate current literary theory. (See *poststructuralism.) Holland's next book, *The Brain of Robert Frost* (1988), tests his theories of subjectivity in the context of Frost as author/subject/reader. Chapter 6 is a hypothetical examination of the way academics read and argue about poetry. The book is also informed by Holland's interest in cognitive psychology. His most recent book, *Holland's Guide to Psychoanalytic Psychology and Literature-and-Psychology* (1990), an introductory handbook to both psychoanalytic and psychological interpretation, is clearly designed to stimulate a wide range of research methodologies and interdisciplinary uses.

Holland's work has suffered the misfortune of being overshadowed by the psychoanalytic revisions of *Jacques Lacan, whose theories of subjectivity and language have been highly influential. By moving away from the text and towards the individual reader, Holland has restricted the very possibility of theorizing literary language and *textuality. As Elizabeth Wright has pointed out, 'the oddity of Holland's transaction is that he leaves out in theory what he takes account of in practice, the influence of the text on the reader' (*Psychoanalytic Criticism* 67). Holland has remained hostile to poststructuralist attempts to expand the domains of textuality. In a response to Lacan's seminar on Poe's 'The Purloined Letter,' he reminisces about the boyhood copy of the text he still holds in his hand; his transaction with the text is intensely personal: 'Is not a transactive criticism truer to the human dynamics of literary response than the linguistic glides of a Lacan or the deconstructions of a Derrida? Is it not better to have a literary and especially a psychoanalytic criticism that is grounded in the body and the family?' ('Re-

covering "The Purloined Letter"' 317). (See
*deconstruction, *Jacques Derrida.) Holland's
transactive criticism opens a window to what
actually goes on in the reading and teaching of
literature but, it can be argued, a criticism
'grounded in the body' is in danger of losing
sight of the text altogether.

GREGOR CAMPBELL

Primary Sources

Holland, Norman N. *The Brain of Robert Frost*. New
York: Routledge, 1988.
– *The Dynamics of Literary Response*. New York: Ox-
ford UP, 1968.
– *5 Readers Reading*. New Haven: Yale UP, 1975.
– 'Hamlet – My Greatest Creation.' *Journal of Ameri-
can Academy of Psychoanalysis* 3 (1975): 419–27.
– *Holland's Guide to Psychoanalytic Psychology and
Literature-and-Psychology*. New York: Oxford UP,
1990.
– 'Human Identity.' *Critical Inquiry* 4 (Spring 1978):
451–69.
– *The I*. New Haven: Yale UP, 1985.
– 'I-ing Film.' *Critical Inquiry* 12 (Summer 1986):
654–71.
– *Laughing: A Psychology of Humor*. Ithaca: Cornell
UP, 1982.
– 'Literature as Transaction.' In *What is Literature?*
Ed. Paul Hernadi. Bloomington: Indiana UP, 1978,
206–18.
– *Poems in Persons: An Introduction to The Psycho-
analysis of Literature*. New York: Norton, 1973.
– *Psychoanalysis and Shakespeare*. New York: Mc-
Graw Hill, 1966.
– 'Re-covering "The Purloined Letter": Reading as a
Personal Transaction.' In *The Purloined Poe: Lacan,
Derrida, and Psychoanalytic Reading*. Ed. John P.
Muller and William J. Richardson. Baltimore:
Johns Hopkins UP, 1988, 307–22.
– *The Shakespearean Imagination*. New York: Macmil-
lan, 1964.
– 'UNITY IDENTITY TEXT SELF.' *PMLA* 90.5 (Oct. 1975):
813–22.

Secondary Sources

Bleich, David. *Subjective Criticism*. Baltimore: Johns
Hopkins UP, 1978.
Freud, Sigmund. *The Standard Edition of the Complete
Psychological Works*. Trans. and ed. James
Strachey. 24 vols. London: Hogarth P, 1953–74.
Kaplan, Morton, and Robert Kloss. *The Unspoken
Motive: A Guide to Psychoanalytic Literary Criti-
cism*. New York: Free P, 1973.
Suleiman, Susan, and Inge Crosman, eds. *The Reader
in the Text: Essays on Audience and Interpretation*.
Princeton: Princeton UP, 1980.
Tompkins, Jane P., ed. *Reader-Response Criticism:
From Formalism to Poststructuralist Criticism*. Balti-
more: Johns Hopkins UP, 1980.
Wright, Elizabeth. *Psychoanalytic Criticism: Theory in
Practice*. London: Methuen, 1984.

Husserl, Edmund

(b. Moravia, 1859–d. 1938) Philosopher. Edmund Husserl studied mathematics at Leipzig,
Berlin and Vienna. After a brief period as
assistant to the distinguished mathematician
Karl Theodor Weierstrass in Berlin, Husserl
returned to Vienna to work under Franz
Brentano, a prominent empirical psychologist.
Like many mathematicians of his day, Husserl
sought an adequate theoretical grounding for
mathematics and he looked to the new psychological science for that foundation. Brentano introduced him to the British empiricists,
particularly to David Hume and John Stuart
Mill, who, together with René Descartes and
Immanuel Kant, had a profound influence on
Husserl's philosophical development. After de-
ciding on a career in philosophy, he taught at
the Universities of Halle (1887–1901), Göttingen (1901–16) and Freiburg (1916–29). Few
important intellectual movements in recent
European thought from existentialism to
*poststructuralism have not been influenced
to some extent by Husserl's ideas. Most recently, Husserl has become of considerable
interest to language theorists, who look to him
to resolve some of the most pressing problems in meaning theory.

Husserl's central insight is that consciousness is essentially *intentional*, that is, in relationship with an object, and hence it is
unnecessary to inquire about objects outside of
a relation to consciousness or about consciousness without an object of which it is conscious.
(See *intention/intentionality, *subject/object.)
Husserl devoted the first volume of his first
truly phenomenological work, *Logische Untersuchungen [Logical Investigations* 1900], to dismembering the position he had espoused in
the *Philosophie der Arithmetik [Philosophy of
Arithmetic* 1891]. He still searched for the theoretical foundations of mathematics and of science, but realized that one cannot understand
the nature of pure mathematics without developing a theory of thought itself, specifically of
logical thought. Thereafter he concerned himself with basic questions concerning the nature

of knowledge and of science. *Investigations* is best described as a phenomenological study in which ordinary metaphysical commitments (for example, about the existence of non-conscious entities) are set out of action, allowing the data, the phenomena, to be attended to without being distorted by the beliefs and circumstances of the investigator, that is, by psychological data. In this respect Husserl's phenomenology is 'transcendental': the results of such an approach will be valid for all possible instances rather than just for a limited set of concrete cases. The achievement of the *Investigations* is a sketch of a 'pure logic,' a descriptive analytic account of basic cognitive activities (intentionality, understanding, perception, memory) and of fundamental cognitive objects (meaning, truth, proposition), particularly those involved in scientific thinking. (See *phenomenological criticism.)

The central *text of phenomenology is Husserl's *Ideen zu einer reinen Phänomenologie und phänomenologischen Philosophie [Ideas Pertaining to a Pure Phenomenology and to a Phenomenological Philosophy* 1913]. In it Husserl further articulates his method for analysing intentional structures. Also, much to the dismay of some of his admirers, he makes of phenomenology a 'transcendental idealism,' which seems to declare transcendental consciousness (the conditions for the possibility of experience) the chief datum investigated by the phenomenologist. In fact, Husserl made a much weaker but more tenable claim resting on the insight that all understanding, including understanding about the existence or non-existence of things in addition to one's consciousness, originates in the immediate experience of the individual possessing that understanding and declaring that this can be investigated in a way that transcends the practical limits within which the psychologist must proceed. By insisting that phenomenology is an idealism Husserl is merely declaring his intent to restrict the scope of the discipline to a concern with ideas (which he variously equates with essences, meanings, the structural laws of categories of possible objects). This is not to deny the existence of real as opposed to ideal objects; it simply avoids the complex of insoluble problems involved in justifying truth claims about objects considered outside of a relationship to consciousness.

Husserl's late works introduce some significant modifications and some changed em-

phases. In the *Cartesianische Meditationen [Cartesian Meditations* 1931], he counters the charge that a philosophy centring on the notion of transcendental consciousness must be incapable of dealing with one of the most important aspects of experience – the social or intersubjective dimension. In *Formale und transzendentale Logik [Formal and Transcendental Logic* 1929] and *Die Krisis der europäischen Wissenschaft und die transzendentale Phänomenologie [The Crisis of European Sciences and Transcendental Phenomenology* 1936] he stresses much more than he had done previously the 'constitutive' function of consciousness. That is, although he is not a 'subjective idealist' who reduces reality to ideas, he insists that consciousness contributes to sense. Consciousness has its own characteristics and it always has a determinate perspective from which it interrelates with things and that influences the character of the ideas which a determinate consciousness has. Philosophical analysis now has as its aim to retrace the genesis of concepts and networks of concepts from their origins in pre-theoretical experience. This seems to bring Husserl very far away from the concerns of earlier phenomenology. Another important late idea developed in the *Krisis* is 'lived experience' (*Lebenswelt). Husserl never forgot that the point of theorizing is to better understand experience. The notion of lived experience contains the idea of the primacy of pre-theoretical experience, an idea that *Martin Heidegger and *Maurice Merleau-Ponty put at the centre of their philosophies.

Although Husserl was too engaged with shoring up the foundations of all thought to attend directly to the nature of art or *literature or to the specific forms of intentionality at work in literary experience, many theorists have found much in Husserl's philosophy that is peculiarly apt for literary thinking. For example, his restricted consideration of ideal (or purely possible) objects may be related to literature, which also contains ideal objects (possible worlds or components of them). His method of describing and analysing them suggests the possibility of an analogous literary critical procedure. Imagination plays a major role in the phenomenologist's method which, for purposes of analysis, transforms the material of ordinary belief into fictions. A description of that role elucidates the process of literary production. Finally, Husserl's insights into temporality – specifically into the retentional and protentional nature of consciousness help clarify the 'time arts,' music and literature.

Many contemporary literary theorists are indebted to Husserl, perhaps none more self-consciously than *Roman Ingarden. Ingarden makes critical use of the notions of intentionality and meaning and of the theory of meaning constitution. He sees the phenomenological method as peculiarly apt for the description of aesthetic experience and aesthetic objects and has used it to considerable effect in the contentious cause of a scientific understanding of literature and literary cognition. Mikel Dufrenne, also deeply influenced by Husserl's late works, believes that his own phenomenology or aesthetic experience rectifies false moves made by Husserl and Ingarden, particularly their prejudice in favour of the cognitive at the expense of the sensuous and affective dimensions of the aesthetic. *E.D. Hirsch's thesis that an interpretation of a text is a reconstitution of the author's intended sense rests on the assumption that texts are Husserlian intentional objects. Finally, *Paul Ricoeur's work on time and narrative rests squarely on Husserl's phenomenology of time consciousness, a theory which Ricoeur both supplements and supplants.

MARGARET VAN DE PITTE

Primary Sources

Husserl, Edmund. *Cartesian Meditations. An Introduction to Phenomenology.* Trans. Dorion Cairns. New York: Humanities P, 1966.
– *The Crisis of European Sciences and Transcendental Phenomenology.* Trans. David Carr. Evanston: Northwestern UP, 1973.
– 'Formale und transzendentale Logik: Versuch einer Kritik der logischen Vernunft.' In *Jahrbuch* 10 (1929): 1–298. Trans. Dorion Cairns. *Formal and Transcendental Logic.* The Hague: Martinus Nijhoff, 1969.
– *The Idea of Phenomenology.* Trans. W.P. Alston and G. Nakhnikian. The Hague: Martinus Nijhoff, 1983.
– *Ideen zu einer reinen Phänomenologie und phänomenologischen Philosophie 1.* Halle: Max Niemeyer, 1913. *Ideas Pertaining to a Pure Phenomenology and to a Phenemenological Philosophy.* Trans. F. Kersten. Hague, Boston, Lancaster: Martinus Nijhoff, 1983.
– *Logical Investigations.* Trans. J.N. Findlay. 2 vols. New York: Humanities P, 1970.

– *The Phenomenology of Internal Time-Consciousness.* Ed. Martin Heidegger. Trans. J.S. Churchill. Bloomington: Indiana UP, 1966.

Secondary Sources

Elliston, Frederick, and Peter McCormick, eds. *Husserl: Expositions and Appraisals.* Notre Dame/London: U of Notre Dame P, 1977.
Natanson, Maurice. *Edmund Husserl: Philosopher of Infinite Tasks.* Evanston: Northwestern UP, 1973.
Ricoeur, Paul. *Husserl: An Analysis of His Phenomenology.* Evanston: Northwestern UP, 1967.
Sokolowski, Robert. *Husserlian Meditations.* Evanston: Northwestern UP, 1974.
Zaner, Richard M. *The Way of Phenomenology: Criticism as a Philosophical Discipline.* Indianapolis: Bobbs-Merrill, 1970.

Ingarden, Roman

(b. Poland, 1893–d. 1970) Philosopher and literary theorist. Born in Cracow, Ingarden studied in Lvov under Twardowski before becoming a student of *Edmund Husserl at Göttingen. He later followed Husserl to Freiburg where he received his doctorate with a dissertation on Henri Bergson (1918). Returning to Poland, Ingarden became a *Privatdozent* at Lvov in 1924, professor in 1933. While at Lvov he published his two major works in aesthetics, *The Literary Work of Art* (1931) and *The Cognition of the Literary Work of Art* (1937). During the German occupation Ingarden taught German *literature and literary theory at the University of Lvov (1940–1) and mathematics at the secondary school level. He also finished his major work in ontology, *Spór o istnienie świata* [*The Controversy over the Existence of the World* 1947–8]. In 1945 Ingarden was expelled from eastern Poland after the Soviet annexation. Settling in Cracow, he was afterwards (1949–56) forbidden to teach by the Polish government because of the 'idealist' direction of his philosophy. Reinstated in 1956, Ingarden became professor emeritus in 1963.

Ingarden's work is a contribution to the development of phenomenology in the Husserlian tradition. (See *phenomenological criticism.) In reaction against psychologism and positivism, Husserl undertook to establish the principles and methodology of a science of phenomena, allowing the things themselves to show themselves to the observer. The goal of phenomenology is to describe the structures of different kinds of objects, in each case identifying the ways in which they give themselves to consciousness. While Ingarden shares this enterprise with Husserl, he broke with him as early as 1918 in consequence of Husserl's transcendental turn, which led the founder of phenomenology to concentrate on the analysis of the structures of pure consciousness. For his part, Ingarden insisted on the necessity of establishing the existence of the material world as independent of consciousness. This disagreement remained decisive for Ingarden's philosophical path.

Since Ingarden's interest in aesthetics grew out of his attempt to develop his ontological position, his investigation of the work of art serves as an ontology of one kind of object and attempts to determine the common features of this class. The artwork, moreover, is particularly suited to Ingarden's central concern – to show the existence of the real as independent of the ideal – because it is a heteronomous structure, neither simply real (in the world) nor ideal (universals, for example). The work of art, Ingarden proposes, is an intentional structure; it is 'a purely intentional formation which has the source of its being in the creative acts of consciousness of its author and its physical foundation in the text set down in writing ... By virtue of the dual stratum of its language the work is both intersubjectively accessible and reproducible, so that it becomes an intersubjective intentional object, related to a community of readers. (See *intention/intentionality.) As such it is not a psychological phenomenon and is transcendent to all experiences of consciousness, those of the author as well as those of the reader' (The Cognition of the Literary Work of Art 14). The literary work, then, has its origin in the intentional acts of its author who creates a linguistic model of real objects and the real world. While the work, as intentional, has no independent existence in relation to the concrete reality of which it is a model, it is nonetheless autonomous of that reality and mere subjective experience by virtue of 'two entirely heterogeneous objectivities.' For it has the basis of its existence, on the one hand, in 'ideal concepts and ideal qualities (essences), and, on the other hand ... in real "word signs"' (The Literary Work of Art 361). (See *sign.) The work of art therefore has three ontic foundations: (1) the material thing, (2) acts of consciousness, and (3) ideal entities. The ideal meanings are

actualized by acts of consciousness in sentence formation and these intended meanings bring the work into being.

In The Literary Work of Art, Ingarden develops this threefold heterogenous foundation of the work in terms of four strata which in their polyphonic harmony allow the aesthetic object to be produced. Simply put, the first two strata refer respectively to the levels of 'sound' and of 'sense.' The third stratum refers to the fact that the work presents us with aspects, or views, of the objects intended. Hence, just as we never perceive an object in the real world whole but only as a succession of partial views, so the work allows us, by means of a series of 'schemata' organized temporally by its sentences, to constitute an object. The fourth refers to the objects represented in the work and can best be understood by the way of essential distinctions between represented objects and objects experienced in the real world. Objects represented differ from real objects in at least these respects: (1) every real object is absolutely individual, but the represented object is always somewhat general; (2) real objects are completely determined, but 'literary objects' are given by nominal expressions having multiple interpretations. Literary works leave represented objects underdetermined – they present schemata. The work's nominal expressions set the limits of interpretation; but the represented object can never be fully determined because the limits set by nominal expressions allow for 'spaces of indeterminacy.' The notion of lacunae or indeterminacies has proven especially fruitful in subsequent reflections on the structure of the literary work deriving from Ingarden. (See *indeterminacy.)

The Cognition of the Literary Work of Art supplements this investigation by explicating the ways in which the work, given its internal structure, can be apprehended. The distinction Ingarden makes between the work itself and the work as aesthetic object can illuminate his main concern in this *text. The pre-aesthetic cognition of the work implicates the apprehension of its structure prior to *concretization, hence knowledge of the work in itself. This kind of cognition, as well as other forms, is determined by the intention according to which the work is apprehended. While the pre-aesthetic attitude reflects a scholarly mode of cognition, the natural attitude of the reader tends toward an aesthetic concretization of the work. The concretization fills in the places of indeterminacy we have noted, whereas the pre-aesthetic attitude attempts to leave these lacunae open in order to establish the structure of the work in and for itself. The aesthetic objectification of the work brings all of the four strata of the text into play and intends their unity. This is one way in which the literary work is distinguished from the scientific because in the latter only the stratum of meanings is developed to the exclusion of the others. The aesthetic object thus intended calls forth an explicitly aesthetic emotion generated by the quality of the representation itself rather than by what is represented. The value of the work is determined by its ability to call for concretizations and aesthetic emotions of complexity and intensity.

Ingarden's aesthetics have entered the mainstream of the Anglo-American tradition through *René Wellek and Austin Warren's influential *Theory of Literature*, which draws heavily on Ingarden. His most direct and decisive influence to date, however, has been on practitioners of *reader-response criticism, especially as developed by the *Constance School of Reception Aesthetics (*Wolfgang Iser, *Hans Robert Jauss). In *The Act of Reading*, Iser draws on Ingarden's concept of the structural indeterminacy of the text to develop his own position. Given that intentional objects are to simulate the determinateness of real objects (as Iser interprets Ingarden's argument), then their concretization tends towards a determinateness which actualizes the pre-aesthetically inherent structure of the work. Iser argues that the gaps allow for a range of concretizations – one cannot judge some false, others true, especially because, as Iser proposes, closing one set of indeterminacies gives rise to another. This is particularly borne out by examples from modern literature. Ingarden's development of the concept of indeterminacy is still tied to classical aesthetics and the notion of the closure of the work. (See *closure/dis-closure.) This also becomes evident by the priority Ingarden gives to the concept of aesthetic emotion. The 'original' emotion, described as a kind of hunger for completion generated by the work, allows it to be transformed into a specifically aesthetic object. In Iser's reading of Ingarden, this emotion guides the concretization of the work in a way more fundamental than the indeterminacies, now relegated to the status of secondary effects. Consequently, Iser calls for a more systematic development of the role of indeterminacies in our reading of the literary text.

While these and other questions are raised by Ingarden's work, there is no doubt as to the seminal role which the systematic investigations he initiated have played and continue to play.

BERNHARD RADLOFF

Primary Sources

Ingarden, Roman. *Erlebnis, Kunstwerk und Wert. Vorträge zur Aesthetik* 1937–67. Tübingen: Max Niemeyer, 1969.
– *Das Literarische Kunstwerk. Eine Untersuchung aus dem Grenzgebiet der Ontologie, Logik und Literaturwissenschaft.* Halle: Max Niemeyer, 1931. *The Literary Work of Art. An Investigation on the Borderlines of Ontology, Logic and the Theory of Literature.* Trans. George G. Grabowicz. Evanston: Northwestern UP, 1973.
– *O poznawaniu dzieła literackiego.* Lvov: Ossolineum, 1937. Rev. German trans. *Vom Erkennen des literarischen Kunstwerks.* Tübingen: Max Niemeyer, 1968. *The Cognition of the Literary Work of Art.* Trans. Ruth Ann Crowly and Kenneth R. Olson. Evanston: Northwestern UP, 1973.
– *Selected Papers in Aesthetics.* Ed. Peter J. McCormick. Munich: Philosophia Verlag, 1985.
– *Spór o istnienie świata* [*The Controversy over the Existence of the World*]. Vols. 1–2. Krakow: PAU, 1947–8. *Der Streit um die Existenz der Welt.* Tübingen: Max Niemeyer, 1964. Partial English trans. Helen R. Michejda, *Time and Modes of Being.* Springfield: American Lectures in Philosophy, 1964.
– *Untersuchungen zur Ontologie der Kunst: Musikwerk, Bild, Architektur, Film.* Tübingen: Max Niemeyer, 1962.

Secondary Sources

Falk, E.H. *The Poetics of Roman Ingarden.* Chapel Hill: U of North Carolina P, 1981.
Fielder, T. 'Taking Ingarden Seriously: Critical Reflections on *The Cognition of the Literary Work of Art.' Journal of the British Society for Phenomenology* 2 (1975): 131–40.
Graff, P., and S. Krzemień-Ojak, eds. *Roman Ingarden and Contemporary Polish Aesthetics.* Warsaw: Polish Scientific Publishers, 1975.
Hamm, V. 'The Ontology of the Literary Work of Art: Roman Ingarden's *Das Literarische Kunstwerk.'* In *The Critical Matrix.* Washington: Georgetown UP, 1961, 171–209.
Hamrick, W.S. 'Ingarden on Aesthetic Experience and Aesthetic Object.' *Journal of the British Society for Phenomenology* 1 (1974): 71–80.

Iser, Wolfgang. *Der Akt des Lesens. Theorie ästhetischer Wirkung.* Wilhelm Fink Verlag, 1976. *The Act of Reading. A Theory of Aesthetic Response.* Baltimore: Johns Hopkins UP, 1978.

McCormick, P., and B. Dziemidok, eds. *On the Aesthetics of Roman Ingarden.* Boston: Martinus Nijhoff, 1989.

Rudnick, H.H. 'Roman Ingarden's Literary Theory.' In *Ingardeniana, Analecta Husserliana,* IV (1976): 105–19.

Wellek, René, and Austin Warren. *Theory of Literature,* 3rd ed. New York: Harcourt, 1956.

Irigaray, Luce

(b. Belgium, c. 1934–) Feminist theorist, philosopher, psychoanalyst, linguist. After completing a Licence en philosophie et lettres (1954), Irigaray wrote a thesis at the Université de Louvain (Belgium) on 'La Notion de pureté chez Paul Valéry, le mot pur, la pensée pure, la poésie pure' (1955) and prepared for secondary school teaching (1956). She taught in Brussels (1956–9), then studied for a Licence de psychologie at the Université de Paris (1961), completing a Diploma in Psychopathology the following year. In 1962, she joined FNRS (Belgian scientific research), moving in 1964 to its French counterpart (CNRS) where, since 1982, she has been Maître de recherches. With her doctorat de 3ème cycle (Université de Paris X-Nanterre 1968), Irigaray switched to linguistics, publishing her thesis, *Le Langage des déments* (1973), on the ways schizophrenia and other mental disturbances can be discerned in the syntax of language. From 1969 to 1974, Irigaray taught at the Université de Paris VIII-Vincennes where she was attached to the Ecole freudienne de Paris of *Jacques Lacan. *Speculum de l'autre femme,* her thesis for the doctorat d'état ès lettres (Paris VIII, 1974), developed a feminist critique of psychoanalysis and philosophy and sparked controversy about the politicizing of psychoanalysis. Irigaray was subsequently expelled from the Ecole freudienne, lost her teaching position, continuing, though, with her psychoanalytic practice. In recent years Irigaray has been a visiting professor in a number of countries including Holland, Denmark, the U.S.A., Canada, and Italy. (See *Sigmund Freud, *psychoanalytic theory.)

Reputed to be the most difficult of French feminists for her 'sibylline prose' (Whitford 11), Irigaray challenges through her densely allusive approach and disciplinary range, drawing on the history of classical and Continental philosophy as reworked by contemporary French theorists. (See French *feminist criticism.) Her work encompasses several fields. In linguistics, it has been largely empirical. Noting in the analytic session the tendency of women to hysterical and of men to obsessional *discourse, Irigaray modified the tests administered to the mentally ill for *Le Language des déments* so as to test for gender differences in syntactic structures. Drawing on the *semiotics of *Emile Benveniste, especially his work on deictics (shifters) where subjectivity is constituted in and by language, Irigaray's empirical research demonstrates how women, in contrast to men, fail to assume a subject position in language, effacing themselves in favour of men or of the world of objects through shifts in syntax. (See *subject/object.) The theoretical work on sexual markers in discourse is published in *Parler n'est jamais neutre* (1985), while the conclusions of her research are reported in 'Le Sexe linguistique' (1987) and *Sexes et genres à travers les langues* (1990).

The development of psychoanalytic theory is the best known aspect of Irigaray's work on the ways language and culture position men and women differently through the Oedipal configuration of the symbolic. (See *imaginary/symbolic/real.) Using a deconstructive approach, she critiques psychoanalysis from within, using psychoanalytic theory against itself to expose its contradictions and its gendered presuppositions. (See *deconstruction.) Crucial here is her demonstration in *Speculum de l'autre femme* (1974) of the 'blind spot of an old dream of symmetry' (11), how Freud's argument about the construction of female sexuality is predicated on the norm of development of the boy and assumes that a similar model applies to the girl. Subsumed under similarity, the Selfsame, sexual difference is indifference. Irigaray's critique of Freud is not a rejection of psychoanalysis. On the contrary, her use of psychoanalysis marks a major divergence between her theorization of sexual difference and that of *Simone de Beauvoir, whose idea of Woman as Other she develops. (See *self/other.) Irigaray posits an otherness for women that is self-defined, a difference not to be transcended but to be given symbolic and social representation by and for women. Each sex could then be the 'other' for the other sex in the reciprocity of exchange whose absence de Beauvoir analysed.

To theorize this exchange, Irigaray adapts Lacanian psychoanalysis and its concern with the Oedipal configuration of the Symbolic, of the unconscious as a semiotic system in which libidinal economies orchestrate the signifier in excess of the signified so that meaning always evades the subject, never rational or fully self-present. (See *signified/signifier/signification.) Psychoanalysis nonetheless is a discourse fixed by a transcendent signified, the Phallus. Irigaray critiques Lacan's metaphorization of psychoanalysis as a masculine body and his unexamined presupposition of prior sexual difference. She challenges his focus on the subject's cathexis, on the Other as object, on definitions of terms rather than on relations between them; that is, the privileging of metaphor over metonymy. (See *metonymy/metaphor.)

In contrast to the Lacanian lack, Irigaray posits contiguity, the metonymy of two lips touching, what moves and destabilizes the Lacanian system that attempts to pin woman down, immobilize and domesticate her within a system containing her within the maternal function as a resource for the masculine subject. This dominant fantasy of the mother as 'not-all' is a volume, a closed container, a 'receptacle for the (re)production of sameness' and the support of all forms of (re)production, particularly discourse. The symbolic, she charges, is the masculine imaginary transformed into the social. Postulated as a virtuality, as a becoming, not a being, a fluid heterogeneity, 'awoman' hints at the Utopian possibility for women's desire to be represented for-itself in a non-completable process of becoming form. This would open the possibility for a feminine symbolic, representations of the feminine for-itself, structures of mediation for relations between women and reciprocal intercourse between maternal and paternal genealogies.

Irigaray's strategy is to deploy Lacan's theory of discourse against itself, through quotation, repetition, interrogation, exposing its contradictions, that it is not the discourse of analysis, but the discourse of mastery. Tracing the discourse of various masters, she turns it through *irony from Truth to ambiguity to suggest the possibilities of an other discourse, 'speaking (as) woman,' attempting 'to provide a place for the 'other' as feminine' (This Sex

135). Miming alterity, Irigaray stages a dialogue with the dominant discourse that is not a dialectic collapsing difference into the same. She employs this discursive strategy and theorizes it in her attempt to 'psychoanalyze philosophy,' her major project which, until very recently, has received little critical attention. Speculum is Irigaray's summum. Like *Jacques Derrida, she engages in a critique of metaphysics in the tradition of Western philosophy which, privileging analogy and the gaze, has valorized identity and the same (both words translate as même). (See *metaphysics of presence.) However, Irigaray diverges from Derrida, to critique his work for being implicated in a gendered discourse of closure. (See *closure/dis-closure.) At the founding moment of philosophical discourse is an act of matricide, not one of parricide, Irigaray counters Freud (Le Corps-à-corps 81), a matricide in which Derrida with his focus on the sun/son is implicated. Her interpretive re-reading of Plato for the 'grammar' of his metaphors focuses on the allegory of the cave, a cave that is not a cave but an enceinte (enclosure/pregnant womb). The philosophical project is one of giving birth that denies 'sensible' origins in favour of 'intelligible' or created origins (Godard).

While Plato ironically uses a mimetic mode to denounce *mimesis, Irigaray's exposure of this double bind occurs in repetition not representation, as 'mimetism' or 'mimicry,' that is, as staged re-presentation. That she refuses mimesis, with its logic of the same, is signalled in her title, which holds not a mirror up to truth as likeness but the concave speculum, whose curved surface, folded back on itself, explores female birthing passages in a delusion of interiority. This intervention to 'disturb the staging of representation' is addressed in more detail in Ce Sexe qui n'en est pas un [This Sex Which Is Not One 1977; 1985, 155], a series of essays and talks that expand and clarify the theoretical work of Speculum.

Framed as the repetition of a repetition of a repetition (Souter's Alice Through the Looking Glass as viewed by *Gilles Deleuze), the *text enacts the topological logic it discerns, eschewing 'ownership and property,' but not the 'proximate' or contiguity, in decentring the 'logic of meaning' from the 'logic of the Self-same.' (See *centre/decentre.) This logic of the recursive paradigm is a logic of non-sense, *paradox, where binary distinctions between inside/outside, surface/depth, and word/

meaning no longer operate. (See *binary opposition.) While some of the texts address specific audiences and clarify Irigaray's concern with gender and the symbolic ('Questions'), and others reiterate her concern with the power relations mediated by discourse and the problems for a women's politics in a phallocratic order ('The Power of Discourse and the Subordination of the Feminine'), many of the texts in *Ce Sexe* elaborate Irigaray's theory of an economy organized by metonymic relations of exchange. Particularly important is her linking of models of semiotic exchange with those of economic production and exchange. In 'Women on the Market' and 'Commodities Among Themselves,' Irigaray challenges Marxism for its failure to theorize the gendered organization of the social contract where exogamy functions as endogamy among men, as unexamined 'hom(m)osexuality,' excluding women from participating in exchange among themselves. (See *Marxist criticism.)

This attempt to figure a feminine imaginary as an assumed fiction, in what Jane Gallop calls Irigaray's 'vulvomorphic display' (96), was more generally termed 'writing the body' and condemned by Anglo-American feminists as essentialist (Jones 367; Moi 139). (See feminist criticism, *Anglo-American; *essentialism.) Irigaray explained that these sections (and her other lyrical texts *Et l'une ne bouge pas sans l'autre* [1979], *Corps-à-corps avec la mère* [1981], and *Passions élémentaires* [1982]) do 'not imply a regressive retreat to the anatomical' for 'women have two lips several times over]' Rather this is a deliberately assumed metonymy, borrowed from *Maurice Merleau-Ponty (*Ethiques de la différence sexuelle* 156), to break out of the 'tautological systems of discourse' through another 'morphologic' (*Irigaray Reader* 97), one without closure, an economy of loss, not sexualized only by the phallic function as the maternal metaphor. It is, moreover, a questioning of bisexuality which Irigaray, in contrast to *Hélène Cixous and *Julia Kristeva, sees as a way of evading the question of 'relations with the same body or the same sex' (ibid. 100). This question of women's relations to other women is a major one for Irigaray. It is not a metaphysical project of identities but an ethical one of relations, of the ways in which the gendered socio-symbolic order produced by exogamy has failed to constitute women as a group, has no symbology for the 'feminine plural.'

For Irigaray, it matters who is speaking, since relations of material and historical contingency – prior to and in excess of – mediate signification. This is evident in her later work, still in the process of translation into English, in which she engages in a kind of 'amorous relations' between the sexes (*Sexes et parentés* 191) that has supplemented the model of psychoanalytic dialogue where the question of transference is as central as that of desire. Irigaray's philosophical discourse aims to expose the provisionality of the truth claims of all philosophical discourse and to open the possibility for the circulation of other discourses, undermining the singularity of power. Her engagement is with philosophers who advance her own aim, as in the case of *Nietzsche's critique of truth as 'unveiling.' However, his focus on repetition as the 'eternal return' is yet another murder of the maternal, a strategic turning away from the unrepeatable moment of birth. Nietzsche's feminine asserts the 'being of becoming.' Is this also the 'becoming of being,' Irigaray asks? Merleau-Ponty's phenomenology of the body privileges the visible and a scopic economy of sight, insight, truth, over the tangible, touching, contiguity, and assemblage, and so participates in philosophy's paternal genealogy. (See *phenomenological criticism.) So too does Emmanuel Levinas whose phenomenology of the caress provides openings for Irigaray's theorization of the 'lovhers'' dialogue as exchange between irreducible others, while the feminine functions as horizon for the masculine's transcendent project; there is no horizon, no symbology for women.

Following her work on the ethics of radical alterity, Irigaray turned, in *Sexes et parentés* (1987), to theories of exchange as these engage the sacred and the primal violence of the female sacrifice analysed by *René Girard. Irigaray reiterates the necessity of a feminine symbolic in order to mediate relations between women, whose death drives are not deflected, with the result that there is only violence and a lack of respect among them or they are buried alive in the culture. Social-symbolic forms are needed to construct a feminine genealogy. In essays such as *Divine Women* (1986), Irigaray argues for the necessity of a spiritual and divine dimension for the maternal as a horizon of possibility. Other forms of representation also need to be constructed and disseminated. Among the forms of representation requiring redistribution is language. Beginning in *Parler n'est jamais neutre* (1985), Irigaray returned to the issues of her early research in psycholinguistics to outline the difficulties of and necessity for women to represent themselves as subjects in language. Discourse is not the only mode of representation that requires transformation. All forms of socio-symbolic mediation need to be radically realigned to allow feminine alterity. Unlike *Michel Foucault, Irigaray's attention is not directed at the institutions fixing discourse into hierarchical relations of power. She analyses systems of representation to show how their truths are contingent on the interests of those constructing them. This is an epistemological and ethical project, not the identity politics of much feminism.

Irigaray's influence as a feminist theorist has been considerable in Europe, where German and Italian feminists have responded to her concern to establish a symbolic order for women (Ecker, Bono). She has also had a significant impact in Quebec, where feminist writer/theorists such as Nicole Brossard and France Théoret have engaged in *écriture au féminin*, that is, writing that works upon discourse and the symbolic (Théoret 143). (See *feminist criticism, Quebec.) In France, however, Irigaray was grouped with Cixous, Kristeva and others working with psychoanalysis as 'cultural feminism,' feminism of 'difference': 'a new attack with the good old rhetoric on sex differences but this time uttered by women, which eliminates historical and dialectical materialism in order to give voice to the naked truth of women's eternal bodies' *(Questions féministes* 225, 218). This 'neo-femininity' was denounced by radical materialist feminists in their founding manifesto of *Questions féministes*, where they attacked the focus on a 'woman's language' and advocated an analysis of the 'history of our oppression' (223) and the institutions, laws, and socio-economic structures oppressing women (217).

The specific arguments against Irigaray are rehearsed by Monique Plaza in a later issue of the periodical, where she charges Irigaray to be guilty of the logic of the same: her '"new" concept of woman' is merely the return of 'the eternal feminine' in what is the 'patriarchal vicious circle' – women's 'anti-feminism' that allows 'the perpetuation of patriarchy' (Plaza 94, 98, 90). Irigaray is concerned with 'oppressive theory,' with '"woman" of masculine dis-

course' not with a 'theory of oppression,' with describing 'women' as they are under patriarchy (Plaza 90). Although Irigaray states that a political questioning of psychoanalysis should be carried out through an investigation of 'the historical determinations of this destiny' *(Ce Sexe* 62; Plaza 82), she does not undertake it, carrying out a psychological reduction and generalization to position the 'womb' in the realm of the 'tangible' and make its concealment the foundation of 'the Western Logos' (Plaza 78). Woman is concealed by discourse. Constructing her is, Plaza affirms, 'a question of projecting her in a conditional perspective.' Irigaray has done so, she suggests, by searching for woman before the process of 'transformation-deformation,' that is, to posit a 'feminine "essence"' 'outside of [prior to] the oppressive social framework, that is to say, *in the body of woman*' (Plaza 73). This critical assessment overlooks the question of Irigaray's quotation of philosophers' metaphors of the female body to expose their sexism.

Irigaray's reception in anglophone milieux has been mixed. Three short lyric texts appeared in English translation in *Signs* almost simultaneously with the French materialist critiques of her work in the English version of the periodical *Feminist Issues*. Divorced from the analysis of the institution of philosophy in Irigaray's longer works, these lyrical effusions imaging two lips seemed to support the description of 'writing the body' and lend credence to the attacks.

This has been the orthodox Anglo-American feminist response to Irigaray's work despite the defence of Gayatri Chakravorty Spivak of the method of '*symptomatic reading' for contradictions. *Toril Moi criticizes Irigaray for not exploring the political context of women's oppression in the domestic economy alongside the specular discursive economy (Moi 147). Moreover, Moi writes, Irigaray enters into the binary logic of the same to figure 'fluidity as a positive alternative,' thus 'fall[ing] into the very essentialist trap of defining woman that she set out to avoid' (Moi 142), developing idealist categories when the historical determinants are not made precise, and the quotation marks in her mockery of patriarchal constructions are not visible. What Moi addresses here is the problem of irony in feminist discourse and the potential for divergent readings it entails.

A number of recent studies by feminist philosophers examine the full range of Irigaray's texts within a tradition of philosophical discourse. Elizabeth Grosz reads Irigaray's work as concerned with creativity and production, with 'what is new, what remains unthought, the space for the projection of possible futures' (Grosz 162), the space for forging social transformations. This is to read Irigaray's construction of women in a conditional perspective, not as a retreat into an atemporal past, but as the utopian horizon of feminist change. Such an interpretation of Irigaray finds support in the work of Rosi Braidotti, who underlines the conditional tense of women's becoming that entails a constant process of recreation (Braidotti 257, 263), and in that of Judith Butler, who argues for the importance of masquerade and miming as engagements with the cultural inscription of gender in a project to renew cultural history as a possibility that includes never becoming 'woman.' Gender here is a 'performative' (Butler 141). This development in philosophy rereads materialism to include the embodiment of the subject as a 'critique of dualism as a form of violence' (Braidotti 264), a direction in which Irigaray has taken the lead. Since most of her work is only now appearing in translation, Irigaray's significance as a feminist theorist is in constant mutation. (See also *materialist criticism, *desire/lack.)

BARBARA GODARD

Primary Sources

Irigaray, Luce. *Amante marine. De Friedrich Nietzsche.* 1980. *Marine Lover.* Trans. Gillian Gill. New York: Columbia, 1991.
– *Ce Sexe qui n'en est pas un.* 1977. *This Sex Which Isn't One.* Trans. Catherine Porter. Ithaca: Cornell UP, 1985. 'When Our Lips Speak Together.' Trans. Carolyn Burke. *Signs* 6.1 (Autumn 1980): 69–79. 'This Sex Which Is Not One.' 'When the Goods Get Together.' Trans. Claudia Reeder. *New French Feminisms.* Ed. Elaine Marks and Isabelle de Courtivron. Amherst: U of Massachusetts P, 1980, 99–106, 107–10.
– *Le Corps-à-corps avec la mère.* Montreal: La Pleine Lune, 1981.
– *La Croyance même.* Paris: Galilée, 1983.
– 'Egales ou différentes?' 1986. Repr. in *Je, tu, nous.* 1990. 'Equal or Different?' Trans. David Macey. In *The Irigaray Reader.* Ed. Margaret Whitford. Oxford: Basil Blackwell, 1991, 30–3.
– *Ethiques de la différence sexuelle.* Paris: Minuit, 1984.
– *Et l'une ne bouge pas sans l'autre.* 1979. 'And the One Doesn't Stir Without the Other.' Trans.

Hélène Wenzel. *Signs* 7.1 (Autumn 1981): 56–67.
– 'Femmes divines.' *Critique* 454 (March 1985): 294–308. Repr. in *Sexes et parentés,* 67–85. *Divine Women.* Trans. Stephen Muecke. Sydney: Local Consumption, 1986.
– *The Irigaray Reader.* Ed. Margaret Whitford. Oxford: Basil Blackwell, 1991.
– *Je, tu, nous: Pour une culture de la différence.* Paris: Grasset, 1990.
– *Le Langage des déments.* Paris: Mouton, 1973.
– *L'Oubli de l'air chez Martin Heidegger.* Paris: Minuit, 1983.
– *Parler n'est jamais neutre.* Paris: Minuit, 1985.
– *Passions élémentaires.* Paris: Minuit, 1982.
– 'Questions to Emmanuel Levinas.' Trans. Margaret Whitford. In *Rereading Levinas.* Ed. Robert Bernasconi and Simon Critchley. Bloomington: Indiana UP, 1991.
– *Sexes et genres à travers les langues.* Paris: Grasset, 1990.
– *Sexes et parentés.* Paris: Minuit, 1987.
– *Speculum de l'autre femme.* 1974. *Speculum of the Other Woman.* Trans. Gillian Gill. Ithaca: Cornell UP, 1985.
– *Le Temps de la différence.* Paris: Livre de Poche, 1989.
– 'Le Sexe linguistique.' *Langages* 89 (March 1987).

Secondary Sources

Bono, Paola, and Sandra Kemp, eds. *Italian Feminist Thought.* Oxford: Blackwell, 1991.
Braidotti, Rosi. *Patterns of Dissonance: A Study of Women in Contemporary Philosophy.* Trans. Elizabeth Guild. New York: Routledge, 1991.
Brossard, Nicole. *L'Amer ou le chapitre effrité.* Montreal: Quinze, 1977. *These Our Mothers.* Trans. Barbara Godard. Toronto: Coach House, 1983.
Butler, Judith. *Gender Trouble: Feminism and the Subversion of Identity.* New York: Routledge, 1990.
Deleuze, Gilles. *Logique du sens.* Paris: Minuit, 1969.
Ecker, Gisela, ed. *Feminist Aesthetics.* London: Women's P, 1985.
Gallop, Jane. 'The Body Politic.' 1982, 1983. In *Thinking Through the Body.* New York: Columbia UP, 1988, 91–118.
Girard, René. *Violence and the Sacred.* Trans. P. Gregory. Baltimore: Johns Hopkins UP, 1977.
Godard, Barbara. 'Translating (With) the *Speculum.*' *Traduction, Terminologie, Rédaction* 4.2 (Winter 1991), 85–121.
Grosz, Elizabeth. *Sexual Subversions: Three French Feminists.* Sydney: Allen and Unwin, 1989.
Moi, Toril. *Sexual/Textual Politics: Feminist Literary Theory.* London and New York: Methuen, 1985.
Plaza, Monique. '"Phallomorphic" Power and the Psychology of "Woman."' *Feminist Issues* (Summer 1980): 71–102.
Questions féministes Collective. 'Variations on Common Themes.' *Questions féministes* 1 (Nov. 1977).

Trans. Yvonne Rochette-Ozzello. In *New French Feminisms*. Ed. Elaine Marks and Isabelle de Courtivron. Amherst: U of Massachusetts P, 1980, 212–30.

Spivak, Gayatri Chakravorty. 'French Feminism in an International Frame.' *Yale French Studies* 62 (1981): 154–84.

Théoret, France. 'Le Déplacement du symbolique.' *Entre raison et déraison*. Montreal: Les Herbes Rouges, 1987.

Whitford, Margaret. *Philosophy in the Feminine*. London: Routledge, 1991.

Iser, Wolfgang

(b. Germany, 1926–) Literary theorist and professor of English and comparative literature. Iser studied at the University of Heidelberg and has taught there and at Würzburg, Cologne, Constance (since 1967) and the University of California, Irvine (since 1978). He has also held various visiting professorships and fellowships. One of the central figures of the *Constance School of Reception Aesthetics, he is best known for his work on reader reception theory, strongly influenced by the phenomenology of *Roman Ingarden and *Edmund Husserl and by the *hermeneutics of *Hans-Georg Gadamer. (See *reader-response criticism, *phenomenological criticism.)

Iser's earlier work focuses on English literature, including an examination of the aesthetics of Walter Pater and a study of Lawrence Sterne's *Tristram Shandy*. His inaugural lecture at the University of Constance was subsequently published under the title *Die Appellstruktur der Texte. Unbestimmtheit als Wirkungsbedingung literarischer Prosa* [Indeterminacy and the Reader's Response 1970]. Textual *indeterminacy and reader response also stand at the centre of his *Theorie ästhetischer Wirkung* [Theory of Aesthetic Response 1976], subsequently developed in *Der implizite Leser* [The Implied Reader 1972] and *Der Akt des Lesens* [The Act of Reading 1976].

The Implied Reader outlines a phenomenological approach to the reading process. Iser here conceives of the *text as an intentional object whose communicatory effect can be brought about only by the reader's active assumption of a role designated by the text itself. (See *intention/intentionality.) This role is mapped out by strategies that act as instructions enabling the real reader to fulfil the intention of the text. This role is characterized by Iser as that of an '*implied reader,' which he conceives of as a construct that can be applied in both a synchronic and diachronic framework, thus accommodating both thematically and historically conditioned changes and variations in reader response. In the terms of *communication theory, to which Iser repeatedly refers, the model presupposes a sender and a receiver sharing the same linguistic and cultural *code, the deformations of which in the text perform their communicatory functions by their allusion to the normative functions of these codes.

During the reading process the reader's activity is bent on realizing the communicative potential of the text, which consists of determinate or given elements surrounded by blanks or gaps, which must be filled in by the reader according to the instructions encoded in the text. This process of *concretization, achieved by the elimination of indeterminacy (blanks or gaps), permits the consistency-building which ultimately leads to the constitution of meaning. In contrast to the traditional quest for a meaning presumed to be hidden in the text, the constitution of meaning is seen as an experience resulting from the interaction between text and reader throughout the entire reading process.

It is precisely in the reader's activity and participation, necessitated by the indeterminacies of the text, that Iser situates the aesthetic, or the text as a work of art. He defines the aesthetic as an empty principle, a potential effect, which is realized by a structuring of outside realities that enables the reader to construct a world no longer exclusively determined by the hitherto familiar. In contrast to Ingarden's 'place of indeterminacy,' which implies a textual deficiency, Iser's use of the term designates not only the selectivity and segmentation inevitable in the representation of the fictional world of the text; it is also a vacancy in the overall system of the text which must be occupied to bring about the interaction of textual patterns necessary for the text to achieve its effect. Indeterminacy in the Iserian sense is thus the ideational impulse that both enables and drives the reader to interact with the text. The reader does so by filling in gaps, occupying vacancies, connecting segments, and negating the given according to the 'instructions' encoded in the text, which can be intersubjectively agreed upon.

While Iser's theory of aesthetic effect places less emphasis on *Rezeptionsgeschichte* [history of reception] than does the work of *Hans Robert Jauss, Iser also insists on a cumulative approach to non-contemporary literature, maintaining that past interpretations form a part of the contemporary response to a text. Iser demonstrates changes in reader response to historical texts in *The Implied Reader,* which includes a number of essays on individual prose works from Bunyan to Beckett. Here Iser also develops a typology of perspectival relationships, identifying the paradigms predominating during a given historical period. This typology, further refined in *The Act of Reading,* has a synchronic as well as a diachronic dimension as it permits the identification and description of particular strategies in creating certain kinds of effects.

Iser's work on norm repertoires and perspectivization, which accommodates 'affirmative' as well as 'negative' or critical texts more easily than Jauss' model and insists on negativity as a principle of aesthetic effect, has had considerable impact on various aspects of socioliterary study, including periodization and *sociocriticism. Although discussions of Iserian theory have centred on his notion of indeterminacy, Iser himself has been focusing increasingly on the sociological and anthropological implications of his model.

The appeal of Iser's work is often seen in its emancipatory potential, in its highly refined exposure and articulation of the interaction between subject and world as it occurs in the processing of a fictive text. His theory of indeterminacy offers a solution to the unresolved issue of interpretative validation by accounting for deviant readings (by acknowledging that different readers will fill up the schematically outlined *Gestalten* in various ways), while misreadings can be excluded owing to intersubjectively agreed upon 'instructions' encoded as strategies in the text. While it is Iser's work on indeterminacy that has been in large part responsible for his theoretical appeal, it is also an issue on which he has been challenged, notably by *Stanley Fish, who contests Iser's distinction between the determinate and the indeterminate.

Since the publication of his initial theoretical position, Iser has become a central figure in international theoretical debate. As with his Constance colleague Jauss, his influence in

Germany was initially due perhaps as much to his acknowledgment of the crisis in which the *literary institution – indeed the academic institution as a whole – found itself in the late 1960s as it was to the theoretical model by which he proposed to seek a way out of this impasse. The early recognition of the importance of his work in English-speaking countries was facilitated by the rapid appearance of good-quality English translations. The French response to Iser's work (and to German reception theory as a whole) was somewhat belated, in part owing to the lack of ready accessibility to modern German hermeneutics in which reception theory is largely grounded, as witnessed in the lateness, lack, or, in some cases, problematic nature of French translations of seminal German works. The importance of Iser's contribution to literary theory is generally seen in his construction of a model that permits acknowledgment of both textual intentionality and the diversity of individual reader response and in his meticulous description of the act of reading as a consciousness-altering, socially formative and hence historically formative event.

ROSMARIN HEIDENREICH

Primary Sources

Iser, Wolfgang. *Der Akt des Lesens. Theorie ästhetischer Wirkung.* Munich: Fink, 1976. *The Act of Reading. A Theory of Aesthetic Response.* Baltimore: Johns Hopkins UP, 1978.
– *Die Appellstruktur der Texte. Unbestimmtheit als Wirkungsbedingung literarischer Prosa.* Konstanz: Universitätsverlag, 1970. 'Indeterminacy and the Reader's Response.' In *Aspects of Narrative.* Ed. J. Hillis Miller. New York: Columbia UP, 1971, 1–45.
– *Das Fiktive und das Imaginäre. Grundzüge einer Literaturanthropologie.* Frankfurt: Suhrkamp, 1991.
– *Der implizite Leser. Kommunikationsformen des Romans von Bunyan bis Beckett.* Munich: Fink, 1972. *The Implied Reader. Patterns of Communication in Prose Fiction from Bunyan to Beckett.* Baltimore: Johns Hopkins UP, 1974.
– *Lawrence Sterne: Tristram Shandy.* Cambridge UP, 1988.
– *Prospecting. From Reader Response to Literary Anthropology.* Baltimore: Johns Hopkins UP, 1989.
– *Walter Pater. Die Autonomie des ästhetischen.* Tübingen: 1960. *Walter Pater. The Aesthetic Moment.* Cambridge UP, 1987.

Jakobson, Roman Osipovich

(b. Russia, 1896–d. U.S.A., 1982) Linguist, literary scholar, semiotician. In 1914 Jakobson entered Moscow University where he took his first degree; he moved to Czechoslovakia in 1920 and completed his studies at the University of Prague where he received his doctorate, teaching at Masaryk University from 1935 until the Nazi occupation in 1939, when he fled to Scandinavia. He emigrated to the U.S.A. in 1941, and subsequently taught at the Ecole Libre des Hautes Etudes in New York (1942–6), Columbia (1946), Harvard (1949) and the Massachusetts Institute of Technology (1957). He was a founding member of the Moscow Circle in 1915 and the Prague Linguistic Circle (1926). (See Russian *formalism, *Semiotic Poetics of the Prague School.) His work is based on the principles of the linguistics of *Ferdinand de Saussure, on the phenomenology of *Edmund Husserl, and on the extension and application of the *semiotics of *Charles Sanders Peirce. (See also *phenomenological criticism.)

Jakobson's best-known achievements in linguistics are closely allied to his lifelong work in literary research; he argued that these two disciplines should be studied in conjunction. The founding of the Moscow Linguistic Circle in 1915 provided an unprecedented forum for research into the relations of *literature and language, since such research had remained outside the scope of the Neogrammarian linguistics then dominating language studies. The work of the Circle promoted research into prosody, *myth and both traditional and contemporary folklore ('Retrospect,' *Selected Writings* 1: 631; *SW* 5: 569; 'Toward the History of the Moscow Linguistic Circle,' *SW* 7: 279–82). Jakobson counted among his collaborators and friends many leading avant-garde poets and painters, such as Vladimir Maiakovskii, Velimir Khlebnikov, and Kasimir Malevich, whom he would often credit for their formative influence on his work. The close affiliation of the Circle with the Petrograd-based OPOIAZ (Society for the Study of Poetic Language) provided a context in which scholarly and historical research proceeded hand in hand with contemporary literature.

De Saussure's linguistics ('Retrospect,' *SW* 1: 631) provided Jakobson from the beginning of the 1920s with a model for the systematic investigation of language in terms of relational concepts such as synchrony/diachrony, *langue/parole* and *signans/signatum*. Throughout his career, however, Jakobson sought to replace Saussure's notion of the synchrony/diachrony relation with a permanently dynamic synchrony and with a diachrony containing static invariants. Jakobson would thus investigate language as a structural network of dynamic relations and, as if to reiterate the intersemiotic and creative aspects of this work, Jakobson often quoted the Cubist painter Georges Braque, who claimed himself not to believe in things, but only in the relations between things ('Retrospect,' *SW* 1: 631). Modern painting, in Jakobson's view, in its exploration of abstraction and of multiple temporal and visual perspectives, stresses the relation of *signans* and *signatum* (see *signifier/signified/signification), forcing one to discriminate more clearly between the *signatum* and the *designatum* (see *sign). Such painting, and poetic work in general, focus not on the object of reference, but on the relations of the signifying elements in the sign itself. In thus emphasizing the set *(Einstellung)* towards the message itself, poetry foregrounds the *code, or the Saussurean *langue*, at the expense of the object of reference ('Futurizm,' 717–22; 'On the Relation between Visual and Auditory Signs,' 338–44). (See *reference/referent.)

As early as 1919 Jakobson proposed the notion of 'literariness' (*literaturnost'*) to characterize the literary fact, making 'literariness,' and not literature itself, the proper focus of research' (see *Noveishaia russkaia poeziia* [*Modern Russian Poetry*] and 'Retrospect,' *SW* 3: 766). In formalist terms, the artistic work was seen as an agglomeration of self-focusing or autotelic 'devices.' (See *Shklovskii.) Primary among the devices is *defamiliarization or the 'making strange' *(ostranenie)* that results from the marking of previously unmarked signs. Jakobson would further refine the notion of the device by arguing that the work is a system of devices organized into a hierarchy forming a global sign, with one device serving as the 'dominant' within a relational network. The model of the constellation of devices could thus include not only individual works, but also poetic genres and their dynamic changes in diachrony ('The Dominant,' 751–6). The notion of the dominant moves the emphasis from the materiality of the individual device to the function of that device within a network of related elements. This in turn corresponds to a shift from a formalist emphasis on the immanence of the poetic work to a structuralist understanding of the work as an autonomous structure that is in turn necessarily linked in a hierarchy to other signifying structures and codes (with Iurii Tynianov, 'Problemy skumania literatury i iazyka,' 3–6). (See *Tynianov.)

His studies in language acquisition and aphasia, the first of which were presented in the late 1930s ('Les Lois phoniques du langage enfantin et leur place dans la phonologie générale,' SW 1: 317–27; 'Kindersprache Aphasie und allgemeine Lautgesetze' ['Children's Language, Aphasia, and General Phonology'] SW 1: 328–96) led to his formulation of the notion of the metaphoric and metonymic poles of linguistic ('Two Aspects of Language,' 229–59). (See *metonymy/metaphor.) Building upon the Saussurean doctrine of the paradigmatic and syntagmatic axes of language, Jakobson argued that the operations of selection and combination should be understood in terms of the rhetorical categories of metaphor and metonymy. Language loss and language acquisition, which mirror each other, are thus related to the subject's ability to manage selection and combination, or similarity and contiguity. In the terms of this model, metaphor and metonymy are intrinsic to the working of language at every level, and are not simply a consciously wrought ornamentation subordinate to the referential function. Jakobson extended his argument to claim that a typology of individual literary works, the corpus of a given author, and the stylistic conventions of periods and genres could be given as a function of the frequency of metaphoric or metonymic figures. The model is thus an ambitious attempt to link together literary, neurolinguistic and psychopathological materials.

In the 1950s Jakobson's work in distinctive feature analysis developed into a comprehensive structural description of the ultimate constituents of phonemes and phonological systems, based on the notion of binary oppositions. (See *binary opposition.) During that same decade he also brought together the mathematical theory of communication and the semiotics of Charles Sanders Peirce with his own work in poetics and *communication theory in two important papers: 'Shifters, Verbal Categories, and the Russian Verb,' from 1950–7, and 'Linguistics and Poetics,' originally delivered as the closing statement to a scholarly conference in 1958. The 'closing statement' includes not only a full working out of the factors and functions of his communication model, but also the formulation of the poetic function: 'The poetic function projects the principle of equivalence from the axis of selection into the axis of combination' (27). To each of the six factors that must be present in order for communication to take place (addresser, addressee, code, message, contact, context) there corresponds one of six functions that describe the orientation of the speech act (emotive, conative, metalingual, poetic, referential, and phatic). As the poetic function is oriented to the message itself, similarity at the level of the code becomes the constitutive principle of the sequence. The referential function, in contrast, is oriented to the context and to the relation of the code to the designatum. In expository prose, therefore, although the referential function would be the dominant, the poetic function could be an important subdominant in the hierarchy of functions; whereas in verse, where similarity at the level of the code predominates, the order of the dominants would be inverted. Similarity, stemming from congruities in the various paradigms at the level of the code, may encompass phonological, semantic or syntactic likeness. These in turn may all be described as parallelisms, whether on the sound level as rhyme and paronomasia, on the semantic level as synonymy and antynomy, or on the syntactic level as parallel and antithetical sequences and rhythm. The 'grammar of poetry' consists in the foregrounding of similarities intrinsic to the code or language itself, that is, in the 'poetry of grammar.' Lyric poetry, which is tightly bound to language-specific parallelism, is more difficult, if not impossible, to translate, than is expository prose in which the referential function is the dominant.

Jakobson's later theoretical contributions are accompanied by a very rich body of short studies of poems from many languages and periods, including works by Shakespeare, Blake, Yeats, Khlebnikov, Maiakovskii, Pushkin, Klee, Brecht, Hölderlin, Pessoa, Dante, Du Bellay, and Baudelaire. These 'readings,' many of which are collected in the third volume of the Selected Works, constitute a repertoire of the critical art as he formulates it in such essays as 'Poetry of Grammar and Grammar of Poetry,' 'Language in Operation' and 'Subliminal Verbal Patterning in Poetry,' in which he develops Gerard Manley Hopkins' insight concerning the primary role of repetition and parallelism in the poetic work.

Jakobson's work has also been the centre of controversy. *Michael Riffaterre, responding to Jakobson's and *Lévi-Strauss' analysis of Baudelaire's 'Les Chats,' touched off a protracted and at times heated controversy about the role that linguistic knowledge might properly play in the interpretation of a literary work. *Jonathan Culler has also engaged in a polemic with Jakobson, anticipating in *Structuralist Poetics* some of the premises of deconstructive criticism. (See *deconstruction.)

Jakobson's significance to modern literary research is profound and wide-ranging. His assessment of metaphor and metonymy informs Lacanian criticism (see *Lacan), the notion of binary oppositions as the elements of structure are essential to Claude Lévi-Strauss' structural anthropology, and the phonological model is basic not only to the transformational grammar of *Noam Chomsky, but also by extension to critical work, such as that of *Julia Kristeva, which develops the transformational model of deep and surface structure into the corresponding notions of *genotext and phenotext. It is impossible to understand the background and the contemporary development of *dialogical criticism and the work of *Mikhail Bakhtin, as well as the Tartu and the Moscow Schools, without a knowledge of the controversies surrounding the formalist research of the Moscow Linguistic Circle. (See *Tartu School.) At the same time, many of the specific issues, such as the notion of literariness, have all but disappeared from critical debate, and Jakobson's pioneering work on metaphor seems to have been absorbed largely without acknowledgment in the recent work of the North American cognitivists.

Jakobson's most enduring contribution may be, in the sense of *Roland Barthes, a fusion of scientific and of creative thought. Jakobson's career is a testimony to his belief that language is the predominant human trait, and that as a linguist, nothing to do with the study of language lay outside his interests.

RICHARD KIDDER

Primary Sources

Jakobson, Roman. 'The Dominant.' 1935/1971. Repub. in *SW* 3 (1981): 751–6.
- *The Framework of Language.* Intro. by Ladislaw Matejka. Ann Arbor: Michigan Studies in the Humanities, 1980.
- 'Futurizm.' 1919. Repub. in *SW* 3 (1981): 717–22. Eng. trans. *Language in Literature*, 28–33.
- *Language in Literature.* Ed. Krystyna Pomorska and Stephen Rudy. Belknap-Harvard UP, 1987.
- 'Language in Operation.' 1964. Repub. in *SW* 3 (1981): 7–17.
- 'Linguistics and Poetics.' 1960. Repub. in *SW* 3 (1981): 18–51.
- *Noveishaia russkaia poeziia. Nabrosok pervyi. Viktor Khlebnikov.* 1921. Repub. in *SW* 5 (1985): 299–344. Excerpted as 'Modern Russian Poetry: Velimir Khlebnikov.' In *Major Soviet Writers*, Oxford UP, 1972, and in *Questions de poétique* (see below).
- 'On the Relation between Visual and Auditory Signs.' 1967. Repub. in *SW* 2 (1971): 338–44.
- 'Poeziia grammatiki i grammatika poezii.' 1961. Repub. in *SW* 3 (1981): 163–86. Eng. version. 'Poetry of Grammar and Grammar of Poetry.' 1968. Repub. in *SW* 3 (1981): 87–97.
- *Questions de poétique.* Deuxième édition, revue et corrigée par l'auteur. Publié sous la direction de Tzvetan Todorov. Collection Poétique. Paris: Seuil, 1973.
- 'Retrospect.' Repub. in *SW* 1 (1962): 631–58.
- *Selected Writings.* 7 vols. The Hague; Paris; New York; Berlin; Amsterdam; New York: Mouton, 1962–85.
- 'Shifters, Verbal Categories, and the Russian Verb.' 1957. Repub. in *SW* 2 (1971): 130–47.
- 'Subliminal Verbal Patterning in Poetry.' 1970. Repub. in *SW* 3 (1981): 136–47.
- 'Toward the History of the Moscow Linguistic Circle.' In *SW* 7 (1985): 279–82.
- 'Two Aspects of Language and Two Types of Aphasic Disturbance.' 1956. Repub. in *SW* 2 (1971): 229–59.
- *Verbal Art, Verbal Sign, Verbal Time.* Ed. Krystyna Pomorska and Stephen Rudy. Assisted by Brent Vine. Minneapolis: U of Minnesota P, 1985.
Jakobson, Roman, and Claude Lévi-Strauss. 'Les Chats' de Charles Baudelaire.' *L'Homme* 2 (1962): 5–21. Repub. in *SW* 3 (1981): 447–64.
Jakobson, Roman, and Krystyna Pomorska. *Dialogues.* Trans. Mary Fretz. Paris: Flammarion, 1980.
Jakobson, Roman, and Iurii Tynianov. 'Problemy skumania literatury i iazyka.' *Novj Lef* 12 (1928): 36–7. Eng. trans. 'Epigraph: Problems in the Study of Literature and Language.' Repub. in *SW* 3 (1981): 3–6.
Jakobson, Roman, and Linda Waugh. *The Sound Shape of Language.* Assisted by Martha Taylor. Bloomington: Indiana UP, 1979.

Secondary Sources

Barthes, Roland. 'Avant-propos.' *Cahiers Cistre* 5 (1978): 9–10.

Culler, Jonathan. *Structuralist Poetics: Structuralism, Linguistics and the Study of Literature.* Ithaca: Cornell UP, 1976.

Delcroix, M., and W. Geerts, eds. *"Les Chats" de Baudelaire: Une confrontation de méthode.* Namur: Presses Universitaires de Namur, 1980.

Eco, Umberto. 'The Influence of Roman Jakobson on the Development of Semiotics.' In *Roman Jakobson: Echoes of His Scholarship.* Ed. Daniel Armstrong and C.H. van Schooneveld. Lisse: Peter de Ridder, 1977, 39–58.

Grzybek, Peter. 'Some Remarks on the Notion of Sign in Jakobson's Semiotics and in Czech Structuralism.' *Znakolog: An International Yearbook of Slavic Semiotics.* 1 (1989): 113–28. Bochum: Initiative zur Forderung Interkultureller und Slavischer Semiotik (IFISS).

– *Studien zum Zeichenbegriff der Sowjetischen Semiotik Moskauer und Tartauer Schule.* Bochumer Beitrage zur Semiotik. Bochum: Brockmeyer, 1989.

Holenstein, Elmar. *Roman Jakobsons Phänomenologischer Strukturalismus.* Frankfurt am Main: Suhrkamp, 1975.

Luria, A.R. 'The Contribution of Linguistics to the Theory of Aphasia.' In *Roman Jakobson: Echoes of His Scholarship.* Ed. Daniel Armstrong and C.H. van Schooneveld. Lisse: Peter de Ridder, 1977, 237–51.

Pomorska, Krystyna, et al., eds. *Language, Poetry and Poetics. The Generation of the 1890s: Jakobson, Trubetzkoy, Majakovskij.* Proceedings of the First Roman Jakobson Colloquium, at the Massachussetts Institute of Technology, October 5–6, 1984. Berlin, New York, and Amsterdam: Mouton de Gruyter, 1987.

– 'The Autobiography of a Scholar.' In *Language, Poetry and Poetics,* 3–13.

Riffaterre, Michael. 'Describing Poetic Structures: Two Approaches to Baudelaire's "Les Chats."' *Yale French Studies* 36–7 (1966): 200–42.

Rudy, Stephen. *Roman Jakobson: A Complete Bibliography of His Writings.* Ed. and comp. by Stephen Rudy. Berlin and New York: Mouton de Gruyter, 1990.

Todorov, Tzvetan. 'Poétique générale.' *Roman Jakobson: Echoes of His Scholarship.* Ed. Daniel Armstrong and C.H. van Schooneveld. Lisse: Peter de Ridder, 1977, 473–84.

Waugh, Linda R. 'The Poetic Function and the Nature of Language.' In *Verbal Art, Verbal Sign, Verbal Time.* Ed. Krystyna Pomorska and Stephen Rudy. Assisted by Brent Vine. Minneapolis: U of Minnesota P, 1985, 143–68.

– 'On the Sound Shape of Language: Mediacy and Immediacy.' In *Language, Poetry and Poetics,* 157–73.

– *Roman Jakobson's Science of Language.* Lisse: Peter de Ridder, 1976.

Winner, Thomas G. 'The Aesthetic Semiotics of Roman Jakobson.' In *Language, Poetry and Poetics,* 257–74.

– 'Roman Jakobson and Avant-garde Art.' In *Roman Jakobson: Echoes of His Scholarship.* Ed. Daniel Armstrong and C.H. van Schooneveld. Lisse: Peter de Ridder, 1977, 503–14.

James, Henry

(b. U.S.A., 1843–d. England, 1916) Novelist, writer of short stories and novellas, literary critic, man of letters. Born into a wealthy family, Henry James travelled widely and attended a variety of schools, including two in Switzerland and Germany. The result was a cosmopolitan and European perspective that convinced him to discontinue his law studies at Harvard in 1862 for a life of writing. His first story, 'A Tragedy of Error,' appeared in *The Atlantic Monthly* in 1864. Thereafter, William Dean Howells, who became editor of the *Monthly* in 1871, gave James a number of assignments. As a result of a lengthy journey in Europe in 1869, James discovered a congenial cultural milieu. In 1875, both Henry and his brother William travelled first to Paris and then to London where Henry lived until his death. It was during this time that James met such important literary figures as Flaubert, de Maupassant, the Goncourt brothers and Turgenev, whose writing became a model for James' later work. In this international atmosphere he produced much of the work that established his reputation as a major novelist, short story and novella writer, literary critic, and theoretician.

In his *20th Century Literary Criticism* (1988), *David Lodge states that 'more than any other single writer, James may be said to have presided over the transformation of the Victorian novel into the modern novel, and at the same time to have laid the foundations of modern criticism of the novel.' A writer of imaginative *literature, James also wrote important criticism and theory, at least in part to explain his fictive purposes. His ideas are rooted in organic forms with a synthetic focus that stems particularly from Aristotle and Longinus. An additional influence stems from the work of his brother William. William James' studies in psychology and his creation of such terms as 'stream of consciousness,' a metaphor which marks a whole new approach to fiction, as well as his pragmatism and ethical sense are keystones of Henry's work. (See *metonymy/metaphor.)

Also reflected in the writings of Henry James is the criticism of Matthew Arnold. In mid-19th-century England, Arnold was bemoaning the philistine mentality and Anglo-Saxon attitudes of English writers of the first half of the century, especially in poetry, whereas James was decrying the 'naivete' and 'vulgarity' of American and English literature, particularly in the novel of the second half of that century. Both men contrasted that literature with the tradition from the Continent that stemmed from Greek and later European examples that had intellectual and philosophical dimensions they found lacking in English and American literature. Both looked to that tradition to modernize and deepen sensibilities, and to broaden awareness of the comparative virtues of other literature. For James, the Victorian novel was lesser than the best European examples because 'it had no air of having a theory, a conviction, a consciousness of itself behind it – of being the expression of an artistic faith, the result of choice or comparison' ('The Art of Fiction'). Even in tone James' criticism mirrors Arnold's, but their major agreement concerned what they saw as the absence of formal and ethical values in English literature. A point they both emphasized again and again was that it should be the function of the imaginative writer and critic (as Arnold puts it when he defines 'criticism') as a 'disinterested endeavor to learn and propogate the best that is known and thought in the world' ('The Function of Criticism'). If Arnold could be accused of 'kid-gloved arrogance' in his criticism, James could be described as a man whose standards were elitist, intellectual and demanding of a deep and abiding knowledge of the great literature of the past, of the tradition of ideas that it reflects in the so-called *canon.

Though it is much less read than his fiction, James' literary criticism is both an invaluable chronicle of literary and cultural life in the late 19th century and an essential adjunct to his fiction. Much of his criticism is contained in informal reviews collected in a Library of America edition. He wrote on American writers such as Hawthorne, Howells, Lowell, and Parkman; English writers such as Arnold, Robert Browning, George Eliot, Trollope; French writers Balzac, Daudet, Flaubert, and Taine; and other Europeans such as Goethe, Turgenev, and D'Annunzio. These reviews give insights into the intellectual milieu of the century but they do not have the same status in criticism and theory as do the sections in the Library of America edition entitled 'The Prefaces to the New York Edition' (the collected edition of his novels) and 'Essays on Literature,' containing a number of essays such as 'The Science of Criticism' (1891: 93), 'The Future of the Novel' (1899), 'The Present Literary Situation in France' (1899), and especially 'The Art of Fiction' (1884: 88).

'The Prefaces to the New York Edition' encapsulate James' 'theory' in a methodological sense, the entries in his 'Notebooks' in a practical sense. 'The Art of Fiction' is a general statement about James' philosophy of creation, expressing his deep commitment to pluralism, humanism and the life of the mind. Each of the 'Prefaces' concerns his studies of 'point of view,' that is, the narrative methods in his novels. 'The Art of Fiction' is a statement about the nature of art and the responsibility of the artist to his art. On the experimental requirement and capacity, he writes that the novelist 'must write from his experience, that his characters must be real and such as might be met with in actual life.' On organicism in form and content: 'A novel is a living thing, all one and continuous, like any other organism, and in proportion as it lives will it be found, I think, that in each of the parts there is something of each of the other parts.' That intellect, ethics, and aesthetics are required in good works of literature: 'No good novel will ever proceed from a superficial mind that seems to me an axiom which, for the artist in fiction, will cover all needful moral ground.'

James insisted on study of the crucial philosophical ideas, on being aware of the techniques of fiction, on being cultured, and on having the generosity, self-discipline, and disinterest to allow the artist his donnée, his gift and his perspectives.

REED MERRILL

Primary Sources

Arnold, Matthew. 'The Function of Criticism at the Present Time.' In Essays in Criticism. Boston: Ticknor and Fields, 1865, 1–38.

James, Henry, Jr. The Complete Notebooks of Henry James. Ed. Leon Edel and L.H. Powers. New York: Oxford UP, 1987.

– Henry James Letters 1843–1916. 4 vols. Ed. Leon Edel. Cambridge, Mass.: Harvard UP, 1974–84.

- *Henry James: Literary Criticism* ('Essays on Litera-
  ture,' 'American Writers'). Ed. Leon Edel. New
  York: Library of America, 1984.
- *Henry James: Literary Criticism* ('French Writers,'
  'Other European Writers,' 'The Prefaces to the
  New York Edition'). Ed. Leon Edel. New York: Li-
  brary of America, 1984.
- *Selected Letters of Henry James.* Ed. Leon Edel.
  Cambridge, Mass.: Harvard UP, 1987.

Secondary Sources

Beach, Joseph Warren. *The Method of Henry James.*
  Philadelphia: A. Salter, 1954.
Blackmur, R.P. 'Introduction.' *The Art of the Novel:
  Critical Prefaces* [from the New York edition]. New
  York: Scribner, 1934.
Daugherty, Sarah B. *The Literary Criticism of Henry
  James.* Athens: Ohio UP, 1981.
Edel, Leon. *Henry James: A Life.* New York: Harper
  and Row, 1985.
- *The Modern Psychological Novel.* New York: Gros-
  set and Dunlap, 1955.
- Dan H. Laurence and James Rambeau. *A Bibliog-
  raphy of Henry James.* Oxford: Oxford UP, 1982.
Gass, William. 'The High Brutality of Good Inten-
  tions.' In Henry James, *The Portrait of a Lady.* New
  York: W.W. Norton, 1975, 704–13.
Leavis, F.R. *The Great Tradition.* New York: New
  York UP, 1967.
Lubbock, Percy. *The Craft of Fiction.* New York: Vi-
  king, 1957.
Roberts, Morris. *Henry James's Criticism.* Cambridge:
  Harvard UP, 1929.
Veeder, William. 'Image and Argument: Henry
  James and the Style of Criticism.' *Henry James Re-
  view* 6 (1985): 172–81.
Wellek, René. *A History of Modern Criticism 1750–
  1950.* New Haven: Yale UP, 1965.
Wimsatt, William K., Jr., and Cleanth Brooks. *Liter-
  ary Criticism: A Short History.* New York: Alfred A.
  Knopf, 1957.

Jameson, Fredric R.

(b. U.S.A., 1934–) Literary critic. Fredric Jame-
son received his B.A. from Haverford College
(1954), his M.A. (1956) and Ph.D. (1960) from
Yale University and also studied at the Uni-
versities of Aix, Munich and Berlin. His doc-
toral dissertation became his first book, *Sartre:
The Origins of a Style* (1961). After teaching at
Harvard and elsewhere, he is now the William
A. Lane Professor of Comparative Literature at
Duke University, co-editor of *Social Text* and a
contributing editor of the *Minnesota Review*.
One of the leading Marxist literary theorists

and cultural critics in the Anglo-American
world, Jameson seeks a genuinely dialectical
engagement with Marxist theorists like *Theodor Adorno, *Walter Benjamin, Herbert Marcuse, Ernst Bloch, *Georg Lukács, and *Jean-
Paul Sartre (see *Marxism and Form*), but also
confronts from a resolutely Marxist perspective
the theoretical challenge posed by *structuralism, *poststructuralism and *postmodernism.
(See also *Marxist criticism, *materialist criticism.)

Jameson's thought is in a Hegelian or Western Marxist tradition. Thus certain themes or
tendencies assert themselves in his writings:
(1) a concern with the interaction between
subject and object or the 'data of individual
experience and the vaster forms of institutional
society'; (2) the recapitulation of this 'opposition' at the aesthetic level in the relation between form and content; and (3) the conception of reality as a 'totality.' (See *subject/
object, *theme.) Jameson brings to these
themes a very personal mode of dialectical
analysis that does not attempt simply to answer a question but rather to reflect on the
very existence of the question itself, a mode of
reflection that leads back, ultimately, to a concrete underlying historical reality. Thus, for example, instead of accepting the concept of
'point of view' as a universal formal category
of fiction, the dialectical critic will recognize its
roots in a determinate social reality: a condition of isolated subjectivity and individualism
characteristic of early capitalism. Similarly,
faced with the obscurity of modern poetry, the
dialectically trained reader will avoid interpreting or restoring to transparency the verbal
opacity he or she is confronted with but will
instead question its status, quality and structure, as well as his or her own mental processes in responding to it.

In *Marxism and Form*, his first major theoretical work, Jameson explores the dialectical relation between form and content, which he
understands not merely in a literary and formalist sense but as a historical and dialectical
constituent of all cultural institutions and symbolic acts. Form and content are dialectically
interchangeable: what at one level of interpretation is perceived as form turns out at another
level of insight to be content. This *paradox
arises from the fact that form is simply the
abstraction or transformation of an already
meaningful content, namely, the components

of our concrete social life and of history. The manifest content of that form (here Jameson adapts Freudian terminology to his own purposes) is the abstraction and distortion of the real that we call *ideology. (See *Freud.) Interpretation works to reverse this process, to reveal the latent, concrete, already meaningful content behind the form. Jameson calls for a Marxist hermeneutic to undertake this process of restoration. Just as a religious hermeneutic seeks to recover meaning in texts and cultures resistant or inimical to its outlook, so too a political hermeneutic will preserve access to revolutionary energies in repressive times and cultures. This hermeneutical operation has a negative and positive aspect, not only the task of *demystification and the destruction of illusions, but also the restoration of the genuine utopian impulse behind alien and antagonistic cultural forms. The work of a conservative like *T.S. Eliot or a writer with fascist leanings like Wyndham Lewis must be stripped of its illusory character, but equally the utopian, prophetic cry that lies buried beneath the surface of the *text must be freed and reconverted to the political aims for which it rightfully calls. (See *hermeneutics, *metacriticism.) Jameson's *Fables of Aggression: Wyndham Lewis, the Modernist as Fascist* (1979) is a critical work that takes up this double hermeneutic task.

The Prison-House of Language (1982) accepts the challenge of structuralism, which is to consider language as a model and to 'rethink everything through once again in terms of linguistics.' Here Jameson shows how Saussurean linguistics, Russian *formalism and French structuralism all constitute fundamentally ahistorical theories that value synchronic analysis over diachrony and ignore the role of the observer in the structures they describe. (See *Saussure.) In order to become a genuine hermeneutic, the structuralist model must re-emphasize the place of the analyst and open itself to 'all the winds of history' (216). This Jameson himself attempts to do by showing how structuralism and formalist analysis are products of a determinate historical moment and social reality.

Jameson's most ambitious theoretical work to date, *The Political Unconscious: Narrative as a Socially Symbolic Act* (1981), attempts to develop an authentically dialectical criticism. Jameson argues that Marxism is no mere substitute for other approaches but constitutes an ' "untranscendable horizon" that subsumes ...

apparently antagonistic or incommensurable critical operations, assigning them an undoubted sectoral validity within itself, and thus at once cancelling and preserving them' (10). Other methods have a local validity, reflecting one or another element within the complex cultural superstructure and offering 'strategies of containment' that promote the illusion of complete and self-sufficient readings. Only Marxism can claim to comprehend the totality, whose ultimate ground is the unity of History itself. The historical past and its relation to current reality can be grasped only if they are understood as parts of a single great collective story, a story of humankind's fall from an original plenitude whose shattered fragments generate humanity's need for narrative and interpretation. But many elements of that fundamental story – the collective struggle for freedom – have been distorted and suppressed: hence, Jameson's preoccupation with the concept of a political unconscious. History can be apprehended only in textual form; in other words, like the concepts of time and space, 'narrative' is a fundamental epistemological category that structures our experience of the world and represents in its form the contours of human desire. As a 'socially symbolic act,' the narrative of a literary text demands interpretation and Jameson adapts the four-fold medieval allegorical framework (as reworked by *Frye in *The Anatomy of Criticism*) to the requirements of a Marxist hermeneutic. Thus interpretation moves through three concentric frameworks or horizons: first, the immediate historical context of the work; second, the social order in the broadest sense (especially as constituted by class struggle); and third, the 'ultimate horizon of human history as a whole.' (See also *ideological horizon.)

Jameson is pre-eminently a cultural rather than a literary critic, as his recent writings on modernism and postmodernism indicate. His greatest strength as a theorist is perhaps his ability to synthesize (synthesis being the dialectician's hallmark) the work of others – *Althusser, *Greimas, *Gadamer, and *Lévi-Strauss, among others. Some indication of his critical influence may be gleaned from the debate that his work has generated. But Jameson's position as a Marxist thinker in the postwar Anglo-American world has meant that he has remained, as Eagleton puts it, an intellectual 'client of Europe.' This is not to undervalue his powerful creativity of thought, but simply to comment dialectically on his historical position as a theorist.

FRANS DE BRUYN

Primary Sources

Jameson, Fredric R. *Fables of Aggression: Wyndham Lewis, the Modernist as Fascist.* Berkeley: U of California P, 1979.
- *The Ideologies of Theory: Essays 1971–1986.* 2 vols. Theory and History of Literature 48 and 49. Minneapolis: U of Minnesota P, 1988.
- *Marxism and Form: 20th Century Dialectical Theories of Literature.* Princeton: Princeton UP, 1971.
- 'Modernism and Imperialism.' In *Nationalism, Colonialism, and Literature.* Minneapolis: U of Minnesota P, 1990, 43–66.
- *The Political Unconscious: Narrative as a Socially Symbolic Act.* Ithaca: Cornell UP, 1981.
- *Postmodernism, or, the Cultural Logic of Late Capitalism.* Durham: Duke UP, 1991.
- *The Prison-House of Language: A Critical Account of Structuralism and Russian Formalism.* Princeton: Princeton UP, 1982.
- *Sartre: The Origins of a Style.* New Haven: Yale UP, 1961.

Secondary Sources

Eagleton, Terry. 'Fredric Jameson: The Politics of Style.' *Diacritics* 12 (Fall 1982): 14–22.
Frow, John. *Marxism and Literary History.* Cambridge, Mass.: Harvard UP, 1986.
LaCapra, Dominick. *Rethinking Intellectual History: Texts, Contexts, Language.* Ithaca and London: Cornell UP, 1983.
Lyotard, Jean-François. 'The Unconscious, History, and Phrases: Notes on The Political Unconscious.' *New Orleans Review* 11 (Spring 1984): 73–9.
Mohanty, S.P. 'History at the Edge of Discourse: Marxism, Culture, Interpretation.' *Diacritics* 12 (Fall 1982): 33–46.
Scholes, Robert. *Textual Power: Literary Theory and the Teaching of English.* New Haven and London: Yale UP, 1985.
Sprinker, Michael. 'The Part and the Whole.' *Diacritics* 12 (Fall 1982): 57–71.
Watkins, Evan. *The Critical Act: Criticism and Community.* New Haven and London: Yale UP, 1978, 158–87.
Weber, Samuel. *Institution and Interpretation.* Theory and History of Literature 31. Minneapolis: U of Minnesota P, 1987, 46–58.
White, Hayden. 'Getting Out of History.' *Diacritics* 12 (Fall 1982): 2–13.

Jauss, Hans Robert

(b. Germany, 1921–) Professor of Romance languages and literary theorist. Jauss studied at Heidelberg and taught at Heidelberg, Munster and Giessen before his appointment at the University of Constance in 1966. He is one of the central figures in the *Constance School and is best known for the aesthetics of reception *(Rezeptionsästhetik)*, a hermeneutically based approach to *literature and literary history influenced primarily by the Russian formalists and by Jauss' teacher *Hans-Georg Gadamer (1900–). (See *hermeneutics, Russian *formalism.)

Jauss' early work concerned aspects of French literature, particularly the medieval period. In 1967 he attracted the attention of literary theorists with his inaugural address at Constance, 'Was heisst und zu welchem Ende studiert man Literaturgeschichte?' [What is and for what purpose does one study literary history?]. This talk was subsequently published as *Literaturgeschichte als Provokation der Literaturwissenschaft* [Literary History as a Provocation to Literary Scholarship]. In this work Jauss outlined the main precepts of the aesthetics of reception, which attempted to combine the best features of two putatively opposing schools of criticism: Russian formalism and *Marxist criticism. From the former he takes the insight that perception is fundamental to our encounter with literary texts and to change in literary history. From the latter he draws the notion that literature is thoroughly historical and can only be understood as a product of historical mediations. The aesthetics of reception thus places the perceiving subject at the centre of a literary historiography that locates texts in a larger artistic, social and political context. (See *reader-response criticism, *text.)

The main tool which Jauss employs to accomplish this re-definition of interpretation and historiography is the *horizon of expectation *(Erwartungshorizont)*. Never explicitly defined by Jauss, the term evidently refers to a system or structure of expectations that are literary, cultural and social. Jauss proposes that literary scholarship should try to determine the *Erwartungshorizont* for any particular work and then measure the distance between the two. Only those works that violate or break the horizon of expectation evidence artistic merit. A guide to aesthetic distance can be found in the array of reactions to a given work by its initial audience and by literary critics, and later by other writers and literary scholarship. The aesthetics of reception thus postulates novelty or a deviation from an established standard as both a criterion for evaluation and as the motive force for change in literary history.

By the early 1970s, however, Jauss had revised his deviationist stance. In his *Kleine Apologie der Ästhetischen Erfahrung* [*Small Apology for Aesthetic Experience* 1972] and in other essays from this period, he criticized what he called the 'aesthetics of negativity.' Reacting to the posthumous publication of *Theodor Adorno's *Aesthetic Theory* (1970), for Jauss the paradigmatic case of negative aesthetics, he reconsidered the implications of his own 'negativity' as well. The aesthetics of negativity is deficient in two areas. First, it unnecessarily reduces the progressive role of art in society by admitting a positive social function only when the work negates the society in which it is produced. There is no room for affirmative art and consequently only elitist and hermetic works are declared authentic. Second, the aesthetics of negativity tends to deny the pleasure art gives. It thereby denies the primary function of art through the ages and is unable to appreciate the artistic value of a wide range of literary works, from medieval heroic epics to the classics of 'affirmative' literature.

Applying this criticism to his own theses from the 'Provocation' essay, Jauss developed a more differentiated notion of reception. In his magnum opus *Ästhetische Erfahrung und literarische Hermeneutik* [*Aesthetic Experience and Literary Hermeneutics* 1977; 1982], he was centrally concerned with doing justice to the variety of responses to works of art. To avoid the deleterious consequences of negative aesthetics, he places the notion of pleasure or enjoyment *(Genuss)* at the centre of his theory. In the aesthetic realm we distance ourselves from the object that we produce by an act of consciousness. The key to aesthetic experience for Jauss is self-enjoyment in the enjoyment of something else *(Selbstgenuss im Fremdgenuss)*. It consists of three moments: *poesis, aisthesis* and *catharsis*. The first refers to the productive aspect of our encounter with literature and art, the pleasure that stems from the application of our own creative abilities. *Aisthesis* is Jauss' designation for the receptive side of aesthetic experience. By supplying common perceptions for members of a community, *aisthesis* contrib-

utes to social unity. Finally, *catharsis* can be understood as the communicative component between art and recipient. It can best be illustrated by the various ways (associative, admiring, sympathetic, cathartic, ironic) in which we interact and identify with the hero.

Despite the subtlety and refinement of his later theoretical work, Jauss' early work had more of an impact in Germany, influencing an entire generation of younger scholars and sparking lively international debates. His importance in the English-speaking world, by contrast, is a phenomenon of the 1980s, when his work became more generally available in translation. His acclaim in both, however, is due to his ability to apply the principles of Gadamerian hermeneutics to the sphere of literature and poetic theory.

ROBERT C. HOLUB

Primary Sources

Jauss, Hans Robert. *Ästhetische Erfahrung und literarische Hermeneutik.* Munich: Fink, 1977. Rev. and exp. Frankfurt: Suhrkamp, 1982. *Aesthetic Experience and Literary Hermeneutics.* Theory and History of Literature 3. Minneapolis: U of Minnesota P, 1982.
– *Kleine Apologie der Ästhetischer Erfahrung.* Konstanzer Universitätsreden 59. Constance: UP, 1972.
– *Literaturgeschichte als Provokation der Literaturwissenschaft.* Frankfurt: Suhrkamp, 1970.
– *Toward an Aesthetic of Reception.* Theory and History of Literature 2. Minneapolis: U of Minneapolis P, 1982.

Jung, Carl Gustav

(b. Switzerland, 1875–d. 1961) Founder of analytical psychology, mythologist and psychiatrist. After studying science at the University of Basel, Jung received his medical doctorate (1900), then specialized in psychiatry at the Burgholzli Clinic in Zurich. His early word-association experiments resulted in his discovery of the basic elements of personality, 'the feeling-toned complexes,' autonomous networks of emotionally charged associations organized around a specific core (a mother complex, father complex and so on). This work led to a meeting with *Freud in 1907 and a collaboration that culminated in their 1909 lectures at Clark University and in Jung's installation as first president of the International Psychoanalytic Association (1910–14). Jung began private psychoanalytic practice in 1909. His developing interest in the mythic dimension of dreams and fantasies led to his increasing difficulty in accepting Freud's Oedipus complex as the underlying *universal of all neuroses and to a conviction that the single-drive (sexual) theory of libido was inadequate (see *Wandlungen und Symbole der Libido* 1911–12; trans. *Symbols of Transformation, Collected Works* 5). (See *myth.) Further differences with Freud over the role of transference in analysis, the nature of dream symbolism, and the meaning of seduction fantasies (*Freud and Psychoanalysis, CW* 4) resulted in their break in 1913 and in Jung's subsequent designation of his own researches as analytical psychology.

As a structuralist and formalist thinker, Jung stands outside the linguistically oriented mainstream of Continental structuralist theory, although his work is related to it and in his own terms would be 'compensatory,' since it explores the domain systematically excluded by structuralist linguistics. (See *structuralism.) Jung's thought is thus mythocentric rather than logocentric: it is concerned with essence rather than function; with the symbolic rather than the semiotic and with the diachronic or historically continuous aspect of language (as mediated through recurring images) rather than with its synchronic aspect. (See *logocentrism, *semiotics.) As the 'talking cure,' psychoanalysis in general must also be concerned with what *Saussure termed *parole*, the subjective and individual utterance, rather than with *langue*, the abstract language-system underlying individual and individualizing speech. (See *langue/parole*.)

As a psychological structuralist, Jung located the instinct to formulate structures, as well as the primary patterns upon which all structures are formulated, in the human psyche. He first designated the basic organizing patterns 'primordial images,' after Jacob Burkhardt's concept of eternally recurring motifs or mythologems. Later, Jung adopted the term *archetype, inspired by Plato, St. Augustine and Kant, and used it generally in his writings after 1919. As innate, a priori impulses to organize images and ideas, archetypes are tendencies to produce form, relatable to instincts and representing 'the precipitate of the psychic functioning of the whole ancestral line, the accumulated experiences of organic life in gen-

eral, a million times repeated, and condensed into types' (*CW* 6: 659). 'Just as his instincts compel man to a specifically human mode of existence, so the archetypes force his ways of perception and apprehension into specifically human patterns' (*CW* 7: 270). The instincts and the archetypes together form the 'collective unconscious,' different from the 'personal unconscious' (which Freud dealt with) because it is not made up of individual, unique or repressed contents, but of those that are inborn, universal and recurring. Crucial to an understanding of Jung is the distinction he makes between the archetype itself and the archetypal image, the concrete representation of the archetype's energic potential. While the archetype as such is irrepresentable and transcendent, it is mediated through spontaneously arising images, which are projected as the symbols comprising fantasies, 'big' dreams and myths and also found in the mystical, gnostic and alchemical texts in which Jung immersed himself (*Four Archetypes: Mother/Rebirth/Spirit/Trickster, CW* 9: i). Some post-Jungians, notably James Hillman, have suggested the distinction between the archetype and its image is irrelevant. *Northrop Frye, a literary structuralist, and *Claude Lévi-Strauss, an anthropological structuralist, apply the term archetype to what Jung designates as its image, thus locating their 'archetype' within a closed system of textual or mythic phenomena that excludes the psyche.

That archetypes are unconscious structures is central to Jung's psychology. As the agency that patterns and directs all psychic activity, the archetype, being projectable in an infinite variety of images, acts to correct or compensate for conscious attitudes and values that are one-sided, fixated or development-inhibiting. Both on the individual and cultural level, the archetype is an equilibrium-inducing and balancing factor. Its image-symbols mediate and resolve the oppositions of a human consciousness that must differentiate (and so create opposites) in order to function; its symbols also heal the division of a psyche split phylogenetically with the 'coming of light' and individually with the birth of consciousness into binary parts. The most important archetype is the 'self,' its most culturally significant image that of Christ on the cross; as a *quaternio*, the crucified Christ is also a mandala, the circle as perfected form and the common feature of all archetypal images of the self (see *Aion, CW* 9:

ii). (See *self/other.) The self directs individuation, the process through which the individual achieves distinction from and transcendent relationship to collective humanity. As the archetype of wholeness and perfected form, the self resolves or synthesizes the opposites confronted on the individuation journey. Jung's analytical psychology posits as the ultimate goal of its therapy the activation of the self archetype, full realization of which would constitute an experience of redemption and divinity. (See also *psychoanalytic theory.)

As a record of individual and cultural psychic process, *literature occupies a privileged place in Jungian thought. Myth offers an archive of archetypal images that aid the amplification of dreams and fantasies, while narrative projects, through the figure of the hero/ine, an image-record of the development of ego-consciousness in its successive stages. The classic and most comprehensive application by an analytical psychologist of Jung's thought on myth is Erich Neumann's *The Origins and History of Human Consciousness* (1952), an interpretation of the psychic significance of the universal patterns and figures of heroic quest cycles. The seminal Jungian study of poetry is that of the literary critic *Maud Bodkin, whose *Archetypal Patterns in Poetry* appeared in 1934. Since then, Jung's influence on literary criticism, while pervasive, has been diffuse and, until recently, evident chiefly in the use of such standard Jungian concepts as the 'shadow' (the unassimilated, negative element of the personality) and *animus* and *anima*, the contrasexual components, respectively, of the female and male psyches. Since 1980, major Jungian studies of Shakespeare, Blake, Yeats, Beckett, Robertson Davies, and Doris Lessing have appeared, as have Jungian approaches to American romanticism and to women writers. Applications of Jungian thought to the visual arts and to film have also been published, as have books on Jung and theology and the Bible. (See also *archetypal criticism.)

JEAN COATES CLEARY

Primary Sources

Major writings by Jung are from *The Collected Works of C.G. Jung*, 20 vol., Bollingen Series 20, Princeton UP, 2nd ed., 1970.

Jung, C.G. *Aion: Researches into the Phenomenology of the Self.* 1951. Vol. 9.

- 'The Analysis of Dreams.' 1909. *Freud and Psychoanalysis.* Vol. 4.
- *The Archetypes and the Collective Unconscious.* 1934–5. Vol. 9.
- 'Freud and Jung: Contrasts.' 1929. *Freud and Psychoanalysis.* Vol. 4.
- *Letters.* 2 vols. Bollingen Series 95. Princeton: Princeton UP, 1973.
- *Memories, Dreams, Reflections.* New York: Vintage Books, 1965.
- 'On the Criticism of Psychoanalysis.' 1910. *Freud and Psychoanalysis.* Vol. 4.
- *The Spirit in Man, Art, and Literature.* 1929–32. Vol. 15.
- *Symbols of Transformation.* 1911–12/1952. Vol. 5
- 'The Theory of Psychoanalysis.' 1913. *Freud and Psychoanalysis.* Vol. 4.

McGuire, William, ed. *The Freud/Jung Letters.* Bollingen Series 94. Princeton: Princeton UP, 1974.

Von Franz, Marie-Louise. *C.G. Jung: His Myth in Our Time.* Boston and Toronto: Little Brown, 1975.

Wehr, Gerhard. *Jung: A Biography.* Boston: Shambala, 1988.

Secondary Sources

1. Applications of Jungian Thought: Myth, Literature, Art

Barrett, Gregory. *Archetypes in Japanese Film: The Sociopolitical and Religious Significance of the Principal Heroes and Heroines.* London and Toronto: Associated UPs, 1989.

Bickman, Martin. *The Unsounded Centre: Jungian Studies in American Romanticism.* Chapel Hill: U of North Carolina P, 1980.

Bodkin, Maud. *Archetypal Patterns in Poetry.* London: Oxford UP, 1934.

Cederstrom, Lorelei. *Fine-tuning the Feminine Psyche: Jungian Patterns in the Novels of Doris Lessing.* New York: Peter Lang, 1990.

Doll, Mary A. *Beckett and Myth: An Archetypal Approach.* Syracuse: Syracuse UP, 1988.

Driscoll, James P. *Identity in Shakespearean Drama.* Lewisburg: Bucknell UP; London and Toronto: Associated UPs, 1983.

Edinger, Edward F. *Encounter with the Self: A Jungian Commentary on William Blake's Illustrations of the Book of Job.* Toronto: Inner City Books, 1986.

Jung, Emma, and M.L. Von Franz. *The Grail Legend.* 2nd ed. Boston: Sigo Press; London: Coventure, 1986.

Knapp, Bettina L. *A Jungian Approach to Literature.* Carbondale: Southern Illinois UP, 1984.

- *Women in 20th Century Literature: A Jungian View.* University Park and London: Pennsylvania State UP, 1987.

Monk, Patricia. *The Smaller Infinity: The Jungian Self in the Novels of Robertson Davies.* Toronto: U of Toronto P, 1982.

385

Neumann, Erich. *The Archetypal World of Henry Moore.* Bollingen Series 67. Princeton: Princeton UP, 1959.
- *Art and the Creative Unconscious.* Bollingen Series 61. Princeton: Princeton UP, 1959.
- *The Origins and History of Human Consciousness.* Bollingen Series 42. Princeton UP, 1954–70.
Olney, James. *The Rhizome and the Flower: The Perennial Philosophy – Yeats and Jung.* Berkeley: U of California P, 1980.
Pratt, Annis. *Archetypal Patterns in Women's Fiction.* Bloomington: Indiana UP, 1981.
Richards, David G. *The Hero's Quest for the Self: An Archetypal Approach to Hesse's Demian and Other Novels.* Lanham, Md.: UP of America, 1987.
Slusser, Gerald H. *From Jung to Jesus: Myth and Consciousness in the New Testament.* Atlanta: John Knox P, 1986.
Weaver, Rix. *Spinning on a Dream Thread: Herman Hesse: His Life and Work, and His Contact with C.G. Jung.* Perth: Wyvern Publications, 1977.

2. Post-Jungian Archetypal Theory

Goldenberg, Naomi R. 'Archetypal Theory after Jung.' *Spring* (1975): 199–220.
Hillman, James. *Archetypal Psychology.* Dallas: Spring Publications, 1985.
Lauter, Estella, and Carol Schreier Rupprecht. *Feminist Archetypal Theory: Interdisciplinary Re-Visions of Jungian Thought.* Knoxville: U of Tennessee P, 1985.
Samuels, Andrew. *Jung and the Post-Jungians.* London and Boston: Routledge and Kegan Paul, 1985.

Kermode, Frank

(b. England, 1919–) Literary critic. Frank Kermode went from a B.A. (1941) and M.A. (1947) at Liverpool University into a teaching career in English *literature highlighted by numerous distinguished chairs. As early as 1958–65 he was J.E. Taylor Professor of English at Manchester, then Winterstoke Professor at Bristol (1965–7), Lord Northcliffe Professor at University College London (1967–74), and finally King Edward Professor of English Literature at Cambridge (1974–82). Subsequently he accepted invitations to distinguished visiting lectureships at Columbia (1983, 1985). Retired at Cambridge, he has continued to write acclaimed works of literary criticism covering a wide range of subjects in literary and aesthetic history.

Early books of note reflect Kermode's teaching interests: *Romantic Image* (1957), *John Donne* (1957), *Wallace Stevens* (1960), *William Shakespeare: The Final Plays* (1963), and *D.H. Lawrence* (1973) are all indicative of his critical intelligence and lucid expository style. Moreover, each work in its own way expresses Kermode's unflagging practical commitment to a Leavisite *canon and aesthetic celebration of the 'Great Tradition,' and thus anticipates his principle legacy to Anglo-American criticism of what is generally called *hermeneutics or interpretation theory. (See *F.R. Leavis.)

The first of his more theoretical books, *The Sense of an Ending: Studies in the Theory of Fiction,* is the published form of the Flexner lectures given by Kermode at Bryn Mawr College in 1965. Here he explores the 'apocalyptic' impulse in historical fiction, that characteristic tendency to want to see the world and the structure of fiction as making most sense retrospectively from its point of closure as optimal signifier. The Bible, in this view, offers the most familiar modelling of meaningful history: starting with 'In the beginning' (Genesis), ending with a vision of the end (Apocalypse), it provides the ideal of 'a wholly concordant structure' (6).

But the impulse evident in the structure of the biblical anthology Kermode finds echoed in varying degrees everywhere in literature. A fundamental principle in Western hermeneutic – that the end alone should declare the purpose of the beginning and order the meaning of all that follows up to that end – is thus taken by Kermode to provide the heuristic motive in our 'explanatory fictions' (35–6). Yet for the modern reader this meaning is not often welcomed as 'our' meaning. Modernist resistance to closure, and indeed the implications of the notion of a beginning before *our* beginning, creates in both our history and fiction a rejection of the metafictional implications of sequence: modern literature is thus tense with a counter-impulse, separating history from chronicle, novel from simple narrative. (See *closure/dis-closure.)

In *The Genesis of Secrecy: On the Interpretation of Narrative* (1979) Kermode turned his focus from the question of meaning as realized structure to the issue of 'insider' versus 'outsider' *discourse in the pursuit and disclosure of meaning. Turning his attention to the Gospel of Mark and Jesus' explanation of his use of parable at once to instruct the insider and confound 'those without' – those who have 'eyes to see and see not, ears to hear and hear not' – Kermode invokes the historical relationship between biblical exegesis and literary theory to juxtapose criticism as elite priestcraft with interpretation more broadly conceived as a vernacular means of negotiating life. In this book the sharply theoretical potential in his agenda is subtly metamorphosed into questions of strategic praxis and culturally responsible, contextualized interpretation. The question of institutional control of interpretation, raised in this work, is explored in an important article in *Salmagundi* (43: 72–86), and returned to again in 'Canons' (1988; cf. his essay in Alter and Kermode [1987]), each time in a manner still largely affirming of preoccupations already articulated in an earlier book, *The Classic: Literary Images of Permanence and Change* (1975).

Kermode's continuing reflections have led him to consider periodization, aesthetic standards and the relation of history and value. In *Forms of Attention* (1985), *History and Value* (1988), *Poetry, Narrative, History* (1989), and in his editorial collaboration with Robert Alter in *The Literary Guide to the Bible* (1987), Kermode elaborates essentially traditional views of canon (he edited, with John Hollander, *The Oxford Anthology of English Literature* [1973]). Assessment of the formation of hierarchies of value, and of social determinacy versus subjective *indeterminacy in establishing meaning are set in illuminating relation to an aesthetic curriculum still basically Arnoldian in its ambitions. Frank Lentricchia, in his preface to *Forms of Attention*, identifies what is in effect a premise in Kermode's critical writing, that 'all commentary on canonical texts varies from generation to generation because it must meet different needs, and that the canonical text proves itself canonical by being able to withstand changing assaults of interpretation without ever seeming to be exhausted.' This characteristic grants to such a *text what Kermode calls 'perpetual modernity.'

The Uses of Error (1990), a collection of review essays, declares Kermode's traditionalist venerations and hermeneutical stance as a critic who sees his writing as subordinate, as second-order discourse. In the essay 'Disentangling Knowledge from Opinion' he concludes that 'the preservation of canonical works is achieved by means of argument that may not be truly worthy of that name, and which is, at best, incapable of resisting later criticism.'

Kermode's mature work is marked by a keen sense of the distinct enterprises of what the Germans call *Tageskritik* (reviewing) and *Literaturwissenschaft* (formal literary study). As one who has persistently done both tasks, and argued for their necessary complementarity in the English tradition, he wagers his own effort on a diachronist's faith in the future of literary history: 'The success of interpretative argument as a means of conferring or endorsing value,' he contends, 'is, accordingly, not to be measured by the survival of the comment but by the survival of its object.'

DAVID LYLE JEFFREY

Primary Sources

Kermode, Frank. 'Apocalypse and the Modern.' In *Visions of Apocalypse: End or Rebirth?* Ed. Saul Friedlander et al. New York: Holmes, 1985, 84–106.
- *An Appetite for Poetry.* Cambridge, Mass.: Harvard UP, 1989.
- 'Can We Say Absolutely Anything We Like?' In *Art, Politics, and Will: Essays in Honor of Lionel Trilling.* Ed. Quentin Anderson et al. New York: Basic, 1977, 159–72.
- 'Canons.' *Dutch Quarterly Review of Anglo-American Letters* 18.4 (1988): 258–70.
- *The Classic: Literary Images of Permanence and Change.* New York: Viking, 1975.
- *Continuities.* London: Routledge and Kegan Paul, 1968.
- 'The Decline of the Man of Letters.' *Partisan Review* 52.3 (1985): 195–209.
- *D.H. Lawrence.* London: Fontana, 1973.
- *Essays on Fiction 1971–1982.* London: Routledge and Kegan Paul, 1983.
- 'Fighting Freud.' *New York Review of Books*, 29 April 1976: 39–41.
- 'Figures in the Carpet: On Recent Theories of Narrative Discourse.' *Comparative Criticism: A Yearbook* 2 (1980): 291–301.
- *Forms of Attention.* Chicago: U of Chicago P, 1985.
- *The Genesis of Secrecy: On the Interpretation of Narrative.* Cambridge, Mass.: Harvard UP, 1979.
- 'Hawthorne's Modernity.' *Partisan Review* 41 (1974): 428–41.
- *History and Value.* Oxford: Clarendon P, 1988.
- 'Institutional Control of Interpretation.' *Salmagundi* 43 (1979): 72–86.
- 'Interpretive Continuities and the New Testament.' *Raritan* 1.4 (1982): 33–49.
- *John Donne.* London, New York: Longmans, Green, and Co., 1957.
- 'The Last Classic.' *Yale Review* 78.2 (1989): 147–65.
- 'Literary Value and Transgression.' *Raritan* 7.3 (1988): 34–53.

- 'The Model of a Modern Modernist.' *New York Review of Books*, 1 May 1975: 20–3.
- 'Modern Poetry and Tradition.' *Yearbook of Comparative and General Literature* 14 (1965): 5–15.
- 'A Modern Way with the Classic.' *New Literary History* 5 (1974): 415–34.
- 'Novel, History and Type.' *Novel* 1(1968): 231–38.
- *Novel and Narrative.* Glasgow: U of Glasgow P, 1972.
- 'Novel and Narrative.' In *The Theory of the Novel: New Essays.* Ed. John Halperin. New York: Oxford UP, 155–74.
- 'On Being an Enemy to Humanity.' *Raritan* 2.2 (1982): 87–102.
- *On Shakespeare's Learning.* Middletown, Conn.: Wesleyan UP, 1965.
- *The Patience of Shakespeare.* New York: Harcourt, Brace and World, 1964.
- 'The Plain Sense of Things.' In *Midrash and Literature.* Ed. G. Hartman and S. Budick. New Haven: Yale UP, 1986, 179–94.
- *Poetry, Narrative, History.* Oxford: Blackwell, 1990.
- *Puzzles and Epiphanies: Essays and Reviews 1958–1961.* New York: Chilmark P, 1962.
- 'A Reply to Denis Donoghue.' *Critical Inquiry* 1 (1975): 699–700.
- 'Revolution: The Role of the Elders.' In *Liberations: New Essays on the Humanities in Revolution.* Ed. I. Hassan. Middletown, Conn.: Wesleyan UP, 1971.
- *Romantic Image.* London: Routledge and Kegan Paul, 1957.
- *The Sense of an Ending: Studies in the Theory of Fiction.* New York: Oxford UP, 1967.
- *Shakespeare, Spenser, Donne: Renaissance Essays.* London: Routledge and Kegan Paul, 1971.
- 'The Structure of Fiction.' *Modern Language Notes* 84 (1969): 891–915.
- 'The University and the Literary Public.' In *The Humanities and the Understanding of Reality.* Ed. Thomas B. Stroup. Lexington: U of Kentucky P, 1965.
- 'The Use of the Codes.' In *Approaches to Poetics.* New York and London: Columbia UP, 1974, 51–79.
- *The Uses of Error.* London: Collins, 1990.
- *Wallace Stevens.* Edinburgh: Oliver and Boyd, 1960.
- *William Shakespeare: The Final Plays.* London: Longmans, Green, and Co., 1963.
- 'World Without End or Beginning.' *Malahat Review* 1 (1967): 113–29.
- *The Living Milton.* London: Routledge and Kegan Paul, 1960.
- and Robert Alter, eds. *The Literary Guide to the Bible.* Cambridge, Mass.: Harvard UP, 1987.
- and John Hollander, eds. *The Oxford Anthology of English Literature.* New York and London: Oxford UP, 1973.
- Foreword to Guiraud, Pierre. *Semiology.* Trans. George Gross. London: Routledge, 1975.

Secondary Sources

Arac, Jonathan. 'History and Mystery: The Criticism of Frank Kermode.' *Salmagundi* 55 (1982): 135–55. [With a response by Frank Kermode, 156–62].

Kierkegaard, Søren Aabye

(b. Denmark, 1813–d. 1855) Philosopher and religious thinker. Søren Kierkegaard originally studied at the Borgerdyskole in Copenhagen and was taught Latin and Greek by his father, who also initiated him into religious studies. Kierkegaard's early rejection of traditional Christianity led him to years of doubt and dissoluteness filled with self-hatred and guilt. At the University of Copenhagen, and under the influence of George Hamann, he completed his theological studies in anticipation of the Lutheran ministry. His dissertation, *The Concept of Irony with Constant Reference to Socrates* (1841), remains an important work on the subject of *irony as well as a source for his lifelong dedication to the maieutic-dialectical method of the master ironist, Socrates. After a short journey to Germany in 1841, Kierkegaard returned to Copenhagen in 1842, dedicating his remaining years to restoring what he considered to be Christ's ideas as opposed to the orthodoxies created in Christ's name, which he believed were antithetical to real Christian ideals.

As was the case with so many other 19th-century students of philosophy, Kierkegaard was confronted by the idealism of Hegel only to reject it and other kinds of absolutism as being unrealistic and opposed to intellectual freedom. He began a new investigation of the idea of a philosophy of the inner self structured upon an intensive and practical awareness by the individual of life's choices and responsibilities. His philosophy of the discovery of the inner self, one of the important contributions to 19th-century philosophy, occupies the many volumes written from 1841–55.

Scholarly discussion of Kierkegaard's ideas constitutes an impressive body of writing, but his importance for literary theory and criticism has been remarkably neglected, perhaps because his ideas are not a priori but rather based on the varieties of human experience in a world of infinite possibility and flux. His philosophy of life's choices and stages is also exemplified by his use of fiction itself (his 'novel' *Either/Or*, which remains an important analysis of aesthetic existence) and of such fictional characters as Don Juan, Faust and Ahasuerus (the Wandering Jew) as analogues of lived experience and decision-making. In addition, his contribution to such literary matters as point of view, indirect discourse, irony, and narrative are yet to be fully discussed in criticism.

Kierkegaard emphasizes that each individual must be aware of choices and their consequences – that is, to create one's own values through the use of one's intellect. He maintains that 'the crucial thing is to find a truth which is true for me, to find the idea for which I am willing to live or die.' Because of numerous facile readings of Kierkegaard which suggest that his subjectivity begets relativism, it needs emphasizing that he was insistent upon one's ethical awareness of the myriad choices of existence. Neither did he accept relativism nor immoralism as valid positions. Kierkegaard believed that although it is filled with doubt and endless paradoxes, only 'passionate certitude' and 'blind faith' in God can transcend the turmoil of finite existence. (See *paradox.) He argues that 'men are not so corrupt that they actually desire evil, but they are blind and really do not know what they are doing. Everything centers on drawing them out into the area of decision.'

To illustrate the choices of the reflective person, Kierkegaard's works depict those decisions and their implications in an open and flexible discussion of free choice and its realm of possibility with Christianity as its base. Although Kierkegaard uses traditional philosophical and theological terms, he does not think about the self in 'pure speculation but constantly relies upon his actual experience for problems and confirmation' (Collins), while also making numerous allusions to literary works, music and history.

Kierkegaard's *oeuvre* falls into two groups that parallel in chronology in writing and publication what he intended to be a description of the ascending value of 'life's choices,' 'categories,' or 'stages on life's way.' Many of his books are narrated by 'pseudonymous authors' whose indirect discourses and individual points of view concern the relative advantages and disadvantages of existential decision-making. Of these his most important works are *The Concept of Irony with Constant Reference to*

Socrates (1841); *Either/Or* (1843), a study of aestheticism based on the example of Don Giovanni; *Fear and Trembling* (1843), concerning absurdist faith and Abraham and Isaac, as well as classical tragedy and its ethical requirements; *Philosophical Fragments* (1844), describing the psychology of his radical transcendent Christian faith; and *Stages on Life's Way* (1845), and *Concluding Unscientific Postscript* (1846), perhaps the two most important works that synthesize his categories. The stages/categories are the 'aesthetic,' 'ethical' and 'religious,' with borderline categories of 'irony' (between the aesthetic and ethical), and 'humour' (between the ethical and religious). The narrators find examples from their own intellectual dialectics to justify their positions. Each of these narratives is placed within a framework much like the confessional; each 'author' defends his position while, at the same time, being aware of its contingencies and limitations.

The second group of Kierkegaard's writings largely consists of his own first-person, direct discussions of the freedom and paradox inherent in one's coming to faith, the conditions that inhere in that understanding. Here again he emphasizes the necessity for personal choice in the discovery of faith and the freedom that it implies, but he also stresses the solitude and doubt that comes of the 'one-to-one' faith in the primacy of God and the debilitation of the believer. These 'personal' discussions of the new faith are introduced in *The Point of View of My Work as an Author* (1859), an important *text for an understanding of Kierkegaard because it gives direct expression to his revolutionary ideas about Christianity, its requirements, and its transcendent value over other choices of existence. It serves as his 'Apology.' Among the other works that illustrate the category of religious choice are *Edifying Discourses in Various Spirits* (1847), *Works of Love* (1848), *The Sickness Unto Death* (1849), and *Training for Christianity* (1850).

Even though Kierkegaard contributed to theories of comedy, irony and humour, virtually nothing has been written to date about this crucial body of ideas. The same holds for his writings on tragedy, and particularly for his profound understanding and elucidation of the ideas of Socrates, who dominated his life and served as his intellectual mentor and 'friend.' Whether or not one accepts Kierkegaard's idea of the paradox of Christian faith, his discursive analyses of the psychology of possibility and probability have continuing importance for critical analysis. The accessibility and application of his ideas are also of value for literary as well as individual study of the psychology of the free intellect.

REED MERRILL

Primary Sources

Kierkegaard, Søren Aabye. *The Concept of Anxiety* [Dread]. Trans. Walter Lowrie. Princeton, NJ: Princeton UP, 1944.

– *The Concept of Irony, with Constant Reference to Socrates*. Trans. Lee M. Capel. Bloomington: Indiana UP, 1968.

– *Concluding Unscientific Postscript*. Trans. David Swenson and Walter Lowrie. Princeton, NJ: Princeton UP, 1941.

– *Edifying Discourse*, I–IV. Trans. David and Lillian Swenson. Minneapolis, Minn.: Augsburg Publishing, 1943–6.

– *Either/Or*. 2 vols. Trans. Howard and Edna Hong. Princeton, NJ: Princeton UP, 1987.

– *Fear and Trembling/Repetition*. Trans. Howard and Edna Hong. Princeton, NJ: Princeton UP, 1983.

– *Philosophical Fragments, or a Fragment of Philosophy*. Trans. Howard and Edna Hong. Princeton, NJ: Princeton UP, 1983.

– *The Point of View of My Work as an Author: A Report to History*. Trans. Walter Lowrie. New York: Harper Torchbooks, 1962.

– *The Present Age*. Trans. Walter Dru and Walter Lowrie. London: Oxford UP, 1940.

– *The Sickness Unto Death*. Trans. Walter Lowrie. Princeton, NJ: Princeton UP, 1970.

– *Søren Kierkegaard's Journals and Papers*. 7 vols. Trans. and ed. Howard and Edna Hong. Bloomington: Indiana UP, 1967–78.

– *Stages on Life's Way*. Trans. Howard and Edna Hong. Princeton, NJ: Princeton UP, 1989.

– *Training for Christianity*. Trans. Walter Lowrie. Princeton, NJ: Princeton UP, 1964.

– *Works of Love*. Trans. Howard and Edna Hong. New York: Harper and Row, 1964.

Secondary Sources

Adorno, Theodor W. *Kierkegaard: Construction of the Aesthetic*. Trans. Robert Hullot-Kentor. Minneapolis: U of Minnesota P, 1989.

Collins, James. *The Mind of Kierkegaard*. Princeton: Princeton UP, 1983.

Diem, Hermann. *Kierkegaard's Dialectic of Existence*. Trans. Harold Knight. London: Oliver and Boyd, 1959.

Fabro, Cornelio. *Some of Kierkegaard's Main Categories*. Copenhagen: Reitzels, 1988.

Heywood, Thomas J. *Subjectivity and Paradox: Kierkegaard*. Oxford: Oxford UP, 1957.

Lapointe, François. *Søren Kierkegaard and His Critics: An International Bibliography*. Westport, Conn.: Greenwood P, 1980.

Lowrie, Walter. *Kierkegaard*. New York and Oxford: Oxford UP, 1938.

Malantscuk, Gregor. *The Controversial Kierkegaard*. Trans. Howard and Edna Hong. Waterloo, Ont.: Wilfrid Laurier UP, 1980.

– *Kierkegaard's Thought*. Trans. Howard and Edna Hong. Princeton: Princeton UP, 1971.

– *Kierkegaard's Way to Truth: An Introduction to the Authorship of Søren Kierkegaard*. Minneapolis: Minnesota UP, 1963.

Shestov, Lev. *Kierkegaard and the Existential Philosophy*. Trans. Elinor Hewitt. Athens: Ohio UP, 1969.

Taylor, M.C. *Journey to Selfhood: Hegel and Kierkegaard*. Berkeley: U of California P, 1980.

– *Kierkegaard's Pseudonymous Authorship: A Study of Time and Self*. Princeton: Princeton UP, 1975.

Thulstrup, Niels, and Howard A. Johnson. *Kierkegaard's Relation to Hegel*. Trans. George Stengren. Princeton: Princeton UP, 1969.

Wyschograd, Michael. *Kierkegaard and Heidegger: The Ontology of Existence*. New York: Harper Torchbooks, 1969.

Koestler, Arthur

(b. Hungary, 1905–d. England, 1983) Man of letters, political and social chronicler, essayist, and theorist. After studying science and psychology at the Technische Hochschule in Vienna (1922–6), Arthur Koestler became a foreign correspondent in Palestine and Paris for the Ullstein syndicate, and later foreign and science editor for the *Vossische Zeitung* in Berlin. Between 1930 and 1932 he was a member of the Communist party. In covering the Spanish Civil War as a correspondent for the London *News Chronicle*, he was captured and sentenced to death. After he was released from prison he was again imprisoned in France, finally escaping to England in 1940. This period is recalled in his two-volume autobiography *Arrow in the Blue* (1952) and *The Invisible Writing* (1954).

Before 1952, Koestler's interests were largely political. However, as early as 1931, his disillusionment with the 'Great Experiment,' especially its Stalinist manifestations, led him to question political values in general and eventually to become an important critic of dialectical materialism and other political ideologies as well as of absolutist systems. (See *ideology.) His political scepticism is evidenced in the prose fiction trilogy *The Gladiators* (1939), his most famous work, *Darkness at Noon* (1941), and *Arrival and Departure* (1943) – all dedicated to describing the negative effects of political expediency – and landmarks in the political novel as a genre. Koestler also contributed an essay to *The God That Failed* (1950), a collection by other disaffected ex-communists such as André Gide, Ignazio Silone and Richard Wright. His total output is 33 volumes, encompassing six novels; one play; literary, political and critical essays; and five volumes of autobiography.

After 1952, Koestler abandoned politics and set about finding solutions to contemporary problems in the sciences and humanities. He referred to himself as a 'trespasser in an age of specialists.' Because of his 'educated generalist's' approach and for speculating and theorizing at the expense of rigorous method, he was often in conflict with academics from various disciplines.

Koestler's literary essays, which largely consist of reviews published in English and Continental newspapers and literary journals (many published in the journal *Encounter)*, are collected in such volumes as *The Trail of the Dinosaur* (1955), *Drinkers of Infinity* (1968), *The Heel of Achilles* (1974), and *Kaleidoscope* (1981). They reveal a polymath whose range of knowledge encompasses the arts and sciences as well as crucial contemporary historical, social and economic issues. The expression of a humanist sharing common intellectual interests with the largest possible educated audience, his informal essays are impressionistic in the same vein as those of *Edmund Wilson or V.S. Pritchett, while his formal and critical works show the clear influence of his background as a scientist whose literary analyses often reflect his scientific perspectives.

Perhaps Koestler's two most important contributions to literary criticism and theory come from his attempt to discover common elements in the diversities of the sciences and humanities. The first contribution concerns the creative process in the arts and sciences, particularly in regard to the psychology of creativity and its relation to humour. The second, which is only tangentially literary criticism, concerns *pluralism as opposed to reductionism, positivism and behaviourism, subjects addressed both in the collection of essays *Beyond Reductionism: New Perspectives in the Life

Sciences edited with J.R. Smythies, and including Ludwig von Bertalanffy, F.A. Hayek, C.H. Waddington and Holger Hydén, among others; and most directly in a withering attack on Skinnerian-Watsonian-Pavlovian behaviourism and positivism in *The Ghost in the Machine* (1967), foreshadowed in his early novel *The Age of Longing* (1951).

Koestler's lifelong attempt to find commonalities between the arts and sciences is first found in his 'bisociation' theory: that there is a consistent pluralisitic and 'Janus-faced' relationship between theories in all the disciplines. His first volume on the subject was *Insight and Outlook: An Inquiry into the Common Foundations of Science, Art, and Social Ethics* (1949). The bisociation hypothesis is much more fully developed in his 'tri-valent creative process,' or 'holon' systems theory (an 'open hierarchic' association theory), a three-layered ontological paradigm that attempts to synthesize and organize the arts and sciences. This desire to find a universal systems theory is also reflected in *The Act of Creation* (1964), in the second part of *The Ghost in the Machine* and in *Janus: A Summing Up* (1978).

Koestler's most direct contribution to criticism and theory is in his discussions of the interrelatedness of comedy and tragedy. Although there is no evidence that Koestler knew *Friedrich Nietzsche's views of the connectedness of comedy and tragedy, he extends Nietzsche's perspective to include the common elements in artistic and scientific creativity as well. Like *Freud's, Koestler's theory of comedy and humour is largely affective (hedonistic and psychological) at the expense of its philosophical implications. In his studies on the comic, Koestler borrows Freud's term, the 'Janus effect,' to describe the complexity of the comic transaction. According to Koestler, the creative act consists of comparing and contrasting matrices (much like attempting to synthesize a theory) and creating new wholes. This process is best demonstrated in the 'laughter reflex' of comedy that occurs when seemingly incongruous elements are combined, creating an unexpected but surprisingly congruous result. Laughter is the shock of recognition resulting from the creation of new patterns in the face of normal patterns of expectation. This process of creativity occurs in a world that consists of hierarchies of systems ('holons') that tend to be conservative and to have organic consistency, 'biological, social, and cognitive,' but that can at the same time adjust to obviously superior changes (theories).

Koestler's holon metaphor is the matrix within which the various bisociative processes occur and changes take place. (See *metonymy/metaphor.) The Janus image illustrates how subordinate elements of any holon (in this case of comic and tragic genres) function individually and collectively as parts of larger wholes. Each organism contains potentially opposite and essentially antithethical elements which, at their polar extremes, tend to be conservative or radical (static or dynamic). The 'integrative tendency' of each unit functions in harmony with the 'self-assertive' tendency. According to Koestler, although there is a basic polarity between the self-assertive and integrative tendencies of holons at all levels, 'under favorable conditions the two basic elements are more or less equally balanced, and the holon lives in a kind of dynamic equilibrium within the whole – the two faces of Janus complement each other.' The 'comic effect' is self-assertive in that it is a collision of 'self-consistent but incompatible frames of reference' which are resolved in laughter. The opposite end of the pole is that of 'artistic and aesthetic creativity,' which is self-transcending in its need to resolve the self in a community, a religious creed or political cause, Nature or Art.

Koestler's works remain of importance because of his argument that monological systems invariably lead to autocratic and destructive ends and that a valid theory will always contain the constituents of creative freedom in an open universe.

REED MERRILL

Primary Sources

Koestler, Arthur. *The Act of Creation: A Study of the Conscious and Unconscious Processes in Humor, Scientific Discovery and Art.* London: Hutchinson, 1964.
– *The Age of Longing.* London: Collins, 1951.
– *Arrow in the Blue: An Autobiography.* London: Collins with Hamish Hamilton, 1952.
– *Darkness at Noon.* Trans. Daphne Hardy. London: Jonathan Cape, 1941.
– *Drinkers of Infinity: Essays 1955–67.* London: Hutchinson, 1968.
– *The Ghost in the Machine.* London: Hutchinson, 1967.
– *The Heel of Achilles: Essays 1968–1973.* London: Hutchinson, 1974.
– 'Humour and Wit.' In *Encyclopaedia Britannica,* 15th ed., 1974, 5–11.
– *Insight and Outlook: An Inquiry into the Common Foundations of Science, Art, and Social Ethics.* London: Macmillan, 1949.
– *The Invisible Writing.* London: Collins with Hamish Hamilton, 1954.
– *Janus: A Summing Up.* London: Hutchinson, 1978.
– *Kaleidoscope.* London: Hutchinson, 1981.
– *Reflections on Hanging.* London: Victor Gollancz, 1956.
– *The Trail of the Dinosaur.* London: Collins, 1955.
– with Alistair Hardy and Robert Harvie. *The Challenge of Chance.* London: Hutchinson, 1973.
– and J.R. Smythies. *Beyond Reductionism: New Perspectives in the Life Sciences: The Alpbach Symposium.* London: Hutchinson, 1969.
– et al. *The God That Failed.* Ed. Richard Crossman. London: Hamish Hamilton, 1950.

Secondary Sources

Calder, Jenni. *Chronicles of Conscience: A Study of George Orwell and Arthur Koestler.* London: Secker and Warburg, 1968.
Debray-Ritzen, Pierre, ed. *Arthur Koestler.* Paris: Editions de l'Herne, 1975.
Harris, Harold, ed. *Astride Two Cultures: Arthur Koestler at 70.* London: Hutchinson, 1976.
Levene, Mark. *Arthur Koestler.* New York: Ungar, 1984.
Merleau-Ponty, Maurice. *Humanism and Terror.* Trans. John O'Neill. Boston: Beacon P, 1969.
Merrill, Reed, and Thomas Frazier. *Arthur Koestler: An International Bibliography.* Ann Arbor, Mich.: Ardis Publications, 1979.
Sperber, Murray A., ed. *Arthur Koestler: A Collection of Critical Essays.* Englewood Cliffs, NJ: Prentice-Hall, 1977.
Strachey, John. *The Strangled Cry.* London: Routledge and Kegan Paul, 1962.
Swingewood, Alan. *The Novel and Revolution.* London: Macmillan, 1975.

Krieger, Murray

(b. U.S.A., 1923–) Literary critic. Murray Krieger earned his Ph.D. from Ohio State University in 1952. He has been University Professor of English at the University of California, Irvine, since 1974, is the founding director of the University of California Humanities Research Institute (1987–), and was director of the School of Criticism and Theory from 1976–81. His many honours include election to the Council of the American Academy of Arts and Science in 1987.

While remaining strongly rooted in the assumptions of formalism and *New Criticism, particularly the belief in the unique otherness of literary language, Krieger's work has nonetheless evolved in response to the shifting theoretical terrain. *The New Apologists for Poetry* (1956) modified formalist theory along more rigorously philosophical lines. *The Tragic Vision* (1960) reread modernist *literature from the point of view of existentialism. *A Window to Criticism* (1964) further qualified formalism with what Krieger called 'contextualism,' a term signifying a concern with the historical contexts of the literary *text. The opening essay in that book, originally titled 'After the New Criticism,' provided Frank Lentricchia with the title of his study of 'four exemplary careers,' of which Krieger's is one. Contextualism is also the guiding methodology of the essays collected in *The Play and Place of Criticism* (1967). *Poetic Presence and Illusion* (1979) and *Words about Words about Words* (1988) contain essays responding to poststructural and New Historical concerns. (See *poststructuralism, *New Historicism.)

Krieger has resisted what he considers to be the 'leveling' tendencies of theories which reduce literary language to ordinary language or which turn the text into merely a social document. The danger to culture of theories that would absorb the literary text into a generalized *écriture* or *textuality is the central focus of *Arts on the Level* (1981). Because of Krieger's defence of the unique literary text, Frank Lentricchia (perhaps unfairly seeking a social allegory in Krieger's literary beliefs) has accused him of being undemocratic. Krieger's defence of the literary text as an élite object and Lentricchia's attack on this position as being a displaced form of social élitism is one of the significant debates in late-20th-century cultural studies. Grant Webster, failing to appreciate Krieger's ongoing revisions of his previous positions, particularly his incorporation of developments in phenomenology and reception theory, has insisted on seeing him as a belated New Critic. (See *phenomenological criticism, *Constance School of Reception Aesthetics.) But Webster's objections, which privilege fashion and opportunism, do not initiate the examination of the place and function of literary studies that the Krieger-Lentricchia confrontation does.

Those who influenced Krieger most in his formative stage were Eliseo Vivas, *Erich Auerbach, Leo Spitzer, Sigurd Burckhardt, and Rosalie Colie. Vivas' idea of the subsistent, insistent and existent aspects of the literary work are central to *A Window to Criticism*, and Krieger refers to Rosalie Colie's theories of metaphor even in his most recent work, seeing her formulations as anticipating the problematics of *deconstruction. (See *metonymy/metaphor, *problematic.) Throughout his work, in fact, Krieger's strong grasp of the history of theoretical issues and positions has been a corrective to the notion of the radical newness of concerns designated by such terms as *structuralism, poststructuralism, deconstruction, and neo-Marxism. (See also *Marxist criticism.)

Krieger has done much to further the teaching of literary criticism, theory and history in the university curriculum, most notably as the director of the School of Criticism and Theory. (See also *theory and pedagogy.) His book-length study of the history of critical theory, *Theory of Criticism* (1976), explains the evolution of the critical and theoretical tradition as an ongoing conflict between formal and mimetic positions. Any history is also an argument, and Krieger does not hide his formal biases – 'imitation theory is the enemy' (67). Any attempt to formulate a tradition will inevitably proscribe and exclude, and such figures as Marx, *Nietzsche and *Freud receive scant attention in Krieger's history, which has therefore been criticized for its conservatism.

His departures from a conservative, formalist poetics can be seen in 'An Apology for Poetics' and in the colloquy devoted to the discussion of this essay at the University of Konstanz in 1982. Both are reprinted in *Words about Words about Words*. Krieger's interest in the role of desire and in the provisional 'as if' status of literary truth are distinctly 'postmodern,' as is his concern with the question of 'presence.' While his willingness to accept *paradox in literary theory (see 'Both Sides Now' in *Words*) has elicited charges of logical inconsistency, this aspect of his poetics is entirely in harmony with the postmodern suspicion of totalizing or monologic theories. (See *postmodernism, *totalization, *metaphysics of presence, *desire/lack.)

Krieger, a broad, synoptic literary critic, has functioned at once as a historian and a trenchant commentator on the contemporary critical scene, all the while developing and refining a critical theory of his own that has grappled

Kristeva

with the new developments in Continental philosophy and the human sciences.

BRUCE HENRICKSEN

Primary Sources

Krieger, Murray. *Arts on the Level: The Fall of the Elite Object.* Knoxville: U of Tennessee P, 1981.
– *The Classic Vision: The Retreat from Extremity in Modern Literature.* Baltimore: Johns Hopkins UP, 1971.
– *The New Apologists for Poetry.* Minneapolis: U of Minnesota P, 1956.
– *The Play and Place of Criticism.* Baltimore: Johns Hopkins UP, 1967.
– *Poetic Presence and Illusion: Essays in Critical History and Theory.* Baltimore: Johns Hopkins UP, 1979.
– *Theory of Criticism: A Tradition and Its System.* Baltimore: Johns Hopkins UP, 1976.
– *The Tragic Vision: Variations on a Theme in Literary Interpretation.* New York: Holt, Rinehart and Winston, 1960.
– *Visions of Extremity in Modern Literature.* Vol. 1: *The Tragic Vision: The Confrontation of Extremity.* Vol. 2: *The Classic Vision: The Retreat from Extremity.* Paperback repr. with new Introduction. Baltimore: Johns Hopkins UP, 1973.
– *A Window to Criticism: Shakespeare's Sonnets and Modern Poetics.* Princeton: Princeton UP, 1964.
– *Words about Words about Words: Theory, Criticism, and the Literary Text.* Baltimore: Johns Hopkins UP, 1988.

Secondary Sources

Free, William J. 'Murray Krieger and the Place of Poetry.' *Georgia Review* 22.2 (1968): 236–46.
Graff, Gerald. 'Tongue-in-Cheek Humanism: A Response to Murray Krieger.' *ADE Bulletin* 69 (Fall 1981): 18–21.
Henricksen, Bruce, ed. *Murray Krieger and Contemporary Critical Theory.* New York: Columbia UP, 1986.
Joseph, Terri B. 'Murray Krieger as Pre- and Post-Deconstructionist.' *New Orleans Review* 12.4 (1985): 18–26.
Kartiganer, Donald M. 'The Criticism of Murray Krieger: The Expansions of Contextualism.' *boundary 2* 2.2 (1974): 584–607.
Leitch, Vincent. *American Literary Criticism from the 30s to the 80s.* New York: Columbia UP, 1988, 45–52.
Lentricchia, Frank. *After the New Criticism.* Chicago: U of Chicago P, 1980, 212–54.
Morris, Wesley. 'The Critic's Responsibility "To" and "For."' *Western Humanities Review* 31.3 (1977): 265–72.

– *Toward a New Historicism.* Princeton: Princeton UP, 1972, 187–209.
Raaberg, Gwen. '*Ekphrasis* and the Temporal/Spatial Metaphor in Murray Krieger's Critical Theory.' *New Orleans Review* 12.4 (1985): 34–43.
Webster, Grant. *The Republic of Letters: A History of Postwar American Literary Opinion.* Baltimore: Johns Hopkins UP, 1979, 190–202.
Weinsheimer, Joel. 'On Going Home Again: New Criticism Revisited.' *PTL: A Journal of Descriptive Poetics and Theory of Literature* 3 (1977): 563–77.

Kristeva, Julia

(b. Bulgaria, 1941–) Psychoanalyst, linguist, semiotician. After an early education in Bulgaria and a brief career as a journalist, Kristeva emigrated to Paris in 1965 to pursue doctoral studies under *Lucien Goldmann and *Roland Barthes at L'Ecole Pratique des Hautes Etudes. She soon joined the 'Tel Quel group' (headed by Philippe Sollers, whom she later married), and through it became active in leftist French politics, including the upheavals of May 1968. During her early years in Paris, she published numerous articles in *Tel Quel*, joining its editorial board in 1970. As well, she began to follow the seminars offered by the psychoanalytic theorist *Jacques Lacan. In 1973 she gained her state doctorate in Paris for the defence of a 620-page thesis, published the following year as *La Révolution du langage poétique: L'Avant-garde à la fin du XIXe siècle: Lautréamont et Mallarmé [Revolution in Poetic Language 1984]. Since 1974, she has held the chair of linguistics at the University of Paris VII, as well as visiting appointments at Columbia University in New York. She has been a practising psychoanalyst since 1979. Her writing represents a complex synthesis of materialist and psychoanalytic theories in an attempt to develop a poststructuralist understanding of language and the self. (See *psychoanalytic theory, *materialist criticism, *poststructuralism, *self/other.)

Like other works of the Tel Quel collective, Kristeva's publications of the later 1960s both delineate her opposition to Western culture's theory of language as product or representation and suggest an alternative understanding of language as a material practice which can support political revolution. For example, the essays collected in *Séméiôtiké: Recherches pour*

394

un sémanalyse (1969) critique the scientific-rationalist model of *semiotics which was developing at the time out of structuralist linguistics. Kristeva proposes that semiotics should develop as a method she calls 'semanalysis,' a way of analysing the text as material production. *Le Texte du roman: Approche sémiologique d'une structure discursive transformationelle* (1970) experiments with this method of 'semanalysis' in order to demonstrate shifting conceptions of the *text in the early modern prose works of Antoine de la Sale. These early publications indicate Kristeva's debt to the futurists and to Russian *formalism, especially the work of *Mikhail Bakhtin, from whom she develops the concepts of '*intertextuality' (every text as the product of the intersection of several texts) and 'poetic language' (language of materiality, which is open to the scene of its production).

La Révolution de langage poétique (1974) extends her method of 'semanalysis' to include psychoanalytic theory. In critical dialogue with a number of major thinkers, including Hegel, Marx, *Husserl, *Heidegger, and *Derrida, Kristeva interprets the theories of *Freud and Lacan as opening structuralist linguistics to the problematics of the production of meaning in relation to the body of the linguistic subject. (See *problematic, *subject/object.) The book develops her notion of language as a dialectical struggle between two poles, the 'semiotic' (a pre- or trans-linguistic modality of psychic inscriptions controlled by the primary processes of 'displacement' and 'condensation') and the 'symbolic' (propositions or representations constitutive of language as a system of signs). Kristeva maintains that although language always includes both of these modalities, modern Western society has consistently refused the 'semiotic,' thereby dissociating the subject from language and adopting a unidimensional model of language and self. Intending to challenge this unitary model, she elaborates a theory of subject identity as produced in language, in dialectical process ('on trial') between the 'semiotic' and 'symbolic' poles. This theory involves her proposing a number of specialized terms, including '*chora,' 'thetic,' 'signifying practice,' 'genotext,' and 'phenotext.' (See *genotext/phenotext.) The French publication of *La Révolution* includes detailed textual analysis of inscriptions of the 'semiotic' in the writing of Lautréamont and Mallarmé,

paralleling the literary activism of the avant-garde with political revolution.

The essays collected in *Polylogue* (1977) continue Kristeva's analysis of visual and literary texts as manifestations of both the 'semiotic' and 'symbolic' dimensions of language and self. *Desire in Language: A Semiotic Approach to Literature and Art* (1980) presents some of these essays in English translation. In these and other essays Kristeva addresses the question of 'female identity' through her theory of the subject of language. From her first publications, she has attempted both an analysis of historical valorizations of 'woman' and a re-evaluation of the meaning of sexual difference that can be socially transformative. *Pouvoirs de l'horreur: Essai sur l'abjection [Powers of Horror: An Essay on Abjection* 1980; trans. 1982] offers a psychoanalytic discussion of the process of 'abjection' (expulsion, rejection of the other) which she ties to the historical exclusion of women. In *Histoires d'amour [Tales of Love* 1983; trans. 1987], she examines historical myths of love in order to probe the significance of idealization for the autonomizing of a subject in language, again with particular attention to the meaning of 'woman.' *Au commencement était l'amour: Psychanalyse et foi [In the Beginning was Love: Psychoanalysis and Faith* 1985; trans. 1987] compares psychoanalytic and religious understandings of love, sexuality and desire. (See *desire/lack.) *Soleil Noir: Dépression et mélancolie [Black Sun: Depression and Melancholy* 1987; trans. 1989] offers a semiotics of melancholy as the underside not only of amorous *discourse but of every positing of meaning in language. *Etrangers à nous-mêmes [Strangers to Ourselves* 1988; trans. 1991] is a semanalysis of estrangement. The book examines the 'foreigner' in *literature and philosophy as well as continuing Kristeva's psychoanalytic exploration of an 'otherness' within the self. *Les Samouraïs*, a novel, appeared in French in 1990.

Kristeva has emerged as one of France's major contemporary theorists. Her writing has achieved international recognition across a number of academic disciplines and has stimulated significant theoretical activity within literary criticism and feminism. (See *feminist criticism, French.)

DAWNE MCCANCE

Primary Sources

Kristeva, Julia. *Au commencement était l'amour: Psychanalyse et foi.* Paris: Hachette, Textes du XXe siècle, 1985. *In the Beginning was Love: Psychoanalysis and Faith.* Trans. Arthur Goldhammer. New York: Columbia UP, 1987.

– *Des Chinoises.* Paris: Editions des femmes, 1974. *About Chinese Women.* Trans. Anita Barrow. New York: Marion Boyars, 1977.

– *Desire in Language: A Semiotic Approach to Literature and Art.* Ed. Leon Roudiez. Trans. Thomas Gora, Alice Jardine, Leon Roudiez. New York: Columbia UP, 1980.

– *Etrangers à nous-mêmes.* Paris: Fayard, 1988. *Strangers to Ourselves.* Trans. Leon Roudiez. New York: Columbia UP, 1991.

– *Histoires d'amour.* Paris: Denoël, 1983. *Tales of Love.* Trans. Leon Roudiez. New York: Columbia UP, 1987.

– *Le Langage, cet inconnu.* Paris: Seuil, 1981.

– *Polylogue.* Paris: Seuil, 1977. Eight essays trans. in *Desire in Language: A Semiotic Approach to Literature and Art.* New York: Columbia UP, 1980.

– *Pouvoirs de l'horreur: Essai sur l'abjection.* Paris: Seuil, 1980. *Powers of Horror: An Essay on Abjection.* Trans. Leon Roudiez. New York: Columbia UP, 1982.

– *La Révolution du langage poétique: L'Avant-garde à la fin du XIXe siècle.* Paris: Seuil, 1974. *Revolution in Poetic Language.* Trans. Margaret Waller. New York: Columbia UP, 1984.

– *Les Samouraïs.* Paris: Fayard, 1990.

– *Sémeiôtiké: Recherches pour une sémanalyse.* Paris: Seuil, 1969. Two essays trans. in *Desire in Language: A Semiotic Approach to Literature and Art.* New York: Columbia UP, 1980.

– *Soleil Noir: Dépression et mélancolie.* Paris: Editions Gallimard, 1987. *Black Sun: Depression and Melancholy.* Trans. Leon Roudiez. New York: Columbia UP, 1989.

– *Le Texte du roman: Approche sémiologique d'une structure discursive transformationelle.* The Hague/Paris: Mouton, 1970.

– ed. *Essays in Semiotics/Essais de sémiotique.* The Hague/Paris: Mouton, 1971.

– Jean-Claude Milner and Nicolas Ruwet, eds. *Langue Discours Société: Pour Emile Benveniste.* Paris: Seuil, 1975.

– and Jean-Michel Ribette, eds. *Folle vérité: Vérité et vraisemblance du texte psychotique.* Paris: Seuil, 1979.

– Collective publication of *Tel Quel. La Traversée des signes.* 1975.

Moi, Toril, ed. *The Kristeva Reader.* New York: Columbia UP, 1986.

Secondary Sources

Caws, Mary Ann. 'Tel Quel: Text and Revolution.' *Diacritics* 3.1 (1973): 2–8.

Coward, Rosalind, and John Ellis. *Language and Materialism: Developments in Semiology and the Theory of the Subject.* Boston, London: Routledge and Kegan Paul, 1977.

Fletcher, John, and Andrew Benjamin, eds. *Abjection, Melancholia, and Love: The Work of Julia Kristeva.* London and New York: Routledge, 1990.

Gallop, Jane. *The Daughter's Seduction: Feminism and Psychoanalysis.* London: Macmillan, 1982.

Jardine, Alice. 'Theories of the Feminine: Kristeva.' *Enclitic* 4:2 (1980): 5–15.

Lechte, John. *Julia Kristeva.* London and New York: Routledge, 1990.

Lewis, Philip. 'Revolutionary Semiotics.' *Diacritics* 4.3 (1974): 28–32.

Rose, Jacqueline. *Sexuality in the Field of Vision.* London: NLB/Verso, 1986.

Roudiez, Leon. 'Twelve Points from Tel Quel.' *L'Esprit Créateur* 14.4 (1974): 291–303.

Zepp, Evelyn. 'The Criticism of Julia Kristeva: A New Mode of Critical Thought.' *Romanic Review* 73.1 (1982): 80–97.

Lacan, Jacques-Marie Emile

(b. France, 1901–d. 1981) Jacques-Marie Lacan was awarded his *diplôme de médicine légiste*, qualifying him as a forensic psychiatrist in 1931 and his *doctorat d'état* in 1932. Initially, Lacan's psychoanalytic writings inspired the surrealists of Paris more than the psychologists, and for several years from 1933 onward he published a number of articles on paranoia in the French surrealist publication *Minotaure*. A practising psychoanalyst, sometimes accused of using unorthodox methods, from 1953 onward Lacan conducted a weekly seminar at the University of Paris which influenced a generation of French intellectuals. His influence has since spread beyond psychoanalysis to the literary world, where it has acquired increasing popularity especially among many feminist critics. (See *psychoanalytic theory, *feminist criticism.)

Both the original French versions and the English translations of Lacan's papers are problematic for some readers because of Lacan's lack of conventional linear or logical expression. Translators such as John P. Muller and William J. Richardson suggest that Lacan's writing can be thought of as a type of rebus or puzzle. In fact, *Ecrits*, the title given to his work, is a misnomer, since the articles included in the two volumes are based on transcripts of his lectures given over a number of years. They are neither 'writings' per se nor do they represent a well-organized whole. Lacan claimed that he structured his papers in a particular manner in order to suggest the shifting structures of dreams and the unconscious. His predilection for language play, puns and associative leaps in logic illustrates and enacts the relationship of mind to language. However, his opacity remains a challenge for many readers.

Lacan's theory, rooted in the linguistic models of *Ferdinand de Saussure and *Roman Jakobson as well as the psychoanalytic methods of *Sigmund Freud, has affected the work of many poststructural literary critics. (See *poststructuralism.) His fundamental thesis is that language is a manifestation of structures in the unconscious and that linguistic patterns reveal important characteristics of the individual subject's psychic state. However, where Saussure regards the relationship between signifier/signified as being relatively fixed, Lacan argues that the signifier can shift in meaning and that the signified is always provisional. (See *signified/signifier/signification.)

Freud maintains that desire is biological, driven by a sexual force, and that the healthy human eventually grows toward a psychic unity. (See *desire/lack.) By contrast, Lacan sees desire as a drive for an ontological unity which can never be achieved because of a psychic split resulting first from the *mirror stage (the individual subject's primal encounter with a mirror which precipitates the 'I' in primordial form) and then the Oedipal phase (characterized by the male subject's desire for the taboo mother).

For Lacan, as for Freud, the individual is socialized by passing through the three phases of the Oedipal complex: (1) the 'seduction' phase in which the subject is attracted to the object of desire or mother; (2) the 'primal stage' in which the subject views the mother having sexual intercourse with the father; and (3) the 'castration' phase in which the father's 'No]' or law prohibiting sexual access to the mother is accompanied by threat of castration. The father's law or the '*Name-of-the-Father' inspires a deflection of desire from the 'mother' to what Lacan calls the 'Other.' (See *self/other, *subject/object.) The Other can be thought of as the locus of desire which can be projected

onto a human counterpart by the subject. More precisely, it is a hypothetical place or space, that of a pure signifier, rather than a physical entity, which resides in the subject's unconscious. It is significant that, according to Lacan, this 'Other' can never truly be grasped because the nature of desire is such that its object is always out of reach. This unfulfilled desire contributes to a *Spaltung* or 'split' in the subject's psyche. It should be noted that instead of understanding Freud's theory of the Oedipal complex on the level of biology, Lacan views it on the level of language. Thus, the 'law' in the 'Name-of-the-Father' is a linguistic phenomenon which serves to socialize the subject.

For Lacan, the three Oedipal phases have an indirect relationship to three psychic levels or 'registers:' (1) the 'imaginary' (which has nothing to do with the imagination per se) corresponds to variations in the unconscious initiated by the formation of the ego, the result of the mirror encounter; (2) the 'symbolic' (which has little to do with symbolism as we generally understand it) corresponds to the metonymic substitutions of the conscious mind; the symbolic register serves an organizing function, particularly on a linguistic level, and thus provides a means by which the subject can enter society through language; and (3) the 'real' (which has nothing to do with reality, objectivity or empiricism) which serves a function of constancy and is beyond the realm of speech; it can be thought of as the ineffable world of objects and experiences, or as that which is lacking in the symbolic order and which may be approached but never grasped. Ellie Ragland-Sullivan's *Jacques Lacan and the Philosophy of Psychoanalysis* offers a cogent extended discussion of the significance of these registers. (See *imaginary/symbolic/real.)

The mirror stage involves two recognitions. First, the subject as child recognizes its own physical unity in the mirror. The subject's first encounter with its idealized self-image in the mirror is fundamentally narcissistic. The mirror encounter serves a catalytic function which initiates a development of the ego and a sense of self-awareness. Second, the subject mis-identifies the spectral 'Other' in the mirror as the object of desire. This *méconnaisance* or misunderstanding of the mirror image further contributes to the split in the subject's psyche.

Simultaneous with the mirror stage is the subject's acquisition of language. Lacan maintains that the subject defines itself on the level of *discourse. Language serves a metonymic function that is analagous to the mirror image insofar as words (signifiers) stand in for things (signifieds), but are not the things themselves. (See *metonymy/metaphor.) It is through an endless metonymic chain of language that the subject pursues the ever-elusive object of desire. Lacan points out that by studying a subject's dreams and speech patterns (including the use of particular figures of speech or slips of the tongue), one can illuminate features of the split in the subject's imaginary register.

For Lacan, the phallus is the universal signifier; not the male sexual organ, rather, a metonymic presence which is indicative of the *manque à être* (a fundamental lack or absence) that can only be fulfilled by the (forever unattainable) object of desire. This *manque* can be either masculine or feminine. It is through language that the subject seeks to evoke the presence of the absent Other or the object of desire. Lacan himself admitted that he had focused primarily on male experience and that he had failed to account successfully for the formation of the female psyche and feminine desire in *Ecrits*. With limited success he tried to deal with this phenomenon in his later book *Feminine Sexuality* (1982).

Lacan's personal contribution to literary criticism is limited but significant. For example, his Seminar on Poe's 'The Purloined Letter,' the first essay in *Ecrits*, demonstrates, among other things, that fiction creates its own rules and therefore aligns itself with and exemplifies the workings of the symbolic register which systematizes language and attempts to order consciousness. His argument that the letter is the 'true subject' of the story is of particular interest to poststructuralist critics.

The range of scholarship on Lacan is extensive. Marxist critic *Louis Althusser applies Lacanian theories on the relationship between language and *power in society in his famous and (some would argue) overly deterministic essay 'Ideology and Ideological State Apparatuses.' (See *Ideological State Apparatuses, *Marxist criticism.) In 'Le Facteur de la vérité' ['The Purveyor of Truth], *Jacques Derrida aggressively attacks Lacan's essay on Poe, arguing that Lacan's interpretation is phonologocentric, that is, it gives priority to an unveiling or revelation of truth through speech. Other reactions to Lacan, especially feminist re-

sponses, can in part be attributed to the fact that the non-biological notion of the Other as it relates to a sense of *manque* is universally applicable. Feminists acknowledge that Lacan has raised the important issue of subjectivity in psychoanalysis and language but that he has done so from a phallocentric perspective. (See *phallocentrism.) *Julia Kristeva has adapted Lacanian concepts to her theory of *semiotics, which considers unconscious patterns of language in regard to the destabilization of the 'thetic' subject in literature. *Hélène Cixous' theory owes something to Lacan's imaginary register in which a prelinguistic unity exists between mother and child. Elizabeth Grosz offers a detailed analysis of various feminist responses to Lacan and points out that his phallo(logo)-centrist perspective opens the door to alternative critical perspectives precisely because it articulates presumptions that are socially dominant but which had hitherto remained largely unarticulated. In spite of any shortcomings, the study and application of Lacanian and post-Lacanian theory is flourishing in Europe and North America.

Lacan's *Television* (1974) includes his challenge to the psychoanalytic establishment. His on-going concern for the informing yet perplexing instability of language is revealed in his opening comments on the television program: 'I always speak the truth. Not the whole truth, because there's no way to say it all. Saying it all is literally impossible: words fail. Yet it's through this very impossibility that the truth holds onto the real.'

KARL E. JIRGENS

Primary Sources

Lacan, Jacques. *Ecrits I*. Paris: Editions du Seuil, 1966.
- *Ecrits II*. Paris: Editions du Seuil, 1971.
- *Ecrits: A Selection*. Trans. Alan Sheridan. New York: W.W. Norton and Co., 1977.
- *Feminine Sexuality*. Trans. Jacqueline Rose. Ed. Juliet Mitchell and Jacqueline Rose. New York: W.W. Norton and Co., 1985.
- *The Four Fundamental Concepts of Psycho-Analysis*. Trans. Alan Sheridan. Ed. Jacques-Alain Miller. New York: W.W. Norton and Co., 1978.
- *Speech and Language in Psychoanalysis*. Trans. with notes by Anthony Wilden. Baltimore: Johns Hopkins UP, 1968.
- *Television: A Challenge to the Psychoanalytic Establishment*. Trans. Denis Hollier, Rosalind Krauss,

Annette Michelson and Jeffrey Mehlman. Ed. Joan Copjec. New York: W.W. Norton & Co., 1990.

Secondary Sources

Bowie, Malcolm. *Freud, Proust and Lacan: Theory as Fiction.* Cambridge: Cambridge UP, 1987.

Davis, Robert Con. *Lacan and Narration: The Psychoanalytic Difference in Narrative Theory.* Baltimore: Johns Hopkins UP, 1983.

– ed. *The Fictional Father: Lacanian Readings of the Text.* Amherst: U of Massachusetts P, 1981.

Freedman, Barbara. *Staging the Gaze: Postmodernism, Psychoanalysis, and Shakespearean Comedy.* Ithaca: Cornell UP, 1991.

Gallop, Jane. *Reading Lacan.* Ithaca: Cornell UP, 1985.

Grosz, Elizabeth. *Jacques Lacan: A Feminist Introduction.* New York: Routledge, 1990.

Hogan, Patrick Colm, and Lalita Pandit, eds. *Lacan and Criticism: Essays and Dialogue on Language, Structure and the Unconscious.* Athens: U of Georgia P, 1990.

Jameson, Fredric. 'Postmodernism and Consumer Society.' In *The Anti-Aesthetic: Essays on Postmodern Culture.* Ed. Hal Foster. Port Townsend, Wash.: Bay P, 1983.

Kristeva, Julia. *Desire in Language: A Semiotic Approach to Literature and Art.* Trans. Thomas Gora, Alice Jardine and Leon S. Roudiez. Ed. Leon S. Roudiez. New York: Columbia UP, 1980.

Lemire, Anika. *Jacques Lacan.* Trans. David Macey. New York: Routledge and Kegan Paul, 1970.

MacCannell, Juliet Flower. *Figuring Lacan: Criticism and the Cultural Unconscious.* London: Croom Helm P, 1986.

Macey, David. *Lacan in Contexts.* London: Verso, 1988.

Muller, John P., and William J. Richardson. *Lacan and Language: A Reader's Guide to Ecrits.* New York: International Universities P Inc., 1982.

– eds. *The Purloined Poe.* Baltimore: Johns Hopkins UP, 1988.

Ragland-Sullivan, Ellie. *Jacques Lacan and the Philosophy of Psychoanalysis.* Chicago: U of Illinois P, 1987.

– and Mark Bracher, eds. *Lacan and the Subject of Language.* New York: Routledge, 1991.

Lawrence, D(avid) H(erbert)

(b. England, 1885–d. 1930) Novelist, poet, dramatist, essayist, and critic. D.H. Lawrence was the fourth of five children born to a passionate but uneducated man and a serious, intellectually alive, and religiously devout woman. His mother's Congregationalist views influenced Lawrence's later attitudes toward his role as a writer and are important for their paradoxically positive shaping effect on his conception of appropriate conduct, especially sexual.

Lawrence's education was haphazard; however, his wide reading and interest in languages, as well as his lifetime of world travel nurtured by an appetite to learn, expanded his knowledge considerably. During his years as a teacher at the Davidson Road School, Croydon (1908–12), Lawrence's life changed dramatically because of two events: his mother's death, which was traumatic for him; and his introduction (in 1912) to the wife of his French teacher, Frieda Weekly, with whom he eventually ran off.

Throughout his life, Lawrence struggled to find a balance between passion and thought, body and spirit, and the creative and destructive powers flowing around and through human existence. It was his intense desire to find ways of living to achieve such a balance – also embodied in his efforts as a poet, dramatist, critical thinker, and novelist – that shaped his attitudes toward *literature and other writers. Lawrence the philosopher/critic was an extension of and complement to Lawrence the creative writer; his critical positions, both theoretical and practical, can be found both in individual, specifically critical works (such as his *Study of Thomas Hardy*) and in scattered comments throughout his other texts.

Difficult to classify as a critic, Lawrence was deliberately subjective, but not impressionistic, in his judgments of artists. His opinions were based on a definite set of moral rather than purely aesthetic principles; yet his morality was not conventional. He states his position most succinctly in *Lady Chatterley's Lover*: 'It [the novel properly handled] can inform and lead into new places the flow of our sympathetic consciousness, and it can lead our sympathy away in recoil from things gone dead ... for it is in the passional secret places of life ... that the tide of sensitive awareness needs to ebb and flow, cleansing and freshening' (104).

In his conviction that the novelist can influence cultural development through the proper exercise of his imagination and intuitive powers, Lawrence had an affinity for aesthetic historicists like *Benedetto Croce and R.G. Collingwood. Their emphasis on creative imagination and intuition separated them from coeval positivist and determinist approaches to cultural history. The influence of the Italian futurist Marinetti on Lawrence's well-known description of the technique of *The Rainbow*, dealing with 'that which is psychic – non-human, in humanity,' suggests much about his evolving theory of the novel and of art in general: successful art is the product of an intuitive process rooted in an awakening awareness of elemental human nature and elemental human needs that must be balanced; in 'The Crown' essays he identifies these as the force of love and the drive of power or, alternatively, as the female, the unicorn and light opposed to the male, the lion and darkness, each struggling for dominance in the individual and in the human community; as long as there is no triumph, and balance (which he calls the 'Holy Ghost') holds, then fulfilment is possible. He judges novels and art generally according to the artist's ability to represent humanity living the processes and consequences of the struggle. This is also what helps to make inevitable his notion that the novel is the highest literary form.

According to *Terry Eagleton, Lawrence belongs with the Romantic humanist critics. For Lawrence, the literary artist is a visionary who reveals an elemental truth through a passionately vivid use of language. Lawrence judges other writers according to the power their *text has to affect him personally rather than according to a standard imposed on the work to measure its aesthetic value. In some cases, such criticism results in scathing commentary – such as in his views on Wordsworth (*Phoenix II* 447–8).

The implied critical theory and method of Lawrence's idiosyncratic reading of the Bible in *Apocalypse* has been compared both to *Wilhelm Dilthey's *hermeneutics and to deconstructive criticism: his 'archaeological metaphor for the text of Revelation ... strikingly resembles terms used by Gayatri Spivak to describe Derrida's notion of a text' (Bonds 107–8). A true precursor of neither contemporary deconstructive or hermeneutic criticism, Lawrence as a critic defies any neat categorization. (See also *deconstruction, *Jacques Derrida.)

Lawrence's own definition of literary criticism as a 'reasoned account of the feeling produced upon the critic by the book he is criticizing' and his description of the proper critic as someone 'able to *feel* the impact of a work in all its complexity and force ... [who]

must be a man of force and complexity himself' (*Phoenix* 539) associates him with Romantic expressionism; modernist conceptions of the artist and of his work shape Lawrence's vision as well but, as with the rest of his life and work, the shape is unique.

LAWRENCE GAMACHE

Primary Sources

Lawrence, D.H. *Apocalypse*. London: Penguin, 1977.
– *D.H. Lawrence: Selected Literary Criticism*. Ed. Anthony Beal. New York: Viking, 1966. [Contains *Study of Thomas Hardy*.]
– *Lady Chatterley's Lover*. Harmondsworth, Middlesex: Penguin, 1961.
– *Phoenix: The Posthumous Papers of D.H. Lawrence*. Ed. Edward D. McDonald. New York: Viking, 1968. [Contains 'Pornography and Obscenity,' Lawrence prefaces, introductions and reviews of books; *Study of Thomas Hardy*; 'Surgery for the Novel – OR a Bomb'; 'Art and Morality'; 'Morality and the Novel'; 'Why the Novel Matters'; 'John Galsworthy'; 'Introduction to These Paintings'; and 'The Novel and the Feelings.']
– *Phoenix II: Uncollected, Unpublished, and Other Prose Works by D.H. Lawrence*. Ed. Warren Roberts and Harry T. Moore. New York: Viking, 1968. [Contains 'Rachel Annand Taylor'; 'Art and the Individual'; uncollected reviews and introductions; 'The Crown'; and 'The Novel.']
– *Studies in Classic American Literature*. London: Penguin, 1977.

Secondary Sources

Arnold, Armin. *D.H. Lawrence and America*. London: Linden P, 1958.
Bien, Peter. 'The Critical Philosophy of D.H. Lawrence.' *D. H. Lawrence Review* 17.2 (1984): 127–34.
Bonds, Diane. 'Review of Peter Faulkner, ed. *The English Modernist Reader*.' *D.H. Lawrence Review* 20.1 (1988): 106–8.
Foster, Richard. 'Criticism as Rage: D.H. Lawrence.' In *A D.H. Lawrence Miscellany*. Ed. Harry T. Moore. Carbondale: Southern Illinois UP, 1959: 312–25.
Gordon, David J. *D.H. Lawrence as a Literary Critic*. New Haven: Yale UP, 1966.
Peters, Joan D. 'The Living and the Dead: Lawrence's Theory of the Novel and the Structure of *Lady Chatterley's Lover*.' *D.H. Lawrence Review* 20.1 (1988): 5–20.
Sharma, K.K. *Modern Fictional Theorists: Virginia Woolf and D.H. Lawrence*. Atlantic Highlands, NJ: Humanities P, 1982.
Singh, Tagindar. *The Literary Criticism of D.H. Lawrence*. New Delhi: Sterling, 1984.

Sitesh, Aruna. *D.H. Lawrence: The Crusader as Critic.* New Delhi: Macmillan, 1975.

Wellek, René. 'The Literary Criticism of D.H. Lawrence.' *Sewanee Review* 91 (1983): 598–613.

Leavis, F(rank) R(aymond)

(b. England, 1895–d. 1978) Literary critic. After service as a stretcher-bearer in the First World War, Leavis entered Emmanuel College, Cambridge (1918), initially to study history, though he later moved into the newly founded English program. He gained his Ph.D. in 1924 with a thesis on 'The Relationship of Journalism to Literature' and taught regularly at Cambridge thereafter, although he was not appointed as college lecturer at Downing College until 1935 or as a member of the University Faculty Board until 1954. He made a reputation as a brilliant if controversial teacher, known in particular for his impassioned advocacy of 'criticism in practice,' his editing of the critical journal *Scrutiny* (1932–53), and his championing of 'English' as a discipline of thought totally distinct from philosophical *discourse. After retiring from Cambridge in 1962, he was visiting professor for some years at the University of York and served more briefly in a similar capacity at Wales and Bristol.

Leavis' importance in the development of literary criticism in England in the middle decades of the 20th century lay in his unceasing insistence on the priority of practice over theory and of the centrality of evaluation within the critical process. Ideally, he argued, the critic should 'say nothing that cannot be related immediately to judgments about producible texts' (*Revaluation* 3). Moreover, mature literary discussion can manifest itself only within an informed human community: 'The form of a judgment is "This is so, isn't it?", the question asking for confirmation that the thing *is* so, but prepared for an answer in the form, "Yes, but –", the "but" standing for corrections, refinements, precisions, amplifications' (*Living Principle* 35). Collaboration is essential, he maintains, because a work of art can exist only in what he calls 'the "Third Realm" – the realm of that which is neither public in the ordinary sense nor merely private' (*Living Principle* 36).

The collaborative nature of criticism is continually underlined in Leavis' own practice, most obviously in the collaborations with his wife, Queenie Dorothy Leavis, in *Lectures in America* and *Dickens the Novelist*. Leavis' early work, indeed, was considerably influenced by her *Fiction and the Reading Public* (1932), a work originating as a thesis directed by *I.A. Richards that focused on the rise of 'popular' journalism, the concept of the best-seller and the cultural attenuation that such developments implied. A further example of collaboration was the influence of Leavis upon his students at Downing, many of whom introduced his methods and principles in schools and universities where they subsequently taught. Above all, it showed itself in the founding of *Scrutiny*, which provided an important if embattled centre and outlet for a wide range of committed and often astringent critical comment.

Dependent upon his view of *literature is the concept of tradition and the necessity of an educated public to maintain cultural continuity. A living culture draws upon the best from the past, adapting it to new situations and new needs, but maintaining its essence; an educated public performs an irreplaceable function by upholding standards that have been established in the past, not as a deadening proliferation of set conventions but as a revivifying series of alterations and challenges. Leavis begins from a strong sense that in his own time English culture had entered a period of crisis, exemplified in the title of an early pamphlet, *Mass Civilization and Minority Culture* (1930). Traditional standards and therefore the all-important continuity were threatened; 'new bearings' were desperately needed.

His writings attempt to address the situation on a number of fronts: in books that sought out the major figures in contemporary writing, both poetry and fiction (*New Bearings in English Poetry, D.H. Lawrence: Novelist*); in others that mapped out their significant literary precursors (*Revaluation, The Great Tradition*); in short books and pamphlets offering practical programs for improved teaching and educational change (*Culture and Environment* with Denys Thompson 1933; *Education and the University*); and, above all, in *Scrutiny*, of which Leavis was the dominating figure. In his later life, in books like *Nor Shall My Sword, The Living Principle* and the posthumously published *Critic as Anti-Philosopher*, he consolidated his position with forceful and often acerbic analyses of the further threats to cultural standards that came in the 1960s and 1970s with the expansion of universities (accompanied, Leavis maintained, by a disastrous decline in standards and seriousness) and the increased emphasis placed by government on science and (especially) technology. (See also *theory and pedagogy.)

Leavis' critical principles have always attracted controversy and are often misunderstood. While his attitudes bear some superficial resemblance to those of the *New Criticism flourishing contemporaneously in the United States, he was never antihistoricist. Because literature and life are for Leavis inextricably connected – 'I don't believe in any "literary values," and you won't find me talking about them; the judgments the literary critic is concerned with are judgments about life' (Nor Shall My Sword 97) – a work of art cannot be separated from the culture that produced it (though a great work from the past is not confined in significance to its historical context).

Similarly, while he has been criticized for failing to define his terms, Leavis argues that words like 'life' or 'standards' or 'sensibility' cannot be 'so fixed by definition as not to shift when we use' them, since this is 'a peculiarity of important words – words we find we can't do without – in the field of our distinctive discipline of intelligence' (English Literature 85). The last phrase is crucial. Major creative writers are concerned, he insists, with a 'necessary kind of thought' (Living Principle 20) but this is not the thought of mathematicians or philosophers or experimental scientists. Creativity is important because it is heuristic, 'concerned with discovery, or new realization' (Critic as Anti-Philosopher 14). Leavis' increasing desperation in his later years stemmed from his awareness that because the modern 'Technologico-Benthamite' world values only what can be scientifically measured, human creativity, as embodied in major writers, was itself threatened.

W.J. KEITH

Primary Sources

Leavis, F.R. 'Anna Karenina' and Other Essays. London: Chatto and Windus, 1967.
– The Common Pursuit. London: Chatto and Windus, 1952.
– The Critic as Anti-Philosopher. Ed. G. Singh. London: Chatto and Windus, 1982.
– D.H. Lawrence: Novelist. London: Chatto and Windus, 1955.
– Education and the University: A Sketch for an 'English School.' London: Chatto and Windus, 1943.
– English Literature in Our Time and the University. London: Chatto and Windus, 1969.
– The Great Tradition: George Eliot, Henry James, Joseph Conrad. London: Chatto and Windus, 1948.
– Letters in Criticism. Ed. John Tasker. London: Chatto and Windus, 1974.
– The Living Principle: 'English' as a Discipline of Thought. London: Chatto and Windus, 1975.
– Mass Civilization and Minority Culture. 1930. Repr. in For Continuity. Cambridge: Minority P, 1933.
– New Bearings in English Poetry. London: Chatto and Windus, 1932.
– Nor Shall My Sword: Discourses on Pluralism, Compassion and Social Hope. London: Chatto and Windus, 1972.
– Revaluation: Tradition and Development in English Poetry. London: Chatto and Windus, 1936.
– A Selection from 'Scrutiny.' 2 vols. Cambridge: Cambridge UP, 1968.
– et al., eds. Scrutiny: A Quarterly Review. 1933–52. Repr. in 20 vols. Cambridge: Cambridge UP, 1963.
– Thought, Words and Creativity: Art and Thought in D.H. Lawrence. London: Chatto and Windus, 1976.
– Valuation in Criticism, and Other Essays. Ed. G. Singh. Cambridge: Cambridge UP, 1986.
– and Q.D. Leavis. Dickens the Novelist. London: Chatto and Windus, 1970.
– and Q.D. Leavis. Lectures in America. London: Chatto and Windus, 1969.
– and Denys Thompson. Culture and Environment. London: Chatto and Windus, 1933.

Secondary Sources

Bilan, R.P. The Literary Criticism of F.R. Leavis. Cambridge: Cambridge UP, 1979.
Boyars, Robert. F.R. Leavis: Judgment and the Discipline of Thought. Columbia: U of Missouri P, 1978.
Hayman, Ronald. Leavis. London: Heinemann; Totowa, NJ: Rowan and Littlefield, 1976.
Leavis, Q.D. Fiction and the Reading Public. London: Chatto and Windus, 1932.
McKenzie, D.F., and M–P. Allum. F.R. Leavis: A Checklist, 1924–64. London: Chatto and Windus, 1966.
Mulhern, Francis. The Moment of 'Scrutiny.' London: New Left Books, 1979.
Robertson, P.J.M. The Leavises on Fiction: An Historic Partnership. New York: St. Martin's P, 1981.
Thompson, Denys, ed. The Leavises: Recollections and Impressions. Cambridge: Cambridge UP, 1984.
Walsh, William. F.R. Leavis. London: Chatto and Windus, 1980.
Watson, Garry. The Leavises, the 'Social,' and the Left. Swansea: Brynmill, 1977.

Lévi-Strauss, Claude

(b. Brussels, 1908–) Cultural anthropologist. Although he received his *agrégation* in philosophy and law in 1931, Claude Lévi-Strauss found neither discipline satisfying. In Brazil from 1935–9 he taught sociology at the University of São Paolo and conducted fieldwork among the Caduveo and Bororo tribes. Following a short period of military service on his return to France, he emigrated to the U.S.A., where he taught at the New School for Social Research in New York (1941–5). During this period he met and worked with *Roman Jakobson. He returned to France in 1947 and, in 1948, received the doctorat ès lettres from the University of Paris. From 1953 to 1960, Lévi-Strauss was secretary general of the International Council of Social Science. After his election to the chair of anthropology at the Collège de France in 1960, he co-founded *L'Homme*, a journal of anthropology. In 1973, he was elected to the Académie Française. He continued to teach at the Collège de France until his retirement in 1982.

From his early studies of kinship systems through to his exploration of systems of mythology, Lévi-Strauss has attempted to uncover universal structures existing in the unconscious that are capable of generating, through transformation, all possible systems. (See *universal.) At the same time, he is a differentialist and rejects the universalism of the 18th century. All cultures are equivalent and produce a social and political equilibrium which has to be respected. Basic to his method is the assumption that in any study of a system, the models constructed by individuals existing within the system 'are not intended to explain the phenomena but to perpetuate them' *(Structural Anthropology* 281); thus consciously created models of a structure must constitute part of the data of the analysis but cannot be assumed to be the structure itself. Conscious models consider kinship terms or mythological elements as containing meaning in and of themselves; at the unconscious level, elements gain meaning only through their relationship with other elements. All elements in a system are interdependent; no element 'can undergo a change without effecting changes in all the other elements' *(Structural Anthropology* 279). The shift in focus from the conscious to the unconscious mind and the emphasis on meaning as generated by relationship place Lévi-Strauss' work within the domain of *structuralism. Although he had independently formulated a method of structural analysis, his meeting with Roman Jakobson in 1941 presented him with a discipline, structural linguistics, that had formal principles similar to his own method and an existing vocabulary that could be transferred from the study of language to the study of other cultural phenomena.

In *Elementary Structures of Kinship* (1949), Lévi-Strauss develops Marcel Mauss' principle of reciprocity *(Essai sur le don* 1924). This principle ensures the stability of society through the exchange of gifts between groups. Gifts express symbolic value, becoming 'vehicles and instruments for realities of another order, such as power, influence, sympathy, status, and emotion' (54). In the systems generated by the structural principle of reciprocity, food, material goods, and women become signs in a symbolic system, having no intrinsic meaning: 'each term is defined by its position within the system' (49). (See *sign.) Lévi-Strauss proposes an analogy between kinship systems and language, subsuming both under the category of communication and suggesting that, in the system of marriage exchange, 'women themselves are treated as signs, which are *misused* when not put to the use reserved to signs, which is to be communicated' (497).

Since the late 1950s, Lévi-Strauss has focused his attention on the study of *myth. He concedes that the principles governing social relationships may be 'the reflection in men's minds of certain social demands that [have] been objectified in institutions' *(The Raw and the Cooked* 10). Myths, on the other hand, are not constrained by the demands of social necessity or by the need to reflect the logic of objective reality. The mind that creates myth 'is in a sense reduced to imitating itself as object' (10). Following a discussion of principles and terminology in 'The Structural Study of Myth' *(Structural Anthropology,* ch. 11), he demonstrates his method with an analysis of the Oedipus myth. Positing that the character of mythological time is simultaneously synchronic and diachronic, Lévi-Strauss concludes that a myth consists of the accumulation of all its versions, that is, there is no single authentic or authoritative version. A sufficient analysis of a myth includes all of its known variants. The correlation of the similarities and differences between versions reveals the gross constituent elements of myth which he terms *mythemes*, on analogy with *phonemes*. In *The Savage Mind* (1962), he discusses the nature of mythical thought, which accumulates a store of images from the observation and classification of natural objects on the basis of their distinctive features. These images perform the function of signifier in a sign system (18). (See *signified/signifier/signification.) Mythical thought is analogous to *bricolage*. Like the *bricoleur* who chooses his materials and tools from an existing inventory that bears no necessary relationship to his immediate purpose (17), the 'primitive' mind considers the existing set of images and recombines them through a series of transformations into new systems of meaning. In *The Raw and the Cooked* (1964), the first of a series of four volumes *(Mythologiques)*, Lévi-Strauss analyses 187 myths that demonstrate the transformation of one *theme, the transition from nature to culture, through the continual reordering of image sets whose content is the opposition of sensory qualities: the raw and the cooked, noise and silence, rotten and burned. (See *binary opposition.)

Lévi-Strauss' work 'has been the main stimulus to the development of structuralism as an intellectual movement' (Clarke 118). Although his works have been criticized for their often obscure formulations and on the basis that his selection of data for analysis has been directed by a preconceived purpose, his application of the methods of structural linguistics to anthropological data demonstrates the adaptability of the system of analysis to other semiotic domains. (See *semiotics.) His formulation of the logical relationships and principles underlying the transformation of myth through various permutation groups constitutes, according to *Jonathan Culler, a theory of reading that, because the texts on which it is based are unfamiliar, 'makes clear just how much we rely, in the reading of texts from Western culture, on a series of codes and conventions of which we are not fully aware' (53). (See *code.)

NANCY FARADAY

Primary Sources

Lévi-Strauss, Claude. *Anthropologie structurale*. Vol. 1. Paris: Plon, 1958. *Structural Anthropology*. Trans. Claire Jacobson and Brooke G. Schoepfe. New York: Basic Books, 1963.
– *Le Cru et le cuit*. Paris: Plon 1964. *The Raw and the Cooked*. Trans. John and Doreen Weightman. New York: Harper and Row, 1969.
– *Leçon inaugurale*. 1960 lecture. *The Scope of Anthropology*. Trans. Sherry Ortner Paul and Robert A. Paul. London: Jonathan Cape, 1967.
– *La Pensée sauvage*. Paris: Plon, 1962. *The Savage Mind*. Trans. London: Weidenfeld and Nicolson, 1966.
– *Les Structures élémentaires de la parenté*. Paris: PUF, 1949. 2nd ed. The Hague: Mouton, 1967. *The Elementary Structures of Kinship*. Ed. Rodney Needham. Trans. James Harle Bell and John R. von Sturmer. Boston: Beacon P, 1969.
– and Didier Eribon. *De Près et de loin*. Paris: Editions Odile Jacob, 1988. *Conversations with Claude Lévi-Strauss*. Trans. Paula Wissing. Chicago: U of Chicago P, 1991.
– and Roman Jakobson. 'Charles Baudelaire's "Les Chats."' *L'Homme* 2 (1962): 5–21. Trans. F.M. De George. In *The Structuralists: From Marx to Lévi-Strauss*. Ed. Richard T. DeGeorge and Fernande M. DeGeorge. New York: Doubleday, 1972.

Secondary Sources

Champagne, Roland A. *Claude Lévi-Strauss*. Boston: Twayne Publishers, 1987.
Clarke, Simon. *The Foundations of Structuralism: A Critique of Lévi-Strauss and the Structuralist Movement*. Totowa, NJ: Barnes and Noble, 1981.
Culler, Jonathan. *Structuralist Poetics: Structuralism, Linguistics and the Study of Literature*. London: Routledge and Kegan Paul, 1975.
Derrida, Jacques. 'Structure, Sign, and Play in the Discourse of the Human Sciences.' In *The Languages of Criticism and the Sciences of Man: The Structuralist Controversy*. Ed. Richard Macksey and Eugenio Donato. Baltimore: Johns Hopkins UP, 1970.
Gardner, Howard. 'The Structural Analysis of Protocols and Myths.' *Semiotica* V 1 (1972): 31–57.
Hayes, Eugene, and Tanya Hayes, eds. *Claude Lévi-Strauss: The Anthropologist as Hero*. Cambridge: MIT P, 1970
Lapointe, François, and Claire Lapointe. *Claude Lévi-Strauss and His Critics*. New York: Garland, 1977.
Leach, Edmund. *Claude Lévi-Strauss*. New York: Viking, 1970.
Lentricchia, Frank. *After the New Criticism*. Chicago: U of Chicago P, 1980.
Pace, David. *Claude Lévi-Strauss: The Bearer of Ashes*. Boston: Routledge and Kegan Paul, 1983.
Riffaterre, Michael. 'Describing Poetic Structures.' In *Structuralism*. Ed. Jacques Ehrmann. Garden City, NY: Doubleday, 1970, 188–230.
Scheffler, Harold W. 'Structuralism in Anthropology.' In *Structuralism*. Ed. Jacques Ehrmann. Garden City, NY: Doubleday, 1970, 57–79.
Steiner, George. 'Orpheus with His Myths: Claude

Lévi-Strauss.' In *Language and Silence: Essays on Language, Literature, and the Inhuman.* New York: Atheneum, 1977.

Lewis, C(live) S(taples)

(b. N. Ireland, 1898–d. England, 1963) Literary historian and critic, novelist, essayist, and religious apologist. C.S. Lewis' most formative experiences were his mother's death in 1908, his residence from 1914 to 1917 with a tutor, W.T. Kirkpatrick, whom he called a 'logic-engine,' and boyhood reading of Norse myths and the prose romances of William Morris and George MacDonald. From these he derived his devotion to *literature of the past, especially *myth and fantasy; his interest in other worlds; in part, his return from agnosticism to orthodox Christianity; and his impersonal, 'either-or' style of argument.

Lewis entered University College, Oxford, was wounded while serving in France, then read classics and philosophy ('Greats'), taking a double first in 1922 and another first, in English, in 1923. He was Lecturer in English and Fellow of Magdalen College (1925–54). His lectures on medieval literature drew large attendances even before his *Allegory of Love* (1936) won general acclaim. This study of chivalric romance and allegory was followed by one of the epic poem, *A Preface to Paradise Lost* (1942). In the latter he attacked *T.S. Eliot's claim that poets could best judge poetry. He had already disputed E.M.W. Tillyard's claim that poets knew 'hells and heavens' unknown to the common reader as leading to 'poetolatry,' and the belief that the poem revealed the poet's experience and personality in their controversy, *The Personal Heresy*, published in 1939.

Lewis sought to rehabilitate Shelley, Scott and Morris, and wrote both science-fiction and fairy tale. He was denied promotion even for his monumental *English Literature in the 16th Century, Excluding Drama* (1954), apparently because of his engagement in religious controversy. His *Pilgrim's Regress* (1933) allegorized his conversion to Christianity. Published broadcasts espousing orthodoxy made him a national figure, and ridicule of feminism and scientific positivism in his novel *That Hideous Strength* (1945) made him enemies in Oxford who helped to defeat his 1951 bid for election

as Professor of Poetry. In 1954 he accepted a specially created chair in Medieval and Renaissance Literature at Cambridge. Ill health compelled him to resign it in 1963.

Some 60 books by Lewis attract separate readerships, the largest for his apologetics and children's classics *The Chronicles of Narnia*, with smaller ones for his critical works. Of his novels the most penetrating is *Till We Have Faces* (1956), based on the Cupid and Psyche myth and improved by consultation with Joy Davidman, with whom he enjoyed a brief but happy marriage from 1956 to 1960. Nearly all his works were first tried out upon his fellow-Christian authors and friends, notably J.R.R. Tolkien. Together, the 'Inklings,' as they called themselves, developed a 'mythopoeic' strain of fantasy. Tolkien's *The Lord of the Rings* is the most famous example.

Lewis' career progressed from *genre criticism through literary and religious controversy (at Oxford) to a preoccupation at Cambridge with language and the act of reading. His often-overlooked contribution to literary theory (a term he used in 1936) can best be conveyed by an account of his principles.

Lewis maintained that no 'expert' assessments or extraneous biographical, ideological or other pre-considerations should distract that reader from 'enjoying' first-hand reading. Nor should premature 'contemplation' be required of the reader. For their part, authors practised the art applicable to a given form, using language as their instrument. The modern idol of 'originality' therefore was neither attainable nor desirable; the value of literary works resided not in truth but in concreteness and formal consistency. They aimed to demonstrate what a more or less imaginary way of life was like and also to entertain. Unlike the daydreams in popular novels, the best myths, fantasies, or romances could apply to life in all ages and cultures. They offered the reader a liberation from his own circumstance and from conditioning by the 20th-century *Zeitgeist*. Deprecating evaluative criticism, especially if negative, in *The Discarded Image* (1964) Lewis sought to assist the would-be reader by depicting earlier models of the cosmos as 'prolegomena' to the reading of unfamiliar texts.

In insisting on first-hand reading, in viewing a work as an object or *poiema* and in opposing commercialism and technocracy Lewis had much in common with *F.R. Leavis and the New Critics. (See *New Criticism.) Yet, he was at odds with them in valuing an author's intention, in his antipathy to modernism, positivism and feminism, and in his contention that an author developed his skill by imitating his precursors. (See *feminist criticism.) Early disabused by Owen Barfield of 'chronological snobbery,' Lewis condemned the application of any reductionist *ideology or psychology to texts and authors. In his *Abolition of Man* (1943), he argued that to denigrate non-referential diction was to impoverish the student's imagination and vocabulary.

In his *Experiment in Criticism* (1961), Lewis proposed the evaluation of texts according to their power to sustain a 'literary' reading. The 'unliterary' read a *text but once, while the 'literary' re-read and absorb texts into their consciousness of life. Though resembling *Wayne Booth's '*implied reader,' Lewis' 'literary' reader differs in being a psychological type evident from childhood. Thus his form of reader-response theory focuses on the individual rather than on the ideal figure. (See *reader-response criticism.) Significantly, Lewis differs from Leavis in ascribing no superior 'maturity' or virtue to his literary reader.

Though criticized for his prejudices in favour of friends and the authors of his youth, and against women and contemporary literature, Lewis remains valuable as a scholar-critic because of his range of reading, his incisive questioning of 20th-century assumptions, his lively and sensitive studies of Spenser, Milton and Chaucer, in particular, and his gift for lucid and witty exposition.

LIONEL ADEY

Primary Sources

Lewis, C.S. *The Abolition of Man, or Reflections on Education with Special Reference to the Teaching of English in ... Schools.* Riddell Memorial Lectures. London: Oxford UP, 1943.
– *The Allegory of Love: A Study in Medieval Tradition.* Oxford: Clarendon P, 1936.
– *The Discarded Image: An Introduction to Medieval and Renaissance Literature.* Cambridge: Cambridge UP, 1964.
– *English Literature in the 16th Century, Excluding Drama.* Oxford History of English Literature, vol. 3. Oxford: Clarendon P, 1954.
– *An Experiment in Criticism.* Cambridge: Cambridge UP, 1961.
– *That Hideous Strength: A Modern Fairy-Tale for Grown-ups.* London: Bodley Head, 1945. (See also *Out of the Silent Planet*, 1938; *Perelandra*, 1943.)
– *Of Other Worlds: Essays and Stories.* Ed. Walter Hooper. London: Bles, 1966.
– *Of This and Other Worlds: Essays.* Ed. Walter Hooper. London: Collins, 1982.
– *The Pilgrim's Regress: An Allegorical Apology for Christianity, Reason and Romanticism.* London: Dent, 1933.
– *A Preface to 'Paradise Lost': Being the Ballard Matthews Lectures.* Rev. and enlarged. London: Oxford UP, 1942.
– *'Rehabilitations,' and Other Essays.* London: Oxford UP, 1939.
– *Selected Literary Essays.* Ed. Walter Hooper. Cambridge: Cambridge UP, 1969.
– *Spenser's Images of Life.* Ed. Alastair Fowler. Cambridge: Cambridge UP, 1967.
– *Studies in Medieval and Renaissance Literature.* Collected by Walter Hooper. Cambridge: Cambridge UP, 1966.
– *Studies in Words.* Cambridge: Cambridge UP, 1960.
– *They Asked for a Paper: Papers and Addresses.* London: Bles, 1962.
– *Till We Have Faces: A Myth Retold.* London: Bles, 1956.
– and E.M.W. Tillyard. *The Personal Heresy: A Controversy.* London: Oxford UP, 1939.

Secondary Sources

Carpenter, Humphrey. *The Inklings: C.S. Lewis, J.R.R. Tolkien, Charles Williams, and Their Friends.* London: Allen and Unwin, 1978. Boston: Houghton Mifflin, 1979.
Como, James, ed. *'C.S. Lewis at the Breakfast Table' and Other Reminiscences.* Incl. bibliography of works by Lewis. New York: Macmillan, 1979.
Gibb, Jocelyn, ed. *Light on C.S. Lewis.* London: Bles, 1965.
Green, R.L., and W. Hooper. *C.S. Lewis: A Biography.* London: Collins, 1974.
Hart, Dabney Adams. *Through the Open Door: A New Look at C.S. Lewis.* University, Ala.: U of Alabama P, 1984.
Manlove, C.N. *C.S. Lewis: His Literary Achievement.* New York: St. Martin's P, 1987.
– *Modern Fantasy: Five Studies.* Cambridge: Cambridge UP, 1975.
Sayer, George. *Jack: C.S. Lewis and His Times.* San Francisco: Harper and Row, 1988.
Schakel, Peter. *Reason and Imagination in C.S. Lewis: A Study of 'Till We Have Faces.'* Grand Rapids, Mich.: Eerdmans, 1984.
Walsh, Chad. *The Literary Legacy of C.S. Lewis.* New York: Harcourt, Brace, Jovanovich, 1979.
Wilson, A.N. *C.S. Lewis: A Biography.* New York: Norton, 1990.

Lodge, David John

(b. England 1935–) Literary critic and novelist. David Lodge studied at the University of London, where he received his B.A. (1955) and his M.A. (1959). For the latter he wrote a thesis on the English Roman Catholic novel. He has been at the University of Birmingham since 1960 and was appointed Professor of Modern English Literature in 1976. He has published well-received novels as well as books of criticism.

Lodge's criticism has been concerned almost exclusively with the English novel of the 19th and 20th centuries and with the poetics of the novel. *Language of Fiction* (1966), his first book, shows the influence of, among others, *Wayne Booth, Mark Schorer, *W.K. Wimsatt, and Ian Watt, and attempts to go beyond Anglo-American *New Criticism by using rhetorical analysis to suggest the possibility of a poetics of fiction. (See *rhetorical criticism.) Lodge follows J.M. Cameron in insisting that the term or category 'poetry' include poetry and prose and be defined on the basis of its purpose, which is the deliberate making of fictions.

Although Lodge rightly calls himself a formalist critic, his work emphasizes, even when influenced by *Roman Jakobson, *Roland Barthes and *Gérard Genette as it is in *The Modes of Modern Writing* (1977) and *Working with Structuralism* (1981), that 'it is the essential characteristic of literature that it concerns values' (*Language of Fiction* 57). His later books show Lodge responding sympathetically to *structuralism, though not to *deconstruction. In his major contribution to critical theory, *The Modes of Writing*, he presents an ontology and typology of literary *discourse based on Jakobson's comments on metaphor and metonomy in his classic essay 'Two Aspects of Language and Two Types of Aphasic Disturbances.' (See *metonymy/metaphor.) On the basis of close readings of 20th-century stories and novels, Lodge argues that the major modernists develop from a metonymic to a metaphoric representation of reality and that ultimately all discourse oscillates between the two terms. One of the consequences of his argument is that prose in general and realistic fiction in particular are more firmly grounded in Jakobson's definition of the poetic. Another is a challenge to Barthes' views on the non-referentiality and autonomy of literary discourse.

Lodge's work on the novel brings together in an interesting synthesis New Criticism, the moral and evaluative criticism of Matthew Arnold and *F.R. Leavis, structuralism, and the dialogism of *Mikhail Bakhtin. With the exception of Lodge's extended engagement with Jakobson's essay, however, the influence of critical theory is evident primarily in some key terms and concepts from Barthes (the death of the author, the five codes in *S/Z*) and Genette (analepsis and the three categories of time in narrative) and, most recently, Bakhtin's dialogism and polyphony). (See *polyphony/dialogism, *code.) His novel *Small World: An Academic Romance* (1984) is a satiric look at contemporary criticism, theory and the academic profession.

SAM SOLECKI

Primary Sources

Lodge, David. *After Bakhtin: Essays on Fiction and Criticism*. New York: Routledge, 1990.
– *Changing Places: A Tale of Two Campuses*. London: Secker and Warburg, 1975.
– *Evelyn Waugh*. New York: Columbia UP, 1971.
– *Graham Greene*. New York: Columbia UP, 1966.
– *Language of Fiction*. London: Routledge and Kegan Paul, 1966.
– *The Modes of Modern Writing: Metaphor, Metonymy, and the Typology of Modern Literature*. London: Arnold, 1977.
– *Nice Work*. London: Secker and Warburg, 1988.
– *The Novelist at the Crossroads and Other Essays on Fiction and Criticism*. London: Routledge and Kegan Paul, 1971.
– *Paradise News*. London: Secker and Warburg, 1992.
– *Small World: An Academic Romance*. London: Secker and Warburg, 1984.
– *Working with Structuralism: Essays and Reviews on 19th and 20th Century Literature*. London: Routledge and Kegan Paul, 1981.
– *Write On! Occasional Essays '65–'85*. London: Secker and Warburg, 1986.

Lotman, Iurii Mikhailovich

(b. R.S.S.R., 1922–) Semiotician. After early training in philology and history of Russian Literature, Lotman remained at the University of Leningrad to complete his doctorate in philology. He then went on to teach at Tartu State

University in Estonia. In 1963 he was named head of the Department of Russian Literature in the same university and began to organize seminars on art, culture, *myth, and religion as sign systems. The results were published in the series *Semeotikė: Trudy po znakovym sistemam [Semeotikė: Works on Sign Systems]*. His *Letnaia shkola* – Summer School on Secondary Modelling Systems – was internationally famous. Lotman's talent for research and organization quickly identified him as the foremost representative of the Russian structural semiotic approach to *literature, art and culture, as well as the founder of the *Tartu School. That regional label is deceptively restrictive. The school included important input from Moscow semioticians such as *Boris Uspenskii. (See also *semiotics, *semiosis, *sign.)

Lotman's structural semiotic approach follows from the work of the Russian formalists, particularly *Iurii Tynianov's 'system of genres' and *Roman Jakobson's 'system of systems.' (See Russian *formalism, *genre criticism.) Lotman's work is also related to the Czech structuralists, notably to *Jan Mukařovský's notion of the value of aesthetic functions in culture, as well as the importance of '*intertextuality' (Mukařovský 1936). (See *Semiotic Poetics of the Prague School, *structuralism.) He also follows Mukařovský on the opposition between the synchronic and the diachronic, pointing out their relative and heuristic rather than existential nature (Winner 1978). Lotman locates his own works within the tradition of *Ferdinand de Saussure's concept of semiotics, which stresses language and not 'individual sign' ('Introduction,' Lotman and Uspenskii, *The Semiotics of Russian Culture)*, but he supplements this with ideas drawn from information theory, mathematics and cybernetics. (See also *communication theory.)

Lotman's structural semiotics is based on the central and unifying concept of 'secondary modelling system' (SMS): all cultural systems other than language such as literature, cinema, art, music, religion, and myth. These systems are 'secondary' to natural language, the 'primary modelling system.' Based on natural language, SMSs have a far more complex structure *(Struktura khudozhestvennovo teksta. Structure of the Artistic Text)* and are subdivided into a non-artistic (myth, religion and folklore) and an artistic series. Moreover, the latter series is organized hierarchically according to the degree to which the art in question is related to the natural language structure (Lotman and Uspenskii, 'O semiotitcheskom mechanizme kul'tury.' 'On the Semiotic Mechanism of Culture.'). As a result, Lotman distinguishes between the semiotics of verbal and non-verbal arts (that is, between the symbolic, future-oriented, aspects of verbal arts and the iconic, past-oriented, dimensions of visual arts).

As carriers of information, SMSs penetrate all levels of communication networks. However, the artistic model, because of its specific and distinct structure, and unlike other models (such as scientific models), allows for a much more complex form of modelling. Information in an artistic work is different from that contained in everyday language because of a 'surplus value' directly related to both the very structure of the work and the process that produces its structure *(Analiz poeticheskovo teksta: Struktura stikha. Analysis of the Poetic Text: Verse Structure)*. The reading of a literary *text will necessarily be double, as the text is both an autonomous entity and an expression of something more significant. For Lotman SMSs add up a complex semiotic totality: culture. Thus the work of art is itself a sign within the sign system of culture.

Conceiving culture as a secondary language demanded the expansion of the notion of text to the notion of 'culture text.' Culture is then conceived as a unique text which includes non-verbal systems, while text is conceived as part of a culture text. The 'culture text' represents the most abstract model of reality for a culture.

'Non-text,' one with a decreased semantic value, is produced for no cognitive or pragmatic aim. The opposition between text and 'non-text' allows Lotman to develop a typology of cultures ('O metaiazyke tipologicheskikh opisanii kul'tury'; 'On the Metalanguage of a Typological Description of Culture'). (See *metalanguage.)

Lotman defines culture as the 'totality of non-hereditary information which is accumulated, stored and transmitted by various groups within human society.' Following Jakobson's distinction in linguistics between 'code' (a system of constraints) and 'message' (content), he further distinguishes between the content of culture texts and the structure of their 'language,' between the *langue* of a culture and its *parole* – a distinction that forms an essential grounding of any analysis or typology of culture. (See *langue/parole*, code.) This approach leads him to represent the history of cultures as a 'paradigmatic series' in which each structural type is deduced from its relationship with signs, with semiotics and with other characteristics of language.

By defining culture as the accumulation, storage and transmission of non-hereditary information, Lotman equates its birth with that of history when humanity became the 'addressee' of information. Raising the questions of time and of duration, he accentuates the two principal mechanisms of culture: memory (a set of texts, conservation functions) and program (dynamic systems to reproduce information; generation of new knowledge) (Lotman, Ivanov et al. 1973).

The structural period of Lotman's research was initiated by *Lektsii po struktural'noi poetike* [*Lectures in Structural Poetics*]. Broadening his line of investigation in *Struktura khudozhestvennovo teksta*, Lotman applied his method to Russian poetry in *Analiz poeticheskovo teksta: Struktura stikha*. His conception of culture led to the study of texts of various cultures and periods, a trend well illustrated by 'O semioticheskom mechanizme kul'tury.' He treated cinema in *Semiotika kino i problemy kinoestetiki* [*Semiotics of Cinema and the Problems of Cinema Esthetics*]. The 'montage' process – the collision among elements coming from various texts and producing a maximum polysemic effect, seemed to provide Lotman with the archetypal example of intertextuality. Lotman's masterpiece of analysis and commentary in this vein is *Roman A.S. Pushkina 'Evgenii Onegin.' Kommentarii* [*On Pushkin's Novel 'Evgenii Onegin.' A Commentary*].

While Lotman's achievements were central to Russian structural semiotics and the Tartu-Moscow collaboration, they are now informing Western semiotic investigations, especially those in the U.S.A., but also in Italy, Germany and France. His work is distinguished by his constant application of theory to concrete historical materials of varied artistic forms, by the supreme role granted to text and by his emphasis on the diachronic aspects of the semiotics of culture.

EVA LE GRAND

Primary Sources

Lotman, Iu. M. *Analiz poeticheskovo teksta: Struktura stikha*. Leningrad, 1972. *Analysis of the Poetic Text: Verse Structure*. Ann Arbor: Ardis, 1976.

– 'Dinamicheskaia model' semiotitcheskoi sistemy.' *Predvaritel'nye publikatsii* 60 (Moscow, 1974): 1–23. 'The Dynamic Model of a Semiotic System.' *Semiotica* 21.3–4 (1977): 193–210.
– *Lektsii po struktural'noi poetike: Vvedenie, teoriia stikha*. Tartu, 1964. *Lectures in Structural Poetics: Introduction, Verse Theory*. Repr. Brown University Slavic Reprint Series. Providence: Brown UP, 1968.
– 'O metaiazyke tipologicheskikh opisanii kul'tury.' *Trudy* 4 (Tartu, 1969). 'On the Metalanguage of a Typological Description of Culture.' *Semiotica* 14.2 (1975): 97–123.
– 'O modeliruischem znatchenii poniatii "kontsa" – "nachala" v khudozhestvennykh tekstakh.' *Tezisy* (Tartu, 1966): 89–95. 'The Modelling Significance of the Concept "End" and "Beginning" in Artistic Texts.' *Poetics in Translation* 3. Colchester: U of Essex, 1976, 7–11.
– 'O nekotorykh printsipal'nykh trudnostiakh v strukturalnom opisanii teksta.' *Trudy* 4 (Tartu, 1969). 'On Some Principle Difficulties in the Structural Description of a Text.' *Linguistics* 121 (1974): 57–63.
– 'The Origin of Plot in the Light of Typology.' *Poetics Today* 1:1–2 (1979): 161–84. [Orig.: *In Stat'i po tipologii kul'tury*. Vol. 2. Tartu, 1973.]
– *Roman A.S. Pushkina 'Evgenii Onegin.' Kommentarii. [On Pushkin's Novel 'Evgenii Onegin.' A Commentary.]* Leningrad: Prosveshchenie, 1980.
– *Semiotika kino i problemy kinoestetiki*. Tallin, 1973. *The Semiotics of Cinema and the Problems of Cinema Esthetics*. Ann Arbor: Michigan Slavic Contributions 5, 1976.
– *Stat'i po tipologii kul'tury. [Articles on the Typology of Culture.]* 2 vols. Tartu, 1970, 1973.
– *Struktura khudozhestvennovo teksta*. Moscow: Iskusstvo, 1970. *Structure of the Artistic Text*. Repr. Brown UP, 1971. Ann Arbor: Michigan Slavic Contributions 7, 1977.
– 'Zametki o strukture khudozhestvennovo teksta.' *Trudy* 5 (Tartu, 1971). 'Notes on the Structure of a Literary Text.' *Semiotica* 15.3 (1975): 199–205.
– and B.A. Uspenskii. *The Semiotics of Russian Culture*. Ed. Ann Shukman. Ann Arbor: Michigan Slavic Contributions 11, 1984.
– and B.A. Uspenskii. *The Semiotics of Russian Cultural History: Essays by Lotman, Ginsburg and Uspenskii*. Ed. A.D. Nakhimovsky and A.S. Nakhimovsky. Ithaca and London: Cornell UP, 1985.
– and B.A. Uspenskii. 'O semioticheskom mechanizme kul'tury.' *Trudy* 5 (Tartu, 1971): 144–6. 'On the Semiotic Mechanism of Culture.' *New Literary History* 9.2 (Soviet Semiotics and Criticism: An Anthology), 1978.
– and B.A Uspenskii et al. *Travaux sur les systèmes de signes. Ecole de Tartu*. Bruxelles: Editions Complexe, 1976.
– and A.M. Piatigorskii. 'Tekst i funktsiia.' Tartu 1968. 'Text and Function.' *New Literary History* 9.2

(1978). 'Le Texte et la fonction.' *Semiotica* 1.2 (1969): 205–17.

– and V.V. Ivanov et al. 'Tezisy k semioticheskomu izucheniiu kultur: v primenii k slavianskim tekstam.' In *Stati po tipologii kultury.* Tartu, 1973, 74–89. 'Thesis on the Semiotic Study of Culture: as Applied to Slavic Texts.' In *The Tell-Tale Sign: A Survey of Semiotics.* Ed. Thomas A. Sebeok. Lisse: Ridder P, 1975.

Secondary Sources

Bailey, R.W., L. Matejka and P. Steiner, eds. *The Sign Semiotics Around the World.* Ann Arbor: Michigan Slavic Contributions 9, 1978.

Baran, H., ed. *Semiotics and Structuralism : Readings from the Soviet Union.* White Plains, NY: International Arts and Sciences, 1974.

Eimermacher, K., and S. Shishkoff. *Subject Bibliography of Soviet Semiotics: The Moscow-Tartu School.* Ann Arbor: Michigan Slavic Publications Bibliographic Series 37, 1977.

Halle, M., et al. *Semiosis: Semiotics and History of Culture (In Honorem Georgii Lotman).* Ann Arbor: Michigan Slavic Contributions 10, 1984.

Margolin, U. 'Lotman on the Creation of Meaning in Literature.' *Canadian Review of Comparative Literature* 2.1–3 (Fall 1975): 262–82.

Matejka, L., S. Shishkoff, M.E. Suino, and I.R. Titunik, eds. *Reading in Soviet Semiotics (Russian Texts).* Ann Arbor: Michigan Slavic Publications, 1977.

Mukařovský, Jan. *Aesthetic Function, Norm and Value as Social Facts.* Trans. Mark E. Suino. Ann Arbor: Michigan Slavic Contributions 3, 1970. [Orig.: *Estetická funkce, norma a hodnota jako sociální fakty* 1936.] Prague: Borovy, 1936.

Shukman, A. *Literature and Semiotics: A Study of the Writings of Ju.M. Lotman.* Amsterdam: North Holland Publishers, 1977.

Winner, I. Portis. 'Cultural Semiotics and Anthropology.' In *The Sign Semiotics Around the World,* 335–63.

Lubbock, Percy

(b. England, 1879–d. 1965) Man of letters, critic. Percy Lubbock was educated at Eton and King's College, Cambridge, where he gained a first in the classical tripos. From 1906 to 1908 he was Pepys librarian at Magdalen College, Cambridge, a position which led to his publication in 1909 of *Samuel Pepys,* an introduction to the *Diary.* In 1906 he had published *Elizabeth Barrett Browning in Her Letters.* Between 1908 and 1914 Lubbock was a frequent contributor to the *TLS* and during these years he met *Henry James. After James' death

Lubbock wrote prefaces for editions of the unfinished works, *The Ivory Tower, The Sense of the Past* and *The Middle Years.* In 1920 he edited a two-volume edition of James' letters.

The influence of the novelist on the critic is apparent in Lubbock's *The Craft of Fiction* (1921). This very popular work was Lubbock's chief contribution to the theory and criticism of the novel. In it he examines works by Tolstoy, Flaubert, Thackeray, and James, among others, from the point of view of novelistic technique. 'How it is made is the only question I shall ask,' he claims, and proceeds with a critical study of the form and design of the various novels. His assumption is that the novel must be seen as a work of art, that its linear nature makes it difficult for the reader to grasp its form, and that the intelligent reader, in trying to fix in mind the form of any novel, is cooperating with the novelist in creating the art work. The terms he uses to discriminate novelistic methods of presentation – 'scenic,' 'panoramic,' 'point of view,' 'pictorial,' 'dramatic,' 'scene,' 'summary' – have become staples of *rhetorical criticism of the novel and have helped prepare for more extensive and subtle treatments such as *Wayne Booth's *The Rhetoric of Fiction.*

WALTER O'GRADY

Primary Sources

Booth, Wayne. *The Rhetoric of Fiction.* Chicago: U of Chicago P, 1961.

James, Henry. *The Ivory Tower.* London: Collins, 1917.

– *Letters.* Ed. Percy Lubbock. London: Macmillan, 1920.

– *The Middle Years.* London: Collins, 1917.

– *The Sense of the Past.* London: Collins, 1917.

Lubbock, Percy. *The Craft of Fiction.* London: Jonathan Cape, 1921.

– *Elizabeth Barrett Browning in Her Letters.* London: Smith, Elder, 1906.

– *Samuel Pepys.* London: Hodder and Stoughton, 1909.

Lukács, Georg (György)

(b. Hungary, 1885–d. 1971) Literary critic, philosopher and political thinker. Georg Lukács was born György von Lukács into an upper-middle-class family of German-Jewish descent. He studied philosophy and *literature in Budapest, Berlin and Heidelberg, where he met Georg Simmel and Max Weber. 'The impact of German philosophy lasted my whole life,' he later acknowledged *(Record of a Life)*. Opposing the prevailing neo-Kantian philosophy, Lukács was attracted by the more historically minded thought of Hegel. To this period of intense study of German modern philosophy and of a passionate examination of the contemporary 'tragedy of culture' (as defined by Georg Simmel) belong such works as *Soul and Form* (1911) and the *Theory of the Novel* (1916), as well as the unfinished 'Heidelberg Aesthetics' (1916–18), in which the young Lukács tried to find an answer to the crises of the bourgeois society that formed the cultural background of the First World War.

His study of German philosophy, as well as his deep discontent with issues of current policies and culture in war-torn Central Europe led Lukács to Marx; after the advent of the Russian Revolution he finally committed himself to Marxism and joined the Communists. (See *Marxist criticism.) A member of the Hungarian Communist party since December 1918, he became a leading member of the Revolutionary Governing Council and a Red Army commissar in the short-lived Bela Kuhn 'proletarian' dictatorship of 1919.

After the defeat of the 'Red Republic,' Lukács lived in exile, first in Vienna and Berlin, where he continued to actively participate in shaping Communist politics and *ideology, writing his most influential works of political ideology *(History and Class Consciousness, The Blum Theses)*. A leading figure in the constitution of Western Marxism, which proposes the renewal of Marxism by critically reappropriating its 'traditional' categories in terms of democratic rationality, Lukács opposed more dogmatic forms of Marxism, developed mainly by the Stalinist 'ideological' apparatus and the Comintern. During his Moscow exile, in the 1930s, Lukács had to limit his activity to literary and philosophical work, occasionally publishing short texts of literary criticism. In these years he wrote *The Historical Novel* (1937) and *The Young Hegel*, published only in 1948. In 1945, Lukács returned to Hungary and finally became a university professor; his main disciples formed the future Budapest School: Agnes Heller, Ferenc Feher, Istvan Meszaros, Mihaly Vajda. In 1956 Lukács, as minister of culture and education, participated in the ill-fated Imre Nagy government, historically the first

East European attempt at constructing a truly democratic state structure outside a dictatorial Stalinist frame. After the crush of that democratic 'revolt,' brought about by Soviet and Warsaw Pact military intervention, Lukács, as well as the other members of the doomed democratic government, was briefly imprisoned in Romania. Unlike Imre Nagy's, his life was spared and in 1959 Lukács was allowed to return to Hungary, although his civil liberties were seriously restricted until 1967, when the liberalization of the regime also brought about a more tolerant assessment of Lukács' lifelong activity.

The *Theory of the Novel* integrates the development of the epic into a general frame of philosophy of history: Lukács reads the history of the epic genre into a Fichte-inspired epochal frame that explains the actual realization of narrative forms, culminating with the novel. Lukács regarded Western civilization as undergoing a transitional phase, where the loss of normativity (of standards of belief and conduct) made it an age of 'absolute sinfulness' *(vollendete Sündhaftigkeit)*. The novel opposes the Homeric epic, proper to an age of innocence and homogeneity between transcendence and immanence, where the hero is an Eponymous, non-individual I, at peace with the values of his own world; the novel, however, is a work proper to an age of crisis, being 'the literary form of the transcendent homelessness of the idea.' From Cervantes' *Don Quixote* to Tolstoy and Dostoevsky the novel mirrors the quest for a new normativity: thus, the Western novel depicts a world dominated by desire, lacking unity and tragically destroying the alienated individual subject who is heroically searching for an immanent meaning. The character's never-ending quest for an immanent meaning in a 'bourgeois world,' unable to provide it, is what gives the novelistic hero his 'demonic nature'; at the same time, the modern author, inasmuch as he perceives the perpetual break between the character's vision and his or her failure caused by a deceiving reality, is invariably placed in a position of *irony.

The *Historical Novel* continues Lukács' preoccupation with the fate of the Western novel, this time within a Marxist-oriented *discourse. Lukács proposes to constitute historical authenticity as a main category of aesthetic evaluation and, in this way, the complexity of the social-historical understanding in terms of

Lukács

'accuracy' is seen as the main value of the literary *text. Regardless of this somewhat muddled aesthetic, the volume contains interesting examinations of Balzac, Walter Scott, Leon Feuchtwanger, Heinrich Mann, and Tolstoy. Lukács' analysis of Scott's novels is exemplary, showing how the 'veridic analysis' of the social representation is constituted as the main criterion of aesthetic judgment. Scott is seen as a radical innovator because he succeeds in showing how the historical meaning of human destiny is constituted as concrete narrrativity. Lukács indicates a number of central points that support his opinion: the plot of the novel usually concerns an important historical crisis, the novel succeeds in depicting and involving social strata of complex structure and, finally, the main character (like Frank Osbaldiston in *Rob Roy)* is more often than not chosen from a middle-class environment, so as to act as a mediating element within the social conflicts depicted in the novel.

Largely ignored by West European thinkers, the later Lukács has its importance. The impressive *Eigenart des Ästhetischen* [*The Specificity of the Aesthetic* 1963], a synthesis of his lifelong thinking on art, integrates art and science into a comprehensive Marxist phenomenology of the Spirit and subsequently examines its social and historical function as a form of spirituality. (See *phenomenological criticism.) Art is defined as man's self-awareness as a species involving the anthropomorphic representation of the world *(Selbstbewusstsein-von).* The work of art thus integrates the fragmented parts of the real and represents the human subject as a totality *(Mensch ganz).*

Lukács' is the most coherent attempt at building a 20th-century systematic aesthetic of Marxist conceptualizations (as compared with similar attempts made by *Adorno, Bloch or *Benjamin). Its merits and its limits have yet to be fully assessed, but it is already evident that such a project deserves a judgment that is able to take into account the whole impact of an age of modern thought on the development of the Marxist doctrine in the field of cultural studies. For this reason Lukács seems more and more a forefather whose work has contributed to the postmodern ability of auto-critique and delegitimation of the totalizing social subject. (See also *reification, *postmodernism, *totalization, *subject/object, *materialist criticism.)

MIRELA SAIM

Primary Sources

Lukács, Georg. *Ästhetic.* Frankfurt am Main: Luchterhand, 1972.
– 'Eigenart des Ästhetischen.' Orig. pub. as 'Ästhetik' in *Werke,* vols. 11–12. Berlin: Luchterhand, 1962–86.
– *Essays on Realism.* Trans. David Fernbach. Cambridge: MIT P, 1981.
– *Essays on Thomas Mann.* Trans. Stanley Mitchell. New York: Grosset and Dunlap, 1965.
– *Goethe and His Age.* Trans. Robert Anchor. New York: Howard Fertig, 1978.
– 'Heidelberger Ästhetik.' 1916–18. In *Werke,* vol. 17. Berlin: Luchterhand, 1962–86.
– *The Historical Novel.* Trans. Hannah Mitchell and Stanley Mitchell. Boston: Beacon P, 1962.
– *History and Class Consciousness: Studies in Marxist Dialectics.* 1923. Trans. Rodney Livingstone. Cambridge: MIT P, 1971.
– *Realism in Our Times.* Trans. John Mander and Necke Mander. New York: Harper and Row, 1964.
– *Record of a Life: An Autobiographical Sketch.* Trans. Rodney Livingstone. London: Verso, 1983.
– *Solzhenitsyn.* Trans. William David Graff. Cambridge: MIT P, 1971.
– *Soul and Form.* Trans. Anna Bostock. Cambridge: MIT P, 1974.
– *Studies in European Realism.* New York: Grosset and Dunlap, 1964.
– *Theory of the Novel.* Trans. Anna Bostock. Cambridge: MIT P, 1971.
– *The Young Hegel: Studies in the Relation Between Dialectics and Economics.* Trans. Rodney Livingstone. London: Merlin P, 1975.

Secondary Sources

Feher, Ferenc, and Agnes Heller. *Reconstructing Aesthetics: Writings of the Budapest School.* Oxford: Basil Blackwell, 1986.
Goldmann, Lucien. *Lukács et Heidegger.* Paris: Donoël/Gonthier, 1983.
Jay, Martin. *Marxism and Totality: The Adventures of a Concept from Lukács to Habermas.* Berkeley and Los Angeles: U of California P, 1984.
Kadarkay, Arpad. *Georg Lukács: Life, Thought and Politics.* Oxford: Basil Blackwell, 1991.
Rockmore, Tom. *Irrationalism: Lukács and the Marxist View of Reason.* Philadelphia: Temple UP, 1992.
Tertulian, Nicolas. *Georges Lukács: Etapes de sa pensée esthétique.* Paris: Le Sycomore, 1980.

Lyotard, Jean-François

(b. France, 1924–) Philosopher. A man of 'peregrinations' *(Peregrinations* 1988), physical as
well as intellectual, Jean-François Lyotard
taught in Algeria, Brazil and California; he was
named professor of philosophy at the University of Paris in 1968 and became director of
the Collège International de Philosophie in
1985. Lyotard acquired an international reputation with *The Postmodern Condition* (1979), a
report on the condition of knowledge written
at the request of the Government of Quebec.

The unity of Lyotard's work is not found in
a single method or analysis or a single political
outlook but in its very activity or in what he
calls the 'effort of thinking' – the effort necessitated by those situations where thought is
least able to deliver definite or incontrovertible
conclusions. He reflects on what is undecid-
able in judgment, on the knots, the double
binds, the paradoxes or the 'paralogisms' of
*discourse. (See also *paradox.) Lyotard has
tried to restore the place of those who, like the
Sophists, resist or complicate finalistic or ontological assertions. Among such thinkers, Lyotard especially refers to 'artists': not only
writers, but also painters, cinematographers
and musicians. One of the first in France to
write about *Theodor Adorno's aesthetics, he
was also the curator of Les Immatériaux
(1985), a vast exhibition at the Beaubourg Museum, which examined new technologies in
*postmodernism. His work on Duchamp *(Les
Transformateurs Duchamp* 1977) and on painting *(Que peindre?* 1987) helped shape theory
and practice in the visual arts.

Like many thinkers of his generation, Lyotard has tried to connect and to reconcile the
philosophical questions raised by avant-garde
or modernist art with the political militancy of
the Left. His work is punctuated by successive
formulations of these problems which give rise
to new styles of analysis. Between his early
study of phenomenology *(La Phénoménologie*
1954) and the later *Discours/figure* (1971),
Lyotard was principally engaged in political
militancy and journalism (Appendix, *Peregrinations).* (See *phenomenological criticism.)
Along with Cornelius Castoriadis and Claude
Lefort, Lyotard created the journal *Socialisme
ou barbarie* [Socialism or Barbarism] and subsequently wrote for the newspaper *Pouvoir ouv-
rier* [The Power of the Worker]. The struggle

for Algerian independence and a growing dis-
satisfaction with Soviet Marxism resulted in
Lyotard's scepticism about the fulfilment of the
Marxist utopian ideal. (See *Marxist criticism.)

In *Discours/figure* Lyotard turned to aesthetics. A criticism of phenomenology, the book
marks the introduction of psychoanalysis in
his work and also critiques *Jacques Lacan's
*structuralism (the attempt to conceive of the
unconscious on a linguistic or discursive
model) and instead uses the Freudian dream-
work (which casts the dream thought into visual form) as the model of the incidence of the
figural in the discursive. The place of desire
becomes the place of constant gap between
form and content; the truth of desire can
therefore never discover a completely adequate
expression. (See *Sigmund Freud, *psychoanalytic theory, *desire/lack.)

In this period, the phenomenological *theme
of the flesh is replaced by the psychoanalytic
theme of desire and its vicissitudes – of a 'libidinal economy' *(Des Dispositifs pulsionnels*
1973 and *Economie libidinale* 1974). Also, Lyotard attempted to rethink Marxism from the
standpoint of a figural unconscious of 'intensities' in the manner of *Gilles Deleuze and
*Félix Guattari. Such 'intensities' consisted in
those sites of energy which can't be measured
or programmed and which are prior to interpretation.

Yet another beginning occurred with the realization that his metaphysics of 'intensities'
'didn't work' *(Au Juste* 1979, 170) because it
could not account for the problem of injustice
– the problem of political judgment: of what to
do or what side to take. In response, Lyotard,
rather in the style of *Ludwig Wittgenstein,
devised a theory of different regimes of sentences *(énoncés)* which he elaborates in *Le Différend* (1983). (See *énonciation/énoncé.) A
différend arises when there must be a decision
made among incommensurable regimes of sentences, as distinct from a *tort* (a wrong), where
there is only the question of the application of
received principles. The question of injustice
brings Lyotard to the Kantian theme of reflective judgment: judgment in the absence of
criteria or in the case where the method of
judging always forms part of the judgment.

Lyotard then turns to a detailed exposition
of the place of the sublime in Kant's critical
philosophy. The sublime is the concept
through which Kant introduces the *problematic of representing the unrepresentable, an

idea central to modernist art and thought ('The Sublime and the Avant-garde' 1984).

Le Différend, the fruit of a ten-year labour begun immediately after *Economie libidinale*, supplies the framework for the sociological diagnosis of *The Postmodern Condition*: the collapse of legitimation based on grand historical schemes *(les grands récits)*. The debate that crystallized around the theme of the end of the *grands récits* perhaps points to the philosophical core of Lyotard's work: the problem of the kind of legitimacy that theory can have when it is not based on a priori principles or on a progressive, holistic history.

Lyotard has chosen to draw attention to those events which disrupt and alter our thinking: 'Auschwitz, Berlin 1953, Budapest 1956, Czechoslovakia 1968, May 1968, Poland 1980, and Kolyma.' In *Heidegger and the Jews* (1988), Lyotard later elaborated the theme of Auschwitz as such an event in the context of the debate over *Martin Heidegger.

ANNE BOYMAN

Primary Sources

Lyotard, Jean-François. *La Condition postmoderne.* Paris: Minuit, 1979. *The Postmodern Condition.* Trans. Geoffrey Bennington and Brian Massumi. Minneapolis: Minnesota UP, 1984.
– *Dérive à partir de Freud et Marx.* Paris: UGE, 1973.
– *Des Dispositifs pulsionnels.* Paris: UGE, 1973.
– *Le Différend.* Paris: Minuit, 1983.
– *Discours/figure.* Paris: Klincksieck, 1971.
– *Economie libidinale.* Paris: Minuit, 1974.
– *L'Enthousiasme, la critique kantienne de l'histoire.* Paris: Galilée, 1986.
– *Heidegger and the Jews.* Minneapolis: Minnesota UP, 1988.
– *Peregrinations: Law, Form, Event.* New York: Columbia UP, 1988.
– *La Phénoménologie.* Paris: PUF, 1954.
– *Que Peindre?* Paris: Editions de la Différence, 1987.
– 'The Sublime and the Avant-garde.' Trans. L. Liebmann, G. Bennington, and M. Hobson. *Paragraph* 6 (1985): 1–18.
– *Les Transformateurs Duchamp.* Paris: Galilée. 1977.
– and Jean-Loup Thébaud. *Au Juste.* Paris: Christian Bourgois, 1979. *Just Gaming.* Trans. Wlad Godzich. Minneapolis: Minnesota UP, 1986.

Secondary Sources

Carroll, David. *Paraesthetics.* New York: Methuen, 1987.
Bennington, Geoffrey. *Lyotard: Writing the Event.* Manchester: Manchester UP, 1988.

Macherey, Pierre

Pierre Macherey (b. France 1938–) Marx theorist. Best known in the anglophone world as the author of *Pour une théorie de la production littéraire [A Theory of Literary Production* 1966; trans. 1978], Macherey worked with *Louis Althusser in the 1960s, has published books on Spinoza, Comte and Hegel and, most recently, renewed his interest in sociological criticism and philosophy with *A quoi pense la littérature?* (1990).

*Terry Eagleton has referred to Macherey as the 'first Althusserian critic' *(Against the Grain* 2), and certainly Macherey's work owes much to the work in Marxist philosophy carried out by Althusser in the 1960s. While there is a tendency in the North American academy to meld the various 'structuralisms' of *Jacques Lacan, *Claude Lévi-Strauss, *Roland Barthes, and Althusser into one enormous project based on Saussurean linguistics and Freudian theories of the unconscious, Althusser's work, and therefore Macherey's, cannot be assimilated into any homogeneous form of 'French structuralism.' (See *structuralism, *Sigmund Freud, *Ferdinand de Saussure.)

Althusser sought to engage with Karl Marx's actual *writings* as *text; and he worked to *disengage* Marxist theory from what he then saw as the trap of a false humanism. (See *Marxist criticism.) The first strategy necessitated a 'return to Marx,' culminating in the theory of an 'epistemic rupture' between the earlier, humanist Marx of the *Economic and Philosophical Manuscripts of* 1844 and the later, scientific Marx of *The German Ideology* and *Capital.* (See *episteme.) The second strategy, then, meant breaking out of the concerns with alienation and *reification associated with the work of Hungarian Marxist *Georg Lukács, as well as attempting to steer the French Communist party away from the valorization of humanism, of 'man' as the 'agent of history.' The most radical and influential effect of Althusser's works (including *For Marx* and the collectively written *Reading Capital*, both 1965) has been his theory of *ideology not as a 'false consciousness' or commonly swallowed lie, but rather as the way in which a society will 'reproduce' its own continuation. Ideology, then, is like Freud's 'manifest content': merely the most visible form of the social real, which must then be analysed.

What Althusser's work means for Macherey's theory is apparent in the first section of *A Theory of Literary Production*, where Macherey confronts the 'elementary concepts' that underwrite literary criticism – that is, primarily, three fallacies: the empirical fallacy, the normative fallacy and the interpretive fallacy (19). Macherey sets out to show that criticism is bedevilled by ideological constraints and is itself an ideology. Thus, first of all, criticism will assume unquestioningly the empirical status of its given object – the literary work of art. Macherey's later work (particularly the essay 'On Literature as an Ideological Form' 1981) shows clearly how *literature is a product of social desire. (See *desire/lack.) Criticism will strive 'to modify the work in order to assimilate it more thoroughly, denying its factual reality as being merely the provisional version of an unfulfilled intention' (19). By seeking some truth in the literary work, interpretation will 'resolve a problem in a way that simply gets rid of it' (38), without, that is, showing how the problem came, historically, to be a part of the text.

While Macherey has been characterized as a poststructuralist, his readings of V.I. Lenin and structuralism in *A Theory of Literary Production* sternly disallow such miscalculation. (See *poststructuralism.) In 'Lenin, Critic of Tolstoy,' Lenin's articles on Tolstoy are interpreted as subtle meditations on the relationship between an individual writer, history and ideology: in effect, Lenin becomes a precursor of the Althusserian critique of humanist Marxism. Most convincingly, Macherey argues that Lenin's criticism offers a way out of naive reflection theory, a topic Macherey returns to in 'The Problem of Reflection' (1976). For Macherey, art is a mirror in the same way that ideology is a mirror. The *trope is psychoanalytic and Lacanian, and signifies the role of the unconscious in the book: 'there is an internal displacement of ideology by virtue of this *redoubling*; this is not ideology contemplating itself, but the mirror effect which exposes its insufficiency' (133). A work of art is ideological by dint of its contradictions, but the point is not for the materialist critic simply to point out some contradictions in a work to 'deconstruct' it. (See also *materialist criticism, *deconstruction, *psychoanalytic theory.)

This is the point at which Macherey leaves the realms of garden-variety Marxist criticism and deconstruction. The critic who seeks, as does Barthes in *Mythologies,* to show the cracks in an ideological edifice is not too different from the old-style critic with his 'normative fallacy' mentioned above: both types of criticism are forms of Platonism. Macherey is unambiguous on this point: 'it is futile to denounce the presence of a contradiction in ideology' (194). So it is not contradiction that the Machereyan critic will tease out in a literary work, but rather gaps or absences, for these gaps indicate a break with the ideological circumstances of the work.

Such an understanding underlies Macherey's reading of Jules Verne's work and particularly the lesson Macherey draws from the novel *The Mysterious Island.* While Verne's works can be said to reflect the bourgeois ideology of scientific expansionism of the Third Republic, this reflection is an active, critical process. The figure of Robinson Crusoe functions as the novel's own 'unconscious' – just as European explorers were not colonizing 'virgin' territory but the homelands of others, so Verne's characters are merely repeating, in a modernized version, the adventures of Daniel Defoe's hero. Jules Verne's narratives are 'faulty' *(en défaut)* in a geological sense: absent but powerful presences – Crusoe as imaginary father, Captain Nemo as ideological one – in the end determine the narrative.

Macherey returns in his later work to problems he first enunciated in *A Theory of Literary Production.* In 'The Problem of Reflection', he poses the *problematic in terms of aesthetics in general. He seeks strenuously to distance materialist aesthetics from Hegelian expressionism, or the notion that 'art "expresses" social reality' (7), or even aesthetic pleasure (10). For Macherey, reflection theory depends upon naive distinctions of subject-object and form-content: his way out of mechanical and abstract aesthetics is first of all to refer to Althusser's work on *Ideological State Apparatuses, and then to Renée Balibar's work on how literature is bound up with national (French) educational practices. (See *subject/object.)

Macherey returns briefly to the question of reflection in 'On Literature as an Ideological Form' (1981), co-written with Etienne Balibar, but here the two critics engage most directly questions of how the educational system in France, with its rigid hierarchy 'reproduces the social division of a society based on the sale and purchase of individual labour-power' (85). The division, Macherey and Balibar argue, is primarily linguistic, and accomplished most forcefully in terms of the teaching of literature – the *français élémentaire* of primary school and *français littéraire* of advanced education. The uses of literature, on the one hand, to teach grammar, and on the other, as example of truth and beauty, are interdependent, the critics argue, as tools of class domination.

The more philosophical bent of Macherey's recent work is accessible in his essay 'In a Materialist Way' (1983). Here he formulates materialism not as a body of knowledge but in the tradition of the critique. He seeks to 'make philosophy admit its historicity' (139), and flirts with *Antonio Gramsci's ideas of a philosophy that re-works 'common sense' as practice. The brief essay is both a summary of Macherey's work on Hegel and Spinoza, and an indication of where he sees a materialist philosophy going, ceaselessly interrogating its multiple and inexorable conditions and struggles.

Two major book-length works by Macherey have not yet been translated into English, and yet the directions implicit even in the *Theory* of 1966 can be seen in the later works. *Hegel ou Spinoza* continues the Althusserian fascination with Baruch de Spinoza – Althusser remarked once that to be a Spinozist or Marxist is essentially the same thing (*Lenin and Philosophy* 175). Spinoza's appeal lies, Christopher Norris has suggested, in his reflections on the difference between lived experience and a transcendent epistemology (44). Macherey is interested in how Spinoza, unlike Hegel, refuses to see philosophy as a reflection of some predetermined reality: 'For Spinoza, ideas are not images or passive representations, and they do not reproduce, in a more or less correct fashion, external realities' (79). Hegel fundamentally *misreads* Spinoza: unlike Hegel's Absolute Spirit, 'the God of the *Ethics* is not a totality of determinations, arranged in a rational order by the logic of their development or their system' (223). Macherey's work suggests a way for 'materialist philosophy' to continue to work out of the anthropological Marxism still predominant today.

A quoi pense la littérature? synthesizes Macherey's concerns at the intersection of literature and philosophy. Here Macherey is most successful when he engages with writers precisely on such boundaries: Raymond Roussel, de Sade, Georges Bataille, Mme de Stael, and Raymond Queneau.

Macherey has been quite influential on British Marxist and leftist criticism – Catherine Belsey and Tony Bennett devote substantial space in their first books to his work, and Eagleton was perhaps the first 'Machereyan critic' in such works as *Criticism and Ideology* and *Marxism and Literary Criticism*. It is easy to see why this should be so. By harnessing both a sophisticated Althusserian theory of ideology and a neo-Freudian or Lacanian idea of the unconscious to a close critical attentiveness, Macherey set the agenda for materialist literary criticism.

CLINT BURNHAM

Primary Sources

Macherey, Pierre. *A quoi pense la littérature?* Paris: PUF, 1990.
– *Hegel ou Spinoza.* Paris: Maspero, 1979.
– 'In a Materialist Way.' Trans. Lorna Scott Fox. In *Philosophy in France Today*. Ed. Alan Montefiore. Cambridge: Cambridge UP, 1983, 136–54.
– 'Interview.' *Red Letters: Communist Party Literature Journal* 5 (Summer 1979): 3–9.
– 'Interview: Etienne Balibar and Pierre Macherey.' By James H. Kavanagh and Thomas E. Lewis. *Diacritics* (1982) 12: 46–62.
– *Pour une théorie de la production littéraire.* Paris: Maspero, 1966. *A Theory of Literary Production.* Trans. by Geoffrey Wall. London: Routledge, 1978.
– 'The Problem of Reflection.' Trans. Susan Sniader Lanser. *Sub-Stance* (1976) 15: 6–20.
– and Etienne Balibar. 'On Literature as an Ideological Form.' Trans. Ian McLeod, John Whitehead and Ann Wordsworth. In *Untying the Text*. Ed. Robert Young. London: Routledge, 1981, 79–99.

Secondary Sources

Althusser, Louis. *Lenin and Philosophy and Other Essays.* Trans. Ben Brewster. New York: Monthly Review, 1971.
Barker, Frances. 'Ideology, Production, Text: Pierre Macherey's Materialist Criticism.' *Praxis* 5 (1980): 99–108.
Belsey, Catherine. *Critical Practice.* London: Methuen, 1980.
Bennett, Tony. *Formalism and Marxism.* London: Methuen, 1979.
Eagleton, Terry. *Criticism and Ideology: A Study in Marxist Literary Theory.* London: Verso, 1976.
– 'Macherey and Marxist Literary Theory.' In *Against the Grain: Selected Essays 1975–1985*. London: Verso, 1986, 9–22.
– *Marxism and Literary Criticism.* London: Methuen, 1976.

Elliot, Gregory. *Althusser: The Detour of Theory.* London: Verso, 1987.

Frow, John. 'Structuralist Marxism.' *Southern Review* 15.2 (1982): 208–17.

Kavanagh, James H. 'Marx's Althusser: Towards a Politics of Literary Theory.' *Diacritics* 12 (1982): 25–45.

Lewis, Thomas E. 'Aesthetic Effect/Ideological Effect.' *Enclitic* 7.2 (1983): 4–16.

Norris, Christopher. *Spinoza and the Origins of Modern Critical Theory.* Oxford: Blackwell, 1991.

Poole, Roger. 'Generating Believable Entities: Post-Marxism as a Theological Enterprise.' *Comparative Criticism: A Yearbook* 7 (1985): 49–71.

Maritain, Jacques

(b. France 1882–d. 1973) Philosopher. At the Sorbonne, where he was studying natural sciences, Jacques Maritain met Raïssa Oumansoff. They were married in 1904 and their intellectual development progressed in tandem under three main influences. One was that of Henri Bergson. Believing that scientists held the supreme principles of the intelligence in little esteem, they began to attend the lectures of this philosopher, whose intuitionism combated the reductive tendencies of the scientific mind. A second influence was the writer Léon Bloy, who led them towards Catholicism and served as their godfather when they were received into the Church in 1906. It was a major step for them to take, since Maritain came from a liberal Protestant background and Raïssa was Jewish, and since the prevailing intellectual climate made them feel that in embracing the Church they were abandoning philosophy forever.

In Heidelberg, however, where he had gone to study the state of biological sciences in the German universities, Maritain came under a third influence, that of Thomas Aquinas. The *Summa Theologia* came to him as 'a luminous flood'; from that time on he became a leading exponent of Thomism in the modern world, considering that the doctrine of St. Thomas would provide a method for fruitful discussion of such contemporary questions as the relations between science and wisdom, the person and the common good, and Christianity and democracy. Beginning in 1912, he taught at the Collège Stanislas in Paris and the following year he spoke on Bergson and Christian philosophy, the first of many series of lectures

at the Institut Catholique (also in Paris). Subsequently he was to teach at Columbia, Chicago, Notre Dame, and especially Princeton; and from 1933 on he was on the faculty of the Institute (later, Pontifical Institute) of Mediaeval Studies in Toronto.

Among his 60 books, there were a number on aesthetics, beginning with one suggested to him by the work of a modern painter, Georges Rouault. In this book, *Art and Scholasticism* (1920), Maritain notes that the schoolmen composed no special treatise on the philosophy of art; their theories about it have to be sought in austere dissertations on problems of logic. St. Thomas, he writes, defined the beautiful as that which gives pleasure on sight. Art belongs to the order of making, the practical realm rather than the speculative. Nevertheless it is stamped with the character of a man, a rational animal, and therefore is intellectual: its activity consists in impressing an idea upon matter.

Like James Joyce, Maritian describes the three qualities of the beautiful in intellectual terms: integrity, because the intellect is pleased with fullness of being; proportion or consonance, because the intellect is pleased with order and unity; and radiance or clarity, because the intellect is pleased with what causes intelligence to see. The fine arts depend upon things; they have a certain relation to imitation, which is difficult to define. (See *mimesis.) But a work of art is more than an object; it possesses a transcendental nature. Aquinas said that 'the beauty of anything created is nothing else than a similitude of divine beauty participated in things,' and this is especially true of the work of art.

Man is grossly in error, Maritain thought, when he seeks to build his existence around art as a supreme end in itself. In *The Degrees of Knowledge* (1932), he wrote that it is wrong to attribute to psychology, the speculative science of the human being, the profound insights of a Pascal or a Shakespeare. Properly speaking, they are not psychologists but moralists; they study the dynamism of the human being, his use of free will and his disposition towards a sovereign good. In six lectures he gave on the responsibility of the artist at Princeton in 1951, Maritain discussed such matters in a systematic way. From the viewpoint of art, he said, the artist seeks only the good of his work. From the viewpoint of morality, to assume that it does not matter what one writes is permissible only to the insane: the artist is responsible to the good of human life, in himself and in his fellow men.

In *Art and Scholasticism*, he explained that he intended to consider the essentials of art rather than the nature of poetry; but 'later on it was this mysterious nature that I became more and more eager to scrutinize.' He did so in *Art and Poetry* (1935) and in a much more ambitious work, *Creative Intuition in Art and Poetry* (1953). In the background of his reflection was the idea that, though poetry is by its process of creation an art, poetry and poetic knowledge infinitely transcend art merely conceived of as the craftsman's virtue. Dante in the Middle Ages and Baudelaire in the modern age both see the spiritual as immanent in the real world: the mysteries of the world and of the spirit embrace each other.

St. Thomas lists art among the intellectual virtues; it is a *habitus* or capacity involving reason. As Armand Maurer points out, Maritain and another leading Thomist, Etienne Gilson, differed about what this implied. Maritain sees art as intellectual in essence; manual skill is no part of it. The source of every work of fine art is creative intuition; the whole work, 'the totality of the work to be engendered,' is present in intuition before it is fashioned. For Gilson, this makes the artist too like a God. He agreed that knowledge accompanied artistic production but not that art is a form of knowing rather than making. For him the artist's *habitus* is in the hands as well as the mind; the art is in the execution, not in the intellect alone.

Maritain had a wide acquaintance among poets, painters and musicians; and paradoxically, on the basis of Thomistic principles, he was able to provide an interpretation and defence of their art. The major innovation of modern art, he thought, lay in its exploration of the self, especially of the preconscious and subconscious activity of the mind. (See *self/other.) Wallace Fowlie writes that the success of *Art and Scholasticism* was due to a surprising concurrence of its conclusions with the beliefs of modern artists, especially those outside any religious persuasion. They were pleased to see confirmation of their belief that the lesson of art is as useful to philosophers as to artists, and that the movement of modern art is a valid illustration of modern ideas and ideologies. (See *ideology.)

At the same time, Maritain saw that the pride of the artist could lead him astray. He deplored modern art's tendency towards 'angelism,' by which he meant its tendency to divorce form from content and seek a 'pure' form of art – an absolute which, by its very nature, art is capable of producing. While praising many abstract artists, he wished to see their work anchored in the real; some provided us with elements of contemplation only by quitting the realm of the human. Still he paid tribute to art and artists for continuing to surprise and delight us: 'Poetry is capable of worming its way in anywhere.'

As employed by Maritain, Thomistic aesthetics was not so much a coherent system as a surprisingly novel approach to both age-old and entirely new problems.

DAVID J. DOOLEY

Primary Sources

Maritain, Jacques. *Art et scholastique*. Paris: Art catholique, 1920. *Art and Scholasticism*. Trans. J.F. Scanlan. New York: Charles Scribner's Sons, 1930.
- *Court traité de l'existence et l'existant*. Paris: P. Hartmann, 1947. *Existence and the Existent*. Trans. Lewis Galantière and Gerald B. Phelan. New York: Imagen Books, 1957.
- *Creative Intuition in Art and Poetry*. New York: Pantheon Books, 1953.
- *Distinguer pour unir: ou, les degrés du savoir*. Paris: Desclée de Brouwer, 1932. *The Degrees of Knowledge*. Trans. Bernard Wall and Margot R. Adamson. London: Geoffrey Bles, 1937.
- *Le Docteur angélique*. Paris: P. Hartmann, 1929. *St. Thomas Aquinas, Angel of the Schools*. Trans. J.F. Scalan. London: Sheed and Ward, 1933.
- *Frontières de la poésie et autres essais*. Paris: L. Rouart, 1935. *Art and Poetry*. Trans. E. de P. Matthews. New York: Philosophical Library, 1943.
- *Humanisme intégral: Problèmes temporals et spirituels d'une nouvelle chrétienté*. Paris: F. Aubier, 1936. *Integral Humanism: Temporal and Spiritual Problems of a New Christendom*. Trans. Joseph W. Evans. New York: Scribner, 1968.
- *Neuf leçons sur les notions premières de la philosophie morale*. Paris: Pierre Téqui, 1950. *An Introduction to the Basic Problem of Moral Philosophy*. Trans. Cornelia N. Borgerhoff. Albany, NY: Magi Books, 1990.
- *Le Paysan de la Garonne: Un Vieux laïc s'interroge à propos du temps présent*. Paris: Desclée de Brouwer, 1930. *The Peasant of the Garonne: An Old Layman Questions Himself about the Present Time*. Trans. Michael Cuddihy and Elizabeth Hughes. New York: Holt, Rinehart and Winston, 1968.
- *Religion et culture*. Paris: Desclée de Brouwer,

1930. *Religion and Culture*. Trans. J.F. Scalan. London: Sheed and Ward, 1931.

– *Réponse à Jean Cocteau*. Paris: Stock, 1926.

– *The Responsibility of the Artist*. New York: Scribner's, 1960.

– *Sept leçons sur l'être: et les premiers principes de la raison spéculative*. Paris: P. Téqui, 1934.

– and Julian Green. *The Story of Two Souls. The Correspondence of Jacques Maritain and Julien Green*. Trans. Bernard Doering. New York: Fordham UP, 1988.

– and Raïssa Maritain. *Situation de la poésie*. Paris: Desclée de Brouwer, 1938. *The Structure of Poetry*. Trans. Marshall Suther. New York: Philosophical Library, 1955.

Secondary Sources

Editors of *La Revue Thomiste. Jacques Maritain: Son oeuvre philosophique*. Paris: Desclée de Brouwer, 1949. (See especially Charles Journet, 'D'une philosophie chrétienne de l'histoire et de la culture.')

Evans, Joseph. *Jacques Maritain: The Man and His Achievement*. New York: Sheed and Ward, 1963. (See especially Wallace Fowlie, 'Maritain the Writer,' and Francis Fergusson, 'Poetic Intuition and Action in Maritain's Creative Intuition in Art and Poetry.')

Fowlie, Wallace. *Jacob's Night: The Religious Renascence in France*. New York: Sheed and Ward, 1947.

Gilson, Etienne. *The Arts of the Beautiful*. New York: Scribner's, 1965.

– *Painting and Reality*. New York: Pantheon Books, 1957.

Hamm, Victor M. *Language, Truth and Poetry*. The Aquinas Lectures, 1960. Milwaukee: Marquette UP, 1960.

Hanke, John W. *Maritain's Ontology of the Work of Art*. The Hague: Martinus Nijhoff, 1973.

Maritain, Raïssa. *Les Grandes amitiés: Souvenirs*. 2 vols. New York: Editions de la maison française, 1941–4.

Maurer, Armand A. *About Beauty: A Thomistic Interpretation*. Houston: Center for Thomistic Studies, 1983.

McInerny, Ralph. *Art and Prudence: Studies in the Thought of Jacques Maritain*. Notre Dame, Ind.: Notre Dame P, 1988.

Redpath, Peter A., ed. *From Twilight to Dawn: The Cultural Vision of Jacques Maritain*. Mickawaka, Ind.: U of Notre Dame P, 1990.

Rover, Thomas Dominic. *The Poetics of Maritain: A Thomistic Critique*. Washington: Thomist P, 1965.

Simonsen, Vagn Lundgaard. *L'Esthétique de Jacques Maritain*. Copenhagen: Munsgaard, 1956.

Speaight, Robert. 'The Springs of Poetry.' *New Scholasticism*. Maritain issue 46 (1972): 51–69.

Mauron, Charles

(b. France, 1899–d. 1966) Literary critic and theorist of *psychocritique*. Trained as a chemist, Mauron's increasing blindness (detached retinas) forced a radical change in career plans before even beginning his first job. At the insistence of the British formalist art critic of post-impressionism, Roger Fry, Mauron began translating *E.M. Forster's *A Passage to India* with the aid of his first wife, Marie. This was to be the first of many translations, including work by Laurence Sterne, *D.H. Lawrence, Katherine Mansfield, *Virginia Woolf, and T.E. Lawrence. Through his friendship with Fry and Forster, Mauron absorbed a very British – and not at all French – literary aesthetic. His first two books, *The Nature of Beauty in Art and Literature* (1927) and *Aesthetics and Psychology* (1935), were published by Virginia and Leonard Woolf at the Hogarth Press and translated by Fry. Mauron finally received his doctorat ès Lettres from the Sorbonne when he was 64 years old. He taught briefly at the Université d'Aix before his death.

In his first two English books, Mauron began to develop a concept of aesthetics as the science that treated of the conditions of sensuous perception and therefore as a form of psychology that empirically examined the nature of aesthetic creation and judgment. While attracted to the theories of *Sigmund Freud (well before most French critics), he felt the need to posit a higher reality, a spiritual sensibility, as the source of art and as a counter to the instinctive, libidinal unconscious. Freud's system, as its critics have delighted in pointing out, is the historical result of an amalgam of 18th-century deterministic rationalism, Romantic irrationalism and 19th-century biologism. When adapted to literary studies, psychoanalysis opens the door to expressive and affective theories of criticism that both tend to value subjectivity and intuition as ways to knowledge. (See *psychoanalytic theory.) This is precisely what appealed to Mauron. His added fascination with the Eastern mystics grew directly out of his early distrust of rationalism and his appreciation of the accounts by Claude Bernard and Henri Poincaré of the role of intuitive insight, even in such codified systems of knowledge as experimental medicine and mathematics. But by 1950, with the publication of *L'Introduction à la psychanalyse de Mal-*

larmé [*Introduction to the Psychoanalysis of Mallarmé*] Mauron had formulated *psychocritique*, his own compromise between what he saw as the 'subjective' and the 'objective,' between aesthetics and psychology.

Psychocritique aims to increase our knowledge of literary works by isolating (and then studying) textual structures whose origin is attributed to the 'unconscious personality' of the author. It does not deny the existence (or the significance) of consciously intended or elaborated textual structure; nor does it underestimate the force of influences. Placing himself always in the position of what he calls the 'man of science,' Mauron insisted that his experimental method demands that the critic acknowledge three variables within the poet's free act of creation – milieu, language and the artist's personality – and the third was his major interest. Using Freud's concept of the unconscious latent source of the manifest form and content of the work of art, Mauron posited, beneath the overt, surface unity to the text, a hidden and more significant one. He did not fall into the reductionist trap of confusing the work of art with either a dream or a symptom. Psychoanalysis or 'scientific psychology' offers, he felt, insights into imaginative fantasies, into the creative process, and into ego-object relations that the literary critic ignores at his or her peril.

Mauron was aware that the methods of psychoanalysis, unlike its insights into the structure of the psyche, must be adapted for use in literary criticism. With no patient to analyse on a couch, with no free associations to work with, the psychocritic must substitute a textually based method, one which Mauron felt must seek to unite the advantages of the patient's free associations (the voluntary suspension of conscious control) and the vigilance of the analyst (ready to seize upon repetitive structures). The method he invented involved the mental superimposition of texts, which are more or less known by heart. (See *text.) The critic allows his/her conscious attention to float and permits coincidences to suggest themselves as the texts are called to mind, though in no conscious or chronological order. Such coincidences are noted and, if the cause does not seem to be in the formal surface unities of the text, they are deemed to be unconscious, latent, and thus of interest. These are now grouped together into what are called 'obsessive metaphors' (though not all are tech-

nically metaphors) or networks of associations that 'resonate.' (Auditory images are common in the blind Mauron's theory; indeed, his blindness is central to his thinking about literary method.) These networks are said to represent unconscious groupings within the author's psyche, groupings of relations to internal and external objects; that is, they are attempts to create a unified vision of the inner fragmented world – as described by Melanie Klein. But in Mauron's work as a whole, the important role of systems of relations in art took root well before his discovery in the 1950s of the object-relation theorists. Its source is in the *formalism which Mauron espoused as early as the 1920s through his contact with Bloomsbury and Fry. This formalism only took its final form, however, after the discovery of Klein. Her theories of projection, of the internalization of desired objects or, more generally, of the dynamic nature of psychic interrelations, allowed Mauron to make dynamic the static associative networks which the process of textual superimposition can single out. He then argued (summarized later in *Des Métaphores obsédantes au mythe personnel* 1962) that a psychic 'force field' is created by the networks of images, a field of conflicts, anguish and defences which become affectively polarized into mythic figures. These then act out certain dramatic roles which represent Kleinian internalized objects and identifications. In other words, underlying the networks of obsessive images, there is an obsessive fantasy – the 'personal myth' – which is the dramatic representation of the structures of the psyche and their interrelations. (See *myth.)

Mauron's early interest was in lyric poets whose works lend themselves well to superimpositions, revealing networks of obsessive metaphors. However, the postulation of the dramatic nature of the personal myth allowed the subsequent extension of his method to the study of dramatic and epic works, as seen in *L'Inconscient dans l'oeuvre et la vie de Racine* (1954). With his attempt to carry out a *psychocritique* of the work of Molière, however, Mauron was forced to consider both generic structures and the possible function of the unconscious of the audience: that is, when Molière's personal myth turned out to coincide with the formal structures of comedy in general, Mauron undertook an analysis of the comic genre as a whole (*Psychocritique du genre comique* 1964), combining the theories of

Freud on jokes, *Carl Gustav Jung on the collective unconscious, and Klein and Anna Freud on defence mechanisms. (See *genre criticism.)

Mauron's psychocritical work, taken as a whole, reveals a constant tension between his desire to elucidate the created object itself and his interest in the creator's psyche. In a sense this is but another formulation of the early conflict between aesthetics and psychology. For a brief time in the early 1960s, Mauron became embroiled in the battle over the *nouvelle critique* – over the importation of the frameworks from the social sciences into French literary criticism. At the time, he was alternately admired and condemned for the rigour of the particular methodology he derived from psychoanalysis. Today his work tends to be considered out of date in France, or else is rewritten – not without considerable distortion – in Lacanian terms. (See *Jacques Lacan.) But his contribution both to critical methodology and to the reading of the work of individual writers (and painters, as well) is perhaps clear in that the term *psychocritique* is still reserved in French for his particular complex psychoanalytic theorizing of the creative process.

LINDA HUTCHEON

Primary Sources

Mauron, Charles. *Aesthetics and Psychology.* Trans. Roger Fry and Katherine John. London: Hogarth P, 1935.
– *Introduction à la psychanalyse de Mallarmé.* 1950. Repr. Paris, Neuchâtel: La Baconnière, 1968. *Introduction to the Psychoanalysis of Mallarmé.* Trans. Archibald Henderson, Jr., and Will McLendon. Berkeley: U of California P, 1963.
– *Mallarmé l'obscur.* Paris: Denoël, 1941.
– *The Nature of Beauty in Art and Literature.* Trans. Robert Fry. London: Hogarth P, 1927.
– *L'Inconscient dans l'oeuvre et la vie de Racine.* 1954 thesis; Paris: José Corti, 1969.
– *Des Métaphores obsédantes au mythe personnel: Introduction à la psychocritique.* Paris: José Corti, 1962, 1964.
– *Psychocritique du genre comique.* Paris: José Corti, 1964.
– *Mallarmé par lui-même.* Paris: Seuil, 1964.
– *Le Dernier Baudelaire.* Paris: José Corti, 1966.
– *Le Théâtre de Giraudoux.* Paris: José Corti, 1971.

Secondary Sources

Clancier, Anne. 'Charles Mauron.' In *Psychanalyse et critique littéraire.* Toulouse: Privat, 1973, 191–221.

Cruickshank, John. 'Psychocriticism and Literary Judgment.' *British Journal of Aesthetics* 4.2 (1964): 155–9.
Hutcheon, Linda. *Formalism and the Freudian Aesthetic: The Example of Charles Mauron.* Cambridge, London, New York: Cambridge UP, 1984.
LeSage, Laurent. 'Charles Mauron in Retrospect.' *L'Esprit Créateur* 14.3 (1974): 265–76.
Mehlman, Jeffrey. 'Entre psychanalyse et psychocritique.' *Poétique* 1.3 (1970): 365–83.

McLuhan, (Herbert) Marshall

(b. Canada, 1911–d. 1980) Literary critic, culturologist, educator. Marshall McLuhan spent his youth in Winnipeg, where he attended Kelvin Technical H.S. and regularly assisted at Baptist church services. He earned degrees in English from the University of Manitoba (B.A. 1933; M.A., thesis on George Meredith, 1934), after an initial year in the Engineering program. During his years as an IODE Scholar at Cambridge (B.A. 1936), McLuhan studied under *F.R. Leavis and *I.A. Richards, and had his perception of the poetic process further shaped by readings in *T.S. Eliot, Ezra Pound and James Joyce. No less formative were the writings of the 'practical mystic' G.K. Chesterton. In 1937, while working at the University of Wisconsin, McLuhan was received into the Roman Catholic church. Teaching in the English Department of St. Louis University (1937–9, 1940–4) afforded him the opportunity to install the *New Criticism there and to develop, within the ambiance of 'Saint-Louis Thomism,' his sense of intellectual processes as the perceiving of 'nets of analogy.' McLuhan was awarded his doctorate from Cambridge in 1943 for 'Thomas Nashe and His Place in the Learning of His Time.' A correspondence struck up that same year with Wyndham Lewis, then in Windsor, Ontario, led to McLuhan's moving there in 1944, to teach at Assumption College. He joined the Department of English at St. Michael's College (of the University of Toronto) in 1946 and was the first (and last) Director of the Centre for Culture and Technology (1963–80).

McLuhan's polymorphic oeuvre turns on one *theme, the genesis and effects of the 'dissociation of sensibility' in Western culture. As characterized in his doctoral dissertation, that breakdown can be traced to the supplanting of grammar and rhetoric by logic in the curriculum of the late Renaissance. Nashe (1567–1601?), it is proposed, retained something of the unified sensibility of the rhetorical tradition extending from Cicero through Augustine to Dante. Indifferent to 'logical copulae' and rich in wordplay and inclusive digression, Nashe's 'polyphonic prose' is praised for the way in which it snubs the dialecticians and their fragmenting 'lineal decorum.' The many essays in literary criticism from McLuhan in the 1940s and 1950s extend his initial reading of psycho-intellectual trauma. Similarly concerned with the cultural and scientific context of writing, they focus on pun, analogy, *paradox, metaphor, *myth, and symbol as media fitted by their alogicality for the restoration of synthetic perception and communication. (See also *metonomy/metaphor.) Like Richards, *Cleanth Brooks and Allen Tate, McLuhan favours 'concrete poetry,' a *literature of indirection striving for comprehensiveness, over a poetry of statement and partiality. Joyce's writing is especially remarked for its polysemic qualities: his 'trivial' puns restore that fulness of sense lost to the 'abcedmindedness' of linear perception, while his adaptation of the newspaper page as an art form synchronous in its action and paratactical in its arrangement recalls the symbolist poetry of Stéphane Mallarmé and, more distantly, the cyclopaedic art of medieval manuscript culture.

The writings which brought McLuhan celebrity in the 1960s also show the impress of H.A. Innis, a Canadian political economist interested in the effects of communications media in history. Adopting a 'mosaic or field approach' in The Gutenberg Galaxy: The Making of Typographic Man (1962), McLuhan develops his own variations on Innis' central teaching, that the growth of literacy, from the invention of the phonetic alphabet to the instauration of moveable type, spelled the decline of spoken *discourse and the sense of community which that medium incorporated. The radical effect of alphabet and typography, according to McLuhan, was to isolate the visual, linear sense: 'Literacy, in translating man out of the closed world of tribal depth and resonance, gave man an eye for an ear and ushered him into a visual open world of specialized and divided consciousness.' This notion is given more stirring expression yet in Understanding Media: The Extensions of Man (1964). Making his own the non-discursive techniques he prizes in artists –

puns, metaphor, paradox and juxtaposition – McLuhan plays to provoke the reader into groping towards a consciousness of the ways in which media transform perception. The englobing circuitry of the electronic age holds out for McLuhan the possibility or promise of a return to the plenary consciousness and communal sense lost since the coming of typographic man and the age of mechanism.

Though it sometimes gives the impression of making a virtue of unreason and analphabetism, McLuhan's work is impelled by a calculated moral intention: 'study the modes of media, in order to hoick all assumptions out of the subliminal, nonverbal realm for scrutiny and for prediction and control of human purposes.' In his first book, The Mechanical Bride: Folklore of Industrial Man (1951), McLuhan jokingly exposes the exploitative mythology buried in newspaper ads. The admen resemble the symbolist poets in their reliance on indirection and parataxis; but, unlike genuine artists, who serve as 'antennae of the race' (Pound) or agents of deep cognition (Wyndham Lewis), they achieve their purpose by maintaining the public in a subliminal trance. Part Freudian 'analyst,' part Erasmian jester and Joycean prophet, McLuhan is always an educator. (See also *Sigmund Freud, *psychoanalytic theory.) As he explains in Explorations in Communication (1960), his aim is 'to develop an awareness about print and the newer technologies so that we can ... get the best out of each in the educational process.' Even in The Gutenberg Galaxy and Understanding Media, the most disinterested and arguably the least ethically unambiguous of McLuhan's faceted theses regarding the dissociative effects of formal logic and literacy, the educational intention is manifest. 'Our extended faculties [in the electronic age],' he writes in his account of typographic man, 'now constitute a single field of experience which demands that they become collectively conscious.' For McLuhan, the essence of education is 'civil defense against media fall-out.' Of his many books in the 1970s, several are intended to enlighten a world of corporate business locked into the modes of specialization.

The charges levelled at McLuhan have zeroed in on his apparent indifference to the niceties of logical analysis and systematic research. He has been said to be inventive to the point of whimsicality, his work a virtual nonsense. McLuhan's response as a watcher of analogical patterns from, he insists, no fixed point of view: 'I explore, I don't explain.' He is not given to consecutive argument. In this respect, McLuhan more resembles Ralph Waldo Emerson than he does Aquinas or Chesterton or even Joyce. McLuhan's importance, as even the staunchest of his opponents acknowledge, is in having prompted a long-neglected cross-disciplinary discussion of the ways in which mass media have shaped and continue to modify human sensibility. (See also *communication theory.)

CAMILLE R. LA BOSSIÈRE

Primary Sources

McLuhan, H. Marshall. *Counterblast*. New York: Harcourt, Brace and World, 1968.
– *Culture Is Our Business*. New York: McGraw-Hill, 1970.
– *The Gutenberg Galaxy*. Toronto: U of Toronto P, 1962.
– *The Interior Landscape: The Literary Criticism of Marshall McLuhan 1943–1962*. Ed. E. McNamara. New York: McGraw-Hill, 1969.
– *Letters of Marshall McLuhan*. Ed. Matie Molinaro, Corinne McLuhan and William Toye. Toronto: Oxford UP, 1987.
– *The Mechanical Bride*. New York: Vanguard P, 1951.
– *Understanding Media*. New York: McGraw-Hill, 1964.
– *Verbi-Voco-Visual Explorations*. New York: Something Else P, 1967.
– and Quentin Fiore. *The Medium Is the Message*. New York: Bantam Books, 1967.
– and Quentin Fiore. *War and Peace in the Global Village*. New York: Bantam Books, 1968.
– and Barrington Nevitt. *Take Today: The Executive as Dropout*. New York: Harcourt, Brace, Jovanovich, 1972.
– and Harley Parker. *Through the Vanishing Point: Space in Poetry and Painting*. New York: Harper and Row, 1968.
– and E.S. Carpenter, eds. *Explorations in Communication*. Boston: Beacon P, 1960.

Secondary Sources

Duffy, Dennis. *Marshall McLuhan*. Toronto: McClelland and Stewart, 1969.
Finkelstein, Sidney. *Sense and Nonsense of McLuhan*. New York: International Publishers, 1968.
Rosenthal, Raymond, ed. *McLuhan: Pro and Con*. Baltimore, Md.: Penguin Books, 1968.
Sanderson, George, and McDonald, Frank, eds. *Marshall McLuhan: The Man and His Message*. Golden, Col.: Fulcrum, Inc., 1989.
Stearn, Gerald, ed. *McLuhan, Hot and Cool*. New York: Dial P, 1967.
Theall, Donald F. *The Medium Is the Rear View Mirror: Understanding McLuhan*. Montreal: McGill-Queen's UP, 1971.

Merleau-Ponty, Maurice

(b. France, 1908–d. 1961) Philosopher. Raised in Paris, Merleau-Ponty was educated at the lycées Janson-de-Sailly and Louis-le-Grand and the Ecole Normale Supérieure. After taking his *agrégation* in philosophy in 1930, he taught at lycées in Beauvais and Chartres until 1935 and, from 1933 to 1934, held a research grant from the Caisse Nationale de la Recherche Scientifique. From 1935 until the outbreak of the Second World War, he taught at the l'Ecole Normale Supérieure. He served in the infantry until 1940 and then returned to teaching philosophy while remaining active in the resistance. During this period he became acquainted with *Jean-Paul Sartre and carried out the research that would produce his first major works: *La Structure du comportement* [*The Structure of Behaviour* 1942, trans. 1963] and *Phénoménologie de la perception* [*Phenomenology of Perception* 1945, trans. 1962]. In 1945 he joined the faculty of the Université de Lyon and began working with Sartre and *Simone de Beauvoir as unofficial co-editor of *Les Temps modernes*, a charge he held until 1953. In 1950 he was called to the Sorbonne to teach general and child psychology. Two years later he began lecturing in philosophy at the Collège de France as successor to Edouard Le Roy, Henri Bergson and Louis Lavelle. Although only 53 when he died, he had already made significant contributions to phenomenology, existentialism and *structuralism. His working notes were edited and published posthumously as *Le Visible et l'invisible* [*The Visible and the Invisible* 1964]. (See also *phenomenological criticism.)

Often described as an enigmatic philosophy of ambiguity, Merleau-Ponty's thought can be understood as an exploration of the region between philosophy's subjective and objective extremes. In his first major works he rejects empiricist and intellectualist accounts of consciousness in favour of a notion of human awareness rooted in the corporeal dimension of existence that is always situated in concrete lived experience. (See *Lebenswelt.)* Although closest to the phenomenology of *Edmund Husserl and *Martin Heidegger, Merleau-Ponty's point of departure in the prereflective perceiving body allows him to move freely between existentialism and structuralism and into the field of visual art. For Merleau-Ponty, our body is not just one object among many. It is a dynamic region of sensory awareness that is oriented toward the world. Through the body, consciousness is free to reach out to and intermingle with our environment, giving it meaning and form. Everyday perceptions and gestures therefore have a creative and symbolic quality. To this direction from the perceiver to the world corresponds a second direction from the world to the perceiver *(Sens et non-sens 1948, trans. Sense and Non-sense 1964, and L'Oeil et l'esprit 1964,* trans. 'Eye and Mind,' in *The Primacy of Perception and Other Essays 1964).* The world also acts upon us, for we perceive those aspects of the world that 'call our attention.' In turn, all that calls our attention and upon which we focus is outlined or framed by what is not perceived. Merleau-Ponty understands existence in terms of the visible and the invisible rather than in terms of being and nothing. The two directions mediating body and world give perception a to-and-fro character similar to a conversation, while the interdependence of what we perceive and what we do not perceive is reflected in the meaningful interdependence of each spoken work and the whole system of language.

Although Merleau-Ponty's approach to language often converges with the linguistics of *Ferdinand de Saussure, Merleau-Ponty tends to focus on the individual act of expression rather than on the *langue* or system ('La Conscience et l'acquisition du langage' 1964; *Consciousness and the Acquisition of Language* 1973). (See *langue/parole.)* There is also a two-way relationship mediating language and perceptual life. On the one hand, the speaking subject is rooted in the natural expressivity of the body situated in its perceptual field. On the other hand, the lived experience of the body as motor subject transcends itself through language and enters a linguistic field beyond its immediate perceptual one *(Phénoménologie de la perception).* In that words are essentially related to the things that come into our existence through them, the linguistic field offers the truth of our field of perception. In

this transcendental layer of existence, writers carry out the task of transforming life into its truth. Since the meaning of a word exists in the silent mediation between it and the other words of language, a writer must express new meaning by 'intertwining' words together in such a way as to reveal a new configuration of the silent 'chiasm' lying between them *(Le Visible et l'invisible.)*

Language, for Merleau-Ponty, is an intersubjective, cultural phenomenon that mediates mind and world. Unlike Sartre, he does not propose that consciousness is absolutely free. He moves closer to the structuralism of *Claude Lévi-Strauss when he affirms that human consciousness is intertwined with the preconscious structures of intersubjective and collective meaning ('La Conscience et l'acquisition du langage' and *Signes 1960;* trans. *Signs 1964).* He also differs from Sartre in his understanding of the relation of poetry to prose. Sartre opposes the two by stating that while poetry expresses and refers to itself, prose refers to objects independent of itself. Merleau-Ponty, on the contrary, insists that prose and poetry should be distinguished by degrees of difference.

Although Maurice Merleau-Ponty's philosophy has had an impact on structuralist, existentialist, and phenomenological inquiry in general, it is the phenomenological *hermeneutics of *Paul Ricoeur that has inherited many of its primary concerns. As James M. Edie has noted, Ricoeur offers an important development of Merleau-Ponty's theory of speech by taking it beyond the level of the word to that of the sentence (Edie xxxii). Ricoeur's understanding of symbol and metaphor as well as his explanation of time and narrative bear the mark of Merleau-Ponty's phenomenology. (See *metonymy/metaphor.)* Merleau-Ponty's philosophy, however, remains an unfinished project and its potential lies in the new directions it suggests for literary research. To the degree that terms such as 'narrative perspective' and 'point of view' are inextricably bound to a theory of perception they can be re-examined in the light of Merleau-Ponty's philosophy.

DANIEL CHAMBERLAIN

Primary Sources

Merleau-Ponty, Maurice. 'La Conscience et l'acquisition du langage.' *Bulletin de psychologie* 18.3–6 (1964): 226–59.

- *L'Oeil et l'esprit*. Paris: Gallimard, 1964.
- *Phénoménologie de la perception*. Paris: Gallimard, 1945.
- *La Prose du monde*. Paris: Gallimard, 1969.
- *Résumés de cours. Collège de France 1952–1960*. Paris: Gallimard, 1968.
- *Sens et non-sens*. Paris: Nagel, 1948.
- *Signes*. Paris: Nouvelle Revue Française, Gallimard, 1960.
- *La Structure du comportement*. Paris: PUF, 1942.
- *Le Visible et l'invisible*. Paris: Gallimard, 1964.

Secondary Sources

Chamberlain, Daniel Frank. *Narrative Perspective in Fiction: A Phenomenological Mediation of Reader, Text, and World*. Toronto: U of Toronto P, 1990.

Edie, James M. Intro. *The Primacy of Perception and Other Essays*. By Maurice Merleau-Ponty. Evanston: Northwestern UP, 1964.

Madison, Gary Brent. *La Phénoménologie de Merleau-Ponty: Une recherche des limites de la conscience*. Paris: Editions Klincksieck, 1973. Trans. Gary Brent Madison. *The Phenomenology of Merleau-Ponty: A Search for the Limits of Consciousness*. Athens: Ohio UP, 1981.

Mallin, Samuel Barry. *Merleau-Ponty's Philosophy*. New Haven: Yale UP, 1979.

Schmidt, James. *Maurice Merleau-Ponty: Between Phenomenology and Structuralism*. Houndmills: Macmillan, 1985.

Miller, J(oseph) Hillis

(b. U.S.A., 1928–) Literary critic. As a child, J. Hillis Miller was exposed to an academic environment and to rural Protestant culture, from both of which he derived 'a vigorous respect for truth' and a sense 'that the truth might be dark, ominous' (Salusinszky 231). Miller attended Oberlin College, where he majored in physics before turning to *literature. He then studied with Andrew Bongiorno, an Aristotelian, and encounted the theoretical work of *Kenneth Burke, which he continues to admire. At Harvard, where he 'learned mostly from the other [graduate] students,' Miller wrote a dissertation on Dickens and read *Geoffrey Hartman's *The Unmediated Vision*, which he valued for its 'awareness of continental modes of criticism' (Salusinszky 236–7, Moynihan 102). He taught at Williams College, Johns Hopkins and Yale before becoming University Professor at the University of California, Irvine, in 1986, the same year he served as president of the Modern Language Association of America.

Miller's influence upon Anglo-American literary theory is due to the breadth of appeal of his work: his theoretical positions are typically revealed and sustained within analytic discussions of the literature of the 19th and 20th centuries. Since Miller adheres to his principle that 'what counts for most in literary criticism is the citations made and what the critic says about those citations' (*Fiction and Repetition* 21), readers often need not embrace the literary theories employed in Miller's analyses in order to benefit from his critiques. A major reason for this seems to be Miller's consistent desire to reveal and explain 'how very strange ... works of literature are' by stressing 'not the theory itself but [by] establishing ... tools ... to make an adequate report on what's actually there in a piece of literature' (Moynihan 111, 116). Miller observes that he grew interested in developing additional modes of literary theory primarily because 'the New-Critical method ... was not all that effective as a way to deal with the works that [he] had been hired to teach, namely Victorian ones' (Salusinszky 231). (See *New Criticism.)

The initial phase of Miller's career (ca. 1958–70) is deeply influenced by the Geneva phenomenological critics, among them *Georges Poulet. (See *Geneva School, *phenomenological criticism.) Fundamental to the mode of inquiry of such books as *Charles Dickens: The World of His Novels* (1958), *The Disappearance of God* (1963), *Poets of Reality* (1965) and *The Form of Victorian Fiction* (1968) is the premise that such an entity as a writer's 'mind' exists, is embodied in his words, and is accessible to the mind of another provided the proper techniques of inquiry are used. Miller's analytic technique assumes that 'certain elements persist' in a given author's work, and that, by means of 'such evidence of recurrence,' a critic can 'identify what persists throughout all the swarming multiplicity' and thereby 'assess the specific quality of [an author's] imagination,' perhaps even discover 'a permanent law' and accomplish a 'revelation of that presiding unity hidden at the center' (*Charles Dickens* 328, x–xi). Miller suggests that naive causal sequences binding an author's mind to his works be revised in favour of an understanding of the works as a medium whereby the author creates and sustains himself. Thus in the process of citing diverse passages that contain recurring rhetorical features, Miller does not stress temporal or generic distinctions. (See *genre criticism.) Instead, he creates a mimetic collage consisting of his own observations mingled with an author's words – for example, quotations from a novel, a poem, an essay, a diary, or a private letter – while he fulfils 'the task of the critic' as he now conceives it: 'to identify himself with the subjectivity expressed in the words, to relive that life from the inside, and to constitute it anew in ... criticism' (The Disappearance of God vii).

In Thomas Hardy: Distance and Desire (1970) and in the essays 'Williams' Spring and All and the Progress of Poetry' (1970) and 'Geneva or Paris?' (1971), Miller begins to articulate a departure from his prior phenomenological allegiances. He now judges assumptions about the immanence in texts of 'an impalpable organizing form' (Charles Dickens ix), signature of an authorial mind, to be the result of a mistaken effort 'to explain the text by something extra-linguistic' (Thomas Hardy vii), a 'priority of presence ... associated, finally, with a tendency to take language for granted in literature' ('Geneva or Paris?' 212). This judgment severely qualifies Miller's prior strategy of reading, which presupposed 'that each sentence or paragraph of a novel ... defines a relationship between an imagining mind and its objects' (Charles Dickens ix), for Miller comes to understand the concept of 'mind' itself as merely a *trope that must be identified and interrogated, as 'a fiction arising from the taking literally [of] a metalepsis' (The Linguistic Moment 239). Miller's new understanding changes his own use of certain prominent patterns of rhetoric. (See *rhetorical criticism.) He once applied a rhetoric of *paradox to the perceptual processes that create a mind, a 'person,' who 'contains as well as hides the truth' (Charles Dickens xvi). But later Miller uses such rhetoric more inclusively to define an ontic 'darkness,' a 'metaphysical entity' that lurks 'in every thing and person, underlying them as their secret substance, but also denying them as formlessness denies form' (Poets of Reality 28). And eventually these rhetorical patterns signify for him the essence of language itself, the 'double movement of cancellation and reaffirmation' that 'characterizes ... linguistic action ... as a whole,' that 'both makes ... emblems and at the same time undermines their referential validity' (The Linguistic Moment 35, 337).

Such conceptual development in part reflects the influence upon Miller of Parisian critics who 'innovated' the analytic technique known as *deconstruction (most notably *Jacques Derrida, whose 'La Différance' appeared in 1968). (See *différance/différence.) These critics claim that it has been possible in Western culture for certain kinds of *discourse to function as self-authenticating, sovereign sources of rational truth only because certain texts historically have been exempt from rigorous rhetorical analysis. When they are exposed to such analytic scrutiny, these privileged texts disclose the inescapable essence that they share with all other language: a 'covert dependence on catachresis, the figurative naming of that which has no name' (The Linguistic Moment 141). This essence inherently subverts reasoned coherence because all figurative devices combine disparate categories and therefore annul both the principle of contradiction and the associated system of binary oppositions that makes rational order possible. (See *binary opposition.) Moreover, deconstructive critics deny that a *text can objectively embody invariant structures or patterns that might reveal the presence of an authorizing mind or final metaphysic existing before or beyond rhetorical effects. (See *metaphysics of presence.) As 'a principle of instability and insubstantiality,' the 'self itself is a trope, and it turns everything it encounters into more tropes' (The Linguistic Moment 161). (See *self/other.) The practice of deconstruction ultimately defines two irreconcilable ways of reading: 'A critic must choose either the tradition of presence or the tradition of "difference," for their assumptions about language, about literature, about history, and about the mind cannot be made compatible' ('Geneva or Paris?' 216).

The most dramatic manifestation of Miller's abandonment of the 'tradition of presence' is his unfavourable review of Meyer Abrams' Natural Supernaturalism: Tradition and Revolution in Romantic Literature (1971). Entitled 'Tradition and Difference,' Miller's essay attacks Abrams for his 'taking for granted of languages and figures of speech' and his consequently naive creation of 'a book about Romanticism which is permeated ... with Romantic assumptions' (11, 8). Miller also castigates Abrams for misrepresenting the 'underminers of the Occidental tradition ... Marx, Nietzsche, Freud, Saussure' (8), who subverted the very concept of opposition that Abrams draws upon for both the title of his book and overall critical methodology. (See *Nietzsche, *Freud, *de Saussure.) Most important, the occasion of this review is apparently used by Miller to articulate his own abandonment of 'the grand tradition of modern humanistic scholarship' (6) and subsequent advocacy of deconstructive criticism. In contrast to Abrams, he asserts that 'the continuity of the tradition is not determined by coercive "sources" which have imposed themselves century after century but is a matter of concepts, metaphors, and myths, each generating the others, which are latently there in the lexicon, the grammar, the syntax of our languages' (10). (See *metonymy/metaphor, *myth.)

Miller's aggressive advocacy of deconstruction – or, as he now puts it, 'rhetorically sophisticated reading' focused 'on the role of figurative language in interfering with the straightforward working of grammar and logic' ('Presidential Address 1986' 289; 'The Function of Literary Theory' 105) – possibly began with his reading in 1968 of Jacques Derrida's 'La Différance.' But the rhetoric of 'opaque similarity' (Fiction and Repetition 9), of subtly oblique, perpetually qualifying differences, was a prominent part of his work from the outset of his career, and his encounter with Derridean thought seems to be both a conceptual fulfilment of a linguistic tendency that long had haunted Miller's work as well as a catalyst for sudden and remarkable change. Even in his early criticism Miller repeatedly offers at the end of an analytic sequence a remark that seems to function as a conclusion, only immediately thereafter to qualify or question it. Since repetitive self-scrutiny is a prominent part of Miller's own analytic strategies, enabling him to elude the 'fault of premature closure ... intrinsic to criticism' (Fiction and Repetition 51), it seems inevitable that he eventually focuses explicitly upon techniques of repetition in literary works, stressing the distinction between '"Platonic" repetition,' which assumes the possibility of 'mimetic copy,' and a 'Nietzschean mode, which 'posits a world based upon difference' wherein each thing is 'intrinsically different from every other thing' (Fiction and Repetition 6). (See *mimesis.)

Recently, Miller is concerned with a question that might seem inappropriate for a critic whose work has been profoundly influenced by Derridean deconstruction: Is there an ethics of reading? However, Miller's 'ethics of read-

ing' is in fact made possible by the theoretical contexts created by deconstructors (such as *Paul de Man), who assert the invalidity of hermeneutic techniques of reading, techniques that assume it is appropriate to seek extralinguistic entities to which the words of the text refer. (See *hermeneutics.) Building upon remarks made by de Man in Allegories of Reading, Miller declares in 'Is There an Ethics of Reading?' that 'literature always and universally' makes 'the literal mean something else,' this 'something else' being 'the law of language whereby a work fails to disclose itself fully or coincide unambiguously ... with a single determinable meaning' (20). And the 'ethics of reading, if there is such a thing, must be a response ... to the demand made by that ... "something else" within language' (21).

A crucial issue in any postmodern discussion of ethics is the nature of the subject. (See *postmodernism, *subject/object.) Miller remains firmly within the context of deconstructive theory when he asserts that in 'response to the implacable demand made by the act of reading, the "I" dissolves as a willing and wilful subject and becomes a relay station ... in a purely linguistic transaction,' merely a 'function in a transference from one locus of language to another' (22–3). Consequently, Miller's 'ethics' engages at best obliquely with traditional imperatives of seeking an adequate ethical basis whereupon responsible subjects might predicate decisions to take or avoid significant action. Instead, Miller seems concerned primarily with an ethics of humility that would negate the familiar practice of founding personal moral acts upon messages supposedly embodied in various literary works.

Miller does not deny that certain decisions and acts necessarily follow the event of reading, but he insists that such responses must always be errant because they do not emerge logically from specific knowledge obtained during the reading experience. If referential techniques of interpretation are invalid, Miller at last can appeal only to his claim that, as a consequence of reading, skilled readers will derive merely a humbling and elusive awareness of their own final inability to read and understand. This awareness must then be used to avoid 'the disaster of a misuse of literature for didactic ends for which it offers no sound basis.' Thus teachers of literature should make the primary ethical decision to teach 'the irrelevance of the thematic assertions of even the most apparently morally concerned literature for the making of moral decisions,' since such judgments appear within literary works only as symptoms of the dynamics of language itself, which dictate 'a perpetual obscuring of grammatical and logical clarity' owing to the predominance of tropes (24).

Miller's current application of these perspectives is perhaps best expressed in the recent essay 'The Function of Literary Theory at the Present Time' (1989). He affirms that the study of literature indeed has much to do with the topics of history, society and the individual, but this relationship is not a result of the presence within literature of 'extra-linguistic forces and facts.' Instead, such study provides opportunities to 'identify the nature of language as it may have effects on what de Man calls '''the materiality of history,''' one example of which seems to be 'the new permeability of the university to invasion by industrial research' (104, 107).

WILLIAM BONNEY

Primary Sources

Miller, J. Hillis. 'The Antitheses of Criticism: Reflections on the Yale Colloquium.' *Modern Language Notes* 81 (1966): 557–71.
– 'Ariachne's Broken Woof.' *Georgia Review* 31 (1977): 44–60.
– 'Ariadne's Thread: Repetition and the Narrative Line.' *Critical Inquiry* 3 (1976): 57–77.
– *Charles Dickens: His World of Novels.* Cambridge, Mass.: Harvard UP, 1958.
– 'The Critic as Host.' *Critical Inquiry* 3 (1977): 439–47.
– 'Deconstructing the Deconstructors.' *diacritics* 5 (1975): 24–31.
– *The Disappearance of God: Five 19th Century Writers.* Cambridge, Mass.: Harvard UP, 1963.
– 'Dismembering and Disremembering in Nietzsche's "On Truth and Lies in a Nonmoral Sense."' *boundary* 2 9–10 (1981): 41–54.
– *The Ethics of Reading.* New York: Columbia UP, 1986.
– 'The Fiction of Realism: *Sketches by Boz, Oliver Twist,* and *Cruikshank's Illustrations.*' In *Dickens Centennial Essays.* Ed. Ada Nisbet, Blake Nevius. Berkeley: U of California P, 1971, 85–153.
– *Fiction and Repetition: Seven English Novels.* Cambridge, Mass.: Harvard UP, 1982.
– *The Form of Victorian Fiction.* Notre Dame, Ind.: U of Notre Dame P, 1968.
– 'The Function of Literary Theory at the Present

Time.' In *The Future of Literary Theory.* Ed. Ralph Cohen. New York: Routledge, 1989, 102–11.
– 'Geneva or Paris? The Recent Work of Georges Poulet.' In *The Quest for Imagination.* Ed. O.B. Hardison. Cleveland: Case Western Reserve UP, 1971, 205–24.
– 'The Geneva School: The Criticism of Marcel Raymond, Albert Beguin, Georges Poulet, Jean Rousset, Jean-Pierre Richard, and Jean Starobinski.' *Critical Inquiry* 8 (1966): 302–21.
– 'The Interpretation of *Lord Jim.*' In *The Interpretation of Narrative.* Ed. Morton W. Bloomfield. Cambridge, Mass.: Harvard UP, 1970, 211–28.
– 'Is There an Ethics of Reading?' Tokyo: English Literary Society of Japan, 1986.
– *The Linguistic Moment.* Princeton: Princeton UP, 1985.
– 'The Literary Criticism of Georges Poulet.' *Modern Language Notes* 78 (1963): 471–88.
– 'Narrative and History.' *English Literary History* 41 (1974): 455–73.
– 'Nature and the Linguistic Moment.' In *Nature and the Victorian Imagination.* Ed. U.C. Knoepflmacher, G.B. Tennyson. Berkeley: U of California P, 1977, 440–51.
– *Poets of Reality: Six 20th Century Writers.* Cambridge, Mass.: Harvard UP, 1965.
– 'Presidential Address 1986. The Triumph of Theory, the Resistance to Reading, and the Question of the Material Base.' *Publications of the Modern Language Association* 104 (1987): 281–91.
– 'The Still Heart: Poetic Form in Wordsworth.' *New Literary History* 2 (1971): 297–310.
– 'The Stone and the Shell: Wordsworth's Dream of the Arab.' *Moments premiers.* Paris: Corti, 1973.
– *Thomas Hardy: Distance and Desire.* Cambridge, Mass.: Harvard UP, 1970.
– 'Tradition and Difference.' *Diacritics* 2 (1972): 6–13.
– 'Williams' *Spring and All* and the Progress of Poetry.' *Daedalus* 99 (1970): 405–34.

Secondary Sources

Leitch, Vincent B. 'The Lateral Dance: The Deconstructive Criticism of J. Hillis Miller.' *Critical Inquiry* 6 (1980): 593–607.
Moynihan, Robert. 'J. Hillis Miller.' In *A Recent Imagining.* Camden, Conn.: Shoestring P, 1986, 97–131.
Salusinszky, Imre. 'J. Hillis Miller.' In *Criticism in Society.* New York: Methuen, 1987, 208–40.

Moi, Toril

(b. Norway, 1953–) Feminist literary critic. Toril Moi completed the Dr.Art. (1985) at the University of Bergen, was lecturer at Oxford

University (1983–5), director of the Centre for Feminist Research in the Humanities, University of Bergen (1985–8), and is currently professor of comparative literature, University of Bergen, and professor of literature, Duke University. Since 1986, she has addressed university audiences in the U.S.A., the U.K., Australia, Canada, and Scandinavia. Her engaging, agonistic style of feministic critical practice aims to 'theorize and politicize while remaining historically and materially concrete.'

Moi has published widely in international journals of feminism, critical theory and cultural studies, translated numerous literary works by English women writers into Norwegian, and introduced French feminists *Julia Kristeva, *Luce Irigaray and Michèle Le Doeuff to Anglo-American audiences. (See *feminist criticism.) She is editor of *The Kristeva Reader* (1986) and *French Feminist Thought* (1987).

Sexual/Textual Politics (1985), the first study to chart major trends in contemporary feminist criticism on both sides of the Atlantic, considers the major attitudinal phases of American feminist literary criticism since Kate Millet's *Sexual Politics* (1969) before proceeding to outline the different textual strategies of contemporary French feminist theorists in order of their anti-patriarchal subversiveness. American feminist literary criticism, notes Moi, has become more sophisticated in its approach to the English *canon but without producing an adequate theory of canon formation. Conversely, French feminists have no lack of anti-patriarchal theory but fail to mobilize pro-feminist thought and action: they overlook the existentialist critical initiative of *Simone de Beauvoir, taking their cue instead from *Jacques Lacan and *Jacques Derrida. Moi accepts this genealogy, showing how *Hélène Cixous, Luce Irigaray and Julia Kristeva use men's theory for a feminist textual practice; but ultimately, she contends, this theory fails to enter the historical arena of feminist politics, lured instead by the seductive entrapments of deconstructing phallogocentrism – the ideological/idealist assumption that language is structured by a determining 'centre' or presence – Will, Ego, Cogito, God, Desire – for which it is a symbolic substitute. This centre is essentially masculine, patriarchal and self-referential in terms of a master phallic signifier. (See *patriarchy, *metaphysics of presence, *signified/signifier/signification, *deconstruction, *phallocentrism.)

Moi repeatedly calls for a clarification of the oft-conflated terms 'feminine,' 'feminist' and 'female.' She criticizes some feminists for privileging 'postfeminist'/'feminine' styles at the expense of all feminist positions (1988) and urges feminists to write paradoxically from three historical and political fronts: those of equality (the claim to the same rights, opportunities, recognition as men), difference (the claim to specificity) and the abolition of difference (the struggle to dissolve the categories of male and female and to displace the phallus as *the* signifier of sexual identity with a proliferation of signifiers).

Moi champions a feminist return to *Sigmund Freud, whose writings show how psychoanalytic epistemology and, by implication, any master *discourse is structured by patriarchal bias undermining its claim to universality and objectivity (1981). Moi considers Freud's model of transference as a paradigm for feminist epistemology since it is dialogical and dialectical, subverting and transforming hegemonic oppositions between the phallic 'subject who knows' and the 'castrated' subject who 'lacks' knowledge. (See *hegemony, *subject/object.) Moi urges feminists (1989) to consider Freud's materialist critique of classical epistemology – his notion of 'epistemophilia' – which views knowledge as a drive arising with infantile sexuality and not as a disembodied, disinterested rationalism issuing from a transcendental cogito.

Moi's book on Beauvoir (1989) reviews the hostile reception of the intellectual woman, Beauvoir, before presenting an analysis of her novel *The Woman Destroyed*. The latter draws on Freud's theory of transference and *Emile Benveniste's subject of enunciation to disclose the rhetorical effects of Beauvoir's writing and to show how her *text, contrary to authorial intentions, generates feminist sympathy for, rather than aversion to, her existentialist anti-heroine. (See *énonciation/énoncé.)

Moi is currently preparing a full-length study of Beauvoir which uses the theories of sociologist *Pierre Bourdieu to analyse Beauvoir's 'self'-constitution as an intellectual woman in the specific symbolic, political and economic domain of the 20th-century French academy. (See *self/other.)

DIANNE CHISHOLM

Primary Sources

Moi, Toril. 'Feminism, Postmodernism and Style: Recent Feminist Criticism in the U.S.' *Cultural Critique* 9 (Spring 1988): 3–22.
- *Feminist Theory and Simone de Beauvoir*. Oxford: Blackwell, 1990.
- 'Patriarchal Thought and the Drive for Knowledge.' In *Between Feminism and Psychoanalysis*. Ed. Teresa M. Brennan. London: Routledge, 1989, 185–205.
- 'Representation of Patriarchy: Sexuality and Epistemology in Freud's *Dora.' Feminist Review* 9 (1981): 60–74.
- *Sexual/Textual Politics*. London: Methuen, 1985.
- *French Feminist Thought*. Oxford: Blackwell, 1987.
- *The Kristeva Reader*. Oxford: Blackwell; New York: Columbia UP, 1986.

Mukařovský, Jan

(b. Bohemia, 1891–d. Czechoslovakia, 1975) Structuralist, aesthetician and semiotician. One of the most active members of the Prague School (Prague Linguistic Circle, founded in 1926), Jan Mukařovský differed from his colleagues in the importance and originality of his own work on poetics and structural aesthetics. (See *Semiotic Poetics of the Prague School.) A member of the academy and a professor of Czech literature at Charles IV University in Prague, Mukařovský was nominated rector of the university. However, in Communist-ruled Czechoslovakia, he was forced (in 1951) to disavow all of his earlier structuralist studies. (See *structuralism.) While a few of his texts were later re-edited in the 1960s, his work was fully rehabilitated only after the collapse of the communist government.

It would be both a historical and a cultural mistake to approach the collective studies of the Prague Linguistic Circle or Mukařovský's personal works exclusively as extensions of *Russian formalism. Doing so would mean forgetting the importance of the Czech linguistic and aesthetic tradition stemming from the 'national renaissance' (as early as the end of the 18th century); it would also mean overlooking the cosmopolitan dimensions of the cultural and artistic fever that seized the country between the two world wars. Although the literary theories of the Russian formalists are present in Mukařovský's early works (1928–9), thanks in part to *Roman Jakobson's move

from Moscow to Prague in 1920, Mukařovský's functional form of structuralism differs from Russian formalism in a fundamental manner. He replaces the concept of causality by reciprocity and form by structure; both substitutions easily testify to the fact that *Edmund Husserl's phenomenological vision – he had spoken at conferences organized by the Prague Linguistic Circle – had markedly influenced Mukařovský's theoretical developments. (See *phenomenological criticism.) Mukařovský always managed to have concrete analyses and epistemology intersect in his theoretical studies. Moreover, he, as well as the other members of the Circle, always insisted on discussing their theoretical reflections with the artistic avant-gardes that were then in full effervescence.

Today, it is clear that Mukařovský's thought can also be distinguished from formal methods by his semiological conception of language, art and culture – a conception logically derived from his approach that was both structural and functional. Refusing as early as the 1930s any theory limited to the *text alone (*La Noblesse de la nature de Polák* 1934), Mukařovský conceives of the artistic *sign as a social and therefore contextual phenomenon ('L'Art comme fait sémiologique' 1934). (See *semiotics, *semiosis.) For him, structure generates the very meaning of a work. At the same time, he underscores the double semiological function of any artistic work: as autonomous and as communicational sign. Later, he elaborated the concept of semantic gesture, that is the 'gesture' through which the artist intentionally proceeds to choose the elements of his or her work and makes them converge within a single, meaningful unity. This also brought Mukařovský to develop the problem of intentionality and unintentionality in art along with that of the creative individual. (See *intention/intentionality.) In this way, he reached the question of the reader and that of 'reception.'

However, among all of Mukařovský's texts, *Estetická funkce, norma a hodnota jako sociální fakty* [*Aesthetic Function, Norm and Value as Social Facts* 1936] plays a special role as it revolutionizes European aesthetic theory in fewer than 75 pages. So important is this work that, according to K. Chvatík, the theoretician and historian of Czech structuralism, Mukařovský is to aesthetics what *Wittgenstein was then for philosophy (Chvatík, 'Jan Mukařovský'). In order to rid aesthetics of positivism and of any psychologizing speculation over 'Beauty' as absolute idea, Mukařovský increases the phenomenological (functional) organization of empirical reality. He deconstructs 'beauty' into three components that can be apprehended from a sociological perspective: function, norm and aesthetic value. He extends the aesthetic function practically to forms of human action and conceives of norm as the regulating agent of this action. 'Beauty' thus becomes an agreement between aesthetic and social norms within a given culture. However, it is his conception of aesthetic value that remains most important. Mukařovský divorces it from any emotional or sensual consideration and demonstrates that 'through its negative aesthetic values, the distortion that sets in between a work and the reigning system of aesthetic values could be the source of innovative artistic values' (Chvatík, 'Jan Mukařovský').

Mukařovský wrote many studies on the aesthetic dimensions of almost all artistic forms (such as film, architecture, theatre, folklore), as well as on aesthetic phenomena located outside the artistic system. However, most of his theoretical texts rest upon concrete analyses of modern Czech *literature, notably in poetry (such as intonation as an element of poetical rhythm). This explains a certain difficulty in gaining access to his work outside the small community of Czech literature specialists. Unlike his studies on poetics and on literary theory, *Kapitoly z české poetiky a estetiky I–III* [Chapters in Czech Poetics I–III, 1948], Mukařovský's aesthetic studies and his art theory were never collected in a single volume. This void was filled only when *Studie z estetiky* [Studies in Aesthetics 1966] and *Cestami poetiky a estetiky* [Along the Roads of Poetics and Aesthetics 1971] appeared.

By approaching aesthetic and poetic problems through semiotics and phenomenology, Mukařovský appears closer to *Mikhail Bakhtin than to the formalists. In this regard, it is significant that the semiotic structuralism of *Iurii Lotman, a leading figure of the *Tartu School, is related to Czech structuralism and its functional dimensions, notably through its use of value and of aesthetic function within culture – notions that were elaborated by Mukařovský. In fact, Lotman has written a preface to the Russian translation of Mukařovský's aesthetic tract. Moreover, his aesthetic theory and particularly the questions of 'semantic gesture' and of reception bring him and the whole Prague School a good deal closer to the German *Rezeptionästhetik*. The founding figures of this movement, *Hans Robert Jauss and *Wolfgang Iser, indeed, often refer to Mukařovský's work as well as to Felix Vodička, the semiotician, and another member of the Prague Linguistic Circle. (See *Constance School of Reception Aesthetics.)

EVA LE GRAND

Primary Sources

Mukařovský, Jan. 'L'Art comme fait sémiologique.' *Actes du huitième congrès international de philosophie à Prague 2–7 septembre 1934.* Prague, 1936. Repr. in *Poétique* 3 (1970).
– *Cestami poetiky a estetiky.* [*Along the Roads of Poetics and Aesthetics.*] Prague: Československý spisovatel, 1971.
– 'La Dénomination poétique et le fonction esthétique de la langue.' *Actes du quatrième congrès international des linguistes.* Copenhagen: Einar Munksgaard, 1938. Repr. in *Poétique* 3 (1970).
– *Estetická funkce, norma a hodnota jako sociální fakty.* 1936. *Aesthetic Function, Norm and Value as Social Facts.* Trans. Mark E. Suino. Ann Arbor: Michigan Slavic Publications, 1970.
– 'Intonation comme facteur du rythme poétique.' *Archives néerlandaises de phonétique expérimental* 8–9. In *The Word and Verbal Art: Selected Essays by Jan Mukařovský.* Ed. and trans. John Burbank and Peter Steiner. New Haven: Yale UP, 1977.
– *Kapitoly z české poetiky a estetiky I–III. Chapters on Czech Poetics I–III.* Prague: Svoboda, 1948.
– 'Karel Čapek: Prose as Lyrical Melody and as Dialogue.' In *A Prague School Reader on Aesthetics, Literary Structure and Style.* Ed. Paul L. Garvin. Washington: Georgetown UP, 1964.
– *Polakova vznešnost prirody.* [*La Noblesse de la Nature de Polák.*] Prague: Sborník Filologicky 10, 1934.
– *Máchův Máj: Estetická studie.* [*Mácha's Máj: An Aesthetic Study.*] Prague: Filosofická fakulta University Karlovy, 1928.
– *Příspěvek k estetice českého verše.* [*A Contribution to the Aesthetic of Czech Verse.*] Prague: Filosofická fakulta University Karlovy, 1923.
– *Structure, Sign and Function: Selected Essays by Jan Mukařovský.* Ed. and trans. John Burbank and Peter Steiner. New Haven: Yale UP, 1978.
– *Studie z estetiky.* [*Studies in Aesthetics.*] Prague: Odeon, 1966.
– *Studie z poetiky.* [*Studies in Poetics.*] Prague: Odeon, 1982.

Secondary Sources

Bojtar, Endre. *Slavic Structuralism.* Amsterdam/Philadelphia: Benjamins, 1985.

Burbank, J., and P. Steiner, eds. *Structure, Sign, and Function: Selected Essays by Jan Mukařovský.* New Haven: Yale UP, 1977.

- eds. *The Word and Verbal Art: Selected Essays by Jan Mukařovský.* New Haven: Yale UP, 1977.

Chvatík, K. 'Jan Mukařovský, Roman Jakobson et le Cercle linguistique de Prague.' *Critique* 483–4 (Aug./Sept. 1987).

- *Structuralismus a avantgarda.* Prague: Československý spisovatel, 1970.

Danow, D.K. 'Dialogic Perspectives: Bakhtin and Mukařovský.' In *Semiotics 1984.* Ed. John Deely. Lanham, Md.: UP of America, 1985.

Deak, F. 'Structuralism in the Theatre: The Prague School Contributions.' *The Drama Review* 20.4 (1976): 83–94.

Doležel, L. 'Mukařovský and the Idea of Poetic Truth.' *Russian Literature* 20 (Nort-Holland) 12.3 (1982): 283–98.

Eagle, H.J. 'Verse as a Semiotic System: Tynianov, Jakobson, Mukařovský, Lotman Extended.' *Slavic and East European Journal* 25.4 (1981): 47–61.

Faye, J.P., and L. Ropel. 'Le Cercle de Prague.' *Change* 3 (1969). Special Issue.

Fizer, J. 'Ingarden's and Mukařovský's Binominal Definition of the Literary Works of Art: A Comparative View of Their Respective Ontologies.' *Russian Literature* 20 (Nort-Holland) 13.3 (1983): 269–90.

Galan, F.W. *Historic Structures: The Prague School Project, 1928–1946.* Austin: U of Texas P, 1985.

Garvin, P.L., ed. *A Prague School Reader on Esthetics, Literary Structure, and Style.* Washington: Georgetown UP, 1964.

Jechová, H. 'Conception et fonction du temps dans la pensée théorique de Jan Mukařovský et de Roman Ingarden.' *Russian Literature* 20 (Nort-Holland) (1986): 353–80.

Le Grand, E. 'Hommage à Jan Mukařovský.' *Canadian Review of Comparative Literature/Revue Canadienne de Littérature Comparée.* Special issue on Dialogue. (Winter 1976): 106–12.

Matějka, L., and I.R. Titunik, eds. *Semiotics of Art: Prague School Contributions.* Cambridge: MIT P, 1976.

- eds. *Sound, Sign and Meaning: Cinquagenary of the Prague Linguistic Circle.* Ann Arbor: Michigan Slavic Publications, 1976.

Tobin, Y., ed. *The Prague School and Its Legacy: In Linguistics, Semiotics, Folklore, and Arts.* Amsterdam/Philadelphia: Benjamins, 1988.

Veltruský, J. 'Jan Mukařovský's Structural Poetics and Esthetics.' *Poetics Today* 2.1b (Winter 1980–1): 117–57.

- 'The Prague School Theory of Theatre.' *Poetics Today* 2.3 (1981): 225–35.

Wellek, René. *The Literary Theory and Aesthetics of the Prague School.* Ann Arbor: Michigan Slavic Publications, 1969. Repr. in *Discriminations: Further Concepts of Criticism.* New Haven: Yale UP, 1970, 275–303.

Nietzsche, Friedrich Wilhelm

(b. Prussia, 1844–d. Weimar, 1900) Philosopher, poet, philologist, composer, historiographer, theothanatologist. Born of a line of Lutheran ministers (his father and grandfathers) many of whose ancestors were butchers, Nietzsche was christened Friedrich Wilhelm after the reigning Prussian king whose birthday he shared. The loss of his father (to a brain disease) and his infant brother left the five-year-old Friedrich with his mother, sister, paternal grandmother, and two spinster aunts. An able musician by age 12, he composed, on the event of his confirmation, a fantasia for four-hand piano under the motto 'Pain is the Keynote of Nature.' The 'a priori of doubt' took hold early in Nietzsche, attended by an enthusiasm for Byron's *Manfred*: in his first attempt at philosophical writing, at age 13, he 'made God the father of evil' ('Preface' par. 3, *Genealogy of Morals*). As a student at Pforta (1858–64) he acquired a fine classical education and a predilection for the natural religion of Theognis, Hölderlin and Emerson. After courses in theology and classical philology at the University of Bonn (1864–5), Nietzsche dropped divinity and moved to Leipzig, where he majored in classical *literature but devoted his mind to the reading of Kant, Schopenhauer and F.A. Lange. He accepted the chair of classical philology at the University of Basel in 1869, Leipzig having graced him with doctor's name without examination or thesis. Promotion to full professor came in 1870.

What little charm the world of workaday classical learning held for Nietzsche vanished soon after his arrival at Basel. The tragic pessimism and prophetic power of Schopenhauer's philosophy of will, Burkhardt's history of culture and Wagner's operatic poetry proved headier; the prospect of heroic solitude, more enticing. Like Mathilde Trampedach's refusal of his offer of marriage, his accelerated estrangement from scholarism evidently came as a relief to Nietzsche. Something of his disaffection from the toming philology of the time shines through *The Birth of Tragedy* [*Die Geburt der Tragödie aus dem Geiste der Musik*], a brief yet grand speculation, free of footnotes or

Greek quotations, on the sublime as the artistic conquest of the horrible. To Nietzsche's mind, tragedy was born of the synthesis of two tendencies in the spirit of Greece – 'the Apollonian' (harmony, proportion, restraint) and 'the Dionysian' (ecstatic self-abandon) – then died with the advent of rationalism and moralism, epitomized in Socrates/Plato. Late in life, Nietzsche would repudiate his first book, finding its patterning 'offensively Hegelian,' or moribund with the *logos* of metaphysical idealism ('Why I Write Such Good Books' in *Ecce Homo*).

A series of 'untimely meditations' *(Unzeitgemässe Betrachtungen)* succeeded *The Birth of Tragedy*: on David Strauss as enlightened Darwinian and non-Christian yet still a philistine (1873), on the kinds and uses of history (1874), on Schopenhauer as teacher of self-reliance (1874), and on the return to pre-ethical drama once promised in Wagner (1876). The larger question of the genesis of 'good' and 'evil' in the history of mentalities came increasingly to occupy Nietzsche in the late 1870s. With *Human, All Too Human [Menschliches, Allzumenschliches* 1878], dedicated to Voltaire, he introduced his psychocultural notion of 'moral prejudices' and their bicameral origin in hale 'aristocratic morality' and life-denying 'slave morality,' rival responses to 'the will to power.' By decade's end Nietzsche had taken his distance from a Schopenhauer now found contaminated with the otherworldliness and pity of slave morality and had broken with Wagner on the grounds of nationalism and anti-Semitism, the 'pandering' to Christianity in *Parsifal*. The synthetic amoralism of Heraclitus, the existential contradictoriness of Montaigne and the worldly optimism of Goethe had become more attractive.

Never good, Nietzsche's health so worsened at Basel that he resigned his chair in 1879. A pension, though modest, allowed him to move from place to place in France and Italy over the next ten years, and to prepare (and pay for the publication of) those works that were to make him a power in modern Western *ideology: The Dawn: Reflections on Moral Prejudices [Morgenröthe: Gedanken über die moralischen Vorurteile* 1881], *The Gay Science [Die fröhliche Wissenschaft* 1882], *Thus Spoke Zarathustra [Also Sprach Zarathustra* parts 1–3, 1883–4; part 4, 1891], *Beyond Good and Evil [Jenseits von Gut und Böse* 1886], *On the Genealogy of Morals [Zur Genealogie der Moral* 1887], and *The Twi-light of the Idols [Die Götzen-Dämmerung* 1889]. In 1889, not long after the completion of *Der Antichrist* (1895), Nietzsche lapsed into a complete paralysis of mind and body and was taken to an asylum at Basel; he subsequently passed into the care of his mother at Naumburg, then of his sister at Weimar. The diagnosis of Nietzsche's insanity as tertiary syphilis was to pass into modern legend, thanks in part to the portrait of the artist in Thomas Mann's *Doktor Faustus*. A year after her brother's death in 1900 Elisabeth Nietzsche's selection from his notebooks for 1884–8 appeared as *Der Wille zur Macht [The Will to Power]*. His mocking self-portrait *Ecce Homo* was made public in 1908.

The substantial negativity of Nietzsche's major undertaking, its devaluation and discrediting of intelligibility and truth as such (cf. *Beyond Good and Evil* par. 34; *Will to Power* par. 493), makes any attempt at a discursive account of his oeuvre more than a little uncertain: 'We are not yet rid of God because we still have faith in grammar' *(Twilight of the Idols* par. 5). Founded on a rejection of traditional logic and referential language, the Nietzschean *text at its labyrinthine best builds toward minimal disclosure *(dévoilement)* with maximal unclosure, 'the zero degree of discourse, a philosophy which never takes place' (Jean-Luc Nancy 57). As deconstructionist readings have asserted, interpretation can never accomplish itself in the Nietzschean disordering of things since there is no-thing at bottom to interpret. (See *deconstruction.) Certainly, the brilliantly playful self-concealment and self-contradiction, the endless ironies, maskings and shiftings in the extravaganza of metaphoricity that is *Thus Spoke Zarathustra* are not made to encourage authoritative reading. (See *irony, *metonymy/metaphor.) Nor is a logically coherent apprehension of Nietzsche's musical yet deterministic doctrine of 'the eternal recurrence' – the repetition of what is, has been and will be, times without end (cf. *Thus Spoke* part 3) – very likely to come in the foreseeable future. But the Nietzschean tabling of new and proper values is not altogether innocent, enjoining as it does a universal theory of the will that portends 'the mastery of all being' (Hans-Georg Gadamer 230). When Zarathustra speaks in the language of Luther's Bible he tacitly appropriates at least as much *authority as he burlesques (cf. *André Gide: Journal 1889–1939* [Dijon: Gallimard,

1948, 990). And Nietzsche himself recognized the potential of his works for empowering new absolutisms: 'I am terrified by the thought of the sort of people who may one day invoke my authority' (letter of June 1884 to his sister). Such is the ethical *indeterminacy of Nietzsche's *text, as *Jacques Derrida has acknowledged in his 'Otobiographies,' that virtually any use may be made of it: 'There are no facts, only interpretations' (Will to Power par. 481).

It is a fact, though, that Nietzsche's texts have been interpreted, and perhaps no more tellingly than by Nietzsche himself in the least undiscursive of his aphoristic works, the polemical Genealogy of Morals, which reviews his progress in decoding the ethics of *power ciphered in the history of mentalities. His readings of the origin of good and evil in 'the long hieroglyphical text of the past of human morality' have 'ripened' since Human, All Too Human, have grown 'clearer, more solid' ('Preface'). Part 1 of the Genealogy affords a fairly consecutive account of Nietzsche's matured sense of Western history as the victory of slave over aristocratic morality – that is, of Judea's values over Rome's: 'It is the Jews who, with a terrifying logic, dared invert the equation of aristocratic values (good=noble=beautiful= happy=beloved of the gods) and who maintained this inversion with a bottomless hatred (the hatred of impotence) ... asserting that only the miserable are the good.' The coming of 'vulgar' Jesus with his 'love born of hatred,' 'the instrument of Israel's revenge,' heralded master morality's demise and the triumph of the common man, the effects of which were the mixing of races and values ('a poisoning of the blood') and the nihilism of heavenly ideals. Shaken though it was during the Reformation, when free spirits attempted a restoration of classical values, the slave morality institutionalized in 'the ecumenical synagogue' of 'New Rome' held firm, 'thanks to the movement of fundamentally populist ressentiment' against a worldly church's domination. Judea's victory was more complete yet in the French Revolution, when European nobility bowed before a populace enslaved to resentment. The present hegemony of democratic socialism in Europe represents 'a montrous atavism.'

Part 2 of the Genealogy, on good and bad conscience, characterizes the manly hero to come after two millennia of resentment towards the world and its aristocratic morality.

He is the Übermensch ('Overman') heralded in Thus Spoke Zarathustra ('Of the Bestowing Virtue' par. 3) and Beyond Good and Evil (par. 260), 'the autonomous and supra-moral man' who, true to the instinct to mastery, has given style to his character (cf. Gay Science par. 290), achieved sovereignty over himself. So empowered to say 'yes' to himself, he shuns all nationalisms or parties and the 'bad conscience' that arises from 'the will to mistreat oneself' (cf. Antichrist par. 55). He is perforce irreligious, since 'all religions at the bottom of themselves are systems of cruelty' or self-denial, the gods having been invented for 'the autocrucifixion and the autoprofanation of man.' Likewise anathema to the fully realized man are the moral pose and subjacent idealism of the socialists, anarchists and anti-Semites, who represent 'the man of resentment returned,' yet another triumph for Judea (cf. part 3, par. 26). The hope for the coming of the Overman is secured by the ironic principle that 'every good thing on this earth ends by destroying itself,' including the Judaeo-Christian morality of 'mercy' born of the 'autodestruction of justice' by 'resentment': 'this antichrist and this antinihilist, this conqueror of God and of nothingness – he must come some day ...'

In part 3, Nietzsche reviews his diagnosis of the exhausted ascetical idealism of the West and speculates on the prospects for humanity on its inevitable demise. Like the philosophers and scientists before them, the free thinkers of his time have not broken with the otherworldliness of the herd (Christianity is a Platonism for the people), 'since they still believe in truth.' In their hunger for transcendent verity they have not yet considered 'the value of truth'; nor have they come to see that 'there is no "vision" but perspective, no "knowledge" but perspective.' But the end of their moribund idealism is in sight, since the very acuteness of their illness assures imminent cure. In accordance with the law of life – 'All great things perish of themselves, by an act of self-destruction' – this 'will to truth' in populist Christian metaphysics (a multiple redundancy for Nietzsche) 'will end by drawing the ultimate conclusion, the conclusion against itself,' that there is no God, that 'God,' never more than a semantic fiction, is now empty of meaning (cf. 'Prologue' par. 2, Thus Spoke; Gay Science par. 125). At that moment, all morality must crumble: 'if nothing is true,' as Nietzsche transposes from Dostoevsky's Ivan Karamazov, 'all things are permitted.' Projection into the two centuries to follow the 'unconditional atheism' born of 'the will to truth' affords 'a horrifying spectacle, fraught with the unknown, and perhaps also with the highest hopes ...' His own transvaluation of all received values, so the author of the *Genealogy* anticipates, will have its long day.

The range and force of Nietzsche's impact on high Western culture ('I am no man, I am dynamite'; *Ecce Homo* par. 326) are difficult to overestimate. Its markings are distinctly visible, for example, in the poetry of Rainer Maria Rilke, Gottfried Benn and William Butler Yeats; in the novels of Robert Musil, Hermann Hesse, André Gide, André Malraux, Romain Rolland, Nikos Kazantzakis, Jack London, Ayn Rand, and Susan Sontag; in the elegiac historiography of Oswald Spengler; and in the social theory of Max Horkheimer and *Theodor Adorno. Comparisons of Nietzsche with *Sigmund Freud and *Jacques Lacan on dreamthinking, with *Mircea Eliade on the history of religions, with *José Ortega y Gasset on mass culture and with *Ludwig Wittgenstein on language have become relatively common. But it is in the direct shaping of a variety of existentialisms and phenomenologies that his influence has been most masterful: the writings of Karl Jaspers, Paul Tillich, *Martin Heidegger, Dietrich Bonhoeffer, Martin Buber, Albert Camus, and *Jean-Paul Sartre voluminously comment on the death of transcendent reality announced by Nietzsche. (See also *phenomenological criticism.) The theothanatology of Thomas J. Altizer, William Hamilton and Paul van Buren, prominent members of the U.S. avant-garde of the 1960s, represents an extension of that gloss. Among even the leading Christian existentialists at mid-century, Gabriel Marcel is exceptional in his unambiguous characterization of Nietzschean unreason as suicidal, fatal for theology and philosophy alike.

The importance of Nietzsche for contemporary critical theory is commensurate with his eminence in philosophy. Deconstructionist criticism, as in Derrida, *Roland Barthes, *Paul de Man, *Jean-François Lyotard, *Gilles Deleuze, and *J. Hillis Miller, has found his theothanatology especially virtuous for the propagation of autogeneal, autotelic, 'grammarless' reflection. *Michel Foucault has credited the *Genealogy of Morals* with founding a new approach to 'history.' Given Nietzsche's relentless twitting of 'the flatheads of socialism' *(Beyond Good and*

Evil par. 203), his treatment at the hands of leading Marxist critics has been reasonable: *Georg Lukács, for example, has denounced Nietzsche as the founder of irrationalism in the imperialist period; and *Jürgen Habermas has lamented the effect of his mere aestheticism on the writings of Adorno. (See *Marxist criticism.) Marxist ideology, though, has substantially profited from the Nietzschean rejection of otherworldliness in all its forms: 'with Jehovah buried,' in the words of e.e. cummings, 'Eternity is now a Five Year Plan.' While Nietzsche's inversion of the 'masculine' principle of reason has appealed to *feminist criticism, his actual misogyny understandably has not.

CAMILLE R. LA BOSSIÈRE

Primary Sources

Nietzsche, Friedrich. *Basic Writings of Nietzsche*. Ed. and trans. Walter Kaufmann. New York: Modern Library, 1966.
– *The Portable Nietzsche*. Ed. and trans. Walter Kaufmann. New York: Viking, 1954.
– *Sämtliche Werke: Kritische Studienausgabe*. 15 vols. Ed. Giorgio Colli and Mazzino Montinari. Munich: Deutscher Taschenbuch Verlag; Berlin: Walter de Gruyter, 1980.
– *Selected Letters of Friedrich Nietzsche*. Ed. and trans. Christopher Middleton. Chicago: U of Chicago P, 1969.

Secondary Sources

Behler, Ernst. 'Nietzsches Auffassung der Ironie.' *Nietzsche-Studien* 4 (1975): 1–35.
Buber, Martin. *Eclipse of God*. New York: Harper and Row, 1952.
Copleston, F.C. *Friedrich Nietzsche: Philosopher of Culture*. London: Burns Oates and Washbourne, 1941.
Danto, Arthur C. *Nietzsche as Philosopher*. New York: Columbia UP, 1980.
Deleuze, Gilles. *Nietzsche et sa philosophie*. Paris: PUF, 1965.
Derrida, Jacques. 'Interpreting Signatures (Nietzsche/Heidegger): Two Questions.' In *Looking After Nietzsche*. Ed. Laurence A. Rickels. Albany: SUNY P, 1990, 1–17.
– 'Otobiographies: The Teaching of Nietzsche and the Politics of the Proper Name.' In *The Ear of the Other*. Ed. Christie V. McDonald. New York: Schocken, 1985, 1–38.
– *Spurs: Nietzsche's Styles*. Chicago: U of Chicago P, 1979.
Fink, Eugen. *Nietzsche aujourd'hui*. 2 vols. Paris: Union Générale d'Editions, 1973.

Gadamer, Hans-Georg. 'The Drama of Zarathustra.' In *Nietzsche's New Seas: Explorations in Philosophy, Aesthetics, and Politics.* Ed. Michael Allen Gillespie and Tracy B. Strong. Chicago: U of Chicago P, 1988, 220–31.

Gilman, S.L. *Nietzschean Parody.* Bonn: Bouvier Verlag H. Grundmann, 1976.

Heidegger, Martin. *Nietzsche.* 2 vols. Pfullingen: Neske, 1961.

Heller, Eric. *The Importance of Nietzsche.* Chicago: U of Chicago P, 1988.

Irigaray, Luce. *Amante marine: De Friedrich Nietzsche.* Paris: Editions de Minuit, 1980.

Janz, Curt Paul. *Friedrich Nietzsche: Biographie.* 3 vols. Munich: Hanser, 1978–9.

Jaspers, Karl. *Nietzsche: An Introduction to the Understanding of His Philosophical Activity.* South Bend: Regenery/Gateway, 1965.

Kaufmann, Walter A. *Nietzsche: Philosopher, Psychologist, Antichrist.* Princeton: Princeton UP, 1950.

Magnus, B. *Nietzsche's Existential Imperative.* Bloomington: Indiana UP, 1978.

Murchland, Bernard, ed. *The Meaning of the Death of God.* New York: Vintage, 1967.

Nancy, Jean-Luc. 'Nietzsche's Thesis on Teleology.' In *Looking after Nietzsche.* Ed. Rickels, 49–66.

Nehamas, Alexander. *Nietzsche: Life as Literature.* Cambridge: Harvard UP, 1985.

Rey, Jean-Michel. *L'Enjeu des signes: Lectures de Nietzsche.* Paris: Editions du Seuil, 1971.

Reichert, H.W. *Friedrich Nietzsche's Impact on Modern German Literature.* Chapel Hill: U of North Carolina P, 1975.

Shapiro, Gary. *Nietzschean Narratives.* Bloomington: Indiana UP, 1989.

Thatcher, David S. *Nietzsche in England 1890–1914: The Growth of a Reputation.* Toronto: U of Toronto P, 1970.

Olson, Elder

(b. U.S.A., 1909–) Poet, playwright, critic. Educated at the University of Chicago, Olson taught at Armour Institute of Technology, Chicago (1938–42) and the University of Chicago (1942–77). As founding member of the so-called Chicago School, Olson is a theorist and practitioner of *pluralism (the pursuit of various ways of knowing literary texts by using a variety of methodologies). (See *text.) The philosophical bases of his approach are discussed in 'The Dialectical Foundations of Critical Pluralism' (1976) in which he identifies seven types of dialectic and eight fundamental kinds of criticism. As a practical critic, however, Olson, like the other Chicago critics, is most closely identified with the method of Aristotle. (See *Neo-Aristotelian or Chicago School.)

Olson distinguishes mimetic from didactic literary works. (See *mimesis.) This is not a value judgment (the *Iliad* and *Hamlet* would belong to the former category, *Paradise Lost* and the *Divine Comedy* to the latter) but rather a formal distinction based on the final end or intention of the work. Both sorts of works imitate human actions, but whereas mimetic works do so merely for whatever interest lies in these actions, didactic works do so in order to demonstrate some thesis. Thus didactic works, although they may superficially resemble mimetic works (such as tragedies, comedies, epics), are really works of rhetoric and can only be understood according to rhetorical principles. The author's intention to persuade has powerful consequences for probability of plot and consistency of characterization among other things. Olson provides a good specimen of rhetorical analysis in 'Rhetoric and the Appreciation of Pope' (1976). (See *rhetorical criticism.)

Olson's approach to criticism strongly relies on experience, both of the artist and of the reader: 'I am not sure that art permits of absolute demonstration; I am positive that it entails experiences which are matters of fact and can be generalized' (*Tragedy* 75). As a practical critic, Olson is primarily concerned with tracing the reasoning of artists in forming their works and with the reasons why these works affect us as they do. While he has written on numerous writers, perhaps the best introduction to his work is his *Tragedy and the Theory of Drama* (1961). Olson influenced a wide variety of critics including *Wayne Booth, Sheldon Sacks, Norman Friedman, James Phelan, Walter A. Davis, and James Kinneavy. His strength as a critic lies in his consistent effort to expose the theoretical bases of differences of interpretation so that readers can both formulate and resolve problems of their own.

HOLLIS RINEHART

Primary Sources

Olson, Elder. *On Value Judgements in the Arts and Other Essays.* Chicago and London: U of Chicago P, 1976.
– *The Poetry of Dylan Thomas.* Chicago: U of Chicago P, 1954.
– *The Theory of Comedy.* Bloomington: Indiana UP, 1968.

– *Tragedy and the Theory of Drama.* Detroit: Wayne State UP, 1961.

Secondary Sources

Batterby, James L. *Elder Olson: An Annotated Bibliography.* New York: Garland, 1983.
Crane, R.S., ed. *Critics and Criticism: Ancient and Modern.* Chicago: U of Chicago P, 1952.

Ong, Walter Jackson

(b. U.S.A., 1912–) Literary critic. Walter Jackson Ong is a Jesuit priest, Emeritus University Professor of Humanities, William E. Haren Professor of English, and Professor of Humanities in Psychiatry at Saint Louis University in Missouri. During the 1950s Ong researched and taught at Harvard. His academic credits include Ph.L., 1940; M.A., 1941; S.T.L., 1948 (St. Louis University); Ph.D. 1955 (Harvard University); as well as a number of honorary degrees. He entered the Society of Jesus in 1935 and was ordained a Roman Catholic priest in 1946. Ong lectured extensively in Canada, France and the U.S.A. where he has also appeared on national radio and television. His Terry Lectures at Yale were published in 1968 as *The Presence of the Word* and his Alexander Lectures at the University of Toronto were published as *Hopkins, the Self, and God.*

Ong is a literary critic, a scholar of rhetoric and the European Renaissance, a specialist in the interrelationship between consciousness and communications, a vocal American Catholic and past president of the Modern Language Association. His communications theory which is founded on a unique blend of sociology, anthropology, religious *hermeneutics, classics, and rhetoric, has affinities with French *semiotics and *structuralism. *Orality and Literacy* (1982), his best-selling book to date, has been translated into eight languages. (See also *rhetorical criticism, *communication theory.)

Ong's early essays, including those collected in *The Barbarian Within: And Other Fugitive Essays* (1954) and *In the Human Grain* (1967), deal primarily with literary topics such as the methodologies of the New Critics. (See *New Criticism.) Finding New Critical methods useful but unnecessarily limiting, Ong disputed their view of the *text as autonomous object. His theories – influenced by those of his colleague and former teacher *Marshall McLuhan,

who argued in *The Gutenberg Galaxy* (1962) that the invention of the printing press marked a major shift in human consciousness – trace the relationship between communications media and the human psyche.

In *Orality and Literacy: The Technologizing of the Word,* Ong continues the study that he began in his trilogy which includes *The Presence of the Word* (1967), *Rhetoric, Romance, and Technology* (1971) and *Interfaces of the Word* (1977). In these books he deals historically and anthropologically with three phases in the development of Western verbal communications media: the preliterate or primary oral/aural; the chirographic/typographic; and the electronic or secondary oral/aural. He points to the importance of formulaic composition, which was used as a mnemonic device in preliterate culture and then traces the influence of oral composition and rhetoric on the chirographic/typographic and electronic or secondary oral phases. He perceives logic and rhetoric as two opposing features in Western culture. Rhetoric is founded in preliterate orality, while logic emerges from the visual technology of writing and print. Ong explains that the shift from oral/aural to visual modes of communication and perception marks a fundamental change in human consciousness which features an internalization of the technology of writing and rhetorical modes embedded in language. Ong stresses the importance of Latin in this development and the fact that we are often unconscious of rhetorical features embedded in both language and psyche. He also notes that the three phases bear an uneven resemblance to the Freudian psychosexual stages (oral, anal and genital). (See *Sigmund Freud, *psychoanalytic theory.) Although he does not pursue this resemblance, in *Hopkins, the Self, and God* (1968) he suggests that a complex interbreeding of, for example, Saussurean linguistics and Freudian psychoanalysis as found in *Jacques Lacan might prove most useful in further studies of what he calls the 'interiorizing and anthropologization' of culture and society. (See *Ferdinand de Saussure.)

Ong occasionally applies his theories to a Catholic view of the world. For example, he finds it remarkable that the word of God in the form of Christ entered into the world precisely at the time when it had the 'greatest opportunity to endure and flower,' that is, during a period when primary orality was still predominant but also a time when the alphabet was coming into use, thereby ensuring that the word could be recorded and disseminated.

Fundamental to Ong's view is his study of the Huguenot educationalist and rhetorician Peter Ramus. In *Ramus, Method, and the Decay of Dialogue* (1958) and in *Ramus and Talon Inventory* (1958) Ong suggests that Ramus played a pivotal role in re-shaping Western consciousness through the introduction of visually oriented systems to organize new knowledge. He reminds his readers that the inward turn of human consciousness that appears to have been inspired by Ramus has been studied by psychiatrists Sigmund Freud and *Carl Gustav Jung and by palaentologist-mystic Teilhard de Chardin. Ong also believes that the romantic period has a special significance in the shift in human consciousness since it draws from both primary oral and print-oriented phases of cultural development. While, on the one hand, romanticism favoured the old primary oral world by rejecting typographically grounded rationalism, it also showed an academic or para-academic interest in popular literature, folk ballads and folklore. On the other hand, romanticism relied heavily on rationalism founded in writing and print. Ong points out that the quest for originality, or the new, reveals romanticism as a typographically inspired phenomenon despite its avowed commitment to the oral past. We are still in a typographic world, he reminds us, and the quest for the new is still under way.

In other studies Ong applies his theories specifically to literary matters. In 'The Writer's Audience is Always a Fiction,' Ong discusses the idea of an imagined audience and its relationship to the writer. This essay has contributed significantly to the current debate on reader-response theory. (See *reader-response criticism.) In *Hopkins, the Self, and God*, Ong examines 19th-century English Jesuit poet Gerard Manley Hopkins and his concern with 'inscape' within the context of Christian and Victorian sensibilities. He maintains that Hopkins' sense of self and his related particularism is a pivotal example of the large-scale, centuries-old movement toward greater particularization of the exterior world and interiorization of consciousness that marks the evolution of the human psyche. Ong shows how Hopkins' writing anticipates the predilections of the modern and postmodern movements. (See *self/other, *postmodernism.)

There have been substantial objections to

Ong's view of orality in regard to voice, which situates material *logos* in human *ethos* and finds a partial basis in Longinus' rhetoric and Kant's aesthetics. Anthropologists argue that Ong's view veers toward essentialist primitivism. Deconstructionists object to his phenomenological definition of voice and regard language in a material sense as a reified figure that forever defers meaning. For deconstructionists, voice is a figural deviation; for Ongians, it is an event, itself unstable and indeterminate, always retaining some 'ineluctable interiority' ('Dialectics' 500). (See *deconstruction, *phenomenological criticism.)

A major study of the implications of Ong's theories, *Media, Consciousness, and Culture* (1991), re-examines Ong's writing in reference to electronic media, First and Third World rhetoric, feminist theory, and current critical debate on *discourse and theories of the dialogic self. Critics have only begun to fathom the degree to which Ong's studies have implications for structuralist, deconstructionist, speech act and reader response theories. (See also *feminist criticism, *dialogical criticism, *speech act theory.)

KARL E. JIRGENS

Primary Sources

Ong, Walter J. 'Agonistic Structures in Academia: Past to Present.' *Interchange; A Journal of Education* 5: 1–12. (An earlier abridged version appeared under the same title in *Daedalus: Journal of the American Academy of Arts and Sciences* issued in *Proceedings of the American Academy of Arts and Science* 103.4 (1974): 229–38.)
- *American Catholic Crossroads* (Catholic Book Club Selection). New York: Macmillan, 1959.
- *The Barbarian Within: And Other Fugitive Essays.* New York: Macmillan, 1954.
- 'Communications Media and the State of Theology.' *Cross Currents* 19: 462–80.
- 'A Dialectic of Aural and Objective Correlatives.' In *20th Century Literary Criticism.* Ed. David Lodge. London: Longmans, 1972, 497–508.
- *Fighting for Life: Contest, Sexuality, and Consciousness.* Amherst: U of Massachusetts P, 1981.
- *Frontiers in American Catholicism.* New York: Macmillan, 1957.
- *Hopkins, the Self, and God.* Toronto: U of Toronto P, 1986.
- *Interfaces of the Word: Studies in the Evolution of Consciousness and Culture.* Ithaca and London: Cornell UP, 1977.
- *In the Human Grain: Further Explorations of Contemporary Culture.* New York: Macmillan, 1967.

- *Orality and Literacy: The Technologizing of the Word.* London and New York: Methuen, 1982.
- *The Presence of the Word: Some Prolegomena for Cultural and Religious History.* New Haven: Yale UP, 1967.
- *Ramus, Method, and the Decay of Dialogue: From the Art of Discourse to the Art of Reason.* Cambridge, Mass.: Harvard UP, 1958.
- 'Ramus: Rhetoric and the Pre-Newtonian Mind.' In *English Institute Essays 1952.* Ed. Alan S. Downer. New York: Columbia UP, 1954, 138–70.
- *Ramus and Talon Inventory.* Cambridge, Mass.: Harvard UP, 1958.
- *Rhetoric, Romance, and Technology.* Ithaca: Cornell UP, 1971.
- 'Technology Outside Us and Inside Us.' *Communio* 5 (1978): 100–21.
- 'Truth in Conrad's Darkness.' *Mosaic: A Journal for the Comparative Study of Literature and Ideas* 11 (1978): 151–63.
- *Why Talk? A Conversation about Language.* San Francisco: Chandler and Sharp, 1973.
- 'The Writer's Audience is Always a Fiction.' *PMLA* 90 (1975): 9–21. Also in *20th Century Literary Theory: An Introductory Anthology.* Ed. Vassilis Lambropoulos and David Neal Miller. Buffalo: SUNY P, 1987, 401–22.
- ed. and co-author. *Darwin's Vision and Christian Perspective.* New York: Macmillan, 1960.
- and co-author. *Knowledge and the Future of Man.* New York: Holt, Rinehart, and Winston, 1968.
- ed. *Petrus Ramus and Audomarus Talaeus: Collectaneae praefationes, epistolae, orationes.* [Facsimile of the 1599 Marburg edition.] Hildesheim, Germany: Georg Olms Verlagsbuchhandlung, 1969.
- *Petrus Ramus: Scholae in liberales artes.* [Facsimile of the 1569 Basel edition.] Hildesheim, Germany: Georg Olms Verlagsbuchhandlung, 1970.

Secondary Sources

Gronbeck, Bruce E., Thomas J. Farrell, and Paul A. Soukup, eds. *Media, Consciousness, and Culture: Explorations of Walter Ong's Thought.* Newbury Park, Calif.: Sage Publications, 1991.
Kermode, Frank. 'Father Ong.' In *Modern Essays.* Glasgow: Fontana P, 1990, 99–107.

Ortega y Gasset, José

(b. Spain, 1883–d. 1955) Philosopher, journalist, social critic. Born into a liberal, literary family well-connected with the artistic, political and intellectual élite of Spain, Ortega y Gasset received a privileged education from the Jesuits, and began his studies of philosophy in the Jesuit University of Deusto. From 1898 he studied philosophy at the University of Madrid, where he received his doctorate in 1904. While still a student, he met Miguel de Unamuno, whose initial influence upon him was great, and with whom he began an important correspondence. At this time, he also became friends with Ramiro de Maeztu, with whom he later claimed to have passed through the 'torrid zone' of the thought of *Nietzsche. Despite the deep mark left upon him by French *literature, he chose to continue his studies in Germany, first in Leipzig and Berlin. Later, in Marburg, he was exposed to neo-Kantianism as well as to the thought and personalities of Hermann Cohen and Paul Natorp. The experiences in Germany intensified his interest in language, philosophical and scientific thought and, especially, rigorous intellectual methodology. As he matured, however, he moved away from neo-Kantian idealism.

From 1908 until the outbreak of the Civil War in 1936, Ortega was one of the most influential thinkers in Spain and a significant bridge to contemporary European thought and methods. From his chair as professor of metaphysics at the University of Madrid, he formed a distinguished generation of Spanish intellectuals, among whom the best-known is Julian Marias (1914–). Perhaps still more important, he founded important intellectual journals (*Faro, Europa, España*), specifically conceived as vehicles that would permit a broad range of Spaniards to become familiar with the best of contemporary creative thinking. His most influential journal was the *Revista de Occidente* (1923–36), in which great European thinkers (Einstein, Frank, Frobenius, Huizinga, *Jung, Russell, Simmel) could present their world to Spaniards and in which Spanish thinkers might find an encouraging atmosphere. Virtually all of Ortega's own writing first appeared in a journalistic context and was only later collected into volumes.

With the notable exception of religion, almost no area of thought escaped Ortega's consideration. His most enduring studies of literary and aesthetic creativity appeared between 1914 and 1925, but many of his theories on language and social usage received their fullest treatment in the last decade of his life. His own highly characteristic and plastic literary style made him especially sensitive to a broad range of aesthetic concerns, to which he was able to add a solid intellectual base, so important in a time in which Western artistic practices seemed disoriented and in flux. He argued that the 19th-century concept of beauty as a utilitarian and orderly instinct had to be surpassed by new norms that saw aesthetics and all forms of criticism as indispensable adjuncts to the creative process. Only through responsible criticism, which could add understanding to instinct, could high standards be stimulated. However, in literature, as in painting, Ortega detected an increasing reliance upon technique, at the expense of the feeling and intelligence that engender creativity. Genuine style, he was to argue, is rather a unique perspective dictated by observation or experience, and passed through the filter of artistic individuality.

In 1913–14, Ortega's reservations about the evolution of the thought of *Edmund Husserl and of phenomenology helped him to refine his view that the surface of reality, in which he included artistic creations, presupposes depth, and that an understanding of this fact is imperative to any task. (See *phenomenological criticism.) In a literary *text, for example, the visible surface is characterized by the fact that it both suggests and conceals depth, without which it would not exist, and which the viewer and the critic have the obligation to seek consciously so as to bring it into being. 'Surface,' 'depth,' 'foreshortening,' and 'latency,' as well as the importance of perspective in interpretation acquired an increasingly important role in Ortega's thought, as he derived social consequences from a more intense critical methodology.

This methodology was developed in his first book, *Meditations on Quixote* (1914), published as a philosophical introduction to Cervantes' novel, both as literary and historical object and as an example of the Spanish way of seeing the relationship between the 'I' and its world: 'I am I and my circumstance.' In addition, Ortega offered here his earliest significant views on the novel, in which, as in all art, both context and personal feeling converge in the object of contemplation, and relate it to the individual. Himself a superlative practitioner of imagery, his insight into the functioning of metaphor ('Essay on Aesthetics by Way of a Prologue' 1914), remains an illuminating affirmation of the ability of the 'I' to be executant and dynamic, that is, to create new reality, both actively and as the object of contemplation, in counterposition to the transparency of the aesthetic object. (See *metonymy/meta-

phor.) The miracle of the metaphor flows from the fact that, although it is created out of elements that are perceived as being in some way similar, it is itself radically lacking in sameness, and thus opens onto another possible world.

Through a series of shorter essays in which he examines dance, music and the ludic elements of life, Ortega reaches his great, but often misunderstood, essay *The Dehumanization of Art* (1924–5), in which he sets himself the task, not of dictating artistic criteria, but of understanding and analysing those that underlay such current artistic manifestations as cubism and the literary avant-garde. Of particular interest is his conviction that contemporary art had set as its goal the division of its public into a 'mass,' which could not possibly understand the work, and an 'élite' of the initiated, to whom it was directed. This division was largely achieved by stripping art of its sentimental, 'human,' elements, as well of its transcendence. In *Ideas on the Novel* (1924–5), Ortega offers his analysis of a genre that continued to live in crisis. He posits that since the novel had effectively run out of themes, and the 20th-century reader is more knowledgeable about human nature, the importance of plot may be reduced in favour of a new type of density, especially psychological, that may stimulate the willingness of the reader to become effectively cut off from his daily life upon entering the possible world created by the novel. (See *genre criticism, *theme.)

Especially in the years of his exile (1936–45) and after, Ortega devoted considerable attention to the concept of artistic expression as the vanguard of social change. Highly suggestive are his reflections on the function of 'derealization' in art, that is, its ability to be something other than merely a representation of the object that it claims to represent, or from which it seems to have sprung, as well as his thoughts on the dynamics of social structures and institutions. His writings on 'The Idea of the Theatre' (1946), and especially on the social significance of language and gestures *(Man and People* 1949–55), prefigure many ideas in *semiotics and sociolinguistics that would be developed by others only in the 1960s and 1970s.

VICTOR OUIMETTE

Peirce

Primary Sources

Ortega y Gasset, José. *La Deshumanización del arte.*
Obras completas. Vol. 3. Madrid: Revista de Occidente, 1947–83. 12 vols. *The Dehumanization of
Art.* Trans. Hélène Weyl. In *The Dehumanization of
Art and Other Essays on Art, Culture and Literature.*
Princeton: Princeton UP, 1968.
– 'Ensayo de estética a manera de prólogo.' *Obras
completas.* Vol. 6. Madrid: Revista de Occidente,
1947–83. 'Essay on Aesthetics by Way of a Pro-
logue.' Trans. Philip W. Silver. In *Phenomenology
and Art.* New York: Norton, 1975.
– *El hombre y la gente.* Madrid: Revista de Occidente
en Alianza Editorial, 1980. *Man and People.* Trans.
William R. Trask. New York: W.W. Norton, 1957.
– 'The Idea of the Theatre.' 1946. Trans. Philip W.
Silver. In *Phenomenology and Art.* New York: Norton, 1975.
– *Ideas sobre la novela. Obras completas.* Vol. 3. Madrid: Revista de Occidente, 1947–83. *Ideas on the
Novel.* Trans. Hélène Weyl. In *The Dehumanization
of Art and Other Essays on Art, Culture and Litera-
ture.*
– *Meditaciones del Quijote. Obras completas.* Vol. 1.
Madrid: Revista de Occidente, 1947–83. *Medita-
tions on Quixote.* Trans. Evelyn Rugg and Diego
Marín. New York: W.W. Norton, 1961.

Peirce, C(harles) S(anders)

(b. U.S.A., 1839–d. 1914) Philosopher, logician, scientist, and mathematician. Founder of
modern semiotic theory (1867), pragmatism
(1878), the logic of relations and quantification
(1870–85). At Harvard, where his father was
professor of mathematics, Charles Peirce studied science, mathematics and philosophy.
From 1861 to 1891 he worked as a scientist
for the U.S. Coast and Geodetic Survey and,
throughout an immensely productive life, published many significant papers in mathematics,
physics, astronomy, chemistry, biology, and
other sciences. While he was briefly (1879–84)
a professor of philosophy at Johns Hopkins, he
planned and supervised the first carefully controlled experiments in psychology conducted
in America. Peirce's major achievements are
his original and foundational contributions to
*semiotics, logic, theory of induction, probabil-
ity, measurement, and scientific method and to
the philosophy of pragmatism.
In 1867 Peirce published 'On a New List of
Categories' *(Writings* 2: 49–59), a short, dense,
and profoundly original paper in which he laid

the philosophical foundations for a comprehensive and detailed system of semeiotic (his
preferred spelling). He outlined its three chief
subdivisions (a semeiotic grammar, theory of
truth conditions and rhetoric), defined some of
the major classes of signs or representations
and briefly indicated their application to logic
and scientific reasoning. (See *sign.) He suggested in passing that the semeiotic had bearing on linguistics, *literature, the arts, law and
society. In papers published in 1868 he argued
that the semeiotic confuted the Cartesian theory of the mind and replaced it with the view
that 'man is a sign, so that ... my language
is the sum total of myself' ('Some Consequences,' *Writings* 2: 41). Perception, emotion,
attention, action, and thought are all forms of
semeiosis. After 1890 Peirce embarked on a
fresh and original examination of the basic
principles of semeiotic change and evolution,
arguing that such change is fundamentally teleological. In his correspondence with Victoria
Lady Welby (1903–11), Peirce amplified his
triadic analysis and elliptically sketched a dekadic analysis of signs, distinguishing ten elements essential to the constitution of a sign.
The dekadic semeiotic, if it were ever clarified
and completed, would permit a far subtler and
more precise specification of signs and of sign
change than the earlier triadic analysis. It is
unfortunate that he never wrote a systematic
and comprehensive account of his triadic semeiotic or of his later dekadic semeiotic.
Peirce took the concept of a sign so broadly
that he sometimes spoke of an entire book or
an entire literature as a single complex sign.
He understood anything to be a sign, or *representamen* if, when it is present to an interpreter, some aspect of it is interpreted in
feeling and imagination, in practice, and in
cognition, as standing for something beyond
what is present. A sign or representation is
thus a triad of (a) interpretation or *Interpretant;*
(b) *Object* beyond the sign, for which the sign
is interpreted to stand; and (c) significant aspect, sometimes called the *Ground* of the sign.
A sign can be interpreted only in further signs.
Since each Interpretant is a sign it must itself
beget further interpretants, each of them encompassing an interpretation in imagination
and feeling (the *emotional* interpretant), an
interpretation in action (the *energetic* interpretant), and a cognitive interpretation (the *logical*
interpretant). Self-referring signs excepted,
every sign must be a sign of something be-

441

yond itself, its *object*. Signs arise and function within a real-world context. The Object of a sign is something with which all interpreters of that particular sign must have some collateral and independent acquaintance so that the sign may communicate *further* information. Peirce's semeiotic thus avoids some familiar problems, like reference to non-existent or problematic entities, or signs which do not refer at all – conjunctions, adjectives, samples, natural phenomena like the rainbow or medical symptoms. Peirce further distinguished the Ground, or significant aspect of a sign, from the many material features irrelevant to its functioning as a representamen (sign).

Since each sign is a triad, it can be classified and distinguished from other signs according to the nature of its Ground, relation to its Object and relation to its Interpretant. The Ground of a sign may be a *Qualisign, Sinsign* or *Legisign*, according to whether it is a quality (for example, a colour sample), a singular event or entity (for example, the starter's pistol, a memorial monument), or a general law, rule or function (for example, words and their meaningful combinations, codes, notational systems). A sign is an **icon, *index* or *symbol*, as it is related to its object through qualitative resemblance, forceful interaction or a general rule followed by all its interpretants. Analogously, signs may be related to their interpretants in three different ways, as *rhemes, dicents* and *arguments*. Signs are interpreted by their interpretants to be signs of the characteristics of possible entities (rhemes), signs of actual entities (dicents) or signs of general law (argments). Ground, relation to object and relation to interpretant then combine to form species or classifications of signs. A feeling of empathy with another person is a *rhematic iconic qualisign*. A portrait painting is, if the subject is not identified, a *rhematic indexical sinsign*. If the subject is identified it is a *dicent indexical sinsign*. If it is a portrait of a purely imaginary or fictional subject it is a *rhematic iconic sinsign*. A demonstrative pronoun is a *rhematic indexical legisign*. An autobiography is a *dicent indexical legisign* whose component parts are almost entirely *dicent symbols*.

During Peirce's lifetime, only Josiah Royce recognized the importance of the semeiotic. *T.S. Eliot, a member of Royce's seminar, indicates in *Knowledge and Experience* (103) that he knew something of the semeiotic. Still, it was not until C.K. Ogden and *I.A. Richards de-

voted a section of *The Meaning of Meaning* (1923) to Peirce's later semeiotic that it began to reach a wider literary audience. But it was *Roman Jakobson's frequent admiring and commendatory references to Peirce that brought him to the attention of both the international linguistics community and the community of literary critics and theorists. Peircean semiotics is being pursued and developed notably by Jean Fisette, Maryan Ayim, Richard Tursman, and David Savan in Canada; by Michael and Marianne Shapiro, Joseph M. Ransdell, Raimo Anttila, Tom Short, and many others in the United States; by Max Bense, Elisabeth Walther, Helmut Pape, and *Jürgen Habermas in Germany; by G. Granger, Gérard Deledalle and his school in France; and by *Umberto Eco and others in Italy, and Dan Nesher in Israel.

DAVID SAVAN

Primary Sources

Deledalle, G., ed. and trans. *Ecrits sur le signe*. Paris: Seuil, 1978.
Eisele, C., ed. *New Elements of Mathematics by C.S. Peirce*. 4 vols. The Hague: Mouton, 1976.
Fisch, Max H., et al., eds. *Writings of Charles S. Peirce: A Chronological Edition*. Vols. 1–. Bloomington: Indiana UP, 1982–.
Fouchier-Axelsen, B., and C. Foz, trans. Intro. D. Savan. *Textes fondamentaux de sémiotique: C.S. Peirce*. Paris: Meridiens Klincksieck, 1987.
Hardwick, C.S., ed. *Semiotic and Significs: The Correspondence Between Charles S. Peirce and Victoria Lady Welby*. Bloomington: Indiana UP, 1977.
Hartshorne, C., and Paul Weiss, ed. *Collected Papers of Charles S. Peirce*. 8 vols. Ed. A. Burks; vols. 7, 8. Cambridge, Mass.: Harvard UP, 1931–58.
[The following references are a guide to some of Peirce's chief writings on semeiotic: *Collected Papers* (by volume and paragraph number) 1: 545–67, 2: 227–308, 5: 213–317, 8: 313–5, 317–79; *New Elements* 3: 839–44, 4: 235–63.]
Ogden, C.K., and I.A. Richards. *The Meaning of Meaning: A Study of the Influence of Language upon Thought and of the Science of Symbolism*. London: Kegan Paul, Trench, Trubner, 1923.

Secondary Sources

Bense, Max. *Semiotische Prozesse und Systeme*. Baden-Baden: Agis, 1975.
Deledalle, G. *Théorie et pratique du signe*. Paris: Payot, 1979.
Fisch, M. *Peirce, Semeiotic, and Pragmatism*. Bloomington: Indiana UP, 1986.

Fisette, J. *Introduction à la sémiotique de C.S. Peirce.*
Montreal: XYZ, 1990.

Haley, M.C. *The Semeiosis of Poetic Metaphor.* Bloomington: Indiana UP, 1988.

Langages 58 (juin 1980). *La Sémiotique de C.S. Peirce.*
Special issue.

Ransdell, J.M. *Peirce.* In *Encyclopedic Dictionary of Semiotics.* Berlin and New York: Mouton de Gruyter,
1986.

Savan, D. *An Introduction to C.S. Peirce's Full System
of Semeiotic.* Toronto: Toronto Semiotic Circle,
Monograph Series 1, 1976; rev. 1987–8.

– 'Peirce's Semiotic Theory of Emotion.' In *Proceed-
ings of the C.S. Peirce Bicentennial International
Congress,* K.L. Ketner et al., eds., 319–33. Lubbock:
Texas Tech UP, 1981.

– 'Peirce and the Trivium.' *Cruzeiro Semiotico* 8 (Jan.
1988): 50–6. Associaçao Portuguesa de Semiotica,
Porto.

Shapiro, M. *The Sense of Change: Language as History.*
Bloomington: Indiana UP, 1991.

– *The Sense of Grammar: Language as Semeiotic.*
Bloomington: Indiana UP, 1983.

– with Marianne Shapiro. *Figuration in Verbal Art.*
Princeton: Princeton UP, 1988.

Sheriff, J. *The Fate of Meaning.* Princeton: Princeton
UP, 1989.

Potebnia, Aleksander A.

(b. Ukraine, 1935–d. 1981) Linguist, literary
theorist. Aleksander Potebnia matriculated at
Kharkiv University's faculty of law in 1854.
Two years later he transferred to the faculty of
history and philology and then studied at Berlin University in 1862. Receiving his doctorate
for *Iz zapisok po russkoi grammatike* [*Notes on
Russian Grammar*] in 1874 in Kharkiv, Potebnia
was promoted to professor (1875) and in 1877
elected corresponding member of the Imperial
Academy of Sciences in Petersburg. At Kharkiv University he lectured on literary figures,
literary theory and folklore. Potebnia's significance for literary theory rests upon three of his
works: *Mysl' i iazyk* 1862 [*Thought and Language*], *Iz lektsii po teorii slovesnosti* 1894 [*Lectures on the Theory of Literature*] and *Iz zapisok
po teorii slovesnosti* 1905 [*Notes on the Theory
of Literature.*]

In the disciplines that constituted his intellectual horizon – epistemology, psychology,
philosophy of language, folklore – Potebnia
was akin to scholars of the Berlin school
centred around *Zeitschrift für Sprachwissen-
schaft und Völkerpsychologie:* Wilhelm Humbolt,
Heyman Steinthal and Herman Lotze. Like

Humbolt, Potebnia differentiated between the
autonomous existing empirical world and the
spiritual/cultural reality. Both of these entities,
he thought, exist in a synchretic and contingent bond. While the former emerges and
transforms according to its own energy and
laws, the latter is an object of man's continuous creativity. It emerges and manifests itself
through and by language. It does not precede
language, nor does it proceed from language;
rather it exists within language. Reality and
language are therefore coterminous.

Language is a cognitive energy, a continuous
process of becoming rather than a mere ready-
made instrument of cognition. It is therefore
both the means of generating ever-new knowledge about the empirical world as well as the
impediment to its conclusive apprehension.
Hence, it is not a mere acoustic construct existing at the service of thought. Language and
thought are inseparable. There is no thought
without language and no language without
thought.

According to Potebnia, the minimal unit of
the speech act is the word, defined syntacti-
cally rather than lexically. (See also *speech
act theory.) The word's structural aspects are
the external form, the content or idea, and the
internal form. The external form is inseparable
from the internal one, changing along with it
while retaining its own specificity; the content
is always abstract, hidden and difficult to
grasp; the internal form is the relationship of
the content to consciousness. It is a demonstrated appearance of our thought. The word
contains two levels of signification: the objective or closely etymological, with only one single property of the referred object, event or
occurence; and the subjective or distant, with
potentially many properties. (See *signified/
signifier/signification.) At the moment of the
word's enunciation, the close signification is its
only content. (See *énonciation/énoncé.) At the
same time, however, the close signification,
given the different sensory perception of the
speaker and the recipient, is transformed into a
multitude of referential variants. Thus, if it
were not for the 'ethnic kinship' of the close
signification, the communicative process would
be seriously impeded or even completely broken. If the close signification of the word is
obliterated and thus not recognized dialogically, the external form then becomes the sole
transmitter of signification and communication.
Out of the subjective or distant signification

results a higher objectivity of thought, namely, scholarly and scientific.

The same structural components exist in the poetic work of art as in the word: the external form, the internal form and the content or idea. As in the word, these three components are coextensive and interdependent. This means that they have no separate value; that in perception all three are determined at once rather than sequentially and that such simultaneous determination permits no radical variability in their configuration.

The external form of the poetic work, in order to be a viable component of the poetic structure, must be meaning-generating. The internal form of the poetic word is synonymous with its images. The image is either a progressively constructed collocation of words that is pregnant with explicit or implicit meanings or a transcendent configuration of them. The first resembles the algebraic ground and depends upon the combinatory system of a given syntax or on the modality of combination. The second is a non-additive whole that is intentionally created at strategic points of the *text. Usually the former aims at a realistic or mimetic creation of reality and the latter at a symbolic creation of reality. Images of both types form the leap from representation to signification. (See *mimesis.) As long as they remain constant predicates to their ever-changing subjects, they retain aesthetic valency. Should they, however, become equivalents of the intended reference, they automatically assume a didactic role. They convert the text either to referential prose or to *myth. The poetic image is a linguistic rather than a psychological category. Yet, its relative constancy does not guarantee its permanence. In time, it may, as it often does, lose its palpability and cease to elicit aesthetic responses. In this way, the poetic text becomes a mere historical artefact.

It follows that the content of the poetic work as it appears in our consciousness is not an indiscriminate computation of all of the text's semantic components but instead an intentional correlation of what is being selected, retained, transformed, and amplified by our mind. (See *intention/intentionality.)

Potebnia rendered the poetic text – namely, its being, its creation and its perception – algorithmically. Thus, he may have inadvertently impressed some of his readers and followers that it was theoretically possible to define all variants of poetic text by one all-embracing notation. His algorithm reads as follows: $X = a < A$, in which X stands for the content or idea; a for the text; and A for the writer's and reader's perception.

The reception of the poetic work is an inverted process of its creation, that is, $a < A = X$. Aesthetic reception, however, should not be understood as semantically coextensive with the text's creation. Because a is the only one of the three components involved in both processes that is constant, while X and A are variable, we should infer that a paired measure like this will vary in accordance with the value of the two variables. Should a be perceived as identical with X, the text will become strictly referential, that is prosaic or scientific; should a retain its imaginative character while at the same time mimicking X, the text will be mythological; only when a serves as a *tertium comparationis* between X and A does the text retain its poeticalness. The text as a bare signal of transmission rather than as a polysemous invocation is prosaic. Algorithmically, the three textual modalities are to be written as follows: poetry: $X = a < A$; prose and science: $X = a$; myth: $X = a (A)$.

Potebnia's theory distinguishes between two kinds of poetic forms: one constitutes the very essence of poetic language and is independent of man's creative intentionality; the other results from such an intentionality. Verbal constructs, seen from the perspective of the former, are determined by the semantic function of their internal forms or images; when seen from the perspective of the latter, they are determined by the poet's creative choice.

From among the various generic or intentional forms, Potebnia chose the fable and the proverb as demonstrative models for such complex works as the novel and such simple works as the simple poetic statement. Fable, he thought, was highly representative of the structure of poetic art in general. It consists of two parts: the first is not expressed by words, does not enter the fable directly, and hence in abstraction is easily omitted. It is the *explenandum* of the text. The second, which is usually called fable, is the explaining predicate. As the protracted explanation of ever-new existential predicaments, fable must have four characteristics: (1) it must consist of a series of actions; (2) the actions must form a definite unity; (3) the *actants* must be recognized without description or explanation; and (4) the images must refer to concrete events. (See *actant.)*

The proverb may be formed out of a condensed fable. Such a condensation might occur in one of two ways: first, the fable's two givens – the story and the generalization – are inverted, the latter retained completely and the former either condensed or abandoned altogether. Fables can also be condensed to what are generally known as sayings – allegorical images consisting of one person or one action, but never all *three.* Fables, however, are not the only genre that can be transformed into proverbs. More complex forms, such as comedy, epic, novella, and the novel also can be condensed into one syntactical unit. (See also *genre criticism.)*

In sum, the work of poetic art is a 'form of forms,' a configuration of either intentional or immanent forms. Intentional forms, inherently tied with man's progressing or regressing consciousness, specify either the 'poeticalness' or the 'prosaicness' of the work. Immanent forms, tied with historical conventions and history, as it manifests itself in language, is a resevoir of a never-ceasing creative quest, both poetic and prosaic. Language, in its perennial variation, remains polysemous and therefore multifunctional. Its two seemingly exclusive directions – poetry and prose – are actually complementary. Thus, poetry, myth and science coexist in a state of symbiosis.

This function of poetic art, by involving cognition, emotion and endeavour, is reducible to three equivalent categories: cognitive, expressive and representational. A work of poetic art does not function cognitively without also affecting two other mental faculties. This functional syncretism, however, does not preclude various ratios among the three. Consequently, a view that the work of poetic art generates only emotional catharsis, or invokes only the sense of beauty or repulsion, or arouses only a will to act, is, in Potebnia's view, explicitly reductive.

In retrospect, the significance of Potebnia's theory lies not only in how it actually defined the work of poetic art but also in how it redirected critical theory towards the issues of the text itself. Generally, then, the principal claims of Potebnia's theory are as follows: (1) language and poetic art are genetically related; (2) language and poetry have a triune structure; (3) internal form in language and images in poetry have generative power; (4) poetry's

principal function is cognition; (5) aesthetic perception is productive rather than merely reproductive; (6) poetry and prose, including scholarly and scientific texts, are complementary; (7) generic taxonomy is arbitrary and serves only heuristic purposes; (8) poetic *semiosis is predominantly ethnocentric; (9) poetic signs and their signification are asymmetrical; and (10) mythological, poetic, and scientific function are potentially present in reading, interpretation and aesthetic experiences. As a set of general principles, proposed for the purpose of explaining existing poetic texts, Potebnia's theory has a historical significance, but owing to its by and large deductive character, it retains, if only in part, epistemological cogency. (See also *sign.)*

JOHN FIZER

Primary Sources

Potebnia, A.A. *Iz lektsii po teorii slovesnosti: Basnia, poslovitsa, pogovorka.* Kharkiv: K. Scahsin, 1894.
– *Iz zapisok po teorii slovesnosti: Poeziia i proza. Tropy i figury. Myshlenie poetichneskoe i mificheskoe.* Kharkiv: M.F. Potebnia, Prilozheniia, 1905.
– *Mysl' i iazyk.* In *Estetika i poetika.* Ed. I.V. Ivan'o and A.I. Kolodnaia. Moscow: Iskusstvo, 1976.

Secondary Sources

Fizer, J. *Alexander A. Potebnja's Psycholinguistic Theory of Literature: A Metacritical Inquiry.* Cambridge: Harvard UP, 1988.
Presniakov, O.P. *A.A. Potebnia i russkoe literaturovedenie kontsa 19–nachala 20 veka.* Saratov: Izd. Saratovskogo Universiteta, 1978.
Franchuk, V. Iv. *Oleksander Opanasovych Potebnia.* Kiev: Naukova dumka, 1975.
Shklovskii, V. 'Potebnia.' In *Poetika: Sborniki po teorii poeticheskogo iazyka.* Vol. 1. Petrograd, 1919.

Poulet, Georges

(b. Belgium, 1902–) Theoretician and critic of French *literature. After receiving his doctorate from the University of Liège in 1927, Poulet taught at the University of Edinburgh (1927–51), Johns Hopkins University (1952–7), the University of Zurich (1957–9), and the University of Nice (1968–). The best known of the phenomenological critics associated with the *Geneva School, he popularized an interpretive practice based on the tenets of phenomenology. (See *phenomenological criticism.)*

445

Rather than analyse the formal structures of particular works, his criticism reconstitutes an author's distinctive subjectivity or consciousness of self and world as expressed in the entire corpus of that author's writing. (See *self/other.) Although Poulet's emphasis on author subjectivity runs counter to later structuralist interests, his work paved the way for the rise of theory in the 1970s by initiating American critics into the use of philosophy as a tool for reading and by providing those critics with a powerful alternative to the formalist doctrine of the *New Criticism. His phenomenological approach particularly influenced the early work of the two most visible American proponents of *deconstruction, *Paul de Man and *J. Hillis Miller. (See also *structuralism.)

Poulet gained prominence fairly late in his career with the publication of Etudes sur le temps humain (1949). This collection of essays examines the patterns of consciousness and the sense of selfhood expressed by French authors from the Renaissance to the present. The initial volume under the title was followed by three others: La Distance intérieure (1952), Le Point de départ (1964) and Mesure de l'instant (1968). Unlike the formalist criticism dominating Anglo-American criticism at that time, these studies reject the analysis of individual literary constructs in favour of reanimating the itinerary of an author's consciousness as it consolidates itself into a distinctive identity over time. Poulet reconstructs each author's distinctive expression of the self's relationship to the world and to itself by extrapolating from all of the author's writing – including correspondence, journals, critical essays, fragments, and literary works of various genres – consistent figures of speech, vocabulary choices and ways of emplotting human action within the world.

Rather than specifying the meaning of a particular *text, then, Poulet's method weaves citations from many texts into a narrative of the author's characteristic way of achieving a sense of self. Typically, these narratives precede from a Cartesian origin – that of the writing ego's consciousness of itself as pure consciousness – through an enumeration of the successive reassessments of self-presence which consciousness undergoes as it confronts the problem of its own duration and location in the world. The unifying *theme of temporality or lived time which dominates Etudes sur le temps humain is replaced in other studies,

such as L'Espace proustien (1963) or Les Métamorphoses du cercle (1961), by the experience of space, but Poulet's strategy remains consistent in all of his dozen or so subsequent books.

In La Conscience critique (1971), Poulet extended his phenomenological analysis to include the activity of the critic and reader of literature, interpreting the subjectivity of literary critics from Madame de Staël to *Jean Rousset. His analysis of the reading consciousness in the same volume, 'Phénoménologie de la conscience critique' (repr. 'The Phenomenology of Reading') is perhaps the most succinct introduction to the critical perspective assumed by the critics of the Geneva School. There Poulet traces the way a reader's consciousness becomes absorbed in a literary work and perceives itself to be immersed in the consciousness of another subjectivity while at the same time aware of its own identity. His analysis makes clear the difference between phenomenological criticism, which conceives of the reading experience as a means of apprehending the consciousness of another, and American *reader-response criticism, which seeks the meaning of texts in the interaction between textual structure and reader identity.

In the wake of *poststructuralism, with its devaluation of consciousness and the individual *subject, Poulet's influence waned considerably. More recent critical trends which emphasize cultural history and the study of *ideology have further reduced his prominence. But his work remains important not only as a document of the historical moment when theory began to displace the New Criticism but also as a point of entry into the problematics of subjectivity as they apply to reading and literary criticism.

WILLIAM RAY

Primary Sources

Poulet, Georges. La Conscience critique. Paris: Corti, 1971.
- La Distance intérieure. Etudes sur le temps humain 2. Paris: Plon, 1952. The Interior Distance. Trans. Elliot Coleman. Baltimore: Johns Hopkins UP, 1959.
- Entre moi et moi: Essais critiques sur la conscience de soi. Paris: Corti, 1976.
- L'Espace proustien. Paris: Gallimard, 1963. Proustian Space. Trans. Elliot Coleman. Baltimore: Johns Hopkins UP, 1977.
- Etudes sur le temps humain. Édinburgh: Edinburgh

UP, 1949. *Studies in Human Time*. Trans. Elliott Coleman. Baltimore: Johns Hopkins UP, 1956.
- *Mesure de l'instant*. Etudes sur le temps humain 4. Paris: Plon, 1968.
- *Les Métamorphoses du cercle*. Paris: Plon, 1961. *The Metamorphoses of the Circle*. Trans. Carley Dawson and Elliot Coleman. Baltimore: Johns Hopkins UP, 1966.
- 'The Phenomenology of Reading.' *NLH* 2 (1970): 123–62.
- *La Poésie éclatée: Baudelaire/Rimbaud*. Paris: PUF, 1980. *Exploding Poetry: Baudelaire/Rimbaud*. Trans. Françoise Meltzer. Chicago: U of Chicago P, 1984.
- *Le Point de départ*. Etudes sur le temps humain 3. Paris: Plon, 1964.

Secondary Sources

Alexander, Ian W. *French Literature and the Philosophy of Consciousness*. Cardiff: U of Wales P, 1984.
de Man, Paul. 'The Literary Self as Origin: The Work of Georges Poulet.' In *Blindness and Insight*. New York: Oxford UP, 1971, 79–101.
Miller, J. Hillis. 'The Literary Criticism of Georges Poulet.' *MLN* 78.5 (1963): 471–88.

Praz, Mario

(b. Italy, 1896–d. 1982) Comparatist, critic, educator, translator, scholar, and connoisseur. Mario Praz received his Dr. Juris at the University of Rome in 1918 and his D.Litt. from the University of Florence in 1920. Most of his life was spent as an educator, teaching at a number of universities but largely at the University of Rome. The recipient of honorary degrees and numerous awards, Praz has been called 'one of the last humanists,' indicating his life-long commitment to learning and to perpetuating the ideas and methods of the 'great tradition,' a view undergirding all his writings, which include autobiography, *literature, translation, and comparative studies. Much of Praz's work is dedicated to showing the intellectual and artistic linkages between the 17th and 20th centuries.

Machiavelli and the Elizabethans (1928) is a reception study of Machiavelli's contribution to modern theories of state. Originally a lecture, this short work emphasizes the negative view which Machiavelli's contemporaries had of him and the sinister and amoral Italian Gothic themes thought to have evolved from his influence. (See *theme.) Praz argues that Machiavelli's contemporaries saw in his work

what was already in themselves, never comprehending the political pragmatism of *The Discourse* and *The Prince*.

The Romantic Agony (1933), Praz's most important critical work, is a study of the historical evolution of one strain of romanticism stemming from de Sade, Poe, Baudelaire, Keats, and others, accentuating degeneration and the pathology of romantic ideas, particularly their sexual manifestations. The lasting influence of this point of view is underlined by Praz who argues that 'the sexual idiosyncracies ... offer ... a distorted image of characteristics common to all mankind.'

A comprehensive history of the literature of emblems and devices, *Studies in 17th Century Imagery* (1939) is an analysis of the development of love conceits since the Alexandrian age which also illuminates the history of iconography and religious feeling during the 17th century. 'The connection of emblem and device with epigram and conceit ... are considered here as manifestations of the same spirit which promoted epigrams and conceits.'

Similar synthetic tendencies of reading one art form in the light of another are apparent in *The Hero in Eclipse in Victorian Fiction* (1956), a comparative study of genre painting and its pervasive influence on the fiction of the 18th and 19th centuries. Praz argues that the 'decay of sacred art as the result of Protestantism' generated the portrait, the interior scene and genre painting, as well as generally initiating the birth of realism, which carried with it an increasing sense of disillusionment, decay and artlessness, particularly since nobility of subject-matter no longer seemed necessary.

Although it is similar to his earlier book on Machiavelli, *The Flaming Heart: Essays on Crashaw, Machiavelli, and Other Studies in the Relations Between Italian and English Literature From Chaucer to T.S. Eliot* (1958) is a more comprehensive reception study. Praz shows that the extensive Italian influence on English literature in the 16th century dissipated by the 18th century but for some Gothic images and ideas derived from Italian models. Praz concludes that 'an author is popular in so far as he lends himself to be interpreted in the terms of current vogue or a prevalent tendency of the age.'

Although they have no direct connection with literary criticism and theory, the three works *An Illustrated History of Furnishings, From the Renaissance to the 2oth Century*

(1964), his memoir *The House of Life* (1964), and *Conversation Pieces: A Survey of the Informal Group Portrait in Europe and America* (1971) show the intimate connection between Praz's idea that the good life is that of the man of culture, the connoisseur and aesthete whose pleasures derive from the diversity of artistic creation and from his ability to comprehend and recognize that diversity and its commensurate beauty and affirmation.

In one of his last major works, *Mnemosyne: The Parallel Between Literature and the Visual Arts* (1970), Praz suggests that the greatness of a work of art is reflected in a kind of 'aesthetic memory' of sensations of consciousness. He also maintains that there is an abiding structural affinity between arts and letters until the 18th century, largely because of architectural models. After the 19th century architecture ceases to be the structural foundation of the arts, hence comparisons and contrasts between modern writing and painting are not obvious or valid because the old norms and harmonies no longer exist.

Praz has been criticized for his greatest strength – his synthetic ability to discover common themes and parallel ideas and influences in historical periods, in the arts themselves and in images and icons of common usage as they have appeared since the 17th century. This ability to synthesize important concepts is the result of Praz's enormous range of knowledge, his love of the arts and his dedication to scholarship and the pleasures of connoisseurship. Yet in his memoir, *The House of Life,* Praz seems to anticipate the antihumanist turn of critical fashion when he wistfully views himself as already outmoded: 'I see myself as having myself become an object and an image, a museum piece among museum pieces, already detached and remote, and that, like Adam in the graffito on the marble floor of the church of San Domenico in Siena, I have looked at myself in a convex mirror, and have seen myself as no bigger than a handful of dust.'

REED MERRILL

Primary Sources

Praz, Mario. *Conversation Pieces: A Survey of the Informal Group Portrait in Europe and America.* College Park, Penn.: Pennsylvania State P, 1971.
– *The Flaming Heart: Essays on Crashaw, Machiavelli and Other Studies in the Relations Between Italian and English Literature from Chaucer to T.S. Eliot.* Garden City, NY: Doubleday, 1958. Repr. W.W. Norton, 1973.
– *The Hero in Eclipse in Victorian Fiction.* Trans. Angus Davidson. London: Oxford UP, 1956.
– *The House of Life.* Trans. Angus Davidson. New York: Oxford UP, 1964.
– *An Illustrated History of Furnishings, From the Renaissance to the 20th Century.* Trans. William Weaver. New York: Braziller, 1964. English version: *An Illustrated History of Interior Decorating from Pompei to Art Nouveau.* Trans. William Weaver. London: Thames and Hudson, 1964.
– *Machiavelli and the Elizabethans.* London: Folcroft, 1928. Repr. 1970.
– *Mnemosyne: The Parallel Between Literature and the Visual Arts.* Princeton: Princeton UP, 1970.
– *On Neoclassicism.* Trans. Angus Davidson. Evanston, Ill.: Northwestern UP, 1969.
– *La Poesia metafisica inglese del seicento, John Donne.* Rome: Edizioni Italiane, 1946.
– *Richard Crashaw.* Rome: Morcelliana, 1946.
– *The Romantic Agony.* Trans. Angus Davidson. New York: Oxford UP, 1933; 2nd. ed., 1951.
– *Studies in 17th Century Imagery.* London: Warburg Institute, 1939; 2nd ed., expanded, Rome: Edizioni di Storia e Letteratura, 1964.

Secondary Sources

Gabrieli, Vittorio, ed. *Friendship's Garland: Essays Presented to Mario Praz on His 70th Birthday.* Rome: Edizioni di Storia e Letteratura, 1966.

Prince, Gerald

(b. Egypt, 1942–) Literary theorist. In 1968, Gerald Prince obtained his Ph.D. in French *literature at Brown University. He became a member of the Department of Romance Languages at the University of Pennsylvania in 1967 and was promoted to full professor in 1981. While he has written on 20th-century French literature, most of his work is devoted to literary theory, especially to *narratology.

One of his early books, *A Grammar of Stories* (1973), directly inspired by the first versions of *Noam Chomsky's generative grammar, presents a grammar of narrative with the objective of developing an instrument to simplify the structural analysis of narrative. Prince's proposed grammar consists essentially of three components: the stative event, which expresses a state; the action event, expressing an action; and conjunctive features that encompass all conjunctive elements. The kernel narrative consists of an active event framed by two stative events, all of these united by three conjunctive features. The first feature links the first component to the second on the temporal axis, and the other two connect the second component to the third on the causal and temporal axes. For instance, 'He was happy, then he met a woman, then, as a result, he was unhappy' is a basic structure from which several types of narrative can be elaborated.

To be effective, a narrative grammar must contain two intrinsic qualities: simplicity of use and applicability to all forms of narrative. Prince's grammar possesses neither characteristic, since it is both unwieldy and excludes certain forms of narrative such as that structured by association. Still, *A Grammar of Stories* is rich in insight and touches on themes that the author explores more fully in his later work. (See *theme.)

Narratology: The Form and Functioning of Narrative (1982) presents a synthesis of acquired understanding of narratology, referring to work by other researchers in the field, notably *Roland Barthes, *Gérard Genette, *Tzvetan Todorov, *Wayne Booth, Seymour Chatman, and *Jonathan Culler. Prince's contribution is found in his articulation and development of the concept of *narratee and in his discussion of the functions of metanarrative signs. (See *sign.) Prince shows how the metanarrative sign can take on a great many functions at the level of several narrative codes. (See *code, *narrative code.) In the concluding chapter, inspired by Barthes, Chatman and William Labov, Prince attempts to identify the features needed to ensure a high degree of narrativity in a *text. According to Prince, a narrative is good (from a narrative standpoint) only if the narrated event is individualized, concrete and narrated with assurance. Further, 'good narrative' should attempt to represent a whole; otherwise it becomes a simple concatenation of unrelated events. In addition, all narration must be oriented, that is, the reader must feel an organizing principle at work in the text, awakening the desire to continue reading to the end. Finally, a narrative must have a higher objective than the simple telling of a story. (See *story/plot.) By determining the characteristic elements of narration – the presence of which nevertheless does not guarantee work of high quality – we encourage a better understanding of the functioning of nar-

rative in general and of the meaning of the narrative moment.

The concern for synthesis evident in *Narratology* can also be seen in Prince's next work and most important achievement, *A Dictionary of Narratology* (1987). Intended mainly for beginners, it constitutes an excellent introduction to the field of narratology. However, his major contribution to narrative theory as such remains his development of the concept of the narratee in 'Introduction à l'étude du narrataire' (1973), which inspired a number of scholars who studied the means by which the reader's presence is implied or written in the text. (See *implied reader.)

FRANÇOIS GALLAYS

Primary Sources

Prince, G. *A Dictionary of Narratology*. Lincoln and London: U of Nebraska P, 1987.
– *A Grammar of Stories*. The Hague and Paris: Mouton, 1973.
– 'Introduction à l'étude du narrataire.' *Poétique* 14 (1973): 178–96. 'Introduction to the Study of the Narratee.' In *Essentials of the Theory of Fiction*. Ed. Michael J. Hoffman and Patrick D. Murphy. Durham and London: Duke UP, 1988, 313–34.
– *Narratology: The Form and Functioning of Narrative*. Berlin/New York/Amsterdam: Mouton Publishers, 1982.

Secondary Sources

Brémond, Claude. *Logique du récit*. Paris: Seuil, 1973.
Chambers, Ross. *Story and Situation: Narrative Seduction and The Power of Fiction*. Minneapolis: U of Minnesota P, 1984.
Chatman, Seymour. *Story and Discourse: Narrative Structure in Fiction and Film*. Albany, NY: Cornell UP, 1978.
Cohn, Dorritt. *Transparent Minds: Narrative Modes for Presenting Consciousness in Fiction*. Princeton, NJ: Princeton UP, 1978.
Hamburger, Kate. *The Logic of Literature*. Bloomington: Indiana UP, 1975.
Labov, William. *Language in the Inner City*. Philadelphia: U of Philadelphia P, 1972.

Propp, Vladimir Iakovlevich

(b. Russia 1895–d. 1970) Russian formalist scholar. Born in St. Petersburg to a family of German extraction, Propp studied Russian and German philology from 1913 to 1918 at the

University of St. Petersburg. In the 1920s he worked as a teacher in a secondary school. From 1932 until his death he was a professor at Leningrad University, chairing the Department of Folklore until it was incorporated into the Department of Russian Literature.

As an outstanding folklorist, Propp contributed to the study of the theory and history of Russian folklore. His folkloristic studies concentrated on the fairy tale, heroic epic poetry and historical semantics. Propp's most important contribution to the theory of *literature was his pioneering study of the structural laws of the folktale, *Morfologiia skazki [Morphology of the Folktale* 1928; English trans. 1958]. Propp believed that all folktales are structurally identical if we approach them from the point of view of their composition rather than their characters. What is important in the structure is not the characters and their identities but the actions they perform. He identifed these as 'functions' and defined them from the standpoint of their significance for the course of the action. He distinguished 31 functions that appear in the structure of the folktale and emphasized that they are constant, regardless of how and by whom they are carried out. In addition Propp also formulated some important rules about their sequence. An individual tale, he claimed, can use all the functions or it can dispense with some of them, but the sequence of functions would remain the same. The absence of certain functions, he emphasized, would not interfere with the order of appearance of the others since the sequence of functions is constant.

In 'Transformatsiia volshebnykh skazok' ['Fairy Tale Transformations' 1928; English trans. 1971], he investigated the external circumstances that modify the genre. He argued that we would not grasp the evolution of the genre unless we considered comparative material from the environment of the fairy tale. He singled out two areas of special significance to the transformations of the fairy tale – religion and life in general – and formulated several principles that characterize the interrelations between them: (1) if the same form occurs in both a religious monument and in a fairy tale, the religious form is primary; (2) if the same element has two variants, one of which derives from religious forms and the other from daily life, the religious formation is primary and the one drawn from daily life is secondary; (3) a fantastic element in a fairy tale component is older than its rational treatment; (4) a heroic treatment of a fairy tale is older than a humorous treatment; (5) a form used logically is older than a form used nonsensically; (6) an international form is older than a national one.

Propp's morphological and historical investigations of the structural laws of the folktale had important implications for the theory of literature. Following the model of *Iurii Tynianov, Propp put forward the notion of a literary structure in which all elements are interconnected and interdependent. He introduced the concept of 'function,' defining the role of a narrative element from the point of view of its significance for the course of the action. He combined the synchronic and diachronic approaches by showing the role of the invariant functions at any given point in time, and by analysing the transformations that occur in the historical process.

More than any other Russian formalist, Propp influenced the development of French *structuralism, stimulating responses from *Claude Lévi-Strauss, *Algirdas Greimas, *Claude Bremond, and *Tzvetan Todorov. He also played an important role in the emergence of Russian semiotics, influencing the works of E.M. Meletskii, S.D. Serebrianyi, I.I. Revzin, and others. (See Russian *formalism, *semiotics.)

NINA KOLESNIKOFF

Primary Sources

Propp, V.I. *Morfologiia skazki.* Leningrad: Akademia, 1928. *Morphology of the Folktale.* Bloomington: Indiana UP, 1958.
– *Theory and History of Folklore.* Minneapolis: U of Minnesota P, 1984.
– 'Transformatsiia volshebnykh skazok.' *Poetika: Vremennik otdela slovesnykh iskusstv* 4. Leningrad: Akademia, 1928, 70–89. 'Fairy Tale Transformations.' In *Readings in Russian Poetics: Formalist and Structuralist Views.* Ed. L. Matejka and K. Pomorska. Cambridge, Mass.: MIT P, 1971, 94–116.

Secondary Sources

Bremond, C. *Logique du récit.* Paris: Seuil, 1973.
Greimas, A.J. 'A la recherche des modèles de transformation.' In *Sémantique structurale.* Paris: Larousse, 1966.
Lévi-Strauss, C. 'La Structure et la forme. Réflexions sur un ouvrage de Vladimir Propp.' In *Anthropologie structurale deux.* Paris: Plon, 1973.

Maranda, P., ed. *Soviet Structural Folkloristics*. The Hague: Mouton, 1974.

Shukman, A. 'The Legacy of Propp.' *Essays in Poetics* 1.2 (1976): 82–94.

Todorov, T. 'Les Transformations narratives.' In *Poétique de la Prose*. Paris: Seuil, 1971.

Richards, I(vor) A(rmstrong)

(b. England, 1893–d. 1979) Literary critic and theorist. The English School at the University of Cambridge was established in 1917; I.A. Richards was one of its first teachers. A philosopher by academic training, Richards imposed a theoretical rigour and logical exactitude on the study of English *literature that was unusual for that historical moment. Immersed in psychology, semantics and aesthetics, he tried to give the emerging discipline of literary criticism a scientific grounding. In 1929 Richards left Cambridge for Peking. After spending several years abroad, he eventually settled at Harvard in 1939. His influence on Anglo-American criticism derives mainly from his early work (1922–38), the latter part of his career being devoted to the propagation of Basic English – a prospective universal language that is built on 850 words – and to language-training and pedagogy in general. (See *theory und pedagogy.)

The cornerstone of Richards' theory of literature is the distinction between the referential and emotive uses of language, first developed as early as 1923 with C.K. Ogden *(The Meaning of Meaning* 150). In *Poetries and Sciences,* Richards makes this distinction more precise by using the term 'pseudo-statement' to define an utterance in which the evocative function is dominant and the term 'statement' to define an utterance in which the symbolic function is dominant: a pseudo-statement is justified entirely by its effect in releasing or organizing our impulses and attitudes ... A statement, on the other hand, is justified by its truth, that is its correspondence, in a highly technical sense, with the fact to which it points' *(Poetries and Sciences* 60). Hence an utterance 'may be used for the sake of the *reference,* true or false, which it causes. This is the *scientific* use of language. But it may also be used for the sake of the effects in emotion and attitude produced by the reference it occasions. This is the *emotive* use of language' *(Principles of Literary Criticism* 268). (See *reference/referent.)

Science, therefore, yields a body of undistorted references whose criteria for legitimacy are empirical verifiability and correspondence with objective reality, whereas literature yields a body of possibly distorted references whose criteria for legitimacy are coherence, verisimilitude and sincerity. As science organizes the external realm of reference, so poetry organizes the internal realm of impulse and attitude.

Richards defines attitudes as 'imaginal or incipient activities or tendencies to actions' *(Principles of Literary Criticism* 112). The function of poetry is to integrate these attitudes and impulses, converting 'a welter of responses' into a 'systematized complex response' *(Principles of Literary Criticism* 183) and thus creating in the reader 'a balanced poise, stable through its power of inclusion, not through the force of its exclusions' *(Principles of Literary Criticism* 248). This equilibrium of synaesthesis is the vibrant poise of a completely coordinated individual whose harmonized attitudes are 'imaginal' rather than 'stimulative.' Thus poetry has a compensatory or therapeutic function. It is a momentary stay against the chaos and confusion of 20th-century life, a fictive substitute for a religious belief that has been challenged by science. Like his predecessor Matthew Arnold and his contemporary Wallace Stevens, Richards believes that poetry is a source not only of value and significance but also of harmony and consolation.

Richards' qualitative distinction between referential and emotive language implies a rejection of the 'Proper Meaning Superstition' – 'the common belief ... that a word has a meaning of its own (ideally, only one) independent of and controlling its use and the purpose for which it should be uttered' *(The Philosophy of Rhetoric* 11). Richards contends that such a view is committed to the mistaken proposition that meaning is context-neutral. He proposes as an alternative the context theorem of meaning. 'Freud has taught us that a dream may mean a dozen different things; he has persuaded us that some symbols are, as he says, "over-determined" and mean many different selections from among their causes. This theorem goes further, and regards all discourse – outside the technicalities of science – as over-determined, as having multiplicity of meaning' *(The Philosophy of Rhetoric* 38–9). (See *Freud, *overdetermination, *discourse.) Richards' theorem emphasizes 'the interinanimation of words' in a *text, claiming that 'the senses of an author's words are ... are resultants which we arrive at only through the interplay of the interpretative possibilities of the whole utterance' *(The Philosophy of Rhetoric* 55). The reader must attempt to decipher the 'systematic ambiguity' *(The Philosophy of Rhetoric* 73) of the text.

Richards' dichotomous view of linguistic functions and his concomitant view of literary language as inherently ambiguous influenced not only his students (the most famous of whom were *William Empson and *F.R. Leavis) but also *New Criticism, the formalist school of criticism that reigned supreme in the U.S.A. from the 1940s to the 1970s. New Criticism is grounded in Richards' distinction between scientific and literary language as well as in his valorization of ambiguity, a non-pejorative term for the capacity of language to sustain multiple meanings. The notion that ambiguity is the root condition of all literary discourse as well as the key to its richness, complexity and concentration became an integral aspect of the New Critical view that *irony, *paradox and tension are definitive aspects of the work of art. This movement also owes to Richards the idea that the analysis and assessment of a work of art can take place only with reference to certain intrinsic criteria – form, coherence, poise, organic unity (the interdependence of parts and whole), and so forth. Extrinsic criteria, such as facts that might be gleaned from biography and history, are deemed to be inadmissible. The aesthetic object is to be seen as autonomous and self-contained. Though Richards was more in tune with the psychology of reader response than were his New Critical counterparts (they in fact derisively labelled such audience-oriented concerns the affective fallacy), their whole process of practical criticism – the close reading of individual texts, especially poems, with particular attention to intrinsic verbal texture and structure – derives from Richards' eponymous book, *Practical Criticism*. (See also *reader-response criticism.)

In *Practical Criticism* Richards analyses the responses of his students to poems unfamiliar to them in order to point out ten characteristic errors in understanding, interpretation and evaluation: (1) failure to make out the plain sense of a poem, not to mention its feeling, tone and intention; (2) failure to grasp the sound and rhythm of a poem; (3) failure to

grasp the function of imagery; (4) indulgence in mnemonic irrelevances, personal associations that have nothing to do with the words on the page; (5) stereotyped and stock responses; (6) sentimentality; (7) inhibition; (8) doctrinal adhesions, belief-systems that the reader improperly uses to determine the truth and value of poetic utterances; (9) technical presuppositions such as the view that poetry is not poetry if it neither rhymes nor has a regular meter; and (10) general critical preconceptions, prior demands made upon poetry as a result of theories – conscious or unconscious – about its nature and value. By inductively examining his students' responses to poems that ranged from John Donne's *Holy Sonnets* to the Reverend G.A.Studdert Kennedy's *More Rough Rhymes of a Padre*, Richards demonstrates that the undergraduate élite of Cambridge can go badly wrong in their understanding, interpretation and evaluation of poems they have never seen before. What inferences one draws from his study are open to debate, but Richards concludes that defective pedagogy is responsible for the bizarre misreadings that even intelligent students are capable of producing. What is not open to debate is the fact that Richards' method of practical criticism has been enormously influential and that it is still the method of teaching poetry to undergraduate students, the hegemony of contemporary literary theory notwithstanding.

GREIG HENDERSON

Primary Sources

Richards, I.A. *Beyond*. New York: Harcourt Brace Jovanovich, 1974.
– *Coleridge on Imagination*. London: Kegan Paul, Trench, Trubner, 1934.
– *Complementarities: Uncollected Essays*. Ed. John Paul Russo. Cambridge, Mass.: Harvard UP, 1976.
– *How to Read a Page: A Course in Efficient Reading, with an Introduction to One Hundred Great Words*. New York: Norton, 1942.
– *Interpretation in Teaching*. New York: Harcourt, Brace, 1938.
– *Mencius on the Mind: Experiments in Multiple Definition*. London: Kegan Paul, Trench, Trubner, 1932.
– *The Philosophy of Rhetoric*. New York: Oxford UP, 1965.
– *Practical Criticism: A Study of Literary Judgment*. London: Kegan Paul, Trench, Trubner, 1929.
– *Principles of Literary Criticism*. London: Kegan Paul, Trench, Trubner, 1924.

- *Science and Poetry*. London: Kegan Paul, Trench, Trubner, 1926. 2nd ed., 1935. 3rd ed., *Poetries and Sciences, with a Reorientation and Notes*. New York: Norton, 1970.
- *Speculative Instruments*. Chicago: U of Chicago P, 1955.
- and C.K. Ogden. *The Meaning of Meaning: A Study of the Influence of Language upon Thought and of the Science of Symbolism*. London: Kegan Paul, Trench, Trubner, 1923.
- C.K. Ogden and James Wood. *The Foundations of Aesthetics*. London: Allen and Unwin, 1922.

Secondary Sources

Brower, Reuben, Helen Vendler, and John Hollander, eds. *I.A. Richards: Essays in His Honor*. New York: Oxford UP, 1973.

Empson, William. *The Structure of Complex Words*. London: Chatto and Windus, 1951.

Fekete, John. *The Critical Twilight: Explorations in the Ideology of Anglo-American Literary Theory from Eliot to McLuhan*. London: Routledge and Kegan Paul, 1977.

Fish, Stanley. *Is There a Text in This Class?* Cambridge, Mass.: Harvard UP, 1980.

Graff, Gerald. *Poetic Statement and Critical Dogma*. 2nd. ed. Chicago: U of Chicago P, 1980.

Hotoph, W.H.N. *Language, Thought and Comprehension: A Case Study of the Writings of I.A. Richards*. London: Routledge and Kegan Paul, 1965.

Hyman, Stanley Edgar. *The Armed Vision: A Study of the Methods of Modern Criticism*. New York: Knopf, 1948.

Karnani, Chetan. *Criticism, Aesthetics, and Psychology: A Study of the Writings of I.A. Richards*. New Delhi: Arnold-Heinemann, 1977.

Krieger, Murray. *The New Apologists for Poetry*. Minneapolis: U of Minnesota P, 1956.

Needham, John. *'The Completest Mode': I.A. Richards and the Continuity of English Criticism*. Edinburgh: Edinburgh UP, 1982.

Ransom, John Crowe. *The New Criticism*. Norfolk: New Directions, 1941.

Russo, John Paul. *I.A. Richards: His Life and Work*. Baltimore: Johns Hopkins UP, 1989.

Schiller, Jerome P. *I.A. Richards' Theory of Literature*. New Haven: Yale UP, 1969.

Ricoeur, Paul

(b. France, 1913–) Philosopher and Christian activist. Paul Ricoeur's range of interests is as remarkable as the suggestiveness of his contributions to whichever debate he enters. Ricoeur, whose strongest institutional links are to the universities of Paris and Chicago, is well known for his contributions to philosophical anthropology, Freudian psychoanalysis, ethics, theology, phenomenology, *hermeneutics, and literary theory. His political and social writings are less well known than they deserve to be, but this may change with the changing intellectual climate, the recent publication of a number of his lectures on Marx, *Althusser and Weber, and the growth of interest in connections between historicity and human agency. (See *psychoanalytic theory, *phenomenological criticism.)

In his early volumes devoted to *The Philosophy of the Will* (1950–60), Ricoeur came to recognize with increasing force that the need for a 'poetics of the will' would require a major investigation of the role of language in the expression and recovery of meaning. It is this project, this poetics, which has taken up much of the remainder of his career and has made him an important figure in literary theory. Ricoeur's background in the existentialism of Gabriel Marcel and the phenomenology of *Edmund Husserl might have marooned him in a disciplinary backwater, vainly endeavouring to accommodate the claims of rigour and mystery, intentionality and divinity. (See *intention/intentionality.) However, his study of the symbolism of evil (as stain, sin, guilt) prepared him for a linguistic turn to symbol, metaphor, *text, and narrative, a shift in emphasis from the rigours of phenomenological description to a hermeneutic phenomenology. (See *metonymy/metaphor.) If, as hermeneutics traditionally affirms, understanding precedes explanation, how can those distinct activities performed in that sequence be used to connect semantic innovation with a more inclusive *semiosis where knowing and communicating, sense but also reference, are both possible and intelligible?

Well versed in the theories of reflexivity enunciated by Descartes, Husserl and *Heidegger, and yet still affirmative in his emphasis on the productive rather than the partial nature of signifying systems, Ricoeur proceeds to consider semantic innovation first on the level of the figure, rewriting Aristotle's *Poetics* in *The Rule of Metaphor* (1978), perhaps his most difficult yet rewarding book. This work consists of eight 'studies,' patient and generous engagements with some of the most influential ancient and modern work on linguistic meaning. Ricoeur distinguishes between a semantics of the word and a semantics of the sentence, showing how 20th-century emphases on the latter 'cannot but assign the phenomena of meaning-change to the history of word usage' (*Rule* 5). French *structuralism shares with Saussurean linguistics a valid but (from the standpoint of a poetics of the will) insufficiently purposive theory of meaning, despite its recognition of the primacy of the word in the process of semantic innovation. Ricoeur feels the need to move from the semantic to the hermeneutic level, shifting his focus from the sentence both back to the word and forward to discourse. (See *Ferdinand de Saussure.)

Metaphor can be situated in the scene of interpretation, where the fact of its contributing to both sense and reference justifies a renewed claim for *literature as heuristic, a mode of learning reality. Ricoeur does not argue that metaphor affords the sole access to reality, or that hermeneutics offers the only means of accounting for figuration. However, Aristotle was shrewder than most of his successors for esteeming metaphor as highly as he did and for reasons which Ricoeur painstakingly reconstructs. Metaphor is crucial because it originates in the 'tension' between the existential and relational functions of the verb *to be* (248); it rules a definable and valuable domain, where particular forms of *discourse variously encourage us to experience this figure not simply or predominantly as 'aberrant attribution' (*Rule* 21) or 'ontological *vehemence*' (249) but as the appropriate and inevitable dynamism of meaning (Aristotle's *epiphora*).

The dynamism of metaphorical meaning is for Ricoeur not a flight from identity but its necessary reconstitution in relation to that textual identity which moves 'between the Charybdis of logical identity and the Scylla of the identity of identity and difference' ('The Text' 175). The text is the product of invention (both discovery and creation [*Rule* 306]) for its author and for its readers, and this process is distinguished by a 'dialectical structure' (*Interpretation Theory* 72) in both instances. The text comes into being as written signs whose materiality marks in an especially graphic way the 'exteriorization of discourse' (43); however, the text thus distanced from its author can be appropriated by the reader through a productive dialectic between otherness and ownness, distanciation and appropriation. (See *sign.)

In his *Lectures on Ideology and Utopia*, Ricoeur clarifies the relation between his dynamic, dialectical hermeneutics and theories of meaning and action promoted by Marx, Weber, Mannheim, and others. The early Marx, up to and including *The German Ideology*, is interpreted as moving from consciousness to *praxis in a way that anticipates Ricoeur's own itinerary. However, Ricoeur is not willing to follow Marx in limiting the role of representation to ideological distortion in the scene of praxis; nor can he accept Marx's reductive appeal to 'the language of real life.' Linguistic representation, whether considered as rhetoric or *ideology, helps constitute praxis and must therefore be understood as part of rather than apart from (and opposed to) what really happens.

This does not mean that Ricoeur has joined the camp of (to use his own designation) 'modern pre-Socratics' like *Derrida or antihumanist Marxists like Althusser. There is no withdrawal of interest from the living individual and the poetics of the human will. The problematic mediation of the actual creates a need for articulation of the potential (utopia), and the dynamic transformation that distinguishes metaphor on the level of the figure is hence replayed on the level of discourse as a dialectic between ideology and utopia. What ensues is not the cynicism or quietism that too readily attends the deconstructionist logic of the supplement but rather a sense of possibility and purpose authorized by a poetics of the complement. (See *deconstruction, *supplementarity.) Ideology confers identity and wholeness on that which is merely a prefiguration of those attributes; utopia entails a transfiguration of reality whereby what has been prefigured comes to pass. In these lectures ideology is no longer the other of science, subject to a 'hermeneutics of suspicion' in the interpretative tradition of Marx, *Nietzsche and *Freud (*Freud and Philosophy* 35), but a term in the pair ideology/utopia which illuminates 'the unsolved general question of imagination as a philosophical problem' (*Ideology and Utopia* 1).

In the three volumes of *Time and Narrative* Ricoeur completes the project begun in *The Rule of Metaphor*. He had concluded the earlier work by insisting on the links between temporality and narrativity, invention and distanciation, while examining the philosophical grounds of his own arguments. His points of departure in the trilogy are Augustine (Book XI of the *Confessions*) and Aristotle's *Poetics* once again. The notion of *aporia so prominent in deconstructionist discourse is freshly inflected as part of a characteristic move from mise-en-abîme to mise-en-intrigue, from serial *indeterminacy to sequence and story. (See *story/plot.) With a systematic austerity worthy of Althusser, Ricoeur distinguishes three kinds of imitation as temporal functions: prefiguration (past; the order of action), configuration (current; the order of narrative), and refiguration (future; the order of life).

The power of this model is made clear through a review of the treatment of time in analytical philosophy, and an assessment of modern theories of historiography. Ricoeur recognizes the tendency to think of fiction as 'owning' narative while history 'owns' reference, but he resists such claims to exclusive title by showing how rhetoric and narrative feature in even the most sober attempts to reconstruct rather than redescribe reality. Aligning the imagination with continuity rather than causality, Ricoeur reaffirms that that which is narratable is always already symbolically mediated, and those mediations are challengingly exemplified in fiction. He thus concentrates in part 3 on 'The Configuration of Time in Fictional Narrative,' endeavouring to 'characterize the nature of the narrative function without giving in to any sort of essentialism' (2: 4). (See *essentialism.) The only 'transcendence' allowable is that which moves from the work (in whatever medium the fiction is made) to the world it projects outside itself, and thence to the 'life-world of the reader' (2: 160). He shows himself to be an accomplished reader of classics by *Woolf, Mann and Proust, before returning to metaphor (2: 148). The 'novel about time ... preserves, in my opinion, an indelible privilege ... [as] the 'silent sister' of the epic of death and the tragedy of culture' (2: 117), Ricoeur says, thus confirming his commitment to a generously inclusive and engaged poetics.

The fourth and concluding part of Time and Narrative begins with an elaboration of the view (derived from Augustine) that 'there has never been a phenomenology of temporality free of every aporia, and that in principle there can never be one' (3: 3). The return to Augustine (and to Husserl and Heidegger) is a return to the 'phenomenology of time-consciousnesss' and the risky business of philosophy which helps radicalize the activities of 'historiography and narratology.' An aporetics of temporality

squares off against a poetics of historical and fictional narrative in order to show how Ricoeur's linguistic turn has maintained its 'relatedness to the real' (3: 5). He has been motivated by a discursive necessity rather than an aestheticist or otherwise escapist impulse. To analyse temporality is to multiply aporias, while to configure it in narrative is to claim aporia for dénouement.

However, Ricoeur is not intent on denying 'the ultimate unrepresentability of time' (3: 243), but only on establishing the opportunities as well as the limitations deriving from that fact. He readily admits that there is no compelling reason for resorting to narrative forms as antidotes to indeterminacy, and his final caveat appropriately blends will and humility while looking forward to the human subject of Soi-même comme un autre: 'It ought not to be said that our eulogy to narrative unthinkingly has given life again to the claims of the constituting subject to master all meaning' (3: 274; emphasis added).

Throughout his life, from his internment as a prisoner of war to his installation in high academic office, Paul Ricoeur has remained faithful to a credo that appears to have room for us all – if on exacting conditions, yet without prejudice: 'Beyond every possible suspicion, we must have confidence in the powerful institution of language. This is a wager that brings its own justification' (Time and Narrative 2: 22).

LEN FINDLAY

Primary Sources

Ricoeur, Paul. *The Conflict of Interpretations: Essays in Hermeneutics.* Trans. and intro. Don Ihde. Evanston, Ill.: Northwestern UP, 1974.
– *Fallible Man.* Trans. C. Kelbley. Chicago: Henry Regnery, 1965.
– *Freedom and Nature: The Voluntary and the Involuntary.* Trans. E.V. Kohak. Evanston, Ill.: Northwestern UP, 1966.
– *Freud and Philosophy: An Essay on Interpretation.* Trans. D. Savage. New Haven: Yale UP, 1970.
– *From Text to Action: Essays in Hermeneutics, II.* Trans. Kathleen Blamey and John B. Thompson. Evanston, Ill.: Northwestern UP,1991.
– *Hermeneutics and the Human Sciences: Essays on Language, Action and Interpretation.* Ed. and trans. John B. Thompson. Cambridge: Cambridge UP, 1981.
– *History and Truth.* Trans. and intro. C. Kelbley. Chicago: Chicago UP, 1965.

- *Husserl: An Analysis of His Phenomenology.* Evanston, Ill.: Northwestern UP, 1967.
- *Interpretation Theory: Discourse and the Surplus of Meaning.* Fort Worth: Texas Christian UP, 1976.
- *Lectures on Ideology and Utopia.* Ed. George H. Taylor. New York: Columbia UP, 1986.
- *Political and Social Essays.* Ed. D. Stewart and J. Bien. Trans. D. Siewert et al. Athens: Ohio UP, 1974.
- *The Reality of the Historical Past.* Milwaukee: Marquette UP, 1984.
- *A Ricoeur Reader: Reflection and Imagination.* Ed. Mario J. Valdés. Toronto and Buffalo: U of Toronto P, 1991.
- *The Rule of Metaphor: Multi-disciplinary Studies of the Creation of Meaning in Language.* Trans. Robert Czerny with Kathleen McLaughlin and John Costello, SJ. London: Routledge and Kegan Paul, 1978; Cambridge UP, 1981.
- *Soi-même comme un autre.* Paris: Seuil, 1990.
- *The Symbolism of Evil.* Trans. E. Buchanan. Boston: Beacon P, 1969.
- 'The Text as Dynamic Identity.' In *The Identity of the Literary Text.* Ed. Mario J. Valdés and Owen Miller. Toronto: U of Toronto P, 1985, 175–86.
- *Time and Narrative.* Trans. Kathleen McLaughlin Blamey and David Pellauer. 3 vols. Chicago: Chicago UP, 1984–8.

Secondary Sources

Carr, David. *Time, Narrative, and History.* Bloomington: Indiana UP, 1986.

Ihde, Don. *Hermeneutic Phenomenology: The Philosophy of Paul Ricoeur.* Evanston, Ill.: Northwestern UP, 1971.

Kemp, T. Peter, and David M. Rasmussen, eds. *The Narrative Path: The Later Works of Paul Ricoeur.* Cambridge, Mass.: MIT P, 1989.

Klemm, David E. *The Hermeneutical Theory of Paul Ricoeur: A Constructive Analysis.* Lewisburg, Pa.: Bucknell UP, 1983.

Reagan, Charles E., ed. *Studies in the Philosophy of Paul Ricoeur.* Athens: Ohio UP, 1979.

Thompson, John B. *Critical Hermeneutics: A Study in the Thought of Paul Ricoeur and Jürgen Habermas.* Cambridge: Cambridge UP, 1981.

University of Ottawa Quarterly 55.4 (Oct.–Dec., 1985). *A la recherche du sens/In search of meaning.* A special issue on Ricoeur.

Valdés, Mario J. Introduction. *A Ricoeur Reader: Reflection and Imagination.* Toronto and Buffalo: U of Toronto P, 1991, 3–40.

Riffaterre, Michael

(b. France, 1924–) Literary theorist. After studies at the University of Lyons and the University of Paris in the 1940s, Riffaterre emigrated to the U.S.A. and completed his Ph.D. at Columbia University in 1955. His dissertation, *Le Style des Pléiades de Gobineau: Essai d'application d'une méthode stylistique*, won the Ansley Award and was published by Columbia University Press (1957). After teaching at New York University until 1964, he took up an appointment at Columbia, where he held the Blanche W. Knopf Chair in French Literature from 1975 to 1982, chaired the Department of French (1974–83), and was appointed University Professor in 1982. He has held several prestigious visiting professorships in the U.S.A., Canada and France. He is general editor of the *Romanic Review* and, since 1987, directs the School of Theory and Criticism at Dartmouth College.

Riffaterre's principal concern in his theoretical writings has been to re-orient the search for the definition of literariness in the reading process itself. A priori theorizing on the nature of *literature or attempts to apply categories and methods borrowed from other disciplines – no matter how closely related – can only displace properties specific to literature or risk overshadowing them with concerns pertinent mostly to those other disciplines. Only by focusing on the very practice of literature, the actual reading process, Riffaterre argues, can the categories and the modes of operation specific to the literary *text be delineated.

Beginning with the stylistic tradition which has always presented literary discourse's particularity as heightened expressivity by deviation from normal usage, Riffaterre argues that whatever norms or rules from which literary discourse diverges are not pre-existing linguistic or grammatical ones but norms set up within the text itself in patterns perceived by readers engaged in the reading process. (See *discourse.) His concepts of the 'average reader' and of the 'superreader' are not meant as substitutes for any actual reader or for some abstract set of functions of communication. Both of these concepts are in fact collections of readers' responses to specific segments of literary texts. (See *reader-response criticism.) What elicits these responses are sudden breaks with a perceived pattern (grammatical, semantic, rhetorical) established within the text itself. These stylistic devices (consisting of both the pattern and its break) constrain the reading process by intensifying attention on some points rather than others. For Riffaterre, all aspects of literariness are determined and defined in and through the reading process. The sense of 'estrangement' (*defamiliarization) which some of the Russian formalists identified as the essence of literature is not an effect experienced through a contrast with norms available in reality or in some coherent sense of everyday experience. (See Russian *formalism.) For Riffaterre, such norms are generated within the text itself – often, precisely at the same time as they are contravened. Similarly, the reader's presumed expectations are not to be determined through the a priori constitution of a Weltanschauung (cf. *Wolfgang Iser) but are produced in the reading process itself, by the text's ability to summon the reader's idiomatic and textual memory in relation to itself.

Particularly successful sets of stylistic devices become clichés and descriptive systems. They are integrated into the reader's linguistic competence so much so that modifying them becomes a new stylistic device in itself referring the reader back to the original cliché as a kind of *hypogram, a text already present in the cultural baggage the reader brings to bear in attempting to decipher the text. (See *competence/performance.)

Describing and mapping out all stylistic devices is primary to the analysis which takes place at a second, hermeneutic stage of the reading process. (See *hermeneutics.) This second stage is, according to Riffaterre, a requirement particular to literary texts.

In the first, heuristic stage the reader relies essentially on basic linguistic competence to get the 'meaning' of the text (whatever realities the text at first appears to be about). In this first interpretation literary language is still conceived of as practical, as primarily mimetic: it is still experienced as referring to reality despite the indirection imposed by the text's use of tropes and figures. (See *mimesis, *trope.)

Reality is infinitely diverse, whereas what characterizes literary discourse, according to Riffaterre, is its unity, its integrity. Literary texts survive long after the realities they point to or describe have lost all interest or pertinence; and it is this aspect of literariness which literary theory needs to investigate.

Readers remain aware – no matter how far-ranging or how complex its references may appear – that the text is about one thing. What Riffaterre calls the text's 'significance' is the active process through which the reader is constantly oriented back, beyond the text's mimetic diversity, to its essential unity of form and meaning. Riffaterre emphasizes the experiential nature of significance: to attain it, readers must go through a second, retroactive reading in which they attempt to resolve the discrepancies and contradictions they perceive in the first reading. What creates both the discrepancies and the reader's sense of an ultimate unity is the fact that the text is organized around an absent key word or sentence, a matrix, which makes its presence felt by constantly generating variants of itself through the text's mimesis. Because the matrix also substitutes its own structure for that of the reality the text seems to be about at the mimetic level, its variants appear as 'ungrammaticalities,' as misfits, in the first reading. It is precisely through this perceived ungrammaticality that the matrix becomes available to analysis. Because the ungrammaticalities have to be resolved into latent equivalents (generated by a form of intertextual interference), readers become aware of the presence of another level of meaning in the text. What Riffaterre calls *semiosis consists of all the elements which participate in this promotion of a text's signs from the mimetic level to the level of significance. (See *intertextuality, *sign.)

GABRIEL MOYAL

Primary Sources

Riffaterre, Michael. 'Describing Poetic Structures: Two Approaches to Baudelaire's *les Chats.' Yale French Studies* 36–7 (1966): 188–230.
- *Essais de stylistique structurale.* Paris: Flammarion, 1971.
- *Fictional Truth.* Baltimore and London: Johns Hopkins UP, 1990.
- *La Production du texte.* 1979. *Text Production.* New York: Columbia UP, 1983.
- *The Semiotics of Poetry.* Bloomington/London: Indiana UP, 1978.

Secondary Sources

de Man, Paul. 'Hypogram and Inscription: Michael Riffaterre's Poetics of Reading.' *Diacritics* 9.4 (1981): 17–35.

Robertson, Durant Waite, Jr.

(b. U.S.A., 1914–92) Medievalist and historical critic. Beginning his graduate career at the University of North Carolina with an extensive M.A. thesis which studied the Renaissance controversy over 'katharsis' in Aristotle's definition of tragedy, D.W. Robertson proceeded with a textual examination of a Middle English confessional manual, Robert Mannyng's *Handlynge Synne,* for his Ph.D. (1946). Robertson became aware of substantial discrepancies between modern evaluations of classical and medieval texts and interpretative reflections on them written during the Middle Ages and Renaissance. (See *text.) Central to his early work was his recognition that for medieval readers the Bible and its traditional commentaries were, with medieval versions of certain Roman classics, foundational to a richly intertextual medieval praxis. (See *intertextuality.) Among formative interpreters for the Middle Ages of scriptural tradition, he discovered St. Augustine to be of primary influence, and that Augustinian formulations on aesthetic and hermeneutic as much as theological matters had, until well after the 14th century, almost canonical status among medieval authors. (See *hermeneutics, *canon.)

Especially after going to Princeton (1948), Robertson wrote a number of influential articles, largely on Anglo-Norman and medieval French texts, illustrating something of the character of medieval intertextuality and literary self-consciousness. In 1951, with his then colleague B.F. Huppé, he brought together the substance and method of his earlier work in *'Piers Plowman' and Scriptural Tradition.* This study, dependent for its insights upon primary textual materials available to the 14th-century author, stirred almost immediate controversy. *Fruyt and Chaff* (1963), actually first drafted by Robertson and Huppé in this same period, undertook the same approach to Chaucer. Adversarial critics called the authors 'neo-Augustinians' or 'neo-exegetes.' When Huppé shortly thereafter left Princeton, the derogatory appellation 'Robertsonian' soon began to attach itself to any who seemed to follow Robertson's inclination to approach medieval texts from the perspective afforded by medieval works of literary theory, textual commentary, pictorial iconography, and scriptural exegesis. Robertson himself called his approach 'Histori-

cal Criticism,' which he defined as 'that kind of literary analysis which seeks to reconstruct the intellectual attitudes and the cultural ideals of a period in order to reach a fuller understanding of its literature' *(English Institute Essays;* repr. *Essays in Medieval Culture* [1980] 3). This he distinguished from literary history, as then conceived, citing the literary historian's preoccupation 'with purely literary rather than with intellectual traditions.' But in the 1950s, when adherents of *New Criticism still dominated medieval literary scholarship, Robertson's effectual 'Catholicization' of medieval vernacular texts (by referring their idiom to contemporary intellectual traditions) seems to have been the chief irritant in many quarters.

By *A Preface to Chaucer* (1962), when he had extended his study of medieval iconography considerably, his interest in 'stylistic history' had begun to evidence the influence of art historians Emile Mâle, and Heinrich Wölfflin, as well as the 'psychological history' of phenomenologist J.H. Van den Berg. This European-oriented interest in the intellectual history of style was further developed in *Abelard and Heloise* (1972) in which he considered the reception history of the famous correspondence from medieval to modern times, using it as a guide to understanding the evolution of aesthetic attitudes as revealed in *literature. In 1969, in the first volume of *New Literary History,* Robertson had already published 'Some Observations on Method in Literary Studies.' These pages affirm some of the general insights of *Michel Foucault (while wishing for more historical precision in Foucault's 'evidences'). The relationship of Robertson's method to that of Foucault may be contextualized usefully by Robertson's prefatory comment to the article's third reprinting (1980): 'It seems to me that students are often taught to be skeptical about the beliefs and ideas of the past without being taught also that current beliefs are equally contingent and transitory. This does not mean that verbal "truths," which always have a date and place, should not be respected when they have operational validity, but that their contingent nature should be recognized, and their practical function (if any) in the society that produces them should be considered. If they are or were useful tools, they deserve the utmost respect. And this is true in spite of the fact that verbal formulations useful at some time in the past may no longer be useful.' Robertson's 'Robertsonianism,' often as distinct from that of those associated with it by influence, is most concisely articulated, as theory and as method, in his 'Historical Criticism' (1950) and 'Observations on Method' (1969) essays. (See also *phenomenological criticism.)

DAVID LYLE JEFFREY

Primary Sources

Robertson, D.W., Jr. *Abelard and Heloise.* New York: Dial P, 1972.
– *Chaucer's London.* New York: Wiley P, 1968.
– *Essays in Medieval Culture.* Princeton: Princeton UP, 1980.
– *The Literature of Medieval England.* New York: McGraw-Hill, 1970.
– *A Preface to Chaucer.* Princeton: Princeton UP, 1962.
– 'Some Observations on Method in Literary Studies.' *New Literary History* 1 (1969): 21–33.
– and B.F. Huppé. *Fruyt and Chaff: Studies in Chaucer's Allegories.* Princeton: Princeton UP, 1963.
– and B.F. Huppé. *'Piers Plowman' and Scriptural Tradition.* Princeton: Princeton UP, 1951.

Secondary Sources

Utley, Francis L. 'Robertsonian Redivivus.' *Romance Philology* 19 (1965): 250–60.

Rorty, Richard

(b. U.S.A., 1931–) Philosopher. Rorty took his B.A. and M.A. at the University of Chicago (1949, 1952) and his doctorate at Yale University (1956). After military service (1957–8) his first appointment was at Wellesley College (1958–61); the bulk of his career was at Princeton University (1961–82). His increasingly critical view of analytic philosophy was publicly voiced in his American Philosophical Association presidential address (Eastern Division 1979), published in his *Philosophy and the Mirror of Nature* (1979) and *Consequences of Pragmatism* (1982), and consummated in his departure from Princeton's philosophy department to become the University of Virginia's Kenan Professor of Humanities (1982). Early recognition included a MacArthur Foundation Prize (1981–6), visiting fellowships at Stanford University's Center for Advanced Study (1982–3) and the Australian National University's Humanities Research Centre (1982), and election to the American Academy of Arts and Sciences (1983). A visiting fellowship at the Wissenschaftskolleg zu Berlin (1986–7) showed his European popularity. Rorty's views enjoy regular discussion in publications ranging from disciplinary journals to New York's *The Village Voice.*

Rorty's contribution to postmodernist thought has three aspects: the first is his critique of traditional and analytic philosophy's epistemological assumption that human knowledge is grounded in necessity or a 'given' or principles of reason (foundationalism) and its conception of truth as the correspondence of sentences to facts and so of language as essentially referential and descriptive (correspondism). (See *postmodernism.) The second aspect is Rorty's endorsement of 'edifying' philosophy: revolutionary thought as exemplified by *Wittgenstein's and *Heidegger's later work. The third is Rorty's efforts to establish connections between his vision of a post-philosophical culture and his political liberalism and individualism. These efforts seem prompted equally by interest in and by criticism of apparent politically conservative and even resignatory implications in his thought.

Rorty's most important contribution lies in his critique of traditional and analytic philosophy's self-bestowed status as repository of capital-T Truth and capital-R Reason and hence as supreme overseer of intellectual inquiry. His impeccable analyst's credentials lent special weight to his criticism and even though the bulk of analytic philosophers have tried to dismiss his writings and lectures as hopelessly relativistic, Rorty's impact on students has been exceeded only by his impact on disciplines ranging from political studies to comparative *literature and film.

Rorty finds in W.V.O. Quine's critique of analytic truth and Wilfrid Sellars' critique of elemental perceptual 'givens' exposure of the *myth that philosophy has access to ahistorical Necessity and Certainty. He is unwilling to accept the idea that philosophy has a fundamental criterion for correctness in sameness of meaning or that awareness of a problematic world begins – and ends – with 'internal' phenomenal elements which are the raw material of conceptualized thought and perception. In this connection Rorty also relies heavily on Donald Davidson's rejection of conceptual-scheme *pluralism, insisting that we do not have diverse and incommensurable ways of organizing a common but somehow perspective-neutral reality. In replacing the correspondence theory of truth with 'conversational' standards, spurning foundationalism in favour of established practices and unmasking capital-R Rationality as only entrenched history, Rorty denies epistemology its claimed special subject-matter and criteria for correctness. He argues that philosophy is only, in Michael Oakeshott's phrase, another voice in the conversation of mankind.

The rejection of correspondence, foundationalism, and so of philosophy's rational-adjudicator role, turns on Rorty's pragmatism and is encapsulated in the pivotal mirror metaphor of his first monograph – which echoes *Nietzsche's complaint in *Daybreak* that the history of epistemology is like a series of confused efforts to either grasp the things reflected in the mirror or to see the mirror independently of what it reflects. (See *metonymy/metaphor.) Rorty mocks the conception of knowledge and language as mirroring nature, of knowledge as 'internal' replication of reality and of language as vehicle for faithful facsimiles which are amenable to testing for representational accuracy. Rorty reminds us that we cannot escape language: that truth is always internal to language and that we cannot establish a 'correspondence' or iconic fidelity between what is thought or said and what *is*, when these are conceived as distinct *relata*.

Rorty's pragmatism is evident in his critical style, for he does not – and cannot – offer philosophical *arguments* against traditional positions. Instead he comes at his targets from many sides and in many different ways and moods to show us the tenuousness or vacuity of the positions he attacks. But though he extols the classical pragmatists, he under-emphasizes John Dewey's commitment to progress in inquiry. In place of advancement of knowledge he offers newness of 'vocabularies' or discourses; in place of progress he offers greater 'productivity,' not through betterment of past and current discourses but from novel construals of our predecessors' construals of history. (See *discourse.) Even more than the political implications of his views (Richard Bernstein), this area of Rorty's thought has prompted the sharpest philosophical criticism. Many read Rorty as having embraced a 'discourse relativism' which leaves him without standards for inquiry (Charles Taylor) and reduces intellectual activity to 'just talk' (John Caputo). Though his critique of philosophy as self-styled 'adjudicator of reason' is very powerful, some feel that Rorty's conception of modern science as just another discourse is unacceptable because of the explanatory power of scientific theories and the fact that the scientific notion of 'objectivity' is itself a product of the scientific enterprise and not a confused philosophical imposition (Bernard Williams). The continuity of scientific progress does seem to be more than just our history of science and manifests what Dewey characterized as progress in inquiry. It is also doubtful that Rorty has either basis for his confidence in our ability to endlessly generate discourses novel enough to sustain virtually continuous intellectual revolution or grounds for his implicit view that the world will support near-infinitely varying 'discourses.'

C.G. PRADO

Primary Sources

Rorty, Richard. *Consequences of Pragmatism*. Minneapolis: U of Minnesota P, 1982.
– *Contingency, Irony and Solidarity*. Cambridge: Cambridge UP, 1989.
– *Essays on Heidegger and Others. Philosophical Papers*, vol. 2. Cambridge: Cambridge UP, 1991.
– *Objectivity, Relativism and Truth. Philosophical Papers*, vol. 1. Cambridge: Cambridge UP, 1991.
– *Philosophy and the Mirror of Nature*. Princeton: Princeton UP, 1979 (with minor corrections 1980).
– *The Linguistic Turn*. Chicago: U of Chicago P, 1967.

Secondary Sources

Kolenda, Konstantin. *Rorty's Humanistic Pragmatism*. Tampa: U of South Florida P, 1990.
Malachowski, Alan, ed. *Reading Rorty*. Oxford: Blackwell, 1990.
Prado, C.G. *The Limits of Pragmatism*. Atlantic Highlands: Humanities P, 1987.

Rousset, Jean

(b. Switzerland, 1910–) Literary critic. Jean Rousset studied law and arts at the University of Geneva, worked as a *lecteur de français* at the University of Munich and, after four years of research and study in Paris (1946–50), became assistant and then professor of French *literature in the Faculty of Arts at Geneva. In his critical work he first focused on the 17th century as the context for a study of the baroque movement in literature and the visual arts. He then turned to genre studies, in particular the epistolary novel and the personal diary. His critical approach, based on hermeneutic *structuralism, centred on the links between form and textual interpretation. Akin to *Georges Poulet, *Jean Starobinski and Jean-Pierre Richard, but closest to Marcel Raymond, Jean Rousset has been associated with the *Geneva School. (See also *genre criticism, *phenomenological criticism, *hermeneutics.)

His first work, *La Littérature de l'âge baroque en France* (1953), sets out Rousset's main critical interests: careful attention to the themes and symbols of literary genres, authors and periods; preoccupation with the self and the place of the artist's inner world; and the desire to bring together various forms of art. (See *theme, *self/other.)

His master's thesis, *Forme et signification* (1962), best defines Rousset's critical approach. He views 'art as the creation of forms revealing their meaning' (vii). Meaning does not precede the work: it can only be discovered through the formal network that supports it. Form is an ordered series of repetitions and transformations – 'a simultaneously occurring network of reciprocal relations' (xiii). Thus the critic must look solely to the work to discern its meaning. In this perspective, the critic becomes a 'historian of the imagination' (7). Mimetic reading will therefore allow the reader to grasp the concept of the work mediated by its formal source, rather than the author's intended meaning. (See *mimesis.) Subsequent essays on 17th-century poetry and theatre, *L'Intérieur et l'extérieur* (1968), continued to adhere to the principle that the morphology of a work reveals the author's own perception of the world.

With the exception of *Le Mythe de Don Juan* (1978) and *Leurs yeux se rencontrèrent* (1981) Rousset examines, in the former, myths from a structural standpoint and, in the latter, the *scène de première vue* as a fundamental Romanesque structure – Rousset next approached the problems of the self, the personal and the diary. (See *myth.) These issues are also evident in his first work on the baroque period, and are developed in *Narcisse romancier* (1973) and *Le Lecteur intime* (1986), as well as in several articles, in particular in 'Préambule semi-théorique' (*Narcisse romancier*), which outlines the typology of the first-person narrative from the standpoint of narrative *discourse.

Of all the members of the Geneva School, Rousset was the most sensitive to form. His critical work constitutes an oveview of literary study since 1950. While Rousset follows a rationalist tendency that sometimes obscures individual characteristics, favouring transparency over an equally significant opacity, he never converts relations into fixed elements, and he always captures their movement and dynamic. His skill can be seen in *Passages* (1990), a series of essays on intercrossings, exchanges and interferences in the narrative. In the final analysis, as he said of the novelists he examined in *Passages*, Jean Rousset practised a 'sémiologie amoureuse.'

PIERRE HÉBERT

Primary Sources

Rousset, Jean. *Anthologie de la poésie baroque française*. Paris: Armand Colin, 1961.
– *Forme et signification*. Paris: José Corti, 1962.
– *L'Intérieur et l'extérieur: Essais sur la poésie et sur le théâtre au XVIIe siècle*. Paris: José Corti, 1968.
– *Le Lecteur intime: De Balzac au journal*. Paris: José Corti, 1986.
– *Leurs yeux se rencontrèrent: La scène de première vue dans le roman*. Paris: José Corti, 1981.
– *La Littérature de l'âge baroque en France: Circé et le paon*. Paris: José Corti, 1953.
– *Le Mythe de Don Juan*. Paris: Armand Colin, 1978.
– *Narcisse romancier: Essai sur la première personne dans le roman*. Paris: José Corti, 1973.
– *Passages, échanges et transpositions*. Paris: José Corti, 1990.

Said, Edward W.

(b. Palestine, 1935–) Literary critic. Edward Said was awarded his A.B. by Princeton in 1957, his A.M. by Harvard in 1960 and his Ph.D., also by Harvard, in 1964. With the exception of acting as a tutor at Harvard and various visiting appointments at other American universities, his entire career has been at Columbia University, where he is now Parr Professor of English and Comparative Literature. His influence in the American academy has been primarily as one of the pre-eminent introducers of contemporary European critical theory, particularly as a critical supporter of *Michel Foucault and opponent of *Jacques Derrida, but his international prestige is based on his position as perhaps the best-known post-colonial critic. (See *post-colonial theory.)

Said's reputation was established by his first book, *Joseph Conrad and the Fiction of Autobiography* (1966), originally his doctoral dissertation. Still very important as Conrad scholarship it is perhaps most interesting as a precursor of various issues Said has followed throughout his criticism. His study depends greatly on Conrad's correspondence and presents as central the relationship between Conrad's development of self and the fiction which he authored. Said denies a simplistic view of intention, that the meaning of the fiction is merely what Conrad intended to say, but posits that the product must be seen as the result of an intent, in this case to create a control seldom available in Conrad's life. (See *self/other, *intention/intentionality.)

Beginnings: Intention and Method (1975) remains Said's major contribution to literary criticism in general. His own assessment of the book's historical position, in his preface to the 1985 edition, gives a perceptive look at its value. There he emphasizes a *binary opposition which has continued to be central to his thought, that between filiation and affiliation. Filiation reflects a biological inevitability, the fact of son-ness, of being the product of a parent. Affiliation is instead a choice, in which something chooses to be associated with a metaphorical parent, or even sibling.

Thus *Beginnings* is concerned with the very possibility of beginning. If, as has been claimed by many contemporary critics, *literature is filiation, always controlled by that literature which has gone before, there is no beginning, only a series of false origins. But is it possible to consider any *text, any thing, without asserting that it has an at least arguable 'beginning?' Said's answer is that regardless of the validity, which he admits, of various contemporary arguments about the impossibility of the original, there is always something which can be said to be the origin.

Said finds this in the intention of the author. As in his study of Conrad, this is not a simple intention, but one shaped by all the forces of society, one which never makes the author into an individual independent of the multitude of forces of the author's world. Said states that his interest is in the text as writing, rather than reading, so he emphasizes what he calls 'the intentional beginning act' which 'authorizes' the text. One of Said's primary objects of study is Freud's *Interpretation of Dreams*, which he chooses expressly because it creates a narrative in opposition to what are presented as pre-existent material events. (See *Sigmund Freud.) For Said, Freud's textual method represents the logic of narrative structure based on a beginning in a subject's intention. As Said notes, Freud's problem of creating a verbal representation of a dream demonstrates what seems the inevitable failure of the relationship between author's intention and the resulting text.

Beginnings shows Said the introducer. It is an early example of a work identifiably within the American critical tradition which explores many of the major European poststructuralist thinkers. (See *poststructuralism.) As well, in the conclusion Said makes Vico into a commentator of explicit relevance for the 1970s, a view which has continued in much contemporary criticism since. Through Vico Said explores the possibility of 'relevance' in contemporary criticism, ending with *Noam Chomsky.

Orientalism (1978) might be seen as a major shift for Said, a venture away from the purely literary but, as the comments at the end of *Beginnings* show, the social context has always been central to Said's concerns. In *Orientalism* Said examines a number of European representations of the Middle East and shows how concepts of orientalism shaped what purported to be scientific objective observations. Said argues that these did not represent reality but rather were representations which reflected real conditions. He looks at orientalism as an economy controlled by a series of values. Thus many of the elements associated with orientalism are 'standard commodities.' For example, the assumed greater emphasis on sexuality in 'oriental' cultures meant that texts had to exhibit such sexuality in order to be valued as oriental. Said shows that the attacks on such sexuality and the yearning for it were but swings of the same pendulum.

Orientalism is an example of what has come to be called 'colonial critique.' Some, including Said, have called it 'post-colonial criticism,' but it might be contrasted with the latter in terms of its object of study. Colonial critique considers the set of problems provided by imperialist views of the colonies. Post-colonial criticism instead examines the products of the post-colonial societies, usually texts by authors such as Ngugi wa Thiongo or George Lamming, who perceive themselves in direct opposition to colonialism.

Said's recent work has followed two apparently disparate but philosophically closely related paths. In one, best seen at length in the collection of essays titled *The World, the Text and the Critic* (1983), Said has become a general commentator on the need for a criticism which responds to society. In a discussion at a symposium in 1985 in which Gerald Graff raised serious questions about the value of French theory, Graff went on to suggest that Said is one of the more important recent examples of Anglo-American social criticism. Appropriately, *Beginnings* was the winner of the first Lionel Trilling Memorial Award. (See *Lionel Trilling.)

The other side of Said's publications has been as a spokesman for Palestinian causes. This has led to him becoming arguably the most controversial American academic after Noam Chomsky. Said's political position was clear quite early, most particularly in 'Chomsky and the Question of Palestine' (1975), but it is best seen in his book *The Question of Palestine* (1979). In some ways a companion volume to *Orientalism*, *Question* is Said's statement of the 'truth' of the Middle East.

A word such as 'truth' might seem out of place in a poststructuralist age but it suits Said. His concern that authors be aware of their own positions has, however, never led to an intense self-reflexivity on his part. While always quick to assert his identity as a Palestinian he seldom considers his gender or his position within the academic establishment. Said's various public statements take an almost Arnoldian view of the function of criticism but never with Arnoldian disinterestedness. While he may not claim to be neutral, he seems to believe his observations have a truth well beyond that controlled by his interested subjectivity.

All of those ideas might be seen in connection with those early comments on Conrad and intention. In *Orientalism* Said praises Foucault but also emphasizes his rejection of Foucault's view of the author as only a discursive function. For Said the author must be an always active and responsible subject in the text. Thus the critic must not just present a dissemination, as in Said's version of Derrida, but an assessment of what is – the text as a manifestation of the world.

Said's influence as a literary critic continues through the lasting presence of *Beginnings*. His importance as a spokesman for Palestinian causes may seem in the future to have been only a moment in a political development but it will have been a moment of historical importance. However, his most discussed work, *Orientalism*, might come to have much less influence than expected. Post-colonial criticism has rapidly gone beyond colonial critique, from criticism of the imperial self's view of the other to exploration of the other as self. Said's comments on post-colonial writers have been brief, almost always limited to the major figures, but also limited by Said's own intention, as in the following: 'I don't want to over-interpret what Rushdie means, nor do I want to put ideas in his prose that he may not have intended.' Said offers few practical suggestions about how the oppositional critic can function in support of a text rather than in opposition to it.

Said's most recent book, *Musical Elaborations* (1991), has been considered by some an aberration, in which he allows his accomplishments as a pianist to lead him into an intellectual field not his own. Still, some continuity with his other work may be discerned, such as his assessment of *Paul de Man and of his possible connections to Zionism. Much of the book's criticism reflects the work of *Theodor Adorno. At the centre of the book is an extended consideration of that very strange figure Glenn Gould, great pianist, thinker, misanthrope, and Cassandra. As Said shows, the musician in performance is at once moving beyond and locked within society; hence the need for the polemical social critic.

TERRY GOLDIE

Primary Sources

Said, Edward. *Beginnings: Intention and Method.* New York: Basic Books, 1975.
– *Covering Islam: How the Media and the Experts Determine How We See the Rest of the World.* New York: Pantheon, 1981.
– *Joseph Conrad and the Fiction of Autobiography.* Cambridge: Harvard UP, 1966.
– *Musical Elaborations.* New York: Columbia UP, 1991.
– *Orientalism.* New York: Pantheon, 1978.
– *The Palestine Question and the American Context.* Beirut: Institute for Palestine Studies, 1979.
– *The Question of Palestine.* New York: New York Times Books, 1979.
– *The World, the Text and the Critic.* Cambridge: Harvard UP, 1983.

Sartre, Jean-Paul

(b. France, 1905–d. 1980) Novelist, dramatist, philosopher, literary critic. Jean-Paul Sartre's studies at the Louis-le-Grand preparatory school (1922–4) led to training in philosophy at the Ecole Normale Supérieure (1924–9) where he met his lifelong companion, *Simone de Beauvoir. In Berlin, having obtained a scholarship for study at the French Institute, he plunged into the phenomenology of *Edmund Husserl (1932–3). (See *phenomenological criticism.) After a sporadic career as *lycée* philosophy professor (1931–9), Sartre abandoned teaching altogether to devote himself to what he considered his 'neurosis': writing. A brief detention as prisoner-of-war (1940–1) left a lasting effect on Sartre's world-view.

Sartre's debut as a dramatist (followed shortly by the liberation of France), his role as journalist and political analyst, and the founding with de Beauvoir of the influential journal *Les Temps modernes* (1945) were main factors contributing to the meteoric rise of existentialism as the predominant mode of thought for a postwar generation. At the very moment that the revelations of Stalinism's misdeeds convinced many fellow-travelling French intellectuals to sever all ties with the Communist party, Sartre (who had until then remained aloof, if not altogether critical) was closing ranks with the party's program for 'revolutionary action.' Thus, diverging political philosophies in the midst of the Cold War precipitated infamous breaks with Albert Camus as well as with two notable members of the journal's editorial board, Raymond Aron and *Maurice Merleau-Ponty. In 1964, Sartre refused a Nobel Prize on moral grounds. Although remaining a feverish writer of criticism and a political activist, Sartre's influence as *maître à penser* began to wane in the mid-1960s as *structuralism, Althusserianism and a looming *deconstruction took their place as dominant critical approaches. (See *Louis Althusser.)

For a majority of readers, Sartre is best known as an author of fiction and theatre. Indeed, he himself believed that the writer committed to engaging the general public in the debate of ideas needed to exploit literary forms whose impact was as immediate and far-reaching as possible. Sartre's literary works illustrate the principal notions of his philosophy. Thus,

Roquentin, the diary-writing anti-hero of *Nausea* (1938), describes the anguishing experience of discovering man's contingent existence. *The Wall* (1939), a collection of five short stories, deals variously with the exercise of freedom in face of a condemnation to death, the gratuitous act, madness and love, weakness, and conformity fostered by a bourgeois upbringing. The fresco of characters in Sartre's unfinished saga novel, *The Roads to Freedom* (1945, 1949), constitutes an attempt to map out the various choices open to the individual in the context of world war. Among his plays, *Dirty Hands* (1948), *The Devil and the Good Lord* (1951) and *The Condemned of Altona* (1959) in particular are concerned with questions of ethics.

An early and a late Sartre may be discerned based on his two principal contributions to philosophy: *Being and Nothingness* (1943) and *Critique of Dialectical Reason* (1960). But although a shift is noticeable from the emphasis on a solitary subject in the former to a more socialized one in the latter, human consciousness, according to Sartre, tends to follow a uniformly predictable path beginning with the discovery of contingency, through a triumphant realization of radical freedom (*The Flies* 1943) and ending ideally in a practice of universal responsibility. The difficulties and variations of this path are examined in Sartre's fiction, theatre and, most poignantly, in the autobiography of his childhood, *The Words* (1964). The contingent nature of the for-itself (the consciousness of humans as lack of being) is reinforced upon our anguished realization of the essential being of the in-itself (things). Thus Hegel's 'unhappy consciousness' becomes a repulsion (*Nausea*) so powerful that the subject may be driven to an illusion of human essence: 'bad faith,' in Sartrean terminology. But while things simply *are*, humans *exist* (due to the faculty of negation), thereby escaping determination. This leads Sartre to his conceptualization of choice of being or the free creation of oneself with its overtones of moral responsibility. Constantly threatened by the presence of the other, freedom is the most precarious given of human existence (*No Exit* 1944). (See *self/other.) In the *Critique*, the individual's struggle against the practico-inert requires a *praxis of group action (the 'group in fusion') in order to overcome, if only temporarily, economic need and political oppression.

Sartre's essays on contemporary writers (1938–45) collected in *Situations, I* (1947)

transformed literary study and interpretation by manoeuvring these practices closer to philosophical considerations. Indeed the work of several writers analysed in those essays – *Blanchot, Bataille, Ponge, Camus – may be situated at the crossroads of philosophy and *literature. In *What Is Literature?* (1947), Sartre contends that a committed literature (one that addresses the controversies of the historical present) can be produced authentically only through the medium of the novel and related art forms deeply rooted in realism. Yet Sartre repeatedly questions this very thesis in a series of literary biographies that stirred controversy for their methodology and polemical thrust (*Baudelaire* 1947, *Saint Genet* 1952, *The Family Idiot* 1971–2). The redemptive activity of aesthetic creation, of which these literary subjects are emblematic, undermines Sartre's rejection of poetry as ahistorical art for art's sake. Sartre also wrote extensively on the theatre, being particularly fascinated by Diderot's notion of the 'actor's paradox,' where the consummate actor sheds his own character to don another, more noble one.

Sartre's early work is as much a reaction against Bergson and French neo-Kantians as it is a positive response to phenomenology, dialectical materialism and certain tenets from *Freud and *Nietzsche. The crucial role that descriptive methods borrowed from Hegel and Husserl were to play in Sartre's thought is evident from the first sentence of *Being and Nothingness* where he praises phenomenology for having reduced 'the existent to the series of appearances that manifest it.' Sartre perceives an aesthetic operation of 'derealization' at work in what Husserl called 'phenomenological reduction.' As early as *The Transcendence of the Ego* (1936), he radicalizes Husserl's notion of intentionality by claiming that all consciousness is consciousness *of* something, thus ridding it of any interiority. (See *intention/intentionality.) His later reading of *Heidegger would make him aware of certain historical and ontological implications of this radicalization. While rejecting Freud's theory of the unconscious, Sartre transposed much of his thought and applied 'existential psychoanalysis,' coupled later with the progressive-regressive sociological method, adapted from Henri Lefebvre, in virtually all of his critical work. (See also *psychoanalytic theory.)

Sartre's political philosophy, developed late in his career, is coextensive with his suddenly public role after the Second World War. An on-going debate with Marxist philosophers eventually led to his period of fellow-travelling in the early 1950s. Sartre's break with the Communist party after the invasion of Hungary did not dampen his affinity for revolutionary movements, particularly in 'Third World' countries, or his openness to the ideas of certain Marxist critics (*Antonio Gramsci, *Georg Lukács, the *Frankfurt School, *Lucien Goldmann, Lefebvre). Viewing structuralism as a form of antihumanistic neo-positivism, Sartre's plan to counter the advent of competing positions by writing an existentialist-Marxist ethics late in life was ceaselessly deferred by his political activism and, eventually, by poor health. (See also *Marxist criticism, *materialist criticism.)

The complexity of assessing Sartre's influence derives from a thought whose theoretical expressions are intimately enmeshed with a mode of existence that is (through activism, documentary films and de Beauvoir's memoirs) equally well known. A judgment on any one aspect of Sartre's work or on any one of his contributions to contemporary thought is inevitably inflected by his simultaneous 'presence' in some other realm of culture. The unusually long peak-period of Sartre's activity (1945–65), during which he tirelessly put his critical theories to practice, profoundly influenced the shaping of several generations of European thinking.

In the 1960s, Sartre's abhorrence of pure theory without grounding in action and lived experience ('situation') placed him at odds with Althusserian scientism and Lacanian psychoanalysis, as it had, in the 1950s, with *Lévi-Strauss and other early structuralists. (See *Jacques Lacan.) Yet Sartre's humanism, his fundamental notion of desire as lack and his profound conviction that Marxism was the one unavoidable philosophy of our time situates him paradoxically close to the concerns of these arch-rivals. (See *desire/lack.) And his repeated and varied attempts to address the incommensurables deriving from the Cartesian ontology of split being foreshadows today's general repudiation of all dualistic metaphysics. Owing principally to his prolonged dominance on the French cultural stage, a wave of anti-Sartrean reaction followed his death. This atmosphere of collective dismissal appears to be dissipating, however, giving way to a general recognition of his unique contributions to Western thought.

ROBERT HARVEY

Primary Sources

Sartre, Jean-Paul *Les Chemins de la liberté*. Paris: Gallimard, 1945, 1949.
– *Critique de la raison dialectique*. Paris: Gallimard, 1960.
– *Le Diable et le Bon Dieu*. Paris: Gallimard, 1951.
– *L'Etre et le Néant: Essai d'ontologie phénoménologique*. Paris: Gallimard, 1943.
– *Huis clos*. Paris: Gallimard, 1945.
– *L'Idiot de la famille*. Paris: Gallimard, 1971–2.
– *Les Mains sales*. Paris: Gallimard, 1948.
– *Les Mots*. Paris: Gallimard, 1964.
– *Les Mouches*. Paris: Gallimard, 1943.
– *Le Mur*. Paris: Gallimard, 1939.
– *La Nausée*. Paris: Gallimard, 1938.
– *Qu'est-ce que la littérature?* Paris: Gallimard, 1947.
– *Saint Genet: Comédien et martyr*. Paris: Gallimard, 1952.
– *Les Séquestrés d'Altona*. Paris: Gallimard, 1959.
– *Situations, I*. Paris: Gallimard, 1947.
– *La Transcendance de l'ego*. Paris: Vrin, [1936,] 1965.
– ed. *Baudelaire*. Paris: Gallimard, 1947.

Secondary Sources

Buisine, Alain. *Laideurs de Sartre*. Lille: Presses Universitaires de Lille, 1986.
Burnier, Michel-Antoine. *Les Existentialistes et la politique*. Paris: Gallimard, 1966.
Cohen-Solal, Annie. *Sartre: 1905–1908*. Paris: Gallimard, 1985.
Collins, Douglas. *Sartre as Biographer*. Cambridge, Mass.: Harvard UP, 1980.
Contat, Michel, and Michel Rybalka. *Les Ecrits de Sartre*. Paris: Gallimard, 1970.
Froment-Meurice, Marc. *Sartre et l'existentialisme*. Paris: Nathan, 1984.
George, François. *Deux études sur Sartre*. Paris: Christian Bourgois, 1976.
Harvey, Robert. *Search for a Father: Sartre, Paternity and the Question of Ethics*. Ann Arbor: U of Michigan P, 1991.
Hollier, Denis. *Politique de la prose: Sartre et l'an quarante*. Paris: Gallimard, 1982.
Jameson, Fredric. *Sartre: The Origins of a Style*. New York: Columbia UP, 1984.
Jeanson, Francis. *Sartre*. Paris: Seuil, 1955.
Pacaly, Josette. *Sartre au miroir*. Paris: Klincksieck, 1980.
Poster, Mark. *Existential Marxism in Postwar France: From Sartre to Althusser*. Princeton, NJ: Princeton UP, 1975.
Sicard, Michel. *Essais sur Sartre*. Paris: Galilée, 1989.

de Saussure, Ferdinand

(b. Switzerland, 1857–d. 1913) Linguist. Ferdinand de Saussure studied physics and try at the University of Geneva (1875–6) and then linguistics at the Universities of Leipzig (1880) and Berlin (1878–9), receiving his doctorate from Leipzig (1880). Saussure taught historical linguistics at the Ecole Pratique des Hautes Etudes, Paris (1881–91), and later Sanskrit and historical linguistics at the University of Geneva. His major impact came through three series of lectures on general linguistics (1907; 1908–9; 1910–11). Saussure's unpublished notes were combined with students' notes in a posthumous book, *Cours de linguistique générale*, edited by Charles Bally and Albert Sechehaye, which forms the basis for the claim that he is the founder of modern linguistics.

Mémoire sur le système primitif des voyelles dans les langues indo-européennes, the only book published in his lifetime, underlies current views on the phonological system of Proto-Indo-European. While not as explicitly presented as in the *Cours*, *Mémoire* is based on the premise that language is a set of signs whose values are determined by relationships in a specific system. (See *sign.) Viewing that system rigorously in accordance with mathematical principles, Saussure proposes that verbal roots in the parent language of the Indo-European family, e.g. *sed* – 'sit,' had a structure consisting of C(onsonant) V(owel) C(onsonant), with *e* as the basic vowel. Roots not showing this structure, such as *ag-* 'lead' and *(s) ta-* 'stand,' he accounted for by positing earlier consonants that he labelled *coefficients sonantiques*, subsequently called laryngeals. In this way he accounted for vowel variations called ablauts in different forms of a root, such as those still evident on verbs such as *sing, sang, sung*, as well as for subsequent assumptions about the consonant system. The *coefficients* that he posited purely by internal analysis were confirmed in 1927, when Jerzy Kurylowicz determined that Hittite sounds transliterated as *h* corresponded to such coefficients. Besides clarifying the phonological system Saussure put the method of internal reconstruction in historical linguistics on a solid base side by side with the comparative method.

Although Saussure's teaching and his chief

publications dealt with the historical developments of language, in his series of lectures on
general linguistics he set out to identify the
fundamental problems of linguistics and to
suggest ways to solve them, in an effort to
make linguistics a science. In contrast to the
predominant attention of the time to the psychological shape of language, Saussure considered linguistics to be concerned with a social
institution. He identified language as a system
of signs. And in contrast to earlier views classifying it with the physical sciences, he proposed a distinct set of sciences within semiology, now generally known as *semiotics.
The proposal is assumed to be original with
Saussure, although during the same period
the notable American philosopher *Charles
Sanders Peirce was also laying the groundwork for semiotics as it is now pursued.

Signs for Saussure are arbitrary; they have
no direct relationship with their referent, as
may be illustrated by variation from language
to language. (See *reference/referent.) English
house, for example, corresponds to Japanese *ie*,
to Turkish *ev*, to Latin *domus*. Signs gain their
value through oppositions. English *house* corresponds also to German *Haus*, but that has a
broader set of values, corresponding also to
English *building*, (business) *firm*, and so on.
Because English *know*, on the other hand, has
a smaller set of oppositions than do the German correspondences *wissen* 'know (facts),'
kennen 'know (people),' *können* 'know (languages),' its value is broader than any of the
German equivalents.

To determine the value of any linguistic entity, one must locate its position in its system.
A language then is a structure where everything is interrelated or, in the phrase of Saussure's most famous student, Antoine Meillet,
où tout se tient. As Harris has pointed out,
Saussure determined the place of elements in
semiotics itself by oppositions, often not providing his essential terms with definitions.
Among crucial oppositions are language *(langue)* as an abstract system maintained by a
social group in contrast to speech *(parole)*, the
manifestations of that system. (See *langue/
parole.)* Elements are then characterized by a
duality. By another opposition continuing a
contrast of earlier philosophy, we perceive
substance in use of language but its essence is
form, that is, a social convention consisting of
abstractions.

Signs are dual entities of *signifier (signifiants,*

that is, sound patterns) and *signified (signifiés,*
that is, concepts). (See *signified/signifier/
signification.) The essential of language is its
union of sound patterns and concepts, both of
which are mental. Moreover, while linear, language, especially as subsequently treated by
*Roman Jakobson, consists of a *syntagmatic*
and a *paradigmatic* plane. That is to say, relationships are significant through sequences, for
example, *pot: top, she did: did she*, on the syntagmatic axis, and through substitutions of the
paradigmatic axis, for example, *pit: pot, he
does: he did.*

The *Cours* secured a position as a science for
a social convention. Its success led to comparable procedures for other humanistic pursuits,
such as *literature; the approach came to be
known as *structuralism, with Saussure as its
founder.

Yet, the *Cours* has also been variously interpreted. Received without excitement by linguists in the decade after its publication, later it
was elevated by linguists to the position of an
almost messianic document. In the devoted attention to it, the editors have been criticized
for inadequately representing the full complexities of Saussure's theories as well as for the
book's inconsistencies. Saussure raised other
debated questions, such as his search for anagrams, chiefly in Latin literature. One type of
anagram mirrors proper nouns in syllables of
words in the text, as Saussure is mirrored in
the italic syllables of the next sentence. He
*sough*t these largely for proper names, though
it is un*cert*ain whether they are based on pronunciation or spelling, even though Saussure
himself proposed anaphony as a more accurate
term than anagram (Starobinski 1979: 14).
Another type spells out key words, such as
proper nouns, by choice of initial sounds or
letters, as do the letters in italic in the following sentence. Similarly without *a*nswer even
*u*nder *s*ubsequent *s*tudy is whether they are
*u*nintended *r*ather than *e*ssential patterns of
the text produced by an author. Jakobson,
though sympathetic, leaves such questions unresolved (1970: 30). *Jonathan Culler (1976:
106–14) suggests that Saussure may have been
seeking to cut through Western *logocentrism,
as a kind of forerunner of *deconstruction, directing attention towards phonological segments of language rather than words.

The *Cours* concentrates on only one segment
of language, its phonology. Further, even historical study of language is poorly incorpora-

ted in the new conception of linguistics. Saussure may be regarded as a teacher who in an initial series of courses posed a number of questions about the essentials of his field, but through accidents of health and other interests never proceeded to a final formulation. The queries of admiring leaders of the field, as well as the misunderstanding generated especially by translations, illustrate the difficulties of understanding his work. But its success in identifying fundamental problems and initiating important investigations as well as in securing for linguistics a position as an independent science justifies the continuing high regard for Saussure.

WINFRED P. LEHMANN

Primary Sources

Saussure, Ferdinand de. *Cours de linguistique générale.* Ed. Charles Bally and Albert Sechehaye in collaboration with Albert Riedlinger. Lausanne and Paris: Payot, 1916. 3rd corrected ed. Paris: Payot, 1931. 5th ed. T. de Mauro. Paris: Payot, 1972. *Course in General Linguistics.* Ed. and annotator, Roy Harris. London: Duckworth, 1983. Cf. earlier trans. by Wade Baskin. New York: Philosophical P, 1959; McGraw-Hill, 1966.
- *Mémoire sur le système primitif des voyelles dans les langues indo-européennes.* Leipzig: Teubner, 1879.
- *Recueil des publications scientifiques.* Ed. Charles Bally and Léopold Gautier. Geneva: Editions Sonor; Lausanne: Payot; Heidelberg: Winter, 1922. Repr. Geneva: Slatkine, 1970.

Secondary Sources

Culler, Jonathan. *Ferdinand de Saussure.* London: Fontana, 1976. Rev. ed., 1986.
Godel, Robert. *Les Sources manuscrites du Cours de linguistique générale de Ferdinand de Saussure.* Geneva: Droz, 1957.
Harris, Roy. *Reading Saussure: A Critical Commentary on the 'Cours de linguistique générale.'* London: Duckworth, 1987.
Jakobson, Roman, and Lawrence G. Jones. *Shakespeare's Verbal Art in Th'Expense of Spirit.* The Hague: Mouton, 1970.
Koerner, E.F. Konrad. *Bibliographia Saussureana 1870–1970.* Metuchen, NJ: Scarecrow, 1972.
- *Ferdinand de Saussure: Origin and Development of His Linguistic Theory in Western Studies of Language.* Braunschweig: Vieweg, 1973.
Starobinski, Jean. *Words upon Words. The Anagrams of Ferdinand de Saussure.* Trans. Olivia Emmet. New Haven: Yale UP, 1979.

Scholes, Robert

(b. U.S.A., 1929–) Literary critic, educator. Educated at Yale (B.A., 1950) and Cornell (M.A., 1956; Ph.D., 1959), Robert Scholes began his teaching career at the University of Virginia (1959) and subsequently taught at the University of Wisconsin, the University of Iowa and Brown University where he is now Andrew W. Mellon Professor of Humanities. Scholes is not essentially a formulator of critical theory; his influence has come rather from the lucidity with which he has explained, applied and evaluated major trends in critical theory over the last quarter of a century. Primarily interested in narrative, Scholes' work combines extensive knowledge of the history of narrative, an essentially ethical perspective and a vital awareness of the possibilities of new critical approaches to *literature.

The foundation of his comprehensive understanding of narrative is found in *The Nature of Narrative* (1966), co-authored by Robert Kellogg. The volume explores the meaning of narrative ('meaning' is here defined as the relationship between the fictional and the 'real' worlds), modes of creating characters, forms of plot, and point of view in narrative fiction to the middle of the present century. (See *story/plot.) The distinctions first developed here between 'relational' and 'representative' relations to experience, between 'empirical' and 'fictional' narrative, and between the historical and mimetic modes of the former and the romantic and didactic modes of the latter, while constantly reworked, have remained central to Scholes' thought.

Thus, *The Nature of Narrative* associates romantic fiction with a primarily aesthetic impulse and the fable with a primarily didactic one, while in *The Fabulators* (1967) contemporary fabling (described with relish as 'fabulation') is regarded as partaking of both the aesthetic and the didactic, its strong tendency toward fantasy representing the illustrative rather than the representative. For Scholes, 'fabulation' is represented by 'new literary artifacts' (14) of the kind produced by Lawrence Durrell, Kurt Vonnegut, John Hawkes, Iris Murdoch, and John Barth as well as by a range of earlier texts exhibiting similar characteristics. A significantly expanded version of *The Fabulators* appeared in 1979 under the title *Fabulation and Metafiction.* (See *text.)

Structuralism in Literature (1974) was immediately successful as an introduction to structuralist theory, surveying diverse applications to narrative by André Jolles, Etienne Souriau, *Vladimir Propp, *Claude Lévi-Strauss, *Tzvetan Todorov, *Roland Barthes, and *Gérard Genette. Scholes' preoccupation with *structuralism during the 1970s led to the argument of *Structuralist Fabulation* (1975) that while 19th- and early 20th-century realism is no longer viable (structuralist theory having been one of the forces that has undermined the realist program), science fiction solves both the metaphysical and practical problems of contemporary fiction and further offers the possibility of ethical transformation through the provision of alternative models of the future: 'The future of fiction lies in the future' (17). Scholes' division of the functions of fiction into 'sublimation' and 'cognition' in this volume is a partial transformation of his earlier distinction between the romantic and the didactic. His interest in fabulation is extended in the useful introduction to the field of science fiction, *Science Fiction: History, Science, Vision*, co-authored by Eric Rabkin (1977).

Semiotics and Interpretation (1982) is a series of essays applying *semiotics (defined here as 'the study of codes') to literary works; in essence the essays are experiments in moving beyond structuralism to poststructuralist perspectives. (See *poststructuralism, *code.) The ethical concern and especially the pedagogical question of the function of the teacher of the humanities evident in *Semiotics and Interpretation* is developed further in *Textual Power: Literary Theory and the Teaching of English* (1985), which specifically sets out strategies for teaching students to interpret literature. (See *theory and pedagogy.) Such interpretation involves the assumption of authorial intention – as Scholes here explicitly recognizes. Correlatively, the volume also includes specific criticism of elements of the poststructuralist thought of *Jacques Derrida, *Jonathan Culler and *Stanley Fish in arguments intended to balance the claims of culturally influenced interpretation with those of the structures of the text itself.

The direction of this argument is pursued more fully in *Protocols of Reading* (1989), which grants Derridean *deconstruction its achievement in raising necessary questions but criticizes Derrida and some of his followers for

a failure to recognize that ethics can neither be derived from nor denied by theories of language or rhetoric. 'Rhetoric will help us follow the exchange of pleasure and power in any textual situation. It will not tell us whether these exchanges are right or wrong' (133). (See *power.) The ethical reading for which Scholes argues is to be achieved by a dialectical process of reading 'centripetally' toward the 'original intention located at the center' of the text and 'centrifugally' in relation to one's own life and experience (8).

Scholes' major contributions have been in maintaining a historical perspective on narrative while exploring and testing new modes of analysis and commentary. The ethical function of literature, regarded in its broadest aspect as the enhancement of readers' understanding of experience and of the possibilities for improving the condition of human life, has assumed an increasingly central role in his writing; at the same time he has come to reject those elements of structuralist and poststructuralist thought that deny the possibility of evaluating either texts or human action in terms of moral standards. His position is summarized in the last paragraph of *Protocols of Reading*: 'If we have no Truth with a capital *T*, we must stop using the notion of such Truth – in whatever guise – to measure what we then take to be our failure to attain it. But we must not give up distinguishing between truth and lies within whatever framework we can construct to make such determinations' (154).

WENDELL V. HARRIS

Primary Sources

Scholes, Robert. *Fabulation and Metafiction*. Urbana: U of Illinois P, 1979.

– *The Fabulators*. New York: Oxford UP, 1967.

– *Protocols of Reading*. New Haven: Yale UP, 1989.

– *Semiotics and Interpretation*. New Haven: Yale UP, 1982.

– *Structural Fabulation: As Essay on the Fiction of the Future*. Notre Dame, Ind.: U of Notre Dame P, 1975.

– *Structuralism in Literature: An Introduction*. New Haven: Yale UP, 1974.

– *Textual Power: Literary Theory and the Teaching of English*. New Haven: Yale UP, 1985.

– and Robert Kellogg. *The Nature of Narrative*. New York: Oxford UP, 1966.

– and Eric Rabkin. *Science Fiction: History, Science, Vision*. New York: Oxford UP, 1977.

– and Richard M. Kain, eds. *The Workshop of Daeda-*

lus: James Joyce and the Raw Materials for 'A Portrait of the Artist as a Young Man.' Evanston: Northwestern UP, 1964.

Searle, John R.

(b. U.S.A., 1932–) Philosopher of language. John Searle is generally known as a student of *J.L. Austin. During his 1955 William James Lectures at Harvard University (pub. as *How to Do Things with Words* 1962), Austin drew the attention of language philosophers to sentences that do not simply report states of affairs in the world. Certain types of sentences – commands, instructions, expressions of feeling, declarations of intent, promises – actually seem to bring about changes in the world. Their truth conditions involve complex calculations of the sincerity of mental states (intentions) and of actual consequences. In a series of papers published throughout the 1960s, Searle explored the philosophical implications of performative language – speech acts uttered in the various contexts of human agency. In *Speech Acts* (1969), based on his 1959 D.Phil. thesis at Oxford, Searle expanded an analysis of speech acts into a comprehensive philosophy of language. For Searle, 'speaking a language is engaging in a (highly complex) rule-governed form of behavior.' A coherent theory of speech acts could account for all of language. (See *speech act theory.) Searle was able to produce a much more consistent and far-ranging speech act theory than J.L. Austin's. Uttering a word is performing an 'utterance act'; referring and predicating are 'propositional acts'; openly performative speech acts – 'stating, questioning, commanding, promising' – are, following Austin, 'illocutionary acts.'

Searle's theory of speech acts offers literary critics fresh insight into the way words are able to refer to the world. Reference itself is a speech act but speech acts are also governed by the conventions and rules of language. (See *reference/referent.) The need to distinguish the representational function of language from its overall logical and grammatical coherence – which may have little to do with reference – led Searle to posit a realm of 'institutional facts' (x married y; team z beat team r) from non-conventional or 'brute' facts. Reference is never just a game, since 'whatever is referred to must exist.' Fictional *discourse presents an obvious problem for Searle's speech act theory. In a later paper ('The Logical Status of Fictional Discourse' 1975) Searle solved the problem by an ingenious argument: by pretending to refer, novelists create fictional characters. While the *act* of referring is real, the object of the reference might not be. Sherlock Holmes, for example, need not exist for a statement about him to be true or false.

In 1977 Searle came to the attention of literary theorists as the result of a debate with *Jacques Derrida waged in the first issue of *Glyph.* In 'Signature Event Context,' Derrida questioned the assumptions underlying Austin's notion of a speech act, particularly the idea that the intentionality of a speaking subject is a determining factor in the production of linguistic meaning. (See *intention/intentionality, *subject/object.) How could there be speech acts when language itself is largely a matter of convention? In his response, 'Re-iterating the Differences: A Reply to Derrida,' Searle accused Derrida of seriously misinterpreting Austin. While pointing out that Austin died before working out a general theory of speech acts, Searle defends Austin against virtually all of Derrida's objections. According to Searle, Derrida's idea that parasitic discourse is internal to the notion of language does not contradict Austin's view of the role conventionality and iterability play in speech acts. Searle concludes his rebuttal with a renewed emphasis on the role of intentionality in speech acts, an importance strengthened, not (as Derrida claimed) weakened, by the iterability of linguistic forms. In the next issue of *Glyph,* Derrida responded in a highly unusual piece entitled 'Limited Inc abc ... ' in which he sometimes refers to Searle as 'Sarl.' Searle did not reply.

Apart from his fame as a speech act theorist, Searle has established himself as an informed commentator on crises within the university. His widely reprinted 1968 article concerning student uprisings became the first chapter of *The Campus War* (1971). 'Minds, Brains and Programs' (1980) challenged the assumption that Artificial Intelligence models could mirror the structure of the mind. Using the analogy of a Chinese room, Searle argued that human consciousness is fully intentional and thus unique and distinct from all existing AI models, an idea expanded in *Intentionality: An Essay in the Philosophy of Mind* (1983). Searle's speech act theory remains influential among literary theorists, communication action theorists such as *Jürgen Habermas, and linguists (especially those interested in pragmatics), while his more recent work in the philosophy of mind attests to the continued vitality of Anglo-American analytic philosophy. (See *communicative action.)

The literary applications of speech act theory were anticipated, in a sense, by *Kenneth Burke's. five key terms of 'dramatism' as outlined in *A Grammar of Motives* (1945): act, scene, agent, agency, purpose. Human speech acts are produced by agents, acting within contexts or scenes, using language as agency for some purpose. In drama, the illocutionary force of speech acts can be measured against on-stage consequences to determine whether characters mean what they say. Literary works clearly contain representations of speech acts: the status of works as a whole is a different question. In *Toward a Speech Act Theory of Literary Discourse* (1977), Mary Louise Pratt laid the groundwork for applying the theories of Austin, Searle and other speech act philosophers to the question of literary texts. (See *text.) The initial question faced by theorists is simply one of classification: how is language used in *literature? For Pratt, literature is circumscribed by its context: 'as with any utterance, the way people produce and understand literary works depends enormously on unspoken, culturally-shared knowledge of the rules, conventions, and expectations that are at play when language is used in that context' (86). Features of the literary speech situation include reader/audience reception, preparation and selection before utterance, and what Pratt calls 'the tellability of what is being asserted' – the quality of stories that makes us sit up and take notice. As we learn more about the contexts of literature, its ongoing reception history, and its ability to communicate, we will be in a better position to evaluate the applicability of Searle's work to literary criticism. Intentionality may very well return as an issue in the production of literary texts. As it stands currently, the work of Austin and Searle is largely an untapped resource for literary theory.

GREGOR CAMPBELL

Primary Sources

Searle, John R. *The Campus War*. New York: World Publishing Company, 1971.

- 'Consciousness, Unconsciousness and Intentionality.' *Philosophical Topics* 17 (1989): 193–209.
- *Expression and Meaning: Studies in the Theory of Speech Acts*. Cambridge: Cambridge UP, 1979.
- *Intentionality: An Essay in the Philosophy of Mind*. Cambridge: Cambridge UP, 1983.
- 'The Logical Status of Fictional Discourse.' *New Literary History* 6 (1975): 319–32.
- 'Meaning, Communication and Representation.' In *Philosophical Grounds of Rationality, Intentionality, Categories and Ends*. Ed. R. Grandy and R. Warner. Oxford: Clarendon P, 1986.
- 'Minds, Brains and Programs.' *Behavioral and Brain Sciences* 3 (1980): 417–57. Repr. in *The Mind's I*. Ed. D.R. Hofstadter and D.C. Dennet. New York: Basic Books, 1981.
- *Minds, Brains and Science*. Cambridge, Mass.: Harvard UP, 1985.
- 'Re-iterating the Differences: A Reply to Derrida.' *Glyph* 1 (1977): 198–208.
- *Speech Acts: An Essay in the Philosophy of Language*. Cambridge: Cambridge UP, 1969.

Secondary Sources

Austin, J.L. *How to Do Things with Words*. Ed. J.O. Urmson and Marina Sbisà. Cambridge, Mass.: Harvard UP, 1962.
Derrida, Jacques. 'Signature Event Context.' Trans. Samuel Weber and Jeffrey Mehlman. *Glyph* 1 (1977): 172–97.
- 'Limited Inc abc ... ' *Glyph* 2 (1977): 162–254.
Fish, Stanley E. 'How to Do Things with Austin and Searle: Speech Act Theory and Literary Criticism.' *MLN* 91 (1976): 983–1025.
- 'With the Compliments of the Author: Reflections on Austin and Derrida.' *Critical Inquiry* 8 (1982): 693–721.
Lepore, Ernest, and Robert Van Gulick, eds. *John Searle and His Critics*. Oxford: Basil Blackwell, 1991.
Ohmann, Richard. 'Speech Acts and the Definition of Literature.' *Philosophy and Rhetoric* 4 (1971): 1–19.
- 'Speech, Literature and the Space Between.' *New Literary History* 5 (1974): 37–63.
Petrey, Sandy. *Speech Acts and Literary Theory*. London: Routledge, 1990.
Pratt, Mary Louise. *Toward a Speech Act Theory of Literary Discourse*. Bloomington: Indiana UP, 1977.

Shklovskii, Viktor Borisovich

(b. Russia, 1893–d. 1984) Russian formalist scholar and novelist. Upon graduating from St. Petersburg University, Shklovskii taught at the Institute of Art History. In 1916 with Osip Brik and Lev Iakubinskii he organized OPOIAZ (acronym for the Society for the Study of Poetic Language), whose members aimed to examine and define the distinctive features of *literature rather than the external conditions under which literature is created. OPOIAZ became the main centre of Russian *formalism and Shklovskii its chief spokesman and theoretician. In the late 1920s he became the chief target of the antiformalist campaign, responding with a self-critical article, 'Pamiatnik nauchnoi oshibke' ['A Monument to Scientific Error' 1930]. After the suppression of the formalist school, he worked in relative obscurity publishing sociologically oriented studies of Tolstoy. He re-emerged in the 1960s with several reprints of his earlier works and memoirs of OPOIAZ and its members.

Shklovskii was the most influential critic in the first phase of Russian formalism. 'Iskusstvo kak priem' ['Art as Technique' 1917] served as the manifesto of the new school, introducing the concept of *ostranenie* [*defamiliarization]. At first, Shklovskii used the concept of defamiliarization to describe a new and startling perception of outside reality in a work of art. Later he modified the concept to refer to the process of renewal of old literary forms by new ones.

Shklovskii developed a coherent theory of prose in 'Sviaz' priemov siuzhetoslozheniia s obshchimi priemami stilia' ['On the Connection between Devices of Syuzhet and General Stylistic Devices' 1919], *Razvertyvanie siuzheta* [*The Unfolding of the Plot* 1921] and *Tristram Shendi Sterna i teoriia romana* [*Sterne's Tristram Shandy and the Theory of the Novel* 1921], later reprinted in *O teorii prozy* [*On the Theory of Prose* 1925]. He introduced the concepts of 'material' and 'device,' corresponding to the pre-aesthetic and aesthetic phases of the literary process; *fabula* [story] and *siuzhet* [plot], describing the chronological and causal order of events as opposed to their artistic rearrangement; and 'new forms' and 'old clichés,' referring to the continuous renewal of literary forms. (See *story/plot.)

Shklovskii concentrated on the analysis of plot composition, distinguishing such structures as 'a staircase construction' that breaks the action into episodes with the use of repetition, tautology, and parallelism; double plotting that interpolates heterogeneous material into the story; and 'hook-like composition' that

relies on contrast, opposition and a false ending. He outlined his favourite technique of 'laying bare' a device, breaking the tradition of realistic motivation in fiction and deliberately revealing the basic technique of narration itself.

The chief appeal of Shklovskii's works lies in his discovery of the internal laws of prose through a careful examination of the literary techniques employed by individual writers. The weakness of his approach was his tendency to dismiss all thematic connections. (See *theme.) Despite his own insistence on the continuous renewal of literary forms, he also failed to place texts in their larger historical context, thus excluding diachrony from the synchronic analysis of literary devices.

NINA KOLESNIKOFF

Primary Sources

Shklovskii, V.B. 'Iskusstvo kak priem.' In *Sborniki po teorii poeticheskogo iazyka* 2. Petrograd, 1919, 3–14. 'Art as Technique.' In *Russian Formalist Criticism: Four Essays*. Ed. L. Lemon and M. Reis. Lincoln: U of Nebraska P, 1966, 3–24.
– 'Pamiatnik nauchnoi oshibke.' *Literaturnaia gazeta*, 27 January 1930, 1.
– *Razvertyvanie siuzheta*. Petrograd, 1921.
– 'Sviaz' priemov siuzhetoslozheniia s obschimi priemami stilia.' In *Poetika. Sborniki po teorii poeticheskogo iazyka*. Petrograd, 1919, 115–50. 'On the Connection Between Devices of Syuzhet and General Stylistic Devices.' In *Russian Formalism: A Collection of Articles and Texts in Translation*. Ed. S. Bann and J. Bowlt. Edinburgh: Scottish Academic P, 1973, 48–72.
– *O teorii prozy*. Moscow, 1925.
– *Tristram Shendi Sterna i teoriia romana*. Petrograd, 1921. 'Sterne's *Tristram Shandy* and the Theory of the Novel.' In *Russian Formalist Criticism: Four Essays*, 25–60.

Secondary Sources

Sheldon, Richard. 'The Formalist Poetics of Viktor Shklovsky.' *Russian Literature Triquarterly* 2 (1972): 351–72.
– *Viktor Shklovsky: An International Bibliography of Works by Him and about Him*. Ann Arbor: Ardis, 1976.
– 'Viktor Shklovsky and the Device of Ostensible Surrender.' *Slavic Review* 34.1 (1975): 86–108.
Sherwood, R.J. 'Early Formalist Theories in Modern Context.' *Essays in Poetics* 1.1 (1976): 1–31.
– 'Viktor Shklovsky and the Development of Early Formalist Theory on Prose Literature.' In *Russian*

Formalism: A Collection of Articles and Texts in *Translation*. Ed. S. Bann and J. Bowlt. Edinburgh: Scottish Academic P, 1973, 26–40.

Showalter, Elaine

(b. U.S.A., 1941–) Feminist literary critic. Elaine Showalter received her B.A. from Bryn Mawr College in 1962, her M.A. from Brandeis University in 1964, and her Ph.D. from the University of California, Davis, in 1970. She is, at present, professor of English at Princeton University.

Showalter's work as a feminist literary critic has had three continuing emphases: recovering a women's literary and cultural history; charting the evolution of feminist literary criticism; and calling for far-ranging curricular and pedagogical reform. All three projects are founded upon an idea of women's culture as 'muted' in relation to the dominant masculine culture (*A Literature of Their Own* 11). (See *feminist criticism.) Showalter rejects the notion of an innate female literary imagination or style, emphasizing instead women's shared cultural and sociohistorical experiences.

Showalter argues that a women's literary subculture, like those of other minority groups, evolves through three major phases: imitation and internalization of dominant literary modes; protest against those standards and advocacy of minority rights and values; and self-discovery, a search for self-identity. Within a women's literary tradition, Showalter calls these phases feminine, feminist and female and, in *A Literature of Their Own* (1977), she explores the evolution of such a female tradition in the works of a number of 19th- and 20th-century English women writers ranging from Charlotte Brontë to Doris Lessing. *The Female Malady* (1985) is a more broadly cultural analysis of the ways in which female insanity has been defined, detected and treated in 19th- and 20th-century England, and of the long cultural associations between femininity and madness. Both *A Literature of Their Own* and *The Female Malady* suggest that attention to gender and sexual difference reveals 'another plot' ('Review Essay: Literary Criticism'), another literary or cultural history hitherto submerged in that of the dominant, masculine culture. *Sexual Anarchy* (1990) draws parallels between *fin de siècle* preoccupations and representations in both 19th– and 20th-century culture, focusing,

as the title suggests, on 'myths, metaphors and images of sexual crises and apocalypse.' (See *myth, *metonymy/metaphor.)

After *A Literature of Their Own*, Showalter turned her attention to charting the relationship both between feminist and other modes of literary criticism and between varieties of feminist criticism. 'Toward a Feminist Poetics' (1979) responds to charges that feminist criticism lacks rigour and a clearly articulated theory by outlining a 'taxonomy' of feminist criticism which distinguishes between feminist critique and 'gynocritics.' Feminist critique is concerned with woman as reader, especially of male-authored texts, and is 'political and polemical'; because of its dependence on existing male texts and critical models, the potential for feminist critique to produce a feminist literary theory is limited. Gynocritics, on the other hand, is concerned with woman as writer and seeks 'to construct a female framework for the analysis of women's literature.' In its emphasis on a female culture, gynocritics has much in common with feminist research in such fields as anthropology, history and sociology. 'Feminist Criticism in the Wilderness' (1981) further distinguishes between four models of gynocriticism, listed in order of their perceived value: biological, linguistic, psychoanalytic, and cultural. (See also *psychoanalytic theory.) Showalter draws from the work of Oxford anthropologists Shirley and Edwin Ardener to reinforce her argument that feminist examinations of the 'wild zone' or uncharted space of a female culture, 'muted' in relation to the dominant culture, offer the greatest promise for the construction of a women's literary *canon and the evolution of a feminist literary theory.

Showalter's interest in curricular and pedagogical issues has remained constant throughout her career. (See *theory and pedagogy.) In 'Women and the Literary Curriculum' (1970) she emphasized the importance of women's studies courses, which would 'serve as the academic equivalent of decontamination chambers.' More recently, Showalter has argued for the need to institute curricular change which would incorporate 'gender as a fundamental category of literary analysis' ('The Other Bostonians'), not only by installing women writers but also by defamiliarizing or problematizing masculinity; that is, by showing how masculinity, like femininity, is socially constructed. (See *defamiliarization.)

Showalter has been criticized by some feminist critics for her negative reading of *Virginia Woolf in *A Literature of Their Own* and for what is sometimes seen as her theoretical naiveté – what *Toril Moi calls her 'traditional humanism.' In part, her work attracts such criticism because it is seen as representative of trends in specifically American feminist criticism, regarded as less sophisticated because more empirical and sociohistorical than French feminist criticism, which draws heavily from psychoanalysis (especially that of *Jacques Lacan) and *deconstruction (especially that of *Jacques Derrida). However, there is no doubt that Showalter's literary and critical histories have served an important function in synthesizing and contextualizing many of the major debates in feminist literary criticism. (See also *feminist criticism, Anglo-American.)

JO-ANN WALLACE

Primary Sources

Showalter, Elaine. *The Female Malady: Women, Madness and English Culture, 1830–1980.* New York: Pantheon Books, 1985.
– 'Feminist Criticism in the Wilderness.' *Critical Inquiry* 8 (1981): 179–205.
– *A Literature of Their Own: British Women Novelists From Brontë to Lessing.* Princeton: Princeton UP, 1977.
– 'The Other Bostonians: Gender and Literary Study.' *Yale Journal of Criticism* 1 (1988): 179–87.
– 'Review Essay: Literary Criticism.' *Signs: Journal of Women in Culture and Society* 1 (1975): 435–60.
– *Sexual Anarchy: Gender and Culture at the Fin de Siècle.* New York: Viking, 1990.
– 'Toward a Feminist Poetics.' In *Women's Writing and Writing About Women.* Ed. Mary Jacobus. London: Croom Helm, 1979.
– 'Women and the Literary Curriculum.' *College English* 32 (1970): 855–62.
– 'Women's Time, Women's Space: Writing the History of Feminist Criticism.' *Tulsa Studies in Women's Literature* 3 (Spring-Fall 1984–5): 29–43.
– *The New Feminist Criticism: Essays on Women, Literature and Theory.* New York: Pantheon Books, 1985.
– *Speaking of Gender.* New York: Routledge, 1989.

Secondary Sources

Kaplan, Sydney Janet. 'Varieties of Feminist Criticism.' In *Making a Difference: Feminist Literary Criticism.* Ed. Gayle Greene and Coppélia Kahn. London: Methuen, 1985.
Moi, Toril. *Sexual/Textual Politics: Feminist Literary Theory.* London: Methuen, 1985.
Todd, Janet. *Feminist Literary History.* New York: Routledge, 1988.

Starobinski, Jean

(b. Switzerland 1920–) Professor and critic. Jean Starobinski studied at the University of Geneva (1942–9) where he received his doctorat ès lettres and doctorat en médecine and served as assistant to Marcel Raymond, leader of the *Geneva School. After interning in medicine and psychiatry, he became assistant professor of French at the Johns Hopkins University (1954–6) and attended clinics and seminars in the history of medicine. Although he abandoned medicine as a profession in 1958, he continues to write on the history and theory of medicine and psychology. At present, Starobinski is a professor of French *literature at the University of Geneva and president of the Rencontres Internationales de Genève and the Société J.-J. Rousseau. He has received many honorary doctorates and prizes and has been elected to several foreign academies including the American Academy of Arts and Sciences.

Preferring the word *'relation'* and not 'theory' or 'method' to describe his criticism, Starobinski argues that theory may be applied in the physical sciences but in literary criticism it merely legitimizes the critic's a posteriori illusions. For Starobinski, *relation* is a transcoding, a free transcription of various data presented in the 'interior' of the *text (*L'Oeil vivant* 2: 158–9). Successful criticism will not come from preconceived methods which unfold automatically. Instead, Starobinski looks for *relations* in the text, for the driving force behind the text.

His conviction that the evidence immanent in the text is sufficient data for criticism parallels the primacy and interiority of texts demanded by his professor Marcel Raymond and the Geneva School. Since data must be derived from the text, the text must be 'definitive.' Starobinski insists that philology be applied to verify texts, to understand words according to their historical meanings and to evaluate the distance between the exceptional and the common word (*Pour un Temps* 11). Starobinski's edition of Jean-Jacques Rousseau's *Discours sur l'origine et les fondements de l'inégalité* and his study of Ferdinand de Saussure's notes, published as *Les Mots sous les mots*, provide examples of exacting standards for textual editions. (See *Ferdinand de Saussure, *genetic criticism.)

Once the text's reliability is established, the critic turns to its form, particularly to repeated patterns, the exterior signs of what is hidden in the preconscious of the creator of the text. This is anamnesis, following the psychoanalyst's practice of tracing to discover the inner individual or the society hidden behind such devices as masks, allegory and ornate language. Since his first publication in the 1940s, Starobinski has dealt with these artifices of hiding manifested in works from antiquity to the present.

Starobinski's main focus has been 18th-century texts. *Montesquieu par lui-même* (1966) describes Montesquieu as believing that all obscure, hidden truths can be unveiled and then viewed in the light of reason. *Jean-Jacques Rousseau: La Transparence et l'obstacle* (1971) traces each work of Rousseau back to a childhood experience of injustice. The child's inability to make his innocence transparent led to Rousseau's later conclusion that such opacities are found throughout the history of mankind. Rousseau's obstacle/transparence conflict continues, culminating in *Rêveries du promeneur solitaire* (1782), when the lonely author offers his innocence up to the hostile world. Drawing upon architecture and art, Starobinski studies the opposition of darkness and light in *1789: Les Emblèmes de la raison* (1973).

The systematic exploration of darkness and opacities found in the subconscious associates Starobinski with surrealism, founded by André Breton and Louis Aragon. His search for the one psychological state to explain the entire work of an individual or century recalls Taine's *faculté maîtresse* and produces such convincing studies as Stendhal's pseudonyms and Claude Simon's oneness of the past and present. Yet, the brilliance and clarity of simplification must be accepted as only one point of view.

Starobinski's influence in the U.S.A. may be suggested by the numerous translations of his works. (See also *phenomenological criticism.)

MARTHA O'NAN

Primary Sources

Starobinski, Jean, ed. *Discours sur l'origine et les fondements de l'inégalité.* Paris: Gallimard, 1964.

Vol. 3 of *Oeuvres complètes de Jean-Jacques Rousseau.* 4 vols. 1959–69.
– 'Entretien avec Jacques Bonnet.' In *Pour un Temps.* Ed. Jacques Bonnet. Cahiers pour un Temps. Paris: Centre Georges Pompidou, 1985, 9–23.
– *L'Invention de la liberté.* Collection Art Idées Histoire. Geneva: Skira, 1964.
– *Jean-Jacques Rousseau: La Transparence et l'obstacle* followed by *Sept essais sur Rousseau.* Collection Tel. Paris: Gallimard, 1971.
– 'La Journée dans "Histoire."' In *Sur Claude Simon.* Communications au Colloque Claude Simon. Paris: Minuit, 1987, 9–32.
– *1789: Les Emblèmes de la raison.* Paris: Flammarion, 1973.
– *Montaigne en mouvement.* Bibliothèque des Idées. Paris: Gallimard, 1982.
– *Montesquieu par lui-même.* Ecrivains de toujours. Paris: Seuil, 1966.
– *Les Mots sous les mots: Les Anagrammes de Ferdinand de Saussure.* Collection Le Chemin. Paris: Gallimard, 1971.
– *L'Oeil vivant.* 2 vols. Collection Le Chemin. Paris: Gallimard, 1961–8.
– *Portrait de l'artiste en saltimbanque.* Les Sentires de la Création. Geneva: Skira, 1970.
– *Trois fureurs.* Collection Le Chemin. Paris: Gallimard, 1974.
– and Nicolas Bouvier. *Histoire de la médecine.* Lausanne: Rencontre, 1963.

Secondary Sources

Bonnet, Jacques, ed. *Pour un temps.* Cahiers pour un Temps. Paris: Centre Georges Pompidou, 1985.
Carrard, Philippe. 'Starobinski, Rousset et la question du récit.' *Swiss-French Studies/Etudes Romades* 1.2 (1980): 24–61.
Demougin, Jacques, ed. *Dictionnaire de la littérature française et francophone.* 3 vols. Paris: Larousse, 1988.
Lawall, Sarah. *Critics of Consciousness: The Existential Structures of Literature.* Cambridge, Mass.: Harvard UP, 1968.
Reichler, Claude. 'Jean Starobinski et la critique genevoise.' *Critique* 43: 481–2 (1987): 606–11.
Spears, Monroe K. 'Montaigne Our Contemporary.' *Hudson Review* 41 (1988): 301–18.

Steiner, George Francis

(b. France, 1929–) Literary critic. Born in France, George Steiner spent his youth in the United States. He was educated at the Sorbonne (Bachelier ès Lettres 1947), the University of Chicago (B.A. 1948), Harvard University (M.A. 1950), and Balliol College,

Oxford (D.Phil. 1955). In 1961 he was appointed a fellow at Churchill College, Cambridge, and in 1974 he became professor of English and comparative literature at the University of Geneva. Steiner is a literary critic but prefers the terms *Kulturkritiker* and *Sprachphilosoph*, since these better suggest the wide range of his interests: criticism, *hermeneutics, philosophy and philosophies of language, and theories of culture. He has published poetry and fiction, including *The Portage to San Cristobal of A.H.* (1981), a controversial novel about Hitler and the Holocaust which develops some suggestions from Freud's *Moses and Monotheism.* (See *Sigmund Freud.)

Steiner's first two books, *Tolstoy or Dostoevsky* (1959) and *The Death of Tragedy* (1961), express two of the basic assumptions of his criticism: metaphysical, religious and political concerns are central both in great *literature and in criticism, and the best criticism uses, in *Kenneth Burke's words (quoted by Steiner), 'all that there is to use.' In Steiner's early work this idea is directed against the *New Criticism; in *After Babel* (1975) and *Real Presences* (1989) it is central to his critique of *deconstruction. The first two books also introduce the apocalyptic note characteristic of his work, with their insistence that Western civilization is in decline and that evidence of this can be found in the fact that its literature is rarely tragic or religious.

In *Language and Silence* (1967) and *In Bluebeard's Castle* (1971) Steiner argues that modern barbarism – the Holocaust, in particular – indicates that the phase of Western civilization which began in Periclean Athens is over. Although he insists throughout his criticism on the value of Western civilization, Steiner, developing *Walter Benjamin's 'Theses on History,' nevertheless asks disturbing questions about the extent to which that culture's values, ideals and supreme achievements have been implicated in events ostensibly their antithesis.

Steiner's concern with language is developed in *Extraterritorial* (1971), a collection of essays, and in his most substantial work, *After Babel.* The latter is a history of language, a critique of theories of language and an inquiry into topics such as 'counter-factuality,' the multiplicity of languages, and the debate between linguistic relativists (Humboldt, Sapir and Whorf) and universalists (*Chomsky). The book's central concern is translation. Particularly important for students of literature is Steiner's engage-

ment with hermeneutics which results in a four-fold model for translation. While sympathetic to linguistics, Steiner nevertheless suggests that it is only of limited use in the study of literature and translation. Both here and in his later work, Steiner acknowledges his debt to Benjamin and *Martin Heidegger, especially Heidegger's interest in hermeneutics and the relationship between language and being. (See theories of *translation.)

Steiner followed *After Babel* with *Heidegger* (1978) and *Antigones* (1984). The first offers a sympathetic reading of a philosopher many of whose major themes are also Steiner's. The second, in its concern with the translations of a major text, looks back to *After Babel*; but in its emphasis on the classic's 'presence' and its dimension of transcendence it anticipates the critique of deconstruction in *Real Presences.*

Real Presences is Steiner's *summa.* Arguing against *poststructuralism's view of literature as play and its deconstruction of 'presence,' Steiner insists that art and reading are a 'wager' on meaning and transcendence and that 'the final stakes are theological' (4, 87). Central to Steiner's argument are the example of music, the well-known aporias (impasses of thought) in Descartes, Kant, and 'axiomatic systems' in mathematics (213–14). (See theories of *play/freeplay, *aporia, *metaphysics of presence.)

Steiner belongs to no critical school and is more syncretic than original. His critical masters are *George Lukács, Hermann Broch, Martin Heidegger, Walter Benjamin, *Edmund Wilson, and *F.R. Leavis. He is without any apparent disciples in the universities but has a wide influence on the general educated public through his reviews and essays in *The New Yorker* and the London *Sunday Times* which show him to be a very effective popularizer of contemporary trends and ideas.

Some critics have argued that Steiner conducts his argument at too abstract a level with few references to texts or facts. Others argue that some of his larger, more provocative questions are either unanswerable ('Why is there not just one language?') or meaningless ('Is there a lie, anywhere, in Mozart?'). Like most conservatives he idealizes the past. On the other hand, the case for Steiner can perhaps be best stated by emphasizing the extent to which in an age of narrow specialization, he has attempted to make literary and cultural criticism not only comparative and interdisciplinary but relevant to the large human issues art has always addressed. His introduction to *The George Steiner Reader* (1984) is an excellent summary of his views on culture and criticism.

SAM SOLECKI

Primary Sources

Steiner, George. *After Babel: Aspects of Language and Translation*. New York: Oxford UP, 1975.
- *Anno Domini: Three Stories*. New York: Atheneum, 1967.
- *Antigones*. New York: Oxford UP, 1984.
- *The Death of Tragedy*. New York: Knopf, 1961.
- *Extraterritorial: Papers on Literature and the Language Revolution*. New York: Atheneum, 1971.
- *The George Steiner Reader*. New York: Oxford UP, 1984.
- *Heidegger*. London: Fontana and Collins, 1978.
- *In Bluebeard's Castle: Some Notes Towards the Redefinition of Culture*. New Haven: Yale UP, 1971.
- *Language and Silence: Essays on Language, Literature and the Inhuman*. New York: Atheneum, 1967.
- *On Difficulty and Other Essays*. New York: Oxford UP, 1978.
- *The Portage to San Cristobal of A.H.* New York: Simon and Schuster, 1981.
- *Proofs and Three Parables*. London: Faber and Faber, 1992.
- *Real Presences*. Chicago: U of Chicago P, 1989.
- *Tolstoy or Dostoevsky: An Essay in the Old Criticism*. New York: Knopf, 1959.

Todorov, Tzvetan

(b. Bulgaria, 1939–) Literary structuralist and semiotician. Todorov studied Slavic philology for his first degree (1961) at the University of Sofia and then migrated to France to study language and *literature at the University of Paris. His doctoral thesis (1966) on Choderlos de Laclos' epistolary novel *Les Liaisons dangereuses* was written under the direction of *Roland Barthes and later published as *Littérature et signification* (1967). In 1970 he was awarded the doctorat ès lettres. From 1964 to 1967, he was a research assistant at the Ecole Pratique des Hautes Etudes en Sciences Sociales; and from 1968 to the present he has held a research appointment at the Centre National de la Recherche Scientifique (CNRS) in Paris. He has also served as member of the board of directors of the Centre de Recherches sur les Arts et le Langage and as the editor (1970–9) of the journal *Poétique: Revue de théorie et*

d'analyse littéraires. Together with *Hélène Cixous and *Gérard Genette, Todorov directed the publication of an important collection of studies on poetics, which include, in addition to some of his own work, several influential studies by Genette (*Figures I, Figures II* and *Figures III*). Todorov has taught at several universities in the U.S.A., including Yale, Iowa, NYU, Wisconsin, and Columbia. Three works in particular have made him a leading theorist of the structuralist movement in France. One is his influential study *The Fantastic: A Structural Approach to a Literary Genre* (1973); the other two, which are more general in scope, are the *Poetics of Prose* (1977) and *Introduction to Poetics* (1981). His *Theories of the Symbol* (1982) is a historical study of the *semiotics of literary symbolic expression and his *Encyclopedic Dictionary of the Sciences of Language* (1979), written in collaboration with *Oswald Ducrot, discusses many of the schools, fields and concepts of modern, semiotically oriented, language study. (See also *structuralism.)

Todorov's work is based in part on the poetics of the Russian formalists (especially *Vladimir Propp, *Roman Jakobson and *Mikhail Bakhtin), the textual analyses of the German Morphological School, the epistemology of *Claude Lévi-Strauss, and – more recently – the poststructuralist arguments of Roland Barthes and *Jacques Derrida. (See Russian *formalism, *poststructuralism.) For Todorov, the proper subject-matter of poetics is not 'interpretation' (or the naming of a work's meaning) but the structures that are generally inherent in literary *discourse. In other words, poetics is concerned with explaining the essence of literariness rather than the significance of literary texts. (See *text.) The particular structures described by poetics concern three aspects of literary discourse as a system: the semantic, the syntactic and the verbal. Literary semantics takes for granted a semiotic distinction between signification and symbolization and is concerned with 'discourse registers.' (See *signified/signifier/signification.) These are formed by certain features of language, especially its degree of abstractness, 'figurality,' 'intertextual valence,' and 'subjectivity.' (See *intertextuality.) Literary syntactics concerns the types of relation – logical, temporal and spatial – that can obtain among minimal units of thematic structure. The 'verbal' aspect of discourse concerns the characterizing of information through its mode ('the

477

degree of exactitude with which ... [a] discourse evokes its referent'), its presentation of time (the relation between the temporal line of a fictional discourse and the temporal line of its corresponding fictive universe), its perspectival vision (the point of view from which an object is observed and the quantity and quality of the information received), and its voice (the properties of fictional discourse analysed as a speech act) (*Introduction to Poetics* 13–58). (See also *speech act theory, *discourse analysis theory.)

Todorov distinguishes between scientific poetics and other types of criticism to which he refers generally as 'projection.' In his view, some forms of projection – especially biographical, psychoanalytic, sociological, and *phenomenological criticism – treat the literary text as essentially a transposition from some non-literary essence: an author's life, a psychological reality, a social condition, or a writer's mind. (See also *psychoanalytic theory.) Other forms of projection, including commentary, *explication de texte*, and paraphrase, merely discuss a text as the expression of a certain meaning (*Poetics of Prose* 234–46). Still other forms can be grouped under the general heading of *archetypal criticism. These involve a projection of certain philosophical, psychological and ethical concepts necessarily implicit in the definition of myths and the constructive use of these concepts to elaborate descriptive taxonomies. (See *myth.) Todorov argues that projective criticism has little explanatory power (*The Fantastic* 9–21).

Todorov also distinguishes between a linguistically oriented poetics and 'reading.' Poetics is an instrument of investigation for the description of an individual textual system; it takes for granted the pre-existence of all categories of literary discourse, all linguistic categories, and an 'atemporal material structure.' Reading, on the other hand, involves an individual's encounter with a particular text and consists 'in relating each element of ... [a] text to all others, these being inventoried not in their general signification but with a view to this unique usage.' Reading thus involves a 'certain destruction of the text's apparent order' as well as the overlaying of linguistic levels and of figuration. As any reading, moreover, necessarily 'privileges' certain elements of the text, an 'indefinite number' of readings of any text are possible (*Poetics of Prose* 237–40). Todorov, it may be noted,

strongly disagrees with certain American types of poststructuralism. He is especially critical of the pragmatism advocated by *Stanley Fish and the *deconstruction advanced by *J. Hillis Miller (*Literature and Its Theorists* 182–91).

JAMES STEELE

Primary Sources

Todorov, Tzvetan. *The Conquest of America*. Trans. Richard Howard. New York: Harper and Row, 1982.
– *The Fantastic: A Structural Approach to a Literary Genre*. Trans. Richard Howard. Ithaca: Cornell UP, 1973.
– *Grammaire du Décaméron*. The Hague: Mouton, 1969.
– *Introduction to Poetics*. Trans. Richard Howard. Minneapolis: U of Minneapolis P, 1981.
– 'Language and Literature.' In *The Structuralist Controversy: The Languages of Criticism and Sciences of Man*. Ed. Richard Macksey and Eugenio Donato. Baltimore: Johns Hopkins UP, 1970.
– *Literature and Its Theorists*. Ithaca: Cornell UP, 1984.
– *Littérature et signification*. Paris: Larousse, 1967.
– *Mikhail Bakhtin, Le principe dialogique*. Paris: Editions du Seuil, 1981.
– *The Poetics of Prose*. Trans. Richard Howard. Ithaca: Cornell UP, 1977.
– *Theories of the Symbol*. Trans. Catherine Porter. Ithaca: Cornell UP, 1982.
– and Oswald Ducrot. *Encyclopedic Dictionary of the Sciences of Language*. Trans. Catherine Porter. Baltimore and London: Johns Hopkins UP, 1979.
– *Théorie de la littérature*. Paris: Editions du Seuil, 1965.

Secondary Sources

Brooks, Peter. *Reading for the Plot: Design and Intention in Narrative*. New York: Vintage (Random House), 1984.
Culler, Jonathan. *The Pursuit of Signs: Semiotics, Literature, Deconstruction*. Ithaca: Cornell UP, 1981.
– *Structuralist Poetics: Structuralism, Linguistics, and the Study of Literature*. London: Routledge and Kegan Paul, 1975.
Genette, Gérard. *Figures of Literary Discourse*. Trans. Alan Sheridan. New York: Columbia UP, 1982.
Davis, Lennard J. *Resisting Novels: Ideology and Fiction*. London: Methuen, 1987.
Fokkema, D.W., and Elrud Kunne-Ibsch. *Theories of Literature in the 20th Century: Structuralism, Marxism, Aesthetics of Reception, Semiotics*. London: C. Hurst and Co., 1977.
Jefferson, Ann, and David Robey, eds. *Modern Literary Theory: A Comparative Introduction*. London: B.T. Batsford, 1982.

Merquior, J.G. *From Prague to Paris: A Critique of Structuralist and Post-Structuralist Thought.* London: Verso, 1986.

Scholes, Robert. *Semiotics and Interpretation.* New Haven: Yale UP, 1982.

– *Structuralism in Literature: An Introduction.* New Haven: Yale UP, 1974.

Selden, Raman. *A Reader's Guide to Contemporary Literary Theory.* Lexington: UP of Kentucky, 1985.

Tomashevskii, Boris Viktorovich

(b. Russia, 1890–d. 1957) Russian formalist scholar. Graduating from the University of Liège with a degree in electrical engineering, Tomashevskii attended the Sorbonne, studying 17th- and 18th-century French poetry. Upon returning to Russia, he studied Russian philology at St. Petersburg University and in 1918 joined OPOIAZ (acronym for the Society for the Study of Poetic Language) in which he played a significant role in developing the formalist theory of versification. From the mid-1920s he taught poetics and stylistics at Leningrad University. Forced to give up teaching in the 1930s, he became involved in editorial activities, preparing critical editions of Pushkin, Gogol, Dostoevsky, and Chekhov. In his last years he was allowed both to resume teaching at Leningrad University and to prepare some of his works on poetics and stylistics for publication. (See Russian *formalism.)

As a theorist, Tomashevskii was concerned primarily with questions of versification and poetics. His *Russkoe stikhoslozhenie. Metrika* [*Russian Versification. Metrics* 1923] is a concise introduction to the problems of Russian versification, defining poetic speech as speech organized in its phonetic aspect and concentrating on the role of stress and intonation in the metric division of verse. But he also saw the need to investigate the interrelations between intonation and syntax, sound and semantics, thus paving the way for the functional approach to the study of metrics.

The best examples of this approach to versification are his two articles 'Problema stikhotvornogo ritma' ['The Problem of Verse Rhythm' 1923] and 'Stikh i ritm' ['Verse and Rhythm' 1925] included in his 1929 book *O stikhe. Stat'i* [*On Verse: Articles*]. He differentiated between the concepts of the traditional

metric *canon and rhythm, the real phonetic form of a given poem, and distinguished the primary signs of rhythm (stress) from the secondary (intonation and euphony). He also elaborated *Boris Eikhenbaum's idea of the *dominanta,* a device which dominates in a poem and creates a certain artistic and rhythmical impression. In 'Stikh i ritm' he stressed the need to go beyond the analysis of phonetic elements (lexical stress) to the analysis of the phrase construction (phrase stress). He introduced the concept of a 'rhythmical impulse,' the preference of a given poet or poetic school for certain rhythmic devices, and also proposed their detailed study in poetry.

Tomashevskii successfully applied his theory to the study of the rhythmical patterns of the leading Russian poets, especially Pushkin. His articles 'Ritmika chetyrekhstopnogo iamba po nabliudeniiam *Evgeniia Onegina*' ['The Rhythm of the Four-Foot Iamb Based on Observations of *Eugene Onegin*' 1917] and 'Piatistopnyi iamb Pushkina' ['The Five-Foot Iamb in Pushkin' 1919] are still regarded as penetrating investigations of Pushkin's use of the iambic forms and of the Russian syllabo-accentual verse in general.

In both these articles Tomashevskii formulated those applications of statistical analysis to poetic rhythm which served as the basis for the modern linguistic-statistical approach to the study of Russian verse developed in the Soviet Union in the 1960s by scholars of the Tartu-Moscow school, such as M.L. Gasparov, P.A. Rudnev and A.N. Kolmogorov. (See *Tartu School.)

NINA KOLESNIKOFF

Primary Sources

Tomashevskii, B.V. 'Literatura i biografiia.' *Kniga i revolutsiia* 4 (1923). Trans. 'Literature and Biography.' In *Readings in Russian Poetics: Formalist and Structuralist Views.* Ed. L. Matejka and K. Pomorska. Cambridge, Mass.: MIT P, 1971, 47–55.

– 'Piatistopnyi iamb Pushkina.' *Ocherki po poetike Pushkina.* Berlin, 1923.

– 'Problema stikhotvornogo ritma.' *Literaturnaia mysl'* 2 (1923): 124–40.

– *Russkoe stikhoslozhenie. Metrika.* Leningrad, 1923.

– 'Stikh i ritm.' In *O stikhe. Stat'i.* Leningrad, 1929.

– *Teoriia literatury. Poetika.* Leningrad, 1925. Sections trans. as 'Thematics.' In *Russian Formalist Criticism: Four Essays.* Ed. L. Lemon and M. Reis. Lincoln: Nebraska UP, 1965, 61–98. Sections trans. as 'Literary Genres.' *Russian Poetics in Translation* 5 (1978): 52–93.

Secondary Sources

Gasparov, M.L. 'Quantitative Methods in Russian Metrics: Achievements and Prospects.' *Russian Poetics in Translation* 7 (1980): 1–19.
Jakobson, R. 'B.V. Tomashevskii.' *International Journal of Russian Linguistics and Poetics* 1–2 (1959): 313–14.
Striedter, J. 'The Russian Formalist Theory of Literary Evolution.' *PTL: A Journal for Descriptive Poetics and Theory of Literature* 3 (1978): 1–24.
Turner, C.J.G. 'Tomashevsky's Literary Theory.' *Symposium* 26 (1972): 67–77.

Trilling, Lionel

(b. U.S.A., 1905–d. 1975) Literary critic. Trilling obtained a B.A. and M.A. in English from Columbia University and began to teach there in 1931 while working on his Ph.D. Newly married and a young instructor, he was faced with the burden of supporting his indigent parents. Turning against the economic system that had betrayed his immigrant parents' dream of success, he became a political and cultural radical. As a committed Marxist, he wrote reviews for the left-liberal magazines *The Nation* and *The New Republic*. He was the first Jew to teach at Columbia, and that, plus his adherence to Marxism and, later on, Freudianism, nearly resulted in his being dismissed from the highly conservative 'WASP'-dominated department of English. (See *Marxist criticism, *Sigmund Freud.)

During the late 1930s Trilling drew away from Marxism and developed the humanistic liberal political and social attitude that from then on dominated his criticism. He became a model Columbia University English professor, teaching the humanities through the tradition of the great books of Western civilization and analysing modern British and American writers and cultural matters. From Marxism, however, he took a dialectical approach to *literature: dialectic is 'just another word for form, and has for its purpose, in philosophy or in art, the leading of the mind to some conclusion' *(The Liberal Imagination* 283). His first two books, *Matthew Arnold* (1939) and *E.M. Forster* (1943), are characterized by this approach.

Trilling's most important work is found in his various collections of critical essays, the best known of which is *The Liberal Imagination*. He states his position in the preface. 'These are not political essays,' he writes, 'they are essays in literary criticism. But they assume the inevitably intimate, if not always obvious, connection between literature and politics' (xi–xii). Trilling goes on to observe that one of the tendencies of liberalism is to simplify issues, to be overly rational. 'The job of criticism would seem to be, then,' he concludes, 'to recall liberalism to its first essential imagination of variousness and possibility, which implies the awareness of complexity and difficulty' (xv). In the essays that follow he attacks those writers whom he believes have, ideologically or formally, oversimplified, like Dreiser and Sherwood Anderson, and praises those writers, like *Henry James and Scott Fitzgerald, who were aware of complexity and difficulty. Other essays in *The Liberal Imagination* indicate the range of Trilling's interests; 'Freud and Literature,' 'Tacitus Now' and 'The Kinsey Report.'

Trilling was not a literary theorist although he liked to reflect philosophically on literature and life. He believed primarily in the evaluative function of criticism. 'The word criticism,' he wrote in 'What is Criticism?' 'derives from the Greek word meaning judgment. A critic does more things with literature than judge it, but his judicial function is involved in everything that he does' *(The Last Decade: Essays and Reviews, 1965–75* 57). Trilling was in the tradition of that vigorous group of Jewish intellectuals, including Meyer Schapiro, Harold Rosenberg, Philip Rahv, and Clement Greenberg, who, coming out of a radical background, saw criticism not as an academic exercise but as a means of reforming art and society. In his later years, Trilling, like other liberals, felt that his idea of culture and intellect had been fatally undermined by the mobility and transience of the postindustrial age. As Daniel T. O'Hara has said, 'The spectral politics of the shaped self that Trilling practiced for so long have been outmoded by the global economy of the disintegrated self' (288). Trilling became 'the subversive patriarch' of American culture, 'the stylish terminator of modern culture itself' (O'Hara 291). Be that as it may, Lionel Trilling will continue to be read for the acuity of his literary criticism, for his urbane moderation and for the elegance of his style, all of which have brought him a devoted audience in and beyond the universities.

PETER BUITENHUIS

Primary Sources

Trilling, Lionel. *Beyond Culture: Essays on Literature and Learning.* New York: Viking, 1956.
– *E.M. Forster.* London: Hogarth P, 1943. New York: New Directions P, 1964.
– *A Gathering of Fugitives.* Boston: Beacon P, 1956.
– *The Last Decade: Essays and Reviews, 1965–75.* New York: Harcourt, Brace, Jovanovich, 1979.
– *The Liberal Imagination: Essays on Literature and Society.* New York: Viking, 1950.
– *Matthew Arnold.* New York: Columbia UP, 1939.
– *The Middle of the Journey.* New York: Viking, 1947.
– *Mind in the Modern World.* New York: Viking, 1973.
– *Of This Time, Of That Place and Other Stories.* New York: Harcourt, Brace, Jovanovich, 1979.
– *The Opposing Self: Nine Essays in Criticism.* New York: Viking, 1955.
– *Prefaces to the Experience of Literature.* New York: Harcourt, Brace, Jovanovich, 1979.
– *Sincerity and Authenticity.* Cambridge, Mass.: Harvard UP, 1972.
– *Speaking of Literature and Society.* New York: Harcourt, Brace, Jovanovich, 1980.

Secondary Sources

Boyers, Robert. *Lionel Trilling: Negative Capability and the Wisdom of Avoidance.* Columbia: U of Missouri P, 1977.
Chace, William M. *Lionel Trilling: Criticism and Politics.* Stanford: Stanford UP, 1980.
Krupnick, Mark. *Lionel Trilling and the Fate of Cultural Criticism.* Evanston, Ill.: Northwestern UP, 1986.
O'Hara, Daniel T. *Lionel Trilling: The Work of Liberation.* Madison: U of Wisconsin P, 1988.
Shoben, Edward Joseph. *Lionel Trilling.* New York: Ungar Publishing Co., 1981.

Tynianov, Iurii Nikolaevich

(b. Russia, 1894–d. 1943) Russian formalist scholar. After completing his studies in Russian philology in 1918, Tynianov remained at St. Petersburg University. In 1919 he joined OPOIAZ (acronym for the Society for the Study of Poetic Language). From 1921 till 1930 he was a professor at the Leningrad Institute of the History of the Arts. In the 1920s he published his most important studies. From 1925 he started to write historical novels and also worked as a film scriptwriter.

The leading theoretician of the second stage of formalism, Tynianov developed a system of principles on the nature of *literature, literary structure and literary history. (See *Russian formalism.) *Problema stikhotvornogo iazyka* [*The Problem of Verse Language* 1924] advanced the concept of a dynamic structure, in which unity is achieved not by means of combination and merger but through interaction and the foregrounding of one group of elements at the expense of another. He defined the dominant element in a literary work as 'the constructive factor' and described it as the element organizing and subordinating all others.

Tynianov distinguished rhythm as the constructive principle of verse subordinating and deforming all other elements and outlined four important factors promoting rhythmical grouping and subordinating the rules of semantics: (1) the unity of the series – the tendency in verse for isolation and independence of individual lines and the failure of the rhythmical boundaries to converge with the boundaries of the syntactical unit; (2) the compactness of the series, resulting from syntactical isolation of lines, forcing each word to enter into more intimate and deforming relations with every other word; (3) the 'dynamization' of vocal material – the process of sharpening the principal meaning of the word in response to the rhythmical significance of the series; and (4) the successiveness of vocal material – the appearance of certain secondary or oscillating signs of meaning as a result of a word filling in a rhythmical gap in a given series.

Tynianov proceeded to investigate the relations between the elements of a given literary structure and the whole literary system, as well as extraliterary systems. 'O literaturnoi evolutsii' ['On Literary Evolution' 1927] differentiated between two constructive functions: the 'syn-function,' the interconnection of an element with other elements in the same work, and the 'auto-function,' the interrelation of an element with similar elements in other literary works and in other systems.

Initially, he examined intraliterary relations and formulated the principle of literary dynamics, that is, the continuous process of disautomatization and renewal of literary forms. Later, he explored the area of extraliterary relations and stressed their importance in determining the path of literary evolution. He argued for a closer investigation of the correlation between literature and the most immediate systems, especially social systems.

Tynianov's contribution to the development of formalism was immense. He almost single-handedly advanced the formalist theory toward *structuralism by formulating the principles of dynamic structure and the constructive factor and of literary dynamics and evolution. Many of these concepts were taken up and developed by the Prague Linguistic Circle, becoming a vital part of a coherent structuralist theory of literature. (See *Semiotic Poetics of the Prague School.)

NINA KOLESNIKOFF

Primary Sources

Tynianov, I.N. *Arkhaisty i novatory.* Leningrad, 1929.
– *Dostoevsky i Gogol'. K teorii parodii.* Petrograd, 1921.
– 'O literaturnoi evolutsii.' *Na literaturnom postu* 4 (1927). 'On Literary Evolution.' In *Readings in Russian Poetics: Formalist and Structuralist Views.* Ed. L. Matejka and K. Pomorska. Cambridge, Mass.: MIT P, 1971, 66–78.
– *Problema stikhotvornogo iazyka.* Leningrad, 1924. *The Problem of Verse Language.* Ann Arbor: Ardis, 1981.
– and R. Jakobson. 'Problemy izucheniia literatury i iazyka.' *Novyi lef* 12 (1928): 36–7. 'Problems in the Study of Literature and Language.' In *Readings in Russian Poetics: Formalist and Structuralist Views,* 79–81.

Secondary Sources

Erlich, Victor. *Russian Formalism: History-Doctrine.* The Hague: Mouton, 1955.
Steiner, Peter. *Russian Formalism: A Metapoetics.* Ithaca: Cornell UP, 1984.
Striedter, Jurij. 'The Russian Formalist Theory of Literary Evolution.' *PTL: A Journal for Descriptive Poetics and Theory of Literature* 3 (1978): 1–24.
– 'The Russian Formalist Theory of Prose.' *PTL: A Journal for Descriptive Poetics and Theory of Literature* 2 (1977): 429–70.

Uspenskii, Boris Andreevich

(b. U.S.S.R., 1937–) Semiotician and structuralist critic. After studying general and comparative linguistics at Moscow University, Boris Uspenskii wrote a dissertation on the structural typology of languages, *The Principles of Structural Typology* (1965; trans. 1968). His second dissertation was on the relation between the histories of traditional Russian church pronunciation and literary Russian pronunciation. In 1961 he studied at the University of Copenhagen's Institut for Lingvistik og Fonetik, where he consulted with the Danish structuralist Louis Hjelmslev. (See *structuralism, *semiotics.)

Returning to Moscow in 1962, he participated in the Moscow Symposium on Semiotic Analysis, a colloquium which marked the formation of the Soviet school of structural semiotics. He subsequently participated in the Tartu Summer Symposia, organized by *Iurii Lotman in 1964, 1966, 1968, and 1970 to discuss problems relating to structuralism and semiotics. (See *Tartu School.) While developing his ideas on structuralist semiotics, Uspenskii engaged in research at the Institute of African Languages (a part of the U.S.S.R.'s Academy of Sciences) and at the Laboratory of Computational Linguistics at Moscow University. He also lectured at Moscow University on the typology of languages and the history of Russian literary language. Although most of his work has been published in Russian only, three of his books have been translated into English. Two of these – *A Poetics of Composition* (1973) and *The Semiotics of the Russian Icon* (1976) – are concerned with the semiotics of artistic expression and one *(The Semiotics of Russian Culture* 1984, written jointly with Lotman) with the semiotics of certain historical movements.

Uspenskii's structuralist orientation is a synthesis of the semiotics of *C.S. Pierce and Charles Morris, the concepts of syntagmatics and paradigmatics advanced by *Ferdinand de Saussure, the pragmatic notions of the Prague School, and certain critical insights of *Mikhail Bakhtin and V.N. Voloshinov. (See *Semiotic Poetics of the Prague School.) His topics for semiotic analyses have included matters as diverse as fortune-telling by cards, the medieval icon, the songs of the Siberian Ket people, the management of direct speech in Tolstoy's *War and Peace,* modelling systems for understanding the dynamics of Russian culture, and certain compositional principles inherent in artistic texts. (See *text.)

In *A Poetics of Composition,* Uspenskii is concerned with analysing types of 'point of view' (which he defines as 'an ideological and evaluative position') and the kinds of relationship that may obtain among them. Point of view, he observes, operates as a functional unit of *discourse on several textual planes and forms part of the 'syntax' of artistic composition. On a deep, semantic plane, which involves a writer's general conception of the world, point of view may be understood as the position or positions 'from which the narrative is conducted.' This viewpoint may be either concealed or openly acknowledged, and it may be expressed by the author, by a narrator, or by a character, or by some combination of these. It may, likewise, be either a simple structure, in which all subordinate viewpoints are dominated by a single perspective, or a polyphonic structure containing multiple, non-subordinated viewpoints. (See *polyphony/dialogism.) On the 'phraseological plane' (or the level of speech characteristics), point of view may be expressed by such means as diction, shifts in 'functional sentence perspective,' kinds of naming, and the management of direct and indirect speech. On the spatial and temporal planes, it is manifested through verbally established relations between the describing subject (the author) and the described event (the object). The spatial position of the author may either concur (in different ways) or not concur with that of the characters described. Time, which is always a fundamental dimension of a literary text, may be ordered either from the position of one or more characters, or in accordance with an author's transcendent schema, or on the basis of some combination of these two systems. On the plane of 'psychology,' narrative can be constructed through the 'deliberately subjective viewpoint of a particular individual's consciousness' or 'objectively' on the basis of 'facts' known to the author. It can also involve two methods of description: (1) external description, or description from the point of view of an outside observer who describes only what he sees; and (2) internal description, or description from the point of view of an omniscient observer who can see into conciousness itself. Uspenskii notes that all forms of representational art – including pictorial art, *literature, film and theatre – are structurally 'isomorphic,' that is to say, they are all essentially 'framed' constructions combining, in one way or another, both 'external' and 'internal' points of view.

Uspenskii elaborates on this last point in *The Semiotics of the Russian Icon* – an exploration of some general semiotic conventions subsuming 'the language of art' in the medieval period. He argues that the 'internal' point of view in the art of this period is typically expressed by means of 'a system of inverted perspective,' which is the very opposite of 'perspective' as it came to be understood in the modern period, and that the organizing principle of medieval art is 'summation' – either explicitly by the artist or implicitly by the viewer – of a multiplicity of ('inverted') visual positions. Although this richly suggestive book is mainly concerned with the spatial organization of pictorial art, many of the principles discussed are also relevant to an understanding of the literary art of this period.

JAMES STEELE

Primary Sources

Lotman, Iu. M., and B.A. Ouspenskii, eds. *Travaux sur les systèmes de signes: Ecole de Tartu.* Trans. Anne Zouboff. Bruxelles: Editions Complexe, 1976.
Nakhimovsky, Alexander D., and Alice Stone Nakhimovsky, eds. *The Semiotics of Russian Cultural History: Essays by Iurii M. Lotman, Lidiia Ia. Ginsburg, Boris A. Uspenskii.* Ithaca/London: Cornell UP, 1985.
Uspenskii, Boris. 'The Language Situation and Linguistic Consciousness in Muscovite Rus': The Perception of Church Slavonic and Russian.' *California Slavic Studies* 12 (1984): 365–85.
– '"Left" and "Right" in Icon-Painting.' *Semiotica* 13.1 (1975): 33–9.
– *A Poetics of Composition: The Structure of the Artistic Text and Typology of a Compositional Form.* Trans. Valentina Zavarin and Susan Wittig. Berkeley/Los Angeles/London: U of California P, 1973.
– *The Principles of Structural Typology.* The Hague: Mouton, 1968.
– *The Semiotics of the Russian Icon.* Ed. Stephen Rudy. Lisse: Peter de Ridder P, 1976.
– 'Structural Isomorphism of Verbal and Visual Art.' *Poetics* 5 (1972): 5–39.
– and M.I. Lekomceva. 'A Description of a Semiotic System with Simple Syntax.' *Semiotica* 18.2 (1976): 157–69.
– and Yu. M. Lotman. *The Semiotics of Russian Culture.* Ed. Ann Shukman. Michigan Slavic Contributions, no.11. Ann Arbor: Department of Slavic Languages and Literatures, U of Michigan, 1984.

Secondary sources

Bakhtin, M. *Problems of Dostoevsky's Poetics.* Trans. R.W. Rotsel. Ann Arbor: Ardis, 1973.
Eisenstein, S. *The Film Form: Essays in Film Theory.* Cleveland: World Publishing, 1957.
Lotman, Ju. M. *The Structure of the Artistic Text.* Trans. Ronald Vroon and Gail Vroon. Michigan

Slavic Contributions, no. 7. Ann Arbor: Department of Slavic Languages and Literatures, U of Michigan, 1977.

Matejka, Ladislav, and Krystyna Pomorska, eds. *Russian Poetics: Formalist and Structuralist Views*. Cambridge, Mass.: MIT P, 1971.

Saussure, Ferdinand de. *Course in General Linguistics*. Ed. Charles Bally and Albert Sechehaye in collaboration with Albert Riedlinger. Trans. Wade Baskin. New York/Toronto/London: McGraw-Hill, 1966.

Voloshinov, V.N. *Marxism and the Philosophy of Language*. Trans. L. Matejka and I.R. Titunik. New York: Seminar P, 1973.

Wellek, René

(b. Austria, 1903–) Theoretician of *literature and comparative literature, historian of modern literary criticism. Wellek studied in Prague, England (1924–5) and the United States (1927–30). From 1930 to 1935, he was an active junior member of the Prague Linguistic Circle; from 1935 to 1939 he lectured on Czech language and literature at the University of London. (See *Semiotic Poetics of the Prague School.) Wellek left for the United States after Hitler's invasion of Czechoslovakia. Director of comparative literature at Yale University from 1946 to his retirement in 1972, a prolific scholar whose work is translated into 23 languages, Wellek has been part of the institution of comparative literature since its rebirth shortly after the Second World War.

From Kant, Wellek derives his concept of literature as an autonomous aesthetic phenomenon; from the Prague Linguistic Circle, especially *Jan Mukařovský and *Roman Jakobson, he takes the idea of the work as a linguistic sign system related to historical norms and values. (See *sign.) He adapts theories of the Polish phenomenologist *Roman Ingarden in his definition of literature as a stratified system of norms. Wellek introduced Slavic phenomenological theory in the United States and spurred the conceptualization of literary studies there. (See *phenomenological criticism.) His discussion of literary-critical concepts in an international context helped define comparative literature as an academic discipline.

From his earliest major essay, the 'Theory of Literary History' (1936), he ponders the idea of literary history throughout his career. He is best known, however, for the part of his work associated with formalist *New Criticism: a set of theoretical assertions in the 1949 *Theory of Literature* (co-authored with Austin Warren) that challenged positivist scholarship tied to extraliterary disciplines and encouraged readers to envisage literature as an object of study in itself. Wellek proposed to study works as autonomous aesthetic wholes, *monuments* rather than historical *documents*, and he distinguished *intrinsic* approaches that studied the work's aesthetic structure from *extrinsic* approaches that subordinated literature to another discipline such as sociology or psychology. Literary analysis was to depend on a coherent theory of literature which Wellek proposed in a discussion of the 'mode of existence of the literary work of art' that included a description of Ingarden's 'stratified system of norms.'

Wellek's insistence on methodological priorities and his rejection of historical positivism have helped define modern comparative literature studies. In 'The Crisis of Comparative Literature' (1958), a polemical lecture delivered at the second International Comparative Literature Association Congress, he attacked an arid factualism of literary study that relied on quantitative analysis and exclusive domains of expertise. To current French definitions of comparative literature as the documentable study of literary influence, Wellek responded that the proper subject of comparative literature was the study of *literariness* across national boundaries and the analysis of a work as a stratified structure of signs and meanings with its own aesthetic value and 'substantial identity' throughout various readings.

'Perspectivism' is Wellek's term for the correlation of history, theory and criticism, and of absolute and relative points of view, that is necessary to grasp this stratified structure of meanings. A perspectivist view of literary history examines patterns of norms or 'regulatory ideas'; it rejects both atomistic description and rigid paradigms such as the division by centuries. Essays like 'The Concept of Romanticism in Literary History' (*Concepts of Criticism* 1963) attempt to grasp larger frameworks while taking into account the aesthetic identity of individual texts. (See *text.) Wellek considers his chief work the monumental *History of Modern Criticism: 1750–1950* (1955–) which adapts the perspectivist approach to a study of major Western literary critics. When he published the first volume he planned to demonstrate a gradual evolution of critical theory. By 1973 ('The Fall of Literary History'), he no longer believed in such an evolution and described his *History* instead as a series of debates on recurrent problems of literary analysis.

The immediate impact and global popularity of *Theory of Literature* has overshadowed much of Wellek's other work. Published in the same decade as many New Critical books, sharing with New Criticism a belief in artistic autonomy and aesthetic value, offering clearly phrased philosophical distinctions, and proposing in the first edition a reform of graduate literary study, *Theory of Literature* was received as the philosophical foundation for New Criticism. Wellek has repeatedly rejected this identification and reasserted his own preoccupation with literary history. Nonetheless, *Theory*'s insistence on literature as an object of study in its own right and on the rejection of extrinsic or extraliterary criteria for literary judgment has continued to define the book for many readers. Complicating discussion is the fact that the examples of extrinsic criticism are those available in 1949.

Less recognized is Wellek's historiographical side: his perspectivism and the notion of literary history as a process governed by a dialectical relationship between the norms of the autonomous literary work and systems of norms in history. This aspect, clearly derived from Prague *structuralism, has elements in common with current approaches such as reception theories and *New Historicism that rely on historical positioning to examine different dialectical relationships between *text and history. (See *Constance School, *Hrvatsko filolosko drustvo.) A major difference, however, lies in Wellek's insistence on the work's autonomous aesthetic value. Upon similar grounds he rejects deconstructionist criticism, in which he sees the same risk of infinite semiotic regress criticized earlier in Mukařovský. (See *deconstruction, *semiotics.)

Wellek is the 20th century's best known and most influential comparatist. His emphasis on conceptualizing literary study helped shape analytical criticism in the U.S.A and Europe, including those current theories of *textuality that reject Wellek's aesthetic and work-centred view as part of an older humanistic model. His breadth, liberalism and insistence on the need to coordinate different modes of inquiry helped define the broadly literary-critical

stance of American studies of comparative literature. Although his frame of reference is the Western tradition which he sees as a unity, the clarity and applicability of his analyses have caused his work to be translated and used as a standard reference around the world.

SARAH LAWALL

Primary Sources

Wellek, René. *The Attack on Literature*. Chapel Hill: U of North Carolina P, 1982.
– *Concepts of Criticism*. Ed. Stephen G. Nichols, Jr. New Haven: Yale UP, 1963.
– *Confrontations: Studies in the Intellectual and Literary Relations between Germany, England, and the United States during the 19th Century*. Princeton: Princeton UP, 1965.
– *Discriminations: Further Concepts of Criticism*. New Haven: Yale UP, 1970.
– *Four Critics: Croce, Valéry, Lukács, and Ingarden*. Seattle/London: U of Washington P, 1981.
– *A History of Modern Criticism: 1750–1950*. Vol. 1: *The Later 18th Century*, 1955. Vol. 2: *The Romantic Age*, 1955. Vol. 3: *The Age of Transition*, 1965. Vol. 4: *The Later 19th Century*, 1965. Vol 5: *English Criticism, 1900–1950*, 1986. Vol. 6: *American Criticism, 1900–1950*, 1986. New Haven: Yale UP; London: J. Cape.
– *The Rise of English Literary History*. Chapel Hill: U of North Carolina P, 1941.
– 'The Theory of Literary History.' *Travaux du Cercle linguistique de Prague* 6 (1936): 179–91.
– and Austin Warren. *Theory of Literature*. New York: Harcourt, 1949.

Secondary Sources

Bucco, Martin. *René Wellek*. Boston: Twayne, 1981.
Creed, Walter G. 'René Wellek and Karl Popper on the Mode of Existence of Ideas in Literature and Science.' *Journal of the History of Ideas* 44.4 (Oct. 1983): 639–56.
Fietz, Lothar. 'René Welleks Literaturtheorie und der Prager Strukturalismus.' In *Englische und amerikanische Literaturtheorie*. Ed. Rudiger Ahrens and Erwin Wolff. 2 vols. Heidelberg, 1978–9.
Lawall, Sarah. 'René Wellek: Phenomenological Literary Historian.' In *Literary Theory and Criticism: Festschrift in Honor of René Wellek*. Ed. Joseph Strelka. Zurich: Peter Lang, 1984, 393–416.
– 'René Wellek and Modern Literary Criticism.' *Comparative Literature* 40.1 (Winter 1988): 3–24.
Wellek, René. 'Collaborating with Austin Warren on *Theory of Literature*.' In *Teacher and Critic: Essays by and about Austin Warren*. Ed. Myron Simon and Harvey Gross. Los Angeles: Plantin P, 1976, 68–75.

- 'My Early Life.' In *Contemporary Authors Autobiography Series*, vol. 7. Ed. Adele Sarkissian. Detroit: Gale Research, 1988, 205–26.
Winner, Thomas G., and John P. Kasik. 'René Wellek's Contribution to American Literary Scholarship.' *Forum* 2 (1977): 21–31.

White, Hayden

(b. U.S.A., 1928–) Historian and philosopher of history. White studied at Wayne State University and at the University of Michigan, where he received his Ph.D. in 1956. He has taught at the University of Rochester, UCLA and Wesleyan University, and since 1978 has been professor in the History of Consciousness Program, University of California at Santa Cruz.

White is best known for applying concepts derived from literary theory to the analysis of historical writings. In his major work, *Metahistory* (1973), he discusses 19th-century historians (Michelet, Ranke, Toqueville, and Burckhardt) and philosophers of history (Hegel, Marx, *Nietzsche, and *Croce). This study is introduced by an idealized 'theory of the historical work' which describes the process by which historians select and arrange the data from the 'unprocessed historical record' in order to render that record 'more comprehensible to an *audience* of a particular kind' (5). The process involves three modes of explanation which are combined in each historian's work: explanation by emplotment, by formal argument and by ideological implication. White follows *Northrop Frye (*Anatomy of Criticism*) in speaking of four modes of emplotment: romance, tragedy, comedy, and satire. There are also four modes of formal argument (following Stephen Pepper's *World Hypotheses*): formalist, organicist, mechanistic, and contextualist. Explanations by ideological implication (this time following Karl Mannheim's *Ideology and Utopia*) are either anarchist, conservative, radical, or liberal. Each of the works White discusses exhibits a particular combination of these modes which is the expression of its author's 'coherent vision or presiding image' of the whole historical field. Underlying this vision is a distinctive style whose grounds are 'poetic, and specifically linguistic, in nature' (30). The historian 'prefigures' the field in terms that correspond to the traditional tropes identified by poetic theory: metaphor, meto-

nymy, *synecdoche, and *irony. (See *trope, *metonymy/metaphor.) 'The theory of tropes provides a way of characterizing the dominant modes of historical thinking which took shape in Europe in the 19th century' (38).

White draws his ideas from many sources but he is perhaps most strongly influenced by structuralist theories of literature. (See *structuralism.) Though he speaks of the historian's poetic 'acts' or 'choices,' he thinks of these as culturally determined and unconscious ('precognitive and precritical in the economy of the historian's own consciousness' 31).

White's work has been influential in the literary study of historical texts but the focus of his work is not literary criticism or theory. It must be understood in the context of the debate over the epistemological status of historical knowledge. Some 19th- and 20th-century historians and positivistic philosophers have tried to make history into an objective explanatory discipline which tells what happened and why it happened in the manner of the natural sciences. In opposition to this view of history, White stresses the creative and constructive character not merely of historical writing but of historical knowledge itself.

In essays published since *Metahistory* (some collected in two volumes mentioned below), White has continued his literary treatment of history in general and historians in particular, on the whole not adhering to the overly rigid theoretical grid presented in his major work but more generally taking the concept of narrative as his point of departure.

DAVID CARR

Primary Sources

White, Hayden. *The Content of the Form: Narrative Discourse and Historical Representations*. Baltimore: Johns Hopkins UP, 1987.
– *Metahistory: The Historical Imagination in 19th Century Europe*. Baltimore: Johns Hopkins UP, 1973.
– *Tropics of Discourse: Essays in Cultural Criticism*. Baltimore: Johns Hopkins UP, 1978.

Williams, Raymond

(b. Wales, 1921–d.1988) Man of letters, literary critic, cultural theorist, and political activist. Williams was born and raised in a working-class family in Wales. As his critique of English culture sharpened through a long engagement with its *literature and institutions and through a growing affinity for Continental currents of thought, he came to settle on a cultural identity as a Welsh European. His death interrupted an ambitious and impressive work in progress concerning his deepest roots; what is left is a 1500-page fragment of a Welsh historical novel tracking 'The People of Black Mountain' as far as the Middle Ages. This is the region Williams left in his late teens. From Abergavenny Grammar School he moved to Trinity College, Cambridge, as an undergraduate on scholarship (1939), married his life-long companion and co-worker, Joyce (Joy) Dalling (1942), rose to the rank of captain in an anti-tank regiment during the war, and completed his degree just thereafter. He worked in adult education at Oxford (1946–61), promoting the theme of democratic permanent education, and published several books to direct students toward the social and political contexts of drama and fiction.

From 1961 to his retirement in 1983, Williams found his place at Jesus College, Cambridge. The position of Professor of Drama was created for him in 1974. As a political writer, Williams engaged in numerous discourses and media, including the academic, the artistic and the journalistic, producing more than 600 publications.

In all his cultural work, Williams was writing against two traditions: 'one which has totally spiritualized cultural production, the other which has relegated it to secondary status' (Politics and Letters 352–3). At his death, both opposing traditions had been much weakened. Williams was committed to the view that the prevailing 'categories of literature and criticism were so deeply compromised that they had to be challenged in toto' (Politics and Letters 326). He meant that the whole enterprise of 'imaginative literature,' confined to a specialized reserve secluded from other writing and other activity, had become so complicit in the capitalist system of meanings, values and divisions of labour that it had become an obstacle in the path of the long revolution toward a fuller attainment of (cultural, political and economic) value which he had documented and on behalf of which he always pressed his arguments.

His most important legacy is the interdisciplinary field of cultural studies which he pioneered and consolidated. As part of his contribution, he articulated and refined such key concepts as 'structure of feeling,' 'knowable community,' '*hegemony,' and '*cultural materialism.' Along with New Left Review and the Birmingham Centre for Contemporary Cultural Studies, for both of which he served as a kind of spiritual father at one time or another over two decades, Williams actively built bridges to such converging currents of cultural studies as the *Frankfurt School, the neo-Gramscians, and other renewals of Western cultural Marxism, as well as French and East European historical semiology, Foucauldian genealogy, and the McLuhan-inspired Canadian *discourse on communications technology. (See *Marxist criticism, *materialist criticism, *semiotics, *Foucault, *Gramsci, *McLuhan, *communication theory.)

In the 1950s and early 1960s, in Culture and Society, The Long Revolution and Communications, Williams established the frameworks for placing literary debates in larger contexts. He traced the culture and society argument from the 18th century to the 20th as a critique of the developing capitalist *social formation. Where the argument in its early stages had been critical of industrialism, in its modern versions, especially as embraced by *T.S. Eliot and *F.R. Leavis, who both loomed large in the cultural milieu where Williams was active, the argument could become evidently anti-democratic. Williams argued instead for the democratization of culture through the reform of cultural institutions.

By studying 'culture' in active and indissoluble relationship with such other key words as 'class,' 'industry,' 'democracy,' and 'art,' he opposed the influence that Eliot and Leavis had mobilized on behalf of minority cultural forms and argued that culture and democracy must be assisted to develop together. His scholarly analyses of the institutions of culture – for example, the forms of drama and fiction, the standardization of the language, the press, education, and literacy – provided evidence that the changes and conflicts of a way of life are deeply implicated in its systems of learning and communication, and supported his contention that relationships of *power, property and production are no more fundamental to a society than relationships in describing, learning, modifying, exchanging, and preserving experiences. Williams asserted, further, that these latter, far from being secondary communications about some other primary reality, are 'a central and necessary part of our humanity' (*Communications* 18–19).

In the later 1960s and early 1970s, encouraged by a newly politicized generation, Williams produced revaluations of fiction, drama and television: *Modern Tragedy, Drama from Ibsen to Brecht, The Country and the City,* and *Television.* He historicized and democratized such categories as 'tragedy,' read texts in their historical context and discussed cultural institutions within a critical sociology of society. In the later 1970s Williams turned to rewriting Marxist literary and cultural theory. No longer a renegade or fellow traveller (who had taken considerable distance from the crude anticultural Marxism of the received orthodox traditions) he became a respected innovator.

In *Marxism and Literature, Politics and Letters, Problems in Materialism and Culture,* and *Culture,* Williams elaborated his mature theory of cultural materialism, thematizing culture as a productive process and a constitutive signifying system whose institutions and practices are delimitable from the anthropological sense of culture as a whole way of life. Through the reworked category of 'hegemony,' he also showed that domination saturates the whole process of living culture, but always incompletely, and is therefore always resisted, based as it is in selective traditions of inclusion and exclusion. The result of Williams' theory of culture, in contrast to the formalist model of a cultural order of privileged objects and stable modes of composition and response, is a dynamic picture of a contested culture of practices and formations with varied and variable affiliations. It is a model that is capable of sustaining the gesture for which he was to become celebrated after *The Long Revolution:* the consistent Gramscian call for a regroupment of the optimism of the will and for 'making hope practical, rather than despair convincing' (*Towards 2000* 240).

JOHN FEKETE

Primary Sources

Williams, Raymond. *Border Country.* London: Chatto and Windus, 1960.
– *Cobbett.* Past Masters series. New York: Oxford UP, 1983.
– *Communications: Britain in the Sixties.* Penguin special 207. 1962. Rev. ed., Penguin special 831. Harmondsworth: Pelican-Penguin, 1968.

– *The Country and the City.* London: Chatto and Windus, 1973.
– *Culture.* New Sociology series. London: Fontana, 1981.
– *Culture and Society 1780–1950.* London: Chatto and Windus, 1958.
– *Drama from Ibsen to Brecht.* Rev. and exp. successor to *Drama from Ibsen to Eliot.* 1952. London: Chatto and Windus, 1968.
– *The English Novel from Dickens to Lawrence.* London: Chatto and Windus, 1970.
– *The Fight for Manod.* London: Chatto and Windus, 1979.
– *Keywords: A Vocabulary of Culture and Society.* Communications series. London: Fontana, 1976. Rev. and exp. ed. London: Flamingo-Fontana, 1983.
– *The Long Revolution.* London: Chatto and Windus, 1961.
– *Marxism and Literature.* Marxist Introductions series. London, New York: Oxford UP, 1977.
– *May Day Manifesto 1968.* Harmondsworth: Penguin, 1968.
– *Modern Tragedy.* London: Chatto and Windus, 1966.
– *Orwell.* Modern Masters series. London: Fontana/Collins, 1971.
– *Politics and Letters: Interview with New Left Review.* London: New Left Books, 1979.
– *Preface to Film.* London: Film Drama, 1954.
– *Problems in Materialism and Culture: Selected Essays.* London: Verso, 1980.
– *Second Generation.* London: Chatto and Windus, 1964.
– *Television: Technology and Cultural Form.* Technosphere series. London: Fontana and Collins, 1974.
– *Towards 2000.* London: Chatto and Windus, 1983. Harmondsworth: Penguin, 1985.
– *Writing in Society.* London: Verso, 1984.

Secondary Sources

Barnett, Anthony. 'Raymond Williams and Marxism: A Rejoinder to Terry Eagleton.' *New Left Review* 99 (1976): 47–64.
Christgau, Robert. 'Living in a Material World: Raymond Williams' *Long Revolution.*' *The Village Voice Literary Supplement* (Apr. 1985): 1, 12–18.
Eagleton, Terry. 'Criticism and Politics: The Work of Raymond Williams.' *New Left Review* 95 (1976): 3–23. Repr. in *Criticism and Ideology: A Study in Marxist Literary Theory.* London: New Left Books, 1976, 21–43.
– ed. *Raymond Williams: Critical Perspectives.* Oxford: Polity P, 1989.
Gorak, Jan. *The Alien Mind of Raymond Williams.* Literary Frontiers edition, no. 32. Columbia: U of Missouri P, 1988.
Green, Michael. 'Raymond Williams and Cultural Studies.' *Cultural Studies* 6 (1975): 31–48.

Hall, Stuart. 'Cultural Studies: Two Paradigms.' *Media, Culture and Society* 2 (1980): 57–72.

Heath, Stephen, and Gillian Skirrow. 'An Interview with Raymond Williams.' In *Studies in Entertainment: Critical Approaches to Mass Culture*. Ed. Tania Modleski. Bloomington and Indianopolis: Indiana UP, 1986, 3–17.

Higgins, John. 'Raymond Williams and the Problem of Ideology.' In *Postmodernism and Politics*. Ed. Jonathan Arac. Minneapolis: U of Minnesota P, 1986, 112–22. Repr. from *boundary 2* 11(1982–3): 145–54.

Inglis, Fred. 'Culture and Politics: Richard Hoggart, the *New Left Review*, and Raymond Williams.' In *Radical Earnestness: English Social Theory 1880–1980*. Oxford: Martin Robertson, 1982.

Johnson, Lesley. *The Cultural Critics: From Matthew Arnold to Raymond Williams*. London: Routledge and Kegan Paul, 1979.

Johnson, Richard. 'What Is Cultural Studies Anyhow?' *Social Text* 16 (1986–7): 38–80.

Lockwood, Bernard. 'Four Contemporary British Working-Class Novelists: A Thematic and Critical Approach to the Fiction of Raymond Williams, John Braine, David Storey and Alan Sillitoe.' Diss. U of Wisconsin, 1966.

O'Connor, Alan. *Raymond Williams: Writing, Culture, Politics*. Oxford and New York: Basil Blackwell, 1989.

Pinkney, Tony. *Raymond Williams*. Bridgend, Mid Glamorgan, Wales: Seren Books, 1992.

Watkins, Evan. 'Raymond Williams and Marxist Criticism.' *boundary 2* 4 (1975–6): 933–46.

Ward, J.P. *Raymond Williams*. Writers of Wales series. Cardiff: U of Wales P for the Welsh Arts Council, 1981.

Zinman, Rosalind. 'Raymond Williams: Towards a Sociology of Culture.' Diss. Concordia U (Montreal), 1984.

Wilson, Edmund

(b. U.S.A., 1895–d. 1972) Literary critic and chronicler, social historian, novelist, playwright, poet, diarist, man of letters. After attending university Edmund Wilson worked briefly as a reporter, then served in Europe in the First World War. He became a writer and editor for *Vanity Fair* (1920–1), was a book-review editor for *The New Republic* (1926–31), and a regular contributor to *The New Yorker* (1944–60). Wilson's relationships with many of the most famous intellectuals of the 50 years between 1920 and 1970, his indefatigable interest in languages, European *literature, cultures and ideas outside mainstream America, and his massive literary output make him an important figure in the history of American letters.

Although most of Wilson's literary production concerned belles-lettres, his catholic interests encompassed social and political topics as well. Seldom deliberately theoretical except in a few of his earlier works, Wilson's writing is rather in the tradition of Matthew Arnold, Saintsbury and such contemporary critics as V.S. Pritchett: impressionistic but grounded in pragmatic sensibility, it is dedicated to clarity of expression and to reaching the largest possible audience.

Wilson's first significant publication of critical essays, *Axel's Castle: A Study in the Imaginative Literature of 1870–1930* (1931) is a now rather dated but pioneering study of the Symbolist movement, its influence on early 20th-century literature and on such major figures as Joyce, Valéry, Yeats, Proust, Rimbaud, *Eliot, and Stein. *The Triple Thinkers* (1938), essays largely collected from periodicals, contains some of his most influential work, such as 'The Ambiguity of Henry James' and 'Marxism and Literature,' one of the first American studies of socialist realism. (See *Henry James, *Marxist criticism.)

To the Finland Station: A Study in the Writing and Acting of History (1940), is an account of the rise of socialism from its roots in Saint-Simon, Michelet and Taine to the ideas of Marx, Lenin and Trotsky and the social movement that changed the world.

The Wound and the Bow (1941), essays on such diverse figures as Dickens, Kipling, Hemingway, and Sophocles, emphasizes the Freudian concept of creation and neurosis. (See *Sigmund Freud.) *The Shock of Recognition: The Development of Literature in the United States Recorded by the Men Who Made It* (1943), a collection of essays about famous American literary figures by other famous figures, includes such classics as Mark Twain's 'Fenimore Cooper's Literary Offences' and pieces by Henry Adams, T.S. Eliot and others. *Classics and Commercials: A Literary Chronicle of the Forties* (1950) displays the diversity of Wilson's interests about European literary and artistic figures such as Dali, Kafka and Waugh – then little-known in the U.S.A. – in addition to his famous essay on the paucity of literary production from the American West Coast writers, 'The Boys in the Back Room.' *The Shores of Light: A Literary Chronicle of the Twenties and Thirties* (1952) remains a significant contribution to American criticism and literary history, especially because Wilson was so intimately associated with many of the major literary figures of those periods including F. Scott Fitzgerald and Hemingway. *The American Earthquake: A Documentary of the Twenties and Thirties* (1958), although largely compiled of articles on social events, is also important as a literary history of the times, as is *Patriotic Gore: Studies in the Literature of the American Civil War* (1962), a study of such then little-known American literary figures as Bierce, Cabell, Lanier, and Chopin.

The Bit Between My Teeth: A Literary Chronicle of 1950–65 (1965), another collection of Wilson's essays largely from *The New Yorker*, also contains two now-famous essays on Pasternak's *Doctor Zhivago* which caused a series of vitriolic exchanges between Wilson and Nabokov.

Another controversial article, 'The Fruits of MLA' (1967), satirizes American English department academics as scholars and methodologists, particularly for what he saw as their cumbersome and often ludicrous editing policies. *The Dead Sea Scrolls: 1947–69* (1969) is one of the first attempts to evaluate the theological ideas contained in the scrolls, as well as being a study of methods of biblical exegesis, and of ecclesiastical responses to the texts. Although much of the work was published in *The New Yorker*, and like many of Wilson's works can be considered a kind of 'journalism,' his facility in relating complex ideas without downplaying their implications and overtones marks his special contribution to the field of literary history and criticism.

The final work Wilson published during his lifetime is *A Window on Russia: For the Use of Foreign Readers* (1972), another collection of essays on Russian writers that Wilson wrote between 1943 and 1971 on Pushkin, Tiutchev, Gogol, Chekhov, Tolstoy, and others, as well as his essay on Nabokov's four-volume translation of *Eugene Onegin*, 'The Strange Case of Pushkin and Nabokov.' After Wilson's death in 1972, Leon Edel assumed the task of publishing Wilson's remaining works, the ones most directly connected with literary criticism being *The Devils and Canon Barham: Ten Essays on Poets, Novelists and Monsters* (1973), and *Letters on Literature and Politics*, edited by Elena Wilson (1976).

Thanks to the care of Edel, Wilson's diaries, letters and personal journals are being col-

lected and issued posthumously. The most recent of these collections is *The Fifties* (1988). Wilson's contribution to literary criticism, intellectual history and most particularly to American letters is complex. He placed the American stamp on the thought of the world as well as broadening the interest of American scholarship. His works remain essential for any student of 20th-century American letters and intellectual history.

REED MERRILL

Primary Sources

Wilson, Edmund. *The American Earthquake: A Documentary of the Twenties and Thirties.* Garden City, NJ: Doubleday and Company, 1958.
– *The American Jitters: A Year of the Slump.* New York: Charles Scribner's Sons, 1932.
– *Axel's Castle: A Study in the Imaginative Literature of 1870–1930.* 1931. New York: Charles Scribner's Sons, 1965.
– *The Bit Between My Teeth: A Literary Chronicle of 1950–1965.* New York: Farrar, Straus and Giroux, 1965.
– *Classics and Commercials: A Literary Chronicle of the Forties.* New York: Farrar, Straus and Company, 1950.
– *The Devils and Canon Barham: Ten Essays on Poets, Novelists and Monsters.* New York: Farrar, Straus and Giroux, 1973.
– *Europe Without Baedeker: Sketches Among the Ruins of Italy, Greece, and England.* Garden City, NJ: Doubleday and Company, 1947.
– *The Fifties.* Ed. Leon Edel. New York: Farrar, Straus and Giroux, 1986.
– *The Forties.* Ed. Leon Edel. New York: Farrar, Straus and Giroux, 1983.
– 'The Fruits of MLA I. Their Wedding Journey.' *New York Review of Books* 2.5, 26 Sept. 1968.
– *The Dead Sea Scrolls 1947–69.* New York: Oxford UP, 1969. Repub. in *Israel and the Dead Sea Scrolls.* New York: Farrar, Straus and Giroux, 1978.
– *Letters on Literature and Politics.* Ed. Elena Wilson. New York: Farrar, Straus and Giroux, 1977.
– *The Nabokov-Wilson Letters: 1940–1971.* New York: Harpers, 1979.
– *O Canada: An American's Notes on Canadian Culture.* New York: Farrar, Straus and Giroux 1965.
– *Patriotic Gore: Studies in the Literature of the American Civil War.* New York: Oxford UP, 1962.
– *Red, Black, Blond and Olive: Studies in Four Civilizations: Zuni, Haiti, Soviet Russia, and Israel.* New York, Oxford, 1956.
– *The Shores of Light: A Literary Chronicle of the Twenties and Thirties.* New York: Farrar, Straus and Young, 1952.

- *The Thirties.* Ed. Leon Edel. New York: Farrar, Straus and Giroux, 1980.
- *To the Finland Station: A Study in the Writing and Acting of History.* New York: Harcourt, Brace and Company, 1940.
- *The Triple Thinkers: Essays on Literature.* New York: Harcourt, Brace and Company, 1938.
- *The Twenties.* Ed. Leon Edel. New York: Farrar, Straus and Giroux, 1975.
- *A Window on Russia: For the Use of Foreign Readers.* New York: Farrar, Straus and Giroux, 1972.
- *The Wound and the Bow: Seven Studies in Literature.* New York: Oxford UP, 1941.
- ed. *The Crack-Up: With Other Uncollected Pieces, Note-Books and Unpublished Letters Together with Letters to Fitzgerald from Gertrude Stein, Edith Wharton, T.S. Eliot, Thomas Wolfe and John Dos Passos and Essays and Poems by Paul Rosenfeld, Glenway Wescott, John Dos Passos, John Peale Bishop and Edmund Wilson.* New York: New Directions, 1945.
- *The Shock of Recognition: The Development of Literature in the United States Recorded by the Men Who Made It.* Garden City, NJ: Doubleday Doran and Co., 1943.

Secondary Sources

Castronovo, David. *Edmund Wilson.* New York: Ungar, 1984.
Douglas, George H. *Edmund Wilson's America.* Lexington: U of Kentucky P, 1983.
Groth, Janet. *Edmund Wilson: A Critic for Our Time.* Athens: Ohio UP, 1989.
Kriegel, Leonard. *Edmund Wilson.* Carbondale: Southern Illinois UP, 1971.
Paul, Sherman. *Edmund Wilson: A Study of Literary Vocation in Our Time.* Urbana: U of Illinois P, 1967.
Ramsey, Richard David. *Edmund Wilson: A Bibliography.* New York: David Lewis, 1971.
Wain, John, ed. *An Edmund Wilson Celebration.* London: Phaidon, 1978.

Wimsatt, William Kurtz, Jr.

(b. U.S.A., 1907–d. 1975) Literary critic. William Kurtz Wimsatt completed his B.A. (1928) and M.A. (1929) at Georgetown University. From 1930–5 he was head of the English department and a teacher of Latin at the Portsmouth Priory School in Portsmouth, Rhode Island; from 1935–6 he studied and taught at the Catholic University of America before embarking on a Ph.D. in English at Yale. He gained his doctorate in 1939 with a dissertation on 'The Prose Style of Samuel Johnson' and from then until his death he remained at Yale, rising from his initial position of instructor to become Frederick Clifford Ford Professor of English (1965) and Sterling Professor of English (1974). He established a reputation both as an eminent scholar of 18th-century English *literature and as a radical exponent of the New Critical theory of 'objectivism,' focusing on the work of art itself, independent of its origins and its effects, as the central concern of literary criticism. Although inaccurately, Wimsatt became known as one of the 'Yale formalists,' together with *Cleanth Brooks and *René Wellek. (See *New Criticism.)

Wimsatt's 18th-century scholarship includes books on Johnson's style and vocabulary (1941, 1948), an edition of a volume in the Yale Boswell papers (1959), articles on Alexander Pope and an edition of his selected works (1951), and studies of developments in poetry from the Augustan to the Romantic eras. His natural penchant for wit and humour and his lively interest in style as 'a level of meaning' *(The Verbal Icon* xii) inform all his practical criticism. His concern to demonstrate the iconic status of representation ranges from a compilation of all the known portraits of Pope (1966) to repeated investigations into the nature of verbal *mimesis, the subject of his final published paper. Here he argues, against *Ferdinand de Saussure's contention that language is merely conventional, that language has 'natural' powers, 'both imagistic and diagrammatic' *(Day of the Leopards* 73). Wimsatt's discussions of the metrics and sound-patterns of poetry are undergirded by this same belief in the inseparability of form and meaning *(Hateful Contraries* 240) and in the essential reference of language to reality.

Wimsatt's stance is remarkably consistent over the 30-odd years of his published work, perhaps partly as a result of his constant awareness of the historical contexts of literary criticism. His longest book, *Literary Criticism: A Short History* (1957), on which he collaborated with Cleanth Brooks though writing 25 of the 32 chapters himself, is a narrative history of criticism from its classical origins to contemporary times. All of Wimsatt's major concerns are suggested here: he insists on the principle of 'continuity and intelligibility in the history of literary argument' (vii) because of 'the continuity and real community of human experience' (viii); he declares that the historian 'believes that he has in fact a coherent, a real and unequivocal subject matter' (ix) and offers 'the history of one kind of thinking about values' (vii). Thus although Wimsatt is often considered the foremost exponent of the American New Criticism which flourished in the late 1930s and 1940s, he is both historical and resolutely referential in his convictions. He did not himself adopt the name of New Critic but described himself variously as an 'objective' or 'modern' critic concerned with 'cognitive' and 'explicatory' literary criticism in order to 'defend literature as a form of knowledge' (The Verbal Icon xii). Although he affirmed the famous New Critical dogma that 'a poem should not mean but be,' he qualified it by declaring that a poem is a human act of knowing rather than a literal object (The Verbal Icon 50), and that its relation to the real world is determined by a complex of interactions between 'dramatic speaker' and audience, consisting in a 'discourse ... about the emotive quality of objects' (The Verbal Icon 38).

Most of Wimsatt's essays are collected in three volumes roughly a decade apart: The Verbal Icon (1954), Hateful Contraries (1965) and Day of the Leopards (1976 – a posthumous publication). Wimsatt himself stressed the historical sequence of these titles, in that the notion of the poem as a verbal icon must be understood to contain conflicting parts held in a tension whose potential imbalance is as destructive as its maintenance is creative (Day of the Leopards xi). The two most influential papers in The Verbal Icon are 'The Intentional Fallacy' (1946) and 'The Affective Fallacy' (1949), written in collaboration with Monroe Beardsley; together these papers are seen as the fullest account of the doctrines of New Criticism and their arguments are ones that Wimsatt continued to expound and clarify throughout his career. Wimsatt contends that since the intentional fallacy centres on the sincerity of the poet and the affective fallacy centres on the sincerity of the critic, in both cases the poem itself tends to disappear (The Verbal Icon 29). Critical inattention to the relation of technique to content, he suggests, has often led to these fallacious approaches to the poem; the first 'begins by trying to derive the standard of criticism from the psychological causes of the poem and ends in biography and relativism,' whereas the second 'begins by trying to derive the standard of criticism from the psychological effects of the poem and ends in impressionism and relativism' (The Verbal

Icon 21). Neither biographical inquiry nor audience response is true literary criticism, which must focus on evidence internal to the poem – with the addition, however, of the 'intermediate evidence' offered by an awareness of the associations particular words may have had for the poet. In this sense 'historical causes [may] enter in a pronounced way into the very meaning of literary works' (The Verbal Icon 254).

Wimsatt is essentially and significantly synchretistic: 'I find no embarrassment,' he declares in the introduction to Day of the Leopards, 'in having taken both sides of the debate' (xi). The central tenet of his poetics is perhaps most clearly diagrammed in 'Horses of Wrath' (Hateful Contraries 36): he locates his 'tensional' theory of literary criticism at the midway point of two intersecting poles: one, the pole separating contentual, didactic criticism from formal, stylistic criticism; the other, the pole separating intentional, speaker-based from affective, audience-based theories. He therefore sees metaphor as 'the principle of all poetry' (The Verbal Icon 49), since its 'logical impurity ... is a ready slant, a twist, of abstract idea toward the inclinations of speaker or audience or of both' (Hateful Contraries 41) – the locus of the essential relationship between poetry and the real world. (See *metonymy/metaphor.)

Wimsatt's understanding of art as tension has a moral as well as a formal base because the tensional element is part of the moral quality of experience and can therefore justly be repeated in art (Hateful Contraries 47). He sees poetic and moral value as distinct, insofar as poetic value inheres in the 'imaginative power of [poetry's] presentation' (The Verbal Icon 98) so that what is wrong with a bad poem is that it does not make sense, either in explicit statement or in implicit suggestion through image (Explication as Criticism 16). However, both poetic and moral value are related to the notion of evil as negation or a gap in order and to good as positive – 'in the natural order the designed complexity of what ... most has being' (The Verbal Icon 100), so that 'the complexity and unity of the poem is also its maturity or sophistication or richness or depth' (The Verbal Icon 82); 'the greatest poetry will be morally right' (The Verbal Icon 100). In the conclusion to his critical history, Wimsatt confesses to his Christian stance in locating the ultimately satisfactory metaphysical expression of tension in the mix of suffering, optimism and mystery inherent in the Incarnation (*Literary Criticism* 746).

The relation of Wimsatt to other literary critics demonstrates his considered eclecticism. He offers guarded affirmation of *I.A. Richards' concern for explication, for literary value and for moral significance, but rejects Richards' separation of emotive and referential meaning (*Day of the Leopards* 236). He applauds the structuralists' defence of the literary object, but warns against their absolutism (*Day of the Leopards* 201–2). (See *structuralism.) He appreciates the verbal energy of *Northrop Frye while berating him for using it as a cover for the illogicality of his ahistoricism and fanciful megalomania (*Day of the Leopards* 90, 93). He denounces the *Geneva School for their subjectivity, the Chicago critics for their overemphasis on poetic species rather than specifics, and those who hold to the doctrine of 'autonomous visionary imagination' for subscribing to a solipsistic 'antidoctrine' that cannot yield 'a valid account of the relation between poetic form and poetic meaning' (*Hateful Contraries* 243–4). (See *Neo-Aristotelian or Chicago School.) *Day of the Leopards* expresses his distress over what in the 1960s he sees as the kidnapping of poetry for political ends and the surrender to unreason in academic criticism, most specifically and painfully for him among the Yale deconstructionists. (See *deconstruction.) As he had said from the beginning of his career, he is concerned that once emotion overrules the cognitive qualities of the context, 'the sequence of licenses is endless' (*The Verbal Icon* 27). Such a sequence he would have perceived in *poststructuralism, schools of criticism which Wimsatt would argue 'batter the object' (*Day of the Leopards* 183).

DEBORAH BOWEN

Primary Sources

Wimsatt, W.K., Jr. *Day of the Leopards: Essays in Defense of Poems*. New Haven and London: Yale UP, 1976.
– *Hateful Contraries: Studies in Literature and Criticism.* [With an essay on English meter written with Monroe C. Beardsley.] Lexington: U of Kentucky P, 1965.
– *Philosophic Words: A Study of Style and Meaning in the 'Rambler' and 'Dictionary' of Samuel Johnson.* New Haven, Conn.: Yale UP, 1948.
– *The Portraits of Alexander Pope.* New Haven, Conn.: Yale UP, 1965.

– *The Prose Style of Samuel Johnson.* New Haven, Conn.: Yale UP, 1941.
– *The Verbal Icon: Studies in the Meaning of Poetry.* [With two preliminary essays written with Monroe C. Beardsley.] Lexington: U of Kentucky P, 1954.
– and Cleanth Brooks. *Literary Criticism: A Short History.* New York: Knopf, 1957.
– ed. *Alexander Pope: Selected Poetry and Prose.* New York: Rinehart, 1951. Rev. ed., 1972.
– *Explication as Criticism: Selected Papers from the English Institute 1941–52.* New York and London: Columbia UP, 1963.
– and F.A. Pottle, eds. *Boswell for the Defence, 1769–1774.* New York: McGraw-Hill, 1959. London: Heinemann, 1959.

Secondary Sources

Bagwell, J. Timothy. *American Formalism and the Problem of Interpretation.* Houston: Rice UP, 1986.
Beardsley, Monroe C. 'Textual Meaning and Authorial Meaning.' *Genre* 1.3 (July 1968): 169–81.
Berman, Art. *From the New Criticism to Deconstruction: The Reception of Structuralism and Post-Structuralism.* Urbana and Chicago: U of Illinois P, 1988.
Bloom, Harold. *The Anxiety of Influence: A Theory of Poetry.* New York: Oxford UP, 1973.
Borklund, Elmer. *Contemporary Literary Critics.* London: Macmillan, 1977, 526–32.
Bradbury, Malcolm, and David Palmer, eds. *Contemporary Criticism.* London: Edward Arnold, 1970.
Brady, Frank, John Palmer and Martin Price, eds. *Literary Theory and Structure: Essays in Honor of William K. Wimsatt.* New Haven and London: Yale UP, 1973.
Brooks, Cleanth. *The Well Wrought Urn: Studies in the Structure of Poetry.* New York: Harcourt, Brace, and World, 1947.
de Man, Paul. 'The Rhetoric of Temporality.' In *Interpretation: Theory and Practice.* Ed. C.S. Singleton. Baltimore: Johns Hopkins UP, 1969.
Fish, Stanley. 'Literature in the Reader: Affective Stylistics.' *New Literary History* 2.1 (Autumn 1970): 123–62.
Graff, Gerald. *Literature Against Itself: Literary Ideas in Modern Society.* Chicago: U of Chicago P, 1979.
Hirsch, E.D., Jr. *Validity in Interpretation.* New Haven and London: Yale UP, 1967.
Krieger, Murray. *The Play and Place of Criticism.* Baltimore: Johns Hopkins UP, 1967.
Lentricchia, Frank. *After the New Criticism.* Chicago: U of Chicago P, 1980.
Lodge, David. 'Review of *Hateful Contraries.' Modern Language Review* 61.4 (Oct. 1966): 647–8.
Pagliaro, Harold E. 'The Affective Question.' *Bucknell Review* 20 (1972): 3–20.
Pradhan, S.V. 'The Positivist Fallacy: "Cognitive Translatability" in Criticism.' *British Journal of Aesthetics* 27.2 (Spring 1987): 138–44.

Richards, I.A. *Principles of Literary Criticism.* 1924. Repr. ed. New York: Harcourt, Brace and Co., 1959.

Robey, David. 'Anglo-American New Criticism.' In *Modern Literary Theory: A Comparative Introduction.* Ed. Ann Jefferson and David Robey. Totawa, NJ: Barnes and Noble, 1982, 65–83.

Wellek, René. 'The Literary Theory of William K. Wimsatt.' *The Yale Review* 66 (Winter 1976): 178–92.

Winters, (Arthur) Yvor

(b. U.S.A., 1900–d. 1968) Poet and literary critic. At the University of Chicago (1917–18), Yvor Winters joined the Poetry Club and met fellow poets Glenway Westcott, Elizabeth Maddox Roberts and Harriet Monroe, who published some of his earliest work in her *Poetry Magazine.* After three years in a tuberculosis sanitorium, he taught school for two years in the mining communities of Madrid and Los Cerillos, New Mexico. He gained his B.A. and M.A. degrees in Romance languages with a minor in Latin at the University of Colorado at Boulder, and then taught at the University of Idaho. Following marriage to the poet Janet Lewis, Winters began doctoral work at Stanford on the post-romantic reaction in lyrical verse, completing it in 1935. Winters spent the rest of his teaching and writing life at Stanford from where he retired as Albert Guérard Professor of English in 1966.

Winters' importance in literary criticism in the U.S.A. during the middle decades of the 20th century lies in his revaluation of the romantic-modernist aesthetics he originally espoused. In his Imagist manifesto 'The Testament of a Stone, Being Notes on the Mechanics of the Poetic Image' (1924), he argues that a poem 'is a stasis in a world of flux and indecision, a permanent gateway to waking oblivion, which is the only infinity and the only rest' (*Uncollected Essays* 195). However, his wish to emulate the poets he regarded as the best recent practitioners – Baudelaire, Valéry, Bridges, Hardy, Dickinson, and Stevens – led Winters to reject free verse and return to the traditional forms in which these poets had written their best work. Winters provides a definitive statement of his mature view of the poem in 'Problems for the Modern Critic of Literature' (1956): 'I believe that a poem (or other work of artistic literature) is a statement in words about a human experience ... In each work there is a content which is rationally apprehensible, and each work endeavors to communicate the emotion which is appropriate to the rational apprehension of the subject. The work is thus a judgment, rational and emotional of the experience – that is a complete moral judgment in so far as the work is successful' (*The Function of Criticism* 26).

Winters' criticial views of poetry emanate from his own practical experience as poet and were also influenced by his many contacts with other poets, including Marianne Moore and Hart Crane. His marriage to Janet Lewis was a lifelong critical and poetic collaboration. Crane's suicide in 1932 became for Winters frightening evidence of the bankruptcy of Emersonian-Whitmanian romanticism; Crane was 'a Gawayne who succumbed' (*New Republic,* 2 June 1937, 104). At Stanford, William Dinsmore Briggs (an editor of Ben Jonson) became a strong influence on Winters, leading him to read St. Thomas Aquinas and to deepen his interest in American *literature and in the English poetry of the Renaissance. Winters wrote several poems in honour of Briggs, most movingly his 'Dedication for a Book of Criticism' (*Collected Poems of Yvor Winters* 145).

During his years as a teacher at Stanford (1928–66) Winters himself influenced many students who became colleagues and fellow poets, some of whose work he included in two series of *Poets of the Pacific* (1937; 1949). His last critical act was to co-edit with Kenneth Fields *Quest for Reality: An Anthology of Short Poems in English* (1969), the companion volume to *Forms of Discovery* (1967).

Winters' revaluation of his original romantic-modernist aesthetics led him to become an Aristotelian-Thomist who followed the progress of scholastic logic into Renaissance short poems in the plain style. Also, he became a sharp critic of the degeneration of New England Calvinism into Unitarianism and Transcendentalism. Winters' final view of the development of the short poem in English was that 'the two great periods in the poetry of our language are the period from Wyatt to Dryden, inclusive, and the period from Jones Very to the present, and the second period does not seem to have come to an end' (*Forms of Discovery* 358). Winters believed that of these two periods the second, which he terms 'post-Symbolist,' with its 'carefully controlled association' 'offers the possibility, at least, of greater flexibility and greater inclusiveness of matter (and without confusion) than we can find in the Renaissance structures; the post-Symbolist imagery provides a greater range of thinking and perceiving than we have ever had before' (*Forms of Discovery* 253).

Winters has been characterized as an anti-modernist; but he is a defender of reason and a critic of the Shaftesburian sentimentalism, associationism and deism that led to romanticism. He shows himself in the vanguard of those who sought to revolutionize the teaching of literature in America. Though associated with the *New Criticism, Winters was reluctant to accept association with its 'learned paraphrasing' (*The Function of Criticism* 81). Writing of Winters, Terry Comito quotes Winters' characterization of Sturge Moore as applicable to Winters himself. He attempted 'to understand the tradition into which he was born, and, at one and the same time, to save himself from it and to make something of it' (*Forms of Discovery* 249).

JOHN FERNS

Primary Sources

Winters, Yvor. *The Anatomy of Nonsense*. Norfolk, Conn.: New Directions, 1943.
– *The Bare Hills*. Boston: Four Seas, 1927.
– *Before Disaster*. Tyron, NC: Tyron Pamphlets, 1934.
– *Collected Poems*. Denver: Alan Swallow, 1952.
– *The Collected Poems of Yvor Winters*. Intro. Donald Davie. Manchester: Carcanet, 1978; Athens: Swallow P, U of Ohio P, 1980.
– *Edwin Arlington Robinson*. Norfolk, Conn.: New Directions, 1946.
– *Forms of Discovery: Critical and Historical Essays on the Forms of the Short Poem in English*. Chicago: Alan Swallow, 1967.
– *The Function of Criticism: Problems and Exercises*. Denver: Alan Swallow, 1957.
– *In Defense of Reason*. Denver and New York: Alan Swallow P and W. Morrow, 1947.
– *Maule's Curse: Seven Studies in the History of American Obscurantism*. Norfolk, Conn.: New Directions, 1938.
– *Primitivism and Decadence: A Study of American Experimental Poetry*. New York: Arrow Editions, 1937.
– *The Proof*. New York: Coward-McCann, 1930.
– *Twelve Poets of the Pacific*. Stanford: Stanford UP, 1937. Repr. *Poets of the Pacific*. Stanford: Stanford UP, 1949.
– *Uncollected Essays and Reviews*. Ed. Francis Murphy. Chicago: Swallow P, 1973.
– and Kenneth Fields. *Quest for Reality: An Anthology of Short Poems in English*. Chicago: Swallow P, 1969.

Secondary Sources

Comito, Terry. *In Defense of Winters: The Poetry and Prose of Yvor Winters*. Madison: U of Wisconsin P, 1986.
Davis, Dick. *Wisdom and Wilderness: The Achievement of Yvor Winters*. Athens: U of Georgia P, 1983.
Lohf, Kenneth A., and Eugene P. Sheehy. *Yvor Winters: A Bibliography*. Denver: Alan Swallow, 1959.
Parkinson, Thomas, ed. *Hart Crane and Yvor Winters: Their Literary Correspondence*. Berkeley: U of California P, 1978.
Powell, Grosvenor. *Language as Being in the Poetry of Yvor Winters*. Baton Rouge: Louisiana State UP, 1980.
– *Yvor Winters: An Annotated Bibliography 1919–1982*. Metuchen, NJ: Scarecrow P, 1983.

Wittgenstein, Ludwig

(b. Austria, 1884–d. England, 1951) Philosopher. Ludwig Wittgenstein was educated at home until the age of 14. After three years in school, he entered the Technische Hochschule in Berlin in 1906 to study engineering. From 1908 to 1911 he worked as a research student at the University of Manchester, conducting kite-flying experiments and designing a propeller for a jet turbine. Becoming interested in the foundations of mathematics, he read Bertrand Russell's *Principles of Mathematics* and some of Frege's logical writings. On Frege's advice he entered Trinity College, Cambridge, in 1912 to study with Russell. From late 1913 until the outbreak of war in 1914, he lived in an isolated hut in Norway. During the First World War Wittgenstein saw action on the eastern front. Soon after the war, he renounced his inheritance, trained as an elementary school teacher and spent 1920–6 teaching in remote mountain villages in Lower Austria. In 1926 he worked as a gardener's assistant in a monastery and then returned to Vienna, where he designed and oversaw the construction of a modernist house throughout 1927–8. During this time he discussed philosophy, mathematics and poetry with Moritz Schlick, Rudolf Carnap and other members of what would become the Vienna Circle of logical positivists. In 1929 he returned to Cambridge, where he submitted the *Tractatus Logico-Philosophicus* (written in prison camp) as his Ph.D.

thesis, in 1930 becoming research fellow of Trinity College. He was made professor of philosophy in 1939. His writings during this period were extensive and some, notably *The Blue Book* of 1933–4 and the *The Brown Book* of 1935, were circulated in stencilled copies. Revisions of *The Brown Book* formed the first part of *Philosophical Investigations*, which Wittgenstein prepared for publication but did not complete to his satisfaction. He became a British citizen in 1937, after Austria's annexation by Germany, and served as a hospital orderly during the Second World War. Returning to Cambridge he soon resigned his post in order to live in a seaside hut in Ireland but later returned to England once again. *Philosophical Investigations* was published posthumously, followed by a steady stream of published notebooks, manuscripts, lecture notes, and memoirs.

The *Tractatus* is a severe modernist work, concerned with marking out strict distinctions among disciplines. Its positions originate in the criticism of the philosophies of logic of Frege and Russell, particularly of the idea that there can be discoveries in logic that are of the order of discoveries in the natural sciences. Unlike science, Wittgenstein argued, the propositions of logic say nothing, are senseless; instead they show how certain propositions may be substituted for others that are tautologically equivalent. Logic is the framework of thought, language and the world. It does not describe arrangements of objects *in* the world. The distinction between description of the world and other kinds of language was extended to characterize ethics, aesthetics, metaphysics, and the rest of philosophy as nonsense. Goodness, beauty, the metaphysical subject, and the will stand outside the world and experience. They may, in a way, suffuse it or stand as its absolute presuppositions, but about how this is so nothing can be said. These things 'are what is mystical' (6.522).

Though its castings of science as concerned with facts, logic and mathematics as concerned with frameworks, and all of traditional philosophy as nonsense were congenial to and influential upon the Vienna positivists, it is doubtful that Wittgenstein himself ever shared their scientism. Throughout the 1930s he came to doubt that truth-table analysis, which he had invented in the *Tractatus*, could elucidate all the framework principles to which we keep in ordinary speech. This doubt led him to investigate various, more specific *Satzsysteme* or discourse schemes employed in ordinary language, the precursors of the language-games (*Sprachspiele*) of *Philosophical Investigations*.

Like the *Tractatus*, *Philosophical Investigations* distinguishes philosophy from other systems of thought and seeks to curb its pretensions. Philosophy's aim is clarity, not discovery. It has no privileged relation to the essence of the world, for the world has no essence. It cannot guide practice on the basis of deep knowledge, for practices and language-games are autonomous. At best it can uncover and dismiss nonsense. 'Philosophy may in no way interfere with the actual use of language; it can in the end only describe it. For it cannot give it any foundation either. It leaves everything as it is' (sec. 124). These metaphysical theses are combined with patient and trenchant criticism of paradigmatic types of traditional philosophical confusion about thinking, representation, the mind, and the will. The paradoxical aim of these criticisms is to chasten us, perhaps ceaselessly, into a kind of naturalness and away from seeking explanations of our humanity or experience in general.

The anti-foundationalism and moralism about the ordinary in Wittgenstein's later philosophy have received a number of interpretations. Four are distinctive and significant. (1) *Richard Rorty has affiliated Wittgenstein's antifoundationalism with the *deconstruction and *poststructuralism of *Jacques Derrida, allying Wittgenstein in this with *Martin Heidegger and John Dewey as critics of philosophical theorizing. Here changes in language-games are seen as things that just happen, at best for local reasons and never in response to the deep nature of things. Unconstrained proliferation of language-games is seen as valuable expansion of human possibilities. It is doubtful whether this line of development is faithful to Wittgenstein's impatience with nonsense and tendencies to criticize scientism, European culture and casualness in life. (2) *M.H. Abrams has argued that Wittgenstein's account of language-games offers us a pragmatic refutation of poststructuralism. Within language-games, for example, the language-game of literary criticism, there are constraints upon what we can sensibly say, even though no language-games themselves have any absolute foundation. One difficulty here is that Wittgenstein himself left little indication of the way the borders of language-games are to be traced, so that it is not clear how criticism is to be distinguished from sociology of *literature or psychoanalysis or creative revision. (See *psychoanalytic theory.) (3)*Terry Eagleton has noted that Wittgenstein's concentration on practice has affinities with the Marxist tradition and he has traced similarities between Wittgenstein's remarks about language and the antiscientific Marxisms of *Mikhail Bakhtin and *Theodor Adorno. (See *Marxist criticism.) Despite his emphasis on practice, however, Wittgenstein's philosophical writings show little specific historical consciousness and no concern for class. The confusions that occupy him are more on the order of perennial temptations. (4) Stanley Cavell has suggested that Wittgenstein's unending criticisms of and fascination with philosophical explanation-seeking enact and make us conscious of our persistent ambivalence toward language and community. Language, community and ordinary practice are necessary backgrounds for human thought and individuality and they are, at the same time, when ossified, inimical to them in their stereotypings of human responsiveness. Here Cavell sees in Wittgenstein the Kantian *theme of human reason endlessly warring with itself. Human avoidance and acknowledgment are the intertwined effects of this ambivalence. This way of receiving Wittgenstein has yet to gain wide currency.

RICHARD ELDRIDGE

Primary Sources

Wittgenstein, Ludwig. *The Blue and Brown Books.* Oxford: Basil Blackwell, 1958.
– *Culture and Value.* Ed. G.H. von Wright and Heikki Nyman. Trans. Peter Winch. Oxford: Basil Blackwell, 1980.
– *Lectures and Conversations on Aesthetics, Psychology, and Religious Belief.* From notes taken by Yorick Smythies, Rush Rhees and James Taylor. Ed. Cyril Barrett. Berkeley: U of California P, 1966.
– *On Certainty.* Ed. G.E.M. Anscombe and G.H. von Wright. Trans. D. Paul and G.E.M. Anscombe. Oxford: Basil Blackwell, 1969.
– *Philosophical Grammar.* Ed. R. Rhees. Trans. A.J.P. Kenny. Oxford: Basil Blackwell, 1974.
– *Philosophical Investigations.* Ed. G.E.M. Anscombe and R. Rhees. Trans. G.E.M. Anscombe. 3rd ed. Oxford: Basil Blackwell, 1958.
– *Philosophical Remarks.* Ed. R. Rhees. Trans. R. Hargreaves and R. White. Oxford: Basil Blackwell, 1975.
– *Remarks on the Foundations of Mathematics.* Ed. G.H. von Wright, R. Rhees and G.E.M. Anscombe. Trans. G.E.M. Anscombe. 3rd ed. Oxford: Basil Blackwell, 1978.
– *Tractatus Logico-Philosophicus.* Trans. D.F. Pears and B.F. McGuinness. London: Routledge and Kegan Paul, 1961.
Engelmann, Paul. *Letters from Ludwig Wittgenstein, with a Memoir.* Oxford: Basil Blackwell, 1967.

Secondary Sources

Abrams, M.H. *Doing Things with Texts: Essays in Criticism and Critical Theory.* Ed. Michael Fischer. New York: W.W. Norton and Co., 1989.
Anscombe, G.E.M. *An Introduction to Wittgenstein's Tractatus.* Philadelphia: U of Pennsylvania P, 1959.
Baker, Gordon. *Wittgenstein, Frege, and the Vienna Circle.* Oxford: Basil Blackwell, 1988.
– and P.M.S. Hacker. *Wittgenstein: Understanding and Meaning – An Analytical Commentary on the Philosophical Investigations.* Vol. 1. Oxford: Basil Blackwell, 1980.
– and P.M.S. Hacker. *Wittgenstein: Rules, Grammar and Necessity – An Analytical Commentary on the Philosophical Investigations.* Vol. 2. Oxford: Basil Blackwell, 1985.
Bartley, William Warren, III. *Wittgenstein.* London: Quartet Books, 1974.
Block, Irving, ed. *Perspectives on the Philosophy of Wittgenstein.* Oxford: Basil Blackwell, 1981.
Bloor, David. *Wittgenstein: A Social Theory of Knowledge.* New York: Columbia UP, 1983.
Bogen, James. *Wittgenstein's Philosophy of Language.* London: Routledge and Kegan Paul, 1972.
Cavell, Stanley. *The Claim of Reason.* New York: Oxford UP, 1979.
– *This New Yet Unapproachable America: Lectures After Emerson After Wittgenstein.* Albuquerque, NM: Living Batch P, 1989.
Eagleton, Terry. 'Wittgenstein's Friends.' *New Left Review* 135 (Sept.–Oct. 1982): 64–90.
Edwards, James C. *Ethics Without Philosophy: Wittgenstein and the Moral Life.* Tampa: U Presses of Florida, 1982.
Fann, K.T. *Wittgenstein's Conception of Philosophy.* Berkeley: U of California P, 1969.
Fogelin, Robert J. *Wittgenstein.* London: Routledge and Kegan Paul, 1976.
Griffin, James. *Wittgenstein's Logical Atomism.* London: Oxford UP, 1964.
Grayling, A.C. *Wittgenstein.* Oxford: Oxford UP, 1988.
Hacker, P.M.S. *Insight and Illusion: Themes in the Philosophy of Wittgenstein.* Rev. ed. Oxford: Clarendon P, 1986.
Janik, Allan, and Stephen Toulmin. *Wittgenstein's Vienna.* New York: Simon and Schuster, 1973.

Kenny, Anthony. *Wittgenstein.* Cambridge, Mass.: Harvard UP, 1973.

Kripke, Saul A. *Wittgenstein on Rules and Private Language.* Cambridge, Mass.: Harvard UP, 1982.

Luckhardt, C.G., ed. *Wittgenstein: Sources and Perspectives.* Ithaca, NY: Cornell UP, 1979.

Malcolm, Norman. *Ludwig Wittgenstein: A Memoir.* London: Oxford UP, 1958.

– *Nothing is Hidden: Wittgenstein's Criticism of His Early Thought.* Oxford: Basil Blackwell, 1986.

McGinn, Colin. *Wittgenstein on Meaning.* Oxford: Basil Blackwell, 1984.

McGuinness, Brian, ed. *Wittgenstein and His Times.* Oxford: Basil Blackwell, 1982.

– *Wittgenstein: A Life – Young Ludwig, 1889–1921.* Berkeley: U of California P, 1988.

Monk, Ray. *Ludwig Wittgenstein: The Duty of Genius.* New York: Macmillan, 1990.

Pears, David. *The False Prison: A Study of the Development of Wittgenstein's Philosophy.* 2 vols. Oxford: Clarendon P, 1987, 1988.

– *Ludwig Wittgenstein.* New York: Viking, 1970.

Pitcher, George, ed. *Wittgenstein: The Philosophical Investigations.* Garden City, NY: Doubleday Books, 1966.

Rhees, Rush, ed. *Recollections of Wittgenstein.* Oxford: Oxford UP, 1984.

Rorty, Richard. *Consequences of Pragmatism.* Minneapolis: U of Minnesota P, 1982.

– *Philosophy and the Mirror of Nature.* Princeton: Princeton UP, 1979.

Rubinstein, David. *Marx and Wittgenstein: Social Praxis and Social Explanation.* London: Routledge and Kegan Paul, 1981.

Specht, Ernest Konrad. *The Foundation of Wittgenstein's Late Philosophy.* Trans. D.E. Walford. Manchester: Manchester UP, 1969.

Stenius, Erik. *Wittgenstein's Tractatus.* Ithaca, NY: Cornell UP, 1960.

Vesey, Godfrey, ed. *Understanding Wittgenstein.* London: Macmillan, 1974.

von Wright, Georg Henrik. *Wittgenstein.* Minneapolis: U of Minnesota P, undated.

Woolf, Virginia Stephen

(b. England, 1882–d. 1941) Novelist, literary critic and feminist. Adeline Virginia Stephen was educated by tutelage at home; although she had the unusual freedom, for a woman, of uncensored access to an extensive family library, she was acutely aware of the effects of exclusion from the university education naturally acquired by her brothers and their male friends. In 1912 she married Leonard Woolf with whom she later founded the Hogarth Press. As a novelist, Woolf was noted for her innovations in narrative technique, and her reputation as one of the leading modernists became securely established with the publication of *To the Lighthouse* (1927) and *The Waves* (1931). In keeping with her principle of remaining outside the patriarchal *hegemony, Woolf refused all honours, including honorary degrees from Manchester and Liverpool universities and a nomination for Companion of Honour. As a critic and theorist, Woolf has been considered in relation to her Victorian heritage and to other members of the Bloomsbury group (especially to the novelist *E.M. Forster and art critics Roger Fry and Clive Bell); more recently, discussions of Woolf relate her to various women writers and artists and to an increasing number of postmodernist critics. (See *feminist criticism, *postmodernism.)

Virginia Woolf's career as a literary journalist began with the publication of an unsigned review in the *Guardian* in 1904; she rapidly became established, especially after 1916, as a prolific reviewer and essayist for the *Times Literary Supplement.* In total, she published over 500 pieces in more than 30 periodicals. Woolf published two collections of essays in her lifetime, *The Common Reader* (1925) and *The Common Reader: Second Series* (1932); two longer feminist works, *A Room of One's Own* (1929) and *Three Guineas* (1938); plus several pamphlets issued separately by the Hogarth Press. Several volumes of essays have been published posthumously; beginning in 1986, Andrew McNeillie has been editing and publishing the complete essays.

To study Woolf as a literary critic means to go beyond traditional categories of genre. (See *genre criticism.) Much of her fiction conveys literary theory, while her non-fiction employs fictional techniques. Self-reflexive and metafictional elements in her novels comment upon theoretical issues. *Jacob's Room* (1922), for example, is significant for ideas about the nature of character; *Orlando* (1928) for theories of biography and the relation of style to historical context; and *Between the Acts* (1941) for the relation between writer and audience, and the concept of decentred *text. (See *centre/decentre.) In a similar conflation of genres, the essay-lecture *A Room of One's Own* employs multiple fictional narrators and embodies much of its argument in anecdote and image. In its theoretical implications, this style attests to Woolf's rejection of the authoritative stance of the author and her commitment to a suggestive and pluralistic, rather than definitive and monologic, use of language. (See *monologism.)

Woolf's essays also convey theory through rhetorical strategy; they can best be described as metacritical, since they examine and comment upon their own form, their own thought processes. (See *metacriticism.) The style Woolf most frequently employs is dialogic, or as Woolf herself once called it, a 'turn and turn about method.' The method allows her to be evaluative and to formulate general principles yet, at the same time, to undercut her theories with the contradictory impulse or to situate them clearly with regard to her subject position. Not surprisingly, two opposite impulses inform her critical approach: one must attempt to formulate general laws or one will be, like Mr. Priestley, merely an 'appreciator' ('Appreciations'); one must also situate such 'rules' as individual philosophy or one will, like Mr. Patmore, run the danger of elevating the 'freaks of prejudice and partisanship' into infallible 'oracular' doctrine ('Mr. Patmore's Criticism').

Woolf's statement that 'we think back through our mothers if we are women' (Room) is a fitting comment on her significance for feminist literary criticism. Her essays on various women writers begin to chart a female literary tradition; in turn, she herself has become a generative mother-figure for contemporary feminist thought.

As a feminist critic, Woolf directs attention to the ways in which material conditions – economic and social – have limited the possibilities for women as artists. She advocates the emancipation of both women and men from restrictive gender roles and she points out how ideological bias in social and political terms affects the interpretation and evaluation of *literature. (See *ideology.) It is her consistent claim that the values of life are inseparable from the values of art; prevailing values influence a critic's response both to the subject-matter of a literary work – we have taken for granted that there is more importance in 'what is commonly thought big than in what is commonly thought small' ('Modern Fiction') – and to the style – facts have been privileged over feeling, logic over the unconscious, linearity over pluralism.

Woolf was also a pioneer in what is now known as 'Images of Women' criticism; one particularly influential image embodies her view that female characters in novels written by men represent not women, but projections of male fantasies, desires and fears: 'Women have served all these centuries as looking-glasses' (Room). Finally, Woolf was one of the first to suggest what has been more recently termed écriture féminine, or a distinctive style of women's writing. Debate continues about the extent to which Woolf considers women's writing to be inherently distinctive and the extent to which she attributes differences to socially prescribed gender roles, advocating instead the greater freedom of the androgynous mind. But what is clear is that she challenges conventional thinking by exposing the fallacy of assuming certain values to be universal and absolute, when in reality they reflect a specifically patriarchal and imperialist tradition; to this end, much of her work directs attention to an opposing but neglected female tradition with its 'own inheritance – the difference of view, the difference of standard' ('George Eliot'). (See *universal.)

In addition to her pioneering role in feminist criticism, Woolf's rejection of the authoritative writer and the univocal text, her focus on the active role of the reader, and her analysis of social and historical contexts place her as forerunner of *deconstruction, *reader-response criticism and *New Historicism. Connecting Woolf with postmodernism adds a new dimension to traditional assessments of her critical position. Initially, Woolf was regarded as an impressionistic critic; however, although she praises 'enthusiasm' as the 'life-blood' of criticism ('Winged Phrases') and describes novels as 'not form which you see but emotion which you feel' ('On Re-reading Novels'), her approach is not to record impressions but to analyse the reading process. Certain of her essays ('Mr. Bennett and Mrs. Brown,' 'Modern Fiction') are often treated as modernist manifestos. In these essays, Woolf indeed defends writers who portray the inconclusive inner world of consciousness against writers whom she considers to be 'materialists'; yet her argument is not for one true style but for the style most appropriate to the age. In other contexts, she analyses the strengths of the representational mode ('"Robinson Crusoe"'). Woolf has also been seen as influenced by aestheticism, but again the connection should be qualified. When Woolf suggests that we read to grasp a work's 'perspective' and that the best works present us with a single vision, she seems to approach each work as an autonomous organic unity; nevertheless, her reading is never ahistorical, impersonal or divorced from non-literary issues. Overall, her approach is that literature grows out of and is informed by its total context: 'Masterpieces are not single and solitary births' *(Room)*.

In discussing literary history, Woolf thus approaches the text as a collaborative production involving the writer, the reader and their social, political and cultural contexts. She considers fluctuations in writers' reputations in relation to changes in the historical reader and relates changing conditions of production and consumption to developments in style ('The Patron and the Crocus'). Her analysis frequently emphasizes the interrelatedness of art-writing and life-writing ('The Pastons and Chaucer'); she rejects the predominance of 'historians' histories' – those defining history as great acts by great men – and focuses instead upon the history encoded in such forms as letters, diaries, memoirs, and journals. In doing so, Woolf exposes the *textuality of history, showing that the selection of historical evidence is an act in itself expressive of ideology. Radical for her time, she treats all forms of writing as significant, breaking away from established notions of genre hierarchies: while the critic must be 'exacting' in assessing the strengths and weaknesses of each style, the crucial goal is not the assigning of merit; each work has significance as a stage in the development of an individual writer or of a culture.

Woolf's analysis of reading is similarly contextual: she explores difference in attitudes and emotional response in different historical periods; she discusses the effects of national character and geography, for 'the mind takes its bias from its place of birth' ('The Russian Point of View'). Again her analysis avoids establishing hierarchies. An earlier period, such as the Elizabethan, implies a 'different' but not a more 'elementary' stage of reading development ('Notes on an Elizabethan Play'). Another antihierarchical aspect lies in Woolf's advocacy of the 'common reader.' For Woolf, the common reader is distinct from the professional reader, being motivated by pleasure and a desire for broader human experience, not by the need to propound a theory or advance an argument; furthermore, the common reader's knowledge of literature is far-ranging and

catholic in its scope, rather than narrow and specialized. Woolf's reader is not the ordinary person in the street but the person informed by a passion for reading; nevertheless, her literary model is democratic not elitist. Emphasizing readers' differences, she assumes not that readers share a common view but that they stand on common ground; thus the relationship she establishes with her reader is one of interactive exchange not of authoritarian instruction. Since Woolf is acutely aware of the connection between literature and ideology, her construct of reading likewise may be seen to have political implications. Communal rather than colonialist in its dynamics, Woolf's imaging of the relationship between writer and reader expresses her fundamental opposition to imperialism, fascism and indeed all totalitarian and totalizing regimes. (See *totalization, *patriarchy.)

MELBA CUDDY-KEANE

Primary Sources

Woolf, Virginia. '"Anon" and "The Reader": Virginia Woolf's Last Essays.' Ed. Brenda Silver. *20th Century Literature* 25 (1979): 356–441.
- *Books and Portraits.* Ed. Mary Lyon. London: Hogarth P, 1977.
- *The Captain's Death Bed and Other Essays.* Ed. Leonard Woolf. London: Hogarth P, 1950.
- *Collected Essays.* Ed. Leonard Woolf. 4 vols. London: Hogarth P, 1966–7.
- *The Common Reader: [First Series.]* London: Hogarth P, 1925.
- *The Common Reader: Second Series.* London: Hogarth P, 1932.
- *Contemporary Writers.* Ed. Jean Guiguet. London: Hogarth P, 1965.
- *The Death of the Moth and Other Essays.* Ed. Leonard Woolf. London: Hogarth P, 1942.
- *The Essays of Virginia Woolf.* Ed. Andrew McNeillie. 3 vols. to date. London: Hogarth P, 1986–.
- *Granite and Rainbow: Essays.* Ed. Leonard Woolf. London: Hogarth P, 1958.
- *The Moment and Other Essays.* Ed. Leonard Woolf. London: Hogarth P, 1947.
- *A Room of One's Own.* London: Hogarth P, 1929.
- *Three Guineas.* London: Hogarth P, 1938.
- *Women and Writing.* Ed. Michele Barrett. London: Women's P, 1979.

Secondary Sources

Bell, Barbara Currier, and Carol Ohmann. 'Virginia Woolf's Criticism: A Polemical Preface.' In *Feminist Literary Criticism: Explorations in Theory.* Ed.

Josephine Donovan. Lexington: Kentucky UP, 1975, 48–60.

Brewster, Dorothy. 'The Uncommon Reader as Critic.' In *Virginia Woolf*. New York: New York UP, 1962, 32–78.

Caughie, Pamela. 'Virginia Woolf as Critic: Creating as Aesthetic, Self-Reflexive Criticism.' In *Virginia Woolf and Postmodernism: Literature in Quest and Question of Itself*. Urbana: U of Illinois P, 1991, 169–93.

Daiches, David. 'The Uncommon Reader.' In *Virginia Woolf*. Norfolk, Conn.: New Directions, 1942, 124–92.

Ferebee, Steve. 'Bridging the Gulf: The Reader in and out of Virginia Woolf's Literary Essays.' *College Language Association Journal* 30 (1987): 343–61.

Gillespie, Diane. 'The Common Viewer: Virginia Woolf's Published Art Criticism.' In *The Sisters' Arts: The Writing and Painting of Virginia Woolf and Vanessa Bell*. New York: Syracuse UP, 1988, 63–103.

Goldman, Mark. *The Reader's Art: Virginia Woolf as Literary Critic*. The Hague: Mouton, 1976.

Good, Graham. 'Virginia Woolf: Angles of Vision.' In *The Observing Self: Rediscovering the Essay*. London: Routledge, 1988, 112–34.

Guiguet, Jean. 'Analysis and Argument.' In *Virginia Woolf and Her Works*. London: Hogarth P, 1965, 124–92.

Hill, Katherine C. 'Virginia Woolf and Leslie Stephen: History and Literary Revolution.' *PMLA* 96 (1981): 351–62.

Humm, Maggie. 'Virginia Woolf.' In *Feminist Criticism: Women as Contemporary Critics*. New York: St. Martin's P, 1986, 123–54.

Moi, Toril. *Sexual/Textual Politics: Feminist Literary Theory*. London: Methuen, 1985.

Novak, Jane. 'The Artist as Critic: Judging the Balance.' In *The Razor Edge of Balance: A Study of Virginia Woolf*. Coral Gables: U of Miami P, 1975, 35–50.

Rosenbaum, S.P. 'Intellectual Backgrounds.' In *Victorian Bloomsbury: The Early Literary History of the Bloomsbury Group*. New York: St. Martin's P, 1987, 21–34.

Silver, Brenda R. 'Introduction: The Uncommon Reader.' In *Virginia Woolf's Reading Notebooks*. Ed. B. Silver. Princeton: Princeton UP, 1983, 3–31.

Sharma, Vijay L. *Virginia Woolf as Literary Critic: A Reevaluation*. New Delhi: Arnold-Heinemann, 1977.

Wellek, René. 'Virginia Woolf.' *English Criticism, 1900–1950*. Vol. 5 of *A History of Modern Criticism: 1750–1950*. 6 vols. New Haven: Yale UP, 1986, 5: 65–84.

Zholkovskii, Aleksander K.

(b. U.S.S.R., 1937–) Specialist in Russian and comparative literature, Somali studies, theoretical linguistics, and poetics. Aleksander Zholkovskii attended Moscow University, where he completed a Diploma in 1959 and a Ph.D. in 1969 in African studies. His doctoral dissertation was on the deep and surface structures of Somali syntax. From 1959 to 1970, he was a research fellow in the Laboratory of Machine Translation at the Institute for Foreign Languages (Moscow). For part of this time (1963–5), he held a cross-appointment as a visiting professor of Somali Language at Moscow University's Institute of Oriental Languages. From 1970 to 1978, he was a senior research fellow in Computational Linguistics, first in the Institute for Foreign Languages and then in the Computational Linguistics Department of the Informelectro Institute (also in Moscow). After teaching for two years (1979–81) as a visiting professor at the University of Amsterdam, Zholkovskii migrated to the U.S.A. and took up an appointment as professor of Russian *literature at Cornell University. In 1982 he was appointed chairman of Cornell's Department of Russian.

Zholkovskii is best known for his work on poetics, particularly for a theory of literature developed in collaboration with Iurii K. Shcheglov, the *poetics of expressiveness. This theory (which in its early stages of development was referred to as 'Soviet generative poetics' and the 'Theme-Text' model of literary structure) combines certain structuralist notions of the Russian formalists and of modern linguistics with a systematic elaboration of the insights of the film-maker Sergei Eisenstein concerning the various *expressive devices that can serve to organize artistic form and make it engaging. (See also Russian *formalism, *structuralism, *theme.)

Although most of Zholkovskii's recent work has been in the field of literary theory, he has also made important contributions to the field of computational linguistics. Specifically, he collaborated with I.A. Mel'čuk to develop the concept of lexical functions and, more generally, the 'Meaning-Text Theory' of language – a semantically based dependency grammar that offers solutions to syntactical problems left unresolved by formalist, transformational-generative theories. In certain respects, the poetics of expressiveness is analogous to the multilevelled 'Meaning-Text' model of primary natural language; in other respects, it complements the natural-language model by a offering a delicate metalanguage for describing a secondary (that is, literary) use of the language system.

JAMES STEELE

Primary Sources

Zholkovskii, Aleksander. 'Levels, Domains, Invariants: A Format for the Analysis of Poems.' *The Proceedings of the 8th Annual Meeting of the Semiotic Society of America*. Bloomington: Indiana UP, 1984.
- 'On Three Analogies Between Linguistics and Poetics (Semantic Invariance, Obligatoriness of Grammatical Meanings, Competence vs. Performance).' *Poetics* 6 (1977): 77–106.
- *Themes and Texts: Toward a Poetics of Expressiveness*. Ed. Kathleen Parthé. Trans. from the Russian by the author. Ithaca/London: Cornell UP, 1984.
- and I.A. Melčuk. 'Towards a Functioning Meaning↔Text Model of Language.' *Linguistics* 57 (1970): 10–47.
- and Iu. K. Shcheglov. 'Poetics as a Theory of Expressiveness: Towards a "Theme-Expressiveness Devices-Text" Model of Literary Structure.' *Poetics* 5 (1976): 207–46.
- and Iu. K. Shcheglov 'Structural Poetics Is a Generative Poetics.' *Soviet Semiotics*. Ed. D. Lucid. Baltimore: Johns Hopkins UP, 1978.
- 'Generating the Literary Text.' *Russian Poetics in Translation* 1 (1975): 1–77.
- *Poetics of Expressiveness: A Theory and Applications*. Linguistic and Literary Studies in Eastern Europe, vol. 18. Amsterdam/Philadelphia: John Benjamins, 1987.

Secondary Sources

Culler, Jonathan. *Structuralist Poetics*. Ithaca: Cornell UP, 1975.
Eisenstein, Sergei. *The Film Form: Essays in Film Theory*. Cleveland: World Publishing, 1957.
- *The Film Sense*. Cleveland: World Publishing, 1957.
Fokkema, D.W., and Elrud Kunne-Ibsch. *Theories of Literature in the 20th-Century: Structuralism, Marxism, Aesthetics of Reception, Semiotics*. London: C. Hurst and Company.
Lotman, Ju.M. *The Structure of the Artistic Text*. Trans. Ronald and Gail Vroon. Michigan Slavic Contributions, no. 7. Ann Arbor: Department of Slavic Languages and Literature, U of Michigan, 1977.
Saussure, Ferdinand de. *Course in General Linguistics*. Ed. Charles Bally and Albert Sechehaye in collaboration with Albert Riedlinger. Trans. Wade Baskin. New York/Toronto/London: McGraw-Hill, 1966.
Seyffert, Peter. *Literary Structuralism: Background Debate Issues*. Columbus, Ohio: Slavica, 1985.
Steele, James, ed. *Meaning-Text Theory: Linguistics, Lexicography, and Implications*. Ottawa: U of Ottawa P, 1990.
- 'Re-constructing Structuralism: The Theme-Text Model of Literary Language and F.R. Scott's "Lakeshore."' In *Future Indicative: Literary Theory and Canadian Literature*. Ed. John Moss. Ottawa: U of Ottawa P, 1987.
Tallis, Raymond. *Not Saussure: A Critique of Post-Saussurean Literary Theory*. London: Macmillan, 1988.

3

TERMS

Actant

The term *actant* (literally 'that which accomplishes or undergoes the action') refers, in *semiotics, to the great functions or roles occupied by the various characters of a narrative, be they humans, animals, or simple objects. In the initial state of the Greimassian theory, these functions form three sets: Subject-Object, Sender-Receiver, Helper-Opponent.

*A.J. Greimas borrowed the concept of *actant* from the French linguist Lucien Tesnière, for whom this term designates a syntactic function which can be subject or object. In accordance with a principle already asserted by *Roland Barthes, following which a narrative may be considered as 'a long sentence,' Greimas postulated that this 'global utterance can be decomposed into a series of concatenated narrative utterances (=Propp's "functions")' ('Les actants' 162). (See *Propp.) He then defined the utterance as 'a relation between the actants that constitute it' and borrowed from two sources in order to make an inventory of the *actants* in the narrative. A first source was the seminal work of Vladimir Propp. In his *Morphology of the Folktale*, Propp identified in the Russian folkloric tale 31 basic functions, each function designating the action of a character, defined from the point of view of its signification in the unfolding of the plot. He then regrouped these functions into 7 spheres of actions: the villain, the donor (provider), the helper, the princess (and her father), the dispatcher, the hero, the false hero. Taking his inspiration from this model and from the model of Emile Souriau, Greimas proposed a more compact and more powerful model constituted by three pairs of *actants*.

The axis made by the first pair of *actants*, Subject-Object, refers to the person who is doing the action and what he/she wants to win or acquire. The Sender-Receiver axis refers to the person who gives a mission to the hero and the person for whose benefit this mission is accomplished (the Receiver may be the same as the Sender, or it may be a very general entity, like Humanity, Power or Happiness). The Helper-Opponent axis refers to the support available to the Subject (fairy godmother, horse, sword, magical ring) and to the obstacles he or she will have to overcome (traitor, labyrinth).

In a later version of his theory, Greimas limits the *actants* of the narrative to the two axes Subject-Object and Sender-Receiver, which he sees as fundamental and from which various others may be derived. Each of these four actants is seen as a category which may be projected on the *semiotic square* and thus unfold following its positive or negative poles. (See *seme.) The most common example of this functioning may be seen with the axis formed by the Subject and the Anti-Subject, this latter *actant* playing the role formerly attributed to the Opponent. This reorganization of the theory makes more visible the essentially polemical structure of the narrative and the fact that the so-called Opponent is in competition with the Subject for the possession of a same Object.

One should be careful not to confuse the *actant*, which is a narrative function based in the deep structure, with the *actor*. The actor is the name given to the concrete manifestation of an actant in a given narrative. For example, at the actorial level, which depends upon the superficial discursive structure, one could read a narrative sequence such as 'King Arthur sends Perceval to kill the Dragon in exchange for a beautiful diamond.' One recognizes here the actors Arthur, Perceval, the Dragon, and the Diamond. At the deep level, this corresponds to an actantial sequence in which a Sender sends a Subject to kill an Opponent in exchange for an Object. However, the relation actant-actor is not necessarily one-to-one. The same actor may, at various moments of a narrative, personify various *actants* and, conversely, the same *actant* may be embodied by various actors. As Greimas puts it, 'an articulation of actors constitutes a particular tale; a structure of *actants* constitutes a genre' (*Sémantique structurale* 175).

The concept of *actant* has proved its efficiency in the analysis not only of a narrative but also of a great variety of texts – be they philosophical, religious or scientific. (See *text.) By focusing only on the forces responsible for the action, regardless of their moral or psychological connotations, the notion of *actant* enabled critics to break away from the traditional emphasis put on the psychological status of the characters. As such, this concept is probably one of the most widely used in semiotics today. (See also *narratology.)

CHRISTIAN VANDENDORPE

Primary Sources

Greimas, A.J. *Sémantique structurale.* Paris: Larousse, 1966; Repub. PUF, 1986. *Structural Semantics.* Trans. D. McDowell, R. Schleifer and A. Velie. Lincoln and London: U of Nebraska P, 1983.

– 'Les actants, les acteurs et les figures.' In *Sémiotique narrative et textuelle.* Ed. C. Chabrol and J.C. Coquet. Paris: Larousse, 1973, 161–76. Repr. in *Du Sens II.* Paris: Seuil, 1983, 49–66. *On Meaning.* Trans. Paul Perron and F.H. Collins. Minneapolis: U of Minnesota P, 1987.

– and J. Courtés. *Sémiotique. Dictionnaire raisonné de la théorie du langage.* Paris, 1979. *Semiotics and Language: An Analytical Dictionary.* Trans. L. Crist, D. Patte et al. Bloomington: Indiana UP, 1982.

Secondary Sources

Propp, V. *Morphology of the Folktale.* 2nd ed. Austin: U of Texas P, 1928–68.
Souriau, E. *Les 200 000 situations dramatiques.* Paris: Flammarion, 1950.

Affective stylistics

Affective stylistics is a critical method and theory of literary meaning developed by *Stanley Fish in the late 1960s and early 1970s. A version of *reader-response criticism, affective stylistics is based on the idea that a work's meaning is to be found not in its formal architecture but in the sequence of interpretive decisions which the *text elicits in its reader. The most concise statement of the method and its underlying theoretical assumptions can be found in the 1970 manifesto 'Literature in the Reader: Affective Stylistics,' reprinted with Fish's other theoretical articles from the same period in *Is There a Text in This Class?* (1980). (See *literature.)

The central tenet of affective stylistics is that a work's meaning inheres in the experience of its reading. In opposition to formalist practices which consider the work as a unified structure, Fish examines the parts of the text as they succeed each other in time, concentrating on what the sequence of words does to the reader who attempts to make sense of it. Beneath the surface thematics, he seeks the second-level messages about language and intelligibility which the work promotes subliminally by forcing various decisions, attitudes, judgments, and reversals on its reader. (See also Russian *formalism, *New Criticism, *theme.)

Fish used this approach most impressively in his interpretation of Milton, *Surprised by Sin: The Reader in 'Paradise Lost'* (1967) and his collection of readings of 17th-century texts, *Self-Consuming Artifacts: The Experience of 17th Century Literature* (1972). In the latter work especially, he focused on what he called 'dialectical' works, which bring about a questioning of the reader's opinions and ways of knowing, rather than reinforcing them. However, in subsequent writings Fish became increasingly convinced that such textual effects were themselves conditioned by the critical strategies which even the most unbiased readers unwittingly deploy. Persuaded that even the simplest, most literal meaning is filtered through an interpretive matrix which can never be known, if only because it is the ground of knowing, he ultimately moved away from the cause-effect paradigm that characterized affective stylistics as originally formulated.

WILLIAM RAY

Primary Sources

Fish, Stanley. *Is There a Text in This Class? The Authority of Interpretive Communities.* Cambridge, Mass.: Harvard UP, 1980.

– 'Literature in the Reader: Affective Stylistics.' *New Literary History* 2 (1970): 123–62.

– *Self-Consuming Artifacts: The Experience of 17th Century Literature.* Berkeley: U of California P, 1972.

– *Surprised by Sin: The Reader in 'Paradise Lost.'* New York: Macmillan, 1967.

Anxiety of influence

Anxiety of influence is a theory of poetic influence first formulated by *Harold Bloom. Bloom developed his theory in a major tetralogy – *The Anxiety of Influence* (1973), *A Map of Misreading* (1975), *Kabbalah and Criticism* (1975), and *Poetry and Repression* (1976). It has since provided the theoretical foundation for his practical criticism. Although his debts are esoteric and many, Bloom borrowed primarily from *Freud to devise a theory of influence stressing the paralysing, oppressive burden of the past on later or 'belated' writers. By highlighting not collaboration but literary contestation, the anxiety of influence represents a new, more embattled approach to *intertextuality. According to Bloom, literary influence features not a benign interaction of the present with the past, but the Oedipal struggle of belated poets to conquer or 'transume' their predecessors. Through an act of *misprision – a defensive misreading rendering their precursors less intimidating – 'latecomers' seek to clear a space for their own creations. Wallace Stevens' poetry, for instance, must be read as an anxious struggle against the formidable wealth of Emerson and Whitman. Stevens found their prophetic affirmations so powerful, Bloom maintains, that his own disposition toward the prophetic had to be chastened into poetry of severe, ascetic discipline.

The anxiety of influence does not, however, result in merely arbitrary and random misreadings. Patterns of misprision are always determinate; Bloom had 'mapped' an exotic catalogue of six 'revisionary ratios' or defences. Most 'strong poems,' he argues, enact three successive dialectical substitutions or 'poetic crossings.' That is, the poet first withdraws before the precursor's influence; strong poets counter these 'tropes of limitation' with 'tropes of restitution.' (See *trope.) Clinamen, for instance, is the 'swerve' or revisionary misreading proper to all misprision; it marks the ephebe 's (young poet's) initial disordering of the precursor's vision. In tessera, the ephebe attempts to 'complete' or piece together these broken fragments. Kenosis opens the second dialectical movement; it involves the humbling or emptying out of the precursor by the ephebe. Bloom explains: '"Undoing" the precursor's strength in oneself serves also to "isolate" the self from the precursor's stance ... ' (Anxiety 88). In daemonisation, the ephebe's 'Counter-Sublime' is positioned before the Sublime of the precursor. After the sublime expansion of daemonisation, askesis begins the final crossing with another movement of contraction or limitation. Askesis, like kenosis, involves the precursor's purgation, but by 'curtailing' influence and not denying it outright. In apophrades, the precursor is no longer repressed but in fact seems to return; the ephebe has so staged this return, however, that the precursor is re-introduced not as an important predecessor but as the ephebe 's own ephebe.

PAUL ENDO

Primary Sources

Bloom, Harold. *The Anxiety of Influence: A Theory of Poetry.* New York: Oxford UP, 1973.
– *Kabbalah and Criticism.* New York: Seabury, 1975.
– *A Map of Misreading.* New York: Oxford UP, 1975.
– *Poetry and Repression: Revisionism from Blake to Stevens.* New Haven: Yale UP, 1976.

Aporia

Aporia is a Greek word used to identify an insoluble philosophical problem which nevertheless continues to draw thinkers not so much because it is a challenge but because it is built into the train of thought which philosophers have taken. To bring the question face to face with an aporia is the goal of the Socratic method: only then does the questioner realize that he does not know; the realization of not-knowing is the beginning of concerted searching (*Meno* 80d–86c). For Aristotle the aporia consists in the equal validity of contrary arguments; the methodological function of positing these arguments is to sharpen the statement of the problem and to prepare a solution (*Topics* 6.145.16–20).

In contemporary thought aporia represents a dead-end to a line of thought which calls for the mediation of new ideas or perhaps the reformulation of the questions asked. For example, in *Hermeneutics and the Human Sciences* (1981) *Paul Ricoeur refers to an internal aporia of hermeneutical reflection which calls for a reorientation of *hermeneutics through *semiotics. The hermeneutical inquiry after *Martin Heidegger and *Hans-Georg Gadamer has overcome the aporia of *subject/object through the concept of Being-in-the-world as linguistically constituted, but the aporia has been displaced and not eliminated. Heidegger has displaced the arena from 'how do I know the other' (epistemology) to 'the primacy of belonging in language' (ontology). After Gadamer the aporia becomes how does my world fuse with the text's world? The mediation of the textual sciences offers a possibility of shared meaning not only within language but also within textual analysis. (See also *text.)

MARIO J. VALDÉS

Archetype

Primary Sources

Aristotle. *Topics.*
Ricoeur, Paul. *Hermeneutics and the Human Sciences.*
  Ed. and trans. John B. Thompson. Cambridge:
  Cambridge UP, 1981.
Plato. *Meno.*

Archetype

A literary archetype (from the Greek *arché*, a
beginning, first cause, origin, and *typos*, pattern, model, type) is a typical or recurring
image, character, narrative design, *theme, or
other literary phenomenon that has been in
*literature from the beginning and regularly
reappears. Because archetypes are present in
all literature, though most easily seen and recognized in popular or naive writings, they
provide a basis for connecting one work with
another and enable readers to integrate and
unify literary experience.

The term archetype came into literary criticism from cultural anthropology (James G.
Frazer) and from psychology (*Carl G. Jung).
Frazer's encyclopedic 12-volume *The Golden
Bough* (1890–1915) traced archetypal myths
and rituals in the tales and ceremonies of diverse cultures. Frazer's work provided criticism
(see *archetypal criticism, *myth, *Northrop
Frye) with an extensive collection and description of the kinds of communal human actions
that are the content of drama. His account of
ritual patterns also proved useful in understanding the structure and generic principles of
drama. Jung employed the term archetype to
designate primordial images inherited in the
collective unconscious of the human race, from
where they emerge into myths, religions, literature, the visual arts, dreams and private fantasies. Jung's impact on literary studies has
been primarily on the understanding of the
dream basis of romance literature. In *From Ritual to Romance* (1920) Jessie Weston described
how archetypal rituals concerned with the victory of fertility over the wasteland provide the
imagery of the quest romance. *Maud Bodkin
(*Archetypal Patterns in Poetry* 1934) was one of
the earliest critics consciously to use the concept of the archetype. Since her preliminary
attempts, Robert Graves, G. Wilson Knight, Joseph Campbell, and Northrop Frye, especially
the last of these, have played significant roles

in making the study of archetypes an important part of literary criticism.

Consideration of certain verbal phenomena
as archetypes takes criticism beyond historical
explanations to the study of genres and conventions (see *genre criticism), and to questions of what literature as a whole is. Since the
archetype by definition is perennial and recurrent, it has shaping, communicating force and
so is important in considerations of the social
aspects and uses of literature. Acceptance,
moreover, of the archetypal or conventional
elements in literature makes possible the linking of one work with another, thus facilitating
coherent imaginative training through the
reading of literature.

ALVIN A. LEE

Primary Sources

Bodkin, Maud. *Archetypal Patterns in Poetry: Psycho-
  logical Studies of Imagination.* London: Oxford UP,
  1934.
Campbell, Joseph. *The Hero with a Thousand Faces.*
  New York: Pantheon Books, 1949.
Frazer, James G. *The Golden Bough: A Study in Magic
  and Religion.* 12 vols. London: Macmillan and Co.
  Ltd., 1890–1915. Abr. in 1 vol., 1954.
Frye, Northrop. *Anatomy of Criticism: Four Essays.*
  Princeton: Princeton UP, 1957.
– *Fearful Symmetry: A Study of William Blake.* Prince-
  ton: Princeton UP, 1957.
Graves, Robert. *Greek Myths.* London: Cassell, 1958.
– *The White Goddess: A Historical Grammar of Poetic
  Myths.* Amended and enl. ed. New York: Vintage
  Books; London: Faber and Faber, 1961.
Jung, Carl G. *Collected Works.* 20 vols. London: Rout-
  ledge and Kegan Paul, 1953–79.
Knight, G. Wilson. *The Starlit Dome: Studies in the
  Poetry of Vision.* London: Methuen, 1959.
Weston, Jessie. *From Ritual to Romance.* Garden City,
  NY: Doubleday, 1957.

Arche-writing: *see Différance/
différence*, trace

Aura

Aura is a term used by Marxist critic *Walter
Benjamin to characterize the subjective experience of a work of art or the conditions of production and exhibition that help to generate
such an experience. (See *Marxist criticism.)
Benjamin first mentions the aura in his 'Kleine

Geschichte der Photographie' ['Short History of Photography' 1931], in which he associates it with the aesthetic qualities of uniqueness and 'fullness,' as well as with the peculiar luminosity of early photographs. The essay contains the first hints of what will become the two dominant themes of Benjamin's later writings on the aura. (See *theme.) The first suggestion has to do with the experience of the aura. Whatever the objective basis for the phenomenon, cognizance of the aura, Benjamin suggests, does not arise from formal analysis but occurs in a moment of distraction. Experiencing the auratic object thus involves a 'strange weaving of space and time: the unique appearance or semblance of distance, no matter how close the object may be' (One-Way Street 250). The second suggestion has to do with the plight of the aura in an industrial world. According to Benjamin, producing multiple copies of an auratic object through technological means destroys the aura by divesting the object of its uniqueness. The mixture of intimacy and distance, time and space, is lost as the object is treated as no more than a commodity to be possessed and reproduced over and over again.

Benjamin develops this latter theme in his most famous essay, 'Das Kunstwerk im Zeitalter seiner technischen Reproduzierbarkeit' ['The Work of Art in the Age of Mechanical Reproduction' 1935], in which he uses aura to designate not any formal feature of a work of art, but a special cult value or authenticity that has been attributed to the work because of its rarity, some aspect of its history or the context of its exhibition. In this way, the experience of the aura, though it may still involve feelings of reverence, brings into play a set of responses that have been shaped by ritual, religion or some other form of communal behaviour. An object acquires aura and, by extension, *authority by being inserted into a *canon of equally hallowed works: 'The uniqueness of a work of art is inseparable from its being embedded in the fabric of tradition' (Illuminations 223). Yet this authority is undermined in an industrial world, in part because social relations have been so altered as to inhibit any sense of a traditional community, in part because the aura cannot survive mechanical reproduction. Though Benjamin related the destruction of the aura with some regret, he generally welcomed what he saw as the democratizing effects of mechanical reproduc-

tion, a position which earned him the censure of *Theodor Adorno. In other works, in particular his unfinished 'Arcades Project' of the 1930s, Das Passagenwerk, Benjamin deplored modern efforts to create a bogus aura through glamour, fashion and what Benjamin felt was the false religiosity of aestheticism. In these works, Benjamin seems to suggest that the maintenance of the aura is incompatible with the experience of modernity and that any attempt to restore the aura in art or in life must be rejected as either illusory nostalgia or exploitative despotism.

TREVOR ROSS

Primary Sources

Benjamin, Walter. *Gesammelte Schriften.* Ed. Rolf Tiedemann and Hermann Schweppenhäuser. 6 vols. Frankfurt: Suhrkamp, 1972–85.
– *Illuminations.* Ed. Hannah Arendt. Trans. Harry Zohn. New York: Schocken, 1969.
– *One-Way Street and Other Writings.* Trans. Edmund Jephcott and Kingsley Shorter. London: New Left Books, 1979.

Authority

The term authority is used in three closely related ways in contemporary criticism and critical theory. Most commonly, authority designates that quality of a literary *text which ensures its worth as a credible and reliable expression of meaning. Traditionally, a work acquired authority – and was subsequently granted canonical status – by means of the perceived virtue, enlightenment or grace of its author (auctor). The endowment of authority was earlier concomitant with a favourable judgment of the author's substantial agreement with the system of values deemed correct by the endowing party. Thus, the canons of authoritative writings have fluctuated with changes in social and political climates. (See *canon.) In the Middle Ages, the Bible was thought to be the quintessential authoritative text, a direct transcription of the meaning of a supreme Auctor against whose word the authority (auctoritas), or truth, of all subsequent writing was measured. This kind of understanding of authority is premised on the existence of a determinate, divinely informed meaning and the possibility of the recovery of that meaning. The erosion of such an essentialist epistemology, of the possibility of absolute truth, by the religious and political turbulence of the 15th and 16th centuries was attended by the questioning of the nature of authority and by the search for sources of worth and credibility beyond the scope of medieval Christian doctrine.

In large measure, this search continues to dominate modern theorizing on the nature of authority. No longer confident of the existence of a stable core of truth, literary theorists have not so much discarded the notion of authority as redefined its criteria according to their particular convictions about the source of linguistic meaning. For instance, New Critics systematically divest the author of authority and assign it instead to the text, convinced that the text itself is the only legitimate field of literary study and that it discloses its meaning to the properly trained and suitably distanced reader. (See *New Criticism.) For the hermeneutical critic (see *hermeneutics), centrally concerned with the nature of interpretation and the transmission of tradition(s), authority is thought to be either a quality of the tradition instinctively and universally recognized in the very act of cognition (*Gadamer) or the interested and self-legitimating product of systems of social domination (*Habermas). Not unlike the view of Habermas is that of Marxist and feminist critics, who deliberately refrain from assigning authority to any particular component of the hermeneutic process in the belief that authority is always ideologically charged, that it invariably promotes the interests and perpetuates the dominance of a self-selected group of individuals. (See *Marxist criticism, *feminist criticism, *ideology.) For critics like *E.D. Hirsch, who follow generally the hermeneutical approach in stressing the need for some objective measure of validity in interpretation, authority is restored to authorial intention and the task of criticism is the recovery of this intention with a minimal intrusion of the critic's own historical situation or interpretative bias. By contrast, the proponents of *reader-response criticism maintain that authority rests finally in the reader whose bringing to bear upon a text of the very interpretative bias Hirsch wishes to exorcise is the actual determinant of textual meaning. Finally, and perhaps most radically, critics who practise *deconstruction paradoxically submit that there is no authority in texts or anywhere else, that any configuration of letters which we label a text,

or indeed an interpretation of a text, is already self-subverting, already speaks of the silent 'other' which undermines its own claim to authoritative utterance. (See *subversion, *self/other.) For all these schools of criticism, however different their approaches to the nature of meaning, authority is a key concern. (See also *metacriticism.)

Stemming from these theoretical issues is the related concern with the nature of interpretative authority within the institution of literary criticism. Here the concern is defining the extent to which an expert (or 'authority') in the study of *literature can claim authority in writing about or teaching the interpretation of texts in a critical climate where determining meaning itself is under debate. In view of the recent developments in the theory of verbal communication, literary theorists are turning their attention to re-evaluating the professional practice of literary criticism.

The term authority is also used more narrowly in literary criticism (as distinct from literary theory) to denote the source of *power within the societies depicted in texts. In this usage, the critic emphasizes relationships of force and obedience with a view to exposing the oppressive actions of individuals or social groups seen to control the discursive, conventional and institutional spheres of their respective societies. Authority in this sense is rather inaccurately synonymous with power.

MARTA STRAZNICKY

Primary Sources

Arendt, Hannah. 'What is Authority?' *Between Past and Future: Eight Exercises in Political Thought.* Harmondsworth: Penguin, 1968, 91–141.

Cain, William E. 'Authors and Authority in Interpretation.' *Georgia Review* 34 (1980): 617–34.

Docherty, Thomas. *On Modern Authority: The Theory and Condition of Writing 1500 to the Present Day.* Sussex: Harvester, 1987.

Fraser, John. 'Playing for Real: Discourse and Authority.' *University of Toronto Quarterly* 56 (1987): 416–34.

Miller, Jacqueline T. *Poetic License: Authority and Authorship in Medieval and Renaissance Contexts.* New York: Oxford UP, 1986.

Newton, K.M. 'Interest, Authority, and Ideology in Literary Interpretation.' *British Journal of Aesthetics* 22 (1982): 103–14.

Ricoeur, Paul. 'Hermeneutics and the Critique of Ideology.' Trans. John B. Thompson. *The Hermeneutic Tradition: From Ast to Ricoeur.* Ed. Gayle L.

Ormiston and Alan D. Schrift. Syracuse: SUNY P,
1990, 298–334.

White, Hayden. 'Conventional Conflicts [Authority
and the Profession of Criticism].' *New Literary
History* 13 (1981): 145–60.

Primary Sources

Culler, Jonathan. *Structuralist Poetics: Structuralism,
Linguistics, and the Study of Literature.* Ithaca: Cornell UP, 1975.

Binary opposition

Binary opposition is a term which is central to
dialectic logic and is widely used in theoretical
argument. Binary oppositions provide a way of
bringing dynamics and process into theory. In
a binary opposition the two poles must not
only be opposed to each other but must also
be in exclusive opposition to each other; in
other words, they are bound in polar opposition like the positive and negative charge of an
electric current. Some of the most influential
examples are sense/reference (Gottlob Frege);
synchronic/diachronic, paradigmatic/syntagmatic (*Ferdinand de Saussure); signifier/signified (French *structuralism); *subject/object
(René Descartes); noumena/phenomena (Immanuel Kant); explanation/understanding
(*Wilhelm Dilthey; *Hans-Georg Gadamer;
*Paul Ricoeur). (See also *signified/signifier/
signification.)

To use the last as a model, explanation is a
social act of making some state of affairs
known to another person, understanding is
an individual act of comprehension and appropriation. When the two concepts are coupled
together in binary opposition, the result is a
process of interaction between the individual
and society.

Structural linguistics, which defines language
as a system of functional relations, presupposes binary oppositions of the phonological
elements of language as the basis and model
of its analysis. The advantage of binarism in
structuralist studies, 'but also its principal danger,' as *Jonathan Culler (*Structuralist Poetics*
15) notes, 'lies in the fact that it permits one to
classify anything.' The oppositions posited as
functional in a given analysis ignore qualitative
distinctions which are *not* functional – but
nevertheless real – and for this reason binary
analysis often operates on a level of misleading abstraction from the way in which phenomena present themselves to us.

MARIO J. VALDÉS

Bracketing

A term developed by the German philosopher
*Edmund Husserl bracketing refers to the process of suspending judgment about the existence of the world around us, by placing in
abeyance or parentheses our commonsensical
presuppositions about the world and the relationship between the perceiving consciousness
and objects in external reality ('Phenomenology' 125, 130). (See also *phenomenological
criticism.) Also known as *epoche* or reduction,
this suspension of the natural attitude extends
past the unthinking, unconsidered hypotheses
of the common human being to encompass
those comparable attitudes specific to the sciences, especially the natural sciences and the
science of psychology ('Philosophy as Rigorous
Science' 173–9; Kockelmans 50–2). Bracketing
involves as well, then, the suspension of presuppositions about the knowable implicit in
these sciences ('Phenomenology' 136–8; Sinha,
35–9). In this view (sometimes called scientific-
objectivist), both the objects in the external
world and the relationships between them are
thought to have meaning in and of themselves, with little or no account being taken
of the constitutive role of the perceiving consciousness. (See *subject/object.) In his search
for what he called 'the Archimedean point,'
the source of absolute certainty which would
eliminate the purely contingent aspects of
objects perceived in the natural attitude and
which would, in turn, serve as the foundation
for human knowledge, Husserl fixed upon the
process of bracketing ('Phenomenology' 130).
As the purifying of one's perspective of the
natural attitude, bracketing enables the subject
to accomplish the aim of phenomenology: the
suspension of the non-essential, purely contingent and metaphysical implications of the natural attitude and the subsequent identification
and description of the universal structures of
human consciousness, or essences ('Phenomenology' 125, 126–8). As this description
indicates, the final aim of bracketing is not
simply the unprejudiced description of pure

phenomena: it is also the intuiting of and reflection upon the essential, invariant features
of these objects held in consciousness and the
essential structures of consciousness itself, in
those intentional mental acts which reveal
these essences ('Phenomenology' 123–4).
Simply, in bracketing, reduction or *epoche*,
Husserl believed that one could arrive at the
essence of objects, experiences and consciousness itself. As such, it is the central method of
phenomenological investigation ('Phenomenology' 124). (See *intention/intentionality.)

Bracketing, *epoche* or reduction, however, is
not a denial of the external reality of the objects posited in the natural attitude in favour
of a system of ideal forms or abstractions
which are beyond our perception. Neither is
bracketing a process of radical subjectivism,
where the objects in the external world are
categorically stated to exist *only* as projections
of the subject's consciousness. The bracketing
of the external reality of these objects as they
exist in the natural attitude is a process of exclusion, of delimiting which objects are suitable for phenomenological investigation and
which are not. It is the process through which
phenomenologists from Husserl to Pfander to
Scheler prepare the field for the investigation
and description of phenomena and the universal structures of human consciousness (Schmitt
140). Since bracketing aims at bringing the
realm of pure phenomena to the focus of consciousness, phenomenologists are perfectly
willing to consider non-existent objects (that is,
objects of mental acts which have no correlates in the 'real' world) as suitable objects of
investigation. In their view 'nonexistent objects
have [both] properties and relations' and can
be the object of intentional mental acts, just as
existent ones do and can (Grossmann 140–1).

Bracketing is, then, the general term for a
set of reductions which have as their aim the
production of a non-empirical, and 'unprejudiced' (Husserl, *Cartesian Meditations* 36) series
of statements about phenomena, the production of a knowledge of essences (Schmitt 136–
9). In its goal of seeing and fixing essences in
bracketing, phenomenology suggests the accompanying process of free-imaginative *variation. In this process, the existence of objects
having been bracketed, the subject arrives at
the essence of a phenomenon through the process of exemplification. One first posits and
then varies the description of an example of
the said phenomenon held in consciousness by

adding to or subtracting from the characteristics of the example. Each deletion or addition
is tested against the question of whether it
transforms the object so that it is no longer an
example of the same phenomenon that one
began with in one's mind (Schmitt 141). In
this way, the subject discovers the essence of
an object in consciousness, by identifying both
the 'necessary and invariant' (Schmitt 141) as
well as the contingent and variant features of
an object (*Cartesian Mediations* 29; Hammond
et al. 75–8; Schmitt 140–4). This process which
allows for the identification, investigation and
description of the essence of phenomena and
the correlative description of the essential, universal structures of human consciousness is
known specifically as eidetic reflection, and requires a particular kind of bracketing: eidetic
reduction or eidetic abstraction ('Phenomenology' 126–8). Taken from the Greek, *eidos*,
meaning 'idea' or 'ideal,' the adjective 'eidetic'
indicates Husserl's debt to Platonic philosophy
and its distinction between the ideal (*eidos*) and
the particular for his own comparable distinction between essence and instance. Through
the eidetic reduction, we are able to bracket
the perceived instance and attend to the object's essence. In addition, eidetic reduction
allows us to 'perceive,' in phenomenological
terms intuit, the connections between various
essences. Eidetic reflection does not simply
concentrate on essences alone but on their
interrelationships (Grossmann 103).

Although probably the most important reduction in Husserlian phenomenology, eidetic
reduction is only one among many different
forms of reduction. Each of these other reductions, variously called the psychological reduction (the bracketing of the natural ego and the
claims of the science of psychology to the possession of certainty), the phenomenological reduction, and the philosophical reduction, has
as its aim to allow the subject to pass from the
world of 'realities' posited in the natural attitude to the world of their ultimate presuppositions ('Phenomenology' 122–3, 125; Kockelmans 133–4, 107–8). Since it is obvious, for
example, that the natural ego cannot be the
consciousness which constitutes or intuits the
essential meanings of objects, it is the performance of bracketing upon the natural ego
which leads to the transcendental-phenomenological consciousness or ego (Kockelmans
163–4). Husserl expected that the transcendental ego, in its ability to intuit the essences of

objects and to thereby establish the universal structures of human consciousness, would provide the grounds for procuring absolutely certain and valid knowledge about things and events (Kockelmans 162–3). In this kind of reduction, we perform a reflection upon consciousness itself, concentrating not on specific mental acts, but on their essences. In eidetic reflection we are, for example, interested not in a description of loving any particular thing, but in the essential, invariant features displayed in 'loving-of' itself ('Phenomenology' 122–7). As a result of these reductions, a field of original experiences, what Husserl will later describe as the *Lebenswelt* or life-world, is opened up to philosophical investigation (Kockelmans 252–3, 278–9). In historical terms, Husserl's concept of bracketing is akin to the systematic doubt common to other philosophic approaches like scepticism and Cartesianism, but with several important differences. Husserl indicates his link with ancient Greek scepticism through his adoption of the term *epoche* from this very school (Sinha 28). For the sceptics, this term referred to a kind of radical doubt as a method for achieving certain knowledge. This doubt involves a provisional suspension of any judgment about the validity of an idea until all available evidence has been gathered and examined. In addition, Husserl himself stresses the strong similarities between his procedure of bracketing and the methodical or systematic doubt characteristic of the work of René Descartes, going so far as to say that 'phenomenology might almost be called a new, a 20th century Cartesianism' (*Paris Lectures* 3). He also emphasizes, however, the vast difference between Descartes' radical doubt about existence and his own suspension of belief in existence (Schmitt 140; *Cartesian Mediations* 29–31, 35–6). Unlike in Cartesianism, phenomenology's own peculiar form of methodical doubt 'does not necessarily lead to a system of indubitable metaphysical truths' (Sinha 28); its orientation is more epistemological, since it concentrates primarily upon providing a methodology through which the universal structures of human consciousness can be examined (*Paris Lectures* 11–12; Sinha 26–8; Kockelmans 72–6).

While the work of *Martin Heidegger is heavily influenced by Husserl's methodology, he finds bracketing to be a procedure not wholly suited to his philosophic project. Heidegger's main interest lies in the unique hu-

man phenomenon, defined in terms of the inherently intentional nature of the *Dasein* (being-in-the-world): 'For Husserl, the phenomenological reduction ... is the method of leading phenomenological vision from the natural attitude of the human being whose life is involved in the world of things and persons back to the transcendental life of consciousness ... in which objects are constituted as correlates of consciousness. For us, phenomenological reduction means leading phenomenological vision back from the apprehension of a being, whatever may be the character of that apprehension, to the understanding of the being of this being' (*Basic Problems of Phenomenology* 21). Heidegger's ontological orientation leads him to revise radically Husserl's phenomenological reduction, denying it centrality and primacy in philosophical investigation and suggesting that there are really 'three basic components of phenomenological method: reduction, construction, destruction' (21). In construction, our vision is not simply guided back from beings to being (as in reduction) but 'guided forward towards being itself' (21). Destruction is 'a critical process in which traditional concepts (of ontology), which at first must necessarily be employed, are de-constructed down to the sources from which they were drawn' (23). Like Husserl, Heidegger insists upon a philosophical radicalism, but one which will ensure 'the genuine character of [ontology's] concepts' (23).

Phenomenological literary criticism (particularly of the Husserlian-influenced *Geneva School) adopts and adapts the concepts of bracketing, eidetic reduction and the intuition of essences. Just as the phenomenologist proper places in parentheses the world as perceived in the natural attitude, so the critics of the Geneva School, which includes such theorists as *Georges Poulet, Jean-Pierre Richard and Marcel Raymond, analogously attempt to suspend all presuppositions and to bracket any personal commitment to a particular *ideology or metaphysic (Magliola 8–9, 28–9, 39–42). By placing in brackets such ideology, whether it be Marxist (see *Marxist criticism), feminist (see *feminist criticism) or humanist, the phenomenological literary critic lays claim to a methodology and type of interpretation which is both 'intrinsic' and *universal: 'intrinsic' in that it claims, through bracketing, to treat that intentional object – the *text – alone, the aim of this critical practice being to experience, describe and explicate what is actually in the text, not to place extrinsic categories or expectations upon it; universal in that, in focusing solely upon the text, such criticism claims that any text is an expression of consciousness (defined in terms of intentionality, as 'the reciprocal implication of self and world' [Magliola 35]), a thesis which at least gives the appearance of a thoroughly unbiased approach. (Magliola 29–30, 39–41). Consequent to the critic's bracketing of all ideological and metaphysical assumptions is the employment of a kind of phenomenological reduction where the text is isolated from its historically and culturally specific milieu, although later phenomenological critics believe such a move unnecessary (Magliola 43–4). As the Husserlian subject then intuits the essential features of the bracketed object, so the Geneva critic intuits the essential structure of the literary work, the unified group of intentional subject-object relations which are part of the 'author's Lebenswelt and which he or she imaginatively transforms into the fictive universe of the text' (Magliola 28). The practice of criticism for phenomenological critics is then, in its broadest sense, comparable to the kind of minute description of an object's essence undertaken by Husserl. It is an 'intuiting' of the text in order to experience and then describe as fully as possible 'the text's Lebenswelt [or] phenomenological consciousness' (Magliola 42).

MARIE H. LOUGHLIN

Primary Sources

Grossmann, Reinhardt. *Phenomenology and Existentialism*. London: Routledge, 1984.
Hammond, Michael, Jane Howarth and Russell Keat. *Understanding Phenomenology*. Oxford: Blackwell, 1991.
Heidegger, Martin. *The Basic Problems of Phenomenology*. Trans., intro. and lexicon, Albert Hofstadter. Bloomington: Indiana UP, 1982.
Husserl, Edmund. *Cartesian Mediations: An Introduction to Phenomenology*. Trans. Dorion Cairns. The Hague: Martinus Nijhoff, 1970.
– *The Paris Lectures*. Trans. and intro. Peter Koestenbaum. The Hague: Martinus Nijhoff, 1975.
– 'Phenomenology.' In *Deconstruction in Context: Literature and Philosophy*. Ed. Mark C. Taylor. Chicago: U of Chicago P, 1986.
– 'Philosophy as Rigorous Science.' In *Husserl: Shorter Works*. Ed. Peter McCormick and Frederick A. Elliston. Notre Dame, Ind.: U of Notre Dame P, 1981, 166–97.
Kockelmans, Joseph J. *A First Introduction to Husserl's Phenomenology*. Pittsburgh: Duquesne UP, 1967.
Magliola, Robert. *Phenomenology and Literature: An Introduction*. West Lafayette, Ind.: Purdue UP, 1977.
Schmitt, Richard. 'Phenomenology.' In *The Encyclopedia of Philosophy*. Vol. 5. Ed. Paul Edwards. New York: Macmillan, 1967, 135–51.
Sinha, Debabrata. *Phenomenology and Existentialism: An Introduction*. Calcutta: Progressive Publishers, 1974.

Canon

A canon is a body of writings or other creative works that have been recognized as standard or authoritative. An ancient Greek word, canon originally meant either of two things, a measuring rod or a list. From the first is derived the idea of a model or standard, in particular a standard which can be applied as a rule, law or principle. This sense survives in the notions of 'canon (or ecclesiastical) law' or 'canons of criticism.' From the second comes the concept of canonization, the Roman Catholic practice of admitting an individual to a 'list' of saints. One who assembles such a list or presents the case for canonization is called a postulator. These two original senses of canon have since become fused, in part because list-makers and postulators have routinely claimed value or *authority for their lists.

The idea of a canon of writings first developed in relation to the Bible, in the 4th century of the modern era. Though formed over a long period of time, and often at the service of local secular interests, the biblical canon comprises all the books that the Christian church considers Holy Scripture. The apocrypha, or 'hidden' books, is the term given to a set of writings that relate to the Scriptural canon in form and matter yet whose authenticity has not been officially recognized: the Roman Catholic Bible includes 11 books that Protestants reject as apocryphal. A critical reading that emphasizes the unity of the Bible is sometimes called a canonical interpretation; in contrast, a historical interpretation assumes that the books of Scripture bear the inscriptions of their divergent authors and of the very dissimilar circumstances in which they were produced.

The first applications of canon to a body of secular writings date, in English at least, from the late 16th century. This secular variant initially develops by analogy not, as might be expected, with the Scriptural canon but with the practice of canonization. Elizabethan authors, most notably Donne in his poem 'The Canonization,' express their hope of being canonized, in the sense of achieving fame comparable to that of Catholic saints. William Covell, in his tract *Polimanteia* (1595), is the first to advocate the canonization of secular *literature under the auspices of England's universities. The analogy with the biblical canon comes into play much later, when critics first use the term to designate all the works that can be legitimatelyattributed to a given author, as in 'the Shakespeare canon.' Works inconclusively attributed to that author are dubbed apocryphal, again by analogy with the biblical example. Here the merging of the dual senses of canon becomes particularly apparent: though establishing the canon of an author's works may seem to involve only a listing of proven attributions, the successful ascription of a particular *text to a major author such as Shakespeare will dramatically increase the critical attention lavished on that work and may thus help to increase its value over time.

The idea of 'major' authors brings up the most familiar current usage of canon, as a collective term for the totality of the most highly esteemed works in a given culture. It differs from other collective epithets such as 'World's Classics,' 'The Great Books' or 'Masterpieces of Western Literature' in that its usage is not usually honorific or commendatory. Indeed the term is most often used by critics who wish to emphasize the affinities between the exclusive character of the literary canon and the highly institutionalized and monolithic nature of its biblical equivalent. A literary canon is usually perceived as a static if 'open' totality; hence it is not identical to a tradition, which usually implies a historical scheme. The latter term denotes a series of works or set of customs that manifest formal or thematic resemblances, or lines of influence, that have been maintained over multiple generations. A tradition is also a neutral term and may be used to refer to works that are not necessarily highly esteemed, such as 'the oral tradition.' Yet, as *T.S. Eliot argued in his most famous essay, 'Tradition and the Individual Talent' (1919), the literature of the present cannot be truly appreciated if it is not understood in relation to its antecedents. (See *anxiety of influence.)

The qualities or circumstances that make a work eligible for inclusion in a canon constitute its canonicity. Another term, canon-formation, names the process whereby authors become recognized or valued as standard. The intricacies of this process are a matter of much current debate, as are the criteria of canonicity. The conventional view is that the canonicity of a work is established by a consensus of successive generations of readers, critics and educators, as well as by the extent of its influence on later literature. According to this view, a work deserves a place in the canon if it continues to be read and prized in changing contexts; the work, it is said, must pass 'the test of time.' How much time is unclear: it has been a critical commonplace since Horace's day to set a term of 100 years, but critics have rarely observed the term, as the meteoric canonizations of Proust, Joyce and others in our century may indicate.

There are a number of problems with this belief in a critical consensus. Canon-formation may involve a host of contingencies, not all of which can be directly related to the attitudes of critics and scholars: the accidents of survival in the period before printing, the effects of censorship and the fluctuating availability of published works. Moreover, despite the efforts of literary historians, including the *Constance School of Reception Aesthetics, it is almost impossible to measure with any accuracy the range and relative weight of the divergent values that make up this consensus. It is not always clear, for example, whether later critics are revising the views of earlier generations or merely reiterating received opinion. Above all, this consensus has rarely if ever embraced the values of a broad cultural diversity. On the contrary, canon-formation has frequently been under the control of an official culture that valorizes only those works that in some way assert or reveal its dominant *ideology. Many of our notions of the European canon were developed at the turn of the century and reflect the strong nationalist feelings and prejudices that were current during this period. Our sense of the early English canon, for example, has been heavily influenced by the work of early German philologists, whose nationalistic biases led them to claim an Anglo-Saxon culture superior to the equally substantial Anglo-Norman and Anglo-Latin cultures.

Recent critics have stressed how the literary canon favours works by white European men from the middle and higher classes to the exclusion of most works by women, popular artists or writers from other cultures or races. These critics advocate either a broad revision of the canon to reflect a more pluralistic set of values or the institution of separate canons for each of these literary subgroups. It is now possible to speak of the canon of women's writings, the canon of proletarian literature, and so on. Some critics have even suggested abandoning the idea of the canon altogether because it is inherently exclusive and élitist. The danger in such wholesale rejection of the canon is that it assumes that criticism can do without evaluation, when in fact evaluation is implicit in all forms of interpretation. There is a danger as well in such relativistic arguments of underestimating the complexity of canon-formation; critics who reject the canon as élitist often muddle the question of value by confusing the quality or merit of a work, the attitudes it may express, the ideological functions it may have served in the past, and its relevance to our immediate concerns. Though the canon may serve hegemonic interests, canonical works themselves, as Dominick LaCapra suggests, 'have complex, internally divided relations to their contexts of creation and use' (5).

Though it is often identified with the pedagogical curriculum, the canon is in fact loosely structured and is more akin to the repertoire in drama or music. The process of revising the canon may be slow but it is not impossible. The recent ascendancy of the deconstructionist critics (see *deconstruction) has meant a higher critical standing for the authors they habitually discuss, including the English Romantic poets, Jean-Jacques Rousseau and *Friedrich Nietzsche. In general, it is a simpler task to revise received interpretations of a major author than to attempt to alter that author's status in the canon. The situation may differ for marginal authors or authors unduly overlooked but, on the whole, it may take more than a generation to adjust the relative rankings of canonical authors.

TREVOR ROSS

Primary Sources

Barr, James. *Holy Scripture: Canon, Authority, Criticism.* Oxford: Clarendon P, 1983.

Fiedler, L., and H. Baker, eds. *English Literature: Opening Up the Canon.* Baltimore: Johns Hopkins UP, 1981.

Fowler, Alastair. 'Genre and the Literary Canon.' *New Literary History* 11 (1979): 97–119.

Guillory, John. 'Canonical and Non-canonical: A Critique of the Current Debate.' *ELH* 54 (1987): 483–527.

Harris, Wendell V. 'Canonicity.' *PMLA* 106 (1991): 110–21.

Kermode, Frank. *Forms of Attention.* Chicago: U of Chicago P, 1985.

Kibel, Alvin C. 'The Canonical Text.' *Dedalus* 112 (1983): 239–54.

LaCapra, Dominick. *Soundings in Critical Theory.* Ithaca: Cornell UP, 1989.

Lauter, Paul. *Canons and Contexts.* Oxford: Oxford UP, 1991.

Lindenberger, Herbert. *The History in Literature: On Value, Genre, Institutions.* New York: Columbia UP, 1990.

Robinson, Lilian. 'Treason Our Text: Feminist Challenges to the Literary Canon.' *Tulsa Studies in Women's Literature* 2 (1983): 83–98.

Smith, Barbara Herrnstein. *Contingencies of Value.* Cambridge, Mass.: Harvard UP, 1988.

Von Hallberg, Robert, ed. *Canons.* Chicago: U of Chicago P, 1984.

Carnival

While isolated usages of the word occur in European *literature as early as the medieval period, carnival is a term first used systematically by the Russian scholar *Mikhail Bakhtin. Bakhtin used the example of late medieval and early Renaissance folk culture in developing his theory of laughter. In *Rabelais and his World* (1965; trans. 1968), he offers a new reading of the novels of François Rabelais as embodying the essence of carnival, 'a boundless world of humorous forms and manifestations opposed [to] the official and serious tone of medieval ecclesiastical and feudal culture' (*Rabelais* 4). The life of the people parallels official culture, at once radically subverting state *ideology and offering an outlet for the ongoing role of repression and of élite cultural practices in the unfolding of human history. Focused on the body and on bodily realities such as eating, drinking, evacuation, sex, birth, and death, the carnival possesses its own rituals, whose status as agency and whose mimetic function both remain open to question. (See also *mimesis.)

Bakhtin's notion of the carnival implicitly addresses his own experience and understanding of Stalinism. Originally written in the 1930s as his Ph.D. thesis at the Gorky Institute, *Rabelais and His World* remained unpublished in Russia for three decades. In historic context, its deployment of the concept of carnival has been described as 'a denunciation of what the revolution had become, and a plea for understanding revolution in another way' (Holquist 8). For Linda Hutcheon, 'in discussing the particular case of the medieval carnival, Bakhtin seems to have uncovered [an] underlying principle of all parodic discourse: the paradox of its authorized transgression of norms.' (See *paradox, *disclosure.) Carnival, like *parody, 'posits, as a prerequisite to its very existence, a certain aesthetic institutionalization which entails the acknowledgement of recognizable, stable forms and conventions' (Hutcheon 74–5). *Umberto Eco, like *Julia Kristeva and *Fredric Jameson, offers a psychoanalytic reading of the comedy of carnival as suspect: it means 'enjoying the murder of the father, provided that others, less human than ourselves [i.e., wearing an animal mask], commit the crime' (Eco 2). Thus 'Bakhtin was right in seeing the manifestation of a profound drive towards liberation and *subversion in medieval carnival. The hyper-Bakhtinian ideology of carnival as *actual* liberation may, however, be wrong' (Eco 3). Some have queried Nietzschean or Christian traces in Bakhtin's thought; feminist perspectives on Bakhtin criticize his vision of carnival as unconsciously patriarchal and essentialist, especially in his treatment of the female body and the voices of women. (See *Friedrich Nietzsche, *feminist criticism, *patriarchy, *essentialism.)

Laughter occupies a pre-eminent role in Bakhtin's notion of the carnivalesque. Ritual language and gesture of a theatrical caste explicitly employ the grotesque, exaggeration and transgression in order to parody accepted beliefs and rules in celebrations such as the feast of fools, the feast of the ass, the reign of the boy bishop, and Mardi Gras. (See *grotesque, theories of the.) Carefully wrought literary inversions and spontaneous speech together exhibit 'the social consciousness of all the people' (*Rabelais* 92). The body, foregrounded by means of grotesque realism, reveals a universal levelling tendency, eradicating distinctions not only between classes but also between actor and spectator (*Rabelais* 27). As street theatre, carnival implicates everyone in simultaneous performance, observation, reflection, and celebration. Linguistically, carnival also resists order, closure and the sacrosanct; its language is identifiable by its oaths, billingsgate and the polyglot *heteroglossia of the marketplace. Bawdy parodies of sacred words, texts, rituals, and narratives mark the temporary suspension of all other prohibitions and hypocrisies. Contradiction is acknowledged in Bakhtin's linguistic understanding of carnival in Rabelais, where laughter is marked by expansiveness and excess: by the moment of recognition and the recognition of important moments in individuals' and communities' sense of time and mutability. Laughter and its carnivalesque manifestation are, for Bakhtin as for Rabelais, no less significant philosophically than the tragic, and closely related to it. According to Eco, Bakhtin succeeds in theorizing and recontextualizing Aristotle's missing, apocryphal *text on comedy.

Class conflict, linked to the emerging cultural hybridization of the carnivalesque with and within highbrow culture in Renaissance theatre, has been the focus of Shakespearean scholars in both Europe and America. Robert Weimann was one of the first to argue that 'the popular tradition itself assimilated wholly disparate elements (including classical, courtly and humanist materials) until it became part of a vastly larger cultural and aesthetic synthesis: the 'mingle-mangle' of which John Lyly spoke when he noted that 'the whole worlde is become an Hodge-Podge' (Weimann xviii). Michael Bristol adopts a more theoretical approach, arguing that 'the problem of authority cannot be fully elucidated by focusing exclusively on the relationship between what purports to be a virtual monopoly of significant political power and a few individual centers of avant-garde consciousness uneasily balanced between alternatives of affiliation or critical rejection of the imperatives of a ruling elite' (Bristol 6). In his reading of its politics, 'carnival is a general refusal to understand any fixed and final allocation of authority,' for example in the distribution of social wealth according to an immutable sense of natural order (Bristol 212). (See *authority.)

Thus carnival laughter is public as well as popular, structural as well as transgressive, linked to the feast and the fair. It can be wholly or partly located in art, literature and folklore in many variants. Literary images of carnival are present in the fabliaux; in Sancho Panza's relation to Don Quixote; in Ben Jonson's Falstaffian table talk; in the Shakespearean fool; and in the 'Don Quixote in Nighttown' sequence of James Joyce's *Ulysses*, to name only a few examples. Visual representations of carnival are contained in the paintings of Hieronymus Bosch, Pieter Breugel and Marc Chagall, while mythology and folklore exemplify the carnival in Saturnalia, the charivari, cross-dressing, and the mock wedding. Spontaneous and institutionalized practices ranging from student riots to Melanesian cargo cults all possess strong links with carnival.

MICHÈLE LACOMBE

Primary Sources

Bakhtin, Mikhail. *Rabelais and His World.* Trans. Hélène Iswolsky. Cambridge: MIT P, 1968.

Secondary Sources

Bristol, Michael. *Carnival and Theater: Plebian Culture and the Structure of Authority in Renaissance England.* New York: Methuen, 1985.
Eco, Umberto. 'The Frames of Comic "Freedom."' In *Carnival.* Ed. Thomas A. Sebeok. Berlin: Mouton Publishers, 1984.
Holquist, Michael. 'Bakhtin and Rabelais: Theory as Praxis.' In *boundary 2* 2.1–2 (Fall-Winter 1982): 12–17.
Hutcheon, Linda. *A Theory of Parody: The Teachings of Twentieth-Century Art Forms.* New York: Methuen, 1985.
Kinser, Samuel. 'Bakhtin's Discovery.' In *Rabelais' Carnival: Text, Context, Metatext.* Berkeley: U of California P, 1990.
Morson, Gary Saul, ed. *Bakhtin: Essays and Dialogues on His Work.* Chicago: U of Chicago P, 1986.
Weimann, Robert. *Shakespeare and the Popular Tradition in the Theater: Studies in the Social Dimension of Dramatic Form and Function.* Ed. Robert Schwartz. Baltimore: Johns Hopkins UP, 1978.

Centre/decentre

Each society tends to perceive reality in more or less coherent ways and maintains generally systematic and systemic values. These constitute its foundations or centres and are often viewed as the firm structures which are part of a closed system. If the existence of a centre is assumed, other ways of seeing reality and other values must be ignored, repressed or marginalized. (See *margin.) In other words, reality and values ('presences') are not *universal but are conditional upon specific cultural, social, economic, and political perspectives. Through rethinking of these perspectives, an existing centre can be destabilized, denaturalized, deconstructed, or 'decentred.' (See *deconstruction.) Much poststructural criticism takes as its mandate the decentring of values and perspectives in *literature and the contexts that give birth to it. In *Michel Foucault's words, 'there is no center, but always decenterings, series that register the halting passage from presence to absence, from excess to deficiency' *(Language* 165). (See *poststructuralism.)

In *The Archaeology of Knowledge,* Foucault speaks of three formative ideas that have heavily influenced ways of rethinking dominant concepts of society and self (see *self/other); these include the economic, social and political theories of Karl Marx, the irrationalist and antiteleological philosophy of *Friedrich Nietzsche, and theories of the subject (see *subject/object), self-identity, and self-expression in psychoanalysis, linguistics and ethnology proposed by *Sigmund Freud and *Ferdinand de Saussure, among others. (See *psychoanalytic theory, *structuralism.) To these, *Jacques Derrida adds the Heideggerean critique of metaphysics *(Structure* 250). (See *Heidegger.) In these instances, 'centres' or 'myths, kinship systems, languages, sexuality, or desire' *(Archaeology* 14) are opened up by exploring discontinuities, ruptures and inconsistencies. (See *myth.)

Derrida was among the first of the new breed of French literary and philosophical theoreticians to define the centre and demonstrate the value of decentring. One of his primary essays which achieved general acceptance in North American academic circles was 'Structure, Sign, and Play in the Discourse of the Human Sciences,' delivered at the Johns Hopkins symposium on structuralism held in 1966. Remarkably, this conference and its published proceedings brought structuralism and poststructuralism to North America almost simultaneously. In 'Structure, Sign, and Play' Derrida speaks of the centre as 'a point of presence, a fixed origin' whose function is 'not only to orient, balance, and organize the structure ... but above all to make sure that the organizing principle of the structure would limit what we might call the *free play* of the structure' (247–8). (See theories of *play/freeplay.) By 'centre' he means the organizing principles, the precepts, the 'fundamental immobility and ... reassuring certitude' (248), the assumptions universally held to be true, and the beliefs that create normatives and that cohere to provide a certain opinion or view a privileged position.

Centres, Derrida argues, have been traditionally viewed as part of the structure – its focus, coherence, and raison d'être – but yet outside of it and separate from the mechanisms of structuring as such. Being both inside and outside, centres achieve a transcendent status and, having no apparent origin or end, are thought to be unassailable. Indeed, they preclude opposing viewpoints. Sometimes they are hard to name, so absorbed by culture have they become, but Derrida believes that we can locate these centres by looking at the hierarchizing of one term over another in the typically binary pairings of our social system: speech over writing, game over play, male over female, and nature over culture, for example. (See *game theory, *binary opposition.) By analysing these centres, exploring them as foundations and especially as structures of language, and finding their fault lines, gaps and fissures, Derrida puts the concepts 'under erasure'; that is, he cannot erase or destroy the governing ideas of our culture, but he can situate, rupture or disrupt them by showing how they have been constructed and how certain facts, views or contrary opinions have been left out, pushed aside, relegated to the margins, or 'marginalized.' He is able, by such means, to decentre our positions, to argue persuasively that human beings are themselves structures without centres. To decentre or dislocate is to show how and when 'the structurality of structure' occurs and thereby to deprive the centre of its transcendency (249). Since Derrida assumes that centres are constituted by language and 'that language bears within itself the necessity of its own critique' (254), his task is to find the weaknesses in the arguments that give privilege to certain views.

Derrida undertakes this decentring with a full awareness of his own limitations as an analyst: he is dependent upon the same structures of language and argumentation that he seeks to expose. He also acknowledges that his task is limited insofar as he has no other

centre to install. Consequently, as he states, for example, in *Dissemination, Of Grammatology, Positions,* and *Writing and Difference,* in calling into question Plato's privileging of *logocentrism (values and forms of expression, like speech, that are said to be 'natural'), he does not do so in order to implement graphocentrism (values and forms of expression, like writing, which are said to be characterized by artifice) or to introduce a privileged third area or term. His is not another invigoration of binarity or a new incarnation of a paradoxical dialectic. The deconstructive process calls into question all centres and cannot rest with one centre simply replacing another. Decentring is an unending process for Derrida, not only with respect to the opinions of others but also with respect to his own.

Foucault is also no stranger to the process of decentring, though he relates it less to the structures of logic and argumentation than to the processes of *power. Nearly all of his works take as their subject the nature of knowledge as related to, controlled by, and disseminated through the channels of power. Power, he says, is never simply a matter of governor and governed or, more negatively, of oppressor and oppressed, but it is, nevertheless, centred and focused within a given domain and subordinated to a certain *ideology. Ideology recognizes certain mechanisms of power and constrains others, to make the power relations seem continuous, though power is finally 'something which circulates' or 'functions in the form of a chain,' something that is 'employed and exercised through a net-like organisation' *(Power/Knowledge* 98). Power consists of many different attributes and forms but, as it is exercised through the mechanisms of ideology, only some of these are given prominence. By analysing the network, Foucault decentres the structures of power, shows the growth of power to be discontinuous, dismantles hegemonic practices, and recuperates lost or hidden manifestations of power and knowledge. (See *hegemony.) Some manifestations of power that he has deformed and decentred include criminality and delinquency, the penal system, madness and psychiatric care, and sexuality: while the body politic is ripe for his critique, so is the sexualized body. Some critics, too, have noted that Foucault's own use of language is as decentring as his attack on public institutions and morals. As *Hayden White remarks of Foucault: 'there is no centre to Foucault's discourse. It is all surface – and intended to be so. For even more consistently than Nietzsche, Foucault resists the impulse to seek an origin or transcendental subject which would confer any specific "meaning" on human life. Foucault's discourse is wilfully superficial' (82).

Another who reflects upon centre is *Jacques Lacan, who hypothesizes that individuals no more have centres than does society at large. One of the longest-standing myths, according to Lacan, is that the human subject has a certain essence or self-identity. This liberal-humanist myth presupposes either that humans are born with a certain individually definable totality or that they develop one as they mature; the end result is the same in either case – an emphasis upon the wholeness, balance, rationality, and consistency that supposedly characterize each of us. Lacan speculates that, on the contrary, each person has no centre – only perceptions based on images of others, ranging from early impressions of the mother to others more external to the home. These images constantly shift and change and with them one's view of oneself. The self, then, is fragmentary, constantly shifting, and dependent upon images of other equally fragmentary selves. Each of us desires to have a coherent, centred self and attempts to meet this goal throughout life, but none of us will ever achieve this desire. Until recognizing our conflicting goals, ideas and drives – our very fragmentation, self-division and self-alienation – we can never fully enter the realm of shared social discourses, institutional observances and communal language practices – those things that supposedly mark us as coherent, rational, objective, and centred personalities. There is, for Lacan, no centre of one's self; there is no logical, unified self but only a constantly displaced signifier in search of a signified. (See *signified/signifier/signification.)

According to these views of language, social *discourse, and the self, there is no essential centre. Centres have been artificially created over time, and may even seem permanent in many respects, but are in constant need of *subversion and decentring. To recognize the arbitrariness of their creation and perpetuation is to begin to allow new possibilities to exist, to permit a new awareness of the limitations and possibilities of one's self, and to permit a

new tolerance of others, no matter how different.

GORDON E. SLETHAUG

Primary Sources

Derrida, Jacques. *Dissemination.* Trans. and intro. Barbara Johnson. Chicago: U of Chicago P, 1981.
– *Of Grammatology.* Trans. Gayatri Chakravorty Spivak. Baltimore and London: Johns Hopkins UP, 1976.
– *Positions.* Trans. Alan Bass. Chicago: U of Chicago P, 1981.
– 'Structure, Sign, and Play in the Discourse of the Human Sciences.' In *The Structuralist Controversy: The Languages of Criticism and the Sciences of Man.* Ed. Richard Macksey and Eugenio Donato. Baltimore and London: Johns Hopkins UP, 1972, 247–72.
– *Writing and Difference.* 1967. Trans. Alan Bass. Chicago: U of Chicago P, 1978.
Foucault, Michel. *The Archaeology of Knowledge.* Trans. A.M. Sheridan Smith. London and New York: Routledge, 1972.
– *Language, Counter-Memory, Practice: Selected Essays and Interviews.* Ed. Donald F. Bouchard. Ithaca: Cornell UP, 1977.
– *Power/Knowledge: Selected Interviews and Other Writings 1972–1977.* New York: The Harvester P, 1980.
Lacan, Jacques. *Ecrits: A Selection.* Trans. Alan Sheridan. New York and London: W.W. Norton and Co., 1977.
White, Hayden. 'Michel Foucault.' In *Structuralism and Since: From Lévi-Strauss to Derrida.* Ed. John Sturrock. Oxford and New York: Oxford UP, 1979, 81–115.

Character zones

Character zones are territories or fields of action for a character's speech which encroach in various ways upon the author's voice. Such 'zones' produce many different kinds of *double-voicing (dialogism) in the novel. The sphere of influence of a character zone is not limited to the character's actual words but may begin early in the *text and extend far beyond the boundaries of his direct *discourse. *Mikhail Bakhtin calls the dialogic interaction between the distinct voice of a character and that of the author within a single utterance a 'hybrid construction.' In such a discourse, the words of the author and his character are changed as they pass through each other's sphere of influence and are therefore 'refracted' (modified) in the dialogic interaction. For Bakhtin, there are no empty zones in the novel but instead disputed territories where double-voiced relationships occur.

When the idiosyncratic speech of a character combines with that of the author, it results in 'that special type of novelistic dialogue that realizes itself within the boundaries of constructions that externally resemble monologues' ('Discourse in the Novel' 370). Bakhtin examines character zones in the context of a discussion of the comic novel and subsequently analyses a number of examples in Turgenev. The various languages of the characters are not only concentrated in direct speeches but are also 'diffused throughout the authorial speech that surrounds the characters, creating highly particularized *character zones*' ('Discourse in the Novel' 316). These zones may be formed in various ways – from 'fragments of a character's speech, from various forms for hidden transmission of someone else's word and from scattered words and sayings belonging to someone else's speech' (ibid.).

Character zones describe one more way in which *heteroglossia may be incorporated within the novel. Oblique and subtle traces of a character's voice may be perceived in varied examples of hybrid, internally dialogized, double-voiced discourse. (See also *dialogical criticism.)

PHYLLIS MARGARET PARYAS

Primary Sources

Bakhtin, M.M. *The Dialogic Imagination.* Ed. and trans. Caryl Emerson and Michael Holquist. Austin: U of Texas P, 1981.
– *Problems of Dostoevsky's Poetics.* Ed. and trans. Caryl Emerson. Minneapolis: U of Minnesota P, 1984.
Morson, Gary Saul, and Caryl Emerson. *Mikhail Bakhtin: Creation of a Prosaics.* Stanford: Stanford UP, 1990.

Chora

The term chora is developed by *Julia Kristeva in order to account for the pre-sign or extra-linguistic functioning which she thinks distinguishes language from other sign systems, and which marks the subject's condition in language as dialectical or double. (See *sign, *subject/object.) Kristeva takes the term from

Plato's *Timaeus*, which refers to a receptacle which is hybrid and anterior to identity and naming. In *Revolution in Poetic Language* (1974), she uses the Platonic term in two different but related ways. First, the chora signifies a hypothetical space or phase which precedes the child's acquisition of language, and which is prior to the psychoanalytic *mirror stage. Kristeva describes this preverbal chora as rhythmic, nourishing, maternal, and as formed by what *Sigmund Freud defined as instinctual drives. She emphasizes that because these drives are always already ambiguous, simultaneously assimilating and fragmenting, the chora cannot be thought of as an originary unity.

In a second use of the term, Kristeva associates the chora with the extralinguistic functioning which she contends is a dimension of all *signifying practice. For Kristeva, the child's acquisition of language necessitates a rupture, which is at once a conscious-unconscious division of the emerging subject, and its detachment from the pre-symbolic chora. Yet the chora re-emerges whenever its drives decentre the positioning of a transcendent subject and open language to unconscious heterogeneity. (See *centre/decentre.) According to this use, the term chora is synonymous with what Kristeva calls the semiotic modality of signification, experienced as *jouissance*. (See *semiotics.)

Kristeva suggests that Freud points to the idea of the chora both through his theory of the drives and through his postulation of a rupture or break upon which society is founded. In her development of the term, she also relies on the work of *Jacques Lacan, particularly his theory of the mirror stage. More generally, Kristeva's elaboration of the term chora involves her critique of *Edmund Husserl's phenomenological subject, and her reworking of Hegel's concept of negativity. (See *phenomenological criticism.) In *Revolution in Poetic Language*, Kristeva suggests that *Jacques Derrida's concept of the *trace is suggestive of the choric space or place which escapes structure. Derrida has criticized Kristeva's use of the term and recently ('Comment ne pas parler: Dénégations' 1987) has begun to elaborate his own treatment of the place-space of the chora.

DAWNE McCANCE

Primary Sources

Derrida, Jacques. 'Comment ne pas parler: Dénégations.' In *Psyché: Inventions de l'autre*. Paris: Galilée, 1987. 'How to Avoid Speaking: Denials.' In
*Languages of the Unsayable: The Play of Negativity
in Literature and Literary Theory*. Trans. Ken Frie-
den. Ed. Sanford Budick and Wolfgang Iser. New
York: Columbia UP, 1989.
Kristeva, Julia. *La Révolution du langage poétique:
L'avant-garde à la fin du XIXe siècle*. 1974. *Revolution in Poetic Language*. Trans. Margaret Waller.
New York: Columbia UP, 1984.

Classeme

In Greimassian *semiotics, the classeme is a
contextual *seme, that is, a general and abstract category by means of which a nuclear
seme takes on a specific meaning in a given
context. (See *A.J. Greimas.) The classeme
combines with the seme to form a *sememe*: this
term refers to the minimal effect of meaning
produced by a specific appropriation of a lexeme (that is, an object-term) in a given context. Unlike the nuclear seme, which is a
semantic property inherent to a lexeme, the
classeme manifests itself only in a discursive
unit superior to the word, whether this be a
syntagm, a sentence or a *text. The classeme is
'the denominator common to a whole class of
contexts' (Greimas, *Sémantique* 45).

The concept of classeme appeared necessary
to explain the variations of meaning of a same
term according to the context. For example,
the phrase 'X is barking' can be read as referring to an animal or to a human being, the
verb 'bark' being able to apply to any of the
classemes animality or humanity virtually
present in the word X. When the content of
the subject is made more precise (for example,
'X, the dog, is barking'), the meaning of the
verb 'barking' and that of X can be stabilized
with the help of the classeme animality and
thus form an unequivocal sememe. One can
see by this example that the recurrence of a
same classeme in a given phrase or *discourse
allows the reader to characterize the text as 'a
semantic micro-universe closed on itself' (ibid.,
93). This characteristic of the text is the necessary condition for a reader to be able to make
a uniform and coherent reading of it, once its
*isotopy has been recognized.

At a more general level, classemes lay the

foundations and the frame of the semantic
universe. The outside world is pictured
through the general paradigmatic frames of
reference that are the basis of classemes (for
example, animate and inanimate).

The term 'classeme' is derived from the
studies in componential semantics of Bernard
Pottier (dating back to his doctoral thesis in
1955), from whom Greimas borrowed it in
order to explain the elementary structure of
meaning. Greimas' particular appropriation of
this term has been criticized and rejected by
various semioticians, notably Pierre Lerat and
François Rastier. These critics prefer to adopt
Pottier's definition of the classeme as 'the set
of generic semes in a sememe.'

CHRISTIAN VANDENDORPE

Primary Sources

Greimas, A.J. *Sémantique structurale*. Paris: Larousse,
1966. Repub. PUF, 1986. *Structural Semantics*.
Trans. D. McDowell, R. Schleifer and A. Velie.
Lincoln and London: U of Nebraska P, 1983.
– and J. Courtés. *Sémiotique. Dictionnaire raisonné de
la théorie du langage*. Paris, 1979. *Semiotics and
Language: An Analytical Dictionary*. Trans. L. Crist,
D. Patte, et al. Bloomington: Indiana UP, 1982.
Pottier, B. *Linguistique générale*. Paris: Klincksieck,
1974.

Secondary Sources

Lerat, P. *Sémantique descriptive*. Paris: Hachette,
1983.
Rastier, F. *Sémantique interprétative*. Paris: Hachette,
1987.

Closure/dis-closure

Perhaps the notion of literary closure, or the
sense of an ending (to borrow *Frank Kermode's phrase), originated with Aristotle's
statement in the *Poetics* that a poetic work
should be 'whole' and 'complete.' However,
the term closure emerged in the early 20th
century from the *discourse of Gestalt psychologists such as Kurt Koffka who, in *Principles of
Gestalt Psychology* (1935), examined the nature
and significance of the human tendency to
perceive wholeness. In *The Sense of an Ending*
(1966), the literary critic Frank Kermode suggested that creating endings is a human tendency, evident not only in *literature but also in

life's fictions. As one example of this human desire to impose order, Kermode pointed to the long history of disconfirmed apocalyptic predictions.

More specifically, the term closure gained new currency in the late 1960s as a way of describing textual resolution, most notably with the publication of Barbara Herrnstein Smith's *Poetic Closure*. For Smith, closure is produced by a *text when it creates a sense of 'appropriate cessation' for its reader, when it 'announces and justifies the absence of further development.' That is, closure is a direct result of the text's formal structure: its coherence, integrity and completeness. As such, Smith's use of the term is reminiscent of Aristotle's notion of textual integrity and of Kant's sense of 'internal purposiveness,' both of which proved central to the New Critical concept of the text as closed aesthetic object. (See *New Criticism.)

Although limited to poetry, Smith's study breaks the ground for subsequent analyses of closure, most notably of closure in the novel. However, the potential open-endedness of what *Mikhail Bahktin calls the 'postmythic' novel *(The Dialogic Imagination* 1981) frustrates the formalist desire to find closure integral to the structure of the work, and the corollary assumption that texts can and do achieve closure. One solution to the dilemma is offered by David Richter in *Fable's End* (1974), when he separates the notion of completeness from that of formal closure (the sense of an ending established by the author through such a device as summary). Richter argues that rhetorical or thesis-driven novels (such as Joseph Heller's *Catch* 22) differ fundamentally from plot-driven novels, where thought is subordinate to action. Although potentially open in form, such intentional fictions achieve completeness and closure in the adequate illustration of a particular thesis.

Looking beyond the novel's formal structure to its ethical and sociohistorical context, other critics argue that the defining feature of the 'modern' novel is not its closure but rather its open-endedness. Common to their analyses is the assumption that the novel is not closed off from but is part of its sociopolitical moment, and that novelistic form is not a fixed structure but rather one in 'process.' One such critic was David Daiches who, as early as 1939, positioned himself as a 'maximum-context critic,' and argued that the novel was a form in tran-

sition because of the profound impact of the erosion of the public belief in Western civilization *(The Novel and the Modern World).* In the 1960s, Ihab Hassan *(Radical Innocence)* and Alan Friedman *(The Turn of the Novel)* suggest not only that the form of the novel is still in process but also that the form is one of process. Dominated by what Hassan calls 'the spirit and shape of irony,' and what Friedman calls the 'flux of moral experience,' open-endedness of design in the novel takes on ethical as well as structural and aesthetic dimensions. (See *irony.) Feminist critic Rachel Blau du Plessis, also interested in the ideological implications of novelistic closure, explores the way contemporary women writers have sought alternatives to the traditional endings of romance (marriage or death) in *Writing Beyond the Ending* (1985). (See *feminist criticism, *ideology.)

Twentieth-century communication theorists also use the term closure, or more particularly ideological closure, to identify the way in which a text's rhetorical strategies direct reading. (See *rhetorical criticism, *communication theory.) Although ideological closure is used most frequently in media analysis (to refer to the 'slant' of a newspaper article, for example), it is perceived to be a property of all texts.

That textual closure is not so much a product of literary texts themselves as the result of the reader's desire to master or apply closure to them was an approach to critical closure that also gained a hearing in the late 1960s. Here, the term closure is a product not of the literary text but of the act of interpretation itself. *Stanley Fish, for example, places characteristic emphasis on the reader's role in the production of meaning and suggests that the reader performs a kind of perceptual closure in the act of reading, irrespective of the text's formal structure *(Is There a Text in This Class?).* (See also *reader-response criticism.)

The most radical challenge of textual closure is voiced by the deconstructionists and, in particular, by *Jacques Derrida in 'Structure, Sign and Play in the Language of the Human Sciences' (1966) and, more generally, in *Of Grammatology* and *Writing and Difference.* (See *deconstruction.) Arguing that we exist within the enclosure of language ('il n'y a pas de hors texte'), Derrida asserts that interpretation is without end. If there is no locus of meaning outside the world of language, as Derrida suggests with the concept of *différance*, then the meaning of a literary text can never be fixed. Without a centre to ground the play of meaning, the text is opened to infinity; the critic's attempt to assert closure is an illusion. (See *centre/decentre, theories of *play/freeplay.) In this second sense, closure is used to qualify a verb (for example, to perform closure), its meaning approximating *totalization. For the deconstructionists, and especially for Derrida, the impulse to assert closure is a temptation that must be avoided.

Although some deconstructionist critics lament the impossibility of textual closure as anything other than a heuristic ideal (*Paul de Man), or explore the labyrinthine complexity of a critical language that is continually displaced or borrowed (*J. Hillis Miller), or explore the disintegration of textual and interpretive frames (Barbara Johnson), their discussions reveal the kind of radical dis-closure that they find at the heart of all creative and critical texts. Indeed, the deconstructionist challenge implies not only that texts illustrate dis-closure but, as J. Hillis Miller argues, the instability of meaning makes it impossible to demonstrate closure at all.

One significant celebration of dis-closure is William V. Spanos' 'Breaking the Circle: Hermeneutics as Dis-closure' (1977), which analyses and extends *Martin Heidegger's *Being and Time* (*Sein und Zeit*). (See *hermeneutics.) Spanos refers to the work of the New Critics, but also to the myth criticism of *Northrop Frye, the *structuralism of *Tzvetan Todorov and *Roland Barthes, as well as to what he calls the phenomenological criticism of consciousness of *Georges Poulet' (see also *Geneva School, *phenomenological criticism), all of which share a desire to focus on the formal or spatial aspects of a literary work at the expense of exploring its temporal and processual implications. (See *spatial form.) They 'see' and chart the text, in other words, rather than 'hear' and experience it. The subsequent analysis becomes a kind of vicious circle, whereby the reading merely confirms the reader's expectation that the text is a unified whole that can be perceived in spatial terms. Instead, Spanos asserts that a literary work must be experienced as an event. In this way, 'phenomenological hermeneutics becomes a process of discovery in the sense of *dis-closing* – opening out – the hermeneutic possibilities that the inauthentic spatial impulse of the Western literary consciousness *closes off*, conceals, and

ultimately forgets in coercing the temporality of the text into a circle.' Rather than a kind of closure, then, such a phenomenological hermeneutics allows for a reading that, as the title of Spanos' article suggests, is a kind of dis-closure. Worthy of note, however, is that Spanos finds that Heidegger's own essays on poetry, language and thought do not present a method 'radical enough' to break out of the enclosure.

As a result of the deconstructionist and other assaults on structuralist notions of closure, critics began to think differently about the integrity of a literary text. In 'An Apology for Poetics,' for instance, *Murray Kreiger (1981) moves away from a New Critical stance with its characteristic 'commitment to formal closure as the primary characteristic of the successful literary object.' Instead, he describes closure as the illusion of 'sealing off' which results from both the author's *and* the reader's 'habit' of seeking closure. As a definition of closure, the word 'sealing' (also used by *Geoffrey Hartman in *Saving the Text*) deliberately lacks the kind of formal authority carried by Herrnstein Smith's 'integrity' or Richter's 'completeness.'

NATHALIE COOKE

Primary Sources

Bakhtin, Mikhail. *The Dialogic Imagination*. Ed. Michael Holquist. Trans. Caryl Emerson and Michael Holquist. Texas: U of Texas P, 1981.

Blau du Plessis, Rachel. *Writing Beyond the Ending*. Bloomington: Indiana UP, 1985.

Daiches, David. *The Novel and the Modern World*. Chicago: U of Chicago P, 1939.

Derrida, Jacques. *Of Grammatology*. 1967. Trans. Gayatri Chakravorty Spivak. Baltimore: Johns Hopkins UP, 1976.

– *Writing and Difference*. 1967. Trans. Alan Bass. Chicago: U of Chicago P, 1978.

Fish, Stanley. *Is There a Text in This Class?* Harvard: Harvard UP, 1980.

Friedman, Alan. *The Turn of the Novel*. New York: Oxford UP, 1966.

Hartman, Geoffrey. *Saving the Text*. Baltimore: Johns Hopkins UP, 1981.

Hassan, Ihab. *Radical Innocence*. Princeton: Princeton UP, 1961.

Johnson, Barbara. 'The Frame of Reference: Poe, Lacan, Derrida.' *Yale French Studies* 55.6 (1977): 457–505.

Kermode, Frank. *The Sense of an Ending*. New York: Oxford UP, 1966.

Koffka, Kurt. *Principles of Gestalt Psychology*. New

York: Paul Trench and Trubner, 1935. Repr. London: Routledge and Kegan Paul, 1962.

Krieger, Murray. 'An Apology for Poetics.' In *American Criticism in the Poststructuralist Age*. Ed. Ira Konigsberg. Michigan: U of Michigan P, 1981.

Miller, J. Hillis. 'Ariadne's Thread.' *Critical Inquiry* 3 (Autumn 1976): 56–77.

– 'The Problematic of Ending in Narrative.' *Nineteenth-Century Fiction* 33.1 (June 1978): 3–7.

O'Sullivan, Tim, John Hartley, Danny Saunders and John Fiske, eds. *Key Concepts in Communication*. London and New York: Methuen, 1983.

Richter, David. *Fable's End: Completeness and Closure in Rhetorical Fiction*. Chicago: U of Chicago P, 1974.

Smith, Barbara Herrnstein. *Poetic Closure: A Study of How Poems End*. Chicago: U of Chicago P, 1968.

Spanos, William V. 'Breaking the Circle: Hermeneutics as Dis-closure.' *boundary* 2 2 (Winter, 1977): 421–57.

Code

A code is the sign-system from which any given message is generated. It consists of a set of signs and the rules that govern their combination. (See *sign.) The code may be a simple set of equivalences (Morse code or machine language, for example), or it may be a highly complex structure with rules which are not explicitly formulated and which are operated largely unconsciously. A spoken sentence in a natural language, for example, is produced from the set of syntactic, semantic and phonological rules that constitute a code.

In linguistics the term was first used by *Ferdinand de Saussure in his *Course in General Linguistics* (1916) in a sense which corresponded approximately to his concept of *langue* in the opposition *langue/parole* (language system/individual speech act). *Roman Jakobson later adopted the notion from *communication theory where it referred simply to a repertory of signals. He set out a six-part model of communication in his well-known 'Closing Statement' to the Indiana Conference on Style (1958). In this model, an addresser sends a message to an addressee through some physical channel – the contact. The message requires a context to which it refers, and must use a code sufficiently familiar to both parties for the message to be understood. The opposition code/message derived from this model thus corresponds nearly to Saussure's *langue/parole*.

In *semiotics the term has a broader sense, applying not just to communication but to any system that can be considered a signifying system. Animal tracks, medical symptoms, patterns of DNA in cells, for example, may all be considered as elements in a code. In an even broader application, the notion has been extended to include cultural systems. In his work in anthropology, *Claude Lévi-Strauss proposed that aspects of social life not directly pertaining to communication (kinship systems, for example) could be understood using linguistic models. Human cultural activities such as the cooking and serving of food or modes of dressing could be analysed as the products of cultural codes. Many current studies in semiotics undertake to identify and explain the codes that underlie everyday life. As well as giving impetus to semiotics, Lévi-Strauss' work greatly influenced the development of *structuralism, one of the foremost tenets of which is that every aspect of human experience is inevitably coded.

The concept of code has several applications in literary theory. Structuralist critics such as *A.J. Greimas and *Tzvetan Todorov attempted to describe a system or 'grammar' which generated texts. They saw the *text, to use Saussure's terms, as the *parole* of a *langue* composed of the transformational rules that generate literary texts. *Michael Riffaterre, focusing on poetry, used a theory of codes to describe the conventions which underlie a text, emphasizing the special significance of the reader's recognition of these codes. *Roland Barthes argued that the text is not the 'accomplishment of a code' but is 'traversed' by various codes. In *S/Z*, his reading of Balzac's *Sarrasine*, he identified five codes (hermeneutic, semantic, symbolic, proairetic – pertaining to action – and cultural). His description of these codes has proved too vague for his work to provide the basis of a more general application to other texts. Yet his study, implying that it is the reader rather than the text who is the product of codes, marks an important departure from the structuralist perspective. (See also *reader response criticism, *narrative code.)

MELANIE SEXTON

Primary Sources

Barthes, Roland. *S/Z*. Paris: Seuil, 1970.
Jakobson, Roman. 'Closing Statement: Linguistics

and Poetics.' In T.A. Sebeok, ed. *Style in Language*. Cambridge, Mass.: MIT P, 1960, 350–77.
Saussure, Ferdinand de. *Course in General Lingusitics*. New York: McGraw-Hill, 1966.

Secondary Sources

Culler, Jonathan. *Structuralist Poetics: Structuralism, Linguistics and the Study of Literature*. London: Routledge and Kegan Paul, 1975.
Eagleton, Terry. *Literary Theory*. Oxford: Blackwell, 1983.
Greimas, Algirdas Julien. *Semiotics and Language: An Analytical Dictionary*. Bloomington: Indiana UP, 1982.
Hawkes, Terence. *Structuralism and Semiotics*. Berkeley: U of California P, 1977.

Communicative action

Communicative action is the central concept from which *Jürgen Habermas builds his version of contemporary *critical theory for the *Frankfurt School tradition, a tradition which also includes Max Horkheimer, *Theodor Adorno, *Walter Benjamin, Leo Lowenthal, and Herbert Marcuse.

Communicative action is predicated on the notion that the structuring of meaning between social actors or speakers is a pragmatic task at both the micro and macro levels. In micro communicative action, the speaker, in the process of structuring an utterance, assumes a rational response from the listener. This exchange requires, first of all, the intelligibility of the utterance as well as socialization in the correct communicative competence and the safe transmission of the previous stock of knowledge about communicative competence. On the macro level, social systems or societies also produce objective meanings. Through mass-diffused communicative actions, the coexistence of conflicting communication communities or life-worlds within the same social system remains possible. (See also *communication theory.)

GREG NIELSEN

Primary Sources

Habermas, Jürgen. *The Theory of Communicative Action: Vol. I. Reason and the Rationalization of Society*. Trans. Thomas McCarthy. Boston: Beacon P, 1984.
– *Vol. II. Life-world and System: A Critique of Functionalist Reason*. Boston: Beacon P, 1988.

Competence/performance

'Competence' and 'performance' are terms developed by the American linguist *Noam Chomsky. They are central to transformational generative grammar and have become widely used in linguistics as a whole as well as in psychology, philosophy and literary studies.

'Competence' refers to the implicit knowledge or tacit mastery which adult speakers and hearers have of their native language. It involves an extensive amount of varied linguistic knowledge, including the ability to produce and understand an indefinite number of novel utterances (the creative aspect of language); to recognize relationships between sentences; to resolve ambiguities; and to identify and interpret certain mistakes or deviations in grammatical form. This knowledge is conceived as deriving from a set of mentally represented principles which are in part innately determined rather than learned, a position known as the Innateness Hypothesis. From this perspective, the study of language structure is linked to the study of human psychology and biology, and human nature in general; and linguistics may thus be viewed as part of cognitive science.

For Chomsky, competence must be innately determined at least in part because it constitutes a complex cognitive system mastered quickly and effortlessly by children in spite of the relative poverty of the data they are exposed to in the process of first language acquisition (Plato's problem). Therefore it appears implausible that the required principles are acquired through inductive learning. Rather, a rich innate component or Universal Grammar controls the growth of language in each individual.

Competence interacts with other cognitive systems such as memory and logic to determine performance, that is, our linguistic behaviour, or the specific use of language in concrete situations. Linguistic theory addresses itself to the explicit characterization of competence rather than to the study of actual performance per se. In literary criticism, *Jonathan Culler has extended the meaning of competence to include literary competence: an understanding of the conventions, genres and rules which are required for an understanding of *literature (*Structuralist Poetics*). (See also *genre criticism.)

MARIA-LUISA RIVERO

Primary Sources

Culler, Jonathan. *Structuralist Poetics*. Ithaca: Cornell UP, 1975.

Concretization

A term first used by *Roman Ingarden, concretization designates the activity by which the *text is put together in reading which leads to the reader's cognition of it as meaningful experience. The implicit ground for this concept is that the work of *literature as a written *code is virtual until it is read and imaginatively realized, that is, concretized.

The most important critic to demonstrate the concept of concretization is *Wolfgang Iser in *The Implied Reader* and *The Act of Reading*. Iser develops an extensive analysis of the way the virtual text is concretized in the act of reading. He has given literary criticism such important concepts as textual blanks or gaps (built-in situations that demand reader participation in concretization) and consistency building (the essential coherence a reader must give a text in order to progress in reading).

Concretization is also related to *Paul Ricoeur's term 'configuration' (*Time and Narrative, I* 1984), but the latter adds a strong historical and social component.

The term is sometimes used synonymously with realization, but concretization still carries the strong implication of making actual what was only virtual. (See also *reader-response criticism, *Constance School of Reception Aesthetics.)

MARIO J. VALDÉS

Primary Sources

Iser, Wolfgang. *The Act of Reading*. 1976. Baltimore: Johns Hopkins UP, 1978.
– *The Implied Reader*. 1972. Baltimore: Johns Hopkins UP, 1974.
Ricoeur, Paul. *Time and Narrative*. 3 vols. Trans. Kathleen McLaughlin Blamey and David Pellauer. Chicago: U of Chicago P, 1984–8.

Critical theory

The term critical theory has been developed by successive generations of the *Frankfurt School tradition, where it has taken on a particular significance. While critical theory is the term that best describes the general approach of the tradition, it should not be confused with its meaning as the generic term for literary criticism. The Frankfurt School would define most literary criticism as either a form of *hermeneutics founded on the practical interests of interpretation and the critique or recovery of hidden or deferred meaning in texts (*deconstruction, *reception theory), or as a positivism founded on the technical interests of explanation (*semiotics, *narratology, *genetic criticism) (cf. *Jürgen Habermas). As defined by the Frankfurt tradition, critical theory is seen to respond to the specifically emancipatory interest in aesthetic and social practices. It was first defined by Max Horkheimer around 1932 as an approach that sees all knowledge, be it scientific, moral or aesthetic, as rooted in some set of social interests. Critical theory is thus allied with all those approaches in the humanities and social sciences that seek to provide a theory which will explain the emancipatory interest that enters the order of social practice (cf. Geuss).

In this contemporary sense, critical theory argues that all knowledge is rooted in some set of interests that inform the social and communicative practices of the subjects of class, gender, ethnicity, and race (Fraser). These interests do not remain fixed, singular or static; they may clash, overlap or work together and are in a constant process of change. Critical theory proceeds by juxtaposing possible alternative explanations of the subject of the social practices it is studying. It negates claims of universal explanation made within each approach while gathering and synthesizing explanations from each that help formulate a normative theory of what ought to be done to emancipate the subjects of social practice from domination.

Social practices are reasoned forms of action. They are derived from either the critical or instrumental reason that subjects enter into in their practices (Horkheimer). Instrumental reason is on the side of domination while critical reason is on the side of emancipation. Critical theory seeks to negate instrumental reason and free subjects by bringing them a knowledge about themselves and especially about what they might become. By contrast, instrumental reason seeks an identity between the subjects and the domination that is visited on them. An example of instrumental reason at work is society's attempt to dominate nature, to reduce it to its own interests and to transform it to suit human needs. Critical theory refuses instrumental truth claims based on theories of objectivity that seek to explain human phenomena through the methods of the natural sciences (cf. Adorno et al.). It is also separate from the purely practical interests of the hermeneutic sciences that seek to recover meaning strictly by interpreting the representations of social practices. Critical theory is a self-reflexive but explanatory approach to theorizing because it maintains an interest in the emancipation of the subject of social practices and not simply in its representation. It is therefore always in part about itself and always rooting itself in the processes of change. (See also *subject/object, *universal, *Adorno.)

GREG NIELSEN

Primary Sources

Adorno, Theodor, et al. *De Vienne à Frankfurt: La Querelle allemande des sciences sociales.* Paris: Editions Complexes, 1979.
Fraser, Nancy. *Unruly Practices: Power, Discourse and Gender in Contemporary Social Theory.* Minneapolis: U of Minnesota P, 1989.
Geuss, Raymond. *The Idea of Critical Theory.* Cambridge, Mass.: Cambridge UP, 1981.
Habermas, Jürgen. *Knowledge and Human Interest.* Boston: Beacon P, 1971.
– *The Philosophical Discourse of Modernity.* Cambridge, Mass.: MIT P, 1987.
Horkheimer, Max. *Critical Theory.* New York: Seabury, 1972.
– *Critique of Instrumental Reason.* New York: Seabury, 1974.

Dasein: see Heidegger, Martin; Geneva School; Bracketing; Intention/Intentionality; *Lebenswelt*; Phenomenological criticism

Defamiliarization

Defamiliarization is one of several English renditions of the Russian term *ostranenie*, a concept introduced and developed by *Viktor Shklovskii in 'Iskusstvo kak priem' ['Art as Device'], published in the second formalist publication *Poetika: Sborniki po teorii poeticheskogo iazyka* [*Studies in the Theory of Poetic Language* 1917]. (See Russian *formalism.)

Shklovskii developed the concept of defamiliarization in opposition to *Aleksander Potebnia's theory of art as thinking in images and his arguments that the images are clearer and simpler than what they signify. According to Shklovskii, the opposite is true. The meaning of art is based on the ability to 'defamiliarize' things, to show them in a new, unexpected way. In everyday life, we do not see things and their texture, since our perception has become habitual and automatic. The purpose of art is to impart the sensation of things as they are perceived and not as they are known. Art 'defamiliarizes' objects by making forms strange, and by increasing the difficulty and the length of perception, because the process of perception is an aesthetic end in itself and must be prolonged.

As applied specifically to *literature, defamiliarization, according to Shklovskii, operates on three levels. On the level of language, it makes language difficult and deliberately impeded, as, for example, in the accumulation of difficult sounds and the use of rhythm in poetry. On the level of content, it challenges accepted concepts and ideas, by distorting them and showing them from a different perspective. For example, Leo Tolstoy's story 'The Strider' shows the illogicality of the human world from the point of view of a horse. On the level of literary forms, it 'defamiliarizes' literary conventions, by breaking with the dominant artistic canons and introducing new ones, elevating some subliterary genres such as farce or detective story to the status of fine art. (See *canon, *genre criticism.)

The concept of defamiliarization proved extremely useful in literary criticism. It described a process valid for all literature and distinguished literature from other verbal modes. It allowed the establishment of a hierarchy of elements within the literary work itself, with the principle of defamiliarization acting as the central one and subordinating all other elements to itself. Finally, it led to a new concept of literary history based not on the continuity of tradition but on abrupt breaks with the past and the introduction of new artistic rules.

Shklovskii's theory of defamiliarization influenced Bertold Brecht's notion of *Verfremdungs-Effekt* [the alienation effect], which stressed the need in theatre to alter the events to be presented in order to induce a critical attitude in the spectators towards what they see.

NINA KOLESNIKOFF

Primary Sources

Shklovskii, V.B. 'Iskusstvo kak priem.' In *Poetika: Sborniki po teorii poeticheskogo iazyka*. 1919. 'Art as Device.' In *Russian Formalist Criticism: Four Essays*. Ed. L. Lemon and M.J. Reis. Lincoln: U of Nebraska P, 1965.

Demythologizing

Taking their cue from the French left and the *Frankfurt School, cultural materialists argue that there is a tendency within society to insist that things are inherent, natural, 'the way they are,' and commonsensical, without admitting that the 'natural' is in fact an artefact or process of cultural *ideology, subject to social usage. (See *cultural materialism.) For whatever reasons (and the Marxists, who first used the term 'mystification,' assume those to be linked with capitalism), culture perceives a given thing, act or process as natural rather than cultural, and 'mystifies' it. (See *Marxist criticism.) Moreover, what has been mystified usually conforms to rational-humanist views of absolute values, totalized cultures and unified and stable selves – what *Jacques Derrida calls 'transcendental signifieds' and *Paul de Man calls the self-mystified symbols based upon the coherence of God, self and the word. (See *totalization.) In fact Biblical 'myths' were among the first to come under scrutiny by a German scholar, Rudolf Bultmann, who used the term *Entmythologisierung* or demythologization to refer to the hermeneutical process by which conventional interpretations of Christianity could be reassessed in terms of existential categories. (See *hermeneutics, *metacriticism.) One of the responsibilities of anthropologists, semioticians and cultural materialists is, then, to discover the ways meaning is structured and presented in a given culture, to see

how signs pervade every aspect of life, and to demonstrate how these signs can be regarded as cultural artifices or myths and, consequently, be 'demythologized' and 'demystified.' (See *sign, *myth, *semiotics.)

Such pairs of concepts as nature/culture and mythologize/demythologize (demystify), which are intricately related, have been subjected to scrutiny by a number of thinkers, including the structural anthropologist *Claude Lévi-Strauss, who sees these as part of a relational structure or system of differences and explores their general importance, classifies them and assesses their symbolic associations within that system.

Perhaps the most influential 'demystifier' has been *Roland Barthes, who finds language less an instrument of self-expression and communication than a social means of repression and alienation by the bourgeoisie. Assuming that language maintains the structure of *power over an indefinite period of time and, consequently, that it enforces a certain ideology, he argues that the task of the analyst is to read against the grain of history and culture and expose the production of meaning, to critique cultural myths, to 'unlearn' orthodox social values or *doxa*, and to establish more pluralistic perspectives. Although all of his works to some extent accomplish this task, two of his earliest are dedicated to it: *Writing Degree Zero* (1953) and *Mythologies* (1957). In the first, he writes of *écriture bourgeoise* or classical French writing from the mid-1600s to the mid-1900s. The predictability of this style makes it easy to read or, as Barthes puts it, to consume, rendering it 'natural.' Denaturalizing it by investigating how style is produced lessens its inherent power and control. In the second book, he looks at other kinds of social myths in mass culture (writing being one) in order to decipher their mode of operation on people. The myths include sports, cinema, food and drink, advertising, automobiles, photography, and many others, which are not just innocent by-products of our culture but ways in which the dominant ideology asserts itself.

Jacques Derrida explores language systems, argumentation and logic in order to demystify or deconstruct cultural practices and beliefs. (See *deconstruction.) In general, he says, the beliefs of Western cultures cluster around primary transcendent concepts that he calls logocentric: some ultimate spoken word, presence, centre, fixed origin, truth, or reality. (See *logocentrism.) To demystify these, he examines some of the important texts that have produced a Western metaphysics, including Plato's *Phaedrus*, Saussure's *Course in General Linguistics*, and Lévi-Strauss' *The Raw and the Cooked*. (See *metaphysics of presence, *Ferdinand de Saussure.) By reassessing their supposedly solid assumptions, cohesive structures and foundational values, he discovers the aporiatic moments in which texts demonstrate their own flaws and weaknesses; he finds their ruptures and opens them up to new interpretations (see *aporia). He argues that these texts and conceptions are not really unified but rather consist of self-contradictions, unnoticed oppositions and conflicting statements. Derrida suggests that everything is self-contradictory and self-differing (*différence*) and hence will never yield to a single, socially warranted conclusion; ultimate meaning, if it exists at all, is perpetually deferred (*différance*).

Like Barthes and Derrida, *Michel Foucault ventures into the arena of language and significant social practices to discover what constitutes knowledge, who controls it, how it is coded, and where ideology hides amidst discourses and discursive practices. (See *discourse.) His role and that of others who investigate the relationship of language and cultural ideology is to discover the genealogy (roots) of a culture's main goals and tenets as embedded in language and to decentre them. (See *centre/decentre.) Since 'desire and power' always cling to discourse, it is difficult to demystify, but the difficulties can be overcome in part by accepting the arbitrariness of language and all social conventions. All discursive modes are culturally constructed, systematized, ordered, and given their function and value (their *episteme) within a specific culture and period. (See also *desire/lack.)

Although *Jacques Lacan is known more for his 'return to *Freud' than for pronouncements on demystification, his analysis of personality development depends upon a concept of the self as structured according to images of others. (See *self/other.) It is Lacan's position that just as these images as well as culture change, so does the self. When a child enters the so-called post-*mirror stage at about 18 months and accedes to the Law-of-the-Father (the social and linguistic codes that constitute a given culture), it recognizes the necessity of having to adapt to changing conditions and paradigms. (See *Name-of-the-Father.) The self,

then, is always in flux. For Lacan, the notion of a unified, transcendent self is a myth; the subject is self-divided or split between a wish for wholeness (the Imaginary) and the reality of fragmentation (the Symbolic) and is, consequently, as arbitrary as other cultural norms and institutions. (See *imaginary/symbolic/real.) Since, however, culture clings to a view of a coherent, unified, transcendent self, that view needs demythologizing.

Myths, then, encompass every aspect of existence, including language, conceptions of the self, and social patterns and institutions. All of these, according to the structuralists and poststructuralists, need to be demystified and seen as arbitrary and constituted upon conditions unique to a particular society at a certain time. (See *structuralism, *poststructuralism.) Some critics, however, see the concept of arbitrariness as arbitrary in itself. The relativism that underlies the process of demythologizing is neither attractive nor acceptable to those who believe in enduring values or the need for unifying cultural constructs.

GORDON E. SLETHAUG

Primary Sources

Barthes, Roland. *A Barthes Reader*. Ed. and intro. Susan Sontag. New York: Hill and Wang, 1982.
– *Elements of Semiology*. Trans. A. Lavers and C. Smith. New York: Hill and Wang, 1968.
– *Mythologies*. Trans. A. Lavers. London: Paladin Books, 1973.
– *Writing Degree Zero*. Trans. A. Lavers and C. Smith. New York: Hill and Wang, 1968.
Culler, Jonathan. *Barthes*. Glasgow: Fontana Paperbacks, 1983.
de Man, Paul. 'The Rhetoric of Temporality.' In *Interpretation: Theory and Practice*. Ed. C.S. Singleton. Baltimore: Johns Hopkins UP, 1969.
Derrida, Jacques. *Dissemination*. Trans. and intro. Barbara Johnson. Chicago: U of Chicago P, 1981.
– *Of Grammatology*. Trans. Gayatri Chakravorty Spivak. Baltimore and London: Johns Hopkins UP, 1976.
– 'Structure, Sign, and Play in the Discourse of the Human Sciences.' In *The Structuralist Controversy: The Languages of Criticism and the Sciences of Man*. Ed. Richard Macksey and Eugenio Donato. Baltimore and London: Johns Hopkins UP, 1972, 247–72.
Foucault, Michel. *The Archaeology of Knowledge*. Trans. A.M. Sheridan Smith. London and New York: Routledge, 1972.
Lacan, Jacques. 'Aggressivity in Psychoanalysis' and 'The Function and Field of Speech and Language

in Psychoanalysis.' In *Ecrits: A Selection*. Trans. Alan Sheridan. New York and London: W.W. Norton and Co., 1977.

Lévi-Strauss, Claude. *The Elementary Structures of Kinship*. Trans. J.H. Bell and J.R. von Sturmer. Ed. R. Needham. Boston: Beacon P, 1969.

- *The Raw and the Cooked*. Trans. J. and D. Weightman. New York: Harper and Row, 1969.

- *The Savage Mind*. Chicago: U of Chicago P, 1966.

Saussure, Ferdinand de. *Course in General Linguistics*. Trans. Wade Baskin. New York: McGraw Hill, 1966.

White, Hayden. 'Michel Foucault.' In *Structuralism and Since: From Lévi-Strauss to Derrida*. Ed. John Sturrock. Oxford and New York: Oxford UP, 1979, 81–115.

Desire/lack

According to *Jacques Lacan, the onset of the post-specular (post-mirror) phase in a child's development marks a psychological dialectic or a sustained tension between an Ideal-I and necessary social constructions. (See *mirror stage.) The child adapts to arbitrary and socially constructed cultural practices and yet the formative influences from birth to 18 months cannot be expunged. The first object of desire, the mother (a), cannot be wholly replaced by an Other object of desire (a'): to embrace the ego ideal is to be alienated and to experience 'lack.' As the child grows and cultivates its special skills, it longs for the recollected or imagined feelings of unity and harmony, as well as a stable, unchanging meaning. But, to remain wilfully in the realm of an idealized Imaginary and to avoid adaptation to the cultural when faced with a knowledge of the Symbolic would be a primary form of narcissism. (See *self/other, *symbolic/imaginary/real.)

The post-specular child is a split subject. For Lacan the split subject is constituted upon a gap, both an absence of what was once believed to be truly meaningful and a lack of any assurance of present values – unquestioned, transhistorical social meaning or 'presence.' (See *metaphysics of presence.) In an attempt to fill this gap and to replace what has been lost (the Imaginary), subjects go from one experience to another, trying unsuccessfully to recover the sensation of fullness. What Lacan calls 'demand' is the articulation of desire, a substitution of a set of finite objects for the denied infinite object of desire, the (m)other,

who in more Freudian terms has always desired the phallus. (See *Sigmund Freud.) In 'The Signification of the Phallus,' Lacan remarks that 'if the desire of the mother *is* the phallus, the child wishes to be the phallus in order to satisfy that desire' (*Ecrits* 289). The mother's thwarted desire for the phallus is a mirror image of the child's frustrated desire for the mother. Driven by desire, the subject is ever split.

This split also characterizes the relationship between the id, ego and superego or the conscious and unconscious. The relationship between the Imaginary and Symbolic, or for that matter the conscious and unconscious, is not tidy. If the Imaginary is repressed, it acts like the unconscious, which is likewise repressed, and will negatively affect the subject in strange, incomprehensible ways, because the unconscious is never discernible or wholly interpretable by the conscious. Lacan argues that the unconscious is structured like a language with a system unique to itself (*Ecrits* 234). Hints may be given to the conscious through parapraxis, jokes, dreams, and free associations, but the significance of the unconscious is still enigmatic. Despite this gap, there is, in effect, some exchange of information, knowledge and understanding so that the relative position of the conscious and unconscious is never fixed but always undergoing change. The continual dialectic or process of transference and countertransference between personality areas or between subjects is uncertain but insistent, always changing with new conditions and knowledge.

This ongoing dis-ease of the subject, forever caught in a dialectic between the Imaginary and Symbolic, the fantasized and socially acceptable, and the Self and the Other, provides the clue to the processes of both psychoanalysis and textual interpretation. Since the subject is always defined by language(s) split between the conscious and the unconscious, and since language and context are always arbitrary, the 'I can be identified only in terms of the actual moment of the discourse' and 'is sustained by the discourse *as such* – that is, by the chain of signifiers' (Richardson 60). (See *discourse, *signified/signifier/signification.) The self, then, is itself a signifier and, like the process of signification, is marked by constant metonymical displacement. (See *metonymy/metaphor.) As Lacan argues in 'The Agency of the Letter in the Unconscious or Reason Since

Freud,' this intersubjective approach character-izes both psychoanalyst and textual analyst, for psychoanalysis is closely related to, if not an extension of, literary interpretation; each analyst engages in a dialectic with an object of analysis or 'text,' in which one changes the other and itself in the process. (See *text, *psychoanalytic theory.) An objective reading of patient or text is neither possible nor desirable, and the emergence from the mirror stage (not just a phase but the site of a drama as well) becomes both the activity of this dialectic and a metaphor for it.

This view of the split subject, driven by desire, constituted upon lack, and characterized by transference, has been used as the basis for interpretations that go well beyond psychoanalysis and textual study. The exploration of language is one such area. Indeed, one of Lacan's first commentators, Anika Lemaire, considers Lacan a structuralist who adapted the linguistic model to psychoanalysis (3). (See *structuralism.) When Lacan posits that the mirror stage forms the dividing line between the child's personal language and private communication with the mother (the Imaginary) and the shared language of public discourse represented by the father (the Symbolic), he enters the debate about language practices. The Imaginary represents our wish for a stable sign system in which meaning is totalized, transparent, fixed, and unitary, whereas the Symbolic is a fluid system in which meaning is contextually derived, hazy, slippery, and self-divided. (See *sign, *totalization.) In the Symbolic, signifiers bear meanings that are constantly elusive and floating – hence the terms 'shifters' and 'floating signifiers.' (See *floating signifier.) Indeed, the emphasis here is always on the word or signifier rather than on meaning or signification: Lacan has taken the well-known Saussurean formula for the primacy of meaning and the unity of signifier and signified (s/s or signified/signifier) and changed it to S/s (Signifier/signified) to suggest the primacy of the signifier, the play of language per se, and the bar or gap between signifier and meaning. Lacan's formulation announces that language and meaning cannot be known and mastered and that Saussure's notions of representation and the referentiality of language need to be replaced by an awareness of the chain of empty signifiers. (See *Ferdinand de Saussure, theories of *play/freeplay.)

The desire for unitary meaning of the Imaginary, as opposed to the ever-elusive values of the signifier in the Symbolic, is analogous to the problems inherent in the strictly analytical mode. Lacan himself initiates this discussion when, in 'The Agency of the Letter,' he develops a link between logical positivism and the desire to discover 'the meaning of meaning' (*Ecrits* 150). The desire to master and control knowledge and to perceive unchanging structure and meaning is believed to characterize the Western imaginary ideal of logic and reason. Logic, reason and analysis, especially as employed by ego psychology, are consequently considered by some Lacanians as inferior tools in coming to terms with reality. A better way, and one more in keeping with the uncertainty principle of the Symbolic, is based upon a less abstract process and upon a principle of negotiation and transference within a particular situation. While we might 'desire' the apparent absolutes of a given system of logic, the reality of changing circumstances and positions and the inadequacy of strict logical rules must finally be acknowledged and utilized.

Some semioticians have taken such a concept of 'desire' as the single most important motivating factor in the practice of advertising. (See *semiotics.) Advertisements generally appeal to an idealized style of life supposedly attainable if a certain product or service, for example, is purchased. This goal is, however, falsely founded upon a gap. The ad itself conveys a desire for something that the consumer wishes to believe in or to acquire but that the product cannot deliver. The ad is simultaneously constituted upon lack and desire – the lack of any 'real' meaning and satisfaction and the desire or demand for something that stands in the place of primal satisfaction, the wish to possess the (m)other. As *Roland Barthes has pointed out in many texts, but especially *Mythologies*, advertising often presents itself as 'natural' but is wholly constituted upon, and coded by, culture. (See also *code, *myth.)

GORDON E. SLETHAUG

Primary Sources

Lacan, Jacques. 'Desire and Interpretation of Desire in *Hamlet.' Yale French Studies* 55/56 (1977): 11–52.
– *Ecrits: A Selection.* Trans. Alan Sheridan. New York and London: W.W. Norton and Co., 1977.

- *The Four Fundamental Concepts of Psycho-Analysis.* Ed. Jacques-Alain Miller. Trans. Alan Sheridan. New York and London: W.W. Norton and Co., 1978.
- *The Language of the Self: The Function of Language in Psychoanalysis.* Ed. and trans. Anthony Wilden. Baltimore: Johns Hopkins UP, 1968.
- 'Seminar on "The Purloined Letter."' In *Contemporary Literary Criticism: Literary and Cultural Studies.* Ed. Robert Con Davis and Ronald Schleifer. New York and London: Longman, 1989, 301–20.

Secondary Sources

Lemaire, Anika. *Jacques Lacan.* Trans. David Macey. London and New York: Routledge and Kegan Paul, 1977.
Richardson, William J. 'Lacan and the Subject of Psychoanalysis.' In *Interpreting Lacan.* Ed. Joseph H. Smith and William Kerrigan. New Haven: Yale UP, 1983, 139–59.

Dialogism: *see* Double-voicing/dialogism; Polyphony/dialogism

Diegesis

Diegesis is a term used in narrative study to distinguish the narrator's voice from the speech of the characters or, to use *Henry James' functional definition, to distinguish the 'telling' function from the 'showing' function of a narrative. The word is derived from the Greek word meaning 'narration' and has its roots as far back as book 3 of *The Republic*, where Plato sets out two narrative modes by which he believes reality is imitated verbally. He calls these 'mimesis' and 'diegesis' and attributes to the first the representation of action in the words of the characters, and to the second the representation of action in the poet's own words. The former has obvious immediate dramatic implications, while the latter includes the more mediated and controlling aspects such as authorial report, summary and commentary. (See *mimesis.)

The distinction between immediacy and controlling distance raises questions of narrative authority, and a glance at the history of the relationship of mimesis and diegesis shows the changing part that diegesis has played in such questions. As *David Lodge has noted in *After*

Bakhtin (25–44), pre-novelistic *discourse was characterized by a predominance of diegesis, probably arising out of Plato's moral and ethical disapproval of mimesis and his subsequent advocacy of the need for a controlling authorial hand. In this type of discourse, all voices were assimilated to the dominant linguistic register of the author. This linguistic homogeneity was challenged by the rise of classical realism, which brought with it a more even distribution between mimesis and diegesis, as can be seen in the history of the novel. Although the rise of the English novel in the 18th century began in some cases (Richardson, Defoe) with an emphasis upon the ostensively mimetic portrayal of the act of diegesis ('writing to the moment' in the epistolary form and pseudo-autobiography), other authors such as Fielding and Scott restored the diegetic emphasis, advocating a balance between realistic illusion and immediacy and authorial distance and evaluative control. The classic 19th-century novel did the same but, through the extensive use of indirect reported speech, broke down the clear distinction between the two. This emphasis upon the intermingling, at times fusing, of authorial voice with the voices of the characters was followed by Henry James' privileging of mimesis over diegesis, reported speech over authorial speech, showing over telling, in his famous aesthetic of impersonality. The modernist suppression of the author's voice in an aesthetic of impersonality which implies complete authorial control while giving the illusion of a lack of explicit narrative authority, has been followed in *postmodernism by a renewed foregrounding of diegesis. Impersonality has been replaced by a self-conscious emphasis upon the act of narration itself, what the Russian formalists have called 'exposing the device' in which the narrator's voice can be identified with that of the author. (See Russian *formalism.) This highlighting of the diegetic act as a rhetorical construct carries with it a sense of mitigated narrative *authority. Diegesis can be seen to have lost its original authoritative status. The narrator's (and author's) voice no longer retains its privileged evaluative role but has become a function of the fiction, a rhetorical and textual construct that is itself open to interpretation. (See *rhetorical criticism.)

Although the *concept* of diegesis has always existed in the history of novel and narrative study, the term itself has only recently been reintroduced into critical discourse from the Greek by way of Etienne Souriau's cinematographic theory in *L'Univers filmique* (5–10). In the field of narrative study, narratologists have adopted the term from film theory, but in both cases the meaning has undergone considerable distortion, as *Gérard Genette has pointed out. (See *narratology.) Whereas the original Greek meaning emphasized the formal or verbal aspects of narrative, one of several techniques in the telling of a story, the semiologists of the cinema have redefined it in what they term its 'denotative aspect.' (See *semiosis, *semiotics.) It is, as the film theorist Christian Metz defines it, 'the *distant significate* of the film taken as a whole' ... 'the film's *represented* instance' as distinct from the 'expressed, properly aesthetic, instance' *(Film Language*, 144, 98). The distortion of meaning from the original Greek becomes more apparent when the structuralist story/discourse distinction (to use *Tzvetan Todorov's formulation of the *fabula/siuzhet, histoire/discours* model) is invoked. (See *structuralism, *story/plot.) In film theory, diegesis has moved out of the level of discourse to the story plane of a narrative, the 'deep structure' out of which discourse evolves; it is mimesis in its wider, more familiar sense of the represented world. The 'diegetic time' is the signified time of what is narrated, primarily because the telling is always the result of the invisible camera. In his *Narrative Discourse*, Genette introduces the term to narrative theory in this redefined sense. He equates the term 'diegesis' with Todorov's 'story' (27, n.2), discussing it in the context of 'mood,' what he defines as 'the points of view from which the life or the action is looked at' (161). For him, diegesis and mimesis are not two distinct narrative modes, but rather varying degrees of mimetic representation which differ according to the distance between informer and information; diegesis is defined by a maximum of the presence of the informer and a minimum of the quantity of information, and mimesis by the opposite (166). Genette's elaborate discussion of the diegetic, metadiegetic and pseudo-diegetic planes of a *text and heterodiegetic and homo- or autodiegetic levels of discourse is a manifestation of his preoccupation with this modal aspect of narrative. Yet, it would seem that his self-proclaimed emphasis upon what he terms 'narrative in the limited sense' (27), that is, only discourse which is directly available to textual analysis, limits his treat-

ment of the diegetic aspects of a narrative. True to the structuralist enterprise, there is no place for a discussion of the *context* of telling; Genette's diegetic analysis always remains within the confines of the written text. Perhaps more recent poststructuralist transactive models of narrative, which emphasize the contextual situation between text and reader, and which see semantic possibilities in the telling as well as the told, will allow for a wider understanding of the place of diegesis in the field of narrative theory. (See *poststructuralism.)

LINDA HAUCH

Primary Sources

Genette, Gérard. *Narrative Discourse: An Essay in Method.* Trans. Jane E. Lewin. Ithaca: Cornell UP, 1980.Lodge, David. *After Bakhtin: Essays on Fiction and Criticism.* London: Routledge, 1990.Metz, Christian. *Film Language: A Semiotics of the Cinema.* Trans. Michael Taylor. New York: Oxford UP, 1974.Souriau, Etienne. *L'Univers filmique.* Paris: Flammarion, 1953.

Différance/différence

A term used by *Jacques Derrida to designate the production of difference(s) and endlessly deferred meaning which belongs to language or any signifying system understood as a system of differences. It is the term for which Derrida is probably most famous and is indeed perhaps the most important 'non-concept' in his work. The subject of the essay 'La Différance' (1968), this term is of central importance in *De la grammatologie* [*Of Grammatology* 1967] and is prominently used in the closing passages of *La voix et le phénomène* [*Speech and Phenomena* 1972]. (See *grammatology.)

In 'La Différance,' the aberrant spelling of the French word *différence* makes Derrida's point about writing and difference: the difference in spelling is 'written,' for it can only be read not heard; when spoken the difference is lost. By altering the spelling he wishes to combine the Saussurean idea of diacritical difference with the sense of an active production of difference(s) as well as delay and deferral. (See *Ferdinand de Saussure.) It is as though the word *différance* were a fusion of *différence* and the French present participle – with its active sense – of the verb *différer*, which can mean to differ as well as to defer and delay. Derrida accepts the Saussurean idea of language as a system of differences but extends the principle to its ultimate consequences: if there are only differences then meaning is only produced in the relation among signifiers not through the signified; the signified is thus endlessly deferred and delayed through the differential network. (See *signified/signifier/signification.) This deferral and delay is finally not simply a consequence of an already existing system of differences but represents the active production of differences. This production takes the form of both a temporal delay and what Derrida calls *espacement* or 'spacing,' the temporalization and spatialization which are inconceivable before the advent of the differential mark or writing.

Différance, however, cannot be eradicated through the recovery of an undivided state of immediacy. *Différance* produces presence as one of its effects, as the desire of presence. No presence is conceivable without *différance*, this simultaneous effect of difference, production of difference(s) or spacing, deferral, and delay. (See *metaphysics of presence, *supplementarity.)

Derrida's *différance* has proven very useful in literary theory. One important case of immediate influence is *Roland Barthes' emphasis in *S/Z* (1970) and elsewhere on deferred or delayed meaning and the dilatory expansiveness characteristic of literary texts. There is also a widespread recognition of the relevance of *différance* – the idea of the textual productiveness of delayed and ever-deferred resolution – in numerous recent approaches to narrative and temporal structures in epic, romance and the novel. (See also *text, *textuality.)

JOSEPH ADAMSON

Primary Sources

Barthes, Roland. *S/Z*. 1970. *S/Z*. Trans. Richard Miller. New York: Hill and Wang, 1974.
Derrida, Jacques. *De la Grammatologie*. 1967. *Of Grammatology*. Trans. Gayatri Chakravorty Spivak. Baltimore: Johns Hopkins UP, 1977.
– *La Voix et le phénomène*. 1967. *Speech and Phenomena*. Trans. David B. Allison. Evanston: Northwestern UP, 1973.

Discourse

Discourse is a term whose currency in the humanities and social sciences has greatly increased since the 1960s. In linguistics, it can serve as the rough equivalent of speech, that is, language as actually used by the speaker (*parole*), as opposed to language as a system of signs (*langue*). (See *langue/parole*, *Ferdinand de Saussure, *Emile Benveniste, *sign.)

Discourse analysis studies the syntactic or semantic structures of texts (or of language units longer than one sentence) and considers both their linguistic and sociocultural dimensions. (See *discourse analysis theory, *text.) Anglo-American research has usually concentrated on conversational patterns, speech acts and other forms of oral communication, and this work has led to considerations of the distribution of *power and *authority in verbal exchanges (Coulthard). (See also *speech act theory, *communication theory.)

For *Mikhail Bakhtin and his circle, discourse is the proper object of a new science, metalinguistics (translated by *Tzvetan Todorov as translinguistics), the study of utterances, that is, of actual sentences (or texts) in their context of enunciation. (See *énonciation/énoncé.) This theoretical perspective was elaborated partly through a critique of Saussurean linguistics, which assigned the study of the sociohistorical dimensions of sign systems to semiology, and chose to limit its field of inquiry to the language system as a separate entity. (See *semiotics, *semiosis.) This strategy was denounced by the Bakhtin circle as amounting to the *reification of actual attempts by the State to impose a common, national language in order to centralize and consolidate its power (Bakhtin and Voloshinov). For the circle, the social context is an integral part of any verbal communication: the meaning of an utterance includes the position of the speaker (as social subject, refracted in the other), the horizon (the meaning and values) of the listener, and the historical materiality of language itself (the multiple meanings of words as they are used in other discourses, past, present, and future, for other ends). (See *self/other.) As intrinsically social phenomena, utterances present certain regularities of production and distribution; they are organized by types (discursive genres), working as modelling systems which make sense of the world through structured finalization: 'every significant genre is a complex system of means and methods for the conscious control and finalization of reality'; 'the artist must learn to see reality with the eyes of the genre' (Bakhtin and Medvedev 133, 134). Irreducibly diverse, discursive genres clash and compete in the production of knowledge and this dialogical process constitutes society. (See also *dialogical criticism.) Thus discourse is the space and process where *intersubjectivity is established, objects of knowledge produced, and values assigned: for Bakhtin, discourse is 'almost the totality of human life.'

*Michel Foucault's work in the history of systems of thought explores the articulation of knowledge and power in discourse: 'power and knowledge directly imply one another ... there is no power relation without the correlative constitution of a field of knowledge, nor any knowledge that does not presuppose and constitute at the same time power relations' (*Discipline and Punish* 27). Power-knowledge matrices are established in discourse, that is, in the vast network of conflicting and inter-validating discursive practices constituting reality (ibid., 194). Discursive practices (comprising institutional bases, qualified members and normalized production procedures) assign subject positions for their practitioners and determine their objects of knowledge. (See *subject/object.) Power-knowledge matrices are thus both intentional and non-subjective: pursued by individuals for specific purposes, relations of power remain non-subjective, as the subjects and objects of knowledge, the modes of argumentation, and the rules of validation are imposed by discursive practices. (See *intention/intentionality.)

The French School of Discourse Analysis [*L'Ecole française d'analyse du discours*] works within the perspectives developed by both Bakhtin and Foucault and therefore bears practically no relation to the Anglo-American tradition, in spite of the similar labels for their enterprises (Maingueneau). The French school considers utterances as intrinsically sociohistorical and linguistic phenomena, and studies the elaboration of subjects and objects of knowledge in discourse. Dominique Maingueneau defines discourse as the relation between the discursive formation (the set of historical constraints determining proper semantic production) and the historical dispersion of actual (or virtual) utterances produced according to these constraints: the concept therefore requires textual analyses, a dimension excluded from Foucault's archaeological research. The French school considers its object to be the space of exchanges between several discourses (rather than any single practice), as the interdiscourse (the network of relations between discursive practices) overdetermines the identity of any particular instance. Marc Angenot defines social discourse as 'all that is said and written in a given society ... or rather than this empirical totality ... the generic systems, the repertories of topics, the rules of utterance formation which, in a given society, organize the sayable – the narratable and the verisimilar – and insure the division of discursive labour' (Angenot 13; my trans.). (See *overdetermination.) His analyses demonstrate how social discourse generates both regulated public opinion and marginal originality, how it produces 'current events' and excludes the unsayable, how it selects addressees and functions as a market.

Such analyses of discourse cross disciplinary boundaries and thereby participate in a general reorganization of knowledge now taking place in the humanities and social sciences (Geertz). (See also *sociocriticism.)

MARIE-CHRISTINE LEPS

Primary Sources

Angenot, Marc. *1889. Un Etat du discours social.* Longueuil, Que.: Préambule, 1989.
Bakhtin, M.M. *Speech Genres and Other Late Essays.* Trans. V.W. McGee. Austin: U of Texas P, 1986.
– and P.M. Medvedev. *The Formal Method in Literary Scholarship: A Critical Introduction to Sociological Poetics.* 1928. Trans. A.J. Wehrle. Cambridge, Mass., and London: Harvard UP, 1985.
– and V.N. Voloshinov. *Marxism and the Philosophy of Language.* 1929. Trans. M. Ladislav and I.R. Titunik. Cambridge, Mass., and London: Harvard UP, 1973.
Coulthard, Malcolm. *Introduction to Discourse Analysis.* London: Longman, 1979.
Foucault, Michel. *The Archaeology of Knowledge.* 1969. Trans. A.M. Sheridan Smith. New York: Pantheon Books, 1972.
– *Discipline and Punish: The Birth of the Prison.* 1975. Trans. A. Sheridan. New York: Vintage Books, 1978.
The History of Sexuality. Vol. I: An Introduction. 1976. Trans. R. Hurley. New York: Vintage Books, 1980.
– 'Orders of Discourse.' Trans. Rupert Swyer. *Social Science Information* 10 (April 1971): 7–31. Repr. as 'Appendix: "The Discourse on Language."' In *The*

Archaeology of Knowledge. Trans. A.M. Sheridan Smith. New York: Pantheon Books, 1972.

Geertz, Clifford. 'Blurred Genres: The Refiguration of Social Thought.' *The American Scholar* 49 (1980): 165–79.

Maingueneau, Dominique. *Initiation aux méthodes de l'analyse du discours*. Paris: Hachette, 1976.

– *Nouvelles tendances en analyse du discours*. Paris: Hachette, 1987.

Todorov, Tzvetan. *Mikhail Bakhtin: The Dialogical Principle*. Trans. W. Godzich. Minneapolis: U of Minnesota P, 1984.

Disnarrated

Proposed by *Gerald Prince in 'The Disnarrated' (1988), the disnarrated reveals itself in the terms, sentences and passages that express events that do or did not happen, both from the perspective of the *narrator and the narrative, and from that of the character and his or her actions. The disnarrated is used to evoke purely imaginary worlds, desired or simply suggested, and also to express broken dreams or unjustified beliefs, failures, lost hopes, false assumptions, miscalculations, mistakes, lies, and so on.

The disnarrated has many functions. It can be used, for example, as a means to slow down the narrative, to describe a character, or to define the narrator and narratee as well as their relationship. It may also be used to develop a *theme, create suspense and articulate the story in hermeneutic terms. (See *story/ plot, *hermeneutics.) Still, its most important function is unquestionably rhetorical. (See *rhetorical criticism.) When applied to the act of narration rather than narration itself, the disnarrated brings to the foreground the means available for constructing a situation or ordering an experience, and it underscores the reality of the representation as opposed to the representation of the reality. In addition, when applied to that which is told rather than to the person doing the telling, the disnarrated serves to emphasize the quality and value of the former. In this way, the disnarrated serves as an important vehicle through which the novelist may identify, by negation, that which is worth telling.

Accordingly, we must distinguish between the disnarrated and that which, for various reasons, cannot be narrated – that is, the unnarratable. The distinction must also be drawn between the disnarrated and the unnarrated – that which, in a narrative, remains unsaid, passed over in silence either temporarily or forever. (See *narratology.)

FRANÇOIS GALLAYS

Primary Sources

Prince, Gerald. 'The Disnarrated.' *Style* 22.1 (Spring 1988): 1–8.

Secondary Sources

Sareil, Jean. 'La Description négative.' *Romanic Review* 78 (1987): 1–9.

Double-voicing/dialogism

*Mikhail Bakhtin uses the term double-voicing or dialogism in two senses. In the first sense, double-voicing is a characteristic of all speech in that no *discourse exists in isolation but is always part of a greater whole; it is necessarily drawn from the context of the language world which preceded it. Because language is a social phenomenon, it can never be neutral and free from the intentions of others. Bakhtin uses an architectural metaphor to describe this intrinsic complexity of language. That component of the word which reveals that it has already been cited or talked about in the past is termed 'scaffolding.' The linguistic categories available to analyse speech before Bakhtin's innovative formulations concerning the unique nature of prose are clearly inadequate to account for a phenomenon such as double-voicing which occurs within the word. Bakhtin's creation of a 'prosaics' (Morson and Emerson 15), which enables analysis of the particular qualities of novelistic prose, reveals speech to be 'metalinguistic' (beyond linguistics).

Bakhtin's second sense of the term double-voicing is especially relevant to a study of novelistic prose. Here double-voicing is an element discernible in discourse when the speaker wants the listener to hear the words as though they were spoken with 'quotation marks.' The novel is constructed almost exclusively with this kind of internally dialogized language, that is, language which contains two voices within a single grammatical construction. In *Problems of Dostoevsky's Poetics*, Bakhtin distinguishes between utterances spoken without 'quotation marks' (monologic and single-voiced) and those accented with 'quotation marks' (dialogic and double-voiced utterances).

The single-voiced word is spoken without 'quotation marks' and is perceived by the listener as direct and unmediated. The speaker says directly what he wishes to say without any recognition within the utterance that there is another perspective on his discourse, a contesting or different language of *heteroglossia which might be an equally valid way of addressing the 'referential object' (*Problems of Dostoevsky's Poetics* 185). Professional language is an example of single-voiced discourse. It pronounces authoritatively on the object by suppressing both the scaffolding of pre-existing language which is necessarily cited in any speech as well as the awareness of an alternative point of view which might render the utterance ironic or qualified. Consequently, it is not possible for the listener to detect the 'quotation marks' which indicate another discourse within the utterance, although all speech is inescapably 'shot through with intentions and accents' ('Discourse in the Novel' 293).

Conversely, the double-voiced word includes the pre-existing scaffolding of another's voice and allows it to sound as part of the 'architecture' of the utterance, so that it is perceived by the listener. The second voice is part of the intention of the speech and therefore deliberately incorporated into its construction. Words spoken ironically provide examples from everyday speech. Within the novel, in order for a discourse to be truly double-voiced, the character who speaks must be aware of the second voice within the utterance and enter into dialogue with it. The character may agree or disagree with this second voice but it must be perceptible and a part of the 'project of the utterance.' Bakhtin views the capacity to account for such constructions as crucial to any adequate analysis of prose discourse.

Bakhtin further distinguishes among the different kinds of double-voiced words which exist in the novel. For example, he identifies both passive and active double-voiced discourses but finds the active type of most interest. In the passive variety, the author allows the second voice to sound but is essentially in control of the other's speech within the utterance. Nevertheless, dialogism is present; though the speaker or author may be in control and even ultimately agree with the second voice, the very act of interrogating it and thus

putting it to the test changes the nature of its *authority and produces authentic dialogism.

There is a wide 'spectral dispersion' ('Discourse in the Novel' 277) of infinite gradations in the relationship between the speaker and the other in passive double-voicing. (See *self/other.) However, if the author is more or less in agreement with the second discourse, the utterance is said to be stylized. Disagreement, on the other hand, produces *parody. In stylization, the author's intention is 'to make use of someone else's discourse in the direction of its own particular aspirations.' The author's thought 'does not collide with the other's thought but rather follows after it in the same direction' (*Problems of Dostoevsky's Poetics* 193). Bakhtin terms stylization 'uni-directional' double-voicing. Conversely, parody or ironic discourse sets up an opposition and thus 'vari-directional' double-voicing. (See also *irony.)

Whenever there is an appreciable tension or struggle within the utterance, however, whereby one voice vigorously contests and resists the other's attempt at parody and where it escapes authorial control, the speech becomes a variety of active double-voicing. Such speech is intensely internally dialogized and close attention must be paid to style, syntax and tone in order to locate the competing point of view. Moreover, an essential difference between parody in passive double-voicing and active double-voicing is that in the latter case the other discourse is actually beyond the utterance and thus 'exerts influence from without' (ibid., 199).

Bakhtin discusses many kinds of active double-voicing but his first example should be noted, as it introduces two important attributes – that of 'hidden polemic' and the 'sideward glance.' Here, the author's discourse 'is directed towards its own referential object' but at the same time 'a polemical blow is struck at the other's discourse' (ibid., 195). The speaker is anticipating an antagonistic response from the listener; he seems to 'cringe' or take a 'sideward glance' at another's hostile point of view. This type of discourse is common in everyday speech whenever we employ 'barbed' words, 'make digs at others' or use 'self deprecating overblown speech that repudiates itself in advance' (ibid., 196). Bakhtin's exemplar of this and of many other kinds of double-voicing in the novel is Dostoevsky's Underground Man, who resists dialogically all attempts to fix or finalize him.

The most radical application of double-voicing becomes the word with a loophole. In this formulation, such a word can never be said to be ultimate and final because it retains the potential for another meaning. When a character like the Underground Man possesses a 'loophole of consciousness,' he has the capacity to change the final meaning of his own words. The word with a loophole can be identified by a close examination of its structure because its 'potential other meaning, that is, the loophole left open, accompanies the word like a shadow' (ibid., 233). When double-voicing attains this 'heroic' quality in the polyphonic novel, it approaches Bakhtin's ideal of the unfinalizability of human life and discourse. (See *polyphonic novel, *dialogical criticism.)

PHYLLIS MARGARET PARYAS

Primary Sources

Bakhtin, M.M. *The Dialogic Imagination.* Ed. and trans. Caryl Emerson and Michael Holquist. Austin: U of Texas P, 1981.
– *Problems of Dostoevsky's Poetics.* Ed. and trans. Caryl Emerson. Minneapolis: U of Minnesota P, 1984.
Dostoevsky, Fyodor. *Notes From Underground.* Trans. Andrew R. MacAndrew. New York: Signet, 1961.
Morson, Gary Saul, and Caryl Emerson. *Mikhail Bakhtin: Creation of a Prosaics.* Stanford: Stanford UP, 1990.

Ecriture: see Derrida, Jacques; Deconstruction; Différance/ différence; Intertextuality; Logocentrism; Textuality

Ecriture féminine: see Cixous, Hélène; Irigaray, Luce; Kristeva, Julia; Feminist criticism, French, Quebec; Polyphony/dialogism

Embedding

Embedding is a strategy of dialogic (double-voiced) prose *discourse in which the speech and accents of another person are inserted in the speaker's utterance. The second voice is implied and need not be physically present to the character. *Mikhail Bakhtin notes that the epistolary form in the novel is best suited to embedding or 'the reflected discourse of another,' as the writer is clearly shaping his speech in anticipation of the response of a specific person (*Problems of Dostoevsky's Poetics* 205). Bakhtin cites an example from Dostoevsky's *Poor Folk.* The hero, Makar Devushkin, is writing a letter to Varenka Dobroselova in which he is defensively engaged in a hidden polemic as he confesses the humiliating fact that he lives in a kitchen. It is possible to detect the anxious 'sideward glance' of Devushkin as he anticipates Varenka's negative response to the news of his humble living accommodations, as well as his 'cringe' before the expected rejoinder, 'here he is living in the kitchen.' Thus, the speech of another, Varenka Dobroselova, invades Devushkin's discourse; he recognizes its power to 'fix' or finalize him in a humiliating position and so tries to escape its limiting implications. Consequently, his speech becomes convoluted.

Embedding, as a kind of *double-voicing*, then, allows the character's concept of himself to be penetrated by 'someone else's words about him' (209). This, in turn, gives rise to the characteristic style of the 'sideward glance,' in which a character's speech becomes halting and interrupted by qualifiers and reservations. Embedding is an element of double-voicing that is only perceptible through dialogic analysis and helps to illustrate the subtle complexities of novelistic prose. (See *dialogical criticism.)

PHYLLIS MARGARET PARYAS

Primary Sources

Bakhtin, M.M. *The Dialogic Imagination.* Ed. and trans. Caryl Emerson and Michael Holquist. Austin: U of Texas P, 1981.
– *Problems of Dostoevsky's Poetics.* Ed. and trans. Caryl Emerson. Minneapolis: U of Minnesota P, 1984.
Lodge, David. *After Bakhtin: Essays on Fiction and Criticism.* London: Routledge, 1990.
Morson, Gary Saul, and Caryl Emerson. *Mikhail Bakhtin: Creation of a Prosaics.* Stanford: Stanford UP, 1990.

Enonciation/énoncé

The terms *énonciation* [enunciation] and *énoncé* [utterance] are used in French linguistic and semiotic theory to distinguish between the act of producing an oral or written utterance and the resultant utterance itself. (See *semiotics.) While linguistic studies of the *structuralism period were largely confined to developing underlying laws and features that characterized *Ferdinand de Saussure's concept of *langue*, post-Saussurean linguists have investigated the domain of *parole* (individual acts of *discourse), formerly considered too chaotic and difficult to systematize. (See *langue/parole.) One of the consequences of this interest in *parole* was the development of theories of *énonciation*, as theorists recognized the need for a linguistics that would go beyond the sentence (as its maximal unit of study), and the need to account for dimensions of the *text unexplained by purely structuralist goals and methods.

*Emile Benveniste, who can be credited with much of the early work on *énonciation*, defines this term as an individual act of the use of language (*Problèmes* 2: 80). *Enonciation* is thus to be understood as the act of producing an utterance or text, an act which leaves behind its traces in the resultant utterance. (See *trace.) The *énoncé* is the linguistic object, the oral utterance or written text, which is produced by every individual act of *énonciation*. What is emphasized in most descriptions of the *énoncé* is its closed, static, completed nature, whatever its length may be (Dubois et al. 191). The *énonciation/énoncé* *binary opposition encompasses several others: the dynamic movement and activity of *énonciation* contrasts with the static, completed nature of the *énoncé*, and the openness of *énonciation* is opposed to the closure of the *énoncé*. These definitions demonstrate the interdependence of the two terms, not simply because of the circularity of the definitions (that is, each concept is unavoidably explained in terms of the other) but also because of their mutual necessity: any act of *énonciation* always produces an *énoncé*, which exists solely because of a foregoing *énonciation*.

Given the fleeting character of *énonciation* as a process, as an individual act which never recurs in an identical manner, theoreticians have noted the problem of studying *énonciation* in the strict sense of the term. Since the listener/reader can never arrest an act of *énonciation* in progress or seize hold of its continuous movement in order to observe it, he or she is simply left with the *énoncé*, the object created by this act. Examining *énonciation* in the original sense of the term is consequently a methodological impossibility, an impasse which has resulted in the equation of the term with the traces of this act within the *énoncé* (Kerbrat-Orecchioni 29; Ducrot and Todorov 405). A second semantic slippage of the term is also noted by Kerbrat-Orecchioni, who claims that *énonciation* is often synonymous with the presence of the speaking or writing subject within her or his discourse. (See *subject/object.)

The study of *énonciation* is thus effected in terms of the *énonciation énoncée*, the investigation of the traces of the act of *énonciation* within the *énoncé*, traces which constitute the markers of subjectivity in language. An analysis of an utterance from this perspective focuses on the linguistic traces of the speaker or writer within the *énoncé*, emphasizing the various possible relationships between the speaker or writer (the *locuteur*), the act of *énonciation*, the resultant *énoncé*, and the listener or reader (the *allocutaire*). The two major sites of subjectivity in language are modalization and deictics, each of which is expressed by a series of specific linguistic forms or constructions. Modalization indicates the speaker/writer's attitude, be it disbelief, doubt, uncertainty, and so forth, towards the *énoncé*, expressed during an act of *énonciation* and imprinted within the utterance by means of markers such as modal verbs, adverbs of opinion (for example, 'perhaps,' 'certainly'), modalizing transformations (such as the optional use of the passive voice and impersonal constructions), verbs of opinion, the mood of the verb (the conditional, for example, often expresses uncertainty), evaluative expressions indicating the subject's attitude towards the *énoncé* ('appreciative modalities'), and indicators of doubt (for example, 'so-called,' 'seem'). *A.J. Greimas, who understands modalization as the subject's modification of the predicate (*Du Sens* 67), focuses on the study of modal verbs and their functioning in the syntagmatic progression of the narrative *actant (a structural role in the action of a narrative that may be performed by one or more individual characters or 'acteurs') in the quest for a particular object of value. Greimas has integrated his theory of modalities within the larger framework of his actantial theory and the semiotic square. His study of modalities bears an affinity to modal studies in logic and semantics and locates the functioning of modalities at both deep- and surface-structure levels of the text.

The other major site of subjectivity in language is that of deictic signs (also known as shifters or indicators), whose meaning and referent varies with each act of *énonciation*. (See *reference/referent.) While *C.S. Peirce integrates deictic expressions into his more general category of the indexical *sign, *Roman Jakobson considers deictics as indexical symbols which are situated at the point of coincidence between *code (here, the language in which the message is communicated) and message ('Shifters' 131). (See *index, *communication theory.) According to Benveniste, deictic signs are created in and by an act of *énonciation*, as they exist only in relation to the 'here' and 'now' of the speaker/writer (*Problèmes* 1: 252–4). Unlike other terms and expressions used for purposes of reference, deictics are doubly referential, indicating simultaneously the act of *énonciation* in which they were produced and the designated object(s), the nature of which can solely be determined within the context of the particular instance of discourse containing the deictic expression. Included within the category of deictics are personal pronouns, demonstratives (for example, 'this,' 'that'), certain temporal and spatial adverbs (such as 'here,' 'now,' 'there'), verbal tense (especially the present tense), and, in some instances, the definite article. In their capacity to refer, deictics also reinforce the link between speaker/writer and the addressee/reader, insofar as deictic terms focus the latter's attention on the object, time, place, or person designated by the speaker/writer, provided that addressee/reader can recognize the centre of the deictic field of the utterance (that is, the point of convergence of 'I,' 'here,' and 'now'). Benveniste's studies of pronominal deictics (*Problèmes de linguistique générale* 1, 2) have been particularly instrumental in the understanding of the linguistic and semiotic behaviour of the 'I' and 'you' pronouns and their integral role in the creation of the subject.

The relative presence or absence of these markers of the act of *énonciation* within the resultant *énoncé* allows for the characterization of the *énoncé* in terms of its transparency versus opacity (Récanati). A transparent text or utterance contains few or no obvious markers of its *énonciation*, is virtually devoid of modalizers and deictics, and is characterized by the relative effacement of the speaker/writer from the utterance, and hence by a maximal distance between speaker/writer and text, producing an effect of objectivity for the reader. The highly opaque text, on the other hand, is imbued with numerous enunciative markers, clearly indicating the presence of the speaker/writer within the *énoncé* and her or his minimal distance from this utterance, is self-reflexive, and produces effects of ambiguity and subjectivity.

There is, then, a marked difference between studying a specific text from the point of view of its *énonciation*, an analysis which views the text as movement and process and which accounts for the presence and functions of the enunciative markers as described above, and an analysis of a text from the perspective of its status as an *énoncé*. This latter perspective would consider the text as an entity apart from any referential system or context (its situation of *énonciation*) and separate from the speaking/writing subject which produced it, neglect the role of subjective markers, and emphasize the text's structural divisions, syntactic structures, types of lexical denotation and connotation, modes of description, and so on (Fuchs). Many theoreticians now believe this latter type of analysis to be incomplete and reductionist, and argue for the inclusion of the enunciative, discursive dimension in the study of texts or oral discourse. The passage from the study of the *énoncé* alone to that of its *énonciation* thus involves the consideration of the semantic (the relationship between the utterance and its referents) and pragmatic dimensions (the discursive relationship between the interlocutors, the utterance and the context of the situation of *énonciation*) of the *énoncé*. In this sense, then, studies of *énonciation* are related to the Anglo-Saxon speech act theories of *J.L. Austin and *John R.Searle and to their investigation of the performative and illocutionary aspects of the utterance. (See *speech act theory.)

In addition to the continuing linguistic research into *énonciation* and the *énoncé* (Culioli; Danon-Boileau, *Enonciation*), applications of the theories of *énonciation* and the *énonciation*/ *énoncé* distinction in various disciplines have been numerous and fruitful. The description of enunciative markers has enabled the delineation of various typologies of discourse, often motivated by Benveniste's distinction between the *histoire* (objective) and *discours* (subjective) registers of *énonciation* (*Problèmes* 1: 237–50), a distinction modified for the study of literary texts by critics such as J.-M. Adam, *Gérard Genette, J. Simonin(-Grumbach), and *Tzvetan Todorov. In this sense, theories of *énonciation* have made important contributions to theories of *narratology. Enunciative analyses of literary texts are particularly pertinent in the case of many contemporary novels (such as those in the French 'New Novel' category), texts that are highly imbued with enunciative markers (for example, frequent shifts in narrator from first- to third-person and vice versa, second-person narrators, the layering of several situations of *énonciation)* (cf. Van den Heuvel's study of selected Robbe-Grillet texts). Political speeches, as well as written reports of political events in newspapers and journals, have provided fertile material for *énonciation* analysis, since certain political texts are frequently the rewriting of or the commentary on a previous discourse (Guespin 23). In this metalingual reformulation of a previous discourse according to the beliefs and attitudes of the political analyst or journalist, the markers of the second *énonciation* depict the speaker or writer's attitude towards the original *énoncé.* (See *metalanguage.) Examples of such analyses include Maldidier's study of the Algerian war press coverage, and Courdesses' typology of polemical versus didactic political oratory, where the absence or presence of enunciative markers indicates a particular ideological stance on the part of the speaker.

Concepts relating to *énonciation* and the *énoncé* have also played a significant role in certain psychoanalytic theories, particularly in *Jacques Lacan's work. (See *psychoanalytic theory.) Throughout his writings, Lacan emphasizes not simply the crucial role of language as the mediator of all other signifiers and the subject's participation in signification only after the acquisition of language, but he also claims that the unconscious comes into existence with the subject's access to language, that is, her or his ability to enunciate. (See *signified/signifier/signification.) The Lacanian subject is constituted by the division between the speaking suject *(le sujet de l'énonciation)* and the subject of the utterance *(le sujet de l'énoncé)* (also evident in the division between unconscious and conscious discourse), and is thus simultaneously speaking and spoken. Fur-

ther, the Lacanian conception of subjectivity is relational, as it is formed of a dialogue between ideal representations of the 'I' and 'you' subject positions. The concepts of *énonciation* and the speaking subject as a split subject (here again, the difference between the grammatical subject, the *sujet de l'énoncé,* and the speaking subject, the *sujet de l'énonciation,* is crucial) are basic to *Julia Kristeva's formulation of semanalysis, according to which semiotics must go beyond meaning as a sign system, to study language as a signifying practice, as a discourse produced by a speaking subject ('Le Mot,' 'The System'). Drawing upon linguistic, psychoanalytic and philosophical theories, Kristeva emphasizes the subject in process *(le sujet en procès:* 'Le Sujet,' 'D'une identité'), demonstrating how heterogeneity and the unconscious shape any process of signification, and the importance of the role of poetic language as the site of the irruption of the semiotic dimension into the symbolic (*La Révolution*). Kristeva also proposes a typology of literary discourse, based on the various types of coincidence or non-coincidence of the subject of *énonciation,* the subject of the *énoncé,* and the addressee, in terms of *Mikhail Bakhtin's dialogic/monologic categories ('Le Mot'). (See *dialogical criticism, *monologism, *polyphony/dialogism.) Also working within the framework of linguistics and psychoanalysis, *Luce Irigaray uses the relative presence and absence of enunciative markers to describe the discourses of the hysteric and the obsessive patient ('Approche') (see also the work of Danon-Boileau in linguistics and psychoanalysis: *Le Sujet*).

Specific contributions of *énonciation* theory have also been adapted to the study of cinematic *énonciation:* the *énonciation* situation in filmic discourse has been investigated in terms of the speaking/spoken subject distinction (Silverman), the larger cultural context and the technological apparatus of film-making (de Lauretis and Heath), and the traces of subjectivity in the image (Jost), and by the adaptation of Genette's theories of narrative discourse to cinematic narration (Gaudreault and Jost). Finally, the apparently transparent discourse of scientific writings has been analysed to reveal its underlying and often hidden enunciative markers of subjectivity (Ouellet).

BARBARA HAVERCROFT

Primary Sources

Adam, Jean-Michel. *Linguistique et discours littéraire.* Paris: Larousse, 1976.

Benveniste, Emile. *Problèmes de linguistique générale.* 2 vols. Paris: Gallimard, 1966, 1974. Selections trans. in *Problems in General Linguistics.* Trans. Mary Elizabeth Meek. Coral Gables, Fla.: U of Miami P, 1971.

Courdesses, Lucille. 'Blum et Thorez en mai 1936: Analyse d'énoncés.' *Langue française* 9 (1971): 22–33.

Culioli, Antoine. 'Sur quelques contradictions en linguistique.' *Communications* 20 (1973): 83–91.

– 'Valeurs modales et opérations énonciatives.' *Le Français moderne* 46.4 (1978): 300–17.

Danon-Boileau, Laurent. *Le Sujet de l'énonciation: Psychanalyse et linguistique.* Paris: Ophrys, 1987.

– *Enonciation et référence.* Paris: Ophrys, 1987.

Dubois, Jean, et al. *Dictionnaire de linguistique.* Paris: Larousse, 1973.

Ducrot, Oswald, and Tzvetan Todorov. *Dictionnaire encyclopédique des sciences du langage.* Paris: Seuil, 1972. *Encyclopedic Dictionary of the Sciences of Language.* Trans. Catherine Porter. Baltimore: Johns Hopkins UP, 1979.

Fuchs, Catherine. 'Variations discursives.' *Langages* 70 (1983): 15–33.

Gaudreault, André, and François Jost. *Le Récit cinématographique.* Paris: Nathan, 1990.

Genette, Gérard. 'Frontières du récit.' 1966. *Communications 8, L'Analyse structurale du récit.* Collection Points. Paris: Seuil, 1981, 158–69. 'Frontiers of Narrative.' In Genette, *Figures of Literary Discourse.* Trans. Alan Sheridan. New York: Columbia UP, 1982, 127–44.

– *Figures III.* Paris: Seuil, 1972. Trans. (in part) in *Narrative Discourse: An Essay in Method.* Trans. Jane E. Lewin. Ithaca: Cornell UP, 1980.

Greimas, A.J. *Du Sens II.* Paris: Seuil, 1983. Selections trans. in *On Meaning.* Trans. Paul Perron and Frank Collins. Minneapolis: U of Minnesota P, 1987.

Guespin, Louis. 'Problématique des travaux sur le discours politique.' *Langages* 23 (1971): 3–24.

Irigaray, Luce. 'Approche d'une grammaire de l'énonciation de l'hystérique et de l'obsessionnel.' *Langages* 5 (1967): 99–109. Repub. in *Parler n'est jamais neutre.* Paris: Editions de Minuit, 1985, 55–68.

Jakobson, Roman. 'Shifters, Verbal Categories, and the Russian Verb.' In *Selected Writings.* The Hague: Mouton, 1971. Vol. 2: *Word and Language,* 130–47.

Jost, François. 'Narration(s): En deçà et au-delà.' *Communications* 38 (1983): 192–212.

Kerbrat-Orecchioni, Catherine. *L'Enonciation: De la subjectivité dans le langage.* Paris: Armand Colin, 1980.

Kristeva, Julia. 'D'Une identité à l'autre.' In *Poly-logue.* Paris: Seuil, 1977, 149–72. 'From One Identity to Another.' In *Desire in Language.* Ed. Leon Roudiez. Trans. Thomas Gora, Alice Jardine, and Leon Roudiez. New York: Columbia UP, 1980, 124–47.

– 'Le Mot, le dialogue et le roman.' *Séméiótiké: Recherches pour une sémanalyse.* Paris: Seuil, 1969, 143–73. 'Word, Dialogue, and Novel.' In *Desire in Language,* 64–91.

– *La Révolution du langage poétique.* Paris: Seuil, 1974. *Revolution in Poetic Language.* Trans. Margaret Waller. New York: Columbia UP, 1984.

– 'Le Sujet en procès.' *Tel Quel* 52 (Hiver 1972): 12–30.

– 'The System and the Speaking Subject.' In *The Tell-Tale Sign. A Survey of Semiotics.* Ed. Thomas Sebeok. Lisse, The Netherlands: Peter de Ridder P, 1975, 47–55.

Lacan, Jacques. *Ecrits.* Paris: Seuil, 1966. *Ecrits: A Selection.* Trans. Alan Sheridan. New York: Norton, 1977.

de Lauretis, Teresa, and Stephen Heath, eds. *The Cinematic Apparatus.* New York: St. Martin's P, 1980.

Maldidier, Denise. 'Le Discours politique de la guerre d'Algérie: Approche synchronique et diachronique.' *Langages* 23 (1971): 57–86.

Ouellet, Pierre. 'La Désénonciation: Les instances de la subjectivité dans le discours scientifique.' *Protée* 12.2 (1984): 43–53.

– 'Le Petit fait vrai: La construction de la référence dans le texte scientifique.' In *Les Discours du savoir.* Ed. Pierre Ouellet. Montreal: Les Cahiers de l'ACFAS, 1986, 37–57.

– 'La Voix des faits, approche sémiotique du discours scientifique.' *Protée* 11.3 (1983): 29–41.

Récanati, François. *La Transparence et l'énonciation.* Paris: Seuil, 1979.

Silverman, Kaja. *The Subject of Semiotics.* New York: Oxford UP, 1983.

Simonin, Jenny. 'Les Plans d'énonciation dans *Berlin Alexanderplatz* de Döblin.' *Langages* 73 (1984): 30–56.

Simonin-Grumbach, Jenny. 'Pour une typologie du discours.' In *Langue Discours Société.* Ed. Julia Kristeva, J.-C. Milner, and Nicolas Ruwet. Paris: Seuil, 1975, 85–121.

Todorov, Tzvetan. 'Les Catégories du récit littéraire.' 1966. *Communications 8.* Special issue. L'Analyse structurale du récit. Collection Points. Paris: Seuil, 1981, 131–57.

Van den Heuvel, Pierre. *Parole, Mot, Silence: Pour une poétique de l'énonciation.* Paris: Librairie José Corti, 1985.

Episteme

An episteme is a historically specific, dynamic field of representations of knowledge. *Michel Foucault defines it in *The Archaeology of Knowledge* as 'the total set of relations that unite, at a given period, the discursive practices that give rise to epistemological figures, sciences, and possibly formalized systems' (191). In short, an episteme constitutes the discursive conditions of possibility of an epistemology.

The notion of episteme is most fully developed in Foucault's works of the late 1960s, notably *The Order of Things* [*Les Mots et les choses* 1966] and *The Archaeology of Knowledge* [*L'Archéologie du savoir* 1969]. In the former he attempts a history or an 'archaeology' of the human sciences that avoids producing the traditional sovereign unity of a subject, a spirit or a period. (See *subject/object.) The history of knowledge thus theorized is represented as a dynamic, constantly changing totality. Foucault argues that this non-unitary, de-centred totality of relations among the human sciences can be discovered through analyses of their discourses. (See *centre/decentre, *discourse.) The analysis of a range of fields at a given historical moment demonstrates a set of discursive practices common to all the fields. This analysis of an episteme uncovers the set of constraints and limitations that are imposed on the range of discourses in the human sciences and, by extension, other knowledge practices.

Foucault's description of the 17th-century episteme serves as an example of the kind of analysis carried out in *The Order of Things:* 'I simply noted that the problem of order ... , or rather the need to introduce an order among series of numbers, human beings or values appears simultaneously in many different disciplines in the seventeenth century. This involves a communication between the diverse disciplines, and so it was that someone who proposed, for example, the creation of a universal language in the seventeenth century was quite close in terms of procedure to someone who dealt with the problem of how one could catalogue human beings' (*Foucault Live* 76). Foucault's notion of episteme contributes to a shift from the traditional historical inquiry into 'what' was known at a given moment to the discursive practices that rendered something knowable. Analysis of an episteme displaces epistemology's theorization of the grounds of knowledge by attending to the representational paradigms which organize that theorization.

DANIEL O'QUINN

Primary Sources

Foucault, Michel. *The Archaeology of Knowledge.* Trans. A.M. Sheridan Smith. New York: Pantheon, 1972.
– *Foucault Live.* Trans. John Johnston. New York: Semiotext(e), 1989
– *The Order of Things.* New York: Vintage, 1973.

Essentialism

The recent feminist concern with essentialism arose particularly during the importation of Continental French writing to the United States. Essentialism is a label for certain theoretical and artistic attempts to explore the specificity of 'the feminine.' These explorations usually take place within a literary or psychoanalytic framework. (See *psychoanalytic theory.) As a strategic choice, these writings hope to escape the patriarchal straitjacket of sexual difference through an emphasis on the positive worth of either a biological, linguistic or philosophical female essence. (See *patriarchy.) Although there is a significant difference between writings which concentrate on the female/feminine as a given, and those which attempt to pry gender loose from sex, to allow masculinity and femininity to float free from male and female, all are often branded essentialist. Essentialist is thus both a descriptive and a prescriptive term, and refers as much to a kind of writing and body of thought as it does to a judgment of the success or failure of this strategic posture.

In the United States, most of these efforts are associated with 'New French Feminists,' Continental French theorists like *Luce Irigaray, *Julia Kristeva and *Hélène Cixous who work within a psychoanalytic framework following *Sigmund Freud and *Jacques Lacan. (See French *feminist criticism.) Lesbian writer Monique Wittig has also been included, rather against the grain, in their company. The literary texts of writers like Annie Leclerc and Chantal Chawaf are considered exemplary of this strategy, while Cixous' 'Laugh of the Medusa,' seductive yet problematic, is the best known. These various writings concentrate on a difficult exploration of female sexuality and subjectivity through the concept of *jouissance*, through a metaphorization of fluidity and of 'the mother' or motherhood, by delving into the languages of irrationality, and especially of the hysteric, and by 'writing (with) the body.' They often use *irony and *parody to mock the phallus and patriarchal discourses. (See *discourse.)

During these exchanges a polarization developed which characterized the French feminists as essentialist, reliant on 'male theory' and overly obscurantist, and U.S. feminists as crudely empiricist, naive and caught up in patriarchal forms of discourse. Because of this polarization, the writings of more materialist French feminists were often overlooked, and significant theoretical and strategical differences between 'New French Feminists' themselves were suppressed. As well, this split obscured the extent to which theories of difference and the valorization of 'woman's' biological or cultural essence as a force for change had become part of feminist thinking about gender on both sides of the Atlantic. Judy Chicago's 'The Dinner Party,' or the work of Nancy Chodorow would be American versions of this 'French' strain of thinking in the U.S.A. Jane Gallop's *The Daughter's Seduction* and essays in the special issue of *Signs* 7.1 (1981) devoted to French feminist theory give a sense of the issues involved in this question of essentialism.

Questions concerning the nature of sexual difference and women's equality range widely, and pass through *literature and psychoanalysis to philosophy and legal studies. When women make demands for better maternity-leave legislation, can they argue on grounds of equality, or of the special worth of female difference, or on entirely different terms? In opening a gap between being female and what is feminine, these imported texts and this debate on essentialism have changed the terrain of the question of gender. Is there a specifically female subjectivity? Can we separate the bodies of men and women from the discourses of masculinity and femininity? These questions on sexual difference have been addressed in recent writing by *Men in Feminism* and more interestingly through questions of difference *between* women, questions of race, class an-

dethnicity. It is here that one should look for the continuation of this highly charged debate.

WENDY WARING

Primary Sources

Cixous, Hélène. 'Le Rire de la Méduse.' *L'Arc* 61 (1975): 39–54. 'The Laugh of Medusa.' Trans. Keith and Paula Cohen. *Signs* 1.4 (1976): 875–93.
Gallop, Jane. *The Daughter's Seduction*. Ithaca: Cornell UP, 1974.
Jardine, Alice, and Paul Smith, eds. *Men in Feminism*. New York and London: Methuen, 1987.

Expressive devices

In the *poetics of expressiveness, a theory of literary structure advanced by *Alexander K. Zholkovsky and Yuri Shcheglov, expressive devices are types of transformation that make a work's '*theme' engaging. Zholkovsky has identified ten elementary expressive devices: augmentation, combination, concord, *concretization, contrast, division, preparation, repetition, reduction, and variation. Each device is a precisely defined type of rule and each produces a certain effect or combination of effects. The device of concretization, for example, typically involves a transition from the general to the particular or from an abstraction to an example. It is 'the substitution for an entity X of a more concrete entity X1 which contains all the properties of X together with some accession P.' Thus an 'animal' becomes a 'smiling cat,' with the added property of self-satisfaction; or 'to touch' becomes 'to embrace,' with the added property of love. One possible effect of this kind of transformation is an increased ease of perception as a result of the greater palpability of X1. Augmentation, another type of transformation, is the 'substitution for [an entity] X of its "big" variant X!, exceeding X in some respect (such as size or intensity).' 'Love' thus becomes 'love at first sight'; or 'a shout' becomes 'a scream.' An obvious effect of this second type of transformation is to increase the force of what is being said through stress or emphasis (Zholkovsky 274–5). Certain expressive devices have variant forms (for example, preparation is a general type of transformation that includes presentation, presage or recoil); others may be combined to form devices of a 'complex' kind.

JAMES STEELE

Primary Sources

Shcheglov, Yuri, and Alexander Zholkovsky. 'Poetics as a Theory of Expressiveness: Towards a "Theme-Expressiveness Devices-Text" Model of Literary Structure.' *Poetics* 5 (1976): 207–46.
– *Poetics of Expressiveness: A Theory and Applications.* Linguistic and Literary Studies in Eastern Europe, vol. 18. Amsterdam/Philadelphia: John Benjamins, 1987.
Zholkovsky, Alexander. *Themes and Texts: Toward a Poetics of Expressiveness.* Trans. by the author. Ed. Kathleen Parthé. Ithaca/London: Cornell UP, 1984.

Floating signifier

In his *Course on General Linguistics,* *Ferdinand de Saussure maintains that signs are combinations of forms and concepts, of signifiers and signifieds, operating together. (See *sign, *signified/signifier/signification.) Like two sides of a sheet of paper, they are inseparably bound so that meanings (signifieds) are intricately related to given sounds (signifiers). Since Saussure chooses for the purposes of analysis to consider language as a closed, stable system (though arbitrary and subject to change), these signs are defined as constant and can be scientifically analysed through differentiating signifiers and meanings.

Other structuralists of the period agreed with Saussure, but *Roman Jakobson asserted that some signifiers were not marked in the same way as others and that, as a result, the meaning depended upon the context. Hence, they could not be objectified. These signifiers were called 'shifters.' 'I,' 'you,' and 'she' are good examples, for much more must be known about the situation and personae to identify referents. (See also *structuralism.)

Jakobson's identification of shifters highlighted a weakness in Saussure's linguistic theory, and before long others were observing that the signifying process is much more elusive than previously envisaged. Signifiers include any linguistically or culturally 'marked' units – whether sounds, inscriptions or cultural objects. The meaning of a signifier is rarely known apart from a given cultural context or system of spoken and written relations. To describe this phenomenon anthropologists like *Claude Lévi-Strauss refer to 'mythemes,' culturally coded social units, and linguists refer to phonemes, culturally coded units of sound: these are signifiers whose meanings depend upon particular discursive situations and cannot be given totalizable meanings. (See *code, *totalization.) In a certain sense, all these signifiers are 'floating' because no sign remains diachronically or synchronically constant. When cultures change, so do the values attributed to signifiers, and within a given culture no sign is denotative of one thing only; its connotative value depends upon context.

A recent development in the history of the floating signifier is the notion of *Jacques Lacan. A neo-Freudian, Lacan is aware not only of the slipperiness of self-identity but, since the self or subject is always constituted by language, also of the slipperiness of language. (See *self/other, *subject/object.) Lacan argues that the successful development of the ego brings the child from a narrow dependency upon the mother into the arena and laws of culture at large, from a limited, nearly narcissistic *discourse, to the generally prevailing discursive practices of society. Still, this is the discourse of the ego, and behind or underlying that is the id, which, Lacan says, is not only constituted like a language, but seems to have a mode of expression of its own; this language of the unconscious or discourse of the Other is hinted at through parapraxis, through dreams and slips of the tongue, places where the armour of the conscious reveals a chink. In these slips Lacan locates human subjectivity, which depends upon the particular relations of the conscious and unconscious. This image of the self provides an analogy that becomes important for Lacan's conception of floating signifiers: the conscious (ego) can be known only in relation to the unconscious (id), just as the *language* of the conscious can only be known in relation to the *language* of the unconscious. Since, however, the unconscious and its language are only marginally comprehensible, the self can never be mastered or totalized. At the heart of the self and the language of the self is a split.

This split or rupture characterizes signs as such. Between the signifier and the signified one does not find the glue of Saussure's sheet of paper, but the slash or bar, which renders them unendingly separable. The signified can never be one with the signifier; hence positivistic, transhistorical, or transcendent meaning is never possible. Lacan provides a useful example of this phenomenon in his analysis of Poe's 'Purloined Letter.' The content of the stolen letter is never known, and its value depends upon who holds it, whether the noblewoman from whom it is stolen, the Minister who steals it, Dupin who retrieves it, or the Prefect of Police who organizes the retrieval. As form without inherent meaning, the letter continues to circulate, to be exchanged, or to float, and the signification or meaning is dependent upon who holds it, as well as the context in which it is found. Its 'meaning' is split among the various characters and situations.

This notion of floating signification has been successfully applied to narration. *Text (the conscious) and subtext (the unconscious) may never be one and can never be totalized. The language of the text says one thing, but the subtext says another, so that a gap or slash exists between the two. This split is also true of the acts of writing and of reading a tale.

All language, narrative, and conversation is, then, floating, and the 'real' signification of an illocutionary act is only known some time afterward, or indeed never known. In short, no sign or text is transparent but carries within it a latent subtext that may change or undermine the manifest meaning. The function of narratologists and psychoanalysts is, then, to portray the relation of text to possible subtexts and identify the places where intention and consciousness break down and disclose a further meaning. Such critiques can point out instances of floating signification, and reasons for them, but cannot reveal total, undivided meaning where none exists. (See *narratology, *psychoanalytic theory.)

GORDON E. SLETHAUG

Primary Sources

Derrida, Jacques. *Dissemination.* Trans. and intro. Barbara Johnson. Chicago: U of Chicago P, 1981.
– *Of Grammatology.* Trans. Gayatri Chakravorty Spivak. Baltimore and London: Johns Hopkins UP, 1976.
– 'Structure, Sign, and Play in the Discourse of the Human Sciences.' In *The Structuralist Controversy: The Languages of Criticism and the Sciences of Man.* Ed. Richard Macksey and Eugenio Donato. Baltimore and London: Johns Hopkins UP, 1972, 247–72.
– *Writing and Difference.* Trans. and intro. Alan Bass. Chicago: U of Chicago P, 1978.
Ehrmann, Jacques. 'The Death of Literature.' In *Surfiction: Fiction Now ... and Tomorrow.* Ed. Raymond Federman. Chicago: Swallow, 1981, 229–53.
Jakobson, Roman. *Shifters, Verbal Categories and the Russian Verb.* Cambridge: Harvard UP, 1957.
Lacan, Jacques. 'Aggressivity in Psychoanalysis' and 'The Function and Field of Speech and Language in Psychoanalysis.' In *Ecrits: A Selection.* Trans. Alan Sheridan. New York and London: W.W. Norton and Co., 1977.
– 'Seminar on "The Purloined Letter."' *French Freud: Structural Studies in Psychoanalysis.* In *Yale French Studies* 48 (1972): 38–72.
Laplanche, Jean, and Serge Leclaire. 'The Unconscious: A Psychoanalytic Study.' *French Freud: Structural Studies in Psychoanalysis.* In *Yale French Studies* 48 (1972): 118–75.
Leitch, Vincent. *Deconstructive Criticism: An Advanced Introduction.* New York: Columbia UP, 1983.
Lévi-Strauss, Claude. *Structural Anthropology.* Chicago: U of Chicago P, 1976.
Melman, Jeffrey. 'The "Floating Signifier": From Lévi-Strauss to Lacan.' *French Freud: Structural Studies in Psychoanalysis.* In *Yale French Studies* 48 (1972): 10–37.
– ed. *French Freud: Structural Studies in Psychoanalysis.* In *Yale French Studies* 48 (1972).
Saussure, Ferdinand de. *Course in General Linguistics.* Trans. Wade Baskin. New York: McGraw Hill, 1966.

Genotext/phenotext

In *Sémeiótiké* (1969), *Julia Kristeva notes that she borrowed the terms genotext and phenotext from the Russian linguists Saumjan and Soboleva. Kristeva employs the term genotext to signify the transfers of drive energy that can be detected in a spoken or written text. The use of the term presupposes her *psychoanalytic theory of the *text as engendered through a ceaseless and dynamic oscillation between unconscious drive process and social or structural law. The genotext corresponds to the activities of the unconscious, emanating from what she terms the *chora underlying the text. The text is constituted as the drive process which simultaneously adopts and exceeds structural law. The linguistic structure or surface text which results from this dynamic Kristeva terms the phenotext. According to her, the latter represents only the structural phase of textual practice, whereas the genotext is the process which both adopts and exceeds the structuring of the phenotext. Kristeva suggests that inscriptions of the genotext in the phenotext open textual theory to the generating process, and thereby displace ideas of fixed meaning and unitary self. In particular, she points to the writings of the avant-garde (Mallarmé, Artaud, Joyce, Bataille, Lautréamont) as exemplifying a revolutionary practice of the text.

DAWNE MCCANCE

Primary Sources

Kristeva, Julia. *Séméiôtiké: Recherches pour une sémanalyse.* Paris: Seuil, 1969.

Grammatology

A term coined by *Jacques Derrida in *De la Grammatologie* [*Of Grammatology* 1967] as the name for a 'science of letters or writing' (*logos*, 'science,' and *gramme*, 'letter') no longer governed by *logocentrism, by the metaphysical opposition between speech and writing (see *Ferdinand de Saussure) and the privileging of speech and voice over the written word. In Derrida's very broad interpretation, writing refers to the dependency of meaning on a system of differential marks which includes speech. Since the 'fallen' features traditionally attributed to writing are recognizable in all acts of signification, Derrida points to the existence of something he calls 'arche-writing,' an originary activity presupposed by the global effects common to both writing and speech. (See *signified/signifier/signification.) The new definition Derrida gives to writing does not apply exclusively to what is traditionally denoted as writing; it applies to all meaning and is the necessary, unalterable condition of signification in general. Although Derrida has continued to concern himself consistently with the question of 'writing,' the idea of grammatology as a program for an actual science of writing is something which, for whatever reason, he has not pursued in his later work. (See *deconstruction, *trace.)

JOSEPH ADAMSON

Primary Sources

Derrida, Jacques. *De la Grammatologie.* 1967. *Of Grammatology.* Trans. Gayatri Chakravorty Spivak. Baltimore: Johns Hopkins UP, 1977.

Gynesis

Gynesis is a neologism coined by Alice Jardine (from the Greek *gyne*, woman, and the suffix *sis*, action or process) to describe the metaphorizing of woman in contemporary French theory. (See *metonymy/metaphor.) Jardine, who works at the intersection of French and Anglo-American thought, argues that the postmodern interrogation of European master narratives (history, philosophy, religion, science) produces a rhetorical space that is gendered as feminine within those narratives, a recurrent preoccupation with 'woman' that is called gynesis. (See *postmodernism.) The epistemological crisis since the Second World War made visible the linkage between structures of knowledge and cultural oppression, and the sense of legitimacy offered by traditional conceptual paradigms serves to underwrite not only culture but a specifically patriarchal culture. The rethinking of these master narratives has tended to take attention away from identity and unity and to focus it on difference, concentrating its energies on language and theories of the speaking subject. (See *subject/object, *différance/différence.) It has required an examination not only of the classical foundations of Western thought and the binarities or oppositions that sustain them, but also of the way these dualisms are implicitly gendered (man/woman and thus active/passive, spirit/matter, time/space, soul/body). The resulting critiques are preoccupied with areas that have been excluded from or marginalized within traditional thought, uncontrollable spaces that have been coded as feminine or represented as woman. (See *margin, *binary opposition, *code.)

Texts that study gynesis employ metaphors of the female body or designate social and epistemological structures as feminine, as, for example, *Jacques Derrida's work on writing (his references to the 'invaginated' text, the hymen, or his consideration of the feminine imaging of Truth); *Jacques Lacan's discussion of *desire and subjectivity; *Jean Baudrillard's writings on seduction; *Roland Barthes' analyses of gender and eroticism; and *Michel Foucault's examination of madness and sexuality. Thus, the valorization of the feminine and the metaphorization of 'woman' have become identifying marks of postmodern thought. Yet because the 'feminine' (or woman) is a conceptual category, constructed in opposition to the 'masculine' (or man), there is often a complex relation to or a divergence from biological femaleness and the historical, economic, racial, and sexual diversities of women. Gynesis is not necessarily feminist, for many of the texts are male authored and at times seem to reinscribe traditional representations of the feminine rather than interrogate them. Further, there is no necessary connection between the concept of woman as it appears in the texts of gynesis and the political and historical positioning of actual women. Nevertheless, gynesis offers powerful and important insights for feminists, since it provides alternative ways of understanding the systems of knowledge and representation that have oppressed and may continue to imprison female subjectivity. A number of French women have used gynesis in their feminist theorizing, as, for instance, *Hélène Cixous' use of Derrida's work on writing, *Luce Irigaray's interrogations of *Freud and Lacan, and *Julia Kristeva's work on linguistic phenomena and *psychoanalytic theory. Because gynesis emerges from a French theoretical matrix that questions the possibility of transcendent truth and human essence, it emphasizes the linguistic basis of subjectivity and the way gender is constructed by language and culture. (See *feminist *criticism, Anglo-American, French; *patriarchy.)

ELIZABETH HARVEY

Primary Sources

Jardine, Alice. *Gynesis: Configurations of Woman and Modernity.* Ithaca: Cornell UP, 1985.

Hegemony

The concept of hegemony, developed from the work of the Italian Marxist philosopher *Antonio Gramsci provides a tool for analysing the relations of *literature and society. The concept has been used both to situate writers and in-

tellectuals in relation to society and to analyse the play of social forces within literary texts.

Lenin's emphasis on the consent of subordinate groups to the leadership or hegemony of the proletariat is central to Gramsci's elaboration of the concept in his *Prison Notebooks* (1929–35, English selections 1971). For Gramsci the bourgeoisie exercises hegemony over other classes in capitalist states. While the bourgeoisie may dominate society through political and juridical institutions (its rule enforceable through the police and the military), it leads through hegemony in the private realm by presenting itself as representative of the 'universal' advancement of society. (See *universal.) To the division between the state and civil society, Gramsci assigns the oppositions of force/consent, authority/morality, coercion/persuasion, domination/hegemony. A subordinate group, its identity established in economic terms, will achieve intellectual, ethical and political fulfilment by realizing that its own interests 'transcend the corporate limits of the purely economic class, and can and must become the interests of other subordinate groups too' (181). If the leading group is fundamental to the stage of economic development and if it allies itself with other subordinate groups by making economic sacrifices to them, it will achieve hegemony as a step toward state power.

Hegemony is established and maintained at the intellectual, cultural and ideological levels. Gramsci defines intellectuals as those who perform a directing and organizing function. This definition includes 'traditional' intellectuals attached to superseded social orders; however, 'organic' intellectuals, directly connected with a social class, organize 'the "spontaneous" consent' of the populace to 'the general direction imposed on social life' by that class (12). Organic intellectuals define 'customs, ways of thinking and acting, morality' (242), ensuring that individuals govern themselves in accord with political society. A dominant class has achieved hegemony when its 'world view' is suffused throughout society. Hegemony is not coextensive with *ideology since it is also manifest in non-discursive forms – work ethics, habits, personal relations.

Gramsci presents hegemony as a dynamic process with degrees of completion. A hegemonic group, in its drive to incorporate ever more elements of society, must continually make compromises. Hegemony nonetheless remains selective in terms of which experiences, meanings and values it is able to absorb. Developing this aspect of the concept, *Raymond Williams emphasizes that no society can ever encompass all of human potential. As practices existing outside the dominant order, Williams identifies the residual (attached to a previous social order) and the emergent (generated by the lacunae of the present society). A dominant culture may try to incorporate both residual and emergent, but they may become nuclei for the coalescence of counter-hegemony.

The concept of hegemony is particularly suited to the analysis of modern representative democracies where force is seldom used as a means of social control. The development of civil society in such areas as education and health care, mass media and entertainment, political organizations and trade unions contributes to the regulation of hegemony by the dominant capitalist class, especially since the state has expanded inextricably with these areas. Gramsci's analysis of hegemony thus accords with the work of *Theodor Adorno and Herbert Marcuse on the 'culture industry' as a mechanism through which dissidence is pacified and integrated, and radical ideas are diffused or nullified. Hegemony may also be related to *Michel Foucault's analysis of the articulation of knowledge and *power. By the 1980s the term had such wide currency and was used in such disparate contexts that it began to lose some of its specificity as a concept. *Edward Said uses hegemony to develop his concept of affiliation through which, in the narrowly cultural sphere, writers and critics establish systems of relationship based on shared beliefs and values as alternatives to those relationships they inherit through birth (The World, the Text, and the Critic 1983), but also uses hegemony to clarify the dominance of European culture over what it represents as the Orient. *Terry Eagleton in The Ideology of the Aesthetic (1990) shows how the development of aesthetics is central to middle-class hegemony, but also uses hegemony as a synonym for any type of dominance achieved through consent and coercion. The value of hegemony as a concept would seem to depend on maintaining its connections with both social class and cultural production.

JOHN THURSTON

Primary Sources

Eagleton, Terry. *The Ideology of the Aesthetic.* Oxford: Basil Blackwell, 1990.

Gramsci, Antonio. *Selections from the Prison Notebooks.* Ed. and trans. Quintin Hoare and Geoffrey Nowell Smith. New York: International Publishers, 1971.

Said, Edward. *The World, the Text, and the Critic.* Cambridge: Harvard UP, 1983.

Williams, Raymond. *Marxism and Literature.* Oxford: Oxford UP, 1977.

Hermeneutic circle

Modern *hermeneutics passes through at least three avatars: it is the art and methodology of interpretation (Friedrich Ast; Friedrich Schleiermacher); a general theory of the conditions of possibility of the *Geisteswissenschaften* (*Wilhelm Dilthey); and it allies itself with phenomenology to offer a fundamental ontology of the structures of human being (*Martin Heidegger). (See *phenomenological criticism.) Later developments, especially by *Hans-Georg Gadamer and *Paul Ricoeur, derive from Heidegger's re-orientation of hermeneutics toward language and therefore take the historical inscriptions of human being in the languages of cultural production as the object of their hermeneutic phenomenologies.

Interpretation moves in a circle. In order to understand the word, the sentence must be understood and vice versa; striving to understand an author's work, we attempt to unfold it sentence by sentence; but the sentence remains opaque unless we have already grasped, by a leap in advance, its rhetorical function in the whole of the work. The work begins to render up its sense when we have glimpsed the movement of the author's entire corpus; and the oeuvre is focused in the perspectives of many works. The author's texts are themselves woven into a historical context; *text and context together inscribe aspects of one, unified design. The act of interpretation oscillates between the part and the encompassing whole on this historical level of investigation, as it does on the grammatical, stylistic and rhetorical movements of interpretation, which the historical comprehends.

The circle of understanding within which interpretation comes into play must, moreover, comprehend the historical situation and consciousness of the interpreter, the present of the act of interpretation, and the past of the work interpreted in order for the work to be comprehensible at all. In the act of interpretation, we leap into the circle of our being in which we already, largely unknown to ourselves, more or less securely stand. This prior unity, which is more fundamental than the opposition of subject and object, is grasped in the hermeneutics of Ast, Schleiermacher, and especially Dilthey, as the animating *Geist* [Spirit] common to the mind of the historian and the mind which has been recorded in the work. The interpretor understands himself or herself only by encountering, in a process of self-discovery, his or her own being through the historically determined, in each case finite and particular manifestation of Spirit. Here, too, understanding moves in a circle: human being, far from being a static essence, is determined and determines itself by grasping its own, present being out of the projected horizon of the whole which the past unveils; and the undiscovered country of the past, the whole of the inscription of Spirit, emerges out of the living, analogical being of the interpretor's participation in *Geist*. The way forward – the question posed, the project of self-discovery – is the way back.

Heidegger's philosophy shifts the centre of hermeneutics from the presupposition of a unifying *Geist* which manifests itself through language, to the movement of being-as-language in its radical historicity. Heidegger's hermeneutics of *Dasein* has the interpretation of the structure of human being-in-the-world as its goal. This interpretation is circular inasmuch as it presupposes a preconceptual understanding of being as the condition of its possibility; the interpretation works out in explicit conceptual detail what is already 'known' in the sense of being existentially enacted in the structures of our world without being conceptually articulated. Without moving 'back' into what we already understand, existentially and preconceptually, we cannot move 'forward' into what we seek to know conceptually; but the reverse is also true. Because the work of art, according to the analysis of *Being and Time*, offers preconceptual evidence of our understanding of the modes of being which it, no less than conceptual thought, reveals, the experience of art and the labour of conceptual thought not only complement each other but inscribe the movement of understanding: art is

the existential enactment of the stand in the midst of being that a historically rooted people has taken; 'criticism' is the understanding which brings this 'stand' into the light of conceptual reflection; conceptual thought remains dependent on the preconceptual in which it is rooted, and art nourishes itself on the concept which it bears. (See also *metacriticism.)

BERNHARD RADLOFF

Primary Sources

Ast, Friedrich. *Grundlinien der Grammatik, Hermeneutik und Kritik*. Landshut: Thomann, 1808.
Dilthey, Wilhelm. 'Der Aufbau der Geschichtlichen Welt in den Geisteswissenschaften.' In *Gesammelte Schriften*, vol. 7. Stuttgart: Teubner, 1968.
– *Descriptive Psychology and Historical Understanding*. Trans. Richard M. Zaner and Kenneth L. Heiges. The Hague: Martinus Nijhoff, 1977.
– 'Poetry and Experience.' In *Selected Works*, vol. 5. Ed. Rudolf A. Makkreel and Frithjof Rodi. Trans. Rudolf Makkreel et al. Princeton: Princeton UP, 1985.
– *Selected Writings*. Trans. H.P. Rickman. Cambridge: Cambridge UP, 1976.
Gadamer, Hans-Georg. *Truth and Method*. Trans. Sheed and Ward Ltd. London: Sheed and Ward, 1975.
Heidegger, Martin. *Being and Time*. Trans. John Macquarrie and Edward Robinson. London: SCM P, 1962.
Ricoeur, Paul. *Freud and Philosophy: An Essay in Interpretation*. Trans. Paul Savage. New Haven: Yale UP, 1970.
Schleiermacher, Friedrich. *Hermeneutik*. Ed. Heinz Kimmerle. Heidelberg: Carl Winter, 1959.
– *Hermeneutics: The Handwritten Manuscripts*. Ed. Heinz Kimmerle. Trans. James Duke and Jack Forstmann. Missoula: Scholars P, 1977.

Heteroglossia

Heteroglossia (*reznorechie, reznorechivost'*) is a term created by *Mikhail Bakhtin to describe the myriad discursive strata within all national languages and the ways in which these strata govern the operation of meaning in any utterance. Bakhtin develops the implications of this term most fully in his essay 'Discourse in the Novel' (*The Dialogic Imagination*). Every individual utterance is unitary and concrete, the expression of a particular person at a particular non-recurring moment in time. Yet every utterance also articulates extrapersonal forces, derives from what Bakhtin calls the 'socio-ideological' languages in the culture at large. Because heteroglossia is concerned with the contextual overtones of any given utterance, it is the enemy of systematic linguistics. As Bakhtin puts it, 'it is possible to give a concrete and detailed analysis of any utterance, once having exposed it as a contradiction-ridden, tension-filled unity of two embattled tendencies in the life of language' ('Discourse in the Novel' 272).

Heteroglossia provides Bakhtin with a conceptual scheme for categorizing – and judging – individual authors, schools and genres. All can be characterized according to their allegiances in the struggle between the centripetal and centrifugal forces in language. Those which most fully embrace heteroglossia are consistently valorized in Bakhtin's writings. Thus Dostoevsky is superior to Tolstoy; Romanticism to Classicism; the novel to poetry. The novel is potentially the ideal form for the literary embodiment of heteroglossia, since it allows for the fullest artistic representation of the diversity of social speech types and individual voices in a given culture. But Bakhtin identifies two traditions in the history of the novel, one of which suppresses heteroglossia. This 'monologic' tradition is typified by such forms as the Greek romance, the chivalric romance and all genres which privilege respectable language, such as the idyll, the pastoral and the 18th-century sentimental novel. Heteroglossia is present in these narratives but functions primarily as a kind of linguistic background. Beginning with Rabelais and Cervantes another tradition emerged in which prose narrative foregrounds, intensifies and dramatizes heteroglossia. For Bakhtin, Dostoevsky is both heir and supreme master of this 'polyphonic' tradition. (See *polyphonic novel, *polyphony, *monologism.)

Bakhtin's theory of heteroglossia supplements rather than supplants the authorial-intention tradition of Jamesian formalism. (See *Henry James.) Bakhtin would replace traditional stylistics, for instance, with 'sociological stylistics,' which he claims is the only stylistics capable of dealing with the novel as a genre. (See *genre criticism.) Whatever the artistic intention of a given author, he or she must make use of a pre-existing language that is already informed by the social intentions of other speakers: 'Each word tastes of the context and contexts in which it has lived its socially charged life; all words and forms are populated by intentions. Contextual overtones (generic, tendentious, individualistic) are inevitable in the word' ('Discourse in the Novel' 293). Bakhtin grants the author the power of 'orchestrating' this diversity of social speech types and thereby creating a distinctive style, but he also insists that because of its social, temporal nature, there is something in language outside of the control of the author that influences the meaning of any artistic utterance. This emphasis on multivocality in fictional discourse has achieved the status of a kind of hermeneutic given, as when Alan Singer writes that 'novelistic voice is inherently and notoriously multiple ... Novelistic voice subverts the unitary imperative of the very metaphor of human speech which otherwise endows its rhetorical aptitude' (173). Moreover, the recent proliferation of sociological and ideological analyses of literary texts can be traced to Bakhtin's theoretical example, which has served to foreground the extraliterary dimensions of all literary *discourse.

JAMES DIEDRICK

Primary Sources

Bakhtin, Mikhail. 'Discourse in the Novel.' In *The Dialogic Imagination*. Trans. Caryl Emerson and Michael Holquist. Austin: U of Texas P, 1981, 259–422.

Clark, Katerina, and Michael Holquist. *Mikhail Bakhtin*. Cambridge: Harvard UP, 1984.

Singer, Alan. 'The Voice of History/The Subject of the Novel.' *Novel: A Forum on Fiction* 21 (1988): 173–9.

Horizon of expectation

The horizon of expectation (*Erwartungshorizont*) is a term employed by *Hans Robert Jauss, a central figure in the *Constance School, in his aesthetics of reception (*Rezeptionsästhetik*). Although Jauss is responsible for the popularization of the term, it is not his invention. Both the philosopher Karl Popper and the sociologist Karl Mannheim had used the concept before Jauss. It had also appeared in the work of the art historican *E.H. Gombrich who, under Popper's influence, defined the horizon of expectation in *Art and Illusion* (1960) as a mental set which registers deviations and modifications from a norm with exaggerated sensitivity. Jauss' usage, which is similar to Gombrich's, is more likely derived from the phenomenological and hermeneutical heritage, in which *Edmund Husserl, *Martin Heidegger and *Hans-Georg Gadamer had recourse to the notion of a horizon. (See *phenomenological criticism, *hermeneutics.) For Gadamer, Jauss' teacher and the most important intellectual influence on his early work, the horizon is an essential part of every interpretive situation. It represents a standpoint that limits the possibility of vision, resulting from our necessary situatedness in the world. Yet it is neither a fixed standpoint, nor is it static, but rather it is a continuously evolving vantage point into which we move and which moves with us. It is intimately linked to the prejudices we bring to any situation, since they represent a 'horizon' over which we cannot see. Finally, Gadamer defines understanding (*Verstehen*) as a fusion of one's own horizon (*Horizontverschmelzung*) with the horizon of the other, whether the other be *text or person. (See *self/other.)

Jauss uses the term in a related but slightly different fashion. In his work the horizon of expectation refers to an intersubjective system or structure of expectations that a hypothetical reader might bring to a given text. (See *intersubjectivity.) It is essential for both the interpretation and the evaluation of a literary work. The critic must establish the horizon of expectations for a particular historical moment. This is accomplished most readily with parodistic texts since they often foreground their own horizon. (See *parody.) With other texts the critic must rely on internal features of genre, literary history and language. Once the horizon has been objectified in this fashion, the aesthetic value of a work can be measured by its distance from the horizon. Works that do not deviate from expectations are considered of lesser aesthetic merit; those that violate or break the horizon of expectations are aesthetically more valued. A good indicator of the horizon of expectations is the audience response, the literary criticism and the scholarship for any given period. (See also *reader-response criticism.)

Jauss' more recent work has largely abandoned the horizon of expectation as a negative foil for the innovative qualities of literary work. Although it no longer functions in an aesthetics of negativity, the horizon of expectation has nonetheless been retained in his work during the 1970s and 1980s and applied pro-

ductively to analyse different perceptions of literary texts. Still a tool for historical contextualization and interpretation, the horizon of expectation has ceased to be the sole measure for aesthetic value.

ROBERT C. HOLUB

Primary Sources

Gombrich, E.H. *Art and Illusion.* Oxford: Phaidon P, 1960.
Jauss, Hans Robert. *Aesthetic Experience and Literary Hermeneutics.* Minneapolis: U of Minnesota P, 1982.
– *Toward an Aesthetic of Reception.* Minneapolis: U of Minnesota P, 1982.

Hypogram

The hypogram is related to the anagram and the paragram and is most readily understood in relation to these. An anagram is the process of the transposition of the letters of a given word or string of words to make a new word or string of words (e.g., given word: 'cat'; anagram: 'act'). 'Anagram' may also refer to the word so derived ('act'). In literary theory the anagram owes its recent popularity to *Ferdinand de Saussure's study of anagrams (published posthumously by *Jean Starobinski) in which he shows how, in a series of Latin poems, sounds obey the same principle as anagrams, since the sounds or letters of a proper name are to be found scattered in random order throughout the poems.

'Paragram' is the name given to the type of anagrammatic distribution described by Saussure. Saussure's anagram (the paragram) is seen as a network which provides the text's structure. (See *text.) This structure is unusual, for instead of being linear, it is paragrammatic: that is, the paragram's first sound, or group of sounds, does not lead to its second then to its third, as the text unfolds from beginning to end. Rather, the anagrammatic elements scattered throughout the text are linked in a nonlinear network. These paragrammatic elements coexist in time and space regardless of any pre-established order. The very notion of any fixed order (linear or otherwise) is irrelevant, since the anagram destroys order by separating and isolating the constituent elements, placing them in a diagrammatic arrangement, or disarrangement – one where all elements exist in direct relation to both the key word and one another.

Henri Meschonnic's definition of the activity of creating a paragram (paragrammatism) is useful, since it describes the central role of the original 'theme word.' For him paragrammatism is the 'prosodic organisation of a text by the complete or partial diffraction of the voiced or written elements of a "theme word" within its [textual] context outside the order of these elements in time.'

*Julia Kristeva sees in paragrammatism a new structuring principle, a new dynamic akin to *Mikhail Bakhtin's dialogical perception of the literary text. Dialogism enables contradictions to coexist in a text, for it construes them as voices in dialogue with each other within a dynamic and centrifugal system. A text's paragrammatic structure allows its contradictory aspects to come to the fore, thus enhancing the text's *polyphony.

For Starobinski, the hypogram is another word for the paragram or Saussurean anagram. Saussure defines it thus: 'a hypogram highlights a name or word by artfully repeating its syllables, thus giving it a second, artificial mode of existence, added, as it were, to the word's original form.'

For *Michael Riffaterre, however, the hypogram is not a paragram. Though both are a non-linear, scattered redistribution of a given pretextual entity, both are not made of the same type of components. Whereas the paragram redistributes the 'graphemes' or 'lexemes' derived from the keyword and embeds them in the words of the text, the hypogram involves an altogether larger scale: whole words are embedded in sentences. Furthermore, the hypogram implies the supremacy of form, since it is the hypogram's structure which is evoked by the way words are embedded in sentences and by the very organization of these sentences. (See *embedding.)

Riffaterre defines his hypogram as a structural pre-text, a generator of the poetic text, that is, one in which the poetic function dominates. The hypogram may be a cliché, a quotation, a group of conventional associations, or a thematic complex. It may be a single word, such as 'monster,' and all its associations, or an entire text. For example, Riffaterre sees the linking of 'flower' and 'abyss,' referring to the cliché of the flower on the edge of the abyss as a hypogram in the following texts: 'This meadow flower growing peacefully ... in the heart of Paris, between two streets, in the midst of passersby, shops, cabs and omnibuses ... this *flower* of the fields beside the cobblestones opened up an *abyss* of reverie' (Victor Hugo *Choses vues*). 'Vice in him was not an *abyss*, as in some old men, but a natural *flowering*, for all to see.' (Emile Zola, *La Curée*). The distinctive feature of this particular hypogram is an oxymoron linking opposites and reducing them to equivalents. Thus, in Hugo's example, the 'abyss' is not negative (dark, horrifying, hell-like, evil), but positive; here it suggests infinite reverie.

The author's conscious or unconscious use of a hypogram generates a matrix or keyword, which in turn generates a model (its primary actualization) and series of variants. 'Matrix, model, and text are variants of the same structure,' that is, hypogram, according to Riffaterre. (See *variation.) An adaptation of Riffaterre's analysis of the following, by the Jesuit Athanasius Kircher, provides a brief example: 'Tibi vero gratias agam quo clamore? Amore more ore re.' (How shall I cry out my thanks to Thee? [The Almighty replies:] With thy love, thy customs, thy words, thy deeds.) The hypogram might be termed 'prayer,' implying the latter's dialogic self-generating structure. The matrix is thanksgiving; the question *clamore* (the crying out) is the model for the reply *amore*, and *amore* is a model for the sequence *more, ore, re*, which are its variants. The variants echo the model's syntax (all use the ablative) and morphology (all being a diminishing repetition of *clamore).* Thus *clamore* provides a paradigm which is projected on the syntagmatic axis reinforcing the signification of the matrix.

The reader's *praxis is the reverse of the writer's as he attempts to solve the puzzle of textual significance. Faced with apparent 'ungrammaticalities' (Riffaterre's term), incongruities which block mimetic or referential meaning, he seeks a common element in these variants and thereby the generating model and matrix. When he finally solves the puzzle, everything points to one symbolic focus, one unifying matrix, which itself refers to the pretextual generator: its hypogram. Since this hypogram is perceived as a deeper unifying structure than its different levels of textual manifestation, it seems that Riffaterre also prefers the suffix *hypogram* for its implication of ultimate 'deep-level' meaning, for the prime structuring generator is indeed far more deeply buried than the elements of the less complex paragram from which he distinguishes it.

ANNA WHITESIDE – ST. LEGER LUCAS

Primary Sources

Bakhtin, Mikhail. *Problems of Dostoevsky's Poetics.* Bloomington and London: Indiana UP, 1978.
Kristeva, Julia. *Sémeiôtiké.* Paris: Seuil, 1969.
Riffaterre, Michael. *Semiotics of Poetry.* Bloomington and London: Indiana UP, 1978.
Starobinski, Jean. *Words upon Words: The Anagrams of Ferdinand de Saussure.* New Haven: Yale UP, 1979.

Secondary Sources

Meschonnic, Henri. *Le Signe et le poème.* Paris: Gallimard, 1975.

Icon/iconology

The icon is one of three types of *sign (including symbols and indices) in *Charles Sanders Peirce's classification, based on the type of relationship between the sign and the extra-linguistic world. In the case of the icon the relationship is based on likeness: an icon displays the same property as the object denoted. For example, a road sign depicting children at a crossing displays a visually recognizable silhouette of children; a simplified drawing of an ice cream on a menu denotes ice cream as one of the desserts available in that restaurant.

According to Peirce, the icon, as distinct from the *index and symbol, is 'a sign which refers to the object that it denotes merely by virtue of characters of its own, and which it possesses ... Anything whatever, be it quality, existent individual, or law, is an icon of anything, in so far as it is like that thing and used as a sign of it' (CP 2.247).

In other words, an iconic 'thing' ranges from the hypostasized to the most abstract and may refer to an equally broad range of referents. The governing principle in iconic signs is, then, similitude: similitude which may be recognized according to Peirce's three fundamental categories of 'firstness,' 'secondness' and 'thirdness,' and thus as a 'qualisign,' a 'sinsign' or a 'legisign.' Three categories of icon are, then, theoretically possible. However, the first – the pure iconic qualisign – is a conjectural

hypothetical entity since, were it to exist, it would, by its very existence, become a sinsign rather than a qualisign. Thus, for Peirce, there are in fact two and not three categories of icon: the iconic sinsign and iconic legisign. These may, nevertheless, evoke three categories of similitude of quality, existence and law. In keeping with Peirce's self-perpetuating triadic system, these icons may, in turn, be perceived as falling into three classes: the image, the diagram or the metaphor. (See *metonymy/metaphor.)

Peirce's theory of the icon has proved most useful in applications to concrete or representational texts, such as the ideogram in poetry, and to theatre and drama. In the latter case, Keir Elam discusses how stage props, decor and actors playing characters become icons of what they represent. (See also *communication theory.)

Iconology is quite distinct from Peirce's semiotic theory of the icon. The term was first proposed by Erwin Panofsky to distinguish his broader approach to the analysis of meaning in the visual arts from iconography, which merely identifies subject-matter (e.g., painting X is a portrait of Y, a scene from such and such a battle, a view of such and such a place). According to Panofsky, iconology seeks to understand the total meaning of a work of art in its historical and cultural context. Thus a work of art is to be treated as a concrete historical document in the study of a civilization, or period, to bridge the gap between art history and other historical studies. Critics argue that this is a dangerous method unless allied with aesthetic sensibility and a sense of historical relevance. More recent work on iconology has been done by W.J.T. Mitchell, who examines the links between *ideology and iconology and reveals the fears about imagery, expressed in a 'rhetoric of iconoclasm,' based in notions of class, race and gender.

ANNA WHITESIDE – ST. LEGER LUCAS

Primary Sources

Mitchell, W.J.T. *Iconology: Image, Text, Ideology.* Chicago: U of Chicago P, 1986.
Panofsky, Erwin. *Renaissance and Renascences in Western Art.* New York: Harper and Row, 1960.
Peirce, Charles Sanders. *Collected Papers.* Cambridge, Mass.: Harvard UP, 1931–58.

Secondary Sources

Elam, Keir. *The Semiotics of Theatre and Drama.* London and New York: Methuen, 1980.

Ideal reader

The ideal reader does not exist either in reality or in the *text. The concept is a construct of the imagination, a mental creation that can be attributed, according to Didier Coste in 'Trois conceptions du lecteur' (1980), to an author or interpreter, but is usually ascribed to a producer of fiction. For that producer, the ideal reader is nothing more than a projection of a mode of production in a mode of reception. Isaac Babel expresses this accurately in 'Mes premiers honoraires' (1972), where he states, 'My reader is intelligent and cultivated, with hearty and demanding tastes ... He exists within me, but has been there for so long that I have managed to fashion him in my image and semblance. He may have ended up confusing himself with me.'

FRANÇOIS GALLAYS

Primary Sources

Babel, Isaac. *Mes premiers honoraires.* Paris: Gallimard, 1972.
Coste, Didier. 'Trois conceptions du lecteur et leur contribution à une théorie du texte littéraire.' *Poétique* 43 (September 1980): 354–71.

Ideologeme

An ideologeme is the smallest intelligible unit of *ideology. The term is a parallel construction to, for instance, 'phoneme,' 'philosopheme' or '*seme,' which are the smallest units of phonetics, philosophy and semantics, respectively. An understanding of the ideologeme is a function of an understanding of ideology itself.

One of the most developed discussions of the concept occurs in *Fredric Jameson's *The Political Unconscious.* Jameson defines the ideologeme as 'a historically determinate conceptual or semic complex which can project itself variously in the form of a 'value system' or 'philosophical concept,' or in the form of a protonarrative, a private or collective narrative

fantasy' (115). For Jameson, ideologemes are the 'ultimate raw material' of cultural products, and ideological analysis seeks to understand cultural products as 'a complex work of transformation on ... the ideologeme in question' (87). By means of a 'radical historicization,' the 'essence,' 'spirit' or 'world-view' of a text can be understood as an ideologeme implicated, finally, in the class struggle. In *The Political Unconscious* Jameson attempts to rewrite or restore the class horizon organized, in certain texts, around ideologemes like the Victorian concept of *ressentiment.*

According to Jameson, *ressentiment* was a way to 'explain' the phenomena of revolution in Europe by attributing it to a '"psychological" and non-material ... envy the have-nots feel for the haves' (201). According to the concept, those who incited resistance to the dominant social order did so not out of a legitimate political analysis, but out of 'private dissatisfactions'; they were always 'unsuccessful writers and poets, bad philosophers, bilious journalists, and failures of all kinds' (202). In *literature, *ressentiment* is mainly embodied in characters whose revolutionary tendencies are explained away as symptoms of psychological imbalance.

In contemporary fiction, the *ressentiment* motif can still be seen in, for instance, the novels of Robertson Davies, which contain many minor characters that might be called left-wing or feminist 'buffoons.' These characters – Denyse Hornick and the 'penniless scheme-spinners' in *Fifth Business,* Murray Brown in *The Rebel Angels,* Ismay Glasson and Charlie Fremantle in *What's Bred in the Bone,* Wally Crottel and Al Crane in *The Lyre of Orpheus* – link social activism or criticism of class privilege with ignorance, meanness of character, personal spite, and/or psychological disorder. Linking criticisms of the present order to such discreditable individuals works to discredit the criticisms themselves. The 'buffoon' characters, then, may be read as signs implicating Davies' novels in a wider reactionary ideology; in this sense they, and the concept of *ressentiment* which they embody, operate as ideologemes. (See *sign.)

Jameson's description of the ideologeme is consistent with the semiotic description of the relationship between the sign and the sign system that produces signification. (See *signified/signifier/signification.) In *semiotics, an element of signification functions not by its intrinsic power but because of the network of oppositions that distinguishes and relates it from and to another. As a sign, the ideologeme is also articulated by difference. Individual 'value systems,' 'philosophical concepts' and 'protonarratives' only achieve a signifying force in opposition and relation to other systems, concepts and protonarratives. Moreover, the 'same' ideologeme could have radically different effects depending on the wider ideological system within which it is articulated. Jameson exploits the political possibilities in this complexity by emphasizing the 'dialogical' character of the ideologeme – a term he borrows from *Mikhail Bahktin. For Jameson, the 'normal form of the dialogical is essentially an *antagonistic* one' (84). Ideologemes, then, like individual texts or cultural phenomena in general, are sites upon which opposing discourses (particularly class discourses) struggle for position. (See *text, *discourse, *dialogical criticism.)

A related use of the concept of ideologeme has been made by the Tel Quel group of critics. In her contribution to their *Théorie d'ensemble*, *Julia Kristeva emphasizes the close relation between the ideologeme and *intertextuality: 'We call the ideologeme the communal function that attaches a concrete structure (like the novel) to other structures (like the discourse of science) in an intertextual space' (313). In *Le Texte du roman*, Kristeva describes the ideologeme as both an organizing function within a text and a function that indicates the text's implication in a wider social and historical text. As an organizing function, the ideologeme is materialized at different levels in the structure of a text; it is a thematic or conceptual nexus around which the transformations effected by the text's enunciations can be seized as a whole (12). (See *énonciation/énoncé*.) At the same time, the ideologeme indicates the social and historical coordinates of the text, the implication of the text in the impersonal order of other texts called the 'intertext' (12, 102).

JAMIE DOPP

Primary Sources

Jameson, Fredric. *The Political Unconscious: Narrative as a Socially Symbolic Act*. Ithaca: Cornell UP, 1981.

Kristeva, Julia. *Le Texte du roman: Approche sémiologique d'une structure discursive transformationnelle*. The Hague: Mouton, 1970.
[Tel Quel]. *Théorie d'ensemble*. Paris: Seuil, 1968.

Ideological horizon

Ideological horizon is a term first employed by *Pierre Macherey in his 'Lenin, Critic of Tolstoy,' which forms part of his work known in English as *A Theory of Literary Production*. Macherey uses the term to explain Lenin's reference to mirror and reflection in his analysis of Tolstoy. *Marxist criticism is commonly attacked for its simple reflection theory, in which the critic treats fiction as a direct mirror of the material conditions of history but Macherey asserts that 'Lenin uses the mirror to refer to a concept rather than an image.' Macherey views this concept as an understanding of contradiction: 'It would therefore be incorrect to say that the contradictions of the work are the *reflection* of historical contradictions: rather they are the consequences of the absence of this reflection.' Thus, the critic searches not for a direct representation of history but for the ideological horizon which refers 'to that abyss over which ideology is built. Like a planet revolving around an absent sun, an ideology is made of what it does not mention; it exists because there are things which must not be spoken of.' The ideological horizon is therefore the critic's description of the *ideology which informs the *text but never quite appears in it. For example, a Canadian novel of exploration which makes no reference to Native peoples might be examined in light of that absence.

Although not a synonym for *Louis Althusser's concept of the '*problematic,' the ideological horizon also deals with the revelation of ideology through contradiction.

TERRY GOLDIE

Primary Sources

Macherey, Pierre. *A Theory of Literary Production*. London: Routledge and Kegan Paul, 1978.

Ideological State Apparatuses (ISAS)

The designation of such apparently private institutions as the family and the schools as Ideological State Apparatuses with the public function of constituting subjects suited to perform in specific ways within society has enabled much recent cultural theory. According to French Marxist philosopher *Louis Althusser, *ideology is embodied in the actions of subjects through 'the *material existence of an ideological apparatus*' (168). Building on *Antonio Gramsci's concept of *hegemony and his own concept of the *social formation, Althusser divides the superstructure into 'two "levels" or "instances"': the politico-legal (law and the State) and ideology (the different ideologies, religious, ethical, legal, political, etc.)' (134). The first level, the Repressive State Apparatus (RSA), contains 'the Government, the Administration, the Army, the Police, the Courts, the Prisons, etc.' (142–3). Among Ideological State Apparatuses (ISAS) constitutive of the second level, he identifies churches, schools, the family, political parties, trade unions, the media and cultural institutions, all unified under the dominant ideology. He rejects the allocation of these two levels to the public and private domains as a distinction 'internal to bourgeois law' (144). The reproduction of the relations of production is secured through the superstructure. The RSA, functioning through force (actual or potential), secures 'the political conditions' (149). The ISAS 'largely secure the reproduction specifically of the relations of production' (150). The ISAS perform this function through *interpellation or hailing whereby individuals who are addressed in this manner (mis)recognize themselves as subjects with attributes necessary to the dominant relations of production. The concept of ISA has been widely used in socialist and feminist literary theory and criticism, and in the semiotic analysis of the cinema and advertising. (See *feminist criticism, *semiotics, *Marxist criticism.)

JOHN THURSTON

Primary Sources

Althusser, Louis. 'Ideology and Ideological State Apparatuses (Notes towards an Investigation).' In *Lenin and Philosophy and Other Essays*. Trans. Ben Brewster. New York: Monthly Review P, 1971, 127–86.

Ideology

Though much used in recent literary and cultural criticism, ideology is as slippery a term in criticism as it is in the social sciences. Some critics, including *Raymond Williams have even questioned its usefulness (*Marxism and Literature* 71). In use, the term is often nearly synonymous with Georges Sorel's 'myths,' Vilfredo Pareto's 'derivations' (intellectual systems of justification), *Sigmund Freud's 'rationalization,' *Antonio Gramsci's '*hegemony,' and *Roland Barthes' 'mythologies.' (See also *myth.)

Critics who practise ideological criticism usually discuss texts with reference to issues of political *power, sexuality and class. (See *text.) They assume that a text reflects or embodies, to some degree, the ideologies prevailing in its society. They tend to define ideology either descriptively as an explicit or tacit sharing of certain attitudes, values, assumptions, and ideas; or, more often, evaluatively as a covert means of social oppression and exploitation because it offers 'concepts and categories that distort the whole of reality in a direction useful to the prevailing power' (Scruton 123). In the latter context, ideology is one of the means, perhaps the dominant one, by which a society maintains its economic and political status quo. Because ideology is usually seen as mystifying or distorting or concealing the relations of power within society, an ideological reading of a text is usually contestational and involves revealing lacunae, omissions and distortions. (See also *demythologizing.)

The word was first used by Antoine Destutt de Tracy in his *Eléments d'Idéologie* (1801–5) to refer to a new science of ideas (an idea-logy) involving a rational investigation of the sources of ideas in order to distinguish knowledge from opinion and science from metaphysical and religious prejudices.

Much more influential on contemporary Marxists and non-Marxists alike, however, has been the set of definitions offered by Karl Marx and Friedrich Engels (especially in *The German Ideology* 1845–6 and in Engels' letter to Franz Mehring, 14 July 1893). (See *Marxist criticism.) They used the term disparagingly to refer (1) to the idealism of the Young Hegelians, which was ideological because it disregarded the material origins and determinants of their ideas; (2) to any complex of attitudes and ideas concealing the real nature of social relations and thus helping to justify and perpetuate the oppressive social dominance of one class over others; and (3) to what Engels described as 'false consciousness,' which is any process of thought in which 'the real motive forces impelling [a thinker] remain unknown to him' (Engels to Mehring). In Marxist usage, ideology has pejorative connotations and, more often than not, refers to the thought of others.

The term has also been used more generally to refer in a value-neutral sense to any system of norms or beliefs 'directing the social and political attitudes of a group, a social class, or a society as a whole' (Nüth 377). In this sense one can speak of a feminist ideology or working-class ideology or American ideology. Also worth noting is the usage, less frequent today, which 'identifies ideology with the sphere of ideas in general' (Nüth 378).

It is no exaggeration to say, however, that most subsequent criticism concerned with ideology has been shaped by Marx and Engels' passing remarks on the topic. Many critics who are not Marxists (for instance, *Lionel Trilling, Roland Barthes and many contemporary feminists like *Sandra Gilbert and Mary Jacobus) nevertheless reflect 'the hermeneutics of suspicion' (*Paul Ricoeur's phrase) inseparable from the classical Marxist view of ideology as signifying 'the values, ideas and images which tie [individuals] to their social functions and so prevent them from a true knowledge of society as a whole' (Eagleton Marxism and Literary Criticism 17). (See also *feminist criticism, *hermeneutics.)

While critics concerned with ideology and *literature argue that the latter is inevitably ideological, they nevertheless tend to assume a privileged epistemology for literature to the extent that they think of it as simultaneously marked by ideology and transcending it. However, with the exception of *Terry Eagleton and *Fredric Jameson, both heavily influenced by the French Marxist philosopher *Louis Althusser, few critics have indicated on what theoretical basis they make such an assumption. Developing Marx's insights, Althusser sees ideology as a 'social practice' which helps

conceal the true nature of social reality – economic and political. It is 'a system of representation – composed of ideas, concepts, myths, or images – in which people live their imaginary relations to the real conditions of existence' (Lenin and Philosophy 162). For Althusser, art's roots are in ideology but it isn't purely ideological because its aesthetic forms and devices offer a distance from and perspective on ideology. Where science offers 'knowledge' of reality, art 'alludes' to it (Lenin and Philosophy 204).

Thus, for Althusser and his followers, art presents ideology in a non-ideological form. The critic's task is to offer a 'symptomatic' reading that, beginning with the surface of the text, attempts to find its lacunae and contradictions in order to locate the text's 'problematic' (the body of concepts restricting what can be said). Such a reading is important because it reveals how ideology helps construct ('interpellate') the individual as a social subject willing to accept a particular view of what is, what is good, and what is possible (Thompson 16). (See *symptomatic reading, *interpellation, *problematic.)

In Jameson's criticism, such an analysis is seen as a prelude to the creation of a more just society. Although indebted to *Georg Lukács' History and Class Consciousness (1923) and to the work of *T.W.Adorno and the *Frankfurt School, Jameson goes far beyond their pessimistic comments on ideology's complicit function in capitalist society and art to suggest that 'a Marxist practice of ideological analysis proper' must deal with the utopian impulses within ideological cultural texts' (The Political Unconscious 296). Almost alone among critics of ideology, Jameson insists on seeing a utopian dimension within it.

A theoretical problem less often acknowledged in cultural criticism than in the social sciences pertains to the question of how the intellectual or critic, of whatever political persuasion, is able to escape ideological consciousness (what Engels, though not Marx, called 'false consciousness'). In other words, how does the critic find a point of view outside ideology to observe ideologically marked social discourses and practices in order to judge them ideological? (See *discourse.) If ideology is as pervasive as some critics suggest, how is anyone able to step outside it and avoid the tu quoque response from texts and other critics judged ideological? Marxist critics like Eagleton and Jameson suggest that Marxism is less ideological or 'truer' than other critical approaches because it 'subsumes' them (Jameson 10).

Non-Marxist and non-deconstructionist critics of ideology tend to avoid a theoretical engagement with the issue. (See *deconstruction.) Were they to confront it squarely the debate would probably be similar to the one in the social sciences over Karl Mannheim's now discredited suggestion that intellectuals, because they constitute a classless stratum, are able to achieve disinterested, non-ideological knowledge (*Ideology and Utopia*).

It is worth noting that writers as different as de Tracy, Marx, Mannheim, Daniel Bell, Adorno, *Jürgen Habermas, and Jameson have all speculated about the possibility of an end to ideology. For feminists and Marxists, for instance, ideology will end when ideological criticism has done its work.

In *semiotics, this assumption has resulted in a debate between those, like Roland Barthes and *Umberto Eco, who think that applied semiotics (or text semiotic studies) can demystify ideologies by studying the sign systems transmitting them, and those who argue from a metasemiotic or theoretical viewpoint that an escape from ideology is impossible. (See also *sign, *metacriticism.)

SAM SOLECKI

Primary Sources

Adorno, Theodor, and Horkheimer, Max. *The Dialectic of Enlightenment*. New York: Seabury, 1972.
Althusser, Louis. 'Ideology and Ideological State Apparatuses.' In *Lenin and Philosophy*. London: New Left Books, 1971.
Bell, Daniel. *The End of Ideology*. New York: Free P, 1960.
Eagleton, Terry. *Criticism and Ideology*. London: New Left Books, 1976.
- *Ideology: An Introduction*. London: Verso, 1991.
- *Marxism and Literary Criticism*. London: Methuen, 1976.
Frankfurt Institute for Social Research. 'Ideology.' In *Aspects of Sociology*. London: Heinemann, 1973.
Jameson, Fredric. *The Political Unconscious: Narrative as a Socially Symbolic Act*. Ithaca: Cornell UP, 1981.
Kavanagh, James H. 'Ideology.' In *Critical Terms for Literary Study*. Ed. Frank Lentricchia and Thomas McLaughlin. Chicago: U of Chicago P, 1990.
Mannheim, Karl. *Ideology and Utopia*. London: Routledge and Kegan Paul, 1936.
Marcuse, Herbert. *One-Dimensional Man*. Boston: Beacon P, 1964.
Marx, Karl, and Friedrich Engels. *The German Ideology*. New York: International Publishers, 1970.
McLennan, David. *Ideology*. Minneapolis: U of Minnesota P, 1986.
Nüth, Winfried. *Handbook of Semiotics*. Bloomington: Indiana UP, 1990.
Plamenatz, John. *Ideology*. London: Macmillan, 1970.
Scruton, Roger. 'Ideologically Speaking.' In *The State of Language*. Ed. Christopher Ricks and Leonard Michaels. Berkeley: U of California P, 1990.
Thompson, Kenneth. *Beliefs and Ideologies*. London: Tavistock, 1986.
Williams, Raymond. *Marxism and Literature*. London: Oxford UP, 1977.

Imaginary/symbolic/real

*Jacques Lacan's three major terms – the imaginary, the symbolic and the real – are best understood in conjunction as forming a topology of subjectivity and a radical revision of *psychoanalytic theory. Early in his career, Lacan derived inspiration from Melanie Klein's object relations theory. For Klein, the notion of an object suggests both things in the world and the goal or target of aggressive, inner drives. This dual function of the object, as striding some middle ground between the subjectivity of desire and the 'objectivity' or otherness of the real, defines the realm of the imaginary. (See *desire/lack, *self/other, *subject/object.) As Lacan remarks in his first seminar (1953–4), 'when Melanie Klein tells us that the objects are constituted by the interplay of projections, introjections, expulsions, reintrojections of bad objects ... don't you have the feeling that we are in the domain of the imaginary?' (74).

Klein's pioneering work derived from the psychoanalysis of children; in Lacan's case the imaginary has an empirical base in what he calls the *mirror stage. Sometime between the ages of 6 and 18 months, the infant is able to recognize its own image in a mirror, that is, as an *external* relation. Thus, the formation of an I concept, the ego, occurs within the realm of the imaginary: the subject assumes an image, or, as in another Lacanian formulation, 'the subject becomes object.' In other words, in order for the ego to be a subject, it must internalize a principle of otherness as a consequence of its own desire to be a desiring subject. This is the meaning of another puzzling

Lacanian formulation: desire is the desire of the Other. Lacan is so determined to separate sex drives from any natural or instinctual base – the Other is an effect of *signification – that it is sometimes difficult to know how radical Lacan wants his ontology to be. (See *signified/signifier/signification.) It is nevertheless clear that human desire cannot be satisfied by its objects: the Lacanian system is not utopian. The full implication of Lacan's 'imaginary' marks human identity as endlessly fragmented: 'It is the nature of desire to be radically torn. The very image of man brings in here a mediation which is always imaginary, always problematic, and that is therefore never completely fulfilled' (Seminar Book II 166).

The instability of desire, however, reaches a limit of sorts in the realm of the symbolic. Lacan's stress on the symbolic order is based on his post-Saussurean analysis of the linguistic signifier. The signifier is meaningful not because it refers to a definite signified that determines it, but because it stands in opposition to another signifier. Language, for Lacan, is a system of signifiers that form a closed, autonomous order. To this extent, he is a structuralist. (See *structuralism.) Human subjectivity is caught within this system or chain of signification because (a) language is a self-sustaining, closed system and (b) the unconscious is structured like a language. The human subject will thus remain within 'the prisonhouse of language,' except that in Lacan's understanding of it, language is no ordinary prison. In 'The Function of Language in Psychoanalysis' (1953), Lacan claims not just that 'it is the world of words which creates the world of things' but that 'man speaks ... because the symbol has made him man' (39). The subject is an effect of the symbolic, decentred within the play of signifiers. (See *centre/decentre.) The psychoanalytic consequence of the symbolic order involves a move away from biological or instinctual motivation towards a consideration of particular symbols that rule over and cripple the subject. Freud's Oedipus complex, as primal Law of consciousness, is linked by Lacan to its equivalent signifier in the symbolic order: *the Name-of-the-Father. Although the Oedipal situation involves both imaginary and real relations, it is the symbolic relation which constitutes it essentially. (See also *Sigmund Freud.)

Lacan's notion of the real must be understood within the dictates of his complex and often contradictory theories of subjectivity and signification. The real initially signifies the domain outside of symbolization (spatial metaphors and topological diagrams are heuristically indispensible for Lacan), a space distinct from imaginary relations and language. (See also *spatial form, *metonymy/metaphor.) The real is, to some extent, a problem that Lacan creates for himself when words are given the power to create things and desire rules over all object relations. The real is equally a problem for Lacan's entire post-Hegelian project of placing desire and lack at the core of human subjectivity. Slavoj Žižek, in The Sublime Object of Ideology, defines Lacan's real as 'something that cannot be negated ... because it is already in itself, in its positivity, nothing but an embodiment of a pure negativity, emptiness' (170). The real implies that lack itself is not an illusion or an imaginary relation. Since language is constituted as a system of opposing signifiers for Lacan, the symbolic order by its very nature evokes a certain level of unreality or distortion, equivalent perhaps to the méconnaissance of imaginary relations. It is the insistence on the real, therefore, that preserves Lacan's thought from simply being yet another 20th-century 'prisonhouse of language' philosophy. Critics of Lacan, however, may wonder if his notion of the real is unnecessarily vague and too high a price to pay for his theories of language, reference and subjectivity. (See also *reference/referent.)

GREGOR CAMPBELL

Primary Sources

Lacan, Jacques. 'The Function of Language in Psychoanalysis.' In Speech and Language in Psychoanalysis. Trans. Anthony Wilden. Baltimore: Johns Hopkins UP, 1973.
– The Seminar of Jacques Lacan Book I: Freud's Papers on Technique 1953–1954. Ed. Jacques-Alain Miller. Trans. John Forrester. Cambridge: Cambridge UP, 1988.
– The Seminar of Jacques Lacan Book II: The Ego in Freud's Theory and in the Technique of Psychoanalysis 1954–1955. Ed. Jacques-Alain Miller. Trans. Sylvana Tomaselli. Cambridge: Cambridge UP, 1988.
– Žižek, Slavoj. The Sublime Object of Ideology. London: Verso, 1989.

Implied reader

The implied reader is a term developed by
*Wolfgang Iser, one of the foremost members
of the *Constance School, to describe the interaction between *text and reader. It is an
adaptation of the concept of 'implied author'
which *Wayne Booth had discussed in *The
Rhetoric of Fiction* (1961). For Booth the implied author is different from the persona or
*narrator; the term refers rather to the second-
self of the author, the literary, created version
of the real person. Iser's implied reader is similarly a construct. As it appears in the book
Der implizite Leser (The Implied Reader 1972),
the implied reader designates the active participation of the reader in the reading process.
In keeping with Iser's interactive approach to
the production of meaning, the term implied
reader does not belong to either the text or to
the reader but rather to both. It incorporates
both the prestructuring of the text which allows or facilitates the production of meaning
and the reader's actualization of potential
meaning during the reading process. Iser thus
seeks to distinguish the implied reader from
the various types of readers employed by
reader-response critics. (See *reader-response
criticism.) Iser wants to account for the reader's presence but seeks to avoid both real or
empirical readers and abstract readers whose
qualifications have been determined before
their encounter with any specific literary text.
His model is thus transcendental or phenomenological since his implied reader embodies all
the predispositions necessary to cope with a
given text while excluding empirical interference. (See also *phenomenological criticism.)
   On the one hand, we may think of the implied reader as the particular role offered to
any reader of a text. This role is prestructured
by three basic components: the differing perspectives of the text, the vantage point from
which the reader links these perspectives and
the meeting place where the perspectives converge. According to Iser, during the reading
process readers are forced out of their habitual
vantage point and made to assume a standpoint from which they can produce textual
meaning. The reader is carried through various
perspectives defined by characters and narrative voices and must ultimately fit the diverse
perspectives into a gradually evolving pattern.
But we may also think of the implied reader as

the structured acts accomplished by the reader.
In Iser's theory readers fill in blanks or gaps
(*Leerstellen*) and thereby eliminate *indeterminacy. While the textual perspectives are given,
the final meeting place of these perspectives
has to be imagined. This process of mental action, the creative side of our encounter with
texts, is the other aspect of the implied reader.
Every empirical interaction with a text will
produce a slightly different result; no two
readers will form images or fill in blanks in
precisely the same way. But each actualization
by individual readers partakes in the implied
reader, whose own structure provides a framework within which responses can be compared
and communicated.

ROBERT C. HOLUB

Primary Sources

Booth, Wayne C. *The Rhetoric of Fiction.* Chicago: U
   of Chicago P, 1961. Augmented ed., 1983.
Iser, Wolfgang. *Der implizite Leser.* 1972. *The Implied
   Reader.* Baltimore: Johns Hopkins UP, 1974.

Indeterminacy

Indeterminacy is a term associated primarily
with the phenomenological tradition of literary
criticism. (See *phenomenological criticism.)
*Roman Ingarden, a student of *Edmund Hus-
serl, presents an extensive discussion of indeterminacy in his analysis of literary cognition.
According to Ingarden, a literary work consists
of four interrelated strata – word sounds,
meaning units, represented objects, and sche-
matized aspects – and the two further dimensions of aesthetic value and temporality.
Indeterminacy arises because of the peculiar
way in which these layers and dimensions fit
together. In contrast to objects in the real
world, which are always determinate, objects
as represented in a literary work of art exhibit
points or places of indeterminacy (*Unbes-
timmtheitsstellen*) between aspects or dimensions. Although indeterminacy may take
several forms, it occurs primarily whenever it
is impossible for the reader to determine precisely an attribute of a particular object. For
example, we may never be able to describe ex-
haustively a room in the real world, but no
part of it is theoretically indeterminate. A
room represented in a work of *literature, by

contrast, may be described in voluminous detail but some portion will always escape description and be left to the imagination or ideation of the reader. The central activity of the reader for Ingarden is to eliminate indeterminacy by way of *concretization. By filling in the indeterminacies, the reader thus creates (or co-creates) the literary work. (See *reader-response criticism).

Basing his theory of reading in part on Ingarden's phenomenological model, *Wolfgang Iser has recast indeterminacy in the form of blanks or gaps (*Leerstellen*) in the *text. Blanks occupy a central position in the communicative function of a literary work, defining and delimiting the role of the reader. In their interaction with texts, readers are implicitly called upon to remove or complete various blanks on several levels, from the simplest connections in plot to the more complex relationship between themes that stand out against an implicit horizon. (See *horizon of expectation, *theme.)

Iser's theory of the nature of indeterminacy and determinacy in literary works has been challenged most forcefully by *Stanley Fish. From a metacritical perspective Fish claims that the distinction between the two opposed notions is theoretically incoherent. For him indeterminacy presupposes a free subjectivity operating outside of all interpretive constraints. Since we are always reading a text from within conventions determined by the interpretive community to which we belong, Fish argues that the notion that we are at liberty to supply a meaning is an illusion. Although we can use indeterminacy as a method to generate interpretations of texts, it is ultimately based on an untenable epistemological confusion. (See *metacriticism.)

ROBERT C. HOLUB

Primary Sources

Fish, Stanley. *Doing What Comes Naturally*. Durham: Duke UP, 1989.
– *Is There a Text in This Class?* Cambridge, Mass.: Harvard UP, 1980.
Ingarden, Roman. *O poznawaniu dzieła literackiego*. 1937. *The Cognition of the Literary Work of Art*. English trans. from the German trans. Ruth Ann Crowly and Kenneth R. Olson. Evanston: Northwestern UP, 1973.
Iser, Wolfgang. *Der implizite Leser*. 1972. *The Implied Reader*. Baltimore: Johns Hopkins UP, 1974.

Index

The index is one of three types of *sign (*icon, index and symbol) in *Charles Sanders Peirce's theory of *semiotics. Peirce defines all three in terms of their relationship to the object for which they stand. In the case of the index this relationship is 'natural' and metonymical rather than conventional (as with the symbol). (See *metonymy/metaphor.)

We may distinguish two types of index, each expressing a different aspect of metonymy: (1) the relationship between an index's signifier and signified indicates causality (for example, symptoms are indices, just as fever is an index of illness); (2) the index also implies a relationship of contiguity (for example, dark clouds are an index of impending rain, since they are naturally associated with, and so 'point to,' rain; smoke is an index of fire). (See *signified/signifier/signification.)

In literary *discourse, style is often seen as an index of the author's sociocultural background (real or assumed) or of a character's milieu. In descriptions by, say, 19th-century writers like Flaubert or Dickens, the long detailed descriptions of material things (e.g., decor, costume) may be seen as indexical in a variety of ways. They may indicate a character's wealth, taste, milieu, social success or lack of it. For the modern reader such descriptions may also indicate a literary convention which holds that detailed 'realistic' description is an asset. In science fiction, strange things, people, ways, modes of communication serve to remind us that the context is not our own. Elsewhere, repetition might be an index of obsession; gaps or omissions in, say, an autobiography, an index of a desire to hide something, loss of memory, or the lack of importance the writer attaches to the events omitted.

ANNA WHITESIDE–ST. LEGER LUCAS

Primary Sources

Barthes, Roland. 'The Reality Effect.' In *French Literary Theory Today*. Ed. Tzvetan Todorov. Cambridge: Cambridge UP, 1982.
Peirce, Charles Sanders. *Collected Papers*. Cambridge, Mass.: Harvard UP, 1931–58.

Secondary Sources

Culler, Jonathan. *Structuralist Poetics*. Ithaca: Cornell UP, 1975.

Prieto, Luis. *Pertinence et pratique*. Paris: Minuit, 1975.

Intention/intentionality

Although intention and intentionality have a long history as philosophical terms, the German philosopher *Edmund Husserl first gave them their specifically phenomenological orientation. Often called the key concept in the phenomenological analysis of knowledge and experience, for Husserl, being intentional is not only a characteristic of acts of consciousness: it is the essential characteristic or fundamental structure of consciousness itself. The intentional nature of consciousness means that it is always relational or always has a referent: consciousness is always consciousness *of* something. Every intentional act of consciousness, then, has its intentional object, that towards which consciousness is directed; every act of consciousness has its own particular directedness towards the object it constitutes and is constituted by ('Phenomenology' 122–3). In keeping with phenomenology's aim of intuiting or grasping the essences of objects and, as well, the essence (or essential structures) of human consciousness in this act of intuition, the presented object in this relation need not be actual. Indeed, as long as the object is aimed at in any cognitive (judging, evaluating) or emotive (desiring, hating and so forth) mental act, it is of no consequence if the object of any such intentional experiences exists only in the context of these mental acts (Grossman 140–1). In short, the concept of intentionality focuses attention upon consciousness as a relational act rather than a faculty (Sinha 45). The act which 'intends' and the object which is 'intended' are therefore correlates of one another, emphasizing that phenomenological reflection's main concern is with the intentional consciousness' various and different modes of referentiality ('Phenomenology' 123–4; Sinha 44–7). (See *phenomenological criticism, *reference/referent, *subject/object.)

Although used by Jeremy Bentham in the ordinary non-philosophical sense of 'done purposely' or 'deliberately' (Schmitt 144), the first specialized usage of intentionality must be traced back to the medieval scholastics. According to R.D. Chisholm, for these thinkers intentionality has to do with the nature and status of objects in thought which have no correlates in the actual world known through sensory perception. Such an object, since it can clearly be the object of an intentional act (such as believing, desiring, loving) as much as any object which has a correlate in the 'real' world, cannot simply be dismissed as meaningless. On the other hand, such a non-existent object must have a mode of being which differentiates it from those objects of intentional acts which do have such correlates. The aim of positing this particular mode of being ('intentional inexistence' or 'immanent objectivity') for objects which exist strictly in the context of mental acts, as does the object in the sentence 'I am thinking about a dragon,' is primarily ontological. If the properties of an intentional object match up with an actual object, then the mind can be said to have correctly seen and described the truth of this object (201).

Intention/intentionality were first introduced in terms of consciousness by Husserl's teacher, the Austrian philosopher Franz Brentano, one of the founders of the science of psychology, in his book *Psychology from the Empirical Standpoint* (1874). In desiring a purely descriptive psychology, proceeding without any prior assumptions or established hypotheses, Brentano refined the concept of intentionality to the point where it became the hallmark of all mental phenomena and psychological processes, where these phenomena and processes have their own intrinsic relational character: all have their own particular reference to some content or direction towards some object (Chisholm 202–3; Brentano 53–8). Intentionality, Brentano further argues, is that which separates mental from physical phenomena (Chisholm 203). While Husserl takes from Brentano the concept that all mental phenomena are directed and that, in addition, they all have a peculiar and intrinsic reference character, for Husserl the phenomenological appropriation and reworking of this term empties it of its psychological-empirical orientation. For Husserl, the placing of this term within a phenomenological methodology transforms what was a way of describing particular psychological processes into a way of identifying and investigating the essential, universal structures of human consciousness, structures upon which an absolutely sure foundation for human knowledge could be established (Sinha 44–6). In this way, the referential nature of consciousness is more than the statement of the simple psychological fact that all thoughts have their objects; it has for Husserl an important and largely epistemological aim, since it is this 'kind' of consciousness which allows us to reflect upon our own mental acts and arrive at an unprejudiced description of their essence. As Grossman notes, while Brentano and many of his students had problems with the inclusion of non-existent objects with existent ones as things which can be the objects of intentional acts, Husserl adopts the scholastic view, with some refinements, to the point where such inclusion becomes one of the hallmarks of phenomenological intentionality and a fundamental principle of his definition of the relations between subject and object (49–50, 140–1).

While all phenomenologists and existentialists accept, in some form, the thesis of intentionality, these schools disagree within and among themselves about intentionality's scope and aim. In the works of both *Martin Heidegger and *Maurice Merleau-Ponty the notions of consciousness and intentionality are altered and enlarged. Heidegger's conception of intentionality is particularly influential in that he expands intentionality so that it no longer applies simply and solely to consciousness, to the mental world of humans, but to the *Dasein*, the whole physical as well as mental reality of human beings in the world. Heidegger avoids the mind-body dualism which many critics feel is always a latent feature in Husserl's formulation of intentionality: 'Because the usual separation between a subject with its immanent sphere and an object with its transcendent sphere – because, in general, the distinction between an inner and an outer is constructive and continually gives occasion for further constructions, we shall in future no longer speak of a subject, of a subjective sphere, but shall understand the being to whom intentional comportments belong as *Dasein*' (64). Indeed, intentionality is 'one of the *Dasein's* basic constitutions' (64). For Heidegger, common psychological and philosophical definitions of the intentional subject are 'utterly deficient' since the definition of the subject frequently precedes attempts to define intentionality which is 'the essential ... structure of the subject itself' (65). Intentionality, for Heidegger, is not only the fundamental characteristic relatedness of human being to the world (what he calls *Dasein*); it is also that feature which distinguishes between being and human being, or *Existenz*.

Only a human being can be intentionally related to the world: 'A distinguishing feature between the existent and the extant is found precisely in intentionality ... A window, a chair, in general anything in the broadest sense, does not exist, because it cannot comport toward extant entities in the manner of intentional self-directedness-toward-them' (64). The crucial nature of intentionality as characterizing the entire *Dasein* (being-in-the-world) and not just human consciousness (as in Husserl) is indicated by Heidegger's claim that 'the constitution of the *Dasein's* comportments is precisely the ontological condition of the possibility of every and any transcendence' (65).

The *Geneva School's definition of the literary *text itself and its relationship both to the author and the reader/critic reflects the strong links with Husserlian intentionality. Critics such as *Georges Poulet, Marcel Raymond and Jean-Pierre Richard, as well as later American critics like Paul Brodtkorb and the early *J. Hillis Miller, generally agree that the meaning of a literary text hinges upon the Husserlian thesis that the relationship between subject and object is characterized by its mutual referentiality. Just as Husserl asserted the mutual referentiality of subject and object, just as Merleau-Ponty asserted their analytic inseparability (Magliola 13), so phenomenological theory offers the possibility of erasing the dichotomy between subject and object, of eliminating the necessity of choosing a locus of meaning which is either exclusively within the text or outside of it. Phenomenological literary theory posits the text as an author's imaginative transformation of his or her own personal lifeworld (ibid. 28). As such, it is often said to display a unique phenomenological ego or consciousness. This 'fictive universe' not only contains representations of various intentional acts, but it and all these intentional acts are also dominated and organized by the intentional act of imagining, frequently the privileged intentional act in terms of phenomenological criticism (ibid. 36). The author's *Lebenswelt* and its unique 'network' (28) of subject-object relations become embodied in the literary text in two ways; those intentional acts which are largely cognitive (thinking, remembering, reasoning) are embodied 'in the conceptual layer of language,' while 'nonconceptual modes are embodied' through the use of symbols (36). In the theory of the symbol, 'experience embodied in poetic language somehow represents all the modes of consciousness,' that is, all intentional acts whether emotive or rational (37). In addition, 'the expressions of the nonconceptual modes receive their fundamental embodiment in rhyme, rhythm and other phonemic values; in figurative language and all stylistic traits; and in the whole range of the connotative' (37). The description of the author's consciousness and the discovery of his or her intention vis-à-vis the text is not, however, the goal of phenomenological literary criticism. Critics of this school are careful to make the distinction between the author's ' "actual ego" which is inaccessible' to the reader/critic and his or her 'phenomenological ego,' which is 'immanent in the work' itself or, as some critics put it, between the 'author's empirical ego' and the 'text's phenomenological ego' (67). Even so, critics of phenomenological literary criticism point out that this distinction does not alter the fact that there are aspects of the author's consciousness which are reflected in the literary text. As Magliola argues, 'the patterns of experience sublatent in the former "pass over" into the latter. In this sense the author's "deep self" remains the *fons et origo* of his or her literature' (67).

The thesis of intentionality in terms of phenomenological literary criticism and later reader-response theory raises important questions concerning the process of interpretation, particularly concerning the status of reading as intentional act and text as intentional object. (See *reader-response criticism.) For Georges Poulet, the influential Belgian critic, reading is an experience of 'interiority' where the boundaries between subject and object are dissolved and where subject and object are shown to exist in a dynamic and 'continuous field of experience' (Con Davis 346). Poulet, however, in asserting that 'reading is the act in which the subjective principle, which I call I, is modified in such a way that I no longer have the right, strictly speaking, to consider it as my I. I am on loan to another, and this other feels, suffers and acts within me' (354), also distinguishes between the intentional acts of reading and critiquing. While aiming at the same experience of 'giving way ... to a host of alien words' and 'to the very alien principle which utters and shelters them' (352), the critic nevertheless does not entirely disappear into the mind of the text.

MARIE H. LOUGHLIN

Primary Sources

Brentano, Franz. 'The Distinction Between Mental and Physical Phenomena.' In *Realism and the Background of Phenomenology*. Ed. Roderick M. Chisholm. Glencoe, Ill.: Free P, 1960, 39–61.

Chisholm, Roderick M. 'Intentionality.' In *The Encyclopedia of Philosophy*. Vol. 4. Ed. Paul Edwards. New York: Macmillan, 1967, 201–4.

Con Davis, Robert. 'The Affective Response.' In *Contemporary Literary Criticism: Modernism Through Post-Structuralism*. Ed. Robert Con Davis. New York: Longman, 1986, 345–9.

Grossman, Reinhardt. *Phenomenology and Existentialism: An Introduction*. London: Routledge, 1984.

Heidegger, Martin. *The Basic Problems of Phenomenology*. Trans., intro. and lexicon, Albert Hofstadter. Bloomington: Indiana UP, 1982.

Husserl, Edmund. 'Phenomenology.' In *Deconstruction in Context: Literature and Philosophy*. Ed. Mark C. Taylor. Chicago: U of Chicago P, 1986, 121–40.

Iser, Wolfgang. 'The Reading Process: A Phenomenological Approach.' In *Contemporary Literary Criticism: Modernism Through Post-Structuralism*. Ed. Robert Con Davis. New York: Longman, 1986, 376–91.

Magliola, Robert. *Phenomenology and Literature: An Introduction*. West Lafayette, Ind.: Purdue UP, 1977.

Poulet, Georges. 'Phenomenology of Reading.' In *Contemporary Literary Criticism: Modernism Through Post-Structuralism*. Ed. Robert Con Davis. New York: Longman, 1986, 350–62.

Schmitt, Richard. 'Phenomenology.' In *The Encyclopedia of Philosophy*. Vol. 6. Ed. Paul Edwards. New York: Macmillan, 1967, 135–51.

Sinha, Debabrata. *Phenomenology and Existentialism: An Introduction*. Calcutta: Free P, 1974.

Interpellation

Interpellation, or hailing, is associated with the thought of French Marxist philosopher *Louis Althusser, who employs it as part of his theory of *ideology in order to explain how ideology constitutes and 'centres' subjects in the social world. (See *centre/decentre.) Originally a legislative term in France describing an interruption of the order of the day that demands from a minister explanation of a matter pertaining to his department, interpellation appears to have entered the discourse of literary theory with the account of *myth provided by French semiotician *Roland Barthes in *Mythologies* (1957). (See *semiotics.) As Barthes describes it, myth is characterized by its 'interpellant speech' (*parole interpellative*), that is, by the way in which it addresses itself directly to the subject in order to appear both natural and devoid of history. (See also *subject/object.)

In '*Ideology and Ideological State Apparatuses' (1969), Althusser develops the term in order to demonstrate how ideology is not simply an illusion or false consciousness masking the 'real' nature of society but is instead a material system of social practices (what he calls 'ideological apparatuses') producing certain effects upon individuals and providing them with their social identities. Ideology 'naturalizes' or 'makes obvious' the ways in which people live their lives in society; it is 'a representation of the imaginary relationship of individuals to their real conditions of existence' (152–3).

Interpellation functions in this theory as the ongoing process by which subjects are constituted in ideology. In order to describe this process, Althusser employs insights into the construction of the subject provided by French psychoanalyst *Jacques Lacan. Lacan describes how the infant ego is constituted by the child's identification with or misrecognition (*méconnaissance*) of his own mirror image, which provides him with an imaginary picture of his own autonomy and self-presence. (See *mirror stage, *psychoanalytic theory.) Althusser suggests that such recognition and misrecognition work as well in the social world at the level of the ideological; the human subject is given back, through ideology, an imaginary construction of his own autonomy, unity and self-presence. He argues that ideology 'recruits' individuals and transforms them, through the 'ideological recognition function,' into subjects. This recognition function is the process of interpellation: ideology 'interpellates' or 'hails' individuals, that is, addresses itself directly to them. Althusser gives as his example a policeman hailing an individual by calling, 'Hey, you there!' The hailed individual will turn around, recognize himself as the one who was hailed, and in the process become constituted as a subject. All hailed individuals, recognizing or misrecognizing themselves in the address, are transformed into subjects conceiving of themselves as free and autonomous members of a society that has in fact constructed them.

Although Althusser argues that the structure and functioning of ideology is always the same, the practices which he includes as performing ideological roles have varied with the development of his theories. Prior to his introduction of the concepts of interpellation and ideological state apparatuses, Althusser emphatically stated, '*I do not rank real art among the ideologies.*' Without defining what he meant by 'authentic art,' he specified that certain works of *literature achieve an '*internal distantiation* from ... the very ideology in which they are held.' Whereas 'art makes us *see*' ideology, it needs to be supplemented by science which alone can produce the same object 'in the form of *knowledge*' ('Ideology' 223). This privileging of art derives partly from the literary criticism of *Pierre Macherey. Althusser formulates as a goal for criticism the need 'to produce an adequate (scientific) *knowledge* of the processes which produce the "aesthetic effect" of a work of art.' Macherey is the first to attempt to enact this formula in his *Pour une théorie de la production littéraire* [*A Theory of Literary Production* 1966; trans. 1978]. Althusser's essay on the ideological state apparatuses incorporates his rethinking of the categories of both art and science and places art and literature within 'the cultural ISA.' Subsequently, in collaborative work on literature and society, Macherey and Etienne Balibar denote literature to a position among the ideological apparatuses that constitute subjects. Literature functions as a material practice that interpellates individual readers, furnishing them with an image of their place as subjects in the social world. The absorption of Althusser's and Macherey's work within English literary theory, beginning with Terry Eagleton's *Criticism and Ideology* (1976), has been marked by the hope of endowing literary criticism with a scientific status through the analysis of what literature does with ideology, and by an ambivalence about the position of literature within the *social formation. (See also *Eagleton, *materialist criticism.)

ROSS KING

Primary Sources

Althusser, Louis. 'Ideology and Ideological State Apparatuses (Notes Towards an Investigation).' In *Lenin and Philosophy and Other Essays*. Trans. Ben Brewster. London: New Left Books, 1977, 127–86.
– 'A Letter on Art in Reply to André Daspré (April 1966).' In *Lenin and Philosophy and Other Essays*, 221–7.
Balibar, Etienne, and Pierre Macherey. 'On Literature

as an Ideological Form.' In *Untying the Text: A Post-Structuralist Reader*. Ed. Robert Young. London: Routledge and Kegan Paul, 1981, 79–99.

Barthes, Roland. *Mythologies*. Trans. Annette Lavers. London: Grafton, 1973.

Eagleton, Terry. *Criticism and Ideology*. London: New Left Books, 1976.

Lacan, Jacques. *Ecrits: A Selection*. Trans. Alan Sheridan. New York: W.W. Norton and Co., 1977.

Macherey, Pierre. *A Theory of Literary Production*. 1966. London: Routledge and Kegan Paul, 1978.

Intersubjectivity

Intersubjectivity is a key term in phenomenological *hermeneutics that designates the interaction of communication between subjects. The impasse of Romantic hermeneutics which reached its climax in the works of *Wilhelm Dilthey is the impossibility of accounting for how one subject can know another if all means of knowing must proceed from the knowing subject to others in a dualistic paradigm of *subject/object. The breakthrough came with *Martin Heidegger's concept of Being-in-the-world. Before the subject can know anything, it already belongs to the world whose being is language.

Intersubjectivity therefore is the escape from the confines of subjectivism through language to a process of communicative interaction. The more one attempts to explain one's experience the more will the speaker or writer move away from subjectivity and into intersubjectivity. The source aim of explaining to another is to draw on the common ground of language in such a way that experience can become shared meaning. *Hans-Georg Gadamer's *Truth and Method* (1960) and *Paul Ricoeur's *Hermeneutics and the Human Sciences* (1981) provide fundamental treatments of intersubjectivity. (See also *phenomenological criticism.)

MARIO J. VALDÉS

Primary Sources

Gadamer, Hans-Georg. *Truth and Method*. Trans. Garret Barden and William G. Doerpel. New York: Seabury, 1975.

Ricoeur, Paul. *Hermeneutics and the Human Sciences*. Ed. and trans. John B. Thompson. Cambridge: Cambridge UP, 1981.

Intertextuality

Although *intertexo*, to intermingle while weaving, was used in both proper and figurative senses in Latin, 'intertextuality' (*intertextualité*) is a recent creation of *Julia Kristeva to elaborate a theory of the *text as a network of sign systems situated in relation to other systems of signifying practices (ideologically marked sign usage) in a culture. By 'situ[ating] the literary structure within a social ensemble considered as a textual ensemble' ('Problèmes' 61) intertextuality would overcome the limitations of formalism and *structuralism by orienting the text to its sociohistoric signification in the interaction of the different codes, discourses or voices traversing the text. In short, a text is not a self-sufficient, closed system. (See *sign, *semiotics, *code, *discourse, *signifying practice.)

Kristeva introduced intertextuality as a 'permutation of texts' ('Pour un sémiologie des paragrammes') within the semiotic project of textual stratification and typology to specify different textual arrangements within historical and social texts. The point of intersection of semiotic practices and utterances is the 'ideologeme,' 'the intertextual function read as "materialized" at the different structural levels of each text.' ('The Bounded Text' 36). (See *ideologeme.) Borrowed from members of the Bakhtin circle, ideologeme describes sign production ('social intercourse' or 'semiotic interaction') in a specific social reality as the 'materialized ideological horizon' (*The Formal Method in Literary Scholarship*). (See *ideological horizon, *materialist criticism.) In developing interaction into intertextuality, Kristeva significantly changed *Mikhail Bahktin's theory of dialogism (*Problems of Dostoevsky's Poetics*), which focused on the utterance rather than on the text as dynamic milieu of interchange among diverse social speech genres, a concept also conveyed by his terms '*polyphony,' 'double-voiced word,' '*heteroglossia,' and the carnivalesque. While intertextuality developed from Marxist critiques of Russian formalism's theories of literariness as *defamiliarization (making strange) that neglected diachrony (historical change), in France intertextuality was divorced from the co-term ideologeme, dehistoricized, and came to function synchronically alongside universals such as text and society. (See Russian *formalism, *carnival, *double-voicing/dialogism, *universal.)

For Kristeva, intertextuality was first associated with the 'ideologeme of the sign' which, though an advance over the medieval 'ideologeme of the symbol,' she rejected for its *closure. Between 1966 and 1974 intertextuality was an important concept through which she theorized the text as negativity in a 'redistributive' relationship to the bound structures of novel and sign. Her analysis of the intersection of the subject, signifier and cultural practice in the text focuses on the formulation of the logical rules for the transformations that the producing text makes in its intertext, those of 'opposition,' 'permutation' and 'indefinite transformations' (*La Révolution*). Kristeva is concerned with text generation, with genetics, as suggested in the related concepts 'genotext' (signifiers and speaking subject, dislocating tissue of language) and 'phenotext' (grammatical and semantic surface, residue or trace of this psychic and historical activity). Subsequently, she concentrated on the concept of the self as an intertextual site. (See *subject/object, *genotext/phenotext, *signified/signifier/signification, *self/other.)

Intertextuality functioned as a slogan indicating a certain position taken in the critical debate in France by the Tel Quel group in their critique of structuralism through combination and extension of the work of *Ferdinand de Saussure, Karl Marx and *Sigmund Freud: the challenge to the referent, the death of the author, the death of the subject. (See *reference/referent.) Textual analysis would no longer be concerned with meaning, with the relation of language to a referent, but with signification, the relation of signs and texts in *semiosis (sign interaction) to other signs. The 'fetishism' of meaning was thought, in Marxist terms, to have obscured the *trace of the use value and the work of textual production. Kristeva's concept of text as 'productivity' ('Problèmes de la structuration du texte') was equated with intertextuality as the 'junction of several texts of which it is simultaneously the rereading, accentuation, condensation, displacement and depth' (Sollers 75). Translinguistic 'productivity' as dialectical decentring developed such explanatory force that for *Roland Barthes 'the concept of intertext is what brings to the theory of text the volume of its social dimension: not according to the path of an identifiable filiation, of a voluntary imita-

tion, but according to that of dissemination' ('Texte' 1015). Intertextuality is the untying of the text, the infinite play of semiosis, which effects a 'revolution in poetic language' (Kristeva, *La Révolution)* against the closure of the signifier in representational discourse. While all texts are potentially heterogeneous, the transgressive force of such shattering of symbolic unity is realized only in specific historico-social conjunctures. (See *centre/decentre.)

The term 'intertextuality' migrated quickly in French circles in the 1970s, acquiring conflictual definitions, including the inaccurate, 'banal sense of "study of sources"' (Kristeva, *La Révolution* 59–60). Contradiction is implicit in the concept: the theory of intertextuality is unable to recognize intertextuality: the illimitable can only be known through a missing phenomenon that is measurable (Culler 1382). Consequently, the term developed in divergent contexts, in some emphasizing the disruptive force of pure *textuality as illimitable intertextual transformation, in others seeking to classify the processes of production/reception in the text whereby the rule breaking can be known.

Exponents of 'general' intertextuality, unlimited semiosis or 'dissemination,' follow *Jacques Derrida who proclaims, 'there is no outside text' ('Grammatology' 158). Intertextuality is associated with a concept of the text as 'hyphology' or spider's weaving (Barthes, *Pleasure* 101), a conceptual heterogeneity that violates logical rules of non-contradiction. *Deconstruction is a theory of the necessary intertextuality of all discourse since each text or utterance is an interweaving or 'textile of signifiers' whose signifieds are by definition intertextually determined by other discourses (*Positions*).

Most scholars who use the term have developed a 'restricted' intertextuality which focuses on the relations between several texts. Ironically, this may involve little more than the philological tradition of influence tracing which the term sought to displace. In others, this develops within a frame of a semiotics of non-linear text production, rejecting evolutionary theories of history for a triadic relation among signs that function semiotically. *Umberto Eco considers intertextuality a mode of 'over-coding' (*A Theory of Semiotics*) that sets up frames for relating texts to other similar texts. The related concept 'presupposition' is, however, termed 'extra-coding.' *Michael Riffaterre develops this approach to text production/reception opposed to both deconstruction and historicism by treating the relationship of text to intertext as parallel to that of sign to interpretant in *Charles S. Peirce's theory of semiosis, which demands an interrelational reading. Riffaterre makes a distinction between 'intertext' (the totality of texts that may be related to the text being considered) and 'intertextuality' (the reader's perception of significance, that is of the literariness of the text). Riffaterre's concept combines a semiotic transformation and the inference a reader draws from it when, reading and rereading to locate discrete units in a system, she or he discovers ungrammaticalities (deviations not accountable in the rules of ordinary language), the 'hypogram' or 'matrix' (the hypothetical structure) of a hidden intertext. (See *hypogram.) Riffaterre's formulation of the *problematic addresses the *paradox of intertextuality, that it is only operative in the indissoluble union of 'rule and rule-breaking' ('The Interpretant in Literary Semiotics' 43), but posits undecidability as a passing stage in the reader's progress to interpretation ('Interpretation and Undecidability' 238). The activity of production is displaced from text to reader, whose compulsion to repeat is a tropological rather than psychoanalytical drive in response to an enigma or gap – an epistemological process ('Compulsory Reader Response' 77). (See *trope.) This extension of the concept ultimately results in a restriction of its implications, since the relationships so clarified are microstructural, on the order of a word or phrase, an allusion to another literary text – questions of literary stylistics.

Intertextuality is the normal mode of textual production for Riffaterre as it is also for *Gérard Genette, who describes *literature as a 'second degree' construct made out of pieces of other texts and sets out a generic map for reading. He limits the term 'intertextuality' to quotation, plagiarism and allusion – 'intratextuality' involves these relationships within the work of a single writer – then distinguishes these types of 'transtextual' relations from 'architectuality' (interrelations of types of discourse, modes of enunciation, literary genres) and 'paratextuality' (relations between a literary text and its social text through its title, prefaces, cover, illustrations). (See *énonciation/énoncé.) A fourth type of transtextual relation occurs between 'hypotext' (A) and 'hypertext'

(B) mediated through the third point of a generic model or universal, relations on the order of *parody and pastiche. While the concept of 'palimpsest' is a conceptual advance in terms of the range of textual arrangements it encompasses and the rigour of Genette's taxonomy, through its formalist stance on the classic genus-species model of text production it narrows the interpretive power of the term. It too limits the implications of 'intertextuality' to questions of stylistics and neglects the social (and conflictual) overlapping of texts.

Though his approach to the question is very different, through the hidden libidinal investments of the work of the text, *Harold Bloom develops a theory of influence with a typology of tropes of textual transformation or 'revisionary ratios.' Six types of 'misreading' or 'misprision' map out the possibilities of 'intrapoetic relationships.' The metaphor of 'family romance' makes clear that, in taking up the issues of intentionality and psychologism shunned by other theorists of textual relations, Bloom has reaffirmed, rather than critiqued, the evolutionary model of literary history challenged by the view of literature as a synchronic system of signs. Author/work/tradition are the operative terms in Bloom's theory of textual relations, not text/discourse/culture. (See also *misprison, *anxiety of influence, *intention/intentionality, *metonymy/metaphor.)

German theorists working with the French concept of intertextuality have critiqued its emphasis on textuality by foregrounding Bakhtin's dialogism as a materialist theory of the utterance. They stress the instance of enunciation, especially the activity of reading or interpretation, the *concretization of the play of allusion, parody or motif. Linked to semiotics either through pragmatics (Schmid 141) or through C.S. Peirce's 'interpretant' as *signifiance* (Stemple 89), intertextuality is located in the process of the reader's actualization of the text, the intertextual relation understood as a hermeneutic relation, 'the moment of the identity of texts' (Stierle 23, 16). It is not only to be studied as a *Produktionsästhetische* as Kristeva suggests, but must also be elaborated as a *Rezeptionsästhetische* (Stierle 9) within a theory of communication. Critiquing the supposed materialism of Kristeva's theory of the subjectless text and its claims to decentre the identity of the work, Stierle reframes the question of textuality in terms of identity and *intersubjectivity. (See *communication theory.)

The work of the *Tartu School, especially of *Iurii Lotman in developing a semiotics of culture and theorizing the hierarchization of different levels of structuration that make a 'text,' are different developments of the synchronic view of textual relations. Lotman's concept of 'extratextual' is connected to the conditions of readability of a culture, in the relations of 'the ensemble of fixed elements in the text to the ensemble of elements from which the choice was made' (*The Structure of the Artistic Text* 89–90). 'Parody' and hidden polemic are considered under the term extratextual, which is thus linked to Bakhtin's 'dialogism.'

The term 'intertextuality' is surprisingly absent in the work of a number of theorists of social discourse working on overlapping issues, notes Marc Angenot. Linking 'intertextuality' (circulation and transformation of ideologemes) with 'interdiscursivity' (interaction of contiguous axioms under a *hegemony), he aims to reorient the analysis of textual interrelations toward the location of rules or tendencies defining a particular historical configuration in a social discourse ('Intertextualité, Interdiscursivité, Discours social' 107). Texts are heterogeneous fragments cut from the social discourse which is the juxtaposition within a field of languages marked by a given hegemony. Intertextuality is extended here to multidisciplinary interdiscursivity. With the increasing importance of textual analysis in many disciplines, intertextuality is being associated through the interconnection of historicity and systematicity with the actualization in oral performance of textual structures (Zumthor), the complexities of ethnographic text construction in anthropology (Tyler), the reception of music (Karbusicky), the theorization of heterogeneous art forms such as the illustrated book (Hansen-Löve) or film (Reader) and the transferential relation in psychoanalysis (Hand). (See also *discourse analysis theory.)

Intertextuality is currently used less frequently and more critically, the concept of textuality having in many cases been abandoned for that of discourse (in the Foucauldian sense of an ontologically impure mix of textual structures, practices, institutional sites, and rules of application). (See also *Michel Foucault, *hermeneutics, *metacriticism.)

BARBARA GODARD

Primary Sources

Angenot, Marc. 'Intertextualité, Interdiscursivité, Discours social.' *Texte* 2 (1983): 101–12.

Bakhtin, M.M. *Problems of Dostoevsky's Poetics.* 1929. Trans. Caryl Emerson. Minneapolis: U of Minnesota P, 1984.

– and Pavel M. Medvedev. *The Formal Method in Literary Scholarship.* 1928. Trans. Albert J. Wehrle. Cambridge: Harvard UP, 1983.

Barthes, Roland. *The Pleasure of the Text.* 1973. Trans. Richard Miller. New York: Hill and Wang, 1975.

– 'Texte (théorie du).' *Encyclopedia Universalis.* Vol. 15. Paris: Encyclopaedia Universalis, 1973, 1013–17. 'Theory of the Text.' Trans. Ian Macleod. *Untying the Text.* Ed. Robert Young. Boston/London: Routledge, 1981, 31–47.

Bloom, Harold. *The Anxiety of Influence.* New York: Oxford UP, 1973.

Clayton, Jay, and Eric Rothstein, eds. *Influence and Intertextuality in Literary History.* Madison: Wisconsin UP, 1991.

Culler, Jonathan. 'Presupposition and Intertextuality.' *Modern Language Notes* 91.6 (1976): 1380–97.

Derrida, Jacques. *Of Grammatology.* 1967. Trans. Gayatri Chakravorty Spivak. Baltimore: Johns Hopkins UP, 1976.

– *Positions.* 1972. Trans. Alan Bass. Chicago: U of Chicago P, 1981.

Eco, Umberto. *A Theory of Semiotics.* Bloomington: Indiana UP, 1976.

Genette, Gérard. *Palimpsestes: La Littérature au second degré.* Paris: Seuil, 1982.

Groupe Mu, ed. *Revue d'esthétique* 3/4 (1978).

Hand, Sean. 'Missing You: Intertextuality, Transference and the Language of Love.' In Worton and Still, 79–91.

Hansen-Löve, Aage A. 'Intermedialität und Intertextualität: Probleme der Korrelation von Wort-und-Bildkunst-Am Beispiel der russischen Moderne.' In *Dialog der Texte: Hamburger Kolloquium zur Intertextualität.* Ed. Wolf Schmid and Wolf-Dieter Stempel. Sonderband 11. Vienna: Wiener Slawistischer Almanach, 1983, 291–360.

Karbusicky, Vladimir. 'Intertextualität in der Musik Hinweise zu den Autoren.' In *Dialog der Texte: Hamburger Kolloquium zur Intertextualität.* Ed. Wolf Schmid and Wolf-Dieter Stempel. Sonderband 11. Vienna: Wiener Slawistischer Almanach, 1983, 361–98.

Kristeva, Julia. 'The Bounded Text.' In *Desire In Language: A Semiotic Approach to Literature and Art.* Trans. Thomas Gora, Alice Jardine and Leon S. Roudiez. New York: Columbia UP, 1980, 36–63.

– 'Pour une sémiologie des paragrammes.' *Tel Quel* 29 (printemps 1967): 53–75.

– 'Problèmes de la structuration du texte.' *La Nouvelle Critique.* Special issue. 'Actes du Colloque de Cluny, 16–17 avril 1968' (1968): 55–64.

- 'La Productivité dite texte.' *Communications* 11 (1968): 59–83.
- *La Révolution du langage poétique.* Paris: Seuil, 1974. *Revolution in Poetic Language.* Trans. Margaret Waller. Abr. New York: Columbia UP, 1984.

Jenny, Laurent, ed. *Poétiques* 27 (1976).

Lotman, Juri. *The Structure of the Artistic Text.* 1971. Trans. Donald B. Johnson. Ann Arbor: Ardis, 1977.

Morgan, Thaïs, ed. *American Journal of Semiotics* 3.4 (1985).

Oliver, Andrew, ed. *Texte* 2 (1983).

Reader, Keith A. 'Literature/Cinema/Television: Intertextuality in Jean Renoir's *Le Testament du docteur Cordelier.*' In Worton and Still, 176–89.

Riffaterre, Michael. 'Compulsory Reader Response: The Intertextual Drive.' In Worton and Still, 56–78.

- 'The Interpretant in Literary Semiotics.' *American Journal of Semiotics* 3.4 (1985): 41–55.
- 'Interpretation and Undecidability.' *New Literary History* 12.2 (1981): 227–41.

Schmid, Wolf. 'Sinnpotentiale der diegetischen Allusion: Aleksandr Puškins Posthalternovelle und ihre Prätexte.' In *Dialog der Texte: Hamburger Kolloquium zur Intertextualität.* Ed. Wolf Schmid and Wolf-Dieter Stempel. Sonderband 11. Vienna: Wiener Slawistischer Almanach, 1983, 141–88.

Sollers, Philippe, et al. [Tel Quel.] *Théorie d'Ensemble.* Paris: Seuil, 1968.

Stempel, Wolf-Dieter. 'Intertextualität und Rezeption.' In *Dialog der Texte: Hamburger Kolloquium zur Intertextualität.* Ed. Wolf Schmid and Wolf-Dieter Stempel. Sonderband 11. Vienna: Wiener Slawistischer Almanach, 1983, 85–110.

Stierle, Karlheinz. 'Werk und Intertextualität.' In *Dialog der Texte: Hamburger Kolloquium zur Intertextualität.* Ed. Wolf Schmid and Wolf-Dieter Stempel. Sonderband 11. Vienna: Wiener Slawistischer Almanach, 1983, 7–26.

Tyler, Stephen A. '"Ethnography" Intertextuality and the End of Description.' *American Journal of Semiotics* 3.4 (1985): 83–98.

Worton, Michael, and Judith Still, eds. *Intertextuality: Theories and Practices.* Manchester: Manchester UP, 1990.

Zumthor, Paul. 'Intertextualité et mouvance.' *Littérature* 41 (février 1981): 8–16.

La Nouvelle Critique. No. spéciale (1968).

Irony

The critical history of 'irony' invites a broad distinction between two uses of the term. In its first sense, dominant till the end of the 18th century, the term refers to a rhetorical or verbal mode – the dissimulation of ignorance (Gr. *eironeia*) by one who says other or less than he means *(eiron)* – as exemplified by Socrates in the *Dialogues.* Classical rhetoricians defined irony as a figure and a *trope; medieval theorists did likewise, though, typically, as a subcategory of *allegoria:* 'Allegory is other-speech. One thing is spoken, another is meant' (Isidore of Seville, *Etymologiae).* Samuel Johnson's single definition (with the illustration 'Bolingbroke was a holy man') conforms with traditional usage in limiting 'irony' to 'a mode of speech in which the meaning is contrary to the words.' Irony so defined and practised is inherently corrective and unambiguous, normative and referential: spoken statements are dominated by intended meanings, falsehoods by truths, surface appearances by underlying realities. As recent commentators have emphasized, the 'dyadic *écart*' basic to verbal irony 'was only possible in the stable order of representation that characterizes the classical episteme' (Kuzniar 144). (See *episteme.) *Wayne C. Booth's *A Rhetoric of Irony* (1974) argues for a return to the 'stable irony' enabled by that order.

Use of the term irony in its second, and much more complex, sense, was introduced by German romantic theorists in the late 18th and early 19th centuries. Friedrich Schlegel's redefinition is pivotal: irony is 'the recognition of the fact that the world in its essence is paradoxical and that an ambivalent attitude alone can grasp its contradictory totality' (Wellek 14). (See *paradox.) Irony so conceived, explains Schlegel, is by nature non-corrective in the sense that, like Socratic wisdom, it is self-regarding and endless: 'No things are more unlike than satire, polemic, and irony. Irony in the new sense is self-criticism [*Selbstpolemik*] surmounted; it is never-ending satire' (64). Non-normative and ethically indeterminate by virtue of the self-reflexiveness and synthetic balancing that it enjoins, this new, 'situational' irony (Muecke 42) confers the freedom of a divine authority. 'Supreme Irony,' Karl Wilhelm Solger can agree with his opponent Schlegel, 'reigns in the conduct of God as he creates men and the life of men. In earthly art Irony has this meaning – conduct similar to God's' (cited from Sedgwick 17). For Georg Wilhelm Friedrich Hegel, irony in the Schlegelian sense seems indistinguishable from nihilizing subjective play, while *Søren Kierkegaard sees in the whole of romantic irony an abbreviation of reality to the self-consciousness of the altogether bored human artist. The romantic notion of the artist as divine amoralist and ironic creator has had wide play in modern literary culture, thanks in some measure to the place it occupies in the writings of such figures as Thomas Mann and André Gide, whose irony strives 'to make us at home in indecision' (Burke 104). The ironies that 20th-century scholarship has identified as irony 'of Fate,' 'of events,' 'of Nature,' 'pure irony,' 'cosmic irony,' and 'metaphysical irony' represent, in effect, overlapping extensions or subcategories of the situational irony initially defined by German romanticism. 'Dramatic irony,' a term coined in the 19th century, continues to test the wit of ironologists, since it refers to an irony (as in Sophoclean tragedy) that is at once situational and verbal (see Muecke 104–7; Tittler 38–9).

Irony's full arrival as a modern critical term coincides with the ascendancy of a *New Criticism disposed to privilege situational over verbal irony. Essential to the best poetry, according to *I.A. Richards in 1924, irony is 'the bringing in of ... opposites' in such a way as to achieve a 'balanced poise' (250). Robert Penn Warren's 'Pure and Impure Poetry' (1942) offers to refine Richards' proposition by replacing 'opposites' with the more inclusive 'tensions.' The New Critical sense of irony is further expanded in *Cleanth Brooks' The Well Wrought Urn (1947): not only is 'irony our most general term for indicating that recognition of incongruities – which ... pervades all poetry,' it is also 'the most general term that we have for the kind of qualification which the various elements in a context receive from the context' (209–10). It follows from Brooks' use of the term that no *discourse can be unironical.

Poststructuralist thought tacitly follows the New Critical tendency to value situational at the expense of verbal irony. (See *poststructuralism.) When in his 'The Rhetoric of Temporality' (1969), for example, *Paul de Man dismisses irony, he refers solely to 'the rhetorical mode' (222). In his Metahistory (1973), *Hayden White can affirm the concept of irony that he adapts from *Northrop Frye, but only as 'a mode of thought which is radically self-critical' (37). More often, perhaps because of irony's association with New Criticism, the poststructuralist response to the term has been virtual silence. Though *Jacques Derrida has been read as a master of that irony which consists in 'the power to entertain widely diver-

gent possible interpretations' (O'Hara 362), he rarely uses the term irony, and only in passing. And *J. Hillis Miller, in his discussion of 'undecidability' anthologized in Deconstruction and Criticism (1979), can repeatedly refer to irony without 'explicitly' pronouncing 'the word' (Tittler 44 n6). As Joseph A. Dane observes, 'irony, however defined, suggests an authority' – even if limited to that of the romantic artist's successor, 'the postromantic critic' (11).

CAMILLE R. LA BOSSIÈRE

Primary Sources

Allemann, B. 'Ironie als literarisches Prinzip.' In Ironie und Dichtung. Ed. A. Schaefer. Munich: Beck, 1970, 11–37.

Bloom, Harold, et al. Deconstruction and Criticism. New York: Seabury, 1979.

Booth, Wayne C. A Rhetoric of Irony. Chicago: U of Chicago P, 1974.

Brooks, Cleanth. The Well Wrought Urn: Studies in the Structure of Poetry. New York: Harcourt, Brace, 1947.

Burke, Kenneth. Counter Statement. 2nd ed. Berkeley: U of California P, 1953.

Dane, Joseph A. The Critical Mythology of Irony. Athens: U of Georgia P, 1991.

de Man, Paul. 'The Rhetoric of Temporality.' 1969. Repr. in his Blindness and Insight: Essays in the Rhetoric of Contemporary Criticism. 2nd ed., rev. Minneapolis: U of Minnesota P, 1983, 187–228.

Dyson, A.E. The Crazy Fabric: Essays in Irony. London: Macmillan, 1965.

Handwerk, Gary. Irony and Ethics in Narrative: From Schlegel to Lacan. New Haven: Yale UP, 1985.

Jankélévitch, Vladimir. L'Ironie. 1936. Paris: Flammarion, 1964.

Kierkegaard, Søren. The Concept of Irony with Constant Reference to Socrates. 1841. Trans. Lee M. Capel. Bloomington: Indiana UP, 1965.

Knox, Norman. The Word 'Irony' and Its Context (1500–1755). Durham: Duke UP, 1961.

Kuzniar, Alice A. Review of Marike Finlay, The Romantic Irony of Semiotics. Canadian Review of Comparative Literature 17 (1990): 144–6.

Merrill, Reed. '"Infinite Absolute Negativity": Irony in Socrates, Kierkegaard and Kafka.' Comparative Literature Studies 16 (1979): 222–36.

Muecke, D.C. The Compass of Irony. London: Methuen and Co., 1969.

O'Hara, Daniel. Review of Jacques Derrida, Of Grammatology. Journal of Aesthetics and Art Criticism 36 (1977): 361–4.

Richards, I.A. Principles of Literary Criticism. 1924. New York: Harcourt, Brace and Co., 1938.

Schlegel, Friedrich. Friedrich Schlegel: Literary Notebooks, 1779–1801. Ed. Hans Eichner. London: Athlone P, 1957.

Sedgwick, G.G. *Of Irony, Especially in Drama.* Toronto: U of Toronto P, 1935.

Thompson, A.R. *The Dry Mock: A Study of Irony in Drama.* Berkeley: U of California P, 1948.

Thomson, J.A.K. *Irony: An Historical Introduction.* Cambridge, Mass.: Harvard UP, 1927.

Tittler, Jonathan. 'Approximately Irony.' *Modern Language Studies* 15 (1985): 32–46.

Warren, Robert Penn. 'Pure and Impure Poetry.' 1942. Repr. in *Criticism: The Foundations of Modern Literary Judgment.* Ed. M. Schorer, J. Miles and G. McKenzie. New York: Harcourt, Brace and Co., 1948, 366–78.

Wellek, René. *A History of Modern Criticism (1750–1950): The Romantic Age.* New Haven: Yale UP, 1955.

White, Hayden. *Metahistory: The Historical Imagination in Nineteenth-Century Europe.* Baltimore: Johns Hopkins UP, 1973.

ISAS: *see* Ideological State Apparatuses

Isotopy

Isotopy is 'a redundant set of semantic categories which make possible the uniform reading of a narrative' (*A.J. Greimas; Greimas and Courtés 1970:188). Isotopy depends on 'the permanence of a hierarchical classematic base' (Greimas 1966:96) which one can find in any given text. (See *classeme.)

Conceived as a principle of coherence and at the same time as an actual set of features found in any *text, the phenomenon of isotopy is fundamental to explaining the fact that a given message is always understood as a whole of meaning and that, in the face of ambiguities, a reader will try to resolve them by adopting an unequivocal point of view. This search is particularly evident in the case of jokes and puns, where 'the mental pleasure resides in the discovery of two different isotopies within a supposedly homogeneous narrative' (Greimas 1966:71).

Such a definition of isotopy is clearly semantic: it applies to content (as opposed to expression) and is linked to the notions of meaning and coherence. There is, however, another definition, proposed by François Rastier who sees isotopy as a larger phenomenon

resulting from 'any iteration of a linguistic unit' (82). Such a definition would authorize many types of isotopies: phonetic, prosodic, stylistic, rhetorical, enunciative, syntactic, and so forth. To avoid confusion, many scholars now add the adjective 'semantic' to the word 'isotopy' in order to refer to isotopy in the strict sense of the word.

Greimas and Courtés recognize that 'theoretically ... nothing stands in the way of transposing the concept of isotopy, developed and restricted up until now to the content plane, to the expression plane' (199). But in practical terms they focus their interest on the content plane (which combines, according to Louis Hjelmslev, form and substance). They make a distinction between *grammatical isotopy* (made of recurrent categories like gender and number) and *semantic isotopy*. The junction of these two planes is operated by means of *actorial isotopy* (see *actant). Another distinction is made between *figurative isotopy* (which is situated at the surface level of discourse) and *thematic isotopy* (which is embedded at a deeper level and may appear in numerous discourses). This distinction is developed by Courtés (1981) and has been useful in the analysis of narrative. (See *theme, *embedding, *discourse.)

The meaning of the concept, nevertheless, has not been stabilized and much discussion has taken place since the publication of the dictionary of *semiotics (Greimas and Courtés) as to whether, for example, isotopy is a paradigmatic phenomenon or a syntagmatic one. See notably Pierre Lerat, for whom 'isotopy is a paradigm' and François Rastier, who holds the opposite view. These two authors, along with many others, agree, however, to define isotopy as the recurrence not of classemes, nor of semic categories, but of any specific seme. (See *seme.)

One can find in Adriaens a presentation of this extremely rich concept in relation to narrative grammar. Despite its 'natural lubricity' (Kerbrat-Orecchioni) and the terminologic confusion which plagues it, the concept of isotopy has quickly become essential to semiotics. It has also proved to be useful in the analysis of dramatic works in relation to the distinction between isotopy of the action and isotopy of the representation (Pavis).

CHRISTIAN VANDENDORPE

Primary Sources

Dubois, J., F. Edeline, J.-M. Klinkenberg and P. Min-
guet. *Rhétorique de la poésie: Lecture linéaire, lec-
ture tabulaire*. Bruxelles: Editions Complexe, 1977.
Greimas, A.J. *Sémantique structurale*. Paris: Larousse,
1966. Repub. PUF, 1986. *Structural Semantics*.
Trans. D. McDowell, R. Schleifer and A. Velie.
Lincoln and London: U of Nebraska P, 1983.
– *Du sens*. Paris: Seuil, 1970.
– and J. Courtés. *Sémiotique. Dictionnaire raisonné de
la théorie du langage*. Paris, 1979. *Semiotics and
Language: An Analytical Dictionary*. Trans. L. Crist,
D. Patte, and others. Bloomington: Indiana UP,
1982.
Rastier, F. *Sémantique interprétative*. Paris: Hachette,
1987.

Secondary Sources

Adriaens, M. 'Isotopic Organization and Narrative
Grammar.' *PTL: A Journal for Descriptive Poetics
and Theory of Literature* 4 (1980): 501–44.
Arrivé, M. 'Pour une théorie des textes poly-isoto-
piques.' *Langages* 31 (1973): 53–63.
Courtés, J. 'Contre-note.' *Documents du Groupe de re-
cherche en sémio-linguistique* (Paris) 3.29 (1981):
37–47.
Kerbrat-Orecchioni, C. 'Problématique de l'isotopie.'
In *Linguistique et sémiologie I: L'isotopie*. Lyon:
Presses universitaires de Lyon, 1976, 11–33.
Klinkenberg, J.-M. *Le Sens rhétorique: Essais de sé-
mantique littéraire*. Toronto: Editions du GREF,
1990.
Lerat, P. *Sémantique descriptive*. Paris: Hachette,
1983.
Pavis, P. *Dictionnaire du théâtre*. Paris: Messidor,
1987.
Stati, S. 'Isotopy, Coreference, and Redundancy.' In
Text and Discourse Connectedness. Ed. M.-E. Conte,
J. Petöfi and E. Sozer. Amsterdam and Philadel-
phia: John Benjamins, 1989, 207–22.

Jouissance: see Cixous, Hélène; Irigaray, Luce; Feminist criticism, French; Pleasure/bliss

Langue/parole

*Ferdinand de Saussure made the distinction
between *langue* (language) and *parole* (speech
or utterance) in his *Course in General Linguistics*. In an effort to define the object of linguistics, Saussure noted that what we think of as

language is something 'unrelated to the phonic
character of the linguistic sign' (7). The *subject*
of linguistics consists of everything to do with
human speech, whereas the *object* of linguistics is language as 'a self-contained whole and
a principle of classification' that functions as
'*the norm of all other manifestations of speech*'
(9). (See *subject/object.) Language as such
may be separated from a very large pool of
data concerning speech through a concept of
system or structure: 'It is a system of signs in
which the only essential thing is the union of
meanings and sound-images, and in which
both parts of the sign are psychological' (15).
(See *sign.) As a system, *langue* is shaped by
society – the entire community of language
users – and as such, it is 'outside' the control
of any individual. *Parole*, on the other hand,
occurs as an individual act within the unassailable confines set up by *langue*. In contrast to
speech (*parole*) as action, language (*langue*) is a
completely passive storehouse of signs that appear together in *discourse only through the
agency of speech. *Langue* and *parole* coexist in
communication in the sense that *parole* generates a message and *langue* understands or interprets it. The *langue/parole* distinction and its
awareness of the social kernel of all individual
speech behaviour has been very influential for
French *structuralism.

GREGOR CAMPBELL

Primary Sources

Saussure, Ferdinand de. *Course in General Linguistics*.
Ed. Charles Bally and Albert Sechehaye in collaboration with Albert Riedlinger. Trans. Wade Baskin. New York: McGraw-Hill, 1959.

Lebenswelt

Lebenswelt, a term created by the German philosopher *Edmund Husserl, means literally
'life-world' and refers to the world of immediately lived, 'pre-scientific experience' of
specific individuals, societies and cultures
(Kockelmans 252, 256). This immediately lived
experience constitutes the most basic field of
phenomenological investigation. It is the context within which phenomenology's intuitional
exploration and description of phenomena take
place. The *Lebenswelt* is a concern of Husserl's
throughout his work of the 1920s but becomes

a fully developed concept only in his final works. It is described in his last published work in contradistinction to the objectivist world of science, where the relationship between subject and object is imagined as the unproblematic perception of objects and relationships between objects which are themselves wholly determined and determinable by precise scientific rules. (See *subject/object.) In its naive conception of this relationship, where there is no contribution made to this perception by the constituting consciousness of the subject, this scientific-objectivist world-view is similar to that evinced by the natural attitude (see *bracketing). The *Lebenswelt* can only be described after the world-view of scientific-objectivism or the natural attitude has been bracketed ('Philosophy as Rigorous Science' 172; Kockelmans 256–9, 274–8).

As the whole of Husserl's philosophy is concentrated upon the achievement of absolutely certain grounds for human knowledge, it is hardly surprising that he dismisses the scientific-objectivist world-view as one which can provide the necessary a priori conditions for such a foundation. Since scientific theory is given to abstraction and idealization, Husserl argues, there must be some even more prior realm of objects and experiences from which these idealizations and abstractions proceed (Kockelmans 257, 268; Sinha 64). This realm is precisely that of the *Lebenswelt*. For Husserl, this is one of the telling points which demonstrates that the world-view of scientific objectivism is derivative from and not prior to the *Lebenswelt* (Kockelmans 252; Hammond et al. 154). In addition, the a priori and certain status of the *Lebenswelt* is further secured against the claims of science by the allowance of cultural-historical differences between the ways distinct individuals, societies and cultures view the world. If there are as many world-perspectives as there are different cultures and societies at different points in time, then scientific objectivism is reduced to simply one world-view among many (Kockelmans 270–1). As a result, neither science nor any of the other multiple views of the world, whether in agreement with or formulated in reaction to this objectivist stance, can claim certainty (Kockelmans 256–66). Through an initial bracketing, we turn away from the scientific-objectivist world, the world as we (that is, Western post-Enlightenment humanity) have been taught to perceive it through the natural attitude, and in

this way we have access to the *Lebenswelt* as the original life-world of our immediately lived, 'pre-scientific' experience (Kockelmans 257). The bracketing of this scientific-objectivist world-view does not, of course, lead to the rejection, denial or negation of science or scientific theories themselves, but to a characteristic suspension of any judgments concerning or any cognitive use of such concepts (Kockelmans 275).

Husserl's stress upon the *Lebenswelt*'s character as the world of our immediately lived, 'pre-scientific' experience leads to the lifeworld's essential and radical relativity; it is 'the moving historical field of our lived existence' (Wild 7). To solve this difficulty, since how can the essential features of the *Lebenswelt* be intuited and reflected upon if there are as many *Lebenswelts* as there are individuals, Husserl brackets the *Lebenswelt* itself, brings to bear the method of free-imaginative variation and uses these procedures to arrive at the necessary and invariable features of the *Lebenswelt* as such (Kockelmans 277). This mental 'stepping-back from' the *Lebenswelt* permits an examination of its essential structures, and the essential structures of consciousness which intuit them. One arrives at a description of the *Lebenswelt* itself, 'as a possible world of intersubjective experiences,' the 'actual' existence of which is not an issue, since the structures uncovered are present in every *Lebenswelt*, independent of historical and cultural contingencies (Kockelmans 277, 278–80).

In the philosophies of Husserl's influential followers, such as *Martin Heidegger and *Maurice Merleau-Ponty, the notion of the *Lebenswelt* has been enlarged and transformed in keeping with a similar, and sometimes quite radical, transformation of the concepts of consciousness and intentionality. Heidegger's *Dasein*, for example, is similar to the *Lebenswelt* in terms of its central position in a philosophical-phenomenological system, although its constitution, conception and purpose are quite different. Heidegger undertakes the examination of the *Dasein* or the mode of existence (*Existenz*) of a human being in-the-world through a variation of Husserl's phenomenological method. However, while Husserl's philosophy aims at investigating and describing the *Lebenswelt* in order to arrive at its essential, invariant and universal features, as such, in Heidegger's philosophy, the concept of the *Dasein* stresses, not the arrival at essence, but the investigation of existence as the substance of human being. As such, the *Dasein* is marked by its uniqueness as a concept, but it also clearly takes Husserl's thesis of intentionality as its starting-point. For Husserl, human consciousness is an important part of the array of phenomena which compose the *Lebenswelt*; yet, it is still a part of the *Lebenswelt*. In contrast, for Heidegger, human consciousness or, more specifically, human existence as the *Dasein's* mode of being is ontologically marked by its difference from everything else which exists; it is not simply a part of a larger life-world, not simply a thing among things (Grossmann 170–1). In his redefinition of the oldest problem of philosophy, that of being and in turn that of the relationship between subject and object, Heidegger rejects the traditional conception of this relationship (with its implication that intentionality belongs primarily to inner subjective experience) and turns to the concept of the *Dasein*, the 'being to whom intentional comportments belong' (64). For Heidegger, the subject-object 'problem' disappears once the *Dasein* and its mode of being *(Existenz)* are understood as inherently intentional: 'The statements that the comportments of the *Dasein* are intentional means that the mode of being of our own self, the *Dasein*, is essentially such that this being, so far as it is, is always already dwelling with the extant ... When ... we give the concise name "existence" to the *Dasein's* mode of being, this is to say that the *Dasein* exists and is not extant like a thing. A distinguishing feature between the existent and the extant is found precisely in intentionality' (64). Since there is this stress upon the *Dasein* and its mode or being – *Existenz* – as radically different from all other kinds of being, the *Dasein* is obviously a more ethically oriented concept that the *Lebenswelt*. Indeed, Heidegger comments that the ability to differentiate between the existent and the extant is exclusive to 'the human soul' (319). (See *intention/intentionality.)

Phenomenological literary critics, like those of the *Geneva School, adapt and extend Husserl's concept of the *Lebenswelt* in their theories concerning both the function of the author and the constitution of the literary *text. (See *phenomenological criticism.) *Roman Ingarden, whose *Das literarische Kunstwerk* [*The Literary Work of Art* 1965] was so influential for the Geneva School, was among the first to apply Husserlian reduction or bracketing to the

process of literary interpretation, stating that the reader should aim at 'duplicat[ing] the "sense-bestowing" intentional acts of the author' (Magliola 29). The Geneva School (usually taken to include such critics as Marcel Raymond, *Georges Poulet and Jean-Pierre Richard) also conceives of the text as the author's imaginative and selective transformation of his or her personal life-world, and of the intentional acts which comprise it (Magliola 28, 36). The resultant 'fictive construct' (Magliola 28) or textual *Lebenswelt* is, of course, created through language, but since language is part of the intentional structure of consciousness (in keeping with Merleau-Ponty's extension of the intentional field) and therefore of the individual author's *Lebenswelt*, the text is stamped with the unique 'network' of intentional acts and relations which comprise the author's consciousness. The presence and critical availability of this unique 'network' of authorial intentional acts which in their textual transformation comprise the 'text's *Lebenswelt*' or 'phenomenological ego' is a mainstay of phenomenological literary theory (Magliola 42). The exploration and delineation of what Magliola has called the 'author's unique imprint' (28) and what the Geneva School refers to as the 'author's experiential patterns' comprise phenomenological interpretation. This theory of the textual *Lebenswelt* also allows phenomenological critics to describe an author's oeuvre in terms of the general intentional structures of an entire body of texts (Magliola 32–3). However, this concentration upon the 'author's unique imprint' (28) does not mean that phenomenological criticism is simply a variation on biographical criticism, since the biographical critic treats the author's ego as truly available both outside the text and reflected in it. Phenomenological critics limit themselves solely to the confines of the literary text, specifically, to the confines of the 'text's *Lebenswelt*.' As a result, phenomenological criticism of the early Geneva School, generally places 'off-limits' an author's personal papers (diaries, letters, journals, and so forth), as well as texts in the work's surrounding cultural and historical field (Magliola 29). This 'intrinsic' method refers as well to the phenomenological critic's practice of bracketing his or her natural attitude, a requirement if one is to perceive and describe the 'text's *Lebenswelt*' and not mistake the author's actual ego for the text's phenomenological one. When the phenomenological critic is exploring and describing the intentional structure of a 'text's *Lebenswelt*,' however, this does not mean that he or she is searching for a definitive statement of the intentional acts which the author meant to place there. Instead, he or she attempts to delineate those intentional acts 'which actually appear in the work,' with no regard to authorial intention, in the non-philosophic sense (Magliola 29).

In general terms, Husserl's concept of the *Lebenswelt* proves more productive for the Geneva School than Heidegger's reworking of it. In the view of the Geneva critics, Heidegger's literary criticism is not only rife with metaphysical presuppositions (Magliola 7), but also discounts the importance of the author's *Lebenswelt* in the production of the text's 'phenomenological ego' (Magliola 57, 62–3). While 'Heidegger insists on the radical absence of the author from the completed literary work' (Magliola 77), on the author's character as a 'conduit which receives Being, delivers it to the written word, and then self-destructs' (Magliola 73), he still finds it hard to avoid treating the text as an imaginative reworking of the author's personal life-world (Magliola 66–9). Consequently, many of the Geneva School criticize Heidegger for not maintaining the distinction between authorial and textual *Lebenswelts*.

MARIE H. LOUGHLIN

Primary Sources

Grossman, Reinhardt. *Phenomenology and Existentialism.* London: Routledge, 1984.

Hammond, Michael, Jane Howarth and Russell Keat. *Understanding Phenomenology.* Oxford: Blackwell, 1991.

Heidegger, Martin. *The Basic Problems of Phenomenology.* Trans., intro. and lexicon, Albert Hofstadter. Bloomington: Indiana UP, 1982.

Husserl, Edmund. 'Phenomenology.' In *Deconstruction in Context: Literature and Philosophy.* Ed. Mark C. Taylor. Chicago: U of Chicago P, 1986, 121–40.

– 'Philosophy as Rigorous Science.' In *Husserl: Shorter Works.* Ed. Peter McCormick and Frederick A. Elliston. Notre Dame, Ind.: U of Notre Dame P, 1981, 166–97.

Kockelmans, Joseph J. *A First Introduction to Husserl's Phenomenology.* Pittsburgh: Duquesne UP, 1967.

Magliola, Robert. *Phenomenology and Literature: An Introduction.* West Lafayette, Ind.: Purdue UP, 1977.

Sinha, Debabrata. *Phenomenology and Existentialism: An Introduction.* Calcutta: Progressive Publishers, 1974.

Wild, John. *Preface.* In *What Is Phenomenology? And Other Essays.* By Pierre Thévenaz. Chicago: Quadrangle, 1962.

Leerstellen: *see* Ingarden, Roman; Iser, Wolfgang; Indeterminacy

Liminality

The concept of liminality comes ultimately from Arnold Van Gennep, who synthesized the whole realm of ritual, and in liminality discerned three phases nearly universal: *séparation* or preliminal rites, *marge* or liminal (threshold) rites, and *agrégation* or postliminal incorporation rites. This tripartite structure links public rites, such as those of territorial passage, with personal rites of passage – initiations, marriages, funerals. Each phase has its signs – *séparation* has death symbols (sacrifices, cutting implements); *marge*, inertness and indeterminacy symbols (transvestism, mock death); *agrégation*, incorporation symbols – threshold crossing, shared meals, handclasps, kisses, sexual contact, gift exchange, symbols such as rings and crowns.

As Van Gennep noted, cultures take a special interest in the liminal stage, and anthropologist Victor Turner built on his predecessor's insights to make a veritable specialty of liminality (see especially *The Ritual Process*). For Turner, liminality is no thin line but an expanded zone, in which liminars may spend much time – as in betrothal or the sequestered life of tribal adolescents awaiting initiation. Liminality involves namelessness, absence of property, nakedness or uniform clothing, transvestism, sexual continence, minimized distinctions of sex, rank and wealth, humility, disregard for personal appearance, obedience, silence, sacred instruction, suspended kinship rights and obligations, invoking of mystical powers, foolishness, acceptance of pain, images of death and rebirth, a sense of comradeship (*communitas*) with fellow liminars (Turner, *Process* 106–7).

The concept of liminality passed easily into literary study, and students of *literature have used it to explore indeterminate liminal states in a wide range of literatures and literary periods. For example, literary journeys show liminal features; that the world's pilgrimage sites are on margins or borders, not in main population centres, emphasizes the separation from the world of those liminal travellers, pilgrims (Turner, *Dramas* 195–6), thus the *communitas* of Chaucer's pilgrims (see Pison) and the spiritual instruction in *The Pilgrim's Progress*. Moreover, pilgrimages are just one of many kinds of journey, and Van Gennep's analogy between journeys and life phases helps account for their ubiquity in folk-tale and literature as analogues of growing up (see Bishop, Rivers). Consequently, besides pilgrims, liminal figures include orphans, children and court jesters (Gilead, 'Victorian Novel'; Iijima; Turner, *Process*).

In Shakespeare, liminars and liminality abound. Edward Berry sees the comedies as 'comic rites of passage,' structured like Van Gennep's three-part rites: shipwrecks and banishments effect *séparation*; the 'dislocation and confusions of identity, the ordeals, and the education characteristic of the liminal phase' occur in a green world like 'the sacred forests of initiation'; and *agrégation* shows in 'rites of incorporation prominent in Elizabethan weddings – the exchanging of rings and oaths, kissing, feasting, and dancing.' Berry sees comedic disorientations – dream, error, madness, witchcraft, metamorphosis – as liminal (58; see also Falk); young men's conventional behaviour – 'writing of sonnets, wearing of love-locks, posturing in romantic attitudes – fulfils many of the conditions of a liminal experience' (30). Like Turner, who notes that tribal rites of passage often involve altered language, Marjorie Garber detects language change at maturity in Romeo, Prince Hal and others (80–115); Brian Vickers notes shifts from prose to poetry at coming of age and onset of courtship (49, 53–4). Lear, divested of the defining roles of king and father, tears off his clothes and enters a hovel, like Turner's African king-elect taken the night before accession to a hut outside of town, stripped nearly naked, insulted, then 'born as a new chief' (*Process* 95, 101).

Liminality has been observed in a wide range of other genres. In *Beowulf* the deer trapped between the hounds and the mere images a kingdom caught between natural and unnatural warfare, and mankind caught in middle-earth between salvation and damnation (Higley). The 'liminality of Jacksonian society poised between the traditional agrarian and mercantile social order and the new ways of commercial and industrial capitalism' (Smith-Rosenberg 377) spawned Davey Crockett. In *The Turn of the Screw*, thresholds are the meeting grounds of waking and dreaming, sanity and insanity (Rust). Liminality is pervasive in Victorian fiction: 'this twilight zone pervades most of Dickens's novels' (Greenstein 276), and so is anti-liminality, where 'covertly present ... are narrative events and symbols antithetical to the liminal myths that appear to emerge triumphant' (Gilead, 'Victorian Novel' 190–1): Oliver Twist spends much of his novel as liminal orphan pauper and underworld denizen but even after re-aggregation into middle-class society, he is denied marriage and thus proper consummation of his rites of passage (Anderson). Jane Eyre persists as liminal until she finally joins Rochester in honourable matrimony at Ferndean, but though this 'completes the rites of passage of Jane and Rochester, and the ritualization of the narrative as a whole, Ferndean remains liminal' (Gilead, 'Bronte's Novels' 311). Liminality and anti-liminality thus coexist, at least in the Victorian era (Gilead, 'Victorian Novels' 191ff.).

Liminality has also been applied to the material conditions of literary production: Steven Mullaney argues that the Elizabethan sense of the marginal space occupied by drama, in theatres 'outside the walls of early modern London in the "licentious Liberties,"' was quite different from the ancient Athenians' sense of drama as central to the culture, with the theatre centrally located in Athens (vii, 7–8). In language, too, 'the interstitial space between words and objects' is liminal (Urla 102); in comedy the space between word and meaning in a malapropism recreates lovers' liminal space. Riddles, common in liminality, often attend tribal weddings and literary suitor tests (Gorfain).

Literary applications of liminality blossomed in the later 1980s; the many recent doctoral dissertations using the concept attest to its usefulness, as does its fruitful application to literatures not only in English but also in French, Russian, Hispanic, Caribbean, and Japanese, and to ancient Greek, Egyptian, Mesopotamian, and Hebrew literature (see Kelsey, Chamier, Tiffany, Walker, Deutsch, Firmat, Charles, Turner ['Liminality'], Fiveash, Perdue).

LINDA WOODBRIDGE and
ROLAND ANDERSON

Primary Sources

Anderson, Roland F. 'Structure, Myth, and Rite in *Oliver Twist.' Studies in the Novel* 18 (1986): 238–57.

Berry, Edward. *Shakespeare's Comic Rites.* Cambridge, London, New York: Cambridge UP, 1984.

Bishop, Norma J. 'Liminal Space in Traveller's Tales: Historical and Fictional Passages.' Ph.D. diss., Pennsylvania State U, 1986.

Chamier, Suzanne. 'The Experimental Poetics of Raymond Queneau.' Ph.D. diss., Washington U, 1985.

Charles, Henry James. 'Theological-Ethical Appraisal of the Disclosure of Possibility for the Post-Colonial Caribbean via an Analysis of Selected Literary Texts.' Ph.D. diss., Yale U, 1982.

Deutsch, Judith E. 'The Cossack Hero in Russian Literature: Topoi and Change.' Ph.D. diss., Columbia U, 1985.

Falk, Florence. 'Dream and Ritual Process in *A Midsummer Night's Dream.' Comparative Drama* 14 (1980–1): 263–79.

Firmat, Gustavo Perez. *Literature and Liminality: Festive Readings in the Hispanic Tradition.* Chapel Hill, NC: Duke UP, 1986.

Fiveash, Michael Matthew. 'The Still Point of the Turning World: A Study of the Metaphors of Liminality in Greek Literature and Religion.' Ph.D. diss., Boston U, 1980.

Garber, Marjorie. *Coming of Age in Shakespeare.* London and New York: Methuen, 1981.

Gilead, Sarah. 'Liminality, Anti-liminality, and the Victorian Novel.' *ELH: English Literary History* 53 (1986): 183–97.

– 'Liminality and Antiliminality in Charlotte Bronte's Novels: *Shirley* reads *Jane Eyre.' Texas Studies in Literature and Language* 29 (1987): 302–22.

Gorfain, Phyllis. 'Riddles and Reconciliation: Formal Unity in *All's Well That Ends Well.' Journal of the Folklore Institute* 13 (1976): 263–81.

Greenstein, Michael. 'Liminality in *Little Dorrit.' Dickens Quarterly* 7 (1990): 275–82.

Higley, Sarah Lynn. 'Aldor on Ofre; Or, The Reluctant Hart: A Study of Liminality in *Beowulf.' Neuphilologische Mitteilungen* 87 (1986): 342–53.

Iijima, Yoshiharu. 'Folk Culture and the Liminality of Children.' *Current Anthropology* 28 (1987): 541–8.

Kelsey, Aline Suquet. 'Lancelot ou Le Chevalier de la Charrete: Le Trajet initiatique du heros.' Ph.D. diss., State U of New Jersey, 1986.

Mullaney, Steven. *The Place of the Stage: License, Play and Power in Renaissance England.* Chicago and London: U of Chicago P, 1988.

Perdue, Leo G. 'Liminality as a Social Setting for Wisdom Instructions.' *Zeitschrift für Die Alttestamentliche Wissenschaft* 93 (1981): 114–26.

Pison, Thomas. 'Liminality in *The Canterbury Tales.' Genre* 10 (1977): 157–71.

Rivers, Joseph Tracy III. 'Pattern and Process in Early Christian Pilgrimage.' Ph.D. diss., Duke U, 1983.

Rust, Richard Dilworth. 'Liminality in *The Turn of the Screw.' Studies in Short Fiction* 25 (1988): 441–6.

Smith-Rosenberg, Carroll. 'Davey Crockett as Trickster: Pornography, Liminality and Symbolic Inversion in Victorian America.' *Journal of Contemporary History* 17 (1982): 325–50.

Tiffany, Dana Rodman. 'The Adolescent God: The Entry of Alfred Jarry into the Symbolist Avant-Garde in Paris, 1884–96.' Ph.D. diss., U of California, San Diego, 1984.

Turner, Edith. 'The Literary Roots of Victor Turner's Anthropology.' In *Victor Turner and the Construction of Cultural Criticism: Between Literature and Anthropology.* Ed. Kathleen M. Ashley. Bloomington: Indiana UP, 1990, 163–9.

Turner, Victor. *Dramas, Fields, and Metaphors: Symbolic Action in Human Society.* Ithaca: Cornell UP, 1974.

– 'Liminality and the Performative Genres.' In *Rite, Drama, Festival, Spectacle: Rehearsals Toward a Theory of Cultural Performance.* Ed. John MacAloon. Philadelphia: ISIH, 1984, 19–41.

– *The Ritual Process: Structure and Anti-Structure.* Chicago: Aldine, 1969.

Urla, Jaqueline. 'New Perspectives in Anthropology and Modern Literature.' *Sub-Stance* 22 (1979): 97–106.

Van Gennep, Arnold. *Les Rites du passage.* 1908. *The Rites of Passage.* Trans. Monika B. Vizedom and Gabrielle L. Caffee. London: Routledge and Kegan Paul, 1960.

Vickers, Brian. 'Rites of Passage in Shakespeare's Prose.' *Jahrbuch der Deutschen Shakespeare-Gesellschaft West* (1986): 45–67.

Walker, Jeanne Murray. 'Totalitarian and Liminal Societies in Zamyatin's *We.' Mosaic* 20 (1987): 113–27.

Literary institution

The literary institution is the field in which all literary experience is realized (Bürger, 'The Institution of Art'). It encompasses two inseparable practices that work together to create a tension in literary modes of production. At one pole, the organizing practices bring together all the materials of the technical and organizational infrastructure of the institution. Here, technologies of reproduction and distribution include the oral, print, electronic, and various other media (cf. Innis). The economics of the institution encompass systems of government subsidies as well as the various cultural industries that ascribe an exchange value to the products of the institution. In turn, techniques of reproduction determine possible menus of criticism that bestow value on the literary products. This process is carried out through a vast variety of literary promotions that includes literary criticism itself as well as the more formal rituals of the art such as literary prizes, book festivals, publishers' conventions, and the like. In this way the organizing practices of the literary institution help establish critical acclaim and bestow legitimacy on the products of the institution.

At the other pole, the imaginative or creative practices bring together all the materials of the aesthetic event that are handed down across the millennia – all the codes, norms, genres, themes, narrative styles, and all those artistic forms that give expression to literary content (Bürger *Theory*; Belleau; Marcotte). Assuming that the author, reader and literary critic are co-creative participants already 'inserted' in the literary work, it follows that the creative practice also in part influences the possibilities of reception and criticism. Themes and narrative styles carry a *horizon of expectation that help form the way in which a story is experienced by a reader; a particular genre may be more familiar to readers of a certain age, national origin, social class or gender; and codes and norms of writing change from one epoch to another. None of the creative practices can be explained by reducing them to the organizing practices, but at the same time the two practices work together, sometimes in conflict, sometimes in harmony, but always within the same frame of reference. (See also *code, *genre criticism, *theme, *metacriticism.)

GREG NIELSEN

Primary Sources

Belleau, André. 'Le Conflit des codes dans l'institution littéraire québécoise.' *Liberté* 134 (1981): 105–18.
Bürger, Peter. 'The Institution of Art as a Category in the Sociology of Literature.' *Culture Critique* 2 (1985): 5–33.
– *The Theory of the Avant-Garde*. Minneapolis: U of Minnesota P, 1984.
Dubois, Jacques. *L'Institution de la littérature*. Paris: Fernand Nathan Editions Labor, 1978.
Innis, Harold. *The Empire of Communications*. Toronto: Oxford UP, 1950.
Marcotte, Gilles. 'Institutions et courants d'air.' *Liberté* 134 (1981): 15–21.

Literature

Of all the definitions contained in this volume, the one for literature is easily the most fluid. As the collective term for the many divergent objects of study for most critics and scholars, including most of those named in this work, literature evolves as criticism evolves, and each critical school, as it defines its practice, recreates literature in its own image. That its definition is under constant revision would suggest that the objects it identifies are linked by relationships that are contingent upon historical circumstance or changing critical standards. Yet however much the sense of literature has evolved, there remain many theorists who argue that literary objects are distinctive, that they are conjoined by a defining essence or, at least, by a set of linguistic relationships. Literature has thus all the peculiarities of a sign system, yet one whose workings are as much a matter of disagreement as its referents. (See *sign.)

Derived from the Latin *litteratura*, literature originally denoted either the ability to form letters or, more commonly, the quality of being widely read. The latter sense is intensified in vernacular usages of the term: literature in early modern Europe designated erudition among a broad range of polite learning, while its cognates, literate and, later, literary, referred to the condition of being well-read, what *E.D. Hirsch has recently termed 'cultural literacy.' That it usually implied polite reading meant that literature was identified with a *canon; this normative aspect is to a degree still implicit in the term, as it is unusual in common usage to speak of 'good' or 'bad' literature. Indeed the term is sometimes used honorifically, to denote, say, the most esteemed works within a culture, as in a 'national literature.' Less obvious though no less significant is the degree to which literature still relates to the act of reading. A recent specialized and neutral usage has the term denoting all reading material on a given topic, as in 'campaign literature' or 'computer literature.' Though some anthropologists insist that literature can be present in oral cultures, the term's associations with reading have retarded, in common usage at least, such a broadening of its defining boundaries (Finnegan).

These associations may also help to explain why, in the late 18th century, literature acquires its most familiar modern sense as an aggregate term for imaginative writings, including poems, plays, novels and short stories. Previously, eloquent writings, including select works of prose, had belonged to the rhetorical category of 'poetry,' a term which, being derived from the ancient Greek word for *making* or *craft*, pertained to invention and production. (See *rhetorical criticism.) Literature, in contrast, has to do with consumption: poetry is composed and spoken, literature read and studied. The shift, then, from 'poetry' to 'literature' as the collective noun for imaginative works reflects a complex cultural change in the way works of art are valorized, a change brought about by, among other phenomena, a growth in readership at all social levels, the rise of the commercial book trade and the subsequent commodification of published works. Invention is still prized, as the modern cults of genius and originality may illustrate, but the social function of written art is rarely understood in relation to the practical requirements of either the author or the immediate occasions such art is designed to address. Literature is valued by and for readers, either for its effects or, as some theorists maintain, for *itself*, as if it involved a non-instrumental, imaginative act of reading.

Modern concepts of literature assume this normative shift from invention to reading in the way they supplement older mimetic or pragmatic theories of poetry by focusing less on the truth-value or social function of a *text than on the text in isolation, or the mode of its comprehension by the reader. Literature, like poetry before it, has been understood to be either a fictive art or a verbal art, or both. Yet where Sidney could defend poetic *mimesis by asserting that the poet 'nothing affirms, and therefore never lieth,' modern fictive concepts of literature, such as *I.A. Richards' theory of literature's distinctive 'pseudo-statements,' are concerned less with the ethical nature of the poetic utterance than with problems of reading and interpretation. Even speech act theorists, who have done most recently to equate literature with fictiveness, assume that literary works are merely representations of verbal acts, representations that have no 'illocutionary' force and no self-evident cognitive value;

as such, these theorists claim, literature is an autonomous *discourse that performs no practical function in society (Ohmann, Woodmansee). (See *speech act theory.) Arguments on behalf of a fictive concept of literature have the virtue of claiming as literature works from a variety of cultures and classes, from fabliau to popular fiction to *myth, though they inevitably exclude didactic works, and genres without obvious mimetic properties such as love poetry or the essay. (See *genre criticism.) Hence such arguments usually stipulate that fiction is a common feature of literary works, though not necessarily their defining essence (*Todorov).

Verbal concepts of literature are more varied, though most imply a division between the peculiarly refined or figurative character of literary language and the more functional nature of performative discourses such as science or ordinary speech. Versions of this argument include the Russian formalist theory of literariness, whose defining quality is a special self-reflexive or emotive use of language; New Critical and structuralist doctrines of *irony, ambiguity or verbal structure, doctrines that emphasize the autotelic economy of the literary text; and more recent rhetorical and deconstructionist arguments that apply the term literature to specific verbal features in *any* text which 'resist' assimilation to conventional meanings or systematic thought. (See Russian *formalism, *New Criticism, *structuralism, *deconstruction.) This last argument suggests, for some, that no absolute distinction can be maintained between literary language and other types of discourse; even ordinary speech, it is claimed, may evince a host of figurative qualities (*Fish). Such thinking may resemble earlier, pragmatic notions of literature, though the emphasis of recent *critical theory has been less on the instrumentality than the interpretation of literature. Arguments for a verbal concept of literature often recognize as literary a broad range of works, both fictional and non-fictional, though may not adequately account for the significance and attributes of certain works, such as the realist novel, where linguistic or stylistic properties seem of secondary importance to aspects of narrative or referentiality.

Opposed, perhaps, to both the verbal and fictive concepts is the claim that literature itself is but a conventional grouping, a separate genre in effect, that includes within loose boundaries a range of forms and modes (georgic, short story, essay, and so forth) related not by a defining essence but by contingency, including changing notions of literary value (Fowler). Related to this argument are aesthetic definitions that posit certain normative if conventional criteria, such as 'aesthetic pleasure' or 'perceptiveness,' which a work must satisfy in order to qualify as literature (Lyas). Both these definitions, the generic and the aesthetic, imply a return to the pragmatic theories of old, though even in these arguments the priority of consumption over invention, reading over writing, is apparent: whether literature is treated as a category bounded by convention or subjective criteria, it is a category that has to do with how a work may be read and received, and not with how or why the work is produced.

From there, it is but a short step to institutional and historicist definitions of literature. Because literature in its modern sense is a relatively recent usage, many critics, including Marxists, literary sociologists and cultural materialists, maintain that the concept makes sense only in the context of modern critical and pedagogical practices, the context, that is, of how literature is read and consumed. (See *Marxist criticism, *sociocriticism, *cultural materialism.) The definition and value of literature, they argue, are primarily determined in accordance with the changing disciplinary interests of academic and cultural institutions, interests that have mainly to do with the reception, preservation and cultural reproduction of literary texts (Bennett, Graff, *Williams). Literature, in this view, is everything that is taught in departments of literature or criticized by literary critics, and hence the category of literature narrows or expands with the way critics and teachers perceive the social purpose of their work. Other critics, including New Historicists, use similar historical and sociological arguments to contest theories of the autonomy of the literary text. (See *New Historicism.) These critics consider literature a social practice, one that can never be absolutely distinguished either from other practices or from other, extra- or non-literary discourses. Their arguments most closely resemble classical, pragmatic claims for the social utility of literary invention. Many of these critics reject the term literature as inadequate and replace it

with its antecedents, notably rhetoric and 'poetics,' in the hope of making explicit the productive, instrumental nature of writing.

TREVOR ROSS

Primary Sources

Bennett, Tony. *Outside Literature*. London: Routledge, 1990.

Finnegan, Ruth. *Literacy and Orality: Studies in the Technology of Communication*. Oxford: Basil Blackwell, 1988.

Fish, Stanley E. 'How Ordinary Is Ordinary Language?' *New Literary History* 5 (1973): 41–54.

Fowler, Alastair. *Kinds of Literature: An Introduction to the Theory of Genres and Modes*. Cambridge, Mass.: Harvard UP, 1982.

Graff, Gerald. *Professing Literature: An Institutional History*. Chicago: U of Chicago P, 1987.

Hernadi, Paul, ed. *What Is Literature?* Bloomington: Indiana UP, 1978.

Kernan, Alvin. *The Death of Literature*. New Haven: Yale UP, 1990.

Lyas, Colin. 'The Semantic Definition of Literature.' *Journal of Philosophy* 66.3 (1969): 81–95.

Ohmann, Richard. 'Speech Acts and the Definition of Literature.' *Philosophy and Rhetoric* 4 (1971): 1–19.

Reichert, John. *Making Sense of Literature*. Chicago: U of Chicago P, 1977.

Striedter, Jurij. *Literary Structure, Evolution, and Value: Russian Formalism and Czech Structuralism Reconsidered*. Cambridge, Mass.: Harvard UP, 1989.

Todorov, Tzvetan. 'The Notion of Literature.' *New Literary History* 5 (1973): 5–16.

Wellek, René. *The Attack on Literature and Other Essays*. Chapel Hill: U of North Carolina P, 1982.

Williams, Raymond. *Marxism and Literature*. Oxford: Oxford UP, 1977.

Woodmansee, Martha. 'Speech-Act Theory and the Perpetuation of the Dogma of Literary Autonomy.' *Centrum* 6 (1978): 75–89.

Logocentrism

Logocentrism, a term coined by *Jacques Derrida, was first given publicity in his *De la Grammatologie [Of Grammatology* 1967; trans. 1976] and has occupied a central place in the polemics of Derrida and his deconstructionist followers ever since. (See *deconstruction, *grammatology.) It denotes the position that words, writings, ideas, systems of thought are fixed and sustained by some *authority or centre external to them whose meaning, validation and truth they convey. (See *centre/decentre.) This validation 'from the outside' may consist of something as simple as mere objects 'out there' in the 'real' world beyond language, apparently referred to by words. The everyday, normative logocentric assumption is that language refers and so also does language organized into *text; that signs have *referends* or *signata*, that words make present to the reader or hearer ascertainable, decipherable meanings, that is, they contain and convey some 'presence' or presences from outside or beyond themselves. (See *sign, *metaphysics of presence.) Reference is, in this view, transcendent. (See *reference/referent.) This logocentric assumption about how words and thinking operate has, according to Derrida, been the foundation of the whole history of Western metaphysics and has dominated Western thought and linguistics from Plato until the present. Deconstruction is thus a mode of analysis that sets out to help us see through, to historicize and so to undermine this conceptual mind-set which has been the glue binding all of Western thinking and writing.

'Presence' is variously manifested in Western thinking as 'presence of the thing to the sight as *eidos*, presence as substance/essence/existence *(ousia)*, temporal presence as point *(stigme)* of the now or of the moment *(nun)*, the self-presence of the cogito, consciousness, subjectivity, the co-presence of the other and of the self, intersubjectivity as an intentional phenomenon of the ego, and so forth' (*Of Grammatology* 12). '*Il n'y a pas de hors-texte,*' Derrida's notorious declaration (*Of Grammatology* 158), commonly, though very roughly, translated into English as 'There is nothing outside of the text,' is the best-known slogan for this principled opposition to presence.

One of the most commonly occurring manifestations of presence is in conventional concepts of speech as the words of real speakers who provide an authoritative source and basis of meaning, and of such speaking as the essence of writing – whose meaning is grounded in the authority of 'authors.' This, Derrida has insisted, is the fallacy of *phonocentrism*, a term he uses interchangeably with *logocentrism*. Against logocentrism or phonocentrism Derrida opposes *écriture* (usually, though not very helpfully, translated as *writing). Ecriture* is the textual condition that best answers the allegation of *Ferdinand de Saussure in his *Cours de linguistique générale* that in linguistic systems 'there are only differences, without positive terms.' *Structuralism borrowed from linguistics the term diacritical to indicate this differential (rather than referential) nature of linguistic systems. Derrida's portmanteau French coinage *différance* – conveying all at once the relativist, relational principle of perpetual meaning, *différence* (difference), and also bringing home the perpetual elusiveness or deferredness of meaning – celebrates what is for Derrida the essence of *écriture* and the opposite of, and alternative to, logocentrism or phonocentrism. (See *différance/différence.)

Ecriture is anti-logocentric not least because it manifestly exists and means apart from the originating, fathering, pen-holding hand or author. Western logocentrism, the 'metaphysics of presence,' is referred back to Plato's condemnation in the *Phaedrus* of writing as a bastardized and confusing mode of communication precisely because, in writing, the *logos* or word is separated from the moment or site of origin, the 'father.'

It is just this separation that deconstruction celebrates. Derrida's analysis of the founding Platonic concept of the *logos*, the word, as 'son' of a 'fathering' origin (see 'The Father of the Logos') is designed to place, and accuse, logocentrism as a key aspect of Christian and biblical thought about the Divine Logos, Son of the Divine Father ('In the beginning was the Word'). The term *theologocentrism* is sometimes used to assert the Christian frame of logocentrism – what Derrida (after *Heidegger) labels *ontotheology* (just as *phallogocentrism* is used by feminists, after Derrida's hostile analysis of Lacan's seminar on Poe's *The Purloined Letter* in 'Le Facteur de la vérité,' to assert logocentrism's *phallocentric*, male dominant, patriarchal cast of mind about the authority and origins of meaning). (See *Lacan, *phallocentrism.) The persistent annexation of key terms from within biblical *textuality and *hermeneutics and Christian theology – Logos, Father, Son, Genesis, *Ecriture* (= Scripture), *ousia* (cf. *parousia*, a central New Testament term for the Second Advent or 'appearing' of Christ), discussions of the 'Real Presence' of Christ in the sacrament of the Eucharist – establishes deconstruction as a self-conscious undoer not only of Western metaphysical orthodoxies in general but of Judaeo-Christian orthodoxies in particular.

Many of the difficulties involved in anti-logocentric analysis are well known to Derrida, if not always to other deconstructionists. Indeed the way deconstruction can be observed to contradict and thus undo itself is sometimes heralded as both the proof and the glory of the deconstructive enterprise. From the start Derrida has affirmed his belief that, though he might wish to transcend the hold of logocentrism, to decentre the word, and so on, he and Western metaphysics are simply stuck in and with the logocentricity of tradition. Deconstructionists will also sometimes acknowledge that theirs is a version of the old Cretan Liar *paradox – namely they assert the error of logocentrism and avow the *indeterminacy of meaning by means of a positive lexicon of terms for difference/deferring (not least the central term *différance* itself) in texts offered as authoritative analyses of the Western tradition, through readings of texts (philosophical, poetic, fictional) that are offered as true and final readings, with all of this analytical work reliant on the absolute, always deferred-to authority of language-systematizing and historically fixing texts such as dictionaries (see Derrida's persistent use of Littré in particular). Anti-logocentric practice is on this reckoning extremely logocentric. Further, and this deconstructionists are more reluctant to acknowledge, there is a good deal of force in Derrida's own awareness (see, for example, 'Edmond Jabès and the Question of the Book') that an anti-logocentric, self-deconstructing strain has infected Judaeo-Christian biblicism and theology right from their (putative) origins in Moses' broken Tables of Law, so that the logocentrism under attack is by no means the monolithic conceptual enterprise commonly alleged and, in its theologocentristic aspects, at least, has all the appearance of a polemical straw-man (cf. Handelman).

VALENTINE CUNNINGHAM

Primary Sources

Derrida, Jacques. *De la Grammatologie*. 1967. *Of Grammatology*. Trans. Gayatri Chakravorty Spivak. Baltimore: Johns Hopkins UP, 1977.
– 'Edmond Jabès and the Question of the Book.' In *L'Ecriture et la différance*. 1967. *Writing and Difference*. Trans. Alan Bass. Chicago: U of Chicago P, 1978.
– 'The Father of the Logos.' In *La Dissémination*. 1972. *Dissemination*. Trans. Barbara Johnson. Chicago: U of Chicago P, 1981.
– 'La Facteur de la vérité.' *Poétique* 21 (1975). 'The Purveyor of Truth.' Trans. Willis Domingo, James Hulbert, Moshe Ron, and M.-R. L[ogan]. *Yale French Studies* 52 (1975): 31–113. Perspectives in Literature and Philosophy. Special issue.
– *Speech and Phenomena*. Trans. David B. Allison. Evanston: Northwestern UP, 1973.
– 'Structure, Sign, and Play in the Discourse of the Human Sciences.' In *L'Ecriture et la différance*. 1967. *Writing and Difference*. 1978.
Handelman, Susan. *The Slayers of Moses: The Emergence of Rabbinic Interpretation in Modern Literary Theory*. Albany: State U of New York P, 1982.
Macksey, Richard, and Eugenio Donato, eds. *The Structuralist Controversy: The Languages of Criticism and the Sciences of Man*. Baltimore: Johns Hopkins UP, 1972.

Margin

The term margin has gained theoretical eminence with the work of *Jacques Derrida, for whom centre and margin indicate constructed limitations embedded in a process that exceeds binary and hierarchical oppositions. (See *centre/decentre, *binary opposition.) In a traditional hermeneutic or philological view, the literal margins of a page represent an important if secondary space of understanding and commentary, for annotation and marginalia or correction and censorship. (See *hermeneutics.) While a certain explanatory power is thus attributed to the margin, margin and centre are defined by a clear distribution of boundaries. Against this notion of the margin as a fixed space outside a main *text, Derrida suggests that the excess of the white page over its marks offers but one possible allusion to margins of meaning that operate both inside and outside the marked space. Already in his early *De la Grammatologie* [*Of Grammatology* 1967; trans. 1976], analysing the notion of the supplement in Rousseau's texts, he emphasizes 'the power of exteriority as constitutive of interiority: of speech, of signified meaning, of the present as such' (313). (See *grammatology, *supplementarity.) Derrida's concomitant strategy of *différance* (deferral) challenges the possibility of an identity, sameness, or inside that could be conceived of independently of the altering power of its difference, its other, or its margin (itself depending, in turn, upon further contextual frames of reference), and is related to his critique of the notion of origin (for instance in his book on *Husserl, *La Voix et le phénomène* [*Speech and Phenomena* 1967; trans.

1973]). (See *différance/différence, *self/other.)
Derrida seeks to show that the origin cannot
be thought of as such without its derivative –
which therefore takes on originary powers itself and thus puts the very concept of origin
into question; as Vincent Descombes has observed in *Le Même et l'autre [Modern French
Philosophy* 1979; trans. 1980], 'the second is
not that which merely arrives ... *after* the first,
but that which permits the first to be the first'
(145).

This 'originary delay' already inherent in
any primary term 'displaces' rather than in-
verses the traditional concept of the margin as
the place of the commentary, the added, the
later and the secondary, since it does not make
the marginal into a new origin or centre. The
asymmetrical shifting of oppositions, which
Derrida aims at the unifying Hegelian contraries, unstructures the dividing-line by which
oppositions are determined. Such symmetrical
correspondences are typically transformed and
mobilized in Derridean texts into a series of
incomplete doubles that cannot be arrested or
'grounded' by an ultimate reference (which
Derrida calls a transcendental signified). (See
*signified/signifier/signification.) In 'Structure,
Sign and Play in the Discourse of the Human
Sciences' (*Writing and Difference* 278–93), the
essay by which he became first known in
North America, Derrida discusses the decentring enterprise of ethnology, and in particular *Claude Lévi-Strauss' account of the 'acen-
tric structure' (*Writing and Difference* 286) of
myths in *The Raw and the Cooked*. (See *myth.)
Derrida suggests that the nature of the field of
mythology, language, constitutes a 'field of infinite substitutions' that 'excludes totalization'
not because it is too large, but because 'a center which arrests and grounds the play of substitutions' is missing: 'One cannot determine
the center and exhaust totalization because the
*sign which replaces the center, which supple-
ments it, taking the center's place in its absence – this sign is added, occurs as a surplus,
as a *supplement*. The movement of signification
adds something, which results in the fact that
there is always more' (*Writing and Difference*
289). (See *totalization.)

Derrida's text here extends and displaces a
structuralist critique of empiricism – a critique
that emphasizes the relational functioning of
signifiers among each other while grounding
them with respect to the signified. (See *structuralism.) The unlimited movement and play

of signification motivates the series of mark,
march and margin Derrida develops in 'The
Double Session' (*Dissemination* 173–285). (See
theories of *play/freeplay.) Since each mark is
constituted by its contexts and its limit, it is
seen as mediated by a continual process of
contextual 're-marking' that undoes the oppositions in which it is – necessarily – first approached. Drawing in particular on Mallarmé's
fascination with the 'blank' and the 'fold'
(blanc, pli), Derrida attributes a destabilizing
and de-limiting power of signification to the
'ordered return of the white spaces' (178) that
forces continual re-marking and rereading,
and runs counter to any thematic critical endeavour. This 'surplus mark, this margin of
meaning' (251) and 'onward *march*' (245) of
Mallarmé's text occurs in its 'full' white marks
(snow, swan, paper, virginity), but finds as
well 'one of these representatives representing
nothing in the blankness or margins of the
page' – without becoming itself a 'fundamental
signified or signifier' (252). Textual signification does not occur in the full sense of marks,
but enters between them, in the '"blank"
meaning,' in the 'non-sense of spacing, the
place where nothing takes place but place'
(257). Thus a signifying function but not a
fixed space is attributed to margins.

The liminal role of margins, seemingly outside and yet a part of a text for which they are
a medium (a function which Derrida discusses
as well in *La Vérité en peinture [The Truth in
Painting* 1978; trans. 1987] in terms of the
frame and the 'parergon') is also explored in
Derrida's minute attention to 'marginal' text
types that mark the 'main' text's boundaries,
such as titles, epigraphs, signatures (for instance in 'Signature, Event, Context'), or footnotes. (See *liminality.) In the 'Prefacing' to
his book *Dissemination*, 'Outwork,' Derrida
shows the multiple temporal and logical position of both introductions and conclusions.
Here as elsewhere the study of literal spacing
investigates and displaces knowledge as a network of significations that is utterly dependent
on the positionality of its marks (*Positions* is
the title of a book of interviews with Derrida).
The preface to Derrida's book significantly entitled *Margins of Philosophy*, 'Tympan,' again
enacting and alluding to its own strategy and
uncertain status by a spatial arrangement of
'literary' and 'philosophical' texts, probes the
relationship between knowledge and its margins by investigating philosophy as a *dis-

course propelled by the (inherently impossible) effort to master its other, its own limit and margin. Philosophy 'has always insisted upon assuring itself mastery over the limit *(peras, limes, Grenze)*. It ... has believed that it controls the margin of its volume and that it thinks its other ... Its other: that which limits it, and from which it derives its essence, its definition, its production' (x).

Derrida's rethinking (or re-marking) of marginality has emerged in a period that has broadly questioned the relationship between centres and margins, as evidenced, for example, by *Michel Foucault's influential investigations of strategies of exclusion and *power. These inquiries – generally marked by a certain 'hermeneutics of suspicion' and mistrust towards forms of totalization – have increasingly linked questions of class, race, gender, and colonialism to forms of knowledge *(savoirs)* and its mediations in language as specific discourses. (See *post-colonial theory.) *Edward Said's study *Orientalism* – although often explicitly directed against Derridean *deconstruction – traces the process by which knowledge and learning can essentialize an exotic geographical margin as object, an other that becomes the medium of a collateral self. (See *essentialism.) Said charges that Orientalism and Orientalist discourse (his usage of these terms has influenced, among other studies, several works on 'Africanist' discourse) construct a relationship between knowledge and geography that both helps to 'produce' the Orient (3) and simultaneously 'has less to do with the Orient than it does with "our" world' (12). (See *Black criticism.) Said diagnoses this distribution of places, roles and power as 'radical realism,' a form of knowledge based on representation and the crucial role of the copula 'is' (72). Homi K. Bhabha has analysed the compulsive repetition of this 'mode of representation of otherness' as a fixity necessary for stereotypes which contain both the alluring and the threatening powers of racial, cultural and historical otherness and marginality. Perhaps the most effective analyses of the relationship between representation, essentialism and marginality have been produced by feminist studies and in particular by those feminisms that have refused to reconstruct representations of 'woman' as a symmetrical answer to marginalizations of woman as other in male-dominated discourses. (See *feminist criticism.) While *Luce Irigaray has

analysed, for example in *Speculum de l'autre femme* [*Speculum of the Other Woman* 1974; trans. 1985], the repression of 'woman' as invisible other outside patriarchal representation and its specular, narcissistic logic of the same, *Julia Kristeva rejects 'the very dichotomy man/woman ... as belonging to *metaphysics*' ('Women's Time' 33) and has problematized representation and identity as a religious 'phantasmic necessity' (32) to be challenged by forms of feminism insisting on difference. (See *patriarchy.) The 'rethinking of margins and edges' (Hutcheon 42) has also played an important role in theories of the postmodern and its decentring strategies. (See *postmodernism.)

WINFRIED SIEMERLING

Primary Sources

Bhabha, Homi K. 'The Other Question ... Homi K. Bhabha Reconsiders the Stereotype and Colonial Discourse.' *Screen* 24.6 (1983): 18–36.

Derrida, Jacques. *Dissemination.* 1972. Trans. Barbara Johnson. Chicago: U of Chicago P, 1981.

– *Margins of Philosophy.* 1972. Trans. Alan Bass. Chicago: U of Chicago P, 1982.

– *Of Grammatology.* Trans. Gayatri Chakravorty Spivak. Baltimore and London: Johns Hopkins UP, 1976.

– *Speech and Phenomena.* Trans. David B. Allison. Evanston: Northwestern UP, 1984.

– *The Truth in Painting.* Trans. Geoff Bennington and Ian McLeod. Chicago: U of Chicago P, 1987.

– *Writing and Difference.* 1967. Trans. Alan Bass. Chicago: U of Chicago P, 1978.

Descombes, Vincent. *Modern French Philosophy.* Trans. L. Scott-Fox and J.M. Harding. Cambridge: Cambridge UP, 1980.

Hutcheon, Linda. *A Poetics of Postmodernism: History, Theory, Fiction.* New York and London: Routledge, 1988.

Irigaray, Luce. *Speculum of the Other Woman.* Trans. Gillian C. Gill. Ithaca: Cornell UP, 1985.

Kristeva, Julia. 'Women's Time.' Trans. Alice Jardine and Harry Blake. *Signs* 7.1 (1981): 13–35.

Said, Edward W. *Orientalism.* New York: Random House, 1978.

Metalanguage

Metalanguage is a term first used by the Russian formalists to denote a language that makes assertions about other languages. (See Russian *formalism.) According to *Roman Jakobson, metalinguistic communicative acts are oriented towards the code of communication itself, as when two individuals discuss whether they are understanding each other. (See *code, *communication theory.) The disciplines of linguistics and *semiotics are metalanguages insofar as they each attempt to explain language through a set of coherent and complementary terms and procedures. Literary criticism, in its traditional form, is also a metalanguage – a language that seeks to explain *literature, another language.

Metalanguage has become an issue in critical studies in two ways: (1) poststructuralist critiques have vigorously questioned the possibility of metalanguages; (2) discourse analysis has identified the operation of *ideology with the role of discourses that explain and organize other discourses. (See *poststructuralism, *discourse analysis theory, *discourse.)

Metalanguages seek to rise above their objects in order to examine them, but poststructuralists have questioned the possibility of such disinterested examination. At the end of *The Fashion System*, for instance, *Roland Barthes qualifies the structuralist model he has deployed by situating himself, the analyst, as a component within the analytic system. (See *structuralism.) In so doing he qualifies his own *authority to produce a metalanguage that would explain the sign system of fashion. (See *sign.) The analyst's language is always 'committed,' argues Barthes, which means that its explanation is always preconditioned and hence limited by the analyst's 'historical situation.' As a result, 'the relation between system-object and the analyst's metalanguage does not ... imply any "real" substance to be credited to the analyst, but only a formal validity' (*The Fashion System* 293–4). Because of the historically limited position of the analyst, there is no ultimate critical metalanguage: one analyst's explanation can be another's object of study, and so on in an infinite regress.

The poststructural questioning of metalanguage is best known through the work of *Jacques Derrida. Derrida undermines the claims of metaphysics to be a metalanguage. For Derrida, the problem with metaphysics – as with all metalanguage – is that in order to articulate first principles, to be the language of languages, it has to efface its own status as language. Derrida puts into question the authority of metaphysics by insisting on its status as *writing* – with all the implications the term holds for him. Even the (meta)language of

'being as such' can only present itself, finally, in language.

Certain versions of discourse analysis, while accepting the philosophical impossibility of metalanguages, have maintained the term as part of the ideological study of texts. Colin MacCabe, for instance, argues that classic realist texts work by means of a 'hierarchy of discourses' in which one discourse – the narrative prose – functions as a metalanguage that explains (away) those sections of the text contained in implicit or explicit inverted commas. The authority of the metalanguage is itself assured ideologically, that is, by its appeal to an imaginary 'real' and its simultaneous effacement of its own status as discourse. Writes MacCabe: 'What I have called an unwritten prose (or metalanguage) is exactly that language, which while placing other languages between inverted commas and regarding them as material expressions which express certain meanings, regards those same meanings as finding transparent expression within the metalanguage itself . . . [Metalanguage] is not regarded as material; it is dematerialised to achieve perfect representation – to let the identity of things shine through the window of words' (*Tracking the Signifier* 35).

Though MacCabe concentrates his analysis on classic realism, there is a sense in which all texts construct relations of discursive dominance and subordination. These relations are the effect of the text's rewriting or reproduction of literary and ideological norms. At the same time, it is possible to categorize texts in terms of their greater or lesser insistence on a strict hierarchy of discourses. Roland Barthes' distinction between 'readerly' and 'writerly' texts might be understood from this point of view. (See *readerly/writerly text.) Readerly texts depend very much on the ordering power of a metalanguage. In such texts, the hermeneutic and proairetic codes organize the other textual codes in order to impose their terms 'according to an irreversible order' (*S/Z* 30). Writerly texts, on the other hand, would resist such an ordering in favour of an unlimited polysemia. A key effect of *S/Z* is to show that there is no absolutely irreversible textual order. Even the most apparently readable text contains elements that undermine the organizing authority of its metalanguage.

JAMIE DOPP

Primary Sources

Barthes, Roland. *The Fashion System.* Trans. Matthew Ward and Richard Howard. New York: Hill and Wang, 1983.
– *S/Z.* Trans. Richard Miller. New York: Hill and Wang, 1974.
Derrida, Jacques. 'White Mythology.' In *Margins of Philosophy.* Trans. Alan Bass. Chicago: U of Chicago P, 1982.
Jakobson, Roman, and Morris Halle. *Fundamentals of Language.* The Hague: Mouton P, 1956.
MacCabe, Colin. *Tracking the Signifier.* Minneapolis: U of Minnesota P, 1985.

Metaphysics of presence

*Deconstruction, according to *Jacques Derrida, seeks to expose the often hidden workings of what he calls the 'metaphysics of presence.' This phrase refers to the assumptions of the metaphysical and philosophical tradition which are founded on a belief in 'presence,' that is, on a faith in some unifying transcendental reference point that alone can guarantee the ultimate intelligibility and totalizing power of its *discourse. This centre can take many forms: God, truth, origin, *arche,* finality, or *telos.* According to Derrida, for example, *Ferdinand de Saussure's concept of the signified functions as a metaphysical centre, as does the phallic 'lack' which *Jacques Lacan identifies as the truth of castration grounding the symbolic order. (See *signified/signifier/signification, *desire/lack, *imaginary/symbolic/real, *totalization.)

Derrida points out that the thinking of history has always been grounded in metaphysics and in the West this means that history has always been conceived of as 'a detour between two presences' (*L'Ecriture et la différance* [*Writing and Difference*]), as the interval of an exile from a 'proper' place to which one returns after a period of delay and wandering. In metaphysical terms the 'fall' into history – into time and space and away from original presence – is always at the same time a fall into the order of language and of the *sign. In this 'fallen' realm we dwell in, the signified presence is always absent although both preserved and promised – its advent deferred or postponed until the *parousia* at the end of time. Derrida uses this Greek word which means 'present' or 'being present' as an interchange-

able term for 'presence'; it has a specific theological significance as well, referring to the advent or second coming of Christ on Judgment Day, a meaning which Derrida is clearly playing on. He also uses the temporal sense of 'present,' as well as the idea of being present, or the idea of the subject's presence to himself in consciousness, all meanings which imply, in one way or another, the immediacy of consciousness to its object. (See also *white mythology, *supplementarity, *trace, *logocentrism.)

JOSEPH ADAMSON

Primary Sources

Derrida, Jacques. *L'Ecriture et la différance.* 1967. *Writing and Difference.* Trans. Alan Bass. Chicago: U of Chicago P, 1978.

Metonymy/metaphor

When grouped together, metonymy/metaphor refer to the two modes of arrangement involved in any linguistic utterance: (1) combination (metonymy), the linking of one *sign with another in speech or writing to form a context; (2) selection (metaphor), the choice of one sign from among a group of alternatives similar to it in some respects, different in others. Metonymy thus indicates relations among signs based on external *contiguity;* metaphor refers to relations of internal *similarity.* In a simple sentence like 'The cat is on the mat,' 'cat' is linked to 'on the mat' as *subject* to *predicate.* 'Cat' is itself composed of smaller linguistic units, the *phonemes* (distinctive sounds) /c/, /a/ and /t/. These are relations of contiguity. But 'cat' is chosen from a set of alternative names such as 'feline,' or 'tabby,' or from names of other animals, such as 'dog' or 'horse,' which could have been used as subject of 'is on the mat.' These are relations of similarity.

Until the Russian-American linguist *Roman Jakobson redefined metonymy and metaphor as the two poles of linguistic operation in *Fundamentals of Language* (1956), the terms had been generally used to designate tropes, or figures of speech. (See *trope.) A metonymy (from the Greek for *change of name)* is a figure in which the name of one thing is used for another to which it has a relation of contiguity,

as the use of 'crown' to mean the king. A metaphor (from the Greek for *transfer)* is a trope
in which the meaning of a word or phrase is
shifted to a new domain on the basis of a relation of similarity or analogy, as 'He is a *fox,*' to
mean that he is *sly.*

Jakobson and other Russian formalists had
already argued during the 1920s and 1930s
that literary styles can be understood in terms
of a *binary opposition between metonymy
and metaphor. (See Russian *formalism.) By
expanding the meaning of metonymy/meta-
phor to include all linguistic, indeed all symbolic, functioning, Jakobson asserted that the
processes of contiguity and similarity, which
traditional rhetoric and poetics had long recognized at work in these figures of speech, form
the basis not only of literary styles but also of
all language and thought, including everyday
speech, even unconscious formations such as
dreams. All rhetorical figures can be explained
as variations or combinations of these two
tropes; romanticism and symbolism are metaphorical styles while realism is metonymic; the
'primary process' mechanisms which the founder of psychoanalysis, *Sigmund Freud, isolated in *The Interpretation of Dreams* (1900)
to account for the operations of unconscious
thought are either metonymic – 'displacement'
and 'condensation' – or metaphoric – 'identification' and 'symbolism.' (See *psychoanalytic
theory.)

These latter assimilations were adapted and
revised by the psychoanalyst *Jacques Lacan in
his *Ecrits* (1966). The marriage of linguistics,
poetics and psychoanalysis became one of the
driving forces behind the recent revival of interest in the formerly-moribund field of rhetoric. The Belgian linguists who call themselves
Groupe Mu have undertaken a complete revision of the theory of rhetoric; the historian
*Hayden White has used the expanded notion
of the trope to analyse historical and cultural
writing; the revised rhetoric has stimulated important contributions to the field of literary
criticism by scholars such as *Paul de Man,
Shoshana Felman, *Gérard Genette, *David
Lodge, and *Tzvetan Todorov; the often conflictual relation between *literature and philosophy has been re-examined in studies of
metaphor by *Paul Ricoeur and *Jacques
Derrida; most recently, feminist thinkers
have attacked the sexist implications of binary
oppositions in general, and of that between

metaphor and metonymy in particular (Schor).
(See also *feminist criticism.)

The connection between rhetoric, mind and
language, however, reaches back to antiquity.
Aristotle claims that the ability to find metaphors is the mark of genius, 'since a good metaphor implies an intuitive perception of the
similarity in dissimilars' (*Poetics* 1459a). Quintilian concludes that all language must be
figurative, for rhetoric is the shape (form), or
figure, of the linguistic expression, and all
thoughts must take on some particular form in
order to be uttered (*Institutio Oratoria* 9.1.12).
It was not until the 18th century, however,
that the attempt was made to link a small
number of tropes to what were then considered the basic processes of thought. According
to John Locke and David Hume, there are
three fundamental categories of the association
of ideas – similarity, correspondence (relation
between things associated through habit or
custom) and connection (relation between a
thing and the class that contains it). (In his
treatise *On Memory and Recollection,* Aristotle
had already stated that one is reminded of a
thing by something similar, opposite or contiguous.) Using this system of classification, the
French grammarian Nicholas Beauzée assigned
one trope to each of the categories: metaphor
to similarity; metonymy to correspondence;
and *synecdoche to connection.

In the 19th century Jeremy Bentham revived
the ancient notion that all language is figurative in his *Theory of Fictions* (cf. Ogden). In his
Philosophy of Rhetoric (1936), *I.A. Richards,
combining Aristotle, Bentham and Freud,
claimed that metaphor is the fundamental
property of human thought and life, since
Freud's 'transference' is a synonym for the
Greek 'metaphor,' and the psychoanalytic process he designated by that name entails the
same transfer in human relations that linguistic
metaphor effects in relations of thought. Those
thinkers like Aristotle, Bentham and Richards
who presume that thought takes precedence
over language, generally focus their attention
on metaphor alone; those who assert the primacy of language over thought, such as Jakobson and Lacan, tend to couple metaphor with
metonymy. (See also *rhetorical criticism.)

GILBERT D. CHAITIN

Primary Sources

Aristotle. *The Rhetoric and the Poetics of Aristotle.* New York: Random House, 1984.

Beauzée, Nicholas. 'Trope,' In *Encyclopédie, ou Dictionnaire raisonné des sciences, des arts et des métiers.* Paris: Briasson, 1751–65. Vol. 34: 299–308.

Brooke-Rose, Christine. *A Grammar of Metaphor.* London: Secker and Warburg, 1958.

de Man, Paul. *Allegories of Reading: Figural Language in Rousseau, Nietzsche, Rilke and Proust.* New Haven: Yale UP, 1979.

– *The Rhetoric of Romanticism.* New York: Columbia UP, 1984.

Derrida, Jacques. 'White Mythology.' In *Margins of Philosophy.* Trans. Alan Bass. Chicago: U of Chicago P, 1982.

Felman, Shoshana. *Literature and Psychoanalysis: The Question of Reading, Otherwise.* Baltimore: Johns Hopkins UP, 1982.

Freud, Sigmund. *The Interpretation of Dreams.* Standard Edition, vols. 4 and 5. London: Hogarth P, 1955.

Genette, Gérard. *Figures of Literary Discourse.* Trans. Alan Sheridan. New York: Columbia UP, 1982.

Groupe Mu. *Rhétorique générale.* Paris: Librairie Larousse, 1970.

Henry, Albert. *Métonymie et métaphore.* Brussels: Palais des Académies, 1983.

Hume, David. *A Treatise of Human Nature.* 1739. Oxford: Clarendon P, 1960.

Jakobson, Roman, and Morris Halle. *Fundamentals of Language.* The Hague: Mouton and Company, 1956.

Lacan, Jacques. *Ecrits: A Selection.* 1966. Trans. Alan Sheridan. New York: Norton, 1977.

Locke, John. *An Essay Concerning Human Understanding.* 1690. Oxford: Clarendon P, 1975.

Lodge, David. *The Modes of Modern Writing: Metaphor, Metonymy, and the Typology of Modern Literature.* Ithaca: Cornell UP, 1977.

Nietzsche, Friedrich. 'On Truth and Falsity in the Ultra-Moral Sense.' In *The Complete Works of Friedrich Nietzsche,* vol. 2. New York: Russell and Russell, 1964.

Ogden, Charles K. *Bentham's Theory of Fictions.* New York: Harcourt, Brace and Company, 1932.

Perelman, Chaim, and L. Olbrechts-Tyteca. *The New Rhetoric: A Treatise on Argumentation.* Notre Dame: Notre Dame UP, 1969.

Quintilian. *The Institutio Oratoria of Quintilian, with an English Translation by H.E. Butler.* London: W. Heinemann, 1921–2.

Richards, Ivor A. *The Philosophy of Rhetoric.* London: Oxford UP, 1936.

Ricoeur, Paul. *The Rule of Metaphor: Multidisciplinary Studies of the Creation of Meaning in Language.* Toronto: U of Toronto P, 1977.

Schor, Naomi. *Breaking the Chain: Women, Theory, and French Realist Fiction.* New York: Columbia UP, 1985.

Sorabji, Richard. *Aristotle on Memory.* Providence: Brown UP, 1972.

Todorov, Tzvetan. *The Poetics of Prose.* Trans. Richard Howard. Ithaca: Cornell UP, 1977.

– *Theories of the Symbol.* Trans. Catherine Porter. Ithaca: Cornell UP, 1977.

Vico, Giambattista. *The New Science of Giambattista Vico.* Trans. Thomas G. Bergin and Max H. Frisch. Ithaca: Cornell UP, 1948.

White, Hayden V. *Tropics of Discourse: Essays in Cultural Criticism.* Baltimore: Johns Hopkins UP, 1978.

Mimesis

Mimesis is 'the continuous dynamic relation between a work of art and whatever stands over against it in the actual moral universe, or could conceivably stand over against it' (Whalley, *Studies* 73). Often translated as 'imitation,' mimesis is in fact a transliteration of the original Greek word, rather than a translation, and as such it retains at least a partial independence. That independence is registered in the way the word has never been wholly naturalized in English, despite being listed in most dictionaries, including the *OED*. It declares insistently its Greek origin, not least in the suggestion of action or activity. Though both terms denote an art of representation or resemblance, the emphasis is different. Imitation, a Latinate abstraction, implies something static, a copy, a final product; mimesis involves something dynamic, a process, an active relation with a living reality.

The precise nature of mimesis has been the subject of age-old debate, its scope set out definitively by Plato and Aristotle and its questions tied invariably to questions concerning the nature of the reality to be represented. Literal mimesis is a copying of the concrete world, accessible to the senses. Plato, in part because he viewed the resulting copy as being at two removes from reality, banished the artists from his ideal state in the *Republic* (chap. 10). Metaphysical mimesis is a copying of the eternal forms, accessible only to intellect and reason, as Plato explains in the *Republic* (3, 6) and celebrates in the *Timaeus*. Discussions of Plato's views, as they bear on art, philosophy and religion, can be found in *Hans-Georg Gadamer, Dialogue and Dialectic* (trans. 1980) and in Iris Murdoch, *The Fire and the Sun* (1977).

Aristotle, in the *Poetics*, adds a further dimension to the debate and refutes some of Plato's charges against the poets, but there is considerable overlap between his views of mimesis and those of Plato. Like Plato, Aristotle thinks the fundamental business of mimesis is to reveal universals, a process that in his view makes poetry more philosophical than history. (See *universal.) He is, however, more hopeful than Plato about the ability of poets to do this, and he thinks of universals as more inextricably tied to particular concrete events and characters. This fusion of the particular and the universal is a lead followed by modern defenders of realism in *literature such as *Yvor Winters and *Georg Lukács. Aristotle's distinctive contribution to the topic arises from his special interest in action, not only the action of tragic drama but also the activity of the poet as maker. In organizing the plot, or in orchestrating the dynamic interplay between form and content, the poet makes, as Gerald Else puts it, 'that structure of events in which universals may come to expression.' (See *story/ plot.)

The core of Aristotle's view may be described as enactive mimesis, a term applying not only to the impersonations of the theatre, where it is the actors who do the mimesis, but more generally as well. (See *performance criticism.) In the words of Stephen Halliwell, 'Aristotle's guiding notion of mimesis is implicitly that of enactment: poetry proper (which may include some works in prose) does not describe, narrate or offer argument, but dramatises and embodies human speech and action.' Some, like Thomas Twining in the 18th century, have been led by the emphasis on action to argue that only dramatic poetry is fully mimetic. It is more broadly characteristic of literary works, however, to involve the act of reliving, or living into, the human experiences that give body and substance to reality. *Erich Auerbach explores the relations between reality and the various levels of style in many different genres. And *F.R. Leavis emphasizes the realizing force of poetic enactment.

The activity of mimesis can be seen as moral in two very broad senses. First, the act of attending to reality implies that it is worth attending to and worth respecting as different from, though not necessarily unrelated to, the perceiver. Second, the enactments of literature

explore the implications or consequences of human actions and perception. At its best, mimesis is a method of strengthening and deepening the moral understanding, just as it is also a method of exploring and challenging received notions of the real. The process does not rest simply with what any reader or writer happens to know; it may stretch the limits of the real by entertaining the conceivable as at least provisionally real, or as offering a perspective on aspects of the real that cannot otherwise be seen. Reality is sometimes defined in contradistinction to the imaginary. But that Aristotle has a more comprehensive view of reality than this distinction allows is shown by his witty remark about a likely impossibility being superior to an implausible possibility. (One of the great examples of a likely impossibility is the ideal state in Plato's *Republic*.) This remark also shows that the dichotomy between classic and romantic – as if only the classic were mimetic – needs rethinking. George Whalley argues that Aristotelian mimesis is congruent with what Coleridge calls 'the primary imagination,' which Whalley describes as performing a 'supreme realizing function.'

A well-known example from Shakespeare (*Hamlet* 3.2) illustrates these various senses of mimesis. Hamlet says that the purpose of drama is 'to hold as 'twere the mirror up to nature.' Note that the process involves the act of holding as well as of mirroring. In the play-within-the-play, Shakespeare explores the dynamic relations among the holder (Hamlet), the mirror ('The Mousetrap'), and the beholders: the audience (which includes Claudius). At the climax, one 'Lucianus' pours poison in the ear of the Player-King. At one level, this copies the murder of King Hamlet by Claudius (a past action). But Hamlet interrupts to say that Lucianus is *'nephew* to the King' (italics added), so at another level the scene represents the relation between Hamlet and Claudius (and a possible, or conceivable, future action – like, though not altogether like, the action which concludes the larger play). This fusing of images is of the essence of the play's dynamic, and shows simple imitation combining with more complex purposes in a full mimesis. In the words of Harold Jenkins (1982), 'when Lucianus becomes the image of Hamlet he does not cease to be Claudius too.' The scene depicts crime and punishment simultaneously, and the idea of retributive justice merges with the concrete physical acts. The simultaneity implies that justice is eternal, not time-bound; but Hamlet's act in pointing to this meaning reveals an intense engagement with the process of the action, which must unfold in time and in the lives of specific individuals. Mimesis, as is seen in this brief example, is a congeries of particular events and their meanings – and of the enactments through which these become manifest.

JOHN BAXTER

Primary Sources

Aristotle. *On Poetry and Style.* Trans. G.M.A. Grube. Indianapolis: Bobbs-Merrill, 1958.

Auerbach, Erich. *Mimesis: The Representation of Reality in Western Literature.* Trans. Willard R. Trask. Princeton: Princeton UP, 1953.

Boyd, John D., SJ. 'A New Mimesis?' *Renascence: Essays on Values in Literature* 37 (1985): 133–210.

Else, Gerald F. *Aristotle's Poetics: The Argument.* Cambridge, Mass.: Harvard UP, 1957.

Halliwell, Stephen. *Aristotle's Poetics.* Chapel Hill: U of North Carolina P, 1986.

Jenkins, Harold, ed. *Hamlet.* By William Shakespeare. London: Methuen, 1982.

Leavis, F.R. 'Imagery and Movement.' *Scrutiny* 13 (1945): 119–34.

Lukács, Georg. *Writer and Critic and Other Essays.* Trans. Arthur Kahn. London: Merlin P, 1970.

McKeon, Richard. 'Literary Criticism and the Concept of Imitation in Antiquity.' In *Critics and Criticism.* Ed. R.S. Crane. Chicago: U of Chicago P, 1952.

Whalley, George. 'The Aristotle-Coleridge Axis.' *University of Toronto Quarterly* 42 (1973): 93–109.

– *Studies in Literature and the Humanities: Innocence of Intent.* Kingston and Montreal: McGill-Queen's UP, 1985.

Winters, Yvor. *In Defense of Reason.* Denver and New York: Alan Swallow P and W. Morrow, 1947.

Mirror stage

*Jacques Lacan first posited the existence of the mirror stage in a paper delivered in 1936, developed it in a published exposition in 1949, and expanded it once again in 1951. The mirror stage is the cornerstone of his psychoanalytic theory and is especially significant as a critique of Freudian ego psychology, which posits a belief in rational, individual self-consciousness. For Lacan early childhood development can be divided into three stages: the pre-mirror, the mirror and the post-mirror, or pre-specular, specular and post-specular, each marked by certain kinds of *méconnaissances*, distortions and misrepresentations. (See *psychoanalytic theory, *Sigmund Freud.)

Sometime before the age of 18 months, the human infant recognizes its own image in a mirror. What takes place is a prelinguistic identification of selfhood: 'that image is me.' The infant discovers its identity in a libidinally invested or narcissistic act of imagination and is thereafter constituted by a primordial, eternal lack (*manque*). What the infant sees, in schematic terms, is the Gestalt of a body that is within the world and yet distinct from it: 'that is *me.*' The image of a body unified and separated by an I-concept suggests a moment when the self creates itself.

The mirror is of such importance because the child's ability to recognize his own image somewhat falsely implies the possibility of a certain objectivity, detachment and self-totalization that can lead to the constituting of a self and the ability to distinguish between self and other as well as between subject and object. (See *self/other, *subject/object, *totalization.) The image of the mirror also illustrates how human beings recognize and even create themselves through the images of others, who are, in their own turn, reflections of yet again still others. The mirror, then, is not something in which viewers see an approximately accurate image of self; rather, it figures the way in which we found our identities upon the images of others and the way in which we finally have to recognize otherness and our differences from others. Consequently, while Freud postulates that, once the child has chosen a sexual identity and social role, he or she can grow through the processes of social interaction, Lacan suggests that human beings are an assemblage of ever-changing images mainly without progression.

In psychoanalytic experience, disintegration is the norm and finds expression in dreams and images of fragmented bodies; but this is not Lacan's main point. The mirror stage begins a process of *méconnaissance* or misrecognition that will endlessly circle the primary truth of the subject – lack. After the mirror stage, the subject creates an armour of false identification systems, and even analysis cannot break through them to reveal an authentic, true self; *méconnaissance* is, to this extent, absolute. The mirror stage occurs within an overall drama of Desire that is the basis of Lacan's system. Desire is always the desire of the Other. The illusion of autonomy and identity exemplified by the mirror stage falls apart under the rule of the Lacanian Other (which is language itself) and with the discovery that the world contains other bodies which rob one's own body of its ideal unity. Lacan's imaginary order necessarily confronts and adopts aspects of the symbolic. This leads Lacan in *Ecrits* to conclude that one's ego can never be reduced to experiential identity and further that 'I is an other.' (See *imaginary/symbolic/real, *desire/lack.)

Lacan's mirror stage develops the work of Freud by providing a theory about the development of the self, but it has itself been responsible for new thinking in the areas of psychoanalysis, *narratology, linguistics, *semiotics, and feminism. (See *feminist criticism.) In many ways these diverse fields are joined together by common assumptions about the symbolic order and its implications for the signifying process. Many feminists, for example, agree with Lacan that subjectivity is socially constructed and that theories of the mirror suggest in what ways *power and *authority have been restricted to males. They approve of Lacan in part because he describes the process by which people are subjectified and subjugated and in part because he has given women the concepts and the language whereby they can legitimize their position as women. *Luce Irigaray and *Julia Kristeva explore the qualities that have sometimes been identified with the matriarchal – the non-rational, the unconscious, the body, the feelings, love, self-identity, speech, and the special language of intimacy – and that are said to belong to the imaginary and to have been repressed. Those characteristics that have often been referred to as masculine – the reason, the conscious, the mind, logic, analysis, writing, the language of the market-place – belonging to the symbolic have been elevated. In moving from the imaginary to the symbolic, human beings have gone from the implicitly feminine to the explicitly masculine. French feminists especially suggest that the goal of women should be to question the symbolic and reinvigorate the imaginary, as well as to destabilize the conscious and enfranchise the unconscious, in order to reconstitute the self and demystify the cogito.

Another area in which the mirror stage has been considered is in the development and structures of prose. The imaginary and symbolic, feminine and masculine, 'inside' and 'outside' (*Innenwelt* and *Umwelt*), and the question of the signifier have become ways of talking about a number of things, especially plot and style. (See *signified/signifier/signification.) Lacan himself raises the issue of literary applications in his interpretations of the role of signifiers in *Hamlet* and Edgar Allan Poe's 'The Purloined Letter.' Shoshana Felman similarly uses Lacanian analysis to develop a theory of narrative based upon the unconscious, while Peter Brooks uses Lacan's ideas of metaphor and metonymy to study the function of desire and the death wish in narrative. (See *metonymy/metaphor.) Writers such as Kristeva have identified the symbolic with logic, coherency and the Artistotelian pattern of introduction, complication and crisis, and denouement. Kristeva's own writing style provides an alternative to this master-realist, male narrative. As exemplified by her essay 'Stabat Mater,' her prose is sometimes separated into two columns, one strongly metaphoric, sensuous, affective, and without end point (illustrative of what she calls the semiotic or pre-Oedipal) and the other rational and coherent with certain conclusions (illustrative of what she calls the symbolic or post-Oedipal). The juxtaposition of the two columns suggests a dispersal of desire that is equated with the imaginary and feminine. Prose based upon the imaginary or implicitly feminine should, then, supposedly appear less consciously structured and rationally determined and thus allow for the play of possibilities and proliferation of voices. (See also theories of *play/freeplay.)

GREGOR CAMPBELL and
GORDON E. SLETHAUG

Primary Sources

Lacan, Jacques. 'Desire and Interpretation of Desire in *Hamlet.' Yale French Studies* 55/56 (1977): 11–52.
– *Ecrits: A Selection.* Trans. Alan Sheridan. New York and London: W.W. Norton and Co., 1977.
– *The Four Fundamental Concepts of Psycho-Analysis.* Ed. Jacques-Alain Miller. Trans. Alan Sheridan. New York and London: W.W. Norton and Co., 1978.
– *The Language of the Self: The Function of Language in Psychoanalysis.* Ed. and trans. Anthony Wilden. Baltimore: Johns Hopkins UP, 1968.
– 'Seminar on "The Purloined Letter."' In *Contemporary Literary Criticism: Literary and Cultural Studies.* Ed. Robert Con Davis and Ronald Schlei-

fer. New York and London: Longman, 1989, 301–20.

Secondary Sources

Brooks, Peter. 'Freud's Masterplot: Questions of Narrative.' *Yale French Studies* 55/56 (1977): 280–300.
Felman, Shoshana. 'Turning the Screw of Interpretation.' *Yale French Studies* 55/56 (1977): 94–207.
Grosz, Elizabeth. *Jacques Lacan: A Feminist Introduction.* London and New York: Routledge, 1990.
Irigaray, Luce. *This Sex Which Isn't One.* Trans. Catherine Porter and Carolyn Burke. Ithaca: Cornell UP, 1985.
Kristeva, Julia. 'Stabat Mater.' In *Contemporary Literary Criticism: Literary and Cultural Studies.'* New York and London: Longman, 1989, 186–203.

Misprision

Misprision is a concept devised by *Harold Bloom describing the mechanics of poetic influence. According to Bloom, the making of poetry necessitates a creative misreading (misprision) of earlier works. Partially based on *Sigmund Freud's 'family romance' and emphasizing *intertextuality, misprision outlines a poet's violent struggle to overcome the '*anxiety of influence,' that is, the pressure exerted by precursors, through a creative alteration of earlier pivotal works. This is not to say that poets endlessly repeat each other, but that a poem entails a fundamental dialectic between the recognition of the power of the past and the 'swerving' away (Bloom describes this process as *clinamen*, a metaphor suggested by Lucretius) from its 'tyranny.' Bloom emphasizes that only 'strong' poets are capable of moving against the pressure of the past and he uses Milton's Satan as an allegory to depict his theory. For Bloom, Milton's Satan (as Fallen Strong Poet), recognizes and rejects the circumscription prescribed by God (the omnipotent precursor) and in the process asserts his own, however provisional, identity. The creation of poetry then is analagous to Satan's position: incapable of extrication from the power of literary influence, it becomes a practice of defiance. Wallace Stevens' 'Notes Toward a Supreme Fiction' is saturated with the presence of Walt Whitman, particularly his 'Song of Myself,' but Stevens does not replicate his precursor's work. Rather he engages misprision through a creative misinterpretation of the

previous *text, thereby asserting a distinct identity. In effect Stevens' poem may be said to enact a misreading of Whitman, a reading that transforms the earlier poem to such an extent that it appears as though Stevens 'himself had written the precursor's characteristic work.'

Borrowing the term 'ephebe' from Wallace Stevens to describe the younger poet, Bloom suggests that there are various stages of progressive mastery that the younger poet must pass through in order to become a strong poet. It is important to note that the relationship between a potentially strong poet and a precursor does not necessarily entail conscious acknowledgment of the precursor's influential power and also that the precursor-figure may be a composite of several writers. What is crucial to this relationship is that the strong poet's works cannot be viewed independently as isolated texts; there are no 'original' works. Through misprision a specific poem is shown to exist in a dynamic interconnection with other poems. Misprision also extends to critical analysis. The practice of criticism involves a wilful misreading of poetic texts and it is Bloom's contention that critical and poetical misprision overlap, blurring the edge between the two forms of *discourse.

The concept of misprision traverses much of Bloom's writing. Discussions of misprision take place in *The Anxiety of Influence: A Theory of Poetry* (1973), *A Map of Misreading* (1975), *Kabbalah and Criticism* (1975), and *Poetry and Repression: Revisionism from Blake to Stevens.* (1976). The most practical application of the theory of misprision is demonstrated in *Wallace Stevens: The Poems of Our Climate* (1977).

MICHAEL TRUSSLER

Primary Sources

Bloom, Harold. *The Anxiety of Influence: A Theory of Poetry.* New York: Oxford UP, 1973.
– *Kabbalah and Criticism.* New York: Seabury, 1975.
– *A Map of Misreading.* New York: Oxford UP, 1975.
– *Poetry and Repression: Revisionism from Blake to Stevens.* New Haven: Yale UP, 1976.
– *Wallace Stevens: The Poems of Our Climate.* Ithaca: Cornell UP, 1977.

Secondary Sources

Leitch, Vincent B. *Deconstructive Criticism.* New York: Columbia UP, 1983.

Monologism

Monologism is the reduction of multiple voices and consciousnesses within a *text to a single version of truth imposed by the author. The truths of other consciousnesses or ideologies are never treated equally alongside the author's but are instead refuted or reduced to a common denominator. (See *ideology.) Novelistic prose is best able to contest monologic control through dialogism which is antisystemic and polyphonic, thus exerting a centrifugal (subversive) pressure against authorial dominance. (See *polyphony, *double-voicing/ dialogism, *subversion.) Some genres, claims *Mikhail Bakhtin, like epic and lyric poetry, exemplify monologism because the author retains the power to convey his vision of truth directly; consequently, the author limits the potential meaning of the text. (See *genre criticism.)

In his early formulation of the dialogic principle which culminates in the novel, Bakhtin celebrates Dostoevsky as the exemplar of polyphony, while Tolstoy is cited as a monologic novelist. The initial sentence of *Anna Karenina* is cited as monologic: 'All happy families are like one another; each unhappy family is unhappy in its own way.' Here, the authorial voice is absolute and uncontestable. There is no counterstatement within the text to query the author's truth. Later, Bakhtin comes to see at least the possibility or potential for polyphony in many early texts – the Socratic dialogues, Menippean satire, the medieval mystery play, Shakespeare, Cervantes, Voltaire, Diderot, Balzac, and Hugo. These precursors prepare the way for Dostoevsky's crucial contribution to the polyphonic novel.

Bakhtin views all systems of *binary opposition as monologic, either Hegelian or Marxist. (See *Marxist criticism.) Ironically, in setting up the Dostoevsky (polyphonic) / Tolstoy (monologic) opposition, Bakhtin can be seen to construct a monologic binary model of his own. He nevertheless theoretically eschews the dialectics of binary oppositions in favour of dialogism. Monologic belief systems which posit absolutes locate truth 'in a single institution, such as the state, or in a single object, such as an idol or text, or in a single identity such as God, the ego conceived as an absolute subject, or the artist-genius who produces unique texts' (Clark and Holquist 348). For

Bakhtin, dialogic truth requires two or more contesting voices which are allowed free play within the 'form-shaping ideology' (Morson and Emerson 238) of novelistic prose. The novel, then, contests monologism. (See theories of *play/freeplay.)

Bakhtin's final position views monologism as an early stage in the evolution of genres towards the democratic ideal of Dostoevskyan polyphony. Polyphony does not supplant monologism, rather 'each new genre merely supplements the old ones, merely widens the circle of already existing genres' (*Problems of Dostoevsky's Poetics* 271). (See *dialogical criticism.)

PHYLLIS MARGARET PARYAS

Primary Sources

Bakhtin, M.M. *The Dialogic Imagination.* Ed. and trans. Caryl Emerson and Michael Holquist. Austin: U of Texas P, 1981.
– *Problems of Dostoevsky's Poetics.* Ed. and trans. Caryl Emerson. Minneapolis: U of Minnesota P, 1984.
Clark, Katerina, and Michael Holquist. *Mikhail Bakhtin.* Cambridge: Harvard UP, 1984.
Morson, Gary Saul, and Caryl Emerson. *Mikhail Bakhtin: Creation of a Prosaics.* Stanford UP, 1990.
Tolstoy, Leo. *Anna Karenina.* Trans. David Magarshak. New York: Signet, 1961.

Myth

Myth is a term used widely in literary criticism, especially in historical criticism's accounts of the mythologies used by literary artists and in *archetypal criticism's descriptions of the ways in which certain widespread images, character types and narrative designs persistently recur throughout *literature. (See *archetype.) *Northrop Frye sees myth as the structural foundation of literature and presents a rhetoric of mythology which is similar to *Tzvetan Todorov's grammar of poetic expression. There are many non-literary uses of the concept of myth, perhaps most notably those of *Claude Lévi-Strauss in his structural studies of Amerindian mythology.

In its most ordinary meaning a myth is a story about a god or some other supernatural being; sometimes it concerns a deified human being or a ruler of divine descent. A collection of traditional myths in a particular culture constitutes a mythology which illustrates or explains the origin of the world, why the world was as it once was and how it has changed and why certain things happen. Each myth serves its expository or its explanatory function by reference to the thoughts, desires and actions of the gods and other supernatural beings. From ancestral stories or myths human beings of a particular culture or society learn how they are to live and what meanings to attach to their lives.

Because many writers use the old stories or myths from their own culture or from others, criticism devotes considerable effort to the identification of these recurrent phenomena and to the explication of ways in which they function in literary works. At times the myth occurs in literature simply as a resonant, powerful story; at other times it simply provides ornamental overtones. Still again, as in its etymological meaning in the Greek *mythos* (plot, story, narrative), the myth is the narrative structure itself of the literary work.

Seen from the perspective of archetypal criticism, myths or *mythoi* are the structural principles of literature that make possible verbal communication of narrative and meaning. Drawing on cultural anthropology's interest in ritual and analytic psychology's interest in dreams, literary criticism sees myth as the union in verbal form of ritual and dreams that otherwise would remain inarticulate. Ritual cannot account for itself and dream is a set of coded references to the dreamer's life. Verbalization of the myth gives meaning to the ritual and narrative form to the dream, thus making possible social communication. Myths as generic narrative structures – comedy, romance, tragedy, *irony and satire – are structures of imagery in movement. (See *Carl Gustav Jung, *psychonanalytic theory, *code.)

In the world of myth, writers find an abstract or purely literary storehouse of fictional and thematic design unaffected by canons of plausible adaptation to ordinary human experience. (See *theme, *canon.) Myth provides writers with a world of total metaphor in which everything can be identified with everything else. (See *metonymy/metaphor.) When the writer moves away from the direct use of myth, adaptation to considerations of greater realism emerge.

A completely different concept of myth is explored by *Roland Barthes. In *Mythologies* (1957) he examines the 'myths' or cultural artefacts of French mass culture, including writing, sports, film, advertising, and food. Regarding language not as a transparent vehicle of communication but as a means of repression by the bourgeoisie, Barthes argues that language enforces a certain *ideology. Studying a variety of texts, Barthes advances a 'paradoxical' mode of reading (Ray 173) in which the reader must search out the 'mythic' or new meaning at odds with the surface logic of the language of a *text. The reader must 'unlearn' traditional social values which have seemed 'natural' and must regain more pluralistic perspectives. (See *paradox, *demythologizing.)

ALVIN A. LEE

Primary Sources

Barthes, Roland. *Mythologies*. New York: Hill and Wang, 1972.
Frye, Northrop. *Anatomy of Criticism*. Princeton: Princeton UP, 1957.
Lévi-Strauss, Claude. *The Savage Mind*. London: Weidenfeld and Nicolson, 1966.
Todorov, Tzvetan. *Theories of the Symbol*. Ithaca: Cornell UP, 1982.
Ray, William. *Literary Meaning: From Phenomenology to Deconstruction*. Oxford: Basil Blackwell, 1984.

Name-of-the-Father

Language, for *Jacques Lacan, is an abstract realm of signifiers. (See *signified/signifier/signification.) Human subjectivity takes place in infancy as an effect of language, and even the unconscious is structured like a language. Lacan's interest in language and the symbolic (see *imaginary/symbolic/real) led him to reinterpret Sigmund Freud's Oedipus complex in symbolic terms. (See *Freud.) The patriarchal dominance of an actual Oedipal Father translates into the dominance of the Name-of-the-Father within Lacan's symbolic order. (See *patriarchy.) In *Totem and Taboo* (1913), Freud posited that the historical dominance of the Father must have resulted in his murder, committed by his sons. The incest taboo, or law in general, is thereby sustained by primordial, criminal guilt. The dead Father of culture and memory exerts a stronger force of repression than the living Father, which is a kind of allegory for the power of signifiers and language in general over what is signified. According to Lacan, 'the symbolic Father is, in so far as he signifies the Law, the dead Father.' The Name-of-the-Father is both the source of *authority and the signifier of that authority.

Within the symbolic order as a whole, the Name-of-the-Father functions as a governing Law (in French, *nom* and *non* are homophonic) in the dual function of restricting and prescribing. The Name, which is a series of names (echoing, perhaps, the Christian liturgy 'in the name of the Father, the Son, and the Holy Spirit'), sustains the structure of desire in the very midst of its prohibition. (See *desire/lack.) Sometime around the *mirror stage, the subject enters into the symbolic order, leaving behind an undifferentiated relation to the mother's body. The subject finds itself essentially divided under the threat of punishment through castration. The signifier of desire for the subject, who is now bound by the symbolic order, is the phallus, which remains under the authority of the Name-of-the-Father. The exclusion of an essential signifier from the symbolic order, an event Lacan terms foreclosure, will trigger psychosis in the form of a breakdown of the symbolic order and its ability to actually signify. A patient in this condition will attempt to reconnect signifiers to their signifieds through delusional metaphors. (See *metonymy/metaphor.)

Within the Lacanian genesis of subjectivity, desire is structured by the laws of language and the semiotic trajectory of the phallus as the image or signifier of desire. (See *semiotics.) The Name-of-the-Father, as pure signifier – signifier of signification – is a stand-in for the *power of language (and culture) to rule through the threat of castration (or foreclosure) and thereby establish boundaries for law, desire, gender, and difference. On the level of *text and *discourse, identifying the Name-of-the-Father has the potential for revealing the entire structure of law and desire within a particular culture or discursive formation.

GREGOR CAMPBELL

Primary Sources

Lacan, Jacques. *Ecrits: A Selection.* Trans. Alan Sheridan. New York: Norton, 1977.
– *The Four Fundamental Concepts of Psycho-Analysis.* Ed. Jacques-Alain Miller. Trans. Alan Sheridan. New York: Norton, 1978.
– and the *Ecole freudienne. Feminine Sexuality.* Ed. Juliet Mitchell and Jacqueline Rose. Trans. Jacqueline Rose. New York: Norton, 1982.

Narratee

The concept of the narratee, first proposed by *Gérard Genette but developed and popularized by *Gerald Prince, is the communicative partner of the *narrator, filler of the receiver position in narrative. As is the case with narrators, narratees are actual individuals in non-fictional narratives but textual constructs in fiction.

While the persona of the narrator is constructed on the basis of the question 'Who speaks?' the narratee is the one who hears, the one to whom the narrator is speaking. Both are determined by explicit or implicit textual signs: the use of second-person pronouns, properties attributed by the narrative *discourse to the referent of these pronouns, rhetorical questions, deictics presupposing familiarity with certain objects ('one of those x ...'), allusions to common knowledge (*Prince, Piwowarczyk). Among these however, a distinction must be made between those which refer to a narratee located in the textual world and those which project an *implied reader located in the actual world. 'Reader, I married him' (*Jane Eyre*) is addressed by a first-person narrator to a narratee who believes in the existence of Jane Eyre, but '(Reader), these characters I am talking about never existed' (modified version of a sentence from John Fowles' *The French Lieutenant's Woman*) would be a metafictional comment addressed by the implied author to a hypothetical reader who regards the *text as a novel. So to some extent does this sentence from Balzac's *Le Père Goriot* – even though it is widely regarded as a prototypical sign of the narratee: 'You, my reader, now holding this book in your white hand, and saying to yourself in the depths of your easy chair, "I wonder if this will amuse me!"' (See *reference/referent, *sign.)

Insofar as utterances may be addressed to either a specific person (in conversation, letters) or to the general public (published texts), narratees may be either individuals or collective entities. Individuated narratees participate in the plot in the same way as do individuated narrators: as uninvolved witness, secondary character or main protagonist (recipients of letters in epistolary novels, or the referent of the second-person pronoun in Butor's *La Modification*). (See *story/plot.) When the text is addressed to a collectivity, the narratee is constructed as a set of beliefs presupposed by the text. As is the case with the relations between the impersonal narrator and the implied author, the beliefs of the collective narratee tend to blend with those of the implied reader on all questions other than the truth of the particular narrative facts.

The possibility of unreliable narration reveals an ambiguity in the concept of narratee. When a first-person narrator tries to deceive his audience or personal addressee (as often happens in epistolary novels), there are two ways to reconstruct the narratee: (1) the individual projected by the narrator, who takes his deceptive discourse at face value; or (2) the character 'objectively' addressed by the narrator, whose beliefs do not necessarily correspond to the narrator's declarations. The first construct is a projection of the narrator but the second is a projection of the implied author. This potential discrepancy leads Peter Rabinowitz to postulate an 'ideal narrative audience.' The issue of delineating the scope of narratee against these two concepts remains to be addressed.

MARIE-LAURE RYAN

Primary Sources

Genette, Gérard. *Figures III*. Paris: Seuil, 1973.

Piwowarczyk, Mary Ann. 'The Narratee and the Situation of Enunciation: A Reconsideration of Prince's Theory.' *Genre* 9 (1976): 161–77.

Prince, Gerald. 'Introduction to the Study of the Narratee.' In *Reader Response Criticism*. Ed. Jane P. Tompkins. Baltimore: Johns Hopkins UP, 1980, 7–25.

Rabinowitz, Peter J. 'Truth in Fiction: A Reexamination of Audiences.' *Critical Inquiry* 4.1 (1977): 121–41.

Narrative code

Narrative *code, a concept first proposed by *Roland Barthes in *S/Z* – a close reading of Balzac's short story 'Sarrasine' (1973) – is defined inductively through the enumeration and description of the members of the class. Barthes proposes a list of five narrative codes:

1. The 'proairetic' code or code of actions which organizes the actions of characters into narrative sequences, subsuming each sequence under a generic term which reveals its strategic function. Barthes' examples of generic categories are murder, date, leisurely walk.

2. The 'hermeneutic' code or code of enigmas gathers the semantic units which pertain in one way or another to the formulation and solution of a problem: identifying the enigma, scattering clues, delaying the answer, suggesting false leads, forming and discarding wrong answers, revealing the truth. (See *hermeneutics.)

3. The 'semic' or connotative code consists of extracting some of the semantic features, or 'semes,' which are 'connoted' (that is, implied, rather than signified) by text units of variable size. Recurring 'semes' are grouped into thematic configurations which transcend the linear order of the narrative *discourse. For example, in 'Sarrasine' a party at a private hotel in the Faubourg Saint-Honoré connotes wealth and is linked to other passages suggesting the same feature. The semic code also collects the various features which are attached to proper names, thus allowing the formation of characters. (See *semee.)

4. The 'symbolic' code links particular events and existents to abstract, universal concepts. (See *universal.) Under symbolic code, Barthes also understands the organization of signifieds into rhetorical figures and spatial patterns, such as antithesis and inverse symmetry. For example, in 'Sarrasine,' the castrato Zambinella represents the inverse concepts of super-femininity and sub-masculinity. (See *signified/signifier/signification.)

5. The 'referential' or cultural code is invoked whenever the text invites the reader to use his or her knowledge of the real world in the formation of meaning. This knowledge, presupposed by the realistic *text to be natural and immediately derived from experience, is regarded by Barthes as an already codified image derived from textual sources. For example, the implicit allusion in 'Sarrasine' is to a voice of popular wisdom stating what everybody is supposed to know about certain human types: women, Italians, artists. (See *reference/referent.)

This repertory of narrative codes raises several theoretical questions:

1. Is the list exhaustive? According to Barthes, all *lexies* (units of reading) illustrate one of the codes and no other code is needed to describe the production of narrative meaning. This claim has been occasionally chal-

lenged by exponents of the structuralist doctrine (*Jonathan Culler, *Robert Scholes) but there has been no serious attempt to amend the system. (See *structuralism.)

2. Are the codes created by the text and cracked by the reader or is their mastering a prerequisite of narrative understanding? The answer differs with every category: the proairetic code presupposes familiarity with standard scripts and models for the interpretation of human activity; the cultural code precedes the text but is modified by it; the symbolic code is built on conventional associations (white= purity), but the text proposes its own system of symbolic equivalences.

3. Are these five aspects of textual communication really codes and are they narrative? A code is a set of rules whose knowledge regulates certain types of behaviour. A truly narrative code should regulate the production of narrative meaning. As such it should differ from both the code serving as medium (usually the linguistic code) and from the cultural codes signified by the text (for instance the traffic code in the sentence 'she ran a red light'). None of the five categories proposed by Barthes can be associated with a definite set of rules constitutive of narrative meaning. They are not codes in any formal sense of the term but rather basic types of semantic operations: detecting scripts in the behaviour of human referents and rationalizing their gestures into meaningful actions (proairetic code); analysing complex representations into simple semantic components (semic code); gathering all the features of textual referents and building their mental image (semic code, second interpretation); establishing networks of relations among signifieds and linking these networks to universal themes (symbolic code); using world-knowledge to fill in the informational gaps in the text (referential code); assessing the contribution of the information provided by the text to the solution of an enigma (hermeneutic code). Of these operations, some appear to be universals of discourse processing (referential and semic code), some are favoured by literary texts independently of narrativity (symbolic code), some indeed presuppose a narrative message (proairetic code), and some may be associated with particular narrative genres (dominance of the hermeneutic code in detective novels). If the five narrative codes are reinterpreted as aspects of the cognitive activity involved in the processing of texts, there is no reason to consider the system exhaustive or its elements definitive. (See also *theme, *narrotology.)

MARIE-LAURE RYAN

Primary Sources

Barthes, Roland. *S/Z*. Paris: Seuil, 1970.
– 'Textual Analysis of Poe's "Valdemar."' In *Untying the Text*. Ed. Robert Young. London: Routledge, 1981, 133–61.
Culler, Jonathan. *Structuralist Poetics*. Ithaca: Cornell UP, 1975.
Scholes, Robert. *Structuralism in Literature. An Introduction*. New Haven and London: Yale UP, 1974.

Narrator

In a narrative *text, the narrator is the speaking 'voice' which takes responsibility for the act of narration, telling the story as 'true fact.' In non-fictional narration, this is the actual speaker who physically produces the narrative *discourse. In fiction these two elements of the communication situation are logically distinct. The actual sender – or author – is located in the actual world and transmits a fiction to another member of the actual world, the reader. The narrator is a part of the textual world and communicates a narrative to another member of the textual world, the so-called *narratee. The communicative pairs formed by author/ reader and narrator/narratee are located in separate systems of reality but the systems are bridged through an accepted convention: the author speaks as if he were the narrator, the reader receives the message as if he were the narratee. (See *communication theory, *narratology.)

There may exist a number of different narrators in any narrative text. The various narrative voices are either juxtaposed on the same level or embedded in a hierarchical structure. Juxtaposition is exemplified by the turn-taking of conversation or by the exchange of letters of epistolary novels. *Embedding occurs whenever a primary narrator quotes the discourse of a secondary narrator. Narrative embedding structures the text into a series of discrete levels (called 'diegetic' by *Gérard Genette). (See *diegesis.)

Narrators of both fiction and non-fiction

may be classified according to their mode of involvement in the narrated events. A narrator may be a historian of events not witnessed in person (Genette's 'heterodiegetic' narrator), a reporter of events witnessed as a non-involved observer, a secondary protagonist ('homodiegetic' narrator), or main character ('autodiegetic' narrator). Genette also makes a distinction between 'intradiegetic' narrators, who are part of the narrative world and 'extradiegetic' ones, who represent this world from the outside. What Genette means by this last term is the effacement and impersonality of what is commonly called the 'third person narrator.' Intradiegetic narrators are characters who become narrators on another diegetic level. Scheherazade is a narrating character within the frame story of *The Arabian Nights* and thus an intradiegetic narrator, but within the stories she tells as fiction she loses her identity, to become an impersonal omniscient third-person narrator.

Another variable feature of the manifestation of narrators is their ontological status. While the narrators of non-fiction are always presumed to be fully individuated human beings – whether or not their discourse provides explicit signs of their identity – fictional narrators vary from impersonal voices postulated for purely logical reasons to identified members of the textual world sharing with the other characters the ontological status of a fictive character. Individuated narrators differ in turn through the amount of information they provide about themselves: this information is usually proportional to the degree of narratorial involvement in narrated events. These various modes are traditionally reduced by narratologists to an opposition between third-person narration, which subsumes both non-involvement and radical non-individuation, and first-person narration, which accepts all other forms of narratorial identity and distance. This broad partition is supported by pragmatic and phenomenological considerations. Among the differences between the two types of narrator are the following: (1) First-person narrators are prisoners of an identity, bound to a fixed point of view; their knowledge is limited to what is available to a single human consciousness. Third-person narrators have unlimited knowledge, access to other minds, and the ability to shift their point of view. (2) In first-person narration, the reader attempts to form a portrait of the narrator on the basis of his or her declarations. In third-person narration, the question 'who speaks' is rarely relevant: the impersonal narrator is primarily a logical, not a psychological entity, and the reader does not usually regard his or her discourse as the expression of a personality. (3) The third-person narrator enjoys absolute narratorial authority (Doležel, Martinez-Bonatí). His or her utterances determine what counts as fact in the narrative world. The first-person narrator may be unreliable (*Booth); his or her utterances are subject to correction by another narrator or by the implied author. (4) The opinions of the first-person narrator may conflict with the message of the implied author, while the major disagreement between a third-person narrator and the implied author concerns the truth of the facts asserted in the text. The 'dummy'-like character of the third-person narrator has prompted some theorists (Hamburger, Banfield, Kuroda) to propose a no-narrator theory for this type of narration: the events are 'telling themselves,' rather than being communicated by a human or human-like subject.

MARIE-LAURE RYAN

Primary Sources

Booth, Wayne. *The Rhetoric of Fiction*. Chicago: U of Chicago P, 1961.

Doležel, Lubomír. 'Truth and Authenticity in Narrative.' *Poetics Today* 1.3 (1980): 7–25.

Genette, Gérard. *Figures III*. Paris: Seuil, 1973.

Lanser, Susan Sniader. *The Narrative Act*. Princeton: Princeton UP, 1981.

Martinez-Bonatí, Felix. 'The Act of Writing Fiction.' *New Literary History* 11.3 (1980): 425–34.

– *Fictive Discourse and the Structures of Literature*. Ithaca: Cornell UP, 1981.

Rousset, Jean. *Narcisse romancier: Essai sur la première personne dans le roman*. Paris: José Corti, 1973.

Ryan, Marie-Laure. 'The Pragmatics of Personal and Impersonal Fiction.' *Poetics* 10 (1981): 517–39.

Tamir, Nomi. 'Personal Narration and Its Linguistic Foundation.' *PTL: A Journal for Descriptive Poetics and Theory and Literature* 1 (1976): 403–29.

Warhol, Robyn. 'Toward a Theory of the Engaging Narrator: Earnest Intervention in Gaskell, Stowe, and Eliot.' *PMLA* 101.5 (1986): 811–18.

Overdetermination

Overdetermination is a term first used by *Sigmund Freud in *The Interpretation of Dreams* (1900) to describe those aspects of dreams which have a multiplicity of determinants. Freud developed the concept to cover any aspect of the unconscious which has more than one causal source; and *Jacques Lacan, through his insight that the unconscious is structured like a language, made overdetermination available to *semiotics. While the term thus has currency throughout the range of *psychoanalytic theory, one of its most forceful usages derives from its absorption in *Marxist criticism, with its emphasis on the material determinants in the production of literary texts, through the work of the French Marxist philosopher *Louis Althusser. Building on Mao and Lenin, Althusser describes the orthodox Marxist contradiction between labour and capital as 'inseparable from the total structure of the social body in which it is found ... determining, but also determined ... by the various *levels* and *instances* of the social formation it animates; it might be called *overdetermined in its principle*' (*For Marx* 101). (See *social formation.) He insists that the capital-labour contradiction is always 'specified by the forms of the *superstructure*' and '*by the internal and external historical situation,*' and hence is '*always overdetermined*' (106). He elaborates a concept of the social formation to situate overdetermination.

The concept has been used in literary theory to analyse the way in which economic, political and ideological contradictions may manifest themselves singly or in combination in literary texts through other contradictions conceived of as internal to literary production. For example, the presence of works of mixed genres in colonial literatures may be overdetermined by the primitiveness of colonial economies, the inchoate state of colonial politics and the ideological orientation of colonial societies towards the founding nation. (See *ideology, *text, *post-colonial theory.)

JOHN THURSTON

Primary Sources

Althusser, Louis. 'Contradiction and Overdetermination.' In *For Marx*. Trans. Ben Brewster. London: New Left Books, 1977, 87–128.

Paradox

A paradox (Gr. *paradoxos*, L. *paradoxus:* 'contrary to received opinion') is an apparently self-contradictory or nonsensical proposition that proves, on close inspection, to be well founded or at least partially true. For example: 'There are none so credulous as infidels' (Richard Bentley); 'What ruins mankind is the ignorance of the expert' (G.K. Chesterton). A paradox compressed into two words (e.g.: 'wise fool') is called an oxymoron. As a figure of rhetoric and a figure of thought, it is designed to induce wonder, to surprise or jolt the reader into genuine reflection and insight, or endless bafflement.

The early history of paradox in Western culture invites a distinction between two types: the rhetorical – an encomium or formal defence of a subject that, to conventional understanding at least, is unworthy or indefensible (Lucian's praise of the fly, Isocrates' of Thersites); and the logical – an argument or question that problematizes linear reason by self-contradiction, as epitomized in Eubulides' The Liar ('A man says that he is lying. Is what he says true or false?') and exploited by Socrates, to dazzling effect, in the *Parmenides*. With Renaissance humanism's return to the classical texts came a conflation of the two types, most notably in Nicholas of Cusa's *De docta ignorantia* [*Of Learned Ignorance*], Erasmus' *Moriae Encomium* [*The Praise of Folly*], Montaigne's *Essais* and Donne's *Biathanatos* ['A Declaration of that Paradoxe, or Thesis, that Self-homicide is not so naturally a Sin, that it may never be otherwise']. Trace elements of the paradoxical encomium remain discernible in post-Renaissance literary culture – in the mock-epic, certainly, and in ironic utopian writings such as Swift's *A Modest Proposal* and Yevgeny Zamyatin's *We*. (See *irony.) It is more to the logic of paradox that modern *littérateurs* critical of positive science and drabbing convention have understandably been drawn. Wilde's paradox, that 'a Truth in art is that whose contradictory is also true' ('The Truth of Masks' in *Intentions),* goes uncontradicted by a host of 19th- and 20th-century texts. If the play of self-contradiction in modern *literature tends to the grimly suicidal – as in Carlyle's *The French Revolution*, Melville's *The Confidence-Man*, Conrad's *Heart of Darkness*, Hubert Aquin's *Neige noire* [*Hamlet's Twin*], and Victor-Lévy

Beaulieu's *Don Quichotte de la Démanche* [*Don Quixote in Nighttown*] – it is not by practical necessity. The paradoxy of Lear, Carroll, Chesterton, Joyce, David Jones, Saint-John Perse, *Marshall McLuhan, Antonine Maillet, and Denys Chabot, for example, is made to induce less quizzical incomprehension than positive wonder.

The full arrival of paradox as a modern critical term dates from the period of *Cleanth Brooks' *The Well Wrought Urn* (1947). Following the lead of *T.S. Eliot's criticism, Brooks' study focuses on 'that perpetual slight alteration of language, words perpetually juxtaposed in new and sudden combinations,' which occurs in poetry. 'The language of poetry,' it follows for Brooks, 'is the language of paradox.' A close reading of Donne's 'The Canonization' in conjunction with Wordsworth's 'Composed upon Westminster Bridge' provides the master case. In the Wordsworthian purpose 'to choose incidents and situations from common life' but so to treat them that 'ordinary things should be presented to the mind in an unusual aspect' (Preface to the second edition of *Lyrical Ballads*) Brooks reads the intention to paradox intrinsic to all that he considers poetry. So comprehensive is the use of the term paradox in *The Well Wrought Urn* (and in *New Criticism generally) that it refers, in effect, to virtually any form of *discourse that is expressive and productive of 'awed surprise.'

The association of paradox with New Criticism and the Renaissance tradition of Christian humanism which that criticism more or less explicitly invokes has all but excluded the term from contemporary critical theory. As Rosalie L. Colie remarks of Renaissance paradox, it is 'recreative in the highest sense of that term, ever attempting the imitative recovery of a transcendent "truth," with all its ambivalences' (508). For all the aspiration to ontological wholeness that it bespeaks, though, paradoxy so practised does display features familiar to students of contemporary theory, *deconstruction in particular. The paradoxical form, observes Colie, by its very nature 'denies commitment: breaking out of imprisonment by disciplinary forms and the regulations of schools, it denies limitation, defies "sitting" in any specific philosophical position' (38). It is at once 'self-destructive' (37) and 'self-regarding, self-contained ... self-confirming' (518).

CAMILLE R. LA BOSSIÈRE

Primary Sources

Brooks, Cleanth. *The Well Wrought Urn: Studies in the Structure of Poetry*. New York: Harcourt, Brace and World, 1947.

Colie, Rosalie L. *Paradoxia Epidemica: The Renaissance Tradition of Paradox*. Princeton: Princeton UP, 1966.

Holloway, John. *The Victorian Sage: Studies in Argument*. London: Macmillan, 1953.

Kaiser, Walter. *Praisers of Folly*. Cambridge: Harvard UP, 1963.

Kenner, Hugh. *Paradox in Chesterton*. Intro. Herbert Marshall McLuhan. New York: Sheed and Ward, 1947.

Kreiger, Murray. *A Window to Criticism: Shakespeare's Sonnets and Modern Poetics*. Princeton: Princeton UP, 1964.

La Bossière, Camille R. 'The Monumental Nonsense of Saint-John Perse.' *Folio* 18 (1990): 25–37.

– *The Victorian 'Fol Sage': Comparative Readings on Carlyle, Emerson, Melville and Conrad*. Lewisburg, Pa.: Bucknell UP, 1989.

Land, Stephen K. *Paradox and Polarity in the Fiction of Joseph Conrad*. New York: St. Martin's, 1984.

Miller, Henry Knight. 'The Paradoxical Encomium with Special Reference to Its Vogue in England.' *Modern Philology* 53 (1956): 145–78.

Ornstein, Robert M. 'Donne, Montaigne, and Natural Law.' *Journal of English and Germanic Philology* 55 (1956): 213–29.

Wasserman, Earl. *The Subtler Language*. Baltimore: Johns Hopkins UP, 1959.

Weisinger, Herbert. *Tragedy and the Paradox of the Fortunate Fall*. East Lansing: Michigan State UP, 1953.

Parody

Sometimes considered parasitic of individuality, originality and genius, parody has in the 20th century received a good deal of favourable attention. All adaptation of preceding styles can be considered parody, though in the strictest sense parody is a conscious ironic or sardonic evocation of another artistic model. (See also *irony.) Within classical notions of imitation, writers learned their craft by imitating those works generally considered to be the best, and developed a personal style or voice out of an ability to adopt the styles and voices of others. Writing, then, was taken to be community-based and collective in nature, with individualized new forms and methods not regarded as essential prerequisites for excellence. In this respect, all imitation is parody.

Many modern theorists use such an understanding as a point of departure. *Mikhail Bakhtin, for instance, postulates that all repetition is parodic in nature but he divides repetition into two different types: stylization (un-ironic parody) and unstylized or ironized parody. Both of these types depend upon 'double-voiced discourses' or 'the intersecting of two voices and accents' – the author's and another's. (See *double-voicing/dialogism.) In an un-ironic stylization (or what other authors call imitative recasting, allusion, quotation, or pastiche) an author uses another voice for its own projects, while in other kinds of parody 'the second voice, having lodged in the other speech, clashes antagonistically with the original, host voice and forces it to serve directly opposite aims. Speech becomes a battlefield for opposing intentions' ('Discourse Typology in Prose' 184, 185). For Bakhtin, parody (apart from stylization) is implicitly transgressive and subversive of conventional *ideology, although the nature of the *subversion may not be at all clear to the naive observer who lacks an adequate understanding of the context.

Both of Bakhtin's variations offer a certain tribute to the original in their embodiment of the original voice. Arguably, both also function conservatively and normatively in perpetuating the host forms, figurations and ideas whether or not the original is the object of irony. Un-ironized parody seems, for Bakhtin, to stem from the Russian formalists' view that all *literature is quotation: nothing literary exists apart from the language of previous texts. (See Russian *formalism, *text.) Indeed, similarity of form and figuration can produce wonderfully creative works. Such seminal works as *Don Quixote,* for example, in relying upon and critiquing the conventions of original models, carry the concerns of those models even further. John Barth's depiction of Pocahantas and his evocation of early American colonial history and cultural mythology in *The Sot-Weed Factor* are simultaneously a tribute to and an exaggeration of tradition, a retelling of old narratives and a creation of new ones. Such evocation and displacement situate the work in a literary tradition and celebrate its intertextual links, even while suggesting that the work is, after all, part of a new and different cultural context. Both stylization and parody, especially postmodern metafictive parodic *intertextuality, mine the vein of literature self-referentially; each in its own way is a tribute to a previous form and lengthens the broad avenue of literature, while functioning in a unique manner. (See *postmodernism, *intertextuality.)

What Margaret Rose calls 'transcontextualized repetition' is just as possible as intertextual repetition and ironizes the copy. Exact imitation or repetition may itself, then, constitute part of the parodic. Theorists such as *Jacques Derrida and *Michel Foucault extend this issue even further, arguing that, regardless of discrepancies in time, all repetition is transgressive. Repetition is excess and excess is dissemination or waste, where the original energy and originality are dissipated. By this argument, Bakhtin's notion of a neutral stylization is impossible; all repetition is parodic and transgressive.

Not all imitations or stylizations have been accepted as parody, however. Standard dictionary definitions comment that parodies are pieces that imitate or mimic other works in order to ridicule the original(s) or some other unrelated work, person, thing, or trait. It is even said to be a 'high burlesque' of a famous work or author by the admixture of that style with a less worthy subject (Jump 2). Indeed Dryden's 'Mac Flecknoe' lampoons not only modern writers who are unheroic in their behaviour but also those writers who use heroic literature meanly. Parody sometimes, then, undermines the original form but becomes implicated in satire by targeting poor literary performances or unworthy human actions completely removed from the original work. Such parodies as Dryden's seem to presuppose not only that the reader will comprehend the butt of the satiric attack but also that the reader's derisive laughter will be triggered by comic uses of incongruity, exaggeration and understatement. Models for parody may thus be generally codified forms as well as particular works, features and conventions. These may be drawn from so-called high literature (well-known and exemplary poems, plays and stories), other generally recognized artisticobjects, or popular culture, even political speeches, advertising, sermons, and journalistic pieces.

No longer restricted to 'mere' imitation or to satire, parody in the 20th century reflects new narrative styles, current social patterns and concerns, and modern psychological views, while at the same time drawing comparisons with other texts that have influenced our way of thinking, acting and writing. According to

*Gérard Genette, some kind of obvious inter-textual allusion and play creates the parody, though for Linda Hutcheon it depends upon noticeable similarities of text with important ironic differences that signal the intellectual and artistic distance between the copy and the original. She asserts that ironic inversion is a characteristic of all parody and is fully pre-pared to accept the view that ideology is often a central issue of parody, though she firmly denies that the element of ridicule must be present. Generally speaking, then, most con-temporary critics would agree that parody does more than merely reiterate other texts; its tex-tual or contextual difference from the original is reinforced by a generally ironic and mocking tone. It does not often satirize; it does not in any way set out to reform its audience or 'cor-rect' the original of the artistic work at hand; but it often amuses and sometimes ridicules. (See also *kitsch.)

GORDON E. SLETHAUG

Primary Sources

Alter, Robert. *Partial Magic: The Novel as a Self-Con-scious Genre.* Berkeley: U of California P, 1975.

Bakhtin, Mikhail M. *The Dialogic Imagination: Four Essays.* Ed. Michael Holquist. Trans. Caryl Emer-son and Michael Holquist. Austin: U of Texas P, 1981.

– 'Discourse Typology in Prose.' Trans. Richard Bal-thazar and I.R. Titunik. In *Readings in Russian Po-etics: Formalist and Structuralist Views.* Ed. Ladislav Matejka and Krystyna Pomorska. Cam-bridge, Mass.: MIT P, 1971, 176–96.

– *Rabelais and His World.* Trans. Hélène Iswolsky. Cambridge, Mass.: MIT P, 1968.

Barth, John. *The Friday Book: Essays and Other Non-fiction.* New York: G.P. Putnam's Sons, 1984.

Burke, Kenneth. *The Philosophy of Literary Form: Studies in Symbolic Action.* Baton Rouge: Louisiana State UP, 1967.

Derrida, Jacques. *Dissemination.* Trans. and intro. Barbara Johnson. Chicago: U of Chicago P, 1981.

– *Writing and Difference.* Trans. Alan Bass. Chicago: U of Chicago P, 1978.

Foucault, Michel. *The Archaeology of Knowledge.* Trans. A.M. Sheridan Smith. London and New York: Routledge, 1972.

Genette, Gérard. *Palimpsestes.* Paris: Seuil, 1982.

Gilman, Sander L. *Nietzschean Parody.* Bonn: Bouvier Verlag/Herbert Grundmann, 1976.

Hutcheon, Linda. *A Theory of Parody: The Teachings of Twentieth-Century Art Forms.* New York and London: Methuen, 1985.

Jump, John Davies. *Burlesque.* London: Methuen, 1972.

Rose, Margaret. *Parody/Metafiction.* London: Croom Helm, 1979.

Patriarchy

Literally denoting the rule of the Law-of-the-Father(s), the term patriarchy has gained par-ticular significance primarily in Anglo-Ameri-can *feminist criticism. In this context, a variety of perspectives is offered concerning the origins and manifestations of patriarchy. Generally, feminist criticism regards patriarchy as having arisen from – and continuing to be supported by – the notion that the sociocul-tural concepts of man and woman and of masculinity and femininity are caused by the biological division of human bodies into cate-gories of male and female. The original con-nection between sexuality and biology seems to have been established in prehistory as the superiority in physical strength of the male over the female. Most feminist criticism tends to represent the family as the main legacy of this male advantage and therefore as patriar-chy's primary model and institution. Conse-quently patriarchy has been defined in this context as a general organizing structure ap-parent in most social, cultural and economic practices world-wide, a structure that is con-sidered to promote and perpetuate, in all facets of human existence, the empowerment of men and the disempowerment of women.

Because they have as their foundation de-scriptions and explanations of the dynamics of the family, Freudian psychology, Marxian eco-nomics and the kinship theories of *Claude Lévi-Strauss often are considered in Anglo-American feminist criticism to offer significant insights into the workings of patriarchy. *Sig-mund Freud's formulation of an exclusive father/son axis of *power has been seen as a framework within which the repression of women in patriarchy – and their compliance and or resistance to this repression – can be examined, and not only in the discipline of psychoanalysis or psychotherapy (Gallop). For example, *Sandra Gilbert and Susan Gubar's *The Madwoman in the Attic* adopts a psychoan-alytic framework as a means of interpreting the resistance to patriarchy they consider to be characteristic of 19th-century literary texts by women. (See *psychoanalytic theory, *text.)

The materialist or more strictly Marxist

framework often found in work by British feminists tends to examine the development and functioning of capitalism as a patriarchal economic system in which the father/capitalist gains by and oversees the production – and reproduction – of the family/factory. (See *Marxist criticism, *cultural materialism, *materialist criticism.) In *Women's Oppression Today* Michele Barrett offers a comprehensive overview of many Marxist feminist issues. She points out that many works tend either to identify women as constituting a separate class within a Marxist system or to consider the oppression of women separately within each class (29). In addition to class and gender, Barrett examines some of the conceptual problems arising from the challenges of ethnicity and race to the Marxist feminist framework. To some extent a Marxist framework also informs Lévi-Strauss' studies. Identifying women primarily as a commodity for exchange in kinship systems organized for the economic and social advantage of males, Lévi-Strauss' work often is seen by Anglo-American feminists to be paradigmatic of oppressive anthropological formulations of patriarchy.

Precisely because feminist criticism views patriarchy as structuring all the aspects of any given culture, society or economy, many Anglo-American feminist studies of its dynamics combine any or all of these three overarching theories with methodologies derived from a number of traditionally distinct disciplines such as history, literary studies, religious studies, philosophy, archaeology, and medicine. Interdisciplinarity characterizes Bonnie Anderson and Judith Zinsser's *A History of Their Own*, for example, which traces the establishment of the patrilineal empowerment of men and the suppression of women in various civilizations.

In addition, dualisms or binary oppositions often associated with patriarchy – such as good/evil, strong/weak, master/slave, superior/inferior, authority/obedience – structure as masculine and feminine, respectively, in each case not only the relations between men and women but also the roles and relations between those who are empowered or disempowered (feminized) generally: for example, the relations between an imperialistic power and the culture(s) upon which it feeds. (See *post-colonial theory, *binary opposition.) Moreover, frequently considered by feminist criticism to be the central systemic structuring element at work in, for example, traditional

institutions, common-sense reasoning and the conventions of everyday life, patriarchy appears to render itself invisible, appearing to be part of human nature, part of what is 'natural.' Much Anglo-American feminist criticism concerned with the study of the condition of women attempts to make patriarchal strategies visible, to reveal that they actually are neither natural nor necessary, and thus to enable women and other 'feminized' groups to empower themselves.

Recently, gender-based criticism by men, such as Marlon Ross' *Contours of Masculine Desire*, has begun to analyse the limitations of patriarchal concepts of masculinity for men and to reveal and render problematic the pervasiveness of men's collusion in oppressive practices. Both kinds of criticism presume patriarchy's obsolescence as a power structure.

HEATHER JONES

Primary Sources

Anderson, Bonnie S., and Judith P. Zinsser. *A History of Their Own*. 2 vols. New York: Harper and Row, 1988.

Barrett, Michele. *Women's Oppression Today: The Marxist/Feminist Encounter*. Rev. ed. London and New York: Verso, 1988.

Gallop, Jane. *The Daughter's Seduction: Feminism and Psychoanalysis*. Ithaca: Cornell UP, 1982.

– *Reading Lacan*. Ithaca and London: Cornell UP, 1985.

Gilbert, Sandra M., and Susan Gubar. *The Madwoman in the Attic: The Woman Writer and the Nineteenth-Century Literary Imagination*. New Haven and London: Yale UP, 1984.

Ross, Marlon. *Contours of Masculine Desire: Romanticism and the Rise of Women's Poetry*. New York and Oxford: Oxford UP, 1989.

Phallocentrism

Derived from the psychoanalytic work of Ernest Jones (cited in Gallop 16–18), this term, in its most general sense, denotes a system of power relations which promotes and perpetuates the phallus as the transcendent symbol of empowerment. In Jones' work the phallus was seen to have a direct correspondence with the penis and thus phallocentrism was seen to denote the exclusive empowerment of men. The *psychoanalytic theory of *Jacques Lacan, however, has dissociated the phallus from the notion of a necessary or natural correspondence to the penis (or the clitoris). Seen in strictly symbolic terms, both men and women experience the phallus in its 'veiled' condition as 'the primal repressed' of the castration complex (Gallop 127–56). Lacan's theory of the phallus primarily as a focus – rather than object – of desire (and thus a possible sense of phallocentrism as indicating the moment of the emergence of the subject in the realm of the symbolic) has tended to be set aside, however, by feminist critics. Consequently, phallocentrism has come to be considered virtually synonymous with *patriarchy, denoting a certain kind of male-centred empowerment, a gender-specific system of power relations. (See also *power, *desire/lack, *subject/object, *imaginary/symbolic/real.)

In the work of some women psychoanalytic theorists, such as *Luce Irigaray, who have found the Lacanian theory of the phallus ultimately male-centred and thus oppressive for women, the system of power relations designated by phallocentrism includes, for example, what *Jacques Derrida has called the master narratives of Western *discourse: the classic works of philosophy, science, history, and religion. Seen as a structuring principle of these master narratives, the phallus appears to denote unity, *authority, tradition, and order; phallocentrism thus denotes the participation in and advocacy of associated assumptions, interests and values. Much empirically based *Anglo-American feminist criticism also tends to equate the Lacanian theory with patriarchy, noting the frequency with which persons who have both the penis and the phallus (only men) appear to be those who are empowered most often.

HEATHER JONES

Primary Sources

Gallop, Jane. *The Daughter's Seduction: Feminism and Psychoanalysis.* Ithaca: Cornell UP, 1982.

Phonocentrism: *see* Logocentrism

Pleasure/bliss

The linked and, for the most part, opposed terms pleasure (*plaisir*) and bliss (*jouissance*) are tendered for discussion (if never entirely defined) by *Roland Barthes in *Le Plaisir du texte* [*The Pleasure of the Text* 1973], a book which builds on Barthes' earlier distinction between the readerly and the writerly, and on the fundamental idea of *écriture* or *textuality (writing conceived as process and *text, rather than as object and work). (See *readerly/writerly text.)

The text of pleasure offers confirmation of the reader's knowledge, beliefs and expectations; the text of bliss brings loss, rupture and discomfort. The text of pleasure 'comes from culture and does not break with it' the text of bliss 'unsettles the reader's historical, cultural, psychological assumptions.' The text of pleasure brings contentment; the text of bliss, a disturbing rapture. The text of pleasure confirms our comfortable relation to language as something stable and limited; the text of bliss 'brings to a crisis [the reader's] relation with language' (*Pleasure of the Text* 14).

Barthes asserts, however, that it is impossible to make a firm distinction between pleasure and bliss. This is because in French the term *plaisir* sometimes includes *jouissance* or bliss, sometimes is opposed to it. In the title of Barthes' book, 'pleasure' is used as extending to and including bliss, while at other times the terms are opposed. Barthes declares that he must accept this and proceed in ambiguity and contradiction. The French term *jouissance*, which has as one of its meanings literally to 'come' in orgasm, cannot be fully rendered into English. Stephen Heath has observed that 'bliss' may be a dubious translation since it 'brings with it connotations of religious and social contentment' which are completely at odds with what Barthes meant in French, 'a radically violent pleasure which shatters – dissipates, loses – [the] ego' (*Image – Music – Text* 91). Barthes believes that pleasure and bliss are parallel forces that can never meet. Bliss results from 'cutting,' when in writing 'two edges are created: an obedient, conformist, plagiarizing edge ... and *another edge*, (underline), mobile blank ... Neither culture nor its destruction is erotic; it is the seam between them, the fault, the flaw, which becomes so' (6–7). It is, then, this 'site of a loss,' this seam between the expected and the surprising which is erotic and creates bliss. Barthes' idea is paradoxical and, at its very heart, a celebration of contradiction. (See *paradox.) The reader who would experience bliss must keep both readings of pleasure and of bliss in view; this reader must live in the seam between culture and its destruction, and simultaneously enjoy 'the consistency of his selfhood (that is his pleasure) and [seek] its loss (that is his bliss)' (14). As the 'site of a loss' bliss is, for all its disruptive intensity, close to boredom. Tragedy, for instance, is of all forms most conducive to bliss, because it is not 'dramatic,' because the end is known from the first, and so 'of all readings, that of tragedy is the most perverse,' offering 'an effacement of pleasure and a progression of bliss' (47, 48).

What are the consequences for criticism which would deal with the text of bliss? And how are we to read such criticism? As a *metalanguage, criticism of the text of pleasure or bliss (here again Barthes is using the words synonymously) must be a 'reported' pleasure, and 'how can we take pleasure in a *reported* pleasure?' (17). Only if we can read this reported pleasure as a primary pleasure of its own. We cannot take this reported pleasure, this critical text, on its own terms; we cannot become 'the confidant of this critical pleasure'; we must become its 'voyeur': 'the commentary then becomes in [our] eyes a text, a fiction, a fissured envelope' (17). Presumably, this is how Barthes wishes us to read his own criticism. It is itself a fiction and must be read as such by the reader as 'voyeur,' the reader willing to see it as itself a text of bliss, a 'site of a loss,' and not a finished object. No critical metalanguage can gain access to the text of bliss, unless it be another text of bliss.

Just as the writerly annulled all *ideology, or the valuing of one interpretation, one idea, over all others, so too 'the pleasure of the text does not prefer one ideology to another' (31). (Here, as in the title of his book, Barthes uses pleasure as a larger term that includes bliss.) To the triumphant plural of the writerly, Barthes now adds the 'perversity' of pleasure, the hedonism of 'difference.' In the text of pleasure 'the *moral unity* that society demands of every human product' is 'overcome, split' (31), and in this text therefore 'the opposing forces are no longer repressed but in a state of becoming: nothing is really antagonistic, everything is plural' (31). This hedonist Utopia, then, builds on the Utopia of the writerly plural posited by Barthes in his earlier book *S/Z* (1970).

Barthes is acutely aware that he must be consistently inconsistent and not himself produce a text of pleasure which will be merely confirmatory, comfortable, plagiaristic, or predictable (this is one reason why he refuses to define his terms unambiguously and proceeds in ambiguity and contradiction). Therefore, 'no "thesis" on the pleasure of the text is possible: barely an inspection (an introspection) that falls short' (34). The affirmation of bliss cannot be 'spoken, doctrinal' (44), for bliss depends on no ripening or process of realization. In the text of bliss everything is becoming and nothing is fixed; 'everything is wrought to a transport at one and the same moment' (52). Yet to affirm all this is, of course, precisely to affirm a doctrine, in most seductively virtuosic terms. In his consistent inconsistency Barthes may not have escaped the trap of generating a text of pleasure, a highly confirmatory and comfortable text to the reader who has recuperated its meanings. At the same time, this confirmatory quality in his text may justify his claim that bliss is to be associated with boredom and opposed to the precarious intensities of pleasure. Paradoxically and yet logically, at the extreme of the unexpected, in a site of loss, we find only what we always know. Like the earlier writerly, bliss may very well be a Utopian ideal, never to be glimpsed save from the well-charted shores of pleasure. (See also *recuperation, *intertextuality.)

FRANCIS ZICHY

Primary Sources

Barthes, Roland. *Image-Music-Text.* Selected and trans. Stephen Heath. New York: Hill and Wang, 1977.
– *The Pleasure of the Text.* 1973. Trans. Richard Miller. New York: Hill and Wang, 1975.
– *S/Z.* 1970. Trans. Richard Miller. London: Jonathan Cape, 1974.

Plot: *see* Story

Pluralism

Pluralism is the view that there can be more than one valid reading of a *text; more precisely, especially in the writings of the *Neo-Aristotelian or Chicago school, it refers to what *Wayne Booth has called 'methodological pluralism,' the view that critical questions and statements are relative to the methodological framework or *discourse which generates them and ultimately to the ends for which this framework is employed. Pluralism is thus a form of pragmatism or instrumentalism, which holds that critical doctrines and methods, rather than being positions to be defended, are merely tools useful for arriving at different kinds of knowledge about texts which we may happen 'at one time or another, or for one or another reason, to want' (*Crane). In this view, some critical methods are useful for some purposes, some for others; they are not reducible to one another. Pluralism is sometimes taken to mean that all critical approaches are equally valid but this is very far from the view of either R.S. Crane or Booth. Rather, critical judgments are relative to the principles and methods of inquiry but these principles and methods may be more or less adequate to the job.

Views contrasting with pluralism are dogmatism or monism (the view that only one critical method can be true), scepticism (none are true) and eclecticism (truth is attained by combining the best elements of several systems). Pluralism rejects the notion of a unitary truth implied by each of these views; it would regard whatever theory was produced by the last method (eclecticism) as merely one more weapon in the arsenal of criticism.

HOLLIS RINEHART

Primary Sources

Booth, Wayne C. *Critical Understanding: The Powers and Limits of Pluralism.* Chicago: U of Chicago P, 1979.
Crane, R.S. *The Languages of Criticism and the Structure of Poetry.* Toronto: U of Toronto P, 1953.
'Pluralism and Its Discontents.' Special issue. *Critical Inquiry* 12.3 (Spring 1986).

Polyphonic novel

In *Problems of Dostoevsky's Poetics* (1929) *Mikhail Bakhtin claims that Dostoevsky's novels represented something new and unprecedented in the history of fiction, and coined the term polyphonic novel to describe it. Later, especially in 'Discourse in the Novel' (1934–5), Bakhtin argued that Dostoevsky's art is the purest expression of a tendency implicit within the novel genre. What *heteroglossia is to linguistic theory, *polyphony and the polyphonic novel are to fictional theory. Just as no speaker is free to express his or her linguistic intention unobstructed but must always mediate that intention in relation to other speakers, so the novelist, according to Bakhtin, must grant characters their own intentions, mediate their voices without subsuming them within a single authorial voice. (See *intention/intentionality.) Dostoevsky's novels are not anchored in the ideas, or arguments, of any single character, but in the relation of each character to the words of the others. Their relationship to one another is dialogic, and in fact dialogism and polyphony are virtual synonyms in Bakhtin's vocabulary. As Bakhtin states: 'Every thought of Dostoevsky's heroes ... senses itself to be from the very beginning a *rejoinder* in an unfinalized dialogue. Such thought is not impelled toward a well-rounded, finalized, systematically monologic whole. It lives a tense life on the borders of someone else's thought, someone else's consciousness' (*Problems* 32).

Bakhtin argues that Dostoevsky's achievement represents a kind of 'Copernican turn' both in the history of fiction and in our understanding of self-consciousness. In place of the traditional fictional unity based on an overarching *theme (the need for and acquisition of 'prudence' in *Tom Jones*, for instance), unity in Dostoevsky's novels is dialogic, consisting of 'the artistically organized coexistence and interaction of spiritual *diversity*, not stages of an evolving unified spirit' (*Problems* 30). Dostoevsky creates 'not voiceless slaves ... but *free* people, capable of standing *alongside* their creator, capable of not agreeing with him and even of rebelling against him' (*Problems* 6). By the time he wrote 'Discourse in the Novel,' where he defines the novel as 'a diversity of social speech types (sometimes even diversity of languages) and a diversity of individual voices, artistically organized' (262), Bakhtin had come to see these qualities of Dostoevsky's novels as constitutive elements of the genre itself, and indeed discovers them in a wide range of European novels.

The influence of Bakhtin's theory of fictional *discourse has been significant. *Paul de Man writes that 'it would be possible to line up an impressive list of contemporary theorists of very diverse persuasion, all of which would have a legitimate claim on Bakhtin's dialogism as congenial or even essential to their enterprise' (104). Don Bialostosky notes that 'we may practice dialogics, as well as rhetoric and dialectic, without identifying our practice with an art of that name,' and cites several examples of literary analyses indebted to the intertwined concepts of dialogism and polyphony (796). Peter K. Garrett's *The Victorian Multiplot Novel* is subtitled *Studies in Dialogic Form*, and employs Bakhtin's conceptual framework to analyse the presence in Victorian novels of 'radical, unresolvable differences, of oppositions that cannot be reduced to stable, abstract antinomies or subjected to dialectical mediation' (9). Whatever the fate of his claims for Dostoevsky, the critical terms Bakhtin initially formulated to account for his novels have entered the mainstream of literary heteroglossia. (See *dialogical criticism.)

JAMES DIEDRICK

Primary Sources

Bakhtin, Mikhail. 'Discourse in the Novel.' In *The Dialogic Imagination*. Ed. and trans. Caryl Emerson and Michael Holquist. Austin: U of Texas P, 1981, 259–422.
– *Problems of Dostoevsky's Poetics*. Trans. Caryl Emerson. Minneapolis: U of Minnesota P, 1984.
Bialostosky, Don. 'Dialogics as an Art of Discourse in Literary Criticism.' *PMLA* 101 (1986): 788–97.
Clark, Katerina, and Michael Holquist. *Mikhail Bakhtin*. Cambridge: Harvard UP, 1984.
de Man, Paul. 'Dialogue and Dialogism.' *Poetics Today* 4 (1983): 99–107.
Garrett, Peter K. *The Victorian Multiplot Novel: Studies in Dialogical Form*. New Haven/London: Yale UP, 1980.

Polyphony/dialogism

Polyphony, a term originally derived from music, is a unique characteristic of prose *literature described and illustrated by *Mikhail Bakhtin, whereby several contesting voices representing a variety of ideological positions can engage equally in dialogue, free from authorial judgment or constraint. The author is democratically positioned among or 'alongside' (*Problems of Dostoevsky's Poetics* 6) the speeches of the characters so that no single point of view is privileged. Consequently, the multiple perspectives of unmerged consciousnesses are granted equal validity within the *text; this free play of discourses precludes the dominance of any point of view, including that of the author. The concept of polyphony is central to Bakhtin's theory of dialogism. (See *dialogical criticism, theories of *play/freeplay, *discourse.)

Dissonance and tension within the text are not resolved, as the integrity of independent discourses remains irreducible to a single, harmonious world-view which, in the monologic text, is imposed by the author. (See *monologism.) Polyphony retains therefore a capacity for 'surprisingness' (Morson and Emerson 244), the potential for genuine innovation. Moreover, because of its focus on process (dialogic relationships) rather than product (closure or finalizing), polyphony can be described as essentially a theory of creativity.

The liberation of the characters from authorial control results in a dialogue that is theoretically unfinalizable. There is no last word which can be spoken, no absolute or single interpretation possible. As long as people are alive there can be no final truth and the work of art can never be finished. Nevertheless, a special kind of unity can be achieved consisting of 'a dialogic concordance of unmerged twos and multiples' (289) which Bakhtin describes as a 'unity of the event' (*Problems of Dostoevsky's Poetics* 21). This new unity is situated in the dynamic process of creation rather than in the finished product.

Bakhtin's conception of polyphony remains problematic because although he describes it he never provides a definition. He also reformulates it at different stages in his career without reconciling his understanding of its origins and applications at different stages in his career. In *Problems of Dostoevsky's Poetics*, Bakhtin finds his ideal of authentic polyphony in the novels of Dostoevsky. Later, he modifies and expands his conception of the origins of polyphony and comes to understand it as an inherent characteristic of all novelistic discourse. Polyphony now becomes another word for dialogism as Bakhtin begins to formulate the concept of a prosaics, a neologism coined by Gary Saul Morson and Caryl Emerson to describe Bakhtin's theory of literature that privileges prose and the novel. His study of the development of the novel in literary history, *The Dialogic Imagination*, sees the potential for polyphony in classical prose models which include elements of the *carnival, such as the Socratic dialogues or Menippean satires like Apuleius' *The Golden Ass*. As a result of this revision, Dostoevsky can be seen to have made a major, though not necessarily unique, contribution to the evolution of the polyphonic novel. Polyphony is now viewed as a possibility inherent in all novelistic prose and the art of Dostoevsky is cited as a particularly felicitous realization of its potential.

Criticism inspired by Bakhtin has applied both his more radical and exclusive description of the origins of polyphony and the subsequent revision. Divisions in *feminist criticism between French and Anglo-American approaches perhaps best demonstrate this dichotomy. *Julia Kristeva, for example, appropriates Bakhtin's earlier utopian stance for the French school. In 'The Novel as Polylogue' (1972), she restricts polyphony to the modernist avant-garde text. Kristeva collapses gender in her definition of the 'feminine' as synonymous with all that is marginalized and silenced by the dominant culture, and includes male authors such as Joyce, Artaud and Bataille as creators of *l'écriture féminine*, which she equates with the polyphonic text. (See *margin/ centre.) Joyce's *Finnegans Wake* can thus exemplify a *polyphonic novel. *Hélène Cixous and *Luce Irigaray, on the other hand, attempt to theorize (and even produce) the polyphonic text or *l'écriture féminine* as a utopian women's writing. Margaret Atwood's *Surfacing* (1972) or Irigaray's 'When our lips speak together' (1977) can be seen as attempts to inscribe a polyphonic discourse that reflects the splitting of the feminine subject. (See *subject/object.) A recent extension of this application is Anne Herrmann's concept of a 'female dialogic,' which draws upon Bakhtin and Irigaray to formulate a model that accounts for the divisions in female subjectivity. For these feminist critics, then, it is the modernist or postmodernist text that is polyphonic; the realist tradition is explicitly rejected by Kristeva, for example, as monologic. (See *postmodernism.)

Many Anglo-American feminists, however, are attracted to Bakhtin's emphasis on the crucial significance of the context of discourse and reject the exclusive appropriation of polyphony by French feminists as exemplified in the radical utopianism of *l'écriture féminine*. Joanne S. Frye, for example, speaks for contextual feminists who find the novel's dialogic capacity for 'eternal re-thinking and evaluating' (*Dialogic* 31) within social contexts an encouraging catalyst for cultural change. She sees these attributes in contemporary novels written in the realist tradition; in such novels female charac-

ters may also 'reject the fixity of meaning' (Frye 34).

British author and critic *David Lodge defines prose literature as 'dialogic, or, in an alternative formulation "polyphonic,"' thus equating the two terms (*After Bakhtin* 58). He finds these characteristics not only present in modernist texts such as Joyce's *Ulysses* or *D.H. Lawrence's *Women in Love* but also perceptible in aspects of the classic realist text (George Eliot's *Middlemarch*) and in modern novelists writing in the realist tradition (Evelyn Waugh, Henry Green, Ivy Compton-Burnett). Such works contain 'an amazing variety of discursive texture, and a surprising degree of interpretive freedom for the reader' (Lodge 86).

Polyphony is undoubtedly one of Bakhtin's most original and controversial concepts and continues to inspire innovative investigations into the complexities of novelistic prose.

PHYLLIS MARGARET PARYAS

Primary Sources

Apuleius, Lucius. *The Golden Ass*. Trans. Robert Graves. London: Penguin, 1990.
Atwood, Margaret. *Surfacing*. New York: Simon and Schuster, 1972.
Bakhtin, M.M. *The Dialogic Imagination*. Ed. and trans. Caryl Emerson and Michael Holquist. Austin: U of Texas P, 1981.
– *Problems of Dostoevsky's Poetics*. Ed. and trans. Caryl Emerson. Minneapolis: U of Minnesota P, 1984.
– *Speech Genres and Other Late Essays*. Ed. Caryl Emerson and Michael Holquist. Trans. Vern W. McGee. Austin: U of Texas P, 1986.
Clark, Katerina, and Michael Holquist. *Mikhail Bakhtin*. Cambridge: Harvard UP, 1984.
Dostoevsky, Fyodor. *Notes From Underground*. Trans. Andrew R. MacAndrew. New York: Signet, 1961.
Eliot, George. *Middlemarch*. New York: Bantam, 1985.
Frye, Joanne S. *Living Stories, Telling Lives: Women and the Novel in Contemporary Experience*. Ann Arbor: U of Michigan P, 1986.
Herrmann, Anne. *The Dialogic and Difference: 'An/Other Woman' in Virginia Woolf and Christa Wolf*. New York: Columbia UP, 1989.
Irigaray, Luce. 'When our lips speak together.' Trans. Carolyn Burke. *Signs* 6 (1980): 69–79.
Joyce, James. *Ulysses*. New York: Random House, 1961.
– *Finnegans Wake*. New York: Viking, 1968.
Kristeva, Julia. 'The Novel as Polylogue.' In *Desire in Language: A Semiotic Approach to Literature and Art*. Ed. Leon Roudiez. Trans. Thomas Gora, Alice

Jardine, Leon Roudiez. New York: Columbia UP, 1980.

Lawrence, D.H. *Women in Love*. New York: Viking, 1968.

Lodge, David. *After Bakhtin: Essays on Fiction and Criticism*. London: Routledge, 1990.

Morson, Gary Saul, and Caryl Emerson, eds. *Mikhail Bakhtin: Creation of a Prosaics*. Stanford: Stanford UP, 1990.

– *Rethinking Bakhtin: Extensions and Challenges*. Evanston: Northwestern UP, 1989.

Tolstoi, Leo. *Anna Karenina*. Trans. David Magarshack. New York: Signet, 1961.

Postmodernism

Postmodernism is a period label generally given to cultural forms since the 1960s that display certain characteristics such as reflexivity, *irony and a mixing of popular and high art forms. Although the term first found favour in architecture (Jencks), it is now used to describe *literature, the visual arts, music, dance, film, theatre, philosophy, criticism, historiography, theology, and anything up-to-date in culture in general. Either seen as a continuation of the more radical aspects of modernism or as marking a rupture with such things as modernist ahistoricism or yearning for *closure, postmodernism has been linked to 'the cultural logic of late capitalism' (*Jameson); the general condition of knowledge in times of informational technology (*Lyotard); the replacing of a modernist epistemological focus with an ontological one (McHale); and the substitution of the simulacrum for the real (*Baudrillard). Postmodern literature has been called a literature of replenishment (Barth), on the one hand, and the literature of an inflationary economy (Newman), on the other. In short, there is little agreement on the reasons for its existence or on the evaluation of its effects. Nevertheless, a study of the overlapping concerns of the various art forms and discourses in which the term is used yields certain common denominators that might be seen to define postmodernism.

The first involves the seemingly paradoxical combination of self-consciousness (or formal and thematic reflexivity) and some sort of historical grounding, however ironized. (See *paradox.) For example, what has been called 'historiographic metafiction' (Hutcheon, *Poetics)* is fiction which is both inward and out-ward directed, that is to say, both concerned with its status as fiction, narrative or language, and also grounded in some verifiable historical reality. Postmodern discourses tend to use but also abuse, install but also subvert, conventions, and they usually negotiate these contradictions through irony (Wilde, *Horizons*) and *parody (Hutcheon, *Politics*). (See *subversion.) In employing traditional forms and expectations and at the same time undermining both, postmodern discourses manage to point to conventions as conventions and thus to de-naturalize the things we take as natural or given. Because these include ideological structures such as capitalism, *patriarchy, imperialism, even humanism, postmodern concerns often overlap with those of Marxist, feminist, post-colonial, and poststructuralist analysis. (See *Marxist criticism, *feminist criticism, *post-colonial theory, *poststructuralism.) These should not, however, be conflated: the Marxist, feminist and post-colonial, in particular, possess theories of political action and agency that the postmodern appears to lack. However, beyond the de-naturalizing impulse, the postmodern also shares their positive valuing of the different, the 'other,' in the face of ideological urges to totalize and homogenize. (See *self/other, *totalization.) Postmodern discourses also challenge the fixing of boundaries (Hassan) between genres, between art forms, between theory and art, between high art and mass-media culture. (See *genre criticism, *discourse.) The latter connection with popular culture has proved most problematic to Marxist analysts (Jameson; *Eagleton) but is the basis of many postmodern challenges to modernist hierarchies of cultural value (Huyssen).

The radically disparate interpretations and evaluations of postmodernism are in part the result of its particular politics and the curious 'middle grounds' (Wilde, *Middle*) it occupies, inscribing yet also subverting various aspects of a dominant culture: however critical the subversion, there is still a complicity that cannot be denied. This strategic doubleness or political ambidextrousness is the common denominator of many postmodern discourses, and to see only one side – either the complicity or the critique – is to deny the complexity of the enterprise. It is also one of the reasons for the differences of opinion about the validity and value of the postmodern 'problematizing' of issues such as history, representation, subjectivity, and *ideology. There are other reasons, as well, some rooted in cultural and national differences. Jean-François Lyotard's defining of the postmodern as marking the death of the grand master narratives that used to make sense of our world for us comes out of a different intellectual and historical frame of reference than does *Jürgen Habermas' argument that the modernist project of Enlightenment rationality requires completion first, for in Germany and in Eastern Europe it can certainly be argued that modernity was cut short. The postmodern revaluing of not only the different but the local and particular over the universal and general demands that such disagreements about the definition of postmodernism be both respected and historicized, not disregarded or downplayed.

LINDA HUTCHEON

Primary Sources

Barth, John. 'The Literature of Replenishment.' *Atlantic* 245 (1980): 65–71.
Baudrillard, Jean. *Simulations.* Trans. Paul Foss, Paul Patton, Philip Beitchman. New York: Semiotext(e), 1983.
Eagleton, Terry. 'Capitalism, Modernism and Postmodernism.' *New Left Review* 152 (1985): 60–73.
Habermas, Jürgen. 'Modernity – an Incomplete Project.' *New German Critique* 22 (1981): 3–14.
Hassan, Ihab. *The Postmodern Turn: Essays in Postmodern Theory and Culture.* Columbus: Ohio State UP, 1987.
Hutcheon, Linda. *A Poetics of Postmodernism: History, Theory, Fiction.* London and New York: Routledge, 1988.
– *The Politics of Postmodernism.* London and New York: Routledge, 1989.
Huyssen, Andreas. *After the Great Divide: Modernism, Mass Culture, Postmodernism.* Bloomington: Indiana UP, 1986.
Jameson, Fredric. 'Postmodernism, or the Cultural Logic of Late Capitalism.' *New Left Review* 146 (1984): 53–92.
Jencks, Charles. *The Language of Post-Modern Architecture.* London: Academy P, 1977.
Lyotard, Jean-François. *La Condition postmoderne: Rapport sur le savoir.* Paris: Minuit, 1979.
McHale, Brian. *Postmodernist Fiction.* London and New York: Methuen, 1987.
Newman, Charles. *The Post-Modern Aura: The Act of Fiction in an Age of Inflation.* Evanston: Northwestern UP, 1985.
Wilde, Alan. *Horizons of Assent: Modernism, Postmodernism, and the Ironic Imagination.* Baltimore: Johns Hopkins UP, 1981.
– *Middle Grounds: Studies in Contemporary American Fiction.* Philadelphia: U of Pennsylvania P, 1987.

Power

The term power is fundamental to a major branch of contemporary criticism and critical theory, the analysis of the political dimension of textual practices. This interest in the connection between texts and the power relations of the society in which they are produced has generated studies of power both as something that is represented and as an extratextual force which structures and limits the nature of representation. Many such studies are directly indebted to the work of *Michel Foucault, himself drawing from the work of *Nietzsche, particularly the *Genealogy of Morals*.

Through his research on the social construction of human subjectivity, Foucault was led to reconceptualize the received view of 'power' as the ability to cause change in the world, as a commodity or a position attributable to an individual human subject. Instead, Foucault understands 'power' as a quality of those relations between individuals in which a given society's systems of control are intentionally put into operation. More specifically, the exercise of 'power' (and for Foucault power exists only when it is exercised) is the action of structuring the possible field of action of others by the deployment of one or more reigning institutional codes or 'disciplines,' be they legal, educational, religious, medical, or political. (See *code.) Moreover, Foucault proposed that 'power' is not simply a by-product of these disciplines but that it is in its own right a productive force, that it makes possible specific conceptions of what one can know about oneself which serve, in turn, to maintain the *episteme of a particular society. In this sense, the etymological relationship between 'subjectivity' and 'subjection' is anything but arbitrary. Contrary to its more familar definition, then, power for Foucault is not attached to an individual human subject, not restricted to state institutions, not one-directional, not essentially prohibitive, and not separable from the social relations in which it manifests itself and through which it achieves its ends.

In his attempt to articulate the workings of power as a social and historically determined set of relations, Foucault deliberately resisted giving his combined insights the status of a 'theory' of power. On the contrary, he encouraged his readers always to ground any subsequent study of control relations in detailed historical analysis. This combined emphasis on 'power' and on its historically specific manifestation has strongly influenced the critical practice known as the *New Historicism. For instance, Stephen Greenblatt, the leading theorist and practitioner of New Historicism, has traced significant relationships between the representation of human subjectivity in English Renaissance *literature and the structure of power relations in the monarchical society of Elizabethan and Jacobean England. Foucault's concept of 'power' has also been used by Marxist and feminist critics in their efforts to uncover the mechanisms by which class- and gender-based domination is established and maintained. (See *Marxist criticism, *feminist criticism.)

MARTA STRAZNICKY

Primary Sources

Balbus, Isaac D. 'Disciplining Women: Michel Foucault and the Power of Feminist Discourse.' In *After Foucault: Humanistic Knowledge, Postmodern Challenges*. Ed. Jonathan Arac. New Brunswick: Rutgers UP, 1988, 138–60.
Dreyfus, Hubert L., and Paul Rabinow. 'Power and Truth.' In *Michel Foucault: Beyond Structuralism and Hermeneutics*. Ed. Hubert L. Dreyfus and Paul Rabinow. Chicago: U of Chicago P, 1982, 184–204.
Foucault, Michel. 'On Power.' In *Politics, Philosophy, Culture: Interviews and Other Writings 1977–1984*. Ed. Lawrence D. Kritzman. New York: Routledge, 1988, 96–109.
– *Power/Knowledge: Selected Interviews and Other Writings 1972–1977*. Ed. Colin Gordon. New York: Pantheon, 1980.
– 'The Subject and Power.' Afterword to *Michel Foucault: Beyond Structuralism and Hermeneutics*. Ed. Hubert L. Dreyfus and Paul Rabinow. Chicago: U of Chicago P, 1982, 208–26.
Greenblatt, Stephen. *Renaissance Self-Fashioning: From More to Shakespeare*. Chicago: U of Chicago P, 1980.
Maslan, Mark. 'Foucault and Pragmatism.' *Raritan* 7.3 (1988): 94–114.
Nietzsche, Friedrich. *The Birth of Tragedy and the Genealogy of Morals*. Trans. Francis Golffing. Garden City, NY: Doubleday, 1956.
Said, Edward W. 'Foucault and the Imagination of Power.' In *Foucault: A Critical Reader*. Ed. David Couzens Hoy. Oxford: Blackwell, 1986, 149–55.
Sawicki, Jana. 'Feminism and the Power of Fou-
cauldian Discourse.' In *After Foucault: Humanistic Knowledge, Postmodern Challenges*. Ed. Jonathan Arac. New Brunswick: Rutgers UP, 1988, 161–78.
Warren, Mark. *Nietzsche and Political Thought*. Cambridge, Mass.: MIT P, 1988.
Wolin, Sheldon S. 'On the Theory and Practice of Power.' In *After Foucault: Humanistic Knowledge, Postmodern Challenges*. Ed. Jonathan Arac. New Brunswick: Rutgers UP, 1988, 179–201.

Praxis

The term praxis plays a pivotal role in dialectical materialism, developed by Karl Marx as a critique of idealism and mechanical materialism. Marx contends in the 'Theses on Feuerbach' ('Feuerbachthesen' 1845) – together with *The German Ideology* [*Die deutsche Ideologie* 1845] a turning-point in his work – that philosophy has offered only different interpretations of the world but has not changed it. He defines praxis here as 'human sensuous activity' (Marx 403) and revolutionary praxis as the simultaneous changing of circumstances and of human activity itself (*Selbstveränderung*). For Marx truth is determined by praxis and therefore is not a question of theory. He argues that the very categories of theory correspond to relationships produced in social praxis. The abstract individual analysed by Ludwig Feuerbach, for instance, is shown to belong to a particular form of society. Marx understands 'human essence' accordingly as the external 'ensemble of the social relations' (404) that result from a distinct, historically determined social praxis, not as an abstract quality pertaining to individuals.

This view of praxis contrasts sharply with the Aristotelian tripartite model in which *theoria* refers to contemplation and is the arbiter of eternal truths (inspired by the regularity of natural phenomena); *praxis* refers primarily to politics as the second highest form of activity open to free citizens, and *poiesis* designates the making of objects. The Aristotelian view excludes a theory of praxis, since theory adjudicates truth with respect to determinate objects (and thus is concerned with knowledge in the strict sense), whereas praxis implies freedom and choice between alternatives. The concept of theoretical knowledge as the basis of praxis begins to develop in medieval interpretations of Aristotle. It leads eventually to the idea, expounded by Francis Bacon, that theoretical knowledge has its end in practical application and must prove its results in praxis. Idealism will later derive its belief in human self-determination from the trust in a theoretical knowledge of praxis. Kant thus constructs practical reason (ethics) on the basis of theoretical knowledge and Hegel develops experience as the unfolding of the spirit. This sense of human self-determination viewed independently of material circumstances is still present in the early writings of Marx.

Marxist literary theory and *Marxist criticism use the term praxis as 'denoting the total process and activity by which men in society (as *Subject*) act upon and change the world as their object' (Weimann 3), to draw attention to literary production as social praxis. (See *subject/object.) They examine in particular historical aspects of literary production and reception with respect to social and economic factors. The investigation of such categories as the aesthetic, or as *literature itself, has led in this context to an acceptance of the term literature in an extensive sense, to include texts beyond the established *canon of literary masterworks. The often-related *sociocriticism (distinct from a sociology of literature) seeks to establish the mediations of social praxis and socially produced relationships in the form and structure of literary works.

A phenomenological and existentialist usage of the term praxis in the 1950s and early 1960s (*Maurice Merleau-Ponty, *Jean-Paul Sartre), drawing mainly on the early work of Marx (before 1845), insists on a necessarily indeterminate human existence and thus on its ineluctable freedom. (See *phenomenological criticism.) By contrast later theory and criticism in France, such as works by *Louis Althusser, *Pierre Bourdieu or the group Tel Quel, often replace the term praxis by practice (*pratique*). In *Pour Marx* [*For Marx* 1965; trans. 1969], Althusser formulates the concept of a theoretical practice (*pratique théorique*) as a specific form of a determinate social practice. Theoretical practice thus falls under the general definition of practice as '*transformation* of a determinate given raw material into a determinate *product*, a transformation effected by a determinate human labour, using determinate means (of 'production')' (Althusser 166). The task of theoretical practice is to transform prescientific abstractions, which Althusser calls ideological, into scientific categories. This particular form of practice submits general concepts to the the-

oretical concepts of a science (as its 'means of production') and elaborates a concrete theoretical knowledge (a Hegelian 'concrete' which is the opposite of an empirical object).

*Julia Kristeva, *Roland Barthes and others subsequently use the term *signifying practice (*pratique signifiante*) to posit structuring and de-structuring processes of meaning production as a field of semiotic inquiry, and oppose concepts such as *text and *écriture* to the notion of the literary work. (See *semiotics.) Kristeva defines practice as a 'transformation of natural and social resistances, limitations, and stagnations' (*Revolution* 17). Since for her a signifying practice is 'the establishment and countervailing of a sign system' (*Desire* 18), the speaking subject appears in texts, which constitute one of the forms of signifying practice, as a subject in process/on trial (*sujet en procès*) that undergoes phases of socially defined identity as well as disruptive processes of change and crisis. (See also *sign, *materialist criticism.)

WINFRIED SIEMERLING

Primary Sources

Althusser, Louis. *Pour Marx.* 1965. *For Marx.* Trans. Ben Brewster. New York: Random House, 1969.

Kristeva, Julia. *Desire in Language. A Semiotic Approach to Literature and Art.* Trans. Thomas Gora, Alice Jardine, and Leon S. Roudiez. New York: Columbia UP, 1980.

– *Revolution in Poetic Language.* Trans. Margaret Waller. New York: Columbia UP, 1984.

Lobkowicz, Nicholas. *Theory and Practice: History of a Concept from Aristotle to Marx.* Notre Dame/London: U of Notre Dame P, 1967.

Marx, Karl. 'Theses on Feuerbach.' In Karl Marx and Frederick Engels. *Selected Works in Two Volumes.* Vol. II. Moscow: Foreign Languages Publishing House, 1958, 403–5.

Weimann, Robert. *Structure and Society in Literary History: Studies in the History and Theory of Historical Criticism.* Baltimore/London: Johns Hopkins UP, 1984.

Presence: *see* Metaphysics of pressure

Problematic

This term, in the strict definition given it by French Marxist philosopher *Louis Althusser, has had wide currency in politically committed literary theory and criticism since the early 1970s. A problematic is the unity of a body of thought from which its separate elements cannot be isolated. The problematic conditions both what can and cannot be thought within it. For example, since the New Critical problematic rejects considerations of biography and history, it is possible that specific instances of what it sees as wit or *irony may have been generated by psychological conflict or social contradiction. (See *New Criticism.) An ideological problematic, responsive to questions arising from its historical circumstances, is doubly blind, both to its internal assumptions and to its external determinates. (See *ideology, *ideological horizon.) Since the problematic of a given social scientific *text is as much a matter of absent problems and concepts – questions it is unable to ask, contradictions it cannot see – as it is of those openly dealt with, it can only be reached through a *symptomatic reading which focuses precisely on the text's lacunae and blind spots.

JOHN THURSTON

Primary Sources

Althusser, Louis. *For Marx.* Trans. Ben Brewster. London: New Left Books, 1977.

Readerly/writerly text

The distinction between the readerly and the writerly (*lisible* and *scriptible*) was argued at length by *Roland Barthes in his book *S/Z* (1970), a protracted, detailed reading of Honoré de Balzac's short novel *Sarrasine*, interspersed with explicit meditations on writing and criticism.

As the original French term suggests, the *scriptible* ('that which it is possible to write') is writing as act and unforeclosed process. The writerly *text is triumphantly plural and in it therefore *ideology (the valuing of one meaning over all others) is annulled. The writerly is absolutely plural because language is infinite. The writerly text is not a structure but a structuration, in which 'the reader [is] no longer a consumer, but a producer of the text' (*S/Z* 4). Because of its triumphant plurality, the writerly completely baffles any criticism or *metalanguage, any subsequent commentary or

categories which would seek to cover the text. Only incompletely plural texts can be discussed: 'there may be nothing to say about writerly texts' (4). As virtual object, the writerly may not exist: 'The writerly text is not a thing, we would have a hard time finding it in a bookstore' (5).

This is why, perhaps, Barthes' *S/Z* is a discussion of a 'classic' or readerly text. Readerly texts are finished objects, products and not productions. The readerly, classic narrative 'is basically subject to the logico-temporal order' (52). It 'sets forth the end of every action·(conclusion, interruption, closure, dénouement)' and so 'declares itself to be historical' (its plot is Aristotelian) (52). The classical narrative is also an 'image of the sentence,' since it is 'based on the articulation of question and answer' (it is 'hermeneutic') (76). (See *hermeneutics.) The basic requirement of the readerly is completeness. The readerly strives for plenitude, fullness, but denies thorough 'dissemination' (compare *Jacques Derrida's book, *Dissemination*). In the readerly, 'dissemination is not the random scattering of meanings toward the infinity of the language [this is the "dissemination" of the writerly]' (182). In the readerly everything is eventually recuperated. (See *recuperation.)

Barthes asserts at the outset that the readerly is the 'countervalue' of the writerly, 'its negative, reactive value' (4). This implies that the relation between the readerly and the writerly is dialectical, that one is inconceivable without the other, that to evoke the writerly, it may be best, or even necessary, to discuss a readerly text. This is in fact exactly what Barthes does in *S/Z*, which can be described as 'reactive' criticism, reacting to and 'differentiating' the readerly, 'more or less' plural novel *Sarrasine*. The painstakingly detailed, 'slowed down' reading exposes the gaps in this readerly text and aims to subvert its order or 'chains or causality' (215). (See *subversion.)

Yet it is true that at times Barthes speaks as if certain contemporary texts, of the French poet Phillippe Sollers for instance, really do approach the condition of the writerly and he explicitly asserts that 'this Replete Literature, readerly literature, can no longer be written' (201). In *S/Z* Barthes remains ambiguous about whether the writerly, as virtual text, actually exists. If the writerly text is 'ourselves writing,' it is perhaps best exemplified in what Barthes himself does in such a virtuoso-like manner in *S/Z* (the writerly is his activity, not his text, for the 'writerly text is not a thing'). The project is to write about the readerly without oneself producing another merely readerly text, to oppose the 'cultural code' of the classical readerly without substituting yet another *code of one's own: 'how can one code be superior to another without abusively closing off the plurality of codes? [That is, what is to prevent the idea of the writerly from itself becoming part of an all-too-readerly code?] Only writing, by assuming the largest possible plural in its own task, can oppose without appeal to force the imperialism of each language' (206). The writerly is writing as text (*texte*), as open-ended process; the readerly is writing as work (*oeuvre*), as closed object (to borrow terms from Barthes' essay 'From Work to Text' [1979]). The triumph of the 'writerly plural' is the triumph of *textuality, of writing seen as infinite and 'indeterminable' (with no single determinate meaning) because language is. Barthes' concept of the writerly is thus closely affiliated to the concepts of *écriture* and *intertextuality as defined by critics like Jacques Derrida, *Julia Kristeva and *Michael Riffaterre.

FRANCIS ZICHY

Primary Sources

Barthes, Roland. *S/Z*. 1970. Trans. Richard Miller. London: Jonathan Cape, 1974.
Derrida, Jacques. *Dissemination*. Trans. and intro. Barbara Johnson. Chicago: U of Chicago P, 1981.

Recuperation

In French, the term *récupération* means recovery, salvage, rehabilitation. Its use in literary criticism is most fully elaborated by *Jonathan Culler in his *Structuralist Poetics*. Culler defines what is referred to in structuralist criticism as recuperation, naturalization or *vraisemblablisation* as the reading process which brings the *text 'within the modes of order which culture makes available' (137). (See *structuralism.)

For a text to be intelligible, it must be recuperated into the order of comprehensibility available to the reader. Culler gives as an example the possibility of making a text by Robbe-Grillet easier to read by supposing it 'the musings or speech of a pathological nar-

rator' (138). In this case, the *code, or text, through which the novel is recuperated is that of common beliefs about human psychology. Culler describes the processes of recuperation through five such codes: first, that of 'the socially given text, that which is taken as the "real world."' Next there is the socially given text which differs from the first in being a set of assumptions recognized by those who hold them as subject to modification. Third, there is the knowledge of literary conventions or generic expectations which helps us recognize writing as falling into known patterns. Fourth, a text may be read and understood through the codes and values constructed by and within it or which distinguish it from other works; included in this recuperative category would be the expectations readers have of the work of a given author and the ways a text lives up to those expectations or not. Lastly, Culler describes recuperation through recognition of an intertext; a text is assimilated through recognition of another text, or body of texts, to which it is in some way related, or which it evokes or parodies. (See *intertextuality, *parody.)

Thus recuperation involves the reading of one text, what is written, through another, and this doubleness leads Culler to say, 'Irony, the cynic might say, is the ultimate form of recuperation and naturalization whereby we ensure that the text says only what we want to hear. We reduce the strange and incongruous ... by calling them ironic' (157). (See *irony.)

Culler modifies this statement by claiming that the reader's detection of irony can as easily result in a text which is not foreclosed. The idea, however, that recuperation is the process by which one text is effaced by the text, or code(s) (or knowledge) through which it is recuperated, suggests that *Jacques Derrida's work on metaphor in 'White Mythology' might also apply. (See *metonymy/metaphor, *white mythology.) Derrida discusses the way in which a metaphor can become so powerful that it erases the reality it represents: an example of this is the way in which a playing-field metaphor might erase the horror of the war for which it is substituted. While the recuperative text, like the metaphor, to some extent erases the material text read through it, it is also the condition which makes signification possible. (See *signified/signifier/signification.) The possibility of recuperation is the possibility of *closure of the text; all principles of closure are ultimately a limiting of polysemy: 'Each time that polysemia is irreducible, when no unity of meaning is even promised to it, one is outside language' (248). Derrida extends his discussion beyond Culler's (of the purely literary text) to the use of the metaphor in all discursive activities. In biology, for example, observations are made intelligible through such metaphors as that of the cell.

The recuperative text is the medium through which the 'real' is read, simultaneously effacing it and making it accessible, and is thus comparable to the notion of *ideology found in the work of *Louis Althusser. For Althusser, ideology is a means of knowing the world, a 'code,' reproduced through such institutions as schools, and also the form of knowledge which makes it possible to recognize ourselves as subjects. It thus serves as a principle of closure in the recuperation of the text of our experience. While, for Derrida, what is not recuperated through metaphor is 'outside language,' for Althusser, 'what seems to take place outside ideology (to be precise, in the street), in reality takes place in ideology' (163).

It must be pointed out that recogniton of the process of recuperation depends on a theory of language that claims that 'real' meaning, like the material text, is always effaced, beyond reach, until naturalized, or rewritten, within some pre-existing text. The critic may not be fully conscious of the recuperative codes which separate her from 'language itself' but must admit the possibility of their existence. All criticism is recuperation.

The following is an example of the use of the term: 'What was neither observed by Europe nor documented by it was therefore "lost" until, at some later date it too could be incorporated by the new sciences of anthropology, political economics, and linguistics. It is out of this later recuperation ... that a still later disciplinary step was taken, the founding of the science of world history' (Said 101).

JULIE BEDDOES

Primary Sources

Althusser, Louis. 'Ideology and Ideological State Apparatuses: Notes Toward an Investigation.' In *Lenin and Philosophy and Other Essays*. Trans. Ben Brewster. London: New Left Books, 1971.
Culler, Jonathan. *Structuralist Poetics: Structuralism, Linguistics and the Study of Literature*. London: Routledge and Kegan Paul, 1975.

Derrida, Jacques. 'White Mythology.' *Margins of Philosophy*. Trans. Alan Bass. Chicago: U of Chicago P, 1982.
Said, Edward. 'Orientalism Reconsidered.' *Cultural Critique* 1 (Fall 1985): 89–107.

Reference/referent

'Reference' is the activity of calling attention to something or to some state of affairs as relevant to the context at hand. 'Referent' is that object which is called to the recipient's attention as being relevant. The term reference has been central in modern philosophy of language from Gottlob Frege to *Paul Ricoeur.

There is no problem with ostensive reference; for example, when one points to the door and asks another person to open it. The semantic problem arises with non-ostensive reference in written language and can be examined at the level of the sentence and at the level of the *text.

In Frege, reference is coupled with the term sense; sense is *what* the proposition states and reference is that about which the proposition is stated; the problem arises out of the lack of a one-to-one relationship between sense and reference in ordinary language. *Emile Benveniste expanded Frege's concept from the level of word to that of sentences. He held that reference is established through its use in the sentence, which gives separate words semantic value and thereby their referents. Ricoeur builds on Benveniste's linguistic observations in his consideration of textual reference. In *The Rule of Metaphor* (1977), Ricoeur argues that 'the meaning of a metaphorical statement rises up from the blockage of any literal interpretation of the statement'; inasmuch as 'the primary reference founders' as a result of the semantic impertinence of the metaphor (230), literal *reference* of a direct description gives way to a *sense*, a metaphorical truth which does not describe an existing reality, but which 'discovers' new possible realities. (See *metonymy/metaphor.)

MARIO J. VALDÉS

Primary Sources

Benveniste, Emile. *Problems in General Linguistics*. Trans. Mary Elizabeth Meek. Coral Gables: U of Miami P, 1977.
Ricoeur, Paul. *The Rule of Metaphor: Multi-discipli-*

nary Studies of the Creation of Meaning in Language. Trans. Robert Czerny with Kathleen McLaughlin and John Costello. London: Routledge and Kegan Paul, 1978.

Reification

Reification is a term associated with the work of the Hungarian Marxist philosopher *Georg Lukács, who presented it as part of his dialectical theory of society in History and Class Consciousness (1923). Lukács employs reification (Verdinglichung) to describe the economic process whereby, under capitalism, human social relations or actions take on the appearance of relations or actions among objects or things that are then described in purely mathematical or scientific terms. Such a reification of social relations ultimately comes to produce, in Lukács' view, certain effects on the subject of production.

Reification bears conceptual similarities and owes debts of influence both to Karl Marx's theory of alienation and to Max Weber's theory of rationalization. In Capital, vol. I (1867), Marx examines how the products of man's creation, such as the products of his labour, come to appear and act as alien constraints upon him because of the nature of commodity production. Writing on the 'fetishism of commodities' under capitalism, he explains that the social character of man's labour appears to him only in an objective light, as a 'thinglike' relation between persons, and conversely, that the relations between commodities assume the appearance of social relations. Reification as understood by Lukács is an amplification of this theory, which in the third volume of Capital is given the name Verdinglichung. Lukács claims that in the commodity-structure characteristic of capitalism, the relations between people acquire a 'phantom objectivity' that conceals the fact and the history of social relations.

Also an important influence on Lukács is the thought of German sociologist Max Weber. Weber's theory of rationalization in Wirtschaft und Gesellschaft [History and Society 1922] describes the way in which, under a capitalist economy, reason and science prevail in a manner privileging quantification and calculability. Capitalism is defined for Weber by its rational organization of production and distribution; all units of human action (such as labour) are broken down into measurable, mechanical, standardized processes. According to Weber, such rationalization ultimately results in extreme bureaucratization and standardization.

Lukács' theory of reification has all of these implications but is expanded beyond economic issues in order to explain the structural consequences of reification for the inner as well the outer life of society. He distinguishes two sides of the phenomenon of reification, which he names the 'objective' and the 'subjective.' If the former aspect is the centrepiece of Marx and Weber's discussions, Lukács' important contribution comes with his examination of the effect of reification upon the consciousness of the worker or, more broadly, upon the consciousness of man. With the reification of consciousness, the production process appears to the worker – or the world appears to man – as fragmented and incoherent. Reification results in man's inability to perceive the historicity or the totality of social relations and in his subsequent passivity in the face of what appears to be a fundamentally ungraspable and unchangeable world. But, according to Lukács, the worker will be able to grasp society as a historical totality because he, unlike the bourgeoisie, possesses through his class consciousness a minimal understanding of his alienation and reification.

Lukács' theory of reification holds implications for his literary criticism. In The Meaning of Contemporary Realism (1963) he argues against the aesthetics of literary modernism, such as that he perceives in James Joyce's Ulysses; such a work is understood to be the product of a reified consciousness incapable of perceiving the historical nature of its own disintegration. He favours instead realism and the historical novel, both of which he believes attempt to provide the reader with a perspective on and an understanding of the historical totality that modernism can only describe in fragments. The theory of reification has emerged more recently in the work of the American Marxist literary critic *Fredric Jameson who accepts, in The Political Unconscious (1981), Lukács' association of modernism with reification but who argues that the newly reified consciousness always brings with it a utopian impulse resulting in a formal experimentation (for example, with language) that attempts to give aesthetic intensity to the reified

Self/other

world of capitalism. (See *Marxist criticism, *materialist criticism.)

ROSS KING

Primary Sources

Jameson, Fredric. *Marxism and Form.* Princeton: Princeton UP, 1971.
– *The Political Unconscious: Narrative as a Socially Symbolic Act.* Ithaca: Cornell UP, 1981.
Lukács, Georg. *History and Class Consciousness: Studies in Marxist Dialectics.* London: Merlin P, 1971.
– *The Meaning of Contemporary Realism.* London: Merlin P, 1963.
Marx, Karl. *Capital: A Critique of Political Economy.* 3 vols. Trans. Samuel Moore and Edward Aveling. Ed. Friedrich Engels. London: Lawrence and Wishart, 1887.
Weber, Max. *Economy and Society: An Outline of Interpretive Sociology.* 3 vols. Ed. Günther Roth and Claus Wittich. Trans. Ephraim Fischoff et al. New York: Bedminster P, 1968.

Self/other

The Self/Other opposition posits that at the centre of personal experience is a subjective self which constructs everything alien to it as 'other.' The opposition, sometimes phrased in different terms such as centre/margin or dominant/muted, has played an important role in *feminist criticism since *Simone de Beauvoir employed it to explain the power imbalance between men and women. It has also been used in psychoanalytic *discourse to suggest a fundamental division within the individual consciousness. (See *centre/decentre, *margin, *psychoanalytic theory.)

In *The Second Sex* (1949) Simone de Beauvoir argued that man is the subject, woman is the Other. (See *subject/object.) Whereas man's experience is central and absolute, woman's is perceived as inessential, alien, negative. Thus, in patriarchal society, woman is denied full selfhood, alienated from her own subjectivity. (See *patriarchy.) De Beauvoir believed the Other to be a fundamental category of human thought. The human mind bears an innate hostility to other consciousnesses. Although this holds for everyone, in the case of the sexes there is an imbalance because women, instead of reciprocally classifying men as alien, submit to men's view of them as Other. They do this even though they constitute neither a minority nor a class which has been subjugated by a specific historical event. They submit for several reasons. First, alienated in patriarchal culture, they are estranged from each other and lack the resources to form a consolidated body; women, de Beauvoir says, 'do not say "We"' (xix). Second, they perceive the imbalance of power between men and women to be an unchangeable absolute. Third, they submit because, in many cases, assuming the role men have scripted for them is easier than attempting to divorce themselves from a structure which has traditionally provided them with direction and value.

De Beauvoir's argument derives in part from Hegel who, in *Phenomenology of Spirit* (1807), had argued that the self characterizes anything which is not identical with itself as 'an unessential, negatively characterized object' (113). Her argument also shares close similarities with the philosophy of the existentialists, with whom she was closely connected. Their account of the relationship between the self and others as the relationship which crucially defines the self was central to their philosophy.

De Beauvoir's concept of the Otherness of women has greatly influenced Anglo-American feminist criticism. (See *feminist criticism, Anglo-American.) Examinations of *literature produced in the patriarchal tradition, such as Kate Millett's pioneering work *Sexual Politics* (1969), seek to show how the male norm is constructed and how women are consistently characterized as Other. The more recent focus on literature written by women, demonstrated in works like *Sandra Gilbert and Susan Gubar's *The Madwoman in the Attic* (1979), has concentrated on the problems women encounter when they attempt to inscribe themselves as central. Anglo-American feminist criticism has thus frequently accepted de Beauvoir's category of Otherness as the primary condition of women's existence.

French feminists such as *Luce Irigaray, *Julia Kristeva and *Hélène Cixous have also taken up the idea of the construction of the feminine as lack, negativity and absence but have employed it to different effect. (See *feminist criticism, French; *desire/lack.) They argue that it is precisely from this Otherness, this unexplored 'dark continent,' that the liberating *écriture féminine*, the discourse of marginality, is generated. Kristeva, for example, argues that the semiotic is a language which emerges from women's marginal position as Other. (See *semiotics.) It diverges sharply

620

from the traditional structures of patriarchal language (the symbolic) and moves in a fluid realm of word-play, association and nonsense. Kristeva firmly resists an essentialist link between women and the semiotic, but she does suggest that it is akin to the language shared between mother and child and predates the symbolic language which the child must ultimately enter. (See *imaginary/symbolic/real, *essentialism.) Unlike the Anglo-American feminists, French feminists generally employ the concept of Otherness as a liberating concept and use it to celebrate women's difference rather than to stress women's limitations.

The Self/Other opposition has also entered critical theory through *Jacques Lacan whose notion of Other is a polysemic concept at the heart of his work. Like de Beauvoir's, Lacan's concept of the Other derives from both Hegel (especially his account of the master-slave dialectic) and the existentialist philosophers. Whereas de Beauvoir assumed that men could possess full subjectivity, Lacan finds even the male subject essentially and irrevocably fragmented and incapable of the full occupation of self. During the formative *mirror stage, the child learns to perceive itself as a stable form but it does so only by means of an image which is not truly identical with itself but other and alien. Its self-image is thus structured by a misidentification. During the Oedipal crisis, the symbolic Father (see *Name-of-the-Father), who for Lacan is the primal Other, legislates the separation of the child from its mother and thus introduces a permanent gap between desire and its object as the child enters the realm of the symbolic. The desire which drives individuals often appears to be the desire for an object (what Lacan calls the *objet a* or small-other object) but in fact it is really for the unattainable original presence.

Although Lacan uses the term Other in many different senses, the Other is thus basically a locus of forces which enables the emergence of the subject but, at the same time, leaves the subject permanently fragmented and in perpetual slavery to desire. Lacan differs from de Beauvoir in that he argues that otherness is not an external category but an internal and unchangeable condition of man's existence. In Lacan's terms, when woman becomes man's Other, she becomes a correlative for man's lack and helps affirm him in his selfhood.

MELANIE SEXTON

Primary Sources

Beauvoir, Simone de. *The Second Sex.* Trans. H.M. Parshley. New York: Alfred A. Knopf, 1970.

Gilbert, Sandra M., and Susan Gubar. *The Madwoman in the Attic: The Woman Writer and the Nineteenth-Century Literary Imagination.* New Haven: Yale UP, 1979.

Hegel, G.W.F. *Phenomenology of Spirit.* Trans. A.V. Miller. Oxford: Clarendon P, 1977.

Kristeva, Julia. *Desire in Language: A Semiotic Approach to Literature and Art.* Ed. Leon S. Roudiez. Trans. Thomas Gora, Alice Jardine, Leon S. Roudiez. New York: Columbia UP, 1980.

Lacan, Jacques. *Ecrits.* Paris: Editions de Seuil, 1966.

Millett, Kate. *Sexual Politics.* New York: Equinox, 1971.

Seme

A seme is a semantic *dictinctive feature* (see *Roman Jakobson) by which it is possible to differentiate one element of the signified of a term from another one in a given context of communication. (See *signified/signifier/signification.) The seme is thought to be 'a minimal unit of signification,' comparable at the semantic level to what the phoneme is at the phonological level. Semic analysis allows *A.J. Greimas to see any lexeme (that is, object-term) as a collection of semes which constitute its properties and by which it differs from another one.

The lexemes 'broad' and 'narrow' have in common with 'high' and 'low' the semes spatiality and dimensionality, but they differ from the latter terms by the absence of the seme verticality and the presence of the semes horizontality and laterality. These semes have no reality other than in their mutual relationships and should not be compared to atomic elements. Considering a given seme (for example, spatiality) as a semic axis, one can see that it forms a complex semic system. First, this system consists of antonymic relationships, the semic oppositions represented by the absence or the presence of the seme dimensionality being necessary to make clear the differences between concurring terms, like 'high' and 'vast.' Also, between the semes of the same category, one can observe a hierarchy of relationships, since each semic axis may be divided into many other axes.

While these characteristics apply to the *nu-*

clear *seme*, there is another type of seme, called *contextual seme* or **classeme*. According to Greimas, this latter seme appears only in a discursive context, where its presence allows a uniform reading of a sentence (see **isotopy*). In order to obtain a minimal sense effect, or a *sememe*, it is necessary to combine at least one *nuclear seme* and one *classeme*.

Conceived by Bernard Pottier for his studies in componential semantics (dating back to his doctoral thesis in 1955), this concept was introduced into **semiotics* by Greimas. Unlike Pottier, however, Greimas does not see semic analysis as a mere paraphrase in natural language but as a metalinguistic construction which would, ideally, be composed of minimal units in a coherent organization. (See **metalanguage*.) The study of the fundamental relationships which may coexist between the semes of a given semic axis led to the elaboration of the *semiotic square*. This figure is presented by Greimas as 'the logical development of a binary semic category, like *white* vs *black*, whose terms are mutually in a relationship of contrariety, each of them being susceptible at the same moment to project a new term which would be its contradictory, and contradictory terms being able, in turn, to contract a relationship of implication toward the opposite contrary term' (*Du sens* 1970, 160).

CHRISTIAN VANDENDORPE

Primary Sources

Greimas, A.J. *Sémantique structurale*. Paris: Larousse, 1966; repub. PUF, 1986. *Structural Semantics*. Trans. D. McDowell, R. Schleifer and A. Velie. Lincoln/London: U of Nebraska P, 1983.
– *Du sens*. Paris: Seuil, 1970.
– and J. Courtés. *Sémiotique: Dictionnaire raisonné de la théorie du langage*. Paris, 1979. *Semiotics and Language: An Analytical Dictionary*. Trans. L. Crist, D. Patte et al. Bloomington: Indiana UP, 1982.

Secondary Sources

Pottier, B. *Linguistique générale*. Paris: Klincksieck, 1974.

Semiosis

Semiosis is the term commonly used to refer to the innate capacity of human beings to produce and understand signs of all kinds (from those belonging to simple physiological signalling systems to highly complex symbolic structures). (See **sign*.) The etymology of the term is traceable to the Greek word *sema*, 'mark, sign,' which is also the root of the related terms **semiotics* and *semiology* or 'the science of signs' and *semantics*, 'the study of meaning.' In the theoretical semiotic **literature* the term *semiosis* is consistently used as well in the broader sense of *signification* or *sign process*.

In its oldest usage (Nöth 12–14), the term refers to the observable pattern of physiological symptoms induced by specific diseases. Hippocrates (460?–377? BC) – the founder of medical science – viewed the semiosic characteristics associated with a disease as the basis for an appropriate diagnosis and a suitable prognosis. As Fisch (41) points out, it was soon after Hippocrates' utilization of the term *semiosis* to refer to symptomatic signs that it came to mean – by the time of Aristotle (384–322 BC) – the 'action' of a sign itself, or the correlative act of sign interpretation.

In all the main conceptualizations of semiosis, from Aristotle to **C.S. Peirce* and Thomas Sebeok, the primary components of this mental process are the *sign* (a representative image or **icon*, a word), the *object* referred to (which can be either concrete or abstract), and the *meaning* that results when the sign and the object are linked by association. It would appear that the human cognitive system operates on the basis of this triadic nexus. Indeed, many semioticians now claim that it underlies the very structure of the mind. Thus, for instance, the word *cat* is a verbal sign that relates the animal (its object) to the meaning 'cat' (the domesticated carnivorous mammal with retractable claws, which kills mice and rats). Similarly, the use of the index finger to point to an object in a room creates a concrete existential meaning relation between the so-called indexical sign (the pointing finger) and the object. (See **index*.) Following Charles Sanders Peirce, most semioticians now add the notion of *interpretant* to the process of semiosic competence. This is Peirce's term for the individual's particular interpretation of the triadic relationship that inheres in semiosis: 'A sign addresses somebody, that is, creates in the mind of that person an equivalent sign, or perhaps a more developed sign. The sign which it creates I call the *interpretant* of the first sign' (2: 228).

Peirce and Charles Morris are two of the most authoritative theorists on semiosis. Morris' account adds a behavioural dimension to the theory of signs by emphasizing the physical as well as the mental responses that a sign elicits in the human organism. Morris' account is considered a development of the Peircean idea that all thought 'is in itself essentially of the nature of a sign' (5: 294). More recently, Thomas Sebeok has argued persuasively that semiosis should constitute the cornerstone for a behavioural science of communication. He defines *semiosis* as 'the capacity for containing, replicating and extracting messages, and of extracting their significance' (*Pandora's Box* 452). (See *communication theory.)

In the view of most theorists semiosis is intrinsically related to communicative behaviour. Whereas *unilateral semiosis* involves any organism in isolation as the receiver and processor of physiologically detectable signals in the immediate environment (Meyer-Eppler), *bilateral semiosis* involves the reception and processing of signals by participating organisms in the surrounding environment. The systematic interaction and pattern of responses in which these organisms participate through bilateral semiosis defines the communication system for the species to which they belong. Only in the human species, however, is highly abstract and symbolic bilateral semiosis possible (as, for instance, in verbal communication). The common factor in all biological organisms is the fact that semiosis and communication allow for the instantaneous interpretation of signals present in the immediate environment. As Ruesch has appropriately pointed out, communication is the 'organizing principle of nature' (83). For *Umberto Eco, semiosis is synonymous with the organization of communication systems (316).

There are various theories on the phylogenesis of the semiosic capacity, but perhaps the most plausible one traces it to the mind's capacity to transform sense impressions into memorable experiences through the formation of images. Although all species participate by instinct in the experiential universe, only humans are endowed with the capacity to model their sense impressions in the form of mental images. It is when these iconic transformations of our bodily experiences are codified into signs and sign systems that they become permanently transportable in the form of cognitive units, phenomenologically free from their physiological units of occurrence. Indeed, the work on semiosis has made it possible to relate the world of sensorial experience to the world of abstraction and thought, by showing the latter to be a kind of 'outgrowth' of the former.

MARCEL DANESI

Primary Sources

Eco, Umberto. *A Theory of Semiotics*. Bloomington: Indiana UP, 1976.

Fisch, Max H. 'Peirce's General Theory of Signs.' In *Sight, Sound, and Sense*. Ed. Thomas A. Sebeok. Bloomington: Indiana UP, 1978, 31–70.

Meyer-Eppler, Werner. *Grundlagen und Anwendungen der Informationstheorie*. Berlin: Springer Verlag, 1959.

Morris, Charles W. *Foundations of the Theory of Signs*. Chicago: U of Chicago P, 1938.

Nöth, Winfred. *Handbook of Semiotics*. Bloomington: Indiana UP, 1990.

Peirce, Charles S. *Collected Papers*. Vols. 1–6. Cambridge, Mass.: Harvard UP, 1931–58.

Ruesch, Jürgen. *Semiotic Approaches to Human Relations*. The Hague: Mouton, 1972.

Sebeok, Thomas A. *Contributions to the Doctrine of Signs*. Lanham, Md.: UP of America, 1976.

– 'Pandora's Box: How and Why to Communicate 10,000 Years into the Future.' In *On Signs*. Ed. M. Blonsky. Baltimore: Johns Hopkins UP, 1985, 448–66.

– *The Sign and Its Masters*. Austin: U of Texas P, 1979.

Sign

'The role of the sign is to represent, to stand as a *substitute* for something else' (*Emile Benveniste, *Problems* 51). For example, a red light may signify 'stop,' a siren or smoke that there is a fire. Signs are an essential feature of communication at every level through any sense or combination of senses. Virtually anything, animate or inanimate, real or imaginary, natural or created, may be used or interpreted as a sign, and for any one sign there may be several interpretations. Nor need these interpretations be mutually exclusive. For example, a drawn, written or other representation of the sun may be a sign of light, heat, life, star type, fine weather, or a combination of some or all of these. (See *communication theory.)

A sign signifies within a system of signs which is by definition semiotic. (See *semiotics, *semiosis.) According to Benveniste, the characteristics of such a system are (1) its mode of operation (how a sign is perceived); (2) its context of validity; (3) the nature and number of its signs; and (4) the way the signs relate to each other within a given system. He illustrates this by using a simple system of traffic lights: one red and one green light. The traffic lights (1) operate visually (2) in the context of road traffic; (3) the two lights are colour differentiated; and (4) they alternate. Within this binary system (or *code), red signifies 'stop,' green 'go.' (See *binary opposition.)

A given language is another sort of system, though much more complex. Within any language a genre, group of texts, particular *text or part of it may also constitute a system. For example, we might choose to reduce Hamlet's 'To be or not to be' speech to a simple binary system of signs: its mode of operation would be chiefly auditory, but gestures might add a secondary visual mode; its context would be (a) the particular scene and (b) the rest of the play, since the signs derive their meaning from the scene *and* the play as a whole; the two signs (to be/not to be) are contrastive (one affirmative, the other negative); they alternate (since one state or its contemplation precludes the other).

A sign implies not only a system, however simple, within which a sign can signify, but also a sender and receiver. In the case of the traffic lights, the obvious sender is the light itself; behind it are other senders: switches, electronic circuits, and the operator or person who programmed the light switching. Similarly, the receiver is not only the vehicle driver (his eye and brain and vehicle) for whom the lights are intended as a signal, but anyone else seeing them as a sign. So, in *literature, the sender may be an author, a *narrator, a character, or a character within a character's embedded story; conversely, a similar proliferation of levels of receiver will be implied. (See *embedding.)

Types of sign

According to *Charles Sanders Peirce there are three classes of sign. Since the work of Luis Prieto, the signal is also considered important. Thus there are four types of sign: *icon, *index, symbol, signal. They are usually considered according to criteria of intention to communicate, their relationship to what they represent, and whether they are natural, conventional or arbitrary (to use Saussure's terminology). (See *Ferdinand de Saussure.) Though, as John Lyons has pointed out, conventional and arbitrary are not synonymous.

The index is usually a natural (rather than conventional) phenomenon, indicating another phenomenon not immediately perceptible but having some factual or causal connection with it: thus fever is an index of illness. Generally speaking, an index reveals no intention to communicate, though in literary texts indices may be intentionally set up for the reader. In this case they could be said to act both as indices and signals. In literary *discourse, style is often an index.

The signal, like the index, indicates a phenomenon which is not itself immediately perceptible. The sender of the signal, unlike that of the index, intends to communicate. Furthermore, the person being sent the signal must recognize it as a signal of something. For example, a white flag is a signal of truce in time of war. The truce is not a visible phenomenon but the flag is, and the person displaying the flag does so with the intention of communicating a message to the enemy, who recognizes this as a conventional, unambiguous signal.

Signals, then, are usually conventional signs, and the relationship between signifier and signified is unambiguous and arbitrary. (See *signified/signifer/signification.) The difference between a signal and an index may be seen by comparing two interpretations of the same sign, variously called a 'wink,' if perceived as an intended conventional sign (a signal) or a 'blink' if perceived as an involuntary and natural sign of someone having something in her eye causing the blinking (that is, an index).

The icon resembles, in some recognizable way, what it represents. Thus a stage play's painted decor or a prose description of Venice are icons of Venice; a stage prop, such as a chair, is an iconic representation of a 'real' chair in the imagined 'real' context. Onomatopoeic expressions, stage sounds offstage, stage costumes, make-up and lighting, *Tristam Shandy*'s dark page representing the dark (technopagnia), Rabelais' panegyric printed in the shape of a bottle, and *mise-en-abyme* are all iconic. As John Lyons observes, the resemblance may be natural or conventional (cultural), depending upon the extent to which perception may be culturally defined. The intention to communicate is not a necessary criterion for icons, indices or symbols as it is with signals. But it should be remembered that literary signs tend to be overdetermined with the express intention of being recognized as signs – of whatever sort.

The symbol differs from the icon and index in that the relationship between the sign and its signification is virtually always arbitrary and conventional. This relationship is established because of some implied 'rule' of conventional or habitual association between the symbol and its object or concept. Thus black is a symbol of evil. Words, both spoken and written, are symbols too, conventionally standing for what they signify.

The components of the linguistic sign

Ferdinand de Saussure defined the linguistic sign as a binary entity: it combines the signifier (or acoustic image) and the signified (or concept). (See *structuralism.) Thus the spoken words or their written equivalent, such as, for example, *horse, equus, cheval, cavallo*, a drawing of a horse, or some other representation, are all signifiers denoting the same signified: 'a solid-hoofed quadruped with flowing mane and tail, used for riding on.' Since meanings derive from a particular instance, or instances, and are always related to and coloured by their previous context(s) of reference in our mind's eye, a signified is said to be composed of two parts: its denotation (the concept) and its connotation (associations evoked by a particular sign in a given context).

The linguistic sign has several distinguishing features. The signifier is linear: since it is primarily auditive, it is spread along a temporal axis; rather than hearing all its constituent sounds in a simultaneous jumble, we hear a sequence of differentiated sounds. The same is thus true of the written signifier, be it simple (a single expression) or complex (a whole text). The link between the signifier and signified is arbitrary. There is no logical reason why the sounds *'arbre'* or 'tree' should be used to signify a tree, or 're-,' as in 'rewrite,' should signify 'again'; the link is purely conventional. This is why linguistic signs are classed as symbols. (Onomatopoeic expressions are an exception, since the link between, say, the sound 'boom' and the sound signified is not arbitrary.) Transmitted from generation to generation this link between signifier and signified is fixed within the linguistic system: the signifier

tree cannot signify 'cat' or anything we choose, but conventionally always signifies 'tree.' Likewise, in art and literature, many symbols or situations become conventionally associated with particular meanings. For example, a bucolic scene typically signifies innocence, commedia dell'arte characters their stock roles and attributes. However, since the link between a signifier and a signified can alter over time, it is also flexible; *albus*, meaning 'white' in Latin, has become *album* in modern English. In literary texts the same phenomenon may occur. A cliché may be intentionally destabilized so as to restore meaning, or a *parody may twist a well-worn message.

Saussure held that linguistic signs signify because of their differences: we distinguish sounds and meanings because they are different from one another. But signs are also related to each other. The syntagmatic relationship links elements within a particular utterance according to certain established rules. Their role and meaning derive from this particular relationship. Each of these elements has been selected from a paradigm of other possible but different elements. Thus 'the grey mare' has three paradigms which might be (1) the, a, (2) black, grey, white, brown, pied, (3) stallion, horse, mare, pony, colt, and so forth. *Roland Barthes illustrates the difference by using a menu. A simple menu might use three paradigms: hors d'oeuvre, main dish, dessert. Each paradigm might comprise four possible choices. Three items, one from each paradigm, are chosen for their mutual compatibility and are combined in a meal – comparable to a syntagmatic chain.

Although in literary analysis the syntagmatic relation tends to be more useful in determining the meaning of a given sign (always defined in its relationship to others within a shared context), the paradigmatic relation is helpful in analysing poetry, since in poetry elements from the same paradigm are often used to construct a system of equivalent signs all pointing to the matrix or *hypogram.

The ternary (or triadic) sign

Saussure (and in his wake many French theorists) described the sign as a binary entity, as indeed it was for him, since he saw the referent as an extralinguistic phenomenon. However, most theorists consider the sign as having three parts: signifier, signified, referent.

(See *reference/referent.) The referent is determined by its context and is the actual object, person or state of affairs to which the sign refers. It is an essential element of semantics. Without it there is no precise meaning: for example, 'she,' 'it' or other shifters are empty expressions without a referent.

The American C.S. Peirce was the first to develop a theory of the 'triadic' sign, as he called it. This he did within a most sophisticated all-embracing, but unfinished, theory of signs or semiotics propounded in various writings. Peirce's impact has not long been evident in part because of the unavailability of his works, and in part because of their complexity. Some years later, in Germany in 1892, Gottlob Frege proposed the following ternary sign (as translated into English by Feigl): sign, sense, nominatum (the object to which the sign refers). Despite the terminology, it is clear that here 'sign' actually has the meaning of signifier. In England in 1923 C.K. Ogden and *I.A. Richards in *The Meaning of Meaning* suggested the triad, symbol, thought or reference, referent. Here again 'symbol' may be interpreted as signifier, and 'thought' as signified. Ogden and Richards define the referent as an object or state of affairs in the external world. A somewhat similar sign, despite its different terminology, was presented by the American Charles Morris in 1938: sign vehicle (signifying vehicle), 'designatum' or 'significatum,' 'denotatum' (that is, an object which actually exists), sign vehicle (signifying vehicle).

In 1934 the Czech linguist *Jan Mukařovský elaborated a ternary sign of particular interest to those applying sign-theory to the arts. Like *Roman Jakobson, Mukařovský was interested in the predominantly aesthetic or 'poetic' function of a work of art. For Mukařovský, a work of art (the signifier) derives its meaning (the signified) from a given historical, social and cultural context, known generally as its ideological context. For Mukařovský, each interpreter (spectator, reader) construes the artistic referent as a specific ideological expression of a particular context (a *concretization). Since the *ideology which this referent or concretization depends upon is likely to vary from age to age and culture to culture, so too will the referent and the signified. As *Mikhail Bakhtin has shown, ideologically construed signs imply dialogical relationships operating between sender and receiver, author and reader. (See *dialogical criticism.) Interpretation of aesthetic signs is particularly constrained by the receiver's awareness of the encoded ideological message, and this interpretation is often further coloured by the receiver's idiosyncratic ideological bent. *Louis Althusser, *Michel Foucault and Roland Barthes were all interested in the aesthetic signification of the 'ideological' sign. For them, the signified is as protean as its referent, and may ultimately be seen as an empty form constantly being refilled by a new ideological meaning or 'reality.'

Years before, Peirce had already developed a multi-tiered theory of signs far more complex than any of the above. His vast scheme is based on his three categories of 'firstness' (I), 'secondness' (II), and 'thirdness' (III). Firstness is the possibility of some abstractable quality in what is perceived. Secondness is the 'being-thereness,' existence or occurrence of something. Thirdness is a linking of the two others by some mediating law or process. Peirce's terms in the following triad reflect these three aspects: qualisign (I), sinsign (II), legisign (III). This triadic sign is contained in, and becomes a single element of a more encompassing triadic sign, where the representamen or sign belongs to the first category, the object it represents to the second, and the interpretant, which interprets it meaningfully, to the third: representamen or sign (I), object (II), interpretant (III). Peirce's sophisticated system is proving an extremely rich source of inspiration for practical applications of sign theory to literary texts.

A more recent interpretation of the sign, and having little in common with any of the above, is that proposed by *Jacques Derrida. He does not believe in the sign per se, and refutes the concepts of system and context generally deemed essential for defining the sign. (He does, however, rely, at least in part, on Saussure, whose concepts of oppositional differences he develops.) Rather, his *deconstruction (or deconstruction theory) exploits *aporia by seeking out the break in a given system. He interprets this aporia as an 'anti-sign' of the subversive difference. This difference, now known as '*différance' (Derrida's spelling) is, in itself, significant. Defined by Derrida as both differing *and* deferring, no sign is ever ultimately definable, since meaning is for ever deferred. This view reveals *Nietzsche's strong influence on Derrida. Derrida's signs are not so much signs as traces of them. (See *trace.) The gaps between these traces are a free space for the reader to construe as she or he will: a space/trace forever protean and incomplete, both absent and imminently (immanently) present. The Derridean sign is a mirror structure which never allows any possibility of distinguishing the authentic originating sign since, for him, these signs have no origin.

ANNA WHITESIDE—ST. LEGER LUCAS

Primary Sources

Benveniste, Emile. *Problems in General Linguistics.* Trans. M.E. Meek. Coral Gables: U of Miami P, 1971.

Mukařovský, Jan. *The Word and Verbal Art.* Trans. and ed. J. Burbank and P. Steiner. New Haven and London: Yale UP, 1977.

Peirce, Charles Sanders. *Collected Papers.* Cambridge, Mass.: Harvard UP, 1931–58.

Prieto, Luis. *Messages et signaux.* Paris: PUF, 1966.

Saussure, Ferdinand de. *Course in General Linguistics.* Ed. Charles Bally and Albert Sechehaye. Trans. Roy Harris. La Salle, Ill.: Open Court, 1986.

Secondary Sources

Dubois, Jean, et al. *Dictionnaire de linguistique.* Paris: Larousse, 1973.

Lyons, John. *Semantics 1.* Cambridge: Cambridge UP, 1977.

Signified/signifier/signification

*Ferdinand de Saussure posited the signifier/signified distinction in his *Course in General Linguistics*. For Saussure, 'the linguistic sign unites, not a thing and a name, but a concept and a sound-image' (66). (See *sign.) The signifier, whether audible as speech or visible as writing, is an object of perception: the signified is absent and ontologically indistinct – 'half way between a mental image, a concept and a psychological reality' (Eco 14–15). Signification is the relationship that holds together the signifier and the signified. To emphasize the non-referential (or non-realist) quality of signification, Saussure argued that 'the bond between the signifier and the signified is arbitrary' (67) in contrast to the symbol which is never arbitrary (68). In a revolutionary move beyond traditional philosophical thinking on the problem of language, Saussure did not grant any prior-

ity to the signified: 'in language there are only differences *without positive terms*' (120).

The controversial feature of Saussure's theory is clearly his notion of the signified. For *Tzvetan Todorov, 'whoever speaks of a sign must accept the existence of a radical difference between signifier and signified, between perceptible and imperceptible, between presence and absence' (100). (See *metaphysics of presence.) Signification thus occurs within a generalized principle of difference: an absence or lack that is *marked*. Saussure himself seems to have a slightly less radical notion that signs 'express' ideas that can be located in a human mind, but his emphasis on the systematic proliferation of signs needed for signification suggests that the immanent logic of signifiers is of greater importance for language than any necessary logic of the signified. We could not think without differentiated signs: 'There are no pre-existing ideas, and nothing is distinct before the appearance of language' (Saussure 112).

*Emile Benveniste has challenged Saussure concerning the arbitrary relation of the signifier and signified, arguing that 'the signifier and the signified, the mental representation and the sound image, are ... in reality the two aspects of a single notion' (45). By welding the two aspects of signification together, Benveniste actually strengthens their opposition: '*The absolute character of the linguistic sign ...* commands in its turn the dialectical *necessity* of values of constant opposition, and forms the structural principle of language' (48). For structuralist and poststructuralist thinking as a whole, however, the arbitrary nature of signification has been very important. *Julia Kristeva, for example, speaks of the gap between signifier and signified as opening 'the heretofore unrecognized possibility of envisioning language as a free play, forever without closure' (128). (See *structuralism, *poststructuralism, theories of *play/freeplay, *closure/disclosure.)

GREGOR CAMPBELL

Primary Sources

Benveniste, Emile. *Problems in General Linguistics.* Trans. Mary Elizabeth Meek. Coral Gables: U of Miami P, 1971.

Eco, Umberto. *A Theory of Semiotics.* Bloomington: Indiana UP, 1976.

Kristeva, Julia. *Desire in Language: A Semiotic Approach to Literature and Art. Ed. Leon S. Roudiez. Trans. Thomas Gora, Alice Jardine and Leon S. Roudiez. New York: Columbia UP, 1980.

Saussure, Ferdinand de. Course in General Linguistics. Ed. Charles Bally and Albert Sechehaye in collaboration with Albert Riedlinger. Trans. Wade Baskin. New York: McGraw-Hill, 1959.

Todorov, Tzvetan, and Oswald Ducrot. Encyclopedic Dictionary of the Sciences of Language. Trans. Catherine Porter. Baltimore: Johns Hopkins UP, 1979.

Signifying practice

*Julia Kristeva employs the term signifying practice in reference to language as socially communicable *discourse. For Kristeva, all such language is generated by a process which includes two signifying modalities, which she terms the 'semiotic' (psychic and libidinal drives) and the 'symbolic' (nomination, *sign, syntax; the realm of positions and judgment). Kristeva contends that these two modalities can be combined in different ways to constitute different types of social discourse or signifying practice. As well, she argues that a particular type of signifying practice corresponds to a particular articulation of subject identity. In her view, only certain types of signifying practice explore the revolutionary possibilities of the semiotic for breaking the closure of political structures by destabilizing unified subject identity. (See *semiotics, *semiosis, *closure/dis-closure.)

Kristeva's Revolution in Poetic Language (1974) suggests a typology of signifying practice which she likens to the typology of discourse presented by *Jacques Lacan at his 1969 and 1970 seminars. Kristeva's classification includes four types of signifying practice: narrative, *metalanguage, contemplation, and text-practice. For her, the first three types represent a subordination of the semiotic in favour of the authoritative position of a *narrator, a philosopher or a theoretician. What she calls text-practice, however, does not close off the semiotic modality of language but instead explores the infinity of its processes for transforming society and self. (See *self/other.) Kristeva associates the literary works of Stéphane Mallarmé and James Joyce with this revolutionary practice of the *text.

DAWNE MCCANCE

Primary Sources

Kristeva, Julia. La Révolution du langage poétique: L'avant-garde à la fin du XIXe siècle. 1974. Revolution in Poetic Language. Trans. Margaret Waller. New York: Columbia UP, 1984.

Social formation

Socialist literary theorists have used French Marxist philosopher *Louis Althusser's concept of the social formation to develop a more sophisticated model for the relationship of *literature and society than the reflection theory of *Georg Lukács. Althusser proposes his concept of the social formation as a replacement for what he sees as the idealist notion of society which does not allow for the differentiation and structural complexity of social reality. He divides the social formation into economic, political, ideological, and theoretical levels or instances, each with its own practices. (A practice is any process by which raw material is transformed by labour into a finished product.) Each level enjoys relative autonomy from the others. Althusser avoids the Marxist heresy of pluralism, which deprives the economic base of its primacy in determining the rest of society, by describing the social formation as a 'structure in dominance' governed by *structural causality. The various levels exist within a hierarchical structure, with the economic level determinant in the last instance. For example, in medieval Europe the feudal economy determined that the Catholic church (part of the ideological level) was dominant over the social formation; in contemporary democracies capitalist economics determine that the political is dominant. By allowing relative autonomy for all levels, Althusser frees theoretical practice from pragmatic or dogmatic considerations arising within the other levels. Hence Marxist literary criticism is freed, as the socialist realism criticism of the early years of the Soviet Union had not been, to pursue its own ends regardless of the needs of the state or the Party. Writers do not have to be judged by how realistically they reflect society, but may be seen to stand in a more complex, partly autonomous, relationship to their society, attached to it by the way they produce *ideology. Marxist theoretical practice requires autonomy if it is to avoid the simple and unproductive mimicry of official party policy and instead serve as a guide to political practice in the 'analysis of the structure of a *conjuncture*' or the alignment of the various levels and practices at a specific time (179).

JOHN THURSTON

Primary Sources

Althusser, Louis. 'On the Materialist Dialectic.' In *For Marx.* Trans. Ben Brewster. London: New Left Books, 1977, 219–47.
Jameson, Fredric. 'On Interpretation: Literature as a Socially Symbolic Act.' In *The Political Unconscious: Narrative as a Socially Symbolic Act.* Ithaca: Cornell UP, 1981, 17–102.

Spatial form

The notion of 'spatial form' gained currency with the publication, in 1945, of Joseph Frank's 'Spatial Form in Modern Literature.' Frank was particularly concerned with making a connection between literary High Modernism (*Eliot, Proust, Joyce, Pound) and a tendency within it to prefer simultaneity over sequentiality. While Frank's elaboration of the notion of spatial form remains contentious, spatialization has come, increasingly, to be an important category of debate within contemporary literary theory.

Frank begins his essay by going back to the major post-classical articulation of the space/time distinction, G.E. Lessing's *Laocoon* (1766). Lessing saw a fundamental distinction between painting (and the plastic arts in general) and poetry (the literary arts): painting developed its meaning simultaneously through space, whereas poetry developed its meaning sequentially, through time. While Lessing's purpose in writing the *Laocoon* was to argue against the mixing of genres (as defined by the space/time distinction), the distinction he makes has a wider application when seen as identifying modes of signification. (See *genre criticism.) As Frank puts it, 'what Lessing offered was not a new set of norms but a new approach to aesthetic form' (45). Thus, based on the space/time distinction, Frank seeks to argue that modernist writers 'ideally intend the reader to apprehend their work spatially, in a moment of time, rather than as a sequence' (46).

Frank sees the Imagist movement in poetry as a major turning-point in the direction of spatial form. One of the major theorists of Imagism was T.E. Hulme, who was profoundly influenced by Henri Bergson's notions of time and space (see Gross), and by his sojourn in the Canadian prairies, where he was confronted by an immense spatiality which, he felt, traditional poetry could not capture (cf. Jones). The Imagism that derived from the speculations of Hulme and others described a poetry that was meant to be apprehended 'in an instant of time,' as Pound wrote in *Make It New* (1934). For Eliot, spatial form in poetry, with its juxtapositioning of lines (as in 'Prufrock'), was a sign of the fragmentation of modern urban existence (cf. Lefebvre). Frank argues that the fragmented nature of these poems makes them impossible to understand on a purely sequential basis: 'modern poetry asks its readers to suspend the process of individual reference temporarily until the entire pattern of internal references can be apprehended as a unity' (49), which was, paradigmatically, the case of Proust's *A la recherche du temps perdu.* Frank's major example of this technique is Joyce's *Ulysses*, in which the work's many cross-references gain coherence only when one has a sense of the work as a whole – thus Frank's paradoxical assertion that 'Joyce cannot be read – he can only be reread' (52). (See *paradox.) Frank sees Djuna Barnes' *Nightwood* (1946; his prime example in this essay) as taking this technique as far as it can go (such that its prose merges with poetry), in that 'the unit of meaning in *Nightwood* is usually a phrase or sequence of phrases – at most a long paragraph' (70), rather than an extended narrative.

Criticism of Frank has centred on the exclusion of the temporal from his theory (cf. *hermeneutics) and on his diminution of the importance of the historical element in *literature (a logical extension of his purely formal argument; see *Kermode). The notion that spatialization has as its concomitant the 'end of history' is pursued by Sharon Willis in her critique of *Jean Baudrillard's notion of hyperspace. W.J.T. Mitchell argues at the other extreme that the space/time distinction is a false one, in that the modes of literary apprehension – including the temporal – are fundamentally spatial.

Frank's insistence on the 'ahistorical' implications of spatial form has been related, by some of his critics, to the fascist ideologies with which such writers as Pound were associated (cf. Libby). It is noteworthy, however, that contemporary Marxist theorists (whose precursor in this is the *Walter Benjamin of the Arcades project; cf. Buck-Morss), such as *Fredric Jameson, *Pierre Bourdieu and Henri Lefebvre, have no difficulty in insisting at once on a historical dimension to their critical positions and on the importance of spatial notions within it (cf. Ross). (See *Marxist criticism, *ideology.) But the very presence of notions of spatiality within contemporary Marxist thought indicates the extent to which spatial form has come to be a central concept around which contemporary theory (and not just literary theory) has ranged itself. How this came to be is worth examining.

Coeval with the high modernists of whom Frank speaks was the Swiss linguist *Ferdinand de Saussure. Saussure's insistence that linguistic systems were to be understood synchronically – that is, as self-contained and self-referring – and not diachronically (historically) was both directly and indirectly influential on subsequent literary theories, from notions of 'structure' (*Frye) to concepts of the grapheme (*Derrida). Given that the synchronic aspect of a linguistic system was one in which all aspects of that system were available simultaneously, then the system itself was able to be conceptualized spatially, its meanings being produced by a network of static interrelationships, and not through succession over time. (Saussure's insistence on the synchronic and simultaneous as the major category of linguistic inquiry has an analogy in M.E. Chevreul's *De la loi du contraste simultané des couleurs* 1838; Chevreul's theory influenced the paintings of Seurat [whose work was subsequently to figure as a major example in *Marshall McLuhan's theories of media] and poets such as Apollinaire [precursor of the concrete poets, for whom poetic meaning was predicated on the spatial deployment of text on the page]. See Perloff and Ashton.)

The structuralists developed the notion of synchronicity in iconographical terms, whereby structure became the immutable and ahistorical repository of timeless form. Frye combined this concept of structure with Eliot's notion of literary 'monuments' ('Tradition and the Individual Talent') in *Anatomy of Criticism*, where the fundamental metaphor is architectural (*architectus* being the term Frye employs), as established by Kant in the *Critique of Pure Reason*. (See *metonymy/metaphor.)

Poststructuralist thought sought to proble-

matize structuralist ahistoricity by going back to Saussure and noting the paradox that Saussure was able to posit the synchronic only as a function of the diachronic – it was precisely the fluctuation of language in time which had forced Saussure to posit the synchronic realm as a necessary fiction to enable analysis. (See *structuralism, *poststructuralism.) But in reasserting history within the theoretical matrix, poststructuralism did not abandon the category of space. Rather (taking the work of *Blanchot and *Bachelard as its point of departure), it reconstructed the concept of space, not as a product but as the process of the 'gaze' (cf. Mulvey) so that questions of context ('Who sees?') become of prime importance, as in *Foucault's notion of the panopticon, and Herrmann's concept of women's space. In its extreme form, representational space merges with the cyberspace of pure information.

*Deconstruction sought to examine the notion of structure (including its implications for the practice of architecture; cf. Benedikt) not only by historicizing it (as poststructuralism had done) but by materializing it as well – that is, by taking the metaphor of space literally and problematizing figure and ground (a dynamic whose importance was established by McLuhan in his references to Seurat in *Through the Vanishing Point* and more broadly in *The Gutenberg Galaxy*), whereby the medium of production – the material book (as in Derrida's *Glas*; cf. D.F. McKenzie) or the graphic signs on the page (as in concrete poetry) – is put into play with the message. Derrida's concept of *différance* is thus materialized in a neologism that can *only* be written, the change from 'e' to 'a' being unvocalized. The transparency which structuralist thought accorded to space gives way to opacity, such that the text must be read *through*, rather than unproblematically read (or reread rather than read, to go back to Frank's terms, though in that process one complicates reading with seeing – one *sees* that the first word of *Ulysses*, 'stately,' contains the last, 'yes,' spelt according to another logic).

What deconstructivist space no longer allows is the *totalization inherent in structuralist thought, where a structure was thought to contain all possibilities of that form. The imperialist implications of the structuralist mode have been decolonized within postcolonialist thought: 'This kind of history, which reduces space to a stage, that pays attention to events unfolding in time alone, might be called imperial history,' writes Paul Carter in *The Road to Botany Bay* (xvi). What he proposes instead (in his rewriting of the 'history' of Australia) is a 'spatial history' of 'horizons, possible tracks, bounding spaces' (xxi). Carter's 'postmodern geography' (Soja) has its literary analogue in Ashcroft/Griffiths/Tiffin's contention that postcolonialist texts 'run European history aground in a new and overwhelming space which annihilates time and imperial purpose' (34). This is to return to the debate over history initiated by Frank's essay, and to recontextualize it. (See *materialist criticism, *postmodernism, *post-colonial theory.)

RICHARD CAVELL

Primary Sources

Baudrillard, Jean. *Simulations*. Trans. P. Foss, P. Patton and P. Beitchman. New York: Semiotext(e), 1983.

Derrida, Jacques. *The Truth in Painting*. Trans. G. Bennington and I. McLeod. Chicago: U of Chicago P, 1987.

Foucault, Michel. *Discipline and Punish*. Trans. A. Sheridan. New York: Vintage, 1979.

Frank, Joseph. *The Idea of Spatial Form*. New Brunswick: Rutgers UP, 1991.

Lefebvre, Henri. *The Production of Space*. Trans. D. Nicholson-Smith. Oxford: Blackwell, 1991.

McLuhan, Marshall. *The Gutenberg Galaxy*. Toronto: U of Toronto P, 1962.

– *Through the Vanishing Point*. New York: Harper and Row, 1968.

Mulvey, Laura. 'Visual Pleasure and Narrative Cinema.' *Screen* 16.3 (1975): 6–18.

Saussure, Ferdinand de. *Course in General Linguistics*. Trans. W. Baskin. New York: McGraw-Hill, 1966.

Secondary Sources

Ashcroft, Bill, Gareth Griffiths and Helen Tiffin. *The Empire Writes Back: Theory and Practice in Post-Colonial Literatures*. London: Routledge, 1989.

Ashton, Dore. *A Fable of Modern Art*. London: Thames and Hudson, 1980.

Bachelard, Gaston. *The Poetics of Space*. 1958. Trans. M. Jolas. Boston: Beacon P, 1969.

Benedikt, Michael, ed. *Cyberspace: First Steps*. Cambridge: MIT P, 1991.

– *Deconstructing the Kimbell: An Essay on Meaning and Architecture*. New York: Sites, 1991.

Blanchot, Maurice. *The Space of Literature*. Trans. A. Smock. Lincoln: U of Nebraska P, 1989 [1955].

Bourdieu, Pierre. *Distinction*. Trans. R. Nice. Cambridge: Harvard UP, 1984.

Buck-Morss, Susan. *The Dialectics of Seeing: Walter Benjamin and the Arcades Project*. Cambridge: MIT P, 1989.

Carter, Paul. *The Road to Botany Bay: An Exploration of Landscape and History*. New York: Knopf, 1988.

Frye, Northrop. *Anatomy of Criticism*. Princeton: Princeton UP, 1957.

Gross, David. 'Time, Space and Modern Culture.' *Telos* 50 (Winter 1981–2): 59–78.

Gusevich, Miriam. 'The Architecture of Criticism.' In *Drawing Building Text*. Ed. Andrea Kahn. New York: Princeton Architectural P, 1991, 8–24.

Herrmann, Claudine. *The Tongue Snatchers*. Trans. N. Kline. Lincoln: U of Nebraska P, 1989.

Jameson, Fredric. 'Cognitive Mapping.' In *Marxism and the Interpretation of Culture*. Ed. C. Nelson and L. Grossberg. Urbana: U of Illinois P, 1988: 347–57.

– *Postmodernism, or, The Cultural Logic of Late Capitalism*. Durham: Duke UP, 1991.

Jones, Alun. *Life and Opinions of T.E. Hulme*. Boston: Beacon P, 1960.

Kermode, Frank. 'A Reply to Joseph Frank.' *Critical Inquiry* 4 (1978): 579–88.

– *The Sense of an Ending*. New York: Oxford UP, 1967.

Libby, Anthony. 'Conceptual Space, The Politics of Modernism.' *Chicago Review* 34:2 (1984): 11–26.

McKenzie, D.F. *Bibliography and the Sociology of Texts*. London: British Library, 1986.

Mitchell, W.J.T. 'Spatial Form in Literature: Toward a General Theory.' In *The Language of Images*. Ed. W.J.T. Mitchell. Chicago: U of Chicago P, 1980, 271–99.

Perloff, Marjorie. *The Futurist Moment*. Chicago: U of Chicago P, 1986.

Ross, Kristin. *The Emergence of Social Space*. Minneapolis: U of Minnesota P, 1988.

Sallis, John. *Spacings – of Reason and Imagination in Texts of Kant, Fichte, Hegel*. Chicago: U of Chicago P, 1987.

Smitten, Jeffrey R., and Ann Daghistany, eds. *Spatial Form in Narrative*. Ithaca: Cornell UP, 1981.

Soja, Edward. *Postmodern Geographies: The Reassertion of Space in Critical Social Theory*. London: Verso, 1989.

Willis, Sharon. 'Spectacular Topographies: *Amerique's* Post Modern Spaces.' In *Restructuring Architectural Theory*. Ed. M. Diani and C. Ingraham. Evanston: Northwestern UP, 1989, 60–6.

Story/plot

The concepts of *fabula* [story] and *siuzhet* [plot] were employed by Russian formalists to distinguish between the raw material of *literature and the aesthetic rearrangement of that material in narrative fiction. (See Russian *formalism.) The basic difference between the two stems from a different treatment of chronology and causality. In the 'story' the events are linked together according to their temporal sequence and causality. In the 'plot' they are rearranged, disrupting the chronological order and causal connections. In the precise definition by *Boris Tomashevskii in his *Teoriia literatury* [*Theory of Literature* 1925], 'the story consists of a series of narrative motifs in their chronological sequence, moving from individual cause to effect; whereas the plot represents the same motifs, but in the specific order of occurrence to which they are assigned in the text.'

Another fundamental difference between the story and the plot, according to *Viktor Shklovskii, results from the introduction into the narrative of authorial digressions, comments and observations. In many works, these digressions are motivated realistically but in some they are 'laid bare,' drawing the attention of the reader to their presence rather than their function. For Shklovskii, the best example of the plot technique 'laid bare' was Laurence Sterne's novel *Tristram Shandy* with its continuous disruptions of the action, authorial digressions, displacement of chronology, transposition of chapters, and retardations. In the opinion of Shklovskii, *Tristram Shandy* was the most typical novel in world literature for it revealed the aesthetic laws of plot construction without any realistic justification.

The concept of plot was further developed by *Vladimir Propp in his study of the structural laws of the folk-tale, *Morfologiia skazki* [*Morphology of the Folktale* 1928]. Focusing on the elements of the composition rather than on characters, Propp distinguished 31 elements that appear in the structure of the folk-tale. He perceived these elements as 'functions' and defined them in terms of their significance for the course of the action. He formulated some important rules about the sequence of functions which, he maintained, would appear in the same order even if some of them were absent. (See also *narratology.)

NINA KOLESNIKOFF

Primary Sources

Propp, Vladimir. *Morfologiia skazki.* 1928. *Morphology of the Folktale.* Bloomington: Indiana UP, 1958.
Tomashevskii, Boris. *Teoriia literatury. Poetika.* 1925. In part trans. as 'Thematics.' In *Russian Formalist Criticism: Four Essays.* Ed. L. Lemon and M. Reis. Lincoln: U of Nebraska P, 1965, 61–98. 'Literary Genres.' *Russian Poetics in Translation* 5 (1978): 52–93.

Structural causality

The concept of structural causality, derived from the work of French Marxist philosopher *Louis Althusser, has been most rigorously used by *Fredric Jameson to explain how social forces manifest themselves in literary texts. (See *text.) Althusser endeavours in *Reading Capital* (1965) to establish the centrality of structural causality to Marxist philosophy. Traditional historiography, according to Althusser, has available to it 'only two systems of concepts with which to think effectivity' (186). One, 'a transitive mechanical causality,' is linear and works only within a 'homogenous planar space' (182). This type of causality, which Althusser attributes to political economy, cannot 'think the effectivity of a whole on its elements' (186). The other option, '*expressive causality*' (187), reduces the social totality to an '*inner essence*' and sees the elements of the totality as 'no more than the phenomenal forms of [its] expression' (186). This type of causality, which Althusser attributes to Hegel, only works 'on the absolute condition that the whole [is] not a structure' (187). Marx, conceiving of the *social formation as a 'complex and deep space' (182) and a 'structure in dominance,' needed a new type of historical causality which would allow for the relative independence of the various levels and their different temporalities, and which would yet bind them together in a totality. According to Althusser, this third type of causality and the only one adequate to its object is '*a structural causality*' (186).

Althusser begins *Reading Capital* with the claim that a *symptomatic reading of Marx uncovers one 'important *answer* to a *question that is nowhere posed.*' Marx answers the question 'of the effectivity of a structure on its elements' without having posed it 'because the age Marx lived in did not provide him ... an adequate concept with which to think what he produced.' He answered the question through a proliferation of images and metaphors around the image of *Darstellung* (representation, exhibition, presentation) (29). (See *metonymy/metaphor.) Althusser claims that this image is the keystone of Marx's work and attempts to provide it with its adequate concept. Althusser's argument culminates with the production of the concept of 'structural causality' (186). The social structure is present only in its effects; it has no empirical existence nor is it 'an essence *outside* the economic phenomena' (188). It is 'a cause immanent in its effects in the Spinozist sense of the term, that *the whole existence of the structure consists of its effects*, in short that the structure, which is merely a specific combination of its peculiar elements, is nothing outside its effects' (189).

Jameson interprets structural causality as Althusser's attempt to retain the Marxist commitment to a model of the social formation as a totality in which all levels are related, in contrast with the capitalist 'fragmentation and ... compartmentalization ... of the various regions of social life' (40). Although Althusser explicitly rejects the concept of mediation, Jameson argues that 'Althusserian structural causality is ... just as fundamentally a practice of mediation as is the "expressive causality" to which it is opposed.' The distinctiveness of structural causality is that, while it 'necessarily insists on the interrelatedness of all elements in a social formation[,] ... it relates them by way of their structural *difference* and distance from one another, rather than by their ultimate identity' (41). The relations of the economic, the political and the ideological to the cultural may only be perceived by way of the 'detour of a theory of language through ... structure, as an ultimate cause only visible in its effects or structural elements' (46). Structural causality can also be related to other poststructuralist concerns, initiated largely by the work of *Jacques Derrida, with effective features of textual reality which are present only in their absence. (See *poststructuralism.)

JOHN THURSTON

Primary Sources

Althusser, Louis, and Etienne Balibar. *Reading Capital*. Trans. Ben Brewster. London: New Left Books, 1970.
Jameson, Fredric. 'On Interpretation: Literature as a Socially Symbolic Act.' In *The Political Unconscious: Narrative as a Socially Symbolic Act*. Ithaca: Cornell UP, 1981, 17–102.

Subject/object

The relationship between subject and object is *the* crucial issue for *Edmund Husserl's phenomenology and for those philosophical schools, like existentialism, which spring from it. (See *phenomenological criticism.) Husserl states frequently in his works that the aim of phenomenology is the examination of the necessary conditions for the possibility of absolutely certain knowledge concerning human experience. He writes that philosophy should be 'a science of true beginnings, or origins' and that, in the pursuit of radicalism, it 'must not rest until it has attained its own absolutely clear beginnings, i.e., its absolutely clear problems, the methods preindicated in the proper sense of these problems, and the most basic field of work wherein things are given with absolute clarity' ('Philosophy as Rigorous Science' 196). In his search for this absolutely true and self-validating foundation for human knowledge, Husserl consequently rejects both metaphysics and any empirical investigation of the sense-given world (Sinha 8, 14–15, 22–3). In other words, metaphysical questions concerning the nature of reality are abandoned in favour of an examination of how we come to a knowledge about the world as it appears to us in consciousness (Sinha 24). To us, these two alternatives – metaphysics and empiricism – may appear to exhaust the possibilities for the absolutely sure grounding of philosophy and the natural sciences, respectively. Husserl, however, states that there is a way of avoiding the taking of the vague, probable and variable 'laws' of empirically founded disciplines for the clearly defined, absolute and invariable laws of essential structures. Through the practice of *transcendental phenomenology*, Husserl believed that he could indeed arrive at an absolutely true, a priori and self-validating foundation for human knowledge which reverted neither to the assumptions of metaphysics nor to those of empiricism, and upon which (subsequently) all sciences could be grounded (Kockelmans 271–80).

As the final and most advanced stage of his philosophy, transcendental phenomenology clearly builds upon the more descriptive orientation of Husserl's earlier works. As phenomenology aims at an absolute certainty which it feels that neither metaphysics nor empiricism has been able to provide, we obviously cannot conceive of transcendental-phenomenological subjectivity in either of these two contexts. It is in some ways, then, easier to describe what this concept of subjectivity does not entail. Husserl, having fought his entire life against charges that phenomenology was nothing more than a branch of empirical psychology, takes great pains to distinguish between the 'psychological I' (the self-evident subject as defined in the science of psychology, made up of all the natural, mental events of an individual's particular psychic life) and the 'transcendental I' (that subjectivity which intuits and reflects upon the essential, invariable and universal structures of consciousness and their contents). Clearly, the construction and goal of these two subjectivities are radically different – the former concerned with and affected by concrete individuals' particular psychic lives and psychological quirks; the latter aimed at intuiting the universal structures of consciousness as consciousness. Through transcendental, non-psychological subjectivity alone can the structures of both this intentional world and of this subjectivity itself be understood (Kockelmans 252–3, 278–9, 301–14).

Consequently, unlike those sciences which posit an empirical-psychological subjectivity, transcendental phenomenology suggests that consciousness and subjectivity are characterized first and foremost by intentionality. (See *intention/intentionality.) Intentionality translates the problem of the subject/object relationship and its influence upon the grounding of human knowledge into one of constitution and referentiality. (See *reference/referent.) In the thesis of intentionality, this relationship is conceived of as inherently relational – the objects of the intentional acts of consciousness (the world as bracketed) give themselves to this consciousness which, in turn, confers upon them their meaning ('Phenomenology' 122–4). (See *bracketing.) In this way, Husserl's conception of transcendental subjectivity tries to avoid the pitfalls of objectivism and subjectivism as they are traditionally understood. The crucial notion of intentionality involves a rejection of the former as an uncritical return to empirical data based on sense-perception as the criteria for an absolutely certain theory of knowledge; it involves a rejection of the latter as a reduction of knowledge itself to a purely individual and self-enclosed mental

realm. Subjectivity is only constituted in phenomenological terms in the interrelationship between subject and object, where neither element in this equation has a prime facie status. Transcendental subjectivity, then, is that subjectivity, characterized by intentionality, which governs, orders and gives meaning to the *Lebenswelt, the world of our immediately lived experience, in its existence as the essential content of consciousness (Kockelmans 252–3, 278–9).

*Martin Heidegger and *Maurice Merleau-Ponty, while sharing many of Husserl's assumptions, have very different conceptions concerning the nature of subjectivity and of the relationship between subject and object. Heidegger, while accepting the crucial importance of the thesis of intentionality in any discussion of the subject-object relation, takes Husserl and other phenomenologists to task for their misconceptions concerning this thesis and the resultant misrepresentation of the roles of subject and object in intentional experience. While acknowledging the care taken by other philosophers to maintain the mutually constituted relationship between subject and object, Heidegger points out that, even in suggesting that subject and object are mutually constituted in intentional experience, such philosophers still employ a traditional, inner-outer spatial model, a model which leads to an 'erroneous subjectivizing of intentionality' (64). Heidegger's solution to this problem of constructing subject-object relations as one of inner and outer, where the ego or subject 'is something within a sphere in which its intentional experiences are, as it were, encapsulated' and the object is something outside this self-enclosed intentional realm, is to refuse a definition of intentionality framed in these terms. Instead, he states that 'the subject is first of all determined only on the basis of an unbiased view of intentionality and transcendence' (64). For Heidegger, the achievement of this unbiased view of intentionality and transcendence depends on this rejection and eradication of what he saw as the latent mind/body, subject/object dualism of Husserl's philosophy: 'we shall in future no longer speak of a subject, or a subjective sphere but shall understand the being to whom intentional comportments belong as *Dasein*' (64). Consequently, Heidegger concentrates upon an elucidation of the *Dasein* (being-in-the-world) as a continuous field of intentional experience,

where the *Dasein*'s mode of being is *Existenz,*
'the specific mode of being that belongs to a
transcending, intentionalistic being which projects the world' (Hofstadter xix). The intentionality characteristic of the subject-object relation
in Husserl becomes for Heidegger that which
characterizes the *Dasein* and human *Existenz,*
that which differentiates the being of humans
from the being of stones or trees. But while
the concept of the *Dasein* emphasizes the
uniqueness of human existence, since only a
human can be said to exist whereas all other
objects (books, cats, etc.) are merely 'extant,'
Heidegger avoids reproducing traditional dualisms by asserting that 'the mode of being of
our own self ... is always dwelling with the extant' (64), with that towards which intentional
experience is directed. While it is true that
Husserl himself in his final experience begins
to consider the existential status of transcendental-phenomenological subjectivity when he
notes that no phenomenological reduction can
affect this transcendental ego, he nevertheless
fails to develop this insight in any systematic
way. Heidegger himself as a result of this
radical redefinition of subject-object relations
necessarily rejects Husserl's emphasis upon
transcendental-phenomenological subjectivity
and the reduction which opens it up to phenomenological investigation. For Heidegger,
the *Dasein* and its mode of being (*Existenz*) are
not amenable to phenomenological bracketing
precisely on account of their unique ontological status.

Merleau-Ponty, like Heidegger and *Jean-
Paul Sartre, also rejects Husserl's concept of
transcendental subjectivity, while supporting
and expanding upon the thesis of intentionality. His expansion of the concept is part of an
attempt to resolve the rift between body and
mind which, as Heidegger noted, threatens
Husserl's conception of this relationship as
mutually constituted. Merleau-Ponty, while he
largely agrees with Husserl that the main concern of philosophy should be the search for
meaning in the world, disagrees with Husserl's
concentration upon essences and their intuition
through the transcendental phenomenological
consciousness as constituting this meaning. For
Merleau-Ponty, like Heidegger, there can
never be 'pure ... consciousness' such as that
characteristic of transcendental subjectivity
(Husserl, 'Phenomenology' 126), since the perception of the world occurs through a consciousness which is always, in an appropria-

tion and expansion of some of Heidegger's
ideas about *Existenz,* both physical as well as
mental. Merleau-Ponty claims that '"the true
subject" which emerges from phenomenolgical
description is not "the thinking Ego", but a
body-subject which is "always already in-the-
world"' (in Hammond et al. 161–2).

The *Geneva School, that early and influential group of phenomenological literary critics
whose ranks include *Georges Poulet, Marcel
Raymond and Jean-Pierre Richard, is most
closely tied to the work of Husserl and Merleau-Ponty. Husserl's conception of consciousness as fundamentally intentional and
Merleau-Ponty's expansion of the intentional
field to include language are both of crucial
importance for their literary criticism, as well
as for that of their American colleagues *J. Hillis Miller and Paul Brodtkorb. For the Geneva
School, then, the meaning of a *text arises
from the arrangement of reader/critic and text
as part of a 'continuous field of experience'
(Con Davis 345), where the activities of reading and critiquing contribute to this meaning.
This attempt to deal with a text phenomenologically, however, has often been charged (as
by *W.K. Wimsatt, M.C. Beardsley and *E.D.
Hirsch) with destroying any objective grounds
for the evaluation of a literary work. The Geneva School, however, while urging the critic
to adopt a stance of 'passive receptivity' in relation to the text, also indicates that the degree
to which the critic 'surrenders' to the text's
phenomenological ego 'can and should be controlled' (Magliola 15). The author's task, then,
is 'to enverbalize the spontaneous mutual implications of his *Lebenswelt,* without scientific
regard for subjectivity and objectivity as such.'
Consequently, the difference between the author's epistemological stance and the critic's is
that the 'author's ... is naive [but] the critic's
must be *relatively* objective' (Magliola 15; emphasis mine); that is, the critic must be aware
of and make his or her reader aware of his or
her particular epistemological stance with regard to the text. As a result, there are two distinct stages in the criticism practised by the
Geneva School: (1) an imaginative identification with and 'a vicarious experience of the
author's phenomenological ego (that is, the
ego enverbalized in the literary text)'; and (2)
'a description of this experience (so the description becomes the "interpretation" proper)'
(Magliola 16). The project of phenomenological literary interpretation as taken up by later

critics such as *Wolfgang Iser also focuses upon the 'mutual implication' of author and text, of reader/critic and text. Accordingly, Iser emphasizes 'not only the actual text but also, and in equal measure, the actions involved in responding to that text' (376).

MARIE H. LOUGHLIN

Primary Sources

Con Davis, Robert. 'The Affective Response.' In *Contemporary Literary Criticism: Modernism Through Post-Structuralism*. New York: Longman, 1986, 345–9.

Hammond, Michael, Jane Howarth and Russell Keat. *Understanding Phenomenology*. Oxford: Blackwell, 1991.

Heidegger, Martin. *The Basic Problems of Phenomenology*. Trans., intro. and lexicon, Albert Hofstadter. Bloomington: Indiana UP, 1982.

Hofstadter, Albert. 'Translator's Introduction.' *The Basic Problems of Phenomenology*. By Martin Heidegger. Bloomington: Indiana UP, 1982, xv–xxxi.

Husserl, Edmund. 'Phenomenology.' In *Deconstruction in Context: Literature and Philosophy*. Ed. Mark C. Taylor. Chicago: U of Chicago P, 1986, 121–40.

– 'Philosophy as Rigorous Science.' In *Husserl: Shorter Works*. Ed. Peter McCormick and Frederick A. Elliston. Notre Dame, Ind.: U of Notre Dame P, 1981, 166–97.

Iser, Wolfgang. 'The Reading Process: A Phenomenological View.' In *Contemporary Literary Criticism: Modernism Through Post-Structuralism*. Ed. Robert Con Davis. New York: Longman, 1986, 376–91.

Kockelmans, Joseph J. *A First Introduction to Husserl's Phenomenology*. Pittsburgh: Duquesne UP, 1967.

Magliola, Robert. *Phenomenology and Literature: An Introduction*. West Lafayette, Ind.: Purdue UP, 1977.

Sinha, Debabrata. *Phenomenology and Existentialism: An Introduction*. Calcutta: Progressive Publishers, 1974.

Subversion

Subversion is best understood over against the concept of *ideology, where ideology is defined as the repertoire of images, themes, and ideas disseminated throughout society by and for a dominant culture. (See *theme.) In this context subversion would represent the articulation or 'becoming visible' of any repressed, forbidden or oppositional interpretations of the social order. In *literature, subversive content may be openly manifested as the thematic content of entire works. Alternatively, it might be voiced as an active opposition by one or more characters in a fiction to ideological norms inscribed in a text's structure. (See *text.) Under conditions of persecution and censorship, subversion must perforce become covert. Here the oppositional or dissident message may be encoded in a work's formal organization, often by means of allegorical displacement. (See *code.) Under conditions of extreme persecution such as those described in Leo Strauss' *Persecution and the Art of Writing*, the subversive content of a work may exist only as an esoteric meaning accessible to a limited group of initiates or conspirators.

The writings of *Mikhail Bakhtin provide a very full account of the process of subversion as popular festive form, which embodies the social world-consciousness of marginal or subordinated groups. (See *margin.) Bakhtin's theories of *carnival and the carnivalesque argue for the existence of a complex and very fully worked-out alternative philosophy disseminated throughout popular culture and oriented towards officially sanctioned subversion and cultural dissidence. The social practices of carnival create a 'second life of the people' with its own characteristic interpretations of the social order. These practices are sedimented in literature as the carnivalesque, which uses laughter, the grotesque, and various types of structural inversion or topsy-turvydom to 'uncrown' and demystify the dominant ideology, but always within the context of being allowed and authorized to do so by dominant institutions. (See *demythologizing, theories of the *grotesque.)

In ordinary usage the idea of subversion seems to be that of an actively empowered, conscious protest or insurgency against the *authority of a dominant or ruling élite. Such a view would imply that there is at least a relatively and provisionally 'rational' character to subversion, in the sense that the subversives want to displace a dominant social and cultural order with a structure that more fully represents their own interests. In the work of *New Historicism, however, subversion is understood not as a resistance to *power, but rather as an instrument and also a *sign of power itself. Subversion cannot achieve an active cultural dissidence, since it works in complicity with the authority of official culture. The idea that subversion is a deliberate strategy of the *dominant* culture and that it serves the interests of privileged groups rather than of marginal elements seems at first completely counter-intuitive. New Historicism, however, bases its interpretation of ideology on the ideas of *Michel Foucault and *Louis Althusser, both of whom suggest, though in different ways, that subversion is 'always already' contained by dominant institutions. For Althusser, subversion is contained by ideology, which operates outside the conscious knowledge or 'behind the backs' of social agents so that any subversive agenda is in principle self-defeating. For Foucault, subversion is contained by the insidious and all-but-omniscient activity of 'power.' In Foucault's writing, power seems to be almost a metaphysical entity of some kind rather than simply the aggregate will of those who hold power. In any case, the movement of this abstract power makes meaningful and purposeful resistance impossible. It is not immediately obvious why a legitimated power structure would find it useful to generate subversiveness where none actually existed. The followers of New Historicism usually argue that the production of subversive elements within a power structure is due to the paradoxical nature of power itself. (See *paradox.) The powerful individuals in whom social power is invested – Queen Elizabeth I is an example often cited – feel a deep and chronic anxiety about their situation. This anxiety is mastered by the elaborate 'staging' of subversion and its containment, not only in literary texts, but also in a wide range of spectacles ranging from court masques and civic processions to elaborate public trials and executions.

MICHAEL D. BRISTOL

Primary Sources

Althusser, Louis. 'Ideology and Ideological State Apparatuses.' In *Lenin and Philosophy and Other Essays*. Trans. Ben Brewster. London: New Left Books, 1971.
Bakhtin, Mikhail. *Rabelais and His World*. Trans. Hélène Iswolsky. Cambridge, Mass.: MIT P, 1968.
Foucault, Michel. *Discipline and Punish: The Birth of the Prison*. Trans. Alan Sheridan. Harmondsworth: Penguin Books, 1975.
Greenblatt, Stephen. *Shakespearean Negotiations*. Berkeley: U of California P, 1987.
Strauss, Leo. *Persecution and the Art of Writing*. Chicago: U of Chicago P, 1950.

Supplementarity

Supplementarity is a term coined by *Jacques Derrida to describe the peculiar logic of all discursive signifying structures. Derrida focuses on the contradiction in the concept of the 'supplement.' The word itself is potentially paradoxical for it can mean either something added to complete a thing or something added to a thing already complete in itself. (See *paradox.) In 'La Structure, le signe, et le jeu' (*L'Ecriture et la différance* – *Writing and Difference* 1967), Derrida shows how *Claude Lévi-Strauss posits in a signifying structure a *floating signifier which, having an excess symbolic value, fills a lack on the part of the signified, but which can do so only because it exceeds the total signification of the structure; thus it represents the overabundance of the signifier in relation to the signified. (See *signified/signifier/signification.) These two senses of supplement coexist in a sort of a-logic, for which Derrida uses the analogy of play and games. (See theories of *play/freeplay, *game theory.) The centre – the end or goal of the game – is paradoxically both outside the game and part of it. The movement of supplementarity is evidence of the de-centred 'play' of signification upon which any *discourse depends. (See *centre/decentre.) This play is paradoxically both the necessary condition of logocentric discourse (see *deconstruction), that which makes such discourse possible, and also that which is marginalized as purely chance activity. (See *margin, *logocentrism.)

In *De la Grammatologie* [*Of Grammatology* 1967], Derrida examines the writings of Lévi-Strauss and Jean-Jacques Rousseau and finds supplementarity at work in profound nostalgia for a lost presence. (See *grammatology.) In different ways both writers conceive of a supplementary chain of vicarious substitutions that takes the place of a lost origin or 'presence' (see *metaphysics of presence). At the same time, however, the supplement represents paradoxically both a violent usurpation and a compensatory substitution. Moreover, the fact that supplementarity always seems to predate the disrupted origin implicitly belies the existence of plenitude, the tragic loss of which is cause for pathos and nostalgia.

The implications of this effect of supplementarity go beyond Lévi-Strauss and Rousseau and extend to the entire metaphysical tradition and its underlying conception of the *sign. Within the metaphysical tradition the sign is supplementary in a substitutional sense. The order of the sign is a secondary and compensatory one, a 'fallen' order, and is always indicative of absence, loss, emptiness, and ultimately death. At its best, the sign is a necessary evil consequent on a loss of presence. In metaphysical thinking, the order of language and of structure in general takes the form of a substitutional chain that compensates for the loss of and is impelled towards the eventual restoration of a lost centre.

In Derrida's view, rather than a secondary and vicarious process tragically originating with the loss of presence, the supplementarity that belongs to the chain of substitutions – writing – is always already there. Writing as supplementarity does not compensate for the loss of presence and voice; it is, rather, the origin of presence and voice; it is that which gives birth to the desire of presence in the first place.

JOSEPH ADAMSON

Primary Sources

Derrida, Jacques. *De la Grammatologie.* 1967. *Of Grammatology.* Trans. Gayatri Chakravorty Spivak. Baltimore: Johns Hopkins UP, 1977.
– *L'Ecriture et la différance.* 1967. *Writing and Difference.* Trans. Alan Bass. Chicago: U of Chicago P, 1978.

Symptomatic reading

Symptomatic reading is used in literary criticism as a means of analysing the presence of *ideology in literary texts. French Marxist philosopher *Louis Althusser develops the technique of symptomatic reading in *Reading Capital,* finding the theoretical rationale for the technique in work by *Sigmund Freud and *Jacques Lacan. *Pierre Macherey transfers the technique to literary theory, where it becomes the reading of a scientific criticism for the ideological unconscious of the literary *text. Symptomatic reading has been diffused in English literary theory through the early work of *Terry Eagleton.

A symptomatic reading uncovers the buried *problematic of a text. According to Althusser, Marx's symptomatic reading of the classical economists found that they were answering

unposed questions dictated to them by the ideology within which they worked. In *Capital* Marx posed the questions behind the work of the classical political economists Adam Smith and David Ricardo, and thus broke with its ideological problematic. Since any new problematic must be formulated in terms carried over from the discarded problematic, Althusser reads *Capital* symptomatically in order to clarify in terms adequate to them the principles of its new problematic.

JOHN THURSTON

Primary Sources

Althusser, Louis, and Etienne Balibar. *Reading Capital.* Trans. Ben Brewster. London: New Left Books, 1970.
Eagleton, Terry. *Criticism and Ideology: A Study in Marxist Literary Theory.* London: New Left Books, 1976.
Macherey, Pierre. *A Theory of Literary Production.* Trans. Geoffrey Wall. London: Routledge and Kegan Paul, 1978.

Synecdoche

A term of classical rhetoric from the Greek meaning 'understanding one thing with another,' synecdoche is a *trope whose range of definitions overlaps considerably with that of metonymy, of which it is sometimes considered a kind. (See *metonymy/metaphor.) The term most often refers to the substitution of a part for a whole, or vice versa, as in saying 'sail' to refer to the ship of which it is part. Yet synecdoche also includes, as defined by Quintilian (*Institutio Oratoria* 8.6.19–21) and others, the following relations of substitution: container for contained, cause for effect, effect for cause, sign for the thing signified, material for the thing made, species for genus, and genus for species. (See *signified/signifier/signification.) In these last instances, synecdoche overlaps with the Aristotelian definition of metaphor. Puttenham, in *The Arte of English Poesie,* renders the Greek synecdoche as the 'figure of quick conceite' because it requires the listener or reader to translate from one order to another. Peacham in his *Garden of Eloquence* warns against the use of synecdoche (or the Latin, *intellectio*) with 'ignorant' hearers because its success depends on both knowledge and understanding.

The most significant rethinking of the character and function of synecdoche occurs in the work of *Kenneth Burke who considers synecdoche one of the four master tropes, along with metaphor, metonymy and *irony, and who thinks of metonymy as a 'special classification of synecdoche.' Burke notes that all synecdochal conversions imply 'an integral relationship, a relationship of convertibility, between the two terms' (506). He links the trope of synecdoche with nothing less than the notion of representation in general. (See also *mimesis.)

Many thinkers rely heavily on synecdoche as a trope for thinking the specific possibilities of language, as Coleridge does in defining the symbol, in contrast to allegory, as a part the whole of which it represents and renders intelligible. In this instance and many others, synecdoche operates as a particularly seductive trope, enlisted to represent totalities not available to thought other than through a mode of rhetorical *totalization.

IAN BALFOUR

Primary Sources

Burke, Kenneth. *A Grammar of Motives*. Berkeley and Los Angeles: U of California P, 1945.

Lausberg, Heinrich L. *Handbuch der literarischen Rhetorik*. 2 vols. Munich: Verlag Max Hueber, 1973.

Quintilian. *Institutio Oratoria*. Trans. H.E. Butler. Cambridge, Mass: Harvard UP and London: Heinemann, 1929.

Ricoeur, Paul. *The Rule of Metaphor*. Trans. Robert Czerny. Toronto: U of Toronto P, 1977.

Text

A text is a structure composed of elements of signification by which the greater or lesser unity of those elements makes itself manifest. A text comprises, consequently, elements of signification, the unity of these elements and the manifestation of this unity. In narrower usages 'text' is restricted to linguistic unities, in wider usages any group of phenomena, and even being itself, may be understood as 'text.' (See *signified/signifier/signification.)

Inasmuch as the totality of being is grasped as text, it is understood as a 'language'; this concept derives from a Graeco-Christian ontotheology of the incarnation of the Logos in the world. *Jacques Derrida's philosophy, following *Martin Heidegger, arises as a reflection on the history of that ontotheology and proposes to deconstruct the so-called *logocentrism of Western thinking by way of a functionalization of its fundamental concepts. (See *deconstruction.) To say that 'truth,' for example, is a 'function' of a system, means, for Derrida, that there is nothing, as such, which corresponds to this ideal entity: what we call 'truth' arises out of the interlocking relations of the textually conceived system as their effect, producing, in turn, effects of behaviour, emotion, power, within the signifying terms of the system. And yet Derrida's interpretation of text as *l'écriture* (writing, *textuality) presupposes an understanding of *being-in-its-totality* as a functional system of inscriptions which, in principle, comprehends the entire scale of being. Hence genetic inscription, linguistic and computor-based inscriptions, for example, are equally aspects of the all-encompassing text of 'inscription in general.'

For any attempt to understand 'text,' the question arises as to how, according to what mode of being, the elements of the structured whole are to be defined, for this will determine what we understand by 'language.' Structuralist conceptions dominate the contemporary debate. (See *structuralism.) Founded on phonetics, the linguistics of *Ferdinand de Saussure proposes that language is composed of signs which are determined by their material and non-material differences. (See *sign.) The system of signs, moreover, is conceived as a conventional institution. Unlike the *index, the symbol, the *icon, or the emblem (composed of iconic and signifying elements), then, the sign has neither existential nor analogical relation to what is represented. The interpretation of the text of the world as system of signs (or of signifiers, in poststructuralist thought) limits the mode of manifestation of the things themselves to the purely functional structures which can be captured in the abstract calculus of a formal system. Aspects of a work of art, a social practice, an experience, which cannot be captured, for example, in the formalism of binary analysis, cannot manifest themselves; and what *can* manifest itself has no ontological 'presence,' only a 'simulacrum' of being. Because a function is always a conditioned and conditioning element of a preconceived system, it is never originary: the function combines with other functions to repeat the elements of a system in variations. Any given event is therefore conceived as a re-iteration of the already written. (See *poststructuralism, *metaphysics of presence, *binary opposition, *variation.) Thus it is that the structuralist characterization of language – and, by extension, of *literature – abstracts utterances or cultural 'products' from their existential and historical *situatedness.*

Inasmuch as language, according to structuralist theory, is conceived as imposing form on the formlessness of Nature (*Friedrich Nietzsche, *Roland Barthes), language prefigures Nature, and makes it manifest as the given of a certain structure. The forms of the already given order themselves into the *cultural codes* of language (Barthes); and these codes, in a further development of structuralist-inspired thought, make up the repertoire of a *discourse (*Michel Foucault). The sign, the codes which order the signs into the already said of a culture, and the discourses to which sets of codes belong are the three basic determinants of the structuralist text. (See *code.)

In Roland Barthes' 'From Work to Text,' 'code' refers to all the forms imposed by language on reality to prefigure our perception of it, and of ourselves. Hence we may refer, for example, to syntactic codes of the grammatical form of the sentence, to narrative codes which prescribe a certain logic of cause and effect, and to semantic codes, which govern the culturally determined meanings we perceive. (See also *narrative code.) All of these codes are, in the French sense of the word, 'clichés' – they impose a prefiguring frame on reality. Now, the procedure of literary analysis consists in identifying the governing codes (those above, and others) which constitute the 'methodological field' out of which the literary text is produced. This field composes a set of discourses that includes the entire regime of research – from the bibliographical establishment of the text, through the conditions of its technical, psychological and sociological production, to its criticism and consumption. If, for example, a research project focuses primarily on the sociological conditions of the production of the text, then the identification of semantic codes will dominate the analysis. The text which consequently emerges will be a product of a methodological perspective based on the assumed priority of sociological conditions and the assumption that the historical past and our own being is a code-ordered signifying system

(see *New Historicism). Because the literary text is a function of the methodological field which produces it, the being it has consists in its *operation* as a quantum of power (and, in this sense as a cultural 'value') within the system of the methodological field. Insofar as the methodology of *Marxist criticism, for example, draws on the regime of research to constitute the text, the text is integrated into the Marxist program and functions as an ideological weapon in the class struggle; the literary text of Marxism consequently emerges as the re-iterative interlacing of the semantic codes which constitute (class) consciousness. (See also *ideology, *materialist criticism.)

As opposed to the traditionally conceived 'work,' which is still an object rather than a function, the literary 'text' is not allowed any autonomy, any substantial or monumental quality which would justify our judging it, like the work, on the criterion of formal unity. While the classical work integrates literary 'sources,' generic 'influences,' historical and sociological 'conditions' into the unity of a new thing (supposedly much like a plant transforms the determinants of its existence into its own tissue), the literary text derives its coherence from the codes which integrate it into the whole of signification. Whereas the 'stability,' or self-sameness of the work derives, for instance, from the imitation of a generic form such as the sonnet, the stability of a text depends upon an analysis which takes the work apart to discover the interaction of the codes: the codes remain stable in the flux of textuality which dissolves generic and historical distinctions into one unified field of signification of varying levels of complexity (complexity itself – not to be confused with 'quality' – emerges as a cultural 'value,' and hence the attraction of the literary text). Moreover, the selfhood of the reader, like selfhood as such, is also conceived of as a structure of code-ordered signs; and consequently selfhood consists in the re-iteration of the Already Written of textuality. To be, at least in this account, is to be the more or less complex interface of a set of clichés.

Basic to the prevailing contemporary understanding of text is the assumption that phenomena, whether linguistic or non-linguistic, are to be understood as purely conventional elements of a system of signification. And it follows from such an understanding that whatever is not functional for the economy of a system cannot manifest itself. Because it is the 'function' of a *myth, according to the structuralism of Malinowski, for example, to help maintain the 'efficiency' of a social system, the existential and revealed truth of the 'myth' – for example, of Christianity – is not and cannot be manifested or even conceived within the terms of the anthropological 'text.' This means that a poem, for example, must also be inscribed as the 'function of' linguistic, psychological, ideological discourse, in order to enter the purview of the human sciences. As such, the poem becomes calculable and can be integrated into a system of causes and effects. The contemporary understanding of 'text' therefore implicates the concept of a coherent system of cause/effect relations from which the things themselves derive as elements of an instituted economy of the already known (the consumable). As such, the unique, the incalculable, the not-already-known, is in principle excluded. In this sense, the understanding of 'text' which is pre-eminent today is appropriate to the technological reduction of all entities and their re-inscription into a postmodern economy of production and consumption. (See *postmodernism.)

BERNHARD RADLOFF

Primary Sources

Barthes, Roland. *Elements of Semiology*. Trans. Annette Lavers and Colin Smith. Boston: Beacon P, 1970.
– 'From Work to Text.' In *Image-Music-Text*. Trans. Stephen Heath. New York: Hill and Wang, 1974.
Culler, Jonathan. *Structuralist Poetics*. London: Routledge, 1975.
Derrida, Jacques. 'Difference.' In *Margins of Philosophy*. Trans. Alan Bass. Chicago: U of Chicago P, 1982.
– 'Freud and the Scene of Writing.' Trans. Jeffrey Mehlman. *Yale French Studies* 48 (1972): 74–117.
– *Of Grammatology*. Trans. Gayatri Chakravorty Spivak. Baltimore: Johns Hopkins UP, 1976.
– 'Structure, Sign, and Play in the Discourse of the Human Sciences.' In *The Critical Tradition*. Ed. David H. Richter. New York: Bedford, 1989.
Foucault, Michel. *The Archaeology of Knowledge*. Trans. A.M. Sheridan Smith. London: Routledge, 1989.
Heidegger, Martin. *Being and Time*. Trans. John Macquarrie and Edward Robinson. London: SCM P, 1962.
Malinowski, Bronislaw. *A Scientific Theory of Culture and Other Essays*. Preface by Huntington Cairns. Chapel Hill: U of North Carolina P, 1973.
Nietzsche, Friedrich. 'On Truth and Lying in an Extra-Moral Sense.' In *Friedrich Nietzsche on Rhetoric and Language*. Ed. and trans. Sander L. Gilman et al. Oxford: Oxford UP, 1989.
– *The Will to Power*. Trans. Walter Kaufman and R.J. Hollingdale. New York: Vintage, 1967.
Saussure, Ferdinand de. *Course in General Linguistics*. Ed. Charles Bally and Albert Sechehaye. Trans. Wade Baskin. New York: McGraw-Hill, 1966.

Textuality

In its most limited sense, textuality describes the written condition of the literary object. The term suggests that *literature is a material entity constructed from words rather than an abstract concept. However, as part of structuralist and poststructuralist linguistic theory, particularly in relation to the work of *Jacques Derrida and *Roland Barthes, the term marks both a breakdown of the boundaries between literature and other verbal and non-verbal signifying practices, and a *subversion of the principle that any *text can function as an object whose meaning is coherent and self-contained. (See *structuralism, *poststructuralism, *signifying practice.) Textuality in this context describes the tendency of language to produce not a simple *reference to the world 'outside' language but a multiplicity of potentially contradictory signifying effects that are activated in the reading process. Therefore, the term implies the suspension of interpretive *closure that this multiplicity makes necessary. It thus represents a rejection of *New Criticism's conception of the text as autonomous and autotelic.

A number of what might broadly be called 'worldly' theorists of textuality, among them *Michel Foucault and *Edward Said, have responded to what they perceive as more linguistically inward-looking versions of the concept by making their own theories responsible to political, historical and social frames of reference. As these approaches demonstrate, textuality takes in what might more traditionally be seen as the purview of the social sciences. Objects of study such as historical events, institutional practices, or cross-cultural relationships may therefore be seen as systems of signs to be deciphered and interpreted, rather than as realities to be recorded. (See *sign.) Any simple opposition between 'text' and 'world' is thus refused. Texts, including literary texts, are read in terms of their specific situations in the world, and 'the world' itself is constituted within signifying processes that must be taken into account. Instead of being considered in terms of the boundless potential of significance, therefore, the textuality of such objects is grounded in their various contexts. Attention to context may extend to the gathering and interpretation of data itself. It, too, is 'textualized' if the analyst is herself perceived as a reader whose reading is contingent on her own 'inscription' within historical, social and political situations. Textuality thus absorbs both the subject and object of study, effacing the distinction between the two. (See *subject/object.)

As a general term, textuality incorporates the sense of radical relationship between texts that *Julia Kristeva denotes more specifically as *intertextuality. It also functions as an extension and elaboration of Roland Barthes' use of the word text.

MANINA JONES

Primary Sources

Balibar, Etienne, and Pierre Macherey. 'On Literature as an Ideological Form.' In *Untying the Text: a Post-Structuralist Reader.* Ed. Robert Young. Boston: Routledge, 1981, 79–99.

Barthes, Roland. 'From Work to Text.' In *Image – Music – Text.* Ed. and trans. Stephen Heath. New York: Hill and Wang, 1977, 155–64.

– 'Theory of the Text.' In *Untying the Text: A Post-Structuralist Reader.* Ed. Robert Young. Boston: Routledge, 1981, 31–47.

Derrida, Jacques. *Of Grammatology.* Trans. Gayatri Chakravorty Spivak. Baltimore: Johns Hopkins UP, 1974.

Foucault, Michel. *The Archaeology of Knowledge.* Trans. A.M. Sheridan Smith. New York: Pantheon, 1972.

Fraser, Nancy. 'On the Political and the Symbolic: Against the Metaphysics of Textuality.' *boundary 2* 14.1–2 (Fall–Winter 1985–86): 195–209.

Glogowski, James. 'The Psychoanalytic Textuality of Jacques Lacan.' *Prose Studies* 11.3 (1988): 13–20.

Harari, Josué, ed. *Textual Strategies: Perspectives in Post-Structuralist Criticism.* Ithaca: Cornell UP, 1979.

Jameson, Fredric. 'The Ideology of the Text.' *Salmagundi* 31–32 (Fall 1975–Winter 1976): 204–46.

Kristeva, Julia. *Desire in Language: A Semiotic Approach to Literature and Art.* Ed. Leon S. Roudiez. Trans. Thomas Gora, Alice Jardine and Leon S. Roudiez. New York: Columbia UP, 1980.

LaCapra, Dominic. *Rethinking Intellectual History: Texts, Contexts, Language.* Ithaca: Cornell UP, 1983.

MacCannell, Juliet Flower. 'The Temporality of Textuality.' *Modern Language Notes* 100.5 (Dec. 1985): 968–88.

Margolis, Joseph. 'What Is a Literary Text?' In *At the Boundaries.* Ed. Herbert L. Sussman. Boston: Northeastern UP, 1984, 47–73.

Ray, William. *Literary Meaning: From Phenomenology to Deconstruction.* Oxford: Basil Blackwell, 1984.

Said, Edward W. 'The Problem of Textuality: Two Exemplary Positions.' *Critical Inquiry* 4.4 (1978): 673–714.

– *The World, the Text, and the Critic.* Cambridge, Mass.: Harvard UP, 1983.

Spanos, William V., Paul Bové and Daniel O'Hara. *The Question of Textuality: Strategies of Reading in Contemporary American Criticism.* Bloomington: Indiana UP, 1982.

Sprinkler, Michael. 'Textual Politics: Foucault and Derrida.' *boundary 2* 8.3 (1980): 75–98.

Theme

History

The term theme originally meant the subject around which an orator proposed to construct a speech. Tacitus speaks of themes as equivalent to *topoi*; Quintilian, in his treatment of forensic rhetoric, discusses theme under the rubric of 'invention' as the facts in the case. By the Middle Ages, 'theme' had come also to mean the scriptural text on which a sermon was founded. (Chaucer's Pardoner says, 'My theme is alwey oon, and evere was – / *Radix malorum est Cupiditas.*')

The use of theme as the subject-matter, topic or idea on which a poet bases a poem, visible as early as Aristotle's *Rhetoric*, is common by the Renaissance. Theme is an author-centred term, but from it follows the idea that readers can read theme out of a work and recognize a common theme in many different works. Theme as a critical term is not, however, much in evidence prior to the 20th century. Before that, didactic terms, such as 'moral,' or terms that emphasized ideational content were generally used instead. 'Theme' became a frequently employed term with the rise of 20th-century formalist schools, such as the American New Critics, that emphasized techniques of close interpretive reading. (See *New Criticism.) Formalist critics largely divorced theme from its previous associations with authorial intention and turned it into a text-centred term. Preferring 'theme' over words such as 'idea' because it suggested an element more grounded in the particulars of the literary work and over words such as 'moral' because it seemed more value-free, they reoriented literary analysis to thematic considerations as a way of opposing earlier plot- and character-based discussions. As well as responding to semantic aspects of the *text, formalist thematic statements acknowledged elements such as imagery, tone, style, and structure. (The fragmentary *form* of *The Waste Land* has often been treated as a thematic element.) Formalist interest in theme was reinforced by the use of theme as a principle in musical compositions (music borrowed the idea from rhetoric in the 16th century) and by the way theme as a musical term shaped the writing of some literary modernists (such as Thomas Mann). Influenced by the development of theme in music, some literary critics have preferred to speak of 'theme and variations' or of 'variations on a theme.' (See *variation.)

Among the objections that have been made to the use of 'theme,' one is that the term is too vague to be truly useful. When applied to a single work, 'theme' may not distinguish between dominant content, central subject, unifying 'thought,' or authorial intention. In an introductory essay *Northrop Frye treated theme as indistinguishable from 'structure' ('We can see the whole design of the work as ... a simultaneous pattern radiating out from a center, not a narrative moving in time. The structure is what we call the theme.'), and some critics (such as Barbara Herrnstein Smith) have enlarged the concept so that it becomes equivalent to all the non-formal aspects of a work (including syntax). When drawing several works together for comparison, critics have often employed 'theme' not only for common topics but also for the recurrence of certain type figures and their associated stories (the *Don Juan theme*), or have spoken of repeated *images* as themes. Theme has also often been associated with generic effects – as it is in *The Tragic Vision: Variations on a Theme in Literary Interpretation*, where *Murray Krieger makes it interchangeable with *vision* as well. Indeed, not only does 'theme' have a range of meanings, but the concepts associated with theme have also been invoked by a number of other terms. One of these is *myth, when used

in phrases such as 'the myth of the frontier in American literature.' (See *literature.) The use of 'motif' has further added to terminological difficulties: many literary critics use 'motif' and 'theme' interchangeably; some, however, distinguish between these terms by defining motifs as theme-like units that are smaller than theme (subthemes, of less importance to the text as a whole); while some – chiefly those influenced by folklore studies – treat motif as an extratextual unit of meaning that is larger than theme. In contemporary theory 'theme' has often been reintroduced under new names: *Michael Riffaterre's *hypogram and *Claude Lévi-Strauss' 'mytheme' are very close to the traditional meanings of theme.

The use of theme as a critical tool and the value of a thematic statement as a goal of interpretation have been reassessed by the critical schools that have emerged in the last 20 years, as part of their larger critique of interpretation. Thematic statements have been objected to as insufficiently nuanced, as reductive and as unsatisfying replacements for complex literary artefacts. The use of 'theme' as a critical tool has been attacked as a totalizing approach that implies a view of a literary work as a vehicle for ideas and as having one presiding idea. (See *totalization.) The term remains in common use, however – especially in the classroom and in anthologies designed for teaching, but also in critical *discourse, where it is employed not only by those who engage in interpretive readings of texts but by a large number of contemporary theorists.

Definition and use

Though its use has been imprecise, 'theme' is too valuable a critical concept to abandon. While definitions in handbooks and introductory guides to literary analysis continue to associate 'theme' with the making of brief statements that are the generalizable meaning of chief concern of a work of literature, it is not necessary to simplify its application to this degree. A better way of using 'theme' today would be to view it as the meeting place of the semantic levels of a literary work with formal structural qualities such as rhythm and repetition. Theme might thus be thought of as the semantic dimensions of a work dispersed by and through its formal elements. Defined in this way, theme can continue to be of considerable value.

Furthermore, as reception theory and *reader-reponse criticism imply, critics can make statements of theme without necessarily arguing for intrinsic meanings in literary works (though *Norman Holland is more extreme than most in viewing theme as a subjective projection onto the work, one that arises entirely from the reader). (See also *Constance School of Reception Aesthetics [Reception Theory].) Not only can theme be conceived of as part of the reading experience; reading for theme can be viewed as a technique to which the reader has recourse as a way of organizing that experience. From this perspective, theme would be regarded as negotiated between reader and text, or between reader and implied author (because readers often conceive of themes as arising out of the author's 'vision' or preoccupations). The making of a thematic statement is thus a synthesizing act that follows from identifying a *pattern* of meaning (or a pattern that contains a range of related meanings).

In addition, reading for theme might be thought of as allowing the formulation of statements that enable readers to connect the text with their experience of the world: theme has sometimes been described as mediating between word and world. Since part of the reader's world consists of other texts, thematic readings are intertextual. (See *intertextuality.) Indeed, themes gain saliency when they are recognized as being repeated in more than one work. (The importance of card-playing in a single Russian story takes on heightened meaning for readers who locate it in the context of gambling as a theme in Russian fiction.) Thus thematic readings can be the opposite of reductive: they can give resonance and significance to what might otherwise be overlooked as minor or trivial.

Reading for theme may also be thought of as a coherence device. Features of a text that seem unrelated in any other way can usually be related through theme, which therefore provides the reader with a way of constructing unity (especially important in modern and postmodern works that avoid plot-based or character-based coherence). (See *postmodernism.) This is one of the reasons themes are often felt by readers to provide an enriched way of approaching a literary work: they offer a secondary understanding or response to the overall narrative at a level other than that of plot and an additional level of unity in lyric poetry besides that offered by the dramatization of the speaker. (See *story/plot.)

Since literary works permit a number of thematic statements, different themes that are neither exclusive nor tautological can be perceived by different readers (or even by the same reader) within the same work. In fact, it is almost impossible to reduce a literary work to a single theme, since any expression of theme can usually be recast in terms of its opposite. ('Illusion and reality' is a familiar theme that is expressed in terms of thematic opposition.) There has been some debate about whether a theme can satisfactorily be given only as a brief – typically one-word – statement (as in 'Death is a central theme in *Hamlet*') or must be expressed in the form of a thesis (as in 'The theme of *Hamlet* is that one must recognize the constraints of time and take action'). It is not necessary to give preference to either form, since brief statements can be transformed into thesis statements (and vice versa) by readers familiar with the work.

Though critics today generally view theme as an area of investigation within a work rather than as the final goal of analysis, theme remains a valuable and flexible concept when employed in a way that remains sensitive to the complex nature of literary expression. Thematic statements can serve as metonymic or mnemonic aids to the critical dialogue, providing convenient starting points for discussion. (See *metonymy/metaphor.) Though such statements may seem reductive in themselves, critics can locate them inside arguments that – by qualifying and contextualizing themes within the particulars of a work – recognize and retain the nuances of individual texts.

Critical approaches through theme

Critical approaches based on reading for theme are often referred to as 'thematic criticism' or 'thematics' (a term first used by the Russian formalist *Boris Tomashevskii in an essay called 'Thematics'). However, 'thematics' has never been a unified school or a single way of approaching texts; and it is useful to distinguish between *explicative thematics* and *comparative thematics*.

Explicative thematics seeks to articulate a theme (or several themes) within a single work. It develops its conclusions through consideration of internal textual relations and uses an inductive approach. Explicative thematics was often the goal of the techniques of critical reading ('close reading') associated with American New Criticism. It remains in extensive use, especially in classrooms.

Comparative thematics, sometimes referred to as the study of 'universal themes,' has its origins in *Stoffgeschichte*, the 19th-century German thematic practice that grew out of the study of comparative literature. Resembling archetypal approaches to criticism, it involves the finding of one theme in many texts – potentially as many as the reader has the time and energy to examine – and has quite often been associated with discussions of recurrent literary figures: Ulysses, Quixote, Don Juan, and Faust are among the most-often cited in Western literature. (See *universal, *archetypal criticism.) While some critics have objected that the name of such a figure is not a theme, it has been argued that these figures serve metonymically. ('Don Juan' can be understood as a figure that emblematically stands for the theme of unbridled desire.) Furthermore, the use of such type figures is one way of not reducing theme to statement. The procedure of comparative thematics is principally *deductive* and consists of collection. Comparative thematics is the kind of thematic practice that has most often been attacked, chiefly for remaining extrinsic to texts and for minimizing their distinctive particulars. But defences of the approach could now be made by employing structuralist theory and especially by understanding comparative thematics as a kind of intertextuality. (See *structuralism.)

A third kind of thematics, which could be called *corpus thematics*, stands between explicative and comparative practice. Corpus thematics resembles the comparative approach in that it describes themes that exist in more than one text, but it is more limited in that it examines a specified and bounded body of texts. This body of work may be relatively small (such as the work of one author) or quite broad (the works of a literary period). At its broadest (as in certain kinds of genre thematics) it may be hard to discriminate between corpus and comparative thematics. However, corpus thematics maintains an inductive model and, unlike comparative thematics, is given to reading a body of work as if it were one large composite text.

The most important kind of corpus thematics today is *cultural thematics* – the reading of cultural themes out of national bodies of literature or out of the writing of ethnic or gender-identified groups. Because cultural thematics joins literary studies with other disciplines such as history, sociology and anthropology, it has been common among critics interested in interdisciplinary approaches, and in fields such as American studies (where it has sometimes been referred to as the 'myth and symbol school'), Canadian studies (where it is known simply as 'thematic criticism'), and post-colonial studies. (See *post-colonial theory.)

Structuralist criticism and the recent work done by anthropologists and sociologists influenced by structuralist methodologies may offer perspectives that permit a more sophisticated handling of comparative and corpus thematics than has sometimes occurred. *Poétique* 64 (1985) is a special issue on theme that may be seen as initiating this investigation. Elsewhere, *Alexander Zholkovskii (often in collaboration with Iu. K. Shcheglov) has attempted an elaborate – though not always satisfying – structuralist approach to theme as part of a *poetics of expressiveness.

Although it might seem that explicative thematics is a necessary first step for the practice of either comparative or corpus thematics, the relationship is not as close as one might anticipate. None of the themes suggested by a reading of specific works may turn out to be the theme(s) emphasized by critics seeing those literary works as part of a larger body of texts. For this reason, critics who emphasize individual texts have sometimes complained that comparative and corpus thematics produce results that are circular; they find what they go looking for. Despite such objections (the use of the hermeneutic model of reading with its emphasis on intuitive leaps provides one response to this objection), cultural criticism has valued thematics as a tool, especially for making comparisons between cultures, where analyses of contrasting themes or of contrasting ways of deploying the same theme may reveal a great deal about larger cultural patterns. All well, critics dealing with the writing of the previously 'silenced' (minorities, women, emerging nations) have not only found thematic approaches valuable in themselves but also – since many of the writers in these groups have created works that deliberately invert, ironize or *parody the themes of a dominant culture – see their own thematic discussions as a way of continuing a contestory project already begun by the writers. (See also *irony, *metacriticism, *hermeneutics.)

RUSSELL BROWN

Primary Sources

Beardsley, Monroe C. *Aesthetics: Problems in the Philosophy of Criticism.* New York: Harcourt Brace and World, 1958.
Chatman, Seymour. 'On the Notion of Theme in Narrative.' In *Essays on Aesthetics: Perspectives on the Work of Monroe C. Beardsley.* Ed. John C. Fisher. Philadelphia: Temple UP, 1983, 161–79.
Crane, R.S. *The Languages of Criticism and the Structure of Poetry.* Toronto: U of Toronto P, 1953.
Culler, Jonathan. *Structuralist Poetics.* London: Routledge and Kegan Paul, 1975.
Frye, Northrop. 'Literary Criticism.' In *The Aims and Methods of Scholarship in Modern Languages and Literature.* Ed. James Thorpe. New York: MLA, 1963, 57–69.
Holland, Norman. *5 Readers Reading.* New Haven: Yale UP, 1975.
– 'Unity Identity Text Self.' In *Reader-Response Criticism: From Formalism to Poststructuralism.* Ed. Jane P. Tompkins. Baltimore: Johns Hopkins UP, 1980, 118–33.
Krieger, Murray. *The Tragic Vision: Variations on a Theme in Literary Interpretation.* New York: Holt, Rinehart and Winston, 1960.
Levin, Harry. 'Thematics and Criticism.' In *Grounds for Comparison.* Ed. Cambridge: Harvard UP, 1972.
Levin, Richard. *New Readings vs. Old Plays: Recent Trends in the Reinterpretation of English Renaissance Drama.* Chicago: U of Chicago P, 1979.
Riffaterre, Michael. *Semiotics of Poetry.* Bloomington: Indiana UP, 1978.
Tomashevsky, Boris. 'Thematics.' 1925. Trans. in *Russian Formalist Criticism: Four Essays.* Ed. L.T. Lemon and M.J. Reis. Lincoln: U of Nebraska P, 1965, 61–95.
Wetherill, P.M. *The Literary Text: An Examination of Critical Methods.* Oxford: Basil Blackwell, 1974.
Zholkovskii, Alexander. *Themes and Texts: Toward a Poetics of Expressiveness.* Ithaca: Cornell UP, 1984.

Totalization

Totalization is the homogenizing process by which a dominant *ideology is imposed on any *text (musical, textual, architectural, philosophical), thereby eliding its diverse elements. A term largely employed by poststructuralists (*Michel Foucault, *Jacques Derrida, *Paul de

Man, *J. Hillis Miller, *Edward Said), it refers to the methods of traditional criticism (*New Criticism) for assessing texts on the basis of inherent formal unity and universal appeal. The term draws attention to the assertion of control and the apparent will to *power evident in any unification process. (See *universal, *poststructuralism.)

Most theorists contend that there are gaps within texts (see *Roman Ingarden, *Gérard Genette, *Pierre Macherey, *Wolfgang Iser). These gaps must be elided or disregarded in order to enforce unity but they also offer interesting insights into the text and its production. For example, when readers interpret the Sherlock Holmes stories as exemplifications of pure logic and deduction, they are totalizing the myth of positivism that underpins the stories. However, a reader may also focus on the gaps that exist within them that critique positivist logic. As Catherine Belsey has demonstrated, in Arthur Conan Doyle's writings feminine representation constitutes such a gap. (*Critical Practice* 109–17). Doyle depicts women as indefinable figures, figures who cannot be explained logically. These feminine portrayals thus emphasize the stories' inability to articulate what lies outside of their male-centred *discourse. *Deconstruction is one among many new theoretical approaches which resists totalizing tendencies.

PRISCILLA L. WALTON

Primary Sources

Belsey, Catherine. *Critical Practice.* London: Methuen, 1980.

Trace

Trace is a theoretical term associated primarily with *Jacques Derrida, the leading proponent of *deconstruction. The problem with defining the term is that definition is itself a gesture which runs contrary to Derrida's overall view. Trace is, at best, an evasive term, one Derrida uses in a number of different ways and in a variety of different contexts. The term, in fact, undergoes in his texts a series of what he calls 'nonsynonymic substitutions,' appearing in various forms such as *'différance,'* 'arche-writing' and 'spacing.' Although Derrida insists that these terms are 'nonsynonymic' and will argue that each of them is dictated by and used within a particular context, the degree of overlap between those terms makes defining them all the more slippery a task. In *Of Grammatology*, Derrida writes, 'Writing is one of the representatives of the trace in general, it is not the trace itself. *The trace itself does not exist*' (167). If the trace 'does not exist,' how, then, can we begin to define it? (See *text, *différance/différence*, *grammatology.)

An instructive, if tentative, starting-point might be Derrida's critique of the notion that the being of any entity is determined as presence. (See *metaphysics of presence.) Rejecting the privileged place in Western thought of being and presence, he introduces the term 'trace' in an attempt to show us that the truth about what is allegedly *present* in language at the moment of utterance is always conditioned by absences. Trace, in this sense, is an extension of *Ferdinand de Saussure's formulation of the *sign; it is the name Derrida gives to the absences, the relations of difference, that are involved in the production of the sign. In his *Course in General Linguistics*, Saussure argued that signs mean what they mean not through direct correspondence with external objects, but through their difference from other elements in the system. No element in language is *present* in and of itself, because, as Derrida puts it in *Positions*, 'no element can function as a sign without referring to another element which itself is not simply present. This interweaving results in each "element"... being constituted on the basis of the trace within it of the other elements of the chain or system' (26). Any element thus signifies only through *reference to other absent elements (similar to and/or different from it) which might have filled the same spot in any given linguistic chain. The linguistic sign receives its value only in relation (contrast and difference) to other signs and therefore, according to Derrida, all other signs which might have filled the same spot leave their traces on the sign in question.

The French word *la trace* can also be rendered into English as track, mark, footprint, trail, or clue. Derrida's term resonates with implications of these various translations. For instance, as a mark of the absence of an anterior presence, the footprint too is a kind of trace and it helps us understand the curious double status which traces enjoy. A footprint serves as a physical reminder of something which is no longer there: as a trace it mediates between presence and absence, between that which remains and that which is no longer present. Derrida shows no nostalgia for a lost presence and would deny that anything is ever fully present in language. But the example of the footprint is useful because it shows us just how difficult it is to fix a stable definition on Derrida's notion of the trace. The *presence* of the physical entity, the footprint itself – this despite Derrida's insistence that the trace does not exist – complicates our understanding of the trace by reminding us that, as a concept, it can serve only as a provisional analogy for the production of meaning in language.

Trace is also a term which enjoys currency in the field of psychoanalysis, particularly in relation to the unconscious, which can only be apprehended by its effects. Throughout his writing, *Sigmund Freud saw the structure of human experience as being based on the trace rather than on a notion of presence. Writing about the human capacity for retaining or reviving the experience of things past, Freud uses the term 'memory-trace' to refer to the ways in which the perceptual apparatus of the mind is always already inhabited by incidents inscribed upon the memory. (See also *psychoanalytic theory.)

AJAY HEBLE

Primary Sources

Derrida, Jacques. *De la Grammatologie*. 1967. *Of Grammatology*. Trans. Gayatri Chakravorty Spivak. Baltimore: Johns Hopkins UP, 1977.
– *Positions*. Trans. Alan Bass. Chicago: U of Chicago P, 1981.
Saussure, Ferdinand de. *Course in General Linguistics*. Trans. Wade Baskin. New York: McGraw-Hill, 1966.

Trope

A trope (Gr. 'turn') is a rhetorical figure in which words are used in a way different from their standard or literal usage. The distinction between the tropological and 'literal' aspects of language has, however, been attacked by post-Saussurean thinkers. (See *Ferdinand de Saussure.) They recognize the rhetorical and metaphorical dimension of language as integral to all *discourse, not just poetic and literary language. Although there is some disagreement about the precise definitions, in general, classical rhetoricians (such as Aristotle, Isocrates, Quintilian) distinguished between tropes and schemes, with trope referring to a change in the meaning of a word, and scheme designating a change in a pattern or series of words. (See *rhetorical criticism.) Sixteenth-century rhetoricians like Peter Ramus categorized the basic organizing principle for figures of speech as four major tropes: metaphor, metonymy, *synecdoche, and *irony. (See *metonymy/ metaphor.) Where classical and Renaissance theories of rhetoric saw tropes as linguistic ornaments that embellished language, Giambattista Vico inverted the distinction between rationalist and poetic theories of language, arguing rather that the tropological provides the foundation for abstract thought. In *The New Science* (1725) he employed the four major tropes as a way of organizing the development of human thought and culture, a history in which the originary mythic and tropological consciousness is eventually supplanted by the abstract language of science.

Structuralist criticism, which assumes that linguistic elements provide keys for understanding not only complex structures in language but also patterns of culture and history, uses tropes to analyse structure. (See *structuralism.) *Gérard Genette and *Tzvetan Todorov are concerned with the figurality of language, the way certain tropes or figures operate as an organizing system at various levels within a *text. *Roman Jakobson, in his chapter on metaphoric and metonymic poles in *Fundamentals of Language* (1956), combines psychological linguistics and literary criticism to produce a binary system of explanation. (See *binary opposition.) Through his analysis of speech disturbances, he designates all aphasic disorders as belonging either to the metaphoric or the metonymic pole, the former relating to similarity disorders and the latter to contiguity disorders. Extrapolating from this study, Jakobson goes on to classify literary forms as belonging to one of the two poles: poetry, romanticism and symbolism are correlated with the metaphoric, whereas prose and realism are associated with metonymy. *Claude Lévi-Strauss also uses the metaphor-metonymy dyad for his analysis of *myth, kinship patterns and culture; and *Jacques Lacan applies the distinction to *Sigmund Freud's writing, metaphor becoming associated with condensation, and metonymy with displace-

ment. Following Vico, *Hayden White in *Metahistory* (1973) draws on the four-fold system of tropes to analyse the history of consciousness in 19th-century Europe, thus providing not only a history of thought, but also an argument for the poetic or tropological nature of historical writing in general.

Hayden White's discussion of tropes illuminates the inescapably rhetorical nature of language. The recognition that all language is tropological is one of the features of poststructuralist thought. (See *poststructuralism.) Since, in this view, our access to the world is always mediated by language, a poststructuralist understanding of the world is fundamentally concerned with tropes. In contradistinction to the philosophical view of metaphor as merely ornamental and language as a transparent medium, *Jacques Derrida in 'White Mythology' demonstrates that metaphor is indispensable to the conceptual system that would seek to classify and contain it, for it is impossible to purify language of the tropological. (See *white mythology, *deconstruction.) But rather than seeing the trope as originary and ontologically secure – as Vico did – poststructuralist thinkers view it as both ubiquitous and unstable. The reliability of meaning is continually subverted by tropes, so that language is always 'turning,' revealing new meaning. Texts are thus read against themselves through their tropological structures, a deconstructive strategy employed by such critics as *J. Hillis Miller, *Harold Bloom and *Paul de Man. De Man's sustained work on tropes – which focuses on a wide range of figures such as metaphor and metonymy, prosopopoeia, apostrophe, and catachresis – has profound implications not only for theories of narrative and the lyric, but also for our conception of discourse itself. His analysis of the relationship between rhetoric and grammar in *Allegories of Reading* challenges the semiological work of critics like Genette, Todorov, *Roland Barthes, and *A.J. Greimas, who, he argues, subsume rhetoric under the univocal logic of grammar. Redefining rhetoric not as persuasion, but as the figural potential of language itself, he claims that rhetoric suspends logic, producing a 'semiological enigma' in which it is impossible to decide whether the 'literal' or the figural meaning should prevail. (See *semiosis.) De Man, like Derrida, examines some of the very philosophical texts that seek to protect themselves from the 'dis-figuring' nature of metaphorical language, disclosing the ultimate futility of the desire either to transcend the tropological or to reduce language to a mere *code. By showing how even the putatively pure and rigorous discourses of philosophy and science are ineluctably metaphorical, poststructuralist theory seeks to collapse the distinction between 'literary' and 'ordinary' discourse. (See also *discourse analysis theory, *semiotics, *narratology.)

ELIZABETH HARVEY

Primary Sources

de Man, Paul. *Allegories of Reading.* New Haven/ London: Yale UP, 1979.
Derrida, Jacques. 'White Mythology.' 1972. In *Margins of Philosophy.* Trans. Alan Bass. Chicago: U of Chicago P, 1982.
Jakobson, Roman, and Morris Hall. *Fundamentals of Language.* The Hague: Mouton and Co., 1956.
Vico, Giambattista. *The New Science.* 1725. Trans. Thomas G. Bergin and Max H. Frisch. Ithaca: Cornell UP, 1948.
White, Hayden. *Metahistory.* Baltimore: Johns Hopkins UP, 1973.

Universal

Brief definitions of the term universal – as, for example, 'the element in literature which appeals to readers regardless of period or condition' – have only a limited usefulness. The more abstract and open-ended the ideas behind a critical term, the less likely are its users to have the same ideas in mind. Indefiniteness is only one reason why the term universal, its derivatives (universality, universalize), and related terms (general, generality) have become the 'loose and baggy monsters' of critical terminology. But indefiniteness is not the only reason why the universal and the ideas it refers to are currently unfashionable, and typically if often dismissed as 'totalizations,' or the collective delusions of white males. (See *totalization.)

Other difficulties with the term arise from its long history. In moving from philosophy to criticism the universals of Plato and Aristotle have suffered losses and accretions that blur new and original meanings as the term is applied in a variety of contexts. In *Literary Criticism: A Short History,* *Wimsatt and *Brooks' acute discussion of neo-classicism (330–3) lo-

cates nine distinct meanings of the term. There are others. The idea of universality seeds itself across the range of formal and thematic issues. It can refer to moral, behavioural and generic norms; to what is accepted as likely or only widely applicable. Such universals apply to the content or the form of literary works. (See also *genre criticism, *theme.) Recent criticism that emphasizes 'the reader's part' and sees the creation of meaning in the act of reading implies (however tacitly) that the process of reading is itself an act of universalizing. (See *reader-response criticism.) In *Structuralist Poetics* (175–6), *Jonathan Culler points out that, in order to create a poem out of the note William Carlos Williams left asking his wife's forgiveness for having eaten some plums, 'we deprive the poem of the pragmatic and circumstantial functions of the note ... and we must therefore supply a new function to justify the poem.' The process of replacing pragmatic and circumstantial functions with others (the function of art), is essentially what Aristotle isolates when he distinguishes drama proper from lampoon in the *Poetics.*

Interpreting a particular use of the term universal requires some sense of its philosophical origins and of the historical and critical contexts in which it figures. Philosophy distinguishes universals (abstract propositions and relations) from particulars (concrete objects that exemplify them); the universal 'whiteness,' for example, from the piece of chalk. For Plato and so-called Realists universals exist independently of thought and things; for Aristotle and Nominalists they are a mental artefact, existing only in particulars. (A midway position, Conceptualism, associated with Aquinas and Locke, is less relevant to literary criticism.)

In literary criticism, as in philosophy, universals are inevitably connected with their nominal opposites. Thus a critic's use of 'universal' is often clarified by examining the accompanying use of the 'particular.' From Plato to *I.A. Richards critical discussion opposes 'minute particulars' to universals. Through a Hegelian sleight of hand of terminology the opposites were supposedly reconciled in the phrase 'concrete universal,' which embodied the idea that *literature achieves universality through the concrete depiction of the particular. This formulation, especially popular with mid-century critics, was rejected by poets like John Crowe Ransom, for whom its neatness seemed superficial, untrue to actual poetic achievement, in which luck, irrelevance and other wayward elements played necessary parts.

Typically, the universal and the particular are in a complex relation of opposition and complement. Yet there are also instructive confrontations. For Blake (the phrase 'minute particulars' is his), the authenticity and power of literature lay in particulars rather than in conformity to the abstract aesthetic norms set out by Joshua Reynolds. For Reynolds 'Theory [was] the Knowledge of what is truly Nature.' This man, Blake wrote in the margin of his copy of Reynolds' *Discourses,* would destroy 'character itself.' For Samuel Johnson, on the other hand, 'Nothing [could] please many, and please long, but just representations of general nature.' It seems the case that cultural moments of conformity and consolidation like the neoclassical emphasize universals in discussions of both the form and aim of literature, and moments of scepticism and iconoclasm like the Romantic period or our own ignore them. Yet it is a mistake to expect no exceptions (there are simply too many kinds of universal), or to ignore differences among critics apparently of the same school. Romantics who rejected aesthetic universals held passionately to the idea of a universal 'human nature.' Samuel Johnson and the French critic Rapin, both neoclassicists, appeal to universality as the test of art, but while Rapin's universals were arrived at a priori, Johnson's appealed to experience and consensus.

Until recently, almost no one would have disagreed with *Wayne Booth's assertion in *The Rhetoric of Fiction* that 'the deeper [the Author] sees into permanency the more likely he is to earn the discerning reader's concurrence' (70). But the 'permanency' of literary responses, or of standards of behaviour and values – all cited by Booth – seems increasingly arguable. On the eve of the Second World War Louis Macneice wrote in his *Autumn Journal:* 'Good-bye now, Plato and Hegel, / The shop is closing down, / They don't want any philosopher-kings in England. / There ain't no universals in this man's town': this, not many lines after the poet told us 'how much [I] liked the Concrete Universal.' In additon to the harrowing public events that led to scepticism about human faculties and responses, objections in recent criticism to 'essentialist' ideas of human nature, and to the class, gender and Eurocentric biases underlying literary judgment have challenged the validity of long-accepted moral and psychological universals, especially – as Macneice suggests – those of a Neoplatonic cast. (See also *essentialism.)

Nominalist or Aristotelian universals have been challenged more subtly. A good gloss on 'universal' as Aristotle uses it in the *Poetics* is provided in the translation and commentary by H.G. Apostle, Elizabeth Dobbs and Morris Parslow (153). There the universal is 'a thought or expression predicable of or applicable to an indefinite number of things.' *Deconstruction might well define 'particular' in the same words. In some contexts it is difficult to maintain an absolute distinction between the universal and the particular, a *binary opposition of the sort deconstruction delights in collapsing.

Whatever the difficulties of interpreting particular use of the term universal, the effort can reveal distinctions of importance. For example, in the *Phaedo* Plato urges the poet to make particulars suggest the universal, while Johnson wants the universal in literature to recall the particulars.

The terms 'universal' and 'particular' seem unavoidable. For Aristotle, drama – by extension all 'making,' literature as a whole – begins with a step toward the universal, with the departure from lampoon by the invention of thought and expression applicable to more than an identifiable contemporary target of satire. Whether the step toward universality is attributed to a poet or to an audience, for there to be literature it must be taken; and if the step is attributed to the audience, objections to the falsity of notional distinctions between the literary and non-literary must seem beside the point. More important, however, is the case for the familiar moral and behavioural universals associated with Plato. For modern critics as diverse as *Todorov, *Said and *Habermas, the confusions and biases that are part of the history of universals in criticism cannot outweigh the need for some idea of 'a shared humanity' which, as Todorov (74) says, it would be dangerous to abandon, even more dangerous than ethnocentric universalism.

At this moment in critical debate, the idea of a shared humanity of human nature is open to attack from many quarters as sentimental and undemonstrable, even pernicious. For some modern critics the idea of 'human nature' or indeed any universal simply ignores the complexity of the historical and psychological evidence. Worse still, such ideas may reflect the efforts of those who speak for the dominant forces in a given culture to impose their vision on the culture as a whole and thus validate the status quo. Clearly, ideas of human nature and notions of universality can easily leave out of account the marginalization of the underclasses and the oppressed, among others who do not participate in the cultural consensus. The richness of recent *feminist criticism and of criticism that comes from outside of Eurocentricism suggests the strength of recent critiques of the idea of universals.

SHELDON P. ZITNER

Primary Sources

Aristotle. *Poetics.* Trans. H. Apostle, E. Dobbs, and M. Parslow. Grinnell, Iowa: Grinnell, 1990.
Aron, Richard Ithamar. *The Theory of Universals.* London: Clarendon P, 1967.
Barthes, Roland. 'The Great Family of Man.' In *Mythologies.* Trans. Annette Lavers. Frogmore: Paladin, 1973, 100–2.
Booth, Wayne. *The Rhetoric of Fiction.* Chicago: U of Chicago P, 1961.
Culler, Jonathan. *Structuralist Poetics: Structuralism, Linguistics and the Study of Literature.* Ithaca: Cornell UP, 1975.
Derrida, Jacques. 'White Mythologies.' In *Margins of Philosophy.* Trans. Alan Bass. Chicago: U of Chicago P, 1982.
Gudas, Fabian. 'Concrete Universal.' In *Princeton Encyclopedia of Poetry and Poetics.* Ed. Alex Preminger. Princeton, NJ: Princeton UP, 1974, 149–51.
Hagstrum, Jean. *Samuel Johnson's Literary Criticism.* Chicago: U of Chicago P, 1952.
Todorov, Tzvetan. '"Race," Writing and Culture.' In *'Race,' Writing and Difference.* Ed. Henry Louis Gates, Jr. Chicago: U of Chicago P, 1986, 370–80.
Wimsatt W.K., Jr., and Cleanth Brooks. *Literary Criticism: A Short History.* New York: Alfred A. Knopf, 1957.

Variation

Variation is a compositional technique borrowed from music which aims at creating artistic order through the exploitation and development of a *theme or a motif. Variations became a preferred form of a musical composition at the beginning of the 18th century. They were later taken up by Beethoven who added the possibility of transforming the themes from within (for example, Variations on a Theme by Diabelli, Sonata Opus 111). Indeed, before Beethoven, variation was only one of the external technical methods related to the sonata, which repeats unchanging material (*Adorno). With Beethoven, the variation takes on a new, dynamic dimension and the development process (the subjective reflection of the theme) acquires a central position in the global structure of the musical piece. Thus the variational development of the theme conserves its starting materials while transforming all of its elements. With this new type of variation, music began to entertain a new and paradoxical relationship with *time.* Finally, at the beginning of the 20th century musical variations rested on series instead of on musical themes (Schönberg, Webern).

Outside music, the variational principle has been used in philosophy (the 'imaginary variation' in *Edmund Husserl's phenomenology) and in the visual arts (particularly painting). However, *literature, and especially the 20th-century novel, uses variations by treating them as differentiating repetitions which reveal the deeply phenomenological dimensions of a work (as one object is submitted to various modes of illumination). A recurring theme, therefore, cannot be confused with simple repetition, for the meaning of the theme itself varies at each stage of its development. The whole set of variations found within a work defines the identity of the chosen theme. (See *phenomenological criticism.)

Proust, Broch, Faulkner, Mann, Hartling, Hrabal, and many other authors of 20th-century Western novels explicitly use variations. Milan Kundera goes even further and uses a variation-based aesthetics in a programmatic manner. Over and over again, he brings to light its manner of working within the *text while questioning its formal, aesthetic, as well as philosophical, and playful meanings.

EVA LE GRAND

Primary Sources

Adorno, Theodor W. *Philosophy of Modern Music.* New York: Seabury, 1973.
Aronson, Alex. *Music and the Novel: A Study in 20th-Century Fiction.* Totowa, NJ: Rowan and Littlefield, 1980.
Brand, Glen. 'Kundera and the Dialectics of Repetition.' *Cross Currents – A Yearbook of Central European Culture* 6 (1987): 461–72.

Deleuze, Gilles. *Différance et répétition*. Paris: PUF, 1968.

Kundera, Milan. *The Art of the Novel*. New York: Grove P, 1988.

– *The Book of Laughter and Forgetting*. New York: A.A. Knopf, 1980.

– 'Introduction à une variation.' In *Jacques et son maître*. Paris: Gallimard, 1981.

Le Grand, Eva. 'L'Esthétique de la variation romanesque chez Kundera.' *L'Infini* 5 (1984): 56–64.

Miller, J. Hillis. *Fiction and Repetition*. Cambridge: Harvard UP, 1982.

Pernon, Gerard. 'Variation.' *Dictionnaire de la musique*. Rennes: Ouest-France, 1984.

'Variations sur le thème.' *Communications* 47 (1988). Special issue.

White mythology

The term 'white mythology' derives from *Jacques Derrida's essay of that name in *Marges de la philosophie [Margins of Philosophy* 1972]. It refers to the metaphysical value of metaphor as the movement of a loss and return of 'proper' – literal – meaning (*sens propre*). (See *metonymy/metaphor.)

Derrida begins the essay by examining a series of philosophical 'metaphors' of the process by which metaphors are transformed into concepts through the loss of their original significance. He borrows the phrase 'white mythology' from Anatole France's *Le Jardin d'Epicure*, a dialogue on figurative language. Playing on the sense of *propre* in French as 'clean' and on *sens propre*, 'literal meaning,' Derrida uses the term 'white mythology' as a general rubric for the philosophical dream of a language cleansed of all figurative stain and made absolutely approximate to its *signified.

One traditional metaphor of this effacement (*usure*) is that of a coin, the inscription of which is worn away by excessive use. The meaning of *usure* as an inexorable dwindling involves a play on the economic sense of the word: with the gradual disappearance of the original metaphoric meaning comes the usurious growth in time of a surplus conceptual meaning. For Derrida this process is essential

to metaphysical thinking. At the end of the essay, Derrida focuses on a passage from Hegel in which the movement of the sun becomes a metaphor for the procession of the Spirit away from and back to itself in the course of history. The Spirit imitates the sun's circular westering away from an oriental origin and towards its recovery. This movement involves a detour through metaphor: with the expropriation of the primitive meaning given to things, we fall into a metaphoric mode of understanding; in the course of human history and through the process of *usure* or wearing away of the figurative, a new 'proper' meaning is restored; this new one is the old one effaced and carried to a higher conceptual power, now interiorized and spiritualized. The delayed return of the proper produces interest, a surplus of meaning which is collected at the end of time when the 'proper,' like Hegel's setting sun, returns to itself. Thus Derrida plays on the French word *plus: plus de métaphor*, no more metaphor (metaphor is destroyed as it becomes increasingly conceptual through the process of wearing away or *usure*) and the surplus of metaphor (the surplus of conceptual meaning produced by *usure* as a sort of accrued interest on an outstanding loan).

Derrida thus exposes the link between the traditional philosophical understanding of something as apparently innocent as metaphor and the entire metaphysical epoch of Western culture. Derrida's critique of 'white mythology' is thus a part of his general exposition of the metaphysical suppression of what he calls 'writing' and of the way in which philosophy's restricted 'law of the proper' attempts but fails to contain the margins of its own *discourse. (See *deconstruction, *centre/decentre, *margin, *metaphysics of presence.)

JOSEPH ADAMSON

Primary Sources

Derrida, Jacques. *Marges de la philosophie*. 1972. *Margins of Philosophy*. Trans. Alan Bass. Chicago: U of Chicago P, 1982.

List of entries

Approaches

Scholars

Terms

List of entries